FontBook

© COPYRIGHT 1993
FONTSHOP INTERNATIONAL GMBH BERLIN

All rights reserved. No part of this publication may be reproduced or used in any form or by any means – graphic, electronic, or mechanical, including photocopying, taping or information storage and retrieval systems without the prior written permission of FontShop International.

PRINTED IN GERMANY 1993 · ISBN 3-930023-00-8

FontBook

Digital Typeface Compendium

Edited by
Ed Cleary,
Jürgen Siebert &
Erik Spiekermann

FontShop
International
Berlin
1993

FontShop

Welcome to FontShop's FontBook – the ultimate source for digital typeface information.

Referencing over 8,000 fonts (including Eastern European & non-roman letterforms) and 15,000 symbols & ornaments from more than 30 international font developers, the FontBook is truly unique. Alphabet displays and text patches for all weights and families, together with comprehensive historical and technical data, make the FontBook indispensible for anyone working with type.

The idea for this book and the FontShop network started about five years ago in Berlin with Erik Spiekermann, type designer and typographer. Today the concept is backed by well-known designers such as David Berlow, Erik van Blokland, Lo Breier, Neville Brody, Ed Cleary, Max Kisman, Gerard Unger, Just van Rossum, Pierre di Sciullo and many friends: just look at our divider pages! And each FontShop has an expert behind it who was involved in type and typography long before it became an everyday tool.

Every FontShop stocks all the fonts in this book – including type on CD – for instant availability. Our regular communications announce new typefaces as they are released. As well as selling high-quality fonts from every reputable font developer and providing technical and typographical services, FontShop's own independent FontFont label encourages new designs from type designers who are working with today's electronic design and production tools.

FUSE is our award-winning multimedia publication of experimental typography, conceived and developed by Neville Brody, exclusive to FontShop.

Willkommen zu FontShops FontBook, dem umfassendsten Kompendium digitaler Schriften.

Es berücksichtigt etwa 8000 Schriften von über 30 internationalen Anbietern (einschließlich osteuropäischer und nicht-lateinischer Zeichensätze) und rund 15000 Symbole und Ornamente. Neben der Darstellung kompletter Alphabete und Textproben von jedem Schnitt einer Familie enthält das FontBook historische und technische Informationen, die das Verzeichnis zu einem unverzichtbaren Werkzeug für alle macht, die mit Schriften umgehen.

Den Grundstein für dieses Buch und das FontShop-Netzwerk legte vor rund fünf Jahren der Typograf und Schriftentwerfer Erik Spiekermann in Berlin. Heute stehen hinter diesem Konzept renommierte Designer wie David Berlow, Erik van Blokland, Lo Breier, Neville Brody, Ed Cleary, Max Kisman, Gerard Unger, Just van Rossum, Pierre di Sciullo und viele weitere FontShop-Freunde, wie die Registerseiten in diesem Buch zeigen. Alle FontShops werden von Fachleuten beraten, die sich bereits mit Schrift und Typografie auskannten, bevor diese einfach verfügbare Werkzeuge für jeden waren.

Jeder FontShop kann sämtliche Schriften in diesem Buch sofort liefern, viele davon auf CD-ROM. Regelmäßige Drucksachen stellen Neuveröffentlichungen vor. Neben dem Angebot hochwertiger Originalschriften aller angesehenen Hersteller, neben technischem und typografischem Support veröffentlicht FontShop außerdem eigene Schriften mit neuen Entwürfen unabhängiger Designer: die FontFont-Bibliothek.

FUSE ist FontShops preisgekrönte Multimedia-Publikation zur experimentellen Typografie, erdacht und betreut von Neville Brody, exklusiv bei FontShop.

Bienvenue au FontBook de FontShop, la source ultime d'informations sur les polices de caractères digitales.

Le FontBook est vraiment unique. Il référence plus de 8000 fontes (dont des sets d'accents pour langues de l'europe orientale et des polices de caractères non-latins) et 15000 symboles et ornements en provenance de plus de 30 développeurs internationaux de fontes. Des affichages d'alphabets et des exemples de composition de toutes graisses et familles, ainsi que des informations historiques et techniques, rendent le FontBook indispensable pour chacun qui travaille avec de la typographie.

L'idée originale pour cet ouvrage de référence et le réseau FontShop est née ilya cinq ans à Berlin de l'esprit d'Erik Spiekermann, créateur de fontes et typographe. Aujourd'hui le concept reçoit le support de designers connus tels que David Berlow, Erik van Blokland, Lo Breier, Neville Brody, Ed Cleary, Max Kisman, Gerard Unger, Just van Rossum, Pierre di Sciullo et nombre d'amis : regardez nos pages de division. Et derrière chaque FontShop se trouve un expert qui était déjà passionné par la typographie bien avant qu'elle ne devenait un outil quotidien.

Toutes les fontes mentionnées dans cet ouvrage – les polices de caractères sur CD-ROM inclues – sont continuellement de stock et sont livrables à l'instant. Nos publications régulières annoncent de nouvelles polices de caractères dès leur sortie. Outre la vente de polices de caractères de qualité de fournisseurs réputés et la procuration d'assistance technique et de conseils typographiques, FontShop encourage via son propre label indépendant FontFont, les créations originales de typographes de talent qui exploitent les modes de création et de production électronique contemporains.

FUSE est notre publication multimédia couronnée pour la typographie expérimentale, conçue et développée par Neville Brody, et exclusive de FontShop.

FontShop

Welkom tot het FontBook van FontShop – de ultieme bron van informatie voor gedigitaliseerde lettertypes.

Het FontBook is werkelijk uniek. Het boek rangschikt meer dan 8.000 lettertypes (waaronder lettertypes vor Oost-Europese talen en niet Latijnse alfabetten), 15.000 symbolen en ornamenten afkomstig meer als 30 internationaal lettertype-ontwikkelaars. Voorbeelden van de karakterset per familie en zetvoorbeelden voor ieder gewicht, eveenals historische en technische informatie maken van het FontBook een onmissbaar naslagwek voor iedereen die met typografie in aanraking komt.

Het originele idee voor dit boek en het internationaal FontShop netwerk is onstaan vijf jaar terug en is het werk van Erik Spiekermann, designer en letterontwerper. FontShop krijgt de nodige steun van bekende typographen zoals David Berlow, Erik van Blokland, Lo Breier, Neville Brody, Ed Cleary, Max Kisman, Gerard Unger, Just van Rossum, Pierre di Sciullo en vele vrienden. Kijk maar naar onze tabbladen! Tevens staat achter elke FontShop vestiging een expert op het gebied van typografie.

Alle fonts opgenomen in dit boek – inclusief de lettertypes op CD-ROM – zijn beschikbaar uit onze voorraad. Via een efficient communicatie systeem zorgen wij ervoor dat nieuwe fonts regelmatig worden gepubliceerd. Behalve het verdelen van lettertypes uit bekend typotheken en het verlenen van technisch en artistiek advies, stimuleert FontShop via FontFont, onze eigen typotheek, originele ontwerpen van jong getalenteerde letterontwerpers.

FUSE, ons interactief magazine voor experimentele typografie, naar het idee van Neville Brody is exclusief bij FontShop verkrijgbaar.

Vi presentiamo il nuovo FontBook di FontShop, dove troverete le più complete informazioni su caratteri tipografici per MAC e PC.

Con i suoi oltre 8.000 font (inclusi quelli per lingue dell'Est europeo e i non latini) e i suoi 15.000 simboli e decorazioni creati da più de 30 case produttrici internazionali, il FontBook è unico nel suo genere. Nelle pagine di questo libro, si trovano gli alfabeti completi di ogni famiglia ed esempi di testo per ogni stile, oltre a informazioni storiche e tecniche. Il FontBook è indispensabile per chiunque lavori con i font.

L'idea alla base di questo libro risale alla creazione, nel 1988, del network FontShop, da parte di Erik Spiekermann, disegnatore di caratteri e graphic designer di Berlino. Oggi collaborano al progetto FontShop ben noti designers quali David Berlow, Erik van Blokland, Lo Breier, Max Kisman, Gerard Unger, Just van Rossum, Pierre de Sciullo e tanti altri amici. Basta guardare le pagine divisorie! Ogni FontShop è condotto da un esperto con una lunga esperienza nel mondo dei caratteri.

Tutti i caratteri presentati nel nuovo FontBook, molti dei quali su CD-ROM, sono disponibili per una consegna immediata. Pubblicazioni periodiche informano sui nuovi caratteri appena realizzati.

Oltre alla vendita di font di alta qualità prodotti da noti disegnatori di caratteri, la nostra etichetta indipendente FontFont incoraggia nuove creazioni da coloro che lavorano con il design elettronico e le moderne tecniche di produzione.

FUSE è la nostra publicazione multimediale dedicata alla tipografia sperimentale, concepita e sviluppata da Neville Brody, in esclusiva per FontShop.

Välkommen till FontShops FontBook – den mest omfattande kollektionen av digitaliserade typsnitt.

Innehållande ca. 8000 typsnitt (inklusive östeuropeiska och icke-latinska teckenformer) och ca. 15000 symboler och ornament från över 30 internationella typsnittsutvecklare, är denna FontBook unik. Förutom kompletta alfabet och textprover av varje typgrupp, innehåller FontBook även historiska och tekniska data, vilket gör denna förteckning oumbärlig för den som är typografiskt intresserad.

FontShop idén startades i Berlin för fem år sedan av den välkände designern och typografen Erik Spiekermann. Idag står välkända världsnamn inom typografi och design bakom detta koncept, som David Berlow, Erik van Blokland, Lo Breier, Neville Brody, Ed Cleary, Max Kisman, Gerard Unger, Just van Rossum, Pierre di Sciullo och många andra FontShop vänner. Och varje FontShop har en eller flera av dessa experter knutna till sig. Erfarna experter som har arbetat med typsnitt och typgrafi långt innan det blev ett verktyg för var man.

FontShop lagerför samtliga typsnitt i denna bok, många även på CD-ROM, och genom våra regelbundna trycksaker informerar vi om när nya typsnitt kommer ut på marknaden.

Förutom erbjudandet av högkvalitativa originaltypsnitt från alla välkända producenter, samt teknisk och typografisk support, publicerar FontShop även ny spännande typsnittsdesign från oberoende designers, inom ramen för det egna FontFont biblioteket.

FUSE är dessutom FontShops prisbelönade multimediapublikation för experimentell typografi, utvecklad av Neville Brody exklusivt for FontShop.

FontShop abbreviation	Manufacturer
A	Adobe
C	Agfa
F	Alphabets
BR	Bear Rock
BT	Bitstream
CA	Carter & Cone
CT	Club Type
EF	Elsner + Flake
ED	EmDash
E	Emigre
ET	Electric Typographer
FG	Fifth Generation Systems
FB	The Font Bureau, Inc.
FF	FontFont
G	Lanston Type
ATF	Kingsley/ATF
LP	Letter·Perfect
L	Letraset
LS	Linguist's Software
LG	Lutz Gottschalk
LH	Linotype-Hell
M	Monotype
K	MacCampus
MC	Mecanorma
PG	ParaType
RB	Richard Beatty
SX	s.a.x. Software
SF	Stylus
SG	Mannesmann Scangraphic
SS	Solo Software
TF	Treacyfaces
TO	Type-ø-Tones

✏️ Designer &
year of publication

👁 See also:
similar typefaces

aa*a* Alternative availability:
other manufacturers

📦 Package:
single weights combined

Typographic classification:
① Sans serif
② Serif
③ Slab serif
④ Script
⑤ Graphic
⑥ Display
⑦ Blackletter
⑧ Symbol & ornaments
⑨ Non-latin & special accents

Mac+PC Operating system

BT 1221 Order number:
see list of manufacturers
for abbreviations

Max '*not just a pretty face*' Kisman, Amsterdam, NL

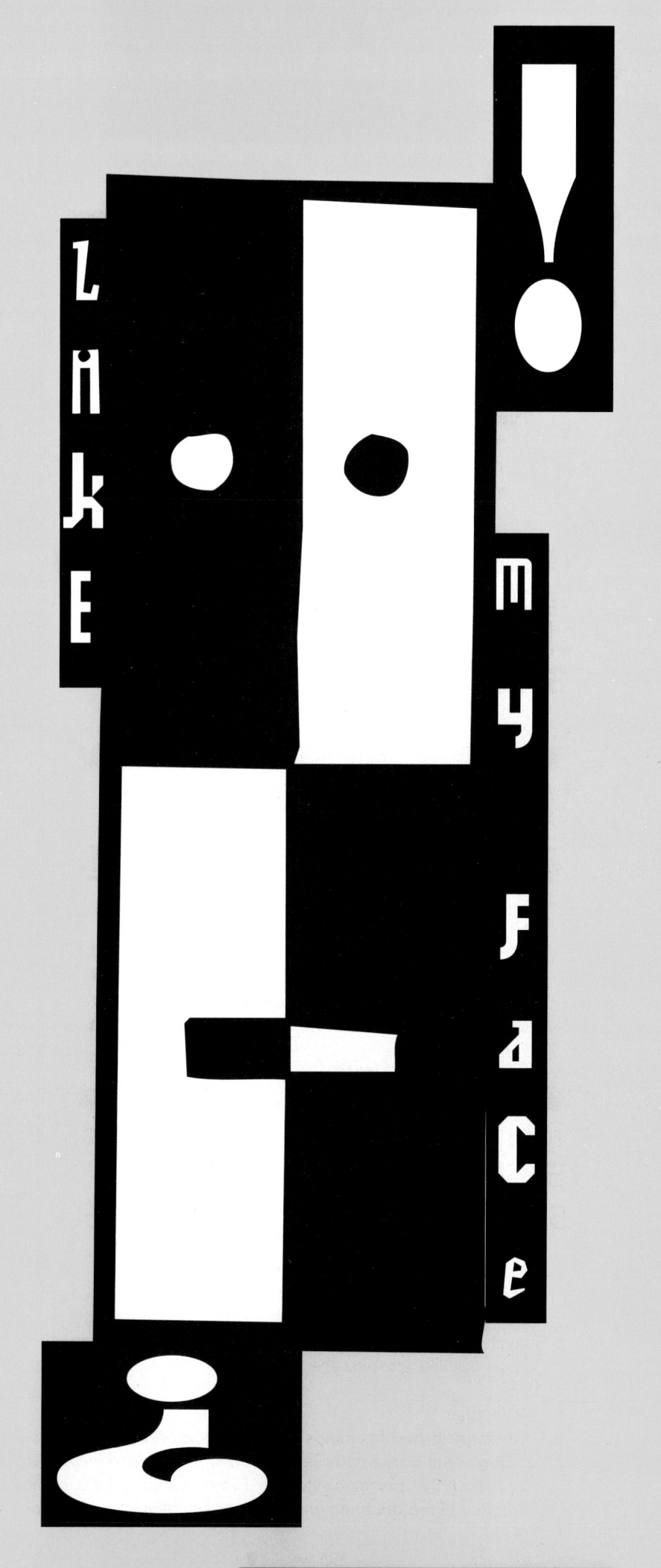

A001 Mac + PC
Aachen Bold

Aachen Bold:
Aachen Bold, Freestyle Script, Revue™, University Roman

BT1221 Mac + PC ③ 1968: Colin Brignall
Aachen™

abcdefghijklmnopqrstuvwxyz[äöüßåøæœç]
ABCDEFGHIJKLMNOPQRSTUVWXYZ
1234567890(.,;:?!$&-*){ÄÖÜÅØÆŒÇ}

aa*a*
A001
Aachen Bold
L6631
Aachen Bold
L6632
Aachen Bold

▶ Regular
The quick brown fox jumps over a Dog. Zwei Boxkämpfer jagen Eva durch Sylt portez ce vieux Whiskey blond qui

▶ Bold
The quick brown fox jumps over a Dog. Zwei Boxkämpfer jagen Eva durch Sylt portez ce vieux Whiskey

---

L6631 Mac ③ 1968: Colin Brignall
Aachen Medium

abcdefghijklmnopqrstuvwxyz[äöüßåøæœç]
ABCDEFGHIJKLMNOPQRSTUVWXYZ
1234567890(.,;:?!$&-*)ÄÖÜÅØÆŒÇ

FB2756 Mac + PC ⑥ 1991: John Benson
Aardvark™

ABCDEFGHIJKLMNOPQRSTUVWXYZ
1234567890(.,;:?!$&-*)[](ÄÖÜÅØÆŒÇ)

Scamp

▶ Regular
THE QUICK BROWN FOX JUMPS OVER A DOG. ZWEI BOXKÄMPFER JAGEN EVA DURCH SYLT PORTEZ CE VIEUX WHISKEY BLOND QUI FUME UNE PIPE ABER ECHT ÜBER DIE MAUER

▶ Bold
THE QUICK BROWN FOX JUMPS OVER A DOG. ZWEI BOXKÄMPFER JAGEN EVA DURCH SYLT PORTEZ CE VIEUX WHISKEY BLOND QUI FUME UNE PIPE ABER

M555 Mac + PC ① 1987: Ong Chong Wah
Abadi® 1

abcdefghijklmnopqrstuvwxyz[äöüßåøæœç]
ABCDEFGHIJKLMNOPQRSTUVWXYZ
1234567890(.,;:?!$&-*){ÄÖÜÅØÆŒÇ}

Angro, Avenir

▶ Extra Light
The quick brown fox jumps over a Dog. Zwei Boxkämpfer jagen Eva durch Sylt portez ce vieux Whiskey blond qui fume une pipe aber echt

▶ Extra Light Italic
The quick brown fox jumps over a Dog. Zwei Boxkämpfer jagen Eva durch Sylt portez ce vieux Whiskey blond qui fume une pipe aber echt

▶ Regular
The quick brown fox jumps over a Dog. Zwei Boxkämpfer jagen Eva durch Sylt portez ce vieux Whiskey blond qui fume une

▶ Italic
The quick brown fox jumps over a Dog. Zwei Boxkämpfer jagen Eva durch Sylt portez ce vieux Whiskey blond qui fume une

© FSI 1993

▼ M555 Mac + PC Abadi® 1

► Bold
The quick brown fox jumps over a Dog. Zwei Boxkämpfer jagen Eva durch Sylt portez ce vieux Whiskey blond qui fume

► Bold Italic
The quick brown fox jumps over a Dog. Zwei Boxkämpfer jagen Eva durch Sylt portez ce vieux Whiskey blond qui fume

M556 Mac + PC ① 1987: Ong Chong Wah
Abadi 2

abcdefghijklmnopqrstuvwxyz[äöüßåøæœç]
ABCDEFGHIJKLMNOPQRSTUVWXYZ
1234567890(.,;:?!$&-*){ÄÖÜÅØÆŒÇ}

Angro, Avenir

► Light
The quick brown fox jumps over a Dog. Zwei Boxkämpfer jagen Eva durch Sylt portez ce vieux Whiskey blond qui fume une pipe

► Light Italic
The quick brown fox jumps over a Dog. Zwei Boxkämpfer jagen Eva durch Sylt portez ce vieux Whiskey blond qui fume une pipe aber

► Extra Bold
The quick brown fox jumps over a Dog. Zwei Boxkämpfer jagen Eva durch Sylt portez ce vieux Whiskey blond

► Extra Bold Italic
The quick brown fox jumps over a Dog. Zwei Boxkämpfer jagen Eva durch Sylt portez ce vieux Whiskey blond qui

M356 Mac + PC ① 1987: Ong Chong Wah
Abadi Condensed

abcdefghijklmnopqrstuvwxyz[äöüßåøæœç]
ABCDEFGHIJKLMNOPQRSTUVWXYZ
1234567890(.,;:?!$&-*){ÄÖÜÅØÆŒÇ}

► Light Condensed
The quick brown fox jumps over a Dog. Zwei Boxkämpfer jagen Eva durch Sylt portez ce vieux Whiskey blond qui fume une pipe aber echt über die Mauer

► Condensed
The quick brown fox jumps over a Dog. Zwei Boxkämpfer jagen Eva durch Sylt portez ce vieux Whiskey blond qui fume une pipe aber echt

► Bold Condensed
The quick brown fox jumps over a Dog. Zwei Boxkämpfer jagen Eva durch Sylt portez ce vieux Whiskey blond qui fume une pipe aber echt

► Extra Bold Condensed
The quick brown fox jumps over a Dog. Zwei Boxkämpfer jagen Eva durch Sylt portez ce vieux Whiskey blond qui fume une pipe aber echt

ET6389 Mac + PC
Abelard / Troubador

Abelard / Troubador:
Abelard™, Troubador™

© FSI 1993

ET6389 Mac + PC ✎ 1992: Judith Sutcliffe
Abelard™

abcdefghijklmnopqrstuvwxyz[äöüßåøæœç]
ABCDEFGHIJKLMNOPQRSTUVWXYZ
1234567890(.,;:?!$&-*){ÄÖÜÅØÆŒÇ}

Abelard / Troubador:
Abelard™, Troubador™

L2977 Mac ✎ 1989: Vince Whitlock
Academy Engraved

abcdefghijklmnopqrstuvwxyz[äöüßåøæœç]
ABCDEFGHIJKLMNOPQRSTUVWXYZ
1234567890(.,;:?!$&-*)ÄÖÜÅØÆŒÇ

MC2891 Mac + PC ⑥
Access™ Medium

ABCDEFGHIJKLMNOPQRSTUVWXYZ
1234567890(.,;:?!$&-*)[]{ÄÖÜÅØÆŒÇ}

MC2892 Mac + PC ⑥
Access Bold

ABCDEFGHIJKLMNOPQRSTUVWXYZ
1234567890(.,;:?!$&-*)
[]{ÄÖÜÅØÆŒÇ}

C590 Mac + PC ② ✎ 1979: Chew Loon
Accolade™

abcdefghijklmnopqrstuvwxyz[äöüßåøæœç]
ABCDEFGHIJKLMNOPQRSTUVWXYZ
1234567890(.,;:?!$&-*){ÄÖÜÅØÆŒÇ}

▶ Light
The quick brown fox jumps over a Dog. Zwei Boxkämpfer jagen Eva durch Sylt portez ce vieux Whiskey blond

▶ Light Italic
The quick brown fox jumps over a Dog. Zwei Boxkämpfer jagen Eva durch Sylt portez ce vieux Whiskey blond

▶ Medium
The quick brown fox jumps over a Dog. Zwei Boxkämpfer jagen Eva durch Sylt portez ce vieux Whiskey

▶ Bold
The quick brown fox jumps over a Dog. Zwei Boxkämpfer jagen Eva durch Sylt portez ce vieux

© FSI 1993

Ad Lib
BT2549 Mac + PC ⑥ 1961: Freeman Craw

abcdefghijklmnopqrstuvwxyz[äöüßåøæœç]
ABCDEFGHIJKLMNOPQRSTUVWXYZ
1234567890(.,;:?!$&-*){ÄÖÜÅØÆŒÇ}

Admark™
CT870 Mac + PC ② 1990: Adrian Williams

abcdefghijklmnopqrstuvwxyz[äöüßåøæœç]
ABCDEFGHIJKLMNOPQRSTUVWXYZ
1234567890(.,;:?!$&-*){ÄÖÜÅØÆŒÇ}

▶ Regular
The quick brown fox jumps over a Dog. Zwei Boxkämpfer jagen Eva durch Sylt portez ce vieux Whiskey blond qui fume

▶ Italic
The quick brown fox jumps over a Dog. Zwei Boxkämpfer jagen Eva durch Sylt portez ce vieux Whiskey blond qui fume une

▶ Medium
The quick brown fox jumps over a Dog. Zwei Boxkämpfer jagen Eva durch Sylt portez ce vieux Whiskey blond qui

▶ Medium Italic
The quick brown fox jumps over a Dog. Zwei Boxkämpfer jagen Eva durch Sylt portez ce vieux Whiskey blond qui fume

▶ Bold
The quick brown fox jumps over a Dog. Zwei Boxkämpfer jagen Eva durch Sylt portez ce vieux Whiskey blond

▶ Bold Italic
The quick brown fox jumps over a Dog. Zwei Boxkämpfer jagen Eva durch Sylt portez ce vieux Whiskey blond qui

Adminster™
C6434 Mac + PC ② 1980: Les Usherwood

abcdefghijklmnopqrstuvwxyz[äöüßåøæœç]
ABCDEFGHIJKLMNOPQRSTUVWXYZ
1234567890(.,;:?!$&-*){ÄÖÜÅØÆŒÇ}

© Minister

▶ Light
The quick brown fox jumps over a Dog. Zwei Boxkämpfer jagen Eva durch Sylt portez ce vieux Whiskey blond qui fume une

▶ Light Italic
The quick brown fox jumps over a Dog. Zwei Boxkämpfer jagen Eva durch Sylt portez ce vieux Whiskey blond qui fume une pipe aber echt

▶ Book
The quick brown fox jumps over a Dog. Zwei Boxkämpfer jagen Eva durch Sylt portez ce vieux Whiskey blond qui fume

▶ Book Italic
The quick brown fox jumps over a Dog. Zwei Boxkämpfer jagen Eva durch Sylt portez ce vieux Whiskey blond qui fume une pipe aber

▶ Bold
The quick brown fox jumps over a Dog. Zwei Boxkämpfer jagen Eva durch Sylt portez ce vieux Whiskey blond

© FSI 1993

Adroit™
C592 Mac + PC ② 1981: Phil Martin

abcdefghijklmnopqrstuvwxyz[äöüßåøæœç]
ABCDEFGHIJKLMNOPQRSTUVWXYZ
1234567890(.,;:?!$&-*){ÄÖÜÅØÆŒÇ}

▶ Light
The quick brown fox jumps over a Dog. Zwei Boxkämpfer jagen Eva durch Sylt portez ce vieux Whiskey blond qui fume une

▶ Light Italic
The quick brown fox jumps over a Dog. Zwei Boxkämpfer jagen Eva durch Sylt portez ce vieux Whiskey blond qui fume

▶ Medium
The quick brown fox jumps over a Dog. Zwei Boxkämpfer jagen Eva durch Sylt portez ce vieux Whiskey blond qui

▶ Medium Italic
The quick brown fox jumps over a Dog. Zwei Boxkämpfer jagen Eva durch Sylt portez ce vieux Whiskey blond qui

Humanist 970 / Ad Sans™
BT745 Mac + PC ① 1959: Walter Tracy — Industry name

abcdefghijklmnopqrstuvwxyz[äöüßåøæœç]
ABCDEFGHIJKLMNOPQRSTUVWXYZ
1234567890(.,;:?!$&-*){ÄÖÜÅØÆŒÇ}

Doric, Sans No. 1, ATF Spartan

▶ Regular
The quick brown fox jumps over a Dog. Zwei Boxkämpfer jagen Eva durch Sylt

▶ Bold
The quick brown fox jumps over a Dog. Zwei Boxkämpfer jagen Eva durch Sylt

FF Advert
FF1536 Mac + PC ① 1991: Just van Rossum

aabcdefghijklmnopqrstuvwxyz[äöüßåøæœç]
ABCDEFGHIJKLMNOPQRSTUVWXYZ
1234567890(.,;:?!$&-*){ÄÖÜÅØÆŒÇ}

▶ Light
The quick brown fox jumps over a Dog. Zwei Boxkämpfer jagen Eva durch Sylt portez ce vieux Whiskey blond qui

▶ Regular
The quick brown fox jumps over a Dog. Zwei Boxkämpfer jagen Eva durch Sylt portez ce vieux Whiskey blond

▶ Bold
The quick brown fox jumps over a Dog. Zwei Boxkämpfer jagen Eva durch Sylt portez ce vieux Whiskey blond

▶ Black
The quick brown fox jumps over a Dog. Zwei Boxkämpfer jagen Eva durch Sylt portez ce vieux Whiskey

FF Advert Rough
FF6182 Mac + PC ① 1992: Just van Rossum

abcdefghijklmnopqrstuvwxyz[äöüßåøæœç]
ABCDEFGHIJKLMNOPQRSTUVWXYZ
1234567890(.,;:?!$&-*){ÄÖÜÅØÆŒÇ}

© FSI 1993

▼ FF6182 Mac + PC   FF Advert Rough

▶ One
The quick brown fox jumps over a Dog. Zwei Boxkämpfer jagen Eva durch Sylt portez ce vieux Whiskey blond

▶ Two
The quick brown fox jumps over a Dog. Zwei Boxkämpfer jagen Eva durch Sylt portez ce vieux Whiskey blond

▶ Three
The quick brown fox jumps over a Dog. Zwei Boxkämpfer jagen Eva durch Sylt portez ce vieux Whiskey blond

▶ Four
The quick brown fox jumps over a Dog. Zwei Boxkämpfer jagen Eva durch Sylt portez ce vieux Whiskey blond

▶ Five
The quick brown fox jumps over a Dog. Zwei Boxkämpfer jagen Eva durch Sylt portez ce vieux Whiskey blond

C2525 Mac + PC   ⑥   1917: Robert Wiebking
Advertisers Gothic™

abcdefghijklmnopqrstuvwxyz[äöüßåøæœç]
ABCDEFGHIJKLMNOPQRSTUVWXYZ
1234567890(.,:;?!$&-*){ÄÖÜÅØÆŒÇ}

Headlines 86S:
Advertisers Gothic™, Ashley Crawford™, Capone Light, Dynamo, Modernistic™

FB593 Mac + PC   ①   1989: (M. F. Benton, 1933) David Berlow
Bureau Agency™

abcdefghijklmnopqrstuvwxyz1234567890[äöüßåøæœç]
ABCDEFGHIJKLMNOPQRSTUVWXYZ(.,:;?!$&-*){ÄÖÜÅØÆŒÇ}

©
Regency Gothic, Huxley Vertical. Aldous Vertical, Phenix American, De Stijl

▶ Regular
The quick brown fox jumps over a Dog. Zwei Boxkämpfer jagen Eva durch Sylt portez ce vieux Whiskey blond qui fume une pipe aber echt über die Mauer gesprungen und auch

▶ Bold
The quick brown fox jumps over a Dog. Zwei Boxkämpfer jagen Eva durch Sylt portez ce vieux Whiskey blond qui fume une pipe aber echt über die Mauer gesprungen und auch

FB6799 Mac + PC   ①   1993: (Edward Johnston) Greg Thompson
Agenda™ 1

abcdefghijklmnopqrstuvwxyz[äöüßåøæœç]
ABCDEFGHIJKLMNOPQRSTUVWXYZ
1234567890(.,:;?!$&-*){ÄÖÜÅØÆŒÇ}

▶ Light
The quick brown fox jumps over a Dog. Zwei Boxkämpfer jagen Eva durch Sylt portez ce vieux Whiskey blond qui fume une pipe aber

▶ Light Italic
The quick brown fox jumps over a Dog. Zwei Boxkämpfer jagen Eva durch Sylt portez ce vieux Whiskey blond qui fume une pipe aber

© FSI 1993

▼ FB6799 Mac + PC   Agenda™ 1

▶ Bold
The quick brown fox jumps over a Dog. Zwei Boxkämpfer jagen Eva durch Sylt portez ce vieux Whiskey blond qui fume une

▶ Black
The quick brown fox jumps over a Dog. Zwei Boxkämpfer jagen Eva durch Sylt portez ce vieux Whiskey blond qui fume

FB6800 Mac + PC   ①   1993: (Edward Johnston) Greg Thompson
Agenda 2

abcdefghijklmnopqrstuvwxyz[äöüßåøæœç]
ABCDEFGHIJKLMNOPQRSTUVWXYZ
1234567890(.,;:?!$&-*){ÄÖÜÅØÆŒÇ}

▶ Medium
The quick brown fox jumps over a Dog. Zwei Boxkämpfer jagen Eva durch Sylt portez ce vieux Whiskey blond qui fume une

▶ Medium Italic
The quick brown fox jumps over a Dog. Zwei Boxkämpfer jagen Eva durch Sylt portez ce vieux Whiskey blond qui fume une pipe aber

▶ Medium Condensed
The quick brown fox jumps over a Dog. Zwei Boxkämpfer jagen Eva durch Sylt portez ce vieux Whiskey blond qui fume une pipe aber echt über die

▶ Bold Condensed
The quick brown fox jumps over a Dog. Zwei Boxkämpfer jagen Eva durch Sylt portez ce vieux Whiskey blond qui fume une pipe aber echt

FB6918 Mac + PC   ①   1993: (Edward Johnston) Greg Thompson
Agenda Extra Condensed

abcdefghijklmnopqrstuvwxyz[äöüßåøæœç]
ABCDEFGHIJKLMNOPQRSTUVWXYZ
1234567890(.,;:?!$&-*){ÄÖÜÅØÆŒÇ}

▶ Light Condensed
The quick brown fox jumps over a Dog. Zwei Boxkämpfer jagen Eva durch Sylt portez ce vieux Whiskey blond qui fume une pipe aber echt über die Mauer

▶ Light Extra Condensed
The quick brown fox jumps over a Dog. Zwei Boxkämpfer jagen Eva durch Sylt portez ce vieux Whiskey blond qui fume une pipe aber echt über die Mauer gesprungen und auch smørebrød en ysjes

▶ Medium Extra Condensed
The quick brown fox jumps over a Dog. Zwei Boxkämpfer jagen Eva durch Sylt portez ce vieux Whiskey blond qui fume une pipe aber echt über die Mauer gesprungen und auch smørebrød en

▶ Bold Extra Condensed
The quick brown fox jumps over a Dog. Zwei Boxkämpfer jagen Eva durch Sylt portez ce vieux Whiskey blond qui fume une pipe aber echt über die Mauer gesprungen und auch

FB6919 Mac + PC   ①   1993: (Edward Johnston) Greg Thompson
Agenda Ultra Condensed

abcdefghijklmnopqrstuvwxyz1234567890[äöüßåøæœç]
ABCDEFGHIJKLMNOPQRSTUVWXYZ(.,;:?!$&-*){ÄÖÜÅØÆŒÇ}

▶ Thin Ultra Condensed
The quick brown fox jumps over a Dog. Zwei Boxkämpfer jagen Eva durch Sylt portez ce vieux Whiskey blond qui fume une pipe aber echt über die Mauer gesprungen und auch smørebrød en ysjes natuurlijk. The quick brown fox jumps over a Dog. Zwei Boxkämpfer jagen Eva durch Sylt portez ce vieux Whiskey blond

▶ Light Ultra Condensed
The quick brown fox jumps over a Dog. Zwei Boxkämpfer jagen Eva durch Sylt portez ce vieux Whiskey blond qui fume une pipe aber echt über die Mauer gesprungen und auch smørebrød en ysjes natuurlijk. The quick brown fox jumps over a Dog. Zwei Boxkämpfer jagen Eva durch

© FSI 1993
▼

▼ FB6919 MAC + PC   Agenda Ultra Condensed

▶ Medium Ultra Condensed
The quick brown fox jumps over a Dog. Zwei Boxkämpfer jagen Eva durch Sylt portez ce vieux Whiskey blond qui fume une pipe aber echt über die Mauer gesprungen und auch smørebrød en ysjes natuurlijk. The quick brown fox jumps over a Dog. Zwei

▶ Bold Ultra Condensed
The quick brown fox jumps over a Dog. Zwei Boxkämpfer jagen Eva durch Sylt portez ce vieux Whiskey blond qui fume une pipe aber echt über die Mauer gesprungen und auch smørebrød en ysjes natuurlijk. The quick brown fox

---

TF2890 MAC + PC   ⑥   ✎ 1992: Joseph Treacy
TF Akimbo™

abcdefghijklmnopqrstuvwxyz1234567890[äöüßåøæœç]

ABCDEFGHIJKLMNOPQRSTUVWXYZ(.,;:?!$&-*){ÄÖÜÅØÆŒÇ}

TF Avian & TF Akimbo:
TF Akimbo™, TF Avian™

AB2941 MAC + PC   ①   ✎ 1963-88: (1898-1953) G. G. Lange
Berthold Akzidenz Grotesk®

abcdefghijklmnopqrstuvwxyz[äöüßåøæœç]
ABCDEFGHIJKLMNOPQRSTUVWXYZ
1234567890(.,;:?!$&-*){ÄÖÜÅØÆŒÇ}

aa*a*
BT1324
Akzidenz Grotesk, Bd, Blk

▶ Light
The quick brown fox jumps over a Dog. Zwei Boxkämpfer jagen Eva durch Sylt portez ce vieux Whiskey blond qui fume une

▶ Light OSF
The quick brown fox jumps over a Dog. 123 4567 890 Zwei Boxkämpfer jagen Eva durch Sylt portez ce vieux Whiskey blond

▶ Regular
The quick brown fox jumps over a Dog. Zwei Boxkämpfer jagen Eva durch Sylt portez ce vieux Whiskey blond qui fume une

▶ Italic
The quick brown fox jumps over a Dog. Zwei Boxkämpfer jagen Eva durch Sylt portez ce vieux Whiskey blond qui fume une

▶ Medium
The quick brown fox jumps over a Dog. Zwei Boxkämpfer jagen Eva durch Sylt portez ce vieux Whiskey blond qui fume

▶ Medium Italic
The quick brown fox jumps over a Dog. Zwei Boxkämpfer jagen Eva durch Sylt portez ce vieux Whiskey blond qui fume

▶ Bold
The quick brown fox jumps over a Dog. Zwei Boxkämpfer jagen Eva durch Sylt portez ce vieux Whiskey blond

▶ Bold Italic
The quick brown fox jumps over a Dog. Zwei Boxkämpfer jagen Eva durch Sylt portez ce vieux Whiskey

▶ Super
The quick brown fox jumps over a Dog. Zwei Boxkämpfer jagen Eva durch Sylt portez ce vieux Whis-

© FSI 1993

AB2943 Mac + PC ① 1958-68: (1896-1953) G. G. Lange
Berthold Akzidenz Grotesk Condensed

abcdefghijklmnopqrstuvwxyz[äöüßåøæœç]
ABCDEFGHIJKLMNOPQRSTUVWXYZ
1234567890(.,;:?!$&-*){ÄÖÜÅØÆŒÇ}

► Light Condensed
The quick brown fox jumps over a Dog. Zwei Boxkämpfer jagen Eva durch Sylt portez ce vieux Whiskey blond qui fume une pipe aber echt über die Mauer gesprungen und auch smørebrød en ysjes

► Condensed
The quick brown fox jumps over a Dog. 123 4567 890 Zwei Boxkämpfer jagen Eva durch Sylt portez ce vieux Whiskey blond qui fume une pipe aber echt über die Mauer

► Medium Condensed
The quick brown fox jumps over a Dog. Zwei Boxkämpfer jagen Eva durch Sylt portez ce vieux Whiskey blond qui fume une pipe aber echt über die Mauer gesprungen und auch smørebrød en ysjes

► Medium Condensed Italic
The quick brown fox jumps over a Dog. Zwei Boxkämpfer jagen Eva durch Sylt portez ce vieux Whiskey blond qui fume une pipe aber echt über die Mauer gesprungen und auch smørebrød en ysjes

► Bold Condensed
The quick brown fox jumps over a Dog. Zwei Boxkämpfer jagen Eva durch Sylt portez ce vieux Whiskey blond qui fume une pipe aber echt über die Mauer

► Extra Bold Condensed
The quick brown fox jumps over a Dog. Zwei Boxkämpfer jagen Eva durch Sylt portez ce vieux Whiskey blond qui fume une pipe aber

► Extra Bold Condensed Italic
The quick brown fox jumps over a Dog. Zwei Boxkämpfer jagen Eva durch Sylt portez ce vieux Whiskey blond qui fume une pipe aber

► Extra Bold
The quick brown fox jumps over a Dog. Zwei Boxkämpfer jagen Eva durch Sylt portez ce vieux Whiskey blond qui fume une

AB2854 Mac + PC ① 1911-1961: (H. Berthold AG)
Berthold Akzidenz Grotesk Extended

abcdefghijklmnopqrstuvwxyz[äöüßåøæœç]
ABCDEFGHIJKLMNOPQRSTUVWXYZ
1234567890(.,;:?!$&-*){ÄÖÜÅØÆŒÇ}

► Light Extended
The quick brown fox jumps over a Dog. Zwei Boxkämpfer jagen Eva durch Sylt portez ce

► Extended
The quick brown fox jumps over a Dog. Zwei Boxkämpfer jagen Eva durch Sylt portez ce

► Medium Extended
The quick brown fox jumps over a Dog. Zwei Boxkämpfer jagen Eva durch Sylt

► Bold Extended
The quick brown fox jumps over a Dog. Zwei Boxkämpfer jagen Eva durch Sylt

► Bold Extended Italic
The quick brown fox jumps over a Dog. Zwei Boxkämpfer jagen Eva durch Sylt

© FSI 1993

A 9

AB6080 Mac + PC   ①   ✎ 1980: G. G. Lange
Berthold Akzidenz Grotesk Book Rounded

abcdefghijklmnopqrstuvwxyz[äöüßåøæœç]
ABCDEFGHIJKLMNOPQRSTUVWXYZ
1234567890(.,:;?!$&-*){ÄÖÜÅØÆŒÇ}

► Regular
The quick brown fox jumps over a Dog. Zwei Boxkämpfer jagen Eva durch Sylt portez ce vieux Whiskey blond qui fume

► Medium
The quick brown fox jumps over a Dog. Zwei Boxkämpfer jagen Eva durch Sylt portez ce vieux Whiskey blond qui fume

► Medium Outline
The quick brown fox jumps over a Dog. Zwei Boxkämpfer jagen Eva durch Sylt portez ce vieux Whiskey blond qui fume

► Bold
The quick brown fox jumps over a Dog. Zwei Boxkämpfer jagen Eva durch Sylt portez ce vieux Whiskey blond

► BoldOutline
The quick brown fox jumps over a Dog. Zwei Boxkämpfer jagen Eva durch Sylt portez ce vieux Whiskey blond qui

► Bold Condensed
The quick brown fox jumps over a Dog. Zwei Boxkämpfer jagen Eva durch Sylt portez ce vieux Whiskey blond qui fume une pipe aber echt

► Bold Cond. Outline
The quick brown fox jumps over a Dog. Zwei Boxkämpfer jagen Eva durch Sylt portez ce vieux Whiskey blond qui fume une pipe aber echt

AB2751 Mac + PC   ①   ✎ 1980: (c. 1898) G. G. Lange
Berthold AG Old Face

abcdefghijklmnopqrstuvwxyz[äöüßåøæœç]
ABCDEFGHIJKLMNOPQRSTUVWXYZ
1234567890(.,:;?!$&-*){ÄÖÜÅØÆŒÇ}

aa*a*
☞ AB6068
Berthold AG Book Stencil, et al

► Regular
The quick brown fox jumps over a Dog. Zwei Boxkämpfer jagen Eva durch Sylt portez ce vieux Whiskey blond qui fume une

► Medium
The quick brown fox jumps over a Dog. Zwei Boxkämpfer jagen Eva durch Sylt portez ce vieux Whiskey blond qui fume

► Bold
The quick brown fox jumps over a Dog. Zwei Boxkämpfer jagen Eva durch Sylt portez ce vieux Whiskey blond qui

► Outline
The quick brown fox jumps over a Dog. Zwei Boxkämpfer jagen Eva durch Sylt portez ce vieux Whiskey blond qui fume une

► Bold Outline
The quick brown fox jumps over a Dog. Zwei Boxkämpfer jagen Eva durch Sylt portez ce vieux Whiskey blond qui

► Shaded
The quick brown fox jumps over a Dog. Zwei Boxkämpfer jagen Eva durch Sylt portez ce vieux Whiskey blond qui fume

© FSI 1993

AB6068 Mac + PC ① ✏ 1984: G. G. Lange
Berthold AG Old Face Shaded

abcdefghijklmnopqrstuvwxyz[äöüßåøæœç]
ABCDEFGHIJKLMNOPQRSTUVWXYZ
1234567890(.,;:?!$&-*){ÄÖÜÅØÆŒÇ}

Berthold AG Book Stencil, et al:
Berthold AG Book Stencil, Berthold AG Old Face Shaded, Berthold Barmeno, Berthold Cosmos, Berthold Formata Outline

---

AB6082 Mac + PC ①
Berthold AG Schoolbook

abcdefghijklmnopqrstuvwxyz[äöüßåøæœç]
ABCDEFGHJJKLMNOPQRSTUVWXYZ
1234567890(.,;:?!$&-*){ÄÖÜÅØÆŒÇ}

▶ Regular
The quick brown fox jumps over a Dog. Zwei Boxkämpfer jagen Eva durch Sylt portez ce vieux Whiskey blond qui fume

▶ Regular A
The quick brown fox jumps over a Dog. Zwei Boxkämpfer jagen Eva durch Sylt portez ce vieux Whiskey blond qui

▶ Medium
The quick brown fox jumps over a Dog. Zwei Boxkämpfer jagen Eva durch Sylt portez ce vieux Whiskey blond qui

▶ Medium A
The quick brown fox jumps over a Dog. Zwei Boxkämpfer jagen Eva durch Sylt portez ce vieux Whiskey blond qui

---

AB6068 Mac + PC
Berthold AG Book Stencil, et al

Berthold AG Book Stencil, et al:
Berthold AG Book Stencil, Berthold AG Old Face Shaded, Berthold Barmeno, Berthold Cosmos, Berthold Formata Outline

---

AB6068 Mac + PC ① ✏ 1985: G. G. Lange
Berthold AG Book Stencil

abcdefghijklmnopqrstuvwxyz[äöüßåøæœç]
ABCDEFGHIJKLMNOPQRSTUVWXYZ
1234567890(.,;:?!$&-*){ÄÖÜÅØÆŒÇ}

Berthold AG Book Stencil, et al:
Berthold AG Book Stencil, Berthold AG Old Face Shaded, Berthold Barmeno, Berthold Cosmos, Berthold Formata Outline

---

G363 Mac + PC ② ✏ 1987: Jim Rimmer
Albertan™ No. 977

abcdefghijklmnopqrstuvwxyz[äöüßåøæœç]
ABCDEFGHIJKLMNOPQRSTUVWXYZ
1234567890(.,;:?!$&-*){ÄÖÜÅØÆŒÇ}

© FSI 1993 ▼

▼ G363 MAC + PC   Albertan™ No. 977

ITC Berkeley Old Style

▶ Regular
The quick brown fox jumps over a Dog. Zwei Boxkämpfer jagen Eva durch Sylt portez ce vieux Whiskey blond qui fume une pipe aber echt

▶ Italic
The quick brown fox jumps over a Dog. Zwei Boxkämpfer jagen Eva durch Sylt portez ce vieux Whiskey blond qui fume une pipe aber echt über die Mauer

▶ Regular OSF
The quick brown fox jumps over a Dog. 123 4567 890 Zwei Boxkämpfer jagen Eva durch Sylt portez ce vieux Whiskey blond qui fume

▶ Italic OSF
The quick brown fox jumps over a Dog. 123 4567 890 Zwei Boxkämpfer jagen Eva durch Sylt portez ce vieux Whiskey blond qui fume une pipe aber echt über

▶ Small Caps
THE QUICK BROWN FOX JUMPS OVER A DOG. 123 4567 890 ZWEI BOXKÄMPFER JAGEN EVA DURCH SYLT PORTEZ CE VIEUX WHISKEY BLOND QUI

▶ Small Caps Italic
THE QUICK BROWN FOX JUMPS OVER A DOG. 123 4567 890 ZWEI BOXKÄMPFER JAGEN EVA DURCH SYLT PORTEZ CE VIEUX WHISKEY BLOND QUI

G2889 MAC + PC   ② 1991: Jim Rimmer

Albertan No. 978 Bold

abcdefghijklmnopqrstuvwxyz[äöüßåøæœç]
ABCDEFGHIJKLMNOPQRSTUVWXYZ
1234567890(.,;:?!$&-*){ÄÖÜÅØÆŒÇ}

ITC Berkeley Old Style

▶ Bold
The quick brown fox jumps over a Dog. Zwei Boxkämpfer jagen Eva durch Sylt portez ce vieux Whiskey blond qui fume une

▶ Bold, Short
The quick brown fox jumps over a Dog. Zwei Boxkämpfer jagen Eva durch Sylt portez ce vieux Whiskey blond qui fume une

▶ Bold Italic
The quick brown fox jumps over a Dog. Zwei Boxkämpfer jagen Eva durch Sylt portez ce vieux Whiskey blond qui fume une pipe

▶ Bold Italic, Short
The quick brown fox jumps over a Dog. Zwei Boxkämpfer jagen Eva durch Sylt portez ce vieux Whiskey blond qui fume une pipe

G2999 MAC + PC   1992: Jim Rimmer

Albertan Inline & Titling

ABCDEFGHIJKLMNOPQRSTUVWXYZ
1234567890(.,;:?!$&-*)[]{ÄÖÜÅØÆŒÇ}

▶ Inline
THE QUICK BROWN FOX JUMPS OVER A DOG. ZWEI BOXKÄMPFER JAGEN EVA DURCH SYLT PORTEZ CE

▶ Inline Italic
THE QUICK BROWN FOX JUMPS OVER A DOG. ZWEI BOXKÄMPFER JAGEN EVA DURCH SYLT PORTEZ CE

▶ Titling
THE QUICK BROWN FOX JUMPS OVER A DOG. ZWEI BOXKÄMPFER JAGEN EVA DURCH SYLT PORTEZ CE

▶ Titling Italic
THE QUICK BROWN FOX JUMPS OVER A DOG. ZWEI BOXKÄMPFER JAGEN EVA DURCH SYLT PORTEZ CE

© FSI 1993

M550 MAC + PC (6) ✏ 1938: Berthold Wolpe
Albertus®

abcdefghijklmnopqrstuvwxyz[äöüßåøæœç]
ABCDEFGHIJKLMNOPQRSTUVWXYZ
1234567890(.,;:?!$&-*){ÄÖÜÅØÆŒÇ}

a a *a*
BT1294
Albertus, Lt, Reg, Bd
📇 A2745
Albertus/Castellar MT
👁
Bitstream Amerigo,
Friz Quadrata

▶ Light
The quick brown fox jumps over
a Dog. Zwei Boxkämpfer jagen
Eva durch Sylt portez ce vieux
Whiskey blond qui fume une

▶ Regular
The quick brown fox jumps over
a Dog. Zwei Boxkämpfer jagen
Eva durch Sylt portez ce vieux
Whiskey blond qui fume une

▶ Italic
*The quick brown fox jumps over a Dog.
Zwei Boxkämpfer jagen Eva durch Sylt
portez ce vieux Whiskey blond qui fume
une pipe aber echt über die Mauer*

Headliners 6:
Albertus®, Castellar™

BT1294 MAC + PC (6) ✏ 1938: Berthold Wolpe   Industry name
Flareserif 821   Albertus

abcdefghijklmnopqrstuvwxyz[äöüßåøæœç]
ABCDEFGHIJKLMNOPQRSTUVWXYZ
1234567890(.,;:?!$&-*){ÄÖÜÅØÆŒÇ}

a a *a*
📇 M550
Headliners 6
📇 A2745
Albertus/Castellar MT
👁
Bitstream Amerigo,
Friz Quadrata

▶ Light
The quick brown fox jumps over
a Dog. Zwei Boxkämpfer jagen
Eva durch Sylt portez ce vieux
Whiskey blond qui fume une

▶ Regular
The quick brown fox jumps
over a Dog. Zwei Boxkämpfer
jagen Eva durch Sylt portez ce
vieux Whiskey blond qui fume

▶ **Bold**
**The quick brown fox jumps
over a Dog. Zwei Boxkämpfer
jagen Eva durch Sylt portez ce
vieux Whiskey blond qui fume**

A2745 MAC + PC
Albertus/Castellar MT

Albertus/Castellar MT:
Albertus MT, Castellar

SG1645 MAC (6) ✏ 1936: Berthold Wolpe
Albertus Demi Bold

abcdefghijklmnopqrstuvwxyz[äöüßåøæœç]
ABCDEFGHIJKLMNOPQRSTUVWXYZ
1234567890(.,;:?!$&-*)ÄÖÜÅØÆŒÇ

© FSI 1993

SG1647 Mac ⑥ ✏ 1936: Berthold Wolpe
Albertus Extra Bold

abcdefghijklmnopqrstuvwxyz[äöüßåøæœç]
ABCDEFGHIJKLMNOPQRSTUVWXYZ
1234567890(.,;:?!$&-*)ÄÖÜÅØÆŒÇ

SG1648 Mac ⑥ ✏ 1936: Berthold Wolpe
Albertus Outline

abcdefghijklmnopqrstuvwxyz[äöüßåøæœç]
ABCDEFGHIJKLMNOPQRSTUVWXYZ
1234567890(.,;:?!$&-*)ÄÖÜÅØÆŒÇ

C594 Mac + PC ⑤ ✏ 1935: Walter Huxley
Aldous™ Vertical

ABCDEFGHIJKLMNOPQRSTUVWXYZ
1234567890(.,;:?!$&-*)[]{ÄÖÜÅØÆŒÇ}

Aldous:
Aldous™ Vertical, Aura, Computer, Eccentric™
👁 Regency Gothic, Huxley Vertical, Phenix American, De Stijl, Bureau Agency

C594 Mac + PC
Aldous

Aldous:
Aldous™ Vertical, Aura, Computer, Eccentric™

A2774 Mac + PC ② ✏ 1954: Hermann Zapf
Aldus™

abcdefghijklmnopqrstuvwxyz[äöüßåøæœç]
ABCDEFGHIJKLMNOPQRSTUVWXYZ
1234567890(.,;:?!$&-*){ÄÖÜÅØÆŒÇ}

👁
Palatino, Zapf
Renaissance

▶ Regular
The quick brown fox jumps over a Dog. Zwei Boxkämpfer jagen Eva durch Sylt portez ce vieux Whiskey blond qui fume une

▶ Regular Small Caps
THE QUICK BROWN FOX JUMPS OVER A DOG. 123 4567 890 ZWEI BOXKÄMPFER JAGEN EVA DURCH SYLT PORTEZ CE VIEUX WHISKEY

▶ Italic
The quick brown fox jumps over a Dog. Zwei Boxkämpfer jagen Eva durch Sylt portez ce vieux Whiskey blond qui fume une

▶ Italic OSF
The quick brown fox jumps over a Dog. 123 4567 890 Zwei Boxkämpfer jagen Eva durch Sylt portez ce vieux Whiskey blond

© FSI 1993

L2815 Mac (6) — 1988: Philip Kelly
Algerian™ Condensed

ABCDEFGHIJKLMNOPQRSTUVWXYZ
1234567890(.,;:?!$&-*)[]ÄÖÜÅØÆŒÇ

BT2872 Mac + PC (6) — 1937: Hans Bohn
Allegro™

abcdefghijklmnopqrstuvwxyz[äöüßåøæœç]
ABCDEFGHIJKLMNOPQRSTUVWXYZ
1234567890(.,;:?!$&-*){ÄÖÜÅØÆŒÇ}

EF6439 Mac + PC (1) — 1903: M. F. Benton
Alternate™ Gothic

abcdefghijklmnopqrstuvwxyz[äöüßåøæœç]
ABCDEFGHIJKLMNOPQRSTUVWXYZ
1234567890(.,;:?!$&-*){ÄÖÜÅØÆŒÇ}

aa*a*
BT783
BT Condensed
Headlines 2
News Gothic, Trade Gothic

▶ No. One
The quick brown fox jumps over a Dog. Zwei Boxkämpfer jagen Eva durch Sylt portez ce vieux Whiskey blond qui fume une pipe aber echt über die Mauer gesprungen und auch smørebrød en ysjes

▶ No. Two
The quick brown fox jumps over a Dog. Zwei Boxkämpfer jagen Eva durch Sylt portez ce vieux Whiskey blond qui fume une pipe aber echt über die Mauer gesprungen und auch

▶ No. Three
The quick brown fox jumps over a Dog. Zwei Boxkämpfer jagen Eva durch Sylt portez ce vieux Whiskey blond qui fume une pipe aber echt über die Mauer gesprungen

M880 Mac + PC (3) — 1990: Ron Carpenter
Amasis™

abcdefghijklmnopqrstuvwxyz[äöüßåøæœç]
ABCDEFGHIJKLMNOPQRSTUVWXYZ
1234567890(.,;:?!$&-*){ÄÖÜÅØÆŒÇ}

▶ Regular
The quick brown fox jumps over a Dog. Zwei Boxkämpfer jagen Eva durch Sylt portez ce vieux Whiskey blond qui fume une

▶ *Italic*
The quick brown fox jumps over a Dog. Zwei Boxkämpfer jagen Eva durch Sylt portez ce vieux Whiskey blond qui fume une pipe aber echt

▶ **Bold**
The quick brown fox jumps over a Dog. Zwei Boxkämpfer jagen Eva durch Sylt portez ce vieux Whiskey blond

▶ ***Bold Italic***
The quick brown fox jumps over a Dog. Zwei Boxkämpfer jagen Eva durch Sylt portez ce vieux Whiskey blond qui fume

© FSI 1993

Amasis Light
M1614　Mac + PC　③　1992: Ron Carpenter

abcdefghijklmnopqrstuvwxyz[äöüßåøæœç]
ABCDEFGHIJKLMNOPQRSTUVWXYZ
1234567890(.,;:?!$&-*){ÄÖÜÅØÆŒÇ}

▶ Light
The quick brown fox jumps over a Dog. Zwei Boxkämpfer jagen Eva durch Sylt portez ce vieux Whiskey blond qui fume une pipe aber

▶ Light Italic
The quick brown fox jumps over a Dog. Zwei Boxkämpfer jagen Eva durch Sylt portez ce vieux Whiskey blond qui fume une pipe aber echt

▶ Medium
The quick brown fox jumps over a Dog. Zwei Boxkämpfer jagen Eva durch Sylt portez ce vieux Whiskey blond qui fume

▶ Medium Italic
The quick brown fox jumps over a Dog. Zwei Boxkämpfer jagen Eva durch Sylt portez ce vieux Whiskey blond qui fume une

▶ Black
The quick brown fox jumps over a Dog. Zwei Boxkämpfer jagen Eva durch Sylt portez ce vieux

▶ Black Italic
The quick brown fox jumps over a Dog. Zwei Boxkämpfer jagen Eva durch Sylt portez ce vieux Whiskey blond

Amazone™
BT848　Mac + PC　④　1958: L. H. D. Smith

abcdefghijklmnopqrstuvwxyz[äöüßåøæœç]
ABCDEFGHIJKLMNOPQRSTUVWXYZ
1234567890(.,;:?!$&-){ÄÖÜÅØÆŒÇ}*

Bitstream Script 1:
Amazone™, Monterey, Piranesi™ Italic

Amelia™
BT781　Mac + PC　⑥　1967: Stanley Davis

abcdefghijklmnopqrstuvwxyz[äöüßåøæœç]
ABCDEFGHIJKLMNOPQRSTUVWXYZ
1234567890(.,;:?!$&-*){ÄÖÜÅØÆŒÇ}

Bitstream Computer:
Amelia™, Orbit-B™

American Text™
BT798　Mac + PC　⑦　1932: M. F. Benton

abcdefghijklmnopqrstuvwxyz[äöüßåøæœç]
ABCDEFGHIJKLMNOPQRSTUVWXYZ
1234567890(.,;:?!$&-*){ÄÖÜÅØÆŒÇ}

© FSI 1993

▼ BT798 Mac + PC **American Text™**

Bitstream Fraktur 1:
American Text™, Cloister Black, Fraktur, London Text™

BT1227 Mac + PC ② 🖉 1965: Richard Isbell, Whedon Davis
Americana™

abcdefghijklmnopqrstuvwxyz[äöüßåøæœç]
ABCDEFGHIJKLMNOPQRSTUVWXYZ
1234567890(.,;:?!$&-*){ÄÖÜÅØÆŒÇ}

aa*a*
A004
Americana, Reg, Ita, Bd, ExtBd

▶ Regular
The quick brown fox jumps over a Dog. Zwei Boxkämpfer jagen Eva durch Sylt portez ce vieux Whis-

▶ *Italic*
The quick brown fox jumps over a Dog. Zwei Boxkämpfer jagen Eva durch Sylt portez ce vieux Whis-

▶ **Bold**
The quick brown fox jumps over a Dog. Zwei Boxkämpfer jagen Eva durch Sylt portez ce vieux

▶ **Extra Bold**
The quick brown fox jumps over a Dog. Zwei Boxkämpfer jagen Eva durch Sylt portez ce vieux

---

BT782 Mac + PC ② 🖉 1965: Richard Isbell, Whedon Davis
Americana Extra Bold Condensed

**abcdefghijklmnopqrstuvwxyz[äöüßåøæœç]
ABCDEFGHIJKLMNOPQRSTUVWXYZ
1234567890(.,;:?!$&-*){ÄÖÜÅØÆŒÇ}**

BT Condensed Headlines 1:
Americana, Serifa 67 Bold Condensed
aa*a* A004
Americana, Reg, Ita, Bd, ExtBd

A003 Mac + PC ③ 🖉 1974: Joel Kaden, Tony Stan
ITC American Typewriter + ITC Machine

ITC American Typewriter + ITC Machine:
ITC American Typewriter, ITC Machine Bold
👁 Courier, Monantı, Olympia, Schreibmaschinenschrift, Prestige, Typewriter, Pica

---

A2540 Mac + PC ③ 🖉 1974: Joel Kaden, Tony Stan
ITC American Typewriter®

abcdefghijklmnopqrstuvwxyz[äöüßåøæœç]
ABCDEFGHIJKLMNOPQRSTUVWXYZ
1234567890(.,;:?!$&-*){ÄÖÜÅØÆŒÇ}

aa*a*
EF365
ITC American Typewriter 1, Lt, Med, Bd
EF367
ITC American Typewriter 3, LtCon, MedCon, BdCon
BT1225
ITC American Typewriter, Lt, Med, Bd
BT1226
ITC American Typewriter Condensed, LtCon, MedCon, BdCon

▶ Light
The quick brown fox jumps over a Dog. Zwei Boxkämpfer jagen Eva durch Sylt portez ce vieux Whiskey

▶ Light Alternate
The quick brown fox jumps over a Dog. Zwei Boxkämpfer jagen Eva durch Sylt portez ce vieux Whiskey

© FSI 1993

▼ A2540 Mac + PC ITC American Typewriter®

Courier, Monanti, Olympia, Schreibmaschinenschrift, Prestige, Typewriter, Pica

▶ Medium
The quick brown fox jumps over a Dog. Zwei Boxkämpfer jagen Eva durch Sylt portez ce vieux

▶ Medium Alternate
The quick brown fox jumps over a Dog. Zwei Boxkämpfer jagen Eva durch Sylt portez ce vieux Whiskey

▶ Bold
The quick brown fox jumps over a Dog. Zwei Boxkämpfer jagen Eva durch Sylt portez ce

▶ Bold Alternate
The quick brown fox jumps over a Dog. Zwei Boxkämpfer jagen Eva durch Sylt portez ce vieux

▶ Light Condensed
The quick brown fox jumps over a Dog. Zwei Boxkämpfer jagen Eva durch Sylt portez ce vieux Whiskey blond qui fume une pipe aber echt

▶ Light Condensed Alternate
The quick brown fox jumps over a Dog. Zwei Boxkämpfer jagen Eva durch Sylt portez ce vieux Whiskey blond qui fume une pipe aber echt

▶ Medium Condensed
The quick brown fox jumps over a Dog. Zwei Boxkämpfer jagen Eva durch Sylt portez ce vieux Whiskey blond qui fume une pipe aber

▶ Medium Condensed Alternate
The quick brown fox jumps over a Dog. Zwei Boxkämpfer jagen Eva durch Sylt portez ce vieux Whiskey blond qui fume une pipe aber

▶ Bold Condensed
The quick brown fox jumps over a Dog. Zwei Boxkämpfer jagen Eva durch Sylt portez ce vieux Whiskey blond qui fume une pipe aber

▶ Bold Condensed Alternate
The quick brown fox jumps over a Dog. Zwei Boxkämpfer jagen Eva durch Sylt portez ce vieux Whiskey blond qui fume une pipe aber

EF366 Mac + PC ③ 1989: Ed Benguiat
ITC American Typewriter 2

abcdefghijklmnopqrstuvwxyz[äöüßåøæœç]
ABCDEFGHIJKLMNOPQRSTUVWXYZ
1234567890(.,;:?!$&-*){ÄÖÜÅØÆŒÇ}

Courier, Monanti, Olympia, Schreibmaschinenschrift, Prestige, Typewriter, Pica

▶ Light Italic
The quick brown fox jumps over a Dog. Zwei Boxkämpfer jagen Eva durch Sylt portez ce vieux Whiskey blond qui

▶ Medium Italic
The quick brown fox jumps over a Dog. Zwei Boxkämpfer jagen Eva durch Sylt portez ce vieux Whiskey

▶ Bold Italic
The quick brown fox jumps over a Dog. Zwei Boxkämpfer jagen Eva durch Sylt portez ce vieux Whis-

MC6357 Mac + PC ⑥ (Victor Hammer)
American Uncial™

abcdefghijklmnopqrstuvwxyz[äöüßåøæœç]
ABCDEFGHIJKLMNOPQRSTUVWXYZ
1234567890(.,;:?!$&-*){ÄÖÜÅØÆŒÇ}

© FSI 1993

BT746 Mac + PC ② 1987: Gerard Unger
Bitstream Amerigo™ 1

abcdefghijklmnopqrstuvwxyz[äöüßåøæœç]
ABCDEFGHIJKLMNOPQRSTUVWXYZ
1234567890(.,;:?!$&-*){ÄÖÜÅØÆŒÇ}

Albertus, Friz Quadrata

▶ Regular
The quick brown fox jumps over a Dog. Zwei Boxkämpfer jagen Eva durch Sylt portez ce vieux Whiskey blond qui fume une pipe

▶ Italic
The quick brown fox jumps over a Dog. Zwei Boxkämpfer jagen Eva durch Sylt portez ce vieux Whiskey blond qui fume une pipe aber echt

▶ Bold
The quick brown fox jumps over a Dog. Zwei Boxkämpfer jagen Eva durch Sylt portez ce vieux Whiskey blond qui fume une

▶ Bold Italic
The quick brown fox jumps over a Dog. Zwei Boxkämpfer jagen Eva durch Sylt portez ce vieux Whiskey blond qui fume une pipe aber echt

BT755 Mac + PC ② 1987: Gerard Unger
Bitstream Amerigo 2

abcdefghijklmnopqrstuvwxyz[äöüßåøæœç]
ABCDEFGHIJKLMNOPQRSTUVWXYZ
1234567890(.,;:?!$&-*){ÄÖÜÅØÆŒÇ}

Albertus, Friz Quadrata

▶ Medium
The quick brown fox jumps over a Dog. Zwei Boxkämpfer jagen Eva durch Sylt portez ce vieux Whiskey blond qui fume une

▶ Medium Italic
The quick brown fox jumps over a Dog. Zwei Boxkämpfer jagen Eva durch Sylt portez ce vieux Whiskey blond qui fume une pipe aber echt

C2521 Mac + PC ④ 1989: Arthur Baker
Amigo™

abcdefghijklmnopqrstuvwxyz[äöüßåøæœç]
ABCDEFGHIJKLMNOPQRSTUVWXYZ
1234567890(.,;:?!$&-*){ÄÖÜÅØÆŒÇ}

Amigo:
Amigo™, Marigold™, Oxford™, Pelican™, Visigoth

C2521 Mac + PC ⑥
Amigo

Amigo:
Amigo™, Marigold™, Oxford™, Pelican™, Visigoth

© FSI 1993

MC6354 Mac + PC ⑥ ✎ K. Kochnowicz
Anatol™

abcdefghijklmnopqrstuvwxyz
1234567890(.,;:?!$£-*){äöüåoœ}

EF498 Mac + PC ① ✎ Erwin Koch
Angro™

abcdefghijklmnopqrstuvwxyz[äöüßåøæœç]
ABCDEFGHIJKLMNOPQRSTUVWXYZ
1234567890(,;:?!$&*){ÄÖÜÅØÆŒÇ}

Abadi, Avenir

▶ Light
The quick brown fox jumps over a Dog. Zwei Boxkämpfer jagen Eva durch Sylt portez ce vieux Whiskey blond qui fume une

▶ Bold
The quick brown fox jumps over a Dog. Zwei Boxkämpfer jagen Eva durch Sylt portez ce vieux Whiskey blond qui fume

EF981 Mac + PC ⑥ ✎ 1990: Daniel Pelavin
ITC Anna™

ABCDEFGHIJKLMNOPQRSTUVWXYZ
1234567890(.,;:?!$&-*)[]{ÄÖÜÅØÆŒÇ}

ITC Anna™, ITC Mona Lisa Recut™
aaa ⌸ C2979
ITC Typographica™

© Bodega, Romeo, Triplex Condensed, Triplex Serif Condensed

EF6440 Mac + PC ⑥
Annlie™

abcdefghijklmnopqrstuvwxyz[äöüßåoæœç]
ABCDEFGHIJKLMNOPQRSTUVWXYZ
1234567890(.,;:?!$&-*)ÄÖÜÅOÆŒÇ

Normande

▶ Extra Bold
The quick brown fox jumps over a Dog. Zwei Boxkämpfer jagen Eva durch Sylt portez ce vieux Whiskey blond qui

▶ Extra Bold Italic
The quick brown fox jumps over a Dog. Zwei Boxkämpfer jagen Eva durch Sylt portez ce vieux Whiskey

F6344 Mac ③ ✎ 1990: (George Nesbitt, 1838) Peter Fraterdeus
Antique Condensed

ABCDEFGHIJKLMNOPQRSTUVWXYZ
1234567890(.,;:?!$&-*)[]{}

A*I Wood Types 1:
A*I Barrel, A*I Box Gothic, A*I French XXX Condensed™, A*I Painter™, A*I Tuscan Egyptian™, Antique Condensed
© Schadow

© FSI 1993

BT809 MAC + PC ③ Industry name
Egyptian 710 Antique No. 3™

abcdefghijklmnopqrstuvwxyz[äöüßåøæœç]
ABCDEFGHIJKLMNOPQRSTUVWXYZ
1234567890(.,;:?!$&-*){ÄÖÜÅØÆŒÇ}

Bitstream Headlines 3:
Antique No. 3™, Futura Black
© Belizio, Clarendon, Egyptian

A162 MAC + PC ① 1962-68: Roger Excoffon
Antique Olive™

abcdefghijklmnopqrstuvwxyz[äöüßåøæœç]
ABCDEFGHIJKLMNOPQRSTUVWXYZ
1234567890(.,;:?!$&-*){ÄÖÜÅØÆŒÇ}

a a *a*
BT1338
Antique Olive 1, Lt,
Reg, Ita, Bd, Blk
C005
Antique Olive™, Reg,
Ita, Med, MedIta

▶ Light
The quick brown fox jumps over a Dog. Zwei Boxkämpfer jagen Eva durch Sylt portez ce vieux Whiskey blond qui

▶ Regular
The quick brown fox jumps over a Dog. Zwei Boxkämpfer jagen Eva durch Sylt portez ce vieux Whiskey

▶ Italic
The quick brown fox jumps over a Dog. Zwei Boxkämpfer jagen Eva durch Sylt portez ce vieux Whiskey

▶ Bold
The quick brown fox jumps over a Dog. Zwei Boxkämpfer jagen Eva durch Sylt portez ce vieux

▶ Black
The quick brown fox jumps over a Dog. Zwei Boxkämpfer jagen Eva durch Sylt portez ce

---

A348 MAC + PC ① 1962-68: Roger Excoffon
Antique Olive 2

abcdefghijklmnopqrstuvwxyz[äöüßåøæœç]
ABCDEFGHIJKLMNOPQRSTUVWXYZ
1234567890(.,;:?!$&-*){ÄÖÜÅØÆŒÇ}

a a *a*
BT1339
Antique Olive 2,
BdCon, Cmp, Nrd,
NrdIta

▶ Bold Condensed
The quick brown fox jumps over a Dog. Zwei Boxkämpfer jagen Eva durch Sylt portez ce vieux Whiskey blond qui fume une pipe aber echt

▶ Compact
The quick brown fox jumps over a Dog. Zwei Boxkämpfer jagen Eva durch Sylt

▶ Nord
The quick brown fox jumps over a Dog. Zwei Boxkämpfer jagen

▶ Nord Italic
The quick brown fox jumps over a Dog. Zwei Boxkämpfer jagen Eva

© FSI 1993

C005 Mac + PC ① 🖉 1962–68: Roger Excoffon
Antique Olive™

abcdefghijklmnopqrstuvwxyz[äöüßåøæœç]
ABCDEFGHIJKLMNOPQRSTUVWXYZ
1234567890(.,;:?!$&-*){ÄÖÜÅØÆŒÇ}

aa*a*
A162
Antique Olive™, Lt, Reg, Ita, Bd, Blk
BT1338
Antique Olive 1, Lt, Reg, Ita, Bd, Blk

▶ Regular
The quick brown fox jumps over a Dog. Zwei Boxkämpfer jagen Eva durch Sylt portez ce vieux

▶ Italic
The quick brown fox jumps over a Dog. Zwei Boxkämpfer jagen Eva durch Sylt portez ce vieux

▶ Medium
The quick brown fox jumps over a Dog. Zwei Boxkämpfer jagen Eva durch Sylt portez ce vieux

▶ Medium Italic
The quick brown fox jumps over a Dog. Zwei Boxkämpfer jagen Eva durch Sylt portez ce vieux

SG1663 Mac ① 🖉 1962–68: Roger Excoffon
Antique Olive Extended

abcdefghijklmnopqrstuvwxyz[äöüßåøæœç]
ABCDEFGHIJKLMNOPQRSTUVWXYZ
1234567890(.,;:?!$&-*)ÄÖÜÅØÆŒÇ

C2780 Mac + PC ⑥ 🖉
Antique Roman

abcdefghijklmnopqrstuvwxyz[äöüßåç]
ABCDEFGHIJKLMNOPQRSTUVWXYZ
1234567890(.,;:?!$&-*){ÄÖÜÅthstÇ}

▶ Solid
The quick brown fox jumps over a Dog. Zwei Boxkämpfer jagen Eva durch Sylt portez ce vieux Whiskey blond qui fume une pipe aber echt über die Mauer gesprungen

▶ Slanted
The quick brown fox jumps over a Dog. Zwei Boxkämpfer jagen Eva durch Sylt portez ce vieux Whiskey blond qui fume une pipe aber echt

Agfa Engravers 1:
Antique Roman, Artisan Roman, Burin Roman, Burin Sans, Classic Roman, Handle Old Style, Roman

A6725 Mac + PC ② 🖉 1964: Adrian Frutiger
Apollo™

abcdefghijklmnopqrstuvwxyz[äöüßåøæœç]
ABCDEFGHIJKLMNOPQRSTUVWXYZ
1234567890(.,;:?!$&-*){ÄÖÜÅØÆŒÇ}

aa*a*
M186
Apollo™, Reg, Ita, SemBd

▶ Regular
The quick brown fox jumps over a Dog. Zwei Boxkämpfer jagen Eva durch Sylt portez ce vieux Whiskey blond qui fume une

▶ Italic
The quick brown fox jumps over a Dog. Zwei Boxkämpfer jagen Eva durch Sylt portez ce vieux Whiskey blond qui fume une pipe aber echt

© FSI 1993

▼ A6725 Mac + PC Apollo™

▶ Semi Bold
The quick brown fox jumps over a Dog. Zwei Boxkämpfer jagen Eva durch Sylt portez ce vieux Whiskey blond qui fume

▶ Small Caps
The quick brown fox jumps over a Dog. 123 4567 890 Zwei Boxkämpfer jagen Eva durch Sylt portez ce vieux Whiskey blond

▶ Italic OSF
The quick brown fox jumps over a Dog. 123 4567 890 Zwei Boxkämpfer jagen Eva durch Sylt portez ce vieux Whiskey blond qui

▶ Semi Bold OSF
The quick brown fox jumps over a Dog. 123 4567 890 Zwei Boxkämpfer jagen Eva durch Sylt portez ce vieux Whiskey

▶ Expert
0123456789 fffiflffiffl-(½⅓¼⅕⅙⅐⅛⅑⅒/₁₂₃₄₅₆₇₈₉₀)$¢Rp₵)ª
THE QUICK BROWN FOX JUMPS OVER A DOG ZWEI BOXKÄMPFER JAGEN

▶ Italic Expert
0123456789 fffiflffiffl-(½⅓¼⅕⅙⅐⅛⅑⅒/₁₂₃₄₅₆₇₈₉₀)$¢Rp₵)ª

▶ Semi Bold Expert
0123456789 fffiflffiffl-(½⅓¼⅕⅙⅐⅛⅑⅒/₁₂₃₄₅₆₇₈₉₀)$¢Rp₵)ª

C178 Mac + PC
Aquarius

Aquarius:
Aquarius™ No. 8, Clarendon Book Condensed, Poster Bodoni

C178 Mac + PC ⑤
Aquarius™ No. 8

abcdefghijklmnopqrstuvwxyz[äöüßåøæœç]
ABCDEFGHIJKLMNOPQRSTUVWXYZ
1234567890(.,;:?!$&-*){ÄÖÜÅØÆŒÇ}

Aquarius:
Aquarius™ No. 8, Clarendon Book Condensed, Poster Bodoni

L2816 Mac ⑥ ✎ 1989: David Quay
Aquinas

abcdefghijklmnopqrstuvwxyz[äöüßåøæœç]
ABCDEFGHIJKLMNOPQRSTUVWXYZ
1234567890(.,;:?!$&-)ÄÖÜÅØÆŒÇ*

© FSI 1993

L6112 MAC ⑥ ✎ 1987: Steven Albert
Aquitaine™ Initials

ABCDEFGHIJKLMNOPQRSTUVWXYZ
1234567890(.,;:?!$&-*)[]ÄÖÜÅØÆŒÇ

E2993 MAC + PC ⑤ ✎ 1992: Jeffrey Keedy
Arbitrary™ Sans

abcdefghijklmnopqrstuvwxyz[äöüßåøæœç]
ABCDEFGHIJKLMNOPQRSTUVWXYZ
1234567890 (.,;:?!$&-*){ÄÖÜÅØÆŒÇ}

▶ Regular
The quick brown fox jumps over a Dog. Zwei Boxkämpfer jagen Eva durch Sylt portez ce vieux Whiskey blond qui fume une pipe

▶ Bold
The quick brown fox jumps over a Dog. Zwei Boxkämpfer jagen Eva durch Sylt portez ce vieux Whiskey blond qui fume une

A652 MAC + PC ⑥ ✎ 1990: Neville Brody
Arcadia™

abcdefghijklmnopqrstuvwxyz1234567890[äöüßåøæœç]
ABCDEFGHIJKLMNOPQRSTUVWXYZ(.,;:?!$&-*){ÄÖÜÅØÆŒÇ}

▶ Regular
The quick brown fox jumps over a Dog. Zwei Boxkämpfer jagen Eva durch Sylt portez ce vieux Whiskey blond qui fume une pipe aber echt über die Mauer gesprungen und auch smorebrod en ysjes natuurlijk. But very long spazierende tekst ist used in dieser catalog waar nicht

▶ Alternates
The quick brown fox jumps over a Dog. Zwei Boxkämpfer jagen Eva durch Sylt portez ce vieux Whiskey blond qui fume une pipe aber echt über die Mauer gesprungen und auch smorebrod en ysjes natuurlijk. The quick brown fox jumps over a Dog. Zwei Boxkämpfer jagen Eva durch Sylt portez ce vieux

Industria:
Arcadia™, Industria™, Insignia™

TF2791 MAC + PC ② ✎ 1992: Joseph Treacy
TF Ardent™ A

abcdefghijklmnopqrstuvwxyz[äöüßåøæœç]
ABCDEFGHIJKLMNOPQRSTUVWXYZ
1234567890(.,;:?!$&-*){ÄÖÜÅØÆŒÇ}

▶ Regular
The quick brown fox jumps over a Dog. Zwei Boxkämpfer jagen Eva durch Sylt portez ce vieux Whiskey blond qui fume

▶ Italic
The quick brown fox jumps over a Dog. Zwei Boxkämpfer jagen Eva durch Sylt portez ce vieux Whiskey blond qui fume une pipe aber echt über die

▶ Extra Bold
The quick brown fox jumps over a Dog. Zwei Boxkämpfer jagen Eva durch Sylt portez ce vieux

▶ Extra Bold Italic
The quick brown fox jumps over a Dog. Zwei Boxkämpfer jagen Eva durch Sylt portez ce vieux Whiskey blond qui fume une

© FSI 1993

M006 Mac + PC ①
Arial® 1

abcdefghijklmnopqrstuvwxyz[äöüßåøæœç]
ABCDEFGHIJKLMNOPQRSTUVWXYZ
1234567890(.,;:?!$&-*){ÄÖÜÅØÆŒÇ}

Helvetica, Unica, News Gothic, Vectora, Univers

▶ Regular
The quick brown fox jumps over a Dog. Zwei Boxkämpfer jagen Eva durch Sylt portez ce vieux Whiskey blond qui fume

▶ Italic
The quick brown fox jumps over a Dog. Zwei Boxkämpfer jagen Eva durch Sylt portez ce vieux Whiskey blond qui fume

▶ Bold
The quick brown fox jumps over a Dog. Zwei Boxkämpfer jagen Eva durch Sylt portez ce vieux Whiskey blond

▶ Bold Italic
The quick brown fox jumps over a Dog. Zwei Boxkämpfer jagen Eva durch Sylt portez ce vieux Whiskey blond

M187 Mac + PC ①
Arial 2

abcdefghijklmnopqrstuvwxyz[äöüßåøæœç]
ABCDEFGHIJKLMNOPQRSTUVWXYZ
1234567890(.,;:?!$&-*){ÄÖÜÅØÆŒÇ}

Helvetica, Unica, News Gothic, Vectora, Univers

▶ Light
The quick brown fox jumps over a Dog. Zwei Boxkämpfer jagen Eva durch Sylt portez ce vieux Whiskey blond qui fume

▶ Light Italic
The quick brown fox jumps over a Dog. Zwei Boxkämpfer jagen Eva durch Sylt portez ce vieux Whiskey blond qui fume

▶ Black
The quick brown fox jumps over a Dog. Zwei Boxkämpfer jagen Eva durch Sylt portez ce

▶ Black Italic
The quick brown fox jumps over a Dog. Zwei Boxkämpfer jagen Eva durch Sylt portez ce

M649 Mac + PC ①
Arial 3

abcdefghijklmnopqrstuvwxyz[äöüßåøæœç]
ABCDEFGHIJKLMNOPQRSTUVWXYZ
1234567890(.,;:?!$&-*){ÄÖÜÅØÆŒÇ}

Helvetica, Unica, News Gothic, Vectora, Univers

▶ Medium
The quick brown fox jumps over a Dog. Zwei Boxkämpfer jagen Eva durch Sylt portez ce vieux Whiskey blond qui

▶ Medium Italic
The quick brown fox jumps over a Dog. Zwei Boxkämpfer jagen Eva durch Sylt portez ce vieux Whiskey blond qui

▶ Extra Bold
The quick brown fox jumps over a Dog. Zwei Boxkämpfer jagen Eva durch Sylt portez ce vieux Whis-

▶ Extra Bold Italic
The quick brown fox jumps over a Dog. Zwei Boxkämpfer jagen Eva durch Sylt portez ce vieux

© FSI 1993

M188 Mac + PC ①
Arial Narrow

abcdefghijklmnopqrstuvwxyz[äöüßåøæœç]
ABCDEFGHIJKLMNOPQRSTUVWXYZ
1234567890(.,;:?!$&-*){ÄÖÜÅØÆŒÇ}

©
Helvetica, Unica, News Gothic, Vectora, Univers

▶ Regular
The quick brown fox jumps over a Dog. Zwei Boxkämpfer jagen Eva durch Sylt portez ce vieux Whiskey blond qui fume une pipe aber echt

▶ Italic
The quick brown fox jumps over a Dog. Zwei Boxkämpfer jagen Eva durch Sylt portez ce vieux Whiskey blond qui fume une pipe aber echt

▶ Bold
The quick brown fox jumps over a Dog. Zwei Boxkämpfer jagen Eva durch Sylt portez ce vieux Whiskey blond qui fume une pipe aber echt

▶ Bold Italic
The quick brown fox jumps over a Dog. Zwei Boxkämpfer jagen Eva durch Sylt portez ce vieux Whiskey blond qui fume une pipe aber echt

M368 Mac + PC ①
Arial Condensed

abcdefghijklmnopqrstuvwxyz[äöüßåøæœç]
ABCDEFGHIJKLMNOPQRSTUVWXYZ
1234567890(.,;:?!$&-*){ÄÖÜÅØÆŒÇ}

©
Helvetica, Unica, News Gothic, Vectora, Univers

▶ Light Condensed
The quick brown fox jumps over a Dog. Zwei Boxkämpfer jagen Eva durch Sylt portez ce vieux Whiskey blond qui fume une pipe aber echt über die

▶ Condensed
The quick brown fox jumps over a Dog. Zwei Boxkämpfer jagen Eva durch Sylt portez ce vieux Whiskey blond qui fume une pipe aber echt

▶ Bold Condensed
The quick brown fox jumps over a Dog. Zwei Boxkämpfer jagen Eva durch Sylt portez ce vieux Whiskey blond qui fume une pipe aber

▶ Extra Bold Condensed
The quick brown fox jumps over a Dog. Zwei Boxkämpfer jagen Eva durch Sylt portez ce vieux Whiskey blond qui fume une pipe aber

M6570 Mac + PC ①
Arial Rounded

abcdefghijklmnopqrstuvwxyz[äöüßåøæœç]
ABCDEFGHIJKLMNOPQRSTUVWXYZ
1234567890(.,;:?!$&-*){ÄÖÜÅØÆŒÇ}

©
AG Rounded, Helvetica Rounded

▶ Light
The quick brown fox jumps over a Dog. Zwei Boxkämpfer jagen Eva durch Sylt portez ce vieux Whiskey blond qui fume

▶ Regular
The quick brown fox jumps over a Dog. Zwei Boxkämpfer jagen Eva durch Sylt portez ce vieux Whiskey blond qui

▶ Bold
The quick brown fox jumps over a Dog. Zwei Boxkämpfer jagen Eva durch Sylt portez ce vieux Whiskey

▶ Extra Bold
The quick brown fox jumps over a Dog. Zwei Boxkämpfer jagen Eva durch Sylt portez ce vieux Whis-

© FSI 1993

A170 Mac + PC
Arnold Böcklin

Arnold Böcklin:
Arnold Böcklin™, Fette Fraktur™, Helvetica Inserat, Present™ Script

A170 Mac + PC ⑥
Arnold Böcklin™

abcdefghijklmnopqrstuvwxyz[äöüßåøæœç]
ABCDEFGHIJKLMNOPQRSTUVWXYZ
1234567890(.,;:?!$&-*){ÄÖÜÅØÆŒÇ}

Arnold Böcklin:
Arnold Böcklin™, Fette Fraktur™, Helvetica Inserat, Present™ Script

BT1091 Mac + PC ② 1991: Richard Lipton
Bitstream Arrus™

abcdefghijklmnopqrstuvwxyz[äöüßåøæœç]
ABCDEFGHIJKLMNOPQRSTUVWXYZ
1234567890(.,;:?!$&-*){ÄÖÜÅØÆŒÇ}

▶ Regular
The quick brown fox jumps over a Dog. Zwei Boxkämpfer jagen Eva durch Sylt portez ce vieux Whiskey blond qui

▶ Italic
The quick brown fox jumps over a Dog. Zwei Boxkämpfer jagen Eva durch Sylt portez ce vieux Whiskey blond qui fume une pipe aber

▶ Bold
The quick brown fox jumps over a Dog. Zwei Boxkämpfer jagen Eva durch Sylt portez ce vieux Whiskey

▶ Bold Italic
The quick brown fox jumps over a Dog. Zwei Boxkämpfer jagen Eva durch Sylt portez ce vieux Whiskey blond qui fume

EF6441 Mac + PC ② 1937: Gerry Powell
Arsis™

abcdefghijklmnopqrstuvwxyz[äöüßåøæœç]
ABCDEFGHIJKLMNOPQRSTUVWXYZ
1234567890(.,;:?!$&-*){ÄÖÜÅØÆŒÇ}

Onyx, Victoria Titling

▶ Regular
The quick brown fox jumps over a Dog. Zwei Boxkämpfer jagen Eva durch Sylt portez ce vieux Whiskey blond qui fume une pipe aber echt über die Mauer gesprungen und auch smørebrød en ysjes natuurlijk. Das kann ja jeder

▶ Italic
The quick brown fox jumps over a Dog. Zwei Boxkämpfer jagen Eva durch Sylt portez ce vieux Whiskey blond qui fume une pipe aber echt über die Mauer gesprungen und auch smørebrød en ysjes natuurlijk. Nun aber los und

C2782 Mac + PC ① 1991: David Quay
Letraset Arta™

abcdefghijklmnopqrstuvwxyz[äöüßåøæœç]
ABCDEFGHIJKLMNOPQRSTUVWXYZ
1234567890(.,;:?!$&-*){ÄÖÜÅØÆŒÇ}

© FSI 1993

Agfa Nadianne, Sayer Spiritual

▼ C2782 Mac + PC   Letraset Arta™

▶ Light
The quick brown fox jumps over a Dog. Zwei Boxkämpfer jagen Eva durch Sylt portez ce vieux Whiskey blond qui fume une pipe aber echt

▶ Light Italic
The quick brown fox jumps over a Dog. Zwei Boxkämpfer jagen Eva durch Sylt portez ce vieux Whiskey blond qui fume une pipe aber echt über die Mauer gesprungen und auch smørebrød en

▶ Book
The quick brown fox jumps over a Dog. Zwei Boxkämpfer jagen Eva durch Sylt portez ce vieux Whiskey blond qui fume une pipe aber

▶ Book Italic
The quick brown fox jumps over a Dog. Zwei Boxkämpfer jagen Eva durch Sylt portez ce vieux Whiskey blond qui fume une pipe aber echt über die Mauer gesprungen und auch

▶ Medium
The quick brown fox jumps over a Dog. Zwei Boxkämpfer jagen Eva durch Sylt portez ce vieux Whiskey blond qui fume une

▶ Medium Italic
The quick brown fox jumps over a Dog. Zwei Boxkämpfer jagen Eva durch Sylt portez ce vieux Whiskey blond qui fume une pipe aber echt über die Mauer

▶ Bold
The quick brown fox jumps over a Dog. Zwei Boxkämpfer jagen Eva durch Sylt portez ce vieux Whiskey blond qui

▶ Bold Italic
The quick brown fox jumps over a Dog. Zwei Boxkämpfer jagen Eva durch Sylt portez ce vieux Whiskey blond qui fume une pipe aber echt über

MC2893 Mac + PC   ⑥   M. Schmidt
Art Deco™

ABCDEFGHIJKLMNOPQRSTUVWXYZ
1234567890(.,;:?!$&-*)[]{ÄÖÜÅØÆŒÇ}

C2780 Mac + PC   ⑥
Artisan Roman

abcdefghijklmnopqrstuvwxyz[äöüßåç]
ABCDEFGHIJKLMNOPQRSTUVWXYZ
1234567890(.,;:?!$&-*){ÄÖÜÅ thst Ç}

Agfa Engravers 1:
Antique Roman, Artisan Roman, Burin Roman, Burin Sans, Classic Roman, Handle Old Style, Roman

L2557 Mac   ④   1991: Martin Wait
Artiste™

ABCDEFGHIJKLMNOPQRSTUVWXYZ
1234567890(.,;:?!$&-*)[]ÄÖÜÅØÆŒÇ

C2983 Mac + PC ⑥
Artistik™

abcdefghijklmnopqrstuvwxyz[äöüßåøæoeç]
ABCDEFGHIJKLMNOPQRSTUVWXYZ
1234567890(.,:;?!$&-*){ÄÖÜÅØÆŒÇ}

Headlines 94S:
Artistik™, Futura Black, Yearbook™

MC2894 Mac + PC ⑥ ✎ J. Dresscher
Art World™

ABCDEFGHIJKLMNOPQRSTUVWXYZ
1234567890(.,;:?!$&-*)[]{ÄÖÜÅØÆŒÇ}

C2525 Mac + PC ⑥ ✎ 1930: Ashley Havinden
Ashley Crawford™

ABCDEFGHIJKLMNOPQRSTUVWXYZ
1234567890(.,:;?!$&-*)[]{ÄÖÜÅØÆŒÇ}

Headlines 86S:
Advertisers Gothic™, Ashley Crawford™, Capone Light, Dynamo, Modernistic™

C2982 Mac + PC ⑥ ✎ 1930: Ashley Havinden
Ashley Inline

ABCDEFGHIJKLMNOPQRSTUVWXYZ
1234567890(.,;:?!$&-*)[]{ÄÖÜÅØÆŒÇ}

Headlines 93S:
Ashley Inline, Beverly Hills, Lotus™, Virile

M264 Mac + PC ④ ✎ 1956: Ashley Havinden
Ashley Script

abcdefghijklmnopqrstuvwxyz[äöüßåøæœç]
ABCDEFGHIJKLMNOPQRSTUVWXYZ
1234567890(.,;:?!$&-*){ÄÖÜÅØÆŒÇ}

Script 2:
Ashley Script, Monoline Script™, New Berolina, Palace Script™
aaa 🕮 A6335
Ashley Script et al

© FSI 1993

A6335 Mac + PC
Ashley Script et al

Ashley Script et al:
Ashley Script, Monoline Script, New Berolina, Palace Script

A237 Mac + PC ② ✏ 1982: (Francesco Simoncini, 1958)
New Aster™

abcdefghijklmnopqrstuvwxyz[äöüßåøæœç]
ABCDEFGHIJKLMNOPQRSTUVWXYZ
1234567890(.,;:?!$&-*){ÄÖÜÅØÆŒÇ}

aaa
BT747
Aster™, Reg, Ita, Bd, Bdlta

▶ Regular
The quick brown fox jumps over a Dog. Zwei Boxkämpfer jagen Eva durch Sylt portez ce vieux Whiskey blond qui

▶ Italic
The quick brown fox jumps over a Dog. Zwei Boxkämpfer jagen Eva durch Sylt portez ce vieux Whiskey blond qui fume

▶ Semi Bold
The quick brown fox jumps over a Dog. Zwei Boxkämpfer jagen Eva durch Sylt portez ce vieux Whiskey blond

▶ Semi Bold Italic
The quick brown fox jumps over a Dog. Zwei Boxkämpfer jagen Eva durch Sylt portez ce vieux Whiskey blond qui

▶ Bold
The quick brown fox jumps over a Dog. Zwei Boxkämpfer jagen Eva durch Sylt portez ce vieux Whiskey

▶ Bold Italic
The quick brown fox jumps over a Dog. Zwei Boxkämpfer jagen Eva durch Sylt portez ce vieux Whiskey

▶ Black
The quick brown fox jumps over a Dog. Zwei Boxkämpfer jagen Eva durch Sylt portez ce vieux

▶ Black Italic
The quick brown fox jumps over a Dog. Zwei Boxkämpfer jagen Eva durch Sylt portez ce vieux

ATF336 Mac
ATF Set 1

ATF Set 1:
Bernhard Fashion™, Cleland Border 1805™, Thompson Quillscript™, Wedding Text™

C2776 Mac + PC ⑥ ✏ 1945: A. Butti, A. Novarese
Athenaeum™

abcdefghijklmnopqrstuvwxyz[äöüåøæœç]
ABCDEFGHIJKLMNOPQRSTUVWXYZ
1234567890(.,;:?!$&-*)ÄÖÜÅØÆŒÇ

▶ Regular
The quick brown fox jumps over a Dog. Zwei Boxkämpfer jagen Eva durch Sylt portez ce vieux Whiskey blond qui fume une pipe aber echt

▶ Italic
The quick brown fox jumps over a Dog. Zwei Boxkämpfer jagen Eva durch Sylt portez ce vieux Whiskey blond qui fume une pipe aber echt

© FSI 1993

▼ C2776 Mac + PC   Athenaeum™

▶ Bold
The quick brown fox jumps over a Dog. Zwei Boxkämpfer jagen Eva durch Sylt portez ce vieux Whiskey blond qui fume une

▶ Initials Positive

▶ Initials Negative

Headlines 85S:
Athenaeum™

C594 Mac + PC   ①   (1928)
Aura

abcdefghijklmnopqrstuvwxyz[äöüßåøæœç]
ABCDEFGHIJKLMNOPQRSTUVWXYZ
1234567890(.,;:?!$&-*){ÄÖÜÅØÆŒÇ}

Aldous:
Aldous™ Vertical, Aura, Computer, Eccentric™
Ⓒ Aurora, Hanseatic, Hadrian, Helvetica Inserat, Helvetica Compressed, Impact, Placard

---

EF499 Mac + PC   ②   1985: Hermann Zapf
Aurelia™

abcdefghijklmnopqrstuvwxyz[äöüßåøæœç]
ABCDEFGHIJKLMNOPQRSTUVWXYZ
1234567890(.,;:?!$&-*){ÄÖÜÅØÆŒÇ}

▶ Light
The quick brown fox jumps over a Dog. Zwei Boxkämpfer jagen Eva durch Sylt portez ce vieux Whiskey blond qui fume

▶ Light Italic
The quick brown fox jumps over a Dog. Zwei Boxkämpfer jagen Eva durch Sylt portez ce vieux Whiskey blond qui fume une pipe aber echt

▶ Book
The quick brown fox jumps over a Dog. Zwei Boxkämpfer jagen Eva durch Sylt portez ce vieux Whiskey blond qui fume

▶ Book Italic
The quick brown fox jumps over a Dog. Zwei Boxkämpfer jagen Eva durch Sylt portez ce vieux Whiskey blond qui fume une pipe aber echt

▶ Bold
The quick brown fox jumps over a Dog. Zwei Boxkämpfer jagen Eva durch Sylt portez ce vieux Whiskey blond qui

© FSI 1993

A1613 Mac + PC ⑥ ✏ 1901-04: Georges Auriol
Auriol™

abcdefghijklmnopqrstuvwxyz[äöüßåøæœç]
ABCDEFGHIJKLMNOPQRSTUVWXYZ
1234567890(.,;:?!$&-*){ÄÖÜÅØÆŒÇ}

a a *a*
BT748
Auriol 1, Reg, Ita, Bd, BdIta
BT749
Auriol 2, Blk, BlkIta

▶ Regular
The quick brown fox jumps over a Dog. Zwei Boxkämpfer jagen Eva durch Sylt portez ce vieux Whiskey blond qui fume une

▶ Italic
The quick brown fox jumps over a Dog. Zwei Boxkämpfer jagen Eva durch Sylt portez ce vieux Whiskey blond qui fume une pipe aber echt

▶ Bold
The quick brown fox jumps over a Dog. Zwei Boxkämpfer jagen Eva durch Sylt portez ce vieux Whiskey blond qui fume

▶ Bold Italic
The quick brown fox jumps over a Dog. Zwei Boxkämpfer jagen Eva durch Sylt portez ce vieux Whiskey blond qui fume une

▶ Black
The quick brown fox jumps over a Dog. Zwei Boxkämpfer jagen Eva durch Sylt portez ce vieux Whiskey blond

▶ Black Italic
The quick brown fox jumps over a Dog. Zwei Boxkämpfer jagen Eva durch Sylt portez ce vieux Whiskey blond

BT751 Mac + PC ① ✏ c. 1928
Aurora Condensed

abcdefghijklmnopqrstuvwxyz[äöüßåøæœç]
ABCDEFGHIJKLMNOPQRSTUVWXYZ
1234567890(.,;:?!$&-*){ÄÖÜÅØÆŒÇ}

©
Aura, Hanseatic, Hadrian, Helvetica Inserat, Helvetica Compressed, Impact, Placard

▶ Condensed
The quick brown fox jumps over a Dog. Zwei Boxkämpfer jagen Eva durch Sylt portez ce vieux Whiskey blond qui fume une pipe aber echt über die Mauer gesprungen und auch smørebrød en ysjes natuurlijk. The quick brown fox jumps over a Dog. Zwei Boxkämp-

▶ Bold Condensed
The quick brown fox jumps over a Dog. Zwei Boxkämpfer jagen Eva durch Sylt portez ce vieux Whiskey blond qui fume une pipe aber echt

BT750 Mac + PC ③ ✏ 1960: Jackson Burke   Industry name
News 706   Aurora™

abcdefghijklmnopqrstuvwxyz[äöüßåøæœç]
ABCDEFGHIJKLMNOPQRSTUVWXYZ
1234567890(.,;:?!$&-*){ÄÖÜÅØÆŒÇ}

©
Aura, Hanseatic, Hadrian, Helvetica Inserat, Helvetica Compressed, Impact, Placard

▶ Regular
The quick brown fox jumps over a Dog. Zwei Boxkämpfer jagen Eva durch Sylt portez ce vieux Whiskey blond qui

▶ Italic
The quick brown fox jumps over a Dog. Zwei Boxkämpfer jagen Eva durch Sylt portez ce vieux Whiskey blond

▶ Bold
The quick brown fox jumps over a Dog. Zwei Boxkämpfer jagen Eva durch Sylt portez ce vieux Whiskey

© FSI 1993

A 32

BT1229 Mac + PC — 1970–77: Lubalin, Carnase; Gschwind, Gürtler, Mengelt
ITC Avant Garde Gothic® 1

abcdefghijklmnopqrstuvwxyz[äöüßåøœeç]
ABCDEFGHIJKLMNOPQRSTUVWXYZ
1234567890(.,:;?!$&-*){ÄÖÜÅØÆŒÇ}

aa*a*
EF369
ITC Avant Garde Gothic 1, ExtLt, Med, Bd
EF370
ITC Avant Garde Gothic 2, ExtLtObl, MedObl, BdObl
EF371
ITC Avant Garde Gothic 3, Bk, BkObl, Demi, DemiObl
A1531
ITC Avant Garde Gothic 2, ExtLt, ExtLtObl, Med, MedObl, Bd, BdObl

▶ Extra Light
The quick brown fox jumps over a Dog. Zwei Boxkämpfer jagen Eva durch Sylt portez ce vieux Whiskey blond qui fume une

▶ Extra Light Oblique
The quick brown fox jumps over a Dog. Zwei Boxkämpfer jagen Eva durch Sylt portez ce vieux Whiskey blond qui fume

▶ Medium
The quick brown fox jumps over a Dog. Zwei Boxkämpfer jagen Eva durch Sylt portez ce vieux Whiskey blond qui

▶ Medium Oblique
The quick brown fox jumps over a Dog. Zwei Boxkämpfer jagen Eva durch Sylt portez ce vieux Whiskey blond qui

▶ Bold
The quick brown fox jumps over a Dog. Zwei Boxkämpfer jagen Eva durch Sylt portez ce vieux Whiskey blond

▶ Bold Oblique
The quick brown fox jumps over a Dog. Zwei Boxkämpfer jagen Eva durch Sylt portez ce vieux Whiskey

BT1230 Mac + PC — 1970–77: Lubalin, Carnase; Gschwind, Gürtler, Mengelt
ITC Avant Garde Gothic 2

abcdefghijklmnopqrstuvwxyz[äöüßåøœeç]
ABCDEFGHIJKLMNOPQRSTUVWXYZ
1234567890(.,:;?!$&-*){ÄÖÜÅØÆŒÇ}

aa*a*
EF369
ITC Avant Garde Gothic 1, ExtLt, Med, Bd
EF370
ITC Avant Garde Gothic 2, ExtLtObl, MedObl, BdObl
EF371
ITC Avant Garde Gothic 3, Bk, BkObl, Demi, DemiObl
A007
ITC Avant Garde Gothic 1, Bk, BkObl, Demi, DemiObl

▶ Book
The quick brown fox jumps over a Dog. Zwei Boxkämpfer jagen Eva durch Sylt portez ce vieux Whiskey blond qui fume

▶ Book Oblique
The quick brown fox jumps over a Dog. Zwei Boxkämpfer jagen Eva durch Sylt portez ce vieux Whiskey blond qui fume

▶ Demi
The quick brown fox jumps over a Dog. Zwei Boxkämpfer jagen Eva durch Sylt portez ce vieux Whiskey blond qui

▶ Demi Oblique
The quick brown fox jumps over a Dog. Zwei Boxkämpfer jagen Eva durch Sylt portez ce vieux Whiskey blond

BT1231 Mac + PC — 1974: Ed Benguiat
ITC Avant Garde Gothic 3

abcdefghijklmnopqrstuvwxyz[äöüßåøœeç]
ABCDEFGHIJKLMNOPQRSTUVWXYZ
1234567890(.,:;?!$&-*){ÄÖÜÅØÆŒÇ}

aa*a*
EF372
ITC Avant Garde Gothic Condensed 4, BkCon, MedCon, DemiCon, BdCon
A462
ITC Avant Garde Gothic Condensed, BkCon, MedCon, DemiCon, BdCon

▶ Book Condensed
The quick brown fox jumps over a Dog. Zwei Boxkämpfer jagen Eva durch Sylt portez ce vieux Whiskey blond qui fume une pipe aber echt

▶ Medium Condensed
The quick brown fox jumps over a Dog. Zwei Boxkämpfer jagen Eva durch Sylt portez ce vieux Whiskey blond qui fume une pipe aber echt

© FSI 1993

▼ BT1231 Mac + PC ITC Avant Garde Gothic 3

▶ Demi Condensed
The quick brown fox jumps over a Dog. Zwei Boxkämpfer jagen Eva durch Sylt portez ce vieux Whiskey blond qui fume une pipe aber

▶ Bold Condensed
The quick brown fox jumps over a Dog. Zwei Boxkämpfer jagen Eva durch Sylt portez ce vieux Whiskey blond qui fume une pipe

SG1671 Mac ① 1970: Herb Lubalin, Tom Carnase
ITC Avant Garde Gothic Extra Light Alternates

SG1674 Mac ① 1970: Herb Lubalin, Tom Carnase
ITC Avant Garde Gothic Book Alternates

SG1677 Mac ① 1970: Herb Lubalin, Tom Carnase
ITC Avant Garde Gothic Medium Alternates

SG1680 Mac ① 1970: Herb Lubalin, Tom Carnase
ITC Avant Garde Gothic Demi Alternate

SG1683 Mac ① 1970: Herb Lubalin, Tom Carnase
ITC Avant Garde Gothic Bold Alternate

A159 Mac + PC ① 1988: Adrian Frutiger
Avenir™ 1

abcdefghijklmnopqrstuvwxyz[äöüßåøæœç]
ABCDEFGHIJKLMNOPQRSTUVWXYZ
1234567890(.,;:?!$&-*){ÄÖÜÅØÆŒÇ}

© Abadi, Angro

▶ Light
The quick brown fox jumps over a Dog. Zwei Boxkämpfer jagen Eva durch Sylt portez ce vieux Whiskey blond qui fume

▶ Light Oblique
The quick brown fox jumps over a Dog. Zwei Boxkämpfer jagen Eva durch Sylt portez ce vieux Whiskey blond qui fume

© FSI 1993

▼ A159　Mac + PC　Avenir™ 1

► Regular
The quick brown fox jumps over a Dog. Zwei Boxkämpfer jagen Eva durch Sylt portez ce vieux Whiskey blond qui fume

► Oblique
The quick brown fox jumps over a Dog. Zwei Boxkämpfer jagen Eva durch Sylt portez ce vieux Whiskey blond qui fume

► Heavy
The quick brown fox jumps over a Dog. Zwei Boxkämpfer jagen Eva durch Sylt portez ce vieux Whiskey blond

► Heavy Oblique
The quick brown fox jumps over a Dog. Zwei Boxkämpfer jagen Eva durch Sylt portez ce vieux Whiskey blond

A160　Mac + PC　①　🖉 1988: Adrian Frutiger
Avenir 2

abcdefghijklmnopqrstuvwxyz[äöüßåøæœç]
ABCDEFGHIJKLMNOPQRSTUVWXYZ
1234567890(.,;:?!$&-*){ÄÖÜÅØÆŒÇ}

ⓒ
Abadi, Angro

► Book
The quick brown fox jumps over a Dog. Zwei Boxkämpfer jagen Eva durch Sylt portez ce vieux Whiskey blond qui fume

► Book Oblique
The quick brown fox jumps over a Dog. Zwei Boxkämpfer jagen Eva durch Sylt portez ce vieux Whiskey blond qui fume

► Medium
The quick brown fox jumps over a Dog. Zwei Boxkämpfer jagen Eva durch Sylt portez ce vieux Whiskey blond qui fume

► Medium Oblique
The quick brown fox jumps over a Dog. Zwei Boxkämpfer jagen Eva durch Sylt portez ce vieux Whiskey blond qui fume

► Black
The quick brown fox jumps over a Dog. Zwei Boxkämpfer jagen Eva durch Sylt portez ce vieux Whiskey blond

► Black Oblique
The quick brown fox jumps over a Dog. Zwei Boxkämpfer jagen Eva durch Sylt portez ce vieux Whiskey blond

TF2890　Mac + PC　⑥
TF Avian & TF Akimbo

TF Avian & TF Akimbo:
TF Akimbo™, TF Avian™

TF2890　Mac + PC　⑥　🖉 1992: Joseph Treacy
TF Avian™

abcdefghijklmnopqrstuvwxyz[äöüßåøæœç]
ABCDEFGHIJKLMNOPQRSTUVWXYZ
1234567890(.,;:?!$&-'){ÄÖÜÅØÆŒÇ}

TF Avian & TF Akimbo:
TF Akimbo™, TF Avian™

© FSI 1993

PLEASE TURN THE PAGE

Gerard Unger, Bussum, NL

| FB6838 | Mac + PC | ⑥ | 1993: Leslie Cabarga |

BadTyp™

ABCDEFGHIJKLMNOPQRSTUVWXYZ[ÄÖÜßÅØÆŒÇ]
ABCDEFGHIJKLMNOPQRSTUVWXYZ
1234567890(.,;:?!$&-*){ÄÖÜÅØÆŒÇ}

FB Display Pack 2:
BadTyp™, Graffiti™, Hip Hop™
C▷ Ad Lib

| A1029 | Mac + PC |

Baker Signet/Impact

Baker Signet/Impact:
Baker Signet™, Impact™

| A1029 | Mac + PC | ⑥ | 1965: Arthur Baker |

Baker Signet™

abcdefghijklmnopqrstuvwxyz[äöüßåøæœç]
ABCDEFGHIJKLMNOPQRSTUVWXYZ
1234567890(.,;:?!$&-*){ÄÖÜÅØÆŒÇ}

Baker Signet/Impact:
Baker Signet™, Impact™
C▷ Signature

| BT752 | Mac + PC | ④ | 1939: Max Kaufmann |

Balloon™

ABCDEFGHIJKLMNOPQRSTUVWXYZ
1234567890(.,;:?!$&-*)[]{ÄÖÜÅØÆŒÇ}

C▷ Flash

▶ Light
THE QUICK BROWN FOX JUMPS OVER A DOG. ZWEI BOXKÄMPFER JAGEN EVA DURCH SYLT PORTEZ CE VIEUX WHISKEY BLOND QUI FUME UNE PIPE ABER ECHT

▶ Bold
THE QUICK BROWN FOX JUMPS OVER A DOG. ZWEI BOXKÄMPFER JAGEN EVA DURCH SYLT PORTEZ CE VIEUX WHISKEY BLOND QUI FUME UNE PIPE ABER ECHT

▶ Extra Bold
THE QUICK BROWN FOX JUMPS OVER A DOG. ZWEI BOXKÄMPFER JAGEN EVA DURCH SYLT PORTEZ CE VIEUX WHISKEY BLOND QUI

| L2558 | Mac | ④ | 1978: Martin Wait |

Balmoral™

abcdefghijklmnopqrstuvwxyz[äöüßåøæœç] 1234567890(.,;:?!$&-*)
ABCDEFGHIJKLM
NOPQRSTUVWXYZ

© FSI 1993

A564 Mac + PC ⑥ 1951: Roger Excoffon
Banco™

ABCDEFGHIJKLMNOPQRSTUVWXYZ
1234567890(.,;:?!$&-*)[]{ÄÖÜÅØÆŒÇ}

German Display 2:
Banco™, Charme™, Flyer™ Condensed, Wilhelm Klingspor Gotisch™
© Ritmo

BT753 Mac + PC ⑤ 1930-33: M. F. Benton
Bank Gothic™

ABCDEFGHIJKLMNOPQRSTUVWXYZ[ÄÖÜSSÅØÆŒÇ]
ABCDEFGHIJKLMNOPQRSTUVWXYZ
1234567890(.,;:?!$&-*){ÄÖÜÅØÆŒÇ}

© Geometric, FF Gothic, Neeskens

▶ Light
THE QUICK BROWN FOX JUMPS OVER A DOG. ZWEI BOXKÄMPFER JAGEN EVA DURCH SYLT PORTEZ CE

▶ Medium
THE QUICK BROWN FOX JUMPS OVER A DOG. ZWEI BOXKÄMPFER JAGEN EVA DURCH SYLT PORTEZ CE

ET1105 Mac + PC ⑦ 1989: Judith Sutcliffe
Barbara™ Sisters

ABcDefGhijklmnopqrstuvwxyz[äöüßåøæœç]
ABCDEFGhIJKLMNOPQRSTUVWXYZ
1234567890(.,;:?!$&-*)[ÄÖÜa]

▶ Barbara Svelte
The quick brown fox jumps over a Dog. Zwei Boxkämpfer jagen Eva durch Sylt portez ce

▶ Santa Barbara
The quick brown fox jumps over a Dog. Zwei Boxkämpfer jagen Eva durch Sylt

▶ Barbara Plump
The quick brown fox jumps over a Dog. Zwei Boxkämpfer jagen Eva durch Sylt

EF6442 Mac + PC ② Hans Eduard Meier
Barbedor 1

abcdefghijklmnopqrstuvwxyz[äöüßåøæœç]
ABCDEFGHIJKLMNOPQRSTUVWXYZ
1234567890(.,;:?!$&-*){ÄÖÜÅØÆŒÇ}

▶ Regular
The quick brown fox jumps over a Dog. Zwei Boxkämpfer jagen Eva durch Sylt portez ce vieux Whiskey blond qui fume une pipe aber

▶ Italic
The quick brown fox jumps over a Dog. Zwei Boxkämpfer jagen Eva durch Sylt portez ce vieux Whiskey blond qui fume une pipe aber echt

© FSI 1993

▼ EF6442 Mac + PC   Barbedor 1

▶ Bold
The quick brown fox jumps over a Dog. Zwei Boxkämpfer jagen Eva durch Sylt portez ce vieux Whiskey blond qui

▶ Bold Italic
The quick brown fox jumps over a Dog. Zwei Boxkämpfer jagen Eva durch Sylt portez ce vieux Whiskey blond qui fume

---

EF6443 Mac + PC   ② ✎ Hans Eduard Meier
Barbedor 2

abcdefghijklmnopqrstuvwxyz[äöüßåøæœç]
ABCDEFGHIJKLMNOPQRSTUVWXYZ
1234567890(.,;:?!$&-*){ÄÖÜÅØÆŒÇ}

▶ Medium
The quick brown fox jumps over a Dog. Zwei Boxkämpfer jagen Eva durch Sylt portez ce vieux Whiskey blond qui fume une

▶ Medium Italic
The quick brown fox jumps over a Dog. Zwei Boxkämpfer jagen Eva durch Sylt portez ce vieux Whiskey blond qui fume une pipe aber

▶ Black
The quick brown fox jumps over a Dog. Zwei Boxkämpfer jagen Eva durch Sylt portez ce vieux Whiskey blond

▶ Black Italic
The quick brown fox jumps over a Dog. Zwei Boxkämpfer jagen Eva durch Sylt portez ce vieux Whiskey blond

---

EF1065 Mac + PC   ⑥ ✎ 1981: Ed Benguiat
ITC Barcelona® 1

abcdefghijklmnopqrstuvwxyz[äöüßåøæœç]
ABCDEFGHIJKLMNOPQRSTUVWXYZ
1234567890(.,;:?!$&-*){ÄÖÜÅØÆŒÇ}

Ⓒ Cortez

▶ Book
The quick brown fox jumps over a Dog. Zwei Boxkämpfer jagen Eva durch Sylt portez ce vieux Whiskey

▶ Book Italic
The quick brown fox jumps over a Dog. Zwei Boxkämpfer jagen Eva durch Sylt portez ce vieux Whiskey

▶ Bold
The quick brown fox jumps over a Dog. Zwei Boxkämpfer jagen Eva durch Sylt portez ce vieux Whiskey

▶ Bold Italic
The quick brown fox jumps over a Dog. Zwei Boxkämpfer jagen Eva durch Sylt portez ce vieux Whiskey

---

EF1066 Mac + PC   ⑥ ✎ 1981: Ed Benguiat
ITC Barcelona 2

abcdefghijklmnopqrstuvwxyz[äöüßåøæœç]
ABCDEFGHIJKLMNOPQRSTUVWXYZ
1234567890(.,;:?!$&-*){ÄÖÜÅØÆŒÇ}

Ⓒ Cortez

▶ Medium
The quick brown fox jumps over a Dog. Zwei Boxkämpfer jagen Eva durch Sylt portez ce vieux

▶ Medium Italic
The quick brown fox jumps over a Dog. Zwei Boxkämpfer jagen Eva durch Sylt portez ce vieux Whiskey

© FSI 1993

▼ EF1066 Mac + PC ITC Barcelona 2

▶ Heavy
The quick brown fox jumps over a Dog. Zwei Boxkämpfer jagen Eva durch Sylt portez ce vieux

▶ Heavy Italic
The quick brown fox jumps over a Dog. Zwei Boxkämpfer jagen Eva durch Sylt portez ce vieux Whiskey

C993 Mac + PC ⑥
Barclay™ Open

abcdefghijklmnopqrstuvwxyz[äöüåøæœç]
ABCDEFGHIJKLMNOPQRSTUVWXYZ
1234567890(.,;:?!$&-*)◊ÄÖÜÅØÆŒÇ♦

Headlines 83S:
Barclay™ Open, Delphian™ Open, Fluidum™ Bold, PL Bernhardt, PL Britannia Bold, PL Fiorello™ Condensed, PL Modern Heavy Condensed, PL Torino Open
ⓒ Chevalier

AB2986 Mac + PC ① ✎ 1983: Hans Reichel
Berthold Barmeno™

abcdefghijklmnopqrstuvwxyz[äöüßåøæœç]
ABCDEFGHIJKLMNOPQRSTUVWXYZ
1234567890(.,;:?!$&-*){ÄÖÜÅØÆŒÇ}

aa*a*
AB6068
Berthold AG Book Stencil, et al

▶ Regular
The quick brown fox jumps over a Dog. Zwei Boxkämpfer jagen Eva durch Sylt portez ce vieux Whiskey blond qui fume une pipe aber

▶ Medium
The quick brown fox jumps over a Dog. Zwei Boxkämpfer jagen Eva durch Sylt portez ce vieux Whiskey blond qui fume une pipe

▶ Bold
The quick brown fox jumps over a Dog. Zwei Boxkämpfer jagen Eva durch Sylt portez ce vieux Whiskey blond qui fume une

▶ Extra Bold
The quick brown fox jumps over a Dog. Zwei Boxkämpfer jagen Eva durch Sylt portez ce vieux Whiskey blond qui fume une

C468 Mac + PC ③ ✎ 1960: Dave West
PL Barnum Block

abcdefghijklmnopqrstuvwxyz[äöüåøæœç]
ABCDEFGHIJKLMNOPQRSTUVWXYZ
1234567890(.,;:?!$&-*)◊ÄÖÜÅØÆŒÇ♦

Headlines 82S:
Neon Extra Condensed™, PL Barnum Block, PL Benguiat Frisky Bold, PL Davison Zip Bold, PL Fiedler Gothic Bold, PL Futura Maxi 2, PL Trophy™ Oblique, Ritmo™ Bold, TC Broadway
ⓒ P. T. Barnum, Egyptian, PL Behemoth

F6344 Mac ⑥
A*I Barrel

ABCDEFGHIJKLMNOPQRSTUVWXYZ[ ]
ABCDEFGHIJKLMNOPQRSTUVWXYZ
1234567890(.,:;?!$&-*){ }

A*I Wood Types 1:
A*I Barrel, A*I Box Gothic, A*I French XXX Condensed™, A*I Painter™, A*I Tuscan Egyptian™, Antique Condensed

---

C997 Mac + PC ② ✎ 1978: André Gürtler
Basilia™

abcdefghijklmnopqrstuvwxyz[äöüßåøæœç]
ABCDEFGHIJKLMNOPQRSTUVWXYZ
1234567890(.,:;?!$&-*){ÄÖÜÅØÆŒÇ}

aa*a*
SG1131
Basilia, Reg
SG1210
Basilia Italic, Ita
SG1211
Basilia Bold
SG1212
Basilia Bold Italic, BdIta
SG1132
Basilia Medium, Med
SG1213
Basilia Medium Italic, MedIta
SG1214
Basilia Black, Blk
SG1215
Basilia Black Italic, BlkIta
©
Walbaum

▶ Roman
The quick brown fox jumps over a Dog. Zwei Boxkämpfer jagen Eva durch Sylt portez ce vieux Whiskey blond qui fume

▶ Medium
The quick brown fox jumps over a Dog. Zwei Boxkämpfer jagen Eva durch Sylt portez ce vieux Whiskey blond qui

▶ Bold
The quick brown fox jumps over a Dog. Zwei Boxkämpfer jagen Eva durch Sylt portez ce vieux Whiskey blond

▶ Black
The quick brown fox jumps over a Dog. Zwei Boxkämpfer jagen Eva durch Sylt portez ce vieux Whiskey

▶ Italic
The quick brown fox jumps over a Dog. Zwei Boxkämpfer jagen Eva durch Sylt portez ce vieux Whiskey blond qui fume

▶ Medium Italic
The quick brown fox jumps over a Dog. Zwei Boxkämpfer jagen Eva durch Sylt portez ce vieux Whiskey blond

▶ Bold Italic
The quick brown fox jumps over a Dog. Zwei Boxkämpfer jagen Eva durch Sylt portez ce vieux Whiskey

▶ Black Italic
The quick brown fox jumps over a Dog. Zwei Boxkämpfer jagen Eva durch Sylt portez ce vieux Whiskey

---

C595 Mac + PC
Basilica

Basilica:
Basilica, Floridian Script, Jasper™, Liberty™

C595 Mac + PC ④
Basilica

abcdefghijklmnopqrstuvwxyz[äöüßåøæœç]
ABCDEFGHIJKLMNOPQRSTUVWXYZ
1234567890(.,:;?!$&-*){ÄÖÜÅØÆŒÇ}

© FSI 1993

B 5

▼ C595   Mac + PC   **Basilica**

Basilica:
Basilica, Floridian Script, Jasper™, Liberty™

EF1064   Mac + PC
Baskerville Old Face

Baskerville Old Face:
Baskerville Old Face™, Old Towne No 536™

EF1064   Mac + PC   ②   ✎ 1768: (Edmund Fry) Isaac Moore
Baskerville Old Face™

abcdefghijklmnopqrstuvwxyz[äöüßåøæœç]
ABCDEFGHIJKLMNOPQRSTUVWXYZ
1234567890(.,;:?!$&-*){ÄÖÜÅØÆŒÇ}

Baskerville Old Face:
Baskerville Old Face™, Old Towne No 536™
aaa ☞ BT807
Bitstream Headlines 1

BT807   Mac + PC   ②   ✎ 1768: (Edmund Fry) Isaac Moore
Fry's Baskerville™

abcdefghijklmnopqrstuvwxyz[äöüßåøæœç]
ABCDEFGHIJKLMNOPQRSTUVWXYZ
1234567890(.,;:?!$&-*){ÄÖÜÅØÆŒÇ}

Bitstream Headlines 1:
Eckmann™, Fry's Baskerville™, Libra™
aaa ☞ EF1064
Baskerville Old Face

AB1528   Mac + PC   ②   ✎ 1980-83: (John Baskerville, 1757) G. G. Lange
Berthold Baskerville Book™

abcdefghijklmnopqrstuvwxyz[äöüßåøæœç]
ABCDEFGHIJKLMNOPQRSTUVWXYZ
1234567890(.,;:?!$&-*){ÄÖÜÅØÆŒÇ}

▶ Regular
The quick brown fox jumps over a Dog. Zwei Boxkämpfer jagen Eva durch Sylt portez ce vieux Whiskey blond qui fume une

▶ Italic
The quick brown fox jumps over a Dog. Zwei Boxkämpfer jagen Eva durch Sylt portez ce vieux Whiskey blond qui fume une pipe aber echt über

▶ Medium
The quick brown fox jumps over a Dog. Zwei Boxkämpfer jagen Eva durch Sylt portez ce vieux Whiskey blond qui fume

▶ Medium Italic
The quick brown fox jumps over a Dog. Zwei Boxkämpfer jagen Eva durch Sylt portez ce vieux Whiskey blond qui fume une pipe

© FSI 1993

AB6379 Mac + PC　②　✎ 1980-83: (John Baskerville, 1757) G. G. Lange
Berthold Baskerville

abcdefghijklmnopqrstuvwxyz[äöüßåøæœç]
ABCDEFGHIJKLMNOPQRSTUVWXYZ
1234567890(.,;:?!$&-*){ÄÖÜÅØÆŒÇ}

▶ Regular
The quick brown fox jumps over a Dog. Zwei Boxkämpfer jagen Eva durch Sylt portez ce vieux Whiskey blond qui fume

▶ Italic
The quick brown fox jumps over a Dog. Zwei Boxkämpfer jagen Eva durch Sylt portez ce vieux Whiskey blond qui fume une pipe aber echt

▶ Medium
The quick brown fox jumps over a Dog. Zwei Boxkämpfer jagen Eva durch Sylt portez ce vieux Whiskey blond

▶ Medium Italic
The quick brown fox jumps over a Dog. Zwei Boxkämpfer jagen Eva durch Sylt portez ce vieux Whiskey blond qui fume une

▶ Bold
The quick brown fox jumps over a Dog. Zwei Boxkämpfer jagen Eva durch Sylt portez ce vieux

M190 Mac + PC　②　✎ 1923: (John Baskerville, 1757)
Baskerville

abcdefghijklmnopqrstuvwxyz[äöüßåøæœç]
ABCDEFGHIJKLMNOPQRSTUVWXYZ
1234567890(.,;:?!$&-*){ÄÖÜÅØÆŒÇ}

aa*a*
BT1232
Baskerville, Reg, Ita, Bd, BdIta

▶ Regular
The quick brown fox jumps over a Dog. Zwei Boxkämpfer jagen Eva durch Sylt portez ce vieux Whiskey blond qui fume une pipe aber

▶ Italic
The quick brown fox jumps over a Dog. Zwei Boxkämpfer jagen Eva durch Sylt portez ce vieux Whiskey blond qui fume une pipe aber echt über die Mauer

▶ Semi Bold
The quick brown fox jumps over a Dog. Zwei Boxkämpfer jagen Eva durch Sylt portez ce vieux Whiskey blond qui

▶ Semi Bold Italic
The quick brown fox jumps over a Dog. Zwei Boxkämpfer jagen Eva durch Sylt portez ce vieux Whiskey blond qui fume

▶ Bold
The quick brown fox jumps over a Dog. Zwei Boxkämpfer jagen Eva durch Sylt portez ce vieux Whiskey blond

▶ Bold Italic
The quick brown fox jumps over a Dog. Zwei Boxkämpfer jagen Eva durch Sylt portez ce vieux Whiskey blond qui

M551 Mac + PC　②　✎ 1923: (John Baskerville, 1757)
Baskerville Expert

ABCDEFGHIJKLMNOPQRSTUVWXYZ(ÄÖÜŠÅØÆŒÇ)
1234567890ffiffiflffl($1_1$$2_2$$3_3$$4_4$$5_5$$6_6$$7_7$$8_8$$9_9$$0_0$) ($$¢Rp₡)ª

▼ M551 Mac + PC **Baskerville Expert**

▶ Expert
0123456789offfiflffiffl-
(¹/₁²/₂³/₃⁴/₄⁵/₅⁶/₆⁷/₇⁸/₈⁹/₉⁰/₀)⁽$¢Rp₵⁾ª
THE QUICK BROWN FOX JUMPS OVER
A DOG ZWEI BOXKÄMPFER JAGEN

▶ Expert Italic
0123456789offfiflffiffl-
(¹/₁²/₂³/₃⁴/₄⁵/₅⁶/₆⁷/₇⁸/₈⁹/₉⁰/₀)⁽$¢Rp₵⁾ª

▶ Expert Semi Bold
0123456789offfiflffiffl-
(¹/₁²/₂³/₃⁴/₄⁵/₅⁶/₆⁷/₇⁸/₈⁹/₉⁰/₀)⁽$¢Rp₵⁾ª

▶ Expert Semi Bold Italic
0123456789offfiflffiffl-
(¹/₁²/₂³/₃⁴/₄⁵/₅⁶/₆⁷/₇⁸/₈⁹/₉⁰/₀)⁽$¢Rp₵⁾ª

▶ Expert Bold
0123456789offfiflffiffl-
(¹/₁²/₂³/₃⁴/₄⁵/₅⁶/₆⁷/₇⁸/₈⁹/₉⁰/₀)⁽$¢Rp₵⁾ª

▶ Expert Bold Italic
0123456789offfiflffiffl-
(¹/₁²/₂³/₃⁴/₄⁵/₅⁶/₆⁷/₇⁸/₈⁹/₉⁰/₀)⁽$¢Rp₵⁾ª

BT1233 Mac + PC ② (John Baskerville, 1757)
Baskerville No. 2

abcdefghijklmnopqrstuvwxyz[äöüßåøæœç]
ABCDEFGHIJKLMNOPQRSTUVWXYZ
1234567890(.,;:?!$&-*){ÄÖÜÅØÆŒÇ}

a a *a*
BT1232
Baskerville, Reg, Ita, Bd, BdIta
M190
Baskerville, Reg, Ita, SemBd, SemBdIta, Bd, BdIta
M551
Baskerville Expert, Exp, ExpIta, ExpSemBd, ExpSemBdIta, ExpBd, ExpBdIta

▶ Regular
The quick brown fox jumps over a Dog. Zwei Boxkämpfer jagen Eva durch Sylt portez ce vieux Whiskey blond qui fume une

▶ Italic
The quick brown fox jumps over a Dog. Zwei Boxkämpfer jagen Eva durch Sylt portez ce vieux Whiskey blond qui fume une pipe aber echt

▶ Bold
The quick brown fox jumps over a Dog. Zwei Boxkämpfer jagen Eva durch Sylt portez ce vieux Whiskey blond qui

▶ Bold Italic
The quick brown fox jumps over a Dog. Zwei Boxkämpfer jagen Eva durch Sylt portez ce vieux Whiskey blond qui fume une

---

A081 Mac + PC ② 1978–82: (J. Baskerville, 1757) J. Quaranta, M. Carter
ITC New Baskerville®

abcdefghijklmnopqrstuvwxyz[äöüßåøæœç]
ABCDEFGHIJKLMNOPQRSTUVWXYZ
1234567890(.,;:?!$&-*){ÄÖÜÅØÆŒÇ}

a a *a*
EF310
ITC New Baskerville 1, Reg, Ita, Bd, BdIta
EF311
ITC New Baskerville 2, SemBd, SemBdIta, Blk, BlkIta
BT1234
ITC New Baskerville 1, Rom, Ita, Bd, BdIta
BT1235
ITC New Baskerville 2, SemBd, SemBdIta, Blk, BlkIta

▶ Regular
The quick brown fox jumps over a Dog. Zwei Boxkämpfer jagen Eva durch Sylt portez ce vieux Whiskey blond qui fume

▶ Italic
The quick brown fox jumps over a Dog. Zwei Boxkämpfer jagen Eva durch Sylt portez ce vieux Whiskey blond qui fume une pipe aber echt

▶ Bold
The quick brown fox jumps over a Dog. Zwei Boxkämpfer jagen Eva durch Sylt portez ce vieux Whiskey blond qui fume

▶ Bold Italic
The quick brown fox jumps over a Dog. Zwei Boxkämpfer jagen Eva durch Sylt portez ce vieux Whiskey blond qui fume une pipe aber echt

© FSI 1993

A1150 Mac + PC ② (J. Baskerville, 1757) J. Quaranta, M. Carter
ITC New Baskerville Small Caps / OSF

ABCDEFGHIJKLMNOPQRSTUVWXYZ[ÄÖÜSSÅØÆŒÇ]
ABCDEFGHIJKLMNOPQRSTUVWXYZ
1234567890(.,:;?!$&-*){ÄÖÜÅØÆŒÇ}

▶ Small Caps / OSF
THE QUICK BROWN FOX JUMPS OVER A DOG. 123 4567 890 ZWEI BOXKÄMPFER JAGEN EVA DURCH SYLT PORTEZ CE VIEUX

▶ Italic OSF
The quick brown fox jumps over a Dog. 123 4567 890 Zwei Boxkämpfer jagen Eva durch Sylt portez ce vieux Whiskey blond qui

▶ Bold Small Caps
THE QUICK BROWN FOX JUMPS OVER A DOG. 123 4567 890 ZWEI BOXKÄMPFER JAGEN EVA DURCH SYLT PORTEZ CE VIEUX

▶ Bold Italic OSF
The quick brown fox jumps over a Dog. 123 4567 890 Zwei Boxkämpfer jagen Eva durch Sylt portez ce vieux Whiskey blond qui

C6426 Mac + PC
Basque, etc

Basque, etc:
Basque, Brophy™ Script, Chevalier™, Uncial

C6426 Mac + PC ⑥
Basque

abcdefghijklmnopqrstuvwxyz[äöüßåøæœç]
ABCDEFGHIJKLMNOPQRSTUVWXYZ
1234567890(.,:;?!$&-*){ÄÖÜÅØÆŒÇ}

Basque, etc:
Basque, Brophy™ Script, Chevalier™, Uncial

A167 Mac + PC ⑤ 1975: (H. Bayer) Ed Benguiat, Vic Caruso
ITC Bauhaus®

abcdefghijklmnopqrstuvwxyz[äöüßåøæœç]
ABCDEFGHIJKLMNOPQRSTUVWXYZ
1234567890(.,:;?!$&-*){ÄÖÜÅØÆŒÇ}

aaa
BT1236
ITC Bauhaus, Lt, Med, Demi, Bd, Hvy
👁
Blippo, ITC Ronda, Horatio, Pump

▶ Light
The quick brown fox jumps over a Dog. Zwei Boxkämpfer jagen Eva durch Sylt portez ce vieux Whiskey blond qui fume une

▶ Medium
The quick brown fox jumps over a Dog. Zwei Boxkämpfer jagen Eva durch Sylt portez ce vieux Whiskey blond qui fume une

▶ Demi
The quick brown fox jumps over a Dog. Zwei Boxkämpfer jagen Eva durch Sylt portez ce vieux Whiskey blond qui fume une

▶ Bold
The quick brown fox jumps over a Dog. Zwei Boxkämpfer jagen Eva durch Sylt portez ce vieux Whiskey blond qui fume une

© FSI 1993

▼ A167 Mac + PC ITC Bauhaus®

▶ Heavy

The quick brown fox jumps over a Dog. Zwei Boxkämpfer jagen Eva durch Sylt portez ce vieux Whiskey blond

---

RB6098 Mac ② 1990: Richard Beatty

Baxter™

abcdefghijklmnopqrstuvwxyz[äöüßåøæœç]
ABCDEFGHIJKLMNOPQRSTUVWXYZ
1234567890(.,:;?!$&-*){ÄÖÜÅØÆŒÇ}

▶ Old Style
The quick brown fox jumps over a Dog. Zwei Boxkämpfer jagen Eva durch Sylt portez ce vieux Whiskey blond qui fume une pipe aber echt

▶ Old Style Italic
The quick brown fox jumps over a Dog. Zwei Boxkämpfer jagen Eva durch Sylt portez ce vieux Whiskey blond qui fume une pipe aber echt über die Mauer

▶ New Style
The quick brown fox jumps over a Dog. Zwei Boxkämpfer jagen Eva durch Sylt portez ce vieux Whiskey blond qui fume une pipe aber echt

▶ New Style Italic
The quick brown fox jumps over a Dog. Zwei Boxkämpfer jagen Eva durch Sylt portez ce vieux Whiskey blond qui fume une pipe aber echt

▶ New Style Demi
The quick brown fox jumps over a Dog. Zwei Boxkämpfer jagen Eva durch Sylt portez ce vieux Whiskey blond qui fume une pipe aber echt

▶ New Style Demi Italic
The quick brown fox jumps over a Dog. Zwei Boxkämpfer jagen Eva durch Sylt portez ce vieux Whiskey blond qui fume une pipe aber echt

▶ Italic Open Caps
THE QUICK BROWN FOX JUMPS OVER A DOG. ZWEI BOXKÄMP FER JAGEN EVA DURCH SYLT PORTEZ CE VIEUX WHISKEY

▶ Demi Italic Open Caps
THE QUICK BROWN FOX JUMPS OVER A DOG. ZWEI BOXKÄMP FER JAGEN EVA DURCH SYLT PORTEZ CE VIEUX WHISKEY

RB6099 Mac ② 1990: Richard Beatty

Baxter SC/OSF

ABCDEFGHIJKLMNOPQRSTUVWXYZ[ÄÖÜÅØÆŒÇ]
ABCDEFGHIJKLMNOPQRSTUVWXYZ
1234567890(.,:;?!$&-*){ÄÖÜÅØÆŒÇ}

▶ Old Style SC/OSF
THE QUICK BROWN FOX JUMPS OVER A DOG. 123 4567 890 ZWEI BOXKÄMPFER JAGEN EVA DURCH SYLT PORTEZ CE VIEUX

▶ Old Style Italic SC/OSF
THE QUICK BROWN FOX JUMPS OVER A DOG. 123 4567 890 ZWEI BOXKÄMPFER JAGEN EVA DURCH SYLT PORTEZ CE VIEUX

▶ New Style SC/OSF
THE QUICK BROWN FOX JUMPS OVER A DOG. 123 4567 890 ZWEI BOXKÄMPFER JAGEN EVA DURCH SYLT PORTEZ CE VIEUX

▶ New Style Italic SC/OSF
THE QUICK BROWN FOX JUMPS OVER A DOG. 123 4567 890 ZWEI BOXKÄMPFER JAGEN EVA DURCH SYLT PORTEZ CE VIEUX

© FSI 1993

▼ RB6099　MAC　Baxter SC/OSF

▶ New Style Demi SC/OSF
THE QUICK BROWN FOX JUMPS OVER A DOG. 123 4567 890 ZWEI BOXKÄMPFER JAGEN EVA DURCH SYLT PORTEZ CE VIEUX

▶ New Style Demi Italic SC/OSF
THE QUICK BROWN FOX JUMPS OVER A DOG. 123 4567 890 ZWEI BOXKÄMPFER JAGEN EVA DURCH SYLT PORTEZ CE VIEUX

▶ Italic Orn. Caps SC/OSF
THE QUICK BROWN FOX JUMPS OVER A DOG. ZWEI BOXKÄMPFER JAGEN EVA DURCH SYLT PORTEZ CE

▶ Demi Italic Ornamental Caps
THE QUICK BROWN FOX JUMPS OVER A DOG. ZWEI BOXKÄMPFER JAGEN EVA DURCH SYLT PORTEZ CE

L2559　MAC　④　✎ 1985: David Harris
Becka™ Script

abcdefghijklmnopqrstuvwxyz[äöüßåøæç]
ABCDEFGHIJKLMNOPQRSTUVWXYZ
1234567890(.,;:?!$₤-*)ÄÖÜÅØÆŒÇ

EF980　MAC + PC　⑥　✎ 1990: Dave Farey
ITC Beesknees™

ABCDEFGHIJKLMNOPQRSTUVWXYZ
1234567890(.,;:?!$₤-*)[]{ÄÖÜÅØÆŒÇ}

ITC Beesknees™, ITC Studio Script™
aa*a* ⌘ C2979
ITC Typographica™

C467　MAC + PC　③　✎ 1960: Dave West
PL Behemoth Semi Condensed

abcdefghijklmnopqrstuvwxyz[äöüåøæç]
ABCDEFGHIJKLMNOPQRSTUVWXYZ
1234567890(.,;:?!$&-*)◊ÄÖÜÅØÆŒÇ◆

Headlines 81S:
Egiziano™ Black, PL Behemoth Semi Condensed, PL Benguiat Frisky, PL Futura Maxi 1, PL Tower™ Condensed, Quirinus™ Bold, Section™ Bold Condensed, Stratford ™Bold, Woodblock
Ⓒ Egyptian, Barnum, Block

FB378　MAC + PC　③　✎ 1987: (A. Novarese, 1958) David Berlow
Belizio™

abcdefghijklmnopqrstuvwxyz[äöüßåøæç]
ABCDEFGHIJKLMNOPQRSTUVWXYZ
1234567890(.,;:?!$&-*){ÄÖÜÅØÆŒÇ}

Ⓒ Antique No. 3, Clarendon, Egyptian

▶ Bold
The quick brown fox jumps over a Dog. Zwei Boxkämpfer jagen Eva durch Sylt portez ce

▶ Bold Italic
The quick brown fox jumps over a Dog. Zwei Boxkämpfer jagen Eva durch Sylt portez ce

© FSI 1993

M515 Mac + PC   ②   1788: Richard Austin
Bell

abcdefghijklmnopqrstuvwxyz[äöüßåøæœç]
ABCDEFGHIJKLMNOPQRSTUVWXYZ
1234567890(.,;:?!$&-*){ÄÖÜÅØÆŒÇ}

▶ Regular
The quick brown fox jumps over a Dog. Zwei Boxkämpfer jagen Eva durch Sylt portez ce vieux Whiskey blond qui fume une pipe

▶ Italic
The quick brown fox jumps over a Dog. Zwei Boxkämpfer jagen Eva durch Sylt portez ce vieux Whiskey blond qui fume une pipe aber echt

▶ Semi Bold
The quick brown fox jumps over a Dog. Zwei Boxkämpfer jagen Eva durch Sylt portez ce vieux Whiskey blond qui fume une pipe

▶ Semi Bold Italic
The quick brown fox jumps over a Dog. Zwei Boxkämpfer jagen Eva durch Sylt portez ce vieux Whiskey blond qui fume une pipe aber echt

▶ Bold
The quick brown fox jumps over a Dog. Zwei Boxkämpfer jagen Eva durch Sylt portez ce vieux Whiskey blond qui fume

▶ Bold Italic
The quick brown fox jumps over a Dog. Zwei Boxkämpfer jagen Eva durch Sylt portez ce vieux Whiskey blond qui fume une

A6085 Mac + PC   ①   1978: Matthew Carter
Bell Centennial

abcdefghijklmnopqrstuvwxyz[äöüßåøæœç]
ABCDEFGHIJKLMNOPQRSTUVWXYZ
1234567890(.,;:?!$&-*){ÄÖÜÅØÆŒÇ}

aa*a*
BT754
Bell Centennial,
Address, NameNumber,
SubCaption, BdListing
©
Bell Gothic, FF Meta,
ITC Officina Sans

▶ Address
The quick brown fox jumps over a Dog. Zwei Boxkämpfer jagen Eva durch Sylt portez ce vieux Whiskey blond qui fume une pipe aber echt

▶ Name & Number
The quick brown fox jumps over a Dog. Zwei Boxkämpfer jagen Eva durch Sylt portez ce vieux Whiskey blond qui fume

▶ SubCaption
The quick brown fox jumps over a Dog. Zwei Boxkämpfer jagen Eva durch Sylt portez ce vieux Whiskey blond qui fume une pipe aber echt

▶ Bold Listing
THE QUICK BROWN FOX JUMPS OVER A DOG. ZWEI BOXKÄMPFER JAGEN EVA DURCH SYLT PORTEZ CE

▶ Bold Listing Alternative
THE QUICK BROWN FOX JUMPS OVER A DOG. ZWEI BOXKÄMPFER JAGEN EVA DURCH SYLT PORTEZ CE

AB2915 Mac + PC   ④   1986: Gustav Jaeger
Berthold Bellevue™

*abcdefghijklmnopqrstuvwxyz[äöüßåøæœç]
ABCDEFGHIJKLMNOPQRSTUVWXYZ
1234567890(.,;:?!$&-*){ÄÖÜÅØÆŒÇ}*

© FSI 1993

▼ AB2915 Mac + PC **Berthold Bellevue™**

Berthold Scripts 1:
Berthold Bellevue™, Berthold Boulevard™, Berthold Script™

BT756 Mac + PC ① ✎ 1938: C. H. Griffith
Bell Gothic

abcdefghijklmnopqrstuvwxyz[äöüßåøæœç]
ABCDEFGHIJKLMNOPQRSTUVWXYZ
1234567890(.,;:?!$&-*){ÄÖÜÅØÆŒÇ}

aa*a*
A6083
Bell Gothic, Lt, Bd, Blk
Ⓒ
Bell Centennial, FF
Meta, ITC Officina Sans

▶ Regular
The quick brown fox jumps over a Dog. Zwei Boxkämpfer jagen Eva durch Sylt portez ce vieux Whiskey blond qui fume une pipe

▶ Bold
The quick brown fox jumps over a Dog. Zwei Boxkämpfer jagen Eva durch Sylt portez ce vieux Whiskey blond qui fume une pipe

▶ Black
The quick brown fox jumps over a Dog. Zwei Boxkämpfer jagen Eva durch Sylt portez ce vieux Whiskey blond qui fume

---

EF6466 Mac + PC ⑥
Belshaw™

abcdefghijklmnopqrstuvwxyz[äöüßåøæœç]
ABCDEFGHIJKLMNOPQRSTUVWXYZ
1234567890(.,;:?!$&-*)ÄÖÜÅØÆŒÇ

E+F Special Headlines 2:
Belshaw™, Camellia™, Carousel™, Cirkulus™, Data 70, Galadriel™
Ⓒ Chesterfield

FB397 Mac + PC ② ✎ 1988–90: (Lucian Bernhard, 1928), David Berlow
Belucian™

abcdefghijklmnopqrstuvwxyz[äöüßåøæœç]
ABCDEFGHIJKLMNOPQRSTUVWXYZ
1234567890(.,;:?!$&-*){ÄÖÜÅØÆŒÇ}

Ⓒ
Bitstream Lucian,
Bernhard Modern

▶ Book
The quick brown fox jumps over a Dog. Zwei Boxkämpfer jagen Eva durch Sylt portez ce vieux Whiskey blond qui fume une pipe aber echt

▶ Book Italic
The quick brown fox jumps over a Dog. Zwei Boxkämpfer jagen Eva durch Sylt portez ce vieux Whiskey blond qui fume une pipe aber echt

▶ Demi
The quick brown fox jumps over a Dog. Zwei Boxkämpfer jagen Eva durch Sylt portez ce vieux Whiskey blond qui fume une pipe aber

▶ Ultra
The quick brown fox jumps over a Dog. Zwei Boxkämpfer jagen Eva durch Sylt portez ce vieux Whiskey blond

© FSI 1993

A010 Mac + PC   ②   1976: (Georg Belwe, 1913) Alan Meeks
Belwe™

abcdefghijklmnopqrstuvwxyz[äöüßåøæœç]
ABCDEFGHIJKLMNOPQRSTUVWXYZ
1234567890(.,;:?!$&-*){ÄÖÜÅØÆŒÇ}

aa*a*
BT1237
Belwe, Lt, Med, Bd, Con

▶ Light
The quick brown fox jumps over a Dog. Zwei Boxkämpfer jagen Eva durch Sylt portez ce vieux Whiskey blond qui fume

▶ Medium
The quick brown fox jumps over a Dog. Zwei Boxkämpfer jagen Eva durch Sylt portez ce vieux Whiskey blond qui

▶ Bold
The quick brown fox jumps over a Dog. Zwei Boxkämpfer jagen Eva durch Sylt portez ce vieux Whiskey

▶ Condensed
The quick brown fox jumps over a Dog. Zwei Boxkämpfer jagen Eva durch Sylt portez ce vieux Whiskey blond qui fume une pipe aber echt

SG1719 Mac   ②   1976: (Georg Belwe, 1913) Alan Meeks
Belwe Italic

abcdefghijklmnopqrstuvwxyz[äöüßåøæœç]
ABCDEFGHIJKLMNOPQRSTUVWXYZ
1234567890(.,;:?!$&-)ÄÖÜÅØÆŒÇ*

L2817 Mac   ③   1989: (Georg Belwe, 1913) Alan Meeks
Belwe Mono

abcdefghijklmnopqrstuvwxyz[äöüßåøæœç]
ABCDEFGHIJKLMNOPQRSTUVWXYZ
1234567890(.,;:?!$&-*)ÄÖÜÅØÆŒÇ

L2818 Mac   ③   1989: (Georg Belwe, 1913) Alan Meeks
Belwe Mono Italic

abcdefghijklmnopqrstuvwxyz[äöüßåøæœç]
ABCDEFGHIJKLMNOPQRSTUVWXYZ
1234567890(.,;:?!$&-)ÄÖÜÅØÆŒÇ*

M011 Mac + PC   ②   1929: (F. Griffo, A. Tagliente)
Bembo® 1

abcdefghijklmnopqrstuvwxyz[äöüßåøæœç]
ABCDEFGHIJKLMNOPQRSTUVWXYZ
1234567890(.,;:?!$&-★){ÄÖÜÅØÆŒÇ}

aa*a*
A886
Bembo 1, Reg, Ita, Bd, BdIta
BT1222
Bembo, Reg, Ita, Bd, BdIta
ⓒ
Poliphilus, Blado

▶ Regular
The quick brown fox jumps over a Dog. Zwei Boxkämpfer jagen Eva durch Sylt portez ce vieux Whiskey blond qui fume une pipe aber

▶ Italic
The quick brown fox jumps over a Dog. Zwei Boxkämpfer jagen Eva durch Sylt portez ce vieux Whiskey blond qui fume une pipe aber echt über

© FSI 1993

B 14

▼ M011 Mac + PC **Bembo® 1**

▶ Bold
The quick brown fox jumps over a Dog. Zwei Boxkämpfer jagen Eva durch Sylt portez ce vieux Whiskey blond qui fume

▶ Bold Italic
The quick brown fox jumps over a Dog. Zwei Boxkämpfer jagen Eva durch Sylt portez ce vieux Whiskey blond qui fume une pipe aber echt

M283 Mac + PC ② 1929: (F. Griffo, A. Tagliente)
Bembo 2

abcdefghijklmnopqrstuvwxyz[äöüßåøæœç]
ABCDEFGHIJKLMNOPQRSTUVWXYZ
1234567890(.,;:?!$&-★){ÄÖÜÅØÆŒÇ}

aa*a*
A887
Bembo 2, SemBd, SemBdIta, ExtBd, ExtBdIta
ⓒ Poliphilus, Blado

▶ Semi Bold
The quick brown fox jumps over a Dog. Zwei Boxkämpfer jagen Eva durch Sylt portez ce vieux Whiskey blond qui fume une

▶ Semi Bold Italic
The quick brown fox jumps over a Dog. Zwei Boxkämpfer jagen Eva durch Sylt portez ce vieux Whiskey blond qui fume une pipe aber echt

▶ Extra Bold
The quick brown fox jumps over a Dog. Zwei Boxkämpfer jagen Eva durch Sylt portez ce vieux Whiskey blond

▶ Extra Bold Italic
The quick brown fox jumps over a Dog. Zwei Boxkämpfer jagen Eva durch Sylt portez ce vieux Whiskey blond qui fume une

M357 Mac + PC ② 1929: (F. Griffo, A. Tagliente)
Bembo Expert

ABCDEFGHIJKLMNOPQRSTUVWXYZ(ÄÖÜŠÅØÆŒÇ)

1234567890fffiflffifflffl($_1^{1}_2^{2}_3^{3}_4^{4}_5^{5}_6^{6}_7^{7}_8^{8}_9^{9}_0$^{0}) ($$¢Rp₡)^a

ⓒ Poliphilus, Blado

▶ Expert
0123456789offfiflffifflffl-
(½⅓¼⅕⅙⅐⅛⅑⅒%‰)($$¢Rp₡)^a THE QUICK BROWN FOX JUMPS OVER A DOG ZWEI BOXKÄMPFER JAGEN EVA

▶ Expert Italic
0123456789offfiflffifflffl-
(½⅓¼⅕⅙⅐⅛⅑⅒%‰)($$¢Rp₡)^a

▶ Expert Bold
0123456789offfiflffifflffl-
(½⅓¼⅕⅙⅐⅛⅑⅒%‰)($$¢Rp₡)^a

▶ Expert Bold Italic
0123456789offfiflffifflffl-
(½⅓¼⅕⅙⅐⅛⅑⅒%‰)($$¢Rp₡)^a

M517 Mac + PC ② 1929: (F. Griffo, A. Tagliente)
Bembo Expert Semi Bold

ABCDEFGHIJKLMNOPQRSTUVWXYZ(ÄÖÜŠÅØÆŒÇ)

1234567890fffiflffifflffl($_1^{1}_2^{2}_3^{3}_4^{4}_5^{5}_6^{6}_7^{7}_8^{8}_9^{9}_0$^{0})

ⓒ Poliphilus, Blado

▶ Expert Semi Bold
0123456789offfiflffifflffl-
(½⅓¼⅕⅙⅐⅛⅑⅒%‰)($$¢Rp₡)^a THE QUICK BROWN FOX JUMPS OVER A DOG ZWEI BOXKÄMPFER JAGEN EVA

▶ Expert Semi Bold Italic
0123456789offfiflffifflffl-
(½⅓¼⅕⅙⅐⅛⅑⅒%‰)($$¢Rp₡)^a

▼ M517 Mac + PC   Bembo Expert Semi Bold

▶ Expert Extra Bold
01234567890fffiflffiffl-
(½⅓⅔¼¾⅕⅖⅗⅘⅙⅚⅐⅛⅜⅝⅞⅑‰)⁽$¢**Rp₵**⁾ª

▶ Expert Extra Bold Italic
01234567890fffiflffiffl-
*(½⅓⅔¼¾⅕⅖⅗⅘⅙⅚⅐⅛⅜⅝⅞⅑‰)⁽$¢**Rp₵**⁾ª*

BT1238 Mac + PC   ② ✎ 1977: Ed Benguiat
ITC Benguiat® 1

abcdefghijklmnopqrstuvwxyz[äöüßåøæœç]
ABCDEFGHIJKLMNOPQRSTUVWXYZ
1234567890(.,;:?!$&-*){ÄÖÜÅØÆŒÇ}

aa*a*
EF1067
ITC Benguiat 1, Bk,
BkIta, Bd, BdIta
🕮 A012
Friz Quadrata

▶ Book
The quick brown fox jumps over a Dog. Zwei Boxkämpfer jagen Eva durch Sylt portez ce vieux Whiskey blond qui

▶ Book Italic
The quick brown fox jumps over a Dog. Zwei Boxkämpfer jagen Eva durch Sylt portez ce vieux Whiskey blond

▶ **Bold**
The quick brown fox jumps over a Dog. Zwei Boxkämpfer jagen Eva durch Sylt portez ce vieux

▶ **Bold Italic**
The quick brown fox jumps over a Dog. Zwei Boxkämpfer jagen Eva durch Sylt portez ce vieux

---

BT1239 Mac + PC   ② ✎ 1977: Ed Benguiat
ITC Benguiat 2

abcdefghijklmnopqrstuvwxyz[äöüßåøæœç]
ABCDEFGHIJKLMNOPQRSTUVWXYZ
1234567890(.,;:?!$&-*){ÄÖÜÅØÆŒÇ}

aa*a*
EF927
ITC Benguiat 2, Med, MedIta

▶ Medium
The quick brown fox jumps over a Dog. Zwei Boxkämpfer jagen Eva durch Sylt portez ce vieux Whiskey blond

▶ Medium Italic
The quick brown fox jumps over a Dog. Zwei Boxkämpfer jagen Eva durch Sylt portez ce vieux Whiskey

---

BT757 Mac + PC   ② ✎ 1978: Ed Benguiat
ITC Benguiat Condensed 1

abcdefghijklmnopqrstuvwxyz[äöüßåøæœç]
ABCDEFGHIJKLMNOPQRSTUVWXYZ
1234567890(.,;:?!$&-*){ÄÖÜÅØÆŒÇ}

▶ Book Condensed
The quick brown fox jumps over a Dog. Zwei Boxkämpfer jagen Eva durch Sylt portez ce vieux Whiskey blond qui fume une pipe aber echt

▶ Book Condensed Italic
The quick brown fox jumps over a Dog. Zwei Boxkämpfer jagen Eva durch Sylt portez ce vieux Whiskey blond qui fume une pipe aber

▶ **Bold Condensed**
The quick brown fox jumps over a Dog. Zwei Boxkämpfer jagen Eva durch Sylt portez ce vieux Whiskey blond qui fume

▶ **Bold Condensed Italic**
The quick brown fox jumps over a Dog. Zwei Boxkämpfer jagen Eva durch Sylt portez ce vieux Whiskey blond qui fume

© FSI 1993

BT877 Mac + PC ② 1978: Ed Benguiat
ITC Benguiat Condensed 2

abcdefghijklmnopqrstuvwxyz(äöüßåøæœç]
ABCDEFGHIJKLMNOPQRSTUVWXYZ
1234567890(.,;:?!$&-*){ÄÖÜÅØÆŒÇ}

▶ Medium Condensed
The quick brown fox jumps over a Dog. Zwei Boxkämpfer jagen Eva durch Sylt portez ce vieux Whiskey blond qui fume une pipe

▶ Medium Condensed Italic
The quick brown fox jumps over a Dog. Zwei Boxkämpfer jagen Eva durch Sylt portez ce vieux Whiskey blond qui fume une

C467 Mac + PC ④ 1960: Ed Benguiat
PL Benguiat Frisky

abcdefghijklmnopqrstuvwxyzäöüåøæœç
ABCDEFGHIJKLMNOPQRSTUVWXYZ
1234567890(.,;:?!$&-*)ÄÖÜÅØÆŒÇ

Headlines 81S:
Egiziano™ Black, PL Behemoth Semi Condensed, PL Benguiat Frisky, PL Futura Maxi 1, PL Tower™ Condensed, Quirinus™ Bold, Section™ Bold Condensed, Stratford ™Bold, Woodblock

C468 Mac + PC ④ 1960: Ed Benguiat
PL Benguiat Frisky Bold

abcdefghijklmnopqrstuvwxyzäöüåøæœç
ABCDEFGHIJKLMNOPQRSTUVWXYZ
1234567890(.,;:?!$&-*)ÄÖÜÅØÆŒÇ

Headlines 82S:
Neon Extra Condensed™, PL Barnum Block, PL Benguiat Frisky Bold, PL Davison Zip Bold, PL Fiedler Gothic Bold, PL Futura Maxi 2, PL Trophy™ Oblique, Ritmo™ Bold, TC Broadway

EF289 Mac + PC ① 1979: Ed Benguiat
ITC Benguiat Gothic® 1

abcdefghijklmnopqrstuvwxyz[äöüßåøæœç]
ABCDEFGHIJKLMNOPQRSTUVWXYZ
1234567890(.,;:?!$&-*){ÄÖÜÅØÆŒÇ}

aa*a*
BT1240
ITC Benguiat Gothic 1,
Bk, BkIta, Bd, BdIta
A888
ITC Benguiat Gothic,
Bk, BkObl, Med,
MedObl, Bd, BdObl,
Hvy, HvyObl

▶ Book
The quick brown fox jumps over a Dog. Zwei Boxkämpfer jagen Eva durch Sylt portez ce vieux Whiskey blond qui fume une

▶ Book Italic
The quick brown fox jumps over a Dog. Zwei Boxkämpfer jagen Eva durch Sylt portez ce vieux Whiskey blond qui fume une

▶ **Bold**
The quick brown fox jumps over a Dog. Zwei Boxkämpfer jagen Eva durch Sylt portez ce vieux Whiskey blond qui fume une

▶ **Bold Italic**
The quick brown fox jumps over a Dog. Zwei Boxkämpfer jagen Eva durch Sylt portez ce vieux Whiskey blond qui fume une

© FSI 1993

EF290 Mac + PC ① 1979: Ed Benguiat
ITC Benguiat Gothic 2

abcdefghijklmnopqrstuvwxyz[äöüßåøæœç]
ABCDEFGHIJKLMNOPQRSTUVWXYZ
1234567890(.,;:?!$&-*){ÄÖÜÅØÆŒÇ}

aa*a*
BT1241
ITC Benguiat Gothic 2,
Med, MedIta, Hvy,
HvyIta
A888
ITC Benguiat Gothic,
Bk, BkObl, Med,
MedObl, Bd, BdObl,
Hvy, HvyObl

▶ Medium
The quick brown fox jumps over a Dog. Zwei Boxkämpfer jagen Eva durch Sylt portez ce vieux Whiskey blond qui fume une

▶ Medium Italic
The quick brown fox jumps over a Dog. Zwei Boxkämpfer jagen Eva durch Sylt portez ce vieux Whiskey blond qui fume une

▶ Heavy
The quick brown fox jumps over a Dog. Zwei Boxkämpfer jagen Eva durch Sylt portez ce vieux Whiskey blond qui fume

▶ Heavy Italic
The quick brown fox jumps over a Dog. Zwei Boxkämpfer jagen Eva durch Sylt portez ce vieux Whiskey blond qui fume une

FF2794 Mac ⑥ 1991: Just van Rossum
FF BeoSans™ Hard

abcdefghijklmnopqrstuvwxyz[äöüßåøæœç]
ABCDEFGHIJKLMNOPQRSTUVWXYZ
1234567890(.,;:?!$&-*){ÄÖÜÅØÆŒÇ}

▶ Regular R 21
The quick brown fox jumps over a Dog. Zwei Boxkämpfer jagen Eva durch Sylt portez ce vieux Whiskey blond qui fume une pipe aber echt

▶ Bold R 21
The quick brown fox jumps over a Dog. Zwei Boxkämpfer jagen Eva durch Sylt portez ce vieux Whiskey blond qui fume une pipe aber echt

▶ Regular R 22
The quick brown fox jumps over a Dog. Zwei Boxkämpfer jagen Eva durch Sylt portez ce vieux Whiskey blond qui fume une pipe aber echt

▶ Bold R 22
The quick brown fox jumps over a Dog. Zwei Boxkämpfer jagen Eva durch Sylt portez ce vieux Whiskey blond qui fume une pipe aber echt

▶ Regular R 23
The quick brown fox jumps over a Dog. Zwei Boxkämpfer jagen Eva durch Sylt portez ce vieux Whiskey blond qui fume une pipe aber echt

▶ Bold R23
The quick brown fox jumps over a Dog. Zwei Boxkämpfer jagen Eva durch Sylt portez ce vieux Whiskey blond qui fume une pipe aber echt

FF2793 Mac ⑥ 1991: Just van Rossum
FF BeoSans Soft

abcdefghijklmnopqrstuvwxyz[äöüßåøæœç]
ABCDEFGHIJKLMNOPQRSTUVWXYZ
1234567890(.,;:?!$&-*){ÄÖÜÅØÆŒÇ}

▶ Regular R 11
The quick brown fox jumps over a Dog. Zwei Boxkämpfer jagen Eva durch Sylt portez ce vieux Whiskey blond qui fume une pipe aber echt

▶ Bold R 11
The quick brown fox jumps over a Dog. Zwei Boxkämpfer jagen Eva durch Sylt portez ce vieux Whiskey blond qui fume une pipe aber echt

© FSI 1993

▼ FF2793 Mac FF BeoSans Soft

▶ Regular R 12
The quick brown fox jumps over a Dog. Zwei Boxkämpfer jagen Eva durch Sylt portez ce vieux Whiskey blond qui fume une pipe aber echt

▶ Bold R 12
The quick brown fox jumps over a Dog. Zwei Boxkämpfer jagen Eva durch Sylt portez ce vieux Whiskey blond qui fume une pipe aber echt

▶ Regular R 13
The quick brown fox jumps over a Dog. Zwei Boxkämpfer jagen Eva durch Sylt portez ce vieux Whiskey blond qui fume une pipe aber echt

▶ Bold R 13
The quick brown fox jumps over a Dog. Zwei Boxkämpfer jagen Eva durch Sylt portez ce vieux Whiskey blond qui fume une pipe aber echt

---

FF475   Mac   ⑥   ✎ 1990: Erik van Blokland, Just van Rossum

FF Beowolf™

abcdefghijklmnopqrstuvwxyz[äöüßåøæœç]
ABCDEFGHIJKLMNOPQRSTUVWXYZ
1234567890(.,:;?!$&-*){ÄÖÜÅØÆŒÇ}

▶ 21
The quick brown fox jumps over a Dog. Zwei Boxkämpfer jagen Eva durch Sylt portez ce vieux Whiskey blond qui fume une pipe

▶ 22
The quick brown fox jumps over a Dog. Zwei Boxkämpfer jagen Eva durch Sylt portez ce vieux Whiskey blond qui fume une pipe

▶ 23
The quick brown fox jumps over a Dog. Zwei Boxkämpfer jagen Eva durch Sylt portez ce vieux Whiskey blond qui fume une pipe

---

L2560   Mac   ④   ✎ 1991: Thomas Finke

Bergell™

abcdefghijklmnopqrstuvwxyz[äöüßåøæœç]
ABCDEFGHIJKLMNOPQRSTUVWXYZ
1234567890(.,:;?!$&-*)

A194   Mac + PC   ②   ✎ 1983: (F. W. Goudy 1938) Tony Stan

ITC Berkeley Oldstyle®

abcdefghijklmnopqrstuvwxyz[äöüßåøæœç]
ABCDEFGHIJKLMNOPQRSTUVWXYZ
1234567890(.,:;?!$&-*){ÄÖÜÅØÆŒÇ}

aa*a*
BT1242
ITC Berkeley Oldstyle 1, Bk, BkIta, Bd, BdIta
BT1243
ITC Berkeley Oldstyle 2, Med, MedIta, Blk, BlkIta
©
Albertan No. 977, Albertan No. 978 Bold

▶ Book
The quick brown fox jumps over a Dog. Zwei Boxkämpfer jagen Eva durch Sylt portez ce vieux Whiskey blond qui fume une pipe

▶ Book Italic
The quick brown fox jumps over a Dog. Zwei Boxkämpfer jagen Eva durch Sylt portez ce vieux Whiskey blond qui fume une pipe aber echt

▶ Medium
The quick brown fox jumps over a Dog. Zwei Boxkämpfer jagen Eva durch Sylt portez ce vieux Whiskey blond qui fume une

▶ Medium Italic
The quick brown fox jumps over a Dog. Zwei Boxkämpfer jagen Eva durch Sylt portez ce vieux Whiskey blond qui fume une pipe aber

© FSI 1993

▼ A194 Mac + PC   ITC Berkeley Oldstyle®

▶ Bold
The quick brown fox jumps over a Dog. Zwei Boxkämpfer jagen Eva durch Sylt portez ce vieux Whiskey blond qui fume

▶ Bold Italic
The quick brown fox jumps over a Dog. Zwei Boxkämpfer jagen Eva durch Sylt portez ce vieux Whiskey blond qui fume une pipe

▶ Black
The quick brown fox jumps over a Dog. Zwei Boxkämpfer jagen Eva durch Sylt portez ce vieux Whiskey blond qui fume

▶ Black Italic
The quick brown fox jumps over a Dog. Zwei Boxkämpfer jagen Eva durch Sylt portez ce vieux Whiskey blond qui fume une

---

AB6651 Mac + PC   ⑥   1979: (1913) Erik Spiekermann
Berliner Grotesk™

abcdefghijklmnopqrstuvwxyz[äöüßåøæœç]
ABCDEFGHIJKLMNOPQRSTUVWXYZ
1234567890(.,;:?!$&-*){ÄÖÜÅØÆŒÇ}

▶ Light
The quick brown fox jumps over a Dog. Zwei Boxkämpfer jagen Eva durch Sylt portez ce vieux Whiskey blond qui fume une pipe aber echt

▶ Medium
The quick brown fox jumps over a Dog. Zwei Boxkämpfer jagen Eva durch Sylt portez ce vieux Whiskey blond qui fume une pipe aber echt

---

BT928 Mac + PC   ②   1951–58: Karl Erik Forsberg   Industry name
Revival 565   Berling™

abcdefghijklmnopqrstuvwxyz[äöüßåøæœç]
ABCDEFGHIJKLMNOPQRSTUVWXYZ
1234567890(.,;:?!$&-*){ÄÖÜÅØÆŒÇ}

aa*a*
A1152
Berling, Reg, Ita, Bd, BdIta
EF1529
Berling, Reg, Ita, Bd
C2520
Berling, Reg, Ita, Bd

▶ Regular
The quick brown fox jumps over a Dog. Zwei Boxkämpfer jagen Eva durch Sylt portez ce vieux Whiskey blond qui fume

▶ Italic
The quick brown fox jumps over a Dog. Zwei Boxkämpfer jagen Eva durch Sylt portez ce vieux Whiskey blond qui fume une

▶ Bold
The quick brown fox jumps over a Dog. Zwei Boxkämpfer jagen Eva durch Sylt portez ce vieux Whiskey blond qui fume

▶ Bold Italic
The quick brown fox jumps over a Dog. Zwei Boxkämpfer jagen Eva durch Sylt portez ce vieux Whiskey blond qui fume

---

FF2957 Mac + PC   ⑥   1992: (Lucian Bernhard) David Berlow
FF Berlinsans™ 1

abcdefghijklmnopqrstuvwxyz[äöüßåøæœç]
ABCDEFGHIJKLMNOPQRSTUVWXYZ
1234567890(.,;:?!$&-*){ÄÖÜÅØÆŒÇ}

▶ Roman
The quick brown fox jumps over a Dog. Zwei Boxkämpfer jagen Eva durch Sylt portez ce vieux Whiskey blond qui fume une

▶ Demi Bold
The quick brown fox jumps over a Dog. Zwei Boxkämpfer jagen Eva durch Sylt portez ce vieux Whiskey blond qui fume

© FSI 1993 ▼

▼ FF2957 Mac + PC   FF Berlinsans™ 1

▶ Roman Expert
THE QUICK BROWN FOOX JUMPS OVER A DOOG. ZWEI BOOXKÄMPFER JAGEN EVA DURCH SYLT POORTEZ CE VIEUX

▶ Demi Bold Expert
THE QUICK BROWN FOOX JUMPS OVER A DOOG. ZWEI BOOXKÄMPFER JAGEN EVA DURCH SYLT POORTEZ CE

FF2958 Mac + PC   ⑥   1992: (Lucian Bernhard) David Berlow
FF Berlinsans 2

abcdefghijklmnopqrstuvwxyz[äöüßåøæoeç]
ABCDEFGHIJKLMNOPQRSTUVWXYZ
1234567890(.,;:?!$&-*){ÄÖÜÅØÆŒÇ}

▶ Light
The quick brown fox jumps over a Dog. Zwei Boxkämpfer jagen Eva durch Sylt portez ce vieux Whiskey blond qui fume une pipe aber echt

▶ Bold
The quick brown fox jumps over a Dog. Zwei Boxkämpfer jagen Eva durch Sylt portez ce vieux Whiskey

▶ Light Expert
THE QUICK BROWN FOOX JUMPS OVER A DOOG. ZWEI BOOXKÄMPFER JAGEN EVA DURCH SYLT POORTEZ CE VIEUX WHISKEY BLOOND

▶ Bold Expert
THE QUICK BROWN FOOX JUMPS OVER A DOOG. ZWEI BOOXKÄMPFER JAGEN EVA DURCH SYLT POORTEZ

▶ Dingbats
✴❖'₂,🙂●▲▼,5'🔅●❉»«✚

M625 Mac + PC   ⑥   (Lucian Bernhard, 1912)
Bernard™ Condensed

abcdefghijklmnopqrstuvwxyz[äöüßåøæœç]
ABCDEFGHIJKLMNOPQRSTUVWXYZ
1234567890(.,;:?!$&-*){ÄÖÜÅØÆŒÇ}

Headliners 5:
Bernard™ Condensed, Compacta Bold, Neographik™, Runic™ Condensed
aaa 🖥 BT799
Bitstream Freeform Gothic

EF6468 Mac + PC   ⑥   1912: Lucian Bernhard
Bernhard Antique Bold Condensed

abcdefghijklmnopqrstuvwxyz[äöüßåøæœç]
ABCDEFGHIJKLMNOPQRSTUVWXYZ
1234567890(.,;:?!$&-*){ÄÖÜÅØÆŒÇ}

E+F Special Headlines 4:
Bernhard Antique Bold Condensed, Cabaret™, Conference™, Countdown™, Einhorn, Highlight

© FSI 1993

ATF336 MAC   ⑥   ✎ 1929: Lucian Bernhard
Bernhard Fashion™

abcdefghijklmnopqrstuvwxyz[äöüßåøæœç]
ABCDEFGHIJKLMNOPQRSTUVWXYZ
1234567890(.,;:?!$&-*){ÄÖÜÅØÆŒÇ}

ATF Set 1:
Bernhard Fashion™, Cleland Border 1805™, Thompson Quillscript™, Wedding Text™
a a *a* BT1244
Bernhard Fashion, Reg
C2778

BT758   MAC + PC   ②   ✎ 1937–38: Lucian Bernhard
Bernhard Modern™

abcdefghijklmnopqrstuvwxyz[äöüßåøæœç]
ABCDEFGHIJKLMNOPQRSTUVWXYZ
1234567890(.,;:?!$&-*){ÄÖÜÅØÆŒÇ}

a a *a*
C1012
Headlines 84S
C6513
Headlines 84S
Belucian, Bitstream Lucian

▶ Regular
The quick brown fox jumps over a Dog. Zwei Boxkämpfer jagen Eva durch Sylt portez ce vieux Whiskey blond qui fume une pipe aber

▶ Italic
The quick brown fox jumps over a Dog. Zwei Boxkämpfer jagen Eva durch Sylt portez ce vieux Whiskey blond qui fume une pipe aber echt

▶ Bold
The quick brown fox jumps over a Dog. Zwei Boxkämpfer jagen Eva durch Sylt portez ce vieux Whiskey blond qui fume

▶ Bold Italic
The quick brown fox jumps over a Dog. Zwei Boxkämpfer jagen Eva durch Sylt portez ce vieux Whiskey blond qui fume une

C1012   MAC + PC   ②   ✎ 1937–38: Lucian Bernhard
Bernhard Modern

abcdefghijklmnopqrstuvwxyz[äöüåøæœç]
ABCDEFGHIJKLMNOPQRSTUVWXYZ
1234567890(.,;:?!$&-*)◊ÄÖÜÅØÆŒÇ◆

Headlines 84S:
Bernhard Modern, Beton Extra Bold, Metropolis Bold, Modern No. 20, Orlando Caps, PL Davison Americana, PL Westerveldt Light, Siena™ Black, TC Europa™ Bold, TC Jasper™
a a *a* BT758
Bernhard Modern™, Reg, Ita, Bd, BdIta

C993   MAC + PC   ⑥   ✎ 1970: (Lucian Bernhard, 1930–31) Ed Benguiat
PL Bernhardt

abcdefghijklmnopqrstuvwxyz[äöüåøæœç]
ABCDEFGHIJKLMNOPQRSTUVWXYZ
1234567890(.,;:?!$&-*)◊ÄÖÜÅØÆŒÇ◆

Kabel, ITC Kabel, Futura Maxi

▶ Light
The quick brown fox jumps over a Dog. Zwei Boxkämpfer jagen Eva durch Sylt portez ce vieux Whiskey blond qui fume

▶ Medium
The quick brown fox jumps over a Dog. Zwei Boxkämpfer jagen Eva durch Sylt portez ce vieux Whiskey blond qui

© FSI 1993

▼ C993 Mac + PC **PL Bernhardt**

▶ Bold

The quick brown fox jumps over a Dog. Zwei Boxkämpfer jagen Eva durch Sylt portez ce vieux Whiskey

Headlines 83S:
Barclay™ Open, Delphian™ Open, Fluidum™ Bold, PL Bernhardt, PL Britannia Bold, PL Fiorello™ Condensed, PL Modern Heavy Condensed, PL Torino Open
ⓒ Kabel, ITC Kabel, Futura Maxi

BT849 Mac + PC ④ 1931–34: Lucian Bernhard

Bernhard Tango™

abcdefghijklmnopqrstuvwxyz [äöüßåøæœç]
ABCDEFGHIJKLMNOPQRSTUVWXYZ
1234567890(.,;:?!$&-*){ÄÖÜÅØÆŒÇ}

Bitstream Script 2:
Bernhard Tango™, Commercial Script, Stuyvesant™
ⓒ Carmine Tango

M264 Mac + PC ④ 1965: Martin Wilke

New Berolina

abcdefghijklmnopqrstuvwxyz [äöüßåøæœç]
ABCDEFGHIJKLMNOPQRSTUVWXYZ
1234567890(.,;:?!$&-*){ÄÖÜÅØÆŒÇ}

Script 2:
Ashley Script, Monoline Script™, New Berolina, Palace Script™
aaa ⌨ A6335
Ashley Script et al

AB2915 Mac + PC ④ 1977: G. G. Lange

Berthold Script™

abcdefghijklmnopqrstuvwxyz [äöüßåøæœç]
ABCDEFGHIJKLMNOPQRSTUVWXYZ
1234567890(.,;:?!$&-*){ÄÖÜÅØÆŒÇ}

▶ Regular

The quick brown fox jumps over a Dog. Zwei Boxkämpfer jagen Eva durch Sylt portez ce vieux Whiskey blond qui fume une pipe aber echt über die Mauer gesprungen

▶ Medium

The quick brown fox jumps over a Dog. Zwei Boxkämpfer jagen Eva durch Sylt portez ce vieux Whiskey blond qui fume une pipe aber echt über die Mauer

Berthold Scripts 1:
Berthold Bellevue™, Berthold Boulevard™, Berthold Script™

L2561 Mac ④ 1991: Martin Wait
Bertram™

ABCDEFGHIJKLMNOPQRSTUVWXYZ
1234567890(.,;:?!$&-*)[]ÄÖÜÅØÆŒÇ

EF1068 Mac + PC ③ 1936: Heinrich Jost
Beton™

abcdefghijklmnopqrstuvwxyz[äöüßåøæœç]
ABCDEFGHIJKLMNOPQRSTUVWXYZ
1234567890(.,;:?!$&-*){ÄÖÜÅØÆŒÇ}

aaa
C1012
Headlines 84S
Memphis, Rockwell,
Stratford Bold, Stymie

▶ Light
The quick brown fox jumps over a Dog. Zwei Boxkämpfer jagen Eva durch Sylt portez ce vieux Whiskey blond qui fume une pipe aber echt

▶ Demi Bold
The quick brown fox jumps over a Dog. Zwei Boxkämpfer jagen Eva durch Sylt portez ce vieux Whiskey blond qui fume une pipe aber echt

▶ Bold
The quick brown fox jumps over a Dog. Zwei Boxkämpfer jagen Eva durch Sylt portez ce vieux Whiskey blond qui fume une

▶ Extra Bold
The quick brown fox jumps over a Dog. Zwei Boxkämpfer jagen Eva durch Sylt portez ce vieux Whiskey blond qui fume

▶ Bold Condensed
The quick brown fox jumps over a Dog. Zwei Boxkämpfer jagen Eva durch Sylt portez ce vieux Whiskey blond qui fume une pipe aber echt

C2982 Mac + PC ⑥
Beverly Hills

ABCDEFGHIJKLMNOPQRSTUVWXYZ
1234567890(.,;:?!$&-*)[]{ÄÖÜÅØÆŒÇ}

Headlines 93S:
Ashley Inline, Beverly Hills, Lotus™, Virile
Broadway, Art Deco

L2562 Mac ④ 1979: Richard Bradley
Bible™ Script

abcdefghijklmnopqrstuvwxyz [äöüßåøæœç]
ABCDEFGHIJKLMNOPQRSTUVWXYZ
1234567890(.,;:?!$&-)ÄÖÜÅØÆŒÇ*

▶ Plain
The quick brown fox jumps over a Dog. Zwei Boxkämpfer jagen Eva durch Sylt portez ce vieux Whiskey blond qui fume une pipe aber echt über die Mauer

▶ Flourishes

© FSI 1993

| L2563 MAC | ④ | ✎ 1986: Alan Meeks |

Bickley™ Script

abcdefghijklmnopqrstuvwxyz[äöüßåøæœç]
ABCDEFGHIJKLMNOPQRSTUVWXYZ
1234567890(.,;:?!$&-*)Ç

| M263 MAC + PC | ④ | |

Biffo™ Script

abcdefghijklmnopqrstuvwxyz(äöüßåøæœç)
ABCDEFGHIJKLMNOPQRSTUVWXYZ
1234567890(.,;:?!$&-*){ÄÖÜÅØÆŒÇ}

Script 1:
Biffo™ Script, Dorchester Script™, Monotype Script Bold™, Pepita®, Swing™ Bold
aaa ☞ A6071
Dorchester Script, et al MT

| BT1302 MAC + PC | ④ | | Industry name |

Freehand 591   Bingham Script

abcdefghijklmnopqrstuvwxyz[äöüßåøæœç]
ABCDEFGHIJKLMNOPQRSTUVWXYZ
1234567890(.,;:?!$&-*){ÄÖÜÅØÆŒÇ}

| M881 MAC + PC | ② | ✎ 1908: (c. 1863) |

Binny Old Style™

abcdefghijklmnopqrstuvwxyz[äöüßåøæœç]
ABCDEFGHIJKLMNOPQRSTUVWXYZ
1234567890(.,;:?!$&-*){ÄÖÜÅØÆŒÇ}

ⓒ
Bookman, Bruce Old Style

▶ Regular
The quick brown fox jumps over a Dog. Zwei Boxkämpfer jagen Eva durch Sylt portez ce vieux Whis-

▶ Italic
The quick brown fox jumps over a Dog. Zwei Boxkämpfer jagen Eva durch Sylt portez ce vieux Whiskey blond qui

| A922 MAC + PC | ⑥ | ✎ 1990: (1879) Lind, Buker, Redick |

Birch™

abcdefghijklmnopqrstuvwxyz1234567890[äöüßåøæœç]
ABCDEFGHIJKLMNOPQRSTUVWXYZ(.,;:?!$&-*){ÄÖÜÅØÆŒÇ}

Wood Type Pack 2:
Birch™, Blackoak™, Madrone™, Poplar™, Willow™, Wood Type Ornaments 2
ⓒ Latin Extra Condensed, Willow

© FSI 1993

B 25

BT762 Mac + PC ④ 1939: Julius Kirn — Industry name
Brush 738 — Bison™

abcdefghijklmnopqrstuvwxyz[äöüßåøæœç]
ABCDEFGHIJKLMNOPQRSTUVWXYZ
1234567890(.,;:?!$&-*){ÄÖÜÅØÆŒÇ}

Bitstream Brush 1:
Bison™, Lydian Cursive, Ondine™, Palette™

L2819 Mac ⑤ 1990: Alan Birch
Bitmax™

ABCDEFGHIJKLMNOPQRSTUVWXYZ
1234567890(.,;:?!$&-*)[]ÄÖÜÅØÆŒÇ

L6584 Mac ⑦ 1983: David Quay
Blackmoor™

abcdefghijklmnopqrstuvwxyz[äöüßåøæœç]
ABCDEFGHIJKLMNOPQRSTUVWXYZ
1234567890(.,;:?!$&-*)ÄÖÜÅØÆŒÇ

A922 Mac + PC ⑥ 1990: Lind, Buker, Redick
Blackoak™

abcdefghijklmnopqrstuvwxyz
ABCDEFGHIJKLMNOPQRS
TUVWXYZ1234567890(.,;:?!$&-*)
[äöüßåøæœç]{ÄÖÜÅØÆŒÇ}

Wood Type Pack 2:
Birch™, Blackoak™, Madrone™, Poplar™, Willow™, Wood Type Ornaments 2

M265 Mac + PC ② 1923: (Stanley Morison)
Blado®

abcdefghijklmnopqrstuvwxyz[äöüßåøæœç]
ABCDEFGHIJKLMNOPQRSTUVWXYZ
1234567890(.,;:?!$&-*){ÄÖÜÅØÆŒÇ}

Poliphilus®:
Blado®, Poliphilus, Van Dijck™
Ⓒ Bembo, Poliphilus

© FSI 1993

Blado Expert
M6697 Mac + PC (2) 1923: (Stanley Morison)

1234567890ffffiflffiffl(¹₁²₂³₃⁴₄⁵₅⁶₆⁷₇⁸₈⁹₉⁰₀)
($¢Rp₡)ª

Poliphilus Expert:
Blado Expert, Poliphilus Expert, Van Dijck Expert
© Bembo, Poliphilus

Blippo™ Black
BT812 Mac + PC (5)

abcdefghijklmnopqrstuvwxyz[äöüßåøæœç]
ABCDEFGHIJKLMNOPQRSTUVWXYZ
1234567890(.,;:?!$&-*){ÄÖÜÅØÆŒÇ}

Bitstream Bold Headlines 1:
Blippo™ Black, Handel Gothic, ITC Bolt Bold®, Trump Mediaeval Black
© ITC Bauhaus, ITC Ronda, Horatio, Pump

Berthold Block®
AB6654 Mac + PC (6) 1979: (H. Hoffmann, 1922) E.Spiekermann

abcdefghijklmnopqrstuvwxyz[äöüßåøæœç]
ABCDEFGHIJKLMNOPQRSTUVWXYZ
1234567890(.,;:?!$&-*){ÄÖÜÅØÆŒÇ}

aa*a*
BT799
Bitstream Freeform Gothic
©
Berliner Grotesk, FF Berlinsans

▶ Regular
The quick brown fox jumps over a Dog. Zwei Boxkämpfer jagen Eva durch Sylt portez ce vieux Whiskey blond qui fume une

▶ Italic
The quick brown fox jumps over a Dog. Zwei Boxkämpfer jagen Eva durch Sylt portez ce vieux Whiskey blond qui fume une

▶ Heavy
The quick brown fox jumps over a Dog. Zwei Boxkämpfer jagen Eva durch Sylt portez ce vieux

▶ Condensed
The quick brown fox jumps over a Dog. Zwei Boxkämpfer jagen Eva durch Sylt portez ce vieux Whiskey blond qui fume une pipe aber echt

▶ Extra Condensed
The quick brown fox jumps over a Dog. Zwei Boxkämpfer jagen Eva durch Sylt portez ce vieux Whiskey blond qui fume une pipe aber echt über die Mauer gesprungen

▶ Extra Condensed Italic
The quick brown fox jumps over a Dog. Zwei Boxkämpfer jagen Eva durch Sylt portez ce vieux Whiskey blond qui fume une pipe aber echt über die Mauer gesprungen

FF Blur™
FF2795 Mac + PC (5) 1991: Neville Brody

abcdefghijklmnopqrstuvwxyz[äöüßåøæœç]
ABCDEFGHIJKLMNOPQRSTUVWXYZ
1234567890(.,;:?!$&-*){ÄÖÜÅØÆŒÇ}

© FSI 1993

▼ FF2795 Mac + PC **FF Blur™**

▶ Light
The quick brown fox jumps over a Dog. Zwei Boxkämpfer jagen Eva durch Sylt portez ce vieux Whiskey blond qui fume une pipe aber echt

▶ Medium
The quick brown fox jumps over a Dog. Zwei Boxkämpfer jagen Eva durch Sylt portez ce vieux Whiskey blond qui fume

▶ Bold
The quick brown fox jumps over a Dog. Zwei Boxkämpfer jagen Eva durch Sylt portez ce vieux Whiskey

---

FB1053 Mac + PC ① 1991: Greg Thompson
Bodega™ Sans

abcdefghijklmnopqrstuvwxyz[äöüßåøæœç]
ABCDEFGHIJKLMNOPQRSTUVWXYZ
1234567890(.,;:?!$&-*){ÄÖÜÅØÆŒÇ}

ITC Anna, Romeo, Triplex Condensed, Triplex Serif Condensed

▶ Light
The quick brown fox jumps over a Dog. Zwei Boxkämpfer jagen Eva durch Sylt portez ce vieux Whiskey blond qui fume une pipe aber echt über die Mauer gesprungen und auch smørebrød en ysjes natuurlijk

▶ Light Old Style
The quick brown fox jumps over a Dog. Zwei Boxkämpfer jagen Eva durch Sylt portez ce vieux Whiskey blond qui fume une pipe aber echt über die Mauer gesprungen und auch smørebrød en ysjes natuurlijk

▶ Black
The quick brown fox jumps over a Dog. Zwei Boxkämpfer jagen Eva durch Sylt portez ce vieux Whiskey blond qui fume une pipe aber echt über die Mauer

▶ Black Old Style
The quick brown fox jumps over a Dog. Zwei Boxkämpfer jagen Eva durch Sylt portez ce vieux Whiskey blond qui fume une pipe aber echt über die Mauer

---

FB2877 Mac + PC ① 1991: Greg Thompson
Bodega Sans 2

abcdefghijklmnopqrstuvwxyz[äöüßåøæœç]
ABCDEFGHIJKLMNOPQRSTUVWXYZ
1234567890(.,;:?!$&-*){ÄÖÜÅØÆŒÇ}

ITC Anna, Romeo, Triplex Condensed, Triplex Serif Condensed

▶ Medium
The quick brown fox jumps over a Dog. Zwei Boxkämpfer jagen Eva durch Sylt portez ce vieux Whiskey blond qui fume une pipe aber echt über die Mauer gesprungen und auch smørebrød en

▶ Medium Old Style
The quick brown fox jumps over a Dog. Zwei Boxkämpfer jagen Eva durch Sylt portez ce vieux Whiskey blond qui fume une pipe aber echt über die Mauer gesprungen und auch smørebrød en

---

FB2878 Mac + PC ① 1991: Greg Thompson
Bodega Sans Small Caps

ABCDEFGHIJKLMNOPQRSTUVWXYZ[ÄÖÜÅØÆŒÇ]
ABCDEFGHIJKLMNOPQRSTUVWXYZ
1234567890(.,;:?!$&-*){ÄÖÜÅØÆŒÇ}

ITC Anna, Romeo, Triplex Condensed, Triplex Serif Condensed

▶ Light Small Caps
THE QUICK BROWN FOX JUMPS OVER A DOG. ZWEI BOXKÄMPFER JAGEN EVA DURCH SYLT PORTEZ CE VIEUX WHISKEY BLOND QUI FUME UNE PIPE ABER ECHT ÜBER DIE MAUER GESPRUNGEN UND AUCH SMØREBRØD EN YSJES NATUURLIJK

▶ Medium Small Caps
THE QUICK BROWN FOX JUMPS OVER A DOG. ZWEI BOXKÄMPFER JAGEN EVA DURCH SYLT PORTEZ CE VIEUX WHISKEY BLOND QUI FUME UNE PIPE ABER ECHT ÜBER DIE MAUER GESPRUNGEN UND AUCH SMØREBRØD EN

© FSI 1993

▼ FB2878   Mac + PC   Bodega Sans Small Caps

▶ Black Small Caps
The quick brown fox jumps over a Dog. Zwei Boxkämpfer jagen Eva durch Sylt portez ce vieux Whiskey blond qui fume une pipe aber echt über die Mauer

FB2879   Mac + PC   ③   1991: Greg Thompson

Bodega Serif

abcdefghijklmnopqrstuvwxyz[äöüßåøæœç]
ABCDEFGHIJKLMNOPQRSTUVWXYZ
1234567890(.,;:?!$&-*){ÄÖÜÅØÆŒÇ}

▶ Light
The quick brown fox jumps over a Dog. Zwei Boxkämpfer jagen Eva durch Sylt portez ce vieux Whiskey blond qui fume une pipe aber echt über die Mauer gesprungen und auch smørebrød en ysjes natuurlijk. The quick brown fox jumps

▶ Light Old Style
The quick brown fox jumps over a Dog. Zwei Boxkämpfer jagen Eva durch Sylt portez ce vieux Whiskey blond qui fume une pipe aber echt über die Mauer gesprungen und auch smørebrød en ysjes natuurlijk. The quick brown fox jumps over

▶ Black
The quick brown fox jumps over a Dog. Zwei Boxkämpfer jagen Eva durch Sylt portez ce vieux Whiskey blond qui fume une pipe aber echt über die Mauer

▶ Black Old Style
The quick brown fox jumps over a Dog. Zwei Boxkämpfer jagen Eva durch Sylt portez ce vieux Whiskey blond qui fume une pipe aber echt über die Mauer

FB2880   Mac + PC   ③   1991: Greg Thompson

Bodega Serif 2

abcdefghijklmnopqrstuvwxyz[äöüßåøæœç]
ABCDEFGHIJKLMNOPQRSTUVWXYZ
1234567890(.,;:?!$&-*){ÄÖÜÅØÆŒÇ}

▶ Medium
The quick brown fox jumps over a Dog. Zwei Boxkämpfer jagen Eva durch Sylt portez ce vieux Whiskey blond qui fume une pipe aber echt über die Mauer gesprungen und auch smørebrød

▶ Medium Old Style
The quick brown fox jumps over a Dog. Zwei Boxkämpfer jagen Eva durch Sylt portez ce vieux Whiskey blond qui fume une pipe aber echt über die Mauer gesprungen und auch smørebrød en

FB2881   Mac + PC   ③   1991: Greg Thompson

Bodega Serif Small Caps

ABCDEFGHIJKLMNOPQRSTUVWXYZ[ÄÖÜÅØÆŒÇ]
ABCDEFGHIJKLMNOPQRSTUVWXYZ
1234567890(.,;:?!$&-*){ÄÖÜÅØÆŒÇ}

▶ Light Small Caps
The quick brown fox jumps over a Dog. Zwei Boxkämpfer jagen Eva durch Sylt portez ce vieux Whiskey blond qui fume une pipe aber echt über die Mauer gesprungen und auch smørebrød en ysjes natuurlijk. The quick brown fox jumps

▶ Medium Small Caps
The quick brown fox jumps over a Dog. Zwei Boxkämpfer jagen Eva durch Sylt portez ce vieux Whiskey blond qui fume une pipe aber echt über die Mauer gesprungen und auch smørebrød en

▶ Black Small Caps
The quick brown fox jumps over a Dog. Zwei Boxkämpfer jagen Eva durch Sylt portez ce vieux Whiskey blond qui fume une pipe aber echt über die Mauer

© FSI 1993

A013 Mac + PC ② 1914–16: (Giambattista Bodoni, c. 1790)
Bodoni 1

abcdefghijklmnopqrstuvwxyz[äöüßåøæœç]
ABCDEFGHIJKLMNOPQRSTUVWXYZ
1234567890(.,;:?!$&-*){ÄÖÜÅØÆŒÇ}

aa*a*
BT1246
Bodoni 2, Bd, BdIta, BdCon
Ⓒ
Bodoni (Monotype), Berthold Bodoni, Bauer Bodoni

▶ Regular
The quick brown fox jumps over a Dog. Zwei Boxkämpfer jagen Eva durch Sylt portez ce vieux Whiskey blond qui fume

▶ Italic
The quick brown fox jumps over a Dog. Zwei Boxkämpfer jagen Eva durch Sylt portez ce vieux Whiskey blond qui fume

▶ Bold
The quick brown fox jumps over a Dog. Zwei Boxkämpfer jagen Eva durch Sylt portez ce vieux Whiskey blond qui fume

▶ Bold Italic
The quick brown fox jumps over a Dog. Zwei Boxkämpfer jagen Eva durch Sylt portez ce vieux Whiskey blond qui fume

▶ Poster Bodoni
The quick brown fox jumps over a Dog. Zwei Boxkämpfer jagen Eva durch Sylt portez ce

A374 Mac + PC ② 1914–16: (Giambattista Bodoni, c. 1790)
Bodoni 2

abcdefghijklmnopqrstuvwxyz[äöüßåøæœç]
ABCDEFGHIJKLMNOPQRSTUVWXYZ
1234567890(.,;:?!$&-*){ÄÖÜÅØÆŒÇ}

aa*a*
BT1245
Bodoni, Bk, BkIta, Reg, Ita

▶ Book
The quick brown fox jumps over a Dog. Zwei Boxkämpfer jagen Eva durch Sylt portez ce vieux Whiskey blond qui fume une pipe aber

▶ Book Italic
The quick brown fox jumps over a Dog. Zwei Boxkämpfer jagen Eva durch Sylt portez ce vieux Whiskey blond qui fume une pipe aber echt

▶ Poster Bodoni Italic
The quick brown fox jumps over a Dog. Zwei Boxkämpfer jagen Eva durch Sylt portez ce

▶ Poster Bodoni Compressed
The quick brown fox jumps over a Dog. Zwei Boxkämpfer jagen Eva durch Sylt portez ce vieux Whiskey blond qui fume une pipe aber echt über die Mauer gesprungen und auch smørebrød en

▶ Bold Condensed
The quick brown fox jumps over a Dog. Zwei Boxkämpfer jagen Eva durch Sylt portez ce vieux Whiskey blond qui fume une pipe aber echt über die Mauer

M2967 Mac + PC ② 1921: (Giambattista Bodoni, c. 1790)
Bodoni (Monotype)®

abcdefghijklmnopqrstuvwxyz[äöüßåøæœç]
ABCDEFGHIJKLMNOPQRSTUVWXYZ
1234567890(.,;:?!$&-*){ÄÖÜÅØÆŒÇ}

© FSI 1993

▼ M2967 Mac + PC   Bodoni (Monotype)®

Poster Bodoni, Onyx

▶ Regular
The quick brown fox jumps over a Dog. Zwei Boxkämpfer jagen Eva durch Sylt portez ce vieux Whiskey blond qui fume une

▶ Italic
The quick brown fox jumps over a Dog. Zwei Boxkämpfer jagen Eva durch Sylt portez ce vieux Whiskey blond qui fume une pipe aber

▶ Bold
The quick brown fox jumps over a Dog. Zwei Boxkämpfer jagen Eva durch Sylt portez ce vieux Whiskey blond qui fume une

▶ Bold Italic
The quick brown fox jumps over a Dog. Zwei Boxkämpfer jagen Eva durch Sylt portez ce vieux Whiskey blond qui

---

M196 Mac + PC
Bodoni (Monotype) 2

Bodoni (Monotype) 2:
Bodoni (Monotype) 2, Onyx

M196 Mac + PC   ②   ✎ 1921: (Giambattista Bodoni, c. 1790)
Bodoni (Monotype) 2

abcdefghijklmnopqrstuvwxyz[äöüßåøæœç]
ABCDEFGHIJKLMNOPQRSTUVWXYZ
1234567890(.,;:?!$&-*){ÄÖÜÅØÆŒÇ}

aaa
A374
Bodoni 2, Bk, BkIta, PosBodIta, PosBodCompressed, BdCon
BT1245
Bodoni, Bk, BkIta, Reg, Ita

Poster Bodoni, Berthold Bodoni, Bauer Bodoni, Bodoni, WTC Our Bodoni

▶ Book
The quick brown fox jumps over a Dog. Zwei Boxkämpfer jagen Eva durch Sylt portez ce vieux Whiskey blond qui fume une pipe aber

▶ Book Italic
The quick brown fox jumps over a Dog. Zwei Boxkämpfer jagen Eva durch Sylt portez ce vieux Whiskey blond qui fume une pipe aber

▶ Ultra Bold
The quick brown fox jumps over a Dog. Zwei Boxkämpfer jagen Eva durch Sylt portez ce

▶ Ultra Bold Italic
The quick brown fox jumps over a Dog. Zwei Boxkämpfer jagen Eva durch Sylt portez ce

Bodoni (Monotype) 2:
Bodoni (Monotype) 2, Onyx
aaa A374
Bodoni 2, Bk, BkIta, PosBodIta, PosBodCompressed, BdCon
BT1245

M266 Mac + PC   ②   ✎ 1921: (Giambattista Bodoni, c. 1790)
Bodoni (Monotype) 1

abcdefghijklmnopqrstuvwxyz[äöüßåøæœç]
ABCDEFGHIJKLMNOPQRSTUVWXYZ
1234567890(.,;:?!$&-*){ÄÖÜÅØÆŒÇ}

Poster Bodoni, Onyx

▶ Bold Condensed
The quick brown fox jumps over a Dog. Zwei Boxkämpfer jagen Eva durch Sylt portez ce vieux Whiskey blond qui fume une pipe aber echt über die Mauer

▶ Bold Condensed Italic
The quick brown fox jumps over a Dog. Zwei Boxkämpfer jagen Eva durch Sylt portez ce vieux Whiskey blond qui fume une pipe aber echt über die Mauer

© FSI 1993

▼ M266 MAC + PC   Bodoni (Monotype) 1

▶ Black
The quick brown fox jumps over a Dog. Zwei Boxkämpfer jagen Eva durch Sylt portez ce vieux Whiskey

▶ Black Italic
The quick brown fox jumps over a Dog. Zwei Boxkämpfer jagen Eva durch Sylt portez ce

---

AB1087 MAC + PC   ② 1930–1985: (Giambattista Bodoni, c. 1790)
Berthold Bodoni-Antiqua®

abcdefghijklmnopqrstuvwxyz[äöüßåøæœç]
ABCDEFGHIJKLMNOPQRSTUVWXYZ
1234567890(.,;:?!$&-*){ÄÖÜÅØÆŒÇ}

Bauer Bodoni, Bodoni, WTC Our Bodoni, Monotype Bodoni

▶ Light
The quick brown fox jumps over a Dog. Zwei Boxkämpfer jagen Eva durch Sylt portez ce vieux Whiskey blond qui fume une

▶ Light Italic
The quick brown fox jumps over a Dog. Zwei Boxkämpfer jagen Eva durch Sylt portez ce vieux Whiskey blond qui fume une pipe aber

▶ Regular
The quick brown fox jumps over a Dog. Zwei Boxkämpfer jagen Eva durch Sylt portez ce vieux Whiskey blond qui fume une

▶ Italic
The quick brown fox jumps over a Dog. Zwei Boxkämpfer jagen Eva durch Sylt portez ce vieux Whiskey blond qui fume une pipe aber

▶ Medium
The quick brown fox jumps over a Dog. Zwei Boxkämpfer jagen Eva durch Sylt portez ce vieux Whiskey blond qui fume

▶ Medium Italic
The quick brown fox jumps over a Dog. Zwei Boxkämpfer jagen Eva durch Sylt portez ce vieux Whiskey blond qui fume

▶ Bold
The quick brown fox jumps over a Dog. Zwei Boxkämpfer jagen Eva durch Sylt portez ce vieux Whis-

▶ Bold Italic
The quick brown fox jumps over a Dog. Zwei Boxkämpfer jagen Eva durch Sylt portez ce vieux Whis-

---

AB2984 MAC + PC   ② 1930–1985: (Giambattista Bodoni, ca. 1790)
Berthold Bodoni-Antiqua Expert

ABCDEFGHIJKLMNOPQRSTUVWXYZ[ÄÖÜSSÅØÆŒÇ]
ABCDEFGHIJKLMNOPQRSTUVWXYZ
1234567890(.,;:?!$&-*){ÄÖÜÅØÆŒÇ}

▶ Light Small Caps
THE QUICK BROWN FOX JUMPS OVER A DOG. 123 4567 890 ZWEI BOXKÄMPFER JAGEN EVA DURCH SYLT PORTEZ CE VIEUX WHISKEY BLOND

▶ Light Expert
0123456789offiflffiffl-
($^{1}/_{1}$$^{2}/_{2}$$^{3}/_{3}$$^{4}/_{4}$$^{5}/_{5}$$^{6}/_{6}$$^{7}/_{7}$$^{8}/_{8}$$^{9}/_{9}$%) ($\$_¢$Rp₡)ᵃ
THE QUICK BROWN FOX JUMPS OVER A DOG ZWEI BOXKÄMPFER JAGEN EVA

▶ Light Italic OSF
The quick brown fox jumps over a Dog. 123 4567 890 Zwei Boxkämpfer jagen Eva durch Sylt portez ce vieux Whiskey blond qui

▶ Light Italic Expert
0123456789offiflffiffl-
($^{1}/_{1}$$^{2}/_{2}$$^{3}/_{3}$$^{4}/_{4}$$^{5}/_{5}$$^{6}/_{6}$$^{7}/_{7}$$^{8}/_{8}$$^{9}/_{9}$%) ($\$_¢$Rp₡)ᵃ

▼ AB2984 Mac + PC Berthold Bodoni-Antiqua Expert

▶ Regular Small Caps
The quick brown fox jumps over a Dog. 123 4567 890 Zwei Boxkämpfer jagen Eva durch Sylt portez ce vieux Whiskey blond

▶ Regular Expert
0123456789offififlffiffl-
(1/12/23/34/45/56/67/78/89/90/0)($$€Rp₡)a
the quick brown fox jumps over a dog zwei boxkämpfer jagen eva

▶ Italic OSF
The quick brown fox jumps over a Dog. 123 4567 890 Zwei Boxkämpfer jagen Eva durch Sylt portez ce vieux Whiskey blond

▶ Italic Expert
*0123456789offififlffiffl-
(1/12/23/34/45/56/67/78/89/90/0)($$€Rp₡)a*

▶ Medium Small Caps
The quick brown fox jumps over a Dog. 123 4567 890 Zwei Boxkämpfer jagen Eva durch Sylt portez ce vieux Whiskey

▶ Medium Expert
**0123456789offififlffiffl-
(1/12/23/34/45/56/67/78/89/90/0)($$€Rp₡)a
the quick brown fox jumps over a dog zwei boxkämpfer**

▶ Medium Italic OSF
The quick brown fox jumps over a Dog. 123 4567 890 Zwei Boxkämpfer jagen Eva durch Sylt portez ce vieux Whiskey

▶ Medium Italic Expert
*0123456789offififlffiffl-
(1/12/23/34/45/56/67/78/89/90/0)($$€Rp₡)a*

▶ Bold OSF
The quick brown fox jumps over a Dog. 123 4567 890 Zwei Boxkämpfer jagen Eva durch

▶ Bold Expert
**0123456789offififlffiffl-
(1/12/23/34/45/56/67/78/89/90/0)($$€Rp₡)**

▶ Bold Italic OSF
The quick brown fox jumps over a Dog. 123 4567 890 Zwei Boxkämpfer jagen Eva durch Sylt portez ce

▶ Bold Italic Expert
***0123456789offififlffiffl-
(1/12/23/34/45/56/67/78/89/90/0)($$€Rp₡)a***

AB6320 Mac + PC ② 1930–1985: (Giambattista Bodoni, c. 1790)
Berthold Bodoni-Antiqua Condensed

abcdefghijklmnopqrstuvwxyz[äöüßåøæœç]
ABCDEFGHIJKLMNOPQRSTUVWXYZ
1234567890(.,:;?!$&-*){ÄÖÜÅØÆŒÇ}

▶ Regular Condensed
The quick brown fox jumps over a Dog. Zwei Boxkämpfer jagen Eva durch Sylt portez ce vieux Whiskey blond qui fume une pipe aber echt über die Mauer gesprungen und auch

▶ Condensed Italic
The quick brown fox jumps over a Dog. Zwei Boxkämpfer jagen Eva durch Sylt portez ce vieux Whiskey blond qui fume une pipe aber echt über die Mauer gesprungen und auch

▶ Medium Condensed
The quick brown fox jumps over a Dog. Zwei Boxkämpfer jagen Eva durch Sylt portez ce vieux Whiskey blond qui fume une pipe aber echt über die

▶ Medium Condensed Italic
The quick brown fox jumps over a Dog. Zwei Boxkämpfer jagen Eva durch Sylt portez ce vieux Whiskey blond qui fume une pipe aber echt

▼ AB6320 Mac + PC Berthold Bodoni-Antiqua Condensed

▶ Bold Condensed
The quick brown fox jumps over a Dog. Zwei Boxkämpfer jagen Eva durch Sylt portez ce vieux Whiskey blond qui fume une pipe aber echt

▶ Bold Condensed Italic
The quick brown fox jumps over a Dog. Zwei Boxkämpfer jagen Eva durch Sylt portez ce vieux Whiskey blond qui fume une pipe aber echt

AB6308 Mac + PC ② 1986: (G. Bodoni, c. 1790) Günter Gerhard Lange
Berthold Bodoni Old Face

abcdefghijklmnopqrstuvwxyz[äöüßåøæœç]
ABCDEFGHIJKLMNOPQRSTUVWXYZ
1234567890(.,;:?!$&-*){ÄÖÜÅØÆŒÇ}

© Berthold Bodoni Antiqua, Bodoni, WTC Our Bodoni, Monotype Bodoni

▶ Regular
The quick brown fox jumps over a Dog. Zwei Boxkämpfer jagen Eva durch Sylt portez ce vieux Whiskey blond qui fume

▶ Italic
The quick brown fox jumps over a Dog. Zwei Boxkämpfer jagen Eva durch Sylt portez ce vieux Whiskey blond qui fume une pipe aber

▶ Medium
The quick brown fox jumps over a Dog. Zwei Boxkämpfer jagen Eva durch Sylt portez ce vieux Whiskey blond qui

▶ Medium Italic
The quick brown fox jumps over a Dog. Zwei Boxkämpfer jagen Eva durch Sylt portez ce vieux Whiskey blond qui fume

▶ Bold
The quick brown fox jumps over a Dog. Zwei Boxkämpfer jagen Eva durch Sylt portez ce vieux Whiskey blond

▶ Bold Italic
The quick brown fox jumps over a Dog. Zwei Boxkämpfer jagen Eva durch Sylt portez ce vieux Whiskey

AB6367 Mac + PC ② 1986: (G. Bodoni, c. 1790) Günter Gerhard Lange
Berthold Bodoni Old Face Expert

ABCDEFGHIJKLMNOPQRSTUVWXYZ[ÄÖÜSSÅØÆŒÇ]
ABCDEFGHIJKLMNOPQRSTUVWXYZ
1234567890(.,;:?!$&-*){ÄÖÜÅØÆŒÇ}

▶ Regular SC
THE QUICK BROWN FOX JUMPS OVER A DOG. 123 4567 890 ZWEI BOXKÄMPFER JAGEN EVA DURCH SYLT PORTEZ CE VIEUX WHISKEY

▶ Italic SC
THE QUICK BROWN FOX JUMPS OVER A DOG. 123 4567 890 ZWEI BOXKÄMPFER JAGEN EVA DURCH SYLT PORTEZ CE VIEUX WHISKEY

▶ Medium SC
THE QUICK BROWN FOX JUMPS OVER A DOG. 123 4567 890 ZWEI BOXKÄMPFER JAGEN EVA DURCH SYLT PORTEZ CE VIEUX WHISKEY

▶ Medium Italic OSF
The quick brown fox jumps over a Dog. 123 4567 890 Zwei Boxkämpfer jagen Eva durch Sylt portez ce vieux Whiskey blond

▶ Bold OSF
The quick brown fox jumps over a Dog. 123 4567 890 Zwei Boxkämpfer jagen Eva durch Sylt portez ce vieux

▶ Bold Italic OSF
The quick brown fox jumps over a Dog. 123 4567 890 Zwei Boxkämpfer jagen Eva durch Sylt portez ce vieux

© FSI 1993

▼ AB6367 Mac + PC **Berthold Bodoni Old Face Expert**

▶ Regular Expert
0123456789offififlffiffl-
(1/12/23/34/45/56/67/78/89/90/0)($$¢Rp₵)ᵃ
THE QUICK BROWN FOX JUMPS
OVER A DOG ZWEI BOXKÄMPFER

▶ Italic Expert
0123456789offififlffiffl-
(1/12/23/34/45/56/67/78/89/90/0)($$¢Rp₵)ᵃ
THE QUICK BROWN FOX JUMPS
OVER A DOG ZWEI BOXKÄMPFER

▶ Medium Expert
0123456789offififlffiffl-
(1/12/23/34/45/56/67/78/89/90/0)($$¢Rp₵)ᵃ
THE QUICK BROWN FOX JUMPS
OVER A DOG ZWEI BOXKÄMPFER

▶ Medium Italic Expert
0123456789offififlffiffl-
(1/12/23/34/45/56/67/78/89/90/0)($$¢Rp₵)ᵃ

▶ Bold Expert
0123456789offififlffiffl-
(1/12/23/34/45/56/67/78/89/90/0)
($$¢Rp₵)ᵃ

▶ Bold Italic Expert
0123456789offififlffiffl-
(1/12/23/34/45/56/67/78/89/90/0)
($$¢Rp₵)ᵃ

A191 Mac + PC ② ✎ 1926: (Giambattista Bodoni, c. 1790)
Bauer Bodoni™ 1

abcdefghijklmnopqrstuvwxyz[äöüßåøæœç]
ABCDEFGHIJKLMNOPQRSTUVWXYZ
1234567890(.,;:?!$&-*){ÄÖÜÅØÆŒÇ}

a a *a*
BT1247
Bauer Bodoni 1, Reg,
Ita, Bd, BdIta, Titling
⊚
Berthold Bodoni
Antiqua, Bodoni, WTC
Our Bodoni, Monotype
Bodoni

▶ Regular
The quick brown fox jumps over a Dog. Zwei Boxkämpfer jagen Eva durch Sylt portez ce vieux Whiskey blond qui fume

▶ Italic
The quick brown fox jumps over a Dog. Zwei Boxkämpfer jagen Eva durch Sylt portez ce vieux Whiskey blond qui fume une

▶ Bold
The quick brown fox jumps over a Dog. Zwei Boxkämpfer jagen Eva durch Sylt portez ce vieux Whiskey blond qui

▶ Bold Italic
The quick brown fox jumps over a Dog. Zwei Boxkämpfer jagen Eva durch Sylt portez ce vieux Whiskey blond qui fume

---

A373 Mac + PC ② ✎ 1926: (Giambattista Bodoni, c. 1790)
Bauer Bodoni 2

abcdefghijklmnopqrstuvwxyz[äöüßåøæœç]
ABCDEFGHIJKLMNOPQRSTUVWXYZ
1234567890(.,;:?!$&-){ÄÖÜÅØÆŒÇ}*

a a *a*
BT1248
Bauer Bodoni 2, Blk,
BlkIta, BdCon, BlkCon
⊚
Poster Bodoni, Onyx

▶ Black
The quick brown fox jumps over a Dog. Zwei Boxkämpfer jagen Eva durch Sylt portez ce vieux

▶ Black Italic
The quick brown fox jumps over a Dog. Zwei Boxkämpfer jagen Eva durch Sylt portez ce vieux

▶ Bold Condensed
The quick brown fox jumps over a Dog. Zwei Boxkämpfer jagen Eva durch Sylt portez ce vieux Whiskey blond qui fume une pipe

▶ Black Condensed
The quick brown fox jumps over a Dog. Zwei Boxkämpfer jagen Eva durch Sylt portez ce vieux Whiskey blond qui fume une pipe

© FSI 1993

A1007 Mac + PC ② 1926: (Giambattista Bodoni, c. 1790)
Bauer Bodoni Small Caps/OSF

ABCDEFGHIJKLMNOPQRSTUVWXYZ[ÄÖÜSSÅØÆŒÇ]
ABCDEFGHIJKLMNOPQRSTUVWXYZ
1234567890(.,;:?!$&-*){ÄÖÜÅØÆŒÇ}

▶ Regular SC
THE QUICK BROWN FOX JUMPS OVER A DOG. 123 4567 890 ZWEI BOXKÄMPFER JAGEN EVA DURCH SYLT PORTEZ CE VIEUX WHISKEY BLOND

▶ Italic OSF
The quick brown fox jumps over a Dog. 123 4567 890 Zwei Boxkämpfer jagen Eva durch Sylt portez ce vieux Whiskey blond

▶ Bold OSF
The quick brown fox jumps over a Dog. 123 4567 890 Zwei Boxkämpfer jagen Eva durch Sylt portez ce vieux Whiskey

▶ Bold Italic OSF
The quick brown fox jumps over a Dog. 123 4567 890 Zwei Boxkämpfer jagen Eva durch Sylt portez ce vieux Whiskey

BT783 Mac + PC ⑥ (R. H. Middleton, 1936) Industry name
Modern 735 — Bodoni Campanile™

abcdefghijklmnopqrstuvwxyz1234567890[äöüßåøæœç]
ABCDEFGHIJKLMNOPQRSTUVWXYZ(.,;:?!$&-*){ÄÖÜÅØÆŒÇ}

BT Condensed Headlines 2:
Alternate Gothic™ No.2, Bodoni Campanile™, Hanseatic, Latin Extra Condensed
Ⓒ Poster Bodoni, Onyx, Victoria Titling

FB6372 Mac + PC ② 1992: (Sol. Hess: 1934) Richard Lipton
Bodoni Bold Condensed

abcdefghijklmnopqrstuvwxyz[äöüßåøæœç]
ABCDEFGHIJKLMNOPQRSTUVWXYZ
1234567890(.,;:?!$&-*){ÄÖÜÅØÆŒÇ}

FBI Condensed Classics™:
Bodoni Bold Compressed, Bodoni Bold Condensed, Caslon Bold Condensed, Century Bold Condensed, Cheltenham Bold Condensed
Ⓒ Berthold Bodoni Antiqua Condensed

FB6372 Mac + PC ② 1992: (Sol. Hess: 1934) Richard Lipton
Bodoni Bold Compressed

abcdefghijklmnopqrstuvwxyz[äöüßåøæœç]
ABCDEFGHIJKLMNOPQRSTUVWXYZ
1234567890(.,;:?!$&-*){ÄÖÜÅØÆŒÇ}

FBI Condensed Classics™:
Bodoni Bold Compressed, Bodoni Bold Condensed, Caslon Bold Condensed, Century Bold Condensed, Cheltenham Bold Condensed
Ⓒ Berthold Bodoni Antiqua Condensed

© FSI 1993

G1516 Mac + PC ② 1911: (G. Bodoni, 1790)

Bodoni No. 175™

abcdefghijklmnopqrstuvwxyz[äöüßåøæœç]
ABCDEFGHIJKLMNOPQRSTUVWXYZ
1234567890(.,:;?!$&-*){ÄÖÜÅØÆŒÇ}

Berthold Bodoni Antiqua, Bodoni, WTC Our Bodoni, Monotype Bodoni

▶ Regular
The quick brown fox jumps over a Dog. 123 4567 890 Zwei Boxkämpfer jagen Eva durch Sylt portez ce vieux Whiskey

▶ Italic
The quick brown fox jumps over a Dog. 123 4567 890 Zwei Boxkämpfer jagen Eva durch Sylt portez ce vieux Whiskey blond

▶ Small Caps
THE QUICK BROWN FOX JUMPS OVER A DOG. 123 4567 890 ZWEI BOXKÄMPFER JAGEN EVA DURCH SYLT PORTEZ CE VIEUX WHIS-

▶ Italic Small Caps
THE QUICK BROWN FOX JUMPS OVER A DOG. 123 4567 890 ZWEI BOXKÄMPFER JAGEN EVA DURCH SYLT PORTEZ CE VIEUX WHIS-

▶ Regular OSF
The quick brown fox jumps over a Dog. 123 4567 890 Zwei Boxkämpfer jagen Eva durch Sylt portez ce vieux Whiskey

▶ Italic OSF
The quick brown fox jumps over a Dog. 123 4567 890 Zwei Boxkämpfer jagen Eva durch Sylt portez ce vieux Whiskey blond

▶ Small Caps OSF
THE QUICK BROWN FOX JUMPS OVER A DOG. 123 4567 890 ZWEI BOXKÄMPFER JAGEN EVA DURCH SYLT PORTEZ CE VIEUX

▶ Italic Small Caps OSF
THE QUICK BROWN FOX JUMPS OVER A DOG. 123 4567 890 ZWEI BOXKÄMPFER JAGEN EVA DURCH SYLT PORTEZ CE VIEUX

▶ Regular, Short
The quick brown fox jumps over a Dog. 123 4567 890 Zwei Boxkämpfer jagen Eva durch Sylt portez ce vieux Whiskey

▶ Italic, Short
The quick brown fox jumps over a Dog. 123 4567 890 Zwei Boxkämpfer jagen Eva durch Sylt portez ce vieux Whiskey blond

▶ Small Caps, Short
THE QUICK BROWN FOX JUMPS OVER A DOG. 123 4567 890 ZWEI BOXKÄMPFER JAGEN EVA DURCH SYLT PORTEZ CE VIEUX WHIS-

▶ Italic Small Caps, Short
THE QUICK BROWN FOX JUMPS OVER A DOG. 123 4567 890 ZWEI BOXKÄMPFER JAGEN EVA DURCH SYLT PORTEZ CE VIEUX WHIS-

▶ Regular OSF, Short
The quick brown fox jumps over a Dog. 123 4567 890 Zwei Boxkämpfer jagen Eva durch Sylt portez ce vieux Whiskey

▶ Italic OSF, Short
The quick brown fox jumps over a Dog. 123 4567 890 Zwei Boxkämpfer jagen Eva durch Sylt portez ce vieux Whiskey blond

▶ Small Caps OSF, Short
THE QUICK BROWN FOX JUMPS OVER A DOG. 123 4567 890 ZWEI BOXKÄMPFER JAGEN EVA DURCH SYLT PORTEZ CE VIEUX

▶ Italic Small Caps OSF, Short
THE QUICK BROWN FOX JUMPS OVER A DOG. 123 4567 890 ZWEI BOXKÄMPFER JAGEN EVA DURCH SYLT PORTEZ CE VIEUX

© FSI 1993

G6342 Mac + PC (2) 1911: (G. Bodoni, 1790)
Bodoni No. 2175™ Bold

abcdefghijklmnopqrstuvwxyz[äöüßåøæœç]
ABCDEFGHIJKLMNOPQRSTUVWXYZ
1234567890(.,;:?!$&-*){ÄÖÜÅØÆŒÇ}

Berthold Bodoni Antiqua, Bodoni, WTC Our Bodoni, Monotype Bodoni

▶ Bold
The quick brown fox jumps over a Dog. Zwei Boxkämpfer jagen Eva durch Sylt portez ce vieux Whiskey blond qui fume

▶ Bold SC
THE QUICK BROWN FOX JUMPS OVER A DOG. 123 4567 890 ZWEI BOXKÄMPFER JAGEN EVA DURCH SYLT PORTEZ CE VIEUX

▶ Bold Short
The quick brown fox jumps over a Dog. Zwei Boxkämpfer jagen Eva durch Sylt portez ce vieux Whiskey blond qui fume

▶ Bold Short SC
THE QUICK BROWN FOX JUMPS OVER A DOG. 123 4567 890 ZWEI BOXKÄMPFER JAGEN EVA DURCH SYLT PORTEZ CE

G2785 Mac + PC (2) 1950: (Sol. Hess, 1911)
Bodoni No. 26

abcdefghijklmnopqrstuvwxyz[äöüssåøæœç]
ABCDEFGHIJKLMNOPQRSTUVWXYZ
1234567890(.,;:?!$&-*){äöüåøæœç}

SF6635 Mac (6) 1993: Rod McDonald
Bodoni Open Condensed

abcdefghijklmnopqrstuvwxyz1234567890[äöüßåøæœç]

ABCDEFGHIJKLMNOPQRSTUVWXYZ(.,;:?!$&-*){ÄÖÜÅØÆŒÇ}

Stylus Headlines 1:
Bodoni Open Condensed, Fanfare Recut, Goudy Globe Gothic, Loyalist™ Condensed

C178 Mac + PC (2) 1920: (Giambattista Bodoni, c. 1790) Chauncey H. Griffith
Poster Bodoni

abcdefghijklmnopqrstuvwxyz[äöüßåøæœç]
ABCDEFGHIJKLMNOPQRSTUVWXYZ
1234567890(.,;:?!$&-*){ÄÖÜÅØÆŒÇ}

aaa
BT1248
Bauer Bodoni 2, Blk, BlkIta, BdCon, BlkCon
Bodoni, Falstaff, Normande, Annlie

▶ Regular
The quick brown fox jumps over a Dog. Zwei Boxkämpfer jagen Eva durch Sylt portez ce

▶ Italic
The quick brown fox jumps over a Dog. Zwei Boxkämpfer jagen Eva durch Sylt portez ce

Aquarius:
Aquarius™ No. 8, Clarendon Book Condensed, Poster Bodoni
aaa BT1248
Bauer Bodoni 2, Blk, BlkIta, BdCon, BlkCon

© FSI 1993

B 38

C995 MAC + PC ② 1989: (G. Bodoni, c. 1790) M. Vignelli, T. Carnase
WTC Our Bodoni™

abcdefghijklmnopqrstuvwxyz[äöüßåøæœç]
ABCDEFGHIJKLMNOPQRSTUVWXYZ
1234567890(.,;:?!$&-*){ÄÖÜÅØÆŒÇ}

© Monotype Bodoni, Bodoni Bauer Bodoni, Berthold Bodoni Antiqua

▶ Light
The quick brown fox jumps over a Dog. Zwei Boxkämpfer jagen Eva durch Sylt portez ce vieux Whiskey blond qui fume une

▶ Light Italic
The quick brown fox jumps over a Dog. Zwei Boxkämpfer jagen Eva durch Sylt portez ce vieux Whiskey blond qui fume une

▶ Regular
The quick brown fox jumps over a Dog. Zwei Boxkämpfer jagen Eva durch Sylt portez ce vieux Whiskey blond qui fume

▶ Italic
The quick brown fox jumps over a Dog. Zwei Boxkämpfer jagen Eva durch Sylt portez ce vieux Whiskey blond qui fume

▶ Medium
The quick brown fox jumps over a Dog. Zwei Boxkämpfer jagen Eva durch Sylt portez ce vieux Whiskey blond

▶ Medium Italic
The quick brown fox jumps over a Dog. Zwei Boxkämpfer jagen Eva durch Sylt portez ce vieux Whiskey blond

▶ Bold
The quick brown fox jumps over a Dog. Zwei Boxkämpfer jagen Eva durch Sylt portez ce vieux

▶ Bold Italic
The quick brown fox jumps over a Dog. Zwei Boxkämpfer jagen Eva durch Sylt portez ce vieux Whiskey

BT812 MAC + PC ⑥ 1970: Tom Carnase, Ronne Bonder
ITC Bolt Bold®

**abcdefghijklmnopqrstuvwxyz[äöüßåøæœç]
ABCDEFGHIJKLMNOPQRSTUVWXYZ
1234567890(.,;:?!$&-*){ÄÖÜÅØÆŒÇ}**

Bitstream Bold Headlines 1:
Blippo™ Black, Handel Gothic, ITC Bolt Bold®, Trump Mediaeval Black

BT759 MAC + PC ② 1936: C. H. Griffith (1860: A. C. Phemister)
Bookman™

abcdefghijklmnopqrstuvwxyz[äöüßåøæœç]
ABCDEFGHIJKLMNOPQRSTUVWXYZ
1234567890(.,;:?!$&-*){ÄÖÜÅØÆŒÇ}

© Binny Old Style, Bruce Old Style

▶ Regular
The quick brown fox jumps over a Dog. Zwei Boxkämpfer jagen Eva durch Sylt portez ce vieux Whiskey blond qui fume

▶ Italic
The quick brown fox jumps over a Dog. Zwei Boxkämpfer jagen Eva durch Sylt portez ce vieux Whiskey blond qui fume

© FSI 1993

Bookman Headline
BT760 Mac + PC — 1936: C. H. Griffith (1860: A. C. Phemister)

abcdefghijklmnopqrstuvwxyz[äöüßåøæœç]
ABCDEFGHIJKLMNOPQRSTUVWXYZ
1234567890(.,;:?!$&-*){ÄÖÜÅØÆŒÇ}

Binny Old Style, Bruce Old Style

▶ Regular
The quick brown fox jumps over a Dog. Zwei Boxkämpfer jagen Eva durch Sylt portez ce vieux Whiskey blond qui

▶ Italic
The quick brown fox jumps over a Dog. Zwei Boxkämpfer jagen Eva durch Sylt portez ce vieux Whiskey blond

ITC Bookman® 1
A014 Mac + PC — 1975: Ed Benguiat

abcdefghijklmnopqrstuvwxyz[äöüßåøæœç]
ABCDEFGHIJKLMNOPQRSTUVWXYZ
1234567890(.,;:?!$&-*){ÄÖÜÅØÆŒÇ}

aa*a*
BT1250
ITC Bookman 1, Lt, LtIta, Demi, DemiIta

▶ Light
The quick brown fox jumps over a Dog. Zwei Boxkämpfer jagen Eva durch Sylt portez ce vieux Whiskey

▶ Light Italic
The quick brown fox jumps over a Dog. Zwei Boxkämpfer jagen Eva durch Sylt portez ce vieux Whiskey blond

▶ Demi
The quick brown fox jumps over a Dog. Zwei Boxkämpfer jagen Eva durch Sylt portez ce vieux

▶ Demi Italic
The quick brown fox jumps over a Dog. Zwei Boxkämpfer jagen Eva durch Sylt portez ce

ITC Bookman 2
A482 Mac + PC — 1975: Ed Benguiat

abcdefghijklmnopqrstuvwxyz[äöüßåøæœç]
ABCDEFGHIJKLMNOPQRSTUVWXYZ
1234567890(.,;:?!$&-*){ÄÖÜÅØÆŒÇ}

aa*a*
BT1251
ITC Bookman 2, Med, MedIta, Bd, BdIta

▶ Medium
The quick brown fox jumps over a Dog. Zwei Boxkämpfer jagen Eva durch Sylt portez ce vieux Whiskey

▶ Medium Italic
The quick brown fox jumps over a Dog. Zwei Boxkämpfer jagen Eva durch Sylt portez ce vieux Whiskey

▶ Bold
The quick brown fox jumps over a Dog. Zwei Boxkämpfer jagen Eva durch Sylt portez ce

▶ Bold Italic
The quick brown fox jumps over a Dog. Zwei Boxkämpfer jagen Eva durch Sylt portez ce

© FSI 1993

L2820 Mac ⑥ ✏ 1987: David Quay
Bordeaux® Display
abcdefghijklmnopqrstuvwxyz[äöüßåøæœç]1234567890
ABCDEFGHIJKLMNOPQRSTUVWXYZ(.,;:?!$&-`)ÄÖÜÅØÆŒÇ

L2564 Mac ② ✏ 1987: David Quay
Bordeaux™ Roman
abcdefghijklmnopqrstuvwxyz[äöüßåøæœç]1234567890
ABCDEFGHIJKLMNOPQRSTUVWXYZ(.,;:?!$&-`)ÄÖÜÅØÆŒÇ

L2565 Mac ② ✏ 1987: David Quay
Bordeaux Italic
abcdefghijklmnopqrstuvwxyz[äöüßåøæœç]1234567890
ABCDEFGHIJKLMNOPQRSTUVWXYZ(.,;:?!$&-`)ÄÖÜÅØÆŒÇ

L6113 Mac ② ✏ 1990: David Quay
Bordeaux Roman Bold
abcdefghijklmnopqrstuvwxyz[äöüßåøæœç]1234567890
ABCDEFGHIJKLMNOPQRSTUVWXYZ(.,;:?!$&-`)ÄÖÜÅØÆŒÇ

L6114 Mac ④ ✏ 1987: David Quay
Bordeaux Script
abcdefghijklmnopqrstuvwxyz[äöüßåøæœç]1234567890(.,;:?!$&-`)
ABCDEFGHIJKLMNOPQRSTUVWXYZ

AB6652 Mac + PC ③ ✏ 1986: Albert Boton
Boton™
abcdefghijklmnopqrstuvwxyz[äöüßåøæœç]
ABCDEFGHIJKLMNOPQRSTUVWXYZ
1234567890(.,;:?!$&-*){ÄÖÜÅØÆŒÇ}

© PMN Caecilia, Glypha, Serifa, Calvert

▶ **Light**
The quick brown fox jumps over a Dog. Zwei Boxkämpfer jagen Eva durch Sylt portez ce vieux Whiskey blond qui fume une

▶ **Light Italic**
The quick brown fox jumps over a Dog. Zwei Boxkämpfer jagen Eva durch Sylt portez ce vieux Whiskey blond qui fume une

▶ **Regular**
The quick brown fox jumps over a Dog. Zwei Boxkämpfer jagen Eva durch Sylt portez ce vieux Whiskey blond qui fume

▶ **Italic**
The quick brown fox jumps over a Dog. Zwei Boxkämpfer jagen Eva durch Sylt portez ce vieux Whiskey blond qui fume

© FSI 1993

▼ AB6652   Mac + PC   Boton™

▶ Medium
The quick brown fox jumps over a Dog. Zwei Boxkämpfer jagen Eva durch Sylt portez ce vieux Whiskey blond qui

▶ Medium Italic
The quick brown fox jumps over a Dog. Zwei Boxkämpfer jagen Eva durch Sylt portez ce vieux Whiskey blond

▶ Bold
The quick brown fox jumps over a Dog. Zwei Boxkämpfer jagen Eva durch Sylt portez ce vieux Whiskey blond

▶ Bold Italic
The quick brown fox jumps over a Dog. Zwei Boxkämpfer jagen Eva durch Sylt portez ce vieux Whiskey

---

SG1801   Mac   (6)   🖉 1972: Tony Wenman
Bottleneck™

abcdefghijklmnopqrstuvwxyz1234567890
ABCDEFGHIJKLMNOPQRSTUVWXYZ
[äöüßåøæœç](.,;:?!$&-*)ÄÖÜÅØÆŒÇ

AB2915   Mac + PC   (4)   🖉 1955: G. G. Lange
Berthold Boulevard™

abcdefghijklmnopqrstuvwxyz[äöüßåøæœç]1234567890(.,;:?!$&-)*
ABCDEFGHIJKLMNOPQ
RSTUVWXYZ{ÄÖÜÅØÆŒÇ}

Berthold Scripts 1:
Berthold Bellevue™, Berthold Boulevard™, Berthold Script™
Ⓒ Francis

F6344   Mac   (6)
A*I Box Gothic

ABCDEFGHIJKLMNOPQRSTUVWXYZ
ABCDEFGHIJKLMNOPQRSTUVWXYZ
1234567890(.,;:?!$&-*){ }[ ]

A*I Wood Types 1:
A*I Barrel, A*I Box Gothic, A*I French XXX Condensed™, A*I Painter™, A*I Tuscan Egyptian™, Antique Condensed

---

M267   Mac + PC   (6)   🖉 1930: W. A. Woolley
Braggadocio™

abcdefghijklmnopqrstuvwxyz[äöüßåøæœç]
ABCDEFGHIJKLMNOPQRSTUVWXYZ
1234567890(.,;:?!$&-*){ÄÖÜÅØÆŒÇ}

Headliners 3:
Braggadocio™, Figaro®, Forte™, Klang™
Ⓒ Futura Black

© FSI 1993

C596 Mac + PC — Letraset™ Bramley™
1980: Alan Meeks

abcdefghijklmnopqrstuvwxyz[äöüßåøæœç]
ABCDEFGHIJKLMNOPQRSTUVWXYZ
1234567890(.,;:?!$&-*){ÄÖÜÅØÆŒÇ}

▶ Light
The quick brown fox jumps over a Dog. Zwei Boxkämpfer jagen Eva durch Sylt portez ce vieux Whiskey blond qui fume une

▶ Medium
The quick brown fox jumps over a Dog. Zwei Boxkämpfer jagen Eva durch Sylt portez ce vieux Whiskey blond qui

▶ Bold
The quick brown fox jumps over a Dog. Zwei Boxkämpfer jagen Eva durch Sylt portez ce vieux Whiskey blond

▶ Extra Bold
The quick brown fox jumps over a Dog. Zwei Boxkämpfer jagen Eva durch Sylt portez ce vieux Whiskey

C016 Mac + PC — Branding Iron

abcdefghijklmnopqrstuvwxyz[äöüßåøæœç]
ABCDEFGHIJKLMNOPQRSTUVWXYZ
1234567890(.,;:?!$&-*){ÄÖÜÅØÆŒÇ}

Branding Iron:
Branding Iron, Isabella™, McCollough, Raphael™
© P. T. Barnum, Barnum Block, Figaro, Egyptian

C016 Mac + PC — Branding Iron

Branding Iron:
Branding Iron, Isabella™, McCollough, Raphael™

C2524 Mac + PC — Brasilia Three

abcdefghijklmnopqrstuvwxyz[äöüßåøæœç]
ABCDEFGHIJKLMNOPQRSTUVWXYZ
1234567890(.,;:?!$&-*)◊ÄÖÜÅØÆŒÇ♦

Headlines 88S:
Brasilia Seven, Brasilia Three, Latin Bold, Latin Elongated, Radiant™

C2524 Mac + PC — Brasilia Seven

abcdefghijklmnopqrstuvwxyz[äöüßåøæœç]
ABCDEFGHIJKLMNOPQRSTUVWXYZ
1234567890(.,;:?!$&-*)◊ÄÖÜÅØÆŒÇ♦

© FSI 1993

▼ C2524 Mac + PC Brasilia Seven

Headlines 88S:
Brasilia Seven, Brasilia Three, Latin Bold, Latin Elongated, Radiant™

K2834 Mac + PC   ⑦   ✎ 1991: Sebastian Kempgen
Breitkopf™ Fraktur

abcdefghijklmnopqrstuvwxyz[äöüßåøæœç]
ABCDEFGHIJKLMNOPQRSTUVWXYZ
1234567890(.,;:?!§&-*){ÄeÖeÜeÅDÆŒÇ}

FB6370 Mac + PC   ⑥   ✎ 1992: Richard Lipton
Bremen

ABCDEFGHIJKLMNOPQRSTUVWXYZ[ÄÖÜÅØÆŒÇ]
ABCDEFGHIJKLMNOPQRSTUVWXYZ
1234567890(.,;:?!$&-*){ÄÖÜÅØÆŒÇ}

© Munich

▶ Light
THE QUICK BROWN FOX JUMPS OVER A DOG. ZWEI BOXKÄMPFER JAGEN EVA DURCH SYLT PORTEZ CE VIEUX WHISKEY

▶ Bold
THE QUICK BROWN FOX JUMPS OVER A DOG. ZWEI BOXKÄMPFER JAGEN EVA DURCH SYLT PORTEZ CE

▶ Black
THE QUICK BROWN FOX JUMPS OVER A DOG. ZWEI BOXKÄMPFER JAGEN EVA DURCH SYLT PORTEZ CE

SG1806 Mac   ⑥   ✎ 1979: Alan Bright
Brighton™ Light

abcdefghijklmnopqrstuvwxyz[äöüßåøæœç]
ABCDEFGHIJKLMNOPQRSTUVWXYZ
1234567890(.,;:?!$&-*)ÄÖÜÅØÆŒÇ

SG1807 Mac   ⑥   ✎ 1979: Alan Bright
Brighton Light Italic

abcdefghijklmnopqrstuvwxyz[äöüßåøæœç]
ABCDEFGHIJKLMNOPQRSTUVWXYZ
1234567890(.,;:?!$&-*)ÄÖÜÅØÆŒÇ

SG1808 Mac   ⑥   ✎ 1979: Alan Bright
Brighton Bold

abcdefghijklmnopqrstuvwxyz[äöüßåøæœç]
ABCDEFGHIJKLMNOPQRSTUVWXYZ
1234567890(.,;:?!$&-*)ÄÖÜÅØÆŒÇ

© FSI 1993

SG1809 Mac ⑥ ✏ 1979: Alan Bright
Brighton Extra Bold

abcdefghijklmnopqrstuvwxyz[äöüßåøæœç]
ABCDEFGHIJKLMNOPQRSTUVWXYZ
1234567890(.,;:?!$&-*)ÄÖÜÅØÆŒÇ

MC2895 Mac + PC ④ ✏ V. Fenocchio
Brio™

abcdefghijklmnopqrstuvwxyz[äöüßåøæœç]
ABCDEFGHIJKLMNOPQRSTUVWXYZ
1234567890(.,;:?!$&-*){ÄÖÜÅØÆŒÇ}

C993 Mac + PC ⑥
PL Britannia Bold

abcdefghijklmnopqrstuvwxyz[äöüßåøæœç]
ABCDEFGHIJKLMNOPQRSTUVWXYZ
1234567890(.,;:?!$&-*)◊ÄÖÜÅØÆŒÇ♦

Headlines 83S:
Barclay™ Open, Delphian™ Open, Fluidum™ Bold, PL Bernhardt, PL Britannia Bold, PL Fiorello™ Condensed, PL Modern Heavy Condensed, PL Torino Open

EF2517 Mac + PC ①
Britannic™

abcdefghijklmnopqrstuvwxyz[äöüßåøæœç]
ABCDEFGHIJKLMNOPQRSTUVWXYZ
1234567890(.,;:?!$&-*){ÄÖÜÅØÆŒÇ}

👁 Mtronome Gothic, Radiant

▶ **Extra Light**
The quick brown fox jumps over a Dog. Zwei Boxkämpfer jagen Eva durch Sylt portez ce vieux Whiskey blond qui fume une pipe aber echt über die Mauer

▶ **Light**
The quick brown fox jumps over a Dog. Zwei Boxkämpfer jagen Eva durch Sylt portez ce vieux Whiskey blond qui fume une pipe aber echt

▶ **Medium**
The quick brown fox jumps over a Dog. Zwei Boxkämpfer jagen Eva durch Sylt portez ce vieux Whiskey blond qui fume une pipe aber

▶ **Bold**
The quick brown fox jumps over a Dog. Zwei Boxkämpfer jagen Eva durch Sylt portez ce vieux Whiskey blond qui fume

▶ **Ultra**
The quick brown fox jumps over a Dog. Zwei Boxkämpfer jagen Eva durch Sylt portez ce vieux Whiskey blond

Broadway™
BT1252 Mac + PC ⑥ — 1928: M. F. Benton

abcdefghijklmnopqrstuvwxyz[äöüßåøæœç]
ABCDEFGHIJKLMNOPQRSTUVWXYZ
1234567890(.,:;?!$&-*){ÄÖÜÅØÆŒÇ}

TC Broadway
C468 Mac + PC ⑥ — (M. F. Benton, 1928)

abcdefghijklmnopqrstuvwxyz[äöüåøæœç]
ABCDEFGHIJKLMNOPQRSTUVWXYZ
1234567890(.,:;?!$&-*)◊ÄÖÜÅØÆŒÇ♦

Headlines 82S:
Neon Extra Condensed™, PL Barnum Block, PL Benguiat Frisky Bold, PL Davison Zip Bold, PL Fiedler Gothic Bold, PL Futura Maxi 2, PL Trophy™ Oblique, Ritmo™ Bold, TC Broadway
ⓒ Beverly Hills, Art Deco

Broadway Engraved
BT789 Mac + PC ⑥ — 1928: Sol. Hess

abcdefghijklmnopqrstuvwxyz[äöüßåøæœç]
ABCDEFGHIJKLMNOPQRSTUVWXYZ
1234567890(.,:;?!$&-*){ÄÖÜÅØÆŒÇ}

Bitstream Decorative 1:
Broadway Engraved, Davida, P. T. Barnum™, Playbill®
ⓒ Beverly Hills, Chic, Jazz

Brody™
EF1069 Mac + PC ④ — 1953: Harold Broderson

abcdefghijklmnopqrstuvwxyzäöüßåøæœç
ABCDEFGHIJKLMNOPQRSTUVWXYZ
1234567890(.,:;?!$&-*){ÄÖÜÅØÆŒÇ}

Brody™, Commercial Script
ⓒ Brophy, Brush, Flash

FF Brokenscript™
FF734 Mac + PC ⑦ — 1991: Just van Rossum

abcdefghijklmnopqrstuvwxyz[áőüßåøæœç]
ABCDEFGHIJKLMNOPQRSTUVWXYZ
1234567890(.,:;?!$¢-*){ÁŐÜÅØÆŒÇ}

▶ Bold
The quick brown fox jumps over a Dog. Zwei Boxkämpfer jagen Eva durch Sylt portez ce vieux Whis-

▶ Bold Rough
The quick brown fox jumps over a Dog. Zwei Boxkämpfer jagen Eva durch Sylt portez ce vieux Whis-

© FSI 1993

▼ FF734 Mac + PC   FF Brokenscript™

► Bold Condensed
The quick brown fox jumps over a Dog. Zwei Boxkämpfer jagen Eva durch Sylt portez ce vieux Whiskey blond qui fume une pipe

► Bold Condensed Rough
The quick brown fox jumps over a Dog. Zwei Boxkämpfer jagen Eva durch Sylt portez ce vieux Whiskey blond qui fume une pipe

L2566 Mac   ④   ✎ 1986: David Quay
Bronx™

abcdefghijklmnopqrstuvwxyz
ABCDEFGHIJKLMNOPQRSTUVWXYZ
1234567890(.,:;?!$&-*)[äöüßåøæœç]

C6426 Mac + PC   ④   ✎ (1953: Harold Broderson)
Brophy™ Script

abcdefghijklmnopqrstuvwxyz[äöüßåøæœç]
ABCDEFGHIJKLMNOPQRSTUVWXYZ
1234567890(.,:;?!$&-*){ÄÖÜÅØÆŒÇ}

Basque, etc:
Basque, Brophy™ Script, Chevalier™, Uncial
© Brody, Brush, Flash

BT761 Mac + PC   ②   ✎ 1909: (1869) Sol. Hess
Bruce Old Style

abcdefghijklmnopqrstuvwxyz[äöüßåøæœç]
ABCDEFGHIJKLMNOPQRSTUVWXYZ
1234567890(.,:;?!$&-*){ÄÖÜÅØÆŒÇ}

© Binny Old Style, Bookman

► Regular
The quick brown fox jumps over a Dog. Zwei Boxkämpfer jagen Eva durch Sylt portez ce vieux Whiskey blond qui fume

► Italic
The quick brown fox jumps over a Dog. Zwei Boxkämpfer jagen Eva durch Sylt portez ce vieux Whiskey blond qui fume une

A018 Mac + PC   ④   ✎ 1942: Robert E. Smith
Brush Script™

abcdefghijklmnopqrstuvwxyz[äöüßåøæœç]
ABCDEFGHIJKLMNOPQRSTUVWXYZ
1234567890(.,:;?!$&-*){ÄÖÜÅØÆŒÇ}

Hobo:
Brush Script™, Hobo, Stencil™
aaa ⌨ BT762
Bitstream Brush 1
⌨ BT1253

© FSI 1993

B 47

BT762 Mac + PC
Bitstream Brush 1

Bitstream Brush 1:
Bison™, Lydian Cursive, Ondine™, Palette™

BT763 Mac + PC
Bitstream Brush 2

Bitstream Brush 2:
Impress™, Impuls™, Jefferson™, Mandate™

TF6628 Mac + PC (2) — 1983-92: Joseph Treacy
TF Bryn Mawr A

abcdefghijklmnopqrstuvwxyz[äöüßåøæœç]
ABCDEFGHIJKLMNOPQRSTUVWXYZ
1234567890(.,;:?!$&-*){ÄÖÜÅØÆŒÇ}

▶ Light
The quick brown fox jumps over a Dog. Zwei Boxkämpfer jagen Eva durch Sylt portez ce vieux Whiskey blond qui fume une pipe aber

▶ Light Italic
The quick brown fox jumps over a Dog. Zwei Boxkämpfer jagen Eva durch Sylt portez ce vieux Whiskey blond qui fume une pipe

▶ Medium
The quick brown fox jumps over a Dog. Zwei Boxkämpfer jagen Eva durch Sylt portez ce vieux Whiskey blond qui

▶ Medium Italic
The quick brown fox jumps over a Dog. Zwei Boxkämpfer jagen Eva durch Sylt portez ce vieux Whiskey blond qui

TF6629 Mac + PC (2) — 1983-92: Joseph Treacy
TF Bryn Mawr B

abcdefghijklmnopqrstuvwxyz[äöüßåøæœç]
ABCDEFGHIJKLMNOPQRSTUVWXYZ
1234567890(.,;:?!$&-*){ÄÖÜÅØÆŒÇ}

▶ Book
The quick brown fox jumps over a Dog. Zwei Boxkämpfer jagen Eva durch Sylt portez ce vieux Whiskey blond qui fume une

▶ Book Italic
The quick brown fox jumps over a Dog. Zwei Boxkämpfer jagen Eva durch Sylt portez ce vieux Whiskey blond qui fume une

▶ Bold
The quick brown fox jumps over a Dog. Zwei Boxkämpfer jagen Eva durch Sylt portez ce vieux Whiskey

▶ Bold Italic
The quick brown fox jumps over a Dog. Zwei Boxkämpfer jagen Eva durch Sylt portez ce vieux Whiskey

CT871 Mac + PC (1) — 1990: Adrian Williams
Bulldog™

abcdefghijklmnopqrstuvwxyz[äöüßåøæœç]
ABCDEFGHIJKLMNOPQRSTUVWXYZ
1234567890(.,;:?!$&-*){ÄÖÜÅØÆŒÇ}

© FSI 1993

▼ CT871 Mac + PC Bulldog™

Bureau Grotesque,
Headline Bold,
Grotesque

▶ Regular
The quick brown fox jumps over a Dog. Zwei Boxkämpfer jagen Eva durch Sylt portez ce vieux Whiskey blond qui fume une pipe aber echt

▶ Italic
The quick brown fox jumps over a Dog. Zwei Boxkämpfer jagen Eva durch Sylt portez ce vieux Whiskey blond qui fume une pipe aber echt

▶ Medium
The quick brown fox jumps over a Dog. Zwei Boxkämpfer jagen Eva durch Sylt portez ce vieux Whiskey blond qui fume une pipe aber echt

▶ Medium Italic
The quick brown fox jumps over a Dog. Zwei Boxkämpfer jagen Eva durch Sylt portez ce vieux Whiskey blond qui fume une pipe aber echt

▶ Bold
The quick brown fox jumps over a Dog. Zwei Boxkämpfer jagen Eva durch Sylt portez ce vieux Whiskey blond qui fume une pipe

▶ Bold Italic
The quick brown fox jumps over a Dog. Zwei Boxkämpfer jagen Eva durch Sylt portez ce vieux Whiskey blond qui fume une pipe

BT764 Mac + PC ② ✎ 1927–28: (William Martin, 1790) M. F. Benton

Bulmer

abcdefghijklmnopqrstuvwxyz[äöüßåøæœç]
ABCDEFGHIJKLMNOPQRSTUVWXYZ
1234567890(.,;:?!$&-*){ÄÖÜÅØÆŒÇ}

Wessex

▶ Regular
The quick brown fox jumps over a Dog. Zwei Boxkämpfer jagen Eva durch Sylt portez ce vieux Whiskey blond qui fume une pipe aber echt

▶ Italic
The quick brown fox jumps over a Dog. Zwei Boxkämpfer jagen Eva durch Sylt portez ce vieux Whiskey blond qui fume une pipe aber echt

C2780 Mac + PC ⑥

Burin Roman

abcdefghijklmnopqrstuvwxyz[äöüßåç]
ABCDEFGHIJKLMNOPQRSTUVWXYZ
1234567890(.,;:?!$&-*){ÄÖÜÅ^{thst}Ç}

Agfa Engravers 1:
Antique Roman, Artisan Roman, Burin Roman, Burin Sans, Classic Roman, Handle Old Style, Roman

C2780 Mac + PC ⑥

Burin Sans

abcdefghijklmnopqrstuvwxyz[äöüßåç]
ABCDEFGHIJKLMNOPQRSTUVWXYZ
1234567890(.,;:?!$&-*){ÄÖÜÅ^{thst}Ç}

Agfa Engravers 1:
Antique Roman, Artisan Roman, Burin Roman, Burin Sans, Classic Roman, Handle Old Style, Roman

© FSI 1993

L2567 Mac ⑥ ✎ 1985: Alan Meeks
Burlington™

abcdefghijklmnopqrstuvwxyz[äöüßåøæœç]
ABCDEFGHIJKLMNOPQRSTUVWXYZ
1234567890(.,:;?!$&-*)ÄÖÜÅØÆŒÇ

BT765 Mac + PC ⑤ ✎ 1970: Herb Lubalin
ITC Busorama®

ABCDEFGHIJKLMNOPQRSTUVWXYZ
1234567890(.,:;?!$&-*)[]{ÄÖÜÅØÆŒÇ}

▶ Light
THE QUICK BROWN FOX JUMPS OVER A DOG. ZWEI BOXKÄMPFER JAGEN EVA DURCH SYLT PORTEZ CE VIEUX WHISKEY BLOND QUI

▶ Medium
THE QUICK BROWN FOX JUMPS OVER A DOG. ZWEI BOXKÄMPFER JAGEN EVA DURCH SYLT PORTEZ CE VIEUX WHISKEY

▶ Bold
THE QUICK BROWN FOX JUMPS OVER A DOG. ZWEI BOXKÄMPFER JAGEN EVA DURCH SYLT PORTEZ CE VIEUX WHISKEY

© FSI 1993

Rian Hughes, London, UK

EF6468 Mac + PC (6)
Cabaret™

abcdefghijklmnopqrstuvwxyzäöüßåøæç
ABCDEFGHIJKLMNOPQRSTUVWXYZ
1234567890(.,;:?!$&-*)ÄÖÜÅØÆŒÇ

E+F Special Headlines 4:
Bernhard Antique Bold Condensed, Cabaret™, Conference™, Countdown™, Einhorn, Highlight
aaa L6115
Cabaret™

A1526 Mac + PC (3) 1991: Peter Matthias Noordzij
PMN Caecilia™

abcdefghijklmnopqrstuvwxyz[äöüßåøæœç]
ABCDEFGHIJKLMNOPQRSTUVWXYZ
1234567890(.,;:?!$&-*){ÄÖÜÅØÆŒÇ}

© Glypha, Serifa, Boton

▶ 45 Light
The quick brown fox jumps over a Dog. Zwei Boxkämpfer jagen Eva durch Sylt portez ce vieux Whiskey blond

▶ 46 Light Italic
The quick brown fox jumps over a Dog. Zwei Boxkämpfer jagen Eva durch Sylt portez ce vieux Whiskey blond qui fume

▶ 55 Regular
The quick brown fox jumps over a Dog. Zwei Boxkämpfer jagen Eva durch Sylt portez ce vieux Whiskey

▶ 56 Italic
The quick brown fox jumps over a Dog. Zwei Boxkämpfer jagen Eva durch Sylt portez ce vieux Whiskey blond qui fume

▶ 75 Bold
The quick brown fox jumps over a Dog. Zwei Boxkämpfer jagen Eva durch Sylt portez ce vieux Whiskey

▶ 76 Bold Italic
The quick brown fox jumps over a Dog. Zwei Boxkämpfer jagen Eva durch Sylt portez ce vieux Whiskey blond qui

▶ 85 Heavy
The quick brown fox jumps over a Dog. Zwei Boxkämpfer jagen Eva durch Sylt portez ce vieux

▶ 86 Heavy Italic
The quick brown fox jumps over a Dog. Zwei Boxkämpfer jagen Eva durch Sylt portez ce vieux Whiskey blond

A1154 Mac + PC (3) 1991: Peter Matthias Noordzij
PMN Caecilia Small Caps / OSF

ABCDEFGHIJKLMNOPQRSTUVWXYZ[ÄÖÜSSÅØÆŒÇ]
ABCDEFGHIJKLMNOPQRSTUVWXYZ
1234567890(.,;:?!$&-*){ÄÖÜÅØÆŒÇ}

© Glypha, Serifa, Boton

▶ 45 Light Small Caps OSF
THE QUICK BROWN FOX JUMPS OVER A DOG. 123 4567 890 ZWEI BOXKÄMPFER JAGEN EVA DURCH SYLT PORTEZ CE VIEUX

▶ 46 Light Italic Small Caps
THE QUICK BROWN FOX JUMPS OVER A DOG. 123 4567 890 ZWEI BOXKÄMPFER JAGEN EVA DURCH SYLT PORTEZ CE VIEUX

© FSI 1993

▼ A1154 Mac + PC PMN Caecilia Small Caps / OSF

▶ 55 Regular Small Caps
THE QUICK BROWN FOX JUMPS OVER A DOG. 123 4567 890 ZWEI BOXKÄMPFER JAGEN EVA DURCH SYLT PORTEZ CE VIEUX

▶ 56 Regular Italic Small Caps
THE QUICK BROWN FOX JUMPS OVER A DOG. 123 4567 890 ZWEI BOXKÄMPFER JAGEN EVA DURCH SYLT PORTEZ CE VIEUX

▶ 75 Bold Small Caps
THE QUICK BROWN FOX JUMPS OVER A DOG. 123 4567 890 ZWEI BOXKÄMPFER JAGEN EVA DURCH SYLT PORTEZ CE

▶ 76 Bold Italic Small Caps
THE QUICK BROWN FOX JUMPS OVER A DOG. 123 4567 890 ZWEI BOXKÄMPFER JAGEN EVA DURCH SYLT PORTEZ CE VIEUX

▶ 85 Heavy Small Caps
THE QUICK BROWN FOX JUMPS OVER A DOG. 123 4567 890 ZWEI BOXKÄMPFER JAGEN EVA DURCH SYLT PORTEZ CE

▶ 86 Heavy Italic Small Caps
THE QUICK BROWN FOX JUMPS OVER A DOG. 123 4567 890 ZWEI BOXKÄMPFER JAGEN EVA DURCH SYLT PORTEZ CE VIEUX

FB6917 Mac + PC ⑥ 1993: Tobias Frere-Jones

Cafeteria™

abcdefghijklmnopqrstuvwxyz[äöüßåøæœç]
ABCDEFGHIJKLMNOPQRSTUVWXYZ
1234567890(.,;:?!$&-*){ÄÖÜÅØÆŒÇ}

▶ Light
The quick brown fox jumps over a Dog. Zwei Boxkämpfer jagen Eva durch Sylt portez ce vieux Whiskey blond qui fume une pipe aber echt über die Mauer gesprungen und auch smørebrød en ysjes

▶ Regular
The quick brown fox jumps over a Dog. Zwei Boxkämpfer jagen Eva durch Sylt portez ce vieux Whiskey blond qui fume une pipe aber echt über die Mauer gesprungen und auch

▶ Bold
The quick brown fox jumps over a Dog. Zwei Boxkämpfer jagen Eva durch Sylt portez ce vieux Whiskey blond qui fume une pipe aber echt über die Mauer gesprungen und auch

▶ Black
The quick brown fox jumps over a Dog. Zwei Boxkämpfer jagen Eva durch Sylt portez ce vieux Whiskey blond qui fume une pipe aber echt über die Mauer

A082 Mac + PC ② 1978: (W. A.. Dwiggins 1938–40) John Quaranta

New Caledonia™

abcdefghijklmnopqrstuvwxyz[äöüßåøæœç]
ABCDEFGHIJKLMNOPQRSTUVWXYZ
1234567890(.,;:?!$&-*){ÄÖÜÅØÆŒÇ}

aa*a*
BT766
Caledonia, Reg, Ita, Bd, BdIta

▶ Regular
The quick brown fox jumps over a Dog. Zwei Boxkämpfer jagen Eva durch Sylt portez ce vieux Whiskey blond qui fume une

▶ Regular Italic
The quick brown fox jumps over a Dog. Zwei Boxkämpfer jagen Eva durch Sylt portez ce vieux Whiskey blond qui fume une pipe

▶ Semi Bold
The quick brown fox jumps over a Dog. Zwei Boxkämpfer jagen Eva durch Sylt portez ce vieux Whiskey blond qui fume

▶ Semi Bold Italic
The quick brown fox jumps over a Dog. Zwei Boxkämpfer jagen Eva durch Sylt portez ce vieux Whiskey blond qui fume

© FSI 1993

▼ A082   Mac + PC   New Caledonia™

▶ Bold
The quick brown fox jumps over a Dog. Zwei Boxkämpfer jagen Eva durch Sylt portez ce vieux Whiskey blond qui

▶ Bold Italic
The quick brown fox jumps over a Dog. Zwei Boxkämpfer jagen Eva durch Sylt portez ce vieux Whiskey blond qui

▶ Black
The quick brown fox jumps over a Dog. Zwei Boxkämpfer jagen Eva durch Sylt portez ce vieux Whiskey

▶ Black Italic
The quick brown fox jumps over a Dog. Zwei Boxkämpfer jagen Eva durch Sylt portez ce vieux Whiskey

A1153   Mac + PC   ②   ✎ 1978: (W. A.. Dwiggins 1938–40) John Quaranta

New Caledonia Small Caps / OSF

ABCDEFGHIJKLMNOPQRSTUVWXYZ[ÄÖÜSSÅØÆŒÇ]
ABCDEFGHIJKLMNOPQRSTUVWXYZ
1234567890(.,;:?!$&-*){ÄÖÜÅØÆŒÇ}

© Caledonia

▶ Small Caps / OSF
THE QUICK BROWN FOX JUMPS OVER A DOG. 123 4567 890 ZWEI BOXKÄMPFER JAGEN EVA DURCH SYLT PORTEZ CE VIEUX

▶ Italic OSF
The quick brown fox jumps over a Dog. 123 4567 890 Zwei Boxkämpfer jagen Eva durch Sylt portez ce vieux Whiskey blond

▶ Bold Small Caps
THE QUICK BROWN FOX JUMPS OVER A DOG. 123 4567 890 ZWEI BOXKÄMPFER JAGEN EVA DURCH SYLT PORTEZ CE VIEUX

▶ Bold Italic OSF
The quick brown fox jumps over a Dog. 123 4567 890 Zwei Boxkämpfer jagen Eva durch Sylt portez ce vieux

M882   Mac + PC   ②   ✎ 1987: Ron Carpenter

Calisto®

abcdefghijklmnopqrstuvwxyz[äöüßåøæœç]
ABCDEFGHIJKLMNOPQRSTUVWXYZ
1234567890(.,;:?!$&-*){ÄÖÜÅØÆŒÇ}

▶ Regular
The quick brown fox jumps over a Dog. Zwei Boxkämpfer jagen Eva durch Sylt portez ce vieux Whiskey blond qui fume une

▶ Italic
The quick brown fox jumps over a Dog. Zwei Boxkämpfer jagen Eva durch Sylt portez ce vieux Whiskey blond qui fume une pipe aber echt

▶ Bold
The quick brown fox jumps over a Dog. Zwei Boxkämpfer jagen Eva durch Sylt portez ce vieux Whiskey blond qui fume

▶ Bold Italic
The quick brown fox jumps over a Dog. Zwei Boxkämpfer jagen Eva durch Sylt portez ce vieux Whiskey blond qui fume une pipe aber

© FSI 1993

LH6640 Mac + PC ④
Calligraphy for Print

Calligraphy for Print:
Ruling Script™, Sho Roman™, Wiesbaden Swing™ Roman

M203 Mac + PC ③   ✎ 1980: Margaret Calvert
Calvert™

abcdefghijklmnopqrstuvwxyz[äöüßåøæœç]
ABCDEFGHIJKLMNOPQRSTUVWXYZ
1234567890(.,;:?!$&-*){ÄÖÜÅØÆŒÇ}

aa*a*
A6073
Calvert, Lt, Med, Bd
©
PMN Caecilia, Glypha, Boton, Serifa

▶ Light
The quick brown fox jumps over a Dog. Zwei Boxkämpfer jagen Eva durch Sylt portez ce vieux Whiskey blond qui

▶ Medium
The quick brown fox jumps over a Dog. Zwei Boxkämpfer jagen Eva durch Sylt portez ce vieux Whiskey

▶ Bold
The quick brown fox jumps over a Dog. Zwei Boxkämpfer jagen Eva durch Sylt portez ce vieux Whiskey

---

EF6466 Mac + PC ⑥
Camellia™

abcdefghijklmnopqrstuvwxyz
1234567890(.,;:?!$&-*)[] äöüåøæœç

E+F Special Headlines 2:
Belshaw™, Camellia™, Carousel™, Cirkulus™, Data 70, Galadriel™

L6116 Mac ⑥   ✎ 1987: Alan Meeks
Campaign™

ABCDEFGHIJKLMNOPQRSTUVWXYZ
1234567890(.,;:?!$&-*)[]ÄÖÜÅØÆŒÇ

MC2896 Mac + PC ⑥
Campus™

ABCDEFGHIJKLMNOPQRSTUVWXYZ
1234567890(.,;:?!$&-*)[]{ÄÖÜÅØÆŒÇ}

© FSI 1993

L6585 Mac ④ 1982: Alan Meeks
Cancelleresca™ Script

abcdefghijklmnopqrstuvwxyz[äöüßåøæç]1234567890(.,:;?!$&-*)
ABCDEFGHIJKLM
NOPQRSTUVWXYZ

EF6465 Mac + PC ⑥
Candice™

abcdefghijklmnopqrstuvwxyz[äöüßåøæç]
ABCDEFGHIJKLMNOPQRSTUVWXYZ
1234567890(.,:;?!$&-*)ÄÖÜÅØÆŒÇ

E+F Special Headlines 1:
Bernhard Fashion, Candice™, Italia Medium Condensed, Lindsay™, Odin™, Van Dijk

A204 Mac + PC ③ 1936: Jakob Erbar
Candida™

abcdefghijklmnopqrstuvwxyz[äöüßåøæœç]
ABCDEFGHIJKLMNOPQRSTUVWXYZ
1234567890(.,;:?!$&-*){ÄÖÜÅØÆŒÇ}

aa*a*
BT1254
Candida, Reg, Ita, Bd
Joanna, FF Scala

▶ Regular
The quick brown fox jumps over a Dog. Zwei Boxkämpfer jagen Eva durch Sylt portez ce vieux Whiskey blond

▶ Italic
The quick brown fox jumps over a Dog. Zwei Boxkämpfer jagen Eva durch Sylt portez ce vieux Whiskey blond

▶ Bold
The quick brown fox jumps over a Dog. Zwei Boxkämpfer jagen Eva durch Sylt portez ce vieux Whiskey

A6076 Mac + PC ② 1986: Ron Carpenter
Cantoria™ 1

abcdefghijklmnopqrstuvwxyz[äöüßåøæœç]
ABCDEFGHIJKLMNOPQRSTUVWXYZ
1234567890(.,;:?!$&-*){ÄÖÜÅØÆŒÇ}

▶ Regular
The quick brown fox jumps over a Dog. Zwei Boxkämpfer jagen Eva durch Sylt portez ce vieux Whiskey blond qui fume

▶ Italic
The quick brown fox jumps over a Dog. Zwei Boxkämpfer jagen Eva durch Sylt portez ce vieux Whiskey blond qui fume une pipe

▶ Bold
The quick brown fox jumps over a Dog. Zwei Boxkämpfer jagen Eva durch Sylt portez ce vieux Whiskey

▶ Bold Italic
The quick brown fox jumps over a Dog. Zwei Boxkämpfer jagen Eva durch Sylt portez ce vieux Whiskey blond qui fume

© FSI 1993

A6077 Mac + PC ② ✎ 1986: Ron Carpenter
Cantoria 2

abcdefghijklmnopqrstuvwxyz[äöüßåøæœç]
ABCDEFGHIJKLMNOPQRSTUVWXYZ
1234567890(.,;:?!$&-*){ÄÖÜÅØÆŒÇ}

▶ Light
The quick brown fox jumps over a Dog. Zwei Boxkämpfer jagen Eva durch Sylt portez ce vieux Whiskey blond qui fume une pipe aber

▶ Light Italic
The quick brown fox jumps over a Dog. Zwei Boxkämpfer jagen Eva durch Sylt portez ce vieux Whiskey blond qui fume une pipe aber echt

▶ Semi Bold
The quick brown fox jumps over a Dog. Zwei Boxkämpfer jagen Eva durch Sylt portez ce vieux Whiskey blond qui

▶ Semi Bold Italic
The quick brown fox jumps over a Dog. Zwei Boxkämpfer jagen Eva durch Sylt portez ce vieux Whiskey blond qui fume

▶ Extra Bold
The quick brown fox jumps over a Dog. Zwei Boxkämpfer jagen Eva durch Sylt portez ce vieux Whiskey

▶ Extra Bold Italic
The quick brown fox jumps over a Dog. Zwei Boxkämpfer jagen Eva durch Sylt portez ce vieux Whiskey

C2525 Mac + PC ⑥
Capone Light

abcdefghijklmnopqrstuvwxyz[äöüßåøæœç]
ABCDEFGHIJKLMNOPQRSTUVWXYZ
1234567890(.,;:?!$&-*){ÄÖÜÅØÆŒÇ}

Headlines 86S:
Advertisers Gothic™, Ashley Crawford™, Capone Light, Dynamo, Modernistic™

MC2897 Mac + PC ⑥
Card Camio™

ABCDEFGHIJKLMNOPQRSTUVWXYZ
1234567890(.,;:?!$&-)[ ]{ÄÖÜÅØÆŒÇ}*

BT767 Mac + PC ② ✎ 1987: Gudrun Zapf von Hesse
Bitstream Carmina™ 1

abcdefghijklmnopqrstuvwxyz[äöüßåøæœç]
ABCDEFGHIJKLMNOPQRSTUVWXYZ
1234567890(.,;:?!$&-*){ÄÖÜÅØÆŒÇ}

ⓒ
Diotima, Berthold Nofret

▶ Light
The quick brown fox jumps over a Dog. Zwei Boxkämpfer jagen Eva durch Sylt portez ce vieux Whiskey blond qui

▶ Light Italic
The quick brown fox jumps over a Dog. Zwei Boxkämpfer jagen Eva durch Sylt portez ce vieux Whiskey blond qui fume une pipe

© FSI 1993

| BT768 MAC + PC ② ✎ 1987: Gudrun Zapf von Hesse |
| Bitstream Carmina 2 |

abcdefghijklmnopqrstuvwxyz[äöüßåøæœç]
ABCDEFGHIJKLMNOPQRSTUVWXYZ
1234567890(.,;:?!$&-*){ÄÖÜÅØÆŒÇ}

ⓒ
Diotima, Berthold
Nofret

▶ Medium
The quick brown fox jumps over a Dog. Zwei Boxkämpfer jagen Eva durch Sylt portez ce vieux Whiskey blond

▶ Medium Italic
The quick brown fox jumps over a Dog. Zwei Boxkämpfer jagen Eva durch Sylt portez ce vieux Whiskey blond qui fume

▶ Bold
The quick brown fox jumps over a Dog. Zwei Boxkämpfer jagen Eva durch Sylt portez ce vieux Whis-

▶ Bold Italic
The quick brown fox jumps over a Dog. Zwei Boxkämpfer jagen Eva durch Sylt portez ce vieux Whiskey

| BT769 MAC + PC ② ✎ 1987: Gudrun Zapf von Hesse |
| Bitstream Carmina 3 |

**abcdefghijklmnopqrstuvwxyz[äöüßåøæœç]
ABCDEFGHIJKLMNOPQRSTUVWXYZ
1234567890(.,;:?!$&-*){ÄÖÜÅØÆŒÇ}**

ⓒ
Diotima, Berthold
Nofret

▶ Black
The quick brown fox jumps over a Dog. Zwei Boxkämpfer jagen Eva durch Sylt portez ce

▶ Black Italic
The quick brown fox jumps over a Dog. Zwei Boxkämpfer jagen Eva durch Sylt portez ce vieux

| C597 MAC + PC |
| Carmine Tango™ |

Carmine Tango™:
Carmine Tango, Chaplin™, Coronet

| C597 MAC + PC ④ ✎ (Lucian Bernhard, 1934) |
| Carmine Tango |

*abcdefghijklmnopqrstuvwxyz[äöüßåøæœç]
ABCDEFGHIJKLMNOPQRSTUVWXYZ
1234567890(.,;:?!$&-*){ÄÖÜÅØÆŒÇ}*

Carmine Tango™:
Carmine Tango, Chaplin™, Coronet
ⓒ Bernhard Tango

| A1147 MAC + PC ⑥ ✎ 1991: Gottfried Pott |
| Carolina™ & Dfr |

abcdefghijklmnopqrstuvwxyz[äöüßåøæœç]
ABCDEFGHIJKLMNOPQRSTUVWXYZ
1234567890(.,;:?!$&-*){ÄÖÜÅØÆŒÇ}

© FSI 1993

▼ A1147 Mac + PC Carolina™ & Dfr

👁 FF Carolus Magnus, Codex, Berthold Catull

▶ Regular
The quick brown fox jumps over a Dog. Zwei Boxkämpfer jagen Eva durch Sylt portez ce vieux Whiskey blond qui

▶ Dfr
The quick brown fox jumpſ over a Dog. Zwei Boxkämpfer jagen Eva durch Sylt portez ce vieux Whiſkey blond qui

Type Before Gutenberg 2:
Carolina™ & Dfr, Clairvaux™, San Marco™
👁 FF Carolus Magnus, Codex, Berthold Catull

FF1533 Mac + PC ④ ✏ 1991: Manfred Klein
FF Carolus Magnus™

abcdefghijklmnopqrstuvwxyz[áöüßç]
abcdefghijklmnopqrstuvwxyz
1234567890(.,;:?!$&-*){áöü}

FF Scribe Type™:
FF Carolus Magnus™, FF Johannes G™, FF Koberger™, FF Schoensperger™
👁 Carolina

EF6466 Mac + PC ⑥
Carousel™

abcdefghijklmnopqrstuvwxyz[äöüßåøæœç]
ABCDEFGHIJKLMNOPQRSTUVWXYZ
1234567890(.,;:?!$&-*) ÄÖÜÅØÆŒÇ

E+F Special Headlines 2:
Belshaw™, Camellia™, Carousel™, Cirkulus™, Data 70, Galadriel™

MC2898 Mac + PC ⑥
Carplate™

ABCDEFGHIJKLMNOPQRSTUVWXYZ
1234567890(.,;:?!$&-*)[](ÄÖÜÅØÆŒÇ)

C598 Mac + PC
Cartier

Cartier:
Cartier, Holland Seminar

C598 Mac + PC ③ ✏ 1967: Carl Dair
Cartier

abcdefghijklmnopqrstuvwxyz[äöüßåøæœç]
ABCDEFGHIJKLMNOPQRSTUVWXYZ
1234567890(.,;:?!$&-*){ÄÖÜÅØÆŒÇ}

© FSI 1993

C 8

▼ C598　Mac + PC　**Cartier**

Raleigh

▶ Regular
The quick brown fox jumps over a Dog. Zwei Boxkämpfer jagen Eva durch Sylt portez ce vieux Whiskey blond qui fume une pipe aber echt

▶ Italic
The quick brown fox jumps over a Dog. Zwei Boxkämpfer jagen Eva durch Sylt portez ce vieux Whiskey blond qui fume une pipe aber echt über die Mauer gesprungen und auch

Cartier:
Cartier, Holland Seminar
Ⓒ Raleigh

BT1301　Mac + PC　④　1966: Matthew Carter　Industry name

Freehand 471　　　　　　　　　　　　　　**Cascade™ Script**

abcdefghijklmnopqrstuvwxyz[äöüßåøæœç]
ABCDEFGHIJKLMNOPQRSTUVWXYZ
1234567890(.,;:?!$&-*){ÄÖÜÅØÆŒÇ}

BT1259　Mac + PC

Caslon Old Face & Open Face

Caslon Old Face & Open Face:
Caslon Old Face, Caslon Open Face

BT1259　Mac + PC　②　1902: (William Caslon, 1725)

Caslon Old Face

abcdefghijklmnopqrstuvwxyz[äöüßåøæœç]
ABCDEFGHIJKLMNOPQRSTUVWXYZ
1234567890(.,;:?!$&-*){ÄÖÜÅØÆŒÇ}

Ⓒ
Adobe Caslon, Caslon No. 540, Caslon Oldstyle No. 377, Berthold Caslon Book

▶ Regular
The quick brown fox jumps over a Dog. Zwei Boxkämpfer jagen Eva durch Sylt portez ce vieux Whiskey blond qui fume une pipe aber echt

▶ Italic
The quick brown fox jumps over a Dog. Zwei Boxkämpfer jagen Eva durch Sylt portez ce vieux Whiskey blond qui fume une pipe aber echt über die Mauer

▶ Heavy
The quick brown fox jumps over a Dog. Zwei Boxkämpfer jagen Eva durch Sylt portez ce vieux Whiskey blond qui fume

Caslon Old Face & Open Face:
Caslon Old Face, Caslon Open Face
Ⓒ Adobe Caslon, Caslon No. 540, Caslon Oldstyle No. 377, Berthold Caslon Book

---

A145　Mac + PC　⑥　(1915)

Caslon Open Face

abcdefghijklmnopqrstuvwxyz[äöüßåøæœç]
ABCDEFGHIJKLMNOPQRSTUVWXYZ
1234567890(.,;:?!$&-*){ÄÖÜÅØÆŒÇ}

© FSI 1993

BT1258 Mac + PC ② 1905: (William Caslon, 1725)
Caslon Bold

abcdefghijklmnopqrstuvwxyz[äöüßåøæœç]
ABCDEFGHIJKLMNOPQRSTUVWXYZ
1234567890(.,;:?!$&-*){ÄÖÜÅØÆŒÇ}

▶ Bold
The quick brown fox jumps over a Dog. Zwei Boxkämpfer jagen Eva durch Sylt portez ce vieux Whiskey blond

▶ Italic
The quick brown fox jumps over a Dog. Zwei Boxkämpfer jagen Eva durch Sylt portez ce vieux Whiskey blond qui fume une

A021 Mac + PC ②
Caslon No. 3 & 540

Caslon No. 3 & 540:
Caslon 540, Caslon No. 3
aa*a* BT1257
Caslon 540, Reg, Ita

A2542 Mac + PC ②
Caslon No. 3 & 540 Small Caps

Caslon No. 3 & 540 Small Caps:
Caslon 540 Small Caps, Caslon No. 3 Small Caps

A021 Mac + PC ② 1905: (William Caslon, 1725)
Caslon No. 3

abcdefghijklmnopqrstuvwxyz[äöüßåøæœç]
ABCDEFGHIJKLMNOPQRSTUVWXYZ
1234567890(.,;:?!$&-*){ÄÖÜÅØÆŒÇ}

aa*a*
BT1257
Caslon 540, Reg, Ita
Ⓒ
Adobe Caslon, Caslon Oldstyle No. 377, Caslon 540, Berthold Caslon Book

▶ Roman
The quick brown fox jumps over a Dog. Zwei Boxkämpfer jagen Eva durch Sylt portez ce vieux Whiskey blond

▶ Italic
The quick brown fox jumps over a Dog. Zwei Boxkämpfer jagen Eva durch Sylt portez ce vieux Whiskey blond qui fume une

Caslon No. 3 & 540:
Caslon 540, Caslon No. 3
aa*a* BT1257
Caslon 540, Reg, Ita

A2542 Mac + PC ② (William Caslon, 1725)
Caslon No. 3 Small Caps

ABCDEFGHIJKLMNOPQRSTUVWXYZ[ÄÖÜSSÅØÆŒÇ]
ABCDEFGHIJKLMNOPQRSTUVWXYZ
1234567890(.,;:?!$&-*){ÄÖÜÅØÆŒÇ}

▶ Regular Small Caps
THE QUICK BROWN FOX JUMPS OVER A DOG. 123 4567 890 ZWEI BOXKÄMPFER JAGEN EVA DURCH SYLT

▶ Italic OSF
The quick brown fox jumps over a Dog. 123 4567 890 Zwei Boxkämpfer jagen Eva durch Sylt portez ce vieux Whiskey blond

▼ A2542 Mac + PC   Caslon No. 3 Small Caps

Caslon No. 3 & 540 Small Caps:
Caslon 540 Small Caps, Caslon No. 3 Small Caps

A021 Mac + PC   ②   1902: (William Caslon, 1725)
Caslon 540

abcdefghijklmnopqrstuvwxyz[äöüßåøæœç]
ABCDEFGHIJKLMNOPQRSTUVWXYZ
1234567890(.,;:?!$&-*){ÄÖÜÅØÆŒÇ}

a a *a*
BT1257
Caslon 540, Reg, Ita

▶ Regular
The quick brown fox jumps over a Dog. Zwei Boxkämpfer jagen Eva durch Sylt portez ce vieux Whiskey blond qui fume

▶ *Italic*
The quick brown fox jumps over a Dog. Zwei Boxkämpfer jagen Eva durch Sylt portez ce vieux Whiskey blond qui fume une pipe aber echt

Caslon No. 3 & 540:
Caslon 540, Caslon No. 3
a a *a* BT1257
Caslon 540, Reg, Ita

A2542 Mac + PC   ②   1902: (William Caslon, 1725)
Caslon 540 Small Caps

ABCDEFGHIJKLMNOPQRSTUVWXYZ[ÄÖÜSSÅØÆŒÇ]
ABCDEFGHIJKLMNOPQRSTUVWXYZ
1234567890(.,;:?!$&-*){ÄÖÜÅØÆŒÇ}

▶ Regular Small Caps
THE QUICK BROWN FOX JUMPS OVER A DOG. 123 4567 890 ZWEI BOXKÄMPFER JAGEN EVA DURCH SYLT PORTEZ CE VIEUX WHISKEY

▶ *Italic OSF*
The quick brown fox jumps over a Dog. 123 4567 890 Zwei Boxkämpfer jagen Eva durch Sylt portez ce vieux Whiskey blond qui fume

Caslon No. 3 & 540 Small Caps:
Caslon 540 Small Caps, Caslon No. 3 Small Caps

L6586 Mac   ②   1981: (William Caslon, 1725) Freda Sack
Caslon 540 Italic & Swashes

abcdefghijklmnopqrstuvwxyz[äöüßåøæœç]
ABCDEFGHIJKLMNOPQRSTUVWXYZ
1234567890(.,;:?!$&-)ÄÖÜÅØÆŒÇ*

A890 Mac + PC   ②   1990: (William Caslon, 1725) Carol Twombly
Adobe Caslon™

abcdefghijklmnopqrstuvwxyz[äöüßåøæœç]
ABCDEFGHIJKLMNOPQRSTUVWXYZ
1234567890(.,;:?!$&-*){ÄÖÜÅØÆŒÇ}

© FSI 1993

▼ A890 Mac + PC Adobe Caslon™

Caslon No. 3, Caslon Oldstyle No. 377, Caslon 540, Caslon Old Face, Berthold Caslon Book

▶ Regular
The quick brown fox jumps over a Dog. Zwei Boxkämpfer jagen Eva durch Sylt portez ce vieux Whiskey blond qui fume une pipe aber

▶ Italic
The quick brown fox jumps over a Dog. Zwei Boxkämpfer jagen Eva durch Sylt portez ce vieux Whiskey blond qui fume une pipe aber echt

▶ Semi Bold
The quick brown fox jumps over a Dog. Zwei Boxkämpfer jagen Eva durch Sylt portez ce vieux Whiskey blond qui fume une

▶ Semi Bold Italic
The quick brown fox jumps over a Dog. Zwei Boxkämpfer jagen Eva durch Sylt portez ce vieux Whiskey blond qui fume une pipe aber echt

▶ Bold
The quick brown fox jumps over a Dog. Zwei Boxkämpfer jagen Eva durch Sylt portez ce vieux Whiskey blond qui fume une

▶ Bold Italic
The quick brown fox jumps over a Dog. Zwei Boxkämpfer jagen Eva durch Sylt portez ce vieux Whiskey blond qui fume une pipe aber

A891 Mac + PC   ② 1990: (William Caslon, 1725) Carol Twombly

Adobe Caslon Expert Collection

ABCDEFGHIJKLMNOPQRSTUVWXYZ(ÄÖÜŠÅØÆŒÇ)

1234567890fffiflffiffl(^{1}₁^{2}₂^{3}₃^{4}₄^{5}₅^{6}₆^{7}₇^{8}₈^{9}₉^{0}₀) ($$¢Rp₵)ª

▶ Expert Regular
0123456789offfiflffiffl-(½⅓⅔¼¾⅕⅖⅗⅘⅙⅚⅛⅜⅝⅞)($$¢Rp₵)ª THE QUICK BROWN FOX JUMPS OVER A DOG ZWEI BOXKÄMPFER JAGEN

▶ Expert Italic
0123456789offfiflffiffl-(½⅓⅔¼¾⅕⅖⅗⅘⅙⅚⅛⅜⅝⅞)($$¢Rp₵)ª

▶ Expert Semi Bold
0123456789offfiflffiffl-(½⅓⅔¼¾⅕⅖⅗⅘⅙⅚⅛⅜⅝⅞)($$¢Rp₵)ª THE QUICK BROWN FOX JUMPS OVER A DOG ZWEI BOXKÄMPFER

▶ Expert Semi Bold Italic
0123456789offfiflffiffl-(½⅓⅔¼¾⅕⅖⅗⅘⅙⅚⅛⅜⅝⅞)($$¢Rp₵)ª

▶ Expert Bold
0123456789offfiflffiffl-(½⅓⅔¼¾⅕⅖⅗⅘⅙⅚⅛⅜⅝⅞)($$¢Rp₵)ª

▶ Expert Bold Italic
0123456789offfiflffiffl-(½⅓⅔¼¾⅕⅖⅗⅘⅙⅚⅛⅜⅝⅞)($$¢Rp₵)ª

▶ Alternate Regular
ffstctfhfiflft

▶ Alternate Italic
ſsteſtſhſiſlſtvw

▶ Alternate Semi Bold
ffstctfhfikflfft

▶ Alternate Semi Bold Italic
ſsteſtſhkſlſtvw

▼ A891 Mac + PC **Adobe Caslon Expert Collection**

▶ Alternate Bold
ffstcthfiknfft

▶ Alternate Bold Italic
ffstctfhfikflftvw

▶ Italic Swash
ABCDEFGHIJKLM
NOPQRSTUVWXYZ

▶ Semi Bold Italic Swash
ABCDEFGHIJKL
MNOPQRSTUVW
XYZ

▶ Bold Italic Swash
ABCDEFGHIJKL
MNOPQRSTUVW
XYZ

Adobe Caslon Expert Collection, Adobe Caslon Ornaments

G599 Mac + PC ② ✎ 1915: (William Caslon, 1725)

Caslon Oldstyle No. 377™

abcdefghijklmnopqrstuvwxyz[äöüßåøæœç]
ABCDEFGHIJKLMNOPQRSTUVWXYZ
1234567890(.,;:?!$&-*){ÄÖÜÅØÆŒÇ}

Caslon Old Face,
Adobe Caslon

▶ Regular OSF
The quick brown fox jumps over a Dog. 123 4567 890 Zwei Boxkämpfer jagen Eva durch Sylt portez ce vieux Whiskey

▶ Italic OSF
The quick brown fox jumps over a Dog. 123 4567 890 Zwei Boxkämpfer jagen Eva durch Sylt portez ce vieux Whiskey blond qui

▶ Regular
The quick brown fox jumps over a Dog. Zwei Boxkämpfer jagen Eva durch Sylt portez ce vieux Whiskey blond qui fume

▶ Italic
The quick brown fox jumps over a Dog. Zwei Boxkämpfer jagen Eva durch Sylt portez ce vieux Whiskey blond qui fume une pipe

▶ Small Caps OSF
THE QUICK BROWN FOX JUMPS OVER A DOG. 123 4567 890 ZWEI BOXKÄMPFER JAGEN EVA DURCH SYLT PORTEZ CE VIEUX WHIS-

▶ Italic Small Caps OSF
THE QUICK BROWN FOX JUMPS OVER A DOG. 123 4567 890 ZWEI BOXKÄMPFER JAGEN EVA DURCH SYLT PORTEZ CE VIEUX

▶ Swash Italic OSF
QWERTYDGKLBN MU 1234567890. Zwei Boxkämpfer jagen Eva durch Sylt portez ce vieux Whiskey blond qui fume

▶ Swash Italic
QWERTYDGKLBN MhkU The quick brown fox jumps over a Dog. Zwei Boxkämpfer jagen Eva durch Sylt portez ce vieux

▶ Quaint S
fifstßfbfltffiffflfhfk

▶ Quaint S, Swash
ABCDEFGHIJKLMNO
PQRSTUVWXYZfihJkfvwz
ftßfbflfifflfhfk

© FSI 1993

▼ G599 MAC + PC Caslon Oldstyle No. 377™

▶ Regular OSF, Short
The quick brown fox jumps over a Dog. 123 4567 890 Zwei Boxkämpfer jagen Eva durch Sylt portez ce vieux Whiskey

▶ Italic OSF, Short
The quick brown fox jumps over a Dog. 123 4567 890 Zwei Boxkämpfer jagen Eva durch Sylt portez ce vieux Whiskey blond

▶ Regular, Short
The quick brown fox jumps over a Dog. Zwei Boxkämpfer jagen Eva durch Sylt portez ce vieux Whiskey blond qui fume

▶ Italic, Short
The quick brown fox jumps over a Dog. Zwei Boxkämpfer jagen Eva durch Sylt portez ce vieux Whiskey blond qui fume une

▶ Small Caps OSF Short
THE QUICK BROWN FOX JUMPS OVER A DOG. 123 4567 890 ZWEI BOXKÄMPFER JAGEN EVA DURCH SYLT PORTEZ CE VIEUX WHIS-

▶ Small Caps Italic OSF, Short
THE QUICK BROWN FOX JUMPS OVER A DOG. 123 4567 890 ZWEI BOXKÄMPFER JAGEN EVA DURCH SYLT PORTEZ CE VIEUX

▶ Quaint S, Italic, Short
ſiſtßſbſlſiſſſlſkſk

G2748 MAC + PC ② 1915: (William Caslon, 1725)

Caslon Bold No. 537™ & 637™

abcdefghijklmnopqrstuvwxyz[äöüßåøæœç]
ABCDEFGHIJKLMNOPQRSTUVWXYZ
1234567890(.,:;?!$&-*){ÄÖÜÅØÆŒÇ}

Caslon Old Face, Adobe Caslon

▶ Regular OSF
The quick brown fox jumps over a Dog. 123 4567 890 Zwei Boxkämpfer jagen Eva durch Sylt portez ce vieux Whiskey

▶ Italic OSF
The quick brown fox jumps over a Dog. 123 4567 890 Zwei Boxkämpfer jagen Eva durch Sylt portez ce vieux Whiskey

▶ Regular
The quick brown fox jumps over a Dog. Zwei Boxkämpfer jagen Eva durch Sylt portez ce vieux Whiskey blond qui fume

▶ Italic
The quick brown fox jumps over a Dog. Zwei Boxkämpfer jagen Eva durch Sylt portez ce vieux Whiskey blond qui fume une

▶ Italic OSF, Short
The quick brown fox jumps over a Dog. 123 4567 890 Zwei Boxkämpfer jagen Eva durch Sylt portez ce vieux Whiskey

▶ Italic, Short
The quick brown fox jumps over a Dog. 123 4567 890 Zwei Boxkämpfer jagen Eva durch Sylt portez ce vieux Whiskey blond

▶ Regular, Short
The quick brown fox jumps over a Dog. Zwei Boxkämpfer jagen Eva durch Sylt portez ce vieux Whiskey blond qui fume

▶ Regular OSF, Short
Zwei Boxkämpfer jagen Eva durch Sylt. 123 4567 890 Portez ce vieux Whiskey blond qui fume une pipe aber echt über

© FSI 1993

AB6075 Mac + PC ② 　✎ 1977: G. G. Lange
Berthold Caslon Book

abcdefghijklmnopqrstuvwxyz[äöüßåøæœç]
ABCDEFGHIJKLMNOPQRSTUVWXYZ
1234567890(.,;:?!$&-*){ÄÖÜÅØÆŒÇ}

ⓒ
Caslon No. 3, Caslon Oldstyle No. 377, Caslon 540, Caslon Old Face

▶ Regular
The quick brown fox jumps over a Dog. Zwei Boxkämpfer jagen Eva durch Sylt portez ce vieux Whiskey blond qui fume une

▶ Italic
The quick brown fox jumps over a Dog. Zwei Boxkämpfer jagen Eva durch Sylt portez ce vieux Whiskey blond qui fume une pipe aber echt

▶ Medium
The quick brown fox jumps over a Dog. Zwei Boxkämpfer jagen Eva durch Sylt portez ce vieux Whiskey blond qui fume

▶ Bold
The quick brown fox jumps over a Dog. Zwei Boxkämpfer jagen Eva durch Sylt portez ce vieux Whiskey blond

AB6311 Mac + PC ② 　✎ 1977: G. G. Lange
Berthold Caslon Book Expert

ABCDEFGHIJKLMNOPQRSTUVWXYZ[ÄÖÜSSÅØÆŒÇ]
ABCDEFGHIJKLMNOPQRSTUVWXYZ
1234567890(.,;:?!$&-*){ÄÖÜÅØÆŒÇ}

▶ Regular SC
THE QUICK BROWN FOX JUMPS OVER A DOG. 123 4567 890 ZWEI BOXKÄMPFER JAGEN EVA DURCH SYLT PORTEZ CE VIEUX WHISKEY

▶ Italic OSF
The quick brown fox jumps over a Dog. 123 4567 890 Zwei Boxkämpfer jagen Eva durch Sylt portez ce vieux Whiskey blond qui fume

▶ Medium SC
THE QUICK BROWN FOX JUMPS OVER A DOG. 123 4567 890 ZWEI BOXKÄMPFER JAGEN EVA DURCH SYLT PORTEZ CE VIEUX WHISKEY

▶ Bold OSF
The quick brown fox jumps over a Dog. 123 4567 890 Zwei Boxkämpfer jagen Eva durch Sylt portez ce vieux Whiskey

▶ Regular Expert
0123456789offfiflffifl-(½⅓⅔¼¾⅕⅖⅗⅘⅙⅚⅛⅞‰)($¢Rp₵)ª THE QUICK BROWN FOX JUMPS OVER A DOG ZWEI BOXKÄMPFER JAGEN

▶ Italic Expert
0123456789offfiflffifl-(½⅓⅔¼¾⅕⅖⅗⅘⅙⅚⅛⅞‰)($¢Rp₵)ª

▶ Medium Expert
0123456789offfiflffifl-(½⅓⅔¼¾⅕⅖⅗⅘⅙⅚⅛⅞‰)($¢Rp₵)ª THE QUICK BROWN FOX JUMPS OVER A DOG ZWEI BOXKÄMPFER JAGEN

▶ Bold Expert
0123456789offfiflffifl-(½⅓⅔¼¾⅕⅖⅗⅘⅙⅚⅛⅞‰)($¢Rp₵)ª

FB6372 Mac + PC ② 　✎ 1992: Jill Pichotta
Caslon Bold Condensed

abcdefghijklmnopqrstuvwxyz[äöüßåøæœç]
ABCDEFGHIJKLMNOPQRSTUVWXYZ
1234567890(.,;:?!$&-*){ÄÖÜÅØÆŒÇ}

© FSI 1993

C 15

▼ FB6372 Mac + PC   Caslon Bold Condensed

▶ Condensed
The quick brown fox jumps over a Dog. Zwei Boxkämpfer jagen Eva durch Sylt portez ce vieux Whiskey blond qui fume une pipe aber

▶ Extra Condensed
The quick brown fox jumps over a Dog. Zwei Boxkämpfer jagen Eva durch Sylt portez ce vieux Whiskey blond qui fume une pipe aber echt über die Mauer gesprungen und auch

FBI Condensed Classics™:
Bodoni Bold Compressed, Bodoni Bold Condensed, Caslon Bold Condensed, Century Bold Condensed, Cheltenham Bold Condensed

---

SG1817 Mac   (6)   ✏ Dave Farey
Caslon Black

abcdefghijklmnopqrstuvwxyz[äöüßåøæœç]
ABCDEFGHIJKLMNOPQRSTUVWXYZ
1234567890(.,;:?!$&-*)ÄÖÜÅØÆŒÇ

SG1818 Mac   (6)   ✏ (Les Usherwood)
Caslon Graphique™

abcdefghijklmnopqrstuvwxyz[äöüßåøæœç]
ABCDEFGHIJKLMNOPQRSTUVWXYZ
1234567890(.,;:?!$&-*)ÄÖÜÅØÆŒÇ

MC6352 Mac + PC   (6)
Caslon Antique

abcdefghijklmnopqrstuvwxyz[äöüßåøæœç]
ABCDEFGHIJKLMNOPQRSTUVWXYZ
1234567890(.,;:?!$&-*){ÄÖÜÅØÆŒÇ}

A893 Mac + PC   (2)   ✏ 1982: (William Caslon, 1725) Ed Benguiat
ITC Caslon No. 224®

abcdefghijklmnopqrstuvwxyz[äöüßåøæœç]
ABCDEFGHIJKLMNOPQRSTUVWXYZ
1234567890(.,;:?!$&-*){ÄÖÜÅØÆŒÇ}

aaa
EF291
ITC Caslon No. 224, Bk, Bklta, Bd, Bdlta
EF292
ITC Caslon No. 224, Med, Medlta, Blk, Blklta
BT1255
ITC Caslon No. 224 1, Bk, Bklta, Bd, Bdlta
BT1256
ITC Caslon No. 224 2, Med, Medlta, Blk, Blklta

▶ Book
The quick brown fox jumps over a Dog. Zwei Boxkämpfer jagen Eva durch Sylt portez ce vieux Whiskey blond qui fume

▶ Book Italic
The quick brown fox jumps over a Dog. Zwei Boxkämpfer jagen Eva durch Sylt portez ce vieux Whiskey blond qui

▶ Medium
The quick brown fox jumps over a Dog. Zwei Boxkämpfer jagen Eva durch Sylt portez ce vieux Whiskey blond qui fume

▶ Medium Italic
The quick brown fox jumps over a Dog. Zwei Boxkämpfer jagen Eva durch Sylt portez ce vieux Whiskey blond

▶ Bold
The quick brown fox jumps over a Dog. Zwei Boxkämpfer jagen Eva durch Sylt portez ce vieux Whiskey blond qui

▶ Bold Italic
The quick brown fox jumps over a Dog. Zwei Boxkämpfer jagen Eva durch Sylt portez ce vieux Whiskey

© FSI 1993

▼ A893 Mac + PC   ITC Caslon No. 224®

▶ Black
The quick brown fox jumps over a Dog. Zwei Boxkämpfer jagen Eva durch Sylt portez ce vieux Whiskey blond

▶ Black Italic
The quick brown fox jumps over a Dog. Zwei Boxkämpfer jagen Eva durch Sylt portez ce vieux Whiskey

M550 Mac + PC   ⑥   1957: J. Peters
Castellar™

ABCDEFGHIJKLMNOPQRSTUVWXYZ
1234567890(.,:;?!$&-*)[KÄÖÜÅØÆŒÇ}

Headliners 6:
Albertus®, Castellar™
aaa A2745
Albertus/Castellar MT

AB6723 Mac + PC   ②   1982: Gustav Jaeger
Berthold Catull®

abcdefghijklmnopqrstuvwxyz[äöüßåøæœç]
ABCDEFGHIJKLMNOPQRSTUVWXYZ
1234567890(.,:;?!$&-*){ÄÖÜÅØÆŒÇ}

© FF Carolus Magnus, Codex, Carolina

▶ Regular
The quick brown fox jumps over a Dog. Zwei Boxkämpfer jagen Eva durch Sylt portez ce vieux Whiskey blond qui fume une

▶ Italic
The quick brown fox jumps over a Dog. Zwei Boxkämpfer jagen Eva durch Sylt portez ce vieux Whiskey blond qui fume une

▶ Medium
The quick brown fox jumps over a Dog. Zwei Boxkämpfer jagen Eva durch Sylt portez ce vieux Whiskey blond

▶ Bold
The quick brown fox jumps over a Dog. Zwei Boxkämpfer jagen Eva durch Sylt portez ce vieux

A375 Mac + PC   ②   1981: Les Usherwood
TSI Caxton™

abcdefghijklmnopqrstuvwxyz[äöüßåøæœç]
ABCDEFGHIJKLMNOPQRSTUVWXYZ
1234567890(.,:;?!$&-*){ÄÖÜÅØÆŒÇ}

aaa
BT1260
TSI Caxton Light, Lt, LtIta
BT1261
TSI Caxton, Bk, BkIta, Bd, BdIta

▶ Light
The quick brown fox jumps over a Dog. Zwei Boxkämpfer jagen Eva durch Sylt portez ce vieux Whiskey blond qui fume

▶ Light Italic
The quick brown fox jumps over a Dog. Zwei Boxkämpfer jagen Eva durch Sylt portez ce vieux Whiskey blond qui fume

▶ Book
The quick brown fox jumps over a Dog. Zwei Boxkämpfer jagen Eva durch Sylt portez ce vieux Whiskey blond qui

▶ Book Italic
The quick brown fox jumps over a Dog. Zwei Boxkämpfer jagen Eva durch Sylt portez ce vieux Whiskey blond qui

© FSI 1993

▼ A375 Mac + PC TSI Caxton™

▶ Bold
The quick brown fox jumps over a Dog. Zwei Boxkämpfer jagen Eva durch Sylt portez ce vieux Whiskey

▶ Bold Italic
The quick brown fox jumps over a Dog. Zwei Boxkämpfer jagen Eva durch Sylt portez ce vieux Whis-

SG1833 Mac ② 1981: Les Usherwood
TSI Caxton Extra Bold
abcdefghijklmnopqrstuvwxyz[äöüßåøæœç]
ABCDEFGHIJKLMNOPQRSTUVWXYZ
1234567890(.,;:?!$&-*)ÄÖÜÅØÆŒÇ

SG1834 Mac ② 1981: Les Usherwood
TSI Caxton Extra Bold Italic
abcdefghijklmnopqrstuvwxyz[äöüßåøæœç]
ABCDEFGHIJKLMNOPQRSTUVWXYZ
1234567890(.,;:?!$&-*)ÄÖÜÅØÆŒÇ

M736 Mac + PC ② 1928-30: Bruce Rogers, Frederic Warde
Centaur®
abcdefghijklmnopqrstuvwxyz[äöüßåøæœç]
ABCDEFGHIJKLMNOPQRSTUVWXYZ
1234567890(.,;:?!$&-*){ÄÖÜÅØÆŒÇ}

aa*a*
BT1410
Centaur, Reg, Ita
A2534
Centaur, Reg, Ita, ItaAlt, Bd, BdIta
©
Cloister, Hollandse Mediaeval

▶ Regular
The quick brown fox jumps over a Dog. Zwei Boxkämpfer jagen Eva durch Sylt portez ce vieux Whiskey blond qui fume une pipe aber echt

▶ Italic
The quick brown fox jumps over a Dog. Zwei Boxkämpfer jagen Eva durch Sylt portez ce vieux Whiskey blond qui fume une pipe aber echt über die Mauer gesprungen und auch

▶ Bold
The quick brown fox jumps over a Dog. Zwei Boxkämpfer jagen Eva durch Sylt portez ce vieux Whiskey blond qui fume une pipe aber echt

▶ Bold Italic
The quick brown fox jumps over a Dog. Zwei Boxkämpfer jagen Eva durch Sylt portez ce vieux Whiskey blond qui fume une pipe aber echt über die Mauer

M1615 Mac + PC ② 1928-30: Bruce Rogers, Frederic Warde
Centaur Expert

ABCDEFGHIJKLMNOPQRSTUVWXYZ(ÄÖÜŠÅØÆŒÇ)

1234567890ffffiflffiffl(^{1}$_1^{2}_2^{3}_3^{4}_4^{5}_5^{6}_6^{7}_7^{8}_8^{9}_9^{0}_0$)

©
Cloister, Hollandse Mediaeval

▶ Expert Regular
0123456789offfiflffiffl-
($\frac{1}{2}$$\frac{1}{3}$$\frac{2}{3}$$\frac{1}{4}$$\frac{3}{4}$$\frac{1}{5}$$\frac{2}{5}$$\frac{3}{5}$$\frac{4}{5}$$\frac{1}{7}$$\frac{1}{8}$$\frac{3}{8}$$\frac{5}{8}$$\frac{7}{8}$‰%)($ $¢Rp℗^{a} THE QUICK BROWN FOX JUMPS OVER A DOG ZWEI BOXKÄMPFER JAGEN EVA DURCH

▶ Expert Italic
0123456789offfiflffiffl-
($\frac{1}{2}$$\frac{1}{3}$$\frac{2}{3}$$\frac{1}{4}$$\frac{3}{4}$$\frac{1}{5}$$\frac{2}{5}$$\frac{3}{5}$$\frac{4}{5}$$\frac{1}{7}$$\frac{1}{8}$$\frac{3}{8}$$\frac{5}{8}$$\frac{7}{8}$‰%)($ $¢Rp℗^{a}

© FSI 1993
▼

▼ M1615 Mac + PC **Centaur Expert**

▶ Expert Bold
0123456789offiflflffiffl-
(½⅓⅔¼¾⅕⅖⅗⅘⅙⅚⅛⅜⅝⅞‰)(ˢ$₵Rp₡)ᵃ

▶ Expert Bold Italic
0123456789offiflflffiffl-
(½⅓⅔¼¾⅕⅖⅗⅘⅙⅚⅛⅜⅝⅞‰)(ˢ$₵Rp₡)ᵃ

BT1410 Mac + PC ② ✎ 1928-30: Bruce Rogers, Frederic Warde Industry name
Venetian 301 **Centaur**

abcdefghijklmnopqrstuvwxyz[äöüßåøæœç]
ABCDEFGHIJKLMNOPQRSTUVWXYZ
1234567890(.,;:?!$&-*){ÄÖÜÅØÆŒÇ}

aa*a*
M736
Centaur®, Reg, Ita, Bd, BdIta
A2534
Centaur, Reg, Ita, ItaAlt, Bd, BdIta
©
Cloister, Hollandse

▶ Regular
The quick brown fox jumps over a Dog. Zwei Boxkämpfer jagen Eva durch Sylt portez ce vieux Whiskey blond qui fume une pipe aber echt

▶ Italic
The quick brown fox jumps over a Dog. Zwei Boxkämpfer jagen Eva durch Sylt portez ce vieux Whiskey blond qui fume une pipe aber echt über die Mauer gesprungen

---

BT6418 Mac + PC ② ✎ 1928-30: Bruce Rogers, Frederic Warde Industry name
Venetian 301 **Centaur 2**

abcdefghijklmnopqrstuvwxyz[äöüßåøæœç]
ABCDEFGHIJKLMNOPQRSTUVWXYZ
1234567890(.,;:?!$&-*){ÄÖÜÅØÆŒÇ}

©
Cloister, Hollandse Mediaeval

▶ Demi Bold
The quick brown fox jumps over a Dog. Zwei Boxkämpfer jagen Eva durch Sylt portez ce vieux Whiskey blond qui fume une pipe aber echt

▶ Demi Bold Italic
The quick brown fox jumps over a Dog. Zwei Boxkämpfer jagen Eva durch Sylt portez ce vieux Whiskey blond qui fume une pipe aber echt über die Mauer

▶ Bold
The quick brown fox jumps over a Dog. Zwei Boxkämpfer jagen Eva durch Sylt portez ce vieux Whiskey blond qui fume une pipe aber echt

▶ Bold Italic
The quick brown fox jumps over a Dog. Zwei Boxkämpfer jagen Eva durch Sylt portez ce vieux Whiskey blond qui fume une pipe aber echt über die Mauer

---

A140 Mac + PC ② ✎ 1986: Adrian Frutiger
Linotype Centennial™

abcdefghijklmnopqrstuvwxyz[äöüßåøæœç]
ABCDEFGHIJKLMNOPQRSTUVWXYZ
1234567890(.,;:?!$&-*){ÄÖÜÅØÆŒÇ}

▶ 45 Light
The quick brown fox jumps over a Dog. Zwei Boxkämpfer jagen Eva durch Sylt portez ce vieux Whiskey blond qui

▶ 46 Light Italic
The quick brown fox jumps over a Dog. Zwei Boxkämpfer jagen Eva durch Sylt portez ce vieux Whiskey blond

▶ 55 Regular
The quick brown fox jumps over a Dog. Zwei Boxkämpfer jagen Eva durch Sylt portez ce vieux Whiskey blond

▶ 56 Italic
The quick brown fox jumps over a Dog. Zwei Boxkämpfer jagen Eva durch Sylt portez ce vieux Whiskey

▼ A140 Mac + PC Linotype Centennial™

▶ 75 Bold
The quick brown fox jumps over a Dog. Zwei Boxkämpfer jagen Eva durch Sylt portez ce vieux Whiskey

▶ 76 Bold Italic
The quick brown fox jumps over a Dog. Zwei Boxkämpfer jagen Eva durch Sylt portez ce vieux Whiskey

▶ 95 Black
The quick brown fox jumps over a Dog. Zwei Boxkämpfer jagen Eva durch Sylt portez ce vieux

▶ 96 Black Italic
The quick brown fox jumps over a Dog. Zwei Boxkämpfer jagen Eva durch Sylt portez ce vieux Whis-

A1024 Mac + PC ② 1986: Adrian Frutiger

Linotype Centennial Small Caps/OSF

ABCDEFGHIJKLMNOPQRSTUVWXYZ[ÄÖÜSSÅØÆŒÇ]
ABCDEFGHIJKLMNOPQRSTUVWXYZ
1234567890(.,;:?!$&-*){ÄÖÜÅØÆŒÇ}

▶ Light Small Caps / OSF
THE QUICK BROWN FOX JUMPS OVER A DOG. 123 4567 890 ZWEI BOXKÄMPFER JAGEN EVA DURCH SYLT PORTEZ CE VIEUX

▶ Light Italic OSF
The quick brown fox jumps over a Dog. 123 4567 890 Zwei Boxkämpfer jagen Eva durch Sylt portez ce vieux

▶ Regular Small Caps / OSF
THE QUICK BROWN FOX JUMPS OVER A DOG. 123 4567 890 ZWEI BOXKÄMPFER JAGEN EVA DURCH SYLT PORTEZ CE VIEUX

▶ Italic OSF
The quick brown fox jumps over a Dog. 123 4567 890 Zwei Boxkämpfer jagen Eva durch Sylt portez ce vieux

▶ Bold OSF
The quick brown fox jumps over a Dog. 123 4567 890 Zwei Boxkämpfer jagen Eva durch Sylt portez ce vieux

▶ Bold Italic OSF
The quick brown fox jumps over a Dog. 123 4567 890 Zwei Boxkämpfer jagen Eva durch Sylt portez ce vieux

▶ Black OSF
The quick brown fox jumps over a Dog. 123 4567 890 Zwei Boxkämpfer jagen Eva durch Sylt portez ce

▶ Black Italic OSF
The quick brown fox jumps over a Dog. 123 4567 890 Zwei Boxkämpfer jagen Eva durch Sylt portez ce

BT1262 Mac + PC ② 1900-04: (L. B. Benton) M. F. Benton

Century Expanded

abcdefghijklmnopqrstuvwxyz[äöüßåøæœç]
ABCDEFGHIJKLMNOPQRSTUVWXYZ
1234567890(.,;:?!$&-*){ÄÖÜÅØÆŒÇ}

aa*a*
A141
Century Expanded,
Reg, Ita

▶ Regular
The quick brown fox jumps over a Dog. Zwei Boxkämpfer jagen Eva durch Sylt portez ce vieux Whiskey blond qui fume

▶ Italic
The quick brown fox jumps over a Dog. Zwei Boxkämpfer jagen Eva durch Sylt portez ce vieux Whiskey blond qui fume

▼ BT1262 Mac + PC Century Expanded

▶ Bold
The quick brown fox jumps over a Dog. Zwei Boxkämpfer jagen Eva durch Sylt portez ce vieux Whiskey blond qui

▶ Bold Italic
The quick brown fox jumps over a Dog. Zwei Boxkämpfer jagen Eva durch Sylt portez ce vieux Whiskey blond qui

A650 Mac + PC ② 1975–79: (M. F. Benton) Tony Stan
ITC Century®

abcdefghijklmnopqrstuvwxyz[äöüßåøæœç]
ABCDEFGHIJKLMNOPQRSTUVWXYZ
1234567890(.,;:?!$&-*){ÄÖÜÅØÆŒÇ}

a a *a*
EF293
ITC Century 1, Lt, LtIta, Bd, BdIta
EF294
ITC Century 2, Bk, BkIta, Ult, UltIta
BT1264
ITC Century Light, Lt, LtIta
BT1265
ITC Century, Bk, BkIta, Bd, BdIta
BT1266
ITC Century Ultra, Ult, UltIta

▶ Light
The quick brown fox jumps over a Dog. Zwei Boxkämpfer jagen Eva durch Sylt portez ce vieux Whiskey blond qui fume

▶ Light Italic
The quick brown fox jumps over a Dog. Zwei Boxkämpfer jagen Eva durch Sylt portez ce vieux Whiskey blond qui

▶ Book
The quick brown fox jumps over a Dog. Zwei Boxkämpfer jagen Eva durch Sylt portez ce vieux Whiskey blond qui fume

▶ Book Italic
The quick brown fox jumps over a Dog. Zwei Boxkämpfer jagen Eva durch Sylt portez ce vieux Whiskey blond qui fume

▶ Bold
The quick brown fox jumps over a Dog. Zwei Boxkämpfer jagen Eva durch Sylt portez ce vieux Whiskey

▶ Bold Italic
The quick brown fox jumps over a Dog. Zwei Boxkämpfer jagen Eva durch Sylt portez ce vieux Whiskey

▶ Ultra
The quick brown fox jumps over a Dog. Zwei Boxkämpfer jagen Eva durch Sylt portez ce

▶ Ultra Italic
The quick brown fox jumps over a Dog. Zwei Boxkämpfer jagen Eva durch Sylt portez ce

A651 Mac + PC ② 1975–79: (M. F. Benton) Tony Stan
ITC Century Condensed

abcdefghijklmnopqrstuvwxyz[äöüßåøæœç]
ABCDEFGHIJKLMNOPQRSTUVWXYZ
1234567890(.,;:?!$&-){ÄÖÜÅØÆŒÇ}*

a a *a*
EF295
ITC Century Condensed 3, LtCon, LtConIta, BdCon, BdConIta
EF296
ITC Century Condensed 4, BkCon, BkConIta, UltCon, UltConIta
BT1267
ITC Century Light Condensed, LtCon, LtConIta
BT1268
ITC Century Condensed, BkCon, BkConIta, BdCon, BdConIta
BT1269
ITC Century Ultra Condensed, UltCon, UltConIta

▶ Light Condensed
The quick brown fox jumps over a Dog. Zwei Boxkämpfer jagen Eva durch Sylt portez ce vieux Whiskey blond qui fume une pipe aber echt

▶ Light Condensed Italic
The quick brown fox jumps over a Dog. Zwei Boxkämpfer jagen Eva durch Sylt portez ce vieux Whiskey blond qui fume une pipe aber echt

▶ Book Condensed
The quick brown fox jumps over a Dog. Zwei Boxkämpfer jagen Eva durch Sylt portez ce vieux Whiskey blond qui fume une pipe aber echt

▶ Book Condensed Italic
The quick brown fox jumps over a Dog. Zwei Boxkämpfer jagen Eva durch Sylt portez ce vieux Whiskey blond qui fume une pipe aber echt

© FSI 1993

▼ A651   Mac + PC   ITC Century Condensed

▶ Bold Condensed
The quick brown fox jumps over a Dog. Zwei Boxkämpfer jagen Eva durch Sylt portez ce vieux Whiskey blond qui fume une pipe aber

▶ Bold Condensed Italic
The quick brown fox jumps over a Dog. Zwei Boxkämpfer jagen Eva durch Sylt portez ce vieux Whiskey blond qui fume une pipe

▶ Ultra Condensed
The quick brown fox jumps over a Dog. Zwei Boxkämpfer jagen Eva durch Sylt portez ce vieux Whiskey blond

▶ Ultra Condensed Italic
The quick brown fox jumps over a Dog. Zwei Boxkämpfer jagen Eva durch Sylt portez ce vieux Whiskey

M976   Mac + PC   ② — 1906–09: L. B. Benton, M. F. Benton
Century Old Style®

abcdefghijklmnopqrstuvwxyz[äöüßåøæœç]
ABCDEFGHIJKLMNOPQRSTUVWXYZ
1234567890(.,;:?!$&-*){ÄÖÜÅØÆŒÇ}

aa*a*
A023
Century Old Style, Reg, Ita, Bd
BT1263
Century Oldstyle, Reg, Ita, Bd

▶ Regular
The quick brown fox jumps over a Dog. Zwei Boxkämpfer jagen Eva durch Sylt portez ce vieux Whiskey blond qui fume une pipe

▶ Italic
The quick brown fox jumps over a Dog. Zwei Boxkämpfer jagen Eva durch Sylt portez ce vieux Whiskey blond qui fume une pipe aber

▶ Bold
The quick brown fox jumps over a Dog. Zwei Boxkämpfer jagen Eva durch Sylt portez ce vieux Whiskey blond

▶ Bold Italic
The quick brown fox jumps over a Dog. Zwei Boxkämpfer jagen Eva durch Sylt portez ce vieux Whiskey

FB6372   Mac + PC   ②
Century Bold Condensed

abcdefghijklmnopqrstuvwxyz[äöüßåøæœç]
ABCDEFGHIJKLMNOPQRSTUVWXYZ
1234567890(.,;:?!$&-*){ÄÖÜÅØÆŒÇ}

FBI Condensed Classics™:
Bodoni Bold Compressed, Bodoni Bold Condensed, Caslon Bold Condensed, Century Bold Condensed, Cheltenham Bold Condensed

A083   Mac + PC   ② — 1917–23: M. F. Benton
New Century Schoolbook™

abcdefghijklmnopqrstuvwxyz[äöüßåøæœç]
ABCDEFGHIJKLMNOPQRSTUVWXYZ
1234567890(.,;:?!$&-*){ÄÖÜÅØÆŒÇ}

▶ Regular
The quick brown fox jumps over a Dog. Zwei Boxkämpfer jagen Eva durch Sylt portez ce vieux Whiskey blond qui

▶ Italic
The quick brown fox jumps over a Dog. Zwei Boxkämpfer jagen Eva durch Sylt portez ce vieux Whiskey blond qui

© FSI 1993

▼ A083   Mac + PC   New Century Schoolbook™

▶ Bold
The quick brown fox jumps over a Dog. Zwei Boxkämpfer jagen Eva durch Sylt portez ce vieux

▶ Bold Italic
The quick brown fox jumps over a Dog. Zwei Boxkämpfer jagen Eva durch Sylt portez ce vieux

---

BT772   Mac + PC   ②   1917–23: M. F. Benton
Century Schoolbook 1

abcdefghijklmnopqrstuvwxyz[äöüßåøæœç]
ABCDEFGHIJKLMNOPQRSTUVWXYZ
1234567890(.,;:?!$&-*){ÄÖÜÅØÆŒÇ}

▶ Regular
The quick brown fox jumps over a Dog. Zwei Boxkämpfer jagen Eva durch Sylt portez ce vieux Whiskey blond qui

▶ Italic
The quick brown fox jumps over a Dog. Zwei Boxkämpfer jagen Eva durch Sylt portez ce vieux Whiskey blond qui fume

▶ Bold
The quick brown fox jumps over a Dog. Zwei Boxkämpfer jagen Eva durch Sylt portez ce vieux

▶ Bold Italic
The quick brown fox jumps over a Dog. Zwei Boxkämpfer jagen Eva durch Sylt portez ce vieux

---

BT773   Mac + PC   ②   (M. F. Benton, 1917–23)
Century Schoolbook 2

abcdefghijklmnopqrstuvwxyz[äöüßåøæœç]
ABCDEFGHIJKLMNOPQRSTUVWXYZ
1234567890(.,;:?!$&-*){ÄÖÜÅØÆŒÇ}

▶ Bold Condensed
The quick brown fox jumps over a Dog. Zwei Boxkämpfer jagen Eva durch Sylt portez ce vieux Whiskey blond qui fume une pipe aber echt über die Mauer

▶ Monospace
The quick brown fox jumps over a Dog. Zwei Boxkämpfer jagen Eva durch Sylt portez ce

---

L2821   Mac   ④   1982: Martin Wait
Challenge™ Bold

*abcdefghijklmnopqrstuvwxyz[äöüßåøæœç]
ABCDEFGHIJKLMNOPQRSTUVWXYZ
1234567890(.,;:?!$&-*)ÄÖÜÅØÆŒÇ*

L2822   Mac   ④   1982: Martin Wait
Challenge Extra Bold

*abcdefghijklmnopqrstuvwxyz[äöüßåøæœç]
ABCDEFGHIJKLMNOPQRSTUVWXYZ
1234567890(.,;:?!$&-*)ÄÖÜÅØÆŒÇ*

Champers™
L2568 MAC ⑥ 1991: Alan Meeks

abcdefghijklmnopqrstuvwxyz[äöüßåøæœç]
ABCDEFGHIJKLMNOPQRSTUVWXYZ
1234567890(.,;:?!$&-*)ÄÖÜÅØÆŒÇ

Chaplin™
C597 MAC + PC ④ (Willard T. Sniffin, 1933)

abcdefghijklmnopqrstuvwxyz[äöüßåøæœç]
ABCDEFGHIJKLMNOPQRSTUVWXYZ
1234567890(.,;:?!$&-*){ÄÖÜÅØÆŒÇ}

Carmine Tango™:
Carmine Tango, Chaplin™, Coronet
© Mandate

Charlemagne/Trajan
A420 MAC + PC

Charlemagne/Trajan:
Charlemagne®, Trajan™

Charlemagne®
A420 MAC + PC ⑥ 1989: Carol Twombly

ABCDEFGHIJKLMNOPQRSTUVWXYZ
1234567890(.,;:?!$&-*)[ ]{ÄÖÜÅØÆŒÇ}

▶ Regular
THE QUICK BROWN FOX JUMPS OVER A DOG. ZWEI BOXKÄMPFER JAGEN EVA DURCH SYLT

▶ Bold
THE QUICK BROWN FOX JUMPS OVER A DOG. ZWEI BOXKÄMPFER JAGEN EVA DURCH

Charlemagne/Trajan:
Charlemagne®, Trajan™

Charlotte™
L6435 MAC ② 1992: Michael Gills

abcdefghijklmnopqrstuvwxyz[äöüßåøæœç]
ABCDEFGHIJKLMNOPQRSTUVWXYZ
1234567890(.,;:?!$&-*){ÄÖÜÅØÆŒÇ}

▶ Book
The quick brown fox jumps over a Dog. Zwei Boxkämpfer jagen Eva durch Sylt portez ce vieux Whiskey blond qui fume

▶ Book Italic
The quick brown fox jumps over a Dog. Zwei Boxkämpfer jagen Eva durch Sylt portez ce vieux Whiskey blond qui fume une pipe aber echt

© FSI 1993

▼ L6435 MAC Charlotte™

▶ Book SC
THE QUICK BROWN FOX JUMPS OVER A DOG. 123 4567 890 ZWEI BOXKÄMPFER JAGEN EVA DURCH SYLT PORTEZ CE VIEUX WHISKEY

▶ Medium
The quick brown fox jumps over a Dog. Zwei Boxkämpfer jagen Eva durch Sylt portez ce vieux Whiskey blond qui fume

▶ Bold
The quick brown fox jumps over a Dog. Zwei Boxkämpfer jagen Eva durch Sylt portez ce vieux Whiskey blond qui

L6436 MAC ① ✎ 1992: Michael Gills
Charlotte Sans™

abcdefghijklmnopqrstuvwxyz[äöüßåøæœç]
ABCDEFGHIJKLMNOPQRSTUVWXYZ
1234567890(.,;:?!$&-*){ÄÖÜÅØÆŒÇ}

▶ Book
The quick brown fox jumps over a Dog. Zwei Boxkämpfer jagen Eva durch Sylt portez ce vieux Whiskey blond qui fume une pipe aber

▶ Book Italic
The quick brown fox jumps over a Dog. Zwei Boxkämpfer jagen Eva durch Sylt portez ce vieux Whiskey blond qui fume une pipe aber echt

▶ Book SC
THE QUICK BROWN FOX JUMPS OVER A DOG. 123 4567 890 ZWEI BOXKÄMPFER JAGEN EVA DURCH SYLT PORTEZ CE VIEUX WHISKEY BLOND

▶ Medium
The quick brown fox jumps over a Dog. Zwei Boxkämpfer jagen Eva durch Sylt portez ce vieux Whiskey blond qui fume une

▶ Bold
The quick brown fox jumps over a Dog. Zwei Boxkämpfer jagen Eva durch Sylt portez ce vieux Whiskey blond qui fume une

A564 MAC + PC ④ ✎ 1957: H. Matheis
Charme™

abcdefghijklmnopqrstuvwxyz[äöüßåøæœç]
ABCDEFGHIJKLMNOPQRSTUVWXYZ
1234567890(.,;:?!$&-){ÄÖÜÅØÆŒÇ}*

German Display 2:
Banco™, Charme™, Flyer™ Condensed, Wilhelm Klingspor Gotisch™

BT774 MAC + PC ② ✎ 1987: Matthew Carter
Bitstream Charter™ 1

abcdefghijklmnopqrstuvwxyz[äöüßåøæœç]
ABCDEFGHIJKLMNOPQRSTUVWXYZ
1234567890(.,;:?!$&-*){ÄÖÜÅØÆŒÇ}

© FSI 1993

▼ BT774 Mac + PC **Bitstream Charter™ 1**

© Demos, Swift

▶ Regular
The quick brown fox jumps over a Dog. Zwei Boxkämpfer jagen Eva durch Sylt portez ce vieux Whiskey blond qui fume

▶ Italic
The quick brown fox jumps over a Dog. Zwei Boxkämpfer jagen Eva durch Sylt portez ce vieux Whiskey blond qui fume une

▶ Black
The quick brown fox jumps over a Dog. Zwei Boxkämpfer jagen Eva durch Sylt portez ce vieux

▶ Black Italic
The quick brown fox jumps over a Dog. Zwei Boxkämpfer jagen Eva durch Sylt portez ce vieux

---

BT775 Mac + PC ② ✎ 1987: Matthew Carter
Bitstream Charter 2

**abcdefghijklmnopqrstuvwxyz[äöüßåøæœç]
ABCDEFGHIJKLMNOPQRSTUVWXYZ
1234567890(.,;:?!$&-*){ÄÖÜÅØÆŒÇ}**

© Demos, Swift

▶ Bold
The quick brown fox jumps over a Dog. Zwei Boxkämpfer jagen Eva durch Sylt portez ce vieux Whiskey blond qui

▶ Bold Italic
The quick brown fox jumps over a Dog. Zwei Boxkämpfer jagen Eva durch Sylt portez ce vieux Whiskey blond qui fume

---

EF1070 Mac + PC ② ✎ 1902–04: M. F. Benton (1896-1902 Bertram Goodhue)
Cheltenham Old Style™

abcdefghijklmnopqrstuvwxyz[äöüßåøæœç]
ABCDEFGHIJKLMNOPQRSTUVWXYZ
1234567890(.,;:?!$&-*){ÄÖÜÅØÆŒÇ}

📦 Cheltenham Old Style™, Goudy Handtooled
aa*a* BT1270
Cheltenham, Reg, Ita, Bd, BdIta

© Gloucester

BT1270 Mac + PC ② ✎ 1902–04: M. F. Benton (1896-1902 Bertram Goodhue)
Cheltenham

abcdefghijklmnopqrstuvwxyz[äöüßåøæœç]
ABCDEFGHIJKLMNOPQRSTUVWXYZ
1234567890(.,;:?!$&-*){ÄÖÜÅØÆŒÇ}

aa*a*
EF1070
Goudy Handtooled, Reg
Cheltenham Old Style™, Reg
© Gloucester

▶ Regular
The quick brown fox jumps over a Dog. Zwei Boxkämpfer jagen Eva durch Sylt portez ce vieux Whiskey blond qui fume une pipe aber echt

▶ Italic
The quick brown fox jumps over a Dog. Zwei Boxkämpfer jagen Eva durch Sylt portez ce vieux Whiskey blond qui fume une pipe aber echt

▶ Bold
The quick brown fox jumps over a Dog. Zwei Boxkämpfer jagen Eva durch Sylt portez ce vieux Whiskey blond qui fume

▶ Bold Italic
The quick brown fox jumps over a Dog. Zwei Boxkämpfer jagen Eva durch Sylt portez ce vieux Whiskey blond qui fume

© FSI 1993

BT878　Mac + PC　② 1902–04: M. F. Benton (1896-1902 Bertram Goodhue)
Cheltenham 1

abcdefghijklmnopqrstuvwxyz[äöüßåøæœç]
ABCDEFGHIJKLMNOPQRSTUVWXYZ
1234567890(.,;:?!$&-*){ÄÖÜÅØÆŒÇ}

© Gloucester

▶ Bold Condensed
The quick brown fox jumps over a Dog. Zwei Boxkämpfer jagen Eva durch Sylt portez ce vieux Whiskey blond qui fume une pipe aber echt über die Mauer

▶ Bold Condensed Italic
The quick brown fox jumps over a Dog. Zwei Boxkämpfer jagen Eva durch Sylt portez ce vieux Whiskey blond qui fume une pipe aber echt über die Mauer

BT776　Mac + PC　② 1902–04: M. F. Benton (1896-1902 Bertram Goodhue)
Cheltenham 2

abcdefghijklmnopqrstuvwxyz[äöüßåøæœç]
ABCDEFGHIJKLMNOPQRSTUVWXYZ
1234567890(.,;:?!$&-*){ÄÖÜÅØÆŒÇ}

© Gloucester

▶ Bold Headline
The quick brown fox jumps over a Dog. Zwei Boxkämpfer jagen Eva durch Sylt portez ce vieux Whiskey blond qui fume

▶ Bold Italic Headline
The quick brown fox jumps over a Dog. Zwei Boxkämpfer jagen Eva durch Sylt portez ce vieux Whiskey blond qui fume

▶ Bold Extra Condensed
The quick brown fox jumps over a Dog. Zwei Boxkämpfer jagen Eva durch Sylt portez ce vieux Whiskey blond qui fume une pipe aber echt über die Mauer gesprungen und auch

FB6372　Mac + PC　②
Cheltenham Bold Condensed

abcdefghijklmnopqrstuvwxyz[äöüßåøæœç]
ABCDEFGHIJKLMNOPQRSTUVWXYZ
1234567890(.,;:?!$&-*){ÄÖÜÅØÆŒÇ}

📦 FBI Condensed Classics™:
Bodoni Bold Compressed, Bodoni Bold Condensed, Caslon Bold Condensed, Century Bold Condensed, Cheltenham Bold Condensed

A567　Mac + PC　② 1975–79: Tony Stan
ITC Cheltenham® 2

abcdefghijklmnopqrstuvwxyz[äöüßåøæœç]
ABCDEFGHIJKLMNOPQRSTUVWXYZ
1234567890(.,;:?!$&-*){ÄÖÜÅØÆŒÇ}

aaa
BT1271
ITC Cheltenham Light, Lt, LtIta
BT1273
ITC Cheltenham Ultra, Ult, UltIta

▶ Light
The quick brown fox jumps over a Dog. Zwei Boxkämpfer jagen Eva durch Sylt portez ce vieux Whiskey blond qui fume une

▶ Light Italic
The quick brown fox jumps over a Dog. Zwei Boxkämpfer jagen Eva durch Sylt portez ce vieux Whiskey blond qui fume une

© FSI 1993

▼ A567 Mac + PC ITC Cheltenham® 2

▶ Ultra
The quick brown fox jumps over a Dog. Zwei Boxkämpfer jagen Eva durch Sylt portez ce

▶ Ultra Italic
The quick brown fox jumps over a Dog. Zwei Boxkämpfer jagen Eva durch Sylt portez ce vieux

A024 Mac + PC ② 1975–79: Tony Stan
ITC Cheltenham 1

abcdefghijklmnopqrstuvwxyz[äöüßåøæœç]
ABCDEFGHIJKLMNOPQRSTUVWXYZ
1234567890(.,;:?!$&-*){ÄÖÜÅØÆŒÇ}

aa*a*
BT1272
ITC Cheltenham, Bk, BkIta, Bd, BdIta

▶ Book
The quick brown fox jumps over a Dog. Zwei Boxkämpfer jagen Eva durch Sylt portez ce vieux Whiskey blond qui fume

▶ Book Italic
The quick brown fox jumps over a Dog. Zwei Boxkämpfer jagen Eva durch Sylt portez ce vieux Whiskey blond qui fume

▶ Bold
The quick brown fox jumps over a Dog. Zwei Boxkämpfer jagen Eva durch Sylt portez ce vieux Whiskey blond

▶ Bold Italic
The quick brown fox jumps over a Dog. Zwei Boxkämpfer jagen Eva durch Sylt portez ce vieux Whiskey

A894 Mac + PC ② 1975–79: Tony Stan
ITC Cheltenham Condensed

abcdefghijklmnopqrstuvwxyz[äöüßåøæœç]
ABCDEFGHIJKLMNOPQRSTUVWXYZ
1234567890(.,;:?!$&-*){ÄÖÜÅØÆŒÇ}

© Cheltenham Old Style

▶ Light Condensed
The quick brown fox jumps over a Dog. Zwei Boxkämpfer jagen Eva durch Sylt portez ce vieux Whiskey blond qui fume une pipe aber echt über die

▶ Light Condensed Italic
The quick brown fox jumps over a Dog. Zwei Boxkämpfer jagen Eva durch Sylt portez ce vieux Whiskey blond qui fume une pipe aber echt über die

▶ Book Condensed
The quick brown fox jumps over a Dog. Zwei Boxkämpfer jagen Eva durch Sylt portez ce vieux Whiskey blond qui fume une pipe aber echt

▶ Book Condensed Italic
The quick brown fox jumps over a Dog. Zwei Boxkämpfer jagen Eva durch Sylt portez ce vieux Whiskey blond qui fume une pipe aber echt

▶ Bold Condensed
The quick brown fox jumps over a Dog. Zwei Boxkämpfer jagen Eva durch Sylt portez ce vieux Whiskey blond qui fume une

▶ Bold Condensed Italic
The quick brown fox jumps over a Dog. Zwei Boxkämpfer jagen Eva durch Sylt portez ce vieux Whiskey blond qui fume une pipe

▶ Ultra Condensed
The quick brown fox jumps over a Dog. Zwei Boxkämpfer jagen Eva durch Sylt portez ce vieux Whiskey blond qui fume

▶ Ultra Condensed Italic
The quick brown fox jumps over a Dog. Zwei Boxkämpfer jagen Eva durch Sylt portez ce vieux Whiskey blond qui

Chesterfield™
EF6469 Mac + PC (6)

abcdefghijklmnopqrstuvwxyz[äöüßåøæœç]
ABCDEFGHIJKLMNOPQRSTUVWXYZ
1234567890(.,:;?!$&-*) ÄÖÜÅØÆŒÇ

E+F Special Headlines 5:
Chesterfield™, Cortez™, Elefont™, Glastonbury™, Julia™ Script, LCD
© Belshaw

Chevalier™
C6426 Mac + PC (4) — 1946: E. A. Neukomm

ABCDEFGHIJKLMNOPQRSTUVWXYZ
1234567890(.,:;?!$&-*)[ ]{ÄÖÜÅØÆŒÇ}

Basque, etc:
Basque, Brophy™ Script, Chevalier™, Uncial
© Barclay Open, EngraversRoman

Chic™
C2778 Mac + PC (6) — 1928: M. F. Benton

ABCDEFGHIJKLMNOPQRSTUVWXYZ
1234567890(.,:;?!$&-*)[ ]{ÄÖÜÅØÆŒÇ}

Headlines 90S:
Bernhard Fashion, Chic™, Eclipse™, Metronome Gothic, Salut™
© Broadway Engraved

Chicago
MC6346 Mac + PC (6)

abcdefghijklmnopqrstuvwxyz[äöüßåøæœç]
ABCDEFGHIJKLMNOPQRSTUVWXYZ
1234567890(.,:;?!$&-*)(äöüåøæœç)

Childs™
RB6094 Mac (6) — 1991: Richard Beatty

abcdefghijklmnopqrstuvwxyz[äöüßåøæœç]
ABCDEFGHIJKLMNOPQRSTUVWXYZ
1234567890(.,:;?!$&-*)(ÄÖÜÅØÆŒÇ)

Beatty Victoriana™:
Childs™, Hermosa™, Recherché™, Spiral™, Wanted™

© FSI 1993

RB6095 Mac (6) — 1991: Richard Beatty
Childs Alternates

abcdefghijklmnopqrstuvwxyz[äöüßåøæœç]
ABCDEFGHIJKLMNOPQRSTUVWXYZ
1234567890(.,;:?!$&-*)(ÄÖÜÅØÆŒÇ)

Beatty Victoriana Alternates:
Childs Alternates, Hermosa Alternates, Recherché Alternates, Spiral Alternates, Wanted Alternates

MC6364 Mac + PC (6) — Albert Boton
Chinon™

abcdefghijklmnopqrstuvwxyz[äöüßåøæœç]
ABCDEFGHIJKLMNOPQRSTUVWXYZ
1234567890(.,;:?!$&-*)(ÄÖÜÅØÆŒÇ)

BT2550 Mac + PC (4) — 1954: Roger Excoffon — Industry name Choc™
Staccato 555

abcdefghijklmnopqrstuvwxyz[äöüßåøæœç]
ABCDEFGHIJKLMNOPQRSTUVWXYZ
1234567890(.,;:?!$&-*){ÄÖÜÅØÆŒÇ}

AB6319 Mac + PC (2) — 1992: Gustav Jaeger
Christiana™

abcdefghijklmnopqrstuvwxyz[äöüßåøæœç]
ABCDEFGHIJKLMNOPQRSTUVWXYZ
1234567890(.,;:?!$&-*){ÄÖÜÅØÆŒÇ}

▶ Regular
The quick brown fox jumps over a Dog. Zwei Boxkämpfer jagen Eva durch Sylt portez ce vieux Whiskey blond qui fume

▶ Italic
The quick brown fox jumps over a Dog. Zwei Boxkämpfer jagen Eva durch Sylt portez ce vieux Whiskey blond qui fume une

▶ Medium
The quick brown fox jumps over a Dog. Zwei Boxkämpfer jagen Eva durch Sylt portez ce vieux Whiskey blond qui fume

▶ Medium Italic
The quick brown fox jumps over a Dog. Zwei Boxkämpfer jagen Eva durch Sylt portez ce vieux Whiskey blond qui fume

▶ Bold
The quick brown fox jumps over a Dog. Zwei Boxkämpfer jagen Eva durch Sylt portez ce vieux Whiskey blond

▶ Bold Italic
The quick brown fox jumps over a Dog. Zwei Boxkämpfer jagen Eva durch Sylt portez ce vieux Whiskey blond

Barbedor

▶ Regular SC
THE QUICK BROWN FOX JUMPS OVER A DOG. ZWEI BOXER JAGEN EVA DURCH SYLT PORTEZ CE VIEUX WHISKEY BLOND QUI FUME UNE

▶ Regular Expert
01234567890ffiflffl-($^1/_1$$^2/_2$$^3/_3$$^4/_4$$^5/_5$$^6/_6$$^7/_7$$^8/_8$$^9/_9$$^0/_0$)$^{(\$}$$cRp$©$)^a$ THE QUICK BROWN FOX JUMPS OVER A DOG ZWEI BOXKÄMPFER JAGEN EVA

© FSI 1993

L2569 Mac — 1983: David Harris
Chromium™

ABCDEFGHIJKLMNOPQRSTUVWXYZ
1234567890(.,;:?!$&-*)[]ÄÖÜÅØÆŒÇ

MC2925 Mac + PC — 1970: Michael Neugebauer
Circus

abcdefghijklmnopqrstuvwxyz[äöüßåøæœç]
ABCDEFGHIJKLMNOPQRSTUVWXYZ
1234567890[.,;:?!$&-*]{ÄÖÜÅØÆŒÇ}

EF6466 Mac + PC — 1970: Michael Neugebauer
Cirkulus™

abcdefghijklmnopqrstuvwxyz
1234567890(.,;:?!$&-*)[ ]äöüåøæœç

E+F Special Headlines 2:
Belshaw™, Camellia™, Carousel™, Cirkulus™, Data 70, Galadriel™

L2976 Mac — 1990: Trevor Loan
Citation™

ABCDEFGHIJKLMNOPQRSTUVWXYZ
1234567890(.,;:?!$&-*)[]ÄÖÜÅØÆŒÇ

E561 Mac + PC — 1986: Zuzana Licko
Citizen™

abcdefghijklmnopqrstuvwxyz[äöüßåøæœç]
ABCDEFGHIJKLMNOPQRSTUVWXYZ
1234567890(.,;: ?!$&-*){ÄÖÜÅØÆŒÇ}

DIN Mittelschrift

▶ Light
The quick brown fox jumps over a Dog. Zwei Boxkämpfer jagen Eva durch Sylt portez ce vieux Whiskey

▶ Bold
The quick brown fox jumps over a Dog. Zwei Boxkämpfer jagen Eva durch Sylt portez ce vieux Whiskey

AB1051 Mac + PC — 1930: Georg Trump
Berthold City®

abcdefghijklmnopqrstuvwxyz[äöüßåøæœç]
ABCDEFGHIJKLMNOPQRSTUVWXYZ
1234567890(.,;:?!$&-*){ÄÖÜÅØÆŒÇ}

▼ AB1051 Mac + PC Berthold City®

aa*a*
BT777
City, Lt, Med, Bd
Berthold Colossalis,
Retro

▶ Light
The quick brown fox jumps over a Dog. Zwei Boxkämpfer jagen Eva durch Sylt portez ce vieux Whiskey blond qui fume une pipe aber echt

▶ Light Italic
The quick brown fox jumps over a Dog. Zwei Boxkämpfer jagen Eva durch Sylt portez ce vieux Whiskey blond qui fume une pipe aber echt

▶ Medium
The quick brown fox jumps over a Dog. Zwei Boxkämpfer jagen Eva durch Sylt portez ce vieux Whiskey blond qui fume une pipe aber

▶ Medium Italic
The quick brown fox jumps over a Dog. Zwei Boxkämpfer jagen Eva durch Sylt portez ce vieux Whiskey blond qui fume une pipe aber

▶ Bold
The quick brown fox jumps over a Dog. Zwei Boxkämpfer jagen Eva durch Sylt portez ce vieux Whiskey blond qui fume une

▶ Bold Italic
The quick brown fox jumps over a Dog. Zwei Boxkämpfer jagen Eva durch Sylt portez ce vieux Whiskey blond qui fume une

---

C600 Mac + PC
Claire News

Claire News:
Claire News, Triplett

C600 Mac + PC ②
Claire News

abcdefghijklmnopqrstuvwxyz[äöüßåøæœç]
ABCDEFGHIJKLMNOPQRSTUVWXYZ
1234567890(.,;:?!$&-*){ÄÖÜÅØÆŒÇ}

▶ Light
The quick brown fox jumps over a Dog. Zwei Boxkämpfer jagen Eva durch Sylt portez ce

▶ Bold
The quick brown fox jumps over a Dog. Zwei Boxkämpfer jagen Eva durch Sylt

Claire News:
Claire News, Triplett

A1147 Mac + PC ⑥ ✎ 1991: Herbert Maring
Clairvaux™

abcdefghijklmnopqrstuvwxyz[äöüßåøæœç]
ABCDEFGHIJKLMNOPQRSTUVWXYZ
1234567890(.,;:?!$&-*){ÄÖÜÅØÆŒÇ}

Type Before Gutenberg 2:
Carolina™ & Dfr, Clairvaux™, San Marco™

© FSI 1993

BT1274 Mac + PC ③ 🖉 1953: H. Eidenbenz
Clarendon

abcdefghijklmnopqrstuvwxyz[äöüßåøæœç]
ABCDEFGHIJKLMNOPQRSTUVWXYZ
1234567890(.,;:?!$&-*){ÄÖÜÅØÆŒÇ}

aa*a*
📖 M206
Headliners 1
📖 A025
Headliners 1
📖 C178
Aquarius
©
Antique No. 3, Belizio, Egyptian

▶ Light
The quick brown fox jumps over a Dog. Zwei Boxkämpfer jagen Eva durch Sylt portez ce vieux Whiskey

▶ Bold
The quick brown fox jumps over a Dog. Zwei Boxkämpfer jagen Eva durch Sylt portez ce vieux

▶ Regular
The quick brown fox jumps over a Dog. Zwei Boxkämpfer jagen Eva durch Sylt portez ce vieux Whis-

BT779 Mac + PC ③ 🖉 1953: H. Eidenbenz
Clarendon 2

abcdefghijklmnopqrstuvwxyz[äöüßåøæœç]
ABCDEFGHIJKLMNOPQRSTUVWXYZ
1234567890(.,;:?!$&-*){ÄÖÜÅØÆŒÇ}

aa*a*
📖 C178
Aquarius
©
Antique No. 3, Belizio, Egyptian

▶ Black
The quick brown fox jumps over a Dog. Zwei Boxkämpfer jagen Eva durch Sylt portez ce vieux

▶ Heavy
The quick brown fox jumps over a Dog. Zwei Boxkämpfer jagen Eva durch Sylt portez ce vieux

C178 Mac + PC ③
Clarendon Book Condensed

abcdefghijklmnopqrstuvwxyz[äöüßåøæœç]
ABCDEFGHIJKLMNOPQRSTUVWXYZ
1234567890(.,;:?!$&-*){ÄÖÜÅØÆŒÇ}

📦
Aquarius:
Aquarius™ No. 8, Clarendon Book Condensed, Poster Bodoni
aa*a* BT778
Clarendon Condensed 1, Con, BdCon

BT778 Mac + PC ③
Clarendon Condensed 1

abcdefghijklmnopqrstuvwxyz[äöüßåøæœç]
ABCDEFGHIJKLMNOPQRSTUVWXYZ
1234567890(.,;:?!$&-*){ÄÖÜÅØÆŒÇ}

aa*a*
📖 C178
Aquarius
©
Antique No. 3, Belizio, Egyptian

▶ Condensed
The quick brown fox jumps over a Dog. Zwei Boxkämpfer jagen Eva durch Sylt portez ce vieux Whiskey blond qui fume une pipe aber echt über die

▶ Bold Condensed
The quick brown fox jumps over a Dog. Zwei Boxkämpfer jagen Eva durch Sylt portez ce vieux Whiskey blond qui fume une pipe aber echt

© FSI 1993

M206 Mac + PC ③ 1960: (H. Eidenbenz, 1953)
Clarendon

abcdefghijklmnopqrstuvwxyz[äöüßåøæœç]
ABCDEFGHIJKLMNOPQRSTUVWXYZ
1234567890(.,:;:?!$&-*){ÄÖÜÅØÆŒÇ}

Headliners 1:
Clarendon, Egyptian, New Clarendon
aaa BT1274
Clarendon, Lt, Reg, Bd
A025

M206 Mac + PC ③
New Clarendon

abcdefghijklmnopqrstuvwxyz[äöüßåøæœç]
ABCDEFGHIJKLMNOPQRSTUVWXYZ
1234567890(.,:;:?!$&-*){ÄÖÜÅØÆŒÇ}

ⓒ Antique No. 3, Belizio, Egyptian

▶ Regular
The quick brown fox jumps over a Dog. Zwei Boxkämpfer jagen Eva durch Sylt portez ce vieux Whiskey blond qui

▶ Bold
The quick brown fox jumps over a Dog. Zwei Boxkämpfer jagen Eva durch Sylt portez ce vieux

Headliners 1:
Clarendon, Egyptian, New Clarendon
ⓒ Antique No. 3, Belizio, Egyptian

C601 Mac + PC ② 1979: Adrian Williams
Claridge™

abcdefghijklmnopqrstuvwxyz[äöüßåøæœç]
ABCDEFGHIJKLMNOPQRSTUVWXYZ
1234567890(.,:;:?!$&-*){ÄÖÜÅØÆŒÇ}

▶ Regular
The quick brown fox jumps over a Dog. Zwei Boxkämpfer jagen Eva durch Sylt portez ce vieux Whiskey blond

▶ Italic
The quick brown fox jumps over a Dog. Zwei Boxkämpfer jagen Eva durch Sylt portez ce vieux Whiskey blond

▶ Bold
The quick brown fox jumps over a Dog. Zwei Boxkämpfer jagen Eva durch Sylt portez ce vieux

▶ Black
The quick brown fox jumps over a Dog. Zwei Boxkämpfer jagen Eva durch Sylt portez ce

M207 Mac + PC ③
Clarion®

abcdefghijklmnopqrstuvwxyz[äöüßåøæœç]
ABCDEFGHIJKLMNOPQRSTUVWXYZ
1234567890(.,:;:?!$&-*){ÄÖÜÅØÆŒÇ}

© FSI 1993

▼ M207 Mac + PC **Clarion®**

Nimrod

▶ **Regular**
The quick brown fox jumps over a Dog. Zwei Boxkämpfer jagen Eva durch Sylt portez ce vieux Whiskey blond

▶ *Italic*
The quick brown fox jumps over a Dog. Zwei Boxkämpfer jagen Eva durch Sylt portez ce vieux Whiskey blond

▶ **Bold**
The quick brown fox jumps over a Dog. Zwei Boxkämpfer jagen Eva durch Sylt portez ce vieux Whiskey

---

C2780 Mac + PC ⑥
Classic Roman

ABCDEFGHIJKLMNOPQRSTUVWXYZ[ÄÖÜÅÇ]
ABCDEFGHIJKLMNOPQRSTUVWXYZ
1234567890(.,:;?!$&-*){ÄÖÜÅTHSTÇ}

Galba, Felix Titling, Serlio, Trajan

▶ **Light**
THE QUICK BROWN FOX JUMPS OVER A DOG. ZWEI BOXKÄMPFER JAGEN EVA DURCH SYLT PORTEZ CE VIEUX WHISKEY BLOND QUI

▶ **Regular**
THE QUICK BROWN FOX JUMPS OVER A DOG. ZWEI BOXKÄMPFER JAGEN EVA DURCH SYLT PORTEZ CE VIEUX WHISKEY BLOND QUI FUME

Agfa Engravers 1:
Antique Roman, Artisan Roman, Burin Roman, Burin Sans, Classic Roman, Handle Old Style, Roman
Galba, Felix Titling, Serlio, Trajan

M884 Mac + PC
Classical Titling

Classical Titling:
Felix™ Titling, Perpetua Titling

FB6372 Mac + PC
FBI Condensed Classics™

FBI Condensed Classics™:
Bodoni Bold Compressed, Bodoni Bold Condensed , Caslon Bold Condensed, Century Bold Condensed, Cheltenham Bold Condensed

---

MC2928 Mac + PC ④
Classic Script™

abcdefghijklmnopqrstuvwxyz[äöüß åæœç]
ABCDEFGHIJKLMNOPQRSTUVWXYZ
1234567890(.,:;?!$&-){ÄÖÜÅÆŒÇ}*

© FSI 1993

C 35

L6117 Mac — Claude Sans™
1988: Alan Meeks

abcdefghijklmnopqrstuvwxyz[äöüßåøæœç]
ABCDEFGHIJKLMNOPQRSTUVWXYZ
1234567890(.,;:?!$&-*)ÄÖÜÅØÆŒÇ

L6118 Mac — Claude Sans Italic
1988: Alan Meeks

abcdefghijklmnopqrstuvwxyz[äöüßåøæœç]
ABCDEFGHIJKLMNOPQRSTUVWXYZ
1234567890(.,;:?!$&-) ÄÖÜÅØÆŒÇ*

L2823 Mac — Claude Sans Bold Italic
1988: Alan Meeks

abcdefghijklmnopqrstuvwxyz[äöüßåøæœç]
ABCDEFGHIJKLMNOPQRSTUVWXYZ
1234567890(.,;:?!$&-*)ÄÖÜÅØÆŒÇ

M208 Mac + PC — Clearface

Clearface:
Clearface Bold, Clearface Gothic

M208 Mac + PC — Clearface Bold
1905–11: M. F. Benton

abcdefghijklmnopqrstuvwxyz[äöüßåøæœç]
ABCDEFGHIJKLMNOPQRSTUVWXYZ
1234567890(.,;:?!$&-*){ÄÖÜÅØÆŒÇ}

Clearface:
Clearface Bold, Clearface Gothic

BT1275 Mac + PC — ITC Clearface® 1
1978: (M. F. Benton, 1905–11) Victor Caruso

abcdefghijklmnopqrstuvwxyz[äöüßåøæœç]
ABCDEFGHIJKLMNOPQRSTUVWXYZ
1234567890(.,;:?!$&-*){ÄÖÜÅØÆŒÇ}

aa*a*
A027
ITC Clearface, Reg, Ita, Bd, BdIta, Blk, BlkIta, Hvy, HvyIta

▶ Regular
The quick brown fox jumps over a Dog. Zwei Boxkämpfer jagen Eva durch Sylt portez ce vieux Whiskey blond qui fume une pipe aber

▶ Regular Italic
The quick brown fox jumps over a Dog. Zwei Boxkämpfer jagen Eva durch Sylt portez ce vieux Whiskey blond qui fume une pipe

© FSI 1993

▼ BT1275 Mac + PC   ITC Clearface® 1

▶ Heavy
The quick brown fox jumps over a Dog. Zwei Boxkämpfer jagen Eva durch Sylt portez ce vieux Whiskey blond qui fume

▶ Heavy Italic
The quick brown fox jumps over a Dog. Zwei Boxkämpfer jagen Eva durch Sylt portez ce vieux Whiskey blond qui fume

BT1276 Mac + PC ② 1978: (M. F. Benton, 1905–11) Victor Caruso
ITC Clearface 2

abcdefghijklmnopqrstuvwxyz[äöüßåøæœç]
ABCDEFGHIJKLMNOPQRSTUVWXYZ
1234567890(.,;:?!$&-*){ÄÖÜÅØÆŒÇ}

aa*a*
A027
ITC Clearface, Reg, Ita, Bd, BdIta, Blk, BlkIta, Hvy, HvyIta

▶ Bold
The quick brown fox jumps over a Dog. Zwei Boxkämpfer jagen Eva durch Sylt portez ce vieux Whiskey blond qui fume une

▶ Bold Italic
The quick brown fox jumps over a Dog. Zwei Boxkämpfer jagen Eva durch Sylt portez ce vieux Whiskey blond qui fume une

▶ Black
The quick brown fox jumps over a Dog. Zwei Boxkämpfer jagen Eva durch Sylt portez ce vieux Whiskey blond qui

▶ Black Italic
The quick brown fox jumps over a Dog. Zwei Boxkämpfer jagen Eva durch Sylt portez ce vieux Whiskey blond

BT784 Mac + PC ⑥ 1978: Victor Caruso
ITC Clearface Contour

abcdefghijklmnopqrstuvwxyz[äöüßåøæœç]
ABCDEFGHIJKLMNOPQRSTUVWXYZ
1234567890(.,;:?!$&-*){ÄÖÜÅØÆŒÇ}

Bitstream Contour:
ITC Clearface Contour, ITC Eras Outline, ITC Serif Gothic, ITC Souvenir Outline

A2864 Mac + PC ① 1992: (1908: M. F. Benton)
Clearface Gothic

abcdefghijklmnopqrstuvwxyz[äöüßåøæœç]
ABCDEFGHIJKLMNOPQRSTUVWXYZ
1234567890(.,;:?!$&-*){ÄÖÜÅØÆŒÇ}

aa*a*
M208 Clearface
C994 Clearface

▶ 45 Light
The quick brown fox jumps over a Dog. Zwei Boxkämpfer jagen Eva durch Sylt portez ce vieux Whiskey blond qui fume une pipe aber echt über die

▶ 55 Roman
The quick brown fox jumps over a Dog. Zwei Boxkämpfer jagen Eva durch Sylt portez ce vieux Whiskey blond qui fume une pipe aber echt

▶ 65 Medium
The quick brown fox jumps over a Dog. Zwei Boxkämpfer jagen Eva durch Sylt portez ce vieux Whiskey blond qui fume une pipe aber echt

▶ 75 Bold
The quick brown fox jumps over a Dog. Zwei Boxkämpfer jagen Eva durch Sylt portez ce vieux Whiskey blond qui fume une pipe

© FSI 1993

▼ A2864 Mac + PC   Clearface Gothic

▶ 95 Black
The quick brown fox jumps over a Dog. Zwei Boxkämpfer jagen Eva durch Sylt portez ce vieux Whiskey blond qui fume

C994 Mac + PC   ① ✎ 1908: M. F. Benton
Clearface Gothic

**abcdefghijklmnopqrstuvwxyz[äöüßåøæœç]
ABCDEFGHIJKLMNOPQRSTUVWXYZ
1234567890(.,;:?!$&-*){ÄÖÜÅØÆŒÇ}**

aa*a*
☞ M208 Clearface
☞ A2864 Clearface

▶ Light
The quick brown fox jumps over a Dog. Zwei Boxkämpfer jagen Eva durch Sylt portez ce vieux Whiskey blond qui fume une pipe aber echt

▶ Regular
The quick brown fox jumps over a Dog. Zwei Boxkämpfer jagen Eva durch Sylt portez ce vieux Whiskey blond qui fume une pipe aber echt

▶ Medium
The quick brown fox jumps over a Dog. Zwei Boxkämpfer jagen Eva durch Sylt portez ce vieux Whiskey blond qui fume une

▶ Bold
The quick brown fox jumps over a Dog. Zwei Boxkämpfer jagen Eva durch Sylt portez ce vieux Whiskey blond qui fume

▶ Black
The quick brown fox jumps over a Dog. Zwei Boxkämpfer jagen Eva durch Sylt portez ce vieux Whiskey blond qui

FB6602 Mac + PC   ⑤ ✎ 1992: Greg Thompson
Clicker™

**abcdefghijklmnopqrstuvwxyz[äöüßåøæœç]
ABCDEFGHIJKLMNOPQRSTUVWXYZ
1234567890(.,;:?!$&-*){ÄÖÜÅØÆŒÇ}**

▶ Regular
The quick brown fox jumps over a Dog. Zwei Boxkämpfer jagen Eva durch Sylt portez ce vieux Whiskey

▶ Expert
0123456789¹²²³³⁴⁵⁵⁶⁶⁷⁷⁸⁸⁹⁹⁰
0←→↑↓⅞¾⅔⅝½⅜⅓¼⅛
*+:

C602 Mac + PC
Cloister

Cloister:
Cloister™, DeVinne

C602 Mac + PC   ② ✎ 1914: M. F. Benton
Cloister™

abcdefghijklmnopqrstuvwxyz[äöüßåøæœç]
ABCDEFGHIJKLMNOPQRSTUVWXYZ
1234567890(.,;:?!$&-*){ÄÖÜÅØÆŒÇ}

© FSI 1993   ▼

▼ C602   Mac + PC   Cloister™

Column, Centaur, Hollandse Mediaeval, Columbus, Cloister

▶ Regular
The quick brown fox jumps over a Dog. Zwei Boxkämpfer jagen Eva durch Sylt portez ce vieux Whiskey blond qui fume une pipe aber echt

▶ Italic
The quick brown fox jumps over a Dog. Zwei Boxkämpfer jagen Eva durch Sylt portez ce vieux Whiskey blond qui fume une pipe aber echt über die Mauer

Cloister:
Cloister™, DeVinne
Column, Centaur, Hollandse Mediaeval, Columbus, Cloister

SG1118 Mac ② 1914: M. F. Benton
Cloister Old Style Bold

abcdefghijklmnopqrstuvwxyz[äöüßåøæœç]
ABCDEFGHIJKLMNOPQRSTUVWXYZ
1234567890(.,;:?!$&-*)ÄÖÜÅØÆŒÇ

SG1164 Mac ② 1914: M. F. Benton
Cloister Old Style Bold Italic

*abcdefghijklmnopqrstuvwxyz[äöüßåøæœç]
ABCDEFGHIJKLMNOPQRSTUVWXYZ
1234567890(.,;:?!$&-*)ÄÖÜÅØÆŒÇ*

BT805 Mac + PC ⑥ (R. H. Middleton, 1920)
Cloister Open Face

abcdefghijklmnopqrstuvwxyz[äöüßåøæœç]
ABCDEFGHIJKLMNOPQRSTUVWXYZ
1234567890(.,;:?!$&-*){ÄÖÜÅØÆŒÇ}

Bitstream Handtooled:
Cloister Open Face, Goudy Handtooled
Academy Engraved, Cochin, Caslon Open

BT798 Mac + PC ⑦ 1904: Joseph W. Phinney or M. F. Benton
Cloister Black

abcdefghijklmnopqrstuvwxyz[äöüßåøæœç]
ABCDEFGHIJKLMNOPQRSTUVWXYZ
1234567890(.,;:?!$&-*){ÄÖÜÅØÆŒÇ}

Bitstream Fraktur 1:
American Text™, Cloister Black, Fraktur, London Text™

A166 Mac + PC ② 1977: (Sol. Hess, 1917) Matthew Carter
Cochin™

abcdefghijklmnopqrstuvwxyz[äöüßåøæœç]
ABCDEFGHIJKLMNOPQRSTUVWXYZ
1234567890(.,;:?!$&-*){ÄÖÜÅØÆŒÇ}

▼ A166 Mac + PC Cochin™

▶ Regular
The quick brown fox jumps over a Dog. Zwei Boxkämpfer jagen Eva durch Sylt portez ce vieux Whiskey blond qui fume une

▶ Italic
The quick brown fox jumps over a Dog. Zwei Boxkämpfer jagen Eva durch Sylt portez ce vieux Whiskey blond qui fume une pipe aber echt

▶ Bold
The quick brown fox jumps over a Dog. Zwei Boxkämpfer jagen Eva durch Sylt portez ce vieux Whiskey blond qui fume

▶ Bold Italic
The quick brown fox jumps over a Dog. Zwei Boxkämpfer jagen Eva durch Sylt portez ce vieux Whiskey blond qui fume une pipe aber

---

BT2875 Mac + PC ⑥ ✎ 1954: Georg Trump   Industry name
Calligraphic 421   **Codex™**

abcdefghijklmnopqrstuvwxyz[äöüßåøæœç]
ABCDEFGHIJKLMNOPQRSTUVWXYZ
1234567890(.,;:?!$&-*){ÄÖÜÅØÆŒÇ}

M6411 Mac + PC
Colonna/Imprint Shaded

Colonna/Imprint Shaded:
Colonna™, Imprint Shaded

M6411 Mac + PC ⑥
Colonna™

abcdefghijklmnopqrstuvwxyz[äöüßåøæœç]
ABCDEFGHIJKLMNOPQRSTUVWXYZ
1234567890(.,;:?!$&-*){ÄÖÜÅØÆŒÇ}

Colonna/Imprint Shaded:
Colonna™, Imprint Shaded

AB6063 Mac + PC ③ ✎ 1984: Aldo Novarese
Berthold Colossalis™

abcdefghijklmnopqrstuvwxyz[äöüßåøæœç]
ABCDEFGHIJKLMNOPQRSTUVWXYZ
1234567890(.,;:?!$&-*){ÄÖÜÅØÆŒÇ}

👁
Yearbook, Retro, Berthold City

▶ Regular
The quick brown fox jumps over a Dog. Zwei Boxkämpfer jagen Eva durch Sylt portez ce vieux Whiskey blond qui fume une pipe aber echt

▶ Medium
The quick brown fox jumps over a Dog. Zwei Boxkämpfer jagen Eva durch Sylt portez ce vieux Whiskey blond qui fume une pipe aber

▶ Bold
The quick brown fox jumps over a Dog. Zwei Boxkämpfer jagen Eva durch Sylt portez ce vieux Whiskey blond qui fume

▶ Black
The quick brown fox jumps over a Dog. Zwei Boxkämpfer jagen Eva durch Sylt portez ce vieux Whiskey

© FSI 1993

M6307 Mac + PC ② 🖉 1992: Patricia Saunders
Columbus™

abcdefghijklmnopqrstuvwxyz[äöüßåøæœç]
ABCDEFGHIJKLMNOPQRSTUVWXYZ
1234567890(.,:;?!$&-*){ÄÖÜÅØÆŒÇ}

Column, Centaur, Hollandse Mediaeval, Cloister

▶ Regular
The quick brown fox jumps over a Dog. Zwei Boxkämpfer jagen Eva durch Sylt portez ce vieux Whiskey blond qui fume une pipe aber echt

▶ Italic
The quick brown fox jumps over a Dog. Zwei Boxkämpfer jagen Eva durch Sylt portez ce vieux Whiskey blond qui fume une pipe aber echt über die Mauer

▶ Semi Bold
The quick brown fox jumps over a Dog. Zwei Boxkämpfer jagen Eva durch Sylt portez ce vieux Whiskey blond qui fume une pipe

▶ Semi Bold Italic
The quick brown fox jumps over a Dog. Zwei Boxkämpfer jagen Eva durch Sylt portez ce vieux Whiskey blond qui fume une pipe aber echt über

▶ Bold
The quick brown fox jumps over a Dog. Zwei Boxkämpfer jagen Eva durch Sylt portez ce vieux Whiskey blond qui fume

▶ Bold Italic
The quick brown fox jumps over a Dog. Zwei Boxkämpfer jagen Eva durch Sylt portez ce vieux Whiskey blond qui fume une pipe aber echt

M6334 Mac + PC ② 🖉 1992: Patricia Saunders
Columbus Expert

ABCDEFGHIJKLMNOPQRSTUVWXYZ(ÄÖÜŠÅØÆŒÇ)

1234567890offfiflffiffl(^{1}$_1^{2}_2^{3}_3^{4}_4^{5}_5^{6}_6^{7}_7^{8}_8^{9}_9^{0}_0$) ($$¢Rp₡)ª

Column, Centaur, Hollandse Mediaeval, Cloister

▶ Regular Expert
01234567890offfiflffiffl-(½⅓¼⅕⅙⅐⅛%‰)($$¢Rp₡)ª THE QUICK BROWN FOX JUMPS OVER A DOG ZWEI BOXKÄMPFER JAGEN EVA

▶ Italic Expert
01234567890offfiflffiffl-(½⅓¼⅕⅙⅐⅛%‰)($$¢Rp₡)ª

▶ Semi Bold Expert
01234567890offfiflffiffl-(½⅓¼⅕⅙⅐⅛%‰)($$¢Rp₡)ª

▶ Semi Bold Italic Expert
01234567890offfiflffiffl-(½⅓¼⅕⅙⅐⅛%‰)($$¢Rp₡)ª

▶ Bold Expert
01234567890offfiflffiffl-(½⅓¼⅕⅙⅐⅛%‰)($$¢Rp₡)ª

▶ Bold Italic Expert
01234567890offfiflffiffl-(½⅓¼⅕⅙⅐⅛%‰)($$¢Rp₡)ª

▶ Ornaments One

▶ Ornaments Two

© FSI 1993

Column™
CT6090 Mac + PC ② 1992: (1985) Adrian Williams

abcdefghijklmnopqrstuvwxyz[äöüßåøæœç]
ABCDEFGHIJKLMNOPQRSTUVWXYZ
1234567890(.,;:?!$&-*){ÄÖÜÅØÆŒÇ}

© Centaur, Hollandse Mediaeval, Columbus, Cloister

▶ Book
The quick brown fox jumps over a Dog. Zwei Boxkämpfer jagen Eva durch Sylt portez ce vieux Whiskey blond qui fume une pipe aber echt

▶ Book Italic
The quick brown fox jumps over a Dog. Zwei Boxkämpfer jagen Eva durch Sylt portez ce vieux Whiskey blond qui fume une pipe aber echt über die Mauer

▶ Medium
The quick brown fox jumps over a Dog. Zwei Boxkämpfer jagen Eva durch Sylt portez ce vieux Whiskey blond qui fume une pipe

▶ Bold
The quick brown fox jumps over a Dog. Zwei Boxkämpfer jagen Eva durch Sylt portez ce vieux Whiskey blond qui fume

▶ Book Italic Swash
ABCDEFGHIJKLMNOPQR STUVWXYZ0123456789fiflffffifl stn ncte rstvwy~&

Comenius-Antiqua™
AB6318 Mac + PC ② 1980: Hermann Zapf

abcdefghijklmnopqrstuvwxyz[äöüßåøæœç]
ABCDEFGHIJKLMNOPQRSTUVWXYZ
1234567890(.,;:?!$&-*){ÄÖÜÅØÆŒÇ}

© ITC Zapf Book

▶ Regular
The quick brown fox jumps over a Dog. Zwei Boxkämpfer jagen Eva durch Sylt portez ce vieux Whiskey blond qui

▶ Italic
The quick brown fox jumps over a Dog. Zwei Boxkämpfer jagen Eva durch Sylt portez ce vieux Whiskey blond qui fume

▶ Medium
The quick brown fox jumps over a Dog. Zwei Boxkämpfer jagen Eva durch Sylt portez ce vieux

▶ Bold
The quick brown fox jumps over a Dog. Zwei Boxkämpfer jagen Eva durch Sylt portez ce

Comic Strip™
MC2929 Mac + PC ④ J. P. Thaulez

ABCDEFGHIJKLMNOPQRSTUVWXYZ
1234567890[ ](.,;:?!$&-*){ÄÖÜÅØÆŒÇ}

Commerce™
FB2755 Mac + PC ⑥ 1991: Greg Thompson, Rick Valicenti

abcdefghijklmnopqrstuvwxyz[äöüßåøæœç]
ABCDEFGHIJKLMNOPQRSTUVWXYZ
1234567890(.,;:?!$&-*){ÄÖÜÅØÆŒÇ}

© FSI 1993

C 42

▼ FB2755   Mac + PC   Commerce™

▶ Lean
The quick brown fox jumps over a Dog. Zwei Boxkämpfer jagen Eva durch Sylt portez ce vieux Whiskey blond qui

▶ Fat
The quick brown fox jumps over a Dog. Zwei Boxkämpfer jagen Eva durch Sylt portez ce vieux Whiskey

BT849   Mac + PC   ④   1906: M. F. Benton
Commercial Script
abcdefghijklmnopqrstuvwxyz[äöüßåøæœç]
ABCDEFGHIJKLMNOPQRSTUVWXYZ
1234567890(.,;:?!$&-*){ÄÖÜÅØÆŒÇ}

Bitstream Script 2:
Bernhard Tango™, Commercial Script, Stuyvesant™
aaa EF1069
Commercial Script, Reg
Brody™, Reg

L6120   Mac   ⑥   1963: Fred Lambert
Compacta Italic
abcdefghijklmnopqrstuvwxyz[äöüßåøæœç]
ABCDEFGHIJKLMNOPQRSTUVWXYZ
1234567890(.,;:?!$&-*)ÄÖÜÅØÆŒÇ

L6119   Mac   ⑥   1963: Fred Lambert
Compacta
abcdefghijklmnopqrstuvwxyz[äöüßåøæœç]
ABCDEFGHIJKLMNOPQRSTUVWXYZ
1234567890(.,;:?!$&-*)ÄÖÜÅØÆŒÇ

BT780   Mac + PC   ①   1963–65: Fred Lambert
Compacta
abcdefghijklmnopqrstuvwxyz1234567890[äöüßåøæœç]
ABCDEFGHIJKLMNOPQRSTUVWXYZ(.,;:?!$&-*){ÄÖÜÅØÆŒÇ}

▶ Light
The quick brown fox jumps over a Dog. Zwei Boxkämpfer jagen Eva durch Sylt portez ce vieux Whiskey blond qui fume une pipe aber echt über die Mauer gesprungen und auch smørebrød en ysjes natuurlijk. But very long

▶ Regular
The quick brown fox jumps over a Dog. Zwei Boxkämpfer jagen Eva durch Sylt portez ce vieux Whiskey blond qui fume une pipe aber echt über die Mauer gesprungen und auch

▶ Italic
The quick brown fox jumps over a Dog. Zwei Boxkämpfer jagen Eva durch Sylt portez ce vieux Whiskey blond qui fume une pipe aber echt über die Mauer gesprungen und auch

▶ Black
The quick brown fox jumps over a Dog. Zwei Boxkämpfer jagen Eva durch Sylt portez ce

© FSI 1993

BT1220 Mac + PC ① 1963–65: Fred Lambert
Compacta 2

abcdefghijklmnopqrstuvwxyz[äöüßåøæœç]
ABCDEFGHIJKLMNOPQRSTUVWXYZ
1234567890(.,:;?!$&-*){ÄÖÜÅØÆŒÇ}

aa*a*
☞ M625
Headliners 5
☞ L2570
Headliners 5

▶ Bold
The quick brown fox jumps over a Dog.
Zwei Boxkämpfer jagen Eva durch Sylt
portez ce vieux Whiskey blond qui fume
une pipe aber echt über die Mauer

▶ Bold Italic
The quick brown fox jumps over a Dog.
Zwei Boxkämpfer jagen Eva durch Sylt
portez ce vieux Whiskey blond qui fume
une pipe aber echt über die Mauer

C594 Mac + PC ⑥
Computer

ABCDEFGHIJKLMNOPQRSTUVWXYZ
1234567890(.,:;?!$&-*)[]{ÄÖÜÅØÆŒÇ}

Aldous:
Aldous™ Vertical, Aura, Computer, Eccentric™
👁 Amelia, Orbit-B, Data 70

BT781 Mac + PC
Bitstream Computer

Bitstream Computer:
Amelia™, Orbit-B™

A164 Mac + PC ② 1968: Günter Gerhard Lange
Berthold Concorde™

abcdefghijklmnopqrstuvwxyz[äöüßåøæœç]
ABCDEFGHIJKLMNOPQRSTUVWXYZ
1234567890(.,:;?!$&-*){ÄÖÜÅØÆŒÇ}

aa*a*
BT1286
Concorde, Reg, Ita, Bd
👁
Times, Life

▶ Regular
The quick brown fox jumps
over a Dog. Zwei Boxkämpfer
jagen Eva durch Sylt portez
ce vieux Whiskey blond qui

▶ Italic
The quick brown fox jumps
over a Dog. Zwei Boxkämp-
fer jagen Eva durch Sylt por-
tez ce vieux Whiskey blond

▶ Bold
The quick brown fox jumps
over a Dog. Zwei Boxkämp-
fer jagen Eva durch Sylt por-
tez ce vieux Whiskey blond

▶ Bold Italic
The quick brown fox jumps
over a Dog. Zwei Boxkämp-
fer jagen Eva durch Sylt por-
tez ce vieux Whiskey blond

AB6187 Mac + PC ② 1968: G. G. Lange
Concorde Expert

ABCDEFGHIJKLMNOPQRSTUVWXYZ[ÄÖÜSSÅØÆŒÇ]
ABCDEFGHIJKLMNOPQRSTUVWXYZ
1234567890(.,:;?!$&-*){ÄÖÜÅØÆŒÇ}

© FSI 1993

▼ AB6187 Mac + PC Concorde Expert

▶ Regular SC
THE QUICK BROWN FOX JUMPS OVER A DOG. 123 4567 890 ZWEI BOXKÄMPFER JAGEN EVA DURCH SYLT PORTEZ CE VIEUX

▶ Italic OSF
The quick brown fox jumps over a Dog. 123 4567 890 Zwei Boxkämpfer jagen Eva durch Sylt portez ce vieux Whiskey

▶ Medium SC
THE QUICK BROWN FOX JUMPS OVER A DOG. 123 4567 890 ZWEI BOXKÄMPFER JAGEN EVA DURCH SYLT PORTEZ CE

▶ Medium Italic OSF
The quick brown fox jumps over a Dog. 123 4567 890 Zwei Boxkämpfer jagen Eva durch Sylt portez ce vieux Whiskey

▶ Regular Expert
0123456789offfiflffiffl-($\frac{1}{1}\frac{2}{2}\frac{3}{3}\frac{4}{4}\frac{5}{5}\frac{6}{6}\frac{7}{7}\frac{8}{8}\frac{9}{9}\frac{0}{0}$)($\$¢Rp₵$)ª
THE QUICK BROWN FOX JUMPS OVER A DOG ZWEI BOXKÄMPFER

▶ Italic Expert
0123456789offfiflffiffl-($\frac{1}{1}\frac{2}{2}\frac{3}{3}\frac{4}{4}\frac{5}{5}\frac{6}{6}\frac{7}{7}\frac{8}{8}\frac{9}{9}\frac{0}{0}$)($\$¢Rp₵$)ª

▶ Medium Expert
**0123456789offfiflffiffl-($\frac{1}{1}\frac{2}{2}\frac{3}{3}\frac{4}{4}\frac{5}{5}\frac{6}{6}\frac{7}{7}\frac{8}{8}\frac{9}{9}\frac{0}{0}$)($\$¢Rp₵$)ª
THE QUICK BROWN FOX JUMPS OVER A DOG ZWEI BOX-**

▶ Medium Italic Expert
0123456789offfiflffiffl-($\frac{1}{1}\frac{2}{2}\frac{3}{3}\frac{4}{4}\frac{5}{5}\frac{6}{6}\frac{7}{7}\frac{8}{8}\frac{9}{9}\frac{0}{0}$)($\$¢Rp₵$)ª

AB6373 Mac + PC ② 🖉 1972-73: G. G. Lange
Concorde Condensed

abcdefghijklmnopqrstuvwxyz[äöüßåøæœç]
ABCDEFGHIJKLMNOPQRSTUVWXYZ
1234567890(.,;:?!$&-*){ÄÖÜÅØÆŒÇ}

▶ Condensed
The quick brown fox jumps over a Dog. Zwei Boxkämpfer jagen Eva durch Sylt portez ce vieux Whiskey blond qui fume une pipe aber echt

▶ Medium Condensed
The quick brown fox jumps over a Dog. Zwei Boxkämpfer jagen Eva durch Sylt portez ce vieux Whiskey blond qui fume une pipe aber echt

▶ Bold Condensed
The quick brown fox jumps over a Dog. Zwei Boxkämpfer jagen Eva durch Sylt portez ce vieux Whiskey blond qui fume une pipe aber

▶ Bold Condensed Outline
The quick brown fox jumps over a Dog. Zwei Boxkämpfer jagen Eva durch Sylt portez ce vieux Whiskey blond qui fume une pipe aber

---

AB6091 Mac + PC ② 🖉 1975: G. G. Lange
Concorde Nova™

abcdefghijklmnopqrstuvwxyz[äöüßåøæœç]
ABCDEFGHIJKLMNOPQRSTUVWXYZ
1234567890(.,;:?!$&-*){ÄÖÜÅØÆŒÇ}

▶ Regular
The quick brown fox jumps over a Dog. Zwei Boxkämpfer jagen Eva durch Sylt portez ce vieux Whiskey blond qui fume une pipe aber echt

▶ Italic
The quick brown fox jumps over a Dog. Zwei Boxkämpfer jagen Eva durch Sylt portez ce vieux Whiskey blond qui fume une pipe aber echt

© FSI 1993

▼ AB6091 Mac + PC Concorde Nova™

▶ Medium
The quick brown fox jumps over a Dog. Zwei Boxkämpfer jagen Eva durch Sylt portez ce vieux Whiskey blond qui fume une pipe aber

▶ Regular SC
THE QUICK BROWN FOX JUMPS OVER A DOG. 123 4567 890 ZWEI BOXKÄMPFER JAGEN EVA DURCH SYLT PORTEZ CE VIEUX WHISKEY BLOND

▶ Italic OSF
The quick brown fox jumps over a Dog. 123 4567 890 Zwei Boxkämpfer jagen Eva durch Sylt portez ce vieux Whiskey blond qui

▶ Medium SC
THE QUICK BROWN FOX JUMPS OVER A DOG. 123 4567 890 ZWEI BOXKÄMPFER JAGEN EVA DURCH SYLT PORTEZ CE VIEUX WHISKEY

▶ Regular Expert
0123456789offfiflffiffl(¹/₁²/₂³/₃⁴/₄⁵/₅⁶/₆⁷/₇⁸/₈⁹/₉⁰/₀)⁽$$¢Rp₵⁾ᵃ THE QUICK BROWN FOX JUMPS OVER A DOG ZWEI BOXKÄMPFER JAGEN EVA DURCH

▶ Italic Expert
0123456789offfiflffiffl(¹/₁²/₂³/₃⁴/₄⁵/₅⁶/₆⁷/₇⁸/₈⁹/₉⁰/₀)⁽$$¢Rp₵⁾ᵃ

▶ Medium Expert
0123456789offfiflffiffl(¹/₁²/₂³/₃⁴/₄⁵/₅⁶/₆⁷/₇⁸/₈⁹/₉⁰/₀)⁽$$¢Rp₵⁾ᵃ

EF6468 Mac + PC ⑥ ✎ Martin Wait
Conference™

abcdefghijklmnopqrstuvwxyz[äöüßåøæœç]
ABCDEFGHIJKLMNOPQRSTUVWXYZ
1234567890(.,;:?!$&-*) ÄÖÜÅØÆŒÇ

E+F Special Headlines 4:
Bernhard Antique Bold Condensed, Cabaret™, Conference™, Countdown™, Einhorn, Highlight

---

FF2961 Mac + PC ⑥ ✎ 1992: Just van Rossum
FF Confidential™

ABCDEFGHIJKLMNOPQRSTUVWXYZ[ÄÖÜSSÅØÆŒÇ]
ABCDEFGHIJKLMNOPQRSTUVWXYZ
1234567890(.,;:?!$&-*){ÄÖÜÅØÆŒÇ}

FF InstantTypes™:
FF Confidential™, FF Dynamoe, FF Flightcase™, FF Karton™, FF Stamp Gothic™

C603 Mac + PC ③ ✎ 1980: Adrian Williams
Congress™

abcdefghijklmnopqrstuvwxyz[äöüßåøæœç]
ABCDEFGHIJKLMNOPQRSTUVWXYZ
1234567890(.,;:?!$&-*){ÄÖÜÅØÆŒÇ}

© FSI 1993

▼ C603   Mac + PC   Congress™

▶ Regular
The quick brown fox jumps over a Dog. Zwei Boxkämpfer jagen Eva durch Sylt portez ce vieux Whiskey blond qui fume une pipe aber

▶ Italic
The quick brown fox jumps over a Dog. Zwei Boxkämpfer jagen Eva durch Sylt portez ce vieux Whiskey blond qui fume une pipe aber

▶ Bold
The quick brown fox jumps over a Dog. Zwei Boxkämpfer jagen Eva durch Sylt portez ce vieux Whiskey blond qui fume une

▶ Heavy
The quick brown fox jumps over a Dog. Zwei Boxkämpfer jagen Eva durch Sylt portez ce vieux Whiskey blond qui fume

SG1906   Mac   ③   1980: Adrian Williams

Congress Light
abcdefghijklmnopqrstuvwxyz[äöüßåøæœç]
ABCDEFGHIJKLMNOPQRSTUVWXYZ
1234567890(.,;:?!$&-*)ÄÖÜÅØÆŒÇ

SG1909   Mac   ③   1980: Adrian Williams

Congress Medium
abcdefghijklmnopqrstuvwxyz[äöüßåøæœç]
ABCDEFGHIJKLMNOPQRSTUVWXYZ
1234567890(.,;:?!$&-*)ÄÖÜÅØÆŒÇ

CT6089   Mac + PC   ①   1992: Adrian Williams

Congress Sans™
abcdefghijklmnopqrstuvwxyz[äöüßåøæœç]
ABCDEFGHIJKLMNOPQRSTUVWXYZ
1234567890(.,;:?!$&-*){ÄÖÜÅØÆŒÇ}

© ITC Quay Sans

▶ Light
The quick brown fox jumps over a Dog. Zwei Boxkämpfer jagen Eva durch Sylt portez ce vieux Whiskey blond qui fume une

▶ Light Italic
The quick brown fox jumps over a Dog. Zwei Boxkämpfer jagen Eva durch Sylt portez ce vieux Whiskey blond qui fume une

▶ Medium
The quick brown fox jumps over a Dog. Zwei Boxkämpfer jagen Eva durch Sylt portez ce vieux Whiskey blond qui fume

▶ Medium Italic
The quick brown fox jumps over a Dog. Zwei Boxkämpfer jagen Eva durch Sylt portez ce vieux Whiskey blond qui fume

▶ Bold
The quick brown fox jumps over a Dog. Zwei Boxkämpfer jagen Eva durch Sylt portez ce vieux Whiskey blond qui

▶ Bold Italic
The quick brown fox jumps over a Dog. Zwei Boxkämpfer jagen Eva durch Sylt portez ce vieux Whiskey blond qui

▶ Extra Bold
The quick brown fox jumps over a Dog. Zwei Boxkämpfer jagen Eva durch Sylt portez ce vieux Whiskey blond

▶ Extra Bold Italic
The quick brown fox jumps over a Dog. Zwei Boxkämpfer jagen Eva durch Sylt portez ce vieux Whiskey blond

© FSI 1993

BT784 Mac + PC
Bitstream Contour

Bitstream Contour :
ITC Clearface Contour, ITC Eras Outline, ITC Serif Gothic, ITC Souvenir Outline

BT785 Mac + PC (6) ✎ 1986: (Oz Cooper, 1926)
Bitstream Cooper 1

abcdefghijklmnopqrstuvwxyz[äöüßåøæœç]
ABCDEFGHIJKLMNOPQRSTUVWXYZ
1234567890(.,;:?!$&-*){ÄÖÜÅØÆŒÇ}

▶ Light
The quick brown fox jumps over a Dog. Zwei Boxkämpfer jagen Eva durch Sylt portez ce vieux Whiskey blond qui fume

▶ Light Italic
The quick brown fox jumps over a Dog. Zwei Boxkämpfer jagen Eva durch Sylt portez ce vieux Whiskey blond qui fume une

▶ Bold
The quick brown fox jumps over a Dog. Zwei Boxkämpfer jagen Eva durch Sylt portez ce vieux Whiskey

▶ Bold Italic
The quick brown fox jumps over a Dog. Zwei Boxkämpfer jagen Eva durch Sylt portez ce vieux Whiskey

BT786 Mac + PC (6) ✎ 1986: (Oz Cooper, 1926)
Bitstream Cooper 2

abcdefghijklmnopqrstuvwxyz[äöüßåøæœç]
ABCDEFGHIJKLMNOPQRSTUVWXYZ
1234567890(.,;:?!$&-*){ÄÖÜÅØÆŒÇ}

▶ Medium
The quick brown fox jumps over a Dog. Zwei Boxkämpfer jagen Eva durch Sylt portez ce vieux Whiskey blond

▶ Medium Italic
The quick brown fox jumps over a Dog. Zwei Boxkämpfer jagen Eva durch Sylt portez ce vieux Whiskey blond qui

BT1282 Mac + PC (6) ✎ 1986: (Oz Cooper, 1926)
Bitstream Cooper 4

abcdefghijklmnopqrstuvwxyz[äöüßåøæœç]
ABCDEFGHIJKLMNOPQRSTUVWXYZ
1234567890(.,;:?!$&-*){ÄÖÜÅØÆŒÇ}

aa*a*
A031
Cooper Black, Blk, BlkIta

▶ Black
The quick brown fox jumps over a Dog. Zwei Boxkämpfer jagen Eva durch Sylt portez ce

▶ Black Italic
The quick brown fox jumps over a Dog. Zwei Boxkämpfer jagen Eva durch Sylt portez ce

BT787 Mac + PC (6) ✎ 1986: (Oz Cooper, 1926)
Bitstream Cooper 3

abcdefghijklmnopqrstuvwxyz[äöüßåøæœç]
ABCDEFGHIJKLMNOPQRSTUVWXYZ
1234567890(.,;:?!$&-*){ÄÖÜÅØÆŒÇ}

© FSI 1993

▼ BT787 Mac + PC Bitstream Cooper 3

▶ Black Headline
The quick brown fox jumps over a Dog. Zwei Boxkämpfer jagen Eva durch Sylt portez ce

▶ Black Italic Headline
The quick brown fox jumps over a Dog. Zwei Boxkämpfer jagen Eva durch Sylt portez ce

▶ Black Outline
The quick brown fox jumps over a Dog. Zwei Boxkämpfer jagen Eva durch Sylt portez ce

---

SG1914 Mac ⑥ ✎ 1926: Oz Cooper
Cooper Black Condensed

**abcdefghijklmnopqrstuvwxyz[äöüßåøæœç]
ABCDEFGHIJKLMNOPQRSTUVWXYZ
1234567890(.,;:?!$&-*)ÄÖÜÅØÆŒÇ**

A376 Mac + PC ⑥ ✎ 1905: F. W. Goudy, Clarence Marder
Copperplate Gothic

ABCDEFGHIJKLMNOPQRSTUVWXYZ[ÄÖÜSSÅØÆŒÇ]
ABCDEFGHIJKLMNOPQRSTUVWXYZ
1234567890(.,;:?!$&-*){ÄÖÜÅØÆŒÇ}

aa*a*
BT1277
Copperplate Gothic,
Rom, Bd, Hvy, Con,
BdCon
©
Engraver's Gothic,
Spartan

▶ 29AB
THE QUICK BROWN FOX JUMPS OVER A DOG. ZWEI BOXKÄMPFER JAGEN EVA DURCH SYLT PORTEZ CE VIEUX WHISKEY

▶ 30AB
THE QUICK BROWN FOX JUMPS OVER A DOG. ZWEI BOXKÄMPFER JAGEN EVA DURCH SYLT PORTEZ CE VIEUX WHISKEY

▶ 31AB
THE QUICK BROWN FOX JUMPS OVER A DOG. ZWEI BOXKÄMPFER JAGEN EVA DURCH

▶ 32AB
THE QUICK BROWN FOX JUMPS OVER A DOG. ZWEI BOXKÄMPFER JAGEN EVA DURCH SYLT

▶ 29BC
THE QUICK BROWN FOX JUMPS OVER A DOG. ZWEI BOXKÄMPFER JAGEN EVA DURCH SYLT PORTEZ CE VIEUX WHISKEY BLOND QUI FUME UNE PIPE ABER

▶ 30BC
THE QUICK BROWN FOX JUMPS OVER A DOG. ZWEI BOXKÄMPFER JAGEN EVA DURCH SYLT PORTEZ CE VIEUX WHISKEY BLOND QUI FUME UNE PIPE ABER

▶ 31BC
THE QUICK BROWN FOX JUMPS OVER A DOG. ZWEI BOXKÄMPFER JAGEN EVA DURCH SYLT PORTEZ CE VIEUX WHISKEY

▶ 32BC
THE QUICK BROWN FOX JUMPS OVER A DOG. ZWEI BOXKÄMPFER JAGEN EVA DURCH SYLT PORTEZ CE VIEUX WHISKEY

▶ 33BC
THE QUICK BROWN FOX JUMPS OVER A DOG. ZWEI BOXKÄMPFER JAGEN EVA DURCH SYLT PORTEZ CE

© FSI 1993

| L6587 | Mac | ④ | 1992: David Quay |

Coptek™

abcdefghijklmnopqrstuvwxyz[äöüßåøæœç]
ABCDEFGHIJKLMNOPQRSTUVWXYZ
1234567890(.,;:?!$&-*)

| BT1360 | Mac + PC | ③ | 1941: C.H. Griffith | Industry name |

News 705
Corona

abcdefghijklmnopqrstuvwxyz[äöüßåøæœç]
ABCDEFGHIJKLMNOPQRSTUVWXYZ
1234567890(.,;:?!$&-*){ÄÖÜÅØÆŒÇ}

aaa
BT1360
Corona, Reg, Ita, Bd, BdIta
ⓒ
Aurora, Excelsior, Imperial, Ionic, Olympian, Textype

▶ Regular
The quick brown fox jumps over a Dog. Zwei Boxkämpfer jagen Eva durch Sylt portez ce vieux Whiskey

▶ Italic
The quick brown fox jumps over a Dog. Zwei Boxkämpfer jagen Eva durch Sylt portez ce vieux Whiskey

▶ Bold
The quick brown fox jumps over a Dog. Zwei Boxkämpfer jagen Eva durch Sylt portez ce vieux Whiskey

▶ Bold Italic
The quick brown fox jumps over a Dog. Zwei Boxkämpfer jagen Eva durch Sylt portez ce vieux Whiskey

| C597 | Mac + PC | ④ | 1937: R. H. Middleton |

Coronet

abcdefghijklmnopqrstuvwxyz[äöüßåøæœç]
ABCDEFGHIJKLMNOPQRSTUVWXYZ
1234567890(.,;:?!$&-*){ÄÖÜÅØÆŒÇ}

aaa
M885
Script 3
BT1376
Script 3

▶ Regular
The quick brown fox jumps over a Dog. Zwei Boxkämpfer jagen Eva durch Sylt portez ce vieux Whiskey blond qui fume une pipe aber echt über die Mauer gesprungen und auch smørebrød en ysjes

▶ Bold
The quick brown fox jumps over a Dog. Zwei Boxkämpfer jagen Eva durch Sylt portez ce vieux Whiskey blond qui fume une pipe aber echt über die Mauer gesprungen und

Carmine Tango™:
Carmine Tango, Chaplin™, Coronet
aaa M885
Script 3
BT1376

| T06660 | Mac | ⑥ | 1993: Laura Meseguer |

Cortada™

abcdefghijklmnopqrstuvwxyz[äöüßåøæœç]
ABCDEFGHIJKLMNOPQRSTUVWXYZ
1234567890(.,;:?!$&-*){ÄÖ Ü ÅØÆŒÇ}

Type-ø-Tones Pack 3:
Cortada™, Frankie™

© FSI 1993

EF6469 Mac + PC ⑥
Cortez™

abcdefghijklmnopqrstuvwxyz[äöüßåøæœç]
ABCDEFGHIJKLMNOPQRSTUVWXYZ
1234567890(.,;:?!$&-*)ÄÖÜÅØÆŒÇ

E+F Special Headlines 5:
Chesterfield™, Cortez™, Elefont™, Glastonbury™, Julia™ Script, LCD
ⓒ ITC Barcelona

AB6064 Mac + PC ① 1982: Gustav Jaeger
Berthold Cosmos™

abcdefghijklmnopqrstuvwxyz[äöüßåøæœç]
ABCDEFGHIJKLMNOPQRSTUVWXYZ
1234567890(.,;:?!$&-*){ÄÖÜÅØÆŒÇ}

▶ Light
The quick brown fox jumps over a Dog. Zwei Boxkämpfer jagen Eva durch Sylt portez ce vieux Whiskey blond qui fume

▶ Light Italic
The quick brown fox jumps over a Dog. Zwei Boxkämpfer jagen Eva durch Sylt portez ce vieux Whiskey blond qui fume

▶ Medium
The quick brown fox jumps over a Dog. Zwei Boxkämpfer jagen Eva durch Sylt portez ce vieux Whiskey blond

▶ Extra Bold
The quick brown fox jumps over a Dog. Zwei Boxkämpfer jagen Eva durch Sylt portez ce

A424 Mac + PC ⑥ 1990: Buker, Lind, Redick
Cottonwood®

ABCDEFGHIJKLMNOPQRSTUVWXYZ
1234567890(.,;:?!$&-*)[ ]{ÄÖÜÅØÆŒÇ}

Wood Type Pack 1:
Cottonwood®, Ironwood®, Juniper®, Mesquite™, Ponderosa®, Wood Type Ornaments 1

EF6468 Mac + PC ⑥ 1965: Colin Brignall
Countdown™

abcdefghijklmnopqrstuvwxyz[äöüßåøæœç]
ABCDEFGHIJKLMNOPQRSTUVWXYZ
1234567890(.,;:?!$&-*)ÄÖÜÅØÆŒÇ

E+F Special Headlines 4:
Bernhard Antique Bold Condensed, Cabaret™, Conference™, Countdown™, Einhorn, Highlight

M1527 Mac + PC
Courier

Courier:
Courier, Symbol

BT788 Mac + PC ③ 1956: Howard Kettler
Courier

abcdefghijklmnopqrstuvwxyz[äöüßåøæœç]
ABCDEFGHIJKLMNOPQRSTUVWXYZ
1234567890(.,;:?!$&-*){ÄÖÜÅØÆŒÇ}

a a *a*
M1527
Courier
©
ITC American Typewriter, Monanti, Schreibmaschinenschrift, Prestige, Typewriter, Pica

▶ Regular
The quick brown fox jumps over a Dog. Zwei Boxkämpfer jagen Eva durch Sylt portez ce

▶ Italic
The quick brown fox jumps over a Dog. Zwei Boxkämpfer jagen Eva durch Sylt portez ce

▶ Bold
The quick brown fox jumps over a Dog. Zwei Boxkämpfer jagen Eva durch Sylt portez ce

▶ Bold Italic
The quick brown fox jumps over a Dog. Zwei Boxkämpfer jagen Eva durch Sylt portez ce

M979 Mac + PC ③ 1956: Howard Kettler
Courier 12

abcdefghijklmnopqrstuvwxyz[äöüßåøæœç]
ABCDEFGHIJKLMNOPQRSTUVWXYZ
1234567890(.,;:?!$&-*){ÄÖÜÅØÆŒÇ}

Typewriter:
Courier 12, Typewriter
© ITC American Typewriter, Courier, Monanti, Schreibmaschinenschrift, Prestige, Pica

C998 Mac + PC ⑥ 1980: Dick Jones
Letraset Crillee™

abcdefghijklmnopqrstuvwxyz[äöüßåøæœç]
ABCDEFGHIJKLMNOPQRSTUVWXYZ
1234567890(.,;:?!$&-){ÄÖÜÅØÆŒÇ}*

©
Serpentine, Russell Square

▶ Light Italic
The quick brown fox jumps over a Dog. Zwei Boxkämpfer jagen Eva durch Sylt portez ce vieux Whiskey blond qui fume

▶ Italic
The quick brown fox jumps over a Dog. Zwei Boxkämpfer jagen Eva durch Sylt portez ce vieux Whiskey blond

▶ Bold Italic
The quick brown fox jumps over a Dog. Zwei Boxkämpfer jagen Eva durch Sylt portez ce vieux

▶ Extra Bold Italic
The quick brown fox jumps over a Dog. Zwei Boxkämpfer jagen Eva durch Sylt portez ce

© FSI 1993

L6588 Mac ⑥ 1980: Dick Jones
Crillee Italic Inline Shaded

abcdefghijklmnopqrstuvwxyz[äöüßåøæœç]
ABCDEFGHIJKLMNOPQRSTUVWXYZ
1234567890(.,;:?!$&-*)ÄÖÜÅØÆŒÇ

SG1119 Mac ⑥ 1978: Philip Kelly
Croissant™

abcdefghijklmnopqrstuvwxyz(äöüßåøæœç)
ABCDEFGHIJKLMNOPQRSTUVWXYZ
1234567890(.,;:?!$&-*)ÄÖÜÅØÆŒÇ

A896 Mac + PC ② 1982: (c. 1896) Vincent Pacella
ITC Cushing®

abcdefghijklmnopqrstuvwxyz[äöüßåøæœç]
ABCDEFGHIJKLMNOPQRSTUVWXYZ
1234567890(.,;:?!$&-*){ÄÖÜÅØÆŒÇ}

aa*a*
BT1278
ITC Cushing 1, Bk, BkIta, Bd, BdIta
BT1279
ITC Cushing 2, Med, MedIta, Hvy, HvyIta

▶ Book
The quick brown fox jumps over a Dog. Zwei Boxkämpfer jagen Eva durch Sylt portez ce vieux Whiskey blond qui fume une pipe

▶ Book Italic
The quick brown fox jumps over a Dog. Zwei Boxkämpfer jagen Eva durch Sylt portez ce vieux Whiskey blond qui fume une pipe aber echt

▶ Medium
The quick brown fox jumps over a Dog. Zwei Boxkämpfer jagen Eva durch Sylt portez ce vieux Whiskey blond qui fume une

▶ Medium Italic
The quick brown fox jumps over a Dog. Zwei Boxkämpfer jagen Eva durch Sylt portez ce vieux Whiskey blond qui fume une pipe aber

▶ **Bold**
The quick brown fox jumps over a Dog. Zwei Boxkämpfer jagen Eva durch Sylt portez ce vieux Whiskey blond qui fume

▶ *Bold Italic*
The quick brown fox jumps over a Dog. Zwei Boxkämpfer jagen Eva durch Sylt portez ce vieux Whiskey blond qui fume une pipe

▶ **Heavy**
The quick brown fox jumps over a Dog. Zwei Boxkämpfer jagen Eva durch Sylt portez ce vieux Whiskey blond qui

▶ *Heavy Italic*
The quick brown fox jumps over a Dog. Zwei Boxkämpfer jagen Eva durch Sylt portez ce vieux Whiskey blond qui fume une

FF731 Mac + PC ⑤ 1991: Max Kisman
FF Cutout™

abcdefghijklmnopqrstuvwxyz[äöüßåsæœç]
ABCDEFGHIJKLMNOPQRSTUVWXYZ
1234567890(.,;:?!$&-*){ÄÖÜÅØÆŒÇ}

FF Kisman™ 1:
FF Cutout™, FF Network™, FF Scratch™, FF Vortex™

© FSI 1993

ONLY BUT BLACK AND SLIM

D

Neville Brody, London, UK

M2837 Mac + PC ② 1991: (1947-54, Giovanni Mardersteig) Ron Carpenter

Dante™

abcdefghijklmnopqrstuvwxyz[äöüßåøæœç]
ABCDEFGHIJKLMNOPQRSTUVWXYZ
1234567890(.,;:?!$&-*){ÄÖÜÅØÆŒÇ}

▶ Regular
The quick brown fox jumps over a Dog. Zwei Boxkämpfer jagen Eva durch Sylt portez ce vieux Whiskey blond qui fume une pipe aber echt

▶ Italic
The quick brown fox jumps over a Dog. Zwei Boxkämpfer jagen Eva durch Sylt portez ce vieux Whiskey blond qui fume une pipe aber echt über die

▶ Medium
The quick brown fox jumps over a Dog. Zwei Boxkämpfer jagen Eva durch Sylt portez ce vieux Whiskey blond qui fume une pipe aber

▶ Medium Italic
The quick brown fox jumps over a Dog. Zwei Boxkämpfer jagen Eva durch Sylt portez ce vieux Whiskey blond qui fume une pipe aber echt

▶ Bold
The quick brown fox jumps over a Dog. Zwei Boxkämpfer jagen Eva durch Sylt portez ce vieux Whiskey blond qui fume une pipe

▶ Bold Italic
The quick brown fox jumps over a Dog. Zwei Boxkämpfer jagen Eva durch Sylt portez ce vieux Whiskey blond qui fume une pipe aber echt

M6384 Mac + PC ② 1991: (1947-54, Giovanni Mardersteig) Ron Carpenter

Dante Expert

ABCDEFGHIJKLMNOPQRSTUVWXYZ
1234567890(.,;:?!$&-*){ÄÖÜÅØÆŒÇ}

▶ Regular Expert
0123456789 0fffiflffiffl-
(½ ⅓ ⅔ ¼ ¾ ⅕ ⅖ ⅗ ⅘ ⅙ ⅚ ⅐ ⅛ ⅜ ⅝ ⅞ ⅑ ⅒ ‰) ($¢Rp₡)ª THE QUICK BROWN FOX JUMPS OVER A DOG ZWEI BOXKÄMPFER JAGEN EVA DURCH

▶ Italic Expert
*0123456789 0fffiflffiffl-
(½ ⅓ ⅔ ¼ ¾ ⅕ ⅖ ⅗ ⅘ ⅙ ⅚ ⅐ ⅛ ⅜ ⅝ ⅞ ⅑ ⅒ ‰) ($¢Rp₡)ª*

▶ Medium Expert
0123456789 0fffiflffiffl-
(½ ⅓ ⅔ ¼ ¾ ⅕ ⅖ ⅗ ⅘ ⅙ ⅚ ⅐ ⅛ ⅜ ⅝ ⅞ ⅑ ⅒ ‰) ($¢Rp₡)ª

▶ Medium Italic Expert
*0123456789 0fffiflffiffl-
(½ ⅓ ⅔ ¼ ¾ ⅕ ⅖ ⅗ ⅘ ⅙ ⅚ ⅐ ⅛ ⅜ ⅝ ⅞ ⅑ ⅒ ‰) ($¢Rp₡)ª*

▶ Bold Expert
**0123456789 0fffiflffiffl-
(½ ⅓ ⅔ ¼ ¾ ⅕ ⅖ ⅗ ⅘ ⅙ ⅚ ⅐ ⅛ ⅜ ⅝ ⅞ ⅑ ⅒ ‰) ($¢Rp₡)ª**

▶ Bold Italic Expert
***0123456789 0fffiflffiffl-
(½ ⅓ ⅔ ¼ ¾ ⅕ ⅖ ⅗ ⅘ ⅙ ⅚ ⅐ ⅛ ⅜ ⅝ ⅞ ⅑ ⅒ ‰) ($¢Rp₡)ª***

▶ Titling
THE QUICK BROWN FOX
JUMPS OVER A LAZY DOG.
ZWEI BOXKÄMPFER JAGEN
EVA DURCH SYLT. PORTEZ

▼ M6384 MAC + PC Dante Expert

▶ Regular Alternates
1£

▶ Italic Alternates
ggggggzz;£

▶ Medium Alternates
1£

▶ Medium Italic Alternates
ggggggzz;£

▶ Bold Alternates
1£

▶ Bold Italic Alternates
ggggggzz;£

EF6466 MAC + PC ⑥ ✎ 1970: Bob Newman
Data 70

abcdefghijklmnopqrstuvwxyz[äöüßåøæœç]
ABCDEFGHIJKLMNOPQRSTUVWXYZ
1234567890[.,:;?!$&-*]ÄÖÜÅØÆŒÇ

E+F Special Headlines 2:
Belshaw™, Camellia™, Carousel™, Cirkulus™, Data 70, Galadriel™
aaa L6121: Data 70 Reg
👁 Computer, Amelia™, Orbit-B

BT789 MAC + PC ⑥ ✎ 1965: Louis Minott
Davida

ABCDEFGHIJKLMNOPQRSTUVWXYZ
1234567890(.,:;?!$&-*)[]{ÄÖÜÅØÆŒÇ}

Bitstream Decorative 1:
Broadway Engraved, Davida, P. T. Barnum™, Playbill®

C1012 MAC + PC ⑥ ✎ 1950: M. Davison
PL Davison Americana

abcdefghijklmnopqrstuvwxyz[äöüßåøæœç]
ABCDEFGHIJKLMNOPQRSTUVWXYZ
1234567890(.,:;?!$&-*)◊ÄÖÜÅØÆŒÇ♦

Headlines 84S:
Bernhard Modern, Beton Extra Bold, Metropolis Bold, Modern No. 20, Orlando Caps, PL Davison Americana, PL Westerveldt Light, Siena™ Black, TC Europa™ Bold, TC Jasper™
👁 Thunderbird, Tuscan Egyptian

C468 Mac + PC ④ 1950: M. Davison
PL Davison Zip Bold

ABCDEFGHIJKLMNOPQRSTUVWXYZ
1234567890(.,;:?!$&-*)[]◊ÄÖÜÅØÆŒÇ♦

Headlines 82S:
Neon Extra Condensed™, PL Barnum Block, PL Benguiat Frisky Bold, PL Davison Zip Bold, PL Fiedler Gothic Bold, PL Futura Maxi 2, PL Trophy™ Oblique, Ritmo™ Bold, TC Broadway

BT789 Mac + PC
Bitstream Decorative 1

Bitstream Decorative 1:
Broadway Engraved, Davida, P. T. Barnum™, Playbill®

BT790 Mac + PC
Bitstream Decorative 2

Bitstream Decorative 2:
ITC Pioneer®, Maximus™, Profil™, Vineta

G2826 Mac + PC ② 1927-34: Frederic W. Goudy
Deepdene™ No. 315

abcdefghijklmnopqrstuvwxyz[äöüßåøæœç]
ABCDEFGHIJKLMNOPQRSTUVWXYZ
1234567890(.,;:?!$&-*){ÄÖÜÅØÆŒÇ}

▶ **Regular OSF**
The quick brown fox jumps over a Dog. 123 4567 890 Zwei Boxkämpfer jagen Eva durch Sylt portez ce vieux Whiskey blond qui

▶ **Italic OSF**
The quick brown fox jumps over a Dog. 123 4567 890 Zwei Boxkämpfer jagen Eva durch Sylt portez ce vieux Whiskey blond qui fume une pipe aber

▶ **Regular**
The quick brown fox jumps over a Dog. 123 4567 890 Zwei Boxkämpfer jagen Eva durch Sylt portez ce vieux Whiskey blond qui

▶ **Italic**
The quick brown fox jumps over a Dog. 123 4567 890 Zwei Boxkämpfer jagen Eva durch Sylt portez ce vieux Whiskey blond qui fume une pipe aber echt über

▶ **Small Caps OSF**
THE QUICK BROWN FOX JUMPS OVER A DOG. 123 4567 890 ZWEI BOXKÄMPFER JAGEN EVA DURCH SYLT PORTEZ CE VIEUX WHISKEY BLOND

▶ **Italic Small Caps OSF**
THE QUICK BROWN FOX JUMPS OVER A DOG. 123 4567 890 ZWEI BOXKÄMPFER JAGEN EVA DURCH SYLT PORTEZ CE VIEUX WHISKEY BLOND QUI

▶ **Swash Italic OSF**
The quick brown fox jumps over a Dog. 1234567 890 Zwei Boxkämpfer jagen Eva durch Sylt portez ce vieux Whiskey blond qui fume une pipe aber echt über

▶ **Alternate Swash Italic OSF**
The quick brown fox jumps over a Dog. 1234567 890 Zwei Boxkämpfer jagen Eva durch Sylt portez ce vieux Whiskey blond qui fume une pipe aber echt über

© FSI 1993

▼ G2826 Mac + PC Deepdene™ No. 315

▶ Swash Italic
The quick brown fox jumps over a Dog. Zwei Boxkämpfer jagen Eva durch Sylt portez ce vieux Whiskey blond qui fume une pipe aber echt über die Mauer

▶ Alternate Swash Italic
The quick brown fox jumps over a Dog. Zwei Boxkämpfer jagen Eva durch Sylt portez ce vieux Whiskey blond qui fume une pipe aber echt über die Mauer

▶ Alt. Swash Small Caps Italic
THE QUICK BROWN FOX JUMPS OVER A DOG. ZWEI BOXKÄMPFER JAGEN EVA DURCH SYLT PORTEZ CE VIEUX WHISKEY BLOND QUI FUME UNE PIPE

▶ Swash Small Caps Italic
THE QUICK BROWN FOX JUMPS OVER A DOG. ZWEI BOXKÄMPFER JAGEN EVA DURCH SYLT PORTEZ CE VIEUX WHISKEY BLOND QUI FUME UNE PIPE

BT2551 Mac + PC ⑥ ✎ 1902: T. M. Cleland
Della Robbia™

abcdefghijklmnopqrstuvwxyz[äöüßåøæœç]
ABCDEFGHIJKLMNOPQRSTUVWXYZ
1234567890(.,:;?!$&-*){ÄÖÜÅØÆŒÇ}

Footlight

▶ Regular
The quick brown fox jumps over a Dog. Zwei Boxkämpfer jagen Eva durch Sylt portez ce vieux Whiskey blond qui fume une pipe

▶ Bold
The quick brown fox jumps over a Dog. Zwei Boxkämpfer jagen Eva durch Sylt portez ce vieux Whiskey blond qui fume une

---

C993 Mac + PC ⑥ ✎ 1928 : R. H. Middleton
Delphian™ Open

ABCDEFGHIJKLMNOPQRSTUVWXYZ
1234567890(.,:;?!$&-*)[]ÄÖÜÅØÆŒÇ

Headlines 83S:
Barclay™ Open, Delphian™ Open, Fluidum™ Bold, PL Bernhardt, PL Britannia Bold, PL Fiorello™ Condensed, PL Modern Heavy Condensed, PL Torino Open

---

AB6317 Mac + PC ① ✎ 1983: Gustav Jaeger
Delta Jaeger™

abcdefghijklmnopqrstuvwxyz[äöüßåøæœç]
ABCDEFGHIJKLMNOPQRSTUVWXYZ
1234567890(.,:;?!$&-*){ÄÖÜÅØÆŒÇ}

▶ Light
The quick brown fox jumps over a Dog. Zwei Boxkämpfer jagen Eva durch Sylt portez ce vieux Whiskey blond qui fume une

▶ Light Italic
The quick brown fox jumps over a Dog. Zwei Boxkämpfer jagen Eva durch Sylt portez ce vieux Whiskey blond qui fume une pipe aber

▶ Book
The quick brown fox jumps over a Dog. Zwei Boxkämpfer jagen Eva durch Sylt portez ce vieux Whiskey blond qui fume

▶ Book Italic
The quick brown fox jumps over a Dog. Zwei Boxkämpfer jagen Eva durch Sylt portez ce vieux Whiskey blond qui fume

© FSI 1993

▼ AB6317   Mac + PC   Delta Jaeger™

► Medium
The quick brown fox jumps over a Dog. Zwei Boxkämpfer jagen Eva durch Sylt portez ce vieux Whiskey blond

► Medium Italic
The quick brown fox jumps over a Dog. Zwei Boxkämpfer jagen Eva durch Sylt portez ce vieux Whiskey blond

► Bold
The quick brown fox jumps over a Dog. Zwei Boxkämpfer jagen Eva durch Sylt portez ce vieux Whiskey blond

► Bold Italic
The quick brown fox jumps over a Dog. Zwei Boxkämpfer jagen Eva durch Sylt portez ce vieux Whiskey

► Outline
The quick brown fox jumps over a Dog. Zwei Boxkämpfer jagen Eva durch Sylt portez ce vieux Whiskey blond

L2571   Mac   ④   🖉 1984: Jan van Dijk
Demian™

abcdefghijklmnopqrstuvwxyz [äöüßåøæœç]
ABCDEFGHIJKLMNOPQRSTUVWXYZ
1234567890(.,;:?!$&-*)ÄÖÜÅØÆŒÇ

L2572   Mac   ④   🖉 1987: (Jan van Dijk, 1984) Peter O'Donnell
Demian Bold

abcdefghijklmnopqrstuvwxyz [äöüßåøæœç]
ABCDEFGHIJKLMNOPQRSTUVWXYZ
1234567890(.,;:?!$&-*)ÄÖÜÅØÆŒÇ

EF502   Mac + PC   ②   🖉 1976: Gerard Unger
Demos™

abcdefghijklmnopqrstuvwxyz[äöüßåøæœç]
ABCDEFGHIJKLMNOPQRSTUVWXYZ
1234567890(.,;:?!$&-*){ÄÖÜÅØÆŒÇ}

©
ITC Flora, Praxis,
Bitstream Charter,
Hollander, Swift

► Medium
The quick brown fox jumps over a Dog. Zwei Boxkämpfer jagen Eva durch Sylt portez ce vieux Whiskey blond qui

► Medium Italic
The quick brown fox jumps over a Dog. Zwei Boxkämpfer jagen Eva durch Sylt portez ce vieux Whiskey blond qui fume une

► Semi Bold
The quick brown fox jumps over a Dog. Zwei Boxkämpfer jagen Eva durch Sylt portez ce vieux Whiskey blond

► Small Caps
THE QUICK BROWN FOX JUMPS OVER A DOG. 123 4567 890 ZWEI BOXKÄMPFER JAGEN EVA DURCH SYLT PORTEZ CE VIEUX

© FSI 1993

C604 Mac + PC
Derek Italic

Derek Italic:
Derek Italic, Engravure, Gothic Extralite Extended, Holland Title

C604 Mac + PC ① (1890)
Derek Italic

abcdefghijklmnopqrstuvwxyz[äöüßåøæœç]
ABCDEFGHIJKLMNOPQRSTUVWXYZ
1234567890(.,;:?!$&-*){ÄÖÜÅØÆŒÇ}

Derek Italic:
Derek Italic, Engravure, Gothic Extralite Extended, Holland Title

LP6664 Mac + PC ⑥ 1992: Garrett Boge
De Stijl™

ABCDEFGHIJKLMNOPQRSTUVWXYZ[ÄÖÜASØÆŒÇ]
ABCDEFGHIJKLMNOPQRSTUVWXYZ
1234567890(.,;:?!$&-*){ÄÖÜÅØÆŒÇ}

Regency Gothic, Huxley Vertical. Aldous Vertical, Phenix American, Bureau Agency

▶ Regular
The quick brown fox jumps over a Dog. Zwei Boxkämpfer jagen Eva durch Sylt portez ce vieux Whiskey blond qui fume une pipe aber echt über die Mauer gesprungen und auch

▶ Expert
The quick brown fox jumps over a Dog. Zwei Boxkämpfer jagen Eva durch Sylt portez ce vieux Whiskey blond qui fume une pipe aber echt über die Mauer gesprungen und auch

LetterPerfect 6:
De Stijl™, Kryptic™
Regency Gothic, Huxley Vertical, Aldous Vertical, Phenix American, Bureau Agency

C602 Mac + PC ② 1890: Gustav Schroeder
DeVinne

abcdefghijklmnopqrstuvwxyz[äöüßåøæœç]
ABCDEFGHIJKLMNOPQRSTUVWXYZ
1234567890(.,;:?!$&-*){ÄÖÜÅØÆŒÇ}

aa*a*
BT791
DeVinne, Reg, Ita
Modern No. 20, Scotch Roman

▶ Regular
The quick brown fox jumps over a Dog. Zwei Boxkämpfer jagen Eva durch Sylt portez ce vieux Whiskey blond qui fume

▶ Italic
The quick brown fox jumps over a Dog. Zwei Boxkämpfer jagen Eva durch Sylt portez ce vieux Whiskey blond qui fume

Cloister:
Cloister™, DeVinne

© FSI 1993

BT792 Mac + PC ② 1890: Gustav Schroeder
DeVinne Text

abcdefghijklmnopqrstuvwxyz[äöüßåøæœç]
ABCDEFGHIJKLMNOPQRSTUVWXYZ
1234567890(.,;:?!$&-*){ÄÖÜÅØÆŒÇ}

Modern No. 20, Scotch Roman

▶ **Regular**
The quick brown fox jumps over a Dog. Zwei Boxkämpfer jagen Eva durch Sylt portez ce vieux Whiskey blond qui fume une pipe aber

▶ **Italic**
The quick brown fox jumps over a Dog. Zwei Boxkämpfer jagen Eva durch Sylt portez ce vieux Whiskey blond qui fume une pipe aber echt

A6374 Mac + PC ② 1991: Adrian Frutiger
Linotype Didot

abcdefghijklmnopqrstuvwxyz[äöüßåøæœç]
ABCDEFGHIJKLMNOPQRSTUVWXYZ
1234567890(.,;:?!$&-*){ÄÖÜÅØÆŒÇ}

Bodoni, Walbaum, ITC Fenice, Modern

▶ **Roman**
The quick brown fox jumps over a Dog. Zwei Boxkämpfer jagen Eva durch Sylt portez ce vieux Whiskey blond qui fume

▶ **Italic**
The quick brown fox jumps over a Dog. Zwei Boxkämpfer jagen Eva durch Sylt portez ce vieux Whiskey blond qui fume une pipe

▶ **Bold**
The quick brown fox jumps over a Dog. Zwei Boxkämpfer jagen Eva durch Sylt portez ce vieux Whiskey blond qui

▶ **Headline**
The quick brown fox jumps over a Dog. Zwei Boxkämpfer jagen Eva durch Sylt portez ce vieux Whiskey blond qui fume

▶ **Roman OSF**
The quick brown fox jumps over a Dog. 123 4567 890 Zwei Boxkämpfer jagen Eva durch Sylt portez ce vieux Whiskey

▶ **Italic OSF**
The quick brown fox jumps over a Dog. 123 4567 890 Zwei Boxkämpfer jagen Eva durch Sylt portez ce vieux Whiskey blond

▶ **Bold OSF**
The quick brown fox jumps over a Dog. 123 4567 890 Zwei Boxkämpfer jagen Eva durch Sylt portez ce vieux Whiskey

▶ **Headline OSF**
The quick brown fox jumps over a Dog. 123 4567 890 Zwei Boxkämpfer jagen Eva durch Sylt portez ce vieux Whiskey

▶ **Roman Small Caps**
THE QUICK BROWN FOX JUMPS OVER A DOG. 123 4567 890 ZWEI BOXKÄMPFER JAGEN EVA DURCH SYLT PORTEZ CE VIEUX WHISKEY

▶ **Initials**
THE QUICK BROWN FOX JUMPS OVER A DOG ZWEI BOXKÄMPFER JAGEN EVA DURCH SYLT PORTEZ CE

▶ **Ornaments One**

▶ **Ornaments Two**

FF1535　Mac + PC
FF Dig, FF Dog, FF Hip

FF Dig, FF Dog, FF Hip:
FF Dig™, FF Dog™, FF Hip™

FF1535　Mac + PC　⑤　✎ 1991: Paul Sych
FF Dig™

ABCDEFGHIJKLMNOPQRSTUVWXYZ
1234567890(.,:;?!$€-*)){|}ÄÖÜÅØÆŒÇ}

FF Dig, FF Dog, FF Hip:
FF Dig™, FF Dog™, FF Hip™

L2975　Mac　⑤　✎ 1990: David Quay
Digitek™

abcdefghijklmnopqrstuvwxyz1234567890[äöüßåøæœç]
ABCDEFGHIJKLMNOPQRSTUVWXYZ(.,:;?!$&-*)ÄÖÜÅØÆŒÇ

A897　Mac + PC
DIN Schriften

DIN Schriften:
DIN, DIN Neuzeit Grotesk

A897　Mac + PC　①
DIN

abcdefghijklmnopqrstuvwxyz[äöüßåøæœç]
ABCDEFGHIJKLMNOPQRSTUVWXYZ
1234567890(.,:;?!$&-*){ÄÖÜÅØÆŒÇ}

ⓒ Citizen, Erbar, Neuzeit Grotesk, Tempo

▶ Engschrift
The quick brown fox jumps over a Dog. Zwei Boxkämpfer jagen Eva durch Sylt portez ce vieux Whiskey blond qui fume une pipe aber echt über die Mauer gesprungen und auch

▶ Mittelschrift
The quick brown fox jumps over a Dog. Zwei Boxkämpfer jagen Eva durch Sylt portez ce vieux Whiskey blond qui fume une

DIN Schriften:
DIN, DIN Neuzeit Grotesk
ⓒ Citizen, Erbar, Neuzeit Grotesk, Tempo

BT793　Mac + PC　②　✎ 1952–53: Gudrun Zapf von Hesse　　Industry name
Calligraphic 810　　　　　　　　　　　　　　　　　　　　　　　　Diotima™

abcdefghijklmnopqrstuvwxyz[äöüßåøæœç]
ABCDEFGHIJKLMNOPQRSTUVWXYZ
1234567890(.,:;?!$&-*){ÄÖÜÅØÆŒÇ}

© FSI 1993

▼ BT793 Mac + Pc   Diotima™

© Bitstream Carmina, Berthold Nofret

▶ Regular
The quick brown fox jumps over a Dog. Zwei Boxkämpfer jagen Eva durch Sylt portez ce vieux Whiskey

▶ Italic
The quick brown fox jumps over a Dog. Zwei Boxkämpfer jagen Eva durch Sylt portez ce vieux Whiskey blond qui fume une pipe aber

FF6621 Mac + Pc ⑥ ✎ 1993: Jeremy Tankard
FF Disturbance™

abcdefghijkLmnopqrstuvwxyz1234567890
(.,;:?!$&-*)[äöüßåøæœç]{ftQustttfffifl}

© Bodoni No. 26

▶ Regular
the quick brown fox jumps over a dog. zwei boxkämpfer jagen eva durch sylt portez ce vieux whiskey blond qui fume une pipe aber echt

▶ Italic
the quick brown fox jumps over a dog. zwei boxkämpfer jagen eva durch sylt portez ce vieux whiskey blond qui fume une pipe aber echt über die mauer

▶ Bold
the quick brown fox jumps over a dog. zwei boxkämpfer jagen eva durch sylt portez ce vieux whiskey blond qui fume une pipe aber echt

FF1535 Mac + Pc ⑤ ✎ 1991: Paul Sych
FF Dog™

abcdefghijklmnopqrstuvwxyz1234567890(äöüßåæœç)
ABCDEFGHIJKLMNOPQRSTUVWXYZ(.,;:?!$&-*)(ÄÖÜÅØÆŒÇ)

📦 FF Dig, FF Dog, FF Hip:
FF Dig™, FF Dog™, FF Hip™

L2573 Mac ⑥ ✎ 1983: (Max Salzmann, 1922)
Dolmen™

abcdefghijklmnopqrstuvwxyz[äöüßåøæœç]
ABCDEFGHIJKLMNOPQRSTUVWXYZ
1234567890(.,;:?!$&-*)ÄÖÜÅØÆŒÇ

FF1057 Mac + Pc ⑥ ✎ 1991: Tobias Frere-Jones
FF Dolores™

abcdefghijklmnopqrstuvwxyz[äöüßåøæœç]
ABCDEFGHIJKLMNOPQRSTUVWXYZ
1234567890(.,;:?!$&-*){ÄÖÜÅØÆŒÇ}

© Estro, Hip Hop

▶ Light
The quick brown fox jumps over a Dog. Zwei Boxkämpfer jagen Eva durch Sylt portez ce vieux Whiskey blond qui fume une pipe aber echt über die Mauer

▶ Regular
The quick brown fox jumps over a Dog. Zwei Boxkämpfer jagen Eva durch Sylt portez ce vieux Whiskey blond qui fume une pipe aber echt

© FSI 1993

▼ FF1057 Mac + PC FF Dolores™

▶ Bold
The quick brown fox jumps over a Dog. Zwei Boxkämpfer jagen Eva durch Sylt portez ce vieux Whiskey blond qui

▶ Extra Bold
The quick brown fox jumps over a Dog. Zwei Boxkämpfer jagen Eva durch Sylt portez ce vieux

▶ Black
The quick brown fox jumps over a Dog. Zwei Boxkämpfer jagen Eva durch Sylt portez

---

BT1280 Mac + PC ④ 1951: Peter Dombrezian
Dom™ Casual

abcdefghijklmnopqrstuvwxyz[äöüßåøæœç]
ABCDEFGHIJKLMNOPQRSTUVWXYZ
1234567890(.,;:?!$&-*){ÄÖÜÅØÆŒÇ}

aaa
A171
Dom Casual, Reg, Bd
Polka, Impress, Flash

▶ Regular
The quick brown fox jumps over a Dog. Zwei Boxkämpfer jagen Eva durch Sylt portez ce vieux Whiskey blond qui fume une pipe aber echt über die Mauer gesprungen und auch

▶ Bold
The quick brown fox jumps over a Dog. Zwei Boxkämpfer jagen Eva durch Sylt portez ce vieux Whiskey blond qui fume une pipe aber echt über die Mauer

---

BT794 Mac + PC ④ 1952: Peter Dombrezian
Dom Diagonal

abcdefghijklmnopqrstuvwxyz[äöüßåøæœç]
ABCDEFGHIJKLMNOPQRSTUVWXYZ
1234567890(.,;:?!$&-*){ÄÖÜÅØÆŒÇ}

Polka

▶ Regular
The quick brown fox jumps over a Dog. Zwei Boxkämpfer jagen Eva durch Sylt portez ce vieux Whiskey blond qui fume une pipe aber echt über die Mauer gesprungen und auch

▶ Bold
The quick brown fox jumps over a Dog. Zwei Boxkämpfer jagen Eva durch Sylt portez ce vieux Whiskey blond qui fume une pipe aber echt über die Mauer

---

FF6623 Mac + PC ⑤
FF Dome / FF Tyson

FF Dome / FF Tyson:
FF Dome™, FF Tyson™

FF6623 Mac + PC ⑤ 1993: Neville Brody
FF Dome™

abcdefghijklmnopqrstuvwxyz1234567890[äöüßåøæœç]
ABCDEFGHIJKLMNOPQRSTUVWXYZ(.,;:?!$&-*){ÄÖÜÅØÆŒÇ}

FF Tyson, FF Tokyo

▶ Display
The quick brown fox jumps over a Dog. Zwei Boxkämpfer jagen Eva durch Sylt portez ce vieux Whiskey blond qui fume une pipe aber echt über die Mauer gesprungen und auch smørebrød en

▶ Text
The quick brown fox jumps over a Dog. Zwei Boxkämpfer jagen Eva durch Sylt portez ce vieux Whiskey blond qui fume une pipe aber echt über die Mauer gesprungen und auch smørebrød en

© FSI 1993

▼ FF6623 Mac + PC FF Dome™

FF Dome / FF Tyson:
FF Dome™, FF Tyson™

A6071 Mac + PC
Dorchester Script, et al MT

Dorchester Script, et al MT:
Biffo Script MT, Dorchester Script, Monotype Script Bold, Pepita
aaa 🕮 M263
Script 1

M263 Mac + PC ④
Dorchester Script™

abcdefghijklmnopqrstuvwxyz[äöüßåøæœç]
ABCDEFGHIJKLMNOPQRSTUVWXYZ
1234567890(.,;:?!$&-*){ÄÖÜÅØŒŒÇ}

Script 1:
Biffo™ Script, Dorchester Script™, Monotype Script Bold, Pepita®, Swing™ Bold
aaa 🕮 A6071
Dorchester Script, et al MT

A377 Mac + PC
Doric/Maximus

Doric/Maximus:
Doric™ Bold, Maximus™

A377 Mac + PC ① ✏ 1972: Walter Tracy
Doric™ Bold

abcdefghijklmnopqrstuvwxyz[äöüßåøæœç]
ABCDEFGHIJKLMNOPQRSTUVWXYZ
1234567890(.,;:?!$&-*){ÄÖÜÅØÆŒÇ}

Doric/Maximus:
Doric™ Bold, Maximus™
👁 Ad Sans, Sans No. 1, ATF Spartan

FF6183 Mac + PC ⑤ ✏ 1992: Marianne van Ham
FF Double Dutch™

abcdefghijklmnopqrstuvwxyz[äöüßåøæœç]
ABCDEFGHIJKLMNOPQRSTUVWXYZ
1234567890(.,;:?!$&-*){ÄÖÜÅØÆŒÇ}

▶ Smooth
The quick brown fox jumps over a Dog. Zwei Boxkämpfer jagen Eva durch Sylt portez ce vieux Whiskey blond qui fume une

▶ Bitmap
The quick brown fox jumps over a Dog. Zwei Boxkämpfer jagen Eva durch Sylt portez ce vieux Whiskey blond qui fume

© FSI 1993

Dubbeldik™
MC2900　Mac + PC　⑥　✎ A. Werner

abcdefghijklmnopqrstuvwxyz
1234567890(.,;:?!$&-=*)[ ]{ }

FF DuBrush™
FF2960　Mac + PC　④

FF DuBrush™:
FF DuChirico™, FF DuDuchamp™, FF DuGauguin™, FF DuTurner™

Duc De Berry™
A996　Mac + PC　⑦　✎ 1990: Gottfried Pott

abcdefghijklmnopqrstuvwxyz[äöüßåøœç]
ABCDEFGHIJKLMNOPQRSTUVWXYZ
1234567890(.,;:?!$&-*){ÄÖÜÅØÆŒÇ}

▶ Regular
The quick brown fox jumps over a Dog. Zwei Boxkämpfer jagen Eva durch Sylt portez ce vieux Whiskey blond qui fume une pipe aber echt

▶ Deutsch Fraktur
The quick brown fox jumpſ over a Dog. Zwei Boxkämpfer jagen Eva durch Sylt portez ce vieux Whiſkey blond qui fume une pipe aber echt

Type Before Gutenberg 1:
Duc De Berry™, Herculanum™, Omnia™

FF DuChirico™
FF2960　Mac + PC　④　✎ 1992: D. van Meerbeeck

abcdefghijklmnopqrstuvwxyz1234567890[äöüßåøœç]
ABCDEFGHIJKLMNOPQRSTUVWXYZ(.,;:?!$&-*){ÄÖÜÅØÆŒÇ}

FF DuBrush™:
FF DuChirico™, FF DuDuchamp™, FF DuGauguin™, FF DuTurner™

FF DuDuchamp™
FF2960　Mac + PC　④　✎ 1992: D. van Meerbeeck

abcdefghijklmnopqrstuvwxyz1234567890[äöüßåøœç]
ABCDEFGHIJKLMNOPQRSTUVWXYZ(.,;:?!$&-*){ÄÖÜÅØÆŒÇ}

FF DuBrush™:
FF DuChirico™, FF DuDuchamp™, FF DuGauguin™, FF DuTurner™

© FSI 1993

FF2960   Mac + PC   ④   1992: D. van Meerbeeck
FF DuGauguin™

abcdefghijklmnopqrstuvwxyz1234567890[äöüßåøæœç]
ABCDEFGHIJKLMNOPQRSTUVWXYZ.,;:?!$&-){ÄÖÜÅØÆŒÇ}*

FF DuBrush™:
FF DuChirico™, FF DuDuchamp™, FF DuGauguin™, FF DuTurner™

FF2960   Mac + PC   ④   1992: D. van Meerbeeck
FF DuTurner™

abcdefghijklmnopqrstuvwxyz[äöüßåøæœç]
ABCDEFGHIJKLMNOPQRSTUVWXYZ
1234567890(.,;:?!$&-){ÄÖÜÅØÆŒÇ}*

FF DuBrush™:
FF DuChirico™, FF DuDuchamp™, FF DuGauguin™, FF DuTurner™

EF6444   Mac + PC   ⑥   1977: (1930: K. Sommer) Alan Meeks
Dynamo

abcdefghijklmnopqrstuvwxyzäöüßåøæœç
ABCDEFGHIJKLMNOPQRSTUVWXYZ
1234567890(.,;:?!$&-*){ÄÖÜÅØÆŒÇ}

aa*a*
C2525
Headlines 86S

▶ Medium
The quick brown fox jumps over a Dog. Zwei Boxkämpfer jagen Eva durch Sylt portez ce vieux Whiskey blond qui fume une

▶ Bold
The quick brown fox jumps over a Dog. Zwei Boxkämpfer jagen Eva durch Sylt portez ce vieux Whiskey blond qui fume

▶ Bold Shadow
The quick brown fox jumps over a Dog. Zwei Boxkämpfer jagen Eva durch Sylt portez ce vieux Whiskey blond qui fume une

▶ Bold Condensed
The quick brown fox jumps over a Dog. Zwei Boxkämpfer jagen Eva durch Sylt portez ce vieux Whiskey blond qui fume une pipe aber echt

---

FF2961   Mac + PC   ⑥   1992: Just van Rossum
FF Dynamoe

ABCDEFGHIJKLMNOPQRSTUVWXYZ
1234567890(.,;:?!$&-*)[]ÄÖÜÅØÆŒÇ

FF Instant Types™:
FF Confidential™, FF Dynamoe™, FF Flightcase™, FF Karton™, FF Stamp Gothic™

© FSI 1993

iN Buchstabe

... diE HAUptAktEUrE vOn SchriftEn
» SiE schrEibEn GEschichtEn
» TypOgrAfiE ist OhnE siE nicht mÖglich.

abcdefghijk?
lmnopqr
stuvwxyzE
d

Claudia Kipp, Bielefeld | Bamberg, D

C2981 Mac + PC — 1933: M. F. Benton
Eagle Bold

ABCDEFGHIJKLMNOPQRSTUVWXYZ
1234567890[ ](.,;:?!$&-*){ÄÖÜÅØÆŒÇ}

Headlines 92S:
Eagle Bold, Joanna Solotype, Matra™, Modernique, Victorian Silhouette

FB605 Mac + PC — 1989: (M. F. Benton, 1933), David Berlow
Bureau Eagle™

abcdefghijklmnopqrstuvwxyz[äöüßåøœç]
ABCDEFGHIJKLMNOPQRSTUVWXYZ
1234567890(.,;:?!$&-*){ÄÖÜÅØÆŒÇ}

▶ Book
The quick brown fox jumps over a Dog. Zwei Boxkämpfer jagen Eva durch Sylt portez ce vieux Whiskey

▶ Bold
The quick brown fox jumps over a Dog. Zwei Boxkämpfer jagen Eva durch Sylt portez ce vieux

T06104 Mac — 1991: José Manuel Urós, Joan Barjau
Ebu™ Script

abcdefghijklmnopqrstuvwxyz1234567890[äöüßåøæœç]
ABCDEFGHIJKLMNOPQRSTUVWXYZ(.,;:?!$&-*){ÄÖÜÅØÆŒÇ}

Type-ø-Tones Pack 1:
Ebu™ Script, Me mima™

C594 Mac + PC
Eccentric™

ABCDEFGHIJKLMNOPQRSTUVWXYZ
1234567890(.,;:?!$&-*)[]{ÄÖÜÅØÆŒÇ}

Aldous :
Aldous™ Vertical, Aura, Computer, Eccentric™
Galadriel

BT807 Mac + PC — 1900: Otto Eckmann — Industry name
Freeform 710 — Eckmann™

abcdefghijklmnopqrstuvwxyz[äöüßåøœç]
ABCDEFGHIJKLMNOPQRSTUVWXYZ
1234567890(.,;:?!$&-*){ÄÖÜÅØÆŒÇ}

© FSI 1993

▼ BT807 Mac + PC Eckmann™

Bitstream Headlines 1:
Eckmann™, Fry's Baskerville™, Libra™

C2778 Mac + PC ⑥
Eclipse™

ABCDEFGHIJKLMNOPQRSTUVWXYZ

1234567890[ ](.,:;?!$&-*){ÄÖÜÅØÆŒÇ}

Headlines 90s:
Bernhard Fashion, Chic™, Eclipse™, Metronome Gothic, Salut™

FB6836 Mac + PC ⑥   ✎ 1993: (Margaret Chase) Richard Lipton
Ecru™ Display

abcdefghijklmnopqrstuvwxyz[äöüßåøæœç]
ABCDEFGHIJKLMNOPQRSTUVWXYZ
1234567890(.,:;?!$&-*){ÄÖÜÅØÆŒÇ}

FB Display Pack 1:
Ecru™ Display, Elli™ Display, Numskill™ Bold, Nutcracker™

EF505 Mac + PC ③   ✎ 1978: Hermann Zapf
Edison™

abcdefghijklmnopqrstuvwxyz[äöüßåøæœç]
ABCDEFGHIJKLMNOPQRSTUVWXYZ
1234567890(.,:;?!$&-*){ÄÖÜÅØÆŒÇ}

© ITC Zapf International

▶ Book
The quick brown fox jumps over a Dog. Zwei Boxkämpfer jagen Eva durch Sylt portez ce vieux Whiskey

▶ Italic
The quick brown fox jumps over a Dog. Zwei Boxkämpfer jagen Eva durch Sylt portez ce vieux Whiskey blond

▶ Semibold
The quick brown fox jumps over a Dog. Zwei Boxkämpfer jagen Eva durch Sylt portez ce vieux

▶ Semibold Italic
The quick brown fox jumps over a Dog. Zwei Boxkämpfer jagen Eva durch Sylt portez ce vieux Whiskey

▶ Bold Condensed
The quick brown fox jumps over a Dog. Zwei Boxkämpfer jagen Eva durch Sylt portez ce vieux Whiskey blond qui fume une

© FSI 1993

C467 Mac + PC — (Vincent Figgins, 1815)
Egiziano™ Black

abcdefghijklmnopqrstuvwxyz[äöüåoæœç]
ABCDEFGHIJKLMNOPQRSTUVWXYZ
1234567890(.,;:?!$&-*)◊ÄÖÜÅOÆŒÇ♦

Headlines 81S:
Egiziano™ Black, PL Behemoth Semi Condensed, PL Benguiat Frisky, PL Futura Maxi 1, PL Tower™ Condensed, Quirinus™ Bold, Section™ Bold Condensed, Stratford ™Bold, Woodblock

F2946 Mac — (1897)
Egyptian Bold Condensed

abcdefghijklmnopqrstuvwxyz[äöüßåoæœç]
ABCDEFGHIJKLMNOPQRSTUVWXYZ
1234567890(.,;:?!$&-*){ÄÖÜÅOÆŒÇ}

▶ Bold Condensed Large Face
The quick brown fox jumps over a Dog. Zwei Boxkämpfer jagen Eva durch Sylt portez ce vieux Whiskey blond qui fume une

▶ Bold Condensed Small Face
The quick brown fox jumps over a Dog. Zwei Boxkämpfer jagen Eva durch Sylt portez ce vieux Whiskey blond qui fume une pipe aber echt

M206 Mac + PC
Egyptian

abcdefghijklmnopqrstuvwxyz[äöüßåøæœç]
ABCDEFGHIJKLMNOPQRSTUVWXYZ
1234567890(.,;:?!$&-*){ÄÖÜÅØÆŒÇ}

Headliners 1:
Clarendon, Egyptian, New Clarendon
Ⓒ▷ Antique No. 3, Belizio, Clarendon

C180 Mac + PC — 1966: André Gürtler
VGC Egyptian 505™

abcdefghijklmnopqrstuvwxyz[äöüßåøæœç]
ABCDEFGHIJKLMNOPQRSTUVWXYZ
1234567890(.,;:?!$&-*){ÄÖÜÅØÆŒÇ}

aaa
BT1287
VGC Egyptian 505, Lt, Reg, Med, Bd

▶ Light
The quick brown fox jumps over a Dog. Zwei Boxkämpfer jagen Eva durch Sylt portez ce vieux Whiskey blond qui fume une pipe

▶ Regular
The quick brown fox jumps over a Dog. Zwei Boxkämpfer jagen Eva durch Sylt portez ce vieux Whiskey blond qui fume une

▶ Medium
The quick brown fox jumps over a Dog. Zwei Boxkämpfer jagen Eva durch Sylt portez ce vieux Whiskey blond qui fume

▶ Bold
The quick brown fox jumps over a Dog. Zwei Boxkämpfer jagen Eva durch Sylt portez ce vieux Whiskey blond qui fume

© FSI 1993

Egyptienne F™

A2543 Mac + PC ③ ✎ 1956: Adrian Frutiger

abcdefghijklmnopqrstuvwxyz[äöüßåøæœç]
ABCDEFGHIJKLMNOPQRSTUVWXYZ
1234567890(.,;:?!$&-*){ÄÖÜÅØÆŒÇ}

aa*a*
BT795
Egyptienne™, Reg, Ita,
Bd, Blk

▶ Regular
The quick brown fox jumps over a Dog. Zwei Boxkämpfer jagen Eva durch Sylt portez ce vieux Whiskey blond qui

▶ Italic
The quick brown fox jumps over a Dog. Zwei Boxkämpfer jagen Eva durch Sylt portez ce vieux Whiskey blond

▶ Bold
The quick brown fox jumps over a Dog. Zwei Boxkämpfer jagen Eva durch Sylt portez ce vieux Whiskey

▶ Black
The quick brown fox jumps over a Dog. Zwei Boxkämpfer jagen Eva durch Sylt portez ce vieux

Ehrhardt

M268 Mac + PC ②

abcdefghijklmnopqrstuvwxyz[äöüßåøæœç]
ABCDEFGHIJKLMNOPQRSTUVWXYZ
1234567890(.,;:?!$&-*){ÄÖÜÅØÆŒÇ}

aa*a*
A2869
Ehrhardt, Reg, Ita,
SemBd, SemBdIta

▶ Regular
The quick brown fox jumps over a Dog. Zwei Boxkämpfer jagen Eva durch Sylt portez ce vieux Whiskey blond qui fume une pipe aber

▶ Italic
The quick brown fox jumps over a Dog. Zwei Boxkämpfer jagen Eva durch Sylt portez ce vieux Whiskey blond qui fume une pipe aber echt

▶ Semi Bold
The quick brown fox jumps over a Dog. Zwei Boxkämpfer jagen Eva durch Sylt portez ce vieux Whiskey blond qui fume

▶ Semi Bold Italic
The quick brown fox jumps over a Dog. Zwei Boxkämpfer jagen Eva durch Sylt portez ce vieux Whiskey blond qui fume une pipe aber

Ehrhardt Expert

M379 Mac + PC ②

ABCDEFGHIJKLMNOPQRSTUVWXYZ(ÄÖÜŠÅØÆŒÇ)

1234567890offfiflffiffl(^{1}⁄$_1$^{2}⁄$_2$^{3}⁄$_3$^{4}⁄$_4$^{5}⁄$_5$^{6}⁄$_6$^{7}⁄$_7$^{8}⁄$_8$^{9}⁄$_9$^{0}⁄$_0$) $^{(\$}$$_\${¢}$Rp₵$^{)a}$

▶ Expert
0123456789offfiflffiffl-(^{1}⁄$_1$^{2}⁄$_2$^{3}⁄$_3$^{4}⁄$_4$^{5}⁄$_5$^{6}⁄$_6$^{7}⁄$_7$^{8}⁄$_8$^{9}⁄$_9$‰)$^{(\$}$$_\${¢}$Rp₵$^{)a}$ THE QUICK BROWN FOX JUMPS OVER A DOG ZWEI BOXKÄMPFER JAGEN EVA

▶ Expert Italic
0123456789offfiflffiffl-(^{1}⁄$_1$^{2}⁄$_2$^{3}⁄$_3$^{4}⁄$_4$^{5}⁄$_5$^{6}⁄$_6$^{7}⁄$_7$^{8}⁄$_8$^{9}⁄$_9$‰)$^{(\$}$$_\${¢}$Rp₵$^{)a}$

▶ Expert Semi Bold
0123456789offfiflffiffl-(^{1}⁄$_1$^{2}⁄$_2$^{3}⁄$_3$^{4}⁄$_4$^{5}⁄$_5$^{6}⁄$_6$^{7}⁄$_7$^{8}⁄$_8$^{9}⁄$_9$‰)$^{(\$}$$_\${¢}$Rp₵$^{)a}$

▶ Expert Semi Bold Italic
0123456789offfiflffiffl-(^{1}⁄$_1$^{2}⁄$_2$^{3}⁄$_3$^{4}⁄$_4$^{5}⁄$_5$^{6}⁄$_6$^{7}⁄$_7$^{8}⁄$_8$^{9}⁄$_9$‰)$^{(\$}$$_\${¢}$Rp₵$^{)a}$

© FSI 1993

SG1165 Mac — 1980: Alan Meeks
Einhorn

abcdefghijklmnopqrstuvwxyz[äöüßåøæœç]
ABCDEFGHIJKLMNOPQRSTUVWXYZ
1234567890(.,;:?!$&-*)ÄÖÜÅØÆŒÇ

EF297 Mac + PC — 1985: Albert Boton
ITC Elan® 1

abcdefghijklmnopqrstuvwxyz[äöüßåøæœç]
ABCDEFGHIJKLMNOPQRSTUVWXYZ
1234567890(.,;:?!$&-*){ÄÖÜÅØÆŒÇ}

aa*a*
C987
ITC Elan, Bk, BkIta,
Med, MedIta, Bd,
BdIta, Blk, BlkIta

Bitstream Amerigo,
Albertus, ITC Symbol,
Friz Quadrata

▶ Book
The quick brown fox jumps over a Dog. Zwei Boxkämpfer jagen Eva durch Sylt portez ce vieux Whiskey blond qui fume

▶ Book Italic
The quick brown fox jumps over a Dog. Zwei Boxkämpfer jagen Eva durch Sylt portez ce vieux Whiskey blond qui fume

▶ Bold
The quick brown fox jumps over a Dog. Zwei Boxkämpfer jagen Eva durch Sylt portez ce vieux Whiskey blond

▶ Bold Italic
The quick brown fox jumps over a Dog. Zwei Boxkämpfer jagen Eva durch Sylt portez ce vieux Whiskey blond

EF298 Mac + PC — 1985: Albert Boton
ITC Elan 2

abcdefghijklmnopqrstuvwxyz[äöüßåøæœç]
ABCDEFGHIJKLMNOPQRSTUVWXYZ
1234567890(.,;:?!$&-*){ÄÖÜÅØÆŒÇ}

aa*a*
C987
ITC Elan, Bk, BkIta,
Med, MedIta, Bd,
BdIta, Blk, BlkIta

Bitstream Amerigo,
Albertus, ITC Symbol,
Friz Quadrata

▶ Medium
The quick brown fox jumps over a Dog. Zwei Boxkämpfer jagen Eva durch Sylt portez ce vieux Whiskey blond qui

▶ Medium Italic
The quick brown fox jumps over a Dog. Zwei Boxkämpfer jagen Eva durch Sylt portez ce vieux Whiskey blond

▶ Black
The quick brown fox jumps over a Dog. Zwei Boxkämpfer jagen Eva durch Sylt portez ce vieux Whiskey

▶ Black Italic
The quick brown fox jumps over a Dog. Zwei Boxkämpfer jagen Eva durch Sylt portez ce vieux Whiskey

EF531 Mac + PC — 1985: Albert Boton
ITC Elan Small Caps

ABCDEFGHIJKLMNOPQRSTUVWXYZ[ÄÖÜSSÅØÆŒÇ]
ABCDEFGHIJKLMNOPQRSTUVWXYZ
1234567890(.,;:?!$&-*){ÄÖÜÅØÆŒÇ}

Bitstream Amerigo,
Albertus, ITC Symbol,
Friz Quadrata

▶ Book Small Caps
THE QUICK BROWN FOX JUMPS OVER A DOG. 123 4567 890 ZWEI BOXKÄMPFER JAGEN EVA DURCH SYLT PORTEZ CE VIEUX WHISKEY

▶ Medium Small Caps
THE QUICK BROWN FOX JUMPS OVER A DOG. 123 4567 890 ZWEI BOXKÄMPFER JAGEN EVA DURCH SYLT PORTEZ CE VIEUX WHISKEY

© FSI 1993

C1038 Mac + PC ② (W. A. Dwiggins, 1935–44)
Elante

abcdefghijklmnopqrstuvwxyz[äöüßåøæœç]
ABCDEFGHIJKLMNOPQRSTUVWXYZ
1234567890(.,;:?!$&-*){ÄÖÜÅØÆŒÇ}

Electra

▶ Regular
The quick brown fox jumps over a Dog. Zwei Boxkämpfer jagen Eva durch Sylt portez ce vieux Whiskey blond qui fume

▶ Italic
The quick brown fox jumps over a Dog. Zwei Boxkämpfer jagen Eva durch Sylt portez ce vieux Whiskey blond qui fume une

▶ Bold
The quick brown fox jumps over a Dog. Zwei Boxkämpfer jagen Eva durch Sylt portez ce vieux Whiskey blond qui fume

▶ Bold Italic
The quick brown fox jumps over a Dog. Zwei Boxkämpfer jagen Eva durch Sylt portez ce vieux Whiskey blond qui fume

BT796 Mac + PC ② 1935–44: W. A. Dwiggins — Industry name
Transitional 521 — Electra™

abcdefghijklmnopqrstuvwxyz[äöüßåøæœç]
ABCDEFGHIJKLMNOPQRSTUVWXYZ
1234567890(.,;:?!$&-*){ÄÖÜÅØÆŒÇ}

Fairfield

▶ Regular
The quick brown fox jumps over a Dog. Zwei Boxkämpfer jagen Eva durch Sylt portez ce vieux Whiskey blond qui fume une

▶ Cursive
The quick brown fox jumps over a Dog. Zwei Boxkämpfer jagen Eva durch Sylt portez ce vieux Whiskey blond qui fume une pipe aber

▶ Bold
The quick brown fox jumps over a Dog. Zwei Boxkämpfer jagen Eva durch Sylt portez ce vieux Whiskey blond qui fume une

ET1107 Mac + PC
Eclectic Electrics™

Eclectic Electrics™:
Electric Hand™, Electric Uncial™, Lutahline™

ET1107 Mac + PC ④ 1987: Judith Sutcliffe
Electric Hand™

ABCDEFGHIJKLMNOPQRSTUVWXYZ
1234567890(.,; :?!$&-*)[]{}

Eclectic Electrics™:
Electric Hand™, Electric Uncial™, Lutahline™

ET1107 Mac + PC ⑦ ✏ 1990: (V. Hammer, 1943) Judith Sutcliffe
Electric Uncial™

abcdefghijklmnopqrstuvwxyz
äöüßåøç1234567890(.,;:?!$&-*)

Eclectic Electrics™:
Electric Hand™, Electric Uncial™, Lutahline™
© Libra, Omnia

ET1108 Mac + PC
Electric Marlborough™

Electric Marlborough™:
Goudy Newstyle, Italian Electric™

EF6469 Mac + PC ⑥ ✏ Bob McGrath
Elefont™

ABCDEFGHIJKLMNOPQRSTUVWXYZ
1234567890(.,;:?!$&-*)[]ÄÖÜÅØÆŒÇ

E+F Special Headlines 5:
Chesterfield™, Cortez™, Elefont™, Glastonbury™, Julia™ Script, LCD

E380 Mac + PC ⑤ ✏ 1985: Zuzana Licko
Elektrix™

abcdefghijklmnopqrstuvwxyz[äöüßåøæç]
ABCDEFGHIJKLMNOPQRSTUVWXYZ
1234567890(.,;:?!$&-*){ÄÖÜÅØÆŒÇ}

▶ Light
The quick brown fox jumps over a Dog. Zwei Boxkämpfer jagen Eva durch Sylt portez ce vieux Whiskey blond qui fume une pipe aber echt

▶ Bold
The quick brown fox jumps over a Dog. Zwei Boxkämpfer jagen Eva durch Sylt portez ce vieux Whiskey blond qui fume une pipe aber echt

FB6836 Mac + PC ④ ✏ 1993: Jean Evans
Elli™ Display

abcdefghijklmnopqrstuvwxyz[äöüßåøæç]
ABCDEFGHIJKLMNOPQRSTUVWXYZ
1234567890(.,;:?!$&-*){ÄÖÜÅØÆŒÇ}

FB Display Pack 1:
Ecru™ Display, Elli™ Display, Numskill™ Bold, Nutcracker™

© FSI 1993

M469 Mac + PC   ②   1990: Michael Harvey
Ellington®

abcdefghijklmnopqrstuvwxyz[äöüßåøæœç]
ABCDEFGHIJKLMNOPQRSTUVWXYZ
1234567890(.,:;?!$&-*){ÄÖÜÅØÆŒÇ}

aaa
A2991
Ellington, Lt, LtIta, Reg, Ita, Bd, BdIta, ExtBd, ExtBdIta

▶ Light
The quick brown fox jumps over a Dog. Zwei Boxkämpfer jagen Eva durch Sylt portez ce vieux Whiskey blond qui fume une pipe aber echt

▶ Light Italic
The quick brown fox jumps over a Dog. Zwei Boxkämpfer jagen Eva durch Sylt portez ce vieux Whiskey blond qui fume une pipe aber echt

▶ Regular
The quick brown fox jumps over a Dog. Zwei Boxkämpfer jagen Eva durch Sylt portez ce vieux Whiskey blond qui fume une

▶ Italic
The quick brown fox jumps over a Dog. Zwei Boxkämpfer jagen Eva durch Sylt portez ce vieux Whiskey blond qui fume une pipe aber

▶ Bold
The quick brown fox jumps over a Dog. Zwei Boxkämpfer jagen Eva durch Sylt portez ce vieux Whiskey blond qui fume

▶ Bold Italic
The quick brown fox jumps over a Dog. Zwei Boxkämpfer jagen Eva durch Sylt portez ce vieux Whiskey blond qui fume une

▶ Extra Bold
The quick brown fox jumps over a Dog. Zwei Boxkämpfer jagen Eva durch Sylt portez ce vieux Whiskey blond qui

▶ Extra Bold Italic
The quick brown fox jumps over a Dog. Zwei Boxkämpfer jagen Eva durch Sylt portez ce vieux Whiskey blond qui

A6724 Mac + PC   ②   1982: Robert Norton
Else NPL™

abcdefghijklmnopqrstuvwxyz[äöüßåøæœç]
ABCDEFGHIJKLMNOPQRSTUVWXYZ
1234567890(.,:;?!$&-*){ÄÖÜÅØÆŒÇ}

©
Century Old Style

▶ Light
The quick brown fox jumps over a Dog. Zwei Boxkämpfer jagen Eva durch Sylt portez ce vieux Whiskey blond qui fume

▶ Medium
The quick brown fox jumps over a Dog. Zwei Boxkämpfer jagen Eva durch Sylt portez ce vieux Whiskey blond qui fume

▶ SemiBold
The quick brown fox jumps over a Dog. Zwei Boxkämpfer jagen Eva durch Sylt portez ce vieux Whiskey blond qui fume

▶ Bold
The quick brown fox jumps over a Dog. Zwei Boxkämpfer jagen Eva durch Sylt portez ce vieux Whiskey blond qui fume

L6437 Mac   ②   1992: (Oldrich Menhart) Michael Gills
Elysium™

abcdefghijklmnopqrstuvwxyz[äöüßåøæœç]
ABCDEFGHIJKLMNOPQRSTUVWXYZ
1234567890(.,:;?!$&-*){ÄÖÜÅØÆŒÇ}

© FSI 1993

▼ L6437 MAC Elysium™

▶ Book
The quick brown fox jumps over a Dog. Zwei Boxkämpfer jagen Eva durch Sylt portez ce vieux Whiskey blond qui fume

▶ Book Italic
The quick brown fox jumps over a Dog. Zwei Boxkämpfer jagen Eva durch Sylt portez ce vieux Whiskey blond qui fume une pipe aber echt

▶ Medium
The quick brown fox jumps over a Dog. Zwei Boxkämpfer jagen Eva durch Sylt portez ce vieux Whiskey

▶ Bold
The quick brown fox jumps over a Dog. Zwei Boxkämpfer jagen Eva durch Sylt portez ce vieux

▶ Book SC
THE QUICK BROWN FOX JUMPS OVER A DOG. 123 4567 890 ZWEI BOXKÄMPFER JAGEN EVA DURCH SYLT PORTEZ CE VIEUX

BT850 MAC + PC ④
Embassy

abcdefghijklmnopqrstuvwxyz[äöüßåøæœç]
ABCDEFGHIJKLMNOPQRSTUVWXYZ
1234567890(.,;:?!$&-*){ÄÖÜÅØÆŒÇ}

Bitstream Script 3:
Embassy, Englische Schreibschrift™, Liberty, Lucia™
© Englische Schreibschrift, Flemish Script, Kuenstler Script, Palace Script

---

E036 MAC + PC ⑤   ✎ 1985: Zuzana Licko
Emigre™

abcdefghijklmnopqrstuvwxyz[äöüßåøæœç]
ABCDEFGHIJKLMNOPQRSTUVWXYZ
1234567890(.,;:?!$&-*){ÄÖÜÅØÆŒÇ}

© Emigre Special

▶ Eight
The quick brown fox jumps over a Dog. Zwei Boxkämpfer jagen Eva durch Sylt portez ce vieux Whiskey blond qui fume une pipe aber echt über die

▶ Ten
The quick brown fox jumps over a Dog. Zwei Boxkämpfer jagen Eva durch Sylt portez ce vieux Whiskey blond qui fume une pipe aber echt über die

▶ Fourteen
The quick brown fox jumps over a Dog. Zwei Boxkämpfer jagen Eva durch Sylt portez ce vieux Whiskey blond qui fume une pipe aber echt

▶ Fifteen
The quick brown fox jumps over a Dog. Zwei Boxkämpfer jagen Eva durch Sylt portez ce vieux Whiskey blond qui fume une pipe aber echt über die Mauer gesprungen und auch

---

E148 MAC + PC
Emigre Special

abcdefghijklmnopqrstuvwxyz1234567890[äöüßåøæœç]
ABCDEFGHIJKLMNOPQRSTUVWXYZ(.,;:?!$&-*){ÄÖÜÅØÆŒÇ}

▼ E148 MAC + PC Emigre Special

▶ Emigre Fifteen
The quick brown fox jumps over a Dog. Zwei Boxkämpfer jagen Eva durch Sylt portez ce vieux Whiskey blond qui fume une pipe aber echt über die Mauer gesprungen und auch

▶ Emperor Eight
The quick brown fox jumps over a Dog. Zwei Boxkämpfer jagen Eva durch Sylt portez ce vieux Whiskey blond qui fume une pipe aber echt über die Mauer gesprungen und auch smørebrød en

▶ Oakland Six
THE QUICK BROWN FOX JUMPS OVER A DOG. ZWEI BOX-KÄMPFER JAGEN EVA

▶ Universal Nineteen
The quick brown fox jumps over a Dog. Zwei Boxkämpfer jagen Eva durch Sylt portez ce vieux Whiskey blond qui fume une pipe aber echt über die Mauer gesprungen und auch smørebrød en ysjes natuurlijk. But very long

E037 MAC + PC ⑤ 🖉 1985: Zuzana Licko
Emperor™

abcdefghijklmnopqrstuvwxyz1234567890[äöüßåøæœç]
ABCDEFGHIJKLMNOPQRSTUVWXYZ(.,;:?!$£-*){ÄÖÜÅØÆŒÇ}

© Emigre Special

▶ Eight
The quick brown fox jumps over a Dog. Zwei Boxkämpfer jagen Eva durch Sylt portez ce vieux Whiskey blond qui fume une pipe aber echt über die Mauer gesprungen und auch smørebrød en

▶ Ten
The quick brown fox jumps over a Dog. Zwei Boxkämpfer jagen Eva durch Sylt portez ce vieux Whiskey blond qui fume une pipe aber echt über die Mauer gesprungen und auch smørebrød en

▶ Fifteen
The quick brown fox jumps over a Dog. Zwei Boxkämpfer jagen Eva durch Sylt portez ce vieux Whiskey blond qui fume une pipe aber echt über die Mauer gesprungen und auch smørebrød en ysjes natuurlijk. But very long spazierende tekst ist used in dieser

▶ Nineteen
The quick brown fox jumps over a Dog. Zwei Boxkämpfer jagen Eva durch Sylt portez ce vieux Whiskey blond qui fume une pipe aber echt über die Mauer gesprungen und auch smørebrød en ysjes natuurlijk. But very long spazierende tekst ist used in dieser

L2824 MAC ⑥ 🖉 1989: Martin Wait
Emphasis™

ABCDEFGHIJKLMNOPQRSTUVWXYZ
1234567890(.,;:?!$£-)[ÄÖÜÅØÆŒÇ]*

FB606 MAC + PC ① 🖉 1989: (1937), David Berlow
Bureau Empire™

abcdefghijklmnopqrstuvwxyz1234567890[äöüßåøæœç]
ABCDEFGHIJKLMNOPQRSTUVWXYZ(.,;:?!$£-*){ÄÖÜÅØÆŒÇ}

© Silhouette, Obelisk No. 2577, Spire No. 377

▶ Regular
The quick brown fox jumps over a Dog. Zwei Boxkämpfer jagen Eva durch Sylt portez ce vieux Whiskey blond qui fume une pipe aber echt über die Mauer gesprungen und auch

▶ Italic
The quick brown fox jumps over a Dog. Zwei Boxkämpfer jagen Eva durch Sylt portez ce vieux Whiskey blond qui fume une pipe aber echt über die Mauer gesprungen und auch

© FSI 1993

C2980 Mac + PC ⑥
Empire™

ABCDEFGHIJKLMNOPQRSTUVWXYZ
1234567890[ ](.,:;?!$&-*) { ÄÖÜÅØÆŒÇ }

Headlines 91S:
Empire™, Gallia™, Gillies Gothic Bold, Quaint™ Roman, Skjald™

BT850 Mac + PC ④
English 157
Industry name: Englische Schreibschrift™

abcdefghijklmnopqrstuvwxyz[äöüßåøæœç]
ABCDEFGHIJKLMNOPQRSTUVWXYZ
*1234567890(.,:;?!$&- */{ÄÖÜÅØÆŒÇ}*

Bitstream Script 3:
Embassy, Englische Schreibschrift™, Liberty, Lucia™
© Flemish Script, Embassy

A6186 Mac + PC
Engravers / Serlio

Engravers / Serlio:
Engravers Bold Face™, Serlio™

C2780 Mac + PC
Agfa Engravers 1

Agfa Engravers 1:
Antique Roman, Artisan Roman, Burin Roman, Burin Sans, Classic Roman, Handle Old Style, Roman

C2781 Mac + PC
Agfa Engravers 2

Agfa Engravers 2:
Sackers Antique Roman, Sackers Classic Roman, Sackers Gothic, Sackers Roman, Sackers Script, Sackers Square Gothic

M269 Mac + PC
Engraver's

Engraver's:
Engraver's Old English, Engraver's Roman

M269 Mac + PC ② 1899: Robert Wiebking
Engraver's Roman

ABCDEFGHIJKLMNOPQRSTUVWXYZ
1234567890(.,:;?!$&-*)[]{ÄÖÜÅØÆŒÇ}

© FSI 1993

E 11

aaa
BT1288
Engraver's Roman,
Reg, Bd
Engravure, Orlando

▼ M269 Mac + PC   Engraver's Roman

▶ Size One
THE QUICK BROWN
FOX JUMPS OVER A
DOG. ZWEI BOX-
KÄMPFER JAGEN

▶ Size One Bold
THERE IS A QUICK
BROWN FOX HE
JUMPS OVER A
DOG. ZWEI BOX-

Engraver's:
Engraver's Old English, Engraver's Roman

BT1288 Mac + PC ②
Engraver's Roman

ABCDEFGHIJKLMNOPQRSTUVWXYZ[ÄÖÜSSÅØÆŒÇ]

ABCDEFGHIJKLMNOPQRSTUVWXYZ

1234567890(.,;:?!$&-*){ÄÖÜÅØÆŒÇ}

aaa
M269
Engraver's
Engravure, Orlando

▶ Regular
THE QUICK BROWN FOX
JUMPS OVER A DOG. ZWEI
BOXKÄMPFER JAGEN EVA
DURCH SYLT PORTEZ CE

▶ Bold
THE QUICK BROWN FOX JUMPS
OVER A DOG. ZWEI BOXKÄMP-
FER JAGEN EVA DURCH SYLT
PORTEZ CE VIEUX WHISKEY

A6186 Mac + PC ⑥
Engravers Bold Face™

ABCDEFGHIJKLMNOPQRSTUVWXYZ[ÄÖÜSSÅØÆŒÇ]

ABCDEFGHIJKLMNOPQRSTUVWXYZ

1234567890(.,;:?!$&-*){ÄÖÜÅØÆŒÇ}

Engravers / Serlio:
Engravers Bold Face™, Serlio™

C604 Mac + PC ② ✏ (Robert Wiebking, 1899)
Engravure

ABCDEFGHIJKLMNOPQRSTUVWXYZ[ÄÖÜÅØÆŒÇ]

ABCDEFGHIJKLMNOPQRSTUVWXYZ

1234567890(.,;:?!$&-*){ÄÖÜÅØÆŒÇ}

Derek Italic:
Derek Italic, Engravure, Gothic Extralite Extended, Holland Title
Engraver's Roman, Orlando

BT808 Mac + PC ⑥
Engraver's Gothic

ABCDEFGHIJKLMNOPQRSTUVWXYZ[ÄÖÜSSÅØÆŒÇ]

ABCDEFGHIJKLMNOPQRSTUVWXYZ

1234567890(.,;:?!$&-*){ÄÖÜÅØÆŒÇ}

© FSI 1993

E 12

▼ BT808 Mac + PC **Engraver's Gothic**

Bitstream Headlines 2:
Engraver's Gothic, Engraver's Old English
👁 Copperplate Gothic, Spartan

BT808 Mac + PC ⑦ ✎ 1901: Cowan, M. F. Benton
Engraver's Old English

abcdefghijklmnopqrstuvwxyz[äöüßåøæœç]
ABCDEFGHIJKLMNOPQRSTUVWXYZ
1234567890(.,;:?!$&-*){ÄÖÜÅØÆŒÇ}

aa*a*
⌂ M269
Engraver's
👁 Linotext, Old English Text, Wedding Text

▶ Regular
The quick brown fox jumps over a Dog. Zwei Boxkämpfer jagen Eva durch Sylt portez ce vieux Whiskey blond qui fume une pipe aber echt

▶ Bold
The quick brown fox jumps over a Dog. Zwei Boxkämpfer jagen Eva durch Sylt portez ce vieux Whiskey blond qui

Bitstream Headlines 2:
Engraver's Gothic, Engraver's Old English

MC6358 Mac + PC ①
Enroute™

abcdefghijklmnopqrstuvwxyz[äöüßåøæœç]
ABCDEFGHIJKLMNOPQRSTUVWXYZ
1234567890(.,;:?!$&-*)(ÄÖÜÅØÆŒÇ)

L2574 Mac ⑥ ✎ 1982: F. Scott Garland
Enviro™

ABCDEFGHIJKLMNOPQRSTUVWXYZ
1234567890(.,;:?!$&-*)[]ÄÖÜÅØÆŒÇ

L6590 Mac ⑥ ✎ 1992: Colin Brignall
Epokha™

ABCDEFGHIJKLMNOPQRSTUVWXYZ
1234567890(.,;:?!$&-*)[ÄÖÜÅØÆŒÇ]

L6127 Mac ⑥ ✎ 1988: Vince Whitlock
Equinox™

abcdefghijklmnopqrstuvwxyz[äöüßåøæœç]
ABCDEFGHIJKLMNOPQRSTUVWXYZ
1234567890(.,;:?!$&-*)ÄÖÜÅØÆŒÇ

© FSI 1993

BT1289 MAC + PC ① 1977–78: (1969) A. Hollenstein, Albert Boton
ITC Eras® 1

abcdefghijklmnopqrstuvwxyz[äöüßåøæœç]
ABCDEFGHIJKLMNOPQRSTUVWXYZ
1234567890(.,:;?!$&-*){ÄÖÜÅØÆŒÇ}

aa*a*
A038
ITC Eras, Lt, Bk, Med, Demi, Bd, Ult

▶ Light
The quick brown fox jumps over a Dog. Zwei Boxkämpfer jagen Eva durch Sylt portez ce vieux Whiskey blond qui fume une pipe aber

▶ **Bold**
The quick brown fox jumps over a Dog. Zwei Boxkämpfer jagen Eva durch Sylt portez ce vieux Whiskey

▶ Ultra
The quick brown fox jumps over a Dog. Zwei Boxkämpfer jagen Eva durch Sylt portez ce

BT1290 MAC + PC ① 1977–78: (1969) A. Hollenstein, Albert Boton
ITC Eras 2

abcdefghijklmnopqrstuvwxyz[äöüßåøæœç]
ABCDEFGHIJKLMNOPQRSTUVWXYZ
1234567890(.,:;?!$&-*){ÄÖÜÅØÆŒÇ}

aa*a*
A038
ITC Eras, Lt, Bk, Med, Demi, Bd, Ult

▶ Book
The quick brown fox jumps over a Dog. Zwei Boxkämpfer jagen Eva durch Sylt portez ce vieux Whiskey blond qui fume une

▶ Medium
The quick brown fox jumps over a Dog. Zwei Boxkämpfer jagen Eva durch Sylt portez ce vieux Whiskey blond qui fume une

▶ Demi
The quick brown fox jumps over a Dog. Zwei Boxkämpfer jagen Eva durch Sylt portez ce vieux Whiskey blond qui fume

BT784 MAC + PC ⑥ 1977–78: (1969) A. Hollenstein, Albert Boton
ITC Eras Outline

abcdefghijklmnopqrstuvwxyz[äöüßåøæœç]
ABCDEFGHIJKLMNOPQRSTUVWXYZ
1234567890(.,:;?!$&-*){ÄÖÜÅØÆŒÇ}

Bitstream Contour :
ITC Clearface Contour, ITC Eras Outline, ITC Serif Gothic, ITC Souvenir Outline

C607 Mac + PC
Erbar/Torino

Erbar/Torino:
Erbar ™Condensed, Torino

C607 Mac + PC ① ✎ 1928–30: Jakob Erbar
Erbar ™Condensed

abcdefghijklmnopqrstuvwxyz[äöüßåøæœç]
ABCDEFGHIJKLMNOPQRSTUVWXYZ
1234567890(.,:;?!$&-*){ÄÖÜÅØÆŒÇ}

© Futura Condensed, DIN Engschrift, Neuzeit Grotesk, Tempo

▶ Light Condensed
The quick brown fox jumps over a Dog. Zwei Boxkämpfer jagen Eva durch Sylt portez ce vieux Whiskey blond qui fume une pipe aber echt über die Mauer gesprungen und auch smørebrød en

▶ Medium Condensed
The quick brown fox jumps over a Dog. Zwei Boxkämpfer jagen Eva durch Sylt portez ce vieux Whiskey blond qui fume une pipe aber echt über die Mauer gesprungen und auch smørebrød en

Erbar/Torino:
Erbar ™Condensed, Torino
© Futura Condensed, DIN Engschrift, Neuzeit Grotesk, Tempo

FF735 Mac + PC ④ ✎ 1991: Erik van Blokland
FF Erikrighthand™

abcdefghijklmnopqrstuvwxyz[äöüßåøæœç]
ABCDEFGHIJKLMNOPQRSTUVWXYZ
1234567890(.,:;?!$&-*){ÄÖÜÅØÆŒÇ}

© FF Justlefthand, Oz Handicraft

▶ Regular
The quick brown fox jumps over a Dog. Zwei Boxkämpfer jagen Eva durch Sylt portez ce vieux Whiskey blond qui fume une pipe aber echt über die Mauer gesprungen und auch smørebrød

▶ Small Caps
THE QUICK BROWN FOX JUMPS OVER A DOG. 123 4567 890 ZWEI BOXKÄMPFER JAGEN EVA DURCH SYLT PORTEZ CE VIEUX WHISKEY BLOND QUI FUME UNE PIPE ABER ECHT ÜBER DIE MAUER GESPRUNGEN

FF Hands™:
FF Erikrighthand™, FF Justlefthand™
© FF Justlefthand, Oz Handicraft

EF299 Mac + PC ② ✎ 1985: Jovica Veljovic
ITC Esprit® 1

abcdefghijklmnopqrstuvwxyz[äöüßåøæœç]
ABCDEFGHIJKLMNOPQRSTUVWXYZ
1234567890(.,:;?!$&-*){ÄÖÜÅØÆŒÇ}

aa*a*
C986
ITC Esprit, Bk, BkIta, Med, MedIta, Bd, BdIta, Blk, BlkIta
A2870
ITC Esprit, Bk, BkIta, Med, MedIta, Bd, BdIta, Blk, BlkIta

▶ Book
The quick brown fox jumps over a Dog. Zwei Boxkämpfer jagen Eva durch Sylt portez ce vieux Whiskey blond qui fume

▶ Book Italic
The quick brown fox jumps over a Dog. Zwei Boxkämpfer jagen Eva durch Sylt portez ce vieux Whiskey blond qui fume une pipe aber

© FSI 1993
▼

▼ EF299　Mac + PC　ITC Esprit® 1

▶ Bold
The quick brown fox jumps over a Dog. Zwei Boxkämpfer jagen Eva durch Sylt portez ce vieux Whiskey blond

▶ Bold Italic
The quick brown fox jumps over a Dog. Zwei Boxkämpfer jagen Eva durch Sylt portez ce vieux Whiskey blond qui fume

EF300　Mac + PC　②　🖉 1985: Jovica Veljovic
ITC Esprit 2

abcdefghijklmnopqrstuvwxyz[äöüßåøæœç]
ABCDEFGHIJKLMNOPQRSTUVWXYZ
1234567890(.,;:?!$&-*){ÄÖÜÅØÆŒÇ}

a a *a*
C986
ITC Esprit, Bk, BkIta, Med, MedIta, Bd, BdIta, Blk, BlkIta
A2870
ITC Esprit, Bk, BkIta, Med, MedIta, Bd, BdIta, Blk, BlkIta

▶ Medium
The quick brown fox jumps over a Dog. Zwei Boxkämpfer jagen Eva durch Sylt portez ce vieux Whiskey blond qui fume

▶ Medium Italic
The quick brown fox jumps over a Dog. Zwei Boxkämpfer jagen Eva durch Sylt portez ce vieux Whiskey blond qui fume une

▶ Black
The quick brown fox jumps over a Dog. Zwei Boxkämpfer jagen Eva durch Sylt portez ce vieux Whiskey

▶ Black Italic
The quick brown fox jumps over a Dog. Zwei Boxkämpfer jagen Eva durch Sylt portez ce vieux Whiskey

EF532　Mac + PC　②　🖉 1985: Jovica Veljovic
ITC Esprit Small Caps

ABCDEFGHIJKLMNOPQRSTUVWXYZ[ÄÖÜßÅØÆŒÇ]
ABCDEFGHIJKLMNOPQRSTUVWXYZ
1234567890(.,;:?!$&-*){ÄÖÜÅØÆŒÇ}

▶ Book Small Caps
THE QUICK BROWN FOX JUMPS OVER A DOG. 123 4567 890 ZWEI BOXKÄMPFER JAGEN EVA DURCH SYLT PORTEZ CE VIEUX WHISKEY

▶ Medium Small Caps
THE QUICK BROWN FOX JUMPS OVER A DOG. 123 4567 890 ZWEI BOXKÄMPFER JAGEN EVA DURCH SYLT PORTEZ CE VIEUX

MC2918　Mac + PC　⑥　🖉 1961: Aldo Novarese
Estro™

abcdefghijklmnopqrstuvwxyz[äöüßåøæœç]
ABCDEFGHIJKLMNOPQRSTUVWXYZ
1234567890(.,;:?!$&-*){ÄÖÜÅØÆŒÇ}

CT1094　Mac + PC　①　🖉 1991: Adrian Williams
Eurocrat™

abcdefghijklmnopqrstuvwxyz[äöüßåøæœç]
ABCDEFGHIJKLMNOPQRSTUVWXYZ
1234567890(.,;:?!$&-*){ÄÖÜÅØÆŒÇ}

© FSI 1993

ITC Quay Sans

▼ CT1094 MAC + PC   Eurocrat™

▶ Regular
The quick brown fox jumps over a Dog. Zwei Boxkämpfer jagen Eva durch Sylt portez ce vieux Whiskey blond qui fume une pipe aber

▶ Italic
The quick brown fox jumps over a Dog. Zwei Boxkämpfer jagen Eva durch Sylt portez ce vieux Whiskey blond qui fume une pipe aber

▶ Medium
The quick brown fox jumps over a Dog. Zwei Boxkämpfer jagen Eva durch Sylt portez ce vieux Whiskey blond qui fume

▶ Medium Italic
The quick brown fox jumps over a Dog. Zwei Boxkämpfer jagen Eva durch Sylt portez ce vieux Whiskey blond qui fume

▶ Bold
The quick brown fox jumps over a Dog. Zwei Boxkämpfer jagen Eva durch Sylt portez ce vieux Whiskey blond

▶ Bold Italic
The quick brown fox jumps over a Dog. Zwei Boxkämpfer jagen Eva durch Sylt portez ce vieux Whiskey blond

---

C1012 MAC + PC   ⑥
TC Europa™ Bold

**abcdefghijklmnopqrstuvwxyzäöüåøæœç
ABCDEFGHIJKLMNOPQRSTUVWXYZ
1234567890(.,;:?!$&-*)ÄÖÜÅØÆŒÇ**

Headlines 84S:
Bernhard Modern, Beton Extra Bold, Metropolis Bold, Modern No. 20, Orlando Caps, PL Davison Americana, PL Westerveldt Light, Siena™ Black, TC Europa™ Bold, TC Jasper™

A039 MAC + PC   ①   ✎ 1962: Aldo Novarese
Eurostile™ 1

abcdefghijklmnopqrstuvwxyz[äöüßåøæœç]
ABCDEFGHIJKLMNOPQRSTUVWXYZ
1234567890(.,;:?!$&-*){ÄÖÜÅØÆŒÇ}

aa**a**
BT1388
Eurostile 1, Reg, Bd

▶ Regular
The quick brown fox jumps over a Dog. Zwei Boxkämpfer jagen Eva durch Sylt portez ce vieux Whiskey blond

▶ Oblique
The quick brown fox jumps over a Dog. Zwei Boxkämpfer jagen Eva durch Sylt portez ce vieux Whiskey blond

▶ Demi
The quick brown fox jumps over a Dog. Zwei Boxkämpfer jagen Eva durch Sylt portez ce vieux Whiskey

▶ Demi Oblique
The quick brown fox jumps over a Dog. Zwei Boxkämpfer jagen Eva durch Sylt portez ce vieux Whiskey

▶ Bold
The quick brown fox jumps over a Dog. Zwei Boxkämpfer jagen Eva durch Sylt portez ce vieux Whis-

▶ Bold Oblique
The quick brown fox jumps over a Dog. Zwei Boxkämpfer jagen Eva durch Sylt portez ce vieux Whis-

A381 Mac + PC ① 1962: Aldo Novarese
Eurostile 2

abcdefghijklmnopqrstuvwxyz[äöüßåøæœç]
ABCDEFGHIJKLMNOPQRSTUVWXYZ
1234567890(.,;:?!$&-*){ÄÖÜÅØÆŒÇ}

a a *a*
BT1389
Eurostile 2, Con, BdCon
BT1390
Eurostile 3, Ext, BdExt

▶ Condensed
The quick brown fox jumps over a Dog. Zwei Boxkämpfer jagen Eva durch Sylt portez ce vieux Whiskey blond qui fume une pipe aber echt

▶ Bold Condensed
The quick brown fox jumps over a Dog. Zwei Boxkämpfer jagen Eva durch Sylt portez ce vieux Whiskey blond qui fume une pipe aber echt

▶ Extended
The quick brown fox jumps over a Dog. Zwei Boxkämpfer jagen Eva durch Sylt

▶ Bold Extended
The quick brown fox jumps over a Dog. Zwei Boxkämpfer jagen Eva durch

BT1359 Mac + PC ③ 1931: C.H. Griffith   Industry name
News 702   Excelsior

abcdefghijklmnopqrstuvwxyz[äöüßåøæœç]
ABCDEFGHIJKLMNOPQRSTUVWXYZ
1234567890(.,;:?!$&-*){ÄÖÜÅØÆŒÇ}

a a *a*
A040
Excelsior, Reg, Ita, Bd
Aurora, Corona, Imperial, Ionic, Olympian, Textype

▶ Regular
The quick brown fox jumps over a Dog. Zwei Boxkämpfer jagen Eva durch Sylt portez ce vieux Whiskey

▶ Italic
The quick brown fox jumps over a Dog. Zwei Boxkämpfer jagen Eva durch Sylt portez ce vieux Whiskey

▶ Bold
The quick brown fox jumps over a Dog. Zwei Boxkämpfer jagen Eva durch Sylt portez ce vieux

▶ Bold Italic
The quick brown fox jumps over a Dog. Zwei Boxkämpfer jagen Eva durch Sylt portez ce vieux

E6279 Mac + PC ⑤ 1990: Jonathon Barnbrook
Exocet™

ABCDEFGHIJKLMNOPQRS+UVWXYZ[ÄÖÜßÅØÆŒÇ]
ABCDEFGHIJKLMNOPQRSTUVWXYZ
1234567890[.,;:?!$&-*]{ÄÖÜÅØÆŒÇ}

FF Disturbance

▶ Light
THE QUICK BROWN FOX JUMPS OVER A DOG. ZWEI BOXKÄMPFER JAGEN EVA DURCH SYLT

▶ Heavy
THE QUICK BROWN FOX JUMPS OVER A DOG. ZWEI BOXKÄMPFER JAGEN EVA DURCH SYLT

© FSI 1993

F

FACTOR SAYS: RECYCLE*

♻ *But not this book! — Factor Design, Hamburg, D

Fairfield™ 1

A2767 Mac + PC ② 1991: (R. Ruzicka, 1939-45) Alex Kaczun

abcdefghijklmnopqrstuvwxyz[äöüßåøæœç]
ABCDEFGHIJKLMNOPQRSTUVWXYZ
1234567890(.,;:?!$&-*){ÄÖÜÅØÆŒÇ}

aaa
BT797
Fairfield, Med, MedIta
© Electra

▶ 45 Light
The quick brown fox jumps over a Dog. Zwei Boxkämpfer jagen Eva durch Sylt portez ce vieux Whiskey blond qui fume une

▶ 46 Light Italic
The quick brown fox jumps over a Dog. Zwei Boxkämpfer jagen Eva durch Sylt portez ce vieux Whiskey blond qui fume une pipe aber echt

▶ 55 Medium
The quick brown fox jumps over a Dog. Zwei Boxkämpfer jagen Eva durch Sylt portez ce vieux Whiskey blond qui fume

▶ 56 Medium Italic
The quick brown fox jumps over a Dog. Zwei Boxkämpfer jagen Eva durch Sylt portez ce vieux Whiskey blond qui fume une

▶ 75 Bold
The quick brown fox jumps over a Dog. Zwei Boxkämpfer jagen Eva durch Sylt portez ce vieux Whiskey blond qui

▶ 76 Bold Italic
The quick brown fox jumps over a Dog. Zwei Boxkämpfer jagen Eva durch Sylt portez ce vieux Whiskey blond qui fume

▶ 85 Heavy
The quick brown fox jumps over a Dog. Zwei Boxkämpfer jagen Eva durch Sylt portez ce vieux Whiskey

▶ 86 Heavy Italic
The quick brown fox jumps over a Dog. Zwei Boxkämpfer jagen Eva durch Sylt portez ce vieux Whiskey

Fairfield 2

A2768 Mac + PC ② 1991: (R. Ruzicka, 1939-45) Alex Kaczun

ABCDEFGHIJKLMNOPQRSTUVWXYZ[ÄÖÜSSÅØÆŒÇ]
ABCDEFGHIJKLMNOPQRSTUVWXYZ
1234567890(.,;:?!$&-*){ÄÖÜÅØÆŒÇ}

© Electra

▶ 45 Light Small Caps/OSF
THE QUICK BROWN FOX JUMPS OVER A DOG. 123 4567 890 ZWEI BOXKÄMPFER JAGEN EVA DURCH SYLT PORTEZ CE VIEUX WHISKEY

▶ 55 Medium Small Caps/OSFC
THE QUICK BROWN FOX JUMPS OVER A DOG. 123 4567 890 ZWEI BOXKÄMPFER JAGEN EVA DURCH SYLT PORTEZ CE VIEUX WHISKEY

▶ 75 Bold Small Caps/OSF
THE QUICK BROWN FOX JUMPS OVER A DOG. 123 4567 890 ZWEI BOXKÄMPFER JAGEN EVA DURCH SYLT PORTEZ CE VIEUX

▶ 85 Heavy Small Caps/OSF
THE QUICK BROWN FOX JUMPS OVER A DOG. 123 4567 890 ZWEI BOXKÄMPFER JAGEN EVA DURCH SYLT PORTEZ CE

▶ 45 Light Caption
The quick brown fox jumps over a Dog. 123 4567 890 Zwei Boxkämpfer jagen Eva durch Sylt portez ce vieux Whiskey blond

▶ 55 Medium Caption
The quick brown fox jumps over a Dog. 123 4567 890 Zwei Boxkämpfer jagen Eva durch Sylt portez ce vieux Whiskey

© FSI 1993

▼ A2768 Mac + PC Fairfield 2

▶ 75 Bold Caption
The quick brown fox jumps over a Dog. 123 4567 890 Zwei Boxkämpfer jagen Eva durch Sylt portez ce vieux

▶ 85 Heavy Caption
The quick brown fox jumps over a Dog. 123 4567 890 Zwei Boxkämpfer jagen Eva durch Sylt portez ce

▶ 46 Swash Light Italic/OSF
The quick brown fox jumps over a Dog. 123 4567 890 Zwei Boxkämpfer jagen Eva durch Sylt portez ce vieux Whiskey blond qui

▶ 56 Swash Medium Italic/OSF
The quick brown fox jumps over a Dog. 123 4567 890 Zwei Boxkämpfer jagen Eva durch Sylt portez ce vieux Whiskey blond

▶ 76 Bold Italic/OSF
The quick brown fox jumps over a Dog. 123 4567 890 Zwei Boxkämpfer jagen Eva durch Sylt portez ce vieux Whiskey

▶ 86 Swash Heavy Italic/OSF
The quick brown fox jumps over a Dog. 123 4567 890 Zwei Boxkämpfer jagen Eva durch Sylt portez ce

M215 Mac + PC ② (1931)
Falstaff™

abcdefghijklmnopqrstuvwxyz[äöüßåøæœç]
ABCDEFGHIJKLMNOPQRSTUVWXYZ
1234567890(.,:;?!$&-*){ÄÖÜÅØÆŒÇ}

Headliners 2:
Falstaff™, Headline Bold, Placard®
aaa M6330
Falstaff et al
A6087 Falstaff et al Bodoni Poster, Normande, Poster Bodoni

M6330 Mac + PC ⑥
Falstaff et al

Falstaff et al:
Falstaff, Inflex, Monotype Old Style Bold Outline

A6087 Mac + PC ⑥
Falstaff et al

Falstaff et al:
Falstaff, Inflex, Monotype Old Style Bold Outline

SF6635 Mac ⑤ 1993: (L. Oppenheim, 1927) Rod McDonald
Fanfare Recut

abcdefghijklmnopqrstuvwxyz[äöüßåøæœç]
ABCDEFGHIJKLMNOPQRSTUVWXYZ
1234567890(.,:;?!$&-*){ÄÖÜÅØÆŒÇ}

▶ Regular
The quick brown fox jumps over a Dog. Zwei Boxkämpfer jagen Eva durch Sylt portez ce vieux Whiskey

▶ Alternates
The quick brown fox jumps over a Dog. Zwei Boxkämpfer jagen Eva durch Sylt portez ce vieux

Stylus Headlines 1:
Bodoni Open Condensed, Fanfare Recut, Goudy Globe Gothic, Loyalist™ Condensed

© FSI 1993

L2575 Mac ② ✎ 1986: Alan Meeks
Fashion Compressed™ No. 3

abcdefghijklmnopqrstuvwxyz[äöüßåøæœç]
ABCDEFGHIJKLMNOPQRSTUVWXYZ
1234567890(.,;:?!$&-*)ÄÖÜÅØÆŒÇ

L2576 Mac ⑥ ✎ 1991: Alan Meeks
Fashion Engraved

abcdefghijklmnopqrstuvwxyz[äöüßåøæœç]
ABCDEFGHIJKLMNOPQRSTUVWXYZ
1234567890(.,;:?!$&-*)ÄÖÜÅØÆŒÇ

M884 Mac + PC ⑥ ✎ (1934)
Felix™ Titling

ABCDEFGHIJKLMNOPQRSTUVWXYZ
1234567890(.,;:?!$&-*)[]{ÄÖÜÅØÆŒÇ}

Classical Titling:
Felix™ Titling, Perpetua Titling
⊙ Galba, Serlio, Trajan, Classic Roman

A899 Mac + PC ② ✎ 1977–80: Aldo Novarese
ITC Fenice®

abcdefghijklmnopqrstuvwxyz[äöüßåøæœç]
ABCDEFGHIJKLMNOPQRSTUVWXYZ
1234567890(.,;:?!$&-*){ÄÖÜÅØÆŒÇ}

aa*a*
C179
ITC Fenice 1, Reg, Ita, Bd, BdIta
C1039
ITC Fenice 2, Lt, LtIta, Ult, UltIta
EF608
ITC Fenice 1, Lt, LtIta, Bd, BdIta
EF609
ITC Fenice 2, Reg, Ita, Ult, UltIta
BT1292
ITC Fenice 1, Lt, LtIta, Ult, UltIta
BT1293
ITC Fenice 2, Reg, Ita, Bd, BdIta

▶ Light
The quick brown fox jumps over a Dog. Zwei Boxkämpfer jagen Eva durch Sylt portez ce vieux Whiskey blond qui fume une pipe aber

▶ Light Italic
The quick brown fox jumps over a Dog. Zwei Boxkämpfer jagen Eva durch Sylt portez ce vieux Whiskey blond qui fume une pipe aber

▶ Regular
The quick brown fox jumps over a Dog. Zwei Boxkämpfer jagen Eva durch Sylt portez ce vieux Whiskey blond qui fume une

▶ Italic
The quick brown fox jumps over a Dog. Zwei Boxkämpfer jagen Eva durch Sylt portez ce vieux Whiskey blond qui fume une

▶ Bold
The quick brown fox jumps over a Dog. Zwei Boxkämpfer jagen Eva durch Sylt portez ce vieux Whiskey blond qui

▶ Bold Italic
The quick brown fox jumps over a Dog. Zwei Boxkämpfer jagen Eva durch Sylt portez ce vieux Whiskey blond qui

▶ Ultra
The quick brown fox jumps over a Dog. Zwei Boxkämpfer jagen Eva durch Sylt portez ce vieux

▶ Ultra Italic
The quick brown fox jumps over a Dog. Zwei Boxkämpfer jagen Eva durch Sylt portez ce vieux

© FSI 1993

M6410 Mac + PC ⑥ ✏ 1951: Phillip Boydell
Festival™ Titling

ABCDEFGHIJKLMNOPQRSTUVWXYZ
1234567890[ ](.,;:?!$&-*){ÄÖÜÅØÆŒÇ}

📦 Crazy Headlines™:
Festival™ Titling, Kino™, Matura™ Script, Victoria™ Titling Condensed

A170 Mac + PC ⑦
Fette Fraktur™

abcdefghijklmnopqrstuvwxyz[äöüßåøæœç]
ABCDEFGHIJKLMNOPQRSTUVWXYZ
1234567890(.,;:?!$&-*){ÄÖÜÅØÆŒÇ}

📦 Arnold Böcklin:
Arnold Böcklin™, Fette Fraktur™, Helvetica Inserat, Present™ Script

MC2901 Mac + PC ④
Fidelio™

abcdefghijklmnopqrstuvwxyz[äöü ßåøæœç]
ABCDEFGHIJKL MN OPQRSTUVWXYZ
1234567890(.,;:?!$&-*){ÄÖÜÅØÆŒÇ}

C468 Mac + PC ⑤ ✏ Hal Fiedler
PL Fiedler Gothic Bold

abcdefghijklmnopqrstuvwxyz[äöüåøæœç]
ABCDEFGHIJKLMNOPQRSTUVWXYZ
1234567890(.,;:?!$&-*)◊ÄÖÜÅgÆŒÇ♦

📦 Headlines 82S:
Neon Extra Condensed™, PL Barnum Block, PL Benguiat Frisky Bold, PL Davison Zip Bold, PL Fiedler Gothic Bold, PL Futura Maxi 2, PL Trophy™ Oblique, Ritmo™ Bold, TC Broadway

M267 Mac + PC ⑥
Figaro®

abcdefghijklmnopqrstuvwxyz[äöüßåøæœç]
ABCDEFGHIJKLMNOPQRSTUVWXYZ
1234567890(.,;:?!$&-*){ÄÖÜÅØÆŒÇ}

📦 Headliners 3:
Braggadocio™, Figaro®, Forte™, Klang™
© P. T. Barnum, Egyptian, Playbill, Old Towne No. 536, Ponderosa, French XXX Condensed

© FSI 1993

L6438 Mac ② 1992: (1940: Oldrich Menhart) Michael Gills
Figural™

abcdefghijklmnopqrstuvwxyz[äöüßåøæœç]
ABCDEFGHIJKLMNOPQRSTUVWXYZ
1234567890(.,;:?!$&-*){ÄÖÜÅØÆŒÇ}

▶ Book
The quick brown fox jumps over a Dog. Zwei Boxkämpfer jagen Eva durch Sylt portez ce vieux Whiskey blond qui fume

▶ Book Italic
The quick brown fox jumps over a Dog. Zwei Boxkämpfer jagen Eva durch Sylt portez ce vieux Whiskey blond qui fume une pipe aber

▶ Medium
The quick brown fox jumps over a Dog. Zwei Boxkämpfer jagen Eva durch Sylt portez ce vieux Whiskey blond qui

▶ Bold
The quick brown fox jumps over a Dog. Zwei Boxkämpfer jagen Eva durch Sylt portez ce vieux Whiskey blond

▶ Book SC
THE QUICK BROWN FOX JUMPS OVER A DOG. 123 4567 890 ZWEI BOXKÄMPFER JAGEN EVA DURCH SYLT PORTEZ CE VIEUX

L6123 Mac ④ 1987: Richard Bradley
Fine Hand™

abcdefghijklmnopqrstuvwxyz[äöüßåøæœç]
ABCDEFGHIJKLMNOPQRSTUVWXYZ
1234567890(.,;:?!$&-)*

C993 Mac + PC ⑤
PL Fiorello™ Condensed

abcdefghijklmnopqrstuvwxyz1234567890[äöüåþæœç]
ABCDEFGHIJKLMNOPQRSTUVWXYZ[.,;:?!$&-*}fÄÖÜÅÞÆŒ◆

Headlines 83S:
Barclay™ Open, Delphian™ Open, Fluidum™ Bold, PL Bernhardt, PL Britannia Bold, PL Fiorello™ Condensed, PL Modern Heavy Condensed, PL Torino Open
◉ Woodblock

SG1138 Mac ⑥ 1981: Les Usherwood
Flange™ Light

abcdefghijklmnopqrstuvwxyz[äöüßåøæœç]
ABCDEFGHIJKLMNOPQRSTUVWXYZ
1234567890(.,;:?!$&-*)ÄÖÜÅØÆŒÇ

© FSI 1993

SG1168 MAC ⑥ ✏ 1981: Les Usherwood
Flange Light Italic

abcdefghijklmnopqrstuvwxyz[äöüßåøœœç]
ABCDEFGHIJKLMNOPQRSTUVWXYZ
1234567890(.,;:?!$&-)ÄÖÜÅØÆŒÇ*

SG1120 MAC ⑥ ✏ 1981: Les Usherwood
Flange Book

abcdefghijklmnopqrstuvwxyz[äöüßåøæœç]
ABCDEFGHIJKLMNOPQRSTUVWXYZ
1234567890(.,;:?!$&-*)ÄÖÜÅØÆŒÇ

SG1171 MAC ⑥ ✏ 1981: Les Usherwood
Flange Book Italic

abcdefghijklmnopqrstuvwxyz[äöüßåøæœç]
ABCDEFGHIJKLMNOPQRSTUVWXYZ
1234567890(.,;:?!$&-)ÄÖÜÅØÆŒÇ*

SG1169 MAC ⑥ ✏ 1981: Les Usherwood
Flange Medium

abcdefghijklmnopqrstuvwxyz[äöüßåøæœç]
ABCDEFGHIJKLMNOPQRSTUVWXYZ
1234567890(.,;:?!$&-*)ÄÖÜÅØÆŒÇ

SG1170 MAC ⑥ ✏ 1981: Les Usherwood
Flange Medium Italic

abcdefghijklmnopqrstuvwxyz[äöüßåøæœç]
ABCDEFGHIJKLMNOPQRSTUVWXYZ
1234567890(.,;:?!$&-*)ÄÖÜÅØÆŒÇ

SG1172 MAC ⑥ ✏ 1981: Les Usherwood
Flange Bold

abcdefghijklmnopqrstuvwxyz[äöüßåøæœç]
ABCDEFGHIJKLMNOPQRSTUVWXYZ
1234567890(.,;:?!$&-*)ÄÖÜÅØÆŒÇ

SG1173 MAC ⑥ ✏ 1981: Les Usherwood
Flange Bold Italic

abcdefghijklmnopqrstuvwxyz[äöüßåøæœç]
ABCDEFGHIJKLMNOPQRSTUVWXYZ
1234567890(.,;:?!$&-*ÄÖÜÅØÆŒÇ

© FSI 1993

G1517 Mac + PC ④ 1939: Sol. Hess
Flash™ No 373

abcdefghijklmnopqrstuvwxyz[äöüßåøææç]
ABCDEFGHIJKLMNOPQRSTUVWXYZ
1234567890(.,;:?!$&-*){ÄÖÜÅØÆŒÇ}

SG2051 Mac ④ 1939: Sol. Hess
Flash Bold

abcdefghijklmnopqrstuvwxyz[äöüßåøææç]
ABCDEFGHIJKLMNOPQRSTUVWXYZ
1234567890(.,;:?!$&-*)ÄÖÜÅØÆŒÇ

BT851 Mac + PC ④
Flemish Script

abcdefghijklmnopqrstuvwxyz[äöüßåøæœç]
ABCDEFGHIJKLMNOPQRSTUVWXYZ
1234567890(.,;:?!$&-*){ÄÖÜÅØÆŒÇ}

Bitstream Script 4:
Flemish Script, Gando
© Englische Schreibschrift, Embassy, Kuenstler Script, Palace Script

FF2961 Mac + PC ⑥ 1992: Just van Rossum
FF Flightcase™

ABCDEFGHIJKLMNOPQRSTUVWXYZ
1234567890(.,;:?!$&-*)[]ÄÖÜÅØÆŒÇ

FF InstantTypes™:
FF Confidential™, FF Dynamoe, FF Flightcase™, FF Karton™, FF Stamp Gothic™

C989 Mac + PC
ITC Flora & ITC Isadora

ITC Flora & ITC Isadora:
ITC Flora, ITC Isadora

EF382 Mac + PC ④ 1980: Gerard Unger
ITC Flora®

abcdefghijklmnopqrstuvwxyz[äöüßåøæœç]
ABCDEFGHIJKLMNOPQRSTUVWXYZ
1234567890(.,;:?!$&-*){ÄÖÜÅØÆŒÇ}

aa*a*
C989
ITC Flora & ITC Isadora
A2871
ITC Flora & ITC Isadora
©
Demos, Praxis

▶ Regular
The quick brown fox jumps over a Dog. Zwei Boxkämpfer jagen Eva durch Sylt portez ce vieux Whiskey blond qui fume une

▶ **Bold**
The quick brown fox jumps over a Dog. Zwei Boxkämpfer jagen Eva durch Sylt portez ce vieux Whiskey blond qui

© FSI 1993

Florens™
LP2841 — Mac + PC — (3) — 1989: Garrett Boge

abcdefghijklmnopqrstuvwxyz[äöüßåøæœç]
ABCDEFGHIJKLMNOPQRSTUVWXYZ
1234567890(.,;:?!$&-*){ÄÖÜÅØÆŒÇ}

▶ **Regular**
The quick brown fox jumps over a Dog. Zwei Boxkämpfer jagen Eva durch Sylt portez ce vieux Whiskey blond qui fume une pipe aber echt über die Mauer

▶ **Expert**
The quick brown fox jumps over a Dog Zwei Boxkämpfer jagen Eva durch Sylt portez ce vieux Whis key blond qui fume une pipe aber

LetterPerfect 4:
Florens™, Spring™

Floridian Script
C595 — Mac + PC — (4) — (1972)

abcdefghijklmnopqrstuvwxyz[äöüßåøæœç]
ABCDEFGHIJKLMNOPQRSTUVWXYZ
1234567890(.,;:?!$&-*){ÄÖÜÅØÆŒÇ}

Basilica:
Basilica, Floridian Script, Jasper™, Liberty™

Flourish™
ET6390 — Mac + PC — (4) — 1990: Judith Sutcliffe

abcdefghijklmnopqrstuvwxyz[äöüßåøæœç]
ABCDEFGHIJKLMNOPQRSTUVWXYZ
1234567890(.,;:?!$&-*){ÄÖÜÅØÆŒÇ}

▶ **Regular**
The quick brown fox jumps over a Dog. Zwei Boxkämpfer jagen Eva durch Sylt portez ce vieux Whiskey blond qui fume une pipe aber echt über die Mauer

▶ **Bold**
The quick brown fox jumps over a Dog. Zwei Boxkämpfer jagen Eva durch Sylt portez ce vieux Whiskey blond qui fume une pipe aber echt über die

▶ **Special**
The quick brown fox jumps over a Dog. 123 4567 890 Zwei Boxkämpfer jagen Eva durch Sylt portez ce vieux Whiskey blond qui fume une pipe aber echt über

▶ **Bold Special**
The quick brown fox jumps over a Dog. 123 4567 890 Zwei Boxkämpfer jagen Eva durch Sylt portez ce vieux Whiskey blond qui fume une pipe

Fluidum™ Bold
C993 — Mac + PC — (4) — 1951: Aldo Novarese

abcdefghijklmnopqrstuvwxyz[äöüßåøæœç]
ABCDEFGHIJKLMNOPQRSTUVWXYZ
1234567890(.,;:?!$&-*)◊ÄÖÜÅØÆŒÇ♦

© FSI 1993

▼ C993 Mac + PC Fluidum™ Bold

Headlines 83S:
Barclay™ Open, Delphian™ Open, Fluidum™ Bold, PL Bernhardt, PL Britannia Bold, PL Fiorello™ Condensed, PL Modern Heavy Condensed, PL Torino Open

---

A564 Mac + PC ①
Flyer™ Condensed

abcdefghijklmnopqrstuvwxyz[äöüßåøæœç]
ABCDEFGHIJKLMNOPQRSTUVWXYZ
1234567890(.,;:?!$&-*){ÄÖÜÅØÆŒÇ}

▶ Black Condensed
The quick brown fox jumps over a Dog. Zwei Boxkämpfer jagen Eva durch Sylt portez ce vieux Whiskey blond qui fume une pipe

▶ Extra Black Condensed
The quick brown fox jumps over a Dog. Zwei Boxkämpfer jagen Eva durch Sylt portez ce vieux Whiskey blond qui fume une pipe aber echt über die Mauer

German Display 2:
Banco™, Charme™, Flyer™ Condensed, Wilhelm Klingspor Gotisch™

BT1295 Mac + PC ① ✎ 1962: Konrad Bauer, Walter Baum
Folio™ 1

abcdefghijklmnopqrstuvwxyz[äöüßåøæœç]
ABCDEFGHIJKLMNOPQRSTUVWXYZ
1234567890(.,;:?!$&-*){ÄÖÜÅØÆŒÇ}

aa*a*
A173
Folio, Lt, Med, Bd,
BdCon, ExtBd

▶ Light
The quick brown fox jumps over a Dog. Zwei Boxkämpfer jagen Eva durch Sylt portez ce vieux Whiskey blond qui fume une

▶ Light Italic
The quick brown fox jumps over a Dog. Zwei Boxkämpfer jagen Eva durch Sylt portez ce vieux Whiskey blond qui fume

▶ Book
The quick brown fox jumps over a Dog. Zwei Boxkämpfer jagen Eva durch Sylt portez ce vieux Whiskey blond qui fume

▶ Bold
The quick brown fox jumps over a Dog. Zwei Boxkämpfer jagen Eva durch Sylt portez ce vieux

---

BT1296 Mac + PC ① ✎ 1962: Konrad Bauer, Walter Baum
Folio 2

abcdefghijklmnopqrstuvwxyz[äöüßåøæœç]
ABCDEFGHIJKLMNOPQRSTUVWXYZ
1234567890(.,;:?!$&-*){ÄÖÜÅØÆŒÇ}

aa*a*
A173
Folio, Lt, Med, Bd,
BdCon, ExtBd

▶ Medium
The quick brown fox jumps over a Dog. Zwei Boxkämpfer jagen Eva durch Sylt portez ce vieux Whiskey blond qui

▶ Extra Bold
The quick brown fox jumps over a Dog. Zwei Boxkämpfer jagen Eva durch Sylt portez ce

© FSI 1993

▼ BT1296 Mac + PC Folio 2
▶ Bold Condensed
The quick brown fox jumps over a Dog. Zwei Boxkämpfer jagen Eva durch Sylt portez ce vieux Whiskey blond qui fume une pipe aber echt über die

L2577 Mac ⑥ 1991: Alan Meeks
Follies™

ABCDEFGHIJKLMNOPQRSTUVWXYZ
1234567890(.,;:?!$&-*)[]ÄÖÜÅØÆŒÇ

M6477 Mac + PC ③ 1986: Ong Chong Wah
Footlight™

abcdefghijklmnopqrstuvwxyz[äöüßåøæœç]
ABCDEFGHIJKLMNOPQRSTUVWXYZ
1234567890(.,;:?!$&~*){ÄÖÜÅØÆŒÇ}

Della Robbia, Adroit

▶ Regular
The quick brown fox jumps over a Dog. Zwei Boxkämpfer jagen Eva durch Sylt portez ce vieux Whiskey blond qui fume

▶ Italic
The quick brown fox jumps over a Dog. Zwei Boxkämpfer jagen Eva durch Sylt portez ce vieux Whiskey blond qui fume une

▶ Bold
The quick brown fox jumps over a Dog. Zwei Boxkämpfer jagen Eva durch Sylt portez ce vieux Whiskey blond qui

▶ Bold Italic
The quick brown fox jumps over a Dog. Zwei Boxkämpfer jagen Eva durch Sylt portez ce vieux Whiskey blond qui fume

M6383 Mac + PC ③ 1986: Ong Chong Wah
Footlight Light

abcdefghijklmnopqrstuvwxyz[äöüßåøæœç]
ABCDEFGHIJKLMNOPQRSTUVWXYZ
1234567890(.,;:?!$&~*){ÄÖÜÅØÆŒÇ}

Della Robbia, Adroit

▶ Light
The quick brown fox jumps over a Dog. Zwei Boxkämpfer jagen Eva durch Sylt portez ce vieux Whiskey blond qui fume une

▶ Light Italic
The quick brown fox jumps over a Dog. Zwei Boxkämpfer jagen Eva durch Sylt portez ce vieux Whiskey blond qui fume une pipe aber

▶ Extra Bold
The quick brown fox jumps over a Dog. Zwei Boxkämpfer jagen Eva durch Sylt portez ce vieux Whiskey blond

▶ Extra Bold Italic
The quick brown fox jumps over a Dog. Zwei Boxkämpfer jagen Eva durch Sylt portez ce vieux Whiskey blond qui

© FSI 1993

L2578 Mac ⑥ 1978: Martin Wait
Forest™ Shaded

abcdefghijklmnopqrstuvwxyz[äöüßåøæœç]
ABCDEFGHIJKLMNOPQRSTUVWXYZ
1234567890(.,;:?!$&-*)ÄÖÜÅØÆŒÇ

TF657 Mac + PC ① 1985: Joseph W. Treacy
TF Forever™ A

abcdefghijklmnopqrstuvwxyz[äöüßåøæœç]
ABCDEFGHIJKLMNOPQRSTUVWXYZ
1234567890(.,;:?!$&-*){ÄÖÜÅØÆŒÇ}

▶ Regular
The quick brown fox jumps over a Dog. Zwei Boxkämpfer jagen Eva durch Sylt portez ce vieux Whiskey blond qui fume une pipe aber

▶ Italic
The quick brown fox jumps over a Dog. Zwei Boxkämpfer jagen Eva durch Sylt portez ce vieux Whiskey blond qui fume une pipe aber echt

▶ Extra Bold
The quick brown fox jumps over a Dog. Zwei Boxkämpfer jagen Eva durch Sylt portez ce vieux Whiskey blond qui

▶ Extra Bold Italic
The quick brown fox jumps over a Dog. Zwei Boxkämpfer jagen Eva durch Sylt portez ce vieux Whiskey blond qui fume

TF658 Mac + PC ① 1987: Joseph W. Treacy
TF Forever B

abcdefghijklmnopqrstuvwxyz[äöüßåøæœç]
ABCDEFGHIJKLMNOPQRSTUVWXYZ
1234567890(.,;:?!$&-*){ÄÖÜÅØÆŒÇ}

▶ Thin
The quick brown fox jumps over a Dog. Zwei Boxkämpfer jagen Eva durch Sylt portez ce vieux Whiskey blond qui fume une pipe aber

▶ Thin Italic
The quick brown fox jumps over a Dog. Zwei Boxkämpfer jagen Eva durch Sylt portez ce vieux Whiskey blond qui fume une pipe aber echt

▶ Medium
The quick brown fox jumps over a Dog. Zwei Boxkämpfer jagen Eva durch Sylt portez ce vieux Whiskey blond qui fume une pipe

▶ Medium Italic
The quick brown fox jumps over a Dog. Zwei Boxkämpfer jagen Eva durch Sylt portez ce vieux Whiskey blond qui fume une pipe aber

TF659 Mac + PC ① 1989: Joseph W. Treacy
TF Forever C

abcdefghijklmnopqrstuvwxyz[äöüßåøæœç]
ABCDEFGHIJKLMNOPQRSTUVWXYZ
1234567890(.,;:?!$&-*){ÄÖÜÅØÆŒÇ}

▶ Extra Light
The quick brown fox jumps over a Dog. Zwei Boxkämpfer jagen Eva durch Sylt portez ce vieux Whiskey blond qui fume une pipe aber

▶ Extra Light Italic
The quick brown fox jumps over a Dog. Zwei Boxkämpfer jagen Eva durch Sylt portez ce vieux Whiskey blond qui fume une pipe aber echt

© FSI 1993

▼ TF659 Mac + PC **TF Forever C**

▶ Demi Italic
The quick brown fox jumps over a Dog. Zwei Boxkämpfer jagen Eva durch Sylt portez ce vieux Whiskey blond qui fume une pipe

▶ Demi Bold
The quick brown fox jumps over a Dog. Zwei Boxkämpfer jagen Eva durch Sylt portez ce vieux Whiskey blond qui fume une

TF660 Mac + PC ① 1990: Joseph W. Treacy
TF Forever D

abcdefghijklmnopqrstuvwxyz[äöüßåøæœç]
ABCDEFGHIJKLMNOPQRSTUVWXYZ
1234567890(.,;:?!$&-*){ÄÖÜÅØÆŒÇ}

▶ Light
The quick brown fox jumps over a Dog. Zwei Boxkämpfer jagen Eva durch Sylt portez ce vieux Whiskey blond qui fume une pipe aber

▶ Light Italic
The quick brown fox jumps over a Dog. Zwei Boxkämpfer jagen Eva durch Sylt portez ce vieux Whiskey blond qui fume une pipe aber echt

▶ Bold
The quick brown fox jumps over a Dog. Zwei Boxkämpfer jagen Eva durch Sylt portez ce vieux Whiskey blond qui fume

▶ Bold Italic
The quick brown fox jumps over a Dog. Zwei Boxkämpfer jagen Eva durch Sylt portez ce vieux Whiskey blond qui fume une

AB1049 Mac + PC ① 1984: Bernd Möllenstädt
Formata®

abcdefghijklmnopqrstuvwxyz[äöüßåøæœç]
ABCDEFGHIJKLMNOPQRSTUVWXYZ
1234567890(.,;:?!$&-*){ÄÖÜÅØÆŒÇ}

▶ Light
The quick brown fox jumps over a Dog. Zwei Boxkämpfer jagen Eva durch Sylt portez ce vieux Whiskey blond qui fume une

▶ Light Italic
The quick brown fox jumps over a Dog. Zwei Boxkämpfer jagen Eva durch Sylt portez ce vieux Whiskey blond qui fume une

▶ Regular
The quick brown fox jumps over a Dog. Zwei Boxkämpfer jagen Eva durch Sylt portez ce vieux Whiskey blond qui fume

▶ Italic
The quick brown fox jumps over a Dog. Zwei Boxkämpfer jagen Eva durch Sylt portez ce vieux Whiskey blond qui fume

▶ Medium
The quick brown fox jumps over a Dog. Zwei Boxkämpfer jagen Eva durch Sylt portez ce vieux Whiskey blond qui

▶ Medium Italic
The quick brown fox jumps over a Dog. Zwei Boxkämpfer jagen Eva durch Sylt portez ce vieux Whiskey blond

▶ Bold
The quick brown fox jumps over a Dog. Zwei Boxkämpfer jagen Eva durch Sylt portez ce vieux Whiskey blond

▶ Bold Italic
The quick brown fox jumps over a Dog. Zwei Boxkämpfer jagen Eva durch Sylt portez ce vieux Whiskey

© FSI 1993

AB6068　Mac + PC　①　✎ 1988: Bernd Möllenstädt
Berthold Formata Outline

abcdefghijklmnopqrstuvwxyz[äöüßåøæœç]
ABCDEFGHIJKLMNOPQRSTUVWXYZ
1234567890(.,;:?!$&-*){ÄÖÜÅØÆŒÇ}

Berthold AG Book Stencil, et al:
Berthold AG Book Stencil, Berthold AG Old Face Shaded, Berthold Barmeno, Berthold Cosmos, Berthold Formata Outline

AB6653　Mac + PC　①　✎ 1988: Bernd Möllenstädt
Formata Condensed

abcdefghijklmnopqrstuvwxyz[äöüßåøæœç]
ABCDEFGHIJKLMNOPQRSTUVWXYZ
1234567890(.,;:?!$&-*){ÄÖÜÅØÆŒÇ}

▶ Light Condensed
The quick brown fox jumps over a Dog. Zwei Boxkämpfer jagen Eva durch Sylt portez ce vieux Whiskey blond qui fume une pipe aber echt über die

▶ Light Condensed Italic
The quick brown fox jumps over a Dog. Zwei Boxkämpfer jagen Eva durch Sylt portez ce vieux Whiskey blond qui fume une pipe aber echt über die

▶ Regular Condensed
The quick brown fox jumps over a Dog. Zwei Boxkämpfer jagen Eva durch Sylt portez ce vieux Whiskey blond qui fume une pipe aber echt

▶ Condensed Italic
The quick brown fox jumps over a Dog. Zwei Boxkämpfer jagen Eva durch Sylt portez ce vieux Whiskey blond qui fume une pipe aber echt

▶ Medium Condensed
The quick brown fox jumps over a Dog. Zwei Boxkämpfer jagen Eva durch Sylt portez ce vieux Whiskey blond qui fume une pipe aber echt

▶ Medium Condensed Italic
The quick brown fox jumps over a Dog. Zwei Boxkämpfer jagen Eva durch Sylt portez ce vieux Whiskey blond qui fume une pipe aber

▶ Bold Condensed
The quick brown fox jumps over a Dog. Zwei Boxkämpfer jagen Eva durch Sylt portez ce vieux Whiskey blond qui fume une

▶ Bold Condensed Italic
The quick brown fox jumps over a Dog. Zwei Boxkämpfer jagen Eva durch Sylt portez ce vieux Whiskey blond qui fume une

▶ Condensed Outline
The quick brown fox jumps over a Dog. Zwei Boxkämpfer jagen Eva durch Sylt portez ce vieux Whiskey blond qui fume une pipe aber echt

M6331　Mac + PC　④
Forte et al

Forte et al:
Forte, Klang, Mercurius Bold Script

© FSI 1993

A6088 Mac + PC ④
Forte et al

Forte et al:
Forte, Klang, Mercurius Bold Script

M267 Mac + PC ④ 🖉 1962: Carl Reissburger
Forte™

abcdefghijklmnopqrstuvwxyz[äöüßåøæœç]
ABCDEFGHIJKLMNOPQRSTUVWXYZ
1234567890(.,;:?!$&-*){ÄÖÜÅØÆŒÇ}

Headliners 3:
Braggadocio™, Figaro®, Forte™, Klang™
aaa ☞ A6088
Forte et al
☞ M6331

G1103 Mac + PC ② 🖉 1911: F. W. Goudy
Forum No. 274™

abcdefghijklmnopqrstuvwxyz[äöüßåøæœç]
ABCDEFGHIJKLMNOPQRSTUVWXYZ
1234567890(.,;:?!$&*){ÄÖÜÅØÆŒÇ}

© Hadriano

▶ Regular
The quick brown fox jumps over a Dog. Zwei Boxkämpfer jagen Eva durch Sylt portez ce vieux Whiskey blond qui fume

▶ Italic
The quick brown fox jumps over a Dog. Zwei Boxkämpfer jagen Eva durch Sylt portez ce vieux Whiskey blond qui fume une pipe aber echt

---

BT798 Mac + PC
Bitstream Fraktur 1

Bitstream Fraktur 1:
American Text™, Cloister Black, Fraktur, London Text™

BT798 Mac + PC ⑦
Fraktur

abcdefghijklmnopqrstuvwxyz[äöüßåøœç]
ABCDEFGHIJKLMNOPQRSTUVWXYZ
1234567890(.,;:?!$&-*){ÄÖÜÅØÆŒÇ}

Bitstream Fraktur 1:
American Text™, Cloister Black, Fraktur, London Text™

G1518 Mac + PC ④ 🖉 1991: (G. G. Lange, 1954) Jonn B. Frame
Francis No. 982™

abcdefghijklmnopqrstuvwxyz[äöüssåøæoeç]
ABCDEFGHIJKLMNOPQRSTUVWXYZ
1234567890(.,;:?!$&-){ÄÖÜÅØÆŒÇ}*

© FSI 1993

F 14

Frankfurter™
EF6445 Mac + PC ⑥ 1978: Alan Meeks

abcdefghijklmnopqrstuvwxyz[äöüßåøæœç]
ABCDEFGHIJKLMNOPQRSTUVWXYZ
1234567890(.,;:?!$&-*)ÄÖÜÅØÆŒÇ

aa*a*
L2579
Frankfurter Medium, Reg
L6124
Frankfurter, Reg
L6125
Frankfurter Inline, Inline
L6591
Frankfurter Hilite, Hilite
ⓒ
Chromium, Vega, V.A.G. Rounded

▶ Medium
The quick brown fox jumps over a Dog. Zwei Boxkämpfer jagen Eva durch Sylt portez ce vieux Whiskey blond qui fume une

▶ Inline
THE QUICK BROWN FOX JUMPS OVER A DOG. ZWEI BOXKÄMPFER JAGEN EVA DURCH SYLT PORTEZ CE

▶ Solid
THE QUICK BROWN FOX JUMPS OVER A DOG. ZWEI BOXKÄMPFER JAGEN EVA DURCH SYLT PORTEZ CE

▶ Highlight
THE QUICK BROWN FOX JUMPS OVER A DOG. ZWEI BOXKÄMPFER JAGEN EVA DURCH SYLT PORTEZ CE

Frankie™
TO6660 Mac ⑥ 1993: (M. F. Benton, 1904) Meseguer, Dávila

abcdefghijklmnopqrstuvwxyz[äöüßåøæœç]
ABCDEFGHIJKLMNOPQRSTUVWXYZ
1234567890(.,;:?!$&-*){ÄÖÜÅØÆŒÇ}

Type-ø-Tones Pack 3:
Cortada™, Frankie™

ATF Franklin Gothic
BT1298 Mac + PC ① 1904: M. F. Benton

abcdefghijklmnopqrstuvwxyz[äöüßåøæœç]
ABCDEFGHIJKLMNOPQRSTUVWXYZ
1234567890(.,;:?!$&-*){ÄÖÜÅØÆŒÇ}

aa*a*
A217
Franklin Gothic No. 2, Reg, Con, ExtCon

▶ Regular
The quick brown fox jumps over a Dog. Zwei Boxkämpfer jagen Eva durch Sylt portez ce vieux Whis-

▶ Condensed
The quick brown fox jumps over a Dog. Zwei Boxkämpfer jagen Eva durch Sylt portez ce vieux Whiskey blond qui fume une pipe aber

▶ Italic
The quick brown fox jumps over a Dog. Zwei Boxkämpfer jagen Eva durch Sylt portez ce vieux Whiskey blond

▶ Extra Condensed
The quick brown fox jumps over a Dog. Zwei Boxkämpfer jagen Eva durch Sylt portez ce vieux Whiskey blond qui fume une pipe aber echt über die Mauer gesprungen und auch

ITC Franklin Gothic® 1
BT1299 Mac + PC ① 1980: (M. F. Benton, 1904) Vic Caruso

abcdefghijklmnopqrstuvwxyz[äöüßåøæœç]
ABCDEFGHIJKLMNOPQRSTUVWXYZ
1234567890(.,;:?!$&-*){ÄÖÜÅØÆŒÇ}

© FSI 1993

▼ BT1299 Mac + PC ITC Franklin Gothic® 1

aaa
A042
ITC Franklin Gothic, Bk, BkObl, Demi, DemiObl, Hvy, HvyObl

▶ Book
The quick brown fox jumps over a Dog. Zwei Boxkämpfer jagen Eva durch Sylt portez ce vieux Whiskey blond qui fume une

▶ Book Italic
The quick brown fox jumps over a Dog. Zwei Boxkämpfer jagen Eva durch Sylt portez ce vieux Whiskey blond qui fume une

▶ Demi
The quick brown fox jumps over a Dog. Zwei Boxkämpfer jagen Eva durch Sylt portez ce vieux Whiskey blond qui

▶ Demi Italic
The quick brown fox jumps over a Dog. Zwei Boxkämpfer jagen Eva durch Sylt portez ce vieux Whiskey blond qui

BT1300 Mac + PC ① ✎ 1980: (M. F. Benton, 1904) Vic Caruso

ITC Franklin Gothic 2

abcdefghijklmnopqrstuvwxyz[äöüßåøæœç]
ABCDEFGHIJKLMNOPQRSTUVWXYZ
1234567890(.,;:?!$&-*){ÄÖÜÅØÆŒÇ}

aaa
A042
ITC Franklin Gothic, Bk, BkObl, Demi, DemiObl, Hvy, HvyObl

▶ Medium
The quick brown fox jumps over a Dog. Zwei Boxkämpfer jagen Eva durch Sylt portez ce vieux Whiskey blond qui fume

▶ Medium Italic
The quick brown fox jumps over a Dog. Zwei Boxkämpfer jagen Eva durch Sylt portez ce vieux Whiskey blond qui fume

▶ Heavy
The quick brown fox jumps over a Dog. Zwei Boxkämpfer jagen Eva durch Sylt portez ce vieux Whiskey

▶ Heavy Italic
The quick brown fox jumps over a Dog. Zwei Boxkämpfer jagen Eva durch Sylt portez ce vieux Whiskey

EF2762 Mac + PC ① ✎ 1991: (M. F. Benton, 1904) David Berlow

ITC Franklin Gothic 3 Condensed

abcdefghijklmnopqrstuvwxyz[äöüßåøæœç]
ABCDEFGHIJKLMNOPQRSTUVWXYZ
1234567890(.,;:?!$&-*){ÄÖÜÅØÆŒÇ}

▶ Book Condensed
The quick brown fox jumps over a Dog. Zwei Boxkämpfer jagen Eva durch Sylt portez ce vieux Whiskey blond qui fume une pipe aber echt

▶ Book Condensed Italic
The quick brown fox jumps over a Dog. Zwei Boxkämpfer jagen Eva durch Sylt portez ce vieux Whiskey blond qui fume une pipe aber echt

▶ Book Condensed Small Caps
THE QUICK BROWN FOX JUMPS OVER A DOG. 123 4567 890 ZWEI BOXKÄMPFER JAGEN EVA DURCH SYLT PORTEZ CE VIEUX WHISKEY BLOND QUI FUME UNE PIPE ABER

▶ Demi Condensed
The quick brown fox jumps over a Dog. Zwei Boxkämpfer jagen Eva durch Sylt portez ce vieux Whiskey blond qui fume une pipe aber echt

▶ Demi Condensed Italic
The quick brown fox jumps over a Dog. Zwei Boxkämpfer jagen Eva durch Sylt portez ce vieux Whiskey blond qui fume une pipe aber echt

© FSI 1993

EF2763 Mac + PC ① 1991: (M. F. Benton, 1904) David Berlow
ITC Franklin Gothic 4 Condensed

abcdefghijklmnopqrstuvwxyz[äöüßåøæœç]
ABCDEFGHIJKLMNOPQRSTUVWXYZ
1234567890(.,;:?!$&-*){ÄÖÜÅØÆŒÇ}

▶ **Medium Condensed**
The quick brown fox jumps over a Dog. Zwei Boxkämpfer jagen Eva durch Sylt portez ce vieux Whiskey blond qui fume une pipe aber echt

▶ *Medium Condensed Italic*
The quick brown fox jumps over a Dog. Zwei Boxkämpfer jagen Eva durch Sylt portez ce vieux Whiskey blond qui fume une pipe aber echt

▶ **Medium Cond. Small Caps**
THE QUICK BROWN FOX JUMPS OVER A DOG. 123 4567 890 ZWEI BOXKÄMPFER JAGEN EVA DURCH SYLT PORTEZ CE VIEUX WHISKEY BLOND QUI FUME UNE PIPE

EF2764 Mac + PC ① 1991: (M. F. Benton, 1904) David Berlow
ITC Franklin Gothic 5 Compressed

abcdefghijklmnopqrstuvwxyz[äöüßåøæœç]
ABCDEFGHIJKLMNOPQRSTUVWXYZ
1234567890(.,;:?!$&-*){ÄÖÜÅØÆŒÇ}

▶ **Book Compressed**
The quick brown fox jumps over a Dog. Zwei Boxkämpfer jagen Eva durch Sylt portez ce vieux Whiskey blond qui fume une pipe aber echt über die Mauer gesprungen und

▶ *Book Compressed Italic*
The quick brown fox jumps over a Dog. Zwei Boxkämpfer jagen Eva durch Sylt portez ce vieux Whiskey blond qui fume une pipe aber echt über die Mauer gesprungen und

▶ **Demi Compressed**
The quick brown fox jumps over a Dog. Zwei Boxkämpfer jagen Eva durch Sylt portez ce vieux Whiskey blond qui fume une pipe aber echt über die Mauer

▶ ***Demi Compressed Italic***
The quick brown fox jumps over a Dog. Zwei Boxkämpfer jagen Eva durch Sylt portez ce vieux Whiskey blond qui fume une pipe aber echt über die Mauer

EF2765 Mac + PC ① 1991: (M. F. Benton, 1904) David Berlow
ITC Franklin Gothic 6 X-Compressed

abcdefghijklmnopqrstuvwxyz[äöüßåøæœç]
ABCDEFGHIJKLMNOPQRSTUVWXYZ
1234567890(.,;:?!$&-*){ÄÖÜÅØÆŒÇ}

▶ **Book X-Compressed**
The quick brown fox jumps over a Dog. Zwei Boxkämpfer jagen Eva durch Sylt portez ce vieux Whiskey blond qui fume une pipe aber echt über die Mauer gesprungen und auch smørebrød en ysjes natuurlijk. The quick brown fox

▶ **Demi X-Compressed**
The quick brown fox jumps over a Dog. Zwei Boxkämpfer jagen Eva durch Sylt portez ce vieux Whiskey blond qui fume une pipe aber echt über die Mauer gesprungen und auch smørebrød en ysjes natuurlijk. The quick brown fox

BT799 Mac + PC
Bitstream Freeform Gothic

Bitstream Freeform Gothic:
Bernhard, Block Condensed

L2580 Mac   ④   ✎ 1981: Martin Wait
Freestyle Script

abcdefghijklmnopqrstuvwxyz [äöüßåøæœç]
ABCDEFGHIJKLMNOPQRSTUVWXYZ
1234567890(.,;:?!$&-*)ÄÖÜÅØÆŒÇ

L2581 Mac   ④   ✎ 1986: Martin Wait
Freestyle Script Bold

abcdefghijklmnopqrstuvwxyz[äöüßåøæœç]
ABCDEFGHIJKLMNOPQRSTUVWXYZ
1234567890(.,;:?!$&-*)ÄÖÜÅØÆŒÇ

F6344 Mac   ⑥
A*I French XXX Condensed™

ABCDEFGHIJKLMNOPQRSTUVWXYZ/ABCDEFGHIJKLMNOPQRSTUVWXYZ1234567890(.,?!$&-*)!§

A*I Wood Types 1:
A*I Barrel, A*I Box Gothic, A*I French XXX Condensed™, A*I Painter™, A*I Tuscan Egyptian™, Antique Condensed
© P. T. Barnum, Egyptian, Playbill, Old Towne No. 536, Ponderosa, Figaro

A012 Mac + PC
Friz Quadrata

Friz Quadrata:
Friz Quadrata™, ITC Benguiat
© Bitstream Amerigo, Albertus, ITC Symbol, ITC Élan

A012 Mac + PC   ⑥   ✎ 1974: (Ernst Friz, 1965) Victor Caruso
Friz Quadrata™

abcdefghijklmnopqrstuvwxyz[äöüßåøæœç]
ABCDEFGHIJKLMNOPQRSTUVWXYZ
1234567890(.,;:?!$&-*){ÄÖÜÅØÆŒÇ}

aaa
BT1303
Friz Quadrata, Rom, Bd
©
Bitstream Amerigo,
Albertus, ITC Symbol,
ITC Élan

▶ Roman
The quick brown fox jumps over a Dog. Zwei Boxkämpfer jagen Eva durch Sylt portez ce vieux Whiskey blond qui fume

▶ **Bold**
The quick brown fox jumps over a Dog. Zwei Boxkämpfer jagen Eva durch Sylt portez ce vieux Whiskey blond qui fume

Friz Quadrata:
Friz Quadrata™, ITC Benguiat

© FSI 1993

A146 Mac + PC ① ✎ 1976: Adrian Frutiger

Frutiger™

abcdefghijklmnopqrstuvwxyz[äöüßåøæœç]
ABCDEFGHIJKLMNOPQRSTUVWXYZ
1234567890(.,;:?!$&-*){ÄÖÜÅØÆŒÇ}

aaa
BT1366
Nuptial Script, Reg
BT1367
Old Dreadful No. 7™, Reg
ⓒ
Myriad

▶ 45 Light
The quick brown fox jumps over a Dog. Zwei Boxkämpfer jagen Eva durch Sylt portez ce vieux Whiskey blond qui fume une

▶ 46 Light Italic
The quick brown fox jumps over a Dog. Zwei Boxkämpfer jagen Eva durch Sylt portez ce vieux Whiskey blond qui fume une

▶ 55 Regular
The quick brown fox jumps over a Dog. Zwei Boxkämpfer jagen Eva durch Sylt portez ce vieux Whiskey blond

▶ 56 Italic
The quick brown fox jumps over a Dog. Zwei Boxkämpfer jagen Eva durch Sylt portez ce vieux Whiskey blond

▶ 65 Bold
The quick brown fox jumps over a Dog. Zwei Boxkämpfer jagen Eva durch Sylt portez ce vieux Whiskey blond

▶ 66 Bold Italic
The quick brown fox jumps over a Dog. Zwei Boxkämpfer jagen Eva durch Sylt portez ce vieux Whiskey blond

▶ 75 Black
The quick brown fox jumps over a Dog. Zwei Boxkämpfer jagen Eva durch Sylt portez ce vieux

▶ 76 Black Italic
The quick brown fox jumps over a Dog. Zwei Boxkämpfer jagen Eva durch Sylt portez ce vieux

▶ 95 Ultra Black
The quick brown fox jumps over a Dog. Zwei Boxkämpfer jagen Eva durch Sylt portez ce

A2865 Mac + PC ① ✎ 1985: Adrian Frutiger

Frutiger Condensed

abcdefghijklmnopqrstuvwxyz[äöüßåøæœç]
ABCDEFGHIJKLMNOPQRSTUVWXYZ
1234567890(.,;:?!$&-*){ÄÖÜÅØÆŒÇ}

▶ 47 Light Condensed
The quick brown fox jumps over a Dog. Zwei Boxkämpfer jagen Eva durch Sylt portez ce vieux Whiskey blond qui fume une pipe aber echt

▶ 57 Regular Condensed
The quick brown fox jumps over a Dog. Zwei Boxkämpfer jagen Eva durch Sylt portez ce vieux Whiskey blond qui fume une pipe aber echt

▶ 77 Black Condensed
The quick brown fox jumps over a Dog. Zwei Boxkämpfer jagen Eva durch Sylt portez ce vieux Whiskey blond qui fume une

▶ 87 Extra Black Condensed
The quick brown fox jumps over a Dog. Zwei Boxkämpfer jagen Eva durch Sylt portez ce vieux Whiskey blond qui fume

▼ A2865 Mac + PC **Frutiger Condensed**

▶ 97 Extra Black Condensed
The quick brown fox jumps over a Dog. Zwei Boxkämpfer jagen Eva durch Sylt portez ce vieux Whiskey blond qui

---

FS2835 Mac + PC ⑤ 1991: Max Kisman
Fudoni™

abcdefghijklmnopqrstuvwxyz[äöüßåøæœç]
ABCDEFGHIJKLMNOPQRSTUVWXYZ
1234567890(.,:;?!$&-*){ÄÖÜÅØÆŒÇ}

▶ One
The quick brown fox jumps over a Dog. Zwei Boxkämpfer jagen Eva durch Sylt portez ce vieux Whiskey blond qui fume une

▶ Two
The quick brown fox jumps over a Dog. Zwei Boxkämpfer jagen Eva durch Sylt portez ce vieux Whiskey blond qui fume

▶ Three
The quick brown fox jumps over a Dog. Zwei Boxkämpfer jagen Eva durch Sylt portez ce

---

MC2919 Mac + PC ⑥ L. Fumarolo
Fumo Dropshadow™

abcdefghijklmnopqrstuvwxyz[äöüßåøæœç]
ABCDEFGHIJKLMNOPQRSTUVWXYZ
1234567890(.,:;?!$&-*){ÄÖÜÅØÆŒÇ}

A046 Mac + PC ① 1928-32: Paul Renner
Futura™ 1

abcdefghijklmnopqrstuvwxyz[äöüßåøæœç]
ABCDEFGHIJKLMNOPQRSTUVWXYZ
1234567890(.,:;?!$&-*){ÄÖÜÅØÆŒÇ}

aa*a*
EF1071
Futura 1, Lt, LtObl, Bd, BdObl
EF1072
Futura 2, Bk, BkObl, DemiBd, DemiBdObl
BT1304
Futura 1, Lt, LtObl, ExtBlk, ExtBlkObl
BT1305
Futura 2, Med, MedObl, Bd, BdObl

▶ Light
The quick brown fox jumps over a Dog. Zwei Boxkämpfer jagen Eva durch Sylt portez ce vieux Whiskey blond qui fume une

▶ Light Oblique
The quick brown fox jumps over a Dog. Zwei Boxkämpfer jagen Eva durch Sylt portez ce vieux Whiskey blond qui fume une

▶ Book
The quick brown fox jumps over a Dog. Zwei Boxkämpfer jagen Eva durch Sylt portez ce vieux Whiskey blond qui fume

▶ Book Oblique
The quick brown fox jumps over a Dog. Zwei Boxkämpfer jagen Eva durch Sylt portez ce vieux Whiskey blond qui fume

▶ Bold
The quick brown fox jumps over a Dog. Zwei Boxkämpfer jagen, Eva durch Sylt portez ce vieux

▶ Bold Oblique
The quick brown fox jumps over a Dog. Zwei Boxkämpfer jagen Eva durch Sylt portez ce vieux

© FSI 1993

A045 Mac + PC ① ✏ 1928-32: Paul Renner
Futura 2

abcdefghijklmnopqrstuvwxyz[äöüßåøæœç]
ABCDEFGHIJKLMNOPQRSTUVWXYZ
1234567890(.,;:?!$&-*){ÄÖÜÅØÆŒÇ}

aaa
EF1073
Futura 3, Med, MedObl,
Hvy, ExtBd, ExtBdObl
BT1304
Futura 1, Lt, LtObl,
ExtBlk, ExtBlkObl
BT1305
Futura 2, Med, MedObl,
Bd, BdObl
BT1306
Futura 3, Bk, BkObl,
Hvy, HvyObl

▶ Medium
The quick brown fox jumps over a Dog. Zwei Boxkämpfer jagen Eva durch Sylt portez ce vieux Whiskey blond qui fume une

▶ Medium Oblique
The quick brown fox jumps over a Dog. Zwei Boxkämpfer jagen Eva durch Sylt portez ce vieux Whiskey blond qui fume une

▶ Heavy
The quick brown fox jumps over a Dog. Zwei Boxkämpfer jagen Eva durch Sylt portez ce vieux Whiskey blond qui fume

▶ Heavy Oblique
The quick brown fox jumps over a Dog. Zwei Boxkämpfer jagen Eva durch Sylt portez ce vieux Whiskey blond qui fume

▶ Extra Bold
The quick brown fox jumps over a Dog. Zwei Boxk mpfer jagen Eva durch Sylt

▶ Extra Bold Oblique
The quick brown fox jumps over a Dog. Zwei Boxk mpfer jagen Eva durch Sylt

A047 Mac + PC ① ✏ 1928-32: Paul Renner
Futura Condensed

abcdefghijklmnopqrstuvwxyz[äöüßåøæœç]
ABCDEFGHIJKLMNOPQRSTUVWXYZ
1234567890(.,;:?!$&-*){ÄÖÜÅØÆŒÇ}

aaa
EF1074
Futura 4, LtCon,
LtConObl, BdCon,
BdConObl
EF1075
Futura 5, MedCon,
MedConObl, ExtBdCon,
ExtBdConObl
BT1307
Futura 4, LtCon,
MedCon, BdCon,
BdConObl
BT1308
Futura 5, ExtBlkCon,
ExtBlkConObl

▶ Light Condensed
The quick brown fox jumps over a Dog. Zwei Boxkämpfer jagen Eva durch Sylt portez ce vieux Whiskey blond qui fume une pipe aber echt über die Mauer gesprungen und auch

▶ Light Condensed Oblique
The quick brown fox jumps over a Dog. Zwei Boxkämpfer jagen Eva durch Sylt portez ce vieux Whiskey blond qui fume une pipe aber echt über die Mauer gesprungen und auch

▶ Medium Condensed
The quick brown fox jumps over a Dog. Zwei Boxkämpfer jagen Eva durch Sylt portez ce vieux Whiskey blond qui fume une pipe aber echt über die Mauer gesprungen und auch

▶ Medium Condensed Oblique
The quick brown fox jumps over a Dog. Zwei Boxkämpfer jagen Eva durch Sylt portez ce vieux Whiskey blond qui fume une pipe aber echt über die Mauer gesprungen und auch

▶ Bold Condensed
The quick brown fox jumps over a Dog. Zwei Boxkämpfer jagen Eva durch Sylt portez ce vieux Whiskey blond qui fume une pipe aber echt

▶ Bold Condensed Oblique
The quick brown fox jumps over a Dog. Zwei Boxkämpfer jagen Eva durch Sylt portez ce vieux Whiskey blond qui fume une pipe aber echt

▶ Extra Bold Condensed
The quick brown fox jumps over a Dog. Zwei Boxkämpfer jagen Eva durch Sylt portez ce vieux Whiskey blond qui

▶ Extra Bold Condensed Obl.
The quick brown fox jumps over a Dog. Zwei Boxkämpfer jagen Eva durch Sylt portez ce vieux Whiskey blond qui

© FSI 1993

EF1071 Mac + PC   ① 🔗 1928-32: Paul Renner
Futura 1

abcdefghijklmnopqrstuvwxyz[äöüßåøæœç]
ABCDEFGHIJKLMNOPQRSTUVWXYZ
1234567890(.,;:?!$&-*){ÄÖÜÅØÆŒÇ}

aa*a*
A046
Futura™ 1, Lt, LtObl,
Bk, BkObl, Bd, BdObl
BT1304
Futura 1, Lt, LtObl,
ExtBlk, ExtBlkObl
BT1305
Futura 2, Med,
MedObl, Bd, BdObl

▶ Light
The quick brown fox jumps over a Dog. Zwei Boxkämpfer jagen Eva durch Sylt portez ce vieux Whiskey blond qui fume une

▶ Light Oblique
The quick brown fox jumps over a Dog. Zwei Boxkämpfer jagen Eva durch Sylt portez ce vieux Whiskey blond qui fume une

▶ Bold
The quick brown fox jumps over a Dog. Zwei Boxkämpfer jagen Eva durch Sylt portez ce vieux

▶ Bold Oblique
The quick brown fox jumps over a Dog. Zwei Boxkämpfer jagen Eva durch Sylt portez ce vieux

EF1072 Mac + PC   ① 🔗 1928-32: Paul Renner
Futura 2

abcdefghijklmnopqrstuvwxyz[äöüßåøæœç]
ABCDEFGHIJKLMNOPQRSTUVWXYZ
1234567890(.,;:?!$&-*){ÄÖÜÅØÆŒÇ}

aa*a*
A046
Futura™ 1, Lt, LtObl,
Bk, BkObl, Bd, BdObl
BT1305
Futura 2, Med,
MedObl, Bd, BdObl

▶ Book
The quick brown fox jumps over a Dog. Zwei Boxkämpfer jagen Eva durch Sylt portez ce vieux Whiskey blond qui fume

▶ Book Oblique
The quick brown fox jumps over a Dog. Zwei Boxkämpfer jagen Eva durch Sylt portez ce vieux Whiskey blond qui fume

▶ Demi Bold
The quick brown fox jumps over a Dog. Zwei Boxkämpfer jagen Eva durch Sylt portez ce vieux Whiskey blond qui fume

▶ Demi Bold Oblique
The quick brown fox jumps over a Dog. Zwei Boxkämpfer jagen Eva durch Sylt portez ce vieux Whiskey blond qui fume une pipe

EF1073 Mac + PC   ① 🔗 1928-32: Paul Renner
Futura 3

abcdefghijklmnopqrstuvwxyz[äöüßåøæœç]
ABCDEFGHIJKLMNOPQRSTUVWXYZ
1234567890(.,;:?!$&-*){ÄÖÜÅØÆŒÇ}

aa*a*
A045
Futura 2, Med, MedObl,
Hvy, HvyObl, ExtBd,
ExtBdObl
BT1304
Futura 1, Lt, LtObl,
ExtBlk, ExtBlkObl
BT1305
Futura 2, Med, MedObl,
Bd, BdObl
BT1306
Futura 3, Bk, BkObl,
Hvy, HvyObl

▶ Medium
The quick brown fox jumps over a Dog. Zwei Boxkämpfer jagen Eva durch Sylt portez ce vieux Whiskey blond qui fume une pipe aber

▶ Medium Oblique
The quick brown fox jumps over a Dog. Zwei Boxkämpfer jagen Eva durch Sylt portez ce vieux Whiskey blond qui fume une pipe

▶ Heavy
The quick brown fox jumps over a Dog. Zwei Boxkämpfer jagen Eva durch Sylt portez ce vieux Whiskey blond qui fume

▶ Extra Bold
The quick brown fox jumps over a Dog. Zwei Boxkämpfer jagen Eva durch Sylt portez ce vieux Whis-

© FSI 1993

▼ EF1073 Mac + PC Futura 3
► Extra Bold Oblique
The quick brown fox jumps over a Dog. Zwei Boxkämpfer jagen Eva durch Sylt portez ce vieux Whis-

---

EF1074 Mac + PC ① 1928-32: Paul Renner
Futura 4

abcdefghijklmnopqrstuvwxyz[äöüßåøæœç]
ABCDEFGHIJKLMNOPQRSTUVWXYZ
1234567890(.,;:?!$&-*){ÄÖÜÅØÆŒÇ}

aa*a*
A047
Futura Condensed,
LtCon, LtConObl,
MedCon, MedConObl,
BdCon, BdConObl,
ExtBdCon,
ExtBdConObl
BT1307
Futura 4, LtCon,
MedCon, BdCon,
BdConObl

► Light Condensed
The quick brown fox jumps over a Dog. Zwei Boxkämpfer jagen Eva durch Sylt portez ce vieux Whiskey blond qui fume une pipe aber echt über die Mauer gesprungen und auch smørebrød en ysjes

► Light Condensed Oblique
The quick brown fox jumps over a Dog. Zwei Boxkämpfer jagen Eva durch Sylt portez ce vieux Whiskey blond qui fume une pipe aber echt über die Mauer gesprungen und auch smørebrød en ysjes

► Bold Condensed
The quick brown fox jumps over a Dog. Zwei Boxkämpfer jagen Eva durch Sylt portez ce vieux Whiskey blond qui fume une pipe aber echt über die Mauer

► Bold Condensed Oblique
The quick brown fox jumps over a Dog. Zwei Boxkämpfer jagen Eva durch Sylt portez ce vieux Whiskey blond qui fume une pipe aber echt über die Mauer gesprungen

---

EF1075 Mac + PC ① 1928-32: Paul Renner
Futura 5

abcdefghijklmnopqrstuvwxyz[äöüßåøæœç]
ABCDEFGHIJKLMNOPQRSTUVWXYZ
1234567890(.,;:?!$&-*){ÄÖÜÅØÆŒÇ}

aa*a*
A047
Futura Condensed,
LtCon, LtConObl,
MedCon, MedConObl,
BdCon, BdConObl,
ExtBdCon,
ExtBdConObl
BT1307
Futura 4, LtCon,
MedCon, BdCon,
BdConObl
BT1308
Futura 5, ExtBlkCon,
ExtBlkConObl

► Medium Condensed
The quick brown fox jumps over a Dog. Zwei Boxkämpfer jagen Eva durch Sylt portez ce vieux Whiskey blond qui fume une pipe aber echt über die Mauer gesprungen und auch smørebrød en

► Medium Condensed Oblique
The quick brown fox jumps over a Dog. Zwei Boxkämpfer jagen Eva durch Sylt portez ce vieux Whiskey blond qui fume une pipe aber echt über die Mauer gesprungen und auch smørebrød en

► Extra Bold Condensed
The quick brown fox jumps over a Dog. Zwei Boxkämpfer jagen Eva durch Sylt portez ce vieux Whiskey blond qui fume une pipe aber echt

► Extra Bold Condensed Obl.
The quick brown fox jumps over a Dog. Zwei Boxkämpfer jagen Eva durch Sylt portez ce vieux Whiskey blond qui fume une pipe aber echt

---

SG1133 Mac ① (1928: Paul Renner)
Futura Extra Light Headline

abcdefghijklmnopqrstuvwxyz[äöüßåøæoeç]
ABCDEFGHIJKLMNOPQRSTUVWXYZ
1234567890(.,;:?!$&-*)ÄÖÜÅØÆŒÇ

© FSI 1993

SG1216 Mac ① ✎ (1928: Paul Renner)
Futura Extra Light Oblique Headline

abcdefghijklmnopqrstuvwxyz[äöüßåøæœç]
ABCDEFGHIJKLMNOPQRSTUVWXYZ
1234567890(.,;:?!$&-*)ÄÖÜÅØÆŒÇ

SG1134 Mac ① ✎ 1928: Paul Renner
Futura Light Headline

abcdefghijklmnopqrstuvwxyz[äöüßåøæœç]
ABCDEFGHIJKLMNOPQRSTUVWXYZ
1234567890(.,;:?!$&-*)ÄÖÜÅØÆŒÇ

SG1500 Mac ① ✎ 1930: Paul Renner
Futura Light Oblique Headline

abcdefghijklmnopqrstuvwxyz[äöüßåøæœç]
ABCDEFGHIJKLMNOPQRSTUVWXYZ
1234567890(.,;:?!$&-*)ÄÖÜÅØÆŒÇ

SG1135 Mac ① ✎ 1932: Paul Renner
Futura Book Headline

abcdefghijklmnopqrstuvwxyz[äöüßåøæœç]
ABCDEFGHIJKLMNOPQRSTUVWXYZ
1234567890(.,;:?!$&-*)ÄÖÜÅØÆŒÇ

SG1503 Mac ① ✎ 1939: Paul Renner
Futura Book Oblique Headline

abcdefghijklmnopqrstuvwxyz[äöüßåøæœç]
ABCDEFGHIJKLMNOPQRSTUVWXYZ
1234567890(.,;:?!$&-*)ÄÖÜÅØÆŒÇ

SG1217 Mac ① ✎ 1928: Paul Renner
Futura Medium Headline

abcdefghijklmnopqrstuvwxyz[äöüßåøæœç]
ABCDEFGHIJKLMNOPQRSTUVWXYZ
1234567890(.,;:?!$&-*)ÄÖÜÅØÆŒÇ

SG1218 Mac ① ✎ 1930: Paul Renner
Futura Medium Oblique Headline

abcdefghijklmnopqrstuvwxyz[äöüßåøæœç]
ABCDEFGHIJKLMNOPQRSTUVWXYZ
1234567890(.,;:?!$&-*)ÄÖÜÅØÆŒÇ

© FSI 1993

SG1501 Mac ① 1930: Paul Renner
Futura Demi Bold Headline

abcdefghijklmnopqrstuvwxyz[äöüßåøæœç]
ABCDEFGHIJKLMNOPQRSTUVWXYZ
1234567890(.,;:?!$&-*)ÄÖÜÅØÆŒÇ

SG1502 Mac ① 1930: Paul Renner
Futura Demi Bold Oblique Headline

abcdefghijklmnopqrstuvwxyz[äöüßåøæœç]
ABCDEFGHIJKLMNOPQRSTUVWXYZ
1234567890(.,;:?!$&-*)ÄÖÜÅØÆŒÇ

SG1504 Mac ① 1928: Paul Renner
Futura Bold

abcdefghijklmnopqrstuvwxyz[äöüßåøæœç]
ABCDEFGHIJKLMNOPQRSTUVWXYZ
1234567890(.,;:?!$&-*)ÄÖÜÅØÆŒÇ

SG1505 Mac ① 1937: Paul Renner
Futura Bold Oblique Headline

abcdefghijklmnopqrstuvwxyz[äöüßåøæœç]
ABCDEFGHIJKLMNOPQRSTUVWXYZ
1234567890(.,;:?!$&-*)ÄÖÜÅØÆŒÇ

SG1219 Mac ① 1952: (Paul Renner, 1928) Edwin W. Shaar
Futura Extra Bold Headline

abcdefghijklmnopqrstuvwxyz[äöüßåøæœç]
ABCDEFGHIJKLMNOPQRSTUVWXYZ
1234567890(.,;:?!$&-*)ÄÖÜÅØÆŒÇ

SG1220 Mac ① 1955: (Renner, 1928) Edwin W. Shaar, Tommy Thompson
Futura Extra Bold Oblique Headline

abcdefghijklmnopqrstuvwxyz[äöüßåøæœç]
ABCDEFGHIJKLMNOPQRSTUVWXYZ
1234567890(.,;:?!$&-*)ÄÖÜÅØÆŒÇ

SG1136 Mac ① 1928: Paul Renner
Futura Light Condensed Headline

abcdefghijklmnopqrstuvwxyz[äöüßåøæœç]
ABCDEFGHIJKLMNOPQRSTUVWXYZ
1234567890(.,;:?!$&-*)ÄÖÜÅØÆŒÇ

© FSI 1993

SG1506 Mac ① 1928: Paul Renner
Futura Medium Condensed Headline

abcdefghijklmnopqrstuvwxyz[äöüßåøæœç]
ABCDEFGHIJKLMNOPQRSTUVWXYZ
1234567890(.,;:?!$&-*)ÄÖÜÅØÆŒÇ

SG1507 Mac ① 1930: Paul Renner
Futura Bold Condensed Headline

abcdefghijklmnopqrstuvwxyz[äöüßåøæœç]
ABCDEFGHIJKLMNOPQRSTUVWXYZ
1234567890(.,;:?!$&-*)ÄÖÜÅØÆŒÇ

SG1137 Mac ① 1930: Paul Renner
Futura No. 1 Bold Condensed Headline

abcdefghijklmnopqrstuvwxyz[äöüßåøæœç]
ABCDEFGHIJKLMNOPQRSTUVWXYZ
1234567890(.,;:?!$&-*)ÄÖÜÅØÆŒÇ

SG1510 Mac ① (1928: Paul Renner)
Futura No. 1 Bold Condensed Oblique Headline

abcdefghijklmnopqrstuvwxyz[äöüßåøæœç]
ABCDEFGHIJKLMNOPQRSTUVWXYZ
1234567890(.,;:?!$&-*)ÄÖÜÅØÆŒÇ

SG1508 Mac ① 1928: (1928: Paul Renner)
Futura Extra Bold Condensed Headline

abcdefghijklmnopqrstuvwxyz[äöüßåøæœç]
ABCDEFGHIJKLMNOPQRSTUVWXYZ
1234567890(.,;:?!$&-*)ÄÖÜÅØÆŒÇ

SG1509 Mac ① 1928: (1928: Paul Renner)
Futura Extra Bold Condensed Oblique Headline

abcdefghijklmnopqrstuvwxyz[äöüßåøæœç]
ABCDEFGHIJKLMNOPQRSTUVWXYZ
1234567890(.,;:?!$&-*)ÄÖÜÅØÆŒÇ

SG1513 Mac ① 1932: Paul Renner
Futura Display Headline

abcdefghijklmnopqrstuvwxyz[äöüßåøæœç]
ABCDEFGHIJKLMNOPQRSTUVWXYZ
1234567890(.,;:?!$&-*)ÄÖÜÅØÆŒÇ

© FSI 1993

SG1511 Mac — (1928: Paul Renner)
Futura Round Headline

abcdefghijklmnopqrstuvwxyz[äöüßåøœæç]
ABCDEFGHIJKLMNOPQRSTUVWXYZ
1234567890(.,;:?!$&-*)ÄÖÜÅØÆŒÇ

SG1512 Mac — (1928: Paul Renner)
Futura Extra Bold Shaded Headline

abcdefghijklmnopqrstuvwxyz[äöüßåøœæç]
ABCDEFGHIJKLMNOPQRSTUVWXYZ
1234567890(.,;:?!$&-*)ÄÖÜÅØÆŒÇ

BT809 Mac + PC — 1929: Paul Renner
Futura Black

abcdefghijklmnopqrstuvwxyz[äöüßåøœæç]
ABCDEFGHIJKLMNOPQRSTUVWXYZ
1234567890(.,;:?!$&-*){ÄÖÜÅØÆŒÇ}

Bitstream Headlines 3:
Antique No. 3™, Futura Black
aaa C2983
Headlines 94S

C467 Mac + PC — 1960: (Paul Renner, 1928) Vic Caruso
PL Futura Maxi 1

abcdefghijklmnopqrstuvwxyz[äöüåøœæç]
ABCDEFGHIJKLMNOPQRSTUVWXYZ
1234567890(.,;:?!$&-*)◊ÄÖÜÅØÆŒÇ♦

▶ Light
The quick brown fox jumps over a Dog. Zwei Boxkämpfer jagen Eva durch Sylt portez ce vieux Whis-

▶ Demi
The quick brown fox jumps over a Dog. Zwei Boxkämpfer jagen Eva durch Sylt portez ce

Headlines 81S:
Egiziano™ Black, PL Behemoth Semi Condensed, PL Benguiat Frisky, PL Futura Maxi 1, PL Tower™ Condensed, Quirinus™ Bold, Section™ Bold Condensed, Stratford ™Bold, Woodblock

C468 Mac + PC — 1960: (Paul Renner, 1928) Vic Caruso
PL Futura Maxi 2

abcdefghijklmnopqrstuvwxyz[äöüåøœæç]
ABCDEFGHIJKLMNOPQRSTUVWXYZ
1234567890(.,;:?!$&-*)◊ÄÖÜÅØÆŒÇ♦

▶ Book
The quick brown fox jumps over a Dog. Zwei Boxkämpfer jagen Eva durch Sylt portez ce vieux

▶ Bold
The quick brown fox jumps over a Dog. Zwei Boxkämpfer jagen Eva durch Sylt portez ce

© FSI 1993

▼ C468   Mac + PC   PL Futura Maxi 2

Headlines 82S:
Neon Extra Condensed™, PL Barnum Block, PL Benguiat Frisky Bold, PL Davison Zip Bold, PL Fiedler Gothic Bold, PL Futura Maxi 2, PL Trophy™ Oblique, Ritmo™ Bold, TC Broadway

G

Alexander Branczyk, Berlin, D

EF6466 Mac + PC ⑥
Galadriel™

ABCDEFGHIJKLMNOPQRSTUVWXYZ[ÄÖÜSSÅØÆŒÇ]
1234567890(.,;:?!$&-*)ÄÖÜÅØÆŒÇ

E+F Special Headlines 2:
Belshaw™, Camellia™, Carousel™, Cirkulus™, Data 70, Galadriel™
Eccentric

MC2902 Mac + PC ② Claude Mediavilla
Galba™

ABCDEFGHIJKLMNOPQRSTUVWXYZ
1234567890[ ](.,;:?!$&-*){ÄÖÜÅØÆŒÇ}

C2980 Mac + PC ⑥
Gallia™

ABCDEFGHIJKLMNOPQRSTUVWXYZ
1234567890[ ](.,;:?!$&-*){ÄÖÜÅØÆŒÇ}

Headlines 91S:
Empire™, Gallia™, Gillies Gothic Bold, Quaint™ Roman, Skjald™

CA6675 Mac + PC ② 1978-92: Mathew Carter
ITC Galliard CC

abcdefghijklmnopqrstuvwxyz[äöüßåøæœç]
ABCDEFGHIJKLMNOPQRSTUVWXYZ
1234567890(.,;:?!$&-*){ÄÖÜÅØÆŒÇ}

Mantinia CC

▶ Roman
The quick brown fox jumps over a Dog. Zwei Boxkämpfer jagen Eva durch Sylt portez ce vieux Whiskey blond qui fume

▶ Italic
The quick brown fox jumps over a Dog. Zwei Boxkämpfer jagen Eva durch Sylt portez ce vieux Whiskey blond qui fume une pipe aber echt

▶ Roman SC
THE QUICK BROWN FOX JUMPS OVER A DOG. 123 4567 890 ZWEI BOXKÄMPFER JAGEN EVA DURCH SYLT PORTEZ CE VIEUX

▶ Roman OSF
The quick brown fox jumps over a Dog. 123 4567 890 Zwei Boxkämpfer jagen Eva durch Sylt portez ce vieux Whiskey

▶ Italic OSF
The quick brown fox jumps over a Dog. 123 4567 890 Zwei Boxkämpfer jagen Eva durch Sylt portez ce vieux Whiskey blond qui fume une pipe

▶ Roman Alternates
&⸎&.•⁂•⁑•⁂❧❦⚜ct QQst'rff fiflffiffla ctd e h fj m n r st t z àäåéèrę

© FSI 1993

▼ CA6675 Mac + PC ITC Galliard CC

▶ Italic Alternates
&·❦❧✿❀❁❃❆❈QSLffifflfffifflus
asisactdefrgijfjkmnspsttvzà
äåéènt

▶ Roman Expert
(⁰/₁ ¹/₂³/₃⁴/₅⁵/₆⁶/₇⁷/₈⁸/₉⁹/₀)ffiffflfffl
¹/₄²/₄¹/₈³/₈⁵/₈⁷/₈¹/₂ abdehilmnorstv 0123456
789 THE QUICK BROWN FOX
JUMPS OVER A LAZY DOG. PORTE

▶ Italic Expert
0123456789ᵃᵇᶜᵈᵉʰⁱˡᵐⁿᵒʳˢᵗᵛffiffflfffl₵1
Rp¹/₄²/₄¹/₈³/₈⁵/₈⁷/₈¹/₂¹/₄¹/₂³/₄¹/₈³/₈⁵/₈⁷/₈¹/₃
²/₃⁰₀¹₁ ²₂³₃⁴₄⁵₅⁶₆⁷₇⁸₈⁹₉₵$

▶ Roman Fractions
0123456789/1234567890/¹²³⁴⁵⁶⁷
⁸⁹⁰⁄₁₂₃₄₅₆₇₈₉₀/1234567890

▶ Italic Fractions
0123456789/1234567890/¹²³⁴⁵⁶⁷⁸⁹⁰/
/₁₂₃₄₅₆₇₈₉₀

BT802 Mac + PC ② ✎ 1978: Matthew Carter
ITC Galliard 1

abcdefghijklmnopqrstuvwxyz[äöüßåøæœç]
ABCDEFGHIJKLMNOPQRSTUVWXYZ
1234567890(.,;:?!$&-*){ÄÖÜÅØÆŒÇ}

a a *a*
A1001
ITC Galliard 2 , Blk,
BlkIta, Ult, UltIta

▶ Black
The quick brown fox jumps over a Dog. Zwei Boxkämpfer jagen Eva durch Sylt portez ce vieux Whiskey blond

▶ Black Italic
The quick brown fox jumps over a Dog. Zwei Boxkämpfer jagen Eva durch Sylt portez ce vieux Whiskey blond qui fume

BT803 Mac + PC ② ✎ 1978: Matthew Carter
ITC Galliard 2

abcdefghijklmnopqrstuvwxyz[äöüßåøæœç]
ABCDEFGHIJKLMNOPQRSTUVWXYZ
1234567890(.,;:?!$&-*){ÄÖÜÅØÆŒÇ}

a a *a*
A1001
ITC Galliard 2 , Blk,
BlkIta, Ult, UltIta

▶ Ultra
The quick brown fox jumps over a Dog. Zwei Boxkämpfer jagen Eva durch Sylt portez ce vieux

▶ Ultra Italic
The quick brown fox jumps over a Dog. Zwei Boxkämpfer jagen Eva durch Sylt portez ce vieux Whiskey

BT1309 Mac + PC ② ✎ 1978: Matthew Carter
ITC Galliard® 3

abcdefghijklmnopqrstuvwxyz[äöüßåøæœç]
ABCDEFGHIJKLMNOPQRSTUVWXYZ
1234567890(.,;:?!$&-*){ÄÖÜÅØÆŒÇ}

a a *a*
A048
ITC Galliard 1, Rom, Ita,
Bd, BdIta

▶ Roman
The quick brown fox over a Dog. Zwei Boxkämpfer jagen Eva durch Sylt portez ce vieux Whiskey blond qui fume

▶ Italic
The quick brown fox jumps over a Dog. Zwei Boxkämpfer jagen Eva durch Sylt portez ce vieux Whiskey blond qui fume une pipe aber echt

© FSI 1993
▼

▼ BT1309   Mac + PC   ITC Galliard® 3

▶ Bold
The quick brown fox jumps over a Dog. Zwei Boxkämpfer jagen Eva durch Sylt portez ce vieux Whiskey blond qui

▶ Bold Italic
The quick brown fox jumps over a Dog. Zwei Boxkämpfer jagen Eva durch Sylt portez ce vieux Whiskey blond qui fume une

EF301   Mac + PC   ②   ✎ 1986: Jovica Veljovic
ITC Gamma® 1

abcdefghijklmnopqrstuvwxyz[äöüßåøæœç]
ABCDEFGHIJKLMNOPQRSTUVWXYZ
1234567890(.,;:?!$&-*){ÄÖÜÅØÆŒÇ}

▶ Book
The quick brown fox jumps over a Dog. Zwei Boxkämpfer jagen Eva durch Sylt portez ce vieux Whiskey blond qui fume une

▶ Book Italic
The quick brown fox jumps over a Dog. Zwei Boxkämpfer jagen Eva durch Sylt portez ce vieux Whiskey blond qui fume une pipe aber echt

▶ Bold
The quick brown fox jumps over a Dog. Zwei Boxkämpfer jagen Eva durch Sylt portez ce vieux Whiskey blond qui fume

▶ Bold Italic
The quick brown fox jumps over a Dog. Zwei Boxkämpfer jagen Eva durch Sylt portez ce vieux Whiskey blond qui fume

EF302   Mac + PC   ②   ✎ 1986: Jovica Veljovic
ITC Gamma 2

abcdefghijklmnopqrstuvwxyz[äöüßåøæœç]
ABCDEFGHIJKLMNOPQRSTUVWXYZ
1234567890(.,;:?!$&-*){ÄÖÜÅØÆŒÇ}

▶ Medium
The quick brown fox jumps over a Dog. Zwei Boxkämpfer jagen Eva durch Sylt portez ce vieux Whiskey blond qui fume

▶ Medium Italic
The quick brown fox jumps over a Dog. Zwei Boxkämpfer jagen Eva durch Sylt portez ce vieux Whiskey blond qui fume une

▶ Black
The quick brown fox jumps over a Dog. Zwei Boxkämpfer jagen Eva durch Sylt portez ce vieux Whiskey blond qui

▶ Black Italic
The quick brown fox jumps over a Dog. Zwei Boxkämpfer jagen Eva durch Sylt portez ce vieux Whiskey blond qui fume

EF533   Mac + PC   ②   ✎ 1986: Jovica Veljovic
ITC Gamma Small Caps

ABCDEFGHIJKLMNOPQRSTUVWXYZ[ÄÖÜSSÅØÆŒÇ]
ABCDEFGHIJKLMNOPQRSTUVWXYZ
1234567890(.,;:?!$&-*){ÄÖÜÅØÆŒÇ}

▶ Small Caps Book
THE QUICK BROWN FOX JUMPS OVER A DOG. 123 4567 890 ZWEI BOXKÄMPFER JAGEN EVA DURCH SYLT PORTEZ CE VIEUX WHISKEY BLOND

▶ Small Caps Medium
THE QUICK BROWN FOX JUMPS OVER A DOG. 123 4567 890 ZWEI BOXKÄMPFER JAGEN EVA DURCH SYLT PORTEZ CE VIEUX WHISKEY

© FSI 1993

BT851 Mac + PC ④ 1970: Hans-Jörg Hunziker, Matthew Carter
Gando

abcdefghijklmnopqrstuvwxyz[äöüßåøæœç]
ABCDEFGHIJKLMNOPQRSTUVWXYZ
1234567890(.,;:?!$&-*){ÄÖÜÅØÆŒÇ}

Bitstream Script 4:
Flemish Script, Gando

FB2752 Mac + PC ① 1991: Tobias Frere-Jones
Garage Gothic™

abcdefghijklmnopqrstuvwxyz[äöüßåøæœç]
ABCDEFGHIJKLMNOPQRSTUVWXYZ
1234567890(.,;:?!$&-*){ÄÖÜÅØÆŒÇ}

FF Kipp

▶ **Regular**
The quick brown fox jumps over a Dog. Zwei Boxkämpfer jagen Eva durch Sylt portez ce vieux Whiskey blond qui fume une pipe aber echt über die Mauer gesprungen und auch smørebrød en ysjes natuurlijk. The quick brown fox

▶ **Bold**
The quick brown fox jumps over a Dog. Zwei Boxkämpfer jagen Eva durch Sylt portez ce vieux Whiskey blond qui fume une pipe aber echt über die Mauer gesprungen und auch smørebrød en

▶ **Black**
The quick brown fox jumps over a Dog. Zwei Boxkämpfer jagen Eva durch Sylt portez ce vieux Whiskey blond qui fume une pipe aber echt über die Mauer

---

FB2882 Mac + PC ② 1992: (R. Hunter Middleton, 1929-30) Jill Pichotta
Bureau Garamond™

abcdefghijklmnopqrstuvwxyz[äöüßåøæœç]
ABCDEFGHIJKLMNOPQRSTUVWXYZ
1234567890(.,;:?!$&-*){ÄÖÜÅØÆŒÇ}

Garamont

▶ **Roman**
The quick brown fox jumps over a Dog. Zwei Boxkämpfer jagen Eva durch Sylt portez ce vieux Whiskey blond qui fume une pipe aber echt über

▶ *Italic*
The quick brown fox jumps over a Dog. Zwei Boxkämpfer jagen Eva durch Sylt portez ce vieux Whiskey blond qui fume une pipe aber echt über die Mauer gesprungen

---

A219 Mac + PC ② 1989: (Claude Garamond, 1532) Robert Slimbach
Adobe Garamond™

abcdefghijklmnopqrstuvwxyz[äöüßåøæœç]
ABCDEFGHIJKLMNOPQRSTUVWXYZ
1234567890(.,;:?!$&-*){ÄÖÜÅØÆŒÇ}

Garamond No. 3,
Stempel Garamond,
Simoncini Garamond,
Monotype Garamond,
Berthold Garamond,
Granjon

▶ **Regular**
The quick brown fox jumps over a Dog. Zwei Boxkämpfer jagen Eva durch Sylt portez ce vieux Whiskey blond qui fume une pipe aber echt

▶ *Italic*
The quick brown fox jumps over a Dog. Zwei Boxkämpfer jagen Eva durch Sylt portez ce vieux Whiskey blond qui fume une pipe aber echt

© FSI 1993

▼ A219　Mac + PC　Adobe Garamond™

▶ Semi Bold
The quick brown fox jumps over a Dog. Zwei Boxkämpfer jagen Eva durch Sylt portez ce vieux Whiskey blond qui fume une pipe aber

▶ Semi Bold Italic
The quick brown fox jumps over a Dog. Zwei Boxkämpfer jagen Eva durch Sylt portez ce vieux Whiskey blond qui fume une pipe aber echt

▶ Bold
The quick brown fox jumps over a Dog. Zwei Boxkämpfer jagen Eva durch Sylt portez ce vieux Whiskey blond qui fume une

▶ Bold Italic
The quick brown fox jumps over a Dog. Zwei Boxkämpfer jagen Eva durch Sylt portez ce vieux Whiskey blond qui fume une pipe

A220　Mac + PC　②　✎ 1989: (Claude Garamond, 1532) Robert Slimbach

Adobe Garamond Expert Collection

ABCDEFGHIJKLMNOPQRSTUVWXYZ(ÄÖÜÆŒØ)

1234567890ffffiflffiffl(¼½¾⅛⅜⅝⅞⅓⅔)₵Rp

▶ Expert Regular
0123456789offfiflffiffl-¼½¾⅛⅜⅝⅞⅓⅔ THE QUICK BROWN FOX JUMPS OVER A DOG ZWEI BOXKÄMPFER JAGEN EVA

▶ Expert Italic
0123456789offfiflffiffl-¼½¾⅛⅜⅝⅞⅓⅔

▶ Expert Semi Bold
0123456789offfiflffiffl-¼½¾⅛⅜⅝⅞⅓⅔ THE QUICK BROWN FOX JUMPS OVER A DOG ZWEI BOXKÄMPFER JAGEN EVA

▶ Expert Semi Bold Italic
0123456789offfiflffiffl-¼½¾⅛⅜⅝⅞⅓⅔

▶ Expert Bold
0123456789offfiflffiffl-¼½¾⅛⅜⅝⅞⅓⅔

▶ Expert Bold Italic
0123456789offfiflffiffl-¼½¾⅛⅜⅝⅞⅓⅔

▶ Alternate
℮∽QQtaαenrtz

▶ Alternate Italic
&ƒABCDEFGHIJKLMNOPQRSTUVWXYZftv

▶ Titling
THE QUICK BROWN FOX JUMPS OVER A DOG. ZWEI BOXKÄMPFER JAGEN EVA DURCH SYLT PORTEZ CE

AB2759　Mac + PC　②　✎ 1972: (C. Garamond, 1532) G. G. Lange

Berthold Garamond®

abcdefghijklmnopqrstuvwxyz[äöüßåøæœç]
ABCDEFGHIJKLMNOPQRSTUVWXYZ
1234567890(.,;:?!$&-*){ÄÖÜÅØÆŒÇ}

© FSI 1993　▼

▼ AB2759 Mac + PC **Berthold Garamond®**

☞ Garamond No. 3, Stempel Garamond, Simoncini Garamond, Monotype Garamond, Adobe Garamond, Granjon

▶ Regular
The quick brown fox jumps over a Dog. Zwei Boxkämpfer jagen Eva durch Sylt portez ce vieux Whiskey blond qui fume une

▶ Italic
The quick brown fox jumps over a Dog. 123 4567 890 Zwei Boxkämpfer jagen Eva durch Sylt portez ce vieux Whiskey blond qui fume

▶ Medium
The quick brown fox jumps over a Dog. Zwei Boxkämpfer jagen Eva durch Sylt portez ce vieux Whiskey blond qui fume

▶ Medium Italic
The quick brown fox jumps over a Dog. Zwei Boxkämpfer jagen Eva durch Sylt portez ce vieux Whiskey blond qui fume une pipe aber echt

▶ Bold
The quick brown fox jumps over a Dog. Zwei Boxkämpfer jagen Eva durch Sylt portez ce vieux Whiskey blond qui fume

▶ Condensed
The quick brown fox jumps over a Dog. Zwei Boxkämpfer jagen Eva durch Sylt portez ce vieux Whiskey blond qui fume une pipe aber echt über die Mauer

▶ Medium Condensed
The quick brown fox jumps over a Dog. Zwei Boxkämpfer jagen Eva durch Sylt portez ce vieux Whiskey blond qui fume une pipe aber echt

A050 Mac + PC   ② 🖉 1975–77: (1532)(M. F. Benton, 1917) Tony Stan

ITC Garamond® 1

abcdefghijklmnopqrstuvwxyz[äöüßåøæœç]
ABCDEFGHIJKLMNOPQRSTUVWXYZ
1234567890(.,:;?!$&-*){ÄÖÜÅØÆŒÇ}

aa*a*
EF383
ITC Garamond 1, Lt, LtIta, Bd, BdIta
BT1313
ITC Garamond 1, Lt, LtIta, Ult, UltIta
BT1314
ITC Garamond 2, Bk, BkIta, Bd, BdIta

▶ Light
The quick brown fox jumps over a Dog. Zwei Boxkämpfer jagen Eva durch Sylt portez ce vieux Whiskey blond qui fume

▶ Light Italic
The quick brown fox jumps over a Dog. Zwei Boxkämpfer jagen Eva durch Sylt portez ce vieux Whiskey blond qui fume une

▶ Bold
The quick brown fox jumps over a Dog. Zwei Boxkämpfer jagen Eva durch Sylt portez ce vieux Whiskey blond

▶ Bold Italic
The quick brown fox jumps over a Dog. Zwei Boxkämpfer jagen Eva durch Sylt portez ce vieux Whiskey blond

A565 Mac + PC   ② 🖉 1975–77: (1532) (M. F. Benton, 1917) Tony Stan

ITC Garamond 2

abcdefghijklmnopqrstuvwxyz[äöüßåøæœç]
ABCDEFGHIJKLMNOPQRSTUVWXYZ
1234567890(.,:;?!$&-*){ÄÖÜÅØÆŒÇ}

aa*a*
EF384
ITC Garamond 2, Bk, BkIta, Ult, UltIta
BT1313
ITC Garamond 1, Lt, LtIta, Ult, UltIta
BT1314
ITC Garamond 2, Bk, BkIta, Bd, BdIta

▶ Book
The quick brown fox jumps over a Dog. Zwei Boxkämpfer jagen Eva durch Sylt portez ce vieux Whiskey blond qui fume

▶ Book Italic
The quick brown fox jumps over a Dog. Zwei Boxkämpfer jagen Eva durch Sylt portez ce vieux Whiskey blond qui fume

© FSI 1993 ▼

▼ A565 Mac + PC   ITC Garamond 2

▶ Ultra
The quick brown fox jumps over a Dog. Zwei Boxkämpfer jagen Eva durch Sylt portez ce vieux

▶ Ultra Italic
The quick brown fox jumps over a Dog. Zwei Boxkämpfer jagen Eva durch Sylt portez ce vieux

BT2885 Mac + PC   ✏ 1991: (1532) (M. F. Benton, 1917) (Tony Stan)
ITC Garamond Narrow

abcdefghijklmnopqrstuvwxyz[äöüßåøæœç]
ABCDEFGHIJKLMNOPQRSTUVWXYZ
1234567890(.,;:?!$&-*){ÄÖÜÅØÆŒÇ}

▶ Light
The quick brown fox jumps over a Dog. Zwei Boxkämpfer jagen Eva durch Sylt portez ce vieux Whiskey blond qui fume une pipe aber echt über die Mauer

▶ Light Italic
The quick brown fox jumps over a Dog. Zwei Boxkämpfer jagen Eva durch Sylt portez ce vieux Whiskey blond qui fume une pipe aber echt über die Mauer

▶ Book
The quick brown fox jumps over a Dog. Zwei Boxkämpfer jagen Eva durch Sylt portez ce vieux Whiskey blond qui fume une pipe aber echt

▶ Book Italic
The quick brown fox jumps over a Dog. Zwei Boxkämpfer jagen Eva durch Sylt portez ce vieux Whiskey blond qui fume une pipe aber echt

▶ Bold
The quick brown fox jumps over a Dog. Zwei Boxkämpfer jagen Eva durch Sylt portez ce vieux Whiskey blond qui fume une pipe aber echt

▶ Bold Italic
The quick brown fox jumps over a Dog. Zwei Boxkämpfer jagen Eva durch Sylt portez ce vieux Whiskey blond qui fume une pipe aber echt

A483 Mac + PC   ②   ✏ 1975-77: (1532) (M. F. Benton, 1917) Tony Stan
ITC Garamond Condensed

abcdefghijklmnopqrstuvwxyz[äöüßåøæœç]
ABCDEFGHIJKLMNOPQRSTUVWXYZ
1234567890(.,;:?!$&-*){ÄÖÜÅØÆŒÇ}

a a *a*
EF303
ITC Garamond Condensed 1, LtCon, LtConIta, BdCon, BdConIta
EF304
ITC Garamond Condensed 2, BkCon, BkConIta, UltCon, UltConIta
BT1315
ITC Garamond Condensed 1, LtCon, LtConIta, UltCon, UltConIta
BT1316
ITC Garamond Condensed 2, BkCon, BkConIta, BdCon, BdConIta

▶ Light Condensed
The quick brown fox jumps over a Dog. Zwei Boxkämpfer jagen Eva durch Sylt portez ce vieux Whiskey blond qui fume une pipe aber echt über die Mauer

▶ Light Condensed Italic
The quick brown fox jumps over a Dog. Zwei Boxkämpfer jagen Eva durch Sylt portez ce vieux Whiskey blond qui fume une pipe aber echt über die Mauer

▶ Book Condensed
The quick brown fox jumps over a Dog. Zwei Boxkämpfer jagen Eva durch Sylt portez ce vieux Whiskey blond qui fume une pipe aber echt über die Mauer

▶ Book Condensed Italic
The quick brown fox jumps over a Dog. Zwei Boxkämpfer jagen Eva durch Sylt portez ce vieux Whiskey blond qui fume une pipe aber echt

▶ Bold Condensed
The quick brown fox jumps over a Dog. Zwei Boxkämpfer jagen Eva durch Sylt portez ce vieux Whiskey blond qui fume une pipe aber echt

▶ Bold Condensed Italic
The quick brown fox jumps over a Dog. Zwei Boxkämpfer jagen Eva durch Sylt portez ce vieux Whiskey blond qui fume une

© FSI 1993 ▼

▼ A483 Mac + PC   ITC Garamond Condensed

▶ Ultra Condensed
The quick brown fox jumps over a Dog. Zwei Boxkämpfer jagen Eva durch Sylt portez ce vieux Whiskey blond qui fume une pipe

▶ Ultra Condensed Italic
The quick brown fox jumps over a Dog. Zwei Boxkämpfer jagen Eva durch Sylt portez ce vieux Whiskey blond qui fume

M221 Mac + PC ② 1922: (Claude Garamond, 1532)
Monotype Garamond®

abcdefghijklmnopqrstuvwxyz[äöüßåøæœç]
ABCDEFGHIJKLMNOPQRSTUVWXYZ
1234567890(.,;:?!$&-*){ÄÖÜÅØÆŒÇ}

Garamond No. 3, Stempel Garamond, Simoncini Garamond, Granjon, Adobe Garamond

▶ Regular
The quick brown fox jumps over a Dog. Zwei Boxkämpfer jagen Eva durch Sylt portez ce vieux Whiskey blond qui fume une pipe aber echt

▶ Italic
The quick brown fox jumps over a Dog. Zwei Boxkämpfer jagen Eva durch Sylt portez ce vieux Whiskey blond qui fume une pipe aber echt über die Mauer

▶ Original Italic
The quick brown fox jumps over a Dog. Zwei Boxkämpfer jagen Eva durch Sylt portez ce vieux Whiskey blond qui fume une pipe aber echt über die Mauer

▶ Bold
The quick brown fox jumps over a Dog. Zwei Boxkämpfer jagen Eva durch Sylt portez ce vieux Whiskey blond qui fume une

▶ Bold Italic
The quick brown fox jumps over a Dog. Zwei Boxkämpfer jagen Eva durch Sylt portez ce vieux Whiskey blond qui fume une pipe aber echt

M944 Mac + PC ② 1925: (Claude Garamond, 1532)
Monotype Garamond Expert

ABCDEFGHIJKLMNOPQRSTUVWXYZ(ÄÖÜŠÅØÆŒÇ)
1234567890ffffiflffiffl(^{1}^{2}^{3}^{4}^{5}^{6}^{7}^{8}^{9}^{0}$_0$)

▶ Expert
0123456789 offfiflffiffl-(^{1}/$_1$^{2}/$_2$^{3}/$_3$^{4}/$_4$^{5}/$_5$^{6}/$_6$^{7}/$_7$^{8}/$_8$^{9}/$_9$^{0}/$_0$)($ ¢Rp₤)^a THE QUICK BROWN FOX JUMPS OVER A DOG ZWEI BOXKÄMPFER JAGEN EVA

▶ Expert Italic
0123456789offfiflffiffl-(^{1}/$_1$^{2}/$_2$^{3}/$_3$^{4}/$_4$^{5}/$_5$^{6}/$_6$^{7}/$_7$^{8}/$_8$^{9}/$_9$^{0}/$_0$)($ ¢Rp₤)^a

▶ Expert Bold
0123456789offfiflffiffl-(^{1}/$_1$^{2}/$_2$^{3}/$_3$^{4}/$_4$^{5}/$_5$^{6}/$_6$^{7}/$_7$^{8}/$_8$^{9}/$_9$^{0}/$_0$)($ ¢Rp₤)^a

▶ Expert Bold Italic
0123456789offfiflffiffl-(^{1}/$_1$^{2}/$_2$^{3}/$_3$^{4}/$_4$^{5}/$_5$^{6}/$_6$^{7}/$_7$^{8}/$_8$^{9}/$_9$^{0}/$_0$)($ ¢Rp₤)^a

A143 Mac + PC ② 1922: (Claude Garamond, 1532)
Garamond No. 3™

abcdefghijklmnopqrstuvwxyz[äöüßåøæœç]
ABCDEFGHIJKLMNOPQRSTUVWXYZ
1234567890(.,;:?!$&-*){ÄÖÜÅØÆŒÇ}

© FSI 1993

▼ A143   Mac + PC   Garamond No. 3™

a*a*a
BT1310
Garamond No. 3: Reg, Ita, Bd, BdIta
©
Monotype Garamond, Stempel Garamond, Simoncini Garamond, Berthold Garamond, Adobe Garamond, Granjon

▶ Regular
The quick brown fox jumps over a Dog. Zwei Boxkämpfer jagen Eva durch Sylt portez ce vieux Whiskey blond qui fume une pipe aber echt

▶ Italic
The quick brown fox jumps over a Dog. Zwei Boxkämpfer jagen Eva durch Sylt portez ce vieux Whiskey blond qui fume une pipe aber echt über die Mauer

▶ Bold
The quick brown fox jumps over a Dog. Zwei Boxkämpfer jagen Eva durch Sylt portez ce vieux Whiskey blond qui fume

▶ Bold Italic
The quick brown fox jumps over a Dog. Zwei Boxkämpfer jagen Eva durch Sylt portez ce vieux Whiskey blond qui fume une pipe aber

A1002   Mac + PC   ②   1922: (Claude Garamond, 1532)

Garamond No. 3 Small Caps/OSF

ABCDEFGHIJKLMNOPQRSTUVWXYZ[ÄÖÜSSÅØÆŒÇ]
ABCDEFGHIJKLMNOPQRSTUVWXYZ
1234567890(.,;:?!$&-*){ÄÖÜÅØÆŒÇ}

▶ Regular Small Caps
THE QUICK BROWN FOX JUMPS OVER A DOG. 123 4567 890 ZWEI BOXKÄMPFER JAGEN EVA DURCH SYLT PORTEZ CE VIEUX WHISKEY

▶ Italic OSF
The quick brown fox jumps over a Dog. 123 4567 890 Zwei Boxkämpfer jagen Eva durch Sylt portez ce vieux Whiskey blond qui fume une pipe aber

▶ Bold OSF
THE QUICK BROWN FOX JUMPS OVER A DOG. 123 4567 890 ZWEI BOXKÄMPFER JAGEN EVA DURCH SYLT PORTEZ CE VIEUX WHISKEY

▶ Bold Italic OSF
The quick brown fox jumps over a Dog. 123 4567 890 Zwei Boxkämpfer jagen Eva durch Sylt portez ce vieux Whiskey blond qui

A563   Mac + PC   ②   1958–61: (Claude Garamond, 1532) Simoncini, Bilz

Simoncini Garamond™

abcdefghijklmnopqrstuvwxyz[äöüßåøæœç]
ABCDEFGHIJKLMNOPQRSTUVWXYZ
1234567890(.,;:?!$&-*){ÄÖÜÅØÆŒÇ}

a*a*a
BT1312
Simoncini Garamond: Reg, Ita, Bd
©
Monotype Garamond, Stempel Garamond, Garamond No. 3, Berthold Garamond, Adobe Garamond, Granjon

▶ Regular
The quick brown fox jumps over a Dog. Zwei Boxkämpfer jagen Eva durch Sylt portez ce vieux Whiskey blond qui fume une

▶ Italic
The quick brown fox jumps over a Dog. Zwei Boxkämpfer jagen Eva durch Sylt portez ce vieux Whiskey blond qui fume une pipe aber

▶ Bold
The quick brown fox jumps over a Dog. Zwei Boxkämpfer jagen Eva durch Sylt portez ce vieux Whiskey blond qui fume une

© FSI 1993

G 9

SG2122 Mac ② 1958–61: (Claude Garamond, 1532) Simoncini, Bilz
Simoncini Garamond Extra Bold

abcdefghijklmnopqrstuvwxyz[äöüßåøæœç]
ABCDEFGHIJKLMNOPQRSTUVWXYZ
1234567890(.,;:?!$&-*)ÄÖÜÅØÆŒÇ

A144 Mac + PC ② 1925: (Claude Garamond, 1532)
Stempel Garamond™

abcdefghijklmnopqrstuvwxyz[äöüßåøæœç]
ABCDEFGHIJKLMNOPQRSTUVWXYZ
1234567890(.,;:?!$&-*){ÄÖÜÅØÆŒÇ}

aa*a*
BT1317
Stempel Garamond:
Reg, Ita, Bk, BdIta
©
Monotype Garamond,
Simoncini Garamond,
Garamond No. 3,
Berthold Garamond,
Adobe Garamond,
Granjon

▶ Regular
The quick brown fox jumps over a Dog. Zwei Boxkämpfer jagen Eva durch Sylt portez ce vieux Whiskey blond qui fume

▶ Italic
The quick brown fox jumps over a Dog. Zwei Boxkämpfer jagen Eva durch Sylt portez ce vieux Whiskey blond qui fume une

▶ Bold
The quick brown fox jumps over a Dog. Zwei Boxkämpfer jagen Eva durch Sylt portez ce vieux Whiskey blond qui fume

▶ Bold Italic
The quick brown fox jumps over a Dog. Zwei Boxkämpfer jagen Eva durch Sylt portez ce vieux Whiskey blond qui fume

A1151 Mac + PC ② 1925: (Claude Garamond, 1532)
Stempel Garamond Small Caps / OSF

ABCDEFGHIJKLMNOPQRSTUVWXYZ[ÄÖÜSSÅØÆŒÇ]
ABCDEFGHIJKLMNOPQRSTUVWXYZ
1234567890(.,;:?!$&-*){ÄÖÜÅØÆŒÇ}

©
Monotype Garamond,
Simoncini Garamond,
Garamond No. 3,
Berthold Garamond,
Adobe Garamond,
Granjon

▶ Regular Small Caps
THE QUICK BROWN FOX JUMPS OVER A DOG. 123 4567 890 ZWEI BOXKÄMPFER JAGEN EVA DURCH SYLT PORTEZ CE VIEUX

▶ Italic OSF
The quick brown fox jumps over a Dog. 123 4567 890 Zwei Boxkämpfer jagen Eva durch Sylt portez ce vieux Whiskey blond

▶ Bold OSF
The quick brown fox jumps over a Dog. 123 4567 890 Zwei Boxkämpfer jagen Eva durch Sylt portez ce vieux Whiskey

▶ Bold Italic OSF
The quick brown fox jumps over a Dog. 123 4567 890 Zwei Boxkämpfer jagen Eva durch Sylt portez ce vieux Whiskey

SG2123 Mac ② (M. F. Benton, T. M. Cleland, 1917)
Amsterdam Garamont™

abcdefghijklmnopqrstuvwxyz[äöüßåøæœç]
ABCDEFGHIJKLMNOPQRSTUVWXYZ
1234567890(.,;:?!$&-*)ÄÖÜÅØÆŒÇ

© FSI 1993

| SG2124 | Mac | ② | 1927: (M. F. Benton, T. M. Cleland, 1917) |

Amsterdam Garamont Italic

abcdefghijklmnopqrstuvwxyz[äöüßåøæœç]
ABCDEFGHIJKLMNOPQRSTUVWXYZ
1234567890(.,;:?!$&-)ÄÖÜÅØÆŒÇ*

| SG2125 | Mac | ② | 1927: (M. F. Benton, T. M. Cleland, 1917) |

Amsterdam Garamont Medium

abcdefghijklmnopqrstuvwxyz[äöüßåøæœç]
ABCDEFGHIJKLMNOPQRSTUVWXYZ
1234567890(.,;:?!$&-*)ÄÖÜÅØÆŒÇ

| SG2126 | Mac | ② | 1927: (M. F. Benton, T. M. Cleland, 1917) |

Amsterdam Garamont Medium Italic

abcdefghijklmnopqrstuvwxyz[äöüßåøæœç]
ABCDEFGHIJKLMNOPQRSTUVWXYZ
1234567890(.,;:?!$&-)ÄÖÜÅØÆŒÇ*

| C051 | Mac + PC | ② | 1979: Constance Blanchard, Renee le Winter |

Garth Graphic

abcdefghijklmnopqrstuvwxyz[äöüßåøæœç]
ABCDEFGHIJKLMNOPQRSTUVWXYZ
1234567890(.,;:?!$&-*){ÄÖÜÅØÆŒÇ}

aaa
A924
Garth Graphic®, Reg, Ita, Bd, BdIta, ExtBd, Blk, Con, BdCon

▶ Regular
The quick brown fox jumps over a Dog. Zwei Boxkämpfer jagen Eva durch Sylt portez ce vieux Whiskey blond qui

▶ Italic
The quick brown fox jumps over a Dog. Zwei Boxkämpfer jagen Eva durch Sylt portez ce vieux Whiskey blond qui fume une

▶ Bold
The quick brown fox jumps over a Dog. Zwei Boxkämpfer jagen Eva durch Sylt portez ce vieux Whiskey

▶ Bold Italic
The quick brown fox jumps over a Dog. Zwei Boxkämpfer jagen Eva durch Sylt portez ce vieux Whiskey blond

▶ Extra Bold
The quick brown fox jumps over a Dog. Zwei Boxkämpfer jagen Eva durch Sylt portez ce vieux

▶ Black
The quick brown fox jumps over a Dog. Zwei Boxkämpfer jagen Eva durch Sylt portez ce

▶ Condensed
The quick brown fox jumps over a Dog. Zwei Boxkämpfer jagen Eva durch Sylt portez ce vieux Whiskey blond qui fume une pipe aber echt

▶ Bold Condensed
The quick brown fox jumps over a Dog. Zwei Boxkämpfer jagen Eva durch Sylt portez ce vieux Whiskey blond qui fume une pipe aber echt

A2866 Mac + PC (2)
Gazette™

abcdefghijklmnopqrstuvwxyz[äöüßåøœç]
ABCDEFGHIJKLMNOPQRSTUVWXYZ
1234567890(.,;:?!$&-){ÄÖÜÅØÆŒÇ}*

▶ Regular
The quick brown fox jumps over a Dog. Zwei Boxkämpfer jagen Eva durch Sylt portez ce vieux Whiskey

▶ Italic
The quick brown fox jumps over a Dog. Zwei Boxkämpfer jagen Eva durch Sylt portez ce vieux Whiskey

▶ Bold
The quick brown fox jumps over a Dog. Zwei Boxkämpfer jagen Eva durch Sylt portez ce vieux Whiskey

C611 Mac + PC (5)
Geometric™

abcdefghijklmnopqrstuvwxyz[äöüßåøæœç]
ABCDEFGHIJKLMNOPQRSTUVWXYZ
1234567890(.,;:?!$&-*){ÄÖÜÅØÆŒÇ}

© Bank Gothic

▶ Light
The quick brown fox jumps over a Dog. Zwei Boxkämpfer jagen Eva durch Sylt portez ce

▶ Light Italic
The quick brown fox jumps over a Dog. Zwei Boxkämpfer jagen Eva durch Sylt portez ce

▶ Bold
The quick brown fox jumps over a Dog. Zwei Boxkämpfer jagen Eva durch Sylt portez ce

▶ Bold Italic
The quick brown fox jumps over a Dog. Zwei Boxkämpfer jagen Eva durch Sylt portez ce

A564 Mac + PC
German Display 2

German Display 2:
Banco™, Charme™, Flyer™ Condensed, Wilhelm Klingspor Gotisch™

M052 Mac + PC (1) ✎ 1928–32: Eric Gill
Gill Sans® 1

abcdefghijklmnopqrstuvwxyz[äöüßåøæœç]
ABCDEFGHIJKLMNOPQRSTUVWXYZ
1234567890(.,;:?!$&-*){ÄÖÜÅØÆŒÇ}

aa*a*
A739
Gill Sans 1, Lt, LtIta, Reg, Ita, Bd, BdIta
BT1332
Gill Sans 1, Lt, LtIta, ExtBd, UltBd
BT1333
Gill Sans 2, Reg, Ita, Bd, BdIta

▶ Light
The quick brown fox jumps over a Dog. 123 4567 890 Zwei Boxkämpfer jagen Eva durch Sylt portez ce vieux Whiskey blond qui

▶ Light Italic
The quick brown fox jumps over a Dog. 123 4567 890 Zwei Boxkämpfer jagen Eva durch Sylt portez ce vieux Whiskey blond qui fume une

© FSI 1993

▼ M052   Mac + PC   Gill Sans® 1

▶ Regular
The quick brown fox jumps over a Dog. 123 4567 890 Zwei Boxkämpfer jagen Eva durch Sylt portez ce vieux Whiskey blond qui

▶ Italic
The quick brown fox jumps over a Dog. 123 4567 890 Zwei Boxkämpfer jagen Eva durch Sylt portez ce vieux Whiskey blond qui fume

▶ Bold
The quick brown fox jumps over a Dog. 123 4567 890 Zwei Boxkämpfer jagen Eva durch Sylt portez ce vieux

▶ Bold Italic
The quick brown fox jumps over a Dog. 123 4567 890 Zwei Boxkämpfer jagen Eva durch Sylt portez ce vieux Whiskey

M184   Mac + PC   ①   1928–32: Eric Gill

Gill Sans 2

abcdefghijklmnopqrstuvwxyz[äöüßåøæœç]
ABCDEFGHIJKLMNOPQRSTUVWXYZ
1234567890(.,;:?!$&-*){ÄÖÜÅØÆŒÇ}

aa*a*
A925
Gill Sans 2, ExtBd, UltBd, Con, BdCon, UltBdCon
BT1332
Gill Sans 1, Lt, LtIta, ExtBd, UltBd
BT1333
Gill Sans 2, Reg, Ita, Bd, BdIta
BT1334
Gill Sans Condensed, Con, BdCon, UltBdCon

▶ Extra Bold
The quick brown fox jumps over a Dog. Zwei Boxkämpfer jagen Eva durch Sylt portez ce

▶ Ultra Bold
The quick brown fox jumps over a Dog. Zwei Boxkämpfer jagen Eva durch Sylt

▶ Condensed
The quick brown fox jumps over a Dog. Zwei Boxkämpfer jagen Eva durch Sylt portez ce vieux Whiskey blond qui fume une pipe aber echt über die Mauer gesprungen und auch smørebrød en

▶ Bold Condensed
The quick brown fox jumps over a Dog. Zwei Boxkämpfer jagen Eva durch Sylt portez ce vieux Whiskey blond qui fume une

▶ Ultra Bold Condensed
The quick brown fox jumps over a Dog. Zwei Boxkämpfer jagen Eva durch Sylt portez ce vieux Whiskey blond qui fume

M1086   Mac + PC   ①   1928–32: Eric Gill

Gill Sans (Alternate Fig. 1)

abcdefghijklmnopqrstuvwxyz[äöüßåøæœç]
ABCDEFGHIJKLMNOPQRSTUVWXYZ
1234567890(.,;:?!$&-*){ÄÖÜÅØÆŒÇ}

▶ Alternate Light
The quick brown fox jumps over a Dog. 123 4567 890 Zwei Boxkämpfer jagen Eva durch Sylt portez ce vieux Whiskey blond qui

▶ Alternate Light Italic
The quick brown fox jumps over a Dog. 123 4567 890 Zwei Boxkämpfer jagen Eva durch Sylt portez ce vieux Whiskey blond qui fume une

▶ Alternate Regular
The quick brown fox jumps over a Dog. 123 4567 890 Zwei Boxkämpfer jagen Eva durch Sylt portez ce vieux Whiskey blond qui

▶ Alternate Italic
The quick brown fox jumps over a Dog. 123 4567 890 Zwei Boxkämpfer jagen Eva durch Sylt portez ce vieux Whiskey blond qui fume

© FSI 1993

▼ M1086 Mac + PC Gill Sans (Alternate Fig. 1)

▶ Alternate Bold
The quick brown fox jumps over a Dog. 123 4567 890 Zwei Boxkämpfer jagen Eva durch Sylt portez ce vieux

▶ Alternate Bold Italic
The quick brown fox jumps over a Dog. 123 4567 890 Zwei Boxkämpfer jagen Eva durch Sylt portez ce vieux Whiskey

M6698 Mac + PC ① 1928–32: Eric Gill
Gill Sans Display

abcdefghijklmnopqrstuvwxyz[äöüßåøæœç]
ABCDEFGHIJKLMNOPQRSTUVWXYZ
1234567890(.,;:?!$&-*){ÄÖÜÅØÆŒÇ}

▶ Bold
The quick brown fox jumps over a Dog. Zwei Boxkämpfer jagen Eva durch Sylt portez ce vieux Whiskey blond qui fume

▶ Extra Bold
The quick brown fox jumps over a Dog. Zwei Boxkämpfer jagen Eva durch Sylt portez ce

▶ Bold Condensed
The quick brown fox jumps over a Dog. Zwei Boxkämpfer jagen Eva durch Sylt portez ce vieux Whiskey blond qui fume une pipe aber

M6702 Mac + PC ① 1928–32: Eric Gill
Gill Sans Bold Extra Condensed

abcdefghijklmnopqrstuvwxyz[äöüßåøæœç]
ABCDEFGHIJKLMNOPQRSTUVWXYZ
1234567890(.,;:?!$&-*){ÄÖÜÅØÆŒÇ}

L6592 Mac ⑥ (1930: Eric Gill)
Gill Display Compressed

abcdefghijklmnopqrstuvwxyz[äöüßåøæœç]
ABCDEFGHIJKLMNOPQRSTUVWXYZ
1234567890(.,;:?!$&-*)ÄÖÜÅØÆŒÇ

L6126 Mac ⑥ (1930: Eric Gill)
Gill Kayo Condensed

abcdefghijklmnopqrstuvwxyz[äöüßåøæœç]
ABCDEFGHIJKLMNOPQRSTUVWXYZ
1234567890(.,;:?!$&-*)ÄÖÜÅØÆŒÇ

M6386 Mac + PC ⑥ 1930: Eric Gill
Gill Sans Shaded

abcdefghijklmnopqrstuvwxyz[äöüßåøæœç]
ABCDEFGHIJKLMNOPQRSTUVWXYZ
1234567890(.,;:?!$&-*){ÄÖÜÅØÆŒÇ}

© FSI 1993

▼ M6386 Mac + PC   Gill Sans Shaded

▶ Shadowed
The quick brown fox jumps over a Dog. Zwei Boxkämpfer jagen Eva durch Sylt portez ce vieux Whiskey blond

▶ Shadow
THE QUICK BROWN FOX JUMPS OVER A DOG. ZWEI BOXKÄMPFER JAGEN EVA DURCH SYLT PORTEZ CE

▶ Bold Extra Condensed
The quick brown fox jumps over a Dog. Zwei Boxkämpfer jagen Eva durch Sylt portez ce vieux Whiskey blond qui fume une pipe aber echt über die Mauer gesprungen und auch smørebrød en ysjes natuurlijk

---

EF1076 Mac + PC   ④   1935: William S. Gillies

Gillies Gothic

abcdefghijklmnopqrstuvwxyz[äöüßåøæœç]
ABCDEFGHIJKLMNOPQRSTUVWXYZ
1234567890(.,;:?!$&-*){ÄÖÜÅØÆŒÇ}

Kaufmann, Swing, Brio

▶ Light
The quick brown fox jumps over a Dog. Zwei Boxkämpfer jagen Eva durch Sylt portez ce vieux Whiskey blond qui fume une pipe aber echt über die Mauer gesprungen und auch

▶ Bold
The quick brown fox jumps over a Dog. Zwei Boxkämpfer jagen Eva durch Sylt portez ce vieux Whiskey blond qui fume une pipe aber echt über die Mauer

▶ Extra Bold
The quick brown fox jumps over a Dog. Zwei Boxkämpfer jagen Eva durch Sylt portez ce vieux Whiskey blond qui fume une pipe aber echt über die Mauer

---

EF6647 Mac + PC   ④   1935: William S. Gillies

Gillies Gothic

abcdefghijklmnopqrstuvwxyz[äöüßåøæœç]
ABCDEFGHIJKLMNOPQRSTUVWXYZ
1234567890(.,;:?!$&-*) ÄÖÜÅØÆŒÇ

aaa
MC2920
Gillies Gothic Ultra, Ult
MC2921
Gillies Gothic Ultra Shaded, UltShaded
L6128
Gillies Gothic

▶ Ultra Bold
The quick brown fox jumps over a Dog. Zwei Boxkämpfer jagen Eva durch Sylt portez ce vieux Whiskey blond qui fume une pipe aber echt über die Mauer

▶ Ultra Bold Shaded
The quick brown fox jumps over a Dog. Zwei Boxkämpfer jagen Eva durch Sylt portez ce vieux Whiskey blond qui fume une pipe aber echt über die Mauer gesprungen

---

EF305 Mac + PC   ②   1989: Robert Slimbach

ITC Giovanni® 1

abcdefghijklmnopqrstuvwxyz[äöüßåøæœç]
ABCDEFGHIJKLMNOPQRSTUVWXYZ
1234567890(.,;:?!$&-*){ÄÖÜÅØÆŒÇ}

aaa
C988
ITC Giovanni, Bk, BkIta, Bd, BdIta, Blk, BlkIta
A2750
ITC Giovanni, Bk, BkIta, Bd, BdIta, Blk, BlkIta

▶ Book
The quick brown fox jumps over a Dog. Zwei Boxkämpfer jagen Eva durch Sylt portez ce vieux Whiskey blond qui fume

▶ Bold
The quick brown fox jumps over a Dog. Zwei Boxkämpfer jagen Eva durch Sylt portez ce vieux Whiskey blond qui

© FSI 1993

▼ EF305 Mac + PC   ITC Giovanni® 1

▶ Black

The quick brown fox jumps over a Dog. Zwei Boxkämpfer jagen Eva durch Sylt portez ce vieux Whiskey blond

---

EF385 Mac + PC   ② ✏ 1989: Robert Slimbach
ITC Giovanni 2

abcdefghijklmnopqrstuvwxyz[äöüßåøæœç]
ABCDEFGHIJKLMNOPQRSTUVWXYZ
1234567890(.,;:?!$&-*){ÄÖÜÅØÆŒÇ}

aa*a*
C988
ITC Giovanni, Bk, BkIta, Bd, BdIta, Blk, BlkIta
A2750
ITC Giovanni, Bk, BkIta, Bd, BdIta, Blk, BlkIta

▶ Book Italic
The quick brown fox jumps over a Dog. Zwei Boxkämpfer jagen Eva durch Sylt portez ce vieux Whiskey blond qui fume une pipe aber

▶ Bold Italic
The quick brown fox jumps over a Dog. Zwei Boxkämpfer jagen Eva durch Sylt portez ce vieux Whiskey blond qui fume une

▶ Black Italic
The quick brown fox jumps over a Dog. Zwei Boxkämpfer jagen Eva durch Sylt portez ce vieux Whiskey blond qui fume

---

EF534 Mac + PC   ② ✏ 1989: Robert Slimbach
ITC Giovanni Small Caps

ABCDEFGHIJKLMNOPQRSTUVWXYZ[ÄÖÜSSÅØÆŒÇ]
ABCDEFGHIJKLMNOPQRSTUVWXYZ
1234567890(.,;:?!$&-*){ÄÖÜÅØÆŒÇ}

▶ Book Small Caps
THE QUICK BROWN FOX JUMPS OVER A DOG. 123 4567 890 ZWEI BOXKÄMPFER JAGEN EVA DURCH SYLT PORTEZ CE VIEUX WHISKEY

▶ Bold Small Caps
THE QUICK BROWN FOX JUMPS OVER A DOG. 123 4567 890 ZWEI BOXKÄMPFER JAGEN EVA DURCH SYLT PORTEZ CE VIEUX

L6593 Mac   ④ ✏ 1979: Alan Meeks
Glastonbury™

abcdefghijklmnopqrstuvwxyz[äöüßåøæœç]
ABCDEFGHIJKLMNOPQRSTUVWXYZ
1234567890(.,;:?!$&-)Ç*

G1514 Mac + PC   ⑥ ✏ 1900: (Joseph W. Phinney, 1897) M. F. Benton
Globe Gothic No. 240, 239, 230

abcdefghijklmnopqrstuvwxyz[äöüßåøæœç]
ABCDEFGHIJKLMNOPQRSTUVWXYZ
1234567890(.,;:?!$&-*){ÄÖÜÅØÆŒÇ}

© FSI 1993

▼ G1514 Mac + PC   Globe Gothic No. 240, 239, 230

aaa
C183
Globe Gothic, Lt, Demi,
Bd, Ult

▶ Regular No. 240
The quick brown fox jumps over a Dog. Zwei Boxkämpfer jagen Eva durch Sylt portez ce vieux Whiskey blond qui fume

▶ Italic
The quick brown fox jumps over a Dog. Zwei Boxkämpfer jagen Eva durch Sylt portez ce vieux Whiskey blond qui fume

▶ Condensed No. 239
The quick brown fox jumps over a Dog. Zwei Boxkämpfer jagen Eva durch Sylt portez ce vieux Whiskey blond qui fume une pipe aber echt über die Mauer

▶ Condensed Italic
The quick brown fox jumps over a Dog. Zwei Boxkämpfer jagen Eva durch Sylt portez ce vieux Whiskey blond qui fume une pipe aber echt über die Mauer

▶ Extra Condensed No. 230
The quick brown fox jumps over a Dog. Zwei Boxkämpfer jagen Eva durch Sylt portez ce vieux Whiskey blond qui fume une pipe aber echt über die Mauer gesprungen und auch

▶ Extra Condensed Italic
The quick brown fox jumps over a Dog. Zwei Boxkämpfer jagen Eva durch Sylt portez ce vieux Whiskey blond qui fume une pipe aber echt über die Mauer gesprungen und auch

C183 Mac + PC   ⑥   ✎ 1900: (Joseph W. Phinney, 1897) M. F. Benton
Globe Gothic

abcdefghijklmnopqrstuvwxyz[äöüßåøæœç]
ABCDEFGHIJKLMNOPQRSTUVWXYZ
1234567890(.,;:?!$&-*){ÄÖÜÅØÆŒÇ}

aaa
G1514
Globe Gothic No. 240,
239, 230, RegNo240,
Ita, ConNo239, ConIta,
ExtConNo230,
ExtConIta

▶ Light
The quick brown fox jumps over a Dog. Zwei Boxkämpfer jagen Eva durch Sylt portez ce vieux Whiskey blond qui fume une pipe aber echt

▶ Demi
The quick brown fox jumps over a Dog. Zwei Boxkämpfer jagen Eva durch Sylt portez ce vieux Whiskey blond qui fume une pipe aber

▶ Bold
The quick brown fox jumps over a Dog. Zwei Boxkämpfer jagen Eva durch Sylt portez ce vieux Whiskey blond qui fume

▶ Ultra
The quick brown fox jumps over a Dog. Zwei Boxkämpfer jagen Eva durch Sylt portez ce vieux Whiskey blond qui

SF6635 Mac   ⑥   ✎ 1993: (Fred. W. Goudy) Rod McDonald
Goudy Globe Gothic

abcdefghijklmnopqrstuvwxyz[äöüß åøæœç]
ABCDEFGHIJKLMNOPQRSTUVWXYZ
1234567890(.,;:?!$&-*){ÄÖÜÅØÆŒÇ}

Stylus Headlines 1:
Bodoni Open Condensed, Fanfare Recut, Goudy Globe Gothic, Loyalist™ Condensed

M270 Mac + PC   ②
Gloucester Oldstyle™

abcdefghijklmnopqrstuvwxyz[äöüßåøæœç]
ABCDEFGHIJKLMNOPQRSTUVWXYZ
1234567890(.,;:?!$&-*){ÄÖÜÅØÆŒÇ}

© FSI 1993
G 17

Cheltenham

▼ M270   Mac + PC   Gloucester Oldstyle™

► Regular
The quick brown fox jumps over a Dog. Zwei Boxkämpfer jagen Eva durch Sylt portez ce vieux Whiskey blond qui fume une pipe aber echt

► Bold
The quick brown fox jumps over a Dog. Zwei Boxkämpfer jagen Eva durch Sylt portez ce vieux Whiskey blond qui fume une

► Bold Expanded
The quick brown fox jumps over a Dog. Zwei Boxkämpfer jagen Eva durch Sylt

► Bold Condensed
The quick brown fox jumps over a Dog. Zwei Boxkämpfer jagen Eva durch Sylt portez ce vieux Whiskey blond qui fume une pipe aber echt

► Bold Extra Condensed
The quick brown fox jumps over a Dog. Zwei Boxkämpfer jagen Eva durch Sylt portez ce vieux Whiskey blond qui fume une pipe aber echt über die Mauer gesprungen und auch

MC2903   Mac + PC   ⑥   ✎ B. Zochowski
Glowworm™

abcdefghijklmnopqrstuvwxyz[äöüßåøæœç]
ABCDEFGHIJKLMNOPQRSTUVWXYZ
1234567890(.,;:?!$&-*){ÄÖÜÅØÆŒÇ}

MC2904   Mac + PC   ⑥   ✎ B. Zochowski
Glowworm Compressed

abcdefghijklmnopqrstuvwxyz[äöüßåøæœç]
ABCDEFGHIJKLMNOPQRSTUVWXYZ
1234567890(.,;:?!$&-*){ÄÖÜÅØÆŒÇ}

A054   Mac + PC   ③   ✎ 1979: Adrian Frutiger
Glypha® 1

abcdefghijklmnopqrstuvwxyz[äöüßåøæœç]
ABCDEFGHIJKLMNOPQRSTUVWXYZ
1234567890(.,;:?!$&-*){ÄÖÜÅØÆŒÇ}

PMN Caecilia, Boton, Serifa, Calvert

► 55 Regular
The quick brown fox jumps over a Dog. Zwei Boxkämpfer jagen Eva durch Sylt portez ce vieux Whiskey blond

► 55 Oblique
The quick brown fox jumps over a Dog. Zwei Boxkämpfer jagen Eva durch Sylt portez ce vieux Whiskey blond

► 65 Bold
The quick brown fox jumps over a Dog. Zwei Boxkämpfer jagen Eva durch Sylt portez ce vieux Whiskey

► 65 Bold Oblique
The quick brown fox jumps over a Dog. Zwei Boxkämpfer jagen Eva durch Sylt portez ce vieux Whiskey

© FSI 1993

A902 Mac + PC ③ ✎ 1979: Adrian Frutiger
Glypha 2

abcdefghijklmnopqrstuvwxyz[äöüßåøæœç]
ABCDEFGHIJKLMNOPQRSTUVWXYZ
1234567890(.,;:?!$&-*){ÄÖÜÅØÆŒÇ}

© PMN Caecilia, Boton, Serifa, Calvert

▶ 35 Thin
The quick brown fox jumps over a Dog. Zwei Boxkämpfer jagen Eva durch Sylt portez ce vieux Whiskey blond qui fume une

▶ 35 Thin Oblique
The quick brown fox jumps over a Dog. Zwei Boxkämpfer jagen Eva durch Sylt portez ce vieux Whiskey blond qui fume une

▶ 45 Light
The quick brown fox jumps over a Dog. Zwei Boxkämpfer jagen Eva durch Sylt portez ce vieux Whiskey blond qui fume

▶ 45 Light Oblique
The quick brown fox jumps over a Dog. Zwei Boxkämpfer jagen Eva durch Sylt portez ce vieux Whiskey blond qui fume

▶ 75 Black
The quick brown fox jumps over a Dog. Zwei Boxkämpfer jagen Eva durch Sylt portez ce vieux

▶ 75 Black Oblique
The quick brown fox jumps over a Dog. Zwei Boxkämpfer jagen Eva durch Sylt portez ce vieux

EF386 Mac + PC ② ✎ 1989: Engelmann, Jorgensen, Newton
ITC Golden Type® 1

abcdefghijklmnopqrstuvwxyz [äöüßåøæœç]
ABCDEFGHIJKLMNOPQRSTUVWXYZ
1234567890(.,;:?!$&-*){ÄÖÜÅØÆŒÇ}

▶ Original
The quick brown fox jumps over a Dog. Zwei Boxkämpfer jagen Eva durch Sylt portez ce vieux Whiskey blond qui fume une pipe aber echt

▶ Bold
The quick brown fox jumps over a Dog. Zwei Boxkämpfer jagen Eva durch Sylt portez ce vieux Whiskey blond qui fume une pipe aber

▶ Black
The quick brown fox jumps over a Dog. Zwei Boxkämpfer jagen Eva durch Sylt portez ce vieux Whiskey blond qui fume une

EF535 Mac + PC ② ✎ 1989: Engelmann, Jorgensen, Newton
ITC Golden Type Small Caps

ABCDEFGHIJKLMNOPQRSTUVWXYZ [ÄÖÜSSÅØÆŒÇ]
ABCDEFGHIJKLMNOPQRSTUVWXYZ
1234567890(.,;:?!$&-*){ÄÖÜÅØÆŒÇ}

▶ Original Small Caps
THE QUICK BROWN FOX JUMPS OVER A DOG. 123 4567 890 ZWEI BOXKÄMPFER JAGEN EVA DURCH SYLT PORTEZ CE VIEUX WHISKEY BLOND

▶ Bold Small Caps
THE QUICK BROWN FOX JUMPS OVER A DOG. 123 4567 890 ZWEI BOXKÄMPFER JAGEN EVA DURCH SYLT PORTEZ CE VIEUX WHISKEY BLOND

© FSI 1993

ITC Gorilla®
BT813 Mac + PC ⑥ 1970: Tom Carnase, Ronne Bonder

abcdefghijklmnopqrstuvwxyz[äöüßåøæœç]
ABCDEFGHIJKLMNOPQRSTUVWXYZ
1234567890(.,;:?!$@-*){ÄÖÜÅØÆŒÇ}

ITC Headlines:
ITC Gorilla®, ITC Grizzly®, ITC Grouch®, ITC Tom Roman®

FF Gothic™
FF6184 Mac + PC ⑤ 1992: Neville Brody

abcdefghijklmnopqrstuvwxyz[äöüßåøæœç]
ABCDEFGHIJKLMNOPQRSTUVWXYZ
1234567890[.,;:?!$&-*]{ÄÖÜÅØÆŒÇ}

Geometric, Bank Gothic, Neeskens

▶ One One
The quick brown fox jumps over a Dog. Zwei Boxkämpfer jagen

▶ One Two
The quick brown fox jumps over a Dog. Zwei Boxkämpfer jagen

▶ Two One
The quick brown fox jumps over a Dog. Zwei Boxkämpfer jagen

▶ Two Two
The quick brown fox jumps over a Dog. Zwei Boxkämpfer jagen

▶ One One Condensed
The quick brown fox jumps over a Dog. Zwei Boxkämpfer jagen Eva durch Sylt portez ce vieux Whiskey blond qui

▶ One Two Condensed
The quick brown fox jumps over a Dog. Zwei Boxkämpfer jagen Eva durch Sylt portez ce vieux Whiskey blond qui

Gothic
C612 Mac + PC ① (W. A. Dwiggins, 1930-32)

abcdefghijklmnopqrstuvwxyz[äöüßåøæœç]
ABCDEFGHIJKLMNOPQRSTUVWXYZ
1234567890(.,;:?!$&-*){ÄÖÜÅØÆŒÇ}

▶ No. 1
The quick brown fox jumps over a Dog. Zwei Boxkämpfer jagen Eva durch Sylt portez ce vieux Whiskey blond qui fume une pipe aber echt über die Mauer gesprungen und auch smørebrød en

▶ No. 2
The quick brown fox jumps over a Dog. Zwei Boxkämpfer jagen Eva durch Sylt portez ce vieux Whiskey blond qui fume

▶ No. 3
The quick brown fox jumps over a Dog. Zwei Boxkämpfer jagen Eva durch Sylt portez ce vieux Whiskey blond qui fume

▶ No. 4
The quick brown fox jumps over a Dog. Zwei Boxkämpfer jagen Eva durch Sylt portez ce vieux Whiskey blond qui fume une pipe aber echt

© FSI 1993

C604 Mac + PC ①
Gothic Extralite Extended

abcdefghijklmnopqrstuvwxyz[äöüßåøæœç]
ABCDEFGHIJKLMNOPQRSTUVWXYZ
1234567890(.,;:?!$&-*){ÄÖÜÅØÆŒÇ}

Derek Italic:
Derek Italic, Engravure, Gothic Extralite Extended, Holland Title

A165 Mac + PC
Gothic No. 13

Gothic No. 13:
Gothic No. 13™, Tempo™ Heavy Condensed

A165 Mac + PC ①
Gothic No. 13™

abcdefghijklmnopqrstuvwxyz[äöüßåøæœç]
ABCDEFGHIJKLMNOPQRSTUVWXYZ
1234567890(.,;:?!$&-*){ÄÖÜÅØÆŒÇ}

Gothic No. 13:
Gothic No. 13™, Tempo™ Heavy Condensed
aaa BT1325
Gothic No. 13, Reg

A056 Mac + PC ② 1915: F. W. Goudy
Goudy Old Style

abcdefghijklmnopqrstuvwxyz[äöüßåøæœç]
ABCDEFGHIJKLMNOPQRSTUVWXYZ
1234567890(.,;:?!$&-*){ÄÖÜÅØÆŒÇ}

aaa
BT1328
Goudy Old Style, Reg, Ita, Bd, BdIta, ExtBd
©
Goudy Oldstyle No. 394

▶ Old Style
The quick brown fox jumps over a Dog. Zwei Boxkämpfer jagen Eva durch Sylt portez ce vieux Whiskey blond qui fume une pipe

▶ Old Style Italic
The quick brown fox jumps over a Dog. Zwei Boxkämpfer jagen Eva durch Sylt portez ce vieux Whiskey blond qui fume une pipe aber echt

▶ Bold
The quick brown fox jumps over a Dog. Zwei Boxkämpfer jagen Eva durch Sylt portez ce vieux Whiskey blond qui fume une

▶ Bold Italic
The quick brown fox jumps over a Dog. Zwei Boxkämpfer jagen Eva durch Sylt portez ce vieux Whiskey blond qui fume une

A057 Mac + PC ② 1925-32: F. W. Goudy, Sol. Hess
Goudy 2

abcdefghijklmnopqrstuvwxyz[äöüßåøæœç]
ABCDEFGHIJKLMNOPQRSTUVWXYZ
1234567890(.,;:?!$&-*){ÄÖÜÅØÆŒÇ}

aaa
C055
Goudy Heavyface, Reg,
Ita, Con
BT1327
Goudy Heavyface, Reg,
Con

▼ A057 Mac + PC Goudy 2

▶ Extra Bold
The quick brown fox jumps over a Dog. Zwei Boxkämpfer jagen Eva durch Sylt portez ce vieux Whiskey blond qui

▶ Heavyface
The quick brown fox jumps over a Dog. Zwei Boxkämpfer jagen Eva durch Sylt portez ce

▶ Heavyface Italic
The quick brown fox jumps over a Dog. Zwei Boxkämpfer jagen Eva durch Sylt portez ce

A1149 Mac + PC   ②   1915: F. W. Goudy
Goudy Oldstyle Small Caps / OSF

ABCDEFGHIJKLMNOPQRSTUVWXYZ[ÄÖÜSSÅØÆŒÇ]
ABCDEFGHIJKLMNOPQRSTUVWXYZ
1234567890(.,;:?!$&-*){ÄÖÜÅØÆŒÇ}

▶ Old Style Small Caps / OSF
THE QUICK BROWN FOX JUMPS OVER A DOG. 123 4567 890 ZWEI BOXKÄMPFER JAGEN EVA DURCH SYLT PORTEZ CE VIEUX WHISKEY

▶ Old Style Italic OSF
The quick brown fox jumps over a Dog. 123 4567 890 Zwei Boxkämpfer jagen Eva durch Sylt portez ce vieux Whiskey blond qui fume

▶ Bold OSF
The quick brown fox jumps over a Dog. 123 4567 890 Zwei Boxkämpfer jagen Eva durch Sylt portez ce vieux Whiskey blond

▶ Bold Italic OSF
The quick brown fox jumps over a Dog. 123 4567 890 Zwei Boxkämpfer jagen Eva durch Sylt portez ce vieux Whiskey blond

M223 Mac + PC   ②   1915: F. W. Goudy
Monotype Goudy 1

abcdefghijklmnopqrstuvwxyz[äöüßåøæœç]
ABCDEFGHIJKLMNOPQRSTUVWXYZ
1234567890(.,;:?!$&-*){ÄÖÜÅØÆŒÇ}

aaa
BT1326
Goudy Catalogue, Reg
👁
Goudy Oldstyle No. 394, Goudy Handtooled

▶ Old Style
The quick brown fox jumps over a Dog. Zwei Boxkämpfer jagen Eva durch Sylt portez ce vieux Whiskey blond qui fume

▶ Old Style Italic
The quick brown fox jumps over a Dog. Zwei Boxkämpfer jagen Eva durch Sylt portez ce vieux Whiskey blond qui fume une pipe aber echt

▶ Catalogue
The quick brown fox jumps over a Dog. Zwei Boxkämpfer jagen Eva durch Sylt portez ce vieux Whiskey blond qui fume

▶ Catalogue Italic
The quick brown fox jumps over a Dog. Zwei Boxkämpfer jagen Eva durch Sylt portez ce vieux Whiskey blond qui fume une pipe

▶ Bold
The quick brown fox jumps over a Dog. Zwei Boxkämpfer jagen Eva durch Sylt portez ce vieux Whiskey blond qui fume

M224 Mac + PC ② ✒ 1915: F. W. Goudy
Goudy Extra Bold
abcdefghijklmnopqrstuvwxyz[äöüßåøæœç}
ABCDEFGHIJKLMNOPQRSTUVWXYZ
1234567890(.,;:?!$&-*){ÄÖÜÅØÆŒÇ}

Monotype Goudy 2:
Goudy Extra Bold, Goudy Modern, Goudy Text

M224 Mac + PC
Monotype Goudy 2
Monotype Goudy 2:
Goudy Extra Bold, Goudy Modern, Goudy Text
aaa BT1327
Goudy Heavyface, Reg, Con
A057

G915 Mac + PC ② ✒ 1915: F. W. Goudy
Goudy Old Style No. 394™
abcdefghijklmnopqrstuvwxyz[äöüßåøæœç}
ABCDEFGHIJKLMNOPQRSTUVWXYZ
1234567890(.,;:?!$&-*){ÄÖÜÅØÆŒÇ}

© Goudy Handtooled

▶ Regular OSF
The quick brown fox jumps over a Dog. 123 4567 890 Zwei Boxkämpfer jagen Eva durch Sylt portez ce vieux Whiskey

▶ Italic OSF
The quick brown fox jumps over a Dog. 123 4567 890 Zwei Boxkämpfer jagen Eva durch Sylt portez ce vieux Whiskey blond qui

▶ Small Caps OSF
The quick brown fox jumps over a Dog. 123 4567 890 Zwei Boxkämpfer jagen Eva durch Sylt portez ce vieux Whiskey

▶ Italic Small Caps OSF
The quick brown fox jumps over a Dog. 123 4567 890 Zwei Boxkämpfer jagen Eva durch Sylt portez ce vieux Whiskey

▶ Regular
The quick brown fox jumps over a Dog. Zwei Boxkämpfer jagen Eva durch Sylt portez ce vieux Whiskey blond qui fume

▶ Italic
The quick brown fox jumps over a Dog. Zwei Boxkämpfer jagen Eva durch Sylt portez ce vieux Whiskey blond qui fume une pipe aber echt

▶ Regular OSF, Short
The quick brown fox jumps over a Dog. 123 456 7890 Zwei Boxkämpfer jagen Eva durch Sylt portez ce vieux Whiskey

▶ Italic OSF, Short
The quick brown fox jumps over a Dog. 123 456 7890 Zwei Boxkämpfer jagen Eva durch Sylt portez ce vieux Whiskey blond qui

▶ Regular, Short
The quick brown fox jumps over a Dog. 123 4567 890 Zwei Boxkämpfer jagen Eva durch Sylt portez ce vieux Whiskey

▶ Italic, Short
The quick brown fox jumps over a Dog. 123 4567 890 Zwei Boxkämpfer jagen Eva durch Sylt portez ce vieux Whiskey blond qui

© FSI 1993

Goudy Catalogue
BT1326 MAC + PC — 1915: F. W. Goudy

abcdefghijklmnopqrstuvwxyz[äöüßåøæœç]
ABCDEFGHIJKLMNOPQRSTUVWXYZ
1234567890(.,;:?!$&-*){ÄÖÜÅØÆŒÇ}

Goudy Claremont™
RB6102 MAC — 1992: Richard Beatty (Fred. W. Goudy)

abcdefghijklmnopqrstuvwxyz[äöüßåøæœç]
ABCDEFGHIJKLMNOPQRSTUVWXYZ
1234567890(.,;:?!$&-*){ÄÖÜÅØÆŒÇ}

▶ Old Style Roman
The quick brown fox jumps over a Dog. Zwei Boxkämpfer jagen Eva durch Sylt portez ce vieux Whiskey blond qui fume une pipe aber

▶ Old Style Italic
The quick brown fox jumps over a Dog. Zwei Boxkämpfer jagen Eva durch Sylt portez ce vieux Whiskey blond qui fume une pipe aber echt über die Mauer

Goudy Collection 1:
Goudy Claremont™, Goudy Italian Old Style, Goudy Mediaeval

Goudy Claremont SC/OSF
RB6103 MAC — 1992: Richard Beatty (Fred. W. Goudy)

ABCDEFGHIJKLMNOPQRSTUVWXYZ[ÄÖÜÅØÆŒÇ]
ABCDEFGHIJKLMNOPQRSTUVWXYZ
1234567890(.,;:?!$&-*){ÄÖÜÅØÆŒÇ}

▶ Old Style Roman SC
THE QUICK BROWN FOX JUMPS OVER A DOG. 123 4567 890 ZWEI BOXKÄMPFER JAGEN EVA DURCH SYLT PORTEZ CE VIEUX WHISKEY BLOND

▶ Old Style Italic SC
The quick brown fox jumps over a Dog. 123 4567 890 Zwei Boxkämpfer jagen Eva durch Sylt portez ce vieux Whiskey blond qui fume une pipe aber

Goudy Collection 1 SC/OSF:
Goudy Claremont SC/OSF, Goudy Italian Old Style SC/OSF, Goudy Mediaeval Alternates

Goudy Collection 1
RB6102 MAC

Goudy Collection 1:
Goudy Claremont™, Goudy Italian Old Style, Goudy Mediaeval

Goudy Collection 1 SC/OSF
RB6103 MAC

Goudy Collection 1 SC/OSF:
Goudy Claremont SC/OSF, Goudy Italian Old Style SC/OSF, Goudy Mediaeval Alternates

© FSI 1993

BT805 Mac + PC (6) 1932: Charles H Becker; M. F. Benton, W. A. Parker
Goudy Handtooled

abcdefghijklmnopqrstuvwxyz[äöüßåøæœç]
ABCDEFGHIJKLMNOPQRSTUVWXYZ
1234567890(.,;:?!$&-*){ÄÖÜÅØÆŒÇ}

Bitstream Handtooled:
Cloister Open Face, Goudy Handtooled
aaa EF1070
Goudy Handtooled, Reg
Cheltenham Old Style™, Reg

C055 Mac + PC (2) 1925–32: F. W. Goudy, Sol. Hess
Goudy Heavyface

abcdefghijklmnopqrstuvwxyz[äöüßåøæœç]
ABCDEFGHIJKLMNOPQRSTUVWXYZ
1234567890(.,;:?!$&-*){ÄÖÜÅØÆŒÇ}

aaa
A057
Goudy 2, ExtBd,
Heavyface,
Heavyfacelta
BT1327
Goudy Heavyface, Reg,
Con

▶ Regular
The quick brown fox jumps over a Dog. Zwei Boxkämpfer jagen Eva durch Sylt portez ce

▶ Italic
The quick brown fox jumps over a Dog. Zwei Boxkämpfer jagen Eva durch Sylt portez ce

▶ Condensed
The quick brown fox jumps over a Dog. Zwei Boxkämpfer jagen Eva durch Sylt portez ce vieux Whiskey blond qui fume

---

RB6102 Mac (2) 1992: Richard Beatty (Fred. W. Goudy)
Goudy Italian Old Style

abcdefghijklmnopqrstuvwxyz[äöüßåøæœç]
ABCDEFGHIJKLMNOPQRSTUVWXYZ
1234567890(.,;:?!$&-*){ÄÖÜÅØÆŒÇ}

▶ Roman
The quick brown fox jumps over a Dog. Zwei Boxkämpfer jagen Eva durch Sylt portez ce vieux Whiskey blond qui fume une pipe aber echt

▶ Italic
The quick brown fox jumps over a Dog. Zwei Boxkämpfer jagen Eva durch Sylt portez ce vieux Whiskey blond qui fume une pipe aber echt

Goudy Collection 1:
Goudy Claremont™, Goudy Italian Old Style, Goudy Mediaeval

RB6103 Mac (2) 1992: Richard Beatty (Fred. W. Goudy)
Goudy Italian Old Style SC/OSF

ABCDEFGHIJKLMNOPQRSTUVWXYZ[ÄÖÜÅØÆŒÇ]
ABCDEFGHIJKLMNOPQRSTUVWXYZ
1234567890(.,;:?!$&-*){ÄÖÜÅØÆŒÇ}

▼ RB6103 Mac Goudy Italian Old Style SC/OSF

▶ Roman Small Caps
The quick brown fox jumps over a Dog. 123 4567 890 Zwei Boxkämpfer jagen Eva durch Sylt portez ce

▶ Italic Small Caps
The quick brown fox jumps over a Dog. 123 4567 890 Zwei Boxkämpfer jagen Eva durch Sylt portez ce vieux Whiskey blond qui fume

Goudy Collection 1 SC/OSF:
Goudy Claremont SC/OSF, Goudy Italian Old Style SC/OSF, Goudy Mediaeval Alternates

---

RB6102 Mac ⑦ 1992: Richard Beatty (Fred. W. Goudy)
Goudy Mediaeval

abcdefghijklmnopqrstuvwxyz[äöüßåøæœç]
ABCDEFGHIJKLMNOPQRSTUVWXYZ
1234567890(.,;:?!$&-*){ÄÖÜÅØÆŒÇ}

Goudy Collection 1:
Goudy Claremont™, Goudy Italian Old Style, Goudy Mediaeval

RB6103 Mac ⑦ 1992: Richard Beatty (Fred. W. Goudy)
Goudy Mediaeval Alternates

abcdefghijklmnopqrstuvwxyz[äöüßåøæœç]
ABCDEFGHIJKLMNOPQRSTUVWXYZ
1234567890(.,;:?!$&-*){ÄÖÜÅØÆŒÇ}

Goudy Collection 1 SC/OSF:
Goudy Claremont SC/OSF, Goudy Italian Old Style SC/OSF, Goudy Mediaeval Alternates

---

M224 Mac + PC ② 1918: F. W. Goudy
Goudy Modern

abcdefghijklmnopqrstuvwxyz[äöüßåøæœç]
ABCDEFGHIJKLMNOPQRSTUVWXYZ
1234567890(.,;:?!$&-*){ÄÖÜÅØÆŒÇ}

aa*a*
A6081
Scotch Roman, Reg, Ita
Goudy Modern / Scotch Roman
Goudy Modern , Reg, Ita

▶ Regular
The quick brown fox jumps over a Dog. Zwei Boxkämpfer jagen Eva durch Sylt portez ce vieux Whiskey blond qui fume une pipe aber echt

▶ Italic
The quick brown fox jumps over a Dog. Zwei Boxkämpfer jagen Eva durch Sylt portez ce vieux Whiskey blond qui fume une pipe aber echt

Monotype Goudy 2:
Goudy Extra Bold, Goudy Modern, Goudy Text

© FSI 1993

M6329 Mac + PC
Goudy Modern / Scotch Roman

Goudy Modern / Scotch Roman:
Goudy Modern, Scotch Roman

ET1108 Mac + PC — 1921: F. W. Goudy
Goudy Newstyle

abcdefghijklmnopqrstuvwxyz[äöüśtct]
ABCDEFGHIJKLMNOPQRSTUVWXYZ
1234567890(.,:;?!$&-*){ÄÖÜ}

Electric Marlborough™:
Goudy Newstyle, Italian Electric™

RB6100 Mac — 1992: Richard Beatty (Fred. W. Goudy)
Goudy Saks™

abcdefghijklmnopqrstuvwxyz[äöüßåøæœç]
ABCDEFGHIJKLMNOPQRSTUVWXYZ
1234567890(.,:;?!$&-*){ÄÖÜÅØÆŒÇ}

▶ **Roman**
The quick brown fox jumps over a Dog. Zwei Boxkämpfer jagen Eva durch Sylt portez ce vieux Whiskey blond qui fume une pipe aber echt

▶ **Italic**
The quick brown fox jumps over a Dog. Zwei Boxkämpfer jagen Eva durch Sylt portez ce vieux Whiskey blond qui fume une pipe aber echt über die Mauer gesprungen und auch

▶ **Demi Bold**
The quick brown fox jumps over a Dog. Zwei Boxkämpfer jagen Eva durch Sylt portez ce vieux Whiskey blond qui fume une pipe aber echt

▶ **Demi Bold Italic**
The quick brown fox jumps over a Dog. Zwei Boxkämpfer jagen Eva durch Sylt portez ce vieux Whiskey blond qui fume une pipe aber echt über die Mauer gesprungen und

▶ **Roman Titling Caps**
THE QUICK BROWN FOX JUMPS OVER A DOG. ZWEI BOXKÄMPFER JAGEN EVA DURCH SYLT PORTEZ CE

▶ **Demi Bold Titling Caps**
THE QUICK BROWN FOX JUMPS OVER A DOG. ZWEI BOXKÄMPFER JAGEN EVA DURCH SYLT

RB6101 Mac — 1992: Richard Beatty (Fred. W. Goudy)
Goudy Saks SC/OSF

ABCDEFGHIJKLMNOPQRSTUVWXYZ[ÄÖÜÅØÆŒÇ]
ABCDEFGHIJKLMNOPQRSTUVWXYZ
1234567890(.,:;?!$&-*){ÄÖÜÅØÆŒÇ}

▶ **Roman Small Caps**
THE QUICK BROWN FOX JUMPS OVER A DOG. 123 4567 890 ZWEI BOXKÄMPFER JAGEN EVA DURCH SYLT PORTEZ CE VIEUX WHISKEY BLOND

▶ **Italic OSF**
The quick brown fox jumps over a Dog. 123 4567 890 Zwei Boxkämpfer jagen Eva durch Sylt portez ce vieux Whiskey blond qui fume une pipe aber echt über die Mauer gesprungen

© FSI 1993

▼ RB6101 Mac Goudy Saks SC/OSF

▶ Demi Bold SC
The quick brown fox jumps over a Dog. 123 4567 890 Zwei Boxkämpfer jagen Eva durch Sylt portez ce vieux Whiskey blond

▶ Demi Bold Italic OSF
The quick brown fox jumps over a Dog. 123 4567 890 Zwei Boxkämpfer jagen Eva durch Sylt portez ce vieux Whiskey blond qui fume une pipe aber echt über die Mauer gesprungen

▶ Bold Titling Caps
THE QUICK BROWN FOX JUMPS OVER A DOG. ZWEI BOXKÄMPFER JAGEN EVA DURCH SYLT PORTEZ CE

EF306 Mac + PC ① ✎ 1986: (F. W. Goudy, 1929)
ITC Goudy Sans 1

abcdefghijklmnopqrstuvwxyz[äöüßåøæœç]
ABCDEFGHIJKLMNOPQRSTUVWXYZ
1234567890(.,;:?!$&-*){ÄÖÜÅØÆŒÇ}

a a *a*
C984
ITC Goudy Sans, Bk, BkIta, Med, MedIta, Bd, BdIta, Blk, BlkIta
BT1329
ITC Goudy Sans 1, Lt, LtIta, Blk, BlkIta
BT1330
ITC Goudy Sans 2, Med, MedIta, Bd, BdIta

▶ Book
The quick brown fox jumps over a Dog. Zwei Boxkämpfer jagen Eva durch Sylt portez ce vieux Whiskey blond qui fume une pipe aber echt

▶ Book Italic
The quick brown fox jumps over a Dog. Zwei Boxkämpfer jagen Eva durch Sylt portez ce vieux Whiskey blond qui fume une pipe aber echt

▶ Bold
The quick brown fox jumps over a Dog. Zwei Boxkämpfer jagen Eva durch Sylt portez ce vieux Whiskey blond qui fume une

▶ Bold Italic
The quick brown fox jumps over a Dog. Zwei Boxkämpfer jagen Eva durch Sylt portez ce vieux Whiskey blond qui fume une pipe

---

EF307 Mac + PC ① ✎ 1986: (F. W. Goudy, 1929)
ITC Goudy Sans 2

abcdefghijklmnopqrstuvwxyz[äöüßåøæœç]
ABCDEFGHIJKLMNOPQRSTUVWXYZ
1234567890(.,;:?!$&-*){ÄÖÜÅØÆŒÇ}

a a *a*
C984
ITC Goudy Sans, Bk, BkIta, Med, MedIta, Bd, BdIta, Blk, BlkIta
BT1329
ITC Goudy Sans 1, Lt, LtIta, Blk, BlkIta
BT1330
ITC Goudy Sans 2, Med, MedIta, Bd, BdIta

▶ Medium
The quick brown fox jumps over a Dog. Zwei Boxkämpfer jagen Eva durch Sylt portez ce vieux Whiskey blond qui fume une pipe aber echt

▶ Medium Italic
The quick brown fox jumps over a Dog. Zwei Boxkämpfer jagen Eva durch Sylt portez ce vieux Whiskey blond qui fume une pipe aber echt

▶ Black
The quick brown fox jumps over a Dog. Zwei Boxkämpfer jagen Eva durch Sylt portez ce vieux Whiskey blond qui fume

▶ Black Italic
The quick brown fox jumps over a Dog. Zwei Boxkämpfer jagen Eva durch Sylt portez ce vieux Whiskey blond qui fume une

---

EF536 Mac + PC ① ✎ 1986: (F. W. Goudy, 1929)
ITC Goudy Sans 3

ABCDEFGHIJKLMNOPQRSTUVWXYZ[ÄÖÜSSÅØÆŒÇ]
ABCDEFGHIJKLMNOPQRSTUVWXYZ
1234567890(.,;:?!$&-*){ÄÖÜÅØÆŒÇ}

© FSI 1993

▼

▼ EF536 Mac + PC ITC Goudy Sans 3

▶ Book Small Caps
THE QUICK BROWN FOX JUMPS OVER A DOG. 123 4567 890 ZWEI BOXKÄMPFER JAGEN EVA DURCH SYLT PORTEZ CE VIEUX WHISKEY BLOND QUI FUME UNE PIPE

▶ Medium Small Caps
THE QUICK BROWN FOX JUMPS OVER A DOG. 123 4567 890 ZWEI BOXKÄMPFER JAGEN EVA DURCH SYLT PORTEZ CE VIEUX WHISKEY BLOND QUI

M2858 Mac + PC ⑦ 1928-29: Frederic W Goudy
Goudy Text

abcdefghijklmnopqrstuvwxyz[äöüßåøæœç]
ABCDEFGHIJKLMNOPQRSTUVWXYZ
1234567890(.,:;?!$&-*){ÄÖÜÅØÆŒÇ}

aaa
A2749
Goudy Text, Reg,
Alternate,
DeutscheFraktur,
LombardicCapitals
✠ M224
Monotype Goudy 2

▶ Regular
The quick brown fox jumps over a Dog. Zwei Boxkämpfer jagen Eva durch Sylt portez ce vieux Whiskey blond qui fume une pipe aber echt über die Mauer gesprungen

▶ Alternate
BGJEffiflflfflffląßhstſl

▶ Dfr
The quick brown fox jumps over a Dog. Zwei Boxkämpfer jagen Eva durch Sylt portez ce vieux Whiskey blond qui fume une pipe aber echt über die Mauer gesprungen

▶ Lombardic Capitals
THE QUICK BROWN FOX JUMPS OVER A DOG. ZWEI BOXKÄMPFER JAGEN EVA DURCH

G387 Mac + PC ⑦ 1930: F. W. Goudy
Goudy Thirty, No. 392™

abcdefghijklmnopqrstuvwxyz[äöüßåøæœç]
ABCDEFGHIJKLMNOPQRSTUVWXYZ
1234567890(.,:;?!$&-*){ÄÖÜÅØÆŒÇ}

▶ Regular OSF
The quick brown fox jumps over a Dog. 123 4567 890 Zwei Boxkämpfer jagen Eva durch Sylt portez ce vieux Whiskey blond qui fume

▶ Swash OSF
The quick brown fox jumps over a Dog. Zwei Boxkämpfer jagen Eva durch Sylt portez ce vieux Whiskey blond qui fume une pipe aber echt

---

G2773 Mac + PC ② 1936: F. W. Goudy
Goudy Village™

abcdefghijklmnopqrstuvwxyz[äöüßåøæœç]
ABCDEFGHIJKLMNOPQRSTUVWXYZ
1234567890(.,:;?!$&-*){ÄÖÜÅØÆŒÇ}

▶ Regular OSF
The quick brown fox jumps over a Dog. 123 4567 890 Zwei Boxkämpfer jagen Eva durch Sylt portez ce vieux Whiskey blond qui

▶ Italic OSF
The quick brown fox jumps over a Dog. 123 4567 890 Zwei Boxkämpfer jagen Eva durch Sylt portez ce vieux Whiskey blond qui fume une pipe aber

▶ Small Caps OSF
THE QUICK BROWN FOX JUMPS OVER A DOG. 123 4567 890 ZWEI BOXKÄMPFER JAGEN EVA DURCH SYLT PORTEZ CE VIEUX WHISKEY BLOND QUI

▶ Italic Small Caps OSF
THE QUICK BROWN FOX JUMPS OVER A DOG. 123 4567 890 ZWEI BOXKÄMPFER JAGEN EVA DURCH SYLT PORTEZ CE VIEUX WHISKEY BLOND QUI

© FSI 1993

▼ G2773 Mac + PC Goudy Village™

▶ Regular

The quick brown fox jumps over a Dog. 123 4567 890 Zwei Boxkämpfer jagen Eva durch Sylt portez ce vieux Whiskey blond qui

▶ Italic

The quick brown fox jumps over a Dog. 123 4567 890 Zwei Boxkämpfer jagen Eva durch Sylt portez ce vieux Whiskey blond qui fume une pipe aber echt über

▶ Regular Short

The quick brown fox jumps over a Dog. 123 4567 890 Zwei Boxkämpfer jagen Eva durch Sylt portez ce vieux Whiskey blond qui

▶ Italic Short

The quick brown fox jumps over a Dog. 123 4567 890 Zwei Boxkämpfer jagen Eva durch Sylt portez ce vieux Whiskey blond qui fume une pipe aber echt über

▶ Regular Short OSF

The quick brown fox jumps over a Dog. 123 4567 890 Zwei Boxkämpfer jagen Eva durch Sylt portez ce vieux Whiskey blond qui

▶ Italic Short OSF

The quick brown fox jumps over a Dog. 123 4567 890 Zwei Boxkämpfer jagen Eva durch Sylt portez ce vieux Whiskey blond qui fume une pipe aber echt über

FB6838 Mac + PC ⑥ 1993: Leslie Cabarga

Graffiti™

abcdefghijklmnopqrstuvwxyz[äöüßåøæœç]
ABCDEFGHIJKLMNOPQRSTUVWXYZ
1234567890(.,;:?!$&-*){ÄÖÜÅØÆŒÇ}

FB Display Pack 2:
BadTyp™, Graffiti™, Hip Hop™

A1009 Mac + PC ② 1928–31: (C. Garamond, 1532) G. W. Jones, C. H. Griffith

Granjon™

abcdefghijklmnopqrstuvwxyz[äöüßåøæœç]
ABCDEFGHIJKLMNOPQRSTUVWXYZ
1234567890(.,;:?!$&-*){ÄÖÜÅØÆŒÇ}

aa*a*
BT804
Granjon: Reg, Ita, Bd
©
Monotype Garamond, Simoncini Garamond, Garamond No. 3, Berthold Garamond, Adobe Garamond, Stempel Garamond

▶ Regular

The quick brown fox jumps over a Dog. Zwei Boxkämpfer jagen Eva durch Sylt portez ce vieux Whiskey blond qui fume une pipe aber

▶ Italic

The quick brown fox jumps over a Dog. Zwei Boxkämpfer jagen Eva durch Sylt portez ce vieux Whiskey blond qui fume une pipe aber echt

▶ Bold

The quick brown fox jumps over a Dog. Zwei Boxkämpfer jagen Eva durch Sylt portez ce vieux Whiskey blond qui fume une pipe aber

A1027 Mac + PC ② 1928–31: (C. Garamond, 1532) G. W. Jones, C. H. Griffith

Granjon Small Caps/OSF

ABCDEFGHIJKLMNOPQRSTUVWXYZ[ÄÖÜSSÅØÆŒÇ]
ABCDEFGHIJKLMNOPQRSTUVWXYZ
1234567890(.,;:?!$&-*){ÄÖÜÅØÆŒÇ}

© FSI 1993

G 30

▼ A1027 Mac + PC Granjon Small Caps/OSF

▶ Regular Small Caps / OSF
The quick brown fox jumps over a Dog. 123 4567 890 Zwei Boxkämpfer jagen Eva durch Sylt portez ce vieux Whiskey blond

▶ Italic OSF
The quick brown fox jumps over a Dog. 123 4567 890 Zwei Boxkämpfer jagen Eva durch Sylt portez ce vieux Whiskey blond qui fume une pipe

▶ Bold OSF
The quick brown fox jumps over a Dog. 123 4567 890 Zwei Boxkämpfer jagen Eva durch Sylt portez ce vieux Whiskey blond qui

---

C2523 Mac + PC ⑥ ✎ 1927: M. F. Benton
Greeting Monotone™

abcdefghijklmnopqrstuvwxyz[äöüßåøæœç]
ABCDEFGHIJKLMNOPQRSTUVWXYZ
0123456789(.,;:?!$&-*){ÄÖÜÅØÆŒÇ}

Headlines 87S:
Greeting Monotone™, Koloss™, Phenix™ American, Phosphor™, Zeppelin™

L2582 Mac ④ ✎ 1991: Gerhard Schwekendiek
Greyton™ Script

abcdefghijklmnopqrstuvwxyz[äöüßåøæœç]
ABCDEFGHIJKLMNOPQRSTUVWXYZ
1234567890(.,;:?!$§-)Ç*

BT813 Mac + PC ⑥ ✎ 1970: Tom Carnase, Ronne Bonder
ITC Grizzly®

abcdefghijklmnopqrstuvwxyz[äöüßåøæœç]
ABCDEFGHIJKLMNOPQRSTUVWXYZ
1234567890(.,;:?!$&-*){ÄÖÜÅØÆŒÇ}

ITC Headlines:
ITC Gorilla®, ITC Grizzly®, ITC Grouch®, ITC Tom Roman®
Kabel, ITC Kabel

EF503 Mac + PC ①
Digi Grotesk N™

abcdefghijklmnopqrstuvwxyz[äöüßåøæœç]
ABCDEFGHIJKLMNOPQRSTUVWXYZ
1234567890(.,;:?!$&-*){ÄÖÜÅØÆŒÇ}

Digi Grotesk S

▶ Light
The quick brown fox jumps over a Dog. Zwei Boxkämpfer jagen Eva durch Sylt portez ce vieux Whiskey blond qui fume

▶ Bold
The quick brown fox jumps over a Dog. Zwei Boxkämpfer jagen Eva durch Sylt portez ce vieux Whiskey blond qui fume

© FSI 1993

▼ EF503   Mac + PC   Digi Grotesk N™

▶ Semi Bold Condensed
The quick brown fox jumps over a Dog. Zwei Boxkämpfer jagen Eva durch Sylt portez ce vieux Whiskey blond qui fume une pipe aber echt über die Mauer gesprungen und auch smørebrød en ysjes

▶ Bold Condensed
The quick brown fox jumps over a Dog. Zwei Boxkämpfer jagen Eva durch Sylt portez ce vieux Whiskey blond qui fume une

EF504 Mac + PC ①
Digi Grotesk S™

abcdefghijklmnopqrstuvwxyz[äöüßåøæœç]
ABCDEFGHIJKLMNOPQRSTUVWXYZ
1234567890(.,;:?!$&-*){ÄÖÜÅØÆŒÇ}

© Digi Grotesk N

▶ Light
The quick brown fox jumps over a Dog. Zwei Boxkämpfer jagen Eva durch Sylt portez ce vieux Whiskey blond qui fume une pipe aber echt

▶ Semi Bold
The quick brown fox jumps over a Dog. Zwei Boxkämpfer jagen Eva durch Sylt portez ce vieux Whiskey blond qui fume une pipe

FB613 Mac + PC ①   ✎ 1989: Jonathan Hoefler, David Berlow
Bureau Grotesque™ 1

abcdefghijklmnopqrstuvwxyz1234567890[äöüßåøæœç]

ABCDEFGHIJKLMNOPQRSTUVWXYZ(.,;:?!$&-*){ÄÖÜÅØÆŒÇ}

© Bulldog, Headline Bold, Grotesque

▶ No. 13
The quick brown fox jumps over a Dog. Zwei Boxkämpfer jagen Eva durch Sylt portez ce vieux Whiskey blond qui fume une pipe aber echt über die Mauer gesprungen und auch smørebrød en ysjes natuurlijk.

▶ No. 15
The quick brown fox jumps over a Dog. Zwei Boxkämpfer jagen Eva durch Sylt portez ce vieux Whiskey blond qui fume une pipe aber echt über die Mauer gesprungen und auch

▶ No. 17
The quick brown fox jumps over a Dog. Zwei Boxkämpfer jagen Eva durch Sylt portez ce vieux Whiskey blond qui fume une pipe aber echt über die Mauer

▶ No. 37
The quick brown fox jumps over a Dog. Zwei Boxkämpfer jagen Eva durch Sylt portez ce vieux Whiskey blond qui fume une pipe aber

▶ No. 53
The quick brown fox jumps over a Dog. Zwei Boxkämpfer jagen Eva durch Sylt portez ce vieux Whiskey

▶ No. 79
The quick brown fox jumps over a Dog. Zwei Boxkämpfer jagen Eva durch Sylt

FB6603 Mac + PC ①   ✎ 1992: David Berlow
Bureau Grotesque 2

abcdefghijklmnopqrstuvwxyz[äöüßåøæœç]
ABCDEFGHIJKLMNOPQRSTUVWXYZ
1234567890(.,;:?!$&-*){ÄÖÜÅØÆŒÇ}

▶ No. 11
The quick brown fox jumps over a Dog. Zwei Boxkämpfer jagen Eva durch Sylt portez ce vieux Whiskey blond qui fume une pipe aber echt über die Mauer gesprungen und auch smørebrød en ysjes natuurlijk

▶ No. 31
The quick brown fox jumps over a Dog. Zwei Boxkämpfer jagen Eva durch Sylt portez ce vieux Whiskey blond qui fume une pipe aber echt über die Mauer gesprungen und auch smørebrød en

▼ FB6603 Mac + PC **Bureau Grotesque 2**

► No. 33
The quick brown fox jumps over a Dog. Zwei Boxkämpfer jagen Eva durch Sylt portez ce vieux Whiskey blond qui fume une pipe aber echt über die Mauer

► No. 35
The quick brown fox jumps over a Dog. Zwei Boxkämpfer jagen Eva durch Sylt portez ce vieux Whiskey blond qui fume une pipe aber echt über die

► No. 51
The quick brown fox jumps over a Dog. Zwei Boxkämpfer jagen Eva durch Sylt portez ce vieux Whiskey blond qui fume une pipe

► No. 55
The quick brown fox jumps over a Dog. Zwei Boxkämpfer jagen Eva durch Sylt portez ce vieux

SG2168 Mac ①
Grotesque No. 9 Bold Condensed

**abcdefghijklmnopqrstuvwxyz[äöüßåøæœç]
ABCDEFGHIJKLMNOPQRSTUVWXYZ
1234567890(.,;:?!$&-*)ÄÖÜÅØÆŒÇ**

SG2169 Mac ①
Grotesque No. 9 Bold Condensed Italic

***abcdefghijklmnopqrstuvwxyz[äöüßåøæœç]
ABCDEFGHIJKLMNOPQRSTUVWXYZ
1234567890(.,;:?!$ -*)ÄÖÜÅØÆŒÇ***

M284 Mac + PC ①
Grotesque 1

abcdefghijklmnopqrstuvwxyz[äöüßåøæœç]
ABCDEFGHIJKLMNOPQRSTUVWXYZ
1234567890(.,;:?!$&-*){ÄÖÜÅØÆŒÇ}

aa*a*
BT1322
Grotesque, No126Lt, No126LtIta
BT1323
Grotesque, No215, No215Ita, No216Bd, No216BdIta
A6074
Grotesque, Lt, LtIta, Reg, Ita, Bd, BdIta

► No. 126 Light
The quick brown fox jumps over a Dog. Zwei Boxkämpfer jagen Eva durch Sylt portez ce vieux Whiskey blond qui fume

► No. 126 Light Italic
The quick brown fox jumps over a Dog. Zwei Boxkämpfer jagen Eva durch Sylt portez ce vieux Whiskey blond qui fume une

► No. 215
The quick brown fox jumps over a Dog. Zwei Boxkämpfer jagen Eva durch Sylt portez ce vieux Whiskey blond qui fume

► No. 215 Italic
The quick brown fox jumps over a Dog. Zwei Boxkämpfer jagen Eva durch Sylt portez ce vieux Whiskey blond qui fume

► No. 216 Bold
The quick brown fox jumps over a Dog. Zwei Boxkämpfer jagen Eva durch Sylt portez ce vieux Whis-

© FSI 1993

M271 Mac + PC ①
Grotesque 2

abcdefghijklmnopqrstuvwxyz[äöüßåøæœç]
ABCDEFGHIJKLMNOPQRSTUVWXYZ
1234567890(.,;:?!$&-*){ÄÖÜÅØÆŒÇ}

a a a
A6078
Grotesque 2, Blk,
LtCon, Con, ExtCon

▶ Black
The quick brown fox jumps over a Dog. Zwei Boxkämpfer jagen Eva durch Sylt portez ce vieux Whiskey blond qui fume

▶ Light Condensed
The quick brown fox jumps over a Dog. Zwei Boxkämpfer jagen Eva durch Sylt portez ce vieux Whiskey blond qui fume une pipe aber echt über die Mauer

▶ Condensed
The quick brown fox jumps over a Dog. Zwei Boxkämpfer jagen Eva durch Sylt portez ce vieux Whiskey blond qui fume une pipe aber echt über die

▶ Extra Condensed
The quick brown fox jumps over a Dog. Zwei Boxkämpfer jagen Eva durch Sylt portez ce vieux Whiskey blond qui fume une pipe aber echt über die Mauer gesprungen und auch smørebrød en ysjes

BT813 Mac + PC ⑥   ✎ 1970: Tom Carnase, Ronne Bonder
ITC Grouch®

**abcdefghijklmnopqrstuvwxyz[äöüßåøæœç]
ABCDEFGHIJKLMNOPQRSTUVWXYZ
1234567890(.,;:?!$&-*){ÄÖÜÅØÆŒÇ}**

ITC Headlines:
ITC Gorilla®, ITC Grizzly®, ITC Grouch®, ITC Tom Roman®
👁 Caslon Black, Caslon Graphique

A2544 Mac + PC ②   ✎ 1986: Reinhard Haus
Guardi™

abcdefghijklmnopqrstuvwxyz[äöüßåøæœç]
ABCDEFGHIJKLMNOPQRSTUVWXYZ
1234567890(.,;:?!$&-*){ÄÖÜÅØÆŒÇ}

▶ 55 Roman
The quick brown fox jumps over a Dog. Zwei Boxkämpfer jagen Eva durch Sylt portez ce vieux Whiskey blond qui fume

▶ 56 Italic
The quick brown fox jumps over a Dog. Zwei Boxkämpfer jagen Eva durch Sylt portez ce vieux Whiskey blond qui fume une pipe aber

▶ 75 Bold
The quick brown fox jumps over a Dog. Zwei Boxkämpfer jagen Eva durch Sylt portez ce vieux Whiskey

▶ 76 Bold Italic
The quick brown fox jumps over a Dog. Zwei Boxkämpfer jagen Eva durch Sylt portez ce vieux Whiskey blond qui fume

▶ 95 Black
The quick brown fox jumps over a Dog. Zwei Boxkämpfer jagen Eva durch Sylt portez ce vieux

▶ 96 Black Italic
The quick brown fox jumps over a Dog. Zwei Boxkämpfer jagen Eva durch Sylt portez ce vieux Whis-

© FSI 1993

TF6649 Mac + PC   ⑥   1992: Joe Treacy
TF Guestcheck™

abcdefghijklmnopqrstuvwxyz
ABCDEFGHIJKLMNOPQRSTUVWXYZ
1234567890[.,:;?!$&-*]
[äöüßåøœç]{ÄÖÜÅØÆŒÇ}

TF Guestcheck™ / TF Raincheck™:
TF Guestcheck™, TF Raincheck™

TF6649 Mac + PC
TF Guestcheck™ / TF Raincheck™

TF Guestcheck™ / TF Raincheck™:
TF Guestcheck™, TF Raincheck™

Alessio Leonardi, Berlin, D

TF655 MAC + PC   ②   1985: Joseph W. Treacy
TF Habitat® A

abcdefghijklmnopqrstuvwxyz[äöüßåøæœç]
ABCDEFGHIJKLMNOPQRSTUVWXYZ
1234567890(.,;:?!$&-*)[ÄÖÜÅØÆŒÇ]

▶ Regular
The quick brown fox jumps over a Dog. Zwei Boxkämpfer jagen Eva durch Sylt portez ce vieux Whiskey blond qui fume

▶ Italic
The quick brown fox jumps over a Dog. Zwei Boxkämpfer jagen Eva durch Sylt portez ce vieux Whiskey blond qui fume une pipe aber

▶ Bold
The quick brown fox jumps over a Dog. Zwei Boxkämpfer jagen Eva durch Sylt portez ce vieux Whiskey blond qui

▶ Bold Italic
The quick brown fox jumps over a Dog. Zwei Boxkämpfer jagen Eva durch Sylt portez ce vieux Whiskey blond qui fume une

TF6662 MAC + PC   ②   1985: Joseph W. Treacy
TF Habitat B

abcdefghijklmnopqrstuvwxyz[äöüßåøæœç]
ABCDEFGHIJKLMNOPQRSTUVWXYZ
1234567890(.,;:?!$&-*)[ÄÖÜÅØÆŒÇ]

▶ Book
The quick brown fox jumps over a Dog. Zwei Boxkämpfer jagen Eva durch Sylt portez ce vieux Whiskey blond qui fume

▶ Book Italic
The quick brown fox jumps over a Dog. Zwei Boxkämpfer jagen Eva durch Sylt portez ce vieux Whiskey blond qui fume une pipe aber

▶ Demi
The quick brown fox jumps over a Dog. Zwei Boxkämpfer jagen Eva durch Sylt portez ce vieux Whiskey blond qui

▶ Demi Italic
The quick brown fox jumps over a Dog. Zwei Boxkämpfer jagen Eva durch Sylt portez ce vieux Whiskey blond qui fume une pipe

TF656 MAC + PC   ②   1987: Joseph W. Treacy
Habitat A Condensed

abcdefghijklmnopqrstuvwxyz[äöüßåøæœç]
ABCDEFGHIJKLMNOPQRSTUVWXYZ
1234567890(.,;:?!$&-*)[ÄÖÜÅØÆŒÇ]

▶ Condensed
The quick brown fox jumps over a Dog. Zwei Boxkämpfer jagen Eva durch Sylt portez ce vieux Whiskey blond qui fume une pipe aber echt

▶ Condensed Italic
The quick brown fox jumps over a Dog. Zwei Boxkämpfer jagen Eva durch Sylt portez ce vieux Whiskey blond qui fume une pipe aber echt über die Mauer

▶ Bold Condensed
The quick brown fox jumps over a Dog. Zwei Boxkämpfer jagen Eva durch Sylt portez ce vieux Whiskey blond qui fume une pipe aber

▶ Bold Condensed Italic
The quick brown fox jumps over a Dog. Zwei Boxkämpfer jagen Eva durch Sylt portez ce vieux Whiskey blond qui fume une pipe aber echt

© FSI 1993

TF6630 Mac + PC
TF Habitat Bold Contour

TF Habitat Bold Contour:
TF Habitat Bold Contour, TF Simper™ Extrabold

TF6630 Mac + PC ② ✏ 1992: Joseph W. Treacy
TF Habitat Bold Contour

abcdefghijklmnopqrstuvwxyz[äöüßåøæœç]
ABCDEFGHIJKLMNOPQRSTUVWXYZ
1234567890(.,;:?!$&-*){ÄÖÜÅØÆŒÇ}

TF Habitat Bold Contour:
TF Habitat Bold Contour, TF Simper™ Extrabold

EF6470 Mac + PC ④ ✏ Martin Wait
Hadfield™

abcdefghijklmnopqrstuvwxyz[äöüßåøæœç]
ABCDEFGHIJKLMNOPQRSTUVWXYZ
1234567890(.,;:?!$&-*)ÄÖÜÅØÆŒÇ

E+F Special Headlines 6:
Croissant, Hadfield™, Jenson™ Old Style Bold Condensed, Knightsbridge™, Lazybones™

LP942 Mac + PC ⑤ ✏ (1965)
Hadrian™ Bold

abcdefghijklmnopqrstuvwxyz1234567890[äöüßaøæœç]
ABCDEFGHIJKLMNOPQRSTUVWXYZ(.,;:?!$&-*)ÄÖÜÅØÆŒÇ

LetterPerfect 3:
Hadrian™ Bold, Silhouette™
👁 Aura, Aurora, Hanseatic, Helvetica Inserat, Helvetica Compressed, Impact, Placard

G388 Mac + PC ② ✏ 1918: F. W. Goudy
Hadriano No. 309™

ABCDEFGHIJKLMNOPQRSTUVWXYZÄÖÜSSÅØÆŒÇ
ABCDEFGHIJKLMNOPQRSTUVWXYZ
1234567890(.,;:?!$&-*)ÄÖÜÅØÆŒÇ

C991 Mac + PC ② ✏ 1918: F. W. Goudy
Hadriano

abcdefghijklmnopqrstuvwxyz[äöüßåøæœç]
ABCDEFGHIJKLMNOPQRSTUVWXYZ
1234567890(.,;:?!$&-*){ÄÖÜÅØÆŒÇ}

© FSI 1993

Forum

▼ C991 Mac + PC **Hadriano**

▶ Light
The quick brown fox jumps over a Dog. Zwei Boxkämpfer jagen Eva durch Sylt portez ce vieux Whiskey blond qui fume

▶ Bold
The quick brown fox jumps over a Dog. Zwei Boxkämpfer jagen Eva durch Sylt portez ce vieux Whiskey blond

▶ Extra Bold
The quick brown fox jumps over a Dog. Zwei Boxkämpfer jagen Eva durch Sylt portez ce vieux

▶ Extra Bold Condensed
The quick brown fox jumps over a Dog. Zwei Boxkämpfer jagen Eva durch Sylt portez ce vieux Whiskey blond qui

G2747 Mac + PC ⑥   1932: (F. W. Goudy, 1918) Sol. Hess

Hadriano Stonecut™

ABCDEFGHIJKLMNOPQRSTUVWXYZQÄÖÜSSÅØÆŒÇ
ABCDEFGHIJKLMNOPQRSTUVWXYZ
1234567890(.,;:?!$&-*)ÄÖÜÅØÆŒÇ

FB6798 Mac + PC ①   1993: Tom Rickner

Hamilton

abcdefghijklmnopqrstuvwxyz[äöüßåøæœç]
ABCDEFGHIJKLMNOPQRSTUVWXYZ
1234567890(.,;:?!$&-*){ÄÖÜÅØÆŒÇ}

Oz Handicraft

▶ Light
The quick brown fox jumps over a Dog. Zwei Boxkämpfer jagen Eva durch Sylt portez ce vieux Whiskey blond qui fume une pipe aber echt über die Mauer gesprungen und auch smørebrød en ysjes

▶ Medium
The quick brown fox jumps over a Dog. Zwei Boxkämpfer jagen Eva durch Sylt portez ce vieux Whiskey blond qui fume une pipe aber echt über die Mauer

▶ Bold
The quick brown fox jumps over a Dog. Zwei Boxkämpfer jagen Eva durch Sylt portez ce vieux Whiskey blond qui fume une pipe

EF6446 Mac + PC ⑥

Handel Gothic™

abcdefghijklmnopqrstuvwxyz[äöüßåøæœç]
ABCDEFGHIJKLMNOPQRSTUVWXYZ
1234567890(.,;:?!$&- *){ÄÖÜÅØÆŒÇ}

aaa
BT812
Bitstream Bold Headlines 1
Serpentine

▶ Light
The quick brown fox jumps over a Dog. Zwei Boxkämpfer jagen Eva durch Sylt portez ce vieux Whiskey blond qui

▶ Medium
The quick brown fox jumps over a Dog. Zwei Boxkämpfer jagen Eva durch Sylt portez ce vieux Whiskey blond qui

▶ Bold
The quick brown fox jumps over a Dog. Zwei Boxkämpfer jagen Eva durch Sylt portez ce vieux Whiskey

© FSI 1993

C2780 Mac + PC (6)
Handle Old Style

ABCDEFGHIJKLMNOPQRSTUVWXYZ[ÄÖÜÅÇ]
ABCDEFGHIJKLMNOPQRSTUVWXYZ
1234567890(.,;:?!$&-*){ÄÖÜÅÇ}

Agfa Engravers 1:
Antique Roman, Artisan Roman, Burin Roman, Burin Sans, Classic Roman, Handle Old Style, Roman

FF735 Mac + PC
FF Hands™

FF Hands™:
FF Erikrighthand™, FF Justlefthand™

BT805 Mac + PC
Bitstream Handtooled

Bitstream Handtooled:
Cloister Open Face, Goudy Handtooled

BT783 Mac + PC (1)
Swiss 924
Industry name: Hanseatic

abcdefghijklmnopqrstuvwxyz1234567890[äöüßåøæœç]
ABCDEFGHIJKLMNOPQRSTUVWXYZ(.,;:?!$&-*){ÄÖÜÅØÆŒÇ}

BT Condensed Headlines 2:
Alternate Gothic™ No.2, Bodoni Campanile™, Hanseatic, Latin Extra Condensed
© Aura, Aurora, Hadrian, Helvetica Inserat, Helvetica Compressed, Impact, Placard

MC6359 Mac + PC (5) ✏ L. Hansson
Hansson Stencil™

ABCDEFGHIJKLMNOPQRSTUVWXYZ
1234567890(.,;:?!$&-*){ }{ÄÖÜÅØÆŒÇ}

MC6360 Mac + PC (5) ✏ L. Hansson
Hansson Stencil Bold

ABCDEFGHIJKLMNOPQRSTUVWXYZ
1234567890(.,;:?!$&-*){ }{ÄÖÜÅØÆŒÇ}

LP6663　Mac + PC　⑥　✎ 1992: Garrett Boge
Hardwood™

abcdefghijklmnopqrstuvwxyz[äöüßåøæœç]
ABCDEFGHIJKLMNOPQRSTUVWXYZ
1234567890(.,;:?!$&-*){ÄÖÜÅØÆŒÇ}

LetterPerfect 5:
Hardwood™, Koch Original™, Roslyn Bold

EF6471　Mac + PC　⑥　✎ 1977: Colin Brignall
Harlow™

abcdefghijklmnopqrstuvwxyz[äöüßåøæœç]
ABCDEFGHIJKLMNOPQRSTUVWXYZ
1234567890(.,;:?!$&-*)ÄÖÜÅØÆŒÇ

E+F Special Headlines 7:
Harlow™, Harlow Solid, Horndon™, Koloss, Paddington™, Stentor™
aaa L6129
Harlow, Reg

EF6471　Mac + PC　⑥　✎ 1979: Colin Brignall
Harlow Solid

abcdefghijklmnopqrstuvwxyz[äöüßåøæœç]
ABCDEFGHIJKLMNOPQRSTUVWXYZ
1234567890(.,;:?!$&-*)ÄÖÜÅØÆŒÇ

E+F Special Headlines 7:
Harlow™, Harlow Solid, Horndon™, Koloss, Paddington™, Stentor™
aaa L6130
Harlow Solid, Reg

L2825　Mac　⑥　✎ 1989: Dale R. Kramer
Harvey™

ABCDEFGHIJKLMNOPQRSTUVWXYZ
1234567890(.,;:?!$&-*)[ ]ÄÖÜÅØÆŒÇ

EF6467　Mac + PC　⑥　✎
Hawthorn™

abcdefghijklmnopqrstuvwxyz[äöüßåøæœç]
ABCDEFGHIJKLMNOPQRSTUVWXYZ
1234567890(.,;:?!$&-*)ÄÖÜÅØÆŒÇ

E+F Special Headlines 3:
Hawthorn™, Magnus™ Bold, Octopuss™, Octopuss™ Shaded, Piccadilly™, Stop™

© FSI 1993

L6594 Mac ⑥ ✏ 1992: Phil Grimshaw
Hazel™

ABCDEFGHIJKLMNOPQRSTUVWXYZ
1234567890[ ](.,;:?!$&-)ÄÖÜÅØÆŒÇ*

M215 Mac + PC ①
Headline Bold

abcdefghijklmnopqrstuvwxyz[äöüßåøæœç]
ABCDEFGHIJKLMNOPQRSTUVWXYZ
1234567890(.,;:?!$&-*){ÄÖÜÅØÆŒÇ}

Headliners 2:
Falstaff™, Headline Bold, Placard®
👁 Bulldog, Bureau Grotesque, Grotesque No. 9

M206 Mac + PC
Headliners 1

Headliners 1:
Clarendon, Egyptian, New Clarendon

M215 Mac + PC
Headliners 2

Headliners 2:
Falstaff™, Headline Bold, Placard®

M267 Mac + PC
Headliners 3

Headliners 3:
Braggadocio™, Figaro®, Forte™, Klang™

M226 Mac + PC
Headliners 4

Headliners 4:
Inflex™, Monotype Old Style Bold Outline™, Old English™ Text

M625 Mac + PC
Headliners 5

Headliners 5:
Bernard™ Condensed, Compacta Bold, Neographik™, Runic™ Condensed

© FSI 1993

M550 Mac + PC
Headliners 6

Headliners 6:
Albertus®, Castellar™

BT807 Mac + PC
Bitstream Headlines 1

Bitstream Headlines 1:
Eckmann™, Fry's Baskerville™, Libra™

BT808 Mac + PC
Bitstream Headlines 2

Bitstream Headlines 2:
Engraver's Gothic, Engraver's Old English

BT809 Mac + PC
Bitstream Headlines 3

Bitstream Headlines 3:
Antique No. 3™, Futura Black

BT811 Mac + PC
Bitstream Headlines 4

Bitstream Headlines 4:
Thunderbird, University Roman Bold

BT782 Mac + PC
BT Condensed Headlines 1

BT Condensed Headlines 1:
Americana, Serifa 67 Bold Condensed

BT783 Mac + PC
BT Condensed Headlines 2

BT Condensed Headlines 2:
Alternate Gothic™ No.2, Bodoni Campanile™, Hanseatic, Latin Extra Condensed

BT812 Mac + PC
Bitstream Bold Headlines 1

Bitstream Bold Headlines 1:
Blippo™ Black, Handel Gothic, ITC Bolt Bold®, Trump Mediaeval Black

BT813 Mac + PC
ITC Headlines

ITC Headlines:
ITC Gorilla®, ITC Grizzly®, ITC Grouch®, ITC Tom Roman®

© FSI 1993

M6410 Mac + PC
Crazy Headlines™

Crazy Headlines™:
Festival™ Titling, Kino™, Matura ™Script, Victoria™ Titling Condensed

EF6465 Mac + PC
E+F Special Headlines 1

E+F Special Headlines 1:
Bernhard Fashion, Candice™, Italia Medium Condensed, Lindsay™, Odin™, Van Dijk

EF6466 Mac + PC
E+F Special Headlines 2

E+F Special Headlines 2:
Belshaw™, Camellia™, Carousel™, Cirkulus™, Data 70, Galadriel™

EF6467 Mac + PC
E+F Special Headlines 3

E+F Special Headlines 3:
Hawthorn™, Magnus™ Bold, Octopuss™, Octopuss™ Shaded, Piccadilly™, Stop™

EF6468 Mac + PC
E+F Special Headlines 4

E+F Special Headlines 4:
Bernhard Antique Bold Condensed, Cabaret™, Conference™, Countdown™, Einhorn, Highlight

EF6469 Mac + PC
E+F Special Headlines 5

E+F Special Headlines 5:
Chesterfield™, Cortez™, Elefont™, Glastonbury™, Julia™ Script, LCD

EF6470 Mac + PC
E+F Special Headlines 6

E+F Special Headlines 6:
Croissant, Hadfield™, Jenson™ Old Style Bold Condensed, Knightsbridge™, Lazybones™

EF6471 Mac + PC
E+F Special Headlines 7

E+F Special Headlines 7:
Harlow™, Harlow Solid, Horndon™, Koloss, Paddington™, Stentor™

EF6472 Mac + PC
E+F Special Headlines 8

E+F Special Headlines 8:
Le Griffe™

FB6836 Mac + PC
FB Display Pack 1

FB Display Pack 1:
Ecru™ Display, Elli™ Display, Numskill™ Bold, Nutcracker™

FB6838 Mac + PC
FB Display Pack 2

FB Display Pack 2:
BadTyp™, Graffiti™, Hip Hop™

C467 Mac + PC
Headlines 81S

Headlines 81S:
Egiziano™ Black, PL Behemoth Semi Condensed, PL Benguiat Frisky, PL Futura Maxi 1, PL Tower™ Condensed, Quirinus™ Bold, Section™ Bold Condensed, Stratford ™Bold, Woodblock

C468 Mac + PC
Headlines 82S

Headlines 82S:
Neon Extra Condensed™, PL Barnum Block, PL Benguiat Frisky Bold, PL Davison Zip Bold, PL Fiedler Gothic Bold, PL Futura Maxi 2, PL Trophy™ Oblique, Ritmo™ Bold, TC Broadway

C993 Mac + PC
Headlines 83S

Headlines 83S:
Barclay™ Open, Delphian™ Open, Fluidum™ Bold, PL Bernhardt, PL Britannia Bold, PL Fiorello™ Condensed, PL Modern Heavy Condensed, PL Torino Open

C1012 Mac + PC
Headlines 84S

Headlines 84S:
Bernhard Modern, Beton Extra Bold, Metropolis Bold, Modern No. 20, Orlando Caps, PL Davison Americana, PL Westerveldt Light, Siena™ Black, TC Europa™ Bold, TC Jasper™

C2776 Mac + PC
Headlines 85S

Headlines 85S:
Athenaeum™

C2525 Mac + PC
Headlines 86S

Headlines 86S:
Advertisers Gothic™, Ashley Crawford™, Capone Light, Dynamo, Modernistic™

C2523 Mac + PC
Headlines 87S

Headlines 87S:
Greeting Monotone™, Koloss™, Phenix™ American, Phosphor™, Zeppelin™

© FSI 1993

C2524 Mac + PC
Headlines 88S

Headlines 88S:
Brasilia Seven, Brasilia Three, Latin Bold, Latin Elongated, Radiant™

C2777 Mac + PC
Headlines 89S

Headlines 89S:
Miehle™, Parisian, Phyllis, Sinaloa™

C2778 Mac + PC
Headlines 90S

Headlines 90S:
Bernhard Fashion, Chic™, Eclipse™, Metronome Gothic, Salut™

C2980 Mac + PC
Headlines 91S

Headlines 91S:
Empire™, Gallia™, Gillies Gothic Bold, Quaint™ Roman, Skjald™

C2981 Mac + PC
Headlines 92S

Headlines 92S:
Eagle Bold, Joanna Solotype, Matra™, Modernique, Victorian Silhouette

C2982 Mac + PC
Headlines 93S

Headlines 93S:
Ashley Inline, Beverly Hills, Lotus™, Virile

C2983 Mac + PC
Headlines 94S

Headlines 94S:
Artistik™, Futura Black, Yearbook™

SF6635 Mac
Stylus Headlines 1

Stylus Headlines 1:
Bodoni Open Condensed, Fanfare Recut, Goudy Globe Gothic, Loyalist™ Condensed

C6431 Mac + PC ① ✎ Phil Martin
Heldustry®

abcdefghijklmnopqrstuvwxyz[äöüßåøæœeç]
ABCDEFGHIJKLMNOPQRSTUVWXYZ
1234567890(.,;:?!$&-*){ÄÖÜÅØÆŒÇ}

© FSI 1993

H 10

▼ C6431 MAC + PC **Heldustry®**

▶ Regular
The quick brown fox jumps over a Dog. Zwei Boxkämpfer jagen Eva durch Sylt portez ce vieux Whiskey blond qui

▶ Italic
The quick brown fox jumps over a Dog. Zwei Boxkämpfer jagen Eva durch Sylt portez ce vieux Whiskey blond qui

▶ Demi Bold
The quick brown fox jumps over a Dog. Zwei Boxkämpfer jagen Eva durch Sylt portez ce vieux Whiskey

▶ Demi Bold Italic
The quick brown fox jumps over a Dog. Zwei Boxkämpfer jagen Eva durch Sylt portez ce vieux Whiskey

C6568 MAC + PC ④
Helinda Rook™

abcdefghijklmnopqrstuvwxyz[äöüßaç]
ABCDEFGHIJKLMNOPQRSTUVWXYZ
1234567890(.,:;?!$¢-*){ÄÖÜÆ&Ç}

Agfa Scripts 1:
Commercial Script, Helinda Rook™, Old English Text, Original Script™, Quill™, Stuyvesant2, Wedding Text

L2583 MAC ⑥ ✎ 1991: Lee McAuley
Heliotype™

abcdefghijklmnopqrstuvwxyz[äöüßåøæœç]
ABCDEFGHIJKLMNOPQRSTUVWXYZ
1234567890(.,:;?!$&-*)ÄÖÜÅØÆŒÇ

A061 MAC + PC ① ✎ 1957: (Max Miedinger) Erich Schulz-Anker, Arthur Ritzel
Helvetica™ Light/Black

abcdefghijklmnopqrstuvwxyz[äöüßåøæœç]
ABCDEFGHIJKLMNOPQRSTUVWXYZ
1234567890(.,:;?!$&-*){ÄÖÜÅØÆŒÇ}

▶ Light
The quick brown fox jumps over a Dog. Zwei Boxkämpfer jagen Eva durch Sylt portez ce vieux Whiskey blond qui fume

▶ Light Oblique
The quick brown fox jumps over a Dog. Zwei Boxkämpfer jagen Eva durch Sylt portez ce vieux Whiskey blond qui fume

▶ Black
The quick brown fox jumps over a Dog. Zwei Boxkämpfer jagen Eva durch Sylt portez ce

▶ Black Oblique
The quick brown fox jumps over a Dog. Zwei Boxkämpfer jagen Eva durch Sylt portez ce

A2775 MAC + PC ①
Helvetica Narrow

abcdefghijklmnopqrstuvwxyz[äöüßåøæœç]
ABCDEFGHIJKLMNOPQRSTUVWXYZ
1234567890(.,:;?!$&-*){ÄÖÜÅØÆŒÇ}

▼ A2775 Mac + PC Helvetica Narrow

► Regular
The quick brown fox jumps over a Dog. Zwei Boxkämpfer jagen Eva durch Sylt portez ce vieux Whiskey blond qui fume une pipe aber echt

► Oblique
The quick brown fox jumps over a Dog. Zwei Boxkämpfer jagen Eva durch Sylt portez ce vieux Whiskey blond qui fume une pipe aber echt

► Bold
The quick brown fox jumps over a Dog. Zwei Boxkämpfer jagen Eva durch Sylt portez ce vieux Whiskey blond qui fume une pipe aber echt

► Bold Oblique
The quick brown fox jumps over a Dog. Zwei Boxkämpfer jagen Eva durch Sylt portez ce vieux Whiskey blond qui fume une pipe aber echt

A059 Mac + PC ① 🖉 1974: Hans Jorg Hunziker, Matthew Carter
Helvetica Compressed

**abcdefghijklmnopqrstuvwxyz[äöüßåøæœç]
ABCDEFGHIJKLMNOPQRSTUVWXYZ
1234567890(.,;:?!$&-*){ÄÖÜÅØÆŒÇ}**

aa*a*
BT1400
Helvetica Compressed, Compressed, ExtCompressed, UltCompressed
ⓒ
Aura, Aurora, Hanseatic, Hadrian, Helvetica Inserat, Impact, Placard

► Compressed
The quick brown fox jumps over a Dog. Zwei Boxkämpfer jagen Eva durch Sylt portez ce vieux Whiskey blond qui fume une pipe aber echt

► Extra Compressed
The quick brown fox jumps over a Dog. Zwei Boxkämpfer jagen Eva durch Sylt portez ce vieux Whiskey blond qui fume une pipe aber echt über die Mauer gesprungen und auch

► Ultra Compressed
The quick brown fox jumps over a Dog. Zwei Boxkämpfer jagen Eva durch Sylt portez ce vieux Whiskey blond qui fume une pipe aber echt über die Mauer gesprungen und auch smørebrød en ysjes natuurlijk

A060 Mac + PC ① 🖉 1957: (Max Miedinger)
Helvetica Condensed

abcdefghijklmnopqrstuvwxyz[äöüßåøæœç]
ABCDEFGHIJKLMNOPQRSTUVWXYZ
1234567890(.,;:?!$&-*){ÄÖÜÅØÆŒÇ}

► Light Condensed
The quick brown fox jumps over a Dog. Zwei Boxkämpfer jagen Eva durch Sylt portez ce vieux Whiskey blond qui fume une pipe aber echt über die

► Light Condensed Oblique
The quick brown fox jumps over a Dog. Zwei Boxkämpfer jagen Eva durch Sylt portez ce vieux Whiskey blond qui fume une pipe aber echt über die

► Condensed
The quick brown fox jumps over a Dog. Zwei Boxkämpfer jagen Eva durch Sylt portez ce vieux Whiskey blond qui fume une pipe aber echt

► Condensed Oblique
The quick brown fox jumps over a Dog. Zwei Boxkämpfer jagen Eva durch Sylt portez ce vieux Whiskey blond qui fume une pipe aber echt

► Bold Condensed
The quick brown fox jumps over a Dog. Zwei Boxkämpfer jagen Eva durch Sylt portez ce vieux Whiskey blond qui fume une pipe aber

► Bold Condensed Oblique
The quick brown fox jumps over a Dog. Zwei Boxkämpfer jagen Eva durch Sylt portez ce vieux Whiskey blond qui fume une pipe aber

© FSI 1993

▼ A060 MAC + PC **Helvetica Condensed**

▶ Black Condensed
The quick brown fox jumps over a Dog. Zwei Boxkämpfer jagen Eva durch Sylt portez ce vieux Whiskey blond qui fume une pipe aber

▶ Black Condensed Oblique
The quick brown fox jumps over a Dog. Zwei Boxkämpfer jagen Eva durch Sylt portez ce vieux Whiskey blond qui fume une pipe aber

L6131 MAC ⑥
Helvetica Medium Condensed

abcdefghijklmnopqrstuvwxyz[äöüßåøæœç]
ABCDEFGHIJKLMNOPQRSTUVWXYZ
1234567890(.,;:?!$&-*)ÄÖÜÅØÆŒÇ

L6132 MAC ⑥
Helvetica Bold Condensed

**abcdefghijklmnopqrstuvwxyz[äöüßåøæœç]
ABCDEFGHIJKLMNOPQRSTUVWXYZ
1234567890(.,;:?!$&-*)ÄÖÜÅØÆŒÇ**

A170 MAC + PC ①   ✎ 1965: (Max Miedinger)
Helvetica Inserat

**abcdefghijklmnopqrstuvwxyz[äöüßåøæœç]
ABCDEFGHIJKLMNOPQRSTUVWXYZ
1234567890(.,;:?!$&-*){ÄÖÜÅØÆŒÇ}**

Arnold Böcklin:
Arnold Böcklin™, Fette Fraktur™, Helvetica Inserat, Present™ Script
aa*a* BT1401
Helvetica Inserat, Reg

A062 MAC + PC ①   ✎ 1983: (Max Miedinger, 1957)
Neue Helvetica™ 1

abcdefghijklmnopqrstuvwxyz[äöüßåøæœç]
ABCDEFGHIJKLMNOPQRSTUVWXYZ
1234567890(.,;:?!$&-*){ÄÖÜÅØÆŒÇ}

aa*a*
BT1396
Helvetica 4, 95Blk,
96BlkIta, 96BlkNo2

▶ 25 Ultra Light
The quick brown fox jumps over a Dog. Zwei Boxkämpfer jagen Eva durch Sylt portez ce vieux Whiskey blond qui fume une pipe aber echt

▶ 26 Ultra Light Italic
The quick brown fox jumps over a Dog. Zwei Boxkämpfer jagen Eva durch Sylt portez ce vieux Whiskey blond qui fume une pipe aber

▶ 95 Black
The quick brown fox jumps over a Dog. Zwei Boxkämpfer jagen Eva durch Sylt portez ce vieux

▶ 96 Black Italic
The quick brown fox jumps over a Dog. Zwei Boxkämpfer jagen Eva durch Sylt portez ce vieux

© FSI 1993

A063 Mac + PC   ① ✎ 1983: (Max Miedinger, 1957)
Neue Helvetica 2

abcdefghijklmnopqrstuvwxyz[äöüßåøæœç]
ABCDEFGHIJKLMNOPQRSTUVWXYZ
1234567890(.,;:?!$&-*){ÄÖÜÅØÆŒÇ}

a a *a*
BT1393
Helvetica, 35Thin,
36ThinIta, 45Lt, 46LtIta
BT1394
Helvetica 2, 55Reg,
56Ita, 75Bd, 76BdIta

▶ 35 Thin
The quick brown fox jumps over a Dog. Zwei Boxkämpfer jagen Eva durch Sylt portez ce vieux Whiskey blond qui fume une

▶ 36 Thin Italic
The quick brown fox jumps over a Dog. Zwei Boxkämpfer jagen Eva durch Sylt portez ce vieux Whiskey blond qui fume une

▶ 55 Regular
The quick brown fox jumps over a Dog. Zwei Boxkämpfer jagen Eva durch Sylt portez ce vieux Whiskey blond qui fume

▶ 56 Italic
The quick brown fox jumps over a Dog. Zwei Boxkämpfer jagen Eva durch Sylt portez ce vieux Whiskey blond qui fume

▶ 75 Bold
The quick brown fox jumps over a Dog. Zwei Boxkämpfer jagen Eva durch Sylt portez ce vieux Whiskey blond

▶ 76 Bold Italic
The quick brown fox jumps over a Dog. Zwei Boxkämpfer jagen Eva durch Sylt portez ce vieux Whiskey blond

A064 Mac + PC   ① ✎ 1983: (Max Miedinger, 1957)
Neue Helvetica 3

abcdefghijklmnopqrstuvwxyz[äöüßåøæœç]
ABCDEFGHIJKLMNOPQRSTUVWXYZ
1234567890(.,;:?!$&-*){ÄÖÜÅØÆŒÇ}

a a *a*
BT1393
Helvetica, 35Thin,
36ThinIta, 45Lt, 46LtIta
BT1395
Helvetica 3, 65Med,
66MedIta, 85Hvy,
86HvyIta

▶ 45 Light
The quick brown fox jumps over a Dog. Zwei Boxkämpfer jagen Eva durch Sylt portez ce vieux Whiskey blond qui fume une

▶ 46 Light Italic
The quick brown fox jumps over a Dog. Zwei Boxkämpfer jagen Eva durch Sylt portez ce vieux Whiskey blond qui fume une

▶ 65 Medium
The quick brown fox jumps over a Dog. Zwei Boxkämpfer jagen Eva durch Sylt portez ce vieux Whiskey blond qui

▶ 66 Medium Italic
The quick brown fox jumps over a Dog. Zwei Boxkämpfer jagen Eva durch Sylt portez ce vieux Whiskey blond qui

▶ 85 Heavy
The quick brown fox jumps over a Dog. Zwei Boxkämpfer jagen Eva durch Sylt portez ce vieux Whiskey

▶ 86 Heavy Italic
The quick brown fox jumps over a Dog. Zwei Boxkämpfer jagen Eva durch Sylt portez ce vieux Whiskey

A903 Mac + PC   ① ✎ 1983: (Max Miedinger, 1957)
Neue Helvetica Condensed 1

abcdefghijklmnopqrstuvwxyz[äöüßåøæœç]
ABCDEFGHIJKLMNOPQRSTUVWXYZ
1234567890(.,;:?!$&-*){ÄÖÜÅØÆŒÇ}

© FSI 1993

▼ A903 Mac + PC   Neue Helvetica Condensed 1

aa*a*
BT1397
Helvetica Condensed 1,
47LtCon, 48LtConIta,
97BlkCon, 98BlkConIta

▶ 27 Ultra Light Condensed
The quick brown fox jumps over a Dog. Zwei Boxkämpfer jagen Eva durch Sylt portez ce vieux Whiskey blond qui fume une pipe aber echt über die Mauer gesprungen

▶ 28 Ultra Light Condensed Obl.
The quick brown fox jumps over a Dog. Zwei Boxkämpfer jagen Eva durch Sylt portez ce vieux Whiskey blond qui fume une

▶ 97 Black Condensed
The quick brown fox jumps over a Dog. Zwei Boxkämpfer jagen Eva durch Sylt portez ce vieux Whiskey blond qui fume une pipe

▶ 98 Black Condensed Oblique
The quick brown fox jumps over a Dog. Zwei Boxkämpfer jagen Eva durch Sylt portez ce vieux Whiskey blond qui fume une pipe

▶ 107 Extra Black Condensed
The quick brown fox jumps over a Dog. Zwei Boxkämpfer jagen Eva durch Sylt portez ce vieux Whiskey blond qui fume une

▶ 108 Extra Black Cond. Oblique
The quick brown fox jumps over a Dog. Zwei Boxkämpfer jagen Eva durch Sylt portez ce vieux Whiskey blond qui fume une

A904 Mac + PC   ① ✎ 1983: (Max Miedinger, 1957)

Neue Helvetica Condensed 2

abcdefghijklmnopqrstuvwxyz[äöüßåøæœç]
ABCDEFGHIJKLMNOPQRSTUVWXYZ
1234567890(.,;:?!$&-*){ÄÖÜÅØÆŒÇ}

aa*a*
BT1398
Helvetica Condensed 2, 57Con, 58ConIta, 77BdCon, 78BdConIta

▶ 37 Thin Condensed
The quick brown fox jumps over a Dog. Zwei Boxkämpfer jagen Eva durch Sylt portez ce vieux Whiskey blond qui fume une pipe aber echt über die Mauer

▶ 38 Thin Condensed Oblique
The quick brown fox jumps over a Dog. Zwei Boxkämpfer jagen Eva durch Sylt portez ce vieux Whiskey blond qui fume une pipe aber echt über die Mauer

▶ 57 Condensed
The quick brown fox jumps over a Dog. Zwei Boxkämpfer jagen Eva durch Sylt portez ce vieux Whiskey blond qui fume une pipe aber echt

▶ 58 Condensed Oblique
The quick brown fox jumps over a Dog. Zwei Boxkämpfer jagen Eva durch Sylt portez ce vieux Whiskey blond qui fume une pipe aber echt

▶ 77 Bold Condensed
The quick brown fox jumps over a Dog. Zwei Boxkämpfer jagen Eva durch Sylt portez ce vieux Whiskey blond qui fume une pipe aber

▶ 78 Bold Condensed Oblique
The quick brown fox jumps over a Dog. Zwei Boxkämpfer jagen Eva durch Sylt portez ce vieux Whiskey blond qui fume une pipe aber

A905 Mac + PC   ① ✎ 1983: (Max Miedinger, 1957)

Neue Helvetica Condensed 3

abcdefghijklmnopqrstuvwxyz[äöüßåøæœç]
ABCDEFGHIJKLMNOPQRSTUVWXYZ
1234567890(.,;:?!$&-*){ÄÖÜÅØÆŒÇ}

aa*a*
BT1397
Helvetica Condensed 1,
47LtCon, 48LtConIta,
97BlkCon, 98BlkConIta

▶ 47 Light Condensed
The quick brown fox jumps over a Dog. Zwei Boxkämpfer jagen Eva durch Sylt portez ce vieux Whiskey blond qui fume une pipe aber echt

▶ 48 Light Condensed Oblique
The quick brown fox jumps over a Dog. Zwei Boxkämpfer jagen Eva durch Sylt portez ce vieux Whiskey blond qui fume une pipe aber echt

© FSI 1993
▼

▼ A905 Mac + PC   Neue Helvetica Condensed 3

▶ 67 Medium Condensed
The quick brown fox jumps over a Dog. Zwei Boxkämpfer jagen Eva durch Sylt portez ce vieux Whiskey blond qui fume une pipe aber echt

▶ 68 Medium Condensed Obl.
The quick brown fox jumps over a Dog. Zwei Boxkämpfer jagen Eva durch Sylt portez ce vieux Whiskey

▶ 87 Heavy Condensed
The quick brown fox jumps over a Dog. Zwei Boxkämpfer jagen Eva durch Sylt portez ce vieux Whiskey blond qui fume une pipe

▶ 88 Heavy Condensed Oblique
The quick brown fox jumps over a Dog. Zwei Boxkämpfer jagen Eva durch Sylt portez ce vieux Whiskey blond qui fume une

A906 Mac + PC   1984: (Max Miedinger, 1957)
Neue Helvetica Extended 1

abcdefghijklmnopqrstuvwxyz[äöüßåøæœç]
ABCDEFGHIJKLMNOPQRSTUVWXYZ
1234567890(.,;:?!$&-*){ÄÖÜÅØÆŒÇ}

▶ 23 Ultra Light Extended
The quick brown fox jumps over a Dog. Zwei Boxkämpfer jagen Eva durch Sylt portez ce vieux Whiskey blond

▶ 24 Ultra Light Ext. Oblique
The quick brown fox jumps over a Dog. Zwei Boxkämpfer jagen Eva durch Sylt portez ce vieux Whiskey blond

▶ 93 Black Extended
The quick brown fox jumps over a Dog. Zwei Boxkämpfer jagen Eva

▶ 94 Black Extended Oblique
The quick brown fox jumps over a Dog. Zwei Boxkämpfer jagen Eva

A907 Mac + PC   1984: (Max Miedinger, 1957)
Neue Helvetica Extended 2

abcdefghijklmnopqrstuvwxyz[äöüßåøæœç]
ABCDEFGHIJKLMNOPQRSTUVWXYZ
1234567890(.,;:?!$&-*){ÄÖÜÅØÆŒÇ}

aa*a*
BT814
Helvetica Extended,
43LtExt, 53Ext,
63BdExt, 73BlkExt

▶ 33 Thin Extended
The quick brown fox jumps over a Dog. Zwei Boxkämpfer jagen Eva durch Sylt portez ce vieux Whiskey

▶ 34 Thin Extended Oblique
The quick brown fox jumps over a Dog. Zwei Boxkämpfer jagen Eva durch Sylt portez ce vieux Whiskey

▶ 53 Extended
The quick brown fox jumps over a Dog. Zwei Boxkämpfer jagen Eva durch Sylt portez ce vieux

▶ 54 Extended Oblique
The quick brown fox jumps over a Dog. Zwei Boxkämpfer jagen Eva durch Sylt portez ce vieux

▶ 73 Bold Extended
The quick brown fox jumps over a Dog. Zwei Boxkämpfer jagen Eva durch Sylt

▶ 74 Bold Extended Oblique
The quick brown fox jumps over a Dog. Zwei Boxkämpfer jagen Eva durch Sylt

A908　Mac + PC　① ✎ 1984: (Max Miedinger, 1957)

Neue Helvetica Extended 3

abcdefghijklmnopqrstuvwxyz[äöüßåøæœç]
ABCDEFGHIJKLMNOPQRSTUVWXYZ
1234567890(.,;:?!$&-*){ÄÖÜÅØÆŒÇ}

aa*a*
BT814
Helvetica Extended,
43LtExt, 53Ext,
63BdExt, 73BlkExt

▶ 43 Light Extended
The quick brown fox jumps over a Dog. Zwei Boxkämpfer jagen Eva durch Sylt portez ce vieux Whis-

▶ 44 Light Extended Oblique
The quick brown fox jumps over a Dog. Zwei Boxkämpfer jagen Eva durch Sylt portez ce vieux Whis-

▶ 63 Medium Extended
The quick brown fox jumps over a Dog. Zwei Boxkämpfer jagen Eva durch Sylt portez ce

▶ 64 Medium Extended Oblique
The quick brown fox jumps over a Dog. Zwei Boxkämpfer jagen Eva durch Sylt portez ce

▶ 83 Heavy Extended
The quick brown fox jumps over a Dog. Zwei Boxkämpfer jagen Eva durch Sylt

▶ 84 Heavy Extended Oblique
The quick brown fox jumps over a Dog. Zwei Boxkämpfer jagen Eva durch Sylt

BT815　Mac + PC　⑥ ✎ (Max Miedinger, 1957)　　　Industry name

Swiss 721 Outline　　　Helvetica Outline

abcdefghijklmnopqrstuvwxyz[äöüßåøæœç]
ABCDEFGHIJKLMNOPQRSTUVWXYZ
1234567890(.,;:?!$&-*){ÄÖÜÅØÆŒÇ}

aa*a*
A1148
Neue Helvetica,
75BdOutline

▶ 65 Bold Outline
The quick brown fox jumps over a Dog. Zwei Boxkämpfer jagen Eva durch Sylt portez ce vieux Whiskey blond

▶ 75 Black Outline
The quick brown fox jumps over a Dog. Zwei Boxkämpfer jagen Eva durch Sylt portez ce

▶ 67 Bold Condensed Outline
The quick brown fox jumps over a Dog. Zwei Boxkämpfer jagen Eva durch Sylt portez ce vieux Whiskey blond qui fume une pipe aber echt

A909　Mac + PC　① ✎ 1978: (Max Miedinger, 1957)

Helvetica Rounded

abcdefghijklmnopqrstuvwxyz[äöüßåøæœç]
ABCDEFGHIJKLMNOPQRSTUVWXYZ
1234567890(.,;:?!$&-*){ÄÖÜÅØÆŒÇ}

aa*a*
BT1399
Helvetica Rounded, Bd, Blk
©
AG Book Rounded

▶ Bold
The quick brown fox jumps over a Dog. Zwei Boxkämpfer jagen Eva durch Sylt portez ce vieux Whiskey

▶ Bold Oblique
The quick brown fox jumps over a Dog. Zwei Boxkämpfer jagen Eva durch Sylt portez ce vieux Whiskey

© FSI 1993

H 17

▼ A909 Mac + PC Helvetica Rounded

▶ Black
The quick brown fox jumps over a Dog. Zwei Boxkämpfer jagen Eva durch Sylt portez ce

▶ Black Oblique
The quick brown fox jumps over a Dog. Zwei Boxkämpfer jagen Eva durch Sylt portez ce

▶ Bold Condensed
The quick brown fox jumps over a Dog. Zwei Boxkämpfer jagen Eva durch Sylt portez ce vieux Whiskey blond qui fume une pipe aber echt

▶ Bold Condensed Oblique
The quick brown fox jumps over a Dog. Zwei Boxkämpfer jagen Eva durch Sylt portez ce vieux Whiskey blond qui fume une pipe aber echt

---

BT816 Mac + PC ① 🖉 (Max Miedinger, 1957) Industry name

Monospace 821 — Helvetica Monospace

abcdefghijklmnopqrstuvwxyz[äöüßåøæœç]
ABCDEFGHIJKLMNOPQRSTUVWXYZ
1234567890(.,;:?!$&-*){ÄÖÜÅØÆŒÇ}

▶ Regular
The quick brown fox jumps over a Dog. Zwei Boxkämpfer jagen Eva durch Sylt portez ce

▶ Italic
The quick brown fox jumps over a Dog. Zwei Boxkämpfer jagen Eva durch Sylt portez ce

▶ Bold
The quick brown fox jumps over a Dog. Zwei Boxkämpfer jagen Eva durch Sylt portez ce

▶ Bold Italic
The quick brown fox jumps over a Dog. Zwei Boxkämpfer jagen Eva durch Sylt portez ce

---

FB6837 Mac + PC ⑤ 🖉 1993: Matthew Butterick

Herald Gothic™

ABCDEFGHIJKLMNOPQRSTUVWXYZ1234567890[ÄÖÜXÅØŒÇ]
ABCDEFGHIJKLMNOPQRSTUVWXYZ[.,;:?!$&-*]{ÄÖÜÅØÆŒÇ}

▶ Light
THE QUICK BROWN FOX JUMPS OVER A DOG. ZWEI BOXKÄMPFER JAGEN EVA DURCH SYLT PORTEZ CE VIEUX WHISKEY BLOND QUI FUME UNE PIPE ABER ECHT ÜBER DIE MAUER GESPRUNGEN UND AUCH SMØREBRØD EN YSJES NATUURLIJK THE QUICK BROWN FOX JUMPS OVER A DOG. ZWEI BOXKÄMPFER JAGEN EVA

▶ Light Small Caps
The quick brown fox jumps over a Dog. Zwei Boxkämpfer jagen Eva durch Sylt portez ce vieux Whiskey blond qui fume une pipe aber echt über die Mauer gesprungen und auch smørebrød en ysjes natuurlijk The quick brown fox jumps over a Dog. Zwei Boxkämpfer jagen Eva durch Sylt portez ce vieux

▶ Medium
THE QUICK BROWN FOX JUMPS OVER A DOG. ZWEI BOXKÄMPFER JAGEN EVA DURCH SYLT PORTEZ CE VIEUX WHISKEY BLOND QUI FUME UNE PIPE ABER ECHT ÜBER DIE MAUER GESPRUNGEN UND AUCH SMØREBRØD EN YSJES NATUURLIJK THE QUICK BROWN FOX JUMPS OVER A DOG. ZWEI

▶ Medium Small Caps
The quick brown fox jumps over a Dog. Zwei Boxkämpfer jagen Eva durch Sylt portez ce vieux Whiskey blond qui fume une pipe aber echt über die Mauer gesprungen und auch smørebrød en ysjes natuurlijk The quick brown fox jumps over a Dog. Zwei Boxkämpfer jagen Eva

▶ Bold
THE QUICK BROWN FOX JUMPS OVER A DOG. ZWEI BOXKÄMPFER JAGEN EVA DURCH SYLT PORTEZ CE VIEUX WHISKEY BLOND QUI FUME UNE PIPE ABER ECHT ÜBER DIE MAUER GESPRUNGEN UND AUCH SMØREBRØD EN YSJES NATUURLIJK THE QUICK BROWN FOX

▶ Bold Small Caps
The quick brown fox jumps over a Dog. Zwei Boxkämpfer jagen Eva durch Sylt portez ce vieux Whiskey blond qui fume une pipe aber echt über die Mauer gesprungen und auch smørebrød en ysjes natuurlijk The quick brown fox jumps over a Dog. Zwei

© FSI 1993

| EF510 | Mac + PC | ② | Jarosch Wolf |

Heraldus™

abcdefghijklmnopqrstuvwxyz[äöüßåøœeç]
ABCDEFGHIJKLMNOPQRSTUVWXYZ
1234567890(.,;:?!$&-*){ÄÖÜÅØÆŒÇ}

| A996 | Mac + PC | ④ | 1990: Adrian Frutiger |

Herculanum™

ABCDEFGHIJKLMNOPQRSTUVWXYZ[ÄÖÜSSÅØÆŒÇ]
ABCDEFGHIJKLMNOPQRSTUVWXYZ
1234567890(.,;:?!$&-*){ÄÖÜÅØÆŒÇ}

Type Before Gutenberg 1:
Duc De Berry™, Herculanum™, Omnia™

| RB6094 | Mac | ⑥ | 1991: Richard Beatty |

Hermosa™

abcdefghijklmnopqrstuvwxyz[äöüßåøæœç]
ABCDEFGHIJKLMNOPQRSTUVWXYZ
1234567890(.,;:?!$&-*){ÄÖÜÅØÆŒÇ}

Beatty Victoriana™:
Childs™, Hermosa™, Recherché™, Spiral™, Wanted™

| RB6095 | Mac | ⑥ | 1991: Richard Beatty |

Hermosa Alternates

abcdefghijklmnopqrstuvwxyz[äöüßåøæœç]
ABCDEFGHIJKLMNOPQRSTUVWXYZ
1234567890(.,;:?!$&-*){ÄÖÜÅØÆŒÇ}

Beatty Victoriana Alternates:
Childs Alternates, Hermosa Alternates, Recherché Alternates, Spiral Alternates, Wanted Alternates

| L2584 | Mac | ④ | 1978: Tony Watson |

Highlight™

abcdefghijklmnopqrstuvwxyz[äöüßåøœeç]
ABCDEFGHIJKLMNOPQRSTUVWXYZ
1234567890(.,;:?!$&-*)ÄÖÜÅØÆŒÇ

FF Hip™
FF1535 Mac + PC ⑤ 1991: Paul Sych

abcdefghijklmnopqrstuvwxyz1234567890(äöüßåøæœç)
ABCDEFGHIJKLMNOPQRSTUVWXYZ(.,;:?!$¢-*){ÄÖÜÅØÆŒÇ}

FF Dig, FF Dog, FF Hip:
FF Dig™, FF Dog™, FF Hip™

Hip Hop™
FB6838 Mac + PC ⑥ 1993: Jill Pichotta

abcdefghijklmnopqrstuvwxyz[äöüßåøœœç]
ABCDEFGHIJKLMNOPQRSTUVWXYZ
1234567890(.,;:?!$&-*){ÄÖÜÅØÆŒÇ}

▶ Demi
The quick brown fox jumps over a Dog. Zwei Boxkämpfer jagen Eva durch Sylt portez ce vieux Whiskey

▶ Inline
The quick brown fox jumps over a Dog. Zwei Boxkämpfer jagen Eva durch Sylt portez ce

FB Display Pack 2:
BadTyp™, Graffiti™, Hip Hop™

Hiroshige™
A169 Mac + PC ② 1986: Cynthia Hollandsworth

abcdefghijklmnopqrstuvwxyz[äöüßåøæœç]
ABCDEFGHIJKLMNOPQRSTUVWXYZ
1234567890(.,;:?!$&-*){ÄÖÜÅØÆŒÇ}

aa*a*
C2526
Hiroshige, Bk, BkIta,
Med, MedIta, Bd,
BdIta, Blk, BlkIta
©
Guardi

▶ Book
The quick brown fox jumps over a Dog. Zwei Boxkämpfer jagen Eva durch Sylt portez ce vieux Whiskey blond qui fume

▶ Book Italic
The quick brown fox jumps over a Dog. Zwei Boxkämpfer jagen Eva durch Sylt portez ce vieux Whiskey blond qui fume

▶ Medium
The quick brown fox jumps over a Dog. Zwei Boxkämpfer jagen Eva durch Sylt portez ce vieux Whiskey blond

▶ Medium Italic
The quick brown fox jumps over a Dog. Zwei Boxkämpfer jagen Eva durch Sylt portez ce vieux Whiskey blond qui

▶ Bold
The quick brown fox jumps over a Dog. Zwei Boxkämpfer jagen Eva durch Sylt portez ce vieux Whiskey

▶ Bold Italic
The quick brown fox jumps over a Dog. Zwei Boxkämpfer jagen Eva durch Sylt portez ce vieux Whiskey

© FSI 1993

▼ A169 Mac + PC **Hiroshige™**

▶ Black
The quick brown fox jumps over a Dog. Zwei Boxkämpfer jagen Eva durch Sylt portez ce vieux

▶ Black Italic
The quick brown fox jumps over a Dog. Zwei Boxkämpfer jagen Eva durch Sylt portez ce vieux

A018 Mac + PC   ⑥   1910: M. F. Benton
Hobo

abcdefghijklmnopqrstuvwxyz[äöüßåøæœç]
ABCDEFGHIJKLMNOPQRSTUVWXYZ
1234567890(.,;:?!$&-*){ÄÖÜÅØÆŒÇ}

Hobo:
Brush Script™, Hobo, Stencil™
aaa BT1331
Hobo, Reg

A018 Mac + PC
Hobo

Hobo:
Brush Script™, Hobo, Stencil™

FB6669 Mac + PC   ⑥   1993: Richard Lipton
Hoffmann 1™

abcdefghijklmnopqrstuvwxyz[äöüßåøæœç]
ABCDEFGHIJKLMNOPQRSTUVWXYZ
1234567890(.,;:?!$&-*){ÄÖÜÅØÆŒÇ}

© FF Spontan, Lithos, Sayer Spiritual

▶ Book
The quick brown fox jumps over a Dog. Zwei Boxkämpfer jagen Eva durch Sylt portez ce vieux Whiskey blond qui fume

▶ Roman
The quick brown fox jumps over a Dog. Zwei Boxkämpfer jagen Eva durch Sylt portez ce vieux Whiskey blond qui

▶ Book Expert
THE QUICK BROWN FOX JUMPS OVER A DOG. 123 4567 890 ZWEI BOXKÄMPFER JAGEN EVA DURCH SYLT PORTEZ CE VIEUX WHISKEY

▶ Roman Expert
THE QUICK BROWN FOX JUMPS OVER A DOG. 123 4567 890 ZWEI BOXKÄMPFER JAGEN EVA DURCH SYLT PORTEZ CE VIEUX

FB6692 Mac + PC   ⑥   1993: Richard Lipton
Hoffmann 2

abcdefghijklmnopqrstuvwxyz[äöüßåøæœç]
ABCDEFGHIJKLMNOPQRSTUVWXYZ
1234567890(.,;:?!$&-*){ÄÖÜÅØÆŒÇ}

© FF Spontan, Lithos, Sayer Spiritual

▶ Light
The quick brown fox jumps over a Dog. Zwei Boxkämpfer jagen Eva durch Sylt portez ce vieux Whiskey blond qui fume une

▶ Bold
The quick brown fox jumps over a Dog. Zwei Boxkämpfer jagen Eva durch Sylt portez ce vieux Whiskey

© FSI 1993

▼ FB6692 Mac + PC **Hoffmann 2**

▶ Light Expert
The quick brown fox jumps over a Dog. 123 4567 890 Zwei Boxkämpfer jagen Eva durch Sylt portez ce vieux Whiskey

▶ Bold Expert
The quick brown fox jumps over a Dog. 123 4567 890 Zwei Boxkämpfer jagen Eva durch Sylt por-

▶ Black Titling
THE QUICK BROWN FOX JUMPS OVER A DOG. ZWEI BOXKÄMPFER JAGEN EVA DURCH

EF948 Mac + PC ④ 🖉 Harald Brödel
Hogarth™ Script

abcdefghijklmnopqrstuvwxyzäöüßåøæœç
ABCDEFGHIJKLMNOPQRSTUVWXYZ
1234567890(.,;:?!$&-).ÄÖÜÅØÆŒÇ*

C604 Mac + PC ② 🖉 1974: Hollis Holland
Holland Title

abcdefghijklmnopqrstuvwxyz[äöüßåøæœç]
ABCDEFGHIJKLMNOPQRSTUVWXYZ
1234567890(.,;:?!$&-*){ÄÖÜÅØÆŒÇ}

Derek Italic:
Derek Italic, Engravure, Gothic Extralite Extended, Holland Title
ⓒ Albertus

EF512 Mac + PC ② 🖉 1983: Gerard Unger
Hollander™

abcdefghijklmnopqrstuvwxyz[äöüßåøæœç]
ABCDEFGHIJKLMNOPQRSTUVWXYZ
1234567890(.,;:?!$&-*){ÄÖÜÅØÆŒÇ}

ⓒ
Bitstream Charter,
Demos, Swift

▶ Regular
The quick brown fox jumps over a Dog. Zwei Boxkämpfer jagen Eva durch Sylt portez ce vieux Whiskey blond qui

▶ Italic
The quick brown fox jumps over a Dog. Zwei Boxkämpfer jagen Eva durch Sylt portez ce vieux Whiskey blond qui fume une

▶ Bold
The quick brown fox jumps over a Dog. Zwei Boxkämpfer jagen Eva durch Sylt portez ce vieux Whiskey blond

▶ Small Caps
THE QUICK BROWN FOX JUMPS OVER A DOG. 123 4567 890 ZWEI BOXKÄMPFER JAGEN EVA DURCH SYLT PORTEZ CE VIEUX

© FSI 1993

Hollandse Mediaeval

C614 Mac + PC

Hollandse Mediaeval:
Hollandse Mediaeval, Signature

C614 Mac + PC (2) 1912: S.H. de Roos

Hollandse Mediaeval

abcdefghijklmnopqrstuvwxyz[äöüßåøæœç]
ABCDEFGHIJKLMNOPQRSTUVWXYZ
1234567890(.,;:?!$&-*){ÄÖÜÅØÆŒÇ}

▶ Regular
The quick brown fox jumps over a Dog. Zwei Boxkämpfer jagen Eva durch Sylt portez ce vieux Whiskey blond qui fume une pipe aber echt

▶ Bold
The quick brown fox jumps over a Dog. Zwei Boxkämpfer jagen Eva durch Sylt portez ce vieux Whiskey blond qui fume une pipe aber

Hollandse Mediaeval:
Hollandse Mediaeval, Signature

C598 Mac + PC (2) 1974: Hollis Holland

Holland Seminar

abcdefghijklmnopqrstuvwxyz[äöüßåøæœç]
ABCDEFGHIJKLMNOPQRSTUVWXYZ
1234567890(.,;:?!$&-*){ÄÖÜÅØÆŒÇ}

▶ Regular
The quick brown fox jumps over a Dog. Zwei Boxkämpfer jagen Eva durch Sylt portez ce vieux Whiskey blond qui fume une pipe aber echt

▶ Italic
The quick brown fox jumps over a Dog. Zwei Boxkämpfer jagen Eva durch Sylt portez ce vieux Whiskey blond qui fume une pipe aber echt über die Mauer

Cartier:
Cartier, Holland Seminar

EF6447 Mac + PC (1)

Horatio™

abcdefghijklmnopqrstuvwxyz[äöüßåøæœç]
ABCDEFGHIJKLMNOPQRSTUVWXYZ
1234567890(.,;:?!$&-*)ÄÖÜÅØÆŒÇ

©
ITC Bauhaus, Blippo,
ITC Ronda, Pump

▶ Light
The quick brown fox jumps over a Dog. Zwei Boxkämpfer jagen Eva durch Sylt portez ce vieux Whiskey blond qui fume une pipe aber echt

▶ Medium
The quick brown fox jumps over a Dog. Zwei Boxkämpfer jagen Eva durch Sylt portez ce vieux Whiskey blond qui fume une pipe aber echt

▼ EF6447 Mac + PC Horatio™

▶ Bold

The quick brown fox jumps over a Dog. Zwei Boxkämpfer jagen Eva durch Sylt portez ce vieux Whiskey blond qui fume une pipe aber echt

M518 Mac + PC ②
Horley Old Style™ 1

abcdefghijklmnopqrstuvwxyz[äöüßåøæœç]
ABCDEFGHIJKLMNOPQRSTUVWXYZ
1234567890(.,;:?!$&-*){ÄÖÜÅØÆŒÇ}

© Kennerley

▶ Regular
The quick brown fox jumps over a Dog. Zwei Boxkämpfer jagen Eva durch Sylt portez ce vieux Whiskey blond qui fume une

▶ Italic
The quick brown fox jumps over a Dog. Zwei Boxkämpfer jagen Eva durch Sylt portez ce vieux Whiskey blond qui fume une pipe aber

▶ Bold
The quick brown fox jumps over a Dog. Zwei Boxkämpfer jagen Eva durch Sylt portez ce vieux Whiskey blond qui

▶ Bold Italic
The quick brown fox jumps over a Dog. Zwei Boxkämpfer jagen Eva durch Sylt portez ce vieux Whiskey blond qui fume

M949 Mac + PC ②
Horley Old Style 2

abcdefghijklmnopqrstuvwxyz[äöüßåøæœç]
ABCDEFGHIJKLMNOPQRSTUVWXYZ
1234567890(.,;:?!$&-*){ÄÖÜÅØÆŒÇ}

© Kennerley

▶ Light
The quick brown fox jumps over a Dog. Zwei Boxkämpfer jagen Eva durch Sylt portez ce vieux Whiskey blond qui fume une

▶ Light Italic
The quick brown fox jumps over a Dog. Zwei Boxkämpfer jagen Eva durch Sylt portez ce vieux Whiskey blond qui fume une pipe aber echt

▶ Semi Bold
The quick brown fox jumps over a Dog. Zwei Boxkämpfer jagen Eva durch Sylt portez ce vieux Whiskey blond qui fume

▶ Semi Bold Italic
The quick brown fox jumps over a Dog. Zwei Boxkämpfer jagen Eva durch Sylt portez ce vieux Whiskey blond qui fume une pipe

EF6471 Mac + PC ⑥ ✎ Martin Wait
Horndon™

**ABCDEFGHIJKLMNOPQRSTUVWXYZ
1234567890(.,;:?!$&-*)ÄÖÜÅØÆŒÇ**

E+F Special Headlines 7:
Harlow™, Harlow Solid, Horndon™, Koloss, Paddington™, Stentor™

© FSI 1993

MC6355 Mac + PC ⑥ L. Meuffels
Hotel™

ABCDEFGHIJKLMNOPQRSTUVWXYZ
1234567890(.,;:?!$&-*)[]{ÄÖÜÅØÆŒÇ}

TF2790 Mac + PC ⑥ 1992: Joseph Treacy
TF Hôtelmoderne™

abcdefghijklmnopqrstuvwxyz1234567890[äöüßåøœæç]
ABCDEFGHIJKLMNOPQRSTUVWXYZ(.,:?!$&-*){ÄÖÜÅØÆŒÇ}

▶ Medium
The quick brown fox jumps over a Dog. Zwei Boxkämpfer jagen Eva durch Sylt portez ce vieux Whiskey blond qui fume une pipe aber echt über die Mauer gesprungen und auch smørebrød en ysjes natuurlijk The quick brown fox jumps over

▶ Demi
The quick brown fox jumps over a Dog. Zwei Boxkämpfer jagen Eva durch Sylt portez ce vieux Whiskey blond qui fume une pipe aber echt über die Mauer gesprungen und auch smørebrød en ysjes natuurlijk The quick brown fox jumps

▶ Bold
The quick brown fox jumps over a Dog. Zwei Boxkämpfer jagen Eva durch Sylt portez ce vieux Whiskey blond qui fume une pipe aber echt über die Mauer gesprungen und auch smørebrød en ysjes natuurlijk The quick brown fox

▶ Heavy
The quick brown fox jumps over a Dog. Zwei Boxkämpfer jagen Eva durch Sylt portez ce vieux Whiskey blond qui fume une pipe aber echt über die Mauer gesprungen und auch smørebrød en ysjes natuurlijk The quick brown fox

TF6661 Mac + PC ⑥ 1992: Joseph Treacy
TF Hôtelmoderne Serif

abcdefghijklmnopqrstuvwxyz[äöüßåøœæç]
ABCDEFGHIJKLMNOPQRSTUVWXYZ
1234567890(.,:?!$&-*){ÄÖÜÅØÆŒÇ}

▶ Shaded
The quick brown fox jumps over a Dog. Zwei Boxkämpfer jagen Eva durch Sylt portez ce vieux Whiskey blond qui fume une pipe aber echt über die Mauer gesprungen und auch smørebrød en ysjes

▶ Heavy
The quick brown fox jumps over a Dog. Zwei Boxkämpfer jagen Eva durch Sylt portez ce vieux Whiskey blond qui fume une pipe aber echt über die Mauer gesprungen und auch smørebrød en ysjes

BT2873 Mac + PC ⑥ 1935: Walter Huxley
Huxley Vertical™

ABCDEFGHIJKLMNOPQRSTUVWXYZ[ÄÖÜSSÅØŒÇ]
1234567890(.,:?!$&-*){ÄÖÜÅØŒÇ}

Just van Rossum, LeTterror, Den Haag, NL

L2585 Mac ⑥ ✎ 1987: Freda Sack
Ignatius™

abcdefghijklmnopqrstuvwxyz[äöüßåøæœç]
ABCDEFGHIJKLMNOPQRSTUVWXYZ
1234567890(.,;:?!$&-*) ÄÖÜÅØÆŒÇ

AB1048 Mac + PC ① ✎ 1982: Günter Gerhard Lange
Berthold Imago®

abcdefghijklmnopqrstuvwxyz[äöüßåøæœç]
ABCDEFGHIJKLMNOPQRSTUVWXYZ
1234567890(.,;:?!$&-*){ÄÖÜÅØÆŒÇ}

▶ **Light**
The quick brown fox jumps over a Dog. Zwei Boxkämpfer jagen Eva durch Sylt portez ce vieux Whiskey blond qui fume une pipe aber echt

▶ **Light Italic**
The quick brown fox jumps over a Dog. Zwei Boxkämpfer jagen Eva durch Sylt portez ce vieux Whiskey blond qui fume une pipe aber echt

▶ **Book**
The quick brown fox jumps over a Dog. Zwei Boxkämpfer jagen Eva durch Sylt portez ce vieux Whiskey blond qui fume une

▶ **Book Italic**
The quick brown fox jumps over a Dog. Zwei Boxkämpfer jagen Eva durch Sylt portez ce vieux Whiskey blond qui fume une pipe aber

▶ **Medium**
The quick brown fox jumps over a Dog. Zwei Boxkämpfer jagen Eva durch Sylt portez ce vieux Whiskey blond qui

▶ **Medium Italic**
The quick brown fox jumps over a Dog. Zwei Boxkämpfer jagen Eva durch Sylt portez ce vieux Whiskey blond qui

▶ **Extra Bold**
The quick brown fox jumps over a Dog. Zwei Box-kämpfer jagen Eva durch Sylt portez ce vieux Whis-

▶ **Extra Bold Italic**
The quick brown fox jumps over a Dog. Zwei Box-kämpfer jagen Eva durch Sylt portez ce vieux Whis-

A1029 Mac + PC ⑥ ✎ 1965: Geoffrey Lee
Impact™

abcdefghijklmnopqrstuvwxyz(äöüßåøæœç)
ABCDEFGHIJKLMNOPQRSTUVWXYZ
1234567890(.,;:?!$&-*){ÄÖÜÅØÆŒÇ}

Baker Signet/Impact:
Baker Signet™, Impact™
☞ Aura, Aurora, Hanseatic, Hadrian, Helvetica Inserat, Helvetica Compressed, Impact, Placard

BT817 Mac + PC ② ✎ 1957: E. W. Shaar
Imperial™

abcdefghijklmnopqrstuvwxyz[äöüßåøæœç]
ABCDEFGHIJKLMNOPQRSTUVWXYZ
1234567890(.,;:?!$&-*){ÄÖÜÅØÆŒÇ}

© FSI 1993

Aurora, Corona, Excelsior Ionic, Olympian, Textype

▼ BT817 Mac + PC **Imperial**™

▶ Regular
The quick brown fox jumps over a Dog. Zwei Boxkämpfer jagen Eva durch Sylt portez ce vieux Whiskey

▶ Italic
The quick brown fox jumps over a Dog. Zwei Boxkämpfer jagen Eva durch Sylt portez ce vieux Whiskey

▶ Bold
The quick brown fox jumps over a Dog. Zwei Boxkämpfer jagen Eva durch Sylt portez ce vieux Whiskey

---

BT763 Mac + PC ④
Impress™

abcdefghijklmnopqrstuvwxyz[äöüßåøæœç]
ABCDEFGHIJKLMNOPQRSTUVWXYZ
1234567890(.,;:?!$&-*){ÄÖÜÅØÆŒÇ}

Bitstream Brush 2:
Impress™, Impuls™, Jefferson™, Mandate™
Ⓒ Dom Casual, Flash, Polka

C6432 Mac + PC ③ ✎ 1963: Konrad F. Bauer, Walter Baum
Impressum™

abcdefghijklmnopqrstuvwxyz[äöüßåøæœç]
ABCDEFGHIJKLMNOPQRSTUVWXYZ
1234567890(.,;:?!$&-*){ÄÖÜÅØÆŒÇ}

aa*a*
A228
Impressum, Reg, Ita, Bd

▶ Regular
The quick brown fox jumps over a Dog. Zwei Boxkämpfer jagen Eva durch Sylt portez ce vieux Whiskey

▶ Italic
The quick brown fox jumps over a Dog. Zwei Boxkämpfer jagen Eva durch Sylt portez ce vieux Whiskey blond

▶ Bold
The quick brown fox jumps over a Dog. Zwei Boxkämpfer jagen Eva durch Sylt portez ce vieux Whiskey

▶ Bold Italic
The quick brown fox jumps over a Dog. Zwei Boxkämpfer jagen Eva durch Sylt portez ce vieux Whiskey

---

M153 Mac + PC ② ✎ 1913: (Meynell, Mason, Jackson, Johnston)
Imprint™

abcdefghijklmnopqrstuvwxyz[äöüßåøæœç]
ABCDEFGHIJKLMNOPQRSTUVWXYZ
1234567890(.,;:?!$&-*){ÄÖÜÅØÆŒÇ}

aa*a*
BT1281
Imprint, Reg, Ita, Bd

▶ Regular
The quick brown fox jumps over a Dog. Zwei Boxkämpfer jagen Eva durch Sylt portez ce vieux Whiskey blond qui fume

▶ Italic
The quick brown fox jumps over a Dog. Zwei Boxkämpfer jagen Eva durch Sylt portez ce vieux Whiskey blond qui fume une pipe

© FSI 1993

▼ M153 Mac + PC Imprint™

▶ Bold
The quick brown fox jumps over a Dog. Zwei Boxkämpfer jagen Eva durch Sylt portez ce vieux Whiskey blond

▶ Bold Italic
The quick brown fox jumps over a Dog. Zwei Boxkämpfer jagen Eva durch Sylt portez ce vieux Whiskey

M6411 Mac + PC ⑥ 1913: (Meynell, Mason, Jackson, Johnston)
Imprint Shaded

abcdefghijklmnopqrstuvwxyz[äöüßåøæœç]
ABCDEFGHIJKLMNOPQRSTUVWXYZ
1234567890(.,;:?!$&-*){ÄÖÜÅØÆŒÇ}

▶ Regular
The quick brown fox jumps over a Dog. Zwei Boxkämpfer jagen Eva durch Sylt portez ce vieux Whiskey blond qui fume une

▶ Italic
The quick brown fox jumps over a Dog. Zwei Boxkämpfer jagen Eva durch Sylt portez ce vieux Whiskey blond qui fume

Colonna/Imprint Shaded:
Colonna™, Imprint Shaded

BT763 Mac + PC ④ 1954: P. Zimmermann
Impuls™

abcdefghijklmnopqrstuvwxyz[äöüßåøæœç]
ABCDEFGHIJKLMNOPQRSTUVWXYZ
1234567890(.,;:?!$&-){ÄÖÜÅØÆŒÇ}*

Bitstream Brush 2:
Impress™, Impuls™, Jefferson™, Mandate™

A652 Mac + PC
Industria

Industria:
Arcadia™, Industria™, Insignia™

A652 Mac + PC ⑤ 1990: Neville Brody
Industria™

abcdefghijklmnopqrstuvwxyz1234567890[äöüßåøæœç]
ABCDEFGHIJKLMNOPQRSTUVWXYZ[.,;:?!$&-*){ÄÖÜÅØÆŒÇ}

▶ Solid
The quick brown fox jumps over a Dog. Zwei Boxkämpfer jagen Eva durch Sylt portez ce vieux Whiskey blond qui fume une pipe aber echt über die Mauer gesprungen und auch smørebrød en ysjes natuurlijk. But very long

▶ Solid Alternates
The quick brown fox jumps over a Dog. Zwei Boxkämpfer jagen Eva durch Sylt portez ce vieux Whiskey blond qui fume une pipe aber echt über die Mauer gesprungen und auch smørebrød en ysjes natuurlijk. But very long

© FSI 1993

▼ A652 Mac + PC Industria™

► Inline

The quick brown fox jumps over a Dog. Zwei Boxkämpfer jagen Eva durch Sylt portez ce vieux Whiskey blond qui fume une pipe aber echt über die Mauer gesprungen und auch smørebrød en ysjes natuurlijk. But very long

► Inline Alternates

The quick brown fox jumps over a Dog. Zwei Boxkämpfer jagen Eva durch Sylt portez ce vieux Whiskey blond qui fume une pipe aber echt über die Mauer gesprungen und auch smørebrød en ysjes natuurlijk. But very long

Industria:
Arcadia™, Industria™, Insignia™

L2842 Mac   ④   ✎ 1990: Charles Hughes
Indy™ Italic

abcdefghijklmnopqrstuvwxyz[äöüßåøæœç]
ABCDEFGHIJKLMNOPQRSTUVWXYZ
1234567890(.,;:?!$&-)ÄÖÜÅØÆŒÇ*

M226 Mac + PC   ②
Inflex™

abcdefghijklmnopqrstuvwxyz[äöüßåøæœç]
ABCDEFGHIJKLMNOPQRSTUVWXYZ
1234567890(.,;:?!$&-*){ÄÖÜ ÅØ ÆŒÇ}

Headliners 4:
Inflex™, Monotype Old Style Bold Outline™, Old English™ Text
a a a A6087
Falstaff et al
M6330

L2843 Mac   ⑥   ✎ 1989: Martin Wait
Informal™ Roman

abcdefghijklmnopqrstuvwxyz[äöüßåøæœç]
ABCDEFGHIJKLMNOPQRSTUVWXYZ
1234567890(.,;:?!$&-)ÄÖÜÅØÆŒÇ*

A652 Mac + PC   ⑤   ✎ 1990: Neville Brody
Insignia™

abcdefghijklmnopqrstuvwxyz[äöüßåøæœç]
ABCDEFGHIJKLMNOPQRSTUVWXYZ
1234567890(.,;:?!$&-*){ÄÖÜÅØÆŒÇ}

► Regular

The quick brown fox jumps over a Dog. Zwei Boxkämpfer jagen Eva durch Sylt portez ce vieux Whiskey blond qui

► Alternates

The quick brown fox jumps over a Dog. Zwei Boxkämpfer jagen Eva durch Sylt portez ce vieux Whiskey blond qui

Industria:
Arcadia™, Industria™, Insignia™

© FSI 1993

FF2961 Mac + PC ⑥
FF InstantTypes™

FF InstantTypes™:
FF Confidential™, FF Dynamoe, FF Flightcase™, FF Karton™, FF Stamp Gothic™

BT1358 Mac + PC ③
News 701
Industry name
Ionic No. 5

abcdefghijklmnopqrstuvwxyz[äöüßåøæœç]
ABCDEFGHIJKLMNOPQRSTUVWXYZ
1234567890(.,;:?!$&-*){ÄÖÜÅØÆŒÇ}

aa*a*
M230
Ionic™, Reg, Ita, Bd
©
Aurora, Corona, Excelsior Imperial, Olympian, Textype

▶ Regular
The quick brown fox jumps over a Dog. Zwei Boxkämpfer jagen Eva durch Sylt portez ce vieux

▶ Italic
The quick brown fox jumps over a Dog. Zwei Boxkämpfer jagen Eva durch Sylt portez ce vieux Whis-

▶ Bold
The quick brown fox jumps over a Dog. Zwei Boxkämpfer jagen Eva durch Sylt portez ce vieux

---

M230 Mac + PC ③
Ionic™

abcdefghijklmnopqrstuvwxyz[äöüßåøæœç]
ABCDEFGHIJKLMNOPQRSTUVWXYZ
1234567890(.,;:?!$&-*){ÄÖÜÅØÆŒÇ}

aa*a*
BT1358
Ionic No. 5, Reg, Ita, Bd
©
Aurora, Corona, Excelsior, Imperial, Olympian, Textype

▶ Regular
The quick brown fox jumps over a Dog. Zwei Boxkämpfer jagen Eva durch Sylt portez ce vieux

▶ Italic
The quick brown fox jumps over a Dog. Zwei Boxkämpfer jagen Eva durch Sylt portez ce vieux Whiskey

▶ Bold
The quick brown fox jumps over a Dog. Zwei Boxkämpfer jagen Eva durch Sylt portez ce vieux Whiskey

---

BT2874 Mac + PC ② 🖉 1990: John Downer
BT Iowan Old Style™

abcdefghijklmnopqrstuvwxyz[äöüßåøæœç]
ABCDEFGHIJKLMNOPQRSTUVWXYZ
1234567890(.,;:?!$&-*){ÄÖÜÅØÆŒÇ}

©
Stratford

▶ Roman
The quick brown fox jumps over a Dog. Zwei Boxkämpfer jagen Eva durch Sylt portez ce vieux Whiskey blond qui fume

▶ Italic
The quick brown fox jumps over a Dog. Zwei Boxkämpfer jagen Eva durch Sylt portez ce vieux Whiskey blond qui fume une pipe aber

© FSI 1993

▼ BT.2874   Mac + PC   BT Iowan Old Style™

► Bold
The quick brown fox jumps over a Dog. Zwei Boxkämpfer jagen Eva durch Sylt portez ce vieux Whiskey blond

► Bold Italic
The quick brown fox jumps over a Dog. Zwei Boxkämpfer jagen Eva durch Sylt portez ce vieux Whiskey blond qui fume

► Black
The quick brown fox jumps over a Dog. Zwei Boxkämpfer jagen Eva durch Sylt portez ce

► Black Italic
The quick brown fox jumps over a Dog. Zwei Boxkämpfer jagen Eva durch Sylt portez ce vieux Whiskey

---

FB2754   Mac + PC   ⑥   ✎ 1991: John Downer
Ironmonger™

ABCDEFGHIJKLMNOPQRSTUVWXYZ
1234567890(.,:;?!$&-*)[ ]{ÄÖÜÅØÆŒÇ}

► Black
THE QUICK BROWN FOX JUMPS OVER A DOG. ZWEI BOXKÄMPFER JAGEN

► Extended
THE QUICK BROWN FOX JUMPS OVER A DOG. ZWEI BOXKÄMPFER JAGEN

FB2883   Mac + PC   ⑥   ✎ 1991-3: John Downer
Ironmonger 2

ABCDEFGHIJKLMNOPQRSTUVWXYZ
1234567890(.,:;?!$&-*)[ ]{ÄÖÜÅØÆŒÇ}

► X-Condensed
THE QUICK BROWN FOX JUMPS OVER A DOG. ZWEI BOXKÄMPFER JAGEN EVA DURCH SYLT PORTEZ CE VIEUX WHISKEY BLOND QUI FUME UNE PIPE ABER ECHT Ü BER DIE MAUER GESPRUNGEN UND AUCH SMØREBRØD EN YSJES NATUURLIJK MAINFRAME GREETS JOHN HOLMES AND JOHN WAYNE

► Inlaid
THE QUICK BROWN FOX JUMPS OVER A DOG. ZWEI BOXKÄMPFER JAGEN

► 3-D
THE QUICK BROWN FOX JUMPS OVER A DOG. ZWEI BOXKÄMPFER JAGEN

A424   Mac + PC   ⑥   ✎ 1990: Buker, Lind, Redick
Ironwood®

ABCDEFGHIJKLMNOPQRSTUVWXYZ
1234567890(.,:;?!$&-*)[ ]{ÄÖÜÅØÆŒÇ}

Wood Type Pack 1:
Cottonwood®, Ironwood®, Juniper®, Mesquite™, Ponderosa™, Wood Type Ornaments 1

Isabella™
C016 MAC + PC (6) ✎ 1892: Hermann Ihlenburg

abcdefghijklmnopqrstuvwxyz[äöüßåøœœç]
ABCDEFGHIJKLMNOPQRSTUVWXYZ
1234567890(.,;:?!$&-*){ÄÖÜÅØŒOEÇ}

Branding Iron:
Branding Iron, Isabella™, McCollough, Raphael™

ITC Isadora®
EF389 MAC + PC (4) ✎ 1985: Kris Holmes

abcdefghijklmnopqrstuvwxyzäöüßåøœœç
ABCDEFGHIJKLMNOPQRSTUVWXYZ
1234567890(.,;:?!$&-*)ÄÖÜÅØÆŒÇ

aaa
📖 C989
ITC Flora & ITC Isadora
📖 A6067
ITC Flora & ITC Isadora

▶ Regular
The quick brown fox jumps over a Dog. Zwei Boxkämpfer jagen Eva durch Sylt portez ce vieux Whiskey blond qui fume une

▶ Bold
The quick brown fox jumps over a Dog. Zwei Boxkämpfer jagen Eva durch Sylt portez ce vieux Whiskey blond qui fume

ITC Isbell® 1
BT818 MAC + PC (6) ✎ 1981: Richard Isbell, Jerry Campbell

abcdefghijklmnopqrstuvwxyz[äöüßåøæœç]
ABCDEFGHIJKLMNOPQRSTUVWXYZ
1234567890(.,;:?!$&-*){ÄÖÜÅØÆŒÇ}

▶ Book
The quick brown fox jumps over a Dog. Zwei Boxkämpfer jagen Eva durch Sylt portez ce vieux Whiskey blond qui fume

▶ Book Italic
The quick brown fox jumps over a Dog. Zwei Boxkämpfer jagen Eva durch Sylt portez ce vieux Whiskey blond qui fume

▶ Bold
The quick brown fox jumps over a Dog. Zwei Boxkämpfer jagen Eva durch Sylt portez ce vieux Whiskey

▶ Bold Italic
The quick brown fox jumps over a Dog. Zwei Boxkämpfer jagen Eva durch Sylt portez ce vieux Whiskey

ITC Isbell 2
BT819 MAC + PC (6) ✎ 1981: Richard Isbell, Jerry Campbell

abcdefghijklmnopqrstuvwxyz[äöüßåøæœç]
ABCDEFGHIJKLMNOPQRSTUVWXYZ
1234567890(.,;:?!$&-*){ÄÖÜÅØÆŒÇ}

▶ Medium
The quick brown fox jumps over a Dog. Zwei Boxkämpfer jagen Eva durch Sylt portez ce vieux Whiskey blond

▶ Medium Italic
The quick brown fox jumps over a Dog. Zwei Boxkämpfer jagen Eva durch Sylt portez ce vieux Whiskey blond qui

© FSI 1993

BT820　Mac + PC　(6)　1981: Richard Isbell, Jerry Campbell
ITC Isbell 3

abcdefghijklmnopqrstuvwxyz[äöüßåøæœç]
ABCDEFGHIJKLMNOPQRSTUVWXYZ
1234567890(.,;:?!$&-*){ÄÖÜÅØÆŒÇ}

▶ Heavy
The quick brown fox jumps over a Dog. Zwei Boxkämpfer jagen Eva durch Sylt portez ce vieux

▶ Heavy Italic
The quick brown fox jumps over a Dog. Zwei Boxkämpfer jagen Eva durch Sylt portez ce vieux

L2844　Mac　(6)　1990: Michael Gills
Isis™

ABCDEFGHIJKLMNOPQRSTUVWXYZ
1234567890[][.,;:?!$&-*]ÄÖÜÅØÆŒÇ

A066　Mac + PC　(2)　1977: Colin Brignall
Italia™

abcdefghijklmnopqrstuvwxyz[äöüßåøæœç]
ABCDEFGHIJKLMNOPQRSTUVWXYZ
1234567890(.,;:?!$&-*){ÄÖÜÅØÆŒÇ}

a a *a*
BT1340
Italia, Bk, Med, Bd

▶ Book
The quick brown fox jumps over a Dog. Zwei Boxkämpfer jagen Eva durch Sylt portez ce vieux Whiskey blond qui fume

▶ Medium
The quick brown fox jumps over a Dog. Zwei Boxkämpfer jagen Eva durch Sylt portez ce vieux Whiskey blond qui fume

▶ Bold
The quick brown fox jumps over a Dog. Zwei Boxkämpfer jagen Eva durch Sylt portez ce vieux Whiskey blond qui fume

EF6465　Mac + PC　(6)　1979: Colin Brignall
Italia Medium Condensed

abcdefghijklmnopqrstuvwxyz[äöüßåøæœç]
ABCDEFGHIJKLMNOPQRSTUVWXYZ
1234567890(.,;:?!$&-*)ÄÖÜÅØÆŒÇ

E+F Special Headlines 1:
Bernhard Fashion, Candice™, Italia Medium Condensed, Lindsay™, Odin™, Van Dijk

ET1108　Mac + PC　(2)　1988–90: (F. W. Goudy, 1924) J. Sutcliffe, R. Beatty
Italian Electric™

abcdefghijklmnopqrstuvwxyz[äöüßåøæœç]
ABCDEFGHIJKLMNOPQRSTUVWXYZ
1234567890(.,;:?!$&-*){ÄÖÜÅØÆŒÇ}

© FSI 1993

▼ ET1108 Mac + PC Italian Electric™

▶ Regular
The quick brown fox jumps over a Dog. Zwei Boxkämpfer jagen Eva durch Sylt portez ce vieux Whiskey blond qui fume une pipe aber

▶ Italic
The quick brown fox jumps over a Dog. Zwei Boxkämpfer jagen Eva durch Sylt portez ce vieux Whiskey blond qui fume une pipe aber echt

▶ Small Caps
THE QUICK BROWN FOX JUMPS OVER A DOG. 123 4567 890 ZWEI BOXKÄMPFER JAGEN EVA DURCH SYLT PORTEZ CE VIEUX WHISKEY

Electric Marlborough™:
Goudy Newstyle, Italian Electric™
👁 Goudy Italian

M273 Mac + PC ③
Italian Old Style™

abcdefghijklmnopqrstuvwxyz[äöüßåøæœç]
ABCDEFGHIJKLMNOPQRSTUVWXYZ
1234567890(.,;:?!$&-*){ÄÖÜÅØÆŒÇ}

aa*a*
A6084
Italian Old Style, Reg, Ita, Bd, BdIta
👁
Jenson No. 58

▶ Regular
The quick brown fox jumps over a Dog. Zwei Boxkämpfer jagen Eva durch Sylt portez ce vieux Whiskey blond qui fume une

▶ Italic
The quick brown fox jumps over a Dog. Zwei Boxkämpfer jagen Eva durch Sylt portez ce vieux Whiskey blond qui fume une pipe aber echt

▶ Bold
The quick brown fox jumps over a Dog. Zwei Boxkämpfer jagen Eva durch Sylt portez ce vieux Whiskey blond qui

▶ Bold Italic
The quick brown fox jumps over a Dog. Zwei Boxkämpfer jagen Eva durch Sylt portez ce vieux Whiskey blond qui fume une pipe aber

© FSI 1993

Val Fullard, Toronto, CDN

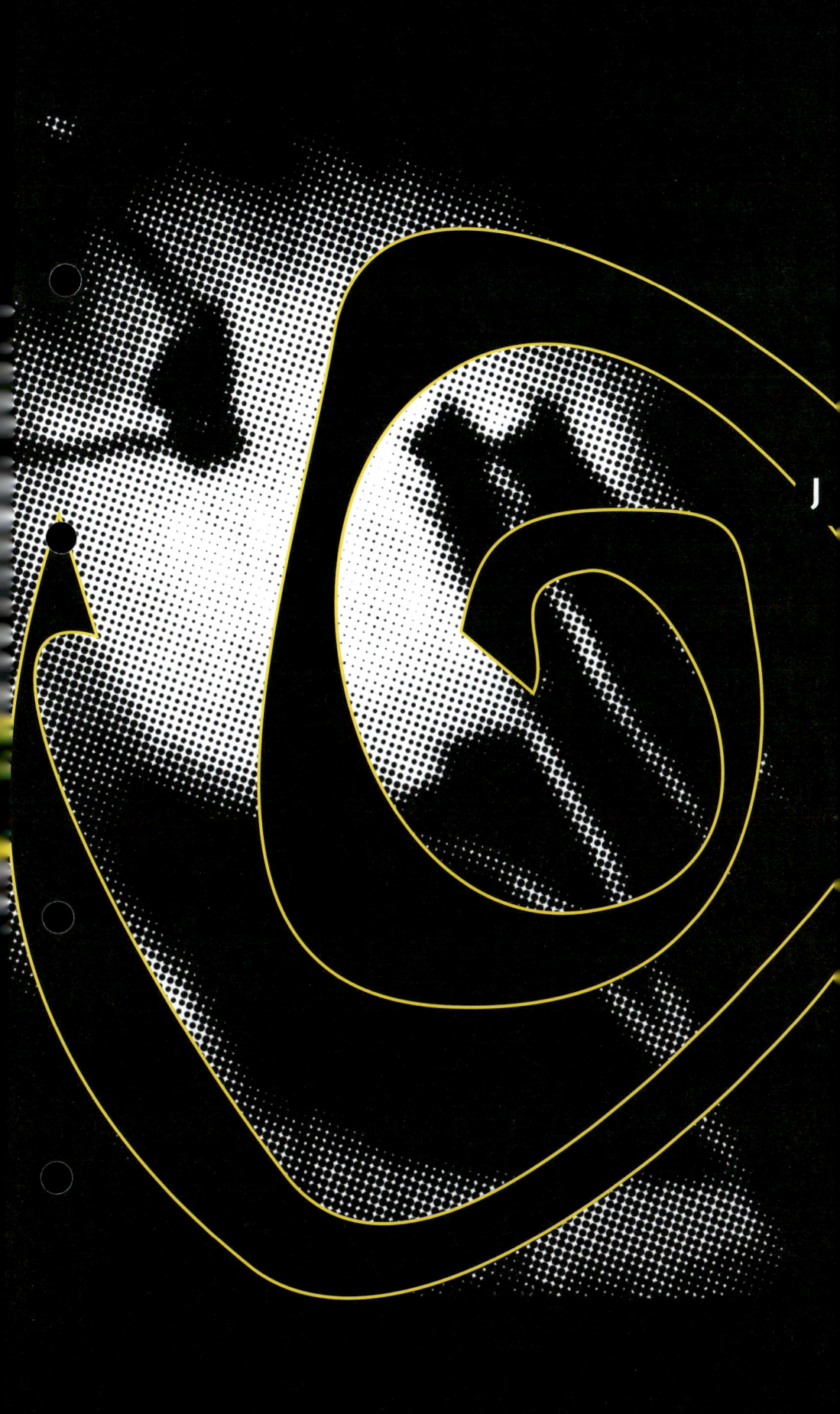

Jackson™
MC2922　Mac + PC　⑥　1971: B. Jacquet

ABCDEFGHIJKLMNOPQRSTUVWXYZ

1234567890(.,;:?!$&-*){[ÄÖÜÅØÆŒÇ}

FF Jacque™
FF1058　Mac + PC　④　1991: Max Kisman

abcdefghijklmnopqrstuvwxyz1234567890[äöüßåøæœç]

ABCDEFGHIJKLMNOPQRSTUVWXYZ(.,;:?!$&-*){ÄÖÜÅØÆŒÇ}

▶ Slim
The quick brown fox jumps over a Dog. Zwei Boxkämpfer jagen Eva durch Sylt portez ce vieux Whiskey blond qui fume une pipe aber echt über die Mauer gesprungen und auch smørebrød en ysjes natuurlijk.

▶ Regular
The quick brown fox jumps over a Dog. Zwei Boxkämpfer jagen Eva durch Sylt portez ce vieux Whiskey blond qui fume une pipe aber echt über die Mauer gesprungen und auch smørebrød en ysjes natuurlijk.

▶ Fat
The quick brown Fox jumps over a Dog. Zwei Boxkämpfer jagen Eva durch Sylt portez ce vieux Whiskey blond qui fume une pipe aber echt

ITC Jamille® 1
EF390　Mac + PC　②　1988: Mark Jamra

abcdefghijklmnopqrstuvwxyz[äöüßåøæœç]
ABCDEFGHIJKLMNOPQRSTUVWXYZ
1234567890(.,;:?!$&-*){ÄÖÜÅØÆŒÇ}

aa*a*
C983
ITC Jamille, Bk, BkIta,
Bd, BdIta, Blk, BlkIta

▶ Book
The quick brown fox jumps over a Dog. Zwei Boxkämpfer jagen Eva durch Sylt portez ce vieux Whiskey blond qui fume une

▶ Bold
The quick brown fox jumps over a Dog. Zwei Boxkämpfer jagen Eva durch Sylt portez ce vieux Whiskey blond qui fume

▶ Black
The quick brown fox jumps over a Dog. Zwei Boxkämpfer jagen Eva durch Sylt portez ce vieux Whiskey blond qui

ITC Jamille 2
EF391　Mac + PC　②　1988: Mark Jamra

abcdefghijklmnopqrstuvwxyz[äöüßåøæœç]
ABCDEFGHIJKLMNOPQRSTUVWXYZ
1234567890(.,;:?!$&-){ÄÖÜÅØÆŒÇ}*

a*aa*
C983
ITC Jamille, Bk, BkIta,
Bd, BdIta, Blk, BlkIta

▶ Book Italic
The quick brown fox jumps over a Dog. Zwei Boxkämpfer jagen Eva durch Sylt portez ce vieux Whiskey blond qui fume une

▶ Bold Italic
The quick brown fox jumps over a Dog. Zwei Boxkämpfer jagen Eva durch Sylt portez ce vieux Whiskey blond qui fume

© FSI 1993

▼ EF391 Mac + PC ITC Jamille 2

▶ Black Italic
The quick brown fox jumps over a Dog. Zwei Boxkämpfer jagen Eva durch Sylt portez ce vieux Whiskey blond qui fume

EF537 Mac + PC ② 🖉 1988: Mark Jamra
ITC Jamille Small Caps

ABCDEFGHIJKLMNOPQRSTUVWXYZ[ÄÖÜSSÅØÆŒÇ]
ABCDEFGHIJKLMNOPQRSTUVWXYZ
1234567890(.,;:?!$&-*){ÄÖÜÅØÆŒÇ}

▶ Book Small Caps
THE QUICK BROWN FOX JUMPS OVER A DOG. 123 4567 890 ZWEI BOXKÄMPFER JAGEN EVA DURCH SYLT PORTEZ CE VIEUX WHISKEY BLOND

▶ Bold Small Caps
THE QUICK BROWN FOX JUMPS OVER A DOG. 123 4567 890 ZWEI BOXKÄMPFER JAGEN EVA DURCH SYLT PORTEZ CE VIEUX WHISKEY

M560 Mac + PC ② 🖉 (Nicholas Kis, 1690)
Monotype Janson®

abcdefghijklmnopqrstuvwxyz[äöüßåøæœç]
ABCDEFGHIJKLMNOPQRSTUVWXYZ
1234567890(.,;:?!$&-*){ÄÖÜÅØÆŒÇ}

▶ Regular
The quick brown fox jumps over a Dog. Zwei Boxkämpfer jagen Eva durch Sylt portez ce vieux Whiskey blond qui fume une pipe aber

▶ Italic
The quick brown fox jumps over a Dog. Zwei Boxkämpfer jagen Eva durch Sylt portez ce vieux Whiskey blond qui fume une pipe aber echt über die Mauer

▶ Bold
The quick brown fox jumps over a Dog. Zwei Boxkämpfer jagen Eva durch Sylt portez ce vieux Whiskey blond qui fume une

▶ Bold Italic
The quick brown fox jumps over a Dog. Zwei Boxkämpfer jagen Eva durch Sylt portez ce vieux Whiskey blond qui fume une pipe aber echt

M6387 Mac + PC ② 🖉 (Nicholas Kis, 1690)
Monotype Janson Expert

ABCDEFGHIJKLMNOPQRSTUVWXYZ(ÄÖÜŠÅØÆŒÇ)

¼½¾⅛⅜⅝⅞⅓⅔ʳffiflffiffl1234567890?!$&₵ᵃᵒᵛ¢Rp

▶ Regular
01234567890ffifflffiffl-
(¼½¾⅛⅜⅝⅞⅓⅔%‰)($¢RpC)ª THE QUICK BROWN FOX JUMPS OVER A DOG ZWEI BOXKÄMPFER JAGEN EVA

▶ Italic
01234567890ffifflffiffl-
(¼½¾⅛⅜⅝⅞⅓⅔%‰)($¢RpC)ª

▶ Bold
01234567890ffifflffiffl-
(¼½¾⅛⅜⅝⅞⅓⅔%‰)($¢RpC)ª

▶ Bold Italic
01234567890ffifflffiffl-
(¼½¾⅛⅜⅝⅞⅓⅔%‰)($¢RpC)ª

© FSI 1993

J 2

A067 Mac + PC ② 1985: (Nicholas Kis, 1690) (Heiderhoff) Frutiger
Janson Text™

abcdefghijklmnopqrstuvwxyz[äöüßåøæœç]
ABCDEFGHIJKLMNOPQRSTUVWXYZ
1234567890(.,;:?!$&-*){ÄÖÜÅØÆŒÇ}

aa*a*
BT1344
Janson, Reg, Ita

▶ Regular
The quick brown fox jumps over a Dog. Zwei Boxkämpfer jagen Eva durch Sylt portez ce vieux Whiskey blond qui fume une

▶ *Italic*
The quick brown fox jumps over a Dog. Zwei Boxkämpfer jagen Eva durch Sylt portez ce vieux Whiskey blond qui fume une pipe aber echt

▶ **Bold**
The quick brown fox jumps over a Dog. Zwei Boxkämpfer jagen Eva durch Sylt portez ce vieux Whiskey blond qui

▶ ***Bold Italic***
The quick brown fox jumps over a Dog. Zwei Boxkämpfer jagen Eva durch Sylt portez ce vieux Whiskey blond qui fume

A1008 Mac + PC ② 1985: (Nicholas Kis, 1690) (Heiderhoff) Frutiger
Janson Text Small Caps/OSF

ABCDEFGHIJKLMNOPQRSTUVWXYZ[ÄÖÜSSÅØÆŒÇ]
ABCDEFGHIJKLMNOPQRSTUVWXYZ
1234567890(.,;:?!$&-*){ÄÖÜÅØÆŒÇ}

▶ Small Caps
THE QUICK BROWN FOX JUMPS OVER A DOG. 123 4567 890 ZWEI BOXKÄMPFER JAGEN EVA DURCH SYLT PORTEZ CE VIEUX WHISKEY

▶ *Italic OSF*
The quick brown fox jumps over a Dog. 123 4567 890 Zwei Boxkämpfer jagen Eva durch Sylt portez ce vieux Whiskey blond qui

▶ **Bold OSF**
The quick brown fox jumps over a Dog. 123 4567 890 Zwei Boxkämpfer jagen Eva durch Sylt portez ce vieux

▶ ***Bold Italic OSF***
The quick brown fox jumps over a Dog. 123 4567 890 Zwei Boxkämpfer jagen Eva durch Sylt portez ce vieux Whiskey

C595 Mac + PC ④ 1939: Frank Riley
Jasper™

abcdefghijklmnopqrstuvwxyz[äöüßåøæœç]
ABCDEFGHIJKLMNOPQRSTUVWXYZ
1234567890(.,;:?!$&-){ÄÖÜÅØÆŒÇ}*

Basilica:
Basilica, Floridian Script, Jasper™, Liberty™

© FSI 1993

C1012 Mac + PC ⑥
TC Jasper™

abcdefghijklmnopqrstuvwxyzäöüåøæœç
ABCDEFGHIJKLMNOPQRSTUVWXYZ
1234567890(.,;:?!$&-*)ÄÖÜÅØÆŒÇ

Headlines 84S:
Bernhard Modern, Beton Extra Bold, Metropolis Bold, Modern No. 20, Orlando Caps, PL Davison Americana, PL Westerveldt Light, Siena™ Black, TC Europa™ Bold, TC Jasper™

L2845 Mac ⑥   1992: Alan Meeks
Jazz™

abcdefghijklmnopqrstuvwxyz[äöüßåøæœç]
ABCDEFGHIJKLMNOPQRSTUVWXYZ
1234567890(.,;:?!$&-*)ÄÖÜÅØÆŒÇ

BT763 Mac + PC ④   Industry name
Freehand 575   Jefferson™

abcdefghijklmnopqrstuvwxyz[äöüßåøæœç]
ABCDEFGHIJKLMNOPQRSTUVWXYZ
1234567890(.,;:?!$&-*){ÄÖÜÅØÆŒÇ}

Bitstream Brush 2:
Impress™, Impuls™, Jefferson™, Mandate™

G392 Mac + PC ②   1890: (N. Jenson, 1470–76) William Morris
Jenson No. 58™

abcdefghijklmnopqrstuvwxyz[äöüßåøæœç]
ABCDEFGHIJKLMNOPQRSTUVWXYZ
1234567890(.,;:?!$&-*){ÄÖÜÅØÆŒÇ}

©
Italian Old Style, ITC
Golden Type

▶ Regular
The quick brown fox jumps over a Dog. Zwei Boxkämpfer jagen Eva durch Sylt portez ce vieux Whiskey blond qui fume

▶ Italic
The quick brown fox jumps over a Dog. Zwei Boxkämpfer jagen Eva durch Sylt portez ce vieux Whiskey blond qui fume

▶ Regular OSF
The quick brown fox jumps over a Dog. 123 4567 890 Zwei Boxkämpfer jagen Eva durch Sylt portez ce vieux Whiskey

▶ Italic OSF
The quick brown fox jumps over a Dog. 123 4567 890 Zwei Boxkämpfer jagen Eva durch Sylt portez ce vieux Whiskey

© FSI 1993

EF6470 Mac + PC ⑥
Jenson™ Old Style Bold Condensed

abcdefghijklmnopqrstuvwxyz[äöüßåøæœç]
ABCDEFGHIJKLMNOPQRSTUVWXYZ
1234567890(.,;:?!$&-*) ÄÖÜÅØÆŒÇ

E+F Special Headlines 6:
Croissant, Hadfield™, Jenson™ Old Style Bold Condensed, Knightsbridge™, Lazybones™

RB6092 Mac ② 1992: Richard Beatty (Nicolas Jenson)
Jenson-Eusebius™

abcdefghijklmnopqrstuvwxyz[äöüßåøæœç]
ABCDEFGHIJKLMNOPQRSTUVWXYZ
1234567890(.,;:?!$&/*){ÄÖÜÅØÆŒÇ}

▶ **Original Roman**
The quick brown fox jumps over a Dog. Zwei Boxkämpfer jagen Eva durch Sylt portez ce vieux Whiskey blond qui fume une pipe aber echt über die Mauer

▶ **Original Roman Italic**
The quick brown fox jumps over a Dog. Zwei Boxkämpfer jagen Eva durch Sylt portez ce vieux Whiskey blond qui fume une pipe aber echt

▶ **New Style Roman**
The quick brown fox jumps over a Dog. Zwei Boxkämpfer jagen Eva durch Sylt portez ce vieux Whiskey blond qui fume une pipe aber echt über die Mauer

▶ **New Style Roman Italic**
The quick brown fox jumps over a Dog. Zwei Boxkämpfer jagen Eva durch Sylt portez ce vieux Whiskey blond qui fume une pipe aber echt

---

RB6093 Mac ② 1992: Richard Beatty (Nicolas Jenson)
Jenson-Eusebius SC/OSF

ABCDEFGHIJKLMNOPQRSTUVWXYZ[ÄÖÜÅØÆŒÇ]
ABCDEFGHIJKLMNOPQRSTUVWXYZ
1234567890(.,;:?!$&/*){ÄÖÜÅØÆŒÇ}

▶ **Original Roman SC**
THE QUICK BROWN FOX JUMPS OVER A DOG. 123 4567 890 ZWEI BOXKÄMPFER JAGEN EVA DURCH SYLT PORTEZ CE VIEUX WHISKEY BLOND

▶ **Original Roman Italic OSF**
The quick brown fox jumps over a Dog. 123 4567 890 Zwei Boxkämpfer jagen Eva durch Sylt portez ce vieux Whiskey blond qui fume

▶ **New Style Roman SC**
THE QUICK BROWN FOX JUMPS OVER A DOG. 123 4567 890 ZWEI BOXKÄMPFER JAGEN EVA DURCH SYLT PORTEZ CE VIEUX WHISKEY BLOND QUI

▶ **New Style Roman Italic OSF**
The quick brown fox jumps over a Dog. 123 4567 890 Zwei Boxkämpfer jagen Eva durch Sylt portez ce vieux Whiskey blond qui fume

---

M231 Mac + PC ③ 1930: Eric Gill
Joanna®

abcdefghijklmnopqrstuvwxyz[äöüßåøæœç]
ABCDEFGHIJKLMNOPQRSTUVWXYZ
1234567890(.,;:?!$&-*) {ÄÖÜÅØÆŒÇ}

© FSI 1993

▼ M231 Mac + PC Joanna®

aa*a*
A2535
Joanna, Reg, Ita,
SemBd, SemBdIta, Bd,
BdIta, ExtBd
Candida, FF Scala

▶ Regular
The quick brown fox jumps over a Dog. Zwei Boxkämpfer jagen Eva durch Sylt portez ce vieux Whiskey blond qui fume une pipe aber

▶ Italic
The quick brown fox jumps over a Dog. Zwei Boxkämpfer jagen Eva durch Sylt portez ce vieux Whiskey blond qui fume une pipe aber echt über die Mauer gesprungen

▶ Bold
The quick brown fox jumps over a Dog. Zwei Boxkämpfer jagen Eva durch Sylt portez ce vieux Whiskey blond qui fume une

▶ Bold Italic
The quick brown fox jumps over a Dog. Zwei Boxkämpfer jagen Eva durch Sylt portez ce vieux Whiskey blond qui fume une pipe aber echt über die Mauer

M232 Mac + PC ③ 1930: Eric Gill
Joanna 2

abcdefghijklmnopqrstuvwxyz[äöüßåøæœç]
ABCDEFGHIJKLMNOPQRSTUVWXYZ
1234567890(.,;:?!$&-*){ÄÖÜÅØÆŒÇ}

aa*a*
A2535
Joanna, Reg, Ita,
SemBd, SemBdIta, Bd,
BdIta, ExtBd
Candida, FF Scala

▶ Semi Bold
The quick brown fox jumps over a Dog. Zwei Boxkämpfer jagen Eva durch Sylt portez ce vieux Whiskey blond qui fume une

▶ Semi Bold Italic
The quick brown fox jumps over a Dog. Zwei Boxkämpfer jagen Eva durch Sylt portez ce vieux Whiskey blond qui fume une pipe aber echt über die Mauer

▶ Extra Bold
The quick brown fox jumps over a Dog. Zwei Boxkämpfer jagen Eva durch Sylt portez ce vieux Whiskey blond qui fume

C2981 Mac + PC ⑥
Joanna Solotype

abcdefghijklmnopqrstuvwxyz[äöüßåøæœç]
ABCDEFGHIJKLMNOPQRSTUVWXYZ
1234567890(.,;:?!$&-*){ÄÖÜÅØÆŒÇ}

Headlines 92S:
Eagle Bold, Joanna Solotype, Matra™, Modernique, Victorian Silhouette

FF1533 Mac + PC ⑦ 1991: Manfred Klein
FF Johannes G™

abcdefghijklmnopqrstuvwxyzäöüßlch
ABCDEFGHIJKLMNOPQRSTUVWXYZ
1234567890(.,;:?!-)ÄÖÜ

FF Scribe Type™:
FF Carolus Magnus™, FF Johannes G™, FF Koberger™, FF Schoensperger™

© FSI 1993

J 6

E936 Mac + PC ③ 1990: Zuzana Licko
Journal™

abcdefghijklmnopqrstuvwxyz[äöüßåøæœç]
ABCDEFGHIJKLMNOPQRSTUVWXYZ
1234567890(.,;:?!$&-*){ÄÖÜÅØÆŒÇ}

▶ Text
The quick brown fox jumps over a Dog. Zwei Boxkämpfer jagen Eva durch Sylt portez ce vieux Whiskey

▶ Italic
The quick brown fox jumps over a Dog. Zwei Boxkämpfer jagen Eva durch Sylt portez ce vieux Whiskey blond qui fume

▶ Ultra
The quick brown fox jumps over a Dog. Zwei Boxkämpfer jagen Eva durch Sylt portez ce

E2760 Mac + PC ③ 1991: Zuzana Licko
Journal Extended

ABCDEFGHIJKLMNOPQRSTUVWXYZ(ÄÖÜŠÅØÆŒÇ)
ABCDEFGHIJKLMNOPQRSTUVWXYZ
1234567890(.,;:?!$&-..)₡e⁹⁰aoˇ¢Rp

▶ Text Small Caps
THE QUICK BROWN FOX JUMPS OVER A DOG. 123 4567 890 ZWEI BOXKÄMPFER JAGEN EVA DURCH SYLT PORTEZ CE VIEUX

▶ Text Fractions
01234567890fffiflffiffl-(½⅓¼⅖⅗⅘⅙⅞⅝⅔⅜)9543Rp₡ oª THE QUICK BROWN FOX JUMPS OVER A DOG ZWEI BOX-

▶ Italic Small Caps
THE QUICK BROWN FOX JUMPS OVER A DOG. 123 4567 890 ZWEI BOXKÄMPFER JAGEN EVA DURCH SYLT PORTEZ CE VIEUX

▶ Italic Fractions
01234567890fffiflffiffl-(½⅓¼⅖⅗⅘⅙⅞⅝⅔⅜)9543Rp₡oª THE QUICK BROWN FOX JUMPS OVER A DOG ZWEI BOXKÄMPFER

▶ Ultra Small Caps
THE QUICK BROWN FOX JUMPS OVER A DOG. 123 4567 890 ZWEI BOXKÄMPFER JAGEN EVA DURCH

▶ Ultra Fractions
01234567890fffiflffiffl-(½⅓¼⅖⅗⅘⅙⅞⅝⅔⅜)9543Rp ₡oa THE QUICK BROWN FOX JUMPS OVER A DOG ZWEI

EF6469 Mac + PC ④ David Harris
Julia™ Script

abcdefghijklmnopqrstuvwxyz[äöüåøæœ]
ABCDEFGHIJKLMNOPQRSTUVWXYZ
1234567890(.,;:?!$&-*)ÄÖÜÅØÆŒÇ

E+F Special Headlines 5:
Chesterfield™, Cortez™, Elefont™, Glastonbury™, Julia™ Script, LCD

© FSI 1993

J 7

Juniper®
A424 Mac + PC (6) — 1990: Buker, Lind, Redick

ABCDEFGHIJKLMNOPQRSTUVWXYZ
1234567890(.,;:?!$&-*)[]{ÄÖÜÅØÆŒÇ}

Wood Type Pack 1:
Cottonwood®, Ironwood®, Juniper®, Mesquite™, Ponderosa®, Wood Type Ornaments 1

FF Justlefthand™
FF735 Mac + PC (4) — 1991: Just van Rossum

abcdefghijklmnopqrstuvwxyz[äöüßåøæœç]
ABCDEFGHIJKLMNOPQRSTUVWXYZ
1234567890(.,;:?!$&-*){ÄÖÜÅØÆŒÇ}

FF Erikrighthand

▶ **Regular**
The quick brown fox jumps over a Dog. Zwei Boxkämpfer jagen Eva durch Sylt portez ce vieux Whiskey blond qui fume une pipe aber echt über die Mauer gesprungen und auch

▶ **Small Caps**
THE QUICK BROWN FOX JUMPS OVER A DOG. 123 4567 890 ZWEI BOXKÄMPFER JAGEN EVA DURCH SYLT PORTEZ CE VIEUX WHISKEY BLOND QUI FUME UNE PIPE ABER ECHT ÜBER DIE MAUER

FF Hands™:
FF Erikrighthand™, FF Justlefthand™
FF Erikrighthand

© FSI 1993

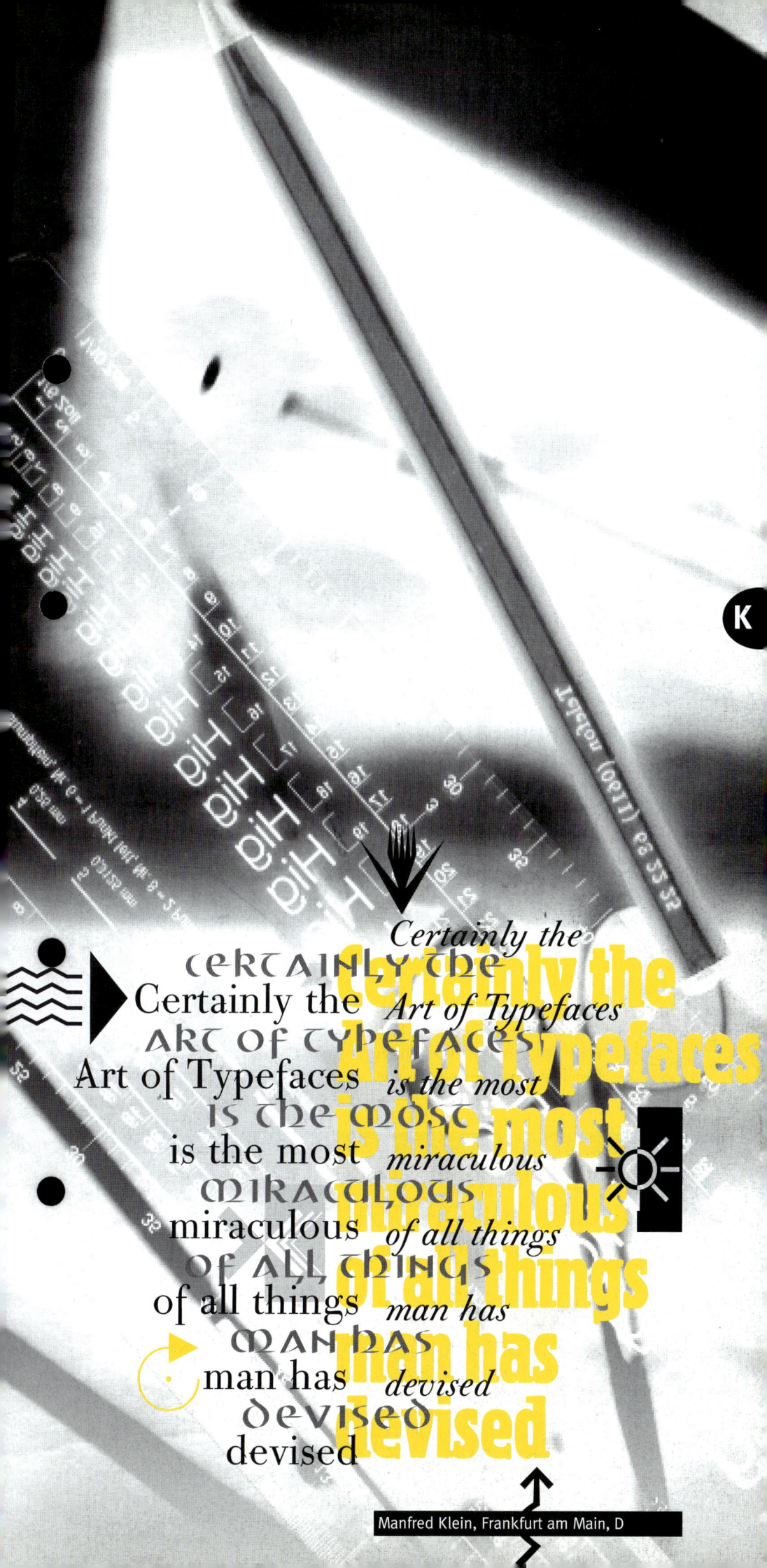

Certainly the Art of Typefaces is the most miraculous of all things man has devised

Manfred Klein, Frankfurt am Main, D

G393 MAC + PC ② 1988: (F. W. Goudy, 1929) Jim Rimmer
Kaatskill No. 976™

abcdefghijklmnopqrstuvwxyz[äöüßåøæœç]
ABCDEFGHIJKLMNOPQRSTUVWXYZ
1234567890(.,;:?!$&-*){ÄÖÜÅØÆŒÇ}

▶ **Regular**
The quick brown fox jumps over a Dog. Zwei Boxkämpfer jagen Eva durch Sylt portez ce vieux Whiskey blond qui fume une pipe aber echt

▶ *Italic*
The quick brown fox jumps over a Dog. Zwei Boxkämpfer jagen Eva durch Sylt portez ce vieux Whiskey blond qui fume une pipe aber echt über die Mauer

▶ **Regular OSF**
The quick brown fox jumps over a Dog. 123 4567 890 Zwei Boxkämpfer jagen Eva durch Sylt portez ce vieux Whiskey blond qui fume

▶ *Italic OSF*
The quick brown fox jumps over a Dog. 123 4567 890 Zwei Boxkämpfer jagen Eva durch Sylt portez ce vieux Whiskey blond qui fume une pipe aber echt über die

▶ **Small Caps**
THE QUICK BROWN FOX JUMPS OVER A DOG. 123 4567 890 ZWEI BOXKÄMPFER JAGEN EVA DURCH SYLT PORTEZ CE VIEUX WHISKEY BLOND QUI

▶ *Small Caps Italic*
THE QUICK BROWN FOX JUMPS OVER A DOG. 123 4567 890 ZWEI BOXKÄMPFER JAGEN EVA DURCH SYLT PORTEZ CE VIEUX WHISKEY BLOND QUI

BT821 MAC + PC ① 1927: Rudolf Koch Industry name
Geometric 231 / Stempel Kabel™

abcdefghijklmnopqrstuvwxyz[äöüßåøæœç]
ABCDEFGHIJKLMNOPQRSTUVWXYZ
1234567890(.,;:?!$&-*){ÄÖÜÅØÆŒÇ}

aaa
A2545
Stempel Kabel, Lt, Bk, Blk, Hvy
©
PL Bernhardt, ITC Kabel, Futura Maxi

▶ **Light**
The quick brown fox jumps over a Dog. Zwei Boxkämpfer jagen Eva durch Sylt portez ce vieux Whiskey blond qui fume une pipe aber echt über die Mauer

▶ **Regular**
The quick brown fox jumps over a Dog. Zwei Boxkämpfer jagen Eva durch Sylt portez ce vieux Whiskey blond qui fume une pipe aber echt über die

▶ **Bold**
The quick brown fox jumps over a Dog. Zwei Boxkämpfer jagen Eva durch Sylt portez ce vieux Whiskey blond qui fume une pipe aber echt

▶ **Heavy**
The quick brown fox jumps over a Dog. Zwei Boxkämpfer jagen Eva durch Sylt portez ce vieux Whiskey blond qui fume

---

A068 MAC + PC ① 1976: (Rudolf Koch, 1927)
ITC Kabel®

abcdefghijklmnopqrstuvwxyz[äöüßåøæœç]
ABCDEFGHIJKLMNOPQRSTUVWXYZ
1234567890(.,;:?!$&-*){ÄÖÜÅØÆŒÇ}

aaa
BT1342
ITC Kabel 2, Med, Demi, Bd
BT1341
ITC Kabel 1, Bk, Ult
©
PL Bernhardt, Kabel, Futura Maxi

▶ **Book**
The quick brown fox jumps over a Dog. Zwei Boxkämpfer jagen Eva durch Sylt portez ce vieux Whiskey blond qui fume une

▶ **Medium**
The quick brown fox jumps over a Dog. Zwei Boxkämpfer jagen Eva durch Sylt portez ce vieux Whiskey blond qui fume

© FSI 1993

▼ A068 Mac + PC ITC Kabel®

▶ Demi
The quick brown fox jumps over a Dog. Zwei Boxkämpfer jagen Eva durch Sylt portez ce vieux Whiskey blond qui fume

▶ Bold
The quick brown fox jumps over a Dog. Zwei Boxkämpfer jagen Eva durch Sylt portez ce vieux Whiskey blond qui fume

▶ Ultra
The quick brown fox jumps over a Dog. Zwei Boxkämpfer jagen Eva durch Sylt portez ce vieux Whiskey blond qui fume

L2846 Mac ⑥ 1992: Ed Bugg
Kanban™

ABCDEFGHIJKLMNOPQRSTUVWXYZ
1234567890 (.,;:?!$&-*) [ ] ÄÖÜÅØÆŒÇ

EF1077 Mac + PC ⑤ 1974: Wolf Jarosch
Kapitellia™ Bold

abcdefghijklmnopqrstuvwxyzäöüßåøæœç
ABCDEFGHIJKLMNOPQRSTUVWXYZ
1234567890(.,;:?!$&-*)ÄÖÜÅØÆŒÇ

FF2961 Mac + PC ⑥ 1992: Just van Rossum
FF Karton™

ABCDEFGHIJKLMNOPQRSTUVWXYZ[ÄÖÜ ÅØÆŒÇ]
ABCDEFGHIJKLMNOPQRSTUVWXYZ
1234567890(.,;:?!$ -) ÄÖÜÅØÆŒÇ

FF InstantTypes™:
FF Confidential™, FF Dynamoe™, FF Flightcase™, FF Karton™, FF Stamp Gothic™

FF6185 Mac + PC ⑥ 1992: Paul H. Neville
FF Kath™ Condensed

ABCDEFGHIJKLMNOPQRSTUVWXYZ1234567890
[ÄÖÜÅØ ÆŒÇ](.,;:?!$&-*){ÄÖÜÅØ ÆŒÇ}

▶ Regular
THE QUICK BROWN FOX JUMPS OVER A DOG. ZWEI BOXKÄMPFER JAGEN EVA DURCH SYLT PORTEZ CE VIEUX WHISKEY BLOND QUI FUME UNE PIPE ABER ECHT ÜBER DIE MAUER GESPRUNGEN UND AUCH SMØRREBRØD EN YSJES NATUURLIJK. BUT VERY LONG SPAZIERENDE TEKST IST USED IN DIESER CATALOG MAAR NICHT SO DURCH SYLT PORTEZ CE VIEUX WHIS-

▶ Inline
THE QUICK BROWN FOX JUMPS OVER A DOG. ZWEI BOXKÄMPFER JAGEN EVA DURCH SYLT PORTEZ CE VIEUX WHISKEY BLOND QUI FUME UNE PIPE ABER ECHT ÜBER DIE MAUER GESPRUNGEN UND AUCH SMØRREBRØD EN YSJES NATUURLIJK. BUT VERY LONG SPAZIERENDE TEKST IST USED IN DIESER CATALOG MAAR NICHT SO DURCH SYLT PORTEZ CE VIEUX WHIS-

▶ Bold
THE QUICK BROWN FOX JUMPS OVER A DOG. ZWEI BOXKÄMPFER JAGEN EVA DURCH SYLT PORTEZ CE VIEUX WHISKEY BLOND QUI FUME UNE PIPE ABER ECHT ÜBER DIE MAUER GESPRUNGEN UND AUCH SMØRREBRØD EN YSJES NATUURLIJK. BUT VERY LONG SPAZIERENDE TEKST IST USED IN

▶ Bold Inline
THE QUICK BROWN FOX JUMPS OVER A DOG. ZWEI BOXKÄMPFER JAGEN EVA DURCH SYLT PORTEZ CE VIEUX WHISKEY BLOND QUI FUME UNE PIPE ABER ECHT ÜBER DIE MAUER GESPRUNGEN UND AUCH SMØRREBRØD EN YSJES NATUURLIJK. BUT VERY LONG SPAZIERENDE TEKST IST USED IN

© FSI 1993

Kaufmann™

A069   Mac + PC   ④   1936: Max R. Kaufmann

abcdefghijklmnopqrstuvwxyz[äöüßåøæœç]
ABCDEFGHIJKLMNOPQRSTUVWXYZ
1234567890(.,;:?!$&-*){ÄÖÜÅØÆŒÇ}

aaa
BT1343 ©
Gillies Gothic, Swing

▶ Regular
The quick brown fox jumps over a Dog. Zwei Boxkämpfer jagen Eva durch Sylt portez ce vieux Whiskey blond qui fume une pipe aber echt über die Mauer

▶ Bold
The quick brown fox jumps over a Dog. Zwei Boxkämpfer jagen Eva durch Sylt portez ce vieux Whiskey blond qui fume une pipe aber echt

Keedy Sans™

E2553   Mac + PC   ⑥   1990: Jeffrey Keedy

abcdefghijklmnopqrstuvwxyz[äöüßåøæœç]
ABCDEFGHiJKLMNOPQRSTUVWXYZ
1234567890(.,;:?!$&-*){ÄÖÜÅØÆŒÇ}

▶ Regular
The quick brown fox jumps over a Dog. Zwei Boxkämpfer jagen Eva durch Sylt portez ce vieux Whiskey

▶ Bold
The quick brown fox jumps over a Dog. Zwei Boxkämpfer jagen Eva durch Sylt portez ce vieux Whiskey

Kennerley™

RB6096   Mac   ②   1991: Richard Beatty (1911-24: Fred. W. Goudy)

abcdefghijklmnopqrstuvwxyz[äöüßåøæœç]
ABCDEFGHIJKLMNOPQRSTUVWXYZ
1234567890(.,;:?!$&-*){ÄÖÜÅØÆŒÇ}

©
Horley Old Style

▶ Original Roman
The quick brown fox jumps over a Dog. Zwei Boxkämpfer jagen Eva durch Sylt portez ce vieux Whiskey blond qui fume une

▶ Original Italic
The quick brown fox jumps over a Dog. Zwei Boxkämpfer jagen Eva durch Sylt portez ce vieux Whiskey blond qui fume une pipe aber

▶ Roman
The quick brown fox jumps over a Dog. Zwei Boxkämpfer jagen Eva durch Sylt portez ce vieux Whiskey blond qui fume une pipe aber

▶ Italic
The quick brown fox jumps over a Dog. Zwei Boxkämpfer jagen Eva durch Sylt portez ce vieux Whiskey blond qui fume une pipe

▶ Bold
The quick brown fox jumps over a Dog. Zwei Boxkämpfer jagen Sylt portez ce vieux Whiskey blond qui fume

▶ Bold Italic
The quick brown fox jumps over a Dog. Zwei Boxkämpfer jagen Eva durch Sylt portez ce vieux Whiskey blond qui fume une

▶ Open
The quick brown fox jumps over a Dog. Zwei Boxkämpfer jagen Eva durch Sylt portez ce vieux Whiskey blond qui fume une pipe aber

© FSI 1993

Kennerley SC/OSF

RB6097 Mac — 1991: Richard Beatty (1911-24: Fred. W. Goudy)

ABCDEFGHIJKLMNOPQRSTUVWXYZ[ÄÖÜÅØÆŒÇ]
ABCDEFGHIJKLMNOPQRSTUVWXYZ
1234567890(.,;:?!$&-*){ÄÖÜÅØÆŒÇ}

Horley Old Style

▶ **Original Roman SC**
THE QUICK BROWN FOX JUMPS OVER A DOG. 123 4567 890 ZWEI BOXKÄMPFER JAGEN EVA DURCH SYLT PORTEZ CE VIEUX

▶ **Original Italic OSF**
The quick brown fox jumps over a Dog. 123 4567 890 Zwei Boxkämpfer jagen Eva durch Sylt portez ce vieux Whiskey blond qui

▶ **Roman SC**
THE QUICK BROWN FOX JUMPS OVER A DOG. 123 4567 890 ZWEI BOXKÄMPFER JAGEN EVA DURCH SYLT PORTEZ CE VIEUX

▶ **Italic OSF**
The quick brown fox jumps over a Dog. 123 4567 890 Zwei Boxkämpfer jagen Eva durch Sylt portez ce vieux Whiskey blond qui

▶ **Bold SC**
THE QUICK BROWN FOX JUMPS OVER A DOG. 123 4567 890 ZWEI BOXKÄMPFER JAGEN EVA DURCH SYLT PORTEZ CE

▶ **Bold Italic OSF**
The quick brown fox jumps over a Dog. 123 4567 890 Zwei Boxkämpfer jagen Eva durch Sylt portez ce vieux Whiskey

▶ **Open SC**
THE QUICK BROWN FOX JUMPS OVER A DOG. ZWEI BOXKÄMPFER JAGEN EVA DURCH SYLT PORTEZ CE VIEUX WHISKEY BLOND QUI

Kennerley No. 268™

G2827 Mac + PC — 1911-24: Frederic W. Goudy

abcdefghijklmnopqrstuvwxyz[äöüßåøæœç]
ABCDEFGHIJKLMNOPQRSTUVWXYZ
1234567890(.,;:?!$&-*){ÄÖÜÅØÆŒÇ}

Horley Old Style

▶ **Regular OSF**
The quick brown fox jumps over a Dog. 123 4567 890 Zwei Boxkämpfer jagen Eva durch Sylt portez ce vieux Whiskey blond qui

▶ **Italic OSF**
The quick brown fox jumps over a Dog. 123 4567 890 Zwei Boxkämpfer jagen Eva durch Sylt portez ce vieux Whiskey blond qui

▶ **Regular**
The quick brown fox jumps over a Dog. Zwei Boxkämpfer jagen Eva durch Sylt portez ce vieux Whiskey blond qui fume une pipe aber

▶ **Italic**
The quick brown fox jumps over a Dog. Zwei Boxkämpfer jagen Eva durch Sylt portez ce vieux Whiskey blond qui fume une pipe aber echt

▶ **Small Caps OSF**
THE QUICK BROWN FOX JUMPS OVER A DOG. 123 4567 890 ZWEI BOXKÄMPFER JAGEN EVA DURCH SYLT PORTEZ CE VIEUX WHISKEY BLOND

▶ **Italic Small Caps OSF**
THE QUICK BROWN FOX JUMPS OVER A DOG. 123 4567 890 ZWEI BOXKÄMPFER JAGEN EVA DURCH SYLT PORTEZ CE VIEUX WHISKEY BLOND

© FSI 1993

▼ G2827 Mac + PC   Kennerley No. 268™

▶ Swash OSF Italic
The quick brown fox jumps over a Dog. 123 4567 890 Zwei Boxkämpfer jagen Eva durch Sylt portez ce vieux Whiskey blond qui

▶ Swash Italic
The quick brown fox jumps over a Dog. Zwei Boxkämpfer jagen Eva durch Sylt portez ce vieux Whiskey blond qui fume une pipe aber echt

M6410 Mac + PC   ⑥   1930: M. Dovey
Kino™

abcdefghijklmnopqrstuvwxyz[äöüßåøæœç]
ABCDEFGHIJKLMNOPQRSTUVWXYZ
1234567890(.,:;?!$&-*){ÄÖÜÅØÆŒÇ}

Crazy Headlines™:
Festival™ Titling, Kino™, Matura ™Script, Victoria™ Titling Condensed

FF6385 Mac + PC   ⑥   1993: Claudia Kipp
FF Kipp™

abcdefghijklmnopqrstuvwxyz[äöüssåøæœç]
ABCDEFGHIJKLMNOPQRSTUVWXYZ
1234567890(.,:;?!$&-*){ÄÖÜÅØÆŒÇ}

© Garage Gothic

▶ No. 1
The quick brown fox jumps over a Dog. Zwei Boxkämpfer jagen Eva durch Sylt portez ce vieux Whiskey blond qui fume une pipe aber echt über die Mauer gesprungen und auch

▶ No. 2
The quick brown fox jumps over a Dog. Zwei Boxkämpfer jagen Eva durch Sylt portez ce vieux Whiskey blond qui fume une pipe aber echt über die Mauer gesprungen und auch

▶ No. 3
The quick brown fox jumps over a Dog. Zwei Boxkämpfer jagen Eva durch Sylt portez ce vieux Whiskey blond qui fume une pipe aber echt über die Mauer gesprungen und auch

▶ No. 4
The quick brown fox jumps over a Dog. Zwei Boxkämpfer jagen Eva durch Sylt portez ce vieux Whiskey blond qui fume une pipe aber echt über die Mauer gesprungen und auch

▶ No. 5 (Overlay elements)

▶ No. 6 (Overlay elements)

▶ No. 7 (Widths only)

FF731 Mac + PC
FF Kisman™ 1

FF Kisman™ 1:
FF Cutout™, FF Network™, FF Scratch™, FF Vortex™

© FSI 1993

M267 Mac + PC — 1955: Will Carter
Klang™

abcdefghijklmnopqrstuvwxyz[äöüßåøæœç]
ABCDEFGHIJKLMNOPQRSTUVWXYZ
1234567890(.,;:?!$&-*){ÄÖÜÅØÆŒÇ}

Headliners 3: Braggadocio™, Figaro®, Forte™, Klang™
aaa ⌨ M6331: Forte et al, ⌨ A6088: Forte et al

L6595 Mac — 1992: Tim Donaldson
Klee™

abcdefghijklmnopqrstuvwxyz[äöüßåøæœç]
ABCDEFGHIJKLMNOPQRSTUVWXYZ
1234567890(.,;:?!$&-*)ÄÖÜÅØÆŒÇ

EF6470 Mac + PC
Knightsbridge™

abcdefghijklmnopqrstuvwxyz[äöüßåøæœç]
ABCDEFGHIJKLMNOPQRSTUVWXYZ
1234567890(.,;:?!$&-*)ÄÖÜÅØÆŒÇ

▶ **Regular**
The quick brown fox jumps over a Dog. Zwei Boxkämpfer jagen Eva durch Sylt portez ce vieux Whiskey blond qui fume une

▶ **Alternates**
The quick brown fox jumps over a Dog. Zwei Boxkämpfer jagen Eva durch Sylt portez ce vieux Whiskey blond qui

E+F Special Headlines 6:
Croissant, Hadfield™, Jenson™ Old Style Bold Condensed, Knightsbridge™, Lazybones™

FF1533 Mac + PC — 1991: Manfred Klein
FF Koberger™

abcdefghijklmnopqrstuvwxyz1234567890äöüßch
ABCDEFGHIJKLMNOPQRSTUVWXYZ
(.,;:?!$&-*)ÄÖÜ

FF Scribe Type™: FF Carolus Magnus™, FF Johannes G™, FF Koberger™, FF Schoensperger™
Carolina

F2945 Mac — (1923): Rudolf Koch
Koch Antiqua™

abcdefghijklmnopqrstuvwxyz[äöüläøæœç]
ABCDEFGHIJKLMNOPQRSTUVWXYZ
1234567890(.,;:?!$&-*)ÄÖÜÅØÆŒÇ

▶ **Light**
The quick brown fox jumps over a Dog. Zwei Boxkämpfer jagen Eva durch Sylt portez ce vieux Whiskey blond qui fume une pipe aber echt über die Mauer

▶ **Demi**
The quick brown fox jumps over a Dog. Zwei Boxkämpfer jagen Eva durch Sylt portez ce vieux Whiskey blond qui fume une pipe aber echt über die Mauer

▶ **Extra Bold**
The quick brown fox jumps over a Dog. Zwei Boxkämpfer jagen Eva durch Sylt portez ce vieux Whiskey blond qui fume une pipe aber echt über die Mauer

© FSI 1993

F6345 Mac — Koch Neuland™
1992: (Rudolf Koch 1923) Lester Dore

ABCDEFGHIJKLMNOPQRSTUVWXYZ[ÄÖÜẞÅØÆ+Ç]
ABCDEFGHIJKLMNOPQRSTUVWXYZ
1234567890(.,;:?!$&-*)(☉☉☉⊕☊♏ŒY}

LP6663 Mac + PC — Koch Original™
1992: Garrett Boge

abcdefghijklmnopqrstuvwxyz[äöüßåøæœç]
ABCDEFGHIJKLMNOPQRSTUVWXYZ
1234567890(.,;:?!$&-*){ÄÖÜÅØÆŒÇ}

LetterPerfect 5:
Hardwood™, Koch Original™, Roslyn Bold
ⓒ Kabel

C2523 Mac + PC — Koloss™
1930: Jakob Erbar

abcdefghijklmnopqrstuvwxyz[äöüßåøæœç]
ABCDEFGHIJKLMNOPQRSTUVWXYZ
1234567890(.,;:?!$&-*){ÄÖÜÅØÆŒÇ}

Headlines 87S:
Greeting Monotone™, Koloss™, Phenix™ American, Phosphor™, Zeppelin™

EF6471 Mac + PC — Koloss
1930: Jakob Erbar

abcdefghijklmnopqrstuvwxyzäöüßåøæœç
ABCDEFGHIJKKLMNOPQRRSTUVWXYZ
1234567890(.,;:?!$&-*){ÄÖÜÅØÆŒÇ}

E+F Special Headlines 7:
Harlow™, Harlow Solid, Horndon™, Koloss, Paddington™, Stentor™

BT1345 Mac + PC — ITC Korinna® 3
1974: (1904) Ed Benguiat, Victor Caruso

abcdefghijklmnopqrstuvwxyz[äöüßåøæœç]
ABCDEFGHIJKLMNOPQRSTUVWXYZ
1234567890(.,;:?!$&-*){ÄÖÜÅØÆŒÇ}

aaa
A070
ITC Korinna, Reg, KursivReg, Bd, KursivBd

▶ Regular
The quick brown fox jumps over a Dog. Zwei Boxkämpfer jagen Eva durch Sylt portez ce vieux Whiskey blond qui fume une

▶ Bold
The quick brown fox jumps over a Dog. Zwei Boxkämpfer jagen Eva durch Sylt portez ce vieux Whiskey blond qui fume

▶ Kursiv Regular
The quick brown fox jumps over a Dog. Zwei Boxkämpfer jagen Eva durch Sylt portez ce vieux Whiskey blond qui fume

▶ Kursiv Bold
The quick brown fox jumps over a Dog. Zwei Boxkämpfer jagen Eva durch Sylt portez ce vieux Whiskey blond qui

© FSI 1993

BT822 MAC + PC ③ 1974: (1904) Ed Benguiat, Victor Caruso
ITC Korinna 1

abcdefghijklmnopqrstuvwxyz[äöüßåøæœç]
ABCDEFGHIJKLMNOPQRSTUVWXYZ
1234567890(.,;:?!$&-*){ÄÖÜÅØÆŒÇ}

aa*a*
A070
ITC Korinna, Reg,
KursivReg, Bd,
KursivBd

▶ Extra Bold
The quick brown fox jumps over a Dog. Zwei Boxkämpfer jagen Eva durch Sylt portez ce vieux Whiskey blond

▶ Kursiv Extra Bold
The quick brown fox jumps over a Dog. Zwei Boxkämpfer jagen Eva durch Sylt portez ce vieux Whiskey

BT823 MAC + PC ③ 1974: (1904) Ed Benguiat, Victor Caruso
ITC Korinna 2

abcdefghijklmnopqrstuvwxyz[äöüßåøæœç]
ABCDEFGHIJKLMNOPQRSTUVWXYZ
1234567890(.,;:?!$&-*){ÄÖÜÅØÆŒÇ}

aa*a*
A070
ITC Korinna, Reg,
KursivReg, Bd,
KursivBd

▶ Heavy
The quick brown fox jumps over a Dog. Zwei Boxkämpfer jagen Eva durch Sylt portez ce

▶ Kursiv Heavy
The quick brown fox jumps over a Dog. Zwei Boxkämpfer jagen Eva durch Sylt portez ce vieux

▶ Bold Outline
The quick brown fox jumps over a Dog. Zwei Boxkämpfer jagen Eva durch Sylt portez ce vieux Whiskey

LP6664 MAC + PC ⑥ 1992: Garrett Boge
Kryptic™

abcdefghijklm
nopqrstuvwxyz
1234567890[.,;:?!$¢+]ÆŒ

LetterPerfect 6:
De Stijl™, Kryptic™

A394 MAC + PC ④ 1957: Hans Bohn
Kuenstler Script™

abcdefghijklmnopqrstuvwxyz[äöüßåøæœç]
ABCDEFGHIJKLMNOPQRSTUVWXYZ
1234567890(.,;:?!$&-){ÄÖÜÅØÆŒÇ}*

Englische
Schreibschrift, Flemish
Script, Embassy, Palace
Script

▶ Medium
The quick brown fox jumps over a Dog. Zwei Boxkämpfer jagen Eva durch Sylt portez ce vieux Whiskey blond qui fume une pipe aber echt

▶ Bold
The quick brown fox jumps over a Dog. Zwei Boxkämpfer jagen Eva durch Sylt portez ce vieux Whiskey blond qui fume une pipe aber echt über die Mauer

© FSI 1993

▼ A394 Mac + PC Kuenstler Script™
► Black

The quick brown fox jumps over a
Dog. Zwei Boxkämpfer jagen
Eva durch Sylt portez ce vieux
Whiskey blond qui fume une pipe

à lire à haute voix avec l'accent de l'ange du bizarre :
"comme le bruit qui sort d'un baril vide
 quand on le frappe avec un gros bâton".

§2. Prestige de l'ekridure ; kose de son asandan
Prestige de l'écriture ; causes de son ascendant   ferdinand de saussure
sur la forme parlé.   kour de linguisdike générale
sur la forme parlée.   Geneve 1915.

◆ langue e ekridure son deu sisdenne de signe disdin ; l'unike
  Langue et écriture   distincts
  rezon d'edre du segon e de reprezandé le prennié ; l'opgé
  raison d'être   représenter
  linguisdik n'e pa defini par la konbinezon du nno ekri e du
                                                           mot écrit
  nno parlé ; se dernié konsdidu a lui seul sed opgé. nne le nno
  mot parlé   cet objet
  ekri se nnéle si indinnennan o nno parlé don til e l'innage, k'il
                intimement   l'image
  fini par uzurpé le role prinsipal ; on an vi-in a doné odan e
                      le rôle
  plus d'inpordanse a la reprezandasi-on du signe vokal k'a se
                     la représentation du signe vocal
  signe lui-nenne. s'e konne si l'on kroi-ié ke, pour konedre
                   c'est comme si l'on croyait que, pour connaître
  kelk'in, il vo nnieu regardé sa fodografi ke son visage. [...]
  quelqu'un   photographie que son visage. [...]

◆ la langue a donk une dradision orale indepandande de
                  une tradition
  l'ekridure, e bien audrennan fikse ; nne le presdige de la forne
                                fixe
  ekride nou anpeche de le voir. le prennié linguisde s'i son
  dronpé, konne auan teu le zunnanisde. [...]

◆ nne konnan s'eksplike se presdige de l'ekridure ?
                         ce prestige de l'écriture ?
  1° d'apor l'innage grafike de nno nou frape konne in opgé
            l'image   des mots nous frappe
  pernnanan e solide, plu propre ke le son a konsdidué l'unidé
  de la langue a drauer le tan. se li-in a po edre superfisiel e
                à travers le temps
  kreé une unidé purennan fakdise : il e bokou plu fasile a
        une unité purement factice
  sezir ke le li-in nadurel, le seul veridaple, selui du son.
          le lien naturel, le seul véritable, celui du son.
  2° ché la blupar de zindividu le zinpresion visuele son plu
                                les impressions visuelles sont plus nettes et plus durables
  nede e plu duraple ke le zinpresion akousdik ; osi s'adache-til
                         que les impressions acoustiques
  de preferanse o prennière. l'innage grafike fini par
  s'inpozé o depan du son.

◆ la langue liderère akro-a enkore l'inpordanse innneridé de
          littéraire   l'importance imméritée de l'écriture
  l'ekridure. ele a se diksionère, se grannnère ; s'e d'apré le
  livre e par le livre k'on ansègne a l'ekole ; la langue aparè
  d'après le livre et par le livre
  règlé par in kode, or se kode e lu-i-nnenne une règle ekride,
  réglée par un code   une règle écrite
  sounnize a in uzage rigoureu : l'ordografe, e voila se ki
  soumise à un usage rigoureux : l'orthographe
  konfère a l'ekridure une inpordanse prinnordi-ale. on fini par
                                       primordiale.
  oublié k'on apran a parlé auan d'aprandre a ekrire, e le
          on apprend à parler avant d'apprendre à écrire
  rapor naturel e ranversé.

FONTS Sintetik Minimum Appex Minimum étroit Appex © Pierre di Sciullo, Paris, F

L6596 Mac ⑥
La Bamba™

abcdefghijklmnopqrstuvwxyz[äöüßåøæœç]
ABCDEFGHIJKLMNOPQRSTUVWXYZ
1234567890(.,;:?!$&-*)ÄÖÜÅØÆŒÇ

L6597 Mac ⑥
Lambada™

abcdefghijklmnopqrstuvwxyz[äöüßåøæœç]
ABCDEFGHIJKLMNOPQRSTUVWXYZ
1234567890(.,;:?!$&-*)ÄÖÜÅØÆŒÇ

L2586 Mac ④ 1987: Martin Wait
Laser™

abcdefghijklmnopqrstuvwxyz[äöüßåøæœç]
ABCDEFGHIJKLMNOPQRSTUVWXYZ
1234567890(.,;:?!$&-*)ÄÖÜÅØÆŒÇ

L6133 Mac ④ 1987: Martin Wait
Laser Chrome

abcdefghijklmnopqrstuvwxyz[äöüßåøæœç]
ABCDEFGHIJKLMNOPQRSTUVWXYZ
1234567890(.,;:?!$&-*)ÄÖÜÅØÆŒÇ

EF6448 Mac + PC ② 1991: Mark Jamra
Latienne 1

abcdefghijklmnopqrstuvwxyz[äöüßåøæœç]
ABCDEFGHIJKLMNOPQRSTUVWXYZ
1234567890(.,;:?!$&-*){ÄÖÜÅØÆŒÇ}

▶ **Roman**
The quick brown fox jumps over a Dog. Zwei Boxkämpfer jagen Eva durch Sylt portez ce vieux Whiskey blond qui fume

▶ **Italic**
The quick brown fox jumps over a Dog. Zwei Boxkämpfer jagen Eva durch Sylt portez ce vieux Whiskey blond qui fume une

▶ **Roman SC**
THE QUICK BROWN FOX JUMPS OVER A DOG. 123 4567 890 ZWEI BOXKÄMPFER JAGEN EVA DURCH SYLT PORTEZ CE VIEUX WHISKEY

▶ **Italic SC**
THE QUICK BROWN FOX JUMPS OVER A DOG. 123 4567 890 ZWEI BOXKÄMPFER JAGEN EVA DURCH SYLT PORTEZ CE VIEUX WHISKEY BLOND

▶ **Italic Swash**
The quick brown fox jumps over a Dog. Zwei Boxkämpfer jagen Eva durch Sylt portez ce vieux Whiskey blond qui fume une

© FSI 1993

EF6449 Mac + PC ② 1991: Mark Jamra
Latienne 2

abcdefghijklmnopqrstuvwxyz[äöüßåøæœç]
ABCDEFGHIJKLMNOPQRSTUVWXYZ
1234567890(.,;:?!$&-*){ÄÖÜÅØÆŒÇ}

▶ Medium
The quick brown fox jumps over a Dog. Zwei Boxkämpfer jagen Eva durch Sylt portez ce vieux Whiskey blond qui

▶ Medium Italic
The quick brown fox jumps over a Dog. Zwei Boxkämpfer jagen Eva durch Sylt portez ce vieux Whiskey blond qui fume

▶ Medium SC
THE QUICK BROWN FOX JUMPS OVER A DOG. 123 4567 890 ZWEI BOXKÄMPFER JAGEN EVA DURCH SYLT PORTEZ CE VIEUX

▶ Medium Italic Swash
The quick brown fox jumps over a Dog. Zwei Boxkämpfer jagen Eva durch Sylt portez ce vieux Whiskey blond qui fume

EF6450 Mac + PC ② 1991: Mark Jamra
Latienne 3

abcdefghijklmnopqrstuvwxyz[äöüßåøæœç]
ABCDEFGHIJKLMNOPQRSTUVWXYZ
1234567890(.,;:?!$&-*){ÄÖÜÅØÆŒÇ}

▶ Bold
The quick brown fox jumps over a Dog. Zwei Boxkämpfer jagen Eva durch Sylt portez ce vieux Whiskey

▶ Bold Italic
The quick brown fox jumps over a Dog. Zwei Boxkämpfer jagen Eva durch Sylt portez ce vieux Whiskey blond

▶ Bold Italic Swash
The quick brown fox jumps over a Dog. Zwei Boxkämpfer jagen Eva durch Sylt portez ce vieux Whiskey blond

M2954 Mac + PC ⑥
Latin Condensed

abcdefghijklmnopqrstuvwxyz1234567890[äöüßåøæœç]
ABCDEFGHIJKLMNOPQRSTUVWXYZ(.,;:?!$&-*){ÄÖÜÅØÆŒÇ}

Latin/Runic/Onyx:
Latin Condensed, Onyx™, Runic Condensed
a a a M625
Headliners 5
A2867
Latin/Runic/Onyx

© FSI 1993

BT783 Mac + PC ⑥
Latin Extra Condensed

ABCDEFGHIJKLMNOPQRSTUVWXYZ
1234567890(.,;:?!$&-*)[]{ÄÖÜÅØÆŒÇ}

BT Condensed Headlines 2:
Alternate Gothic™ No.2, Bodoni Campanile™, Hanseatic, Latin Extra Condensed
ⓒ Birch, Willow, Latin Elongated

C2524 Mac + PC ⑥
Latin Elongated

abcdefghijklmnopqrstuvwxyz1234567890[äöüßåøæœç]

ABCDEFGHIJKLMNOPQRSTUVWXYZ(.,;:?!$&-*)◇ÄÖÜÅØÆŒÇ◆

Headlines 88S:
Brasilia Seven, Brasilia Three, Latin Bold, Latin Elongated, Radiant™
ⓒ Latin Extra Condensed

C2524 Mac + PC ⑥
Latin Bold

abcdefghijklmnopqrstuvwxyz[äöüßåøæœç]
ABCDEFGHIJKLMNOPQRSTUVWXYZ
1234567890(.,;:?!$&-*)◇ÄÖÜÅØÆŒÇ◆

Headlines 88S:
Brasilia Seven, Brasilia Three, Latin Bold, Latin Elongated, Radiant™

MC6363 Mac + PC ⑥ ✎ Jean Larcher
Latina™

abcdefghijklmnopqrstuvwxyz[äöüßåøæœç]
ABCDEFGHIJKLMNOPQRSTUVWXYZ
1234567890(.,;:?!$&-*){ÄÖÜÅØÆŒÇ}

L2587 Mac ② ✎ 1988: David Quay
Latino™ Elongated

ABCDEFGHIJKLMNOPQRSTUVWXYZ
1234567890(.,;:?!$&-*)[]ÄÖÜÅØÆŒÇ

© FSI 1993

M2954 Mac + PC
Latin/Runic/Onyx

Latin/Runic/Onyx:
Latin Condensed, Onyx™, Runic Condensed

A2867 Mac + PC
Latin/Runic/Onyx

Latin/Runic/Onyx:
Latin Condensed, Onyx, Runic Condensed

L2847 Mac   ⑥   1990: Tony Watson
Laura™

abcdefghijklmnopqrstuvwxyz [äöüßåøæœç]
ABCDEFGHIJKLMNOPQRSTUVWXYZ
1234567890(.,:;?!$&-)ÄÖÜÅØÆŒÇ*

EF6470 Mac + PC   ⑥
Lazybones™

abcdefghijklmnopqrstuvwxyzäöüßåøæœç
ABCDEFGHIJKLMNOPQRSTUVWXYZ
1234567890(.,:;?!$&-)ÄÖÜÅØÆŒÇ*

E+F Special Headlines 6:
Croissant, Hadfield™, Jenson™ Old Style Bold Condensed, Knightsbridge™, Lazybones™

L2588 Mac   ⑥   1981: Alan Birch
LCD

ABCDEFGHIJKLMNOPQRSTUVWXYZ
1234567890(.,:;?!$&-*)[]ÄÖÜÅØÆŒÇ

EF395 Mac + PC   ②   1985: Les Usherwood
ITC Leawood® 1

abcdefghijklmnopqrstuvwxyz[äöüßåøæœç]
ABCDEFGHIJKLMNOPQRSTUVWXYZ
1234567890(.,:;?!$&-*){ÄÖÜÅØÆŒÇ}

aa*a*
A910
ITC Leawood, Bk,
BkIta, Med, MedIta, Bd,
BdIta, Blk, BlkIta
BT1350
ITC Leawood 1, Bk,
BkIta, Bd, BdIta

▶ Book
The quick brown fox jumps over a Dog. Zwei Boxkämpfer jagen Eva durch Sylt portez ce vieux Whiskey blond qui

▶ Book Italic
The quick brown fox jumps over a Dog. Zwei Boxkämpfer jagen Eva durch Sylt portez ce vieux Whiskey blond qui fume

▶ Bold
The quick brown fox jumps over a Dog. Zwei Boxkämpfer jagen Eva durch Sylt portez ce vieux

▶ Bold Italic
The quick brown fox jumps over a Dog. Zwei Boxkämpfer jagen Eva durch Sylt portez ce vieux Whiskey

© FSI 1993

EF396 Mac + PC ② 1985: Les Usherwood
ITC Leawood 2

abcdefghijklmnopqrstuvwxyz[äöüßåøæœç]
ABCDEFGHIJKLMNOPQRSTUVWXYZ
1234567890(.,;:?!$&-*){ÄÖÜÅØÆŒÇ}

a a *a*
A910
ITC Leawood, Bk,
BkIta, Med, MedIta,
Bd, BdIta, Blk, BlkIta
BT1351
ITC Leawood 2, Med;
MedIta, Blk, BlkIta

▶ Medium
The quick brown fox jumps over a Dog. Zwei Boxkämpfer jagen Eva durch Sylt portez ce vieux Whiskey

▶ Medium Italic
The quick brown fox jumps over a Dog. Zwei Boxkämpfer jagen Eva durch Sylt portez ce vieux Whiskey blond

▶ Black
The quick brown fox jumps over a Dog. Zwei Boxkämpfer jagen Eva durch Sylt portez ce

▶ Black Italic
The quick brown fox jumps over a Dog. Zwei Boxkämpfer jagen Eva durch Sylt portez ce vieux

EF538 Mac + PC ② 1985: Les Usherwood
ITC Leawood Small Caps

ABCDEFGHIJKLMNOPQRSTUVWXYZ[ÄÖÜSSÅØÆŒÇ]
ABCDEFGHIJKLMNOPQRSTUVWXYZ
1234567890(.,;:?!$&-*){ÄÖÜÅØÆŒÇ}

▶ Book Small Caps
THE QUICK BROWN FOX JUMPS OVER A DOG. 123 4567 890 ZWEI BOXKÄMPFER JAGEN EVA DURCH SYLT PORTEZ CE VIEUX WHISKEY

▶ Medium Small Caps
THE QUICK BROWN FOX JUMPS OVER A DOG. 123 4567 890 ZWEI BOXKÄMPFER JAGEN EVA DURCH SYLT PORTEZ CE VIEUX

EF6700 Mac + PC ① 1992: Ronald Arnholm
ITC Legacy Sans™ 1

abcdefghijklmnopqrstuvwxyz[äöüßåøæœç]
ABCDEFGHIJKLMNOPQRSTUVWXYZ
1234567890(.,;:?!$&-*){ÄÖÜÅØÆŒÇ}

▶ Book
The quick brown fox jumps over a Dog. Zwei Boxkämpfer jagen Eva durch Sylt portez ce vieux Whiskey blond qui fume

▶ Book Italic
The quick brown fox jumps over a Dog. Zwei Boxkämpfer jagen Eva durch Sylt portez ce vieux Whiskey blond qui fume une pipe aber echt

▶ Book SC
THE QUICK BROWN FOX JUMPS OVER A DOG. 123 4567 890 ZWEI BOXKÄMPFER JAGEN EVA DURCH SYLT PORTEZ CE VIEUX WHISKEY

▶ Bold
The quick brown fox jumps over a Dog. Zwei Boxkämpfer jagen Eva durch Sylt portez ce vieux Whiskey blond qui fume

▶ Bold Italic
The quick brown fox jumps over a Dog. Zwei Boxkämpfer jagen Eva durch Sylt portez ce vieux Whiskey blond qui fume une pipe

© FSI 1993

EF6701 Mac + PC ① 1992: Ronald Arnholm
ITC Legacy Sans™ 2

abcdefghijklmnopqrstuvwxyz[äöüßåøæœç]
ABCDEFGHIJKLMNOPQRSTUVWXYZ
1234567890(.,;:?!$&-*){ÄÖÜÅØÆŒÇ}

▶ Medium
The quick brown fox jumps over a Dog. Zwei Boxkämpfer jagen Eva durch Sylt portez ce vieux Whiskey blond qui fume

▶ Medium Italic
The quick brown fox jumps over a Dog. Zwei Boxkämpfer jagen Eva durch Sylt portez ce vieux Whiskey blond qui fume une pipe aber echt

▶ Medium SC
THE QUICK BROWN FOX JUMPS OVER A DOG. 123 4567 890 ZWEI BOXKÄMPFER JAGEN EVA DURCH SYLT PORTEZ CE VIEUX WHISKEY

▶ Ultra
The quick brown fox jumps over a Dog. Zwei Boxkämpfer jagen Eva durch Sylt portez ce vieux Whiskey

EF6703 Mac + PC ① 1992: Ronald Arnholm
ITC Legacy Serif™ 1

abcdefghijklmnopqrstuvwxyz[äöüßåøæœç]
ABCDEFGHIJKLMNOPQRSTUVWXYZ
1234567890(.,;:?!$&-*){ÄÖÜÅØÆŒÇ}

▶ Book
The quick brown fox jumps over a Dog. Zwei Boxkämpfer jagen Eva durch Sylt portez ce vieux Whiskey blond qui fume

▶ Book Italic
The quick brown fox jumps over a Dog. Zwei Boxkämpfer jagen Eva durch Sylt portez ce vieux Whiskey blond qui fume une pipe aber echt

▶ Book SC
THE QUICK BROWN FOX JUMPS OVER A DOG. 123 4567 890 ZWEI BOXKÄMPFER JAGEN EVA DURCH SYLT PORTEZ CE VIEUX WHISKEY

▶ Bold
The quick brown fox jumps over a Dog. Zwei Boxkämpfer jagen Eva durch Sylt portez ce vieux Whiskey blond

▶ Bold Italic
The quick brown fox jumps over a Dog. Zwei Boxkämpfer jagen Eva durch Sylt portez ce vieux Whiskey blond qui fume une

EF6704 Mac + PC ① 1992: Ronald Arnholm
ITC Legacy Serif™ 2

abcdefghijklmnopqrstuvwxyz[äöüßåøæœç]
ABCDEFGHIJKLMNOPQRSTUVWXYZ
1234567890(.,;:?!$&-*){ÄÖÜÅØÆŒÇ}

▶ Medium
The quick brown fox jumps over a Dog. Zwei Boxkämpfer jagen Eva durch Sylt portez ce vieux Whiskey blond qui

▶ Medium Italic
The quick brown fox jumps over a Dog. Zwei Boxkämpfer jagen Eva durch Sylt portez ce vieux Whiskey blond qui fume une pipe

© FSI 1993

▼ EF6704 Mac + PC ITC Legacy Serif™ 2

▶ Medium SC
THE QUICK BROWN FOX JUMPS OVER A DOG. 123 4567 890 ZWEI BOXKÄMPFER JAGEN EVA DURCH SYLT PORTEZ CE VIEUX

▶ Ultra
The quick brown fox jumps over a Dog. Zwei Boxkämpfer jagen Eva durch Sylt portez ce vieux

---

EF6472 Mac + PC ④ 1973: Andre-Michel Lubac
Le Griffe™

abcdefghijklmnopqrstuvwxyz[äöüßåøæœç]
ABCDEFGHIJKLMNOPQRSTUVWXYZ
1234567890(.,;:?!$&-*){ÄÖÜÅØÆŒÇ}

aaa
L6134
Le Griffe, Reg

▶ Regular
The quick brown fox jumps over a Dog. Zwei Boxkämpfer jagen Eva durch Sylt portez ce vieux Whiskey blond qui fume une pipe aber echt über die Mauer gesprungen

▶ Alternates One
The quick brown fox jumps over a Dog. Zwei Boxkämpfer jagen Eva durch Sylt portez ce vieux Whiskey blond qui

▶ Alternates Two
The quick brown fox jumps over a Dog. Zwei Boxkämpfer jagen Eva durch Sylt portez ce vieux Whiskey blond

E+F Special Headlines 8:
Le Griffe™
aaa L6134
Le Griffe, Reg

ET1106 Mac + PC ④ 1990: (L. DaVinci, c. 1512) Judith Sutcliffe
Leonardo Hand™

abcdefghijklmnopqrstuvwxyz[äöüßåøæœç]
ABCDEFGHIJKLMNOPQRSTUVWXYZ
1234567890(.,;:?!$&-*){ÄÖÜÅØÆŒÇ}

Renaissance™:
Leonardo Hand™, Tagliente™

BT1352 Mac + PC ① 1956: Roger Robertson
Letter Gothic 12 Pitch

abcdefghijklmnopqrstuvwxyz[äöüßåøæœç]
ABCDEFGHIJKLMNOPQRSTUVWXYZ
1234567890(.,;:?!$&-*){ÄÖÜÅØÆŒÇ}

aaa
A071
Letter Gothic, Reg, RegSln, Bd, BdSln
Orator

▶ Regular
The quick brown fox jumps over a Dog. Zwei Boxkämpfer jagen Eva durch Sylt portez ce vieux Whiskey blond qui fume une

▶ Italic
The quick brown fox jumps over a Dog. Zwei Boxkämpfer jagen Eva durch Sylt portez ce vieux Whiskey blond qui fume une

© FSI 1993

▼ BT1352　Mac + PC　Letter Gothic 12 Pitch

▶ Bold

The quick brown fox jumps over a Dog. Zwei Boxkämpfer jagen Eva durch Sylt portez ce vieux Whiskey blond qui fume une

▶ Bold Italic

The quick brown fox jumps over a Dog. Zwei Boxkämpfer jagen Eva durch Sylt portez ce vieux Whiskey blond qui fume une

LP2840　Mac + PC
LetterPerfect 1

LetterPerfect 1:
TomBoy™, Wendy™

LP941　Mac + PC
LetterPerfect 2

LetterPerfect 2:
Manito™, Spumoni™

LP942　Mac + PC
LetterPerfect 3

LetterPerfect 3:
Hadrian™ Bold, Silhouette™

LP2841　Mac + PC
LetterPerfect 4

LetterPerfect 4 :
Florens™, Spring™

LP6663　Mac + PC
LetterPerfect 5

LetterPerfect 5:
Hardwood™, Koch Original™, Roslyn Bold

LP6664　Mac + PC
LetterPerfect 6

LetterPerfect 6:
De Stijl™, Kryptic™

L2848　Mac　①
Lexicos™

abcdefghijklmnopqrstuvwxyz[äöüßåøæœç]
ABCDEFGHIJKLMNOPQRSTUVWXYZ
1234567890(.,;:?!$&-')ÄÖÜÅØÆŒÇ

© FSI 1993

Liberty™
C595 Mac + PC ④ 1927: Willard T. Sniffin

abcdefghijklmnopqrstuvwxyz[äöüßåøæœç]
ABCDEFGHIJKLMNOPQRSTUVWXYZ
1234567890(.,;:?!$&-*){ÄÖÜÅØÆŒÇ}

Basilica:
Basilica, Floridian Script, Jasper™, Liberty™
aaa BT850
Bitstream Script 3

Libra™
BT807 Mac + PC ⑦ 1938: S. H. De Roos

abcdefghijklmnopqrstuvwxyz
1234567890(.,;:?!$&-*)[]{äöüåøæœç}

Bitstream Headlines 1:
Eckmann™, Fry's Baskerville™, Libra™
American Uncial, Electric Uncial, Omnia

Life™
BT1353 Mac + PC ② 1965: W. Bilz, F. Simoncini

abcdefghijklmnopqrstuvwxyz[äöüßåøæœç]
ABCDEFGHIJKLMNOPQRSTUVWXYZ
1234567890(.,;:?!$&-*){ÄÖÜÅØÆŒÇ}

aaa
A163
Life, Reg, Ita, Bd
Times, Concorde

▶ Regular
The quick brown fox jumps over a Dog. Zwei Boxkämpfer jagen Eva durch Sylt portez ce vieux Whiskey blond qui fume

▶ Italic
The quick brown fox jumps over a Dog. Zwei Boxkämpfer jagen Eva durch Sylt portez ce vieux Whiskey blond qui fume une

▶ Bold
The quick brown fox jumps over a Dog. Zwei Boxkämpfer jagen Eva durch Sylt portez ce vieux Whiskey blond qui fume

▶ Bold Italic
The quick brown fox jumps over a Dog. Zwei Boxkämpfer jagen Eva durch Sylt portez ce vieux Whiskey blond qui

Lightline Gothic™
SG2208 Mac ① 1908: M. F. Benton

abcdefghijklmnopqrstuvwxyz[äöüßåøæœç]
ABCDEFGHIJKLMNOPQRSTUVWXYZ
1234567890(.,;:?!$&-*)ÄÖÜÅØÆŒÇ

© FSI 1993

L 9

L2589 MAC ④ 1986: Alan Meeks
Limehouse™ Script

abcdefghijklmnopqrstuvwxyz[äöüßåøæœç]
ABCDEFGHIJKLMNOPQRSTUVWXYZ
1234567890(.,;:?!$&-*)ÄÖÜÅØÆŒÇ

EF6465 MAC + PC ⑦ Lindsay Holton
Lindsay™

abcdefghijklmnopqrstuvwxyz[äöüßåøæœç]
ABCDEFGHIJKLMNOPQRSTUVWXYZ
1234567890(.,;:?!$&-*)ÄÖÜÅØÆŒÇ

E+F Special Headlines 1:
Bernhard Fashion, Candice™, Italia Medium Condensed, Lindsay™, Odin™, Van Dijk

L2849 MAC ⑥ 1990: Bob Anderton
Lino Cut™

abcdefghijklmnopqrstuvwxyz[äöüßåøæœç]
ABCDEFGHIJKLMNOPQRSTUVWXYZ
1234567890(.,;:?!$&-*)ÄÖÜÅØÆŒÇ

A6337 MAC + PC ③
LinoLetter™

abcdefghijklmnopqrstuvwxyz[äöüßåøæœç]
ABCDEFGHIJKLMNOPQRSTUVWXYZ
1234567890(.,;:?!$&-*){ÄÖÜÅØÆŒÇ}

▶ Roman
The quick brown fox jumps over a Dog. Zwei Boxkämpfer jagen Eva durch Sylt portez ce vieux Whiskey

▶ Italic
The quick brown fox jumps over a Dog. Zwei Boxkämpfer jagen Eva durch Sylt portez ce vieux Whiskey blond

▶ Medium
The quick brown fox jumps over a Dog. Zwei Boxkämpfer jagen Eva durch Sylt portez ce vieux Whis-

▶ Medium Italic
The quick brown fox jumps over a Dog. Zwei Boxkämpfer jagen Eva durch Sylt portez ce vieux Whiskey

▶ Bold
The quick brown fox jumps over a Dog. Zwei Boxkämpfer jagen Eva durch Sylt portez ce vieux

▶ Bold Italic
The quick brown fox jumps over a Dog. Zwei Boxkämpfer jagen Eva durch Sylt portez ce vieux Whis-

▶ Black
The quick brown fox jumps over a Dog. Zwei Boxkämpfer jagen Eva durch Sylt portez ce

▶ Black Italic
The quick brown fox jumps over a Dog. Zwei Boxkämpfer jagen Eva durch Sylt portez ce vieux

© FSI 1993

A174 Mac + PC
Linoscript/Linotext

Linoscript/Linotext:
Linoscript™, Linotext™

A174 Mac + PC ④ (1903: Morris Fuller Benton)
Linoscript™

abcdefghijklmnopqrstuvwxyz[äöüßåøœæç]
ABCDEFGHIJKLMNOPQRSTUVWXYZ
1234567890(.,;:?!$ & -*){ÄÖÜÅØÆŒÇ}

Linoscript/Linotext:
Linoscript™, Linotext™

A174 Mac + PC ⑦ (1901, Morris Fuller Benton)
Linotext™

abcdefghijklmnopqrstuvwxyz[äöüßåøœæç]
ABCDEFGHIJKLMNOPQRSTUVWXYZ
1234567890(.,;:?!$&-*){ÄÖÜÅØÆŒÇ}

Linoscript/Linotext:
Linoscript™, Linotext™
© Engraver's Old English, Old English Text, Wedding Text

A398 Mac + PC ⑥ 1989: Carol Twombly
Lithos®

ABCDEFGHIJKLMNOPQRSTUVWXYZ
1234567890(.,;:?!$&-*)[]{ÄÖÜÅØÆŒÇ}

© FF Spontan, Sayer Spiritual, Hoffmann

▶ Extra Light
THE QUICK BROWN FOX
JUMPS OVER A DOG.
ZWEI BOXKÄMPFER
JAGEN EVA DURCH SYLT

▶ Light
THE QUICK BROWN FOX
JUMPS OVER A DOG.
ZWEI BOXKÄMPFER
JAGEN EVA DURCH SYLT

▶ Regular
THE QUICK BROWN FOX
JUMPS OVER A DOG.
ZWEI BOXKÄMPFER
JAGEN EVA DURCH SYLT

▶ Bold
THE QUICK BROWN FOX
JUMPS OVER A DOG.
ZWEI BOXKÄMPFER
JAGEN EVA DURCH SYLT

▶ Black
THE QUICK BROWN FOX
JUMPS OVER A DOG.
ZWEI BOXKÄMPFER
JAGEN EVA DURCH SYLT

© FSI 1993

Blackletter 686
BT798 Mac + PC ⑦ — Industry name: London Text™

abcdefghijklmnopqrstuvwxyz [äöüßåøæç]
ABCDEFGHIJKLMNOPQRSTUVWXYZ
1234567890(.,;:?!$&-*){ÄÖÜÅØÆŒÇ}

Bitstream Fraktur 1:
American Text™, Cloister Black, Fraktur, London Text™

Lotus™
C2982 Mac + PC ⑥

ABCDEFGHIJKLMNOPQRSTUVWXYZ

Headlines 93S:
Ashley Inline, Beverly Hills, Lotus™, Virile

Loyalist™ Condensed
SF6635 Mac ⑥ — 1993: Rod McDonald

abcdefghijklmnopqrstuvwxyz1234567890[äöüßåøæç]
ABCDEFGHIJKLMNOPQRSTUVWXYZ(.,;:?!$&-*){ÄÖÜÅØÆŒÇ}

Stylus Headlines 1:
Bodoni Open Condensed, Fanfare Recut, Goudy Globe Gothic, Loyalist™ Condensed

ITC Lubalin Graph 1
BT824 Mac + PC ③ — 1974: Herb Lubalin

abcdefghijklmnopqrstuvwxyz(äöüßåøæoeç)
ABCDEFGHIJKLMNOPQRSTUVWXYZ
1234567890(.,;:?!$&-*){ÄÖÜÅØÆŒÇ}

▶ Extra Light
The quick brown fox jumps over a Dog. Zwei Boxkämpfer jagen Eva durch Sylt portez ce vieux Whiskey

▶ Extra Light Oblique
The quick brown fox jumps over a Dog. Zwei Boxkämpfer jagen Eva durch Sylt portez ce vieux Whiskey

ITC Lubalin Graph 2
BT825 Mac + PC ③ — 1974: Herb Lubalin

abcdefghijklmnopqrstuvwxyz(äöüßåøæoeç)
ABCDEFGHIJKLMNOPQRSTUVWXYZ
1234567890(.,;:?!$&-*){ÄÖÜÅØÆŒÇ}

© FSI 1993

▼ BT825 Mac + PC ITC Lubalin Graph 2

▶ Medium
The quick brown fox jumps over a Dog. Zwei Boxkämpfer jagen Eva durch Sylt portez ce vieux

▶ Medium Oblique
The quick brown fox jumps over a Dog. Zwei Boxkämpfer jagen Eva durch Sylt portez ce vieux

BT1354 Mac + PC ③ 1974: Herb Lubalin
ITC Lubalin Graph® 4

abcdefghijklmnopqrstuvwxyz(äöüßåøœeç)
ABCDEFGHIJKLMNOPQRSTUVWXYZ
1234567890(.,;:?!$&-*){ÄÖÜÅØÆŒÇ}

aaa
A072
ITC Lubalin Graph, Bk, BkObl, Demi, DemiObl

▶ Book
The quick brown fox jumps over a Dog. Zwei Boxkämpfer jagen Eva durch Sylt portez ce vieux Whiskey

▶ Book Oblique
The quick brown fox jumps over a Dog. Zwei Boxkämpfer jagen Eva durch Sylt portez ce vieux Whiskey

▶ Demi
The quick brown fox jumps over a Dog. Zwei Boxkämpfer jagen Eva durch Sylt portez ce vieux

▶ Demi Oblique
The quick brown fox jumps over a Dog. Zwei Boxkämpfer jagen Eva durch Sylt portez ce vieux

BT826 Mac + PC ③ 1974: Herb Lubalin
ITC Lubalin Graph 3

abcdefghijklmnopqrstuvwxyz(äöüßåøœeç)
ABCDEFGHIJKLMNOPQRSTUVWXYZ
1234567890(.,;:?!$&-*){ÄÖÜÅØÆŒÇ}

▶ Bold
The quick brown fox jumps over a Dog. Zwei Boxkämpfer jagen Eva durch Sylt portez ce vieux

▶ Bold Oblique
The quick brown fox jumps over a Dog. Zwei Boxkämpfer jagen Eva durch Sylt portez ce vieux

EF6451 Mac + PC ③ 1992: (1979: Lubalin) Jorgenson, Engelmann
ITC Lubalin Graph Condensed 1

abcdefghijklmnopqrstuvwxyz(äöüßåøœeç)
ABCDEFGHIJKLMNOPQRSTUVWXYZ
1234567890(.,;:?!$&-*){ÄÖÜÅØÆŒÇ}

▶ Book Condensed
The quick brown fox jumps over a Dog. Zwei Boxkämpfer jagen Eva durch Sylt portez ce vieux Whiskey blond qui fume une pipe aber echt

▶ Book Condensed Oblique
The quick brown fox jumps over a Dog. Zwei Boxkämpfer jagen Eva durch Sylt portez ce vieux Whiskey blond qui fume une pipe aber echt

▶ Book Condensed SC
The quick brown fox jumps over a Dog. 123 4567 890 Zwei Boxkämpfer jagen Eva durch Sylt portez ce vieux Whiskey blond qui

▶ Demi Condensed
The quick brown fox jumps over a Dog. Zwei Boxkämpfer jagen Eva durch Sylt portez ce vieux Whiskey blond qui fume une pipe aber

© FSI 1993

▼ EF6451 Mac + PC   ITC Lubalin Graph Condensed 1

▶ Demi Condensed Oblique
The quick brown fox jumps over a Dog. Zwei Boxkämpfer jagen Eva durch Sylt portez ce vieux Whiskey blond qui fume une pipe aber echt

EF6452 Mac + PC   ③   1992: (1979: Lubalin) Jorgenson, Engelmann
ITC Lubalin Graph Condensed 2

abcdefghijklmnopqrstuvwxyz(äöüßåøœœç)
ABCDEFGHIJKLMNOPQRSTUVWXYZ
1234567890(.,:;?!$&-*){ÄÖÜÅØÆŒÇ}

▶ Medium Condensed
The quick brown fox jumps over a Dog. Zwei Boxkämpfer jagen Eva durch Sylt portez ce vieux Whiskey blond qui fume une pipe aber

▶ Medium Condensed Oblique
The quick brown fox jumps over a Dog. Zwei Boxkämpfer jagen Eva durch Sylt portez ce vieux Whiskey blond qui fume une pipe aber echt

▶ Medium Condensed SC
THE QUICK BROWN FOX JUMPS OVER A DOG. 123 4567 890 ZWEI BOX-KÄMPFER JAGEN EVA DURCH SYLT PORTEZ CE VIEUX WHISKEY BLOND

▶ Bold Condensed
The quick brown fox jumps over a Dog. Zwei Boxkämpfer jagen Eva durch Sylt portez ce vieux Whiskey blond qui fume une pipe aber

▶ Bold Condensed Oblique
The quick brown fox jumps over a Dog. Zwei Boxkämpfer jagen Eva durch Sylt portez ce vieux Whiskey blond qui fume une pipe aber

BT850 Mac + PC   ④
Lucia™

*abcdefghijklmnopqrstuvwxyz[äöüßåøœœç]
ABCDEFGHIJKLMNOPQRSTUVWXYZ
1234567890(.,:;?!$&-*){ÄÖÜÅØÆŒÇ}*

Bitstream Script 3:
Embassy, Englische Schreibschrift™, Liberty, Lucia™

BT1092 Mac + PC   ②   1990: (Lucian Bernhard, 1928)
Bitstream Lucian™

abcdefghijklmnopqrstuvwxyz[äöüßåøœœç]
ABCDEFGHIJKLMNOPQRSTUVWXYZ
1234567890(.,:;?!$&-*){ÄÖÜÅØÆŒÇ}

© Belucian, Bernhard Modern

▶ Regular
The quick brown fox jumps over a Dog. Zwei Boxkämpfer jagen Eva durch Sylt portez ce vieux Whiskey blond qui fume une pipe aber

▶ Bold
The quick brown fox jumps over a Dog. Zwei Boxkämpfer jagen Eva durch Sylt portez ce vieux Whiskey blond qui fume une

© FSI 1993

A073 Mac + PC ③ 🖉 1985: C. Bigelow, K. Holmes
Lucida®

abcdefghijklmnopqrstuvwxyz[äöüßåøæœç]
ABCDEFGHIJKLMNOPQRSTUVWXYZ
1234567890(.,;:?!$&-*){ÄÖÜÅØÆŒÇ}

👁 Bitstream Charter, Swift

▶ Regular
The quick brown fox jumps over a Dog. Zwei Boxkämpfer jagen Eva durch Sylt portez ce vieux

▶ Italic
The quick brown fox jumps over a Dog. Zwei Boxkämpfer jagen Eva durch Sylt portez ce vieux Whiskey

▶ Bold
The quick brown fox jumps over a Dog. Zwei Boxkämpfer jagen Eva durch Sylt portez ce

▶ Bold Italic
The quick brown fox jumps over a Dog. Zwei Boxkämpfer jagen Eva durch Sylt portez ce

A074 Mac + PC ① 🖉 1985: C. Bigelow, K. Holmes
Lucida Sans

abcdefghijklmnopqrstuvwxyz[äöüßåøæœç]
ABCDEFGHIJKLMNOPQRSTUVWXYZ
1234567890(.,;:?!$&-*){ÄÖÜÅØÆŒÇ}

▶ Regular
The quick brown fox jumps over a Dog. Zwei Boxkämpfer jagen Eva durch Sylt portez ce vieux Whiskey blond

▶ Italic
The quick brown fox jumps over a Dog. Zwei Boxkämpfer jagen Eva durch Sylt portez ce vieux Whiskey

▶ Bold
The quick brown fox jumps over a Dog. Zwei Boxkämpfer jagen Eva durch Sylt portez ce

▶ Bold Italic
The quick brown fox jumps over a Dog. Zwei Boxkämpfer jagen Eva durch Sylt portez ce

E335 Mac + PC ⑤ 🖉 1988: Zuzana Licko
Lunatix™

abcdefghijklmnopqrstuvwxyz[äöüßåøæœç]
ABCDEFGHIJKLMNOPQRSTUVWXYZ
1234567890(.,;:?!$&-*){ÄÖÜÅØÆŒÇ}

▶ Light
The quick brown fox jumps over a Dog. Zwei Boxkämpfer jagen Eva durch Sylt portez ce vieux Whiskey blond qui fume une

▶ Bold
The quick brown fox jumps over a Dog. Zwei Boxkämpfer jagen Eva durch Sylt portez ce vieux Whiskey blond qui fume une

© FSI 1993

Lutahline™
ET1107 Mac + PC ④ 1990: Judith Sutcliffe

abcdefghijklmnopqrstuvwxyz[äöüßåøæœç]
ABCDEFGHIJKLMNOPQRSTUVWXYZ
1234567890(.,;:?!$&-*){ÄÖÜÅØÆŒÇ}

Eclectic Electrics™:
Electric Hand™, Electric Uncial™, Lutahline™

Lydian™
BT827 Mac + PC ⑥ 1938–39: Warren Chappell

abcdefghijklmnopqrstuvwxyz[äöüßåøæœç]
ABCDEFGHIJKLMNOPQRSTUVWXYZ
1234567890(.,;:?!$&-*){ÄÖÜÅØÆŒÇ}

▶ Regular
The quick brown fox jumps over a Dog. Zwei Boxkämpfer jagen Eva durch Sylt portez ce vieux Whiskey blond qui fume une pipe aber echt

▶ Italic
The quick brown fox jumps over a Dog. Zwei Boxkämpfer jagen Eva durch Sylt portez ce vieux Whiskey blond qui fume une pipe aber echt

▶ Bold
The quick brown fox jumps over a Dog. Zwei Boxkämpfer jagen Eva durch Sylt portez ce vieux Whiskey blond qui fume une pipe aber echt

▶ Bold Italic
The quick brown fox jumps over a Dog. Zwei Boxkämpfer jagen Eva durch Sylt portez ce vieux Whiskey blond qui fume une pipe aber

Lydian Cursive
BT762 Mac + PC ④ 1940: Warren Chappell

*abcdefghijklmnopqrstuvwxyz[äöüßåøæœç]
ABCDEFGHIJKLMNOPQRSTUVWXYZ
1234567890(.,;:?!$&-*){ÄÖÜÅØÆŒÇ}*

Bitstream Brush 1:
Bison™, Lydian Cursive, Ondine™, Palette™

© FSI 1993

L 16

NEVERODDOREVEN
NEVERODDOREVEN

M

Martin Majoor, Arnhem, NL

A1010 Mac + PC ⑤ 🖉 1970: Tom Carnase, Ronne Bonder
ITC Machine®

ABCDEFGHIJKLMNOPQRSTUVWXYZ
1234567890(.,;:?!$&-*)[]{ÄÖÜÅØÆŒÇ}

a a *a*
🖉 A003 ITC American Typewriter + ITC Machine, 🖉 BT1355 ITC American Typewriter + ITC Machine
👁 Princetown, Superstar, Quadrus, Yearbook

▶ Regular
THE QUICK BROWN FOX JUMPS OVER A DOG. ZWEI BOXKÄMPFER JAGEN EVA DURCH SYLT PORTEZ CE VIEUX WHISKEY BLOND QUI FUME UNE PIPE ABER ECHT

▶ Bold
THE QUICK BROWN FOX JUMPS OVER A DOG. ZWEI BOXKÄMPFER JAGEN EVA DURCH SYLT PORTEZ CE VIEUX WHISKEY BLOND QUI FUME UNE PIPE ABER ECHT

BT828 Mac + PC ② 🖉 1965: (H. Hoffmeister, 1909–12) Industry name
Century 725 — Madison 1

abcdefghijklmnopqrstuvwxyz[äöüßåøæœç]
ABCDEFGHIJKLMNOPQRSTUVWXYZ
1234567890(.,;:?!$&-*){ÄÖÜÅØÆŒÇ}

👁 Century

▶ Regular
The quick brown fox jumps over a Dog. Zwei Boxkämpfer jagen Eva durch Sylt portez ce vieux Whiskey blond qui fume

▶ Italic
The quick brown fox jumps over a Dog. Zwei Boxkämpfer jagen Eva durch Sylt portez ce vieux Whiskey blond qui

▶ Bold
The quick brown fox jumps over a Dog. Zwei Boxkämpfer jagen Eva durch Sylt portez ce vieux Whiskey blond qui

---

BT829 Mac + PC ② 🖉 1965: (H. Hoffmeister, 1909–12) Industry name
Century 725 — Madison 2

abcdefghijklmnopqrstuvwxyz[äöüßåøæœç]
ABCDEFGHIJKLMNOPQRSTUVWXYZ
1234567890(.,;:?!$&-*){ÄÖÜÅØÆŒÇ}

👁 Century

▶ Black
The quick brown fox jumps over a Dog. Zwei Boxkämpfer jagen Eva durch Sylt portez ce

▶ Condensed
The quick brown fox jumps over a Dog. Zwei Boxkämpfer jagen Eva durch Sylt portez ce vieux Whiskey blond qui fume une pipe aber echt

▶ Bold Condensed
The quick brown fox jumps over a Dog. Zwei Boxkämpfer jagen Eva durch Sylt portez ce vieux Whiskey blond qui fume une pipe

© FSI 1993

A922 Mac + PC ⑥ 1990: Lind, Buker, Redick
Madrone™

abcdefghijklmnopqrstuvwxyz[äöüßåøæœç]
ABCDEFGHIJKLMNOPQRSTUVWXYZ
1234567890(.,;:?!$&-*){ÄÖÜÅØÆŒÇ}

Wood Type Pack 2:
Birch™, Blackoak™, Madrone™, Poplar™, Willow™, Wood Type Ornaments 2

EF6467 Mac + PC ③ Bruno Grasswill
Magnus™ Bold

abcdefghijklmnopqrstuvwxyz[äöüßåøæœç]
ABCDEFGHIJKLMNOPQRSTUVWXYZ
1234567890(.,;:?!$&-*)ÄÖÜÅØÆŒÇ

E+F Special Headlines 3:
Hawthorn™, Magnus™ Bold, Octopuss™, Octopuss™ Shaded, Piccadilly™, Stop™

L6598 Mac ④ 1992: Alan Meeks
Malibu™

abcdefghijklmnopqrstuvwxyz[äöüßåøæœç]
ABCDEFGHIJKLMNOPQRSTUVWXYZ
1234567890(.,;:?!$&-*)ÄÖÜÅØÆŒÇ

FF2962 Mac + PC ⑥ 1992: Val Fullard
FF Mambo™

abcdefghijklmnopqrstuvwxyz[äöüßåøæœç]
ABCDEFGHIJKLMNOPQRSTUVWXYZ
1234567890(.,;:?!$&-*){ÄÖÜÅØÆŒÇ}

▶ Light
The quick brown fox jumps over a Dog. Zwei Boxkämpfer jagen Eva durch Sylt portez ce vieux Whiskey blond qui fume une pipe aber echt über die Mauer gesprungen

▶ Medium
The quick brown fox jumps over a Dog. Zwei Boxkämpfer jagen Eva durch Sylt portez ce vieux Whiskey blond qui fume une pipe aber echt über die Mauer

▶ Bold
The quick brown fox jumps over a Dog. Zwei Boxkämpfer jagen Eva durch Sylt portez ce vieux Whiskey blond qui fume une pipe aber echt

▶ Initials

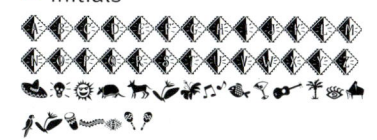

© FSI 1993

BT763 Mac + PC ④ ✎ 1934: R. H. Middleton — Industry name
Freehand 521 / Mandate™

abcdefghijklmnopqrstuvwxyz[äöüßåøæœç]
ABCDEFGHIJKLMNOPQRSTUVWXYZ
1234567890(.,:;?!$&-*){ÄÖÜÅØÆŒÇ}

Bitstream Brush 2:
Impress™, Impuls™, Jefferson™, Mandate™
👁 Chaplin

LP941 Mac + PC ⑥ ✎ 1990: Garrett Boge
Manito™

ABCDEFGHIJKLMNOPQRSTUVWXYZÄÖÜßÅÆŒÇ
ABCDEFGHIJKLMNOPQRSTUVWXYZ
1234567890(.,:;?!$&-*)ÄÖÜÅÆŒÇ

LetterPerfect 2:
Manito™, Spumoni™
👁 Neuland, Totally Glyphic, Koch Neuland

CA6676 Mac + PC ⑥ ✎ 1993: Matthew Carter
Mantinia™ CC

ABCDEFGHIJKLMNOPQRSTUVWXYZ
1234567890(.,:;?!$&&-*){ÄÖÜÅØÆŒÇ}
[TT TU CT H MB ME LA MP MD TY ET W ET]

EF514 Mac + PC ② ✎ 1975: Hermann Zapf
Marconi™

abcdefghijklmnopqrstuvwxyz[äöüßåøæœç]
ABCDEFGHIJKLMNOPQRSTUVWXYZ
1234567890[.,:;?!$&-*]{ÄÖÜÅØÆŒÇ}

👁 ITC Zapf Book

▶ **Book**
The quick brown fox jumps over a Dog. Zwei Boxkämpfer jagen Eva durch Sylt portez ce vieux Whiskey blond qui

▶ *Book Italic*
The quick brown fox jumps over a Dog. Zwei Boxkämpfer jagen Eva durch Sylt portez ce vieux Whiskey blond qui fume

▶ **Semi Bold**
The quick brown fox jumps over a Dog. Zwei Boxkämpfer jagen Eva durch Sylt portez ce vieux Whiskey

▶ ***Semi Bold Italic***
The quick brown fox jumps over a Dog. Zwei Boxkämpfer jagen Eva durch Sylt portez ce vieux Whiskey

▶ Book Small Caps
THE QUICK BROWN FOX JUMPS OVER A DOG. 123 4567 890 ZWEI BOXKÄMPFER JAGEN EVA DURCH SYLT PORTEZ CE VIEUX WHISKEY

© FSI 1993

Marigold™
C2521 MAC + PC ④ 1989: Arthur Baker

abcdefghijklmnopqrstuvwxyz1234567890[äöüßåøæç]

ABCDEFGHIJKLMNOPQRSTUVWXYZ(.,;:?!$&-*){ÄÖÜÅØÆŒÇ}

Amigo:
Amigo™, Marigold™, Oxford™, Pelican™, Visigoth

FF Marten™
FF1060 MAC + PC ⑤ 1991: Martin Wenzel

abcdefghijklmnopqrstuvwxyz[äöüßåøæç]
ABCDEFGHIJKLMNOPQRSTUVWXYZ
1234567890(.,;:?!$&-*){ÄÖÜÅØÆŒÇ}

▶ Regular
The quick brown fox jumps over a Dog. Zwei Boxkämpfer jagen Eva durch Sylt portez ce vieux Whiskey blond qui fume une pipe aber echt über die Mauer gesprungen und auch smørebrød en ysjes natuurlijk

▶ Small Caps
THE QUICK BROWN FOX JUMPS OVER A DOG. 123 4567 890 ZWEI BOXKÄMPFER JAGEN EVA DURCH SYLT PORTEZ CE VIEUX WHISKEY BLOND QUI FUME UNE PIPE ABER ECHT ÜBER DIE MAUER GESPRUNGEN UND AUCH SMØREBRØD EN YSJES

▶ Grotesque
The quick brown fox jumps over a Dog. Zwei Boxkämpfer jagen Eva durch Sylt portez ce vieux Whiskey blond qui fume une pipe aber echt über die Mauer gesprungen und auch smørebrød en ysjes natuurlijk

▶ Grotesque Small Caps
THE QUICK BROWN FOX JUMPS OVER A DOG. 123 4567 890 ZWEI BOXKÄMPFER JAGEN EVA DURCH SYLT PORTEZ CE VIEUX WHISKEY BLOND QUI FUME UNE PIPE ABER ECHT ÜBER DIE MAUER GESPRUNGEN UND AUCH SMØREBRØD EN YSJES

Mastercard™
L2590 MAC ⑥ 1984: John Hamon

ABCDEFGHIJKLMNOPQRSTUVWXYZ
1234567890(.,;:?!$&-*){}ÄÖÜÅØÆŒÇ

Matra™
C2981 MAC + PC ⑥

ABCDEFGHIJKLMNOPQRSTUVWXYZ
1234567890(.,;:?!$&-*){} ÄÖÜÅØÆŒÇ

Headlines 92S:
Eagle Bold, Joanna Solotype, Matra™, Modernique, Victorian Silhouette

Matrix™
E075 MAC + PC ② 1986: Zuzana Licko

abcdefghijklmnopqrstuvwxyz[äöüßåøæç]
ABCDEFGHIJKLMNOPQRSTUVWXYZ
1234567890(.,;:?!$&-*){ÄÖÜÅØÆŒÇ}

© FSI 1993

▼ E075 MAC + PC Matrix™

► Book

The quick brown fox jumps over a Dog. Zwei Boxkämpfer jagen Eva durch Sylt portez ce vieux Whiskey blond qui fume une pipe aber echt

► Regular

The quick brown fox jumps over a Dog. Zwei Boxkämpfer jagen Eva durch Sylt portez ce vieux Whiskey blond qui fume une pipe aber echt

► Bold

The quick brown fox jumps over a Dog. Zwei Boxkämpfer jagen Eva durch Sylt portez ce vieux Whis-key blond qui fume une pipe aber

E234 MAC + PC ② 1987: Zuzana Licko

More Matrix

abcdefghijklmnopqrstuvwxyz[äöüßåøæœç]
ABCDEFGHIJKLMNOPQRSTUVWXYZ
1234567890(.,;:?!$&-*){ÄÖÜÅØÆŒÇ}

► Extra Bold

The quick brown fox jumps over a Dog. Zwei Boxkämpfer jagen Eva durch Sylt portez ce vieux Whiskey blond qui fume

► Narrow

The quick brown fox jumps over a Dog. Zwei Boxkämpfer jagen Eva durch Sylt portez ce vieux Whiskey blond qui fume une pipe aber echt über die Mauer gesprungen und auch smørebrød en ysjes natuurlijk

► Wide

The quick brown fox jumps over a Dog. Zwei Box-kämpfer jagen

E2761 MAC + PC ② 1991: Zuzana Licko

Matrix Extended

ABCDEFGHIJKLMNOPQRSTUVWXYZ(ÄÖÜŠÅØÆŒÇ)
ABCDEFGHIJKLMNOPQRSTUVWXYZ
1234567890(.,;:?!$&-..)₡e90ao˘¢Rp

► Book SmallCaps

THE QUICK BROWN FOX JUMPS OVER A DOG. ZWEI BOXKÄMPFER JAGEN EVA DURCH SYLT PORTEZ CE VIEUX WHISKEY BLOND QUI FUME UNE PIPE ABER ECHT

► Regular Small Caps

THE QUICK BROWN FOX JUMPS OVER A DOG. ZWEI BOXKÄMPFER JAGEN EVA DURCH SYLT PORTEZ CE VIEUX WHISKEY BLOND QUI FUME UNE PIPE ABER ECHT

► Bold Small Caps

THE QUICK BROWN FOX JUMPS OVER A DOG. ZWEI BOXKÄMPFER JAGEN EVA DURCH SYLT PORTEZ CE VIEUX WHIS-KEY BLOND QUI FUME UNE PIPE ABER

► Book Fractions

1/4 1/2 3/4 1/8 3/8 5/8 7/8 1/3 2/3 ffi ffl ABCDEFGHIJK LMNOPQRSTUVWXYZ 1 1 2 2 3 3 4 4 5 5 6 6 7 7 9 9

► Regular Fractions

1/4 1/2 3/4 1/8 3/8 5/8 7/8 1/3 2/3 ffi ffl ABCDEFGHIJ KLMNOPQRSTUVWXYZ 1 1 2 2 3 3 4 4 5 5 6 6 7 7 9 9

► Bold Fractions

1/4 1/2 3/4 1/8 3/8 5/8 7/8 1/3 2/3 ffi ffl ABCDEFG HIJKLMNOPQRSTUVWXYZ 1 1 2 2 3 3 4 4 5 5 6 6 7 7 9 9

Matrix Tall

E937 Mac + PC · 1989: Zuzana Licko

abcdefghijklmnopqrstuvwxyz1234567890[äöüßåøæœç]
ABCDEFGHIJKLMNOPQRSTUVWXYZ(.,;:?!$&-*){ÄÖÜÅØÆŒÇ}

Tall Pack:
Matrix Tall, Senator Tall

Matrix Script

E2994 Mac + PC · 1992: Zuzana Licko

abcdefghijklmnopqrstuvwxyz[äöüßåøæœç]
ABCDEFGHIJKLMNOPQRSTUVWXYZ
1234567890(.,;:?!$&-*){ÄÖÜÅØÆŒÇ}

▶ Book
The quick brown fox jumps over a Dog. Zwei Boxkämpfer jagen Eva durch Sylt portez ce vieux Whiskey blond qui fume une pipe aber echt

▶ Regular
The quick brown fox jumps over a Dog. Zwei Boxkämpfer jagen Eva durch Sylt portez ce vieux Whiskey blond qui fume une pipe aber echt

▶ Bold
The quick brown fox jumps over a Dog. Zwei Boxkämpfer jagen Eva durch Sylt portez ce vieux Whiskey blond qui fume une pipe aber echt

Matrix Inline

E2995 Mac + PC · 1992: Zuzana Licko

abcdefghijklmnopqrstuvwxyz[äöüßåøæœç]
ABCDEFGHIJKLMNOPQRSTUVWXYZ
1234567890(.,;:?!$&-*){ÄÖÜÅØÆŒÇ}

▶ Inline
The quick brown fox jumps over a Dog. Zwei Boxkämpfer jagen Eva durch Sylt portez ce vieux Whiskey blond qui fume

▶ Inline Script
The quick brown fox jumps over a Dog. Zwei Boxkämpfer jagen Eva durch Sylt portez ce vieux Whiskey blond qui fume une pipe aber echt

Matt Antique™

BT830 Mac + PC · 1980: John Matt

abcdefghijklmnopqrstuvwxyz[äöüßåøæœç]
ABCDEFGHIJKLMNOPQRSTUVWXYZ
1234567890(.,;:?!$&-*){ÄÖÜÅØÆŒÇ}

▶ Regular
The quick brown fox jumps over a Dog. Zwei Boxkämpfer jagen Eva durch Sylt portez ce vieux Whiskey blond qui fume

▶ Italic
The quick brown fox jumps over a Dog. Zwei Boxkämpfer jagen Eva durch Sylt portez ce vieux Whiskey blond qui fume

© FSI 1993

▼ BT830 Mac + PC   Matt Antique™

▶ Bold
The quick brown fox jumps over a Dog. Zwei Boxkämpfer jagen Eva durch Sylt portez ce vieux Whiskey blond qui

M6410 Mac + PC   ④   1936: Imre Reiner
Matura ™Script

abcdefghijklmnopqrstuvwxyz[äöüßåøæœç]
ABCDEFGHIJKLMNOPQRSTUVWXYZ
1234567890(.,;:?!$&-*){ÄÖÜÅØÆŒÇ}

Crazy Headlines™:
Festival™ Titling, Kino™, Matura ™Script, Victoria™ Titling Condensed

A377 Mac + PC   ②   1967: Walter Tracy
Maximus™

abcdefghijklmnopqrstuvwxyz[äöüßåøæœç]
ABCDEFGHIJKLMNOPQRSTUVWXYZ
1234567890(.,;:?!$&-*){ÄÖÜÅØÆŒÇ}

Doric/Maximus:
Doric™ Bold, Maximus™

BT790 Mac + PC   ⑤
Maximus™

ABCDEFGHIJKLMNOPQRSTUVWXYZ
1234567890(.,;:?!$&-*)[]{ÄÖÜÅØÆŒÇ}

Bitstream Decorative 2:
ITC Pioneer®, Maximus™, Profil™, Vineta

TO6105 Mac   ⑥   1992: Enric Jardí
Mayayo™

abcdefghijklmnopqrstuvwxyz
1234567890(.,;:?!$&-*)äöüåøæœç

▶ Black
the quick brown fox jumps over a dog. zwei boxkämpfer jagen eva durch sylt portez ce vieux whiskey blond qui fume une pipe

▶ Holes
the quick brown fox jumps over a dog. zwei boxkämpfer jagen eva durch sylt portez ce vieux whiskey blond qui fume une pipe

▼ T06105 Mac Mayayo™

▶ Inline

the quick brown fox jumps over
a dog. zwei boxkämpfer jagen
eva durch sylt portez ce vieux
whiskey blond qui fume une pipe

Type-ø-Tones Pack 2:
Mayayo™, Neeskens™

C016 Mac + PC ⑥ Gustav F. Schroeder
McCollough

abcdefghijklmnopqrstuvwxyz[äöüßåøæœç]
ABCDEFGHIJKLMNOPQRSTUVWXYZ
1234567890(.,;:?!$&-*){ÄÖÜÅØÆŒÇ}

Branding Iron:
Branding Iron, Isabella™, McCollough, Raphael™

A351 Mac + PC ④ 1974: Hermann Zapf
Medici™

*abcdefghijklmnopqrstuvwxyz[äöüßåøæœç]
ABCDEFGHIJKLMNOPQRSTUVWXYZ
1234567890(.,;:?!$&-*){ÄÖÜÅØÆŒÇ}*

Nuptial Script:
Cascade Script, Medici™, Nuptial Script™
↪ ITC Zapf Chancery, Zapf Renaissance

L2591 Mac ⑤ 1988: David Quay
Mekanik™

abcdefghijklmnopqrstuvwxyz1234567890[äöüßåøæœç]
ABCDEFGHIJKLMNOPQRSTUVWXYZ(.,;:?!$&-*)ÄÖÜÅØÆŒÇ

L6135 Mac ⑤ 1988: David Quay
Mekanik Italic

*abcdefghijklmnopqrstuvwxyz1234567890[äöüßåøæœç]
ABCDEFGHIJKLMNOPQRSTUVWXYZ(.,;:?!$&-*)ÄÖÜÅØÆŒÇ*

A076 Mac + PC ③ 1952: Hermann Zapf
Melior™

abcdefghijklmnopqrstuvwxyz[äöüßåøæœç]
ABCDEFGHIJKLMNOPQRSTUVWXYZ
1234567890(.,;:?!$&-*){ÄÖÜÅØÆŒÇ}

© FSI 1993

aaa
BT1418
Melior, Reg, Ita, Bd,
BdIta

▼ A076   Mac + PC   Melior™

▶ Regular
The quick brown fox jumps over a Dog. Zwei Boxkämpfer jagen Eva durch Sylt portez ce vieux Whiskey blond qui

▶ Italic
The quick brown fox jumps over a Dog. Zwei Boxkämpfer jagen Eva durch Sylt portez ce vieux Whiskey blond qui

▶ Bold
The quick brown fox jumps over a Dog. Zwei Boxkämpfer jagen Eva durch Sylt portez ce vieux Whiskey blond

▶ Bold Italic
The quick brown fox jumps over a Dog. Zwei Boxkämpfer jagen Eva durch Sylt portez ce vieux Whiskey

SG2226 Mac ③ 1952: Hermann Zapf   Industry Name
Matrix Medium   Melior Medium

abcdefghijklmnopqrstuvwxyz[äöüßåøæœç]
ABCDEFGHIJKLMNOPQRSTUVWXYZ
1234567890(.,;:?!$&-*)ÄÖÜÅØÆŒÇ

SG2227 Mac ③ 1952: Hermann Zapf   Industry Name
Matrix Medium Italic   Melior Medium Italic

abcdefghijklmnopqrstuvwxyz[äöüßåøæœç]
ABCDEFGHIJKLMNOPQRSTUVWXYZ
1234567890(.,;:?!$&-)ÄÖÜÅØÆŒÇ*

SG2230 Mac ③ 1952: Hermann Zapf   Industry Name
Matrix Extra Bold   Melior Extra Bold

abcdefghijklmnopqrstuvwxyz[äöüßåøæœç]
ABCDEFGHIJKLMNOPQRSTUVWXYZ
1234567890(.,;:?!$&-*)ÄÖÜÅØÆŒÇ

T06104 Mac ④ 1991: José Manuel Urós, Joan Barjau
Me mima™

abcdefghijklmnopqrstuvwxyz[äöüßåøæœç]
ABCDEFGHIJKLMNOPQRSTUVWXYZ
1234567890(.,;:?!$&-*){ÄÖÜÅØÆŒÇ}

▶ Regular
The quick brown fox jumps over a Dog. Zwei Boxkämpfer jagen Eva durch Sylt portez ce vieux Whiskey blond qui fume une pipe aber echt über

▶ Bold
The quick brown fox jumps over a Dog. Zwei Boxkämpfer jagen Eva durch Sylt portez ce vieux Whiskey blond qui fume une pipe aber echt über

Type-ø-Tones Pack 1:
Ebu™ Script, Me mima™

© FSI 1993

BT1318 Mac + PC (3) 1929–38: Rudolf Wolf; C. H. Griffith Industry name
Geometric Slabserif 703 — Memphis™ 1

abcdefghijklmnopqrstuvwxyz[äöüßåøæœç]
ABCDEFGHIJKLMNOPQRSTUVWXYZ
1234567890(.,;:?!$&-*){ÄÖÜÅØÆŒÇ}

aa*a*
A077
Memphis, Lt, LtIta,
Med, MedIta, Bd,
BdIta, ExtBd
©
Beton, Rockwell
Stratford Bold, Stymie

▶ Light
The quick brown fox jumps over a Dog. Zwei Boxkämpfer jagen Eva durch Sylt portez ce vieux Whiskey blond qui fume

▶ Light Oblique
The quick brown fox jumps over a Dog. Zwei Boxkämpfer jagen Eva durch Sylt portez ce vieux Whiskey blond qui fume

▶ Extra Bold
The quick brown fox jumps over a Dog. Zwei Boxkämpfer jagen Eva durch Sylt portez ce vieux Whiskey

▶ Extra Bold Oblique
The quick brown fox jumps over a Dog. Zwei Boxkämpfer jagen Eva durch Sylt portez ce vieux Whiskey

BT1319 Mac + PC (3) 1929: Rudolf Wolf Industry name
Geometric Slabserif 703 — Memphis 2

abcdefghijklmnopqrstuvwxyz[äöüßåøæœç]
ABCDEFGHIJKLMNOPQRSTUVWXYZ
1234567890(.,;:?!$&-*){ÄÖÜÅØÆŒÇ}

aa*a*
A077
Memphis, Lt, LtIta,
Med, MedIta, Bd,
BdIta, ExtBd
©
Beton, Rockwell
Stratford Bold, Stymie

▶ Medium
The quick brown fox jumps over a Dog. Zwei Boxkämpfer jagen Eva durch Sylt portez ce vieux Whiskey blond qui

▶ Medium Oblique
The quick brown fox jumps over a Dog. Zwei Boxkämpfer jagen Eva durch Sylt portez ce vieux Whiskey blond qui fume

▶ Bold
The quick brown fox jumps over a Dog. Zwei Boxkämpfer jagen Eva durch Sylt portez ce vieux Whiskey blond

▶ Bold Oblique
The quick brown fox jumps over a Dog. Zwei Boxkämpfer jagen Eva durch Sylt portez ce vieux Whiskey blond qui

BT831 Mac + PC (3) 1929–38: Rudolf Wolf; C. H. Griffith Industry name
Geometric Slabserif 703 — Memphis 3

abcdefghijklmnopqrstuvwxyz[äöüßåøæœç]
ABCDEFGHIJKLMNOPQRSTUVWXYZ
1234567890(.,;:?!$&-*){ÄÖÜÅØÆŒÇ}

©
Beton, Rockwell,
Stratford Bold, Stymie

▶ Medium Condensed
The quick brown fox jumps over a Dog. Zwei Boxkämpfer jagen Eva durch Sylt portez ce vieux Whiskey blond qui fume une pipe aber echt über die Mauer

▶ Bold Condensed
The quick brown fox jumps over a Dog. Zwei Boxkämpfer jagen Eva durch Sylt portez ce vieux Whiskey blond qui fume une pipe aber echt über die Mauer

▶ Extra Bold Condensed
The quick brown fox jumps over a Dog. Zwei Boxkämpfer jagen Eva durch Sylt portez ce vieux Whiskey blond qui fume une pipe aber echt über die Mauer

© FSI 1993

| EF1609 | Mac + PC | ② | 1990: José Mendoza |

ITC Mendoza™ 1

abcdefghijklmnopqrstuvwxyz[äöüßåøæœç]
ABCDEFGHIJKLMNOPQRSTUVWXYZ
1234567890(.,;:?!$&-*){ÄÖÜÅØÆŒÇ}

aa*a*
C6429
ITC Mendoza, Rom, Ita, Med, MedIta, Bd, BdIta

▶ Book
The quick brown fox jumps over a Dog. Zwei Boxkämpfer jagen Eva durch Sylt portez ce vieux Whiskey blond qui fume une

▶ Book Small Caps
THE QUICK BROWN FOX JUMPS OVER A DOG. 123 4567 890 ZWEI BOXKÄMPFER JAGEN EVA DURCH SYLT PORTEZ CE VIEUX WHISKEY

▶ Book Italic
The quick brown fox jumps over a Dog. Zwei Boxkämpfer jagen Eva durch Sylt portez ce vieux Whiskey blond qui fume une pipe aber echt

| EF1610 | Mac + PC | ② | 1990: José Mendoza |

ITC Mendoza 2

abcdefghijklmnopqrstuvwxyz[äöüßåøæœç]
ABCDEFGHIJKLMNOPQRSTUVWXYZ
1234567890(.,;:?!$&-*){ÄÖÜÅØÆŒÇ}

aa*a*
C6429
ITC Mendoza, Rom, Ita, Med, MedIta, Bd, BdIta

▶ Medium
The quick brown fox jumps over a Dog. Zwei Boxkämpfer jagen Eva durch Sylt portez ce vieux Whiskey blond qui fume

▶ Medium Small Caps
THE QUICK BROWN FOX JUMPS OVER A DOG. 123 4567 890 ZWEI BOXKÄMPFER JAGEN EVA DURCH SYLT PORTEZ CE VIEUX

▶ Medium Italic
The quick brown fox jumps over a Dog. Zwei Boxkämpfer jagen Eva durch Sylt portez ce vieux Whiskey blond qui fume une pipe aber

| EF1611 | Mac + PC | ② | 1990: José Mendoza |

ITC Mendoza 3

abcdefghijklmnopqrstuvwxyz[äöüßåøæœç]
ABCDEFGHIJKLMNOPQRSTUVWXYZ
1234567890(.,;:?!$&-*){ÄÖÜÅØÆŒÇ}

▶ Bold
The quick brown fox jumps over a Dog. Zwei Boxkämpfer jagen Eva durch Sylt portez ce vieux Whiskey blond qui

▶ Bold Italic
The quick brown fox jumps over a Dog. Zwei Boxkämpfer jagen Eva durch Sylt portez ce vieux Whiskey blond qui fume une

| CT873 | Mac + PC | ① | 1989: Adrian Williams |

Mercurius™

abcdefghijklmnopqrstuvwxyz[äöüßåøæœç]
ABCDEFGHIJKLMNOPQRSTUVWXYZ
1234567890(.,;:?!$&-*){ÄÖÜÅØÆŒÇ}

© FSI 1993

▼ CT873 Mac + PC Mercurius™

► Light
The quick brown fox jumps over a Dog. Zwei Boxkämpfer jagen Eva durch Sylt portez ce vieux Whiskey blond qui fume une pipe aber echt über die Mauer

► Light Italic
The quick brown fox jumps over a Dog. Zwei Boxkämpfer jagen Eva durch Sylt portez ce vieux Whiskey blond qui fume une pipe aber echt über die Mauer

► Medium
The quick brown fox jumps over a Dog. Zwei Boxkämpfer jagen Eva durch Sylt portez ce vieux Whiskey blond qui fume une pipe aber

► Medium Italic
The quick brown fox jumps over a Dog. Zwei Boxkämpfer jagen Eva durch Sylt portez ce vieux Whiskey blond qui fume une pipe aber echt

► Black
The quick brown fox jumps over a Dog. Zwei Boxkämpfer jagen Eva durch Sylt portez ce vieux Whiskey blond qui

► Black Italic
The quick brown fox jumps over a Dog. Zwei Boxkämpfer jagen Eva durch Sylt portez ce vieux Whiskey blond qui fume

---

M885 Mac + PC ④   1957: Imre Reiner
Mercurius Bold Script™

abcdefghijklmnopqrstuvwxyz[äöüßåøæœç]
ABCDEFGHIJKLMNOPQRSTUVWXYZ
1234567890(.,:;?!$&-){ÄÖÜÅØÆŒÇ}*

Script 3:
Coronet Bold, Mercurius Bold Script™
aaa A6088
Forte et al
 M6331

A400 Mac + PC ②   1957: Adrian Frutiger
Meridien™

abcdefghijklmnopqrstuvwxyz[äöüßåøæœç]
ABCDEFGHIJKLMNOPQRSTUVWXYZ
1234567890(.,:;?!$&-*){ÄÖÜÅØÆŒÇ}

aaa
BT1348
Meridien 1, Reg, Ita, Bd, BdIta
BT1349
Meridien 2, Med, MedIta
C6433
Meridien, Lt, Ita, Bd, BdIta

► Regular
The quick brown fox jumps over a Dog. Zwei Boxkämpfer jagen Eva durch Sylt portez ce vieux Whiskey blond qui fume

► Italic
The quick brown fox jumps over a Dog. Zwei Boxkämpfer jagen Eva durch Sylt portez ce vieux Whiskey blond qui fume une pipe aber echt

► Medium
The quick brown fox jumps over a Dog. Zwei Boxkämpfer jagen Eva durch Sylt portez ce vieux Whiskey blond qui

► Medium Italic
The quick brown fox jumps over a Dog. Zwei Boxkämpfer jagen Eva durch Sylt portez ce vieux Whiskey blond qui fume une pipe aber echt

► Bold
The quick brown fox jumps over a Dog. Zwei Boxkämpfer jagen Eva durch Sylt portez ce vieux Whis-

► Bold Italic
The quick brown fox jumps over a Dog. Zwei Boxkämpfer jagen Eva durch Sylt portez ce vieux Whiskey blond qui fume

© FSI 1993

A424   Mac + PC   ⑥   🖉 1990: Buker, Lind, Redick
Mesquite™

ABCDEFGHIJKLMNOPQRSTUVWXYZ
1234567890(.,;:?!$&-*)[]{ÄÖÜÅØÆŒÇ}

Wood Type Pack 1:
Cottonwood®, Ironwood®, Juniper®, Mesquite™, Ponderosa®, Wood Type Ornaments 1

FF1059   Mac + PC   ①   🖉 1991: Erik Spiekermann
FF Meta™ 1

abcdefghijklmnopqrstuvwxyz[äöüßåøæœç]
ABCDEFGHIJKLMNOPQRSTUVWXYZ
1234567890(.,;:?!$&-*){ÄÖÜÅØÆŒÇ}

Bell Centennial, Bell Gothic, ITC Officina Sans

▶ Regular
The quick brown fox jumps over a Dog. 123 4567 890 Zwei Boxkämpfer jagen Eva durch Sylt portez ce vieux Whiskey blond

▶ Bold
The quick brown fox jumps over a Dog. 123 4567 890 Zwei Boxkämpfer jagen Eva durch Sylt portez ce vieux Whiskey blond

▶ Small Caps
THE QUICK BROWN FOX JUMPS OVER A DOG. 123 4567 890 ZWEI BOXKÄMPFER JAGEN EVA DURCH SYLT PORTEZ CE VIEUX WHISKEY

FF6181   Mac + PC   ①   🖉 1992: Erik Spiekermann
FF Meta 2

abcdefghijklmnopqrstuvwxyz[äöüßåøæœç]
ABCDEFGHIJKLMNOPQRSTUVWXYZ
1234567890(.,;:?!$&-){ÄÖÜÅØÆŒÇ}*

Bell Centennial, Bell Gothic, ITC Officina Sans

▶ Italic
The quick brown fox jumps over a Dog. 123 4567 890 Zwei Boxkämpfer jagen die Gurkenschriften durch Sylt portez ce

▶ Italic Caps
THE QUICK BROWN FOX JUMPS OVER A DOG. 123 4567 890 ZWEI BOXKÄMPFER JAGEN EVA DURCH SYLT PORTEZ CE VIEUX WHISKEY

▶ Bold Caps
THE QUICK BROWN FOX JUMPS OVER A DOG. 123 4567 890 ZWEI BOXKÄMPFER JAGEN EVA DURCH SYLT PORTEZ CE VIEUX WHISKEY

BT879   Mac + PC   ①   🖉 1930–32: W. A. Dwiggins   Industry name
Geometric 415   Metro™ 1

abcdefghijklmnopqrstuvwxyz[äöüßåøæœç]
ABCDEFGHIJKLMNOPQRSTUVWXYZ
1234567890(.,;:?!$&-*){ÄÖÜÅØÆŒÇ}

© FSI 1993

M 13

▼ BT879 Mac + PC   Metro™ 1

Futura, Spartan, Nobel

▶ Lite
The quick brown fox jumps over a Dog. Zwei Boxkämpfer jagen Eva durch Sylt portez ce vieux Whiskey blond qui fume une

▶ Lite Italic
The quick brown fox jumps over a Dog. Zwei Boxkämpfer jagen Eva durch Sylt portez ce vieux Whiskey blond qui fume une

▶ Medium
The quick brown fox jumps over a Dog. Zwei Boxkämpfer jagen Eva durch Sylt portez ce vieux Whiskey blond qui fume

▶ Medium Italic
The quick brown fox jumps over a Dog. Zwei Boxkämpfer jagen Eva durch Sylt portez ce vieux Whiskey blond qui fume une

BT810 Mac + PC   ①   1930–32: W. A. Dwiggins   Industry name
Geometric 415   Metro 2

abcdefghijklmnopqrstuvwxyz[äöüßåøæœç]
ABCDEFGHIJKLMNOPQRSTUVWXYZ
1234567890(.,:;?!$&-*){ÄÖÜÅØÆŒÇ}

Futura, Spartan, Nobel

▶ Black
The quick brown fox jumps over a Dog. Zwei Boxkämpfer jagen Eva durch Sylt portez ce vieux Whiskey blond qui fume

▶ Black Italic
The quick brown fox jumps over a Dog. Zwei Boxkämpfer jagen Eva durch Sylt portez ce vieux Whiskey blond qui fume

C2778 Mac + PC   ⑥
Metronome Gothic

abcdefghijklmnopqrstuvwxyz1234567890[äöüßåøæœç]
ABCDEFGHIJKLMNOPQRSTUVWXYZ(.,:;?!$&-*) { ÄÖÜÅØÆŒÇ }

Headlines 90S:
Bernhard Fashion, Chic™, Eclipse™, Metronome Gothic, Salut™
Radiant, Britannic

C1012 Mac + PC   ⑥   1928: W. Schwerdtner
Metropolis Bold

abcdefghijklmnopqrstuvwxyz[äöüåøæœç]
ABCDEFGHIJKLMNOPQRSTUVWXYZ
1234567890(.,:;?!$&-*)◊ÄÖÜÅØÆŒÇ♦

Headlines 84S:
Bernhard Modern, Beton Extra Bold, Metropolis Bold, Modern No. 20, Orlando Caps, PL Davison Americana, PL Westerveldt Light, Siena™ Black, TC Europa™ Bold, TC Jasper™

G2784 Mac + PC   ②   1928-30: Bruce Rogers, Frederic Warde
Metropolitan No. 369™

abcdefghijklmnopqrstuvwxyz[äöüßåøæœç]
ABCDEFGHIJKLMNOPQRSTUVWXYZ
1234567890(.,:;?!$&-*){ÄÖÜÅØÆŒÇ}

© FSI 1993

▼

M 14

aaa
M736
Centaur®, Reg, Ita, Bd, BdIta
BT1410
Centaur, Reg, Ita
©
Centaur

▼ G2784 Mac + PC   **Metropolitan No. 369™**

▶ Regular OSF
The quick brown fox jumps over a Dog. 123 4567 890 Zwei Boxkämpfer jagen Eva durch Sylt portez ce vieux Whiskey blond qui fume une pipe aber echt über

▶ Italic OSF
The quick brown fox jumps over a Dog. 123 4567 890 Zwei Boxkämpfer jagen Eva durch Sylt portez ce vieux Whiskey blond qui fume une pipe aber echt über die Mauer gesprungen und

▶ Regular Small Caps OSF
THE QUICK BROWN FOX JUMPS OVER A DOG. 123 4567 890 ZWEI BOXKÄMPFER JAGEN EVA DURCH SYLT PORTEZ CE VIEUX WHISKEY BLOND QUI FUME UNE PIPE ABER

▶ Italic Small Caps OSF
THE QUICK BROWN FOX JUMPS OVER A DOG. 123 4567 890 ZWEI BOXKÄMPFER JAGEN EVA DURCH SYLT PORTEZ CE VIEUX WHISKEY BLOND QUI FUME UNE PIPE ABER

C2777 Mac + PC   ⑥   ✎ 1905: M. F. Benton
Miehle™

abcdefghijklmnopqrstuvwxyz1234567890[äöüßåøæœç]
ABCDEFGHIJKLMNOPQRSTUVWXYZ(.,:;?!$&-*){ÄÖÜÅØÆŒÇ}

Headlines 89S:
Miehle™, Parisian, Phyllis, Sinaloa™

MC2934 Mac + PC   ②
Milton™ Demibold

abcdefghijklmnopqrstuvwxyz[äöüßåøæœç]
ABCDEFGHIJKLMNOPQRSTUVWXYZ
1234567890(.,:;?!$&-*){ÄÖÜÅØÆŒÇ}

A484 Mac + PC   ②   ✎ 1990: Robert Slimbach
Minion™

abcdefghijklmnopqrstuvwxyz[äöüßåøæœç]
ABCDEFGHIJKLMNOPQRSTUVWXYZ
1234567890(.,:;?!$&-*){ÄÖÜÅØÆŒÇ}

▶ Regular
The quick brown fox jumps over a Dog. Zwei Boxkämpfer jagen Eva durch Sylt portez ce vieux Whiskey blond qui fume une pipe aber

▶ Italic
The quick brown fox jumps over a Dog. Zwei Boxkämpfer jagen Eva durch Sylt portez ce vieux Whiskey blond qui fume une pipe aber echt

▶ Display Regular
The quick brown fox jumps over a Dog. 123 4567 890 Zwei Boxkämpfer jagen Eva durch Sylt portez ce vieux Whiskey blond qui

▶ Display Italic
The quick brown fox jumps over a Dog. 123 4567 890 Zwei Boxkämpfer jagen Eva durch Sylt portez ce vieux Whiskey blond qui fume

▶ Semi Bold
The quick brown fox jumps over a Dog. Zwei Boxkämpfer jagen Eva durch Sylt portez ce vieux Whiskey blond qui fume une

▶ Semi Bold Italic
The quick brown fox jumps over a Dog. Zwei Boxkämpfer jagen Eva durch Sylt portez ce vieux Whiskey blond qui fume une pipe aber

© FSI 1993

▼ A484 Mac + PC Minion™

▶ Bold
The quick brown fox jumps over a Dog. Zwei Boxkämpfer jagen Eva durch Sylt portez ce vieux Whiskey blond qui fume une

▶ Bold Italic
The quick brown fox jumps over a Dog. Zwei Boxkämpfer jagen Eva durch Sylt portez ce vieux Whiskey blond qui fume une pipe

▶ Black
The quick brown fox jumps over a Dog. Zwei Boxkämpfer jagen Eva durch Sylt portez ce vieux Whiskey blond qui fume

A485 Mac + PC ② ✎ 1990: Robert Slimbach
Minion Expert

ABCDEFGHIJKLMNOPQRSTUVWXYZ($^{01b}3456789$)Rp

1234567890fffifflffiffl(0123456789) ¼ ½ ¾ ⅛ ⅜ ⅝ ⅞ ⅓ ⅔

▶ Expert Regular
01234567890fffifflffiffl-
(^{01b345678}1234567890Rp₵) THE QUICK BROWN FOX JUMPS OVER A DOG ZWEI BOXKÄMPFER JAGEN

▶ Expert Italic
*01234567890fffifflffiffl-
(^{01b345678}1234567890Rp₵) THE QUICK BROWN FOX JUMPS OVER A DOG ZWEI BOXKÄMPFER JAGEN EVA*

▶ Expert Display
01234567890fffifflffiffl-
(^{01b345678}1234567890Rp₵) THE QUICK BROWN FOX JUMPS OVER A DOG ZWEI BOXKÄMPFER JAGEN EVA

▶ Expert Display Italic
*01234567890fffifflffiffl-
(^{01b345678}1234567890Rp₵) THE QUICK BROWN FOX JUMPS OVER A DOG ZWEI BOXKÄMPFER JAGEN EVA*

▶ Expert Semi Bold
**01234567890fffifflffiffl-
(^{01b345678}1234567890Rp₵) THE QUICK BROWN FOX JUMPS OVER A DOG ZWEI BOXKÄMPFER JAGEN**

▶ Expert Semi Bold Italic
***01234567890fffifflffiffl-
(^{01b345678}1234567890Rp₵) THE QUICK BROWN FOX JUMPS OVER A DOG ZWEI BOXKÄMPFER JAGEN***

▶ Expert Bold
**01234567890fffifflffiffl-
(^{01b345678}1234567890Rp₵)**

▶ Expert Bold Italic
***01234567890fffifflffiffl-
(^{01b345678}1234567890Rp₵)***

▶ Expert Black
**01234567890fffifflffiffl-
(^{01b345678}1234567890Rp₵)**

▶ Swash Italic
ABCDEFGHIJKLMNOPQRST UVWXYZ

▶ Swash Semi Bold Italic
ABCDEFGHIJKLMNOPQRS TUVWXYZ

▶ Swash Display Italic
ABCDEFGHIJKLMNOPQRST UVWXYZ

Minion Expert, Minion Ornaments

© FSI 1993

M 16

Minion Multiple Master

A2969 Mac + PC ②

abcdefghijklmnopqrstuvwxyz[äöüßåøæœç]
ABCDEFGHIJKLMNOPQRSTUVWXYZ
1234567890(.,;:?!$&-*){ÄÖÜÅØÆŒÇ}

3 dimensions: weight, width, display size

▶ **Sample Interpolation 1**
The quick brown fox jumps over a Dog. Zwei Boxkämpfer jagen Eva durch Sylt portez ce vieux Whiskey blond qui fume une pipe aber echt

▶ **Sample Interpolation 2**
The quick brown fox jumps over a Dog. Zwei Boxkämpfer jagen Eva durch Sylt portez ce vieux Whiskey blond qui fume une pipe aber

▶ **Sample Interpolation 3**
The quick brown fox jumps over a Dog. Zwei Boxkämpfer jagen Eva durch Sylt portez ce vieux Whiskey blond qui fume une pipe aber echt

▶ **Sample Interpolation 4**
The quick brown fox jumps over a Dog. Zwei Boxkämpfer jagen Eva durch Sylt portez ce vieux Whiskey blond qui fume une pipe aber echt

▶ **Sample Interpolation 5**
The quick brown fox jumps over a Dog. Zwei Boxkämpfer jagen Eva durch Sylt portez ce vieux Whiskey blond qui fume une

▶ **Sample Interpolation 6**
The quick brown fox jumps over a Dog. Zwei Boxkämpfer jagen Eva durch Sylt portez ce vieux Whiskey blond qui fume une pipe aber echt

▶ **Sample Interpolation 7**
The quick brown fox jumps over a Dog. Zwei Boxkämpfer jagen Eva durch Sylt portez ce vieux Whiskey blond qui fume une

▶ **Italic Sample Interpolation 1**
The quick brown fox jumps over a Dog. Zwei Boxkämpfer jagen Eva durch Sylt portez ce vieux Whiskey blond qui fume une pipe aber echt über die

▶ **Italic Sample Interpolation 2**
The quick brown fox jumps over a Dog. Zwei Boxkämpfer jagen Eva durch Sylt portez ce vieux Whiskey blond qui fume une pipe aber echt

▶ **Italic Sample Interpolation 3**
The quick brown fox jumps over a Dog. Zwei Boxkämpfer jagen Eva durch Sylt portez ce vieux Whiskey blond qui fume une pipe aber echt

▶ **Italic Sample Interpolation 4**
The quick brown fox jumps over a Dog. Zwei Boxkämpfer jagen Eva durch Sylt portez ce vieux Whiskey blond qui fume une pipe aber echt

▶ **Italic Sample Interpolation 5**
The quick brown fox jumps over a Dog. Zwei Boxkämpfer jagen Eva durch Sylt portez ce vieux Whiskey blond qui fume une pipe aber

▶ **Italic Sample Interpolation 6**
The quick brown fox jumps over a Dog. Zwei Boxkämpfer jagen Eva durch Sylt portez ce vieux Whiskey blond qui fume une pipe aber echt

▶ **Italic Sample Interpolation 7**
The quick brown fox jumps over a Dog. Zwei Boxkämpfer jagen Eva durch Sylt portez ce vieux Whiskey blond qui fume une pipe

Minister™

A399 Mac + PC ② 1929: M. Fahrenwaldt

abcdefghijklmnopqrstuvwxyz[äöüßåøæœç]
ABCDEFGHIJKLMNOPQRSTUVWXYZ
1234567890(.,;:?!$&-*){ÄÖÜÅØÆŒÇ}

Adminster

▼ A399 Mac + PC Minister™

▶ Light
The quick brown fox jumps over a Dog. Zwei Boxkämpfer jagen Eva durch Sylt portez ce vieux Whiskey blond qui fume

▶ Light Italic
The quick brown fox jumps over a Dog. Zwei Boxkämpfer jagen Eva durch Sylt portez ce vieux Whiskey blond qui fume une pipe

▶ Book
The quick brown fox jumps over a Dog. Zwei Boxkämpfer jagen Eva durch Sylt portez ce vieux Whiskey blond

▶ Book Italic
The quick brown fox jumps over a Dog. Zwei Boxkämpfer jagen Eva durch Sylt portez ce vieux Whiskey blond qui fume

▶ Bold
The quick brown fox jumps over a Dog. Zwei Boxkämpfer jagen Eva durch Sylt portez ce vieux Whis-

▶ Bold Italic
The quick brown fox jumps over a Dog. Zwei Boxkämpfer jagen Eva durch Sylt portez ce vieux Whiskey blond

▶ Black
The quick brown fox jumps over a Dog. Zwei Boxkämpfer jagen Eva durch Sylt portez ce

▶ Black Italic
The quick brown fox jumps over a Dog. Zwei Boxkämpfer jagen Eva durch Sylt portez ce vieux

BT6414 Mac + PC ② 1992: Carol Twombly
Mirarae™

abcdefghijklmnopqrstuvwxyz[äöüßåøœç]
ABCDEFGHIJKLMNOPQRSTUVWXYZ
1234567890(.,:;?!$&-*){ÄÖÜÅØÆŒÇ}

▶ Roman
The quick brown fox jumps over a Dog. Zwei Boxkämpfer jagen Eva durch Sylt portez ce vieux Whiskey blond qui

▶ Bold
The quick brown fox jumps over a Dog. Zwei Boxkämpfer jagen Eva durch Sylt portez ce vieux Whiskey

BT6415 Mac + PC ⑥ 1992: Jennifer Maestre
Mister Earl™

abcdefghijklmnopqrstuvwxyz[äöüßåøœç]
ABCDEFGHIJKLMNOPQRSTUVWXYZ
1234567890(.,:;?!$&-*){ÄÖÜÅØÆŒÇ}

A349 Mac + PC
Mistral / Reporter

Mistral / Reporter:
Mistral™, Reporter™ No 2

© FSI 1993

M 18

A349　Mac + PC　④　1953: Roger Excoffon
Mistral™

abcdefghijklmnopqrstuvwxyz[äöüßåøæœç]
ABCDEFGHIJKLMNOPQRSTUVWXYZ
1234567890(.,;:?!$&-*){ÄÖÜÅØÆŒÇ}

Mistral / Reporter:
Mistral™, Reporter™ No 2
aaa BT1391
Mistral, Reg

EF308　Mac + PC　①　1985: Aldo Novarese
ITC Mixage® 1

abcdefghijklmnopqrstuvwxyz[äöüßåøæœç]
ABCDEFGHIJKLMNOPQRSTUVWXYZ
1234567890(.,;:?!$&-*){ÄÖÜÅØÆŒÇ}

aa*a*
BT1356
ITC Mixage 1, Bk,
BkIta, Bd, BdIta

▶ Book
The quick brown fox jumps over a Dog. Zwei Boxkämpfer jagen Eva durch Sylt portez ce vieux Whiskey blond qui fume une

▶ Book Italic
The quick brown fox jumps over a Dog. Zwei Boxkämpfer jagen Eva durch Sylt portez ce vieux Whiskey blond qui fume une pipe

▶ Bold
The quick brown fox jumps over a Dog. Zwei Boxkämpfer jagen Eva durch Sylt portez ce vieux Whiskey blond qui fume

▶ Bold Italic
The quick brown fox jumps over a Dog. Zwei Boxkämpfer jagen Eva durch Sylt portez ce vieux Whiskey blond qui fume

EF309　Mac + PC　①　1985: Aldo Novarese
ITC Mixage 2

abcdefghijklmnopqrstuvwxyz[äöüßåøæœç]
ABCDEFGHIJKLMNOPQRSTUVWXYZ
1234567890(.,;:?!$&-*){ÄÖÜÅØÆŒÇ}

aa*a*
BT1357
ITC Mixage 2, Med,
MedIta, Blk, BlkIta

▶ Medium
The quick brown fox jumps over a Dog. Zwei Boxkämpfer jagen Eva durch Sylt portez ce vieux Whiskey blond qui fume

▶ Medium Italic
The quick brown fox jumps over a Dog. Zwei Boxkämpfer jagen Eva durch Sylt portez ce vieux Whiskey blond qui fume une

▶ Black
The quick brown fox jumps over a Dog. Zwei Boxkämpfer jagen Eva durch Sylt portez ce vieux Whiskey blond

▶ Black Italic
The quick brown fox jumps over a Dog. Zwei Boxkämpfer jagen Eva durch Sylt portez ce vieux Whiskey blond

EF539　Mac + PC　②　1985: Aldo Novarese
ITC Mixage Small Caps

ABCDEFGHIJKLMNOPQRSTUVWXYZ[ÄÖÜSSÅØÆŒÇ]
ABCDEFGHIJKLMNOPQRSTUVWXYZ
1234567890(.,;:?!$&-*){ÄÖÜÅØÆŒÇ}

© FSI 1993

▼ EF539 Mac + PC ITC Mixage Small Caps

► Book Small Caps
THE QUICK BROWN FOX JUMPS OVER A DOG. 123 4567 890 ZWEI BOXKÄMPFER JAGEN EVA DURCH SYLT PORTEZ CE VIEUX WHISKEY BLOND

► Medium Small Caps
THE QUICK BROWN FOX JUMPS OVER A DOG. 123 4567 890 ZWEI BOXKÄMPFER JAGEN EVA DURCH SYLT PORTEZ CE VIEUX WHISKEY

C993 Mac + PC ② ✏ 1982: Ed Benguiat
PL Modern Heavy Condensed

abcdefghijklmnopqrstuvwxyz[äöüßåøæœç]
ABCDEFGHIJKLMNOPQRSTUVWXYZ
1234567890(.,;:?!$&-*)◊ÄÖÜÅØÆŒÇ♦

Headlines 83S:
Barclay™ Open, Delphian™ Open, Fluidum™ Bold, PL Bernhardt, PL Britannia Bold, PL Fiorello™ Condensed, PL Modern Heavy Condensed, PL Torino Open

---

M274 Mac + PC ②
Modern™ Extended

abcdefghijklmnopqrstuvwxyz[äöüßåøæœç]
ABCDEFGHIJKLMNOPQRSTUVWXYZ
1234567890(.,;:?!$&-*){ÄÖÜÅØÆŒÇ}

© De Vinne, Scotch Roman, ITC Modern No 216, Modern No 20

► Regular
The quick brown fox jumps over a Dog. Zwei Boxkämpfer jagen Eva durch Sylt portez ce vieux Whiskey blond qui fume

► Italic
The quick brown fox jumps over a Dog. Zwei Boxkämpfer jagen Eva durch Sylt portez ce vieux Whiskey blond qui fume une

► Bold
The quick brown fox jumps over a Dog. Zwei Boxkämpfer jagen Eva durch Sylt portez ce vieux Whiskey blond qui fume une

► Bold Italic
The quick brown fox jumps over a Dog. Zwei Boxkämpfer jagen Eva durch Sylt portez ce vieux Whiskey blond qui fume une

---

BT832 Mac + PC ② ✏ 1969: Walter Tracy   Industry name
Modern 880   Linotype Modern™

abcdefghijklmnopqrstuvwxyz[äöüßåøæœç]
ABCDEFGHIJKLMNOPQRSTUVWXYZ
1234567890(.,;:?!$&-*){ÄÖÜÅØÆŒÇ}

► Regular
The quick brown fox jumps over a Dog. Zwei Boxkämpfer jagen Eva durch Sylt portez ce vieux Whiskey blond qui

► Italic
The quick brown fox jumps over a Dog. Zwei Boxkämpfer jagen Eva durch Sylt portez ce vieux Whiskey blond qui fume

► Bold
The quick brown fox jumps over a Dog. Zwei Boxkämpfer jagen Eva durch Sylt portez ce vieux Whiskey blond qui

© FSI 1993

EF929 Mac + PC ② ✎ 1982: Ed Benguiat
ITC Modern No. 216®

abcdefghijklmnopqrstuvwxyz[äöüßåøæœç]
ABCDEFGHIJKLMNOPQRSTUVWXYZ
1234567890(.,:;?!$&-*){ÄÖÜÅØÆŒÇ}

©
De Vinne, Scotch Roman, ITC Modern 20, Modern Extended

▶ Light
The quick brown fox jumps over a Dog. Zwei Boxkämpfer jagen Eva durch Sylt portez ce vieux Whiskey blond

▶ Light Italic
The quick brown fox jumps over a Dog. Zwei Boxkämpfer jagen Eva durch Sylt portez ce vieux Whiskey blond

▶ Bold
The quick brown fox jumps over a Dog. Zwei Boxkämpfer jagen Eva durch Sylt portez ce vieux

▶ Bold Italic
The quick brown fox jumps over a Dog. Zwei Boxkämpfer jagen Eva durch Sylt portez ce vieux

EF930 Mac + PC ② ✎ 1982: Ed Benguiat
ITC Modern No. 216

abcdefghijklmnopqrstuvwxyz[äöüßåøæœç]
ABCDEFGHIJKLMNOPQRSTUVWXYZ
1234567890(.,:;?!$&-*){ÄÖÜÅØÆŒÇ}

©
De Vinne, Scotch Roman, ITC Modern 20, Modern Extended

▶ Medium
The quick brown fox jumps over a Dog. Zwei Boxkämpfer jagen Eva durch Sylt portez ce vieux Whiskey

▶ Medium Italic
The quick brown fox jumps over a Dog. Zwei Boxkämpfer jagen Eva durch Sylt portez ce vieux Whiskey

▶ Heavy
The quick brown fox jumps over a Dog. Zwei Boxkämpfer jagen Eva durch Sylt portez ce

▶ Heavy Italic
The quick brown fox jumps over a Dog. Zwei Boxkämpfer jagen Eva durch Sylt portez ce

BT2792 Mac + PC ②
Modern 20

abcdefghijklmnopqrstuvwxyz[äöüßåøæœç]
ABCDEFGHIJKLMNOPQRSTUVWXYZ
1234567890(.,:;?!$&-*){ÄÖÜÅØÆŒÇ}

aa*a*
🗎 C1012
Headlines 84S
©
De Vinne, Scotch Roman, ITC Modern No 216, Modern Extended

▶ Regular
The quick brown fox jumps over a Dog. Zwei Boxkämpfer jagen Eva durch Sylt portez ce vieux Whiskey blond qui fume

▶ Italic
The quick brown fox jumps over a Dog. Zwei Boxkämpfer jagen Eva durch Sylt portez ce vieux Whiskey blond qui fume une

© FSI 1993

C1012 Mac + PC ②
Modern No. 20

abcdefghijklmnopqrstuvwxyz[äöüåøæœç]
ABCDEFGHIJKLMNOPQRSTUVWXYZ
1234567890(.,;:?!$&-*){ÄÖÜÅØÆŒÇ}

Headlines 84S:
Bernhard Modern, Beton Extra Bold, Metropolis Bold, Modern No. 20, Orlando Caps, PL Davison Americana, PL Westerveldt Light, Siena™ Black, TC Europa™ Bold, TC Jasper™
Ⓒ▷ De Vinne, Scotch Roman, ITC Modern No 216, Modern Extended

C2981 Mac + PC ⑥
Modernique

abcdefghijklmnopqrstuvwxyz[äöüßåoœæç]
ABCDEFGHIJKLMNOPQRSTUVWXYZ
1234567890(.,;:?!$&-*){ÄÖÜÅØÆŒÇ}

Headlines 92S:
Eagle Bold, Joanna Solotype, Matra™, Modernique, Victorian Silhouette

C2525 Mac + PC ⑥ 1928: W. A. Parker
Modernistic™

ABCDEFGHIJKLMNOPQRSTUVWXYZ
1234567890(.,;:?!$&-*)[]{ÄÖÜÅØÆŒÇ}

Headlines 86S:
Advertisers Gothic™, Ashley Crawford™, Capone Light, Dynamo, Modernistic™

E078 Mac + PC ⑤ 1985: Zuzana Licko
Modular™ Sans

ABCDEFGHIJKLMNOPQRSTUVWXYZ
1234567890(.,;:?!$&-*)[]{ÄÖÜÅØÆŒÇ}

▶ Regular
The quick brown fox jumps over a Dog. Zwei Boxkämpfer jagen Eva durch Sylt portez ce vieux Whiskey blond qui fume une pipe aber echt über die Mauer gesprungen und auch smørebrød en ysjes natuurlijk geht spazieren lange Tekst in diese Katalog mit seine

▶ Bold
The quick brown fox jumps over a Dog. Zwei Boxkämpfer jagen Eva durch Sylt portez ce vieux Whiskey blond qui fume une pipe aber echt über die Mauer gesprungen und auch smørebrød en ysjes natuurlijk. But very long spazierende tekst ist used in

▶ Black
The quick brown fox jumps over a Dog. Zwei Boxkämpfer jagen Eva durch Sylt portez ce vieux Whiskey blond qui fume une pipe aber echt über die Mauer gesprungen und auch smørebrød en ysjes natuurlijk. But very long spazierende

© FSI 1993

E079　Mac + PC　⑤　1988: Zuzana Licko
Modular Serif

abcdefghijklmnopqrstuvwxyz1234567890[äöüßåøæœç]
ABCDEFGHIJKLMNOPQRSTUVWXYZ(.,:;?!$&-*){ÄÖÜÅØÆŒÇ}

▶ **Regular**
The quick brown fox jumps over a Dog. Zwei Boxkämpfer jagen Eva durch Sylt portez ce vieux Whiskey blond qui fume une pipe aber echt über die Mauer gesprungen und auch smørebrød en ysjes natuurlijk. But very long spazierende tekst ist used in

▶ **Bold**
The quick brown fox jumps over a Dog. Zwei Boxkämpfer jagen Eva durch Sylt portez ce vieux Whiskey blond qui fume une pipe aber echt über die Mauer gesprungen und auch smørebrød en ysjes natuurlijk. But very long spazierende tekst ist used in

▶ **Black**
The quick brown fox jumps over a Dog. Zwei Boxkämpfer jagen Eva durch Sylt portez ce vieux Whiskey blond qui fume une pipe aber echt über die Mauer gesprungen und auch smørebrød en ysjes natuurlijk. But very long

E937　Mac + PC　⑤　1989: Zuzana Licko
Modular Tall

abcdefghijklmnopqrstuvwxyz1234567890[äöüßåøæœç]
ABCDEFGHIJKLMNOPQRSTUVWXYZ(.,:;?!$&-*){ÄÖÜÅØÆŒÇ}

Tall Pack:
Matrix Tall, Senator Tall

EF981　Mac + PC　⑥　1990: (Albert Auspurg, 1930)
ITC Mona Lisa Recut™

abcdefghijklmnopqrstuvwxyz[äöüßåøæœç]
ABCDEFGHIJKLMNOPQRSTUVWXYZ
1234567890(.,:;?!$&-*){ÄÖÜÅØÆŒÇ}

ITC Anna™, ITC Mona Lisa Recut™
aa*a*

EF6463　Mac + PC
ITC Mona Lisa Solid / ITC Ozwald

ITC Mona Lisa Solid / ITC Ozwald:
ITC Mona Lisa Solid™, ITC Ozwald™

EF6463　Mac + PC　⑥　1992: (Albert Auspurg, 1930) Pat Hickson
ITC Mona Lisa Solid™

abcdefghijklmnopqrstuvwxyz[äöüßåøæœç]
ABCDEFGHIJKLMNOPQRSTUVWXYZ
1234567890(.,:;?!$&-*){ÄÖÜÅØÆŒÇ}

▼ EF6463 Mac + PC   ITC Mona Lisa Solid™

ITC Mona Lisa Solid / ITC Ozwald:
ITC Mona Lisa Solid™, ITC Ozwald™

EF519 Mac + PC   ③   ✐ 1977: Erwin Koch
Monanti™

abcdefghijklmnopqrstuvwxyz[äöüßåøæœç]
ABCDEFGHIJKLMNOPQRSTUVWXYZ
1234567890(.,;:?!$&-*){ÄÖÜÅØÆŒÇ}

ⓒ
ITC American Typewriter, Courier, Schreibmaschinenschrift, Prestige, Typewriter, Pica

▶ Regular
The quick brown fox jumps over a Dog. Zwei Boxkämpfer jagen Eva durch Sylt portez ce

▶ Semi Bold
The quick brown fox jumps over a Dog. Zwei Boxkämpfer jagen Eva durch Sylt portez ce

---

CT872 Mac + PC   ②   ✐ 1990: Adrian Williams
Monkton™

abcdefghijklmnopqrstuvwxyz[äöüßåøæœç]
ABCDEFGHIJKLMNOPQRSTUVWXYZ
1234567890(.,;:?!$&-*){ÄÖÜÅØÆŒÇ}

▶ Regular
The quick brown fox jumps over a Dog. Zwei Boxkämpfer jagen Eva durch Sylt portez ce vieux Whiskey blond qui fume une pipe aber echt

▶ Italic
The quick brown fox jumps over a Dog. Zwei Boxkämpfer jagen Eva durch Sylt portez ce vieux Whiskey blond qui fume une pipe aber echt

▶ Medium
The quick brown fox jumps over a Dog. Zwei Boxkämpfer jagen Eva durch Sylt portez ce vieux Whiskey blond qui fume une

▶ Medium Italic
The quick brown fox jumps over a Dog. Zwei Boxkämpfer jagen Eva durch Sylt portez ce vieux Whiskey blond qui fume une pipe aber

▶ Bold
The quick brown fox jumps over a Dog. Zwei Boxkämpfer jagen Eva durch Sylt portez ce vieux Whiskey blond qui fume

▶ Bold Italic
The quick brown fox jumps over a Dog. Zwei Boxkämpfer jagen Eva durch Sylt portez ce vieux Whiskey blond qui fume

---

CT6340 Mac + PC   ②   ✐ 1992: Adrian Williams
Monkton Book Expert

abcdefghijklmnopqrstuvwxyz[äöüßåøæœç]
ABCDEFGHIJKLMNOPQRSTUVWXYZ
1234567890(.,;:?!$&-*){ÄÖÜÅØÆŒÇ}

▶ Book
The quick brown fox jumps over a Dog. Zwei Boxkämpfer jagen Eva durch Sylt portez ce vieux Whiskey blond qui fume une pipe aber echt

▶ Expert Book
01234567890fffiflffiffl($\frac{1}{1}$$\frac{2}{2}$$\frac{3}{3}$$\frac{4}{4}$$\frac{5}{5}$$\frac{6}{6}$$\frac{7}{7}$$\frac{8}{8}$$\frac{9}{9}$%)⁽ˢ$3Rp℗ᵃ THE QUICK BROWN FOX JUMPS OVER A DOG ZWEI BOXKÄMPFER JAGEN EVA

▶ Bold, ⓒ CT872

© FSI 1993

M264 Mac + PC ④
Monoline Script™

abcdefghijklmnopqrstuvwxyz[äöüßåøæœç]
ABCDEFGHIJKLMNOPQRSTUVWXYZ
1234567890(.,;:?!$&-*){ÄÖÜÅØÆŒÇ}

Script 2:
Ashley Script, Monoline Script™, New Berolina, Palace Script™
aaa ⌨ A6335
Ashley Script et al

BT848 Mac + PC ④
Monterey

abcdefghijklmnopqrstuvwxyz[äöüßåøæœç]
ABCDEFGHIJKLMNOPQRSTUVWXYZ
1234567890(.,;:?!$&-*){ÄÖÜÅØÆŒÇ}

Bitstream Script 1:
Amazone™, Monterey, Piranesi™ Italic

E6658 Mac + PC ⑥
Motion™

abcdefghijklmnopqrstuvwxyz[äöüßåøæœç]
ABCDEFGHIJKLMNOPQRSTUVWXYZ
1234567890(.,;:?!$&-*){ÄÖÜÅØÆŒÇ}

▶ Light
The quick brown fox jumps over a Dog. Zwei Boxkämpfer jagen Eva durch Sylt portez ce vieux Whiskey blond

▶ Bold
The quick brown fox jumps over a Dog. Zwei Boxkämpfer jagen Eva durch Sylt portez ce vieux Whiskey blond qui

SG1608 Mac ⑥   1976: Otmer Motter
Motter Femina™

abcdefghijklmnopqrstuvwxyz[äöüßåøæœç]
ABCDEFGHIJKLMNOPQRSTUVWXYZ
1234567890(.,;:?!$&-*){ÄÖÜÅØÆŒÇ}

FB6371 Mac + PC ⑥   1992: Richard Lipton
Munich™

ABCDEFGHIJKLMNOPQRSTUVWXYZ[ÄÖÜÅØÆŒÇ]
ABCDEFGHIJKLMNOPQRSTUVWXYZ
1234567890(.,;:?!$&-*){ÄÖÜÅØÆŒÇ}

ⓒ Bremen

▶ Light
THE QUICK BROWN FOX JUMPS OVER A DOG. ZWEI BOXKÄMPFER JAGEN EVA DURCH SYLT PORTEZ CE VIEUX WHISKEY

▶ Bold
THE QUICK BROWN FOX JUMPS OVER A DOG. ZWEI BOXKÄMPFER JAGEN EVA DURCH SYLT PORTEZ CE VIEUX

© FSI 1993

▼ FB6371 Mac + PC   Munich™

▶ Black
THE QUICK BROWN FOX JUMPS OVER A DOG. ZWEI BOXKÄMPFER JAGEN EVA DURCH SYLT PORTEZ CE

BT833 Mac + PC ④   ✎ 1956: Emil Klump
Murray Hill™

abcdefghijklmnopqrstuvwxyz[äöüßåøæœç]
ABCDEFGHIJKLMNOPQRSTUVWXYZ
1234567890(.,:;?!$&-*){ÄÖÜÅØÆŒÇ}

aa*a*
EF1078
Slogan™, Reg
Murray Hill, Reg

▶ Regular
The quick brown fox jumps over a Dog. Zwei Boxkämpfer jagen Eva durch Sylt portez ce vieux Whiskey blond qui fume une pipe aber echt über die Mauer gesprungen und auch smørebrød en ysjes natuurlijk

▶ Bold
The quick brown fox jumps over a Dog. Zwei Boxkämpfer jagen Eva durch Sylt portez ce vieux Whiskey blond qui fume une pipe aber echt über die Mauer gesprungen

C615 Mac + PC ②   ✎ 1968: Tony Geddes
Musketeer™

abcdefghijklmnopqrstuvwxyz[äöüßåøæœç]
ABCDEFGHIJKLMNOPQRSTUVWXYZ
1234567890(.,:;?!$&-*){ÄÖÜÅØÆŒÇ}

©
Milton

▶ Light
The quick brown fox jumps over a Dog. Zwei Boxkämpfer jagen Eva durch Sylt portez ce vieux Whiskey blond qui fume une pipe aber

▶ Regular
The quick brown fox jumps over a Dog. Zwei Boxkämpfer jagen Eva durch Sylt portez ce vieux Whiskey blond qui fume une

▶ Demi Bold
The quick brown fox jumps over a Dog. Zwei Boxkämpfer jagen Eva durch Sylt portez ce vieux Whiskey blond qui fume

▶ Extra Bold
The quick brown fox jumps over a Dog. Zwei Boxkämpfer jagen Eva durch Sylt portez ce vieux

A2862 Mac + PC ①   ✎ 1992: Robert Slimbach, Carol Twombly
Myriad Multiple Master

abcdefghijklmnopqrstuvwxyz[äöüßåøæœç]
ABCDEFGHIJKLMNOPQRSTUVWXYZ
1234567890(.,:;?!$&-*){ÄÖÜÅØÆŒÇ}

2 dimensions:
weight, width

▶ Sample Interpolation 1
The quick brown fox jumps over a Dog. Zwei Boxkämpfer jagen Eva durch Sylt portez ce vieux Whiskey blond qui fume une pipe aber echt über die Mauer gesprungen und auch

▶ Sample Interpolation 2
The quick brown fox jumps over a Dog. Zwei Boxkämpfer jagen Eva durch Sylt portez ce vieux Whiskey blond qui fume une

▶ Sample Interpolation 3
The quick brown fox jumps over a Dog. Zwei Boxkämpfer jagen Eva durch Sylt portez ce vieux Whiskey blond

▶ Sample Interpolation 4
The quick brown fox jumps over a Dog. Zwei Boxkämpfer jagen Eva durch Sylt portez ce vieux Whiskey blond qui fume une pipe aber echt über die

© FSI 1993

▼ A2862 Mac + PC   Myriad Multiple Master

▶ Sample Interpolation 5

The quick brown fox jumps over a Dog. Zwei Boxkämpfer jagen Eva durch Sylt portez ce vieux Whiskey

▶ Sample Interpolation 6

The quick brown fox jumps over a Dog. Zwei Boxkämpfer jagen Eva durch Sylt portez ce vieux Whiskey blond qui fume une pipe aber echt über die Mauer gesprungen und auch smørebrød en

▶ Sample Interpolation 7

The quick brown fox jumps over a Dog. Zwei Boxkämpfer jagen Eva durch Sylt portez ce vieux Whiskey blond qui fume une

▶ Sample Interpolation 8

The quick brown fox jumps over a Dog. Zwei Boxkämpfer jagen Eva durch Sylt portez ce vieux Whiskey blond qui fume

▶ Sample Interpolation 9

The quick brown fox jumps over a Dog. Zwei Boxkämpfer jagen Eva durch Sylt portez ce vieux Whiskey blond qui fume

▶ Sample Interpolation 10

The quick brown fox jumps over a Dog. Zwei Boxkämpfer jagen Eva durch Sylt portez ce vieux Whiskey blond qui fume une pipe aber echt

© FSI 1993

-
-
- typog
- rafyi
- sviole
nce

Words set entirely in capitals are considerably less legible than words in lower case. Italics reduce legibility but, provided the counters of the letters are open, bold face does not. Excessively long lines cause a sharp increase in the number of regressions. Short lines, on the other hand, increase the number of fixation pauses. Leading permits line length to be extended without loss of legibility. There is no appreciable loss of legibility when type is printed in black on tinted paper, provided this is of a low reflectance value or hue. A number of unfavourable factors combined, though not strictly cumulative, may

N

Marianne van Ham, Utrecht, NL

C1202 Mac + PC ④ 1991: Aldo Novarese
Agfa Nadianne™

abcdefghijklmnopqrstuvwxyz[äöüßåøæœç]
ABCDEFGHIJKLMNOPQRSTUVWXYZ
1234567890(.,;:?!$&-*){ÄÖÜÅØÆŒÇ}

▶ Book
The quick brown fox jumps over a Dog. Zwei Boxkämpfer jagen Eva durch Sylt portez ce vieux Whiskey blond qui fume

▶ Medium
The quick brown fox jumps over a Dog. Zwei Boxkämpfer jagen Eva durch Sylt portez ce vieux Whiskey blond

▶ Bold
The quick brown fox jumps over a Dog. Zwei Boxkämpfer jagen Eva durch Sylt portez ce vieux

T06105 Mac ⑤ 1992: Enric Jardí
Neeskens™

abcdefghijklmnopqrstuvwxyz[äöüßåøæœç]
abcdefghijklmnopqrstuvwxyz
1234567890(.,;:?!$&-*)äöüåøæœç

Geometric, Bank Gothic, FF Gothic

▶ Black
the quick brown fox jumps over a dog. Zwei boxkämpfer jagen Eva durch Sylt portez ce vieux Whiskey blond qui fume une pipe aber

▶ Inline
the quick brown fox jumps over a dog. Zwei boxkämpfer jagen Eva durch Sylt portez ce vieux Whiskey blond qui fume une pipe aber

Type-ø-Tones Pack 2:
Mayayo™, Neeskens™

M625 Mac + PC ⑥ 1970: R. Barbor
Neographik™

abcdefghijklmnopqrstuvwxyz[äöüßåøæœç]
ABCDEFGHIJKLMNOPQRSTUVWXYZ
1234567890(.,;:?!$&-*){ÄÖÜÅØÆŒÇ}

Headliners 5:
Bernard™ Condensed, Compacta Bold, Neographik™, Runic™ Condensed

C468 Mac + PC ⑤ 1935: G. de Milano
Neon Extra Condensed™

ABCDEFGHIJKLMNOPQRSTUVWXYZ
1234567890(.,;:?!$&-*)☐ ◇ ÄÖÜÅØÆŒÇ ◆

© FSI 1993

▼ C468   Mac + PC   Neon Extra Condensed™

Headlines 82S:
Neon Extra Condensed™, PL Barnum Block, PL Benguiat Frisky Bold, PL Davison Zip Bold, PL Fiedler Gothic Bold, PL Futura Maxi 2, PL Trophy™ Oblique, Ritmo™ Bold, TC Broadway

---

FF731   Mac + PC   ⑤   🖉 1991: Max Kisman
FF Network™

abcdefghijklmnopqrstuvwxyz1234567890[äöüß ø æœç]

ABCDEFGHIJKLMNOPQRSTUVWXYZ(.,:;?!$&-*){ÄÖÜÅØÆŒÇ}

FF Kisman™ 1:
FF Cutout™, FF Network™, FF Scratch™, FF Vortex™
ⓒ Oblong, FF Vortex, FF Pop

BT834   Mac + PC   ⑥   🖉 1923: Rudolf Koch   Industry name
Informal 011   Neuland™

ABCDEFGHIJKLMNOPQRSTUVWXYZ
1234567890(.,:;!!$&-*)[]{ÄÖÜÅØÆŒÇ}

ⓒ Manito, Totally Glyphic, Koch Neuland

▶ Regular
THE QUICK BROWN FOX JUMPS OVER A DOG. ZWEI BOXKÄMPFER JAGEN EVA DURCH SYLT PORTEZ CE

▶ Black
THE QUICK BROWN FOX JUMPS OVER A DOG. ZWEI BOXKÄMPFER JAGEN EVA DURCH SYLT

A897   Mac + PC   ①   🖉 (1928): Wilhelm Pischner
DIN Neuzeit Grotesk

abcdefghijklmnopqrstuvwxyz[äöüßåøæœç]
ABCDEFGHIJKLMNOPQRSTUVWXYZ
1234567890(.,:;?!$&-*){ÄÖÜÅØÆŒÇ}

ⓒ Nobel

▶ Light
The quick brown fox jumps over a Dog. Zwei Boxkämpfer jagen Eva durch Sylt portez ce vieux Whiskey blond

▶ Bold Condensed
The quick brown fox jumps over a Dog. Zwei Boxkämpfer jagen Eva durch Sylt portez ce vieux Whiskey blond qui fume une pipe aber echt über die Mauer

DIN Schriften:
DIN, DIN Neuzeit Grotesk

BT835   Mac + PC   ①   🖉 1928: Wilhelm Pischner   Industry name
Geometric 706   Neuzeit Grotesk

abcdefghijklmnopqrstuvwxyz[äöüßåøæœç]
ABCDEFGHIJKLMNOPQRSTUVWXYZ
1234567890(.,:;?!$&-*){ÄÖÜÅØÆŒÇ}

© FSI 1993

▼ BT835 Mac + PC   Neuzeit Grotesk

© Nobel

▶ Medium
The quick brown fox jumps over a Dog. Zwei Boxkämpfer jagen Eva durch Sylt portez ce vieux Whiskey blond

▶ Black
The quick brown fox jumps over a Dog. Zwei Boxkämpfer jagen Eva durch Sylt portez ce vieux

BT836 Mac + PC   ①   ✎ 1939: Wilhelm Pischner   Industry name
Geometric 706 Condensed   Neuzeit Grotesk Condensed

abcdefghijklmnopqrstuvwxyz[äöüßåøœç]
ABCDEFGHIJKLMNOPQRSTUVWXYZ
1234567890(.,;:?!$&-*){ÄÖÜÅØÆŒÇ}

© Nobel

▶ Bold Condensed
The quick brown fox jumps over a Dog. Zwei Boxkämpfer jagen Eva durch Sylt portez ce vieux Whiskey blond qui fume une pipe aber echt über die Mauer

▶ Black Condensed
The quick brown fox jumps over a Dog. Zwei Boxkämpfer jagen Eva durch Sylt portez ce vieux Whiskey blond qui fume une pipe aber echt

A474 Mac + PC   ①
Neuzeit-S Book

abcdefghijklmnopqrstuvwxyz[äöüßåøæœç]
ABCDEFGHIJKLMNOPQRSTUVWXYZ
1234567890(.,;:?!$&-*){ÄÖÜÅØÆŒÇ}

▶ Regular
The quick brown fox jumps over a Dog. Zwei Boxkämpfer jagen Eva durch Sylt portez ce vieux Whiskey blond qui

▶ Heavy
The quick brown fox jumps over a Dog. Zwei Boxkämpfer jagen Eva durch Sylt portez ce vieux Whiskey

SG2254 Mac   ④
Nevison Casual™

abcdefghijklmnopqrstuvwxyz[äöüßåøæœç]
ABCDEFGHIJKLMNOPQRSTUVWXYZ
1234567890(.,;:?!$&-*)ÄÖÜÅØÆŒÇ

FF733 Mac + PC   ⑥   ✎ 1991: Peter Verheul
FF Newberlin™

abcdefghijklmnopqrstuvwxyz1234567890[äöüßåøœç]

ABCDEFGHIJKLMNOPQRSTUVWXYZ(.,;:?!$&-*){ÄÖÜÅØÆŒÇ}

▶ Regular
The quick brown fox jumps over a Dog. Zwei Boxkämpfer jagen Eva durch Sylt portez ce vieux Whiskey blond qui fume une pipe aber echt über die Mauer gesprungen und auch

▶ Rough
The quick brown fox jumps over a Dog. Zwei Boxkämpfer jagen Eva durch Sylt portez ce vieux Whiskey blond qui fume une pipe aber echt über die Mauer gesprungen und auch

© FSI 1993

▼ FF733 Mac + PC   FF Newberlin™

▶ Bold
The quick brown fox jumps over a Dog. Zwei Boxkämpfer jagen Eva durch Sylt portez ce vieux Whiskey blond qui fume une pipe aber echt über die Mauer

▶ Bold Rough
The quick brown fox jumps over a Dog. Zwei Boxkämpfer jagen Eva durch Sylt portez ce vieux Whiskey blond qui fume une pipe aber echt über die Mauer

---

C1200 Mac + PC
News/Sans

News/Sans:
News No. 2, News No. 4, Sans No. 1

C1200 Mac + PC   ③
News No. 2

abcdefghijklmnopqrstuvwxyz[äöüßåøæœç]
ABCDEFGHIJKLMNOPQRSTUVWXYZ
1234567890(.,:;?!$&-*){ÄÖÜÅØÆŒÇ}

▶ Regular
The quick brown fox jumps over a Dog. Zwei Boxkämpfer jagen Eva durch Sylt portez ce vieux Whiskey blond

▶ Italic
The quick brown fox jumps over a Dog. Zwei Boxkämpfer jagen Eva durch Sylt portez ce vieux Whiskey

▶ Bold
The quick brown fox jumps over a Dog. Zwei Boxkämpfer jagen Eva durch Sylt portez ce vieux Whiskey

News/Sans:
News No. 2, News No. 4, Sans No. 1

C1200 Mac + PC   ③
News No. 4

abcdefghijklmnopqrstuvwxyz[äöüßåøæœç]
ABCDEFGHIJKLMNOPQRSTUVWXYZ
1234567890(.,:;?!$&-*){ÄÖÜÅØÆŒÇ}

▶ Regular
The quick brown fox jumps over a Dog. Zwei Boxkämpfer jagen Eva durch Sylt portez ce vieux

▶ Italic
The quick brown fox jumps over a Dog. Zwei Boxkämpfer jagen Eva durch Sylt portez ce vieux

▶ Bold
The quick brown fox jumps over a Dog. Zwei Boxkämpfer jagen Eva durch Sylt portez ce vieux

News/Sans:
News No. 2, News No. 4, Sans No. 1

© FSI 1993

M238 Mac + PC — 1908: M. F. Benton (John Renshaw, 1958)
Monotype News Gothic™

abcdefghijklmnopqrstuvwxyz[äöüßåøæœç]
ABCDEFGHIJKLMNOPQRSTUVWXYZ
1234567890(.,;:?!$&-*){ÄÖÜÅØÆŒÇ}

Alternate Gothic, Trade Gothic, Vectora

▶ Regular
The quick brown fox jumps over a Dog. Zwei Boxkämpfer jagen Eva durch Sylt portez ce vieux Whiskey blond qui

▶ Italic
The quick brown fox jumps over a Dog. Zwei Boxkämpfer jagen Eva durch Sylt portez ce vieux Whiskey blond qui fume

▶ Bold
The quick brown fox jumps over a Dog. Zwei Boxkämpfer jagen Eva durch Sylt portez ce vieux Whiskey blond

▶ Condensed
The quick brown fox jumps over a Dog. Zwei Boxkämpfer jagen Eva durch Sylt portez ce vieux Whiskey blond qui fume une pipe aber echt über die

▶ Bold Condensed
The quick brown fox jumps over a Dog. Zwei Boxkämpfer jagen Eva durch Sylt portez ce vieux Whiskey blond qui fume une pipe aber echt

A084 Mac + PC — 1908: M. F. Benton
News Gothic™

abcdefghijklmnopqrstuvwxyz[äöüßåøæœç]
ABCDEFGHIJKLMNOPQRSTUVWXYZ
1234567890(.,;:?!$&-*){ÄÖÜÅØÆŒÇ}

Alternate Gothic, Trade Gothic, Vectora

▶ Regular
The quick brown fox jumps over a Dog. Zwei Boxkämpfer jagen Eva durch Sylt portez ce vieux Whiskey blond qui fume une pipe

▶ Oblique
The quick brown fox jumps over a Dog. Zwei Boxkämpfer jagen Eva durch Sylt portez ce vieux Whiskey blond qui fume une pipe

▶ Bold
The quick brown fox jumps over a Dog. Zwei Boxkämpfer jagen Eva durch Sylt portez ce vieux Whiskey blond

▶ Bold Oblique
The quick brown fox jumps over a Dog. Zwei Boxkämpfer jagen Eva durch Sylt portez ce vieux Whiskey blond

BT1361 Mac + PC — 1909: M. F. Benton
News Gothic 1

abcdefghijklmnopqrstuvwxyz[äöüßåøæœç]
ABCDEFGHIJKLMNOPQRSTUVWXYZ
1234567890(.,;:?!$&-*){ÄÖÜÅØÆŒÇ}

Alternate Gothic, Trade Gothic, Vectora

▶ Light
The quick brown fox jumps over a Dog. Zwei Boxkämpfer jagen Eva durch Sylt portez ce vieux Whiskey blond qui fume une

▶ Light Italic
The quick brown fox jumps over a Dog. Zwei Boxkämpfer jagen Eva durch Sylt portez ce vieux Whiskey blond qui fume une

© FSI 1993

▼ BT1361 MAC + PC   News Gothic 1

▶ Demi
The quick brown fox jumps over a Dog. Zwei Boxkämpfer jagen Eva durch Sylt portez ce vieux Whiskey blond qui fume une

▶ Demi Italic
The quick brown fox jumps over a Dog. Zwei Boxkämpfer jagen Eva durch Sylt portez ce vieux Whiskey blond qui fume une

---

BT1362 MAC + PC   ①   ✎ 1909: M. F. Benton
News Gothic 2

abcdefghijklmnopqrstuvwxyz[äöüßåøæœç]
ABCDEFGHIJKLMNOPQRSTUVWXYZ
1234567890(.,;:?!$&-*){ÄÖÜÅØÆŒÇ}

© Alternate Gothic, Trade Gothic, Vectora

▶ Regular
The quick brown fox jumps over a Dog. Zwei Boxkämpfer jagen Eva durch Sylt portez ce vieux Whiskey blond qui fume une

▶ Italic
The quick brown fox jumps over a Dog. Zwei Boxkämpfer jagen Eva durch Sylt portez ce vieux Whiskey blond qui fume une

▶ Bold
The quick brown fox jumps over a Dog. Zwei Boxkämpfer jagen Eva durch Sylt portez ce vieux Whiskey blond qui fume

▶ Bold Italic
The quick brown fox jumps over a Dog. Zwei Boxkämpfer jagen Eva durch Sylt portez ce vieux Whiskey blond qui fume une

---

BT1363 MAC + PC   ①   ✎ 1909: M. F. Benton
News Gothic Condensed

abcdefghijklmnopqrstuvwxyz[äöüßåøæœç]
ABCDEFGHIJKLMNOPQRSTUVWXYZ
1234567890(.,;:?!$&-*){ÄÖÜÅØÆŒÇ}

© Alternate Gothic, Trade Gothic, Vectora

▶ Condensed
The quick brown fox jumps over a Dog. Zwei Boxkämpfer jagen Eva durch Sylt portez ce vieux Whiskey blond qui fume une pipe aber echt über die Mauer

▶ Condensed Italic
The quick brown fox jumps over a Dog. Zwei Boxkämpfer jagen Eva durch Sylt portez ce vieux Whiskey blond qui fume une pipe aber echt über die Mauer

▶ Bold Condensed
The quick brown fox jumps over a Dog. Zwei Boxkämpfer jagen Eva durch Sylt portez ce vieux Whiskey blond qui fume une pipe aber echt über die

▶ Bold Condensed Italic
The quick brown fox jumps over a Dog. Zwei Boxkämpfer jagen Eva durch Sylt portez ce vieux Whiskey blond qui fume une pipe aber echt

---

BT837 MAC + PC   ①   ✎ 1909: M. F. Benton
News Gothic Extra Condensed

abcdefghijklmnopqrstuvwxyz[äöüßåøæœç]
ABCDEFGHIJKLMNOPQRSTUVWXYZ
1234567890(.,;:?!$&-*){ÄÖÜÅØÆŒÇ}

© Alternate Gothic, Trade Gothic, Phenix American

▶ Extra Condensed
The quick brown fox jumps over a Dog. Zwei Boxkämpfer jagen Eva durch Sylt portez ce vieux Whiskey blond qui fume une pipe aber echt über die Mauer gesprungen und auch

▶ Bold Extra Condensed
The quick brown fox jumps over a Dog. Zwei Boxkämpfer jagen Eva durch Sylt portez ce vieux Whiskey blond qui fume une pipe aber echt über die Mauer gesprungen

© FSI 1993

BT839　Mac + PC　②　🖉 1974: Ray Baker
ITC Newtext ® 2

abcdefghijklmnopqrstuvwxyz[äöüßåøæœç]
ABCDEFGHIJKLMNOPQRSTUVWXYZ
1234567890(.,;:?!$&-*){ÄÖÜÅØÆŒÇ}

▶ Light
The quick brown fox jumps over a Dog. Zwei Boxkämpfer jagen Eva durch Sylt portez ce vieux Whiskey

▶ Light Italic
The quick brown fox jumps over a Dog. Zwei Boxkämpfer jagen Eva durch Sylt portez ce vieux Whiskey blond

BT840　Mac + PC　②　🖉 1974: Ray Baker
ITC Newtext 3

abcdefghijklmnopqrstuvwxyz[äöüßåøæœç]
ABCDEFGHIJKLMNOPQRSTUVWXYZ
1234567890(.,;:?!$&-*){ÄÖÜÅØÆŒÇ}

▶ Book
The quick brown fox jumps over a Dog. Zwei Boxkämpfer jagen Eva durch Sylt portez ce vieux Whiskey

▶ Book Italic
The quick brown fox jumps over a Dog. Zwei Boxkämpfer jagen Eva durch Sylt portez ce vieux Whiskey blond

▶ Demi
The quick brown fox jumps over a Dog. Zwei Boxkämpfer jagen Eva durch Sylt portez ce vieux Whis-

▶ Demi Italic
The quick brown fox jumps over a Dog. Zwei Boxkämpfer jagen Eva durch Sylt portez ce vieux Whiskey

BT838　Mac + PC　②　🖉 1974: Ray Baker
ITC Newtext 1

abcdefghijklmnopqrstuvwxyz[äöüßåøæœç]
ABCDEFGHIJKLMNOPQRSTUVWXYZ
1234567890(.,;:?!$&-*){ÄÖÜÅØÆŒÇ}

▶ Regular
The quick brown fox jumps over a Dog. Zwei Boxkämpfer jagen Eva durch Sylt portez ce vieux Whiskey

▶ Italic
The quick brown fox jumps over a Dog. Zwei Boxkämpfer jagen Eva durch Sylt portez ce vieux Whiskey

FF1532　Mac + PC　⑥　🖉 1991: Gerd Wiescher
FF NewYorkerType™

ABCDEFGHIJKLMNOPQRSTUVWXYZ[ÄÖÜSSÅØÆŒÇ]
ABCDEFGHIJKLMNOPQRSTUVWXYZ
1234567890(.,;:?!$&-*){ÄÖÜÅØÆŒÇ}

▶ Regular
THE QUICK BROWN FOX JUMPS OVER A DOG. ZWEI BOXKÄMPFER JAGEN EVA DURCH SYLT

▶ Bold
THE QUICK BROWN FOX JUMPS OVER A DOG. ZWEI BOXKÄMPFER JAGEN EVA DURCH SYLT

© FSI 1993

Nikis™
EF520 MAC + PC ②

abcdefghijklmnopqrstuvwxyz[äöüßåøæœç]
ABCDEFGHIJKLMNOPQRSTUVWXYZ
1234567890(.,;:?!$&-*){ÄÖÜÅØÆŒÇ}

Sabon

▶ Light
The quick brown fox jumps over a Dog. Zwei Boxkämpfer jagen Eva durch Sylt portez ce vieux Whiskey blond qui fume une pipe aber echt

▶ Light Italic
The quick brown fox jumps over a Dog. Zwei Boxkämpfer jagen Eva durch Sylt portez ce vieux Whiskey blond qui fume une pipe aber echt über

▶ Semi Bold
The quick brown fox jumps over a Dog. Zwei Boxkämpfer jagen Eva durch Sylt portez ce vieux Whiskey blond qui fume une

▶ Semi Bold Italic
The quick brown fox jumps over a Dog. Zwei Boxkämpfer jagen Eva durch Sylt portez ce vieux Whiskey blond qui fume une pipe aber echt

Nimrod®
M154 MAC + PC ③ 1980: Robin Nicholas

abcdefghijklmnopqrstuvwxyz[äöüßåøæœç]
ABCDEFGHIJKLMNOPQRSTUVWXYZ
1234567890(.,;:?!$&-*){ÄÖÜÅØÆŒÇ}

Clarion, Ionic

▶ Regular
The quick brown fox jumps over a Dog. Zwei Boxkämpfer jagen Eva durch Sylt portez ce vieux Whiskey

▶ Italic
The quick brown fox jumps over a Dog. Zwei Boxkämpfer jagen Eva durch Sylt portez ce vieux Whiskey blond

▶ Bold
The quick brown fox jumps over a Dog. Zwei Boxkämpfer jagen Eva durch Sylt portez ce vieux

▶ Bold Italic
The quick brown fox jumps over a Dog. Zwei Boxkämpfer jagen Eva durch Sylt portez ce vieux

Nobel™
FB6670 MAC + PC ① 1992: (1930: S. H. De Roos) Tobias Frere-Jones

abcdefghijklmnopqrstuvwxyz[äöüßåøæœç]
ABCDEFGHIJKLMNOPQRSTUVWXYZ
1234567890(.,;:?!$&-*){ÄÖÜÅØÆŒÇ}

Neuzeit Grotesk

▶ Light
The quick brown fox jumps over a Dog. Zwei Boxkämpfer jagen Eva durch Sylt portez ce vieux Whiskey blond qui fume une pipe aber echt

▶ Regular
The quick brown fox jumps over a Dog. Zwei Boxkämpfer jagen Eva durch Sylt portez ce vieux Whiskey blond qui fume une pipe aber

▶ Italic
The quick brown fox jumps over a Dog. Zwei Boxkämpfer jagen Eva durch Sylt portez ce vieux Whiskey blond qui fume une pipe aber echt

▶ Bold
The quick brown fox jumps over a Dog. Zwei Boxkämpfer jagen Eva durch Sylt portez ce vieux Whiskey blond qui fume

© FSI 1993

▼ FB6670 Mac + PC Nobel™

▶ Condensed
The quick brown fox jumps over a Dog. Zwei Boxkämpfer jagen Eva durch Sylt portez ce vieux Whiskey blond qui fume une pipe aber echt über die Mauer gesprungen und auch

▶ Bold Condensed
The quick brown fox jumps over a Dog. Zwei Boxkämpfer jagen Eva durch Sylt portez ce vieux Whiskey blond qui fume une pipe aber echt über die Mauer gesprungen

AB1050 Mac + PC ②   1986: Gudrun Zapf von Hesse
Nofret®

abcdefghijklmnopqrstuvwxyz[äöüßåøæœç]
ABCDEFGHIJKLMNOPQRSTUVWXYZ
1234567890(.,;:?!$&-*){ÄÖÜÅØÆŒÇ}

© Bitstream Carmina, Diotima

▶ Light
The quick brown fox jumps over a Dog. Zwei Boxkämpfer jagen Eva durch Sylt portez ce vieux Whiskey blond qui fume

▶ Light Italic
The quick brown fox jumps over a Dog. Zwei Boxkämpfer jagen Eva durch Sylt portez ce vieux Whiskey blond qui fume une pipe aber echt

▶ Regular
The quick brown fox jumps over a Dog. Zwei Boxkämpfer jagen Eva durch Sylt portez ce vieux Whiskey blond qui

▶ Italic
The quick brown fox jumps over a Dog. Zwei Boxkämpfer jagen Eva durch Sylt portez ce vieux Whiskey blond qui fume une pipe aber echt

▶ Medium
The quick brown fox jumps over a Dog. Zwei Boxkämpfer jagen Eva durch Sylt portez ce vieux

▶ Medium Italic
The quick brown fox jumps over a Dog. Zwei Boxkämpfer jagen Eva durch Sylt portez ce vieux Whiskey blond

▶ Bold
The quick brown fox jumps over a Dog. Zwei Boxkämpfer jagen Eva durch Sylt portez ce

▶ Bold Italic
The quick brown fox jumps over a Dog. Zwei Boxkämpfer jagen Eva durch Sylt portez ce

BT841 Mac + PC ②
Normande™

abcdefghijklmnopqrstuvwxyz[äöüßåøæœç]
ABCDEFGHIJKLMNOPQRSTUVWXYZ
1234567890(.,;:?!$&-*){ÄÖÜÅØÆŒÇ}

© Bodoni Poster, Falstaff

▶ Regular
The quick brown fox jumps over a Dog. Zwei Boxkämpfer jagen Eva durch Sylt portez ce

▶ Italic
The quick brown fox jumps over a Dog. Zwei Boxkämpfer jagen Eva durch Sylt portez ce

A401 Mac + PC ②   1980: Aldo Novarese
ITC Novarese®

abcdefghijklmnopqrstuvwxyz[äöüßåøæœç]
ABCDEFGHIJKLMNOPQRSTUVWXYZ
1234567890(.,;:?!$&-*){ÄÖÜÅØÆŒÇ}

© FSI 1993

▼ A401　Mac + PC　ITC Novarese®

aaa
EF1520
ITC Novarese 1, Bk, Bklta, Bd, Bdlta
EF1521
ITC Novarese 2, Med, MedIta, Ult
BT1364
ITC Novarese 1, Bk, Bklta, Bd, Bdlta
BT1365
ITC Novarese 2, Med, MedIta, Ult

▶ Book
The quick brown fox jumps over a Dog. Zwei Boxkämpfer jagen Eva durch Sylt portez ce vieux Whiskey blond qui fume une

▶ Book Italic
The quick brown fox jumps over a Dog. Zwei Boxkämpfer jagen Eva durch Sylt portez ce vieux Whiskey blond qui fume une pipe aber echt

▶ Medium
The quick brown fox jumps over a Dog. Zwei Boxkämpfer jagen Eva durch Sylt portez ce vieux Whiskey blond qui fume

▶ Medium Italic
The quick brown fox jumps over a Dog. Zwei Boxkämpfer jagen Eva durch Sylt portez ce vieux Whiskey blond qui fume une pipe aber echt

▶ Bold
The quick brown fox jumps over a Dog. Zwei Boxkämpfer jagen Eva durch Sylt portez ce vieux Whiskey blond qui fume

▶ Bold Italic
The quick brown fox jumps over a Dog. Zwei Boxkämpfer jagen Eva durch Sylt portez ce vieux Whiskey blond qui fume une

▶ Ultra
The quick brown fox jumps over a Dog. Zwei Boxkämpfer jagen Eva durch Sylt portez ce vieux

---

FB6836　Mac + PC　⑥
Numskill™ Bold

abcdefghijklmnopqrstuvwxyz[äöüßåøæœç]
ABCDEFGHIJKLMNOPQRSTUVWXYZ
1234567890(.,:;?!$&-*){ÄÖÜÅØÆŒÇ}

FB Display Pack 1:
Ecru™ Display, Elli™ Display, Numskill™ Bold, Nutcracker™

A351　Mac + PC
Nuptial Script

Nuptial Script:
Cascade Script, Medici™, Nuptial Script™

A351　Mac + PC　④
Nuptial Script™

abcdefghijklmnopqrstuvwxyz[äöüßåøæœç]
ABCDEFGHIJKLMNOPQRSTUVWXYZ
1234567890(.,:;?!$&-){ÄÖÜÅØÆŒÇ}*

Nuptial Script:
Cascade Script, Medici™, Nuptial Script™
aaa BT1366
Nuptial Script, Reg

© FSI 1993

FB6836 Mac + PC ⑥ ✎ 1993: Richard Lipton

Nutcracker™

abcdefghijklmnopqrstuvwxyz[äöüßåøæœç]
ABCDEFGHIJKLMNOPQRSTUVWXYZ
1234567890(.,;:?!$&-*){ÄÖÜÅØÆŒÇ}

FB Display Pack 1:
Ecru™ Display, Elli™ Display, Numskill™ Bold, Nutcracker™

David Berlow, Boston, USA

Oakland™
E086 MAC + PC ⑤ 1985: Zuzana Licko

ABCDEFGHIJKLMNOPQRSTUVWXYZ
1234567890(.,;:?!$&-*){ÄÖÜÅØÆŒÇ}

Emigre Special

▶ Six
THE QUICK BROWN FOX JUMPS OVER A DOG. ZWEI TECHNOMONSTER JAGEN EVA DURCH BERLIN. PORTEZ CE

▶ Eight
The quick brown fox jumps over a Dog. Zwei Boxkämpfer jagen Eva durch Sylt portez ce vieux Whiskey blond qui fume une pipe aber echt über die

▶ Ten
The quick brown fox jumps over a Dog. Zwei Boxkämpfer jagen Eva durch Sylt portez ce vieux Whiskey blond qui fume une pipe aber echt über die

▶ Fifteen
The quick brown fox jumps over a Dog. Zwei Boxkämpfer jagen Eva durch Sylt portez ce vieux Whiskey blond qui fume une pipe aber echt über die Mauer gesprungen und auch smørebrød en

Obelisk No. 2577™
G1104 MAC + PC ⑥ 1991: Jonn B. Frame

ABCDEFGHIJKLMNOPQRSTUVWXYZ1234567890[ÄÖÜSSÅØÆŒÇ]
ABCDEFGHIJKLMNOPQRSTUVWXYZ(.,;:?!$&-*){ÄÖÜÅØÆŒÇ}

Silhouette, Bureau Empire, Spire No. 377

▶ Regular
THE QUICK BROWN FOX JUMPS OVER A DOG. ZWEI BOXKÄMPFER JAGEN EVA DURCH SYLT PORTEZ CE VIEUX WHISKEY BLOND QUI FUME UNE PIPE ABER ECHT ÜBER DIE MAUER GESPRUNGEN UND AUCH SMØREBRØD EN YSJES NATUURLIJK. BUT VERY LONG SPAZIERENDE TEKST IST USED IN DIESER CATALOG MAAR NICHT SO. DURCH

▶ Oblique
THE QUICK BROWN FOX JUMPS OVER A DOG. ZWEI BOXKÄMPFER JAGEN EVA DURCH SYLT PORTEZ CE VIEUX WHISKEY BLOND QUI FUME UNE PIPE ABER ECHT ÜBER DIE MAUER GESPRUNGEN UND AUCH SMØREBRØD EN YSJES NATUURLIJK. BUT VERY LONG SPAZIERENDE TEKST IST USED IN DIESER CATALOG MAAR NICHT SO. DURCH

Oblong™
E087 MAC + PC ⑤ 1989: Rudy VanderLans, Zuzana Licko

abcdefghijklmnopqrstuvwxyz1234567890[äöüßåøæœç]
ABCDEFGHIJKLMNOPQRSTUVWXYZ[.,;:?!$&-*]{ÄÖÜÅØÆŒÇ}

FF Network, FF Vortex, FF Pop

▶ Regular
The quick brown fox jumps over a Dog. Zwei Boxkämpfer jagen Eva durch Sylt portez ce vieux Whiskey blond qui fume une pipe aber echt über die Mauer gesprungen und auch smørebrød en ysjes natuurlijk.

▶ Bold
The quick brown fox jumps over a Dog. Zwei Boxkämpfer jagen Eva durch Sylt portez ce vieux Whiskey blond qui fume une pipe aber echt über die Mauer gesprungen und auch smørebrød en ysjes

Octavian™
M6413 MAC + PC ② 1961: Will Carter, David Kindersley

abcdefghijklmnopqrstuvwxyz[äöüßåøæœç]
ABCDEFGHIJKLMNOPQRSTUVWXYZ
1234567890(.,;:?!$&-*){ÄÖÜÅØÆŒÇ}

aa*a*
A6338
Octavian, Reg, Ita, RegSC, ItaOSF, RegExp, ItaExp

▶ Regular
The quick brown fox jumps over a Dog. Zwei Boxkämpfer jagen Eva durch Sylt portez ce vieux Whiskey blond qui fume une pipe aber echt über

▶ Italic
The quick brown fox jumps over a Dog. Zwei Boxkämpfer jagen Eva durch Sylt portez ce vieux Whiskey blond qui fume une pipe aber echt

© FSI 1993

▼ M6413　Mac + PC　Octavian™

► Regular SC
THE QUICK BROWN FOX JUMPS OVER A DOG. 123 4567 890 ZWEI BOXKÄMPFER JAGEN EVA DURCH SYLT PORTEZ CE VIEUX WHISKEY BLOND

► Italic OSF
The quick brown fox jumps over a Dog. 123 4567 890 Zwei Boxkämpfer jagen Eva durch Sylt portez ce vieux Whiskey blond qui fume une pipe aber

► Regular Expert
0123456789offiflffiffl-(¹/₁²/₂³/₃⁴/₄⁵/₅⁶/₆⁷/₇⁸/₈⁹/₉⁰/₀)⁽$¢Rp₵⁾ᵃ THE QUICK BROWN FOX JUMPS OVER A DOG ZWEI BOXKÄMPFER JAGEN EVA DURCH

► Italic Expert
0123456789offififlffiffl-(¹/₁²/₂³/₃⁴/₄⁵/₅⁶/₆⁷/₇⁸/₈⁹/₉⁰/₀)⁽$¢Rp₵⁾ᵃ

EF6467　Mac + PC　⑥　✎ 1970: Colin Brignall
Octopuss™

abcdefghijklmnopqrstuvwxyz[äöüßåøæœç]
ABCDEFGHIJKLMNOPQRSTUVWXYZ
1234567890(.,;:?!$&-*)ÄÖÜÅØÆŒÇ

E+F Special Headlines 3:
Hawthorn™, Magnus™ Bold, Octopuss™, Octopuss™ Shaded, Piccadilly™, Stop™

EF6467　Mac + PC　⑥　✎ 1974: Colin Brignall
Octopuss™ Shaded

abcdefghijklmnopqrstuvwxyz[äöüßåøæœç]
ABCDEFGHIJKLMNOPQRSTUVWXYZ
1234567890(.,;:?!$&-*)ÄÖÜÅØÆŒÇ

E+F Special Headlines 3:
Hawthorn™, Magnus™ Bold, Octopuss™, Octopuss™ Shaded, Piccadilly™, Stop™

L2592　Mac　⑥　✎ 1988: Peter O'Donnell
Odessa™

abcdefghijklmnopqrstuvwxyz[äöüßåøæœç]
ABCDEFGHIJKLMNOPQRSTUVWXYZ
1234567890(.,;:?!$&-*)ÄÖÜÅØÆŒÇ

EF6465　Mac + PC　⑥　✎ 1972: Bob Newman
Odin™

abcdefghijklmnopqrstuvwxyz[äöüßåøæœç]
ABCDEFGHIJKLMNOPQRSTUVWXYZ
1234567890(.,;:?!$&-*)ÄÖÜÅØÆŒÇ

E+F Special Headlines 1:
Bernhard Fashion, Candice™, Italia Medium Condensed, Lindsay™, Odin™, Van Dijk

© FSI 1993

EF743 Mac + PC ① 1990: Erik Spiekermann

ITC Officina® Sans

abcdefghijklmnopqrstuvwxyz[äöüßåøæœç]
ABCDEFGHIJKLMNOPQRSTUVWXYZ
1234567890(.,;:?!$&-*){ÄÖÜÅØÆŒÇ}

a a *a*
C2783
ITC Officina Sans/Serif,
SansBk, SansBkIta,
SansBd, SansBdIta,
SerifBk, SerifBkIta,
SerifBd, SerifBdIta
Ⓒ
Bell Centennial, Bell Gothic, FF Meta

▶ Book
The quick brown fox jumps over a Dog. Zwei Boxkämpfer jagen Eva durch Sylt portez ce vieux Whiskey blond qui fume une pipe aber echt

▶ Book Italic
The quick brown fox jumps over a Dog. Zwei Boxkämpfer jagen Eva durch Sylt portez ce vieux Whiskey blond qui fume une pipe aber echt

▶ Bold
The quick brown fox jumps over a Dog. Zwei Boxkämpfer jagen Eva durch Sylt portez ce vieux Whiskey blond qui fume une pipe aber

▶ Bold Italic
The quick brown fox jumps over a Dog. Zwei Boxkämpfer jagen Eva durch Sylt portez ce vieux Whiskey blond qui fume une pipe aber echt

EF744 Mac + PC ③ 1990: Erik Spiekermann (Just van Rossum)

ITC Officina Serif

abcdefghijklmnopqrstuvwxyz[äöüßåøæœç]
ABCDEFGHIJKLMNOPQRSTUVWXYZ
1234567890(.,;:?!$&-*){ÄÖÜÅØÆŒÇ}

a a *a*
C2783
ITC Officina Sans/Serif,
SansBk, SansBkIta,
SansBd, SansBdIta,
SerifBk, SerifBkIta,
SerifBd, SerifBdIta

▶ Book
The quick brown fox jumps over a Dog. Zwei Boxkämpfer jagen Eva durch Sylt portez ce vieux Whiskey blond qui fume une pipe aber echt

▶ Book Italic
The quick brown fox jumps over a Dog. Zwei Boxkämpfer jagen Eva durch Sylt portez ce vieux Whiskey blond qui fume une pipe aber echt

▶ Bold
The quick brown fox jumps over a Dog. Zwei Boxkämpfer jagen Eva durch Sylt portez ce vieux Whiskey blond qui fume une

▶ Bold Italic
The quick brown fox jumps over a Dog. Zwei Boxkämpfer jagen Eva durch Sylt portez ce vieux Whiskey blond qui fume une pipe aber

BT1367 Mac + PC ⑥

Old Dreadful No. 7™

abcdefghijklmnopqrstuvwxyz[äöüßåøæœç]
ABCDEFGHIJKLMNOPQRSTUVWXYZ
1234567890(.,;:?!$&-*){ÄÖÜÅØÆŒÇ}

M226 Mac + PC ⑦ (Cowan, M. F. Benton, 1901)

Old English™ Text

abcdefghijklmnopqrstuvwxyz[äöüßåøæœç]
ABCDEFGHIJKLMNOPQRSTUVWXYZ
1234567890(.,;:?!$&-*){ÄÖÜÅØÆŒÇ}

Headliners 4:
Inflex™, Monotype Old Style Bold Outline™, Old English™ Text
a a *a* C6568
Agfa Scripts 1

© FSI 1993

M276 Mac + PC (Alexander Phemister, 1860)
Old Style

abcdefghijklmnopqrstuvwxyz[äöüßåøæœç]
ABCDEFGHIJKLMNOPQRSTUVWXYZ
1234567890(.,;:?!$&-*){ÄÖÜÅØÆŒÇ}

▶ Regular
The quick brown fox jumps over a Dog. Zwei Boxkämpfer jagen Eva durch Sylt portez ce vieux Whiskey blond qui fume

▶ Italic
The quick brown fox jumps over a Dog. Zwei Boxkämpfer jagen Eva durch Sylt portez ce vieux Whiskey blond qui fume une

▶ Bold
The quick brown fox jumps over a Dog. Zwei Boxkämpfer jagen Eva durch Sylt portez ce vieux Whiskey

▶ Bold Italic
The quick brown fox jumps over a Dog. Zwei Boxkämpfer jagen Eva durch Sylt portez ce vieux Whiskey

M226 Mac + PC (Alexander Phemister, 1860)
Monotype Old Style Bold Outline™

abcdefghijklmnopqrstuvwxyz[äöüßåøæœç]
ABCDEFGHIJKLMNOPQRSTUVWXYZ
1234567890(.,;:?!$&-*){ÄÖÜÅØÆŒÇ}

Headliners 4:
Inflex™, Monotype Old Style Bold Outline™, Old English™ Text
aaa M6330
Falstaff et al
A6087 Falstaff et al

A2538 Mac + PC (c. 1870)
Old Style No. 7™

abcdefghijklmnopqrstuvwxyz[äöüßåøæœç]
ABCDEFGHIJKLMNOPQRSTUVWXYZ
1234567890(.,;:?!$&-*){ÄÖÜÅØÆŒÇ}

Century Old Style

▶ Regular
The quick brown fox jumps over a Dog. Zwei Boxkämpfer jagen Eva durch Sylt portez ce vieux Whiskey blond qui fume

▶ Regular Small Caps
THE QUICK BROWN FOX JUMPS OVER A DOG. 123 4567 890 ZWEI BOXKÄMPFER JAGEN EVA DURCH SYLT PORTEZ CE VIEUX

▶ Italic
The quick brown fox jumps over a Dog. Zwei Boxkämpfer jagen Eva durch Sylt portez ce vieux Whiskey blond qui fume une

▶ Italic Small Caps
The quick brown fox jumps over a Dog. 123 4567 890 Zwei Boxkämpfer jagen Eva durch Sylt portez ce vieux Whiskey blond

© FSI 1993

EF1064 Mac + PC ⑥
Old Towne No 536™

abcdefghijklmnopqrstuvwxyz1234567890[äöüßåøæœç]
ABCDEFGHIJKLMNOPQRSTUVWXYZ(.,;:?!$&-*){ÄÖÜÅØÆŒÇ}

Baskerville Old Face:
Baskerville Old Face™, Old Towne No 536™

EF521 Mac + PC ①
Olympia™

abcdefghijklmnopqrstuvwxyz[äöüßåøæœç]
ABCDEFGHIJKLMNOPQRSTUVWXYZ
1234567890(.,;:?!$&-*){ÄÖÜÅØÆŒÇ}

ITC American Typewriter, Courier, Monanti, Schreibmaschinenschrift, Prestige, Typewriter, Pica

▶ Light
The quick brown fox jumps over a Dog. Zwei Boxkämpfer jagen Eva durch Sylt portez ce vieux Whiskey blond qui

▶ Semi bold
The quick brown fox jumps over a Dog. Zwei Boxkämpfer jagen Eva durch Sylt portez ce vieux Whiskey blond qui

A892 Mac + PC ② 1970: Matthew Carter
Olympian™

abcdefghijklmnopqrstuvwxyz[äöüßåøæœç]
ABCDEFGHIJKLMNOPQRSTUVWXYZ
1234567890(.,;:?!$&-*){ÄÖÜÅØÆŒÇ}

aa*a*
BT945
Olympian: Rom, Ita, Bd, BdIta
Aurora, Corona, Excelsior, Imperial, Ionic, Textype

▶ Roman
The quick brown fox jumps over a Dog. Zwei Boxkämpfer jagen Eva durch Sylt portez ce vieux Whiskey

▶ Italic
The quick brown fox jumps over a Dog. Zwei Boxkämpfer jagen Eva durch Sylt portez ce vieux Whiskey

▶ Bold
The quick brown fox jumps over a Dog. Zwei Boxkämpfer jagen Eva durch Sylt portez ce vieux Whiskey

▶ Bold Italic
The quick brown fox jumps over a Dog. Zwei Boxkämpfer jagen Eva durch Sylt portez ce vieux Whiskey

A996 Mac + PC ⑦ 1990: Karlgeorg Hoefer
Omnia™

abcdefghijklmnopqrstuvwxyz
1234567890(.,;:?!$&-*)[]{ÄÖÜÅØÆŒÇ}

Type Before Gutenberg 1:
Duc De Berry™, Herculanum™, Omnia™
American Uncial, Electric Uncial, Libra

© FSI 1993

BT762 Mac + PC ⑦ — 1954: Adrian Frutiger — Industry name
Formal 421 — Ondine™

abcdefghijklmnopqrstuvwxyz[äöüßåøæœç]
ABCDEFGHIJKLMNOPQRSTUVWXYZ
1234567890(.,;:?!$&-*){ÄÖÜÅØÆŒÇ}

Bitstream Brush 1:
Bison™, Lydian Cursive, Ondine™, Palette™

L2593 Mac ④ — 1984: Paul Clarke
One Stroke™ Script

abcdefghijklmnopqrstuvwxyz[äöüßåøæœç]
ABCDEFGHIJKLMNOPQRSTUVWXYZ
1234567890(.,;:?!$&-*)ÄÖÜÅØÆŒÇ

L2594 Mac ④ — 1986: Paul Clarke
One Stroke Script Bold

abcdefghijklmnopqrstuvwxyz[äöüßåøæœç]
ABCDEFGHIJKLMNOPQRSTUVWXYZ
1234567890(.,;:?!$&-*)ÄÖÜÅØÆŒÇ

L2595 Mac ④ — 1987: Paul Clarke
One Stroke Script Shaded

abcdefghijklmnopqrstuvwxyz[äöüßåøæœç]
ABCDEFGHIJKLMNOPQRSTUVWXYZ
1234567890(.,;:?!$&-*)ÄÖÜÅØÆŒÇ

M2954 Mac + PC ② — 1937: Gerry Powell
Onyx™

abcdefghijklmnopqrstuvwxyz1234567890[äöüßåøæœç]
ABCDEFGHIJKLMNOPQRSTUVWXYZ(.,;:?!$&-*){ÄÖÜÅØÆŒÇ}

Latin/Runic/Onyx:
Latin Condensed, Onyx™, Runic Condensed
aaa ⌨ M196
Bodoni (Monotype) 2
⌨ A2867

BT1419 Mac + PC ① — 1958: Hermann Zapf — Industry name
Zapf Humanist 601 — Optima™ 3

abcdefghijklmnopqrstuvwxyz[äöüßåøæœç]
ABCDEFGHIJKLMNOPQRSTUVWXYZ
1234567890(.,;:?!$&-*){ÄÖÜÅØÆŒÇ}

▼ BT1419 Mac + PC Optima™ 3

aaa
A089
Optima, Reg, Obl, Bd, BdObl

▶ Regular
The quick brown fox jumps over a Dog. Zwei Boxkämpfer jagen Eva durch Sylt portez ce vieux Whiskey blond qui fume une

▶ Italic
The quick brown fox jumps over a Dog. Zwei Boxkämpfer jagen Eva durch Sylt portez ce vieux Whiskey blond qui fume une

▶ Bold
The quick brown fox jumps over a Dog. Zwei Boxkämpfer jagen Eva durch Sylt portez ce vieux Whiskey blond qui fume

▶ Bold Italic
The quick brown fox jumps over a Dog. Zwei Boxkämpfer jagen Eva durch Sylt portez ce vieux Whiskey blond qui fume

BT842 Mac + PC   ①   ⬚ 1968: Hermann Zapf   Industry name
Zapf Humanist Demi   **Optima 1**

abcdefghijklmnopqrstuvwxyz[äöüßåøæœç]
ABCDEFGHIJKLMNOPQRSTUVWXYZ
1234567890(.,;:?!$&-*){ÄÖÜÅØÆŒÇ}

▶ Demi
The quick brown fox jumps over a Dog. Zwei Boxkämpfer jagen Eva durch Sylt portez ce vieux Whiskey blond qui fume

▶ Demi Italic
The quick brown fox jumps over a Dog. Zwei Boxkämpfer jagen Eva durch Sylt portez ce vieux Whiskey blond qui fume

BT843 Mac + PC   ①   ⬚ 1968: Hermann Zapf   Industry name
Zapf Humanist Ultra   **Optima 2**

**abcdefghijklmnopqrstuvwxyz[äöüßåøæœç]
ABCDEFGHIJKLMNOPQRSTUVWXYZ
1234567890(.,;:?!$&-*){ÄÖÜÅØÆŒÇ}**

▶ Ultra
The quick brown fox jumps over a Dog. Zwei Boxkämpfer jagen Eva durch Sylt portez ce vieux Whiskey blond qui fume

▶ Ultra Italic
The quick brown fox jumps over a Dog. Zwei Boxkämpfer jagen Eva durch Sylt portez ce vieux Whiskey blond qui fume

BT6420 Mac + PC   ③   ⬚ 1992: Gerard Unger
Oranda™

abcdefghijklmnopqrstuvwxyz[äöüßåøæœç]
ABCDEFGHIJKLMNOPQRSTUVWXYZ
1234567890(.,;:?!$&-*){ÄÖÜÅØÆŒÇ}

©
Bitstream Charter, Demos, Hollander, Swift

▶ Roman
The quick brown fox jumps over a Dog. Zwei Boxkämpfer jagen Eva durch Sylt portez ce vieux Whiskey blond qui fume une pipe aber

▶ Italic
The quick brown fox jumps over a Dog. Zwei Boxkämpfer jagen Eva durch Sylt portez ce vieux Whiskey blond qui fume une pipe aber echt

▶ Bold
The quick brown fox jumps over a Dog. Zwei Boxkämpfer jagen Eva durch Sylt portez ce vieux Whiskey blond qui fume une

▶ Bold Italic
The quick brown fox jumps over a Dog. Zwei Boxkämpfer jagen Eva durch Sylt portez ce vieux Whiskey blond qui fume une pipe aber echt

▼ BT6420 Mac + PC Oranda™

▶ Roman Condensed
The quick brown fox jumps over a Dog. Zwei Boxkämpfer jagen Eva durch Sylt portez ce vieux Whiskey blond qui fume une pipe aber echt

▶ Bold Condensed
The quick brown fox jumps over a Dog. Zwei Boxkämpfer jagen Eva durch Sylt portez ce vieux Whiskey blond qui fume une pipe

MC6353 Mac + PC ② 1962: L. H. D. Smit
Orator

abcdefghijklmnopqrstuvwxyz[äöüßåøæœç]
ABCDEFGHIJKLMNOPQRSTUVWXYZ
1234567890(.,:;?!$&-*){ÄÖÜÅØÆŒÇ}

A090 Mac + PC ①
Orator

ABCDEFGHIJKLMNOPQRSTUVWXYZ[ÄÖÜßÅØÆŒÇ]
ABCDEFGHIJKLMNOPQRSTUVWXYZ
1234567890(.,:;?!$&-*){ÄÖÜÅØÆŒÇ}

Letter Gothic, Olympia

▶ Regular
THE QUICK BROWN FOX JUMPS OVER A DOG. ZWEI BOXKÄMPFER JAGEN EVA DURCH SYLT PORTEZ CE VIEUX WHISKEY

▶ Slanted
THE QUICK BROWN FOX JUMPS OVER A DOG. ZWEI BOXKÄMPFER JAGEN EVA DURCH SYLT PORTEZ CE VIEUX WHISKEY

BT1369 Mac + PC ①
Orator

abcdefghijklmnopqrstuvwxyz[äöüßåøæœç]
ABCDEFGHIJKLMNOPQRSTUVWXYZ
1234567890(.,:;?!$&-*){ÄÖÜÅØÆŒÇ}

Letter Gothic, Olympia

▶ 10 Pitch
The quick brown fox jumps over a Dog. Zwei Boxkämpfer jagen Eva durch Sylt portez ce

▶ 15 Pitch
The quick brown fox jumps over a Dog. Zwei Boxkämpfer jagen Eva durch Sylt portez ce vieux Whiskey blond qui fume une pipe aber echt über die

BT781 Mac + PC ⑤ 1972: S. Biggenden
Orbit-B™

abcdefghijklmnopqrstuvwxyz[äöüßåøæœç]
ABCDEFGHIJKLMNOPQRSTUVWXYZ
1234567890(.,:;?!$&-*){ÄÖÜÅØÆŒÇ}

Bitstream Computer:
Amelia™, Orbit-B™
Data 70, Computer

MC2932 Mac + PC ⑥
Organda™

ABCDEFGHIJKLMNOPQRSTUVWXYZ
1234567890(.,;:?!$&-*)[]{ÃÖÜÅØÆŒÇ}

MC2933 Mac + PC ⑥
Organda Bold

ABCDEFGHIJKLMNOPQRSTUVWXYZ
1234567890(.,;:?!$&-*)[]{ÃÖÜÅØÆŒÇ}

C6568 Mac + PC ④
Original Script™

abcdefghijklmnopqrstuvwxyz[äöüßåç]
ABCDEFGHIJKLMNOPQRSTUVWXYZ
1234567890[.,;:?!$ &-*){ÄÖÜÅthst Ç}

Agfa Scripts 1:
Commercial Script, Helinda Rook™, Old English Text, Original Script™, Quill™, Stuyvesant2, Wedding Text

C1012 Mac + PC ②
Orlando Caps

ABCDEFGHIJKLMNOPQRSTUVWXYZ
1234567890(.,:?!$&-*)[]◊ÄÖÜ ÅØÆŒÇ♦

Headlines 84S:
Bernhard Modern, Beton Extra Bold, Metropolis Bold, Modern No. 20, Orlando Caps, PL Davison Americana, PL Westerveldt Light, Siena™ Black, TC Europa™ Bold, TC Jasper™

L6136 Mac ⑥ ✎ 1986: Freda Sack
Orlando™

ABCDEFGHIJKLMNOPQRSTUVWXYZ
1234567890(.,;:?!$&-*)[]ÄÖÜÅØÆŒÇ

MC2905 Mac + PC ⑥ ✎ J. H. Crook
Ortem™

ABCDEFGHIJKLMNOPQRSTUVWXYZ
1234567890(.,;:?!$&-*)[]{ÄÖÜÅØÆŒÇ}

© FSI 1993

C2521 Mac + PC ④ ✎ 1989: Arthur Baker
Oxford™

abcdefghijklmnopqrstuvwxyz[äöüßåøæœç]
ABCDEFGHIJKLMNOPQRSTUVWXYZ
1234567890(.,;:?!$&-*){ÄÖÜÅØÆŒÇ}

Amigo:
Amigo™, Marigold™, Oxford™, Pelican™, Visigoth

F2947 Mac ⑥
Oz Brush

Oz Brush:
Oz Brush™, Oz Poster™

F2947 Mac ⑥ ✎ 1990-91: (Ozwald B. Cooper) Robert McLamant
Oz Brush™

abcdefghijklmnopqrstuvwxyz[äöüß åøæœç]
ABCDEFGHIJKLMNOPQRSTUVWXYZ
1234567890(.,;:?!$&-*){ÄÖÜÅøÆŒÇ}

▶ Regular
The quick brown fox jumps over a Dog. Zwei Boxkämpfer jagen Eva durch Sylt portez ce vieux Whiskey blond qui fume une pipe aber echt über die Mauer

▶ Italic
The quick brown fox jumps over a Dog. Zwei Boxkämpfer jagen Eva durch Sylt portez ce vieux Whiskey blond qui fume une pipe aber echt über die Mauer

Oz Brush:
Oz Brush™, Oz Poster™

BT1093 Mac + PC ④ ✎ 1991: (Oz Cooper) George Ryan
Bitstream Oz Handicraft™

abcdefghijklmnopqrstuvwxyz1234567890[äöüßåøæœç]
ABCDEFGHIJKLMNOPQRSTUVWXYZ(.,;:?!$&-*){ÄÖÜÅØÆŒÇ}

F2947 Mac ⑥ ✎ 1990-91: (Ozwald B. Cooper) Robert McLamant
Oz Poster™

abcdefghijklmnopqrstuvwxyz[äöüßåøæœç]
ABCDEFGHIJKLMNOPQRSTUVWXYZ
1234567890(.,;:?!$&-*){ÄÖÜÅØÆŒÇ}

▶ Regular
The quick brown fox jumps over a Dog. Zwei Boxkämpfer jagen Eva durch Sylt portez ce vieux Whiskey blond qui fume une

▶ Condensed
The quick brown fox jumps over a Dog. Zwei Boxkämpfer jagen Eva durch Sylt portez ce vieux Whiskey blond qui fume une pipe aber echt über die

© FSI 1993

▼ F2947   Mac   Oz Poster™

Oz Brush:
Oz Brush™, Oz Poster™

EF6463   Mac + PC   ⑥   ✏ 1992: (Oz Cooper) Dave Farey
ITC Ozwald™

abcdefghijklmnopqrstuvwxyz[äöüßåøæœç]
ABCDEFGHIJKLMNOPQRSTUVWXYZ
1234567890(.,;:?!$&-*)(ÄÖÜÅØÆŒÇ)

ITC Mona Lisa Solid / ITC Ozwald:
ITC Mona Lisa Solid™, ITC Ozwald™

© FSI 1993

O 11

Paul Sych, Toronto, Ontario, CDN

G939 Mac + PC — 1902: F. W. Goudy
Pabst Oldstyle No. 45

abcdefghijklmnopqrstuvwxyz[äöüßåøæœç]
ABCDEFGHIJKLMNOPQRSTUVWXYZ
1234567890(.,;:?!$&-*){ÄÖÜÅØÆŒÇ}

EF402 Mac + PC — 1987: Vincent Pacella
ITC Pacella® 1

abcdefghijklmnopqrstuvwxyz[äöüßåøæœç]
ABCDEFGHIJKLMNOPQRSTUVWXYZ
1234567890(.,;:?!$&-*){ÄÖÜÅØÆŒÇ}

aaa
C990
ITC Pacella, Bk, BkIta,
Med, MedIta, Bd,
BdIta, Blk, BlkIta

▶ Book
The quick brown fox jumps over a Dog. Zwei Boxkämpfer jagen Eva durch Sylt portez ce vieux Whiskey blond qui fume une pipe aber

▶ Book Italic
The quick brown fox jumps over a Dog. Zwei Boxkämpfer jagen Eva durch Sylt portez ce vieux Whiskey blond qui fume une pipe aber echt

▶ Bold
The quick brown fox jumps over a Dog. Zwei Boxkämpfer jagen Eva durch Sylt portez ce vieux Whiskey blond qui fume une

▶ Bold Italic
The quick brown fox jumps over a Dog. Zwei Boxkämpfer jagen Eva durch Sylt portez ce vieux Whiskey blond qui fume une

EF403 Mac + PC — 1987: Vincent Pacella
ITC Pacella 2

abcdefghijklmnopqrstuvwxyz[äöüßåøæœç]
ABCDEFGHIJKLMNOPQRSTUVWXYZ
1234567890(.,;:?!$&-*){ÄÖÜÅØÆŒÇ}

aaa
C990
ITC Pacella, Bk, BkIta,
Med, MedIta, Bd,
BdIta, Blk, BlkIta

▶ Medium
The quick brown fox jumps over a Dog. Zwei Boxkämpfer jagen Eva durch Sylt portez ce vieux Whiskey blond qui fume une

▶ Medium Italic
The quick brown fox jumps over a Dog. Zwei Boxkämpfer jagen Eva durch Sylt portez ce vieux Whiskey blond qui fume une pipe aber

▶ Black
The quick brown fox jumps over a Dog. Zwei Boxkämpfer jagen Eva durch Sylt portez ce vieux Whiskey blond qui fume

▶ Black Italic
The quick brown fox jumps over a Dog. Zwei Boxkämpfer jagen Eva durch Sylt portez ce vieux Whiskey blond qui fume

EF540 Mac + PC — 1987: Vincent Pacella
ITC Pacella Small Caps

ABCDEFGHIJKLMNOPQRSTUVWXYZ[ÄÖÜSSÅØÆŒÇ]
ABCDEFGHIJKLMNOPQRSTUVWXYZ
1234567890(.,;:?!$&-*){ÄÖÜÅØÆŒÇ}

▶ Small Caps Book
THE QUICK BROWN FOX JUMPS OVER A DOG. 123 4567 890 ZWEI BOXKÄMPFER JAGEN EVA DURCH SYLT PORTEZ CE VIEUX WHISKEY BLOND

▶ Small Caps Medium
THE QUICK BROWN FOX JUMPS OVER A DOG. 123 4567 890 ZWEI BOXKÄMPFER JAGEN EVA DURCH SYLT PORTEZ CE VIEUX WHISKEY BLOND

© FSI 1993

Paddington™
EF6471 Mac + PC

abcdefghijklmnopqrstuvwxyz[äöüßåøæœç]
ABCDEFGHIJKLMNOPQRSTUVWXYZ
1234567890(.,;:?!$&-*)ÄÖÜÅØÆŒÇ

E+F Special Headlines 7:
Harlow™, Harlow Solid, Horndon™, Koloss, Paddington™, Stentor™

A*I Painter™
F6344 Mac

ABCDEFGHIJKLMNOPQRSTUVWXYZ
ABCDEFGHIJKLMNOPQRSTUVWXYZ
1234567890(.,;:?!$&-*)[ ]{ }

A*I Wood Types 1:
A*I Barrel, A*I Box Gothic, A*I French XXX Condensed™, A*I Painter™, A*I Tuscan Egyptian™, Antique Condensed

Palace Script™
M264 Mac + PC

abcdefghijklmnopqrstuvwxyz[äöüßåøæœç]
ABCDEFGHIJKLMNOPQRSTUVWXYZ
1234567890(.,;:?!$&-*){ÄÖÜÅØÆŒÇ}

Script 2:
Ashley Script, Monoline Script™, New Berolina, Palace Script™
Englische Schreibschrift, Flemish Script, Embassy, Kuenstler Script

Palatino™
A091 Mac + PC — 1948: Hermann Zapf

abcdefghijklmnopqrstuvwxyz[äöüßåøæœç]
ABCDEFGHIJKLMNOPQRSTUVWXYZ
1234567890(.,;:?!$&-*){ÄÖÜÅØÆŒÇ}

aaa
BT1415
Palatino, Reg, Ita, Bd, BdIta
Aldus, Zapf Renaissance

▶ Regular
The quick brown fox jumps over a Dog. Zwei Boxkämpfer jagen Eva durch Sylt portez ce vieux Whiskey blond qui fume

▶ Italic
The quick brown fox jumps over a Dog. Zwei Boxkämpfer jagen Eva durch Sylt portez ce vieux Whiskey blond qui fume une pipe aber

▶ Bold
The quick brown fox jumps over a Dog. Zwei Boxkämpfer jagen Eva durch Sylt portez ce vieux Whiskey blond qui

▶ Bold Italic
The quick brown fox jumps over a Dog. Zwei Boxkämpfer jagen Eva durch Sylt portez ce vieux Whiskey blond qui fume

© FSI 1993

A6072　Mac + PC　② 　1948: Hermann Zapf
Palatino 2

abcdefghijklmnopqrstuvwxyz[äöüßåøæœç]
ABCDEFGHIJKLMNOPQRSTUVWXYZ
1234567890(.,;:?!$&-*){ÄÖÜÅØÆŒÇ}

aa*a*
BT1415
Palatino, Reg, Ita, Bd, BdIta
©
Aldus, Zapf Renaissance

▶ Light
The quick brown fox jumps over a Dog. Zwei Boxkämpfer jagen Eva durch Sylt portez ce vieux Whiskey blond qui fume une

▶ Light Italic
The quick brown fox jumps over a Dog. Zwei Boxkämpfer jagen Eva durch Sylt portez ce vieux Whiskey blond qui fume une pipe aber echt

▶ Medium
The quick brown fox jumps over a Dog. Zwei Boxkämpfer jagen Eva durch Sylt portez ce vieux Whiskey blond qui fume une

▶ Medium Italic
The quick brown fox jumps over a Dog. Zwei Boxkämpfer jagen Eva durch Sylt portez ce vieux Whiskey blond qui fume une

▶ Black
The quick brown fox jumps over a Dog. Zwei Boxkämpfer jagen Eva durch Sylt portez ce vieux Whiskey

▶ Black Italic
The quick brown fox jumps over a Dog. Zwei Boxkämpfer jagen Eva durch Sylt portez ce vieux Whiskey

A1031　Mac + PC　②　1948: Hermann Zapf
Palatino Small Caps/OSF

ABCDEFGHIJKLMNOPQRSTUVWXYZ[ÄÖÜSSÅØÆŒÇ]
ABCDEFGHIJKLMNOPQRSTUVWXYZ
1234567890(.,;:?!$&-*){ÄÖÜÅØÆŒÇ}

©
Aldus, Zapf Renaissance

▶ Small Caps OSF
THE QUICK BROWN FOX JUMPS OVER A DOG. 123 4567 890 ZWEI BOXKÄMPFER JAGEN EVA DURCH SYLT PORTEZ CE VIEUX WHISKEY

▶ Italic OSF
The quick brown fox jumps over a Dog. 123 4567 890 Zwei Boxkämpfer jagen Eva durch Sylt portez ce vieux Whiskey blond qui

▶ Bold OSF
The quick brown fox jumps over a Dog. 123 4567 890 Zwei Boxkämpfer jagen Eva durch Sylt portez ce vieux Whiskey

▶ Bold Italic OSF
The quick brown fox jumps over a Dog. 123 4567 890 Zwei Boxkämpfer jagen Eva durch Sylt portez ce vieux Whiskey

SG2301　Mac　②　1948: Hermann Zapf　　　Industry name
Parlament　　　　　　　　　　　　　　Palatino Heavy

abcdefghijklmnopqrstuvwxyz[äöüßåøæœç]
ABCDEFGHIJKLMNOPQRSTUVWXYZ
1234567890(.,;:?!$&-*)ÄÖÜÅØÆŒÇ

| SG2302 | Mac | ② | 🖉 1948: Hermann Zapf | Industry name |

Paxim — Palatino Headline

abcdefghijklmnopqrstuvwxyz[äöüßåøæœç]
ABCDEFGHIJKLMNOPQRSTUVWXYZ
1234567890(.,;:?!$&-*)ÄÖÜÅØÆŒÇ

| SG2303 | Mac | ② | 🖉 1948: Hermann Zapf | Industry name |

Paxim Bold — Palatino Headline Bold

abcdefghijklmnopqrstuvwxyz[äöüßåøæœç]
ABCDEFGHIJKLMNOPQRSTUVWXYZ
1234567890(.,;:?!$&-*)ÄÖÜÅØÆŒÇ

| BT762 | Mac + PC | ④ | 🖉 1953: Martin Wilke | Industry name |

Brush 445 — Palette™

abcdefghijklmnopqrstuvwxyz[äöüßåøæœç]
ABCDEFGHIJKLMNOPQRSTUVWXYZ
1234567890(.,;:?!$&-){ÄÖÜÅØÆŒÇ}*

Bitstream Brush 1:
Bison™, Lydian Cursive, Ondine™, Palette™

| EF404 | Mac + PC | ① | 🖉 1988: Ed Benguiat | |

ITC Panache® 1

abcdefghijklmnopqrstuvwxyz(äöüßåøæœç)
ABCDEFGHIJKLMNOPQRSTUVWXYZ
1234567890(.,;:?!$&-*){ÄÖÜÅØÆŒÇ}

▶ Book
The quick brown fox jumps over a Dog. Zwei Boxkämpfer jagen Eva durch Sylt portez ce vieux Whiskey blond qui fume une

▶ Bold
The quick brown fox jumps over a Dog. Zwei Boxkämpfer jagen Eva durch Sylt portez ce vieux Whiskey blond qui fume

▶ Black
The quick brown fox jumps over a Dog. Zwei Boxkämpfer jagen Eva durch Sylt portez ce vieux Whiskey

| EF405 | Mac + PC | ① | 🖉 1988: Ed Benguiat | |

ITC Panache 2

abcdefghijklmnopqrstuvwxyz(äöüßåøæœç)
ABCDEFGHIJKLMNOPQRSTUVWXYZ
1234567890(.,;:?!$&-){ÄÖÜÅØÆŒÇ}*

© FSI 1993

▼ EF405 Mac + PC   ITC Panache 2

► Book Italic
The quick brown fox jumps over a Dog. Zwei Boxkämpfer jagen Eva durch Sylt portez ce vieux Whiskey blond qui fume une pipe aber

► Bold Italic
The quick brown fox jumps over a Dog. Zwei Boxkämpfer jagen Eva durch Sylt portez ce vieux Whiskey blond qui fume

► Black Italic
The quick brown fox jumps over a Dog. Zwei Boxkämpfer jagen Eva durch Sylt portez ce vieux Whiskey

EF541 Mac + PC   ① 🖉 1988: Ed Benguiat
ITC Panache Small Caps

ABCDEFGHIJKLMNOPQRSTUVWXYZ(ÄÖÜSSÅØÆŒÇ)
ABCDEFGHIJKLMNOPQRSTUVWXYZ
1234567890(.,;:?!$&-*){ÄÖÜÅØÆŒÇ}

► Book Small Caps
THE QUICK BROWN FOX JUMPS OVER A DOG. 123 4567 890 ZWEI BOXKÄMPFER JAGEN EVA DURCH SYLT PORTEZ CE VIEUX WHISKEY BLOND

► Bold Small Caps
THE QUICK BROWN FOX JUMPS OVER A DOG. 123 4567 890 ZWEI BOXKÄMPFER JAGEN EVA DURCH SYLT PORTEZ CE VIEUX

L6137 Mac   ⑥ 🖉 1983: Chris Costello
Papyrus™

abcdefghijklmnopqrstuvwxyz[äöüßåøæœç]
ABCDEFGHIJKLMNOPQRSTUVWXYZ
1234567890(.,;:?!$&-*)ÄÖÜÅØÆŒÇ

A350 Mac + PC
Parisian / Umbra

Parisian / Umbra:
Parisian™, Umbra™

A350 Mac + PC   ⑥ 🖉 1928: M. F. Benton
Parisian™

abcdefghijklmnopqrstuvwxyz[äöüßåøæœç]
ABCDEFGHIJKLMNOPQRSTUVWXYZ
1234567890(.,;:?!$&-*){ÄÖÜÅØÆŒÇ}

Parisian / Umbra:
Parisian™, Umbra™
aaa BT1370
Parisian, Reg, C2777 Headlines 89S

© FSI 1993

P 5

A092 Mac + PC ④ 🖉 1933: Robert E. Smith
Park Avenue™

abcdefghijklmnopqrstuvwxyz[äöüßåøæœç]
ABCDEFGHIJKLMNOPQRSTUVWXYZ
1234567890(.,;:?!$&-*){ÄÖÜÅØÆŒÇ}

C616 Mac + PC ② 🖉 1975: Tony Stan
Pasquale™

abcdefghijklmnopqrstuvwxyz[äöüßåøæœç]
ABCDEFGHIJKLMNOPQRSTUVWXYZ
1234567890(.,;:?!$&-*){ÄÖÜÅØÆŒÇ}

▶ **Light**
The quick brown fox jumps over a Dog. Zwei Boxkämpfer jagen Eva durch Sylt portez ce vieux Whiskey blond qui fume une

▶ *Light Italic*
The quick brown fox jumps over a Dog. Zwei Boxkämpfer jagen Eva durch Sylt portez ce vieux Whiskey blond qui fume une

▶ **Book**
The quick brown fox jumps over a Dog. Zwei Boxkämpfer jagen Eva durch Sylt portez ce vieux Whiskey blond qui fume

▶ *Book Italic*
The quick brown fox jumps over a Dog. Zwei Boxkämpfer jagen Eva durch Sylt portez ce vieux Whiskey blond qui fume

▶ **Medium**
The quick brown fox jumps over a Dog. Zwei Boxkämpfer jagen Eva durch Sylt portez ce vieux Whiskey blond qui

▶ *Medium Italic*
The quick brown fox jumps over a Dog. Zwei Boxkämpfer jagen Eva durch Sylt portez ce vieux Whiskey blond qui

▶ **Bold**
The quick brown fox jumps over a Dog. Zwei Boxkämpfer jagen Eva durch Sylt portez ce vieux Whiskey blond

▶ *Bold Italic*
The quick brown fox jumps over a Dog. Zwei Boxkämpfer jagen Eva durch Sylt portez ce vieux Whiskey blond

A093 Mac + PC ⑥ 🖉 1937: Adolphe Mouron Cassandre
Peignot™

abcdefghijklmnopqrstuvwxyz[äöüßåøæœç]
ABCDEFGHIJKLMNOPQRSTUVWXYZ
1234567890(.,;:?!$&-*){ÄÖÜÅØÆŒÇ}

aaa
BT1291
Peignot, Lt, Demibold, Bd

▶ **Light**
The quick brown fox jumps over a Dog. Zwei Boxkämpfer jagen Eva durch Sylt portez ce vieux Whiskey blond qui fume une pipe aber echt

▶ **Demi**
The quick brown fox jumps over a Dog. Zwei Boxkämpfer jagen Eva durch Sylt portez ce vieux Whiskey blond qui fume une pipe aber echt

▶ **Bold**
The quick brown fox jumps over a Dog. Zwei Boxkämpfer jagen Eva durch Sylt portez ce vieux Whiskey blond qui fume une pipe

© FSI 1993

C2521 Mac + PC — 1989: Arthur Baker
Pelican™

abcdefghijklmnopqrstuvwxyz[äöüßåøæœç]
ABCDEFGHIJKLMNOPQRSTUVWXYZ
1234567890(.,;:?!$&-*){ÄÖÜÅØÆŒÇ}

Amigo:
Amigo™, Marigold™, Oxford™, Pelican™, Visigoth

L6138 Mac — 1981: Martin Wait
Pendry™ Script

abcdefghijklmnopqrstuvwxyz[äöüßåøæœç]
ABCDEFGHIJKLMNOPQRSTUVWXYZ
1234567890(.,;:?!$&-*)ÄÖÜÅØÆŒÇ

M263 Mac + PC — 1959: Imre Reiner
Pepita®

abcdefghijklmnopqrstuvwxyz[äöüßåøæœç]
ABCDEFGHIJKLMNOPQRSTUVWXYZ
1234567890(.,;:?!$&-*){ÄÖÜÅØÆŒÇ}

Script 1:
Biffo™ Script, Dorchester Script™, Monotype Script Bold™, Pepita®, Swing™ Bold
aaa A6071
Dorchester Script, et al MT

M240 Mac + PC — 1928–35: Eric Gill
Perpetua®

abcdefghijklmnopqrstuvwxyz[äöüßåøæœç]
ABCDEFGHIJKLMNOPQRSTUVWXYZ
1234567890(.,;:?!$&-*){ÄÖÜÅØÆŒÇ}

aaa
A1030
Perpetua, Reg, Ita, Bd, BdIta
BT1347
Perpetua, Reg, Ita, Bd, BdIta, Blk

▶ Regular
The quick brown fox jumps over a Dog. Zwei Boxkämpfer jagen Eva durch Sylt portez ce vieux Whiskey blond qui fume une pipe aber echt

▶ Italic
The quick brown fox jumps over a Dog. Zwei Boxkämpfer jagen Eva durch Sylt portez ce vieux Whiskey blond qui fume une pipe aber echt über die Mauer

▶ Bold
The quick brown fox jumps over a Dog. Zwei Boxkämpfer jagen Eva durch Sylt portez ce vieux Whiskey blond qui fume

▶ Bold Italic
The quick brown fox jumps over a Dog. Zwei Boxkämpfer jagen Eva durch Sylt portez ce vieux Whiskey blond qui fume aber echt

M406 Mac + PC — 1928–35: Eric Gill
Perpetua Expert

ABCDEFGHIJKLMNOPQRSTUVWXYZ(ÄÖÜŠÅØÆŒÇ)
1234567890ffffiflffifl(¹²³⁴⁵⁶⁷⁸⁹⁰)($¢Rp₡)ª

© FSI 1993

a**a***a*
A2987
Perpetua Expert,
RegSC, ItaOSF, BdOSF,
BdItaOSF, RegExp,
ItaExp, BdExp,
BdItaExp

▼ M406 Mac + PC Perpetua Expert

► Expert
01234567890ffiflffiffl-
(½⅓⅔¼¾⅛⅜⅝⅞‰)(⁽$¢Rp₡⁾ᵃ THE
QUICK BROWN FOX JUMPS OVER A
DOG ZWEI BOXKÄMPFER JAGEN EVA

► Expert Italic
*01234567890ffiflffiffl-
(½⅓⅔¼¾⅛⅜⅝⅞‰)(⁽$¢Rp₡⁾ᵃ*

► Expert Bold
**01234567890ffiflffiffl-
(½⅓⅔¼¾⅛⅜⅝⅞‰)(⁽$¢Rp₡⁾ᵃ**

► Expert Bold Italic
***01234567890ffiflffiffl-
(½⅓⅔¼¾⅛⅜⅝⅞‰)(⁽$¢Rp₡⁾ᵃ***

M884 Mac + PC   ⑥   🔗 1928–35: Eric Gill
Perpetua Titling

ABCDEFGHIJKLMNOPQRSTUVWXYZ 1234567890(.,;:?!$&-*)[ ]{ÄÖÜÅØÆŒÇ}

► Light
THE QUICK BROWN FOX
JUMPS OVER A DOG. ZWEI
BOXKÄMPFER JAGEN EVA
DURCH SYLT PORTEZ CE

► Roman
THE QUICK BROWN FOX
JUMPS OVER A DOG. ZWEI
BOXKÄMPFER JAGEN EVA
DURCH SYLT PORTEZ CE

► Bold
**THE QUICK BROWN FOX
JUMPS OVER A DOG.
ZWEI BOXKÄMPFER
JAGEN EVA DURCH SYLT**

Classical Titling:
Felix™ Titling, Perpetua Titling

SG2309 Mac   ⑥   🔗 1928–35: Eric Gill
Perpetua Medium

abcdefghijklmnopqrstuvwxyz[äöüßåøæœç]
ABCDEFGHIJKLMNOPQRSTUVWXYZ
1234567890(.,;:?!$&-*)ÄÖÜÅØÆŒÇ

SG2310 Mac   ⑥   🔗 1928–35: Eric Gill
Perpetua Medium Italic

*abcdefghijklmnopqrstuvwxyz[äöüßåøæœç]
ABCDEFGHIJKLMNOPQRSTUVWXYZ
1234567890(.,;:?!$&-*)ÄÖÜÅØÆŒÇ*

© FSI 1993

SG2314 Mac ⑥ ✎ 1928–35: Eric Gill
Perpetua Heavy

abcdefghijklmnopqrstuvwxyz[äöüßåøæœç]
ABCDEFGHIJKLMNOPQRSTUVWXYZ
1234567890(.,;:?!$&-*)ÄÖÜÅØÆŒÇ

SG2313 Mac ⑥ ✎ 1928–35: Eric Gill
Perpetua Extra Bold

abcdefghijklmnopqrstuvwxyz[äöüßåøæœç]
ABCDEFGHIJKLMNOPQRSTUVWXYZ
1234567890(.,;:?!$&-*)ÄÖÜÅØÆŒÇ

ET6388 Mac + PC
Petroglyph Combo

Petroglyph Combo:
Maskerade™, Petroglyph™, Serpents™

ET6388 Mac + PC ⑥ ✎ 1992: Judith Sutcliffe
Petroglyph™

ABCDEFGHIJKLMNOPQRSTUVWXYZ( )
[pictographic glyphs]
1234567890!.,:?!$ [pictographic glyphs]

Petroglyph Combo:
Maskerade™, Petroglyph™, Serpents™

FB1054 Mac + PC ② ✎ 1991: David Berlow, Just van Rossum
Phaistos™

abcdefghijklmnopqrstuvwxyz[äöüßåøæœç]
ABCDEFGHIJKLMNOPQRSTUVWXYZ
1234567890(.,;:?!$&-*)}ÄÖÜÅØÆŒÇ}

▶ Regular
The quick brown fox jumps over a Dog. Zwei Boxkämpfer jagen Eva durch Sylt portez ce vieux Whiskey blond qui fume une pipe aber echt

▶ Italic
The quick brown fox jumps over a Dog. Zwei Boxkämpfer jagen Eva durch Sylt portez ce vieux Whiskey blond qui fume une pipe aber echt über die Mauer

▶ Bold
The quick brown fox jumps over a Dog. Zwei Boxkämpfer jagen Eva durch Sylt portez ce vieux Whiskey blond qui fume une pipe aber

© FSI 1993

Phenix™ American
C2523 MAC + PC ⑤ 1935: M. F. Benton

abcdefghijklmnopqrstuvwxyz1234567890[äöüßåøæœç]
ABCDEFGHIJKLMNOPQRSTUVWXYZ(.,;:?!$&-*){ÄÖÜÅØÆŒÇ}

Headlines 87S:
Greeting Monotone™, Koloss™, Phenix™ American, Phosphor™, Zeppelin™
Regency Gothic, Huxley Vertical, Aldous Vertical, De Stijl, Bureau Agency

Phosphor™
C2523 MAC + PC ⑥ 1930: Jakob Erbar

ABCDEFGHIJKLMNOPQRSTUVWXYZ
1234567890[ ](.,;:?!$&-*){ÄÖÜÅØÆŒÇ}

Headlines 87S:
Greeting Monotone™, Koloss™, Phenix™ American, Phosphor™, Zeppelin™

Photina® 1
M241 MAC + PC ② 1972: José Mendoza y Almeida

abcdefghijklmnopqrstuvwxyz[äöüßåøæœç]
ABCDEFGHIJKLMNOPQRSTUVWXYZ
1234567890(.,;:?!$&-*){ÄÖÜÅØÆŒÇ}

aa*a*
A6070
Photina, Reg, Ita,
SemBd, SemBdIta, Bd,
BdIta, UltBd, UltBdIta

▶ Regular
The quick brown fox jumps over a Dog. Zwei Boxkämpfer jagen Eva durch Sylt portez ce vieux Whiskey blond qui fume une

▶ Italic
The quick brown fox jumps over a Dog. Zwei Boxkämpfer jagen Eva durch Sylt portez ce vieux Whiskey blond qui fume une pipe aber

▶ Bold
The quick brown fox jumps over a Dog. Zwei Boxkämpfer jagen Eva durch Sylt portez ce vieux Whiskey blond

▶ Bold Italic
The quick brown fox jumps over a Dog. Zwei Boxkämpfer jagen Eva durch Sylt portez ce vieux Whiskey blond qui

Photina 2
M285 MAC + PC ② 1972: José Mendoza y Almeida

abcdefghijklmnopqrstuvwxyz[äöüßåøæœç]
ABCDEFGHIJKLMNOPQRSTUVWXYZ
1234567890(.,;:?!$&-*){ÄÖÜÅØÆŒÇ}

aa*a*
A6070
Photina, Reg, Ita,
SemBd, SemBdIta, Bd,
BdIta, UltBd, UltBdIta

▶ Semi Bold
The quick brown fox jumps over a Dog. Zwei Boxkämpfer jagen Eva durch Sylt portez ce vieux Whiskey blond qui fume

▶ Semi Bold Italic
The quick brown fox jumps over a Dog. Zwei Boxkämpfer jagen Eva durch Sylt portez ce vieux Whiskey blond qui fume

▼ M285 MAC + PC Photina 2

▶ Ultra Bold
The quick brown fox jumps over a Dog. Zwei Boxkämpfer jagen Eva durch Sylt portez ce vieux

▶ Ultra Bold Italic
The quick brown fox jumps over a Dog. Zwei Boxkämpfer jagen Eva durch Sylt portez ce vieux Whiskey

---

EF1079 MAC + PC ④ ✎ 1904: Heinrich Wienyk
Phyllis™

abcdefghijklmnopqrstuvwxyzl äöüßåøæœç 1
ABCDEFGHIJKLMNOPQRSTUVWXYZ
1234567890(.,:;?!$&-)(ÄÖÜÅØÆŒÇ)*

aa*a*
C2777
Headlines 89S

▶ Regular
The quick brown fox jumps over a Dog. Zwei Boxkämpfer jagen Eva durch Sylt portez ce vieux Whiskey blond qui fume une pipe aber echt über die Mauer gesprungen und auch

▶ Initials
The quick brown fox jumps over a Dog. Zwei Boxkämpfer jagen Eva durch Sylt portez ce vieux Whiskey blond qui fume une pipe aber echt über die Mauer gesprungen und

---

BT865 MAC + PC ③
Pica 10 Pitch

abcdefghijklmnopqrstuvwxyz[äöüßåøæœç]
ABCDEFGHIJKLMNOPQRSTUVWXYZ
1234567890(.,;:?!$&-*){ÄÖÜÅØÆŒÇ}

BT Typewriter:
Pica 10 Pitch, Script 12 Pitch
↻ ITC American Typewriter, Courier, Monanti, Schreibmaschinenschrift, Prestige, Typewriter

---

EF6467 MAC + PC ⑥ ✎ 1973: Christopher Mathews
Piccadilly™

ABCDEFGHIJKLMNOPQRSTUVWXYZ
1234567890(.,;:?!$&-*)ÄÖÜÅØÆŒÇ

E+F Special Headlines 3:
Hawthorn™, Magnus™ Bold, Octopuss™, Octopuss™ Shaded, Piccadilly™, Stop™

BT790 MAC + PC ⑥ ✎ 1970: Tom Carnase, Ronne Bonder
ITC Pioneer®

ABCDEFGHIJKLMNOPQRSTUVWXYZ
1234567890(.,;:?!$&-*)[]{ÄÖÜÅØÆŒÇ}

Bitstream Decorative 2:
ITC Pioneer®, Maximus™, Profil™, Vineta

© FSI 1993

BT848 Mac + PC ④ ✏ 1930: M. F. Benton
Piranesi™ Italic

abcdefghijklmnopqrstuvwxyz[äöüßåøæœç]
ABCDEFGHIJKLMNOPQRSTUVWXYZ
1234567890(.,;:?!$&-*){ÄÖÜÅØÆŒÇ}

Bitstream Script 1:
Amazone™, Monterey, Piranesi™ Italic

M215 Mac + PC ①
Placard®

abcdefghijklmnopqrstuvwxyz[äöüßåøæœç]
ABCDEFGHIJKLMNOPQRSTUVWXYZ
1234567890(.,;:?!$&-*){ÄÖÜÅØÆŒÇ}

© Aura, Aurora, Hanseatic, Hadrian, Helvetica Inserat, Helvetica Compressed, Impact

▶ **Condensed**
The quick brown fox jumps over a Dog. Zwei Boxkämpfer jagen Eva durch Sylt portez ce vieux Whiskey blond qui fume une pipe aber echt über die Mauer gesprungen und auch

▶ **Bold Condensed**
The quick brown fox jumps over a Dog. Zwei Boxkämpfer jagen Eva durch Sylt portez ce vieux Whiskey blond qui fume une pipe aber echt

Headliners 2:
Falstaff™, Headline Bold, Placard®
© Aura, Aurora, Hanseatic, Hadrian, Helvetica Inserat, Helvetica Compressed, Impact

---

M094 Mac + PC ② ✏ 1914: (R. Granjon, c. 1700) F. H. Pierpont
Plantin® 1

abcdefghijklmnopqrstuvwxyz[äöüßåøæœç]
ABCDEFGHIJKLMNOPQRSTUVWXYZ
1234567890(.,;:?!$&-★){ÄÖÜÅØÆŒÇ}

a a *a*
A1025
Plantin 1, Reg, Ita, Bd, BdIta
BT1223
Plantin, Reg, Ita, Bd, BdIta
©
Plantin News, Bembo

▶ Regular
The quick brown fox jumps over a Dog. Zwei Boxkämpfer jagen Eva durch Sylt portez ce vieux Whiskey blond qui fume

▶ *Italic*
The quick brown fox jumps over a Dog. Zwei Boxkämpfer jagen Eva durch Sylt portez ce vieux Whiskey blond qui fume une pipe aber

▶ **Bold**
The quick brown fox jumps over a Dog. Zwei Boxkämpfer jagen Eva durch Sylt portez ce vieux Whiskey

▶ ***Bold Italic***
The quick brown fox jumps over a Dog. Zwei Boxkämpfer jagen Eva durch Sylt portez ce vieux Whiskey

---

M242 Mac + PC ② ✏ 1914: (R. Granjon, c. 1700) F. H. Pierpont
Plantin 2

abcdefghijklmnopqrstuvwxyz[äöüßåøæœç]
ABCDEFGHIJKLMNOPQRSTUVWXYZ
1234567890(.,;:?!$&-★){ÄÖÜÅØÆŒÇ}

© FSI 1993

aa*a*
A1519
Plantin 2, Lt, LtIta,
SemBd, SemBdIta,
BdCon
BT1224
Plantin Light, Lt, LtIta,
BdCon
◉
Bembo

▼ M242 Mac + PC   Plantin 2

▶ Light
The quick brown fox jumps over a Dog. Zwei Boxkämpfer jagen Eva durch Sylt portez ce vieux Whiskey blond qui fume

▶ Light Italic
The quick brown fox jumps over a Dog. Zwei Boxkämpfer jagen Eva durch Sylt portez ce vieux Whiskey blond qui fume une pipe aber

▶ Semi Bold
The quick brown fox jumps over a Dog. Zwei Boxkämpfer jagen Eva durch Sylt portez ce vieux Whiskey blond

▶ Semi Bold Italic
The quick brown fox jumps over a Dog. Zwei Boxkämpfer jagen Eva durch Sylt portez ce vieux Whiskey blond

▶ Bold Condensed
The quick brown fox jumps over a Dog. Zwei Boxkämpfer jagen Eva durch Sylt portez ce vieux Whiskey blond qui fume une pipe aber echt

M358 Mac + PC   ②   ✎ 1914: (R. Granjon, c. 1700) F. H. Pierpont
Plantin Expert

ABCDEFGHIJKLMNOPQRSTUVWXYZ(ÄÖÜŠÅØÆŒÇ)

1234567890ffffiflffiffl($^1_1$$^2_2$$^3_3$$^4_4$$^5_5$$^6_6$$^7_7$$^8_8$$^9_9$$^0_0$)

▶ Expert
0123456789offfiflffiffl-
($^1/_1$$^2/_2$$^3/_3$$^4/_4$$^5/_5$$^6/_6$$^7/_7$$^8/_8$$^9/_9$$^0/_0$)$^{(\$¢Rp€)a}$
THE QUICK BROWN FOX JUMPS OVER A DOG ZWEI BOXKÄMPFER

▶ Expert Italic
0123456789offfiflffiffl-
($^1/_1$$^2/_2$$^3/_3$$^4/_4$$^5/_5$$^6/_6$$^7/_7$$^8/_8$$^9/_9$$^0/_0$)$^{(\$¢Rp€)a}$

▶ Expert Bold
0123456789offfiflffiffl-
($^1/_1$$^2/_2$$^3/_3$$^4/_4$$^5/_5$$^6/_6$$^7/_7$$^8/_8$$^9/_9$$^0/_0$)$^{(\$¢Rp€)}$
)a

▶ Expert Bold Italic
0123456789offfiflffiffl-
($^1/_1$$^2/_2$$^3/_3$$^4/_4$$^5/_5$$^6/_6$$^7/_7$$^8/_8$$^9/_9$$^0/_0$)$^{(\$¢Rp€)a}$

M978 Mac + PC   ②   ✎ 1914: (R. Granjon, c. 1700) F. H. Pierpont
Plantin Expert Light

ABCDEFGHIJKLMNOPQRSTUVWXYZ(ÄÖÜŠÅØÆŒÇ)

1234567890ffffiflffiffl($^1_1$$^2_2$$^3_3$$^4_4$$^5_5$$^6_6$$^7_7$$^8_8$$^9_9$$^0_0$)

▶ Expert Light
0123456789offfiflffiffl-
($^1/_1$$^2/_2$$^3/_3$$^4/_4$$^5/_5$$^6/_6$$^7/_7$$^8/_8$$^9/_9$$^0/_0$)$^{(\$¢Rp€)a}$
THE QUICK BROWN FOX JUMPS OVER A DOG ZWEI BOXKÄMPFER

▶ Expert Light Italic
0123456789offfiflffiffl-
($^1/_1$$^2/_2$$^3/_3$$^4/_4$$^5/_5$$^6/_6$$^7/_7$$^8/_8$$^9/_9$$^0/_0$)$^{(\$¢Rp€)a}$

▶ Expert Semi Bold
0123456789offfiflffiffl-
($^1/_1$$^2/_2$$^3/_3$$^4/_4$$^5/_5$$^6/_6$$^7/_7$$^8/_8$$^9/_9$$^0/_0$)$^{(\$¢Rp€)a}$

▶ Expert Semi Bold Italic
0123456789offfiflffiffl-
($^1/_1$$^2/_2$$^3/_3$$^4/_4$$^5/_5$$^6/_6$$^7/_7$$^8/_8$$^9/_9$$^0/_0$)$^{(\$¢Rp€)a}$

© FSI 1993

| M275 MAC + PC ② | (R. Granjon, c. 1700) F. H. Pierpont
Plantin News

abcdefghijklmnopqrstuvwxyz[äöüßåøæœç]
ABCDEFGHIJKLMNOPQRSTUVWXYZ
1234567890(.,;:?!$&-*){ÄÖÜÅØÆŒÇ}

Plantin, Bembo

▶ Regular
The quick brown fox jumps over a Dog. Zwei Boxkämpfer jagen Eva durch Sylt portez ce vieux Whiskey blond qui fume une

▶ Italic
The quick brown fox jumps over a Dog. Zwei Boxkämpfer jagen Eva durch Sylt portez ce vieux Whiskey blond qui fume une pipe aber

▶ Bold
The quick brown fox jumps over a Dog. Zwei Boxkämpfer jagen Eva durch Sylt portez ce vieux Whiskey blond qui fume

▶ Bold Italic
The quick brown fox jumps over a Dog. Zwei Boxkämpfer jagen Eva durch Sylt portez ce vieux Whiskey blond qui fume une

| BT789 MAC + PC ⑥ | 1938: R. Harling
Playbill®

abcdefghijklmnopqrstuvwxyz[äöüßåøæœç]
ABCDEFGHIJKLMNOPQRSTUVWXYZ
1234567890(.,;:?!$&-*){ÄÖÜÅØÆŒÇ}

Bitstream Decorative 1:
Broadway Engraved, Davida, P. T. Barnum™, Playbill®
P. T. Barnum, Egyptian, Old Towne No. 536, Ponderosa, French XXX Condensed, Figaro

| L2596 MAC ⑥ | 1975: Alan Meeks
Plaza™

ABCDEFGHIJKLMNOPQRSTUVWXYZ
1234567890(.,;:?!$&-*)[]ÄÖÜÅØÆŒÇ

| L2597 MAC ⑥ | 1987: Holger Seeling
Pleasure™ Bold Shaded

ABCDEFGHIJKLMNOPQRSTUVWXYZ
1234567890(.,;:?!$&-*)[]ÄÖÜÅØÆŒÇ

| L2598 MAC ⑥ | 1991: Timothy Donaldson
Pneuma™

ABCDEFGHIJKLMNOPQRSTUVWXYZ
1234567890(.,;:?!$&-*)[]ÄÖÜÅØÆŒÇ

© FSI 1993

Poetica™
A6309 Mac + PC — 1992: Robert Slimbach

abcdefghijklmnopqrstuvwxyz[äöüßåøæœç]
ABCDEFGHIJKLMNOPQRSTUVWXYZ
1234567890(.,;:?!$&-*){ÄÖÜÅØÆŒÇ}

▶ **Chancery I**
The quick brown fox jumps over a Dog. Zwei Boxkämpfer jagen Eva durch Sylt portez ce vieux Whiskey blond qui fume une pipe aber echt über die Mauer gesprungen und auch smørebrød en

▶ **Chancery II**
The quick brown fox jumps over a Dog. Zwei Boxkämpfer jagen Eva durch Sylt portez ce vieux Whiskey blond qui fume une pipe aber echt über die Mauer gesprungen und auch smørebrød en

▶ **Chancery III**
The quick brown fox jumps over a Dog. Zwei Boxkämpfer jagen Eva durch Sylt portez ce vieux Whiskey blond qui fume une pipe aber echt über die Mauer gesprungen und auch smørebrød

▶ **Chancery IV**
The quick brown fox jumps over a Dog. Zwei Boxkämpfer jagen Eva durch Sylt portez ce vieux Whiskey blond qui fume une pipe aber echt über die Mauer gesprungen und auch smørebrød en

▶ **Chancery SC**
THE QUICK BROWN FOX JUMPS OVER A DOG. 123 4567 890 ZWEI BOXKÄMPFER JAGEN EVA DURCH SYLT PORTEZ CE VIEUX WHISKEY BLOND QUI FUME

▶ **Chancery SC Alternates**
K L M N N Q R V W X Z K N R X

▶ **Chancery Expert**
0123456789¼½¾⅛⅜⅝⅞½⅔ffffiflffiffl($1 2 3 4 5 5 6 6 7 7 c 8 9 9)Rp¢

Poetica Supplemental
A6310 Mac + PC — 1992: Robert Slimbach

ABCDEFGHIJKLMNOPQRSTUVWXYZ
ABCDEFGHIJKLMNOPQRSTUVWXYZ

▶ **Swash Caps I**
THE QUICK BROWN FOX JUMPS OVER A DOG ZWEI BOXKMPFER JAGEN EVA DURCH SYLT PORTEZ CE

▶ **Swash Caps II**
THE QUICK BROWN FOX JUMPS OVER A DOG ZWEI BOXKMPFER JAGEN EVA DURCH SYLT PORTEZ CE

▶ **Swash Caps III**
THE QUICK BROWN FOX JUMPS OVER A DOG ZWEI BOXKMP FER JAGEN EVA

▶ **Swash Caps IV**
THE QUICK BROWN FOX JUMPS OVER A DOG ZWEI BOXKMP FER JAGEN EVA

▶ **Initial Swash Caps**
A B C D E F G H I J K L M N O P Q R S T U V W X Y Z

▶ **Ampersands**
& & & & & & & & & & & & & & & & & & Q R & & & & & & & & & & & & & & & & & & & & & & &

© FSI 1993

▼ A6310 Mac + PC Poetica Supplemental

► Ligatures

ß ɛ̃ ɛ̃ ɛ̃ ff ff Hi fi ffi fl ffl ft gg
ll ſf ſß ſß ſt ff Th th ch ck ll
ti ct ff ffi fi ffi fl ffl ft gg ll ll ſf ſß
ſp ſſ ſt ſt ſch th

► Ornaments

[ornamental glyphs]

► Lower Case Alternates I

ƀ d̃ g̃ h̃ k̃ T̃ p̃ q v w x y z ƀ d f
g h j k l p Q s T v w x y º

► Lower Case Alternates II

g k p y z d g k p e ſ v w y з

► Lower Case Beginnings I

ƀ c ƒ h i j k l m n p q ſ t cu v
w y ƀ c ƒ h i j k d m n p s t u
v w y

► Lower Case Beginnings II

ƀ e ƒh ɛ ɛj ʃ k ʃl m p ſ ſ ɛ ɛt
gu ɕ gw ʋ ʃ e ʃh ɕ i ʃ ʃ k ʃ l m ɕ n
ɕ ɛ ſ ɕ u v cw ɕ

► Lower Case Endings I

a c d e g h i l m n o r s t u y z

► Lower Case Endings II

a d e h i l m n tƒ w

M265 Mac + PC
Poliphilus®

Poliphilus®:
Blado®, Poliphilus, Van Dijck™
👁 Bembo, Blado

M265 Mac + PC   ②   ✎ 1923: (F. Griffo, 1499)
Poliphilus

abcdefghijklmnopqrstuvwxyz[äöüßåøæœç]
ABCDEFGHIJKLMNOPQRSTUVWXYZ
1234567890(.,;:?!$&-*){ÄÖÜÅØÆŒÇ}

Poliphilus®:
Blado®, Poliphilus, Van Dijck™
👁 Blado

M6697 Mac + PC
Poliphilus Expert

Poliphilus Expert:
Blado Expert, Poliphilus Expert, Van Dijck Expert
👁 Bembo, Blado

M6697 Mac + PC   ②   ✎ 1923: (F. Griffo, 1499)
Poliphilus Expert

ABCDEFGHIJKLMNOPQRSTUVWXYZ(ÄÖÜŠÅØÆŒÇ)

1234567890ffiffifffffl(^{1}^{2}^{3}^{4}^{5}^{6}^{7}^{8}^{9}^{0}) ($$¢Rp₵)ª

Poliphilus Expert:
Blado Expert, Poliphilus Expert, Van Dijck Expert
👁 Bembo, Blado

© FSI 1993

MC2930 Mac + PC ④ ✏ 1954: (Peter Dombrezian, 1951)
Polka™

abcdefghijklmnopqrstuvwxyz1234567890[äöüßåøæœç]

ABCDEFGHIJKLMNOPQRSTUVWXYZ(.,;:?!$&-*){ÄÖÜÅØÆŒÇ}

MC2931 Mac + PC ④ ✏ 1954: (Peter Dombrezian, 1951)
Polka Bold

abcdefghijklmnopqrstuvwxyz1234567890[äöüßåøæœç]

ABCDEFGHIJKLMNOPQRSTUVWXYZ(.,;:?!$&-*){ÄÖÜÅØÆŒÇ}

A424 Mac + PC ⑥ ✏ 1990: Buker, Lind, Redick
Ponderosa™

ABCDEFGHIJKLMNOPQRSTUVWXYZ1234567890(.,;:?!$&-*){ÄÖÜÅØÆŒÇ}

Wood Type Pack 1:
Cottonwood®, Ironwood®, Juniper®, Mesquite™, Ponderosa™, Wood Type Ornaments 1
👁 P. T. Barnum, Egyptian, Playbill, Old Towne No. 536, French XXX Condensed, Figaro

FF2963 Mac ⑤ ✏ 1992: Neville Brody
FF Pop™

abcdefghijklmnopqrstuvwxyz[äöüßåøæœç]
ABCDEFGHIJKLMNOPQRSTUVWXYZ
1234567890(.,;:?!$&-*){ÄÖÜÅØÆŒÇ}

👁 FF Network, Oblong, FF Vortex

▶ Regular
The quick brown fox jumps over a Dog. Zwei Boxkämpfer jagen Eva durch Sylt portez ce vieux Whiskey blond qui fume une pipe aber echt über die Mauer

▶ LED
The quick brown fox jumps over a Dog. Zwei Boxkämpfer jagen Eva durch Sylt portez ce vieux Whiskey blond qui fume une pipe aber echt über die Mauer

A922 Mac + PC ⑥ ✏ 1990: (1830) Lind, Buker, Redick
Poplar™

abcdefghijklmnopqrstuvwxyz[äöüßåøæœç]
ABCDEFGHIJKLMNOPQRSTUVWXYZ
1234567890(.,;:?!$&-*){ÄÖÜÅØÆŒÇ}

Wood Type Pack 2:
Birch™, Blackoak™, Madrone™, Poplar™, Willow™, Wood Type Ornaments 2

© FSI 1993

P 17

Poppl-Exquisit™
MC6365 Mac + PC ④ 1970: Friedrich Poppl

abcdefghijklmnopqrstuvwxyz[äöüßåøæœç]
ABCDEFGHIJKLMNOPQRSTUVWXYZ
1234567890(.,:;?!$&-*){ÄÖÜÅØÆŒÇ}

Poppl-Exquisit Alternates
MC6668 Mac + PC ④ 1970: Friedrich Poppl

abcdefghijklmnopqrstuvwxyz[äöüßåøæœç]
ABCDEFGHIJKLMNOPQRSTUVWXYZ
1234567890(.,:;?!$&-*){ÄÖÜÅØÆŒÇ}

Poppl-Laudatio®
AB6221 Mac + PC ① 1982: Friedrich Poppl

abcdefghijklmnopqrstuvwxyz[äöüßåøæœç]
ABCDEFGHIJKLMNOPQRSTUVWXYZ
1234567890(.,:;?!$&-*){ÄÖÜÅØÆŒÇ}

▶ Light
The quick brown fox jumps over a Dog. Zwei Boxkämpfer jagen Eva durch Sylt portez ce vieux Whiskey blond qui fume

▶ Light Italic
The quick brown fox jumps over a Dog. Zwei Boxkämpfer jagen Eva durch Sylt portez ce vieux Whiskey blond qui fume une

▶ Regular
The quick brown fox jumps over a Dog. Zwei Boxkämpfer jagen Eva durch Sylt portez ce vieux Whiskey blond qui

▶ Italic
The quick brown fox jumps over a Dog. Zwei Boxkämpfer jagen Eva durch Sylt portez ce vieux Whiskey blond qui fume une

▶ Medium
The quick brown fox jumps over a Dog. Zwei Boxkämpfer jagen Eva durch Sylt portez ce vieux Whiskey blond

▶ Medium Italic
The quick brown fox jumps over a Dog. Zwei Boxkämpfer jagen Eva durch Sylt portez ce vieux Whiskey blond qui

▶ Bold
The quick brown fox jumps over a Dog. Zwei Boxkämpfer jagen Eva durch Sylt portez ce vieux Whiskey

▶ Bold Italic
The quick brown fox jumps over a Dog. Zwei Boxkämpfer jagen Eva durch Sylt portez ce vieux Whiskey blond

Poppl-Laudatio Condensed
AB6722 Mac + PC ① 1982: Friedrich Poppl

abcdefghijklmnopqrstuvwxyz[äöüßåøæœç]
ABCDEFGHIJKLMNOPQRSTUVWXYZ
1234567890(.,:;?!$&-*){ÄÖÜÅØÆŒÇ}

▶ Light Condensed
The quick brown fox jumps over a Dog. Zwei Boxkämpfer jagen Eva durch Sylt portez ce vieux Whiskey blond qui fume une pipe aber echt

▶ Condensed
The quick brown fox jumps over a Dog. Zwei Boxkämpfer jagen Eva durch Sylt portez ce vieux Whiskey blond qui fume une pipe aber echt

© FSI 1993

▼ AB6722 Mac + PC   Poppl-Laudatio Condensed

► Medium Condensed
The quick brown fox jumps over a Dog. Zwei Boxkämpfer jagen Eva durch Sylt portez ce vieux Whiskey blond qui fume une

► Bold Condensed
The quick brown fox jumps over a Dog. Zwei Boxkämpfer jagen Eva durch Sylt portez ce vieux Whiskey blond qui fume une

AB2546 Mac + PC   ②   1976: Friedrich Poppl
Poppl-Pontifex™

abcdefghijklmnopqrstuvwxyz[äöüßåøæœç]
ABCDEFGHIJKLMNOPQRSTUVWXYZ
1234567890(.,;:?!$&-*){ÄÖÜÅØÆŒÇ}

► Regular
The quick brown fox jumps over a Dog. Zwei Boxkämpfer jagen Eva durch Sylt portez ce vieux Whiskey blond qui

► Italic
The quick brown fox jumps over a Dog. Zwei Boxkämpfer jagen Eva durch Sylt portez ce vieux Whiskey blond qui fume

► Medium
The quick brown fox jumps over a Dog. Zwei Boxkämpfer jagen Eva durch Sylt portez ce vieux Whiskey

► Medium Condensed
The quick brown fox jumps over a Dog. Zwei Boxkämpfer jagen Eva durch Sylt portez ce vieux Whiskey blond qui fume

► Bold
The quick brown fox jumps over a Dog. Zwei Boxkämpfer jagen Eva durch Sylt portez ce vieux Whiskey

AB2985 Mac + PC   ②   1976: Friedrich Poppl
Poppl-Pontifex Expert

ABCDEFGHIJKLMNOPQRSTUVWXYZ[ÄÖÜSSÅØÆŒÇ]
ABCDEFGHIJKLMNOPQRSTUVWXYZ
1234567890(.,;:?!$&-*){ÄÖÜÅØÆŒÇ}

► Small Caps
THE QUICK BROWN FOX JUMPS OVER A DOG. 123 4567 890 ZWEI BOXKÄMPFER JAGEN EVA DURCH SYLT PORTEZ CE VIEUX

► Regular Expert
0123456789 offififlffiffl- (¹/₁²/₂³/₃⁴/₄⁵/₅⁶/₆⁷/₇⁸/₈⁹/₉⁰/₀)($¢Rp₡)ª
THE QUICK BROWN FOX JUMPS OVER A DOG ZWEI BOX-

► Italic OsF
The quick brown fox jumps over a Dog. 123 4567 890 Zwei Boxkämpfer jagen Eva durch Sylt portez ce vieux Whiskey

► Italic Expert
0123456789 offififlffiffl- (¹/₁²/₂³/₃⁴/₄⁵/₅⁶/₆⁷/₇⁸/₈⁹/₉⁰/₀)($¢Rp₡)ª

► Medium Small Caps
THE QUICK BROWN FOX JUMPS OVER A DOG. 123 4567 890 ZWEI BOXKÄMPFER JAGEN EVA DURCH SYLT POR-

► Medium Expert
**0123456789 offififlffiffl- (¹/₁²/₂³/₃⁴/₄⁵/₅⁶/₆⁷/₇⁸/₈⁹/₉⁰/₀)($¢Rp₡)ª
THE QUICK BROWN FOX JUMPS OVER A DOG ZWEI**

▼ AB2985 Mac + PC Poppl-Pontifex Expert

▶ Medium Cond. Small Caps
The quick brown fox jumps over a Dog. 123 4567 890 Zwei Boxkämpfer jagen Eva durch Sylt portez ce vieux Whiskey

▶ Medium Condensed Expert
01234567890offfiflffiffl-
(¹/₁²/₂³/₃⁴/₄⁵/₅⁶/₆⁷/₇⁸/₈⁹/₉⁰/₀)⁽$¢Rp₵⁾ᵃ
the quick brown fox jumps over a dog zwei boxkämpfer

▶ Bold OSF
The quick brown fox jumps over a Dog. 123 4567 890 Zwei Boxkämpfer jagen Eva durch Sylt portez ce vieux

▶ Bold Expert
01234567890offfiflffiffl-
(¹/₁²/₂³/₃⁴/₄⁵/₅⁶/₆⁷/₇⁸/₈⁹/₉⁰/₀)⁽$¢Rp₵⁾ᵃ

AB2886 Mac + PC ④ 1977: Friedrich Poppl
Poppl-Residenz™

abcdefghijklmnopqrstuvwxyz[äöüßåøæœç]
ABCDEFGHIJKLMNOPQRSTUVWXYZ
1234567890(.,:;?!$&-){ÄÖÜÅØÆŒÇ}*

▶ Light
The quick brown fox jumps over a Dog. Zwei Boxkämpfer jagen Eva durch Sylt portez ce vieux Whiskey blond qui fume une pipe aber echt über die Mauer gesprungen und auch

▶ Regular
The quick brown fox jumps over a Dog. Zwei Boxkämpfer jagen Eva durch Sylt portez ce vieux Whiskey blond qui fume une pipe aber echt über die Mauer gesprungen

CT1095 Mac + PC ② 1991: Adrian WIlliams
Poseidon™

abcdefghijklmnopqrstuvwxyz[äöüßåøæœç]
ABCDEFGHIJKLMNOPQRSTUVWXYZ
1234567890(.,:;?!$&-*){ÄÖÜÅØÆŒÇ}

Sierra

▶ Regular
The quick brown fox jumps over a Dog. Zwei Boxkämpfer jagen Eva durch Sylt portez ce vieux Whiskey blond qui fume une pipe aber echt

▶ Italic
The quick brown fox jumps over a Dog. Zwei Boxkämpfer jagen Eva durch Sylt portez ce vieux Whiskey blond qui fume une pipe aber echt über die Mauer

▶ Medium
The quick brown fox jumps over a Dog. Zwei Boxkämpfer jagen Eva durch Sylt portez ce vieux Whiskey blond qui fume une

▶ Medium Italic
The quick brown fox jumps over a Dog. Zwei Boxkämpfer jagen Eva durch Sylt portez ce vieux Whiskey blond qui fume une pipe aber echt

▶ Bold
The quick brown fox jumps over a Dog. Zwei Boxkämpfer jagen Eva durch Sylt portez ce vieux Whiskey blond qui

▶ Bold Italic
The quick brown fox jumps over a Dog. Zwei Boxkämpfer jagen Eva durch Sylt portez ce vieux Whiskey blond qui fume

A172 Mac + PC ⑦ 1939–1940: Herbert Post
Post Antiqua™

abcdefghijklmnopqrstuvwxyz[äöüßåøæœç]
ABCDEFGHIJKLMNOPQRSTUVWXYZ
1234567890(.,:;?!$&-*){ÄÖÜÅØÆŒÇ}

© FSI 1993

▼ A172 Mac + PC   Post Antiqua™

▶ Regular
The quick brown fox jumps over a Dog. Zwei Boxkämpfer jagen Eva durch Sylt portez ce vieux Whiskey blond qui fume une pipe aber

▶ Bold
The quick brown fox jumps over a Dog. Zwei Boxkämpfer jagen Eva durch Sylt portez ce vieux Whiskey blond qui fume une

---

AB6066 Mac + PC   ②   1944: Herbert Post
Post Mediæval™

abcdefghijklmnopqrstuvwxyz[äöüßåøæœç]
ABCDEFGHIJKLMNOPQRSTUVWXYZ
1234567890(.,;:?!$&-*){ÄÖÜÅØÆŒÇ}

▶ Regular
The quick brown fox jumps over a Dog. Zwei Boxkämpfer jagen Eva durch Sylt portez ce vieux Whiskey blond qui fume une

▶ Italic
The quick brown fox jumps over a Dog. Zwei Boxkämpfer jagen Eva durch Sylt portez ce vieux Whiskey blond qui fume une pipe aber echt über die Mauer

▶ Medium
The quick brown fox jumps over a Dog. Zwei Boxkämpfer jagen Eva durch Sylt portez ce vieux Whiskey blond qui fume

---

L2599 Mac   ⑥   1991: Michael Gills
Prague™

ABCDEFGHIJKLMNOPQRSTUVWXYZ
1234567890(.,;:?!$&-*)[]ÄÖÜÅØÆŒÇ

EF523 Mac + PC   ①   1977: Gerard Unger
Praxis™ 1

abcdefghijklmnopqrstuvwxyz[äöüßåøæœç]
ABCDEFGHIJKLMNOPQRSTUVWXYZ
1234567890(.,;:?!$&-*){ÄÖÜÅØÆŒÇ}

© Demos, ITC Flora

▶ Light
The quick brown fox jumps over a Dog. Zwei Boxkämpfer jagen Eva durch Sylt portez ce vieux Whiskey blond qui fume une pipe aber

▶ Light Small Caps
The quick brown fox jumps over a Dog. 123 4567 890 Zwei Boxkämpfer jagen Eva durch Sylt portez ce vieux Whiskey blond qui

▶ Semi Bold
The quick brown fox jumps over a Dog. Zwei Boxkämpfer jagen Eva durch Sylt portez ce vieux Whiskey blond qui fume

▶ Heavy
The quick brown fox jumps over a Dog. Zwei Boxkämpfer jagen Eva durch Sylt portez ce vieux Whiskey blond qui

© FSI 1993

| EF524 MAC + PC ① | ✎ 1977: Gerard Unger |

Praxis 2

abcdefghijklmnopqrstuvwxyz[äöüßåøæœç]
ABCDEFGHIJKLMNOPQRSTUVWXYZ
1234567890(.,;:?!$&-*){ÄÖÜÅØÆŒÇ}

© Demos, ITC Flora

▶ Regular
The quick brown fox jumps over a Dog. Zwei Boxkämpfer jagen Eva durch Sylt portez ce vieux Whiskey blond qui fume une

▶ Regular Small Caps
THE QUICK BROWN FOX JUMPS OVER A DOG. ZWEI BOXKÄMPFER JAGEN EVA DURCH SYLT PORTEZ CE VIEUX WHISKEY BLOND QUI FUME UNE PIPE

▶ Bold
The quick brown fox jumps over a Dog. Zwei Boxkämpfer jagen Eva durch Sylt portez ce vieux Whiskey blond qui fume

| L2726 MAC ⑥ | ✎ 1969: Colin Brignall |

Premier™ Lightline

abcdefghijklmnopqrstuvwxyz[äöüßåøæœç]
ABCDEFGHIJKLMNOPQRSTUVWXYZ
1234567890(.,;:?!$&-*)ÄÖÜÅØÆŒÇ

| L6139 MAC ⑥ | ✎ 1970: Colin Brignall |

Premier Shaded

ABCDEFGHIJKLMNOPQRSTUVWXYZ
1234567890(.,;:?!$&-*)[]ÄÖÜÅØÆŒÇ

| A170 MAC + PC ④ | ✎ 1974: Friedrich Karl Sallwey |

Present™ Script

abcdefghijklmnopqrstuvwxyz[äöüßåøæœç]
ABCDEFGHIJKLMNOPQRSTUVWXYZ
1234567890(.,;:?!$&-*){ÄÖÜÅØÆŒÇ}

Arnold Böcklin:
Arnold Böcklin™, Fette Fraktur™, Helvetica Inserat, Present™ Script

| BT1372 MAC + PC ③ | ✎ 1953: Clayton Smith |

Prestige 12 Pitch

abcdefghijklmnopqrstuvwxyz[äöüßåøæœç]
ABCDEFGHIJKLMNOPQRSTUVWXYZ
1234567890(.,;:?!$&-*){ÄÖÜÅØÆŒÇ}

▼ BT1372 Mac + PC **Prestige 12 Pitch**

aa*a*
A097
Prestige Elite, Reg,
Sln, Bd, BdSln

▶ Regular
The quick brown fox jumps over a Dog. Zwei Boxkämpfer jagen Eva durch Sylt portez ce

▶ Italic
The quick brown fox jumps over a Dog. Zwei Boxkämpfer jagen Eva durch Sylt portez ce

▶ Bold
The quick brown fox jumps over a Dog. Zwei Boxkämpfer jagen Eva durch Sylt portez ce

▶ Bold Italic
The quick brown fox jumps over a Dog. Zwei Boxkämpfer jagen Eva durch Sylt portez ce

---

BT844 Mac + PC ② ✎ 1953: Rudolf Ruzicka   Industry name
Century 751   Primer

abcdefghijklmnopqrstuvwxyz[äöüßåøæœç]
ABCDEFGHIJKLMNOPQRSTUVWXYZ
1234567890(.,;:?!$&-*){ÄÖÜÅØÆŒÇ}

▶ Regular
The quick brown fox jumps over a Dog. Zwei Boxkämpfer jagen Eva durch Sylt portez ce vieux Whiskey blond qui fume

▶ Italic
The quick brown fox jumps over a Dog. Zwei Boxkämpfer jagen Eva durch Sylt portez ce vieux Whiskey blond qui fume

---

SG1166 Mac ⑤ ✎ 1981: Alan Meeks
Princetown™

ABCDEFGHIJKLMNOPQRSTUVWXYZ
1234567890(.,;:?!$&-*)[]ÄÖÜÅØÆŒÇ

L2850 Mac ⑥ ✎ 1990: Martin Wait
Pritchard™

ABCDEFGHIJKLMNOPQRSTUVWXYZ
1234567890(.,;:?!$&-*)[]ÄÖÜÅØÆŒÇ

L2851 Mac ⑥ ✎ 1990: Martin Wait
Pritchard Line Out

abcdefghijklmnopqrstuvwxyz[äöüßåøæœç]
ABCDEFGHIJKLMNOPQRSTUVWXYZ
1234567890(.,;:?!$&-*)ÄÖÜÅØÆŒÇ

BT790 Mac + PC ⑥ ✎ 1946: Eugen & Max Lenz   Industry name
Decorated 035   Profil™

ABCDEFGHIJKLMNOPQRSTUVWXYZ
1234567890(.,;:?!$&-*)[]{ÄÖÜÅØÆŒÇ}

© FSI 1993
▼

▼ BT790 Mac + PC Profil™

Bitstream Decorative 2:
ITC Pioneer®, Maximus™, Profil™, Vineta
ⓒ Vineta

F2944 Mac ② ✎ 1987-91: Peter Fraterdeus
Prospera™ II

abcdefghijklmnopqrstuvwxyz[äöüßåøæœç]
ABCDEFGHIJKLMNOPQRSTUVWXYZ
1234567890(.,;:?!$&-*){ÄÖÜÅØÆŒÇ}

▶ Regular
The quick brown fox jumps over a Dog. Zwei Boxkämpfer jagen Eva durch Sylt portez ce vieux Whiskey blond qui fume une pipe aber echt

▶ Italic
The quick brown fox jumps over a Dog. Zwei Boxkämpfer jagen Eva durch Sylt portez ce vieux Whiskey blond qui fume une pipe aber echt über die Mauer

▶ Bold
The quick brown fox jumps over a Dog. Zwei Boxkämpfer jagen Eva durch Sylt portez ce vieux Whiskey blond qui fume une pipe aber echt

▶ Bold Italic
The quick brown fox jumps over a Dog. Zwei Boxkämpfer jagen Eva durch Sylt portez ce vieux Whiskey blond qui fume une pipe aber echt

▶ Small Caps
THE QUICK BROWN FOX JUMPS OVER A DOG. 123 4567 890 ZWEI BOXKÄMPFER JAGEN EVA DURCH SYLT PORTEZ CE VIEUX WHISKEY BLOND QUI FUME UNE

BT789 Mac + PC ⑥
P. T. Barnum™

abcdefghijklmnopqrstuvwxyz[äöüßåøæœç]
ABCDEFGHIJKLMNOPQRSTUVWXYZ
1234567890(.,;:?!$&-*){ÄÖÜÅØÆŒÇ}

Bitstream Decorative 1:
Broadway Engraved, Davida, P. T. Barnum™, Playbill®
ⓒ Egyptian, Playbill, Old Towne No. 536, Ponderosa, French XXX Condensed, Figaro

---

EF6453 Mac + PC ⑥
Pump™

abcdefghijklmnopqrstuvwxyz[äöüßåøæœç]
ABCDEFGHIJKLMNOPQRSTUVWXYZ
1234567890(.,;:?!$&-*) ÄÖÜÅØÆŒÇ

aa*a*
L6140
Pump, Reg
L6141
Pump, Demi
ⓒ
ITC Bauhaus, Blippo, ITC Ronda, Horatio, Dubbeldik

▶ Light
The quick brown fox jumps over a Dog. Zwei Boxkämpfer jagen Eva durch Sylt portez ce vieux Whiskey blond qui fume une pipe aber

▶ Medium
The quick brown fox jumps over a Dog. Zwei Boxkämpfer jagen Eva durch Sylt portez ce vieux Whiskey blond qui fume une pipe

© FSI 1993

▼ EF6453 Mac + PC Pump™

▶ Demi
The quick brown fox jumps over a Dog. Zwei Boxkämpfer jagen Eva durch Sylt portez ce vieux Whiskey blond qui fume une pipe

▶ Bold
The quick brown fox jumps over a Dog. Zwei Boxkämpfer jagen Eva durch Sylt portez ce vieux Whiskey blond qui fume une

▶ Triline
The quick brown fox jumps over a Dog. Zwei Boxkämpfer jagen Eva durch Sylt portez ce vieux Whiskey blond qui fume une

Ontwerpbureau Quadraat / Fred Smeijers, NL

FF6180 Mac + PC · ② · 1992: Fred Smeijers

FF Quadraat™

abcdefghijklmnopqrstuvwxyz[äöüßåøæœç]
ABCDEFGHIJKLMNOPQRSTUVWXYZ
1234567890(.,;:?!$&-*){ÄÖÜÅØÆŒÇ}

▶ Regular
The quick brown fox jumps over a Dog. 123 4567 890 Zwei Boxkämpfer jagen Eva durch Sylt portez ce vieux Whiskey blond

▶ Italic
The quick brown fox jumps over a Dog. 123 4567 890 Zwei Boxkämpfer jagen Eva durch Sylt Whiskey blond qui fume une pipe aber

▶ Bold
The quick brown fox jumps over a Dog. 123 4567 890 Zwei Boxkämpfer jagen Eva durch Sylt portez ce vieux Whiskey blond

▶ Regular SC
THE QUICK BROWN FOX JUMPS OVER A DOG. 123 4567 890 ZWEI BOXKÄMPFER JAGEN EVA DURCH SYLT PORTEZ CE VIEUX

L2852 Mac · ⑥ · 1990: Peter Fahrni

Quadrus™

ABCDEFGHIJKLMNOPQRSTUVWXYZ
1234567890(.,;:?!$&-*)[ ]ÄÖÜÅØÆŒÇ

C2980 Mac + PC · ⑥

Quaint™ Roman

abcdefghijklmnopqrstuvwxyz[äöüßåøæœç]
ABCDEFGHIJKLMNOPQRSTUVWXYZ
1234567890(.,;:?!$&-*){ÄÖÜÅØÆŒÇ}

Headlines 91S:
Empire™, Gallia™, Gillies Gothic Bold, Quaint™ Roman, Skjald™

E6666 Mac + PC · ⑥ · 1993: Zuzana Licko

Quartet™

abcdefghijklmnopqrstuvwxyz[äöüßåøæœç]
ABCDEFGHIJKLMNOPQRSTUVWXYZ
1234567890(.,;:?!$&-*){ÄÖÜÅØÆŒÇ}

▶ Regular
The quick brown fox jumps over a Dog. Zwei Boxkämpfer jagen Eva durch Sylt portez ce vieux Whiskey

▶ Bold
The quick brown fox jumps over a Dog. Zwei Boxkämpfer jagen Eva durch Sylt portez ce vieux Whiskey

---

E6667 Mac + PC · ⑥ · 1993: Zuzana Licko

Quartet SC/Fractions

ABCDEFGHIJKLMNOPQRSTUVWXYZ(ÄÖÜŠÅØÆŒÇ)
ABCDEFGHIJKLMNOPQRSTUVWXYZ
1234567890(.,;:?!$&-*)$^{123}/_{467}$

© FSI 1993

▼ E6667 Mac + PC   Quartet SC/Fractions

▶ Regular SC
The quick brown fox jumps over a Dog. 123 4567 890 Zwei Boxkämpfer jagen Eva durch Sylt por-

▶ Bold SC
The quick brown fox jumps over a Dog. 123 4567 890 Zwei Boxkämpfer jagen Eva durch Sylt por-

▶ Regular Fractions
¼ ½ ¾ ⅛ ⅜ ⅝ ⅞ ¹/₃ ²/₃ fflffiff ☚ ★ ¢ ₨

▶ Bold Fractions
¼ ½ ¾ ⅛ ⅜ ⅝ ⅞ ¹/₃ ²/₃ fflffiff ☚ ★ ¢ ₨

EF547 Mac + PC   ①   ✏ 1990: David Quay
ITC Quay Sans® 1

abcdefghijklmnopqrstuvwxyz[äöüßåøæœç]
ABCDEFGHIJKLMNOPQRSTUVWXYZ
1234567890(.,;:?!$&-*){ÄÖÜÅØÆŒÇ}

aa*a*
C2552 ©
Congress Sans, Zelig

▶ Book
The quick brown fox jumps over a Dog. Zwei Boxkämpfer jagen Eva durch Sylt portez ce vieux Whiskey blond qui fume une pipe aber echt

▶ Book Italic
The quick brown fox jumps over a Dog. Zwei Boxkämpfer jagen Eva durch Sylt portez ce vieux Whiskey blond qui fume une pipe aber echt

▶ Book Small Caps
The quick brown fox jumps over a Dog. 123 4567 890 Zwei Boxkämpfer jagen Eva durch Sylt portez ce vieux Whiskey blond qui

---

EF548 Mac + PC   ①   ✏ 1990: David Quay
ITC Quay Sans 2

abcdefghijklmnopqrstuvwxyz[äöüßåøæœç]
ABCDEFGHIJKLMNOPQRSTUVWXYZ
1234567890(.,;:?!$&-*){ÄÖÜÅØÆŒÇ}

aa*a*
C2552 ©
Congress Sans, Zelig

▶ Medium
The quick brown fox jumps over a Dog. Zwei Boxkämpfer jagen Eva durch Sylt portez ce vieux Whiskey blond qui fume une pipe aber

▶ Medium Italic
The quick brown fox jumps over a Dog. Zwei Boxkämpfer jagen Eva durch Sylt portez ce vieux Whiskey blond qui fume une pipe aber echt

▶ Medium Small Caps
The quick brown fox jumps over a Dog. 123 4567 890 Zwei Boxkämpfer jagen Eva durch Sylt portez ce vieux Whiskey blond

---

EF549 Mac + PC   ①   ✏ 1990: David Quay
ITC Quay Sans 3

abcdefghijklmnopqrstuvwxyz[äöüßåøæœç]
ABCDEFGHIJKLMNOPQRSTUVWXYZ
1234567890(.,;:?!$&-*){ÄÖÜÅØÆŒÇ}

© FSI 1993

▼ EF549 Mac + PC ITC Quay Sans 3

aa*a*
C2552
Congress Sans, Zelig

▶ Black
The quick brown fox jumps over a Dog. Zwei Boxkämpfer jagen Eva durch Sylt portez ce vieux Whiskey blond qui fume

▶ Black Italic
The quick brown fox jumps over a Dog. Zwei Boxkämpfer jagen Eva durch Sylt portez ce vieux Whiskey blond qui fume

---

C6568 Mac + PC ④
Quill™

abcdefghijklmnopqrstuvwxyz[äöüßåç]
ABCDEFGHIJKLMNOPQRSTUVWXYZ
1234567890(.,:;?!$&-*){ÄÖÜÅÇ}

Agfa Scripts 1:
Commercial Script, Helinda Rook™, Old English Text, Original Script™, Quill™, Stuyvesant2, Wedding Text

---

C467 Mac + PC ⑥ ✎ 1939: Alessandro Butti
Quirinus™ Bold

abcdefghijklmnopqrstuvwxyzläöüåøæœç|
ABCDEFGHIJKLMNOPQRSTUVWXYZ
1234567890(.,:;?!$&-*)◇ÄÖÜÅØÆŒÇ◆

Headlines 81S:
Egiziano™ Black, PL Behemoth Semi Condensed, PL Benguiat Frisky, PL Futura Maxi 1, PL Tower™ Condensed, Quirinus™ Bold, Section™ Bold Condensed, Stratford ™Bold, Woodblock

---

L2728 Mac ④ ✎ 1991: Vince Whitlock
Quixley™

abcdefghijklmnopqrstuvwxyz[äöüßåøæœç]
ABCDEFGHIJKLMNOPQRSTUVWXYZ
1234567890(.,:;?!$&-*)ÄÖÜÅØÆŒÇ

A407 Mac + PC ② ✎ 1977: Ray Baker
ITC Quorum®

abcdefghijklmnopqrstuvwxyz[äöüßåøæœç]
ABCDEFGHIJKLMNOPQRSTUVWXYZ
1234567890(.,:;?!$&-*){ÄÖÜÅØÆŒÇ}

aa*a*
BT1373
ITC Quorum 1, Lt, Blk
BT1374
ITC Quorum 2, Bk, Med, Bd

▶ Light
The quick brown fox jumps over a Dog. Zwei Boxkämpfer jagen Eva durch Sylt portez ce vieux Whiskey blond qui fume une pipe aber

▶ Book
The quick brown fox jumps over a Dog. Zwei Boxkämpfer jagen Eva durch Sylt portez ce vieux Whiskey blond qui fume une pipe aber

▶ Medium
The quick brown fox jumps over a Dog. Zwei Boxkämpfer jagen Eva durch Sylt portez ce vieux Whiskey blond qui fume une

▶ Bold
The quick brown fox jumps over a Dog. Zwei Boxkämpfer jagen Eva durch Sylt portez ce vieux Whiskey blond qui fume

© FSI 1993

▼ A407 Mac + PC ITC Quorum®
▶ Black
The quick brown fox jumps over a Dog. Zwei Boxkämpfer jagen Eva durch Sylt portez ce vieux Whiskey blond qui fume

Erik van Blokland, LëttErroR, Den Haag, NL

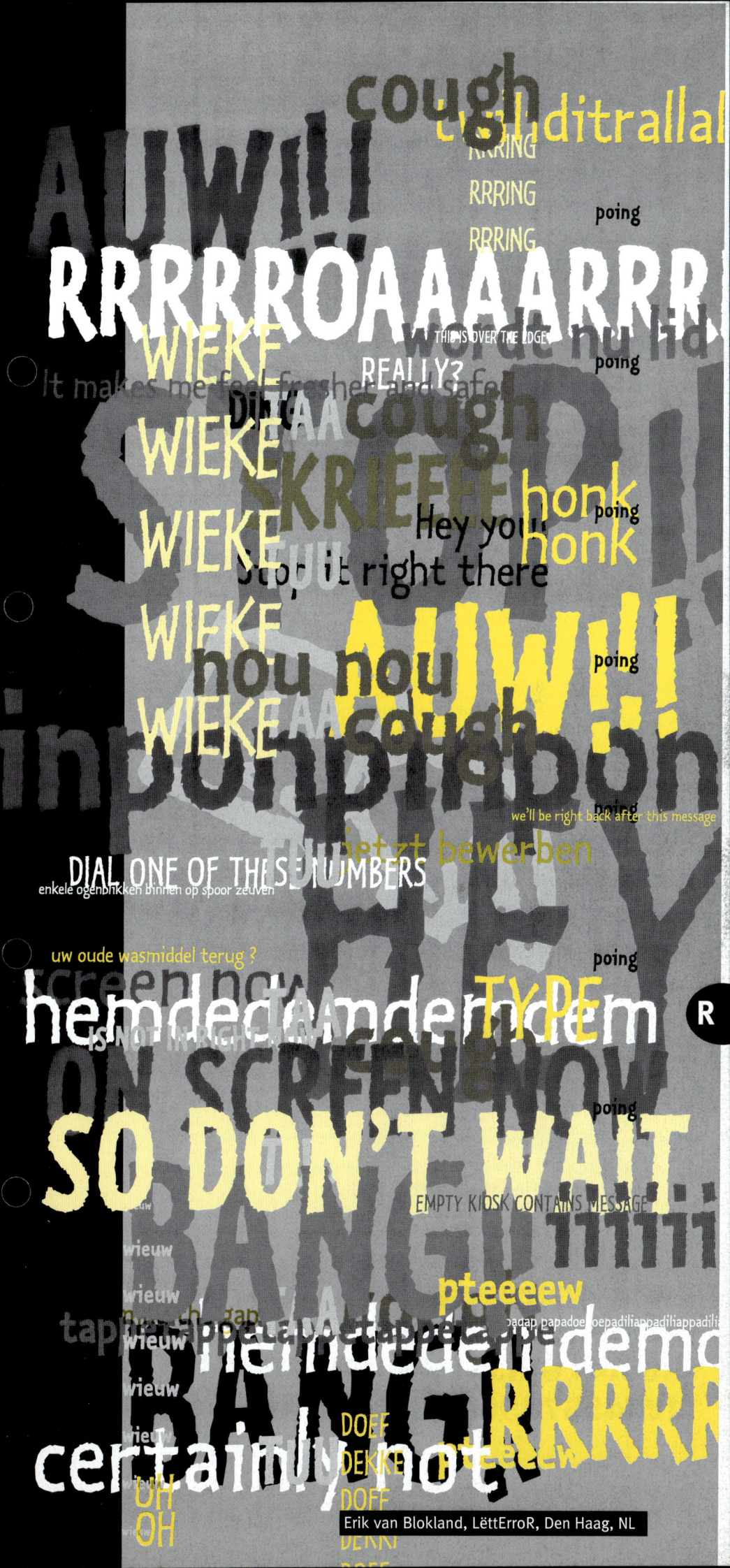

Radiant™
C2524 Mac + PC — 1938: R. H. Middleton

abcdefghijklmnopqrstuvwxyz1234567890[äöüßåøæœç]
ABCDEFGHIJKLMNOPQRSTUVWXYZ(.,:;?!$&-*)◇ÄÖÜÅØÆŒÇ◆

Headlines 88S:
Brasilia Seven, Brasilia Three, Latin Bold, Latin Elongated, Radiant™
Mtronome Gothic, Britannic

Radiant 1 Text
EF6323 Mac + PC — 1938: R. H. Middleton

abcdefghijklmnopqrstuvwxyz[äöüßåøæœç]
ABCDEFGHIJKLMNOPQRSTUVWXYZ
1234567890(.,:;?!$&-*){ÄÖÜÅØÆŒÇ}

Mtronome Gothic, Britannic

▶ Light
The quick brown fox jumps over a Dog. Zwei Boxkämpfer jagen Eva durch Sylt portez ce vieux Whiskey blond qui fume une pipe aber echt

▶ Medium
The quick brown fox jumps over a Dog. Zwei Boxkämpfer jagen Eva durch Sylt portez ce vieux Whiskey blond qui fume une pipe aber echt

▶ Bold
The quick brown fox jumps over a Dog. Zwei Boxkämpfer jagen Eva durch Sylt portez ce vieux Whiskey blond qui fume une pipe aber

Radiant 2 Text
EF6324 Mac + PC — 1938: R. H. Middleton

abcdefghijklmnopqrstuvwxyz[äöüßåøæœç]
ABCDEFGHIJKLMNOPQRSTUVWXYZ
1234567890(.,:;?!$&-*){ÄÖÜÅØÆŒÇ}

Mtronome Gothic, Britannic

▶ Book
The quick brown fox jumps over a Dog. Zwei Boxkämpfer jagen Eva durch Sylt portez ce vieux Whiskey blond qui fume une pipe aber echt

▶ Demi Bold
The quick brown fox jumps over a Dog. Zwei Boxkämpfer jagen Eva durch Sylt portez ce vieux Whiskey blond qui fume une pipe aber

▶ Black
The quick brown fox jumps over a Dog. Zwei Boxkämpfer jagen Eva durch Sylt portez ce vieux Whiskey blond qui fume une

Radiant 3 Display
EF6325 Mac + PC — 1938: R. H. Middleton

abcdefghijklmnopqrstuvwxyz[äöüßåøæœç]
ABCDEFGHIJKLMNOPQRSTUVWXYZ
1234567890(.,:;?!$&-*){ÄÖÜÅØÆŒÇ}

© FSI 1993

▼ EF6325 Mac + PC Radiant 3 Display

Ⓒ Mtronome Gothic, Britannic

▶ Condensed No 1
The quick brown fox jumps over a Dog. Zwei Boxkämpfer jagen Eva durch Sylt portez ce vieux Whiskey blond qui fume une

▶ Condensed No 3
The quick brown fox jumps over a Dog. Zwei Boxkämpfer jagen Eva durch Sylt portez ce vieux Whiskey blond qui fume une pipe aber echt über die Mauer gesprungen und auch

▶ Condensed No 5
The quick brown fox jumps over a Dog. Zwei Boxkämpfer jagen Eva durch Sylt portez ce vieux Whiskey blond qui fume une pipe aber echt über die Mauer gesprungen und auch smørebrød en ysjes natuurlijk

EF6326 Mac + PC ⑥ 1938: R. H. Middleton
Radiant 4 Display

abcdefghijklmnopqrstuvwxyz[äöüßåøæœç]
ABCDEFGHIJKLMNOPQRSTUVWXYZ
1234567890(.,;:?!$&-*){ÄÖÜÅØÆŒÇ}

Ⓒ Mtronome Gothic, Britannic

▶ Condensed No 2
The quick brown fox jumps over a Dog. Zwei Boxkämpfer jagen Eva durch Sylt portez ce vieux Whiskey blond qui fume une pipe aber echt

▶ Condensed No 4
The quick brown fox jumps over a Dog. Zwei Boxkämpfer jagen Eva durch Sylt portez ce vieux Whiskey blond qui fume une pipe aber echt über die Mauer gesprungen und auch smørebrød en ysjes

▶ Condensed No 6
The quick brown fox jumps over a Dog. Zwei Boxkämpfer jagen Eva durch Sylt portez ce vieux Whiskey blond qui fume une pipe aber echt über die Mauer gesprungen und auch smørebrød en ysjes natuurlijk

L2729 Mac ④ 1984: Ron Zwingelberg
Rage™ Italic

abcdefghijklmnopqrstuvwxyz [äöüßåøæœç]
ABCDEFGHIJKLMNOPQRSTUVWXYZ
1234567890 (.,;:?!$&-*)ç

L6142 Mac ⑥ 1987: Alan Meeks
Ragtime™

ABCDEFGHIJKLMNOPQRSTUVWXYZ
1234567890(.,;:?!$&-*)[]ÄÖÜÅØÆŒÇ

TF6649 Mac + PC ⑥ 1992: Joe Treacy
TF Raincheck™

abcdefghijklmnopqrstuvwxyz1234567890[äöüßåøæœç]
ABCDEFGHIJKLMNOPQRSTUVWXYZ(.,;:?!$&-*){ÄÖÜÅØÆŒÇ}

TF Guestcheck™ / TF Raincheck™:
TF Guestcheck™, TF Raincheck™

© FSI 1993

| BT845 Mac + PC ③ 1977: (Dair, 1967) (D. Anderson, 1973) Adrian Williams
Raleigh™ 1

abcdefghijklmnopqrstuvwxyz[äöüßåøæœç]
ABCDEFGHIJKLMNOPQRSTUVWXYZ
1234567890(.,:;?!$&-*){ÄÖÜÅØÆŒÇ}

aa*a*
A408
Raleigh, Reg, Med,
DemiBd, Bd

▶ Light
The quick brown fox jumps over a Dog. Zwei Boxkämpfer jagen Eva durch Sylt portez ce vieux Whiskey blond qui fume une

▶ **Extra Bold**
The quick brown fox jumps over a Dog. Zwei Boxkämpfer jagen Eva durch Sylt portez ce vieux Whiskey blond qui fume

| BT1219 Mac + PC ③ 1977: (Dair, 1967) (D. Anderson, 1973) Adrian Williams
Raleigh 2

abcdefghijklmnopqrstuvwxyz[äöüßåøæœç]
ABCDEFGHIJKLMNOPQRSTUVWXYZ
1234567890(.,:;?!$&-*){ÄÖÜÅØÆŒÇ}

aa*a*
A408
Raleigh, Reg, Med,
DemiBd, Bd

▶ Regular
The quick brown fox jumps over a Dog. Zwei Boxkämpfer jagen Eva durch Sylt portez ce vieux Whiskey blond qui fume une

▶ Medium
The quick brown fox jumps over a Dog. Zwei Boxkämpfer jagen Eva durch Sylt portez ce vieux Whiskey blond qui fume une

▶ Demi bold
The quick brown fox jumps over a Dog. Zwei Boxkämpfer jagen Eva durch Sylt portez ce vieux Whiskey blond qui fume une

▶ **Bold**
The quick brown fox jumps over a Dog. Zwei Boxkämpfer jagen Eva durch Sylt portez ce vieux Whiskey blond qui fume

| C016 Mac + PC ⑥ c. 1885: William F. Jackson
Raphael™

abcdefghijklmnopqrstuvwxyz[äöüßåøæœç]
ABCDEFGHIJKLMNOPQRSTUVWXYZ
1234567890(.,:;?!$&-*){ÄÖÜÅØÆŒÇ}

Branding Iron:
Branding Iron, Isabella™, McCollough, Raphael™

| L2730 Mac ④ 1989: Martin Wait
Rapier™

abcdefghijklmnopqrstuvwxyz [äöüßåøæœç]
ABCDEFGHIJKLMNOPQRSTUVWXYZ
1234567890(.,:: ?!$&-)Ç*

© FSI 1993

RB6094 Mac ⑥ 1991: Richard Beatty
Recherché™

abcdefghijklmnopqrstuvwxyz[äöüßåøæœç]
ABCDEFGHIJKLMNOPQRSTUVWXYZ
1234567890(.,:;?!$&-*){ÄÖÜÅØÆŒÇ}

Beatty Victoriana™:
Childs™, Hermosa™, Recherché™, Spiral™, Wanted™

RB6095 Mac ⑥ 1991: Richard Beatty
Recherché Alternates

abcdefghijklmnopqrstuvwxyz[äöüßåøæœç]
ABCDEFGHIJKLMNOPQRSTUVWXYZ
1234567890(.,:;?!$&-*){ÄÖÜÅØÆŒÇ}

Beatty Victoriana Alternates:
Childs Alternates, Hermosa Alternates, Recherché Alternates, Spiral Alternates, Wanted Alternates

L6143 Mac ⑥ 1988: Martin Wait
Refracta™

ABCDEFGHIJKLMNOPQRSTUVWXYZ
1234567890(.,:;?!$&-*)[ ]ÄÖÜÅØÆŒÇ

L6144 Mac ⑥ 1987: Alan Meeks
Regatta™ Condensed

abcdefghijklmnopqrstuvwxyz[äöüßåøæœç]
ABCDEFGHIJKLMNOPQRSTUVWXYZ
1234567890(.,:;?!$&-*)ÄÖÜÅØÆŒÇ

SF2899 Mac ⑤ 1992: Rod McDonald
Regency Gothic™

ABCDEFGHIJKLMNOPQRSTUVWXYZ1234567890[ÄÖÜÅØÆŒÇ]
ABCDEFGHIJKLMNOPQRSTUVWXYZ(.,:;?!$&-*){ÄÖÜÅØÆŒÇ}

👁
Huxley Vertical, Aldous Vertical, Phenix American, De Stijl, Bureau Agency

▶ One
The quick brown fox jumps over a dog. Zwei Boxkämpfer jagen Eva durch Sylt portez ce vieux Whiskey blond qui fume une pipe aber echt über die Mauer gesprungen und auch smørebrød en ysjes natuurlijk. But very long spazierende tekst ist used in dieser catalog maar nicht

▶ Two
The quick brown fox jumps over a dog. Zwei Boxkämpfer jagen Eva durch Sylt portez ce vieux Whiskey blond qui fume une pipe aber echt über die Mauer gesprungen und auch smørebrød en ysjes natuurlijk. But very long spazierende tekst ist used in dieser catalog

▶ Three
The quick brown fox jumps over a dog. Zwei Boxkämpfer jagen Eva durch Sylt portez ce vieux Whiskey blond qui fume une pipe aber echt über die Mauer gesprungen und auch smørebrød en ysjes natuurlijk. But very long spazierende tekst ist used in dieser

© FSI 1993

E6339 Mac + PC ⑥ 🖉 1992: Frank Heine
Remedy™

abcdefghijklmnopqrstuvwxyz[äöüßåøæœç]
ABCDEFGHIJKLMNOPQRSTUVWXYZ
1234567890(.,;:?!$&-*){ÄÖÜÅØÆŒÇ}

▶ Single
The quick brown fox jumps over a Dog. Zwei Boxkämpfer jagen Eva durch Sylt portez ce vieux Whiskey blond qui fume une pipe

▶ Double
The quick brown fox jumps over a Dog. Zwei Boxkämpfer jagen Eva durch Sylt portez ce vieux Whiskey blond qui fume une pipe

▶ Single Extras
The quick brown fox jumps over a Dog. Zwei Boxkämpfer jagen Eva durch Sylt portez ce vieux

▶ Double Extras
The quick brown fox jumps over a Dog. Zwei Boxkämpfer jagen Eva durch Sylt portez ce vieux

ET1106 Mac + PC
Renaissance™

Renaissance™:
Leonardo Hand™, Tagliente™

EF529 Mac + PC ③ 🖉 1968: (Wolff Olins)
Renault™

abcdefghijklmnopqrstuvwxyz[äöüßåøæœç]
ABCDEFGHIJKLMNOPQRSTUVWXYZ
1234567890(.,;:?!$&-*){ÄÖÜÅØÆŒÇ}

▶ Light
The quick brown fox jumps over a Dog. Zwei Boxkämpfer jagen Eva durch Sylt portez ce vieux Whiskey blond qui fume

▶ Light Italic
The quick brown fox jumps over a Dog. Zwei Boxkämpfer jagen Eva durch Sylt portez ce vieux Whiskey blond qui fume

▶ Bold
The quick brown fox jumps over a Dog. Zwei Boxkämpfer jagen Eva durch Sylt portez ce vieux Whiskey blond

▶ Bold Italic
The quick brown fox jumps over a Dog. Zwei Boxkämpfer jagen Eva durch Sylt portez ce vieux Whiskey

MC2949 Mac + PC ② 🖉 1968: (Wolff Olins)
Renault

abcdefghijklmnopqrstuvwxyz[äöüßåøæœç]
ABCDEFGHIJKLMNOPQRSTUVWXYZ
1234567890(.,;:?!$&-*){ÄÖÜÅØÆŒÇ}

© FSI 1993

Renault Bold
MC2950 Mac + PC ② 1968: (Wolff Olins)

abcdefghijklmnopqrstuvwxyz[äöüßåøæœç]
ABCDEFGHIJKLMNOPQRSTUVWXYZ
1234567890(.,;:?!$&-*){ÄÖÜÅØÆŒÇ}

Reporter™ No 2
A349 Mac + PC ④ 1938: Carlos Winkow

abcdefghijklmnopqrstuvwxyz[äöüßåøæœç]
ABCDEFGHIJKLMNOPQRSTUVWXYZ
1234567890(.,;:?!$&-*){ÄÖÜÅØÆŒÇ}

Mistral / Reporter:
Mistral™, Reporter™ No 2

Retro™ Bold
L2853 Mac ⑤ 1992: Colin Brignall, Andrew Smith

ABCDEFGHIJKLMNOPQRSTUVWXYZ
1234567890[.,;:?!$&-*][]ÄÖÜÅØÆŒÇ

Retro Bold Condensed
L6599 Mac ⑤ 1992: Andrew Smith

ABCDEFGHIJKLMNOPQRSTUVWXYZ
1234567890[.,;:?!$&-*][]ÄÖÜÅØÆŒÇ

Revue™
A001 Mac + PC ⑥ 1969: Colin Brignall

abcdefghijklmnopqrstuvwxyz[äöüßåøæœç]
ABCDEFGHIJKLMNOPQRSTUVWXYZ
1234567890(.,;:?!$&-*){ÄÖÜÅØÆŒÇ}

Aachen Bold:
Aachen Bold, Freestyle Script, Revue™, University Roman
aaa BT1375
Revue, Reg

Ritmo™ Bold
C468 Mac + PC ⑥ 1955: Aldo Novarese

abcdefghijklmnopqrstuvwxyz[äöüåøæœç]
ABCDEFGHIJKLMNOPQRSTUVWXYZ
1234567890(.,;:?!$&-*)◊ÄÖÜÅØÆŒÇ◆

Headlines 82S:
Neon Extra Condensed™, PL Barnum Block, PL Benguiat Frisky Bold, PL Davison Zip Bold, PL Fiedler Gothic Bold, PL Futura Maxi 2, PL Trophy™ Oblique, Ritmo™ Bold, TC Broadway
↻ Banco

© FSI 1993

L2802 Mac · ⑤ · 1989: David Quay
Robotik™
abcdefghijklmnopqrstuvwxyz[äöüßåøæœç]
ABCDEFGHIJKLMNOPQRSTUVWXYZ
1234567890(.,;:?!$&-*)ÄÖÜÅØÆŒÇ

L2803 Mac · ⑤ · 1989: David Quay
Robotik Italic
abcdefghijklmnopqrstuvwxyz[äöüßåøæœç]
ABCDEFGHIJKLMNOPQRSTUVWXYZ
1234567890(.,;:?!$&-*)ÄÖÜÅØÆŒÇ

M099 Mac + PC · ③ · 1934: (F. H. Pierpont)
Rockwell™ 1
abcdefghijklmnopqrstuvwxyz[äöüßåøæœç]
ABCDEFGHIJKLMNOPQRSTUVWXYZ
1234567890(.,;:?!$&-*){ÄÖÜÅØÆŒÇ}

aaa
A738
Rockwell 1, Lt, LtIta,
Reg, Ita, Bd, BdIta
BT1320
Rockwell 1, Lt, LtIta,
ExtBd
BT1321
Rockwell 2, Med,
MedIta, Bd
©
Beton, Memphis,
Stratford Bold, Stymie

▶ Light
The quick brown fox jumps over a Dog. Zwei Boxkämpfer jagen Eva durch Sylt portez ce vieux Whiskey blond qui fume

▶ Light Italic
The quick brown fox jumps over a Dog. Zwei Boxkämpfer jagen Eva durch Sylt portez ce vieux Whiskey blond qui fume une

▶ Regular
The quick brown fox jumps over a Dog. Zwei Boxkämpfer jagen Eva durch Sylt portez ce vieux Whiskey blond qui

▶ Italic
The quick brown fox jumps over a Dog. Zwei Boxkämpfer jagen Eva durch Sylt portez ce vieux Whiskey blond qui fume

▶ Bold
The quick brown fox jumps over a Dog. Zwei Boxkämpfer jagen Eva durch Sylt portez ce vieux Whiskey

▶ Bold Italic
The quick brown fox jumps over a Dog. Zwei Boxkämpfer jagen Eva durch Sylt portez ce vieux Whiskey blond

M185 Mac + PC · ③ · 1934: (F. H. Pierpont)
Rockwell 2
abcdefghijklmnopqrstuvwxyz[äöüßåøæœç]
ABCDEFGHIJKLMNOPQRSTUVWXYZ
1234567890(.,;:?!$&-*){ÄÖÜÅØÆŒÇ}

aaa
A913
Rockwell 2, ExtBd,
Con, BdCon
BT1320
Rockwell 1, Lt, LtIta,
ExtBd
BT1321
Rockwell 2, Med,
MedIta, Bd
©
Beton, Memphis,
Stratford Bold, Stymie

▶ Extra Bold
The quick brown fox jumps over a Dog. Zwei Boxkämpfer jagen Eva durch Sylt

▶ Condensed
The quick brown fox jumps over a Dog. Zwei Boxkämpfer jagen Eva durch Sylt portez ce vieux Whiskey blond qui fume une pipe aber echt über die Mauer gesprungen und auch

▶ Bold Condensed
The quick brown fox jumps over a Dog. Zwei Boxkämpfer jagen Eva durch Sylt portez ce vieux Whiskey blond qui fume une pipe aber echt

© FSI 1993

C2780 Mac + PC ⑥
Roman

ABCDEFGHIJKLMNOPQRSTUVWXYZ[ÄÖÜÅÇ]
ABCDEFGHIJKLMNOPQRSTUVWXYZ
1234567890(.,;:?!$&-*){ÄÖÜÅÇ}

▶ Light
THE QUICK BROWN FOX JUMPS OVER A DOG. ZWEI BOXKÄMPFER JAGEN EVA DURCH

▶ Medium
THE QUICK BROWN FOX JUMPS OVER A DOG. ZWEI BOXKÄMPFER JAGEN EVA DURCH SYLT

Agfa Engravers 1:
Antique Roman, Artisan Roman, Burin Roman, Burin Sans, Classic Roman, Handle Old Style, Roman

EF6454 Mac + PC ②
Romana™ 1

abcdefghijklmnopqrstuvwxyz[äöüßåøæœç]
ABCDEFGHIJKLMNOPQRSTUVWXYZ
1234567890(.,;:?!$&-*){ÄÖÜÅØÆŒÇ}

aa*a*
BT846
Romana, Reg, Bd

▶ Light
The quick brown fox jumps over a Dog. Zwei Boxkämpfer jagen Eva durch Sylt portez ce vieux Whiskey blond qui fume une pipe aber echt

▶ Medium
The quick brown fox jumps over a Dog. Zwei Boxkämpfer jagen Eva durch Sylt portez ce vieux Whiskey blond qui fume une pipe aber echt

▶ Bold
The quick brown fox jumps over a Dog. Zwei Boxkämpfer jagen Eva durch Sylt portez ce vieux Whiskey blond qui fume

EF6455 Mac + PC ②
Romana 2

abcdefghijklmnopqrstuvwxyz[äöüßåøæœç]
ABCDEFGHIJKLMNOPQRSTUVWXYZ
1234567890(.,;:?!$&-*){ÄÖÜÅØÆŒÇ}

aa*a*
BT846
Romana, Reg, Bd

▶ Book
The quick brown fox jumps over a Dog. Zwei Boxkämpfer jagen Eva durch Sylt portez ce vieux Whiskey blond qui fume une pipe aber echt

▶ Demi Bold
The quick brown fox jumps over a Dog. Zwei Boxkämpfer jagen Eva durch Sylt portez ce vieux Whiskey blond qui fume une pipe

▶ Ultra
The quick brown fox jumps over a Dog. Zwei Boxkämpfer jagen Eva durch Sylt portez ce vieux Whiskey blond qui fume

© FSI 1993

Romeo™

FB1055 Mac + PC — 1991: Jill Pichotta, David Berlow

abcdefghijklmnopqrstuvwxyz1234567890[äöüßåøæœç]
ABCDEFGHIJKLMNOPQRSTUVWXYZ(.,;:?!$&-*){ÄÖÜÅØÆŒÇ}

ITC Anna, Bodega, Triplex Condensed, Triplex Serif Condensed

▶ Skinny Condensed
The quick brown fox jumps over a Dog. Zwei Boxkämpfer jagen Eva durch Sylt portez ce vieux Whiskey blond qui fume une pipe aber echt über die Mauer gesprungen und auch smørebrød en ysjes natuurlicht. But very long spazierende text is used in diesen catalog maar nicht

▶ Medium Condensed
The quick brown fox jumps over a Dog. Zwei Boxkämpfer jagen Eva durch Sylt portez ce vieux Whiskey blond qui fume une pipe aber echt über die Mauer gesprungen und auch smørebrød en ysjes

Letraset Romic™

C992 Mac + PC — 1979: Colin Brignall

abcdefghijklmnopqrstuvwxyz[äöüßåøæœç]
ABCDEFGHIJKLMNOPQRSTUVWXYZ
1234567890(.,;:?!$&-*){ÄÖÜÅØÆŒÇ}

▶ Light
The quick brown fox jumps over a Dog. Zwei Boxkämpfer jagen Eva durch Sylt portez ce vieux Whiskey blond qui fume

▶ Light Italic
The quick brown fox jumps over a Dog. Zwei Boxkämpfer jagen Eva durch Sylt portez ce vieux Whiskey blond qui fume

▶ Medium
The quick brown fox jumps over a Dog. Zwei Boxkämpfer jagen Eva durch Sylt portez ce vieux Whiskey blond qui fume

▶ Bold
The quick brown fox jumps over a Dog. Zwei Boxkämpfer jagen Eva durch Sylt portez ce vieux Whiskey blond qui

▶ Extra Bold
The quick brown fox jumps over a Dog. Zwei Boxkämpfer jagen Eva durch Sylt portez ce vieux Whiskey

ITC Ronda®

BT847 Mac + PC — 1970: Tom Carnase, Ronne Bonder

abcdefghijklmnopqrstuvwxyz[äöüßåøæœç]
ABCDEFGHIJKLMNOPQRSTUVWXYZ
1234567890(.,;:?!$&-*){ÄÖÜÅØÆŒÇ}

ITC Bauhaus, Blippo, Horatio, Pump

▶ Light
The quick brown fox jumps over a Dog. Zwei Boxkämpfer jagen Eva durch Sylt portez ce vieux Whiskey blond qui fume

▶ Regular
The quick brown fox jumps over a Dog. Zwei Boxkämpfer jagen Eva durch Sylt portez ce vieux Whiskey blond qui

▶ Bold
The quick brown fox jumps over a Dog. Zwei Boxkämpfer jagen Eva durch Sylt portez ce vieux Whiskey blond qui

© FSI 1993

Rondo™
MC6350 Mac + PC ④ Schlesinger/Dooijes

abcdefghijklmnopqrstuvwxyz[äöüßåøæœç]
ABCDEFGHIJKLMNOPQRSTUVWXYZ
1234567890(.,:;?!$&-*){ÄÖÜÅØÆŒÇ}

FF Rosetta™
FF730 Mac + PC ⑤ 1991: Max Kisman

abcdefghijklmnopqrstuvwxyz1234567890[äöüßåøæœç]
ABCDEFGHIJKLMNOPQRSTUVWXYZ(.,:;?!$&-*){ÄÖÜÅØÆŒÇ}

▶ Regular
The quick brown fox jumps over a Dog. Zwei Boxkämpfer jagen Eva durch Sylt portez ce vieux Whiskey blond qui fume une pipe aber echt über die Mauer gesprungen und auch

▶ Italic
The quick brown fox jumps over a Dog. Zwei Boxkämpfer jagen Eva durch Sylt portez ce vieux Whiskey blond qui fume une pipe aber echt über die Mauer gesprungen und auch

▶ Bold
The quick brown fox jumps over a Dog. Zwei Boxkämpfer jagen Eva durch Sylt portez ce vieux Whiskey blond qui fume

▶ Bold Italic
The quick brown fox jumps over a Dog. Zwei Boxkämpfer jagen Eva durch Sylt portez ce vieux Whiskey blond qui fume

Roslyn Gothic™ Medium
MC6347 Mac + PC ⑥

abcdefghijklmnopqrstuvwxyz[äöüßåøæœç]
ABCDEFGHIJKLMNOPQRSTUVWXYZ
1234567890(.,:;?!$&-*){ÄÖÜÅØÆŒÇ}

Roslyn Gothic Bold
MC6348 Mac + PC ⑥

abcdefghijklmnopqrstuvwxyz[äöüßåøæœç]
ABCDEFGHIJKLMNOPQRSTUVWXYZ
1234567890(.,:;?!$&-*){ÄÖÜÅØÆŒÇ}

Roslyn Gothic Outline
MC6349 Mac + PC ⑥

abcdefghijklmnopqrstuvwxyz[äöüßåøæœç]
ABCDEFGHIJKLMNOPQRSTUVWXYZ
1234567890(.,:;?!$&-*){ÄÖÜÅØÆŒÇ}

© FSI 1993

LP6663 Mac + PC ⑥
Roslyn Bold

abcdefghijklmnopqrstuvwxyz[äöüßåøæœç]
ABCDEFGHIJKLMNOPQRSTUVWXYZ
1234567890(.,:;?!$&-*){ÄÖÜÅØÆŒÇ}

LetterPerfect 5:
Hardwood™, Koch Original™, Roslyn Bold
aaa MC6348
Roslyn Gothic Bold, Bd

A2547 Mac + PC ② 1971: Arthur Ritzel
Rotation™

abcdefghijklmnopqrstuvwxyz[äöüßåøæœç]
ABCDEFGHIJKLMNOPQRSTUVWXYZ
1234567890(.,:;?!$&-*){ÄÖÜÅØÆŒÇ}

▶ Regular
The quick brown fox jumps over a Dog. Zwei Boxkämpfer jagen Eva durch Sylt portez ce vieux Whiskey blond qui fume

▶ Italic
The quick brown fox jumps over a Dog. Zwei Boxkämpfer jagen Eva durch Sylt portez ce vieux Whiskey blond qui fume

▶ Bold
The quick brown fox jumps over a Dog. Zwei Boxkämpfer jagen Eva durch Sylt portez ce vieux Whiskey blond qui fume

C471 Mac + PC ① 1989: Otl Aicher
Rotis™ Sans Serif

abcdefghijklmnopqrstuvwxyz[äöüßåøæœç]
ABCDEFGHIJKLMNOPQRSTUVWXYZ
1234567890(.,:;?!$&-*){ÄÖÜÅØÆŒÇ}

aaa
A1023
Rotis Sans Serif, 45Lt, 46LtIta, 55Reg, 56Ita, 65Bd, 75ExtBd
FF Wunderlich

▶ 45 Light
The quick brown fox jumps over a Dog. Zwei Boxkämpfer jagen Eva durch Sylt portez ce vieux Whiskey blond qui fume une pipe aber echt

▶ 46 Light Italic
The quick brown fox jumps over a Dog. Zwei Boxkämpfer jagen Eva durch Sylt portez ce vieux Whiskey blond qui fume une pipe aber echt

▶ 55 Regular
The quick brown fox jumps over a Dog. Zwei Boxkämpfer jagen Eva durch Sylt portez ce vieux Whiskey blond qui fume une pipe aber echt

▶ 56 Italic
The quick brown fox jumps over a Dog. Zwei Boxkämpfer jagen Eva durch Sylt portez ce vieux Whiskey blond qui fume une pipe aber echt

▶ 65 Bold
The quick brown fox jumps over a Dog. Zwei Boxkämpfer jagen Eva durch Sylt portez ce vieux Whiskey blond qui fume une pipe aber

▶ 75 Extra Bold
The quick brown fox jumps over a Dog. Zwei Boxkämpfer jagen Eva durch Sylt portez ce vieux Whiskey blond qui fume une pipe

© FSI 1993

C472 Mac + PC ① 1989: Otl Aicher
Rotis Semisans

abcdefghijklmnopqrstuvwxyz[äöüßåøæœç]
ABCDEFGHIJKLMNOPQRSTUVWXYZ
1234567890(.,;:?!$&-*){ÄÖÜÅØÆŒÇ}

aa*a*
A1022
Rotis SemiSans, 45Lt, 46LtIta, 55Reg, 56Ita, 65Bd, 75ExtBd

▶ 45 Light
The quick brown fox jumps over a Dog. Zwei Boxkämpfer jagen Eva durch Sylt portez ce vieux Whiskey blond qui fume une pipe aber echt

▶ 46 Light Italic
The quick brown fox jumps over a Dog. Zwei Boxkämpfer jagen Eva durch Sylt portez ce vieux Whiskey blond qui fume une pipe aber echt

▶ 55 Regular
The quick brown fox jumps over a Dog. Zwei Boxkämpfer jagen Eva durch Sylt portez ce vieux Whiskey blond qui fume une pipe aber

▶ 56 Italic
The quick brown fox jumps over a Dog. Zwei Boxkämpfer jagen Eva durch Sylt portez ce vieux Whiskey blond qui fume une pipe aber

▶ 65 Bold
The quick brown fox jumps over a Dog. Zwei Boxkämpfer jagen Eva durch Sylt portez ce vieux Whiskey blond qui fume une

▶ 75 Extra Bold
The quick brown fox jumps over a Dog. Zwei Boxkämpfer jagen Eva durch Sylt portez ce vieux Whiskey blond qui fume une

C473 Mac + PC ② 1989: Otl Aicher
Rotis Serif & SemiSerif

Rotis Serif & SemiSerif:
Rotis SemiSerif, Rotis Serif

C473 Mac + PC ② 1989: Otl Aicher
Rotis SemiSerif

abcdefghijklmnopqrstuvwxyz[äöüßåøæœç]
ABCDEFGHIJKLMNOPQRSTUVWXYZ
1234567890(.,;:?!$&-*){ÄÖÜÅØÆŒÇ}

aa*a*
A1021
Rotis Serif, 55Reg, 56Ita, 65Bd
Rotis SemiSerif, 55Reg, 65Ita
Rotis Serif / SemiSerif

▶ 55 Regular
The quick brown fox jumps over a Dog. Zwei Boxkämpfer jagen Eva durch Sylt portez ce vieux Whiskey blond qui fume une pipe aber

▶ 65 Bold
The quick brown fox jumps over a Dog. Zwei Boxkämpfer jagen Eva durch Sylt portez ce vieux Whiskey blond qui fume une

Rotis Serif & SemiSerif:
Rotis SemiSerif, Rotis Serif
aa*a* A1021
Rotis Serif, 55Reg, 56Ita, 65Bd
Rotis SemiSerif, 55Reg, 65Ita

C473 Mac + PC ② 1989: Otl Aicher
Rotis Serif

abcdefghijklmnopqrstuvwxyz[äöüßåøæœç]
ABCDEFGHIJKLMNOPQRSTUVWXYZ
1234567890(.,;:?!$&-*){ÄÖÜÅØÆŒÇ}

© FSI 1993

▼ C473 Mac + PC   Rotis Serif

aa*a*
A1021
Rotis Serif, 55Reg,
56Ita, 65Bd
Rotis SemiSerif,
55Reg, 65Ita
Rotis Serif / SemiSerif

▶ 55 Regular
The quick brown fox jumps over a Dog. Zwei Boxkämpfer jagen Eva durch Sylt portez ce vieux Whiskey blond qui fume une

▶ 56 Italic
The quick brown fox jumps over a Dog. Zwei Boxkämpfer jagen Eva durch Sylt portez ce vieux Whiskey blond qui fume une

▶ 65 Bold
The quick brown fox jumps over a Dog. Zwei Boxkämpfer jagen Eva durch Sylt portez ce vieux Whiskey blond qui fume

Rotis Serif & SemiSerif:
Rotis SemiSerif, Rotis Serif

TF6921 Mac + PC   ②   1993: Joe Treacy
TF Roux™ ExtraBold

abcdefghijklmnopqrstuvwxyz[äöüßåøæœç]
ABCDEFGHIJKLMNOPQRSTUVWXYZ
1234567890(.,:;?!$&-*){ÄÖÜÅØÆŒÇ}

FB409 Mac + PC   ①   1989–90: John Downer
Bureau Roxy™

abcdefghijklmnopqrstuvwxyz[äöüßåøæœç]
ABCDEFGHIJKLMNOPQRSTUVWXYZ
1234567890(.,:;?!$&-*){ÄÖÜÅØÆŒÇ}

©
FF Wunderlich,
Britannic, Radiant

▶ Medium
The quick brown fox jumps over a Dog. Zwei Boxkämpfer jagen Eva durch Sylt portez ce vieux Whiskey blond qui fume une pipe aber echt

▶ Medium Italic
The quick brown fox jumps over a Dog. Zwei Boxkämpfer jagen Eva durch Sylt portez ce vieux Whiskey blond qui fume une pipe aber echt über die Mauer

---

FB6604 Mac + PC   ①   1992: John Downer
Bureau Roxy 2

abcdefghijklmnopqrstuvwxyz[äöüßåøæœç]
ABCDEFGHIJKLMNOPQRSTUVWXYZ
1234567890(.,:;?!$&-*){ÄÖÜÅØÆŒÇ}

©
FF Wunderlich,
Britannic, Radiant

▶ Light
The quick brown fox jumps over a Dog. Zwei Boxkämpfer jagen Eva durch Sylt portez ce vieux Whiskey blond qui fume une pipe aber echt über die Mauer gesprungen

▶ Light Italic
The quick brown fox jumps over a Dog. Zwei Boxkämpfer jagen Eva durch Sylt portez ce vieux Whiskey blond qui fume une pipe aber echt über die Mauer gesprungen und auch

▶ Black
The quick brown fox jumps over a Dog. Zwei Boxkämpfer jagen Eva durch Sylt portez ce vieux Whiskey blond qui fume une pipe aber

▶ Black Italic
The quick brown fox jumps over a Dog. Zwei Boxkämpfer jagen Eva durch Sylt portez ce vieux Whiskey blond qui fume une pipe aber echt

© FSI 1993

L2804 Mac ④ 1990: Tim Donaldson
Ruach™

abcdefghijklmnopqrstuvwxyz[äöüßåøæç]
ABCDEFGHIJKLMNOPQRSTUVWXYZ
1234567890(.,;:?!$&-*)ÄÖÜÅØÆŒÇ

L2731 Mac ⑥ 1983: Alan Birch
Rubber Stamp™

ABCDEFGHIJKLMNOPQRSTUVWXYZ
1234567890(.,;:?!$&-*)[]ÄÖÜÅØÆŒÇ

LH6640 Mac + PC ④
Ruling Script™

abcdefghijklmnopqrstuvwxyzäöüßåç
ABCDEFGHIJKLMNOPQRSTUVWXYZ
1234567890(.,;:?!&-*)ÄÖÜÅÇ

▶ Regular   ▶ Additions

The quick brown fox jumps over a Dog.   ß£øYæøŒfifl
Zwei Boxkämpfer jagen Eva durch Sylt
portez ce vieux Whiskey blond qui
fume une pipe aber echt über die

Calligraphy for Print:
Ruling Script™, Sho Roman™, Wiesbaden Swing™ Roman

L6145 Mac ⑥ 1987: (1928: Adolf Behrmann)
Rundfunk™

abcdefghijklmnopqrstuvwxyz[äöüßåøæç]
ABCDEFGHIJKLMNOPQRSTUVWXYZ
1234567890(.,;:?!$&-*)ÄÖÜÅØÆŒÇ

M2954 Mac + PC ⑥
Runic Condensed

abcdefghijklmnopqrstuvwxyz1234567890[äöüßåøæç]
ABCDEFGHIJKLMNOPQRSTUVWXYZ(.,;:?!$&-*){ÄÖÜÅØÆŒÇ}

Latin/Runic/Onyx:
Latin Condensed, Onyx™, Runic Condensed
aaa M625
Headliners 5
A2867

© FSI 1993

A1011 Mac + PC ⑤ 1973: John Russell

Beth Russell Square™

abcdefghijklmnopqrstuvwxyz[äöüßåøæœç]
ABCDEFGHIJKLMNOPQRSTUVWXYZ
1234567890(.,;:?!$&-*){ÄÖÜÅØÆŒÇ}

Letraset Crillee, Serpentine

▶ Regular
The quick brown fox jumps over a Dog. Zwei Boxkämpfer jagen Eva durch Sylt portez ce vieux Whiskey blond

▶ Oblique
The quick brown fox jumps over a Dog. Zwei Boxkämpfer jagen Eva durch Sylt portez ce vieux Whiskey blond

© FSI 1993

Hamburgefonts
HAMBURGEFONTS

1990 Isograph
Kurvenlineale
Kopierer

1991 MAC SE 20
Illustrator

Hamburgefonts
HAMBURGEFONTS

Hamburgefonts
HAMBURGEFONTS

Hamburgefonts
HAMBURGEFONTS

Hamburgefonts
HAMBURGEFONTS

1991 MAC SE 30
Ikarus M

Martin Wunderlich, Kiel, D

Sabon™
A168 Mac + PC ② 1966: Jan Tschichold

abcdefghijklmnopqrstuvwxyz[äöüßåøæœç]
ABCDEFGHIJKLMNOPQRSTUVWXYZ
1234567890(.,;:?!$&-*){ÄÖÜÅØÆŒÇ}

aa*a*
M157
Sabon, Reg, Ita, SemBd
BT1311
Sabon, Reg, Ita, Bd, BdIta
©
Nikis

▶ Regular
The quick brown fox jumps over a Dog. Zwei Boxkämpfer jagen Eva durch Sylt portez ce vieux Whiskey blond qui fume

▶ Italic
The quick brown fox jumps over a Dog. Zwei Boxkämpfer jagen Eva durch Sylt portez ce vieux Whiskey blond qui fume

▶ Bold
The quick brown fox jumps over a Dog. Zwei Boxkämpfer jagen Eva durch Sylt portez ce vieux Whiskey blond qui fume

▶ Bold Italic
The quick brown fox jumps over a Dog. Zwei Boxkämpfer jagen Eva durch Sylt portez ce vieux Whiskey blond qui fume

Sabon Small Caps/OSF
A1005 Mac + PC ② 1966: Jan Tschichold

ABCDEFGHIJKLMNOPQRSTUVWXYZ[ÄÖÜSSÅØÆŒÇ]
ABCDEFGHIJKLMNOPQRSTUVWXYZ
1234567890(.,;:?!$&-*){ÄÖÜÅØÆŒÇ}

▶ Small Caps
THE QUICK BROWN FOX JUMPS OVER A DOG. 123 4567 890 ZWEI BOXKÄMPFER JAGEN EVA DURCH SYLT PORTEZ CE VIEUX

▶ Italic OSF
The quick brown fox jumps over a Dog. 123 4567 890 Zwei Boxkämpfer jagen Eva durch Sylt portez ce vieux

▶ Bold OSF
The quick brown fox jumps over a Dog. 123 4567 890 Zwei Boxkämpfer jagen Eva durch Sylt portez ce vieux

▶ Bold Italic OSF
The quick brown fox jumps over a Dog. 123 4567 890 Zwei Boxkämpfer jagen Eva durch Sylt portez ce vieux

Sackers Antique Roman
C2781 Mac + PC ⑥

abcdefghijklmnopqrstuvwxyz[äöüßåç]
ABCDEFGHIJKLMNOPQRSTUVWXYZ
1234567890(.,;:?!$&-*){ÄÖÜÅthstÇ}

▶ Solid
The quick brown fox jumps over a Dog. Zwei Boxkämpfer jagen Eva durch Sylt portez ce vieux Whiskey blond qui fume une pipe aber echt über die Mauer

▶ Open
The quick brown fox jumps over a Dog. Zwei Boxkämpfer jagen Eva durch Sylt portez ce vieux Whiskey blond qui fume une pipe aber echt über die Mauer gesprungen und auch

Agfa Engravers 2:
Sackers Antique Roman, Sackers Classic Roman, Sackers Gothic, Sackers Roman, Sackers Script, Sackers Square Gothic

© FSI 1993

Sackers Classic Roman

ABCDEFGHIJKLMNOPQRSTUVWXYZ[ÄÖÜÅÇ]
ABCDEFGHIJKLMNOPQRSTUVWXYZ
1234567890(.,;:?!$&-*){ÄÖÜÅÇ}

Agfa Engravers 2:
Sackers Antique Roman, Sackers Classic Roman, Sackers Gothic, Sackers Roman, Sackers Script, Sackers Square Gothic

Sackers Gothic

ABCDEFGHIJKLMNOPQRSTUVWXYZ[ÄÖÜÅÇ]
ABCDEFGHIJKLMNOPQRSTUVWXYZ
1234567890(.,;:?!$&-*){ÄÖÜÅÇ}

▶ Light
THE QUICK BROWN FOX JUMPS OVER A DOG. ZWEI BOXKÄMPFER JAGEN EVA DURCH SYLT

▶ Medium
THE QUICK BROWN FOX JUMPS OVER A DOG. ZWEI BOXKÄMPFER JAGEN EVA DURCH SYLT

▶ Heavy
THE QUICK BROWN FOX JUMPS OVER A DOG. ZWEI BOXKÄMPFER JAGEN EVA DURCH SYLT

Agfa Engravers 2:
Sackers Antique Roman, Sackers Classic Roman, Sackers Gothic, Sackers Roman, Sackers Script, Sackers Square Gothic

Sackers Roman

ABCDEFGHIJKLMNOPQRSTUVWXYZ[ÄÖÜÅÇ]
ABCDEFGHIJKLMNOPQRSTUVWXYZ
1234567890(.,;:?!$&-*){ÄÖÜÅÇ}

▶ Light
THE QUICK BROWN FOX JUMPS OVER A DOG. ZWEI BOXKÄMPFER JAGEN EVA

▶ Heavy
THE QUICK BROWN FOX JUMPS OVER A DOG. ZWEI BOXKÄMPFER JAGEN EVA

Agfa Engravers 2:
Sackers Antique Roman, Sackers Classic Roman, Sackers Gothic, Sackers Roman, Sackers Script, Sackers Square Gothic

© FSI 1993

C2781 Mac + PC ④
Sackers Script

abcdefghijklmnopqrstuvwxyz [äöüßåç]
ABCDEFGHIJKLMNOPQRSTUVWXYZ
1234567890(.,;:?!$ & -*){ÄÖÜÅ ʰˢᵗ Ç}

▶ English
The quick brown fox jumps over a Dog. Zwei Boxkämpfer jagen Eva durch Sylt portez ce vieux Whiskey blond qui fume une pipe aber echt über die Mauer gesprungen und

▶ Italian
The quick brown fox jumps over a Dog. Zwei Boxkämpfer jagen Eva durch Sylt portez ce vieux Whiskey blond qui fume une pipe aber echt über die Mauer gesprungen und auch smrebrd en

Agfa Engravers 2:
Sackers Antique Roman, Sackers Classic Roman, Sackers Gothic, Sackers Roman, Sackers Script, Sackers Square Gothic

C2781 Mac + PC ⑥
Sackers Square Gothic

ABCDEFGHIJKLMNOPQRSTUVWXYZ[ÄÖÜÅÇ]
ABCDEFGHIJKLMNOPQRSTUVWXYZ
1234567890(.,;:?!$&-*){ÄÖÜÅᵀᴴˢᵀÇ}

Agfa Engravers 2:
Sackers Antique Roman, Sackers Classic Roman, Sackers Gothic, Sackers Roman, Sackers Script, Sackers Square Gothic

C2778 Mac + PC ⑥ 1931: H. Machler
Salut™

abcdefghijklmnopqrstuvwxyz[äöüßåøæœç]
ABCDEFGHIJKLMNOPQRSTUVWXYZ
1234567890(.,;:?!$&-*){ÄÖÜÅØÆŒÇ}

Headlines 90S:
Bernhard Fashion, Chic™, Eclipse™, Metronome Gothic, Salut™
© Einhorn

FB6839 Mac + PC ① 1993: John Downer
SamSans™

abcdefghijklmnopqrstuvwxyz[äöüßåøæœç]
ABCDEFGHIJKLMNOPQRSTUVWXYZ
1234567890(.,;:?!$&-*){ÄÖÜÅØÆŒÇ}

▶ Thin
The quick brown fox jumps over a Dog. Zwei Boxkämpfer jagen Eva durch Sylt portez ce vieux Whiskey blond qui fume une pipe aber echt über die Mauer gesprungen

▶ Bold
The quick brown fox jumps over a Dog. Zwei Boxkämpfer jagen Eva durch Sylt portez ce vieux Whiskey blond qui fume une pipe aber echt über die Mauer

© FSI 1993

A1147 MAC + PC ⑦ ✎ 1991: Karlgeorg Hoefer
San Marco™

abcdefghijklmnopqrstuvwxyz[äöüßåøæœç]
ABCDEFGHIJKLMNOPQRSTUVWXYZ
1234567890(.,;:?!$&-*){ÄÖÜÅØÆŒÇ}

Type Before Gutenberg 2:
Carolina™ & Dfr, Clairvaux™, San Marco™

C1200 MAC + PC ①
Sans No. 1

abcdefghijklmnopqrstuvwxyz[äöüßåøæœç]
ABCDEFGHIJKLMNOPQRSTUVWXYZ
1234567890(.,;:?!$&-*){ÄÖÜÅØÆŒÇ}

© Ad Sans, Doric, ATF Spartan

▶ No. 1
The quick brown fox jumps over a Dog. Zwei Boxkämpfer jagen Eva durch Sylt portez ce vieux Whiskey

▶ No. 1 Heavy
The quick brown fox jumps over a Dog. Zwei Boxkämpfer jagen Eva durch Sylt portez ce vieux Whiskey

News/Sans:
News No. 2, News No. 4, Sans No. 1
© Ad Sans, Doric, ATF Spartan

L6146 MAC ④ ✎ 1983: David Quay
Santa Fe™

abcdefghijklmnopqrstuvwxyz[äöüßåøæœç]
ABCDEFGHIJKLMNOPQRSTUVWXYZ
1234567890(.,;:?!$&-)Ç*

MC6361 MAC + PC ⑥ ✎ 1953: Hermann Zapf
Saphir™

ABCDEFGHIJKLMNOPQRSTUVWXYZ
1234567890(.,;:?!$&-*)[ ]{ÄÖÜÅØÆŒÇ}

A914 MAC + PC ④ ✎ 1990: Rosemary Sassoon
Sassoon™ Primary

abcdefghijklmnopqrstuvwxyz[äöüßåøæœç]
ABCDEFGHIJKLMNOPQRSTUVWXYZ
1234567890(.,;:?!$&-*){ÄÖÜÅØÆŒÇ}

© FSI 1993

Savoye™
L2805 MAC — 1992: Alan Meeks

abcdefghijklmnopqrstuvwxyz[äöüßåøæœç]
ABCDEFGHIJKLMNOPQRSTUVWXYZ
1234567890(.,;:?!$&-*)Ç

Sayer Interview™
MC2906 MAC + PC — Manfred Sayer

abcdefghijklmnopqrstuvwxyz[äöüßåøæœç]
ABCDEFGHIJKLMNOPQRSTUVWXYZ
1234567890(.,;:?!$&-*){ÄÖÜÅØÆŒÇ}

Sayer Script™ Light
MC2926 MAC + PC — Manfred Sayer

abcdefghijklmnopqrstuvwxyz[äöüßåøæœç]
ABCDEFGHIJKLMNOPQRSTUVWXYZ
1234567890(.,;:?!$&-*){ÄÖÜÅØÆŒÇ}

Sayer Script Bold
MC2927 MAC + PC — Manfred Sayer

abcdefghijklmnopqrstuvwxyz[äöüßåøæœç]
ABCDEFGHIJKLMNOPQRSTUVWXYZ
1234567890(.,;:?!$&-*){ÄÖÜÅØÆŒÇ}

Sayer Script Black
MC2924 MAC + PC — Manfred Sayer

abcdefghijklmnopqrstuvwxyz[äöüßåøæœç]
ABCDEFGHIJKLMNOPQRSTUVWXYZ
1234567890(.,;:?!$&-*){ÄÖÜÅØÆŒÇ}

Sayer Spiritual™
MC2907 MAC + PC — Manfred Sayer

ABCDEFGHIJKLMNOPQRSTUVWXYZ
1234567890(.,;:?!$&-*)[]{ÄÖÜÅØÆŒÇ}

Sayer Spiritual Italic
MC2908 MAC + PC — Manfred Sayer

ABCDEFGHIJKLMNOPQRSTUVWXYZ
1234567890(.,;:?!$&-*)[]{ÄÖÜÅØÆŒÇ}

© FSI 1993

FF Scala™
FF732 MAC + PC ② 1991: Martin Majoor

abcdefghijklmnopqrstuvwxyz[äöüßåøæœç]
ABCDEFGHIJKLMNOPQRSTUVWXYZ
1234567890(.,;:?!$&-*){ÄÖÜÅØÆŒÇ}

Joanna, Candida

▶ Regular
The quick brown fox jumps over a Dog. Zwei Boxkämpfer jagen Eva durch Sylt portez ce vieux Whiskey blond qui fume

▶ Italic
The quick brown fox jumps over a Dog. Zwei Boxkämpfer jagen Eva durch Sylt portez ce vieux Whiskey blond qui fume une pipe aber echt

▶ Bold
The quick brown fox jumps over a Dog. Zwei Boxkämpfer jagen Eva durch Sylt portez ce vieux Whiskey blond qui fume

▶ Small Caps
THE QUICK BROWN FOX JUMPS OVER A DOG. 123 4567 890 ZWEI BOXKÄMPFER JAGEN EVA DURCH SYLT PORTEZ CE VIEUX

Scamp™
FB2753 MAC + PC ④ 1991: Denise Schmidt

ABCDEFGHIJKLMNOPQRSTUVWXYZ1234567890[ÄÖÜSSÅØÆŒÇ]
ABCDEFGHIJKLMNOPQRSTUVWXYZ(.,;:?!$&-*){ÄÖÜÅØÆŒÇ}

Ox Handicraft

▶ Regular
THE QUICK BROWN FOX JUMPS OVER A DOG. ZWEI BOXKÄMPFER JAGEN EVA DURCH SYLT PORTEZ CE VIEUX WHISKEY BLOND QUI FUME UNE PIPE ABER ECHT ÜBER DIE MAUER GESPRUNGEN UND AUCH SMØREBRØD EN YSJES NATUURLIJK. BUT VERY LONG

▶ Fat
THE QUICK BROWN FOX JUMPS OVER A DOG. ZWEI BOXKÄMPFER JAGEN EVA DURCH SYLT PORTEZ CE VIEUX WHISKEY BLOND QUI FUME UNE PIPE ABER ECHT ÜBER DIE MAUER GESPRUNGEN UND AUCH SMØREBRØD EN

▶ Bold Inline
THE QUICK BROWN FOX JUMPS OVER A DOG. ZWEI BOXKÄMPFER JAGEN EVA DURCH SYLT PORTEZ CE VIEUX WHISKEY BLOND QUI FUME UNE PIPE ABER ECHT ÜBER DIE MAUER GESPRUNGEN UND AUCH SMØREBRØD EN YSJES NATUURLIJK. BUT VERY LONG

Schadow™ Black Condensed
BT854 MAC + PC ③ 1938–52: Georg Trump

**abcdefghijklmnopqrstuvwxyz[äöüßåøæœç]
ABCDEFGHIJKLMNOPQRSTUVWXYZ
1234567890(.,;:?!$&-*){ÄÖÜÅØÆŒÇ}**

Stempel Schneidler™
A413 MAC + PC ② 1936: F. H. E. Schneidler

abcdefghijklmnopqrstuvwxyz[äöüßåøæœç]
ABCDEFGHIJKLMNOPQRSTUVWXYZ
1234567890(.,;:?!$&-*){ÄÖÜÅØÆŒÇ}

aa*a*
C6425
Schneidler, Reg, Ita, Bd, BdIta
Schneidler

▶ Light
The quick brown fox jumps over a Dog. Zwei Boxkämpfer jagen Eva durch Sylt portez ce vieux Whiskey blond qui fume

▶ Light Italic
The quick brown fox jumps over a Dog. Zwei Boxkämpfer jagen Eva durch Sylt portez ce vieux Whiskey blond qui fume une pipe aber echt

© FSI 1993

▼ A413 Mac + PC Stempel Schneidler™

▶ Regular
The quick brown fox jumps over a Dog. Zwei Boxkämpfer jagen Eva durch Sylt portez ce vieux Whiskey blond qui fume

▶ Italic
The quick brown fox jumps over a Dog. Zwei Boxkämpfer jagen Eva durch Sylt portez ce vieux Whiskey blond qui fume une pipe aber echt

▶ Medium
The quick brown fox jumps over a Dog. Zwei Boxkämpfer jagen Eva durch Sylt portez ce vieux Whiskey blond qui fume

▶ Medium Italic
The quick brown fox jumps over a Dog. Zwei Boxkämpfer jagen Eva durch Sylt portez ce vieux Whiskey blond qui fume une pipe

▶ Bold
The quick brown fox jumps over a Dog. Zwei Boxkämpfer jagen Eva durch Sylt portez ce vieux Whiskey blond

▶ Bold Italic
The quick brown fox jumps over a Dog. Zwei Boxkämpfer jagen Eva durch Sylt portez ce vieux Whiskey blond qui fume

▶ Black
The quick brown fox jumps over a Dog. Zwei Boxkämpfer jagen Eva durch Sylt portez ce vieux

▶ Black Italic
The quick brown fox jumps over a Dog. Zwei Boxkämpfer jagen Eva durch Sylt portez ce vieux Whiskey

BT1377 Mac + PC   ②   1936: (F. H. E. Schneidler, 1936)

Schneidler 1

abcdefghijklmnopqrstuvwxyz[äöüßåøæœç]
ABCDEFGHIJKLMNOPQRSTUVWXYZ
1234567890(.,;:¿!$&-*){ÄÖÜÅØÆŒÇ}

aa*a*
C6425
Schneidler, Reg, Ita, Bd, BdIta
©
Stempel Schneidler

▶ Light
The quick brown fox jumps over a Dog. Zwei Boxkämpfer jagen Eva durch Sylt portez ce vieux Whiskey blond qui fume

▶ Light Italic
The quick brown fox jumps over a Dog. Zwei Boxkämpfer jagen Eva durch Sylt portez ce vieux Whiskey blond qui fume une pipe aber echt

▶ Black
The quick brown fox jumps over a Dog. Zwei Boxkämpfer jagen Eva durch Sylt portez ce vieux Whis-

▶ Black Italic
The quick brown fox jumps over a Dog. Zwei Boxkämpfer jagen Eva durch Sylt portez ce vieux Whiskey blond

BT1378 Mac + PC   ②   1936: (F. H. E. Schneidler, 1936)

Schneidler 2

abcdefghijklmnopqrstuvwxyz[äöüßåøæœç]
ABCDEFGHIJKLMNOPQRSTUVWXYZ
1234567890(.,;:¿!$&-*){ÄÖÜÅØÆŒÇ}

aa*a*
C6425
Schneidler, Reg, Ita, Bd, BdIta
©
Stempel Schneidler

▶ Regular
The quick brown fox jumps over a Dog. Zwei Boxkämpfer jagen Eva durch Sylt portez ce vieux Whiskey blond qui fume

▶ Regular Italic
The quick brown fox jumps over a Dog. Zwei Boxkämpfer jagen Eva durch Sylt portez ce vieux Whiskey blond qui fume une pipe aber echt

© FSI 1993

▼ BT1378　Mac + PC　Schneidler 2

▶ Bold
The quick brown fox jumps over a Dog. Zwei Boxkämpfer jagen Eva durch Sylt portez ce vieux Whiskey blond

▶ Bold Italic
The quick brown fox jumps over a Dog. Zwei Boxkämpfer jagen Eva durch Sylt portez ce vieux Whiskey blond qui fume

---

BT1379　Mac + PC　②　1936: (F. H. E. Schneidler, 1936)
Schneidler 3

abcdefghijklmnopqrstuvwxyz[äöüßåøæœç]
ABCDEFGHIJKLMNOPQRSTUVWXYZ
1234567890(.,;:?!$&-*){ÄÖÜÅØÆŒÇ}

aa*a*
C6425
Schneidler, Reg, Ita, Bd, BdIta
©
Stempel Schneidler

▶ Medium
The quick brown fox jumps over a Dog. Zwei Boxkämpfer jagen Eva durch Sylt portez ce vieux Whiskey blond qui fume

▶ Medium Italic
The quick brown fox jumps over a Dog. Zwei Boxkämpfer jagen Eva durch Sylt portez ce vieux Whiskey blond qui fume une pipe

---

FF1533　Mac + PC　⑦　1991: Manfred Klein
FF Schoensperger™

abcdefgßijklmnopqrstuvwxyzäöüßſch
ABCDEFGHIJKLMNOPQRSTUVWXYZ
1234567890(.,;:?!$&-*){ÄÖÜ}

FF Scribe Type™:
FF Carolus Magnus™, FF Johannes G™, FF Koberger™, FF Schoensperger™
© Carolina

EF546　Mac + PC　③
Schreibmaschinenschrift™

abcdefghijklmnopqrstuvwxyz [äöüßåøæœç]
ABCDEFGHIJKLMNOPQRSTUVWXYZ
1234567890(.,;:?!$&-*){ÄÖÜÅØÆŒÇ}

FF2797　Mac + PC　①　1991: Just van Rossum
FF Schulbuch™

abcdefghijklmnopqrstuvwxyz[äöüßåøæœç]
ABCDEFGHIJKLMNOPQRSTUVWXYZ
1234567890(.,;:?!$&-*){ÄÖÜÅØÆŒÇ}

▶ Nord Normal
The quick brown fox jumps over a Dog. Zwei Boxkämpfer jagen Eva durch Sylt portez ce vieux Whiskey blond qui fume

▶ Nord Halbfett
The quick brown fox jumps over a Dog. Zwei Boxkämpfer jagen Eva durch Sylt portez ce vieux Whiskey

▶ Süd Normal
The quick brown fox jumps over a Dog. Zwei Boxkämpfer jagen Eva durch Sylt portez ce vieux Whiskey blond qui fume

▶ Süd Halbfett
The quick brown fox jumps over a Dog. Zwei Boxkämpfer jagen Eva durch Sylt portez ce vieux Whiskey

FF2798 Mac + PC ① 1991: Just van Rossum
FF Schulbuch Combi

FF Schulschrift™ A, FF Schulschrift™ B, FF Schulschrift™ C, FF Schulbuch™ Nord, FF Schulbuch™ Süd

FF2796 Mac + PC ④ 1991: Just van Rossum
FF Schulschrift™

abcdefghijklmnopqrstuvwxyz äöüß
ABCDEFGHIJKLMNOPQRSTUVWXYZ
1234567890(.,;:?„-) ÄÖÜ

▶ **Schulschrift A**
The quick brown fox jumps over a Dog. Zwei Boxkämpfer jagen Eva durch Sylt portez ce vieux Whiskey blond qui fume une pipe aberecht über die

▶ **Schulschrift B**
The quick brown fox jumps over a Dog. Zwei Boxkämpfer jagen Eva durch Sylt portez ce vieux Whiskey blond qui fume une pipe aber echt über die Mauer

▶ **Schulschrift C**
The quick brown fox jumps over a Dog. Zwei Boxkämpfer jagen Eva durch Sylt portez ce vieux Whiskey blond qui fume une pipe aber echt über die Mauer gesprungen

M552 Mac + PC ② 1908: (Richard Austin, 1833)
Scotch Roman™

abcdefghijklmnopqrstuvwxyz[äöüßåøæœç]
ABCDEFGHIJKLMNOPQRSTUVWXYZ
1234567890(.,;:?!$&-*){ÄÖÜÅØÆŒÇ}

aa*a*
A6081
Scotch Roman, Reg, Ita, Goudy Modern / Scotch Roman, Goudy Modern, Reg, Ita
◐ De Vinne, Modern No. 20

▶ **Regular**
The quick brown fox jumps over a Dog. Zwei Boxkämpfer jagen Eva durch Sylt portez ce vieux Whiskey blond qui fume

▶ *Italic*
The quick brown fox jumps over a Dog. Zwei Boxkämpfer jagen Eva durch Sylt portez ce vieux Whiskey blond qui fume une

FF731 Mac + PC ⑤ 1991: Max Kisman
FF Scratch™

abcdefghijklmnopqrstuvwxyz[äöüßåøæœç]
ABCDEFGHIJKLMNOPQRSTUVWXYZ
1234567890(.,;:?!$&-*){ÄÖÜÅØÆŒÇ}

▶ **Regular**
The quick brown fox jumps over a Dog. Zwei Boxkämpfer jagen Eva durch Sylt portez ce vieux Whiskey blond qui fume une pipe aber echt über die Mauer

▶ **Outline**
The quick brown fox jumps over a Dog. Zwei Boxkämpfer jagen Eva durch Sylt portez ce vieux Whiskey blond qui fume une pipe aber echt über die

FF Kisman™ 1:
FF Cutout™, FF Network™, FF Scratch™, FF Vortex™

© FSI 1993

L2806 MAC ⑥ 1992: Martin Wait
Scriba™

ABCDEFGHIJKLMNOPQRSTUVWXYZ
1234567890(.,;:?!$&-*)[ ]ÄÖÜÅØÆÇ

FF1533 MAC + PC
FF Scribe Type™

FF Scribe Type™:
FF Carolus Magnus™, FF Johannes G™, FF Koberger™, FF Schoensperger™

M263 MAC + PC ④ 1931: (E. Lautenbach, 1926)
Monotype Script Bold™

abcdefghijklmnopqrstuvwxyz[äöüßåøœæç]
ABCDEFGHIJKLMNOPQRSTUVWXYZ
1234567890(.,;:?!$&-*){ÄÖÜÅØŒOEÇ}

Script 1:
Biffo™ Script, Dorchester Script™, Monotype Script Bold™, Pepita®, Swing™ Bold
aaa

BT865 MAC + PC ④
Script 12 Pitch

abcdefghijklmnopqrstuvwxyz [äöüßåøœæç]
ABCDEFGHIJKLMNOPQRSTUVWXYZ
1234567890(.,;:?!$&-*){ÄÖÜÅØÆŒÇ}

BT Typewriter:
Pica 10 Pitch, Script 12 Pitch

L2978 MAC ⑤ 1992: David Quay
Scriptek™

abcdefghijklmnopqrstuvwxyz[äöüßåøœæç]
ABCDEFGHIJKLMNOPQRSTUVWXYZ
1234567890(.,;:?!$&-*)ÄÖÜÅØÆŒÇ

L2807 MAC ⑤ 1992: David Quay
Scriptek Italic

abcdefghijklmnopqrstuvwxyz[äöüßåøœæç]
ABCDEFGHIJKLMNOPQRSTUVWXYZ
1234567890(.,;:?!$&-*)ÄÖÜÅØÆŒÇ

M263 Mac + PC
Script 1

Script 1:
Biffo™ Script, Dorchester Script™, Monotype Script Bold™, Pepita®, Swing™ Bold

M264 Mac + PC
Script 2

Script 2:
Ashley Script, Monoline Script™, New Berolina, Palace Script™

M885 Mac + PC
Script 3

Script 3:
Coronet Bold, Mercurius Bold Script™

BT848 Mac + PC
Bitstream Script 1

Bitstream Script 1:
Amazone™, Monterey, Piranesi™ Italic

BT849 Mac + PC
Bitstream Script 2

Bitstream Script 2:
Bernhard Tango™, Commercial Script, Stuyvesant™

BT850 Mac + PC
Bitstream Script 3

Bitstream Script 3:
Embassy, Englische Schreibschrift™, Liberty, Lucia™

BT851 Mac + PC
Bitstream Script 4

Bitstream Script 4:
Flemish Script, Gando

C6568 Mac + PC
Agfa Scripts 1

Agfa Scripts 1:
Commercial Script, Helinda Rook™, Old English Text, Original Script™, Quill™, Stuyvesant2, Wedding Text

AB2915 Mac + PC ④
Berthold Scripts 1

Berthold Scripts 1:
Berthold Bellevue™, Berthold Boulevard™, Berthold Script™

Seagull™
BT852 Mac + PC ③ 1978: Adrian Williams, Bob McGrath

abcdefghijklmnopqrstuvwxyz[äöüßåøæœç]
ABCDEFGHIJKLMNOPQRSTUVWXYZ
1234567890(.,;:?!$&-*){ÄÖÜÅØÆŒÇ}

▶ Light
The quick brown fox jumps over a Dog. Zwei Boxkämpfer jagen Eva durch Sylt portez ce vieux Whiskey blond qui fume une

▶ Medium
The quick brown fox jumps over a Dog. Zwei Boxkämpfer jagen Eva durch Sylt portez ce vieux Whiskey blond qui fume

▶ Bold
The quick brown fox jumps over a Dog. Zwei Boxkämpfer jagen Eva durch Sylt portez ce vieux Whiskey blond qui

▶ Heavy
The quick brown fox jumps over a Dog. Zwei Boxkämpfer jagen Eva durch Sylt portez ce vieux Whiskey

Section™ Bold Condensed
C467 Mac + PC ⑤

ABCDEFGHIJKLMNOPQRSTUVWXYZ
1234567890(.,;:?!$&-*)[]◇ÄÖÜÅØÆŒÇ◆

Headlines 81S:
Egiziano™ Black, PL Behemoth Semi Condensed, PL Benguiat Frisky, PL Futura Maxi 1, PL Tower™ Condensed, Quirinus™ Bold, Section™ Bold Condensed, Stratford ™Bold, Woodblock
© Neon

Senator™
E248 Mac + PC ⑤ 1989: Zuzana Licko

abcdefghijklmnopqrstuvwxyz[äöüßåøæœç]
ABCDEFGHIJKLMNOPQRSTUVWXYZ
1234567890(.,;:?!$&-*){ÄÖÜÅØÆŒÇ}

© Modular Serif

▶ Thin
The quick brown fox jumps over a Dog. Zwei Boxkämpfer jagen Eva durch Sylt portez ce vieux Whiskey blond qui fume une pipe aber echt über die Mauer gesprungen und auch

▶ Demi
The quick brown fox jumps over a Dog. Zwei Boxkämpfer jagen Eva durch Sylt portez ce vieux Whiskey blond qui fume une pipe aber echt über die Mauer gesprungen und

▶ Ultra
The quick brown fox jumps over a Dog. Zwei Boxkämpfer jagen Eva durch Sylt portez ce vieux Whiskey blond qui fume une pipe aber echt über die Mauer

© FSI 1993

E937 Mac + PC ⑤ 🖊 1989: Zuzana Licko
Senator Tall

abcdefghijklmnopqrstuvwxyz1234567890[äöüßåøæœç]
ABCDEFGHIJKLMNOPQRSTUVWXYZ(.,;:?!$&-*){ÄÖÜÅØÆŒÇ}

Tall Pack:
Matrix Tall, Senator Tall

BT1380 Mac + PC ⑥ 🖊 1974: Herb Lubalin, Antonio DiSpigna
ITC Serif Gothic® 1

abcdefghijklmnopqrstuvwxyz[äöüßåøæœç]
ABCDEFGHIJKLMNOPQRSTUVWXYZ
1234567890(.,;:?!$&-*){ÄÖÜÅØÆŒÇ}

aaa
A104
ITC Serif Gothic, Lt,
Reg, Bd, ExtBd, Hvy,
Blk

▶ Light
The quick brown fox jumps over a Dog. Zwei Boxkämpfer jagen Eva durch Sylt portez ce vieux Whiskey blond qui fume

▶ Bold
The quick brown fox jumps over a Dog. Zwei Boxkämpfer jagen Eva durch Sylt portez ce vieux Whiskey blond qui fume

▶ Heavy
The quick brown fox jumps over a Dog. Zwei Boxkämpfer jagen Eva durch Sylt portez ce vieux Whiskey blond

BT1381 Mac + PC ⑥ 🖊 1974: Herb Lubalin, Antonio DiSpigna
ITC Serif Gothic 2

abcdefghijklmnopqrstuvwxyz[äöüßåøæœç]
ABCDEFGHIJKLMNOPQRSTUVWXYZ
1234567890(.,;:?!$&-*){ÄÖÜÅØÆŒÇ}

aaa
A104
ITC Serif Gothic, Lt,
Reg, Bd, ExtBd, Hvy,
Blk

▶ Regular
The quick brown fox jumps over a Dog. Zwei Boxkämpfer jagen Eva durch Sylt portez ce vieux Whiskey blond qui fume

▶ Extra Bold
The quick brown fox jumps over a Dog. Zwei Boxkämpfer jagen Eva durch Sylt portez ce vieux Whiskey blond qui fume

▶ Black
The quick brown fox jumps over a Dog. Zwei Boxkämpfer jagen Eva durch Sylt portez ce vieux Whiskey blond

© FSI 1993

BT784 Mac + PC ⑥ ✏ 1974: Herb Lubalin
ITC Serif Gothic Bold Outline

abcdefghijklmnopqrstuvwxyz[äöüßåøæœç]
ABCDEFGHIJKLMNOPQRSTUVWXYZ
1234567890(.,;:?!$&-*){ÄÖÜÅØÆŒÇ}

Bitstream Contour :
ITC Clearface Contour, ITC Eras Outline, ITC Serif Gothic, ITC Souvenir Outline

---

BT1382 Mac + PC ③ ✏ 1967: Adrian Frutiger
Serifa™ 1

abcdefghijklmnopqrstuvwxyz[äöüßåøæœç]
ABCDEFGHIJKLMNOPQRSTUVWXYZ
1234567890(.,;:?!$&-*){ÄÖÜÅØÆŒÇ}

a a *a*
A139
Serifa, 45Lt, 46LtIta,
55Rom, 56Ita, 65Bd,
75Blk
©
PMN Caecilia, Glypha,
Boton, Calvert

▶ 35 Thin
The quick brown fox jumps over a Dog. Zwei Boxkämpfer jagen Eva durch Sylt portez ce vieux Whiskey blond qui fume une

▶ 36 Thin Italic
The quick brown fox jumps over a Dog. Zwei Boxkämpfer jagen Eva durch Sylt portez ce vieux Whiskey blond qui fume une

▶ 45 Light
The quick brown fox jumps over a Dog. Zwei Boxkämpfer jagen Eva durch Sylt portez ce vieux Whiskey blond qui fume une

▶ 46 Light Italic
The quick brown fox jumps over a Dog. Zwei Boxkämpfer jagen Eva durch Sylt portez ce vieux Whiskey blond qui fume une

---

BT1383 Mac + PC ③ ✏ 1967: Adrian Frutiger
Serifa 2

abcdefghijklmnopqrstuvwxyz[äöüßåøæœç]
ABCDEFGHIJKLMNOPQRSTUVWXYZ
1234567890(.,;:?!$&-*){ÄÖÜÅØÆŒÇ}

a a *a*
A139
Serifa, 45Lt, 46LtIta,
55Rom, 56Ita, 65Bd,
75Blk
©
PMN Caecilia, Glypha,
Boton, Calvert

▶ 55 Roman
The quick brown fox jumps over a Dog. Zwei Boxkämpfer jagen Eva durch Sylt portez ce vieux Whiskey blond qui

▶ 56 Italic
The quick brown fox jumps over a Dog. Zwei Boxkämpfer jagen Eva durch Sylt portez ce vieux Whiskey blond qui fume

▶ 65 Bold
The quick brown fox jumps over a Dog. Zwei Boxkämpfer jagen Eva durch Sylt portez ce vieux Whiskey blond

▶ 75 Black
The quick brown fox jumps over a Dog. Zwei Boxkämpfer jagen Eva durch Sylt portez ce vieux

© FSI 1993

BT782 Mac + PC ③ ✎ 1967: Adrian Frutiger
Serifa 67 Bold Condensed

abcdefghijklmnopqrstuvwxyz[äöüßåøæœç]
ABCDEFGHIJKLMNOPQRSTUVWXYZ
1234567890(.,:;?!$&-*){ÄÖÜÅØÆŒÇ}

BT Condensed Headlines 1:
Americana, Serifa 67 Bold Condensed

A6186 Mac + PC ⑥
Serlio™

ABCDEFGHIJKLMNOPQRSTUVWXYZ[ÄÖÜSSÅØÆŒÇ]
ABCDEFGHIJKLMNOPQRSTUVWXYZ
1234567890(.,:;?!$&-*){ÄÖÜÅØÆŒÇ}

Engravers / Serlio:
Engravers Bold Face™, Serlio™
ⓒ Galba, Felix Titling, Trajan, Classic Roman

A566 Mac + PC ⑤
Serpentine™

abcdefghijklmnopqrstuvwxyz[äöüßåøæœç]
ABCDEFGHIJKLMNOPQRSTUVWXYZ
1234567890(.,:;?!$&-*){ÄÖÜÅØÆŒÇ}

ⓒ Letraset Crillee, Handel Gothic, Russell Square

▶ **Light**
The quick brown fox jumps over a Dog. Zwei Boxkämpfer jagen Eva durch Sylt portez ce vieux Whiskey

▶ **Light Oblique**
The quick brown fox jumps over a Dog. Zwei Boxkämpfer jagen Eva durch Sylt portez ce vieux Whiskey

▶ **Medium**
The quick brown fox jumps over a Dog. Zwei Boxkämpfer jagen Eva durch Sylt portez ce

▶ **Medium Oblique**
The quick brown fox jumps over a Dog. Zwei Boxkämpfer jagen Eva durch Sylt portez ce

▶ **Bold**
The quick brown fox jumps over a Dog. Zwei Boxkämpfer jagen Eva durch Sylt portez ce

▶ **Bold Oblique**
The quick brown fox jumps over a Dog. Zwei Boxkämpfer jagen Eva durch Sylt portez ce

---

ET6388 Mac + PC ⑥ ✎ 1992: Judith Sutcliffe
Serpents™

ABCDEFGHIJKLMNOPQRSTUVWXYZ
ABCDEFGHIJKLMNOPQRSTUVWXYZ
CEÆMPOSTØÇ

© FSI 1993

▼ ET6388 Mac + PC Serpents™

Petroglyph Combo:
Maskerade™, Petroglyph™, Serpents™

C105 Mac + PC ① 1982: Kris Holmes, Janice Prescott
Shannon™

abcdefghijklmnopqrstuvwxyz[äöüßåøæœç]
ABCDEFGHIJKLMNOPQRSTUVWXYZ
1234567890(.,;:?!$&-*){ÄÖÜÅØÆŒÇ}

aa*a*
A916
Shannon, Bk, Obl, Bd, ExtBd

▶ Book
The quick brown fox jumps over a Dog. Zwei Boxkämpfer jagen Eva durch Sylt portez ce vieux Whiskey blond qui fume une

▶ Oblique
The quick brown fox jumps over a Dog. Zwei Boxkämpfer jagen Eva durch Sylt portez ce vieux Whiskey blond qui fume une pipe aber

▶ Bold
The quick brown fox jumps over a Dog. Zwei Boxkämpfer jagen Eva durch Sylt portez ce vieux Whiskey blond

▶ Extra Bold
The quick brown fox jumps over a Dog. Zwei Boxkämpfer jagen Eva durch Sylt portez ce vieux Whiskey blond qui fume une

---

C2779 Mac + PC ① 1982: Kris Holmes, Janice Prescott
Shannon Premier

ABCDEFGHIJKLMNOPQRSTUVWXYZ(ÄÖÜŠÅØÆŒÇ)
¼ ½ ¾ ⅛ ⅜ ⅝ ⅞ ⅓ ⅔ fj jj ff fi fl ffi ffl
1234567890(.,;:?!$&-.)¢$¢Rp◀▶○●□■

▶ Book
ff fi fl ffi ffl ij ¼ ½ ¾ ⅛ ⅜ ⅝ ⅞ ⅓ ⅔
THE QUICK BROWN FOX JUMPS OVER A LAZY DOG. 123 4567 890 ZWEI BOXKÄMPFER JAGEN EVA DURCH SYLT

▶ Book Oblique
*ff fi fl ffi ffl ij ¼ ½ ¾ ⅛ ⅜ ⅝ ⅞ ⅓ ⅔
123 4567 890*

▶ Bold
**ff fi fl ffi ffl ij ¼ ½ ¾ ⅛ ⅜ ⅝ ⅞ ⅓ ⅔
123 4567 890**

▶ Extra Bold
**ff fi fl ffi ffl ij ¼ ½ ¾ ⅛ ⅜ ⅝ ⅞ ⅓ ⅔
123 4567 890**

L6600 Mac ⑥ 1973: Vic Carless
Shatter™

abcdefghijklmnopqrstuvwxyz[äöüßåøæœç]
ABCDEFGHIJKLMNOPQRSTUVWXYZ
1234567890(.,;:?!$&-*)ÄÖÜÅØÆŒÇ

A457 Mac + PC ④ 1972: Matthew Carter
Shelley Scripts™

*abcdefghijklmnopqrstuvwxyz[äöüßåøæœç]
ABCDEFGHIJKLMNOPQRSTUVWXYZ
1234567890(.,;:?!$&-*){ÄÖÜÅØÆŒÇ}*

aaa
BT1384
Shelley, Andante,
Allegro, Volante

▼ A457 Mac + PC **Shelley Scripts™**

▶ Shelley Andante
The quick brown fox jumps over a Dog. Zwei Boxkämpfer jagen Eva durch Sylt portez ce vieux Whiskey blond qui fume une pipe aber echt über die Mauer gesprungen

▶ Shelley Allegro
The quick brown fox jumps over a Dog. Zwei Boxkämpfer jagen Eva durch Sylt portez ce vieux Whiskey blond qui fume une pipe aber echt über die Mauer gesprungen

▶ Shelley Volante
The quick brown fox jumps over a Dog. Zwei Boxkämpfer jagen Eva durch Sylt portez ce vieux Whiskey blond qui fume une pipe aber echt über die Mauer

LH6640 Mac + PC ④
Sho Roman™

abcdefghijklmnopqrstuvwxyz[äöüßåøæœç]
ABCDEFGHIJKLMNOPQRSTUVWXYZ
1234567890(.,;:?!$&-*){ÄÖÜÅØÆŒÇ}

Calligraphy for Print:
Ruling Script™, Sho Roman™, Wiesbaden Swing™ Roman

BT855 Mac + PC ⑤ ✎ 1972: J. Looney
Shotgun™

ABCDEFGHIJKLMNOPQRSTUVWXYZ
1234567890(.,;:?!$&-*){ÄÖÜÅØÆŒÇ}

▶ Regular
THE QUICK BROWN FOX JUMPS OVER A DOG. ZWEI BOXKÄMPFER JAGEN EVA DURCH SYLT PORTEZ CE

▶ Blanks
THE QUICK BROWN FOX JUMPS OVER A DOG. ZWEI BOXKÄMPFER JAGEN EVA DURCH SYLT PORTEZ CE

C1012 Mac + PC ⑥
Siena™ Black

abcdefghijklmnopqrstuvwxyz[äöü°åøœæç]
ABCDEFGHIJKLMNOPQRSTUVWXYZ
1234567890(.,;:?!$&-*)◊ÄÖÜÅØÆŒÇ♦

Headlines 84S:
Bernhard Modern, Beton Extra Bold, Metropolis Bold, Modern No. 20, Orlando Caps, PL Davison Americana, PL Westerveldt Light, Siena™ Black, TC Europa™ Bold, TC Jasper™

EF1080 Mac + PC ⑥ ✎ 1989: Kris Holmes
Sierra™

abcdefghijklmnopqrstuvwxyz[äöüßåøæœç]
ABCDEFGHIJKLMNOPQRSTUVWXYZ
1234567890(.,;:?!$&-*){ÄÖÜÅØÆŒÇ}

© FSI 1993

▼ EF1080 Mac + PC Sierra™

© Poseidon

▶ Regular
The quick brown fox jumps over a Dog. Zwei Boxkämpfer jagen Eva durch Sylt portez ce vieux Whiskey blond qui

▶ Italic
The quick brown fox jumps over a Dog. Zwei Boxkämpfer jagen Eva durch Sylt portez ce vieux Whiskey blond qui fume

▶ Bold
The quick brown fox jumps over a Dog. Zwei Boxkämpfer jagen Eva durch Sylt portez ce

▶ Bold Italic
The quick brown fox jumps over a Dog. Zwei Boxkämpfer jagen Eva durch Sylt portez ce vieux Whiskey

---

C614 Mac + PC ⑥ ✎ (Arthur Baker, 1965)
Signature

abcdefghijklmnopqrstuvwxyz[äöüßåøæœç]
ABCDEFGHIJKLMNOPQRSTUVWXYZ
1234567890(.,;:?!$&-*){ÄÖÜÅØÆŒÇ}

© Baker Signet

▶ Light
The quick brown fox jumps over a Dog. Zwei Boxkämpfer jagen Eva durch Sylt portez ce vieux Whiskey blond qui fume une pipe aber echt

▶ Black
The quick brown fox jumps over a Dog. Zwei Boxkämpfer jagen Eva durch Sylt portez ce vieux Whiskey blond qui

Hollandse Mediaeval:
Hollandse Mediaeval, Signature

LP942 Mac + PC ⑤ ✎ 1990: (1937) Garrett Boge
Silhouette™

abcdefghijklmnopqrstuvwxyz1234567890äöüßåøæœç
ABCDEFGHIJKLMNOPQRSTUVWXYZ(.,;:?!$&-*)ÄÖÜÅÆŒÇ

LetterPerfect 3:
Hadrian™ Bold, Silhouette™
© Bureau Empire, Obelisk No. 2577, Spire No. 377, Loyalist

TF6630 Mac + PC ② ✎ 1992: Joseph W. Treacy
TF Simper™ Extrabold

**abcdefghijklmnopqrstuvwxyz[äöüßåøæœç]
ABCDEFGHIJKLMNOPQRSTUVWXYZ
1234567890(.,;:?!$&-*){ÄÖÜÅØÆŒÇ}**

TF Habitat Bold Contour:
TF Habitat Bold Contour, TF Simper™ Extrabold

C2777 Mac + PC ⑤ ✎ 1974: Rosemarie Tissi
Sinaloa™

ABCDEFGHIJKLMNOPQRSTUVWXYZ
1234567890(.,;:?!$&-

© FSI 1993

▼

S 18

▼ C2777 Mac + PC Sinaloa™

Headlines 89S:
Miehle™, Parisian, Phyllis, Sinaloa™
aaa L6643
Sinaloa™, Reg

L2808 Mac ⑥ ✎ 1990: Akira Kobayashi
Skid Row™

ABCDEFGHIJKLMNOPQRSTUVWXYZ
1234567890[ ] (.,;:?!$&-*) ÄÖÜÅØÆŒÇ

C2980 Mac + PC ⑥
Skjald™

abcdefghijklmnopqrstuvwxyz[äöüßåøæœç]
ABCDEFGHIJKLMNOPQRSTUVWXYZ
1234567890(.,;:?!$&-*){ÄÖÜÅØÆŒÇ}

Headlines 91S:
Empire™, Gallia™, Gillies Gothic Bold, Quaint™ Roman, Skjald™

FB2884 Mac + PC ③ ✎ 1992: (Imre Reiner, 1929-34) Jane Patterson
Skyline™

abcdefghijklmnopqrstuvwxyz1234567890|äöüßåøæœç|
ABCDEFGHIJKLMNOPQRSTUVWXYZ(.,;:?!$&-*)ÄÖÜÅØÆŒÇ

▶ Bold Condensed
The quick brown fox jumps over a Dog. Zwei Boxkämpfer jagen Eva durch Sylt portez ce vieux Whiskey blond qui fume une pipe aber echt über die Mauer gesprungen und auch smørrebrød en ysjes natuurlijk The quick brown fox jumps over a Dog. Zwei Box-

▶ Black
The quick brown fox jumps over a Dog. Zwei Boxkämpfer jagen Eva durch Sylt portez ce vieux Whiskey blond qui fume une pipe aber echt über die Mauer

---

EF314 Mac + PC ② ✎ 1987: Robert Slimbach
ITC Slimbach® 1

abcdefghijklmnopqrstuvwxyz[äöüßåøæœç]
ABCDEFGHIJKLMNOPQRSTUVWXYZ
1234567890(.,;:?!$&-*){ÄÖÜÅØÆŒÇ}

aaa
C985
ITC Slimbach, Bk,
BkIta, Med, MedIta, Bd,
BdIta, Blk, BlkIta
A2533
ITC Slimbach, Bk,
BkIta, Med, MedIta, Bd,
BdIta, Blk, BlkIta

▶ Book
The quick brown fox jumps over a Dog. Zwei Boxkämpfer jagen Eva durch Sylt portez ce vieux Whiskey blond qui fume

▶ Book Italic
The quick brown fox jumps over a Dog. Zwei Boxkämpfer jagen Eva durch Sylt portez ce vieux Whiskey blond qui fume une

▶ Bold
The quick brown fox jumps over a Dog. Zwei Boxkämpfer jagen Eva durch Sylt portez ce vieux Whiskey blond qui

▶ Bold Italic
The quick brown fox jumps over a Dog. Zwei Boxkämpfer jagen Eva durch Sylt portez ce vieux Whiskey blond qui fume

© FSI 1993

ITC Slimbach 2
EF315 Mac + PC ② 1987: Robert Slimbach

abcdefghijklmnopqrstuvwxyz[äöüßåøæœç]
ABCDEFGHIJKLMNOPQRSTUVWXYZ
1234567890(.,;:?!$&-*){ÄÖÜÅØÆŒÇ}

aa*a*
C985
ITC Slimbach, Bk,
BkIta, Med, MedIta,
Bd, BdIta, Blk, BlkIta
A2533
ITC Slimbach, Bk,
BkIta, Med, MedIta,
Bd, BdIta, Blk, BlkIta

▶ Medium
The quick brown fox jumps over a Dog. Zwei Boxkämpfer jagen Eva durch Sylt portez ce vieux Whiskey blond qui fume

▶ Medium Italic
The quick brown fox jumps over a Dog. Zwei Boxkämpfer jagen Eva durch Sylt portez ce vieux Whiskey blond qui fume une

▶ Black
The quick brown fox jumps over a Dog. Zwei Boxkämpfer jagen Eva durch Sylt portez ce vieux Whiskey blond qui

▶ Black Italic
The quick brown fox jumps over a Dog. Zwei Boxkämpfer jagen Eva durch Sylt portez ce vieux Whiskey blond qui

ITC Slimbach Small Caps
EF542 Mac + PC ② 1987: Robert Slimbach

ABCDEFGHIJKLMNOPQRSTUVWXYZ[ÄÖÜSSÅØÆŒ]
ABCDEFGHIJKLMNOPQRSTUVWXYZ
1234567890(.,;:?!$&-*){ÄÖÜÅØÆŒÇ}

▶ Book Small Caps
THE QUICK BROWN FOX JUMPS OVER A DOG. 123 4567 890 ZWEI BOXKÄMPFER JAGEN EVA DURCH SYLT PORTEZ CE VIEUX WHISKEY BLOND

▶ Medium Small Caps
THE QUICK BROWN FOX JUMPS OVER A DOG. 123 4567 890 ZWEI BOXKÄMPFER JAGEN EVA DURCH SYLT PORTEZ CE VIEUX WHISKEY

Slipstream™
L2732 Mac ⑥

ABCDEFGHIJKLMNOPQRSTUVWXYZ
1234567890(.,;:?!$&-)[]ÄÖÜÅØÆŒÇ*

Slogan™
EF1078 Mac + PC ④ 1958: H. Matheis

abcdefghijklmnopqrstuvwxyz[äöüßåøæœç]
ABCDEFGHIJKLMNOPQRSTUVWXYZ
1234567890(.,;:?!$&-*){ÄÖÜÅØÆŒÇ}

Murray Hill, Slogan™

Snell Roundhand™ Script
A562 Mac + PC ④ 1965: Matthew Carter

abcdefghijklmnopqrstuvwxyz[äöüßåøæœç]
ABCDEFGHIJKLMNOPQRSTUVWXYZ
1234567890(.,;:?!$&-*){ÄÖÜÅØÆŒÇ}

© FSI 1993

S 20

aaa
BT1385
Snell Roundhand
Script, Reg, Bd, Blk

▼ A562 Mac + PC Snell Roundhand™ Script

▶ Regular
The quick brown fox jumps over a Dog. Zwei Boxkämpfer jagen Eva durch Sylt portez ce vieux Whiskey blond qui fume une pipe aber echt über

▶ Bold
The quick brown fox jumps over a Dog. Zwei Boxkämpfer jagen Eva durch Sylt portez ce vieux Whiskey blond qui fume une pipe

▶ Black
The quick brown fox jumps over a Dog. Zwei Boxkämpfer jagen Eva durch Sylt portez ce vieux Whiskey blond qui

---

CA6920 Mac + PC ⑥ ✎ 1993: Matthew Carter
Sophia™ CC

ABCDEFGHIJKLMNOPQRSTUVWXYZ
1234567890(.,;:?!$&-*)[]{ÄÖÜÅØÆŒÇ}

C617 Mac + PC ① ✎ 1977: George Brian
Souvenir Gothic™

abcdefghijklmnopqrstuvwxyz[äöüßåøæœç]
ABCDEFGHIJKLMNOPQRSTUVWXYZ
1234567890(.,;:?!$&-*){ÄÖÜÅØÆŒÇ}

©
ITC Souvenir

▶ Light
The quick brown fox jumps over a Dog. Zwei Boxkämpfer jagen Eva durch Sylt portez ce vieux Whiskey blond qui fume une pipe aber

▶ Light Italic
The quick brown fox jumps over a Dog. Zwei Boxkämpfer jagen Eva durch Sylt portez ce vieux Whiskey blond qui fume une pipe

▶ Demi
The quick brown fox jumps over a Dog. Zwei Boxkämpfer jagen Eva durch Sylt portez ce vieux Whiskey blond

▶ Demi Italic
The quick brown fox jumps over a Dog. Zwei Boxkämpfer jagen Eva durch Sylt portez ce vieux Whiskey blond qui

---

BT1386 Mac + PC ② ✎ 1977: (M. F. Benton, 1914) Ed Benguiat
ITC Souvenir® 1

abcdefghijklmnopqrstuvwxyz[äöüßåøæœç]
ABCDEFGHIJKLMNOPQRSTUVWXYZ
1234567890(.,;:?!$&-*){ÄÖÜÅØÆŒÇ}

aaa
A107
ITC Souvenir 1, Lt, LtIta, Demi, Demilta

▶ Light
The quick brown fox jumps over a Dog. Zwei Boxkämpfer jagen Eva durch Sylt portez ce vieux Whiskey blond qui fume une

▶ Light Italic
The quick brown fox jumps over a Dog. Zwei Boxkämpfer jagen Eva durch Sylt portez ce vieux Whiskey blond qui fume une

▶ Demi
The quick brown fox jumps over a Dog. Zwei Boxkämpfer jagen Eva durch Sylt portez ce vieux Whiskey blond

▶ Demi Italic
The quick brown fox jumps over a Dog. Zwei Boxkämpfer jagen Eva durch Sylt portez ce vieux Whiskey blond

© FSI 1993

ITC Souvenir 2
BT1387 Mac + PC ② 1977: (M. F. Benton, 1914) Ed Benguiat

abcdefghijklmnopqrstuvwxyz[äöüßåøæœç]
ABCDEFGHIJKLMNOPQRSTUVWXYZ
1234567890(.,;:?!$&-*){ÄÖÜÅØÆŒÇ}

aaa
A410
ITC Souvenir 2, Med,
MedIta, Bd, BdIta

▶ Medium
The quick brown fox jumps over a Dog. Zwei Boxkämpfer jagen Eva durch Sylt portez ce vieux Whiskey blond qui

▶ Medium Italic
The quick brown fox jumps over a Dog. Zwei Boxkämpfer jagen Eva durch Sylt portez ce vieux Whiskey blond qui

▶ Bold
The quick brown fox jumps over a Dog. Zwei Boxkämpfer jagen Eva durch Sylt portez ce vieux

▶ Bold Italic
The quick brown fox jumps over a Dog. Zwei Boxkämpfer jagen Eva durch Sylt portez ce vieux

ITC Souvenir Outline
BT784 Mac + PC ⑥ 1970: (M. F. Benton, 1914) Ed Benguiat

abcdefghijklmnopqrstuvwxyz[äöüßåøæœç]
ABCDEFGHIJKLMNOPQRSTUVWXYZ
1234567890(.,;:?!$&-*){ÄÖÜÅØÆŒÇ}

Bitstream Contour:
ITC Clearface Contour, ITC Eras Outline, ITC Serif Gothic, ITC Souvenir Outline

Geometric 212
BT856 Mac + PC ① 1939–1952: (Renner, 1927) (John Renshaw, Gerry Powell) Industry name: Spartan Classified

abcdefghijklmnopqrstuvwxyz[äöüßåøæœç]
ABCDEFGHIJKLMNOPQRSTUVWXYZ
1234567890(.,;:?!$&-*){ÄÖÜÅØÆŒÇ}

aaa
A917
Spartan Classified, Bk, Hvy
©
Ad Sans, Doric, Sans No. 1

▶ Book
The quick brown fox jumps over a Dog. Zwei Boxkämpfer jagen Eva durch Sylt portez ce

▶ Book Condensed
The quick brown fox jumps over a Dog. Zwei Boxkämpfer jagen Eva durch Sylt portez ce vieux Whiskey blond

▶ Heavy
The quick brown fox jumps over a Dog. Zwei Boxkämpfer jagen Eva durch Sylt portez ce

▶ Heavy Condensed
The quick brown fox jumps over a Dog. Zwei Boxkämpfer jagen Eva durch Sylt portez ce vieux Whiskey blond

Spartan
M411 Mac + PC ⑥

ABCDEFGHIJKLMNOPQRSTUVWXYZ
1234567890(.,;:?!$&-*)☐{ÄÖÜÅØÆŒÇ}

© FSI 1993

▼ M411 Mac + PC Spartan

Copperplate Gothic, Engraver's Gothic

▶ Size One
THE QUICK BROWN FOX JUMPS OVER A DOG. ZWEI BOXKÄMPFER JAGEN EVA DURCH

▶ Size Two
THE QUICK BROWN FOX JUMPS OVER A DOG. ZWEI BOXKÄMPFER JAGEN EVA DURCH SYLT PORTEZ CE

▶ Size Three
THE QUICK BROWN FOX JUMPS OVER A DOG. ZWEI BOXKÄMPFER JAGEN EVA DURCH SYLT PORTEZ CE VIEUX WHISKEY BLOND QUI

▶ Size Four
THE QUICK BROWN FOX JUMPS OVER A DOG. ZWEI BOXKÄMPFER JAGEN EVA DURCH SYLT PORTEZ CE VIEUX WHISKEY BLOND QUI FUME UNE PIPE ABER

M516 Mac + PC ⑥
Spartan Italic

ABCDEFGHIJKLMNOPQRSTUVWXYZ
1234567890(.,;:?!$&-)[]{ÄÖÜÅØÆŒÇ}*

Copperplate Gothic, Engraver's Gothic

▶ Size One
THE QUICK BROWN FOX JUMPS OVER A DOG. ZWEI BOXKÄMP-FER JAGEN EVA

▶ Size Two
THE QUICK BROWN FOX JUMPS OVER A DOG. ZWEI BOXKÄMPFER JAGEN EVA DURCH SYLT PORTEZ CE

▶ Size Three
THE QUICK BROWN FOX JUMPS OVER A DOG. ZWEI BOXKÄMPFER JAGEN EVA DURCH SYLT PORTEZ CE

▶ Size Four
THE QUICK BROWN FOX JUMPS OVER A DOG. ZWEI BOXKÄMPFER JAGEN EVA DURCH SYLT PORTEZ CE VIEUX WHISKEY BLOND QUI FUME UNE

M412 Mac + PC ⑥
Spartan Bold

ABCDEFGHIJKLMNOPQRSTUVWXYZ
1234567890(.,;:?!$&-*)[]{ÄÖÜÅØÆŒÇ}

Copperplate Gothic, Engraver's Gothic

▶ Size One
THE QUICK BROWN FOX JUMPS OVER A DOG. ZWEI BOXKÄMP-FER JAGEN EVA

▶ Size Two
THE QUICK BROWN FOX JUMPS OVER A DOG. ZWEI BOXKÄMPFER JAGEN EVA DURCH SYLT PORTEZ CE

▶ Size Three
THE QUICK BROWN FOX JUMPS OVER A DOG. ZWEI BOXKÄMPFER JAGEN EVA DURCH SYLT PORTEZ CE

▶ Size Four
THE QUICK BROWN FOX JUMPS OVER A LAZY DOG. ZWEI BOXKÄMPFER JAGEN EVA DURCH SYLT PORTEZ CE VIEUX BLOND WHISKEY QUI UND

M6382 Mac + PC ② ✎ 1942: Jan van Krimpen
Spectrum

abcdefghijklmnopqrstuvwxyz[äöüßåøæœç]
ABCDEFGHIJKLMNOPQRSTUVWXYZ
1234567890(.,;:?!$&-*){ÄÖÜÅØÆŒÇ}

a a *a*
M359
Spectrum™, Reg, Ita, SemBd
A6079
Spectrum, Reg, Ita, SemBd, Cap, ItaOsF, ExpIta, SemBdOsF, ExpSemBd

▼ M6382   Mac + PC   Spectrum

▶ Regular

The quick brown fox jumps over a Dog. Zwei Boxkämpfer jagen Eva durch Sylt portez ce vieux Whiskey blond qui fume une pipe aber echt

▶ Italic

The quick brown fox jumps over a Dog. Zwei Boxkämpfer jagen Eva durch Sylt portez ce vieux Whiskey blond qui fume une pipe aber echt über die Mauer gesprungen und auch

▶ Semi Bold

The quick brown fox jumps over a Dog. Zwei Boxkämpfer jagen Eva durch Sylt portez ce vieux Whiskey blond qui fume une pipe

▶ Small Caps

THE QUICK BROWN FOX JUMPS OVER A DOG. 123 4567 890 ZWEI BOXKÄMPFER JAGEN EVA DURCH SYLT PORTEZ CE VIEUX WHISKEY BLOND QUI FUME UNE PIPE

▶ Italic OSF

The quick brown fox jumps over a Dog. 123 4567 890 Zwei Boxkämpfer jagen Eva durch Sylt portez ce vieux Whiskey blond qui fume une pipe aber echt über die Mauer gesprungen und

▶ Expert Italic

0123456789 0 ff fi fl ffi ffl - (⅛ ½ ⅓ ¼ ⅗ ⅘ ⅞ ⅞ ‰) ($ ¢ Rp ₡)ᵃ

▶ Semi Bold OSF

The quick brown fox jumps over a Dog. 123 4567 890 Zwei Boxkämpfer jagen Eva durch Sylt portez ce vieux Whiskey blond

▶ Expert Semi Bold

0123456789 0 ff fi fl ffi ffl - (⅛ ½ ⅓ ¼ ⅗ ⅘ ⅞ ⅞ ‰) ($ ¢ Rp ₡)ᵃ

RB6094   Mac   ⑥   ✏ 1991: Richard Beatty

Spiral™

abcdefghijklmnopqrstuvwxyz(äöüßåøœœç)
ABCDEFGHIJKLMNOPQRSTUVWXYZ
1234567890(.,:;?!$&-*)(ÄÖÜÅØŒŒÇ)

Beatty Victoriana™:
Childs™, Hermosa™, Recherché™, Spiral™, Wanted™

RB6095   Mac   ⑥   ✏ 1991: Richard Beatty

Spiral Alternates

abcdefghijklmnopqrstuvwxyz(äöüßåøœœç)
ABCDEFGHIJKLMNOPQRSTUVWXYZ
1234567890(.,:;?!$&-*)(ÄÖÜÅØŒŒÇ)

Beatty Victoriana Alternates:
Childs Alternates, Hermosa Alternates, Recherché Alternates, Spiral Alternates, Wanted Alternates

---

G1102   Mac + PC   ⑥   ✏ 1937: Sol. Hess

Spire No. 377™

ABCDEFGHIJKLMNOPQRSTUVWXYZ
1234567890(.,:;?!$&-*)[](ÄÖÜÅØÆŒÇ)

© FSI 1993

▼ G1102   Mac + PC   Spire No. 377™

Silhouette, Bureau Empire, Obelisk No. 2577, Loyalist

▶ Regular
THE QUICK BROWN FOX JUMPS OVER A DOG. ZWEI BOXKÄMPFER JAGEN EVA DURCH SYLT PORTEZ CE VIEUX WHISKEY BLOND QUI FUME UNE PIPE ABER ECHT ÜBER DIE MAUER GESPRUNGEN UND AUCH SMØRREBRØD EN YSYES NATUURLIK THE QUICK BROWN FOX JUMPS OVER A DOG. ZWEI BOXKÄMPFER JAGEN EVA

▶ Oblique
THE QUICK BROWN FOX JUMPS OVER A DOG. ZWEI BOXKÄMPFER JAGEN EVA DURCH SYLT PORTEZ CE VIEUX WHISKEY BLOND QUI FUME UNE PIPE ABER ECHT ÜBER DIE MAUER GESPRUNGEN UND AUCH SMØRREBRØD EN YSJES NATUURLIJK THE QUICK BROWN FOX JUMPS OVER A DOG. ZWEI BOXKÄMPFER JAGEN EVA

FF2800   Mac + PC   ⑥   1991: Manfred Klein
FF Spontan™

ABCDEFGHIJKLMNOPQRSTUVWXYZ
1234567890[ÄÖÜßAØÆŒ](.,;:?!$&-*){}

Lithos, Sayer Spiritual, Hoffmann

▶ Plain
THE QUICK BROWN FOX JUMPS OVER A DOG. ZWEI BOXKÄMPFER JAGEN EVA DURCH SYLT

▶ Medium
THE QUICK BROWN FOX JUMPS OVER A DOG. ZWEI BOXKÄMPFER JAGEN EVA DURCH

▶ Black
THE QUICK BROWN FOX JUMPS OVER A DOG. ZWEI BOXKÄMPFER JAGEN EVA DURCH

▶ Initials
JUMPS OVER A DOG ZWEI BOX KÄMPFER JAGEN EVA DURCH SYLT PORTEZ

L2809   Mac   ⑥   1989: Tony Geddes
Spotlight™

abcdefghijklmnopqrstuvwxyz[äöüßåøæç]
ABCDEFGHIJKLMNOPQRSTUVWXYZ
1234567890(.,;:?!$&-*)ÄÖÜÅØÆŒÇ

LP2841   Mac + PC   ④   1988: Garrett Boge
Spring™

abcdefghijklmnopqrstuvwxyz[äöüßåøæç]
ABCDEFGHIJKLMNOPQRSTUVWXYZ
1234567890(.,;:?!$&-*)[ÄÖÜÅØÆŒÇ]

▶ Light
The quick brown fox jumps over a Dog. Zwei Boxkämpfer jagen Eva durch Sylt portez ce vieux Whiskey blond qui fume une pipe aber echt über die Mauer gesprungen

▶ Regular
The quick brown fox jumps over a Dog. Zwei Boxkämpfer jagen Eva durch Sylt portez ce vieux Whiskey blond qui fume une pipe aber echt über die

LetterPerfect 4 :
Florens™, Spring™

© FSI 1993

| SG1167 | Mac | ⑥ | ✏ 1979: Bob McGrath |

Springfield™ Bold

abcdefghijklmnopqrstuvwxyz[äöüßåøæœç]
ABCDEFGHIJKLMNOPQRSTUVWXYZ
1234567890(.,;:?!$&-*)ÄÖÜÅØÆŒÇ

| LP941 | Mac + PC | ⑥ | ✏ 1989: Garrett Boge |

Spumoni™

abcdefghijklmnopqrstuvwxyz[äöüßåøæœç]
ABCDEFGHIJKLMNOPQRSTUVWXYZ
1234567890(.,;:?!$&-*){ÄÖÜÅØÆŒÇ}

LetterPerfect 2:
Manito™, Spumoni™

| MC2909 | Mac + PC | ⑥ | ✏ Jan van Dijk |

Squash™

ABCDEFGHIJKLMNOPQRSTUVWXYZ
1234567890(.,;:?!$&-*)[]{ÄÖÜÅØÆŒÇ}

| MC2910 | Mac + PC | ⑥ | ✏ Jan van Dijk |

Squash Outline

ABCDEFGHIJKLMNOPQRSTUVWXYZ
1234567890(.,;:?!$&-*)[]{ÄÖÜÅØÆŒÇ}

| L2733 | Mac | ④ | ✏ 1980: Michael Neugebauer |

Squire™

abcdefghijklmnopqrstuvwxyz[äöüßåøæœç]
ABCDEFGHIJKLMNOPQRSTUVWXYZ
1234567890(.,;:?!$&-*)ÄÖÜÅØÆŒÇ

| FF2961 | Mac + PC | ⑥ | ✏ 1992: Just van Rossum |

FF Stamp Gothic™

abcdefghijklmnopqrstuvwxyz[äöüßåøæœç]
ABCDEFGHIJKLMNOPQRSTUVWXYZ
1234567890(.,;:?!$&-*){ÄÖÜÅØÆŒÇ}

FF InstantTypes™:
FF Confidential™, FF Dynamoe, FF Flightcase™, FF Karton™, FF Stamp Gothic™

A018 Mac + PC   ⑥   1937: Gerry Powell
Stencil™

ABCDEFGHIJKLMNOPQRSTUVWXYZ
1234567890(.,;:?!$&-*)[]{ÄÖÜÅØÆŒÇ}

Hobo:
Brush Script™, Hobo, Stencil™
aaa BT1392
Stencil, Reg

MC6356 Mac + PC   ⑥
Stencil Antique™

ABCDEFGHIJKLMNOPQRSTUVWXYZ
1234567890(.,;:?!$& *)[]{ÄÖÜÅØÆŒÇ}

EF6471 Mac + PC   ④   1977: Heinz Schumann
Stentor™

abcdefghijklmnopqrstuvwxyz[äöüßåøæœç]
ABCDEFGHIJKLMNOPQRSTUVWXYZ
1234567890(.,;:?!$&-*){ÄÖÜÅØÆŒÇ}

E+F Special Headlines 7:
Harlow™, Harlow Solid, Horndon™, Koloss, Paddington™, Stentor™
Ⓒ Choc

EF1109 Mac + PC   ③   1987: Sumner Stone
ITC Stone Informal®

abcdefghijklmnopqrstuvwxyz[äöüßåøœæç]
ABCDEFGHIJKLMNOPQRSTUVWXYZ
1234567890(.,;:?!$&-*){ÄÖÜÅØÆŒÇ}

aaa
A108
ITC Stone Informal,
Reg, Ita, SemBd,
SemBdIta, Bd, BdIta

▶ Medium
The quick brown fox jumps over a Dog. Zwei Boxkämpfer jagen Eva durch Sylt portez ce vieux Whiskey blond qui fume

▶ Semi Bold
The quick brown fox jumps over a Dog. Zwei Boxkämpfer jagen Eva durch Sylt portez ce vieux Whiskey blond

▶ Bold
The quick brown fox jumps over a Dog. Zwei Boxkämpfer jagen Eva durch Sylt portez ce vieux

EF1110 Mac + PC   ③   1987: Sumner Stone
ITC Stone Informal

abcdefghijklmnopqrstuvwxyz[äöüßåøœæç]
ABCDEFGHIJKLMNOPQRSTUVWXYZ
1234567890(.,;:?!$&-*){ÄÖÜÅØÆŒÇ}

aa*a*
A108
ITC Stone Informal,
Reg, Ita, SemBd,
SemBdIta, Bd, BdIta

▼ EF1110 Mac + PC ITC Stone Informal

▶ Medium Italic
The quick brown fox jumps over a Dog. Zwei Boxkämpfer jagen Eva durch Sylt portez ce vieux Whiskey blond qui fume une pipe

▶ Semi Bold Italic
The quick brown fox jumps over a Dog. Zwei Boxkämpfer jagen Eva durch Sylt portez ce vieux Whiskey blond qui fume une

▶ Bold Italic
The quick brown fox jumps over a Dog. Zwei Boxkämpfer jagen Eva durch Sylt portez ce vieux Whiskey blond qui

EF1111 Mac + PC ③ 1987: Sumner Stone
ITC Stone Informal Small Caps

ABCDEFGHIJKLMNOPQRSTUVWXYZ[ÄÖÜSSÅØÆŒÇ]
ABCDEFGHIJKLMNOPQRSTUVWXYZ
1234567890(.,;:?!$&-*){ÄÖÜÅØÆŒÇ}

▶ Medium Small Caps
THE QUICK BROWN FOX JUMPS OVER A DOG. 123 4567 890 ZWEI BOXKÄMPFER JAGEN EVA DURCH SYLT PORTEZ CE VIEUX WHISKEY

▶ Semi Bold Small Caps
THE QUICK BROWN FOX JUMPS OVER A DOG. 123 4567 890 ZWEI BOXKÄMPFER JAGEN EVA DURCH SYLT PORTEZ CE VIEUX

EF1112 Mac + PC ① 1987: Sumner Stone
ITC Stone Sans®

abcdefghijklmnopqrstuvwxyz[äöüßåøæœç]
ABCDEFGHIJKLMNOPQRSTUVWXYZ
1234567890(.,;:?!$&-*){ÄÖÜÅØÆŒÇ}

aa*a*
A109
ITC Stone Sans, Reg,
Ita, SemBd, SemBdIta,
Bd, BdIta

▶ Medium
The quick brown fox jumps over a Dog. Zwei Boxkämpfer jagen Eva durch Sylt portez ce vieux Whiskey blond qui fume

▶ Semi Bold
The quick brown fox jumps over a Dog. Zwei Boxkämpfer jagen Eva durch Sylt portez ce vieux Whiskey blond qui fume

▶ Bold
The quick brown fox jumps over a Dog. Zwei Boxkämpfer jagen Eva durch Sylt portez ce vieux Whiskey

EF1113 Mac + PC ① 1987: Sumner Stone
ITC Stone Sans

abcdefghijklmnopqrstuvwxyz[äöüßåøæœç]
ABCDEFGHIJKLMNOPQRSTUVWXYZ
1234567890(.,;:?!$&-){ÄÖÜÅØÆŒÇ}*

aa*a*
A109
ITC Stone Sans, Reg,
Ita, SemBd, SemBdIta,
Bd, BdIta

▶ Medium Italic
The quick brown fox jumps over a Dog. Zwei Boxkämpfer jagen Eva durch Sylt portez ce vieux Whiskey blond qui fume une pipe aber

▶ Semi Bold Italic
The quick brown fox jumps over a Dog. Zwei Boxkämpfer jagen Eva durch Sylt portez ce vieux Whiskey blond qui fume une

▼ EF1113 Mac + PC   ITC Stone Sans

▶ Bold Italic

The quick brown fox jumps over a Dog. Zwei Boxkämpfer jagen Eva durch Sylt portez ce vieux Whiskey blond qui fume

---

EF1114 Mac + PC   ① 1987: Sumner Stone
ITC Stone Sans Small Caps

ABCDEFGHIJKLMNOPQRSTUVWXYZ[ÄÖÜSSÅØÆŒÇ]
ABCDEFGHIJKLMNOPQRSTUVWXYZ
1234567890(.,;:?!$&-*){ÄÖÜÅØÆŒÇ}

▶ Medium Small Caps

THE QUICK BROWN FOX JUMPS OVER A DOG. 123 4567 890 ZWEI BOXKÄMPFER JAGEN EVA DURCH SYLT PORTEZ CE VIEUX WHISKEY

▶ Semi Bold Small Caps

THE QUICK BROWN FOX JUMPS OVER A DOG. 123 4567 890 ZWEI BOXKÄMPFER JAGEN EVA DURCH SYLT PORTEZ CE VIEUX

EF1115 Mac + PC   ② 1987: Sumner Stone
ITC Stone Serif®

abcdefghijklmnopqrstuvwxyz[äöüßåøæœç]
ABCDEFGHIJKLMNOPQRSTUVWXYZ
1234567890(.,;:?!$&-*){ÄÖÜÅØÆŒÇ}

aaa
A110
ITC Stone Serif, Reg, Ita, SemBd, SemBdIta, Bd, BdIta

▶ Medium

The quick brown fox jumps over a Dog. Zwei Boxkämpfer jagen Eva durch Sylt portez ce vieux Whiskey blond qui

▶ Semi Bold

The quick brown fox jumps over a Dog. Zwei Boxkämpfer jagen Eva durch Sylt portez ce vieux Whiskey blond qui

▶ Bold

The quick brown fox jumps over a Dog. Zwei Boxkämpfer jagen Eva durch Sylt portez ce vieux

---

EF1116 Mac + PC   ② 1987: Sumner Stone
ITC Stone Serif

abcdefghijklmnopqrstuvwxyz[äöüßåøæœç]
ABCDEFGHIJKLMNOPQRSTUVWXYZ
1234567890(.,;:?!$&-){ÄÖÜÅØÆŒÇ}*

aaa
A110
ITC Stone Serif, Reg, Ita, SemBd, SemBdIta, Bd, BdIta

▶ Medium Italic

The quick brown fox jumps over a Dog. Zwei Boxkämpfer jagen Eva durch Sylt portez ce vieux Whiskey blond qui fume une

▶ Semi Bold Italic

The quick brown fox jumps over a Dog. Zwei Boxkämpfer jagen Eva durch Sylt portez ce vieux Whiskey blond qui fume

▶ Bold Italic

The quick brown fox jumps over a Dog. Zwei Boxkämpfer jagen Eva durch Sylt portez ce vieux Whiskey

© FSI 1993

EF1117 Mac + PC ② 🖉 1987: Sumner Stone
ITC Stone Serif Small Caps

ABCDEFGHIJKLMNOPQRSTUVWXYZ[ÄÖÜSSÅØÆŒÇ]
ABCDEFGHIJKLMNOPQRSTUVWXYZ
1234567890(.,;:?!$&-*){ÄÖÜÅØÆŒÇ}

▶ Medium Small Caps
THE QUICK BROWN FOX JUMPS OVER A DOG. 123 4567 890 ZWEI BOXKÄMPFER JAGEN EVA DURCH SYLT PORTEZ CE VIEUX WHISKEY

▶ Semi Bold Small Caps
THE QUICK BROWN FOX JUMPS OVER A DOG. 123 4567 890 ZWEI BOXKÄMPFER JAGEN EVA DURCH SYLT PORTEZ CE VIEUX

A2868 Mac + PC ⑧ 🖉 1992: (Sumner Stone) John Renner
ITC Stone Phonetic™

abcdefghijklmnopqrstuvwxyz
ɑβçðeɸɢʜɨɿʟɰɲɔʼɾɼʃθʊʋɪχʏʒ
θʌɣʐŋɲkɕʁʀʤʦβɬɸøʑɦɕɥɻ

▶ Sans IPA
abcdefghijklmnopqrstuvwxyza
ɑβçðeɸɢʜɨɿʟɰɲɔʼɾɼʃθʊʋɪχʏʒθʃ
ʌɣʐŋɲkɕʁʀʤʦβɬɸøʑɦɕɥɻɰʍʔ˩
˥œʲɕɦzʌɾʂɖʋʐɳʊʐŋɲkɕʁŋɲkɕʁ

▶ Sans Alternate
b̌č̌đ̌ǝ ƒɥɪ̌ȷ̌χ̌ƛᵐη̣σþɼʳśɪ̣ˬω˳ʸžᵖcʤɛ⁻ ɥɪ̣ɼˀᵏˢʧʋˆω*ɑˎ ɔˑδɀ⎯ ¹∅ ̢λ ˜⁺¹⁰ ⁻ᵃᵘ
ɱˣɀ̲̀ ə˙ ... ˬ ᵥ ᵒ ᴖ ᴖ ʙ ̲ˎ ⁻⁄₀ ⁼⁼²ṣ̈ ⁺ɪ̥ˎ⁻ˎ-ˎ:

▶ Serif IPA
abcdefghijklmnopqrstuvwxyz
ɑβçðeɸɢʜɨɿʟɰɲɔʼɾɼʃθʊʋɪχʏʒ
θʌɣʐŋɲkɕʁʀʤʦβɬɸøʑɦɕɥɰ
ɰʔ˩ɥɪ̣ɿɰɴʜɥɪ̣ɿɰœʲɕɦzʌɾʂ

▶ Serif Alternate
b̌č̌đ̌ǝ ƒɥɪ̌ȷ̌χ̌ƛᵐη̣σþɼʳśɪ̣ˬω˳ʸžᵖcʤ
ɛ⁻ ɥɪ̣ɼˀᵏˢʧʋˆω*ɑˎ ɔˑδɀ⎯ ¹∅ ̢λ ˜⁺¹⁰
ɱˣɀ̲̀ ə˙ ... ˬ ᵥ ᵒ ᴖ ᴖ ʙ ̲ˎ ⁻⁄₀ ⁼⁼²ṣ̈ ⁺ɪ̥ˎ⁻ˎ-ˎ:

EF6467 Mac + PC ⑤ 🖉 Aldo Novarese
Stop™

ABCDEFGHIJKLMNOPQRSTUVWXYZ
1234567890(.,;:?!$&-*){ÄÖÜÅØÆŒÇ}

📦 E+F Special Headlines 3:
Hawthorn™, Magnus™ Bold, Octopuss™, Octopuss™ Shaded, Piccadilly™, Stop™

C467 Mac + PC ③
Stratford ™Bold

abcdefghijklmnopqrstuvwxyz[äöüßåøæœç]
ABCDEFGHIJKLMNOPQRSTUVWXYZ
1234567890(.,;:?!$&-*)◊ÄÖÜÅØÆŒÇ◆

📦 Headlines 81S:
Egiziano™ Black, PL Behemoth Semi Condensed, PL Benguiat Frisky, PL Futura Maxi 1, PL Tower™ Condensed, Quirinus™ Bold, Section™ Bold Condensed, Stratford ™Bold, Woodblock
Ⓒ▷ Beton, Memphis, Rockwell, Stymie

© FSI 1993

SG2400 Mac ② ✎ 1979: Freda Sack
Stratford™
abcdefghijklmnopqrstuvwxyz[äöüßåøæœç]
ABCDEFGHIJKLMNOPQRSTUVWXYZ
1234567890(.,;:?!$&-*)ÄÖÜÅØÆŒÇ

SG2401 Mac ② ✎ 1979: Freda Sack
Stratford Italic
abcdefghijklmnopqrstuvwxyz[äöüßåøæœç]
ABCDEFGHIJKLMNOPQRSTUVWXYZ
1234567890(.,;:?!$&-*)ÄÖÜÅØÆŒÇ

SG2402 Mac ② ✎ 1979: Freda Sack
Stratford Bold
abcdefghijklmnopqrstuvwxyz[äöüßåøæœç]
ABCDEFGHIJKLMNOPQRSTUVWXYZ
1234567890(.,;:?!$&-*)ÄÖÜÅØÆŒÇ

SG2403 Mac ② ✎ 1979: Freda Sack
Stratford Black
abcdefghijklmnopqrstuvwxyz[äöüßåøæœç]
ABCDEFGHIJKLMNOPQRSTUVWXYZ
1234567890(.,;:?!$&-*)ÄÖÜÅØÆŒÇ

L2810 Mac ⑥ ✎ 1990: Vince Whitlock
Strobos™
ABCDEFGHIJKLMNOPQRSTUVWXYZ
1234567890(.,;:?!$&-*) I IÄÖÜÅØÆŒÇ

EF980 Mac + PC ④ ✎ 1990: Pat Hickson
ITC Studio Script™
abcdefghijklmnopqrstuvwxyz[äöüßåøæœç]
ABCDEFGHIJKLMNOPQRSTUVWXYZ
1234567890(.,;:?!$&-*)(ÄÖÜÅØÆŒÇ)

aaa ▶ Regular ▶ Alternates
C2979 The quick brown fox jumps over a Dog. Zwei FMNEFGHILMNOQrsUVWXYI
ITC Typographica™ Boxkämpfer jagen Eva durch Sylt portez ce asrmapserfthnuabodefghiklmnoprstuvwyz
 vieux Whiskey blond qui fume une pipe aber echt
 über die Mauer gesprungen und auch smørebrød

ITC Beesknees™, ITC Studio Script™

© FSI 1993

Stuyvesant™
BT849 Mac + PC ④

abcdefghijklmnopqrstuvwxyz[äöüßåøæœç]
ABCDEFGHIJKLMNOPQRSTUVWXYZ
1234567890(.,:;?!$&-*){ÄÖÜÅØÆŒÇ}

Bitstream Script 2:
Bernhard Tango™, Commercial Script, Stuyvesant™
aa*a* 🖫 C6568
Agfa Scripts 1

Stymie™ 1
BT857 Mac + PC ③ 1935–37: Sol. Hess, Gerry Powell

abcdefghijklmnopqrstuvwxyz[äöüßåøæœç]
ABCDEFGHIJKLMNOPQRSTUVWXYZ
1234567890(.,:;?!$&-*){ÄÖÜÅØÆŒÇ}

aa*a*
EF6456
Stymie 1, Lt, Bd, BdCon
EF6457
Stymie 2, Med, Blk, MedCon
©
Beton, Memphis, Rockwell, Stratford Bold

▶ Light
The quick brown fox jumps over a Dog. Zwei Boxkämpfer jagen Eva durch Sylt portez ce vieux Whiskey blond qui fume

▶ Light Italic
The quick brown fox jumps over a Dog. Zwei Boxkämpfer jagen Eva durch Sylt portez ce vieux Whiskey blond qui fume une

▶ Bold
The quick brown fox jumps over a Dog. Zwei Boxkämpfer jagen Eva durch Sylt portez ce vieux Whiskey blond qui

▶ Bold Italic
The quick brown fox jumps over a Dog. Zwei Boxkämpfer jagen Eva durch Sylt portez ce vieux Whiskey blond qui

---

Stymie 2
BT858 Mac + PC ③ 1935–37: Sol. Hess, Gerry Powell

abcdefghijklmnopqrstuvwxyz[äöüßåøæœç]
ABCDEFGHIJKLMNOPQRSTUVWXYZ
1234567890(.,:;?!$&-*){ÄÖÜÅØÆŒÇ}

aa*a*
EF6456 Stymie 1, Lt, Bd, BdCon, EF6457 Stymie 2, Med, Blk, MedCon
©
Beton, Memphis, Rockwell, Stratford Bold

▶ Medium
The quick brown fox jumps over a Dog. Zwei Boxkämpfer jagen Eva durch Sylt portez ce vieux Whiskey blond qui

▶ Medium Italic
The quick brown fox jumps over a Dog. Zwei Boxkämpfer jagen Eva durch Sylt portez ce vieux Whiskey blond qui fume

---

Stymie 3
BT859 Mac + PC ③ 1935–37: Sol. Hess, Gerry Powell

abcdefghijklmnopqrstuvwxyz[äöüßåøæœç]
ABCDEFGHIJKLMNOPQRSTUVWXYZ
1234567890(.,:;?!$&-*){ÄÖÜÅØÆŒÇ}

aa*a*
EF6456
Stymie 1, Lt, Bd, BdCon
EF6457
Stymie 2, Med, Blk, MedCon
©
Beton, Memphis, Rockwell, Stratford Bold

▶ Extra Bold
The quick brown fox jumps over a Dog. Zwei Boxkämpfer jagen Eva durch Sylt portez ce vieux Whiskey blond qui

▶ Extra Bold Condensed
The quick brown fox jumps over a Dog. Zwei Boxkämpfer jagen Eva durch Sylt portez ce vieux Whiskey blond qui fume une pipe aber echt

© FSI 1993

MC2911 Mac + PC ② ✏ José Mendoza
Sully Jonquieres™

abcdefghijklmnopqrstuvwxyz[äöüßåøæœç]
ABCDEFGHIJKLMNOPQRSTUVWXYZ
1234567890(.,;:?!$&-*){ÄÖÜÅØÆŒÇ}

MC2912 Mac + PC ② ✏ José Mendoza
Sully Jonquieres Bold

abcdefghijklmnopqrstuvwxyz[äöüßåøæœç]
ABCDEFGHIJKLMNOPQRSTUVWXYZ
1234567890(.,;:?!$&-*){ÄÖÜÅØÆŒÇ}

L2734 Mac ⑥ ✏ 1970: Colin Brignall
Superstar™

ABCDEFGHIJKLMNOPQRSTUVWXYZ
1234567890(.,;:?!$&-*)[]ÄÖÜÅØÆŒÇ

MC6351 Mac + PC ⑥
Swaak™ Centennial

ABCDEFGHIJKLMNOPQRSTUVWXYZ
1234567890...:?!ÄÖÜÅ

EF525 Mac + PC ② ✏ 1985: Gerard Unger
Swift™ 1

abcdefghijklmnopqrstuvwxyz[äöüßåøæœç]
ABCDEFGHIJKLMNOPQRSTUVWXYZ
1234567890(.,;:?!$&-*){ÄÖÜÅØÆŒÇ}

Ⓒ Bitstream Charter, Demos

▶ Light
The quick brown fox jumps over a Dog. Zwei Boxkämpfer jagen Eva durch Sylt portez ce vieux Whiskey blond qui fume

▶ Light Italic
The quick brown fox jumps over a Dog. Zwei Boxkämpfer jagen Eva durch Sylt portez ce vieux Whiskey blond qui fume une pipe aber echt

▶ Bold
The quick brown fox jumps over a Dog. Zwei Boxkämpfer jagen Eva durch Sylt portez ce vieux Whiskey blond qui

▶ Extra Bold
The quick brown fox jumps over a Dog. Zwei Boxkämpfer jagen Eva durch Sylt portez ce vieux Whiskey blond

EF526 Mac + PC ② ✏ 1985: Gerard Unger
Swift 2

abcdefghijklmnopqrstuvwxyz[äöüßåøæœç]
ABCDEFGHIJKLMNOPQRSTUVWXYZ
1234567890(.,;:?!$&-*){ÄÖÜÅØÆŒÇ}

© FSI 1993

© Bitstream Charter, Demos, Hollander, Bitstream Oranda

▼ EF526   Mac + PC   Swift 2

▶ Regular
The quick brown fox jumps over a Dog. Zwei Boxkämpfer jagen Eva durch Sylt portez ce vieux Whiskey blond qui fume

▶ Italic
The quick brown fox jumps over a Dog. Zwei Boxkämpfer jagen Eva durch Sylt portez ce vieux Whiskey blond qui fume une pipe aber echt

▶ Small Caps
THE QUICK BROWN FOX JUMPS OVER A DOG. 123 4567 890 ZWEI BOXKÄMPFER JAGEN EVA DURCH SYLT PORTEZ CE VIEUX WHISKEY

▶ Bold Condensed
The quick brown fox jumps over a Dog. Zwei Boxkämpfer jagen Eva durch Sylt portez ce vieux Whiskey blond qui fume

---

M263   Mac + PC   ④   ✎ 1939: (Max Kaufmann, 1936)
Swing™ Bold

abcdefghijklmnopqrstuvwxyz[äöüßåøæœç]
ABCDEFGHIJKLMNOPQRSTUVWXYZ
1234567890(.,;:?!$&-*){ÄÖÜÅØÆŒÇ}

Script 1:
Biffo™ Script, Dorchester Script™, Monotype Script Bold™, Pepita®, Swing™ Bold
aa*a* G414
Swing Bold No. 217™,

EF316   Mac + PC   ②   ✎ 1984: Aldo Novarese
ITC Symbol® 1

abcdefghijklmnopqrstuvwxyz[äöüßåøæœç]
ABCDEFGHIJKLMNOPQRSTUVWXYZ
1234567890(.,;:?!$&-*){ÄÖÜÅØÆŒÇ}

aa*a*
A918
ITC Symbol, Bk, Bklta, Med, Medlta, Bd, Bdlta, Blk, Blklta
C1042
ITC Symbol, Bk, Bklta, Med, Medlta, Bd, Bdlta, Blk, Blklta
BT1402
ITC Symbol 1, Bk, Bklta, Bd, Bdlta
©
Bitstream Amerigo, Albertus, ITC Élan, Friz Quadrata

▶ Book
The quick brown fox jumps over a Dog. Zwei Boxkämpfer jagen Eva durch Sylt portez ce vieux Whiskey blond qui fume une pipe

▶ Book Italic
The quick brown fox jumps over a Dog. Zwei Boxkämpfer jagen Eva durch Sylt portez ce vieux Whiskey blond qui fume une pipe aber

▶ Bold
The quick brown fox jumps over a Dog. Zwei Boxkämpfer jagen Eva durch Sylt portez ce vieux Whiskey blond qui fume

▶ Bold Italic
The quick brown fox jumps over a Dog. Zwei Boxkämpfer jagen Eva durch Sylt portez ce vieux Whiskey blond qui fume

---

EF317   Mac + PC   ②   ✎ 1984: Aldo Novarese
ITC Symbol 2

abcdefghijklmnopqrstuvwxyz[äöüßåøæœç]
ABCDEFGHIJKLMNOPQRSTUVWXYZ
1234567890(.,;:?!$&-*){ÄÖÜÅØÆŒÇ}

aa*a*
A918
ITC Symbol, Bk, Bklta, Med, Medlta, Bd, Bdlta, Blk, Blklta
C1042
ITC Symbol, Bk, Bklta, Med, Medlta, Bd, Bdlta, Blk, Blklta
BT1403
ITC Symbol 2, Med, Medlta, Blk, Blklta
©
Bitstream Amerigo, Albertus, ITC Élan, Friz Quadrata

▶ Medium
The quick brown fox jumps over a Dog. Zwei Boxkämpfer jagen Eva durch Sylt portez ce vieux Whiskey blond qui fume une

▶ Medium Italic
The quick brown fox jumps over a Dog. Zwei Boxkämpfer jagen Eva durch Sylt portez ce vieux Whiskey blond qui fume une

© FSI 1993

▼ EF317 Mac + PC ITC Symbol 2

▶ Black
The quick brown fox jumps over a Dog. Zwei Boxkämpfer jagen Eva durch Sylt portez ce vieux Whiskey blond

▶ Black Italic
The quick brown fox jumps over a Dog. Zwei Boxkämpfer jagen Eva durch Sylt portez ce vieux Whiskey blond

---

EF543 Mac + PC ② 1984: Aldo Novarese
ITC Symbol Small Caps

ABCDEFGHIJKLMNOPQRSTUVWXYZ[ÄÖÜSSÅØÆŒÇ]
ABCDEFGHIJKLMNOPQRSTUVWXYZ
1234567890(.,;:?!$&-*){ÄÖÜÅØÆŒÇ}

© Bitstream Amerigo, Albertus, ITC Élan, Friz Quadrata

▶ Book Small Caps
THE QUICK BROWN FOX JUMPS OVER A DOG. 123 4567 890 ZWEI BOXKÄMPFER JAGEN EVA DURCH SYLT PORTEZ CE VIEUX WHISKEY BLOND QUI

▶ Medium Small Caps
THE QUICK BROWN FOX JUMPS OVER A DOG. 123 4567 890 ZWEI BOXKÄMPFER JAGEN EVA DURCH SYLT PORTEZ CE VIEUX WHISKEY

L6147 Mac ⑤ 1984: Alan R. Birch
Synchro™ Plain

ABCDEFGHIJKLMNOPQRSTUVWXYZ
1234567890(.,;:?!$&-*)[]ÄÖÜÅØÆŒÇ

Synchro™ Plain, Synchro Reversed

L6147 Mac ⑤ 1984: Alan R. Birch
Synchro Reversed

ABCDEFGHIJKLMNOPQRSTUVWXYZ
1234567890(.,;:?!$&-*)[]ÄÖÜÅØÆŒÇ

Synchro™ Plain, Synchro Reversed

EF6458 Mac + PC ② 1992: Hans Eduard Meier
ITC Syndor ™ 1

abcdefghijklmnopqrstuvwxyz[äöüßåøæœç]
ABCDEFGHIJKLMNOPQRSTUVWXYZ
1234567890(.,;:?!$&-*){ÄÖÜÅØÆŒÇ}

▶ Book
The quick brown fox jumps over a Dog. Zwei Boxkämpfer jagen Eva durch Sylt portez ce vieux Whiskey blond qui fume une

▶ Book Italic
The quick brown fox jumps over a Dog. Zwei Boxkämpfer jagen Eva durch Sylt portez ce vieux Whiskey blond qui fume une pipe aber echt

▼ EF6458 Mac + PC ITC Syndor ™ 1
▶ Book SC
THE QUICK BROWN FOX JUMPS
OVER A DOG. 123 4567 890 ZWEI
BOXKÄMPFER JAGEN EVA DURCH
SYLT PORTEZ CE VIEUX WHISKEY

EF6459 Mac + PC ② 1992: Hans Eduard Meier
ITC Syndor 2

abcdefghijklmnopqrstuvwxyz[äöüßåøæœç]
ABCDEFGHIJKLMNOPQRSTUVWXYZ
1234567890(.,;:?!$&-*){ÄÖÜÅØÆŒÇ}

▶ Medium
The quick brown fox jumps over a Dog. Zwei Boxkämpfer jagen Eva durch Sylt portez ce vieux Whiskey blond qui fume

▶ Medium Italic
The quick brown fox jumps over a Dog. Zwei Boxkämpfer jagen Eva durch Sylt portez ce vieux Whiskey blond qui fume une

▶ Medium SC
THE QUICK BROWN FOX JUMPS
OVER A DOG. 123 4567 890 ZWEI
BOXKÄMPFER JAGEN EVA DURCH
SYLT PORTEZ CE VIEUX WHISKEY

EF6460 Mac + PC ② 1992: Hans Eduard Meier
ITC Syndor 3

**abcdefghijklmnopqrstuvwxyz[äöüßåøæœç]
ABCDEFGHIJKLMNOPQRSTUVWXYZ
1234567890(.,;:?!$&-*){ÄÖÜÅØÆŒÇ}**

▶ Bold
The quick brown fox jumps over a Dog. Zwei Boxkämpfer jagen Eva durch Sylt portez ce vieux Whiskey blond qui

▶ Bold Italic
The quick brown fox jumps over a Dog. Zwei Boxkämpfer jagen Eva durch Sylt portez ce vieux Whiskey blond

A415 Mac + PC ① 1968: Hans Eduard Meier
Syntax™

abcdefghijklmnopqrstuvwxyz[äöüßåøæœç]
ABCDEFGHIJKLMNOPQRSTUVWXYZ
1234567890(.,;:?!$&-*){ÄÖÜÅØÆŒÇ}

aa*a*
BT1335
Syntax, Reg, Bd, Blk, UltBlk

▶ Regular
The quick brown fox jumps over a Dog. Zwei Boxkämpfer jagen Eva durch Sylt portez ce vieux Whiskey blond qui fume

▶ Italic
The quick brown fox jumps over a Dog. Zwei Boxkämpfer jagen Eva durch Sylt portez ce vieux Whiskey blond qui fume

▶ Bold
The quick brown fox jumps over a Dog. Zwei Boxkämpfer jagen Eva durch Sylt portez ce vieux Whiskey blond qui fume

▶ Black
The quick brown fox jumps over a Dog. Zwei Boxkämpfer jagen Eva durch Sylt portez ce vieux Whis-

© FSI 1993

▼ A415　Mac + PC　Syntax™
▶ Ultra Black
The quick brown fox jumps over a Dog. Zwei Boxkämpfer jagen Eva durch Sylt portez ce vieux

THE PATH
OF LEAST
RESISTANCE
IS A DEAD END

T

Tobias Frere-Jones, Boston, USA

Tagliente™
ET1106 Mac + PC ④ 1990: (G. Tagliente, c.1524) Judith Sutcliffe

abcdefghijklmnopqrstuvwxyz[äöüßåøæœç]
ABCDEFGHIJKLMNOPQRSTUVWXYZ
1234567890(.,:;?!$&-*){ÄÖÜÅØÆŒÇ}

▶ Regular
The quick brown fox jumps over a Dog. Zwei Boxkämpfer jagen Eva durch Sylt portez ce vieux Whiskey blond qui fume une pipe aber echt uber die Mauer gesprungen und auch smørebrød en ysjes natuurlijk

▶ Initials
ABCDEFGHIJKLM
NOPQRSTUVWXYZ

Renaissance™:
Leonardo Hand™, Tagliente™

Tall Pack
E937 Mac + PC

Tall Pack:
Matrix Tall, Senator Tall

Tango™
BT6417 Mac + PC ⑥ 1974: Colin Brignall

abcdefghijklmnopqrstuvwxyz[äöüßåøæœç]
ABCDEFGHIJKLMNOPQRSTUVWXYZ
1234567890(.,:;?!$&-*){ÄÖÜÅØÆŒÇ}

Tannhauser™
L6148 Mac ⑥ 1984: Alan Meeks

abcdefghijklmnopqrstuvwxyz[äöüßåøæœç]
ABCDEFGHIJKLMNOPQRSTUVWXYZ
1234567890(.,:;?!$&-*)ÄÖÜÅØÆŒÇ

Teknik™
L2735 Mac ⑤ 1989: David Quay

ABCDEFGHIJKLMNOPQRSTUVWXYZ
1234567890[.,:;?!$&-*][]ÄÖÜÅØÆŒÇ

Tekton™
A458 Mac + PC ④ 1989: (Francis D. K. Ching) David Siegel

abcdefghijklmnopqrstuvwxyz[äöüßåøæœç]
ABCDEFGHIJKLMNOPQRSTUVWXYZ
1234567890(.,:;?!$&-*){ÄÖÜÅØÆŒÇ}

© FSI 1993
T 1

▼ A458 Mac + PC   Tekton™

▶ Regular
The quick brown fox jumps over a Dog. Zwei Boxkämpfer jagen Eva durch Sylt portez ce vieux Whiskey blond qui fume une pipe aber

▶ Oblique
The quick brown fox jumps over a Dog. Zwei Boxkämpfer jagen Eva durch Sylt portez ce vieux Whiskey blond qui fume une pipe aber

▶ Bold
The quick brown fox jumps over a Dog. Zwei Boxkämpfer jagen Eva durch Sylt portez ce vieux Whiskey blond qui fume une pipe

▶ Bold Oblique
The quick brown fox jumps over a Dog. Zwei Boxkämpfer jagen Eva durch Sylt portez ce vieux Whiskey blond qui fume une pipe

E1145 Mac + PC   ⑥   1990: Barry Deck
Template Gothic™

abcdefghijklmnopqrstuvwxyz[äöüßåøæœç]
ABCDEFGHIJKLMNOPQRSTUVWXYZ
1234567890(.,;:?!$&-*){ÄÖÜÅØÆŒÇ}

▶ Regular
The quick brown fox jumps over a Dog. Zwei Boxkämpfer jagen Eva durch Sylt portez ce vieux Whiskey blond qui fume une pipe aber

▶ Bold
The quick brown fox jumps over a Dog. Zwei Boxkämpfer jagen Eva durch Sylt portez ce vieux Whiskey blond qui fume une

A165 Mac + PC   ①   1931: R. Hunter Middleton
Tempo™ Heavy Condensed

abcdefghijklmnopqrstuvwxyz[äöüßåøæœç]
ABCDEFGHIJKLMNOPQRSTUVWXYZ
1234567890(.,;:?!$&-*){ÄÖÜÅØÆŒÇ}

DIN Engschrift, Erbar, Neuzeit Grotesk

▶ Regular
The quick brown fox jumps over a Dog. Zwei Boxkämpfer jagen Eva durch Sylt portez ce vieux Whiskey blond qui fume une pipe aber echt über die Mauer

▶ Italic
The quick brown fox jumps over a Dog. Zwei Boxkämpfer jagen Eva durch Sylt portez ce vieux Whiskey blond qui fume une pipe aber echt über die

Gothic No. 13:
Gothic No. 13™, Tempo™ Heavy Condensed
DIN Engschrift, Erbar, Neuzeit Grotesk

BT861 Mac + PC   ③   1929: C.H. Griffith   Industry name
Century 731   Textype™

abcdefghijklmnopqrstuvwxyz[äöüßåøæœç]
ABCDEFGHIJKLMNOPQRSTUVWXYZ
1234567890(.,;:?!$&-*){ÄÖÜÅØÆŒÇ}

▶ Regular
The quick brown fox jumps over a Dog. Zwei Boxkämpfer jagen Eva durch Sylt portez ce vieux Whiskey blond qui

▶ Italic
The quick brown fox jumps over a Dog. Zwei Boxkämpfer jagen Eva durch Sylt portez ce vieux Whiskey blond qui fume

© FSI 1993

▼ BT861 Mac + PC Textype™

▶ Bold
The quick brown fox jumps over a Dog. Zwei Boxkämpfer jagen Eva durch Sylt portez ce vieux Whiskey

▶ Bold Italic
The quick brown fox jumps over a Dog. Zwei Boxkämpfer jagen Eva durch Sylt portez ce vieux Whiskey

ATF336 Mac ④ ✎ 1952: Tommy Thompson
Thompson Quillscript™

abcdefghijklmnopqrstuvwxyz[äöüßåøæœç]
ABCDEFGHIJKLMNOPQRSTUVWXYZ
1234567890(.,;:?!$&-*){ÄÖÜÅØÆŒÇ}

ATF Set 1:
Bernhard Fashion™, Cleland Border 1805™, Thompson Quillscript™, Wedding Text™

EF1085 Mac + PC ⑥
Thunderbird™

ABCDEFGHIJKLM
NOPQRSTUVWXYZ
1234567890(.,;:?!$&-*)
[]{ÄÖÜÅØÆŒÇ}

aa*a*
🕮 BT811
Bitstream Headlines 4
Ⓒ
Davison Americana,
Tuscan Egyptian

▶ Regular
THE QUICK
BROWN FOX
JUMPS OVER
A DOG. ZWEI

▶ Extra Condensed
THE QUICK BROWN FOX JUMPS OVER A DOG. ZWEI BOXKÄMPFER JAGEN EVA DURCH SYLT PORTEZ CE VIEUX WHISKEY BLOND QUI FUME UNE PIPE ABER ECHT ÜBER DIE MAUER GESPRUNGEN UND AUCH SMØREBRØD EN YSYES NATUURLIK

EF416 Mac + PC ② ✎ 1987: Cynthia Hollandsworth
ITC Tiepolo® 1

abcdefghijklmnopqrstuvwxyz[äöüßåøæœç]
ABCDEFGHIJKLMNOPQRSTUVWXYZ
1234567890(.,;:?!$&-*){ÄÖÜÅØÆŒÇ}

aa*a*
C982
ITC Tiepolo, Bk, BkIta,
Bd, BdIta, Blk, BlkIta

▶ Book
The quick brown fox jumps over a Dog. Zwei Boxkämpfer jagen Eva durch Sylt portez ce vieux Whiskey blond qui fume

▶ Bold
The quick brown fox jumps over a Dog. Zwei Boxkämpfer jagen Eva durch Sylt portez ce vieux Whiskey blond qui fume

▶ Black
The quick brown fox jumps over a Dog. Zwei Boxkämpfer jagen Eva durch Sylt portez ce vieux Whiskey blond

EF417 Mac + PC ② ✎ 1987: (Cynthia Hollandsworth)
ITC Tiepolo 2

abcdefghijklmnopqrstuvwxyz[äöüßåøæœç]
ABCDEFGHIJKLMNOPQRSTUVWXYZ
1234567890(.,;:?!$&-*){ÄÖÜÅØÆŒÇ}

© FSI 1993

aa*a*
C982
ITC Tiepolo, Bk, BkIta,
Bd, BdIta, Blk, BlkIta

▼ EF417 Mac + PC ITC Tiepolo 2

▶ Book Italic
The quick brown fox jumps over a Dog. Zwei Boxkämpfer jagen Eva durch Sylt portez ce vieux Whiskey blond qui fume une pipe aber

▶ Bold Italic
The quick brown fox jumps over a Dog. Zwei Boxkämpfer jagen Eva durch Sylt portez ce vieux Whiskey blond qui fume une

▶ Black Italic
The quick brown fox jumps over a Dog. Zwei Boxkämpfer jagen Eva durch Sylt portez ce vieux Whiskey blond qui

EF544 Mac + PC ② 1987: (Cynthia Hollandsworth)
ITC Tiepolo Small Caps

ABCDEFGHIJKLMNOPQRSTUVWXYZ[ÄÖÜSSÅØÆŒÇ]
ABCDEFGHIJKLMNOPQRSTUVWXYZ
1234567890(.,:;?!$&-*){ÄÖÜÅØÆŒÇ}

▶ Book Small Caps
THE QUICK BROWN FOX JUMPS OVER A DOG. 123 4567 890 ZWEI BOXKÄMPFER JAGEN EVA DURCH SYLT PORTEZ CE VIEUX WHISKEY

▶ Bold Small Caps
THE QUICK BROWN FOX JUMPS OVER A DOG. 123 4567 890 ZWEI BOXKÄMPFER JAGEN EVA DURCH SYLT PORTEZ CE VIEUX

BT1404 Mac + PC ② 1974: Ed Benguiat
ITC Tiffany® 1

abcdefghijklmnopqrstuvwxyz[äöüßåøæœç]
ABCDEFGHIJKLMNOPQRSTUVWXYZ
1234567890(.,:;?!$&-*){ÄÖÜÅØÆŒÇ}

aa*a*
A113
ITC Tiffany, Reg, Ita,
Demi, Demilta, Hvy,
Hvylta

▶ Light
The quick brown fox jumps over a Dog. Zwei Boxkämpfer jagen Eva durch Sylt portez ce vieux Whiskey blond qui

▶ Light Italic
The quick brown fox jumps over a Dog. Zwei Boxkämpfer jagen Eva durch Sylt portez ce vieux Whiskey blond qui

▶ Demi
The quick brown fox jumps over a Dog. Zwei Boxkämpfer jagen Eva durch Sylt portez ce vieux Whiskey

▶ Demi Italic
The quick brown fox jumps over a Dog. Zwei Boxkämpfer jagen Eva durch Sylt portez ce vieux Whiskey

BT862 Mac + PC ② 1974: Ed Benguiat
ITC Tiffany 2

abcdefghijklmnopqrstuvwxyz[äöüßåøæœç]
ABCDEFGHIJKLMNOPQRSTUVWXYZ
1234567890(.,:;?!$&-*){ÄÖÜÅØÆŒÇ}

aa*a*
A113
ITC Tiffany, Reg, Ita,
Demi, Demilta, Hvy,
Hvylta

▶ Medium
The quick brown fox jumps over a Dog. Zwei Boxkämpfer jagen Eva durch Sylt portez ce vieux Whiskey blond

▶ Medium Italic
The quick brown fox jumps over a Dog. Zwei Boxkämpfer jagen Eva durch Sylt portez ce vieux Whiskey blond

© FSI 1993

ITC Tiffany 3
BT1405 Mac + PC ② 1974: Ed Benguiat

abcdefghijklmnopqrstuvwxyz[äöüßåøæœç]
ABCDEFGHIJKLMNOPQRSTUVWXYZ
1234567890(.,;:?!$&-*){ÄÖÜÅØÆŒÇ}

aa*a*
A113
ITC Tiffany, Reg, Ita, Demi, Demilta, Hvy, Hvylta

▶ Heavy
The quick brown fox jumps over a Dog. Zwei Boxkämpfer jagen Eva durch Sylt portez ce

▶ Heavy Italic
The quick brown fox jumps over a Dog. Zwei Boxkämpfer jagen Eva durch Sylt portez ce

Tiger Rag™
L2811 Mac ④ 1989: John Viner

abcdefghijklmnopqrstuvwxyz[äöüßåøæœç]
ABCDEFGHIJKLMNOPQRSTUVWXYZ
1234567890(.,;:?!$&-){ÄÖÜÅØÆŒÇ}*

Times New Roman®
M114 Mac + PC ② 1931-35: Stanley Morison, Victor Lardent

abcdefghijklmnopqrstuvwxyz[äöüßåøæœç]
ABCDEFGHIJKLMNOPQRSTUVWXYZ
1234567890(.,;:?!$&-*){ÄÖÜÅØÆŒÇ}

aa*a*
A1530
Times New Roman 1, Reg, Ita, Bd, Bdlta
BT1283
Times 1, Rom, Ita, Bd, Bdlta
©
Times Headline, Times Europa, Times Ten, Life, Concorde

▶ Regular
The quick brown fox jumps over a Dog. Zwei Boxkämpfer jagen Eva durch Sylt portez ce vieux Whiskey blond qui fume une

▶ Bold
The quick brown fox jumps over a Dog. Zwei Boxkämpfer jagen Eva durch Sylt portez ce vieux Whiskey blond qui fume une pipe

▶ Italic
The quick brown fox jumps over a Dog. Zwei Boxkämpfer jagen Eva durch Sylt portez ce vieux Whiskey blond qui fume une pipe

▶ Bold Italic
The quick brown fox jumps over a Dog. Zwei Boxkämpfer jagen Eva durch Sylt portez ce vieux Whiskey blond qui fume une pipe

Times New Roman SC/OSF
A1003 Mac + PC ② 1931-35: Stanley Morison, Victor Lardent

ABCDEFGHIJKLMNOPQRSTUVWXYZ[ÄÖÜSSÅØÆŒÇ]
ABCDEFGHIJKLMNOPQRSTUVWXYZ
1234567890(.,;:?!$&-*){ÄÖÜÅØÆŒÇ}

©
Times Headline, Times Europa, Times Ten, Life, Concorde

▶ Regular Small Caps
THE QUICK BROWN FOX JUMPS OVER A DOG. 123 4567 890 ZWEI BOXKÄMPFER JAGEN EVA DURCH SYLT PORTEZ CE VIEUX WHISKEY

▶ Bold Small Caps
THE QUICK BROWN FOX JUMPS OVER A DOG. 123 4567 890 ZWEI BOXKÄMPFER JAGEN EVA DURCH SYLT PORTEZ CE VIEUX

▶ Italic OSF
The quick brown fox jumps over a Dog. 123 4567 890 Zwei Boxkämpfer jagen Eva durch Sylt portez ce vieux Whiskey blond qui

▶ Bold Italic OSF
The quick brown fox jumps over a Dog. 123 4567 890 Zwei Boxkämpfer jagen Eva durch Sylt portez ce vieux Whiskey blond

© FSI 1993

M553 Mac + PC ② 1931-35: Stanley Morison, Victor Lardent
Times New Roman Expert

ABCDEFGHIJKLMNOPQRSTUVWXYZ(ÄÖÜŠÅØÆŒÇ)

1234567890fffifflffiffl($^1/_1$$^2/_2$$^3/_3$$^4/_4$$^5/_5$$^6/_6$$^7/_7$$^8/_8$$^9/_9$$^0/_0$) ($^$$^¢Rp₡)ᵃ

Times Headline, Times Europa, Times Ten

▶ Expert
0123456789offfifflffiffl-($^1/_1$$^2/_2$$^3/_3$$^4/_4$$^5/_5$$^6/_6$$^7/_7$$^8/_8$$^9/_9$$^0/_0$)($^$$^¢Rp₡)ᵃ
THE QUICK BROWN FOX JUMPS
OVER A DOG ZWEI BOXKÄMPFER

▶ Expert Italic
0123456789offfifflffiffl-
($^1/_1$$^2/_2$$^3/_3$$^4/_4$$^5/_5$$^6/_6$$^7/_7$$^8/_8$$^9/_9$$^0/_0$) ($^$$^¢
Rp₡)ᵃ

▶ Expert Bold
0123456789offfifflffiffl-
($^1/_1$$^2/_2$$^3/_3$$^4/_4$$^5/_5$$^6/_6$$^7/_7$$^8/_8$$^9/_9$$^0/_0$)($^$$^¢Rp₡)ᵃ

▶ Expert Bold Italic
0123456789offfifflffiffl-
($^1/_1$$^2/_2$$^3/_3$$^4/_4$$^5/_5$$^6/_6$$^7/_7$$^8/_8$$^9/_9$$^0/_0$) ($^$$^¢Rp₡)ᵃ

M278 Mac + PC ② 1931-35: Stanley Morison, Victor Lardent
Times New Roman 2

abcdefghijklmnopqrstuvwxyz[äöüßåøæœç]
ABCDEFGHIJKLMNOPQRSTUVWXYZ
1234567890(.,;:?!$&-*){ÄÖÜÅØÆŒÇ}

aa*a*
A919
Times New Roman 2, SemBd, SemBdIta, ExtBd
BT1284
Times 2, SemBd, SemBdIta, ExtBd, ExtBdIta
Times Headline, Times Europa, Times Ten, Life, Concorde

▶ Semi Bold
The quick brown fox jumps over a Dog. Zwei Boxkämpfer jagen Eva durch Sylt portez ce vieux Whiskey blond qui

▶ Semi Bold Italic
The quick brown fox jumps over a Dog. Zwei Boxkämpfer jagen Eva durch Sylt portez ce vieux Whiskey blond qui fume

▶ Extra Bold
The quick brown fox jumps over a Dog. Zwei Boxkämpfer jagen Eva durch Sylt portez ce vieux Whiskey blond qui fume

---

M279 Mac + PC ② 1931-35: Stanley Morison, Victor Lardent
Times New Roman Condensed

abcdefghijklmnopqrstuvwxyz[äöüßåøæœç]
ABCDEFGHIJKLMNOPQRSTUVWXYZ
1234567890(.,;:?!$&-*){ÄÖÜÅØÆŒÇ}

aa*a*
A6086
Times New Roman Condensed MT, Con, ConIta, BdCon
Times Headline, Times Europa, Times Ten, Life, Concorde

▶ Condensed
The quick brown fox jumps over a Dog. Zwei Boxkämpfer jagen Eva durch Sylt portez ce vieux Whiskey blond qui fume une pipe aber echt über

▶ Condensed Italic
The quick brown fox jumps over a Dog. Zwei Boxkämpfer jagen Eva durch Sylt portez ce vieux Whiskey blond qui fume une pipe aber echt über die Mauer

▶ Bold Condensed
The quick brown fox jumps over a Dog. Zwei Boxkämpfer jagen Eva durch Sylt portez ce vieux Whiskey blond qui fume une pipe aber echt

M360 Mac + PC ② 🖉 1931-35: Stanley Morison, Victor Lardent
Times New Roman Small Text

abcdefghijklmnopqrstuvwxyz[äöüßåøæœç]
ABCDEFGHIJKLMNOPQRSTUVWXYZ
1234567890(.,;:?!$&-*){ÄÖÜÅØÆŒÇ}

© Times Headline, Times Europa, Times Ten, Life, Concorde

▶ Regular
The quick brown fox jumps over a Dog. Zwei Boxkämpfer jagen Eva durch Sylt portez ce

▶ Italic
The quick brown fox jumps over a Dog. Zwei Boxkämpfer jagen Eva durch Sylt portez ce

▶ Bold
The quick brown fox jumps over a Dog. Zwei Boxkämpfer jagen Eva durch Sylt portez ce

▶ New Roman Medium
The quick brown fox jumps over a Dog. Zwei Boxkämpfer jagen Eva durch Sylt portez ce vieux Whiskey blond qui fume

▶ New Roman Medium Italic
The quick brown fox jumps over a Dog. Zwei Boxkämpfer jagen Eva durch Sylt portez ce vieux Whiskey blond qui fume une pipe aber

BT1285 Mac + PC ② 🖉 (Stanley Morison, Victor Lardent, 1931-35) Industry name
Dutch 801 | **Times Headline**

abcdefghijklmnopqrstuvwxyz[äöüßåøæœç]
ABCDEFGHIJKLMNOPQRSTUVWXYZ
1234567890(.,;:?!$&-*){ÄÖÜÅØÆŒÇ}

© Times New Roman, Times Europa, Times Ten, Life, Concorde

▶ Roman Headline
The quick brown fox jumps over a Dog. Zwei Boxkämpfer jagen Eva durch Sylt portez ce vieux Whiskey blond qui fume une

▶ Italic Headline
The quick brown fox jumps over a Dog. Zwei Boxkämpfer jagen Eva durch Sylt portez ce vieux Whiskey blond qui fume une pipe aber echt

SG2437 Mac ② 🖉 (Stanley Morison, Victor Lardent, 1931-35)
Times Black

abcdefghijklmnopqrstuvwxyz[äöüßåøæœç]
ABCDEFGHIJKLMNOPQRSTUVWXYZ
1234567890(.,;:?!$&-*)ÄÖÜÅØÆŒÇ

SG2438 Mac ② 🖉 (Stanley Morison, Victor Lardent, 1931-35)
Times Black Italic

abcdefghijklmnopqrstuvwxyz[äöüßåøæœç]
ABCDEFGHIJKLMNOPQRSTUVWXYZ
1234567890(.,;:?!$&-*)ÄÖÜÅØÆŒÇ

© FSI 1993

SG2439 Mac — Times Black Alternates
(1931-35: Stanley Morison, Victor Lardent)

abcdefghijklmnopqrstuvwxyz[äöüßåøæœç]
ABCDEFGHIJKLMNOPQRSTUVWXYZ
1234567890(.,;:?!$&-*)ÄÖÜÅØÆŒÇ

SG2440 Mac — Times Modern Black
(1931-35: Stanley Morison, Victor Lardent)

abcdefghijklmnopqrstuvwxyz[äöüßåøæœç]
ABCDEFGHIJKLMNOPQRSTUVWXYZ
1234567890(.,;:?!$&-*)ÄÖÜÅØÆŒÇ

A116 Mac + PC — Times Ten Roman
1988: (Stanley Morison, Victor Lardent, 1931-35)

abcdefghijklmnopqrstuvwxyz[äöüßåøæœç]
ABCDEFGHIJKLMNOPQRSTUVWXYZ
1234567890(.,;:?!$&-*){ÄÖÜÅØÆŒÇ}

Times New Roman, Times Europa, Times Headline, Life, Concorde

▶ Regular
The quick brown fox jumps over a Dog. Zwei Boxkämpfer jagen Eva durch Sylt portez ce vieux Whiskey blond qui fume

▶ Italic
The quick brown fox jumps over a Dog. Zwei Boxkämpfer jagen Eva durch Sylt portez ce vieux Whiskey blond qui fume

▶ Bold
The quick brown fox jumps over a Dog. Zwei Boxkämpfer jagen Eva durch Sylt portez ce vieux Whiskey blond qui fume

▶ Bold Italic
The quick brown fox jumps over a Dog. Zwei Boxkämpfer jagen Eva durch Sylt portez ce vieux Whiskey blond qui fume

A1004 Mac + PC — Times Ten Small Caps/OSF
1931-35: Stanley Morison, Victor Lardent

ABCDEFGHIJKLMNOPQRSTUVWXYZ[ÄÖÜSSÅØÆŒÇ]
ABCDEFGHIJKLMNOPQRSTUVWXYZ
1234567890(.,;:?!$&-*){ÄÖÜÅØÆŒÇ}

▶ Roman Small Caps
THE QUICK BROWN FOX JUMPS OVER A DOG. 123 4567 890 ZWEI BOXKÄMPFER JAGEN EVA DURCH SYLT PORTEZ CE VIEUX WHISKEY

▶ Italic OSF
The quick brown fox jumps over a Dog. 123 4567 890 Zwei Boxkämpfer jagen Eva durch Sylt portez ce vieux Whiskey

▶ Bold OSF
The quick brown fox jumps over a Dog. 123 4567 890 Zwei Boxkämpfer jagen Eva durch Sylt portez ce vieux Whiskey

▶ Bold Italic OSF
The quick brown fox jumps over a Dog. 123 4567 890 Zwei Boxkämpfer jagen Eva durch Sylt portez ce vieux

© FSI 1993

A1026 MAC + PC ② ✎ 1972: Walter Tracy
Times Europa

abcdefghijklmnopqrstuvwxyz[äöüßåøæœç]
ABCDEFGHIJKLMNOPQRSTUVWXYZ
1234567890(.,;:?!$&-*){ÄÖÜÅØÆŒÇ}

© Times New Roman, Times Headline, Times Ten, Life, Concorde

▶ Regular
The quick brown fox jumps over a Dog. Zwei Boxkämpfer jagen Eva durch Sylt portez ce vieux Whiskey blond

▶ Italic
The quick brown fox jumps over a Dog. Zwei Boxkämpfer jagen Eva durch Sylt portez ce vieux Whiskey blond qui

▶ Bold
The quick brown fox jumps over a Dog. Zwei Boxkämpfer jagen Eva durch Sylt portez ce vieux Whiskey blond

▶ Bold Italic
The quick brown fox jumps over a Dog. Zwei Boxkämpfer jagen Eva durch Sylt portez ce vieux Whiskey blond

---

SG1121 MAC ① ✎ 1988: Volker Küster
Today Sans Serif™ Extra Light

abcdefghijklmnopqrstuvwxyz[äöüßåøæœç]
ABCDEFGHIJKLMNOPQRSTUVWXYZ
1234567890(.,;:?!$&-*)ÄÖÜÅØÆŒÇ

SG1174 MAC ① ✎ 1988: Volker Küster
Today Sans Serif Extra Light Italic

*abcdefghijklmnopqrstuvwxyz[äöüßåøæœç]
ABCDEFGHIJKLMNOPQRSTUVWXYZ
1234567890(.,;:?!$&-*)ÄÖÜÅØÆŒÇ*

SG1122 MAC ① ✎ 1988: Volker Küster
Today Sans Serif Light

abcdefghijklmnopqrstuvwxyz[äöüßåøæœç]
ABCDEFGHIJKLMNOPQRSTUVWXYZ
1234567890(.,;:?!$&-*)ÄÖÜÅØÆŒÇ

SG1177 MAC ① ✎ 1988: Volker Küster
Today Sans Serif Light Italic

*abcdefghijklmnopqrstuvwxyz[äöüßåøæœç]
ABCDEFGHIJKLMNOPQRSTUVWXYZ
1234567890(.,;:?!$&-*)ÄÖÜÅØÆŒÇ*

SG1123 Mac — 1988: Volker Küster
Today Sans Serif Regular

abcdefghijklmnopqrstuvwxyz[äöüßåøæœç]
ABCDEFGHIJKLMNOPQRSTUVWXYZ
1234567890(.,;:?!$&-*)ÄÖÜÅØÆŒÇ

SG1180 Mac — 1988: Volker Küster
Today Sans Serif Italic

abcdefghijklmnopqrstuvwxyz[äöüßåøæœç]
ABCDEFGHIJKLMNOPQRSTUVWXYZ
1234567890(.,;:?!$&-)ÄÖÜÅØÆŒÇ*

SG1175 Mac — 1988: Volker Küster
Today Sans Serif Medium

abcdefghijklmnopqrstuvwxyz[äöüßåøæœç]
ABCDEFGHIJKLMNOPQRSTUVWXYZ
1234567890(.,;:?!$&-*)ÄÖÜÅØÆŒÇ

SG1176 Mac — 1988: Volker Küster
Today Sans Serif Medium Italic

abcdefghijklmnopqrstuvwxyz[äöüßåøæœç]
ABCDEFGHIJKLMNOPQRSTUVWXYZ
1234567890(.,;:?!$&-)ÄÖÜÅØÆŒÇ*

SG1178 Mac — 1988: Volker Küster
Today Sans Serif Bold

abcdefghijklmnopqrstuvwxyz[äöüßåøæœç]
ABCDEFGHIJKLMNOPQRSTUVWXYZ
1234567890(.,;:?!$&-*)ÄÖÜÅØÆŒÇ

SG1179 Mac — 1988: Volker Küster
Today Sans Serif Bold Italic

abcdefghijklmnopqrstuvwxyz[äöüßåøæœç]
ABCDEFGHIJKLMNOPQRSTUVWXYZ
1234567890(.,;:?!$&-*)ÄÖÜÅØÆŒÇ

SG1181 Mac — 1988: Volker Küster
Today Sans Serif Ultra

abcdefghijklmnopqrstuvwxyz[äöüßåøæœç]
ABCDEFGHIJKLMNOPQRSTUVWXYZ
1234567890(.,;:?!$&-*)ÄÖÜÅØÆŒÇ

| SG1182 | Mac | ① | 1988: Volker Küster |

Today Sans Serif Ultra Italic

abcdefghijklmnopqrstuvwxyz[äöüßåøœœç]
ABCDEFGHIJKLMNOPQRSTUVWXYZ
1234567890(.,;:?!$&-*)ÄÖÜÅØÆŒÇ

| FF6624 | Mac + PC | ⑤ | 1993: Neville Brody |

FF Tokyo™

ABCDEFGHIJKLMNOPQRSTUVWXYZ[ÄÖÜBÅØŒŒÇ]
ABCDEFGHIJKLMNOPQRSTUVWXYZ
1234567890(.,;:?!$&-*)(ÄÖÜÅØŒŒÇ)

FF Dome, FF Tyson

▶ One
THE QUICK BROWN FOX JUMPS OVER A
DOG. ZWEI BOXKÄMPFER JAGEN EVA
DURCH SYLT PORTEZ CE VIEUX WHISKEY
BLOND QUI FUME UNE PIPE ABER ECHT

▶ One Solid
THE QUICK BROWN FOX JUMPS OVER A
DOG. ZWEI BOXKÄMPFER JAGEN EVA
DURCH SYLT PORTEZ CE VIEUX WHISKEY
BLOND QUI FUME UNE PIPE ABER ECHT

▶ Two
the quick brown fox jumps over a
dog. zwei boxkämpfer jagen eva
durch sylt portez ce vieux whiskey
blond qui fume une pipe aber echt

▶ Two Solid
the quick brown fox jumps over a
dog. zwei boxkämpfer jagen eva
durch sylt portez ce vieux whiskey
blond qui fume une pipe aber echt

| BT813 | Mac + PC | ⑥ | 1970: Tom Carnase, Ronne Bonder |

ITC Tom Roman®

abcdefghijklmnopqrstuvwxyz[äöüßåøœœç]
ABCDEFGHIJKLMNOPQRSTUVWXYZ
1234567890(.,;:?!$&-*){ÄÖÜÅØÆŒÇ}

ITC Headlines:
ITC Gorilla®, ITC Grizzly®, ITC Grouch®, ITC Tom Roman®

| LP2840 | Mac + PC | ④ | 1990: Garrett Boge |

TomBoy™

abcdefghijklmnopqrstuvwxyz[äöüßåøœœç]
ABCDEFGHIJKLMNOPQRSTUVWXYZ
1234567890(.,;:?!$&-*){ÄÖÜÅØÆŒÇ}

▶ Light
The quick brown fox jumps over a Dog.
Zwei Boxkämpfer jagen Eva durch
Sylt portez ce vieux Whiskey blond qui
fume une pipe aber echt über die

▶ Medium
The quick brown fox jumps over a
Dog. Zwei Boxkämpfer jagen Eva
durch Sylt portez ce vieux Whiskey
blond qui fume une pipe aber echt

▶ Bold
The quick brown fox jumps over a
Dog. Zwei Boxkämpfer jagen Eva
durch Sylt portez ce vieux Whiskey
blond qui fume une pipe aber echt

▼ LP2840 Mac + PC TomBoy™

LetterPerfect 1:
TomBoy™, Wendy™

BT863 Mac + PC (2) 1908: Alessandro Butti Industry name
Industrial 736 / Torino™

abcdefghijklmnopqrstuvwxyz[äöüßåøæœç]
ABCDEFGHIJKLMNOPQRSTUVWXYZ
1234567890(.,;:?!$&-*){ÄÖÜÅØÆŒÇ}

▶ Regular
The quick brown fox jumps over a Dog. Zwei Boxkämpfer jagen Eva durch Sylt portez ce vieux Whiskey blond qui fume une pipe aber echt

▶ Italic
The quick brown fox jumps over a Dog. Zwei Boxkämpfer jagen Eva durch Sylt portez ce vieux Whiskey blond qui fume une pipe aber

---

C607 Mac + PC (2) 1908: Alessandro Butti
Torino

abcdefghijklmnopqrstuvwxyz[äöüßåøæœç]
ABCDEFGHIJKLMNOPQRSTUVWXYZ
1234567890(.,;:?!$&-*){ÄÖÜÅØÆŒÇ}

▶ Condensed
The quick brown fox jumps over a Dog. Zwei Boxkämpfer jagen Eva durch Sylt portez ce vieux Whiskey blond qui fume une pipe aber echt über die Mauer gesprungen und auch smørebrod en ysjes natuurlijk

▶ Bold
The quick brown fox jumps over a Dog. Zwei Boxkämpfer jagen Eva durch Sylt portez ce vieux Whiskey blond qui fume une pipe aber echt über die Mauer

Erbar/Torino:
Erbar ™Condensed, Torino

C993 Mac + PC (6) 1960: (Alesssandro Butti, 1908) Ed Benguiat
PL Torino Open

abcdefghijklmnopqrstuvwxyz[äöü∘åøæœç]
ABCDEFGHIJKLMNOPQRSTUVWXYZ
1234567890(.,;:?!$&-*)◊ÄÖÜÅØÆŒÇ◆

Headlines 83S:
Barclay™ Open, Delphian™ Open, Fluidum™ Bold, PL Bernhardt, PL Britannia Bold, PL Fiorello™ Condensed, PL Modern Heavy Condensed, PL Torino Open

---

E653 Mac + PC (6) 1990: Zuzana Licko
Totally Glyphic™/Totally Gothic™

ABCDEFGHIJKLMNOPQRSTUVWXYZ[ÄÖÜßÅØÆŒÇ]
ABCDEFGHIJKLMNOPQRSTUVWXYZ
1234567890(.,;:?!§&-*){ÄÖÜÅØÆŒÇ}

© FSI 1993

▼ E653 Mac + PC **Totally Glyphic™/Totally Gothic™**

Manito, Neuland

▶ Totally Glyphic
THE QUICK BROWN FOX JUMPS OVER A DOG. ZWEI BOXKÄMPFER JAGEN EVA DURCH SYLT PORTEZ CE VIEUX WHISKEY

▶ Totally Gothic
The quick brown fox jumps over a Dog. Zwei Boxkämpfer jagen Eva durch Sylt portez ce vieux Whiskey blond qui fume une pipe aber echt

▶ Totally Gothic Wide Caps
abcdefghijklmnopqrstuvwxyz
abcdefghijklmnopqrstuvwxyz
1234567890

C467 Mac + PC ⑤ (M. F. Benton, 1934)

PL Tower™ Condensed

abcdefghijklmnopqrstuvwxyz1234567890[äöüåøæœç]

ABCDEFGHIJKLMNOPQRSTUVWXYZ(.,:;?!$&-*)◇ÄÖÜÅØÆŒÇ◆

Headlines 81S:
Egiziano™ Black, PL Behemoth Semi Condensed, PL Benguiat Frisky, PL Futura Maxi 1, PL Tower™ Condensed, Quirinus™ Bold, Section™ Bold Condensed, Stratford ™Bold, Woodblock
👁 Loyalist

A418 Mac + PC ① 1948: Jackson Burke

Trade Gothic™

abcdefghijklmnopqrstuvwxyz[äöüßåøæœç]
ABCDEFGHIJKLMNOPQRSTUVWXYZ
1234567890(.,:;?!$&-*){ÄÖÜÅØÆŒÇ}

Alternate Gothic, News Gothic

▶ Light
The quick brown fox jumps over a Dog. Zwei Boxkämpfer jagen Eva durch Sylt portez ce vieux Whiskey blond qui fume une

▶ Light Oblique
The quick brown fox jumps over a Dog. Zwei Boxkämpfer jagen Eva durch Sylt portez ce vieux Whiskey blond qui fume une

▶ Regular
The quick brown fox jumps over a Dog. Zwei Boxkämpfer jagen Eva durch Sylt portez ce vieux Whiskey blond qui fume

▶ Oblique
The quick brown fox jumps over a Dog. Zwei Boxkämpfer jagen Eva durch Sylt portez ce vieux Whiskey blond qui fume

▶ Bold
The quick brown fox jumps over a Dog. Zwei Boxkämpfer jagen Eva durch Sylt portez ce vieux Whiskey blond qui fume une pipe

▶ Bold Oblique
The quick brown fox jumps over a Dog. Zwei Boxkämpfer jagen Eva durch Sylt portez ce vieux Whiskey blond qui fume une pipe

▶ Bold No. 2
The quick brown fox jumps over a Dog. Zwei Boxkämpfer jagen Eva durch Sylt portez ce vieux Whiskey blond qui fume

▶ Bold No. 2 Oblique
The quick brown fox jumps over a Dog. Zwei Boxkämpfer jagen Eva durch Sylt portez ce vieux Whiskey blond qui fume

A419 Mac + PC ① ✎ 1948: Jackson Burke
Trade Gothic Condensed

abcdefghijklmnopqrstuvwxyz[äöüßåøæœç]
ABCDEFGHIJKLMNOPQRSTUVWXYZ
1234567890(.,;:?!$&-*){ÄÖÜÅØÆŒÇ}

👁 Alternate Gothic, News Gothic

▶ Condensed 18
The quick brown fox jumps over a Dog. Zwei Boxkämpfer jagen Eva durch Sylt portez ce vieux Whiskey blond qui fume une pipe aber echt über die Mauer

▶ Condensed 18 Oblique
The quick brown fox jumps over a Dog. Zwei Boxkämpfer jagen Eva durch Sylt portez ce vieux Whiskey blond qui fume une pipe aber echt über die Mauer

▶ Bold Condensed 20
The quick brown fox jumps over a Dog. Zwei Boxkämpfer jagen Eva durch Sylt portez ce vieux Whiskey blond qui fume une pipe aber echt

▶ Bold Condensed 20 Oblique
The quick brown fox jumps over a Dog. Zwei Boxkämpfer jagen Eva durch Sylt portez ce vieux Whiskey blond qui fume une pipe aber echt

---

A6069 Mac + PC ① ✎ 1948: Jackson Burke
Trade Gothic Extended

abcdefghijklmnopqrstuvwxyz[äöüßåøæœç]
ABCDEFGHIJKLMNOPQRSTUVWXYZ
1234567890(.,;:?!$&-*){ÄÖÜÅØÆŒÇ}

👁 Alternate Gothic, News Gothic

▶ Extended
The quick brown fox jumps over a Dog. Zwei Boxkämpfer jagen Eva durch Sylt portez ce

▶ Bold Extended
The quick brown fox jumps over a Dog. Zwei Boxkämpfer jagen Eva durch Sylt portez ce

---

A420 Mac + PC ⑥ ✎ 1989: Carol Twombly
Trajan™

ABCDEFGHIJKLMNOPQRSTUVWXYZ
1234567890(.,;:?!$&-*)[]{ÄÖÜÅØÆŒÇ}

👁 Galba, Felix Titling, Serlio, Classic Roman

▶ Regular
THE QUICK BROWN FOX JUMPS OVER A DOG. ZWEI BOXKÄMPFER JAGEN EVA DURCH SYLT

▶ Bold
THE QUICK BROWN FOX JUMPS OVER A DOG. ZWEI BOXKÄMPFER JAGEN EVA DURCH SYLT

Charlemagne/Trajan:
Charlemagne®, Trajan™
👁 Galba, Felix Titling, Serlio, Classic Roman

C600 Mac + PC ②
Triplett

abcdefghijklmnopqrstuvwxyz[äöüßåøæœç]
ABCDEFGHIJKLMNOPQRSTUVWXYZ
1234567890(.,;:?!$&-*){ÄÖÜÅØÆŒÇ}

© FSI 1993

▼ C600 Mac + PC **Triplett**

▶ Light
The quick brown fox jumps over a Dog. Zwei Boxkämpfer jagen Eva durch Sylt portez ce vieux Whiskey

▶ Black
The quick brown fox jumps over a Dog. Zwei Boxkämpfer jagen Eva durch Sylt portez ce vieux Whiskey

Claire News:
Claire News, Triplett

E421 Mac + PC ① 1989: Zuzana Licko
Triplex™ Sans

abcdefghijklmnopqrstuvwxyz[äöüßåøæœç]
ABCDEFGHIJKLMNOPQRSTUVWXYZ
1234567890(.,;:?!$&-*) ÄÖÜÅØÆŒÇ

▶ Light
The quick brown fox jumps over a Dog. Zwei Boxkämpfer jagen Eva durch Sylt portez ce vieux Whiskey blond qui fume une pipe aber echt

▶ Bold
The quick brown fox jumps over a Dog. Zwei Boxkämpfer jagen Eva durch Sylt portez ce vieux Whiskey blond qui fume une pipe

▶ Extra Bold
The quick brown fox jumps over a Dog. Zwei Boxkämpfer jagen Eva durch Sylt portez ce vieux Whiskey blond qui fume une

---

E422 Mac + PC ③ 1989: Zuzana Licko
Triplex Serif

abcdefghijklmnopqrstuvwxyz[äöüßåøæœç]
ABCDEFGHIJKLMNOPQRSTUVWXYZ
1234567890(.,;:?!$&-*){ÄÖÜÅØÆŒÇ}

▶ Light
The quick brown fox jumps over a Dog. Zwei Boxkämpfer jagen Eva durch Sylt portez ce vieux Whiskey blond qui fume une pipe aber echt

▶ Bold
The quick brown fox jumps over a Dog. Zwei Boxkämpfer jagen Eva durch Sylt portez ce vieux Whiskey blond qui fume une

▶ Extra Bold
The quick brown fox jumps over a Dog. Zwei Boxkämpfer jagen Eva durch Sylt portez ce vieux Whiskey blond qui fume

---

E938 Mac + PC ⑥ 1985: John Downer
Triplex Italic

abcdefghijklmnopqrstuvwxyz[äöüßåøæœç]
ABCDEFGHIJKLMNOPQRSTUVWXYZ
1234567890(.,;:?!$&-){ÄÖÜÅØÆŒÇ}*

© FSI 1993

▼ E938 Mac + PC Triplex Italic

▶ Italic Light
The quick brown fox jumps over a Dog. Zwei Boxkämpfer jagen Eva durch Sylt portez ce vieux Whiskey blond qui fume une pipe aber

▶ Italic Bold
The quick brown fox jumps over a Dog. Zwei Boxkämpfer jagen Eva durch Sylt portez ce vieux Whiskey blond qui fume une pipe

▶ Italic Extra Bold
The quick brown fox jumps over a Dog. Zwei Boxkämpfer jagen Eva durch Sylt portez ce vieux Whiskey blond qui fume une

---

E1155 Mac + PC ① ✎ 1991Z: Zuzana Licko
Triplex Condensed

abcdefghijklmnopqrstuvwxyz1234567890[äöüßåøæœç]
ABCDEFGHIJKLMNOPQRSTUVWXYZ(.,;:?!$&-*){ÄÖÜÅØÆŒÇ}

ⓒ
ITC Anna, Bodega, Romeo, Triplex Serif Condensed

▶ Regular
The quick brown fox jumps over a Dog. Zwei Boxkämpfer jagen Eva durch Sylt portez ce vieux Whiskey blond qui fume une pipe aber echt über die Mauer gesprungen und auch smørebrød en ysjes natuurlijk. But very long spazierende tekst

▶ Black
The quick brown fox jumps over a Dog. Zwei Boxkämpfer jagen Eva durch Sylt portez ce vieux Whiskey blond qui fume une pipe aber echt über die Mauer gesprungen und auch smørebrød en

---

E1156 Mac + PC ③ ✎ 1991Z: Zuzana Licko
Triplex Serif Condensed

abcdefghijklmnopqrstuvwxyz1234567890[äöüßåøæœç]
ABCDEFGHIJKLMNOPQRSTUVWXYZ(.,;:?!$&-*){ÄÖÜÅØÆŒÇ}

ⓒ
ITC Anna, Bodega, Romeo, Triplex Condensed

▶ Regular
The quick brown fox jumps over a Dog. Zwei Boxkämpfer jagen Eva durch Sylt portez ce vieux Whiskey blond qui fume une pipe aber echt über die Mauer gesprungen und auch smørebrød en ysjes natuurlijk. But very long spazierende

▶ Black
The quick brown fox jumps over a Dog. Zwei Boxkämpfer jagen Eva durch Sylt portez ce vieux Whiskey blond qui fume une pipe aber echt über die Mauer gesprungen und auch

---

FF1534 Mac + PC ⑥ ✎ 1991: Erik van Blokland
FF Trixie™

abcdefghijklmnopqrstuvwxyzäöüßåøæœç
ABCDEFGHIJKLMNOPQRSTUVWXYZ
1234567890(.,;:?!$&-*)ÄÖÜÅØÆŒÇ

▶ Light
The quick brown fox jumps over a Dog. Zwei Boxkämpfer jagen Eva durch Sylt portez ce vieux Whiskey blond qui

▶ Text
The quick brown fox jumps over a Dog. Zwei Boxkämpfer jagen Eva durch Sylt portez ce vieux Whiskey blond qui

▶ Plain
The quick brown fox jumps over a Dog. Zwei Boxkämpfer jagen Eva durch Sylt portez ce vieux Whiskey blond qui

▶ Cameo
The quick brown fox jumps over a dog. Zwei Boxkämpfer jagen Eva durch Sylt. Portez ce vieux

▼ FF1534 Mac + PC FF Trixie™

▶ Extra
the quick brown fox jumps
over a dog zwei box
kaempfer jagen eva durch
sylt portez ce vieux whis

C468 Mac + PC ④ ✎ 1950: Frank Bartuska
PL Trophy™ Oblique

abcdefghijklmnopqrstuvwxyz[äöü°åøœç]
ABCDEFGHIJKLMNOPQRSTUVWXYZ
1234567890(.,;:?!$&-*){ÄÖÜÅØÆŒÇ}

Headlines 82S:
Neon Extra Condensed™, PL Barnum Block, PL Benguiat Frisky Bold, PL Davison Zip Bold, PL Fiedler Gothic Bold, PL Futura Maxi 2, PL Trophy™ Oblique, Ritmo™ Bold, TC Broadway

L6149 Mac ④ ✎ 1988: Vince Whitlock
Tropica™ Script

abcdefghijklmnopqrstuvwxyz[äöüßåøæœç]
ABCDEFGHIJKLMNOPQRSTUVWXYZ
1234567890(.,;:?!$&-*)ç

ET6389 Mac + PC ⑦ ✎ 1992: Judith Sutcliffe
Troubador™

abcdefghijklmnopqrstuvwxyz[äöüßåøœœç]
ABCDEFGHIJKLMNOPQRSTUVWXYZ
1234567890(.,;:?!$&-*){ÄÖÜÅØÆŒÇ}

▶ Regular
The quick brown fox jumps
over a Dog. Zwei Boxkämp-
fer jagen Eva durch Sylt
portez ce vieux Whiskey

▶ Initials

Abelard / Troubador:
Abelard™, Troubador™

A118 Mac + PC ② ✎ 1954: Georg Trump
Trump Mediaeval™

abcdefghijklmnopqrstuvwxyz[äöüßåøæœç]
ABCDEFGHIJKLMNOPQRSTUVWXYZ
1234567890(.,;:?!$&-*){ÄÖÜÅØÆŒÇ}

aa*a*
BT1346
Trump Mediaeval, Reg, Ita, Bd, BdIta

▶ Regular
The quick brown fox jumps
over a Dog. Zwei Boxkämpfer
jagen Eva durch Sylt portez
ce vieux Whiskey blond qui

▶ Italic
*The quick brown fox jumps
over a Dog. Zwei Boxkämp-
fer jagen Eva durch Sylt portez ce vieux Whiskey blond*

© FSI 1993

▼ A118 Mac + PC   Trump Mediaeval™

▶ Bold
The quick brown fox jumps over a Dog. Zwei Boxkämpfer jagen Eva durch Sylt portez ce vieux Whiskey blond qui

▶ Bold Italic
The quick brown fox jumps over a Dog. Zwei Boxkämpfer jagen Eva durch Sylt portez ce vieux Whiskey blond

A1028 Mac + PC   ②   ✎ 1954: Georg Trump
Trump Mediaeval Small Caps/OSF

ABCDEFGHIJKLMNOPQRSTUVWXYZ[ÄÖÜSSÅØÆŒÇ]
ABCDEFGHIJKLMNOPQRSTUVWXYZ
1234567890(.,;:?!$&-*){ÄÖÜÅØÆŒÇ}

▶ Regular Small Caps
THE QUICK BROWN FOX JUMPS OVER A DOG. 123 4567 890 ZWEI BOXKÄMPFER JAGEN EVA DURCH SYLT PORTEZ CE VIEUX

▶ Italic OSF
The quick brown fox jumps over a Dog. 123 4567 890 Zwei Boxkämpfer jagen Eva durch Sylt portez ce vieux

▶ Bold OSF
The quick brown fox jumps over a Dog. 123 4567 890 Zwei Boxkämpfer jagen Eva durch Sylt portez ce vieux

▶ Bold Italic OSF
The quick brown fox jumps over a Dog. 123 4567 890 Zwei Boxkämpfer jagen Eva durch Sylt portez ce vieux

BT812 Mac + PC   ②   ✎ 1954: Georg Trump   Industry name
Kuenstler 480   **Trump Mediaeval Black**

abcdefghijklmnopqrstuvwxyz[äöüßåøæœç]
ABCDEFGHIJKLMNOPQRSTUVWXYZ
1234567890(.,;:?!$&-*){ÄÖÜÅØÆŒÇ}

Bitstream Bold Headlines 1:
Blippo™ Black, Handel Gothic, ITC Bolt Bold®, Trump Mediaeval Black

F6344 Mac   ⑥
A*I Tuscan Egyptian™

ABCDEFGHIJKLMNOPQRSTUVWXYZ
1234567890(.,;:?!$&-*)[ ]{ }

A*I Wood Types 1:
A*I Barrel, A*I Box Gothic, A*I French XXX Condensed™, A*I Painter™, A*I Tuscan Egyptian™, Antique Condensed
👁 Davison Americana, Thunderbird

T06104 Mac
Type-ø-Tones Pack 1

Type-ø-Tones Pack 1:
Ebu™ Script, Me mima™

T06105 Mac
Type-ø-Tones Pack 2

Type-ø-Tones Pack 2:
Mayayo™, Neeskens™

T06660 Mac
Type-ø-Tones Pack 3

Type-ø-Tones Pack 3:
Cortada™, Frankie™

A996 Mac + PC
Type Before Gutenberg 1

Type Before Gutenberg 1:
Duc De Berry™, Herculanum™, Omnia™

A1147 Mac + PC
Type Before Gutenberg 2

Type Before Gutenberg 2:
Carolina™ & Dfr, Clairvaux™, San Marco™

FF2964 Mac + PC ⑤ ✎ 1992: Neville Brody
FF Typeface Four™

abcdefghijklmnopqrstuvwxyz1234567890[äöüßåæç]
ABCDEFGHIJKLMNOPQRSTUVWXYZ(.,;:?!$&-*){ÄÖÜÅØÆŒÇ}

▶ Sans (One)
The quick brown fox jumps over a dog. Zwei Boxkämpfer jagen Eva durch Sylt. Portez ce vieux whiskey blond qui fume une pipe aber echt über die Maori gesprungen und auch smarterra en vsjes nazuntrisi. But very long spazierende Laksi ist used in

▶ Serif (Two)
The quick brown fox jumps over a dog. Zwei Boxkämpfer jagen Eva durch Sylt. Portez ce vieux whiskey blond qui fume une pipe aber echt über die Maori gesprungen und auch smarterra en vsjes nazuntrisi. But very long spazierende Laksi ist used in

FF1061 Mac + PC ⑤ ✎ 1991: Neville Brody
FF Typeface 6 & 7

ABCDEFGHIJKLMNOPQRSTUVWXYZ[ÄÖÜßÅÇ]
ABCDEFGHIJKLMNOPQRSTUVWXYZ
1234567890(.,;:?!$&-*){ÄÖÜÅØÆŒÇ}

▶ Six™
THE QUICK BROWN FOX JUMPS OVER A DOG. ZWEI BOXKÄMPFER JAGEN EVA DURCH SYLT PORTEZ CE

▶ Six Point Five™
THE QUICK BROWN FOX JUMPS OVER A DOG. ZWEI BOXKÄMPFER JAGEN EVA DURCH SYLT PORTEZ CE VIEUX WHISKEY

© FSI 1993

▼ FF1061 Mac + PC   **FF Typeface 6 & 7**

▶ Seven™
THE QUICK BROWN FOX JUMPS OVER A DOG. ZWEI BOXKÄMPFER JAGEN EVA DURCH SYLT PORTEZ CE VIEUX WHISKEY

M979 Mac + PC
Typewriter

Typewriter:
Courier 12, Typewriter

M979 Mac + PC   ③
Typewriter

abcdefghijklmnopqrstuvwxyz[äöüßåøæœç]
ABCDEFGHIJKLMNOPQRSTUVWXYZ
1234567890(.,;:?!$&-*){ÄÖÜÅØÆŒÇ}

©
ITC American Typewriter, Courier, Monanti, Schreibmaschinenschrift, Prestige, Pica

▶ Typewriter
The quick brown fox jumps over a Dog. Zwei Boxkämpfer jagen Eva durch Sylt portez ce

▶ Typewriter Elite
The quick brown fox jumps over a Dog. Zwei Boxkämpfer jagen Eva durch Sylt portez ce

▶ Typewriter Gothic
The quick brown fox jumps over a Dog. Zwei Boxkämpfer jagen Eva durch Sylt portez ce

Typewriter:
Courier 12, Typewriter

BT865 Mac + PC
BT Typewriter

BT Typewriter:
Pica 10 Pitch, Script 12 Pitch

C2979 Mac + PC
ITC Typographica™

ITC Typographica™:
ITC Anna™, ITC Beesknees, ITC Mona Lisa Recut, ITC Studio Script
aaa EF980
ITC Studio Script™, Reg, Alt
ITC Beesknees™, Reg, EF981 ITC Mona Lisa Recut™, Reg, ITC Anna™, Reg

---

BT1406 Mac + PC   ④   ✎ 1905: M. F. Benton
Typo Upright™

abcdefghijklmnopqrstuvwxyz[äöüßåøæœç]
ABCDEFGHIJKLMNOPQRSTUVWXYZ
1234567890(.,;:?!$&-*){ÄÖÜÅØÆŒÇ}

© FSI 1993

FF6623 Mac + PC ⑤ ✎ 1993: Neville Brody
FF Tyson™

abcdefghijklmnopqrstuvwxyz[äöüßåøæœç]
ABCDEFGHIJKLMNOPQRSTUVWXYZ
1234567890(.,;:?!$&-*){ÄÖÜÅØÆŒÇ}

FF Dome / FF Tyson:
FF Dome™, FF Tyson™
FF Dome, FF Tokyo

MC2923 Mac + PC ⑥ ✎ 1973: Albert Boton
Tzigane™

abcdefghijklmnopqrstuvwxyz1234567890[äöüßåøæœç]
ABCDEFGHIJKLMNOPQRSTUVWXYZ(.,;:?!$&-){ÄÖÜÅØÆŒÇ}*

© FSI 1993

i was taken
to a darkened land
led there
by a female hand
the intoxication
of open seas
a wide blue island
of fantasies

across history

the times

I beat
my drum

i heard her voice
carried
on the changing
tide
while on a cliff

the rhythm
counting
my dreams
undone

a dragon breathes
and music plays
lightning strikes
to end those days
and when i woke
all i could see
was the wide blue island
infront of me

Jeremy Tankard, London, UK

L2736 Mac ④ 🖋 1991: Timothy Donaldson
Ulysses™

abcdefghijklmnopqrstuvwxyz[äöüßåøæœç]
ABCDEFGHIJKLMNOPQRSTUVWXYZ
1234567890(.,;:?!$&-)ÄÖÜÅØÆŒÇ*

A350 Mac + PC ⑥ 🖋 1932: R. H. Middleton
Umbra™

ABCDEFGHIJKLMNOPQRSTUVWXYZ
1234567890(.,;:?!$&-*){}[]{ÄÖÜÅØÆŒÇ}

Parisian / Umbra:
Parisian™, Umbra™
aaa BT1407
Umbra, Reg

C6426 Mac + PC ⑦
Uncial

abcdefghijklmnopqrstuvwxyz[äöüßåøœœç]
ABCDEFGHIJKLMNOPQRSTUVWXYZ
1234567890(.,;:?!$&-*){ÄÖÜÅØÆŒÇ}

Basque, etc:
Basque, Brophy™ Script, Chevalier™, Uncial

SG1129 Mac ① 🖋 1981: Gschwind, Gürtler, Mengelt
Unica™ Light

abcdefghijklmnopqrstuvwxyz[äöüßåøæœç]
ABCDEFGHIJKLMNOPQRSTUVWXYZ
1234567890(.,;:?!$&-*)ÄÖÜÅØÆŒÇ

SG1204 Mac ① 🖋 1981: Gschwind, Gürtler, Mengelt
Unica Light Italic

abcdefghijklmnopqrstuvwxyz[äöüßåøæœç]
ABCDEFGHIJKLMNOPQRSTUVWXYZ
1234567890(.,;:?!$&-)ÄÖÜÅØÆŒÇ*

SG1130 Mac ① 🖋 1981: Gschwind, Gürtler, Mengelt
Unica

abcdefghijklmnopqrstuvwxyz[äöüßåøæœç]
ABCDEFGHIJKLMNOPQRSTUVWXYZ
1234567890(.,;:?!$&-*)ÄÖÜÅØÆŒÇ

© FSI 1993

SG1207 MAC ① ✏ 1981: Gschwind, Gürtler, Mengelt
Unica Italic

abcdefghijklmnopqrstuvwxyz[äöüßåøæœç]
ABCDEFGHIJKLMNOPQRSTUVWXYZ
1234567890(.,;:?!$&-)ÄÖÜÅØÆŒÇ*

SG1205 MAC ① ✏ 1981: Gschwind, Gürtler, Mengelt
Unica Medium

abcdefghijklmnopqrstuvwxyz[äöüßåøæœç]
ABCDEFGHIJKLMNOPQRSTUVWXYZ
1234567890(.,;:?!$&-*)ÄÖÜÅØÆŒÇ

SG1206 MAC ① ✏ 1981: Gschwind, Gürtler, Mengelt
Unica Medium Italic

abcdefghijklmnopqrstuvwxyz[äöüßåøæœç]
ABCDEFGHIJKLMNOPQRSTUVWXYZ
1234567890(.,;:?!$&-*)ÄÖÜÅØÆŒÇ

SG1208 MAC ① ✏ 1981: Gschwind, Gürtler, Mengelt
Unica Bold

abcdefghijklmnopqrstuvwxyz[äöüßåøæœç]
ABCDEFGHIJKLMNOPQRSTUVWXYZ
1234567890(.,;:?!$&-*)ÄÖÜÅØÆŒÇ

SG1209 MAC ① ✏ 1981: Gschwind, Gürtler, Mengelt
Unica Bold Italic

abcdefghijklmnopqrstuvwxyz[äöüßåøæœç]
ABCDEFGHIJKLMNOPQRSTUVWXYZ
1234567890(.,;:?!$&-*)ÄÖÜÅØÆŒÇ

A120 MAC + PC ① ✏ 1957: Adrian Frutiger
Univers™

abcdefghijklmnopqrstuvwxyz[äöüßåøæœç]
ABCDEFGHIJKLMNOPQRSTUVWXYZ
1234567890(.,;:?!$&-*){ÄÖÜÅØÆŒÇ}

aa*a*
BT1423
Univers 1, 45Lt,
46LtIta, 75Blk,
76BlkIta, 95ExtBlk
BT1424
Univers 2, 55Reg,
56Ita, 65Bd, 66BdIta
👁
Unica, Helvetica, Neue
Helvetica, Akzidenz-
Grotesk, Vectora, Arial

▶ 45 Light
The quick brown fox jumps over a Dog. Zwei Boxkämpfer jagen Eva durch Sylt portez ce vieux Whiskey blond qui fume

▶ 45 Light Oblique
The quick brown fox jumps over a Dog. Zwei Boxkämpfer jagen Eva durch Sylt portez ce vieux Whiskey blond qui fume

▶ 55 Regular
The quick brown fox jumps over a Dog. Zwei Boxkämpfer jagen Eva durch Sylt portez ce vieux Whiskey blond

▶ 55 Oblique
The quick brown fox jumps over a Dog. Zwei Boxkämpfer jagen Eva durch Sylt portez ce vieux Whiskey blond

© FSI 1993

▼ A120 Mac + PC Univers™

▶ 65 Bold
The quick brown fox jumps over a Dog. Zwei Boxkämpfer jagen Eva durch Sylt portez ce vieux Whiskey blond

▶ 65 Bold Oblique
The quick brown fox jumps over a Dog. Zwei Boxkämpfer jagen Eva durch Sylt portez ce vieux Whiskey blond

▶ 75 Black
The quick brown fox jumps over a Dog. Zwei Boxkämpfer jagen Eva durch Sylt portez ce

▶ 75 Black Oblique
The quick brown fox jumps over a Dog. Zwei Boxkämpfer jagen Eva durch Sylt portez ce

---

A119 Mac + PC ① ⌀ 1957: Adrian Frutiger
Univers Condensed

abcdefghijklmnopqrstuvwxyz[äöüßåøæœç]
ABCDEFGHIJKLMNOPQRSTUVWXYZ
1234567890(.,;:?!$&-*){ÄÖÜÅØÆŒÇ}

aa*a*
BT1425
Univers 3, 47LtCon, 48LtConIta
BT1426
Univers 4, 57Con, 58ConIta, 67BdCon, 68BdConIta

▶ 47 Condensed Light
The quick brown fox jumps over a Dog. Zwei Boxkämpfer jagen Eva durch Sylt portez ce vieux Whiskey blond qui fume une pipe aber echt

▶ 47 Condensed Light Oblique
The quick brown fox jumps over a Dog. Zwei Boxkämpfer jagen Eva durch Sylt portez ce vieux Whiskey blond qui fume une pipe aber echt

▶ 57 Condensed
The quick brown fox jumps over a Dog. Zwei Boxkämpfer jagen Eva durch Sylt portez ce vieux Whiskey blond qui fume une pipe aber

▶ 57 Condensed Oblique
The quick brown fox jumps over a Dog. Zwei Boxkämpfer jagen Eva durch Sylt portez ce vieux Whiskey blond qui fume une pipe aber

▶ 67 Condensed Bold
The quick brown fox jumps over a Dog. Zwei Boxkämpfer jagen Eva durch Sylt portez ce vieux Whiskey blond qui fume une pipe aber

▶ 67 Condensed Bold Oblique
The quick brown fox jumps over a Dog. Zwei Boxkämpfer jagen Eva durch Sylt portez ce vieux Whiskey blond qui fume une pipe aber

---

A1000 Mac + PC ① ⌀ 1957: Adrian Frutiger
Univers Ultra Condensed

abcdefghijklmnopqrstuvwxyz1234567890[äöüßåøæœç]
ABCDEFGHIJKLMNOPQRSTUVWXYZ(.,;:?!$&-*){ÄÖÜÅØÆŒÇ}

aa*a*
BT866
Univers Extra Condensed, 39LtExtCon, 49ExtCon, 59BdExtCon

▶ 39 Thin Ultra Condensed
The quick brown fox jumps over a Dog. Zwei Boxkämpfer jagen Eva durch Sylt portez ce vieux Whiskey blond qui fume une pipe aber echt über die Mauer gesprungen und auch smørebrød en ysjes natuurlijk. But very long spazierende tekst ist used in dieser catalog maar nicht so. Durch Sylt portez ce vieux Whiskey blond qui fume une pipe

▶ 49 Light Ultra Condensed
The quick brown fox jumps over a Dog. Zwei Boxkämpfer jagen Eva durch Sylt portez ce vieux Whiskey blond qui fume une pipe aber echt über die Mauer gesprungen und auch smørebrød en ysjes natuurlijk

▶ 59 Ultra Condensed
The quick brown fox jumps over a Dog. Zwei Boxkämpfer jagen Eva durch Sylt portez ce vieux Whiskey blond qui fume une pipe aber echt über die Mauer gesprungen und auch smørebrød en

▶ 85 Extra Black
The quick brown fox jumps over a Dog. Zwei Boxkämpfer jagen Eva durch Sylt portez ce

© FSI 1993

▼ A1000　Mac + PC　Univers Ultra Condensed

▶ 85 Extra Black Oblique
The quick brown fox jumps over a Dog. Zwei Boxkämpfer jagen Eva durch Sylt portez ce

---

A920　Mac + PC　①　🖉 1957: Adrian Frutiger
Univers Extended

abcdefghijklmnopqrstuvwxyz[äöüßåøæœç]

ABCDEFGHIJKLMNOPQRSTUVWXYZ

1234567890(.,;:?!$&-*){ÄÖÜÅØÆŒÇ}

aa*a*
BT1427
Univers 5, 53Ext,
63BdExt, 73BlkExt,
83UltBlkExt

▶ 53 Extended
The quick brown fox jumps over a Dog. Zwei Boxkämpfer jagen Eva durch Sylt portez ce

▶ 53 Extended Oblique
The quick brown fox jumps over a Dog. Zwei Boxkämpfer jagen Eva durch Sylt portez ce

▶ 63 Bold Extended
The quick brown fox jumps over a Dog. Zwei Boxkämpfer jagen Eva durch Sylt

▶ 63 Bold Extended Oblique
The quick brown fox jumps over a Dog. Zwei Boxkämpfer jagen Eva durch Sylt

▶ 73 Black Extended
The quick brown fox jumps over a Dog. Zwei Boxkämpfer jagen Eva durch Sylt

▶ 73 Black Extended Oblique
The quick brown fox jumps over a Dog. Zwei Boxkämpfer jagen Eva durch Sylt

▶ 83 Extra Black Extended
The quick brown fox jumps over a Dog. Zwei Box- kämpfer jagen Eva

▶ 83 Extra Black Extended Obl.
The quick brown fox jumps over a Dog. Zwei Box- kämpfer jagen Eva

---

SG2464　Mac　①　🖉 (1957: Adrian Frutiger)
Univers No 177

abcdefghijklmnopqrstuvwxyz[äöüßåøæœç]

ABCDEFGHIJKLMNOPQRSTUVWXYZ

1234567890(.,;:?!$&-*)ÄÖÜÅØÆŒÇ

E121　Mac + PC　⑤　🖉 1985: Zuzana Licko
Universal™

abcdefghijklmnopqrstuvwxyz[äöüßåøæœç]

ABCDEFGHIJKLMNOPQRSTUVWXYZ

1234567890(.,;:?!$&-*){ÄÖÜÅØÆŒÇ}

© Emigre Special

▶ Eight
The quick brown fox jumps over a Dog. Zwei Boxkämpfer jagen Eva durch Sylt portez ce vieux Whiskey blond qui fume une pipe aber echt über die Mauer gesprungen

▶ Nineteen
The quick brown fox jumps over a Dog. Zwei Boxkämpfer jagen Eva durch Sylt portez ce vieux Whiskey blond qui fume une pipe aber echt über die Mauer gesprungen und auch smerebred en ysjes natuurlijk

© FSI 1993

| BT1408 | Mac + PC | ⑥ | ✎ 1972: Michael Daines |

University Roman™

abcdefghijklmnopqrstuvwxyz[äöüßåøæœç]
ABCDEFGHIJKLMNOPQRSTUVWXYZ
1234567890(.,;:?!$&-*){ÄÖÜÅØÆŒÇ}

| L2737 | Mac | ⑥ | ✎ 1983: Michael Daines |

University Roman Bold

abcdefghijklmnopqrstuvwxyz[äöüßåøæœç]
ABCDEFGHIJKLMNOPQRSTUVWXYZ
1234567890(.,;:?!$&-*)ÄÖÜÅØÆŒÇ

| C6506 | Mac + PC | ② | ✎ 1984: Les Usherwood |

ITC Usherwood®

abcdefghijklmnopqrstuvwxyz[äöüßåøæœç]
ABCDEFGHIJKLMNOPQRSTUVWXYZ
1234567890(.,;:?!$&-*){ÄÖÜÅØÆŒÇ}

aa*a*
A921
ITC Usherwood, Reg,
Ita, Med, MedIta, Bd,
BdIta, Blk, BlkIta

▶ Book
The quick brown fox jumps over a Dog. Zwei Boxkämpfer jagen Eva durch Sylt portez ce vieux Whiskey blond qui fume

▶ *Italic*
The quick brown fox jumps over a Dog. Zwei Boxkämpfer jagen Eva durch Sylt portez ce vieux Whiskey blond qui fume une pipe

▶ Medium
The quick brown fox jumps over a Dog. Zwei Boxkämpfer jagen Eva durch Sylt portez ce vieux Whiskey blond qui fume

▶ *Medium Italic*
The quick brown fox jumps over a Dog. Zwei Boxkämpfer jagen Eva durch Sylt portez ce vieux Whiskey blond qui fume une

▶ **Bold**
The quick brown fox jumps over a Dog. Zwei Boxkämpfer jagen Eva durch Sylt portez ce vieux Whiskey blond qui fume

▶ ***Bold Italic***
The quick brown fox jumps over a Dog. Zwei Boxkämpfer jagen Eva durch Sylt portez ce vieux Whiskey blond qui fume

▶ **Black**
The quick brown fox jumps over a Dog. Zwei Boxkämpfer jagen Eva durch Sylt portez ce vieux Whiskey

▶ ***Black Italic***
The quick brown fox jumps over a Dog. Zwei Boxkämpfer jagen Eva durch Sylt portez ce vieux Whiskey

| A257 | Mac + PC | ② | ✎ 1989: Robert Slimbach |

Utopia®

abcdefghijklmnopqrstuvwxyz[äöüßåøæœç]
ABCDEFGHIJKLMNOPQRSTUVWXYZ
1234567890(.,;:?!$&-*){ÄÖÜÅØÆŒÇ}

▶ Regular
The quick brown fox jumps over a Dog. Zwei Boxkämpfer jagen Eva durch Sylt portez ce vieux Whiskey blond qui fume

▶ *Italic*
The quick brown fox jumps over a Dog. Zwei Boxkämpfer jagen Eva durch Sylt portez ce vieux Whiskey blond qui fume

▼ A257 Mac + PC Utopia®

▶ Semi Bold
The quick brown fox jumps over a Dog. Zwei Boxkämpfer jagen Eva durch Sylt portez ce vieux Whiskey blond qui

▶ Semi Bold Italic
The quick brown fox jumps over a Dog. Zwei Boxkämpfer jagen Eva durch Sylt portez ce vieux Whiskey blond qui

▶ Bold
The quick brown fox jumps over a Dog. Zwei Boxkämpfer jagen Eva durch Sylt portez ce vieux Whiskey blond qui

▶ Bold Italic
The quick brown fox jumps over a Dog. Zwei Boxkämpfer jagen Eva durch Sylt portez ce vieux Whiskey blond qui

▶ Black
The quick brown fox jumps over a Dog. Zwei Boxkämpfer jagen Eva durch Sylt portez ce vieux

A258 Mac + PC ② 1989: Robert Slimbach
Utopia Expert

ABCDEFGHIJKLMNOPQRSTUVWXYZ(ÄÖÜŠÅØÆŒÇ)

1234567890fffifflffiffl($_1^{1}_2^{2}_3^{3}_4^{4}_5^{5}_6^{6}_7^{7}_8^{8}_9^{9}_0$^{0}) ($^\$$$^\$$$^¢^{Rp}^₵$)^a

▶ Expert Regular
01234567890fffifflffiffl-
(^{1}/$_1$^{2}/$_2$^{3}/$_3$^{4}/$_4$^{5}/$_5$^{6}/$_6$^{7}/$_7$^{8}/$_8$^{9}/$_9$^{0}/$_0$%) ($^\$$$^\$$$^¢^{Rp}^₵$)^a
THE QUICK BROWN FOX JUMPS OVER A DOG ZWEI BOXKÄMPFER

▶ Expert Italic
01234567890fffifflffiffl-
(^{1}/$_1$^{2}/$_2$^{3}/$_3$^{4}/$_4$^{5}/$_5$^{6}/$_6$^{7}/$_7$^{8}/$_8$^{9}/$_9$%) ($^\$$$^\$$$^¢^{Rp}^₵$)^a

▶ Expert Semi Bold
01234567890fffifflffiffl-
(^{1}/$_1$^{2}/$_2$^{3}/$_3$^{4}/$_4$^{5}/$_5$^{6}/$_6$^{7}/$_7$^{8}/$_8$^{9}/$_9$^{0}/$_0$%) ($^\$$$^\$$$^¢^{Rp}^₵$)^a
THE QUICK BROWN FOX JUMPS OVER A DOG ZWEI BOXKÄMPFER

▶ Expert Semi Bold Italic
01234567890fffifflffiffl-
(^{1}/$_1$^{2}/$_2$^{3}/$_3$^{4}/$_4$^{5}/$_5$^{6}/$_6$^{7}/$_7$^{8}/$_8$^{9}/$_9$%) ($^\$$$^\$$$^¢^{Rp}^₵$)^a

▶ Expert Bold
01234567890fffifflffiffl-
(^{1}/$_1$^{2}/$_2$^{3}/$_3$^{4}/$_4$^{5}/$_5$^{6}/$_6$^{7}/$_7$^{8}/$_8$^{9}/$_9$^{0}/$_0$%) ($^\$$$^\$$$^¢^{Rp}^₵$) a

▶ Expert Bold Italic
01234567890fffifflffiffl-
(^{1}/$_1$^{2}/$_2$^{3}/$_3$^{4}/$_4$^{5}/$_5$^{6}/$_6$^{7}/$_7$^{8}/$_8$^{9}/$_9$%) ($^\$$$^\$$$^¢^{Rp}^₵$) a

▶ Expert Black
01234567890fffifflffiffl-
(^{1}/$_1$^{2}/$_2$^{3}/$_3$^{4}/$_4$^{5}/$_5$^{6}/$_6$^{7}/$_7$^{8}/$_8$^{9}/$_9$%) ($^\$$$^\$$$^¢^{Rp}^₵$))a

▶ Titling
A QUICK BROWN FOX JUMPS OVER THE DOG. SYLT WHISKEY BLOND FUME QUI KISUAHELI NEUMYX ZUR

Utopia Expert, Utopia Ornaments

© FSI 1993

TYPOGRAPHIC ORIENTED DIVIDER PAGE

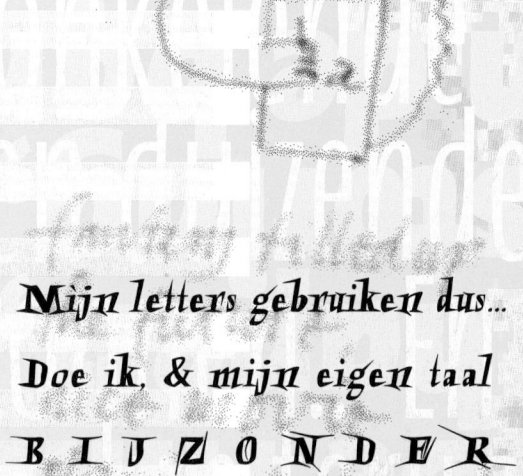

please use your own typefaces

Mijn letters gebruiken dus...
Doe ik, & mijn eigen taal
BIJZONDER
EXCLUSIEF

Arie's ouwe leidse, jammie! Dubbel brood banaan & oe wat is tie fel de maan

But call fontshop Germany NOW, they know where to find me

every
other
day
another
FACE

21
993

V

Luc(as) de Groot, Den Haag & Berlin, NL & D

A175 Mac + PC ①
V.A.G. Rounded

abcdefghijklmnopqrstuvwxyz[äöüßåøœeç]
ABCDEFGHIJKLMNOPQRSTUVWXYZ
1234567890(.,;:?!$&-*){ÄÖÜÅØÆŒÇ}

aa*a*
BT1409
V.A.G. Rounded, Reg
Vega, Futura, Avenir

▶ Thin
The quick brown fox jumps over a Dog. Zwei Boxkämpfer jagen Eva durch Sylt portez ce vieux Whiskey blond qui fume une

▶ Light
The quick brown fox jumps over a Dog. Zwei Boxkämpfer jagen Eva durch Sylt portez ce vieux Whiskey blond qui fume une

▶ Bold
The quick brown fox jumps over a Dog. Zwei Boxkämpfer jagen Eva durch Sylt portez ce vieux Whiskey blond qui fume

▶ Black
The quick brown fox jumps over a Dog. Zwei Boxkämpfer jagen Eva durch Sylt portez ce vieux Whiskey blond qui fume

M265 Mac + PC ② 1935: (Christoffel van Dijck) Jan Van Krimpen
Van Dijck™

abcdefghijklmnopqrstuvwxyz[äöüßåøæœç]
ABCDEFGHIJKLMNOPQRSTUVWXYZ
1234567890(.,;:?!$&-★){ÄÖÜÅØÆŒÇ}

▶ Regular
The quick brown fox jumps over a Dog. Zwei Boxkämpfer jagen Eva durch Sylt portez ce vieux Whiskey blond qui fume une pipe aber echt

▶ Italic
The quick brown fox jumps over a Dog. Zwei Boxkämpfer jagen Eva durch Sylt portez ce vieux Whiskey blond qui fume une pipe aber echt über die Mauer

Poliphilus®:
Blado®, Poliphilus, Van Dijck™

M6697 Mac + PC ② 1935: (Christoffel van Dijck) Jan Van Krimpen
Van Dijck Expert

ABCDEFGHIJKLMNOPQRSTUVWXYZ(ÄÖÜŠÅØÆŒÇ)
1234567890ffiflffiffl($^1{}_1{}^2{}_2{}^3{}_3{}^4{}_4{}^5{}_5{}^6{}_6{}^7{}_7{}^8{}_8{}^9{}_9{}^0{}_0$)($¢Rp₵)ª

▶ Expert
0123456789ffiflffiffl-
(^{1}/$_2$^{2}/$_3$^{3}/$_4$^{4}/$_5$^{5}/$_6$^{6}/$_7$^{7}/$_8$^{8}/$_9$%‰)($¢Rp₵)ª
THE QUICK BROWN FOX JUMPS OVER A DOG ZWEI BOXKÄMPFER JAGEN

▶ Italic Expert
*0123456789ffiflffiffl-
(^{1}/$_2$^{2}/$_3$^{3}/$_4$^{4}/$_5$^{5}/$_6$^{6}/$_7$^{7}/$_8$^{8}/$_9$%‰)($¢Rp₵)ª*

▶ Alternate Figures
0123456789

▶ Alternate Figures Italic
0123456789

Poliphilus Expert:
Blado Expert, Poliphilus Expert, Van Dijck Expert

© FSI 1993

L2738 MAC ④ 1982: Jan van Dijk
Van Dijk™

abcdefghijklmnopqrstuvwxyz[äöüßåøæœç]
ABCDEFGHIJKLMNOPQRSTUVWXYZ
1234567890(.,;:?!$&-*)ÄÖÜÅØÆŒÇ

L2739 MAC ④ 1986: (Jan van Dijk, 1982) Peter O'Donnell
Van Dijk Bold

abcdefghijklmnopqrstuvwxyz[äöüßåøæœç]
ABCDEFGHIJKLMNOPQRSTUVWXYZ
1234567890(.,;:?!$&-*)ÄÖÜÅØÆŒÇ

L2740 MAC ⑥ 1991: Alan Meeks
Varga™

abcdefghijklmnopqrstuvwxyz[äöüßåøæœç]
ABCDEFGHIJKLMNOPQRSTUVWXYZ
1234567890(.,;:?!$&-*)ÄÖÜÅØÆŒÇ

E123 MAC + PC ⑤ 1988: Rudy VanderLans, Zuzana Licko
Variex™

abcdefghijklmnopqrstuvwxyz[äöüßåøæœç]
AbcdefghijklmnopqrstuvwxyZ
1234567890(.,;:?!$&-*){ÄÖÜÅØÆŒÇ}

▶ Light
the quick brown fox jumps over a dog. zwei boxkämpfer jagen eva durch sylt portez ce

▶ Regular
the quick brown fox jumps over a dog. zwei boxkämpfer jagen eva durch sylt

▶ Bold
the quick brown fox jumps over a dog. zwei boxkämpfer jagen eva durch sylt

EF527 MAC + PC ⑥ 1982: Hermann Zapf
Vario™

abcdefghijklmnopqrstuvwxyz äöüßåøæœç
ABCDEFGHIJKLMNOPQRSTUVWXYZ
1234567890(.,;:?!$&-*) ÄÖÜÅØÆŒÇ

▶ Regular
The quick brown fox jumps over a Dog. Zwei Boxkämpfer jagen Eva durch Sylt portez ce vieux Whiskey blond qui fume une pipe aber

▶ Italic
The quick brown fox jumps over a Dog. Zwei Boxkämpfer jagen Eva durch Sylt portez ce vieux Whiskey blond qui fume une pipe aber

© FSI 1993

A2770 Mac + PC
Vectora™
1991: Adrian Frutiger

abcdefghijklmnopqrstuvwxyz[äöüßåøæœç]
ABCDEFGHIJKLMNOPQRSTUVWXYZ
1234567890(.,;:?!$&-*){ÄÖÜÅØÆŒÇ}

Unica, Arial, Univers, News Gothic

▶ 45 Light
The quick brown fox jumps over a Dog. Zwei Boxkämpfer jagen Eva durch Sylt portez ce vieux Whiskey blond qui fume

▶ 46 Light Italic
The quick brown fox jumps over a Dog. Zwei Boxkämpfer jagen Eva durch Sylt portez ce vieux Whiskey blond qui fume

▶ 55 Regular
The quick brown fox jumps over a Dog. Zwei Boxkämpfer jagen Eva durch Sylt portez ce vieux Whiskey blond qui fume

▶ 56 Italic
The quick brown fox jumps over a Dog. Zwei Boxkämpfer jagen Eva durch Sylt portez ce vieux Whiskey blond qui fume

▶ 75 Bold
The quick brown fox jumps over a Dog. Zwei Boxkämpfer jagen Eva durch Sylt portez ce vieux Whiskey

▶ 76 Bold Italic
The quick brown fox jumps over a Dog. Zwei Boxkämpfer jagen Eva durch Sylt portez ce vieux Whiskey

▶ 95 Black
The quick brown fox jumps over a Dog. Zwei Boxkämpfer jagen Eva durch Sylt portez ce vieux

▶ 96 Black Italic
The quick brown fox jumps over a Dog. Zwei Boxkämpfer jagen Eva durch Sylt portez ce vieux

SG1128 Mac
Vega Light

abcdefghijklmnopqrstuvwxyz[äöüßåøæœç]
ABCDEFGHIJKLMNOPQRSTUVWXYZ
1234567890(.,;:?!$&-*) ÄÖÜÅØÆŒÇ

SG1197 Mac
Vega Medium

abcdefghijklmnopqrstuvwxyz[äöüßåøæœç]
ABCDEFGHIJKLMNOPQRSTUVWXYZ
1234567890(.,;:?!$&-*)ÄÖÜÅØÆŒÇ

SG1198 Mac
Vega Standard Bold

abcdefghijklmnopqrstuvwxyz[äöüßåøæœç]
ABCDEFGHIJKLMNOPQRSTUVWXYZ
1234567890(.,;:?!$&-*)ÄÖÜÅØÆŒÇ

© FSI 1993

SG1199 Mac ①
Vega TV

abcdefghijklmnopqrstuvwxyz[äöüßåøæœç]
ABCDEFGHIJKLMNOPQRSTUVWXYZ
1234567890(.,;:?!$&-*)ÄÖÜÅØÆŒÇ

SG1203 Mac ①
Vega VW

abcdefghijklmnopqrstuvwxyz[äöüßåøæœç]
ABCDEFGHIJKLMNOPQRSTUVWXYZ
1234567890(.,;:?!$&-*)ÄÖÜÅØÆŒÇ

L6150 Mac ⑥ 1984: David Quay
Vegas™

abcdefghijklmnopqrstuvwxyz[äöüßåøæœç]
ABCDEFGHIJKLMNOPQRSTUVWXYZ
1234567890(.,;:?!$&-*)

EF1081 Mac + PC ② 1984: Jovica Veljovic
ITC Veljovic® 1

abcdefghijklmnopqrstuvwxyz[äöüßåøæœç]
ABCDEFGHIJKLMNOPQRSTUVWXYZ
1234567890(.,;:?!$&-*){ÄÖÜÅØÆŒÇ}

aa*a*
C620
ITC Veljovic, Reg, Ita, Bd, BdIta
A1146
ITC Veljovic, Bk, BkIta, Med, MedIta, Bd, BdIta, Blk, BlkIta

▶ Book
The quick brown fox jumps over a Dog. Zwei Boxkämpfer jagen Eva durch Sylt portez ce vieux Whiskey

▶ Book Italic
The quick brown fox jumps over a Dog. Zwei Boxkämpfer jagen Eva durch Sylt portez ce vieux Whiskey blond qui

▶ Bold
The quick brown fox jumps over a Dog. Zwei Boxkämpfer jagen Eva durch Sylt portez ce vieux

▶ Bold Italic
The quick brown fox jumps over a Dog. Zwei Boxkämpfer jagen Eva durch Sylt portez ce vieux Whiskey

EF1082 Mac + PC ② 1984: Jovica Veljovic
ITC Veljovic 2

abcdefghijklmnopqrstuvwxyz[äöüßåøæœç]
ABCDEFGHIJKLMNOPQRSTUVWXYZ
1234567890(.,;:?!$&-*){ÄÖÜÅØÆŒÇ}

aa*a*
C620
ITC Veljovic, Reg, Ita, Bd, BdIta
A1146
ITC Veljovic, Bk, BkIta, Med, MedIta, Bd, BdIta, Blk, BlkIta

▶ Medium
The quick brown fox jumps over a Dog. Zwei Boxkämpfer jagen Eva durch Sylt portez ce vieux Whiskey

▶ Medium Italic
The quick brown fox jumps over a Dog. Zwei Boxkämpfer jagen Eva durch Sylt portez ce vieux Whiskey blond

© FSI 1993

▼ EF1082 Mac + PC   ITC Veljovic 2

▶ Black

The quick brown fox jumps over a Dog. Zwei Boxkämpfer jagen Eva durch Sylt portez ce

▶ Black Italic

The quick brown fox jumps over a Dog. Zwei Boxkämpfer jagen Eva durch Sylt portez ce

---

SG1124 Mac   ②   ✎ 1952: Franois Ganeau
Vendome™ Regular

abcdefghijklmnopqrstuvwxyz[äöüßåøæœç]
ABCDEFGHIJKLMNOPQRSTUVWXYZ
1234567890(.,;:?!$&-*)ÄÖÜÅØÆŒÇ

SG1184 Mac   ②   ✎ 1952: Franois Ganeau
Vendome Italic

*abcdefghijklmnopqrstuvwxyz[äöüßåøæœç]
ABCDEFGHIJKLMNOPQRSTUVWXYZ
1234567890(.,;:?!$&-*)ÄÖÜÅØÆŒÇ*

SG1185 Mac   ②   ✎ 1952: Franois Ganeau
Vendome Medium

abcdefghijklmnopqrstuvwxyz[äöüßåøæœç]
ABCDEFGHIJKLMNOPQRSTUVWXYZ
1234567890(.,;:?!$&-*)ÄÖÜÅØÆŒÇ

SG1183 Mac   ②   ✎ 1952: Franois Ganeau
Vendome Medium Italic

*abcdefghijklmnopqrstuvwxyz[äöüßåøæœç]
ABCDEFGHIJKLMNOPQRSTUVWXYZ
1234567890(.,;:?!$&-*)ÄÖÜÅØÆŒÇ*

Vendome Bold
SG1186 Mac — 1952: Franois Ganeau

abcdefghijklmnopqrstuvwxyz[äöüßåøæœç]
ABCDEFGHIJKLMNOPQRSTUVWXYZ
1234567890(.,;:?!$&-*)ÄÖÜÅØÆŒÇ

°Vendome Condensed
SG1187 Mac — 1952: Franois Ganeau

abcdefghijklmnopqrstuvwxyz1234567890[äöüßåøæœç]
ABCDEFGHIJKLMNOPQRSTUVWXYZ(.,;:?!$&-*)ÄÖÜÅØÆŒÇ

Vermont™
L2741 Mac — 1987: Freda Sack

abcdefghijklmnopqrstuvwxyz [äöüßåøæœç]
ABCDEFGHIJKLMNOPQRSTUVWXYZ
1234567890(.,;:?!$&-*)ÄÖÜÅØÆŒÇ

Veronan™
CT874 Mac + PC — 1986: Adrian Williams

abcdefghijklmnopqrstuvwxyz[äöüßåøæœç]
ABCDEFGHIJKLMNOPQRSTUVWXYZ
1234567890(.,;:?!$&-*){ÄÖÜÅØÆŒÇ}

▶ Light
The quick brown fox jumps over a Dog. Zwei Boxkämpfer jagen Eva durch Sylt portez ce vieux Whiskey blond qui fume une pipe

▶ Italic
The quick brown fox jumps over a Dog. Zwei Boxkämpfer jagen Eva durch Sylt portez ce vieux Whiskey blond qui fume une pipe aber

▶ Bold
The quick brown fox jumps over a Dog. Zwei Boxkämpfer jagen Eva durch Sylt portez ce vieux Whiskey blond qui fume

Versailles™
A486 Mac + PC — 1982: Adrian Frutiger

abcdefghijklmnopqrstuvwxyz[äöüßåøæœç]
ABCDEFGHIJKLMNOPQRSTUVWXYZ
1234567890(.,;:?!$&-*){ÄÖÜÅØÆŒÇ}

▶ 45 Light
The quick brown fox jumps over a Dog. Zwei Boxkämpfer jagen Eva durch Sylt portez ce vieux Whiskey blond qui

▶ 46 Light Italic
The quick brown fox jumps over a Dog. Zwei Boxkämpfer jagen Eva durch Sylt portez ce vieux Whiskey blond qui fume

© FSI 1993

▼ A486   Mac + PC   Versailles™

► 55 Regular
The quick brown fox jumps over a Dog. Zwei Boxkämpfer jagen Eva durch Sylt portez ce vieux Whiskey

► 56 Italic
The quick brown fox jumps over a Dog. Zwei Boxkämpfer jagen Eva durch Sylt portez ce vieux Whiskey blond

► 75 Bold
The quick brown fox jumps over a Dog. Zwei Boxkämpfer jagen Eva durch Sylt portez ce vieux

► 76 Bold Italic
The quick brown fox jumps over a Dog. Zwei Boxkämpfer jagen Eva durch Sylt portez ce vieux Whis-

► 95 Black
The quick brown fox jumps over a Dog. Zwei Boxkämpfer jagen Eva durch Sylt portez ce

► 96 Black Italic
The quick brown fox jumps over a Dog. Zwei Boxkämpfer jagen Eva durch Sylt portez ce

---

RB6094   Mac
Beatty Victoriana™

Beatty Victoriana™:
Childs™, Hermosa™, Recherché™, Spiral™, Wanted™

RB6095   Mac
Beatty Victoriana Alternates

Beatty Victoriana Alternates:
Childs Alternates, Hermosa Alternates, Recherché Alternates, Spiral Alternates, Wanted Alternates

---

C2981   Mac + PC   ⑥
Victorian Silhouette

ABCDEFGHIJKLMN
OPQRSTUVWXYZ

Headlines 92S:
Eagle Bold, Joanna Solotype, Matra™, Modernique, Victorian Silhouette

---

M6410   Mac + PC   ⑥
Victoria™ Titling Condensed

ABCDEFGHIJKLMNOPQRSTUVWXYZ
1234567890(.,;:?!$&-*)[]{ÄÖÜÅØÆŒÇ}

Crazy Headlines™:
Festival™ Titling, Kino™, Matura™ Script, Victoria™ Titling Condensed

© FSI 1993

L2812 Mac (6) 1989: Anthony De Meester
Vienna™ Extended

ABCDEFGHIJKLMN
OPQRSTUVWXYZ
1234567890(.,;:?!/&-*)
[]ÄÖÜÅØÆŒÇ

BT790 Mac + PC (6) 1973: Ernst Volker
Vineta

abcdefghijklmnopqrstuvwxyz[äöüßåøæœç]
ABCDEFGHIJKLMNOPQRSTUVWXYZ
1234567890(.,;:?!$&-*){ÄÖÜÅØÆŒÇ}

Bitstream Decorative 2:
ITC Pioneer®, Maximus™, Profil™, Vineta
Profil, Circus

C2982 Mac + PC (6)
Virile

abcdefghijklmnopqrstuvwxyz[äöüßåøæœç]
ABCDEFGHIJKLMNOPQRSTUVWXYZ
1234567890(.,;:?!$&-*) { ÄÖÜÅØÆŒÇ }

▶ Regular
The quick brown fox jumps over a Dog. Zwei Boxkämpfer Jagen Eva durch Sylt portez ce vieux
Whiskey blond qui fume une pipe aber echt über
die Mauer gesprungen und auch smørebrød en

▶ Open
The quick brown fox jumps over a Dog. Zwei Boxkämpfer Jagen Eva durch Sylt portez ce vieux
Whiskey blond qui fume une pipe aber echt über
die Mauer gesprungen und auch smørebrød en

Headlines 93S:
Ashley Inline, Beverly Hills, Lotus™, Virile

C2521 Mac + PC (4) 1989: Arthur Baker
Visigoth

ABCDEFGHIJKLMNOPQRSTUVWXYZ
1234567890(.,;:?!$&-*)[]{ÄÖÜÅØÆŒÇ}

Amigo:
Amigo™, Marigold™, Oxford™, Pelican™, Visigoth

EF1083 Mac + PC (4) 1970: Fritz Peters
Vivaldi™

abcdefghijklmnopqrstuvwxyzäöüßåøæœç
ABCDEFGHIJKLMNOPQRSTUVWXYZ
1234567890(.,;:?!$&-*)ÄÖÜÅØÆŒÇ

© FSI 1993

V 8

EF1084 Mac + PC ③ 1955: K. F. Bauer, Walter Baum
Volta™

abcdefghijklmnopqrstuvwxyz[äöüßåøæœç]
ABCDEFGHIJKLMNOPQRSTUVWXYZ
1234567890(.,;:?!$&-*){ÄÖÜÅØÆŒÇ}

Clarendon

▶ Regular
The quick brown fox jumps over a Dog. Zwei Boxkämpfer jagen Eva durch Sylt portez ce vieux

▶ Medium
The quick brown fox jumps over a Dog. Zwei Boxkämpfer jagen Eva durch Sylt portez ce

▶ Medium Italic
The quick brown fox jumps over a Dog. Zwei Boxkämpfer jagen Eva durch Sylt portez ce vieux

▶ Bold
The quick brown fox jumps over a Dog. Zwei Boxkämpfer jagen Eva

FF731 Mac + PC ⑤ 1991: Max Kisman
FF Vortex™

abcdefghijklmnopqrstuvwxyz1234567890[äöüßåøæœç]
ABCDEFGHIJKLMNOPQRSTUVWXYZ(.,;:?!$&-*){ÄÖÜÅØÆŒÇ}

FF Kisman™ 1:
FF Cutout™, FF Network™, FF Scratch™, FF Vortex™
FF Network, Oblong, FF Pop

Cornel Windlin, London, UK

L2813 Mac ① 1990: Paul Hickson
Wade™ Sans Light

abcdefghijklmnopqrstuvwxyz[äöüßåøæœç]
ABCDEFGHIJKLMNOPQRSTUVWXYZ
1234567890(.,;:?!$&-*)ÄÖÜÅØÆŒÇ

AB2916 Mac + PC ② (J. E. Walbaum, c.1800?) G. G. Lange
Berthold Walbaum (Buch)

abcdefghijklmnopqrstuvwxyz[äöüßåøæœç]
ABCDEFGHIJKLMNOPQRSTUVWXYZ
1234567890(.,;:?!$&-*){ÄÖÜÅØÆŒÇ}

▶ Regular
The quick brown fox jumps over a Dog. Zwei Boxkämpfer jagen Eva durch Sylt portez ce vieux Whiskey blond qui

▶ Italic
The quick brown fox jumps over a Dog. Zwei Boxkämpfer jagen Eva durch Sylt portez ce vieux Whiskey blond qui fume

▶ Medium
The quick brown fox jumps over a Dog. Zwei Boxkämpfer jagen Eva durch Sylt portez ce vieux Whiskey

▶ Medium Italic
The quick brown fox jumps over a Dog. Zwei Boxkämpfer jagen Eva durch Sylt portez ce vieux Whis-

▶ Bold
The quick brown fox jumps over a Dog. Zwei Boxkämpfer jagen Eva durch Sylt portez ce vieux

▶ Bold Italic
The quick brown fox jumps over a Dog. Zwei Boxkämpfer jagen Eva durch Sylt portez ce vieux

A1006 Mac + PC ② 1976: (J. E. Walbaum, c.1800?) G. G. Lange
Berthold Walbaum Small Caps/OSF

ABCDEFGHIJKLMNOPQRSTUVWXYZ[ÄÖÜSSÅØÆŒÇ]
ABCDEFGHIJKLMNOPQRSTUVWXYZ
1234567890(.,;:?!$&-*){ÄÖÜÅØÆŒÇ}

© Basilia

▶ Small Caps
THE QUICK BROWN FOX JUMPS OVER A DOG. 123 4567 890 ZWEI BOXKÄMPFER JAGEN EVA DURCH SYLT PORTEZ CE

▶ Italic OSF
The quick brown fox jumps over a Dog. 123 4567 890 Zwei Boxkämpfer jagen Eva durch Sylt portez ce vieux

▶ Bold OSF
The quick brown fox jumps over a Dog. 123 4567 890 Zwei Boxkämpfer jagen Eva durch Sylt por-

▶ Bold Italic OSF
The quick brown fox jumps over a Dog. 123 4567 890 Zwei Boxkämpfer jagen Eva durch Sylt por-

M280 Mac + PC ② 1933: (J. E. Walbaum, c.1800?)
Monotype Walbaum™

abcdefghijklmnopqrstuvwxyz[äöüßåøæœç]
ABCDEFGHIJKLMNOPQRSTUVWXYZ
1234567890(.,;:?!$&-*){ÄÖÜÅØÆŒÇ}

▼ M280 Mac + PC   Monotype Walbaum™

Basilia, Berthold Walbaum

► **Regular**
The quick brown fox jumps over a Dog. Zwei Boxkämpfer jagen Eva durch Sylt portez ce vieux Whiskey blond qui fume une pipe aber echt

► *Italic*
The quick brown fox jumps over a Dog. Zwei Boxkämpfer jagen Eva durch Sylt portez ce vieux Whiskey blond qui fume une pipe aber echt

► **Medium**
The quick brown fox jumps over a Dog. Zwei Boxkämpfer jagen Eva durch Sylt portez ce vieux Whiskey blond qui fume une pipe aber

► ***Medium Italic***
The quick brown fox jumps over a Dog. Zwei Boxkämpfer jagen Eva durch Sylt portez ce vieux Whiskey blond qui fume une pipe aber

---

SG2477 Mac ⑦ (J. E. Walbaum, c.1800?)
Walbaum Fraktur

abcdefghijklmnopqrstuvwxyz[äöüßåøæœç]
ABCDEFGHIJKLMNOPQRSTUVWXYZ
1234567890(.,;:?!$&-*)ÄÖÜÅØÆŒÇ

RB6094 Mac ⑥ 1991: Richard Beatty
Wanted™

abcdefghijklmnopqrstuvwxyz[äöüßåøæœç]
ABCDEFGHIJKLMNOPQRSTUVWXYZ
1234567890(.,;:?!$&-*){ÄÖÜÅØÆŒÇ}

Beatty Victoriana™:
Childs™, Hermosa™, Recherché™, Spiral™, Wanted™

RB6095 Mac ⑥ 1991: Richard Beatty
Wanted Alternates

abcdefghijklmnopqrstuvwxyz[äöüßåøæœç]
ABCDEFGHIJKLMNOPQRSTUVWXYZ
1234567890(.,;:?!$&-*){ÄÖÜÅØÆŒÇ}

Beatty Victoriana Alternates:
Childs Alternates, Hermosa Alternates, Recherché Alternates, Spiral Alternates, Wanted Alternates

---

MC2913 Mac + PC ⑤
Watch™ Outline

ABCDEFGHIJKLMNOPQRSTUVWXYZ
1234567890(.,;:?!$&-*)[]{ÄÖÜÅØÆŒÇ}

© FSI 1993

L6151 Mac ⑥ 1987: Alan Meeks
Waterloo™ Bold

abcdefghijklmnopqrstuvwxyz[äöüßåøæœç]
ABCDEFGHIJKLMNOPQRSTUVWXYZ
1234567890(.,;:?!$&-*)ÄÖÜÅØÆŒÇ

ATF336 Mac ⑦ 1901: M. F. Benton
Wedding Text™

abcdefghijklmnopqrstuvwxyz[äöüßåøæœç]
ABCDEFGHIJKLMNOPQRSTUVWXYZ
1234567890(.,;:?!$&-*){ÄÖÜÅØÆŒÇ}

ATF Set 1:
Bernhard Fashion™, Cleland Border 1805™, Thompson Quillscript™, Wedding Text™
aa*a* BT1411
Wedding Text, Reg
C6568

EF1522 Mac + PC ② 1983: Kurt Weidemann
ITC Weidemann® 1

abcdefghijklmnopqrstuvwxyz[äöüßåøæœç]
ABCDEFGHIJKLMNOPQRSTUVWXYZ
1234567890(.,;:?!$&-*){ÄÖÜÅØÆŒÇ}

aa*a*
BT1412
ITC Weidemann 1, Bk,
BkIta, Bd, BdIta
A423
ITC Weidemann, Bk,
BkIta, Med, MedIta,
Bd, BdIta, Blk, BlkIta

▶ Book
The quick brown fox jumps over a Dog. Zwei Boxkämpfer jagen Eva durch Sylt portez ce vieux Whiskey blond qui fume une pipe aber echt

▶ Book Italic
The quick brown fox jumps over a Dog. Zwei Boxkämpfer jagen Eva durch Sylt portez ce vieux Whiskey blond qui fume une pipe aber echt

▶ Bold
The quick brown fox jumps over a Dog. Zwei Boxkämpfer jagen Eva durch Sylt portez ce vieux Whiskey blond qui fume une

▶ Bold Italic
The quick brown fox jumps over a Dog. Zwei Boxkämpfer jagen Eva durch Sylt portez ce vieux Whiskey blond qui fume une

EF1523 Mac + PC ② 1983: Kurt Weidemann
ITC Weidemann 2

abcdefghijklmnopqrstuvwxyz[äöüßåøæœç]
ABCDEFGHIJKLMNOPQRSTUVWXYZ
1234567890(.,;:?!$&-*){ÄÖÜÅØÆŒÇ}

aa*a*
BT1413
ITC Weidemann 2,
Med, MedIta, Hvy,
HvyIta
A423
ITC Weidemann, Bk,
BkIta, Med, MedIta, Bd,
BdIta, Blk, BlkIta

▶ Medium
The quick brown fox jumps over a Dog. Zwei Boxkämpfer jagen Eva durch Sylt portez ce vieux Whiskey

▶ Medium Italic
The quick brown fox jumps over a Dog. Zwei Boxkämpfer jagen Eva durch Sylt portez ce vieux Whiskey blond

▶ Heavy
The quick brown fox jumps over a Dog. Zwei Boxk mpfer jagen Eva durch Sylt portez ce vieux Whiskey blond qui fume

▶ Heavy Italic
The quick brown fox jumps over a Dog. Zwei Boxk mpfer jagen Eva durch Sylt portez ce vieux Whiskey blond qui fume

© FSI 1993

EF1524 MAC + PC ② 1983: Kurt Weidemann
ITC Weidemann 3

ABCDEFGHIJKLMNOPQRSTUVWXYZ[ÄÖÜSSÅØÆŒÇ]
ABCDEFGHIJKLMNOPQRSTUVWXYZ
1234567890(.,;:?!$&-*){ÄÖÜÅØÆŒÇ}

▶ Book Small Caps
THE QUICK BROWN FOX JUMPS OVER A DOG. 123 4567 890 ZWEI BOXKÄMPFER JAGEN EVA DURCH SYLT PORTEZ CE VIEUX WHISKEY BLOND QUI

▶ Medium Small Caps
THE QUICK BROWN FOX JUMPS OVER A DOG. 123 4567 890 ZWEI BOXKÄMPFER JAGEN EVA DURCH SYLT PORTEZ CE VIEUX WHISKEY BLOND QUI

A362 MAC + PC ② 1924: Emil Rudolf Weiss
Weiss™

abcdefghijklmnopqrstuvwxyz[äöüßåøæœç]
ABCDEFGHIJKLMNOPQRSTUVWXYZ
1234567890(.,;:?!$&-*){ÄÖÜÅØÆŒÇ}

▶ Regular
The quick brown fox jumps over a Dog. Zwei Boxkämpfer jagen Eva durch Sylt portez ce vieux Whiskey blond qui fume une pipe aber

▶ Italic
The quick brown fox jumps over a Dog. Zwei Boxkämpfer jagen Eva durch Sylt portez ce vieux Whiskey blond qui fume une pipe aber echt über die Mauer

▶ Bold
The quick brown fox jumps over a Dog. Zwei Boxkämpfer jagen Eva durch Sylt portez ce vieux Whiskey blond qui fume une

▶ Extra Bold
The quick brown fox jumps over a Dog. Zwei Boxkämpfer jagen Eva durch Sylt portez ce vieux Whiskey blond qui fume

LP2840 MAC + PC ④
Wendy™

abcdefghijklmnopqrstuvwxyz[äöüßåøæœç]
ABCDEFGHIJKLMNOPQRSTUVWXYZ
1234567890(.,;:?!$&-*){ÄÖÜÅØÆŒÇ}

LetterPerfect 1:
TomBoy™, Wendy™

FB6671 MAC + PC ② 1993: Matthew Butterick
Wessex™

abcdefghijklmnopqrstuvwxyz[äöüßåøæœç]
ABCDEFGHIJKLMNOPQRSTUVWXYZ
1234567890(.,;:?!$&-*){ÄÖÜÅØÆŒÇ}

▶ Roman
The quick brown fox jumps over a Dog. Zwei Boxkämpfer jagen Eva durch Sylt portez ce vieux Whiskey blond qui fume une pipe aber

▶ Italic
The quick brown fox jumps over a Dog. Zwei Boxkämpfer jagen Eva durch Sylt portez ce vieux Whiskey blond qui fume une pipe aber echt

▼ FB6671 Mac + PC   Wessex™

▶ Semi Bold
The quick brown fox jumps over a Dog. Zwei Boxkämpfer jagen Eva durch Sylt portez ce vieux Whiskey blond qui fume une pipe

▶ Roman SC
The quick brown fox jumps over a Dog. 123 4567 890 Zwei Boxkämpfer jagen Eva durch Sylt portez ce vieux Whiskey blond

▶ Roman Titling
THE QUICK BROWN FOX JUMPS OVER A DOG. ZWEI BOXKÄMPFER JAGEN EVA DURCH SYLT PORTEZ CE

C1012 Mac + PC ①
PL Westerveldt Light

abcdefghijklmnopqrstuvwxyz[äöüßåøæœç]
ABCDEFGHIJKLMNOPQRSTUVWXYZ
1234567890(.,;:?!$&-*)◊ÄÖÜÅØÆŒÇ♦

Headlines 84S:
Bernhard Modern, Beton Extra Bold, Metropolis Bold, Modern No. 20, Orlando Caps, PL Davison Americana, PL Westerveldt Light, Siena™ Black, TC Europa™ Bold, TC Jasper™

L2742 Mac ⑥ ✎ 1991: David Westwood
Westwood™

abcdefghijklmnopqrstuvwxyz[äöüßåøæœç]
ABCDEFGHIJKLMNOPQRSTUVWXYZ
1234567890(.,;:?!$&-*)ÄÖÜÅØÆŒÇ

LH6640 Mac + PC ④
Wiesbaden Swing™ Roman

abcdefghijklmnopqrstuvwxyz[äöüßåøæœç]
ABCDEFGHIJKLMNOPQRSTUVWXYZ
1234567890(.,;:?!$&-*){ÄÖÜÅØÆŒÇ}

Calligraphy for Print:
Ruling Script™, Sho Roman™, Wiesbaden Swing™ Roman

C1201 Mac + PC ② ✎ 1990: Cynthia Hollandsworth
Agfa Wile™ Roman

abcdefghijklmnopqrstuvwxyz[äöüßåøæœç]
ABCDEFGHIJKLMNOPQRSTUVWXYZ
1234567890(.,;:?!$&-*){ÄÖÜÅØÆŒÇ}

▶ Book
The quick brown fox jumps over a Dog. Zwei Boxkämpfer jagen Eva durch Sylt portez ce vieux Whiskey blond qui fume une

▶ Italic
The quick brown fox jumps over a Dog. Zwei Boxkämpfer jagen Eva durch Sylt portez ce vieux Whiskey blond qui fume une pipe aber echt

▼ C1201 Mac + PC Agfa Wile™ Roman

► Medium
The quick brown fox jumps over a Dog. Zwei Boxkämpfer jagen Eva durch Sylt portez ce vieux Whiskey blond qui fume une

► Medium Italic
The quick brown fox jumps over a Dog. Zwei Boxkämpfer jagen Eva durch Sylt portez ce vieux Whiskey blond qui fume une pipe aber echt

► Bold
The quick brown fox jumps over a Dog. Zwei Boxkämpfer jagen Eva durch Sylt portez ce vieux Whiskey blond qui fume

► Bold Italic
The quick brown fox jumps over a Dog. Zwei Boxkämpfer jagen Eva durch Sylt portez ce vieux Whiskey blond qui fume une pipe aber echt

► Black
The quick brown fox jumps over a Dog. Zwei Boxkämpfer jagen Eva durch Sylt portez ce vieux Whiskey blond qui fume

► Black Italic
The quick brown fox jumps over a Dog. Zwei Boxkämpfer jagen Eva durch Sylt portez ce vieux Whiskey blond qui fume une

---

A564 Mac + PC ⑦ 1925: Rudolf Koch
Wilhelm Klingspor Gotisch™

abcdefghijklmnopqrstuvwxyz[äöüßåøæœç]
ABCDEFGHIJKLMNOPQRSTUVWXYZ
1234567890(.,;:?!$&-*){ÄÖÜÅØÆŒÇ}

German Display 2:
Banco™, Charme™, Flyer™ Condensed, Wilhelm Klingspor Gotisch™

A2548 Mac + PC ② 1988: Martin Wilke
Wilke™

abcdefghijklmnopqrstuvwxyz[äöüßåøæœç]
ABCDEFGHIJKLMNOPQRSTUVWXYZ
1234567890(.,;:?!$&-*){ÄÖÜÅØÆŒÇ}

► Roman
The quick brown fox jumps over a Dog. Zwei Boxkämpfer jagen Eva durch Sylt portez ce vieux Whiskey blond qui fume

► Italic
The quick brown fox jumps over a Dog. Zwei Boxkämpfer jagen Eva durch Sylt portez ce vieux Whiskey blond qui fume une

► Bold
The quick brown fox jumps over a Dog. Zwei Boxkämpfer jagen Eva durch Sylt portez ce vieux Whiskey blond

► Bold Italic
The quick brown fox jumps over a Dog. Zwei Boxkämpfer jagen Eva durch Sylt portez ce vieux Whiskey

► Black
The quick brown fox jumps over a Dog. Zwei Boxkämpfer jagen Eva durch Sylt portez ce

► Black Italic
The quick brown fox jumps over a Dog. Zwei Boxkämpfer jagen Eva durch Sylt portez ce

© FSI 1993

A922   Mac + PC   ⑥   1953: (1853) Lind, Buker, Redick
Willow™

abcdefghijklmnopqrstuvwxyz1234567890[äöüßåøæœç]
ABCDEFGHIJKLMNOPQRSTUVWXYZ(.,;:?!$&-*)(ÄÖÜÅØÆŒÇ)

Wood Type Pack 2:
Birch™, Blackoak™, Madrone™, Poplar™, Willow™, Wood Type Ornaments 2
ⓒ Birch, Latin Extra Condensed

L2814   Mac   ⑥   1990: Tony Forster
Willow™

ABCDEFGHIJKLMNOPQRSTUVWXYZ
1234567890(.,;:?!$&-*)[]ÄÖÜÅØÆŒÇ

BT1414   Mac + PC   ⑥
Windsor™ 2

abcdefghijklmnopqrstuvwxyz[äöüßåøæœç]
ABCDEFGHIJKLMNOPQRSTUVWXYZ
1234567890(.,;:?!$&-*){ÄÖÜÅØÆŒÇ}

aa*a*
EF6646
Windsor 3, Elongated, ExtBdCon

▶ Light
The quick brown fox jumps over a Dog. Zwei Boxkämpfer jagen Eva durch Sylt portez ce vieux Whiskey blond qui fume une

▶ Regular
The quick brown fox jumps over a Dog. Zwei Boxkämpfer jagen Eva durch Sylt portez ce vieux Whis-

EF530   Mac + PC   ⑥
Windsor

abcdefghijklmnopqrstuvwxyz[äöüßåøæœç]
ABCDEFGHIJKLMNOPQRSTUVWXYZ
1234567890(.,;:?!$&-*){ÄÖÜÅØÆŒÇ}

aa*a*
BT867
Windsor, LtCon, Elongated, Outline
BT1414
Windsor™ 2, Lt, Reg

▶ Light
The quick brown fox jumps over a Dog. Zwei Boxkämpfer jagen Eva durch Sylt portez ce vieux Whiskey blond qui fume une pipe aber

▶ Bold
The quick brown fox jumps over a Dog. Zwei Boxkämpfer jagen Eva durch Sylt portez ce vieux Whiskey blond qui

EF6645   Mac + PC   ⑥
Windsor 2

abcdefghijklmnopqrstuvwxyz[äöüßåøæœç]
ABCDEFGHIJKLMNOPQRSTUVWXYZ
1234567890(.,;:?!$&-*)ÄÖÜÅØÆŒÇ

© FSI 1993

▼ EF6645 Mac + PC Windsor 2

aa*a*
BT867
Windsor, LtCon,
Elongated, Outline
BT1414
Windsor™ 2, Lt, Reg

▶ Ultra Heavy
The quick brown fox jumps over a Dog. Zwei Boxkämpfer jagen Eva durch Sylt portez ce vieux Whiskey blond qui fume

▶ Bold Outline
The quick brown fox jumps over a Dog. Zwei Boxkämpfer jagen Eva durch Sylt portez ce vieux Whiskey blond qui

---

EF6646 Mac + PC   (6)
Windsor 3

**abcdefghijklmnopqrstuvwxyzäöüßåøæœç
ABCDEFGHIJKLMNOPQRSTUVWXYZ
1234567890(.,;:?!$&-*)ÄÖÜÅØÆŒÇ**

aa*a*
BT867
Windsor, LtCon,
Elongated, Outline
BT1414
Windsor™ 2, Lt, Reg

▶ Elongated
The quick brown fox jumps over a Dog. Zwei Boxkämpfer jagen Eva durch Sylt portez ce vieux Whiskey blond qui fume une pipe aber echt über die Mauer gesprungen und auch smørebrød en ysjes natuurlijk

▶ Extra Bold Condensed
The quick brown fox jumps over a Dog. Zwei Boxkämpfer jagen Eva durch Sylt portez ce vieux Whiskey blond qui fume une pipe aber echt über die Mauer

---

BT867 Mac + PC   (6)
Windsor

abcdefghijklmnopqrstuvwxyz[äöüßåøæœç]
ABCDEFGHIJKLMNOPQRSTUVWXYZ
1234567890(.,;:?!$&-*){ÄÖÜÅØÆŒÇ}

aa*a*
EF6646
Windsor 3, Elongated,
ExtBdCon

▶ Light Condensed
The quick brown fox jumps over a Dog. Zwei Boxkämpfer jagen Eva durch Sylt portez ce vieux Whiskey blond qui fume une pipe aber echt über die Mauer

▶ Elongated
The quick brown fox jumps over a Dog. Zwei Boxkämpfer jagen Eva durch Sylt portez ce vieux Whiskey blond qui fume une pipe aber echt über die Mauer gesprungen und auch smørebrød en

▶ Outline
The quick brown fox jumps over a Dog. Zwei Boxkämpfer jagen Eva durch Sylt portez ce vieux Whis-

---

A424 Mac + PC
Wood Type Pack 1

Wood Type Pack 1:
Cottonwood®, Ironwood®, Juniper®, Mesquite™, Ponderosa™, Wood Type Ornaments 1

A922 Mac + PC
Wood Type Pack 2

Wood Type Pack 2:
Birch™, Blackoak™, Madrone™, Poplar™, Willow™, Wood Type Ornaments 2

F6344 Mac
A*I Wood Types 1

A*I Wood Types 1:
A*I Barrel, A*I Box Gothic, A*I French XXX Condensed™, A*I Painter™, A*I Tuscan Egyptian™, Antique Condensed

C467 Mac + PC (6)
Woodblock

ABCDEFGHIJKLMNOPQRSTUVWXYZ
1234567890(.,:;?!$&-*)[]◇ÄÖÜÅØÆŒÇ◆

Headlines 81S:
Egiziano™ Black, PL Behemoth Semi Condensed, PL Benguiat Frisky, PL Futura Maxi 1, PL Tower™ Condensed, Quirinus™ Bold, Section™ Bold Condensed, Stratford™ Bold, Woodblock
© Fiorello

SG1125 Mac (2) ✎ 1974: (1925) Adrian Williams
Worcester Round™

abcdefghijklmnopqrstuvwxyz[äöüßåøæœç]
ABCDEFGHIJKLMNOPQRSTUVWXYZ
1234567890(.,:;?!$&-*)ÄÖÜÅØÆŒÇ

SG1188 Mac (2) ✎ 1974: (1925) Adrian Williams
Worcester Round Italic

abcdefghijklmnopqrstuvwxyz[äöüßåøæœç]
ABCDEFGHIJKLMNOPQRSTUVWXYZ
1234567890(.,:;?!$&-)ÄÖÜÅØÆŒÇ*

SG1189 Mac (2) ✎ 1974: (1925) Adrian Williams
Worcester Round Medium

abcdefghijklmnopqrstuvwxyz[äöüßåøæœç]
ABCDEFGHIJKLMNOPQRSTUVWXYZ
1234567890(.,:;?!$&-*)ÄÖÜÅØÆŒÇ

SG1190 Mac (2) ✎ 1974: (1925) Adrian Williams
Worcester Round Bold

abcdefghijklmnopqrstuvwxyz[äöüßåøæœç]
ABCDEFGHIJKLMNOPQRSTUVWXYZ
1234567890(.,:;?!$&-*)ÄÖÜÅØÆŒÇ

SG1191 Mac (6) ✎ 1974: (1925) Adrian Williams
Worcester Round Bold Outline

abcdefghijklmnopqrstuvwxyz[äöüßåøæœç]
ABCDEFGHIJKLMNOPQRSTUVWXYZ
1234567890(.,:;?!$&-*)ÄÖÜÅØÆŒÇ

© FSI 1993

FF6625　Mac + PC　⑤　1993: Neville Brody

FF World™

abcdefghijklmnopqrstuvwxyz[äöüßåøæœç]
ABCDEFGHIJKLMNOPQRSTUVWXYZ
1234567890(.,;:?!$¢-*){ÄÖÜÅØÆŒÇ}

▶ One
The quick brown fox jumps over a Dog. Zwei Boxkämpfer jagen Eva durch Sylt portez ce

▶ Two
The quick brown fox jumps over a Dog. Zwei Boxkämpfer jagen Eva durch Sylt portez ce

▶ Three
The quick brown fox jumps over a Dog. Zwei Boxkämpfer jagen Eva durch Sylt portez ce

FF6622　Mac + PC　②　1993: Martin Wunderlich

FF Wunderlich™

abcdefghijklmnopqrstuvwxyz[äöüßåøæœç]
ABCDEFGHIJKLMNOPQRSTUVWXYZ
1234567890(.,;:?!$&-*){ÄÖÜÅØÆŒÇ}

Rotis Sans, Roxy

▶ Regular
The quick brown fox jumps over a Dog. Zwei Boxkämpfer jagen Eva durch Sylt portez ce vieux Whiskey blond qui fume une

▶ Italic
The quick brown fox jumps over a Dog. Zwei Boxkämpfer jagen Eva durch Sylt portez ce vieux Whiskey blond qui fume une

▶ Medium
The quick brown fox jumps over a Dog. Zwei Boxkämpfer jagen Eva durch Sylt portez ce vieux Whiskey blond qui fume

▶ Medium Italic
The quick brown fox jumps over a Dog. Zwei Boxkämpfer jagen Eva durch Sylt portez ce vieux Whiskey blond qui fume

▶ Bold
The quick brown fox jumps over a Dog. Zwei Boxkämpfer jagen Eva durch Sylt portez ce vieux Whiskey blond qui fume

▶ Bold Italic
The quick brown fox jumps over a Dog. Zwei Boxkämpfer jagen Eva durch Sylt portez ce vieux Whiskey blond qui

© FSI 1993

Lo Breier, Wien/Hamburg, A/D

X
Y
Z

C2983　Mac + PC　⑤
Yearbook™

ABCDEFGHIJKLMNOPQRSTUVWXYZ
1234567890(.,;:?!$&-*)[] {ÄÖÜÅØÆŒÇ}

▶ Outline
THE QUICK BROWN FOX
JUMPS OVER A DOG. ZWEI
BOXKÄMPFER JAGEN EVA
DURCH SYLT PORTEZ CE

▶ Filler
THE QUICK BROWN FOX
JUMPS OVER A DOG. ZWEI
BOXKÄMPFER JAGEN EVA
DURCH SYLT PORTEZ CE

▶ Solid
**THE QUICK BROWN FOX
JUMPS OVER A DOG. ZWEI
BOXKÄMPFER JAGEN EVA
DURCH SYLT PORTEZ CE**

Headlines 94S:
Artistik™, Futura Black, Yearbook™
Quadrus, Princetown, ITC Machine, Superstar

L6601　Mac　④　✎ 1984: Doyald Young
Young Baroque™

abcdefghijklmnopqrstuvwxyz [äöüßåøæœç]
ABCDEFGHIJKLMNOPQRSTUVWXYZ
1234567890(.,;:?!$$~-)&*

© FSI 1993

MC6362 Mac + PC (6)
Zambesi™

ABCDEFGHIJKLMNOPQRSTUVWXYZ
1234567890(.,;:?!$&-*)[]{ÄÖÜÅØÆŒÇ}

BT868 Mac + PC (2) 🖉 1976: Hermann Zapf
ITC Zapf Book® 1

abcdefghijklmnopqrstuvwxyz[äöüßåøæœç]
ABCDEFGHIJKLMNOPQRSTUVWXYZ
1234567890(.,;:?!$&-*){ÄÖÜÅØÆŒÇ}

aa*a*
EF6461
ITC Zapf Book 1, Lt,
LtIta, Demi, DemiIta
EF6462
ITC Zapf Book 2, Med,
MedIta, Hvy, HvyIta
©
Comenius-Antiqua

▶ Light
The quick brown fox jumps over a Dog. Zwei Boxkämpfer jagen Eva durch Sylt portez ce vieux Whiskey blond qui fume

▶ Light Italic
The quick brown fox jumps over a Dog. Zwei Boxkämpfer jagen Eva durch Sylt portez ce vieux Whiskey blond qui fume

▶ Demi
The quick brown fox jumps over a Dog. Zwei Boxkämpfer jagen Eva durch Sylt portez ce vieux Whiskey blond

▶ Demi Italic
The quick brown fox jumps over a Dog. Zwei Boxkämpfer jagen Eva durch Sylt portez ce vieux Whiskey blond qui

BT869 Mac + PC (2) 🖉 1976: Hermann Zapf
ITC Zapf Book 2

abcdefghijklmnopqrstuvwxyz[äöüßåøæœç]
ABCDEFGHIJKLMNOPQRSTUVWXYZ
1234567890(.,;:?!$&-*){ÄÖÜÅØÆŒÇ}

aa*a*
EF6461
ITC Zapf Book 1, Lt,
LtIta, Demi, DemiIta
EF6462
ITC Zapf Book 2, Med,
MedIta, Hvy, HvyIta
©
Comenius-Antiqua

▶ Medium
The quick brown fox jumps over a Dog. Zwei Boxkämpfer jagen Eva durch Sylt portez ce vieux Whiskey blond qui fume

▶ Medium Italic
The quick brown fox jumps over a Dog. Zwei Boxkämpfer jagen Eva durch Sylt portez ce vieux Whiskey blond qui fume

▶ Heavy
The quick brown fox jumps over a Dog. Zwei Boxkämpfer jagen Eva durch Sylt portez ce vieux Whiskey

▶ Heavy Italic
The quick brown fox jumps over a Dog. Zwei Boxkämpfer jagen Eva durch Sylt portez ce vieux Whiskey

A923 Mac + PC (4) 🖉 1979: Hermann Zapf
ITC Zapf Chancery®

abcdefghijklmnopqrstuvwxyz[äöüßåøæœç]
ABCDEFGHIJKLMNOPQRSTUVWXYZ
1234567890(.,;:?!$&-){ÄÖÜÅØÆŒÇ}*

▶ Light
The quick brown fox jumps over a Dog. Zwei Boxkämpfer jagen Eva durch Sylt portez ce vieux Whiskey blond qui fume une pipe aber echt über die Mauer

▶ Light Italic
The quick brown fox jumps over a Dog. Zwei Boxkämpfer jagen Eva durch Sylt portez ce vieux Whiskey blond qui fume une pipe aber echt über die Mauer

© FSI 1993 ▼

aaa
BT1416
ITC Zapf Chancery 1,
Lt, LtIta, Bd
BT1417
ITC Zapf Chancery 2,
Med, MedIta, Demi
EF425
ITC Zapf Chancery 1,
Lt, Demi, Med, Bd
EF426
ITC Zapf Chancery 2,
LtIta, MedIta
🏛 A125
ITC Zapf Chancery /
ITC Zapf Dingbats
👁
Medici, Zapf
Renaissance

▼ A923 MAC + PC **ITC Zapf Chancery®**

▶ Medium
The quick brown fox jumps over a Dog. Zwei Boxkämpfer jagen Eva durch Sylt portez ce vieux Whiskey blond qui fume une pipe aber echt über die Mauer

▶ Medium Italic
The quick brown fox jumps over a Dog. Zwei Boxkämpfer jagen Eva durch Sylt portez ce vieux Whiskey blond qui fume une pipe aber echt über die Mauer

▶ Demi
The quick brown fox jumps over a Dog. Zwei Boxkämpfer jagen Eva durch Sylt portez ce vieux Whiskey blond qui fume une pipe aber echt

▶ Bold
The quick brown fox jumps over a Dog. Zwei Boxkämpfer jagen Eva durch Sylt portez ce vieux Whiskey blond qui fume une

---

A125 MAC + PC
ITC Zapf Chancery / ITC Zapf Dingbats

ITC Zapf Chancery / ITC Zapf Dingbats:
ITC Zapf Chancery, ITC Zapf Dingbats®

EF621 MAC + PC ② ✎ 1977: Hermann Zapf
ITC Zapf International® 1

abcdefghijklmnopqrstuvwxyz[äöüßåøæœç]
ABCDEFGHIJKLMNOPQRSTUVWXYZ
1234567890(.,;:?!$&-*){ÄÖÜÅØÆŒÇ}

aaa
BT1421
ITC Zapf International 1, Lt, LtIta, Demi, Demilta
C6424
ITC Zapf International, Lt, LtIta, Med, MedIta, Demi, Demilta, Hvy, HvyIta
👁
Edison

▶ Light
The quick brown fox jumps over a Dog. Zwei Boxkämpfer jagen Eva durch Sylt portez ce vieux Whiskey blond

▶ Light Italic
The quick brown fox jumps over a Dog. Zwei Boxkämpfer jagen Eva durch Sylt portez ce vieux Whiskey blond qui

▶ Demi
The quick brown fox jumps over a Dog. Zwei Boxkämpfer jagen Eva durch Sylt portez ce

▶ Demi Italic
The quick brown fox jumps over a Dog. Zwei Boxkämpfer jagen Eva durch Sylt portez ce vieux

---

EF622 MAC + PC ② ✎ 1977: Hermann Zapf
ITC Zapf International 2

abcdefghijklmnopqrstuvwxyz[äöüßåøæœç]
ABCDEFGHIJKLMNOPQRSTUVWXYZ
1234567890(.,;:?!$&-*){ÄÖÜÅØÆŒÇ}

aaa
BT1422
ITC Zapf International 2, Med, MedIta, Hvy, HvyIta
C6424
ITC Zapf International, Lt, LtIta, Med, MedIta, Demi, Demilta, Hvy, HvyIta
👁
Edison

▶ Medium
The quick brown fox jumps over a Dog. Zwei Boxkämpfer jagen Eva durch Sylt portez ce vieux Whiskey

▶ Medium Italic
The quick brown fox jumps over a Dog. Zwei Boxkämpfer jagen Eva durch Sylt portez ce vieux Whiskey blond

▶ Heavy
The quick brown fox jumps over a Dog. Zwei Boxkämpfer jagen Eva durch Sylt portez ce

▶ Heavy Italic
The quick brown fox jumps over a Dog. Zwei Boxkämpfer jagen Eva durch Sylt portez ce

© FSI 1993

SG1126 Mac ② ✎ 1987: Hermann Zapf
Zapf Renaissance™ Light

abcdefghijklmnopqrstuvwxyz[äöüßåøæœç]
ABCDEFGHIJKLMNOPQRSTUVWXYZ
1234567890(.,:;?!$&-*)ÄÖÜÅØÆŒÇ

SG1192 Mac ② ✎ 1987: Hermann Zapf
Zapf Renaissance Light Italic

abcdefghijklmnopqrstuvwxyz[äöüßåøæœç]
ABCDEFGHIJKLMNOPQRSTUVWXYZ
1234567890(.,:;?!$&-)ÄÖÜÅØÆŒÇ*

SG1127 Mac ② ✎ 1987: Hermann Zapf
Zapf Renaissance Light Italic Swash

a̲ bcde f̲ghijklm n̲ opqur̓st ̔ u̓ v̓ wxyz[Aſpffll]
ABCDEFGHIJKLMNOPQRSTUVWXYZ
1234567890❦ vt❦ ¶ ✝vr&zGʒfifffl

SG1193 Mac ② ✎ 1987: Hermann Zapf
Zapf Renaissance Book

abcdefghijklmnopqrstuvwxyz[äöüßåøæœç]
ABCDEFGHIJKLMNOPQRSTUVWXYZ
1234567890(.,:;?!$&-*)ÄÖÜÅØÆŒÇ

SG1194 Mac ② ✎ 1987: Hermann Zapf
Zapf Renaissance Italic

abcdefghijklmnopqrstuvwxyz[äöüßåøæœç]
ABCDEFGHIJKLMNOPQRSTUVWXYZ
1234567890(.,:;?!$&-)ÄÖÜÅØÆŒÇ*

SG1196 Mac ② ✎ 1987: Hermann Zapf
Zapf Renaissance Italic Swash

a̲ bcde f̲ghijklm n̲ opqur̓st ̔ u̓ v̓ wxyz[Aſpffll]
ABCDEFGHIJKLMNOPQRSTUVWXYZ
1234567890❦ vt❦ ¶ ✝vr&zGʒfifffl

SG1195 Mac ② ✎ 1987: Hermann Zapf
Zapf Renaissance Bold

abcdefghijklmnopqrstuvwxyz[äöüßåøæœç]
ABCDEFGHIJKLMNOPQRSTUVWXYZ
1234567890(.,:;?!$&-*)ÄÖÜÅØÆŒÇ

© FSI 1993

Zeitgeist™

M1616 MAC + PC ⑤ 1990: Michael Johnson

abcdefghijklmnopqrstuvwxyz[äöüßåøæœç]
ABCDEFGHIJKLMNOPQRSTUVWXYZ
1234567890(.,:;?!$&-*){ÄÖÜÅØÆŒÇ}

▶ **Regular**
The quick brown fox jumps over a Dog. Zwei Boxkämpfer jagen Eva durch Sylt portez ce vieux Whiskey blond qui fume une pipe aber echt über die Mauer gesprungen und auch

▶ **Alternates**
0234567890
ABCDEFGHIJKLMNOPQRSTUVWXYZ
abcdefggshijckchm n ofspqr stt u v wxy zy

▶ **Italic**
The quick brown fox jumps over a Dog. Zwei Boxkämpfer jagen Eva durch Sylt portez ce vieux Whiskey blond qui fume une pipe aber echt über die Mauer gesprungen und auch

▶ **Bold**
The quick brown fox jumps over a Dog. Zwei Boxkämpfer jagen Eva durch Sylt portez ce vieux Whiskey blond qui fume une pipe aber echt über die Mauer gesprungen und auch

▶ **Condensed**
The quick brown fox jumps over a Dog. Zwei Boxkämpfer jagen Eva durch Sylt portez ce vieux Whiskey blond qui fume une pipe aber echt über die Mauer gesprungen und auch smørrebrød en ysjes natuurlijk

▶ **Crazy Paving**
The quick brown fox jumps over a Dog. Zwei Boxkämpfer jagen Eva durch Sylt portez ce vieux Whiskey blond qui fume une pipe aber echt über die Mauer gesprungen und auch

▶ **Cameo**
The quick brown fox jumps over a Dog. Zwei Boxkämpfer jagen Eva durch Sylt portez ce vieux Whiskey blond qui fume une pipe aber echt über die Mauer gesprungen

▶ **Expert Regular**
0123456789 0ffiflffiffl-
(1/12/23/34/45/56/67/78/89/90) ($¢₨¢)ª THE QUICK BROWN FOX JUMPS OVER A DOG ZWEI BOXKÄMPFER JAGEN EVA DURCH SYLT PORTEZ CE

▶ **Expert Italic**
0123456789 0ffiflffiffl-
(1/12/23/34/45/56/67/78/89/90) ($¢₨¢)ª

▶ **Expert Bold**
0123456789 0ffiflffiffl-
(1/12/23/34/45/56/67/78/89/90) ($¢₨¢)ª

▶ **Expert Condensed**
0123456789 0ffiflffiffl-
(1/12/23/34/45/56/67/78/89/90) ($¢₨¢)ª

▶ **ZeitgeistExpertMT-Cameo**
0123456789 0ffiflffiffl-
(1/12/23/34/45/56/67/78/89/90) ($¢₨¢)ª

Zeppelin™

C2523 MAC + PC ⑥ 1927-29: Rudolf Koch

abcdefghijklmnopqrstuvwxyz[äöüßåøæœç]
ABCDEFGHIJKLMNOPQRSTUVWXYZ
1234567890(.,:;?!$&-*) { ÄÖÜÅØÆŒÇ }

Headlines 87S:
Greeting Monotone™, Koloss™, Phenix™ American, Phosphor™, Zeppelin™
⊙ Kabel, ITC Kabel

© FSI 1993

6 / 6pt FF Lizard / Zero set

7 / 7pt FF Lizard / Zero set

8 / 8pt FF Lizard / Zero set

9 / 9pt FF Lizard / Zero set

10 / 10pt FF Lizard / Zero set

11 / 11pt FF Lizard / Zero set

12 / 12pt FF Lizard / Zero set

14 / 14pt FF Lizard / Zero set

16 / 16pt FF Lizard / Zero set

18 / 18pt FF Lizard / Zero set

24 / 24pt FF Lizard / Zero set

20 / 20pt FF Lizard / Zero set

CHARACTERS IN FONT

8 / 8pt FF Lizard / −20 set, with zero pair kerning

8 / 8pt FF Lizard / −15 set, with zero pair kerning

8 / 8pt FF Lizard / −10 set, with zero pair kerning

8 / 8pt FF Lizard / 0 set, with zero pair kerning

8 / 8pt FF Lizard / −10 set

8 / 9pt FF Lizard / −10 set

8 / 10pt FF Lizard / −10 set

8 / 11pt FF Lizard / −10 set

Ed Cleary, Toronto, CDN

M6412 Mac + PC ⑧
Almanac Pi (Zodiac Symbols)

Monotype Pi Fonts:
Almanac (Zodiac Symbols), Botanical, Circle Frame Pos. & Neg., Directions, Sports One & Two,
Square Frame Pos. & Neg., Transport, Vacation

C2600 Mac + PC ⑧
Agfa Pi & Symbols: Animals

M2836 Mac + PC ⑧
Arabesque Ornaments

▶ One

▶ Two

Rococo Ornaments: Arabesque Ornaments, Rococo Ornaments

ED447 Mac ⑧
Arrowhead Dynamic

▶ Regular

▶ Bold

▶ Heavy

Arrowhead Dynamic:
Arrowhead Dynamic, BulletsNstuff

© FSI 1993

ED447 Mac
Arrowhead Dynamic

Arrowhead Dynamic:
Arrowhead Dynamic, BulletsNstuff

C2601 Mac + PC
Agfa Pi & Symbols: Astrology 1

C2602 Mac + PC
Agfa Pi & Symbols: Astrology 2

C2603 Mac + PC
Agfa Pi & Symbols: Astrology 3

A2539 Mac + PC
Linotype Astrology Pi

▶ One (simple)   ▶ Two (ornate)

A2772 Mac + PC
Audio Pi

Linotype Audio Pi:
Audio Pi, Warning Pi

© FSI 1993

A2772 Mac + PC ⑧
Linotype Audio Pi, Warning Pi

Linotype Audio Pi:
Audio Pi, Warning Pi

LH6641 Mac + PC ⑧ (Georges Auriol, 1901-04)
Auriol Flowers

Auriol

▶ Flowers One

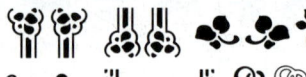

▶ Flowers Two

▶ Vignette Sylvie

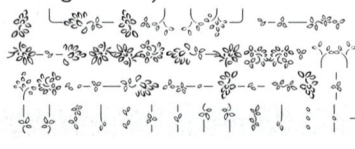

SS2971 PC ⑧
Printbar Barcode 39

SS2970 PC ⑧
Printbar EAN-8/13

▶ EAN-13

▶ EAN-8

SS2972 PC ⑧
Printbar Barcode 2 of 5

SS6842 PC ⑧
Barcode UPC A

0 05500 31695 8

SS6843 PC
Barcode 128

▶ Barcode 128B

▶ Barcode 128C

BR1013 Mac ⑧
Printbar™ (Low-res) UPC/EAN

0 05500 31695 8

▶ UPC-A

0 05500 31695 8

▶ UPC-E

0 123456 5

▶ EAN-8

4031 3511

▶ EAN-13

3 218273 105064

aaa BR1014
Printbar (Hi-res) UPC/EAN, UPCA, UPCE, EAN8/13
BR1015
Printbar (Combo) UPC/EAN, UPCA, UPCE, EAN8/13

BR1014 Mac ⑧
Printbar (Hi-res) UPC/EAN

see above

BR1015 Mac ⑧
Printbar Combi Pack (Low+Hi-res) UPC/EAN

see above

© FSI 1993

BR1158 Mac ⑧
Printbar (Low-res) Barcode 39

PZN-1894063

▶ Barcode 39, high density, human readable

▶ Barcode 39, high density

PZN-1894063

▶ Barcode 39, low density, human readable

PZN-1894063

BR1140 Mac ⑧
Printbar (Hi-res) Barcode 39
see above

BR1159 Mac ⑧
Printbar Combi Pack (Low+Hi-res) Barcode 39
see above

BR1160 Mac ⑧
Printbar (Low-res) Interleaved 2/5

012345

▶ Interleaved 2/5 low density, human readable

▶ Interleaved 2/5 low density

012345

▶ Interleaved 2/5 medium density, human readable

▶ Interleaved 2/5 medium density

012345

BR1161 Mac ⑧
Printbar (Hi-res) Interleaved 2/5
see above

BR1162 Mac ⑧
Printbar (Low+Hi-res) Interleaved 2/5
see above

© FSI 1993

& 5

A898 Mac + PC
Border

Border Pi:
Border, European Pi

A898 Mac + PC
Border Pi

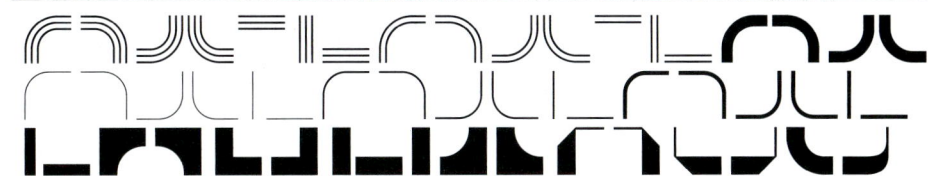

Border Pi:
Border, European Pi

C2604 Mac + PC
Agfa Pi & Symbols: Borders & Ornaments 1

C2605 Mac + PC
Agfa Pi & Symbols: Borders & Ornaments 2

C2606 Mac + PC
Agfa Pi & Symbols: Borders & Ornaments 3

C2607 Mac + PC
Agfa Pi & Symbols: Borders & Ornaments 4

C2608 Mac + PC
Agfa Pi & Symbols: Borders & Ornaments 5

© FSI 1993

C2609 Mac + PC ⑧
Agfa Pi & Symbols: Borders & Ornaments 6

M6412 Mac + PC ⑧
Botanical Pi

Monotype Pi Fonts:
Almanac (Zodiac Symbols), Botanical, Circle Frame Pos. & Neg., Directions, Sports One & Two, Square Frame Pos. & Neg., Transport, Vacation

ED447 Mac ⑧
BulletsNstuff

Arrowhead Dynamic:
Arrowhead Dynamic, BulletsNstuff

A889 Mac + PC ⑧
Bundesbahn Pi

▶ No. 1

▶ No. 2

▶ No. 3

C2610 Mac + PC ⑧
Agfa Pi & Symbols: Business & Services 1

© FSI 1993

C2611 Mac + PC ⑧
Agfa Pi & Symbols: Business & Services 2

C2612 Mac + PC ⑧
Agfa Pi & Symbols: Business & Services 3

FF2799 Mac + PC ⑧ — 1991: Johannes Erler
FF Care Pack™

A020 Mac + PC ⑧ — 1986: Lynne Garell
Carta™

A891 Mac + PC ⑧ — 1990: (William Caslon, 1725) Carol Twombly
Adobe Caslon Ornaments

Adobe Caslon Expert Collection:
Adobe Caslon Expert, Adobe Caslon Ornaments

LH2863 Mac + PC ⑧
Linotype Chemistra Pi

A895 Mac + PC ⑧
Cheq™

M6412 Mac + PC ⑧
Circle Frame Pos. & Neg.

ⒶⒷⒸⒹⒺⒻⒼⒽⒾⒿⓀⓁⓂⓃⓄⓅⓆⓇⓈⓉ
ⓊⓋⓌⓍⓎⓏ⓪①②③④⑤⑥⑦⑧⑨
⓿❶❷❸❹❺❻❼❽❾➊➋➌➍➎➏➐➑➒

▶ Positive
ⒶⒷⒸⒹⒺⒻⒼⒽⒾⒿⓀⓁⓂⓃ
ⓄⓅⓆⓇⓈⓉⓊⓋⓌⓍⓎⓏ
⓪①②③④⑤⑥⑦⑧⑨
⓿❶❷❸❹❺❻❼❽❾➊➋➌➍➎➏➐➑➒

▶ Negative
ⒶⒷⒸⒹⒺⒻⒼⒽⒾⒿⓀⓁⓂⓃ
ⓄⓅⓆⓇⓈⓉⓊⓋⓌⓍⓎⓏ
⓪①②③④⑤⑥⑦⑧⑨
⓿❶❷❸❹❺❻❼❽❾➊➋➌➍➎➏➐➑➒

📦 Monotype Pi Fonts:
Almanac (Zodiac Symbols), Botanical, Circle Frame Pos. & Neg., Directions, Sports One & Two, Square Frame Pos. & Neg., Transport, Vacation

FB1052 Mac + PC ⑧ ✎ 1991: David Berlow
City Ornaments™

📦 Bureau Ornaments™:
City Ornaments™, Town Ornaments™, Village Ornaments™

ATF336 Mac ⑧ ✎ T. M. Cleland
Cleland Border 1805™

📦 ATF Set 1:
Bernhard Fashion, Cleland Border 1805, Thompson Quillscript, Wedding Text

C2613 Mac + PC ⑧
Agfa Pi & Symbols: Commercial 1

C2614 Mac + PC ⑧
Agfa Pi & Symbols: Commercial 2

© FSI 1993

BT1428 Mac + PC
Commercial Pi

C2615 Mac + PC
Agfa Pi & Symbols: Communication 1

C2616 Mac + PC
Agfa Pi & Symbols: Communication 2

C2617 Mac + PC
Agfa Pi & Symbols: Communication 3

C2618 Mac + PC
Agfa Pi & Symbols: Communication 4

C2619 Mac + PC
Agfa Pi & Symbols: Communication 5

C2620 Mac + PC
Agfa Pi & Symbols: Communication 6

© FSI 1993

C2621 Mac + PC ⑧
Agfa Pi & Symbols: Communication 7

C2622 Mac ⑧
Agfa Pi & Symbols: Communication 8

C2623 Mac + PC ⑧
Agfa Pi & Symbols: Credit Cards

C2623 Mac + PC ⑧ — 1989 Joseph Treacy/Carol Treacy
TF Crossword™

TF Crossword™:
TF Puzzle™, TF Solution™

A2537 Mac + PC ⑧
Linotype Decoration Pi

▶ One   ▶ Two

M6412 Mac + PC ⑧
Directions

Monotype Pi Fonts:
Almanac (Zodiac Symbols), Botanical, Circle Frame Pos. & Neg., Directions, Sports One & Two, Square Frame Pos. & Neg., Transport, Vacation

FF2959 Mac + PC ⑧ — 1992: Manfred Klein
FF Double Digits™

© FSI 1993

▼ FF2959 Mac + PC   Double Digits™

▶ Round

▶ Square

▶ Diamond

▶ SuperSquare

C2624 Mac + PC

Agfa Pi & Symbols: Ecology

A2769 Mac + PC

EEC/Olympic Pi

EEC/Olympic Pi:
EEC, Olympic Pi

A2769 Mac + PC

EEC

EEC/Olympic Pi:
EEC, Olympic Pi

A898 Mac + PC

European Pi

▶ One

▶ Two

▶ Three

▶ Four

Border Pi:
Border Pi, European Pi

© FSI 1993

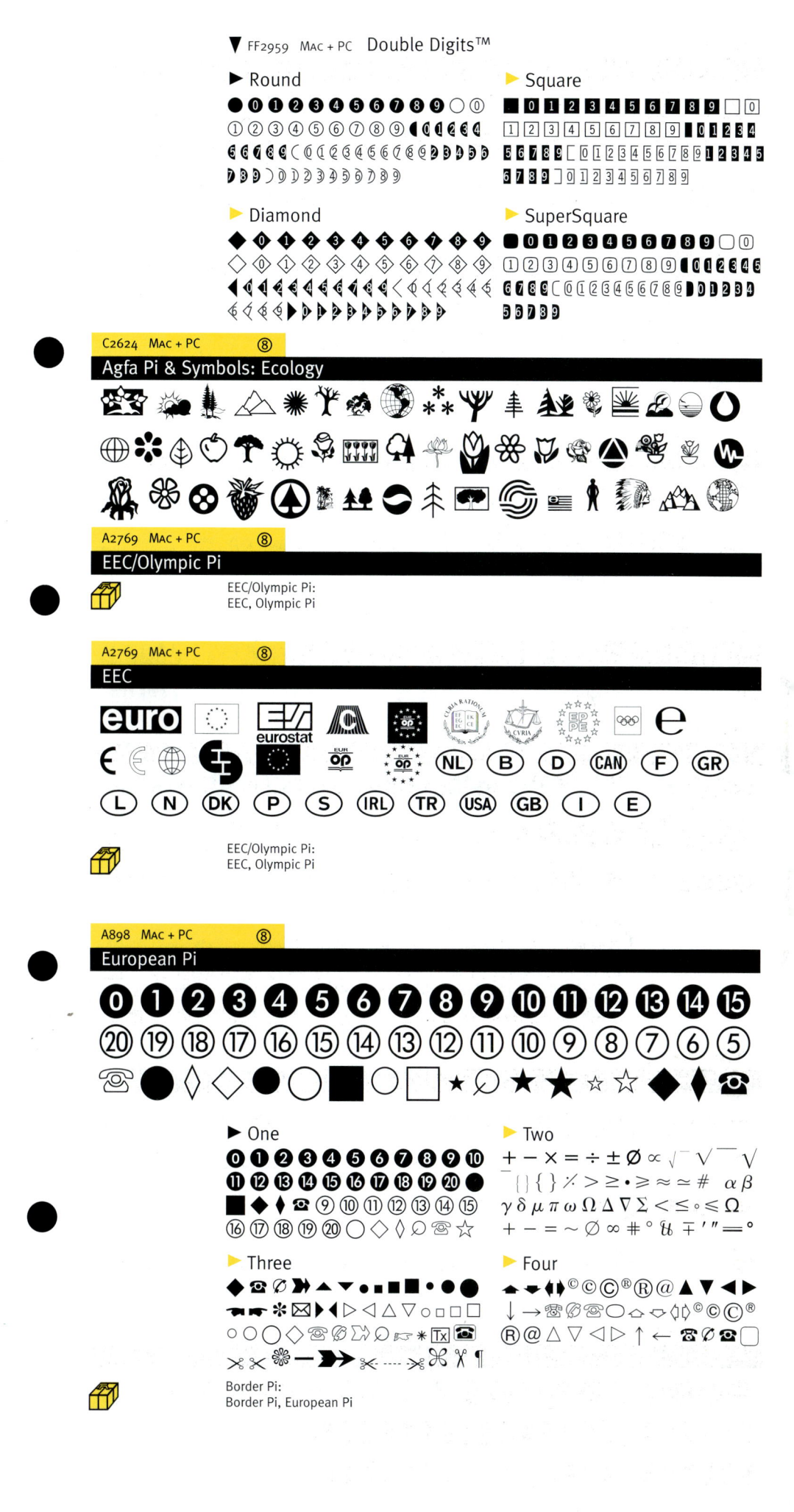

& 12

G1515 Mac + PC ⑧
Figures Square™

$ 0 1 2 3 4 5 6 7 8 9 , .
0 1 2 3 4 5 6 7 8 9 10 11 12 13 14 15
16 17 18 19 , .

G2786 Mac + PC ⑧
Fleurons, Folio 1™

FF6626 Mac + PC ⑧ 1993: Pierre di Sciullo
FF Fléches™

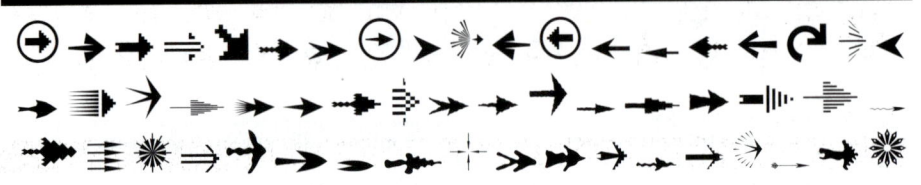

▶ LeftRight

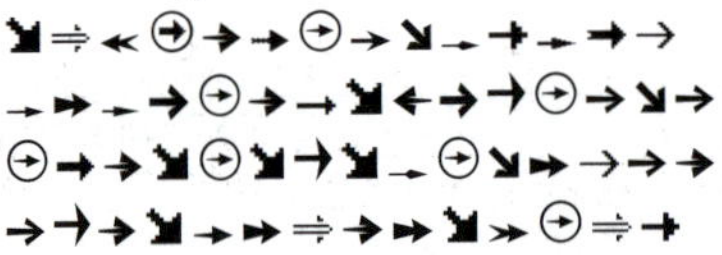

▶ UpDown

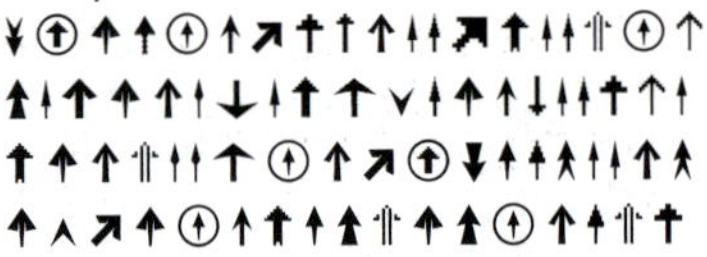

A2743 Mac + PC ⑧
Fractions

1234567890 1234567890 1234567890

1234567890 1234567890

▶ Helvetica Fractions

23^2 169^{23} $13^{2/3}$ 66^6_9 $\frac{232}{999}$ $^{169}/_{123}$
01234567890 1234567890
1234567890 1234567890 1234567890

▶ Helvetica Bold Fractions

23^2 169^{23} $13^{2/3}$ 66^6_9 $\frac{232}{999}$ $^{169}/_{123}$
01234567890 1234567890
1234567890 1234567890 1234567890

▶ New Century Schoolbook Fractions

23^2 169^{23} $13^{2/3}$ 66^6_9 $\frac{232}{999}$ $^{169}/_{123}$
01234567890 1234567890
1234567890 1234567890 1234567890

▶ New Century Schoolbook Bold Fractions

23^2 169^{23} $13^{2/3}$ 66^6_9 $\frac{232}{999}$ $^{169}/_{123}$
01234567890 1234567890
1234567890 1234567890 1234567890

A2744 Mac + PC ⑧
Linotype Game Pi

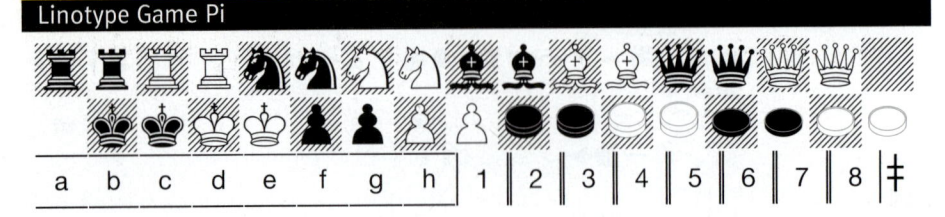

a b c d e f g h 1 2 3 4 5 6 7 8 ‡

© FSI 1993

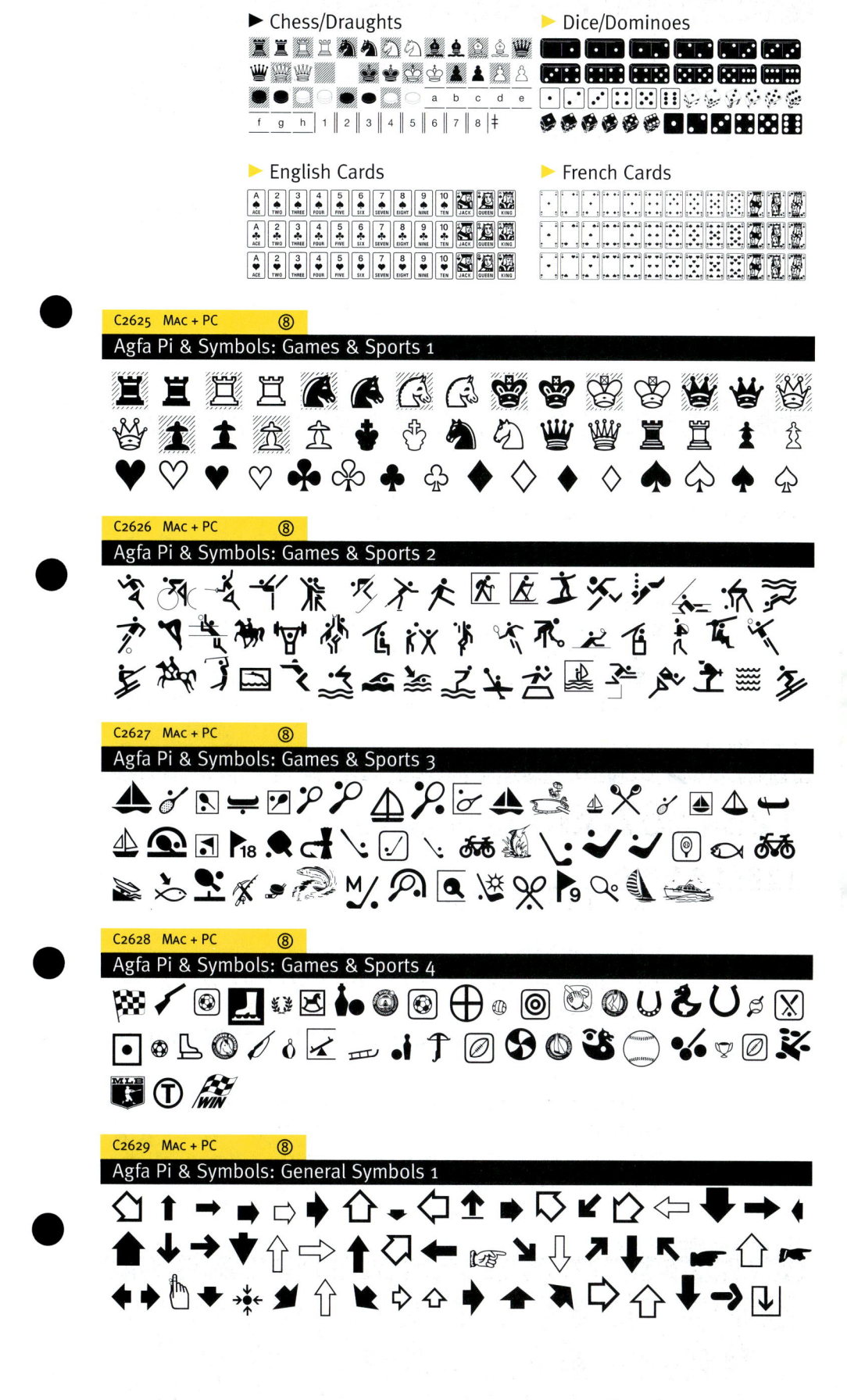

▼ A2744 Mac + PC   Linotype Game Pi

► Chess/Draughts

► Dice/Dominoes

► English Cards

► French Cards

C2625 Mac + PC
Agfa Pi & Symbols: Games & Sports 1

C2626 Mac + PC
Agfa Pi & Symbols: Games & Sports 2

C2627 Mac + PC
Agfa Pi & Symbols: Games & Sports 3

C2628 Mac + PC
Agfa Pi & Symbols: Games & Sports 4

C2629 Mac + PC
Agfa Pi & Symbols: General Symbols 1

© FSI 1993

C2630	Mac + PC	⑧

Agfa Pi & Symbols: General Symbols 2

C2631	Mac + PC	⑧

Agfa Pi & Symbols: General Symbols 3

C2632	Mac + PC	⑧

Agfa Pi & Symbols: General Symbols 4

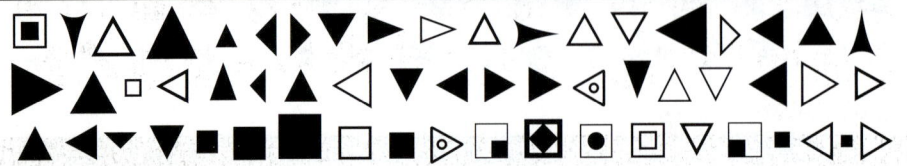

C2633	Mac + PC	⑧

Agfa Pi & Symbols: General Symbols 5

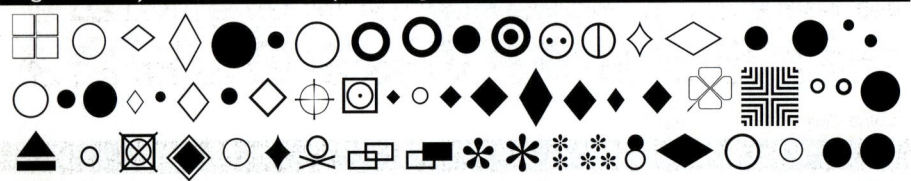

G876	Mac + PC	②	✎ F. W. Goudy

Goudy Initials No. 296™ (EPS)

G624	Mac + PC	③	✎ 1931: C. H. Griffith

Granjon Fleurons

A2536	Mac + PC	⑧

Linotype Holiday Pi

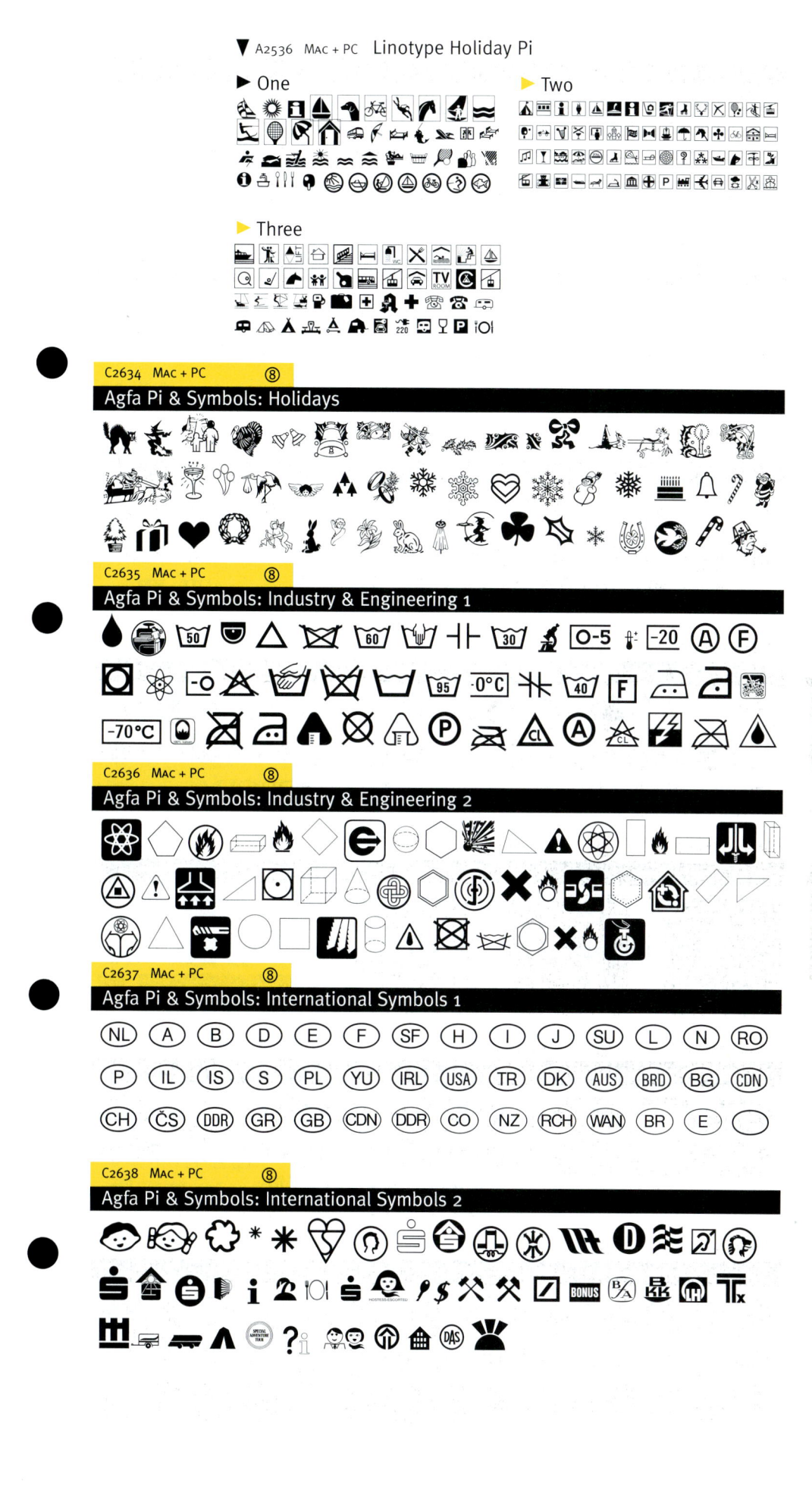

▼ A2536 Mac + PC   Linotype Holiday Pi

► One

► Two

► Three

C2634 Mac + PC
Agfa Pi & Symbols: Holidays

C2635 Mac + PC
Agfa Pi & Symbols: Industry & Engineering 1

C2636 Mac + PC
Agfa Pi & Symbols: Industry & Engineering 2

C2637 Mac + PC
Agfa Pi & Symbols: International Symbols 1

C2638 Mac + PC
Agfa Pi & Symbols: International Symbols 2

LG6106 Mac ⑧
Key Art

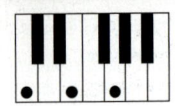

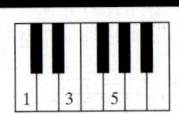

C2639 Mac + PC ⑧
Agfa Pi & Symbols: Legal Trademarks

C2640 Mac + PC ⑧
Agfa Pi & Symbols: Logos - Company 1

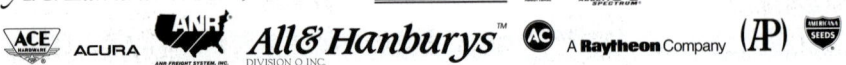

C2641 Mac ⑧
Agfa Pi & Symbols: Logos - Company 2

C2642 Mac + PC ⑧
Agfa Pi & Symbols: Logos - Company 3

C2643 Mac ⑧
Agfa Pi & Symbols: Logos - Company 4

C2644 Mac + PC ⑧
Agfa Pi & Symbols: Logos - Company 5

C2645 Mac
Agfa Pi & Symbols: Logos - Company 6

C2646 Mac
Agfa Pi & Symbols: Logos - Company 7

C2647 Mac + PC
Agfa Pi & Symbols: Logos - Company 8

C2648 Mac
Agfa Pi & Symbols: Logos - Company 9

C2649 Mac + PC
Agfa Pi & Symbols: Logos - Company 10

C2650 Mac
Agfa Pi & Symbols: Logos - Company 11

C2651 Mac + PC
Agfa Pi & Symbols: Logos - Company 12

© FSI 1993

C2652 Mac
Agfa Pi & Symbols: Logos - Company 13

Prudential, Pennzoil, Polaroid, Northeast Savings, Purolator courier, Oral-B, piggly wiggly, ProAd, Pizza Hut, Neff Courier Group, PPG Industries, Phillips 66, Porsche, OLGA, Philips, Philips, Porsche Audi, Oscar Mayer, Polaroid, Pontiac, Paramount, nt, Ortho, Oshawa Foods

C2653 Mac
Agfa Pi & Symbols: Logos - Company 14

Pacific Power, Pepsi-Cola, Oracle, Paramount Communications Company, Syntellect Inc., Philips, PSDI, Pepsi, PBG Pepsi-Cola Bottling Group Food Service, BancOhio National Bank, Paramount Pictures, Pizza Hut, PP, Plus System, PAC-MAN

C2654 Mac
Agfa Pi & Symbols: Logos - Company 15

Qantas, RCA Records, RIGGS, RTL Television, Ralphs, Rogers, Raytheon, Rexall, RDM, Raytheon, Qantas, Ralphs, Southern States, Riverside, Sherwin Williams Automot Finishes, Radio Shack, Roche, Royal 76, PILLOWLINE, Rheem

C2655 Mac
Agfa Pi & Symbols: Logos - Company 16

7up, SINGER, SEARS, Sealy, Sunbeam, SQUIBB Marsam, SONY, Standard, Sherwin Williams, SASSON, Suzuki, SAFEWAY, STP, Schlitz, Smokey, SUNOCO, SPERRY, Shell, $, Puch, BMW, SQUIBB, Serta, SIRE, 7up, SAAB, Schmidt, SENTRY, Sears, Simplicity, SB, SUBARU, SIMMONS, SHELL

C2656 Mac
Agfa Pi & Symbols: Logos - Company 17

SEALED POWER, SUPERIOR GIFT CALENDARS, SIMENS, Seessel's, SOLVAY, Security Savings Bank, STANDARD Lederle PRODUCTS, SUDWEST, SKF, CPC Schneider International, SmithKline Beecham, STATOIL, L·S·AYRES, SAS, STAR BANK

C2657 Mac
Agfa Pi & Symbols: Logos - Company 18

TEXACO, TDI South Yorkshire Passenger Transport Executive, TWA, TEXACO, UNIFORM, Toop, Tertyl, U-HAUL, UNION CARBIDE, UNIROYAL, Tex, USTA Integrity in Tourism, TRW, U.S. ROYAL TIRES, TORO, TA, True Value HARDWARE STORES, UNION CARBIDE, TANDY, AUTHENTIC, TENNECO, TALMAN HOME Talman Insurance Services, Inc., TEXACO, TEKNOWLEDGE

C2658 Mac
Agfa Pi & Symbols: Logos - Company 19

USAA, VHS, UNITED TECHNOL CHEMICA SYSTEMS, VARIG, UC UNITED CASUALTY INSURANCE COMPANY OF AMERICA, UKV, USLIFE, VW, UNIVERS, Vigorena, MAUNA KEA PROPERTIES, UAL, UNITED AIRLINES, ABS, UNITED, GAB, V·A·G, VW, VARIO, ValuRite, Valvoline, V·A·G, VW

C2659 Mac + PC ⑧
Agfa Pi & Symbols: Logos - Company 20

C2660 Mac ⑧
Agfa Pi & Symbols: Logos - Company 21

C2661 Mac ⑧
Agfa Pi & Symbols: Logos - Company 22

C2662 Mac ⑧
Agfa Pi & Symbols: Logos - Company 23

C2663 Mac ⑧
Agfa Pi & Symbols: Logos - Company 24

C2664 Mac + PC ⑧
Agfa Pi & Symbols: Logos - Company 25

C2665 Mac + PC ⑧
Agfa Pi & Symbols: Logos - Company 26

© FSI 1993

| C2666 | Mac + PC | ⑧ |

Agfa Pi & Symbols: Logos - Company 27

| C2667 | Mac + PC | ⑧ |

Agfa Pi & Symbols: Logos - Company 28

| C2668 | Mac | ⑧ |

Agfa Pi & Symbols: Logos - Company 29

| C2669 | Mac + PC | ⑧ |

Agfa Pi & Symbols: Logos - Service 1

| C2670 | Mac + PC | ⑧ |

Agfa Pi & Symbols: Logos - Service 2

| C2671 | Mac | ⑧ |

Agfa Pi & Symbols: Logos - Service 3

| A911 | Mac + PC | ⑧ | ✎ 1988: C. Bigelow, K. Holmes |

Lucida Math

▼ A911 Mac + PC Lucida Math

▶ Expert

{ { [[[ ]] ⟨ ⟨⟨ ⟩⟩ ⟩ ((( )))
Σ Σ ⊔ ⊔ ⊗ ⊗ ∏ ∏ ∪ ∪ ∩

▶ Symbol

∝ ∕ ∞ ∈ ∃ △ ▽ ∀ ⊢ ¬ ∅ ℜ ℑ ⊤ ⊥ ℵ
𝒜 ℬ 𝒞 𝒟 ℰ ℱ 𝒢 ℋ ℐ 𝒥 ‡ ♣ ¶ ◊ ♡
× ∗ ÷ ⋄ ± ∓ ≈ ⊂ ⊃ ≪ ≫ ▷ ◁ ⇐
⇒ ⇑ ⇓ ⇔ ⌢ ⌣ ⊆ ⊇ ≤ ≥ ⊕ ⊖ ⊘ ⊗

▶ Italic

ω ε ϑ ϖ ς φ ▷ ◁ Λ Ξ Π
Σ Υ Φ Ψ Ω α β γ δ ε ζ η θ
ι κ λ μ ν ξ π ρ σ τ υ φ χ
a b c d e f g h i j k l m p

FF2962 Mac + PC ⑧
FF Mambo Initials

FF Mambo:
Mambo Light, Medium, Bold, Initials

ET6388 Mac + PC ⑧ ✎ 1992: Judith Sutcliffe
Maskerade™

Petroglyph Combo:
Petroglyph, Maskerade, Serpents

C2672 Mac + PC ⑧
Agfa Pi & Symbols: Math & Technical 1

C2673 Mac + PC ⑧
Agfa Pi & Symbols: Math & Technical 2

C2674 Mac + PC ⑧
Agfa Pi & Symbols: Math & Technical 3

© FSI 1993

C2675 Mac + PC ⑧
Agfa Pi & Symbols: Math & Technical 4

C2676 Mac + PC ⑧
Agfa Pi & Symbols: Math & Technical 5

C2677 Mac + PC ⑧
Agfa Pi & Symbols: Math & Technical 6

C2678 Mac + PC ⑧
Agfa Pi & Symbols: Math & Technical 7

C2679 Mac + PC ⑧
Agfa Pi & Symbols: Math & Technical 8

C2680 Mac + PC ⑧
Agfa Pi & Symbols: Math & Technical 9

C2681 Mac + PC ⑧
Agfa Pi & Symbols: Math & Technical 10

Α Β Δ Ε Φ Γ Η Ι Κ Λ Μ Ν Ο Π Ω Ρ Σ Τ Υ Ψ Χ Ξ Ζ α β ϑ δ ε φ
φ γ η ι σ κ λ μ ν ο π ϱ s τ υ θ ψ χ ξ ζ + = × ÷ # ╱ ∂ , . : ; − -) —
0 1 2 3 4 5 6 7 8 9

C2682 Mac + PC ⑧
Agfa Pi & Symbols: Math & Technical 11

ΑΒΔΕΦΓΗΙΚΛΜΝΟΠΩΡΣΤΥΘΨΧΞΖ α α β ϑ δ ε φ φ γ η ι ϰ λ μ ν ο π ω ϱ σ τ υ θ ψ χ ξ ζ + = × ÷ # … ╱ : ∂ , . : ; – -) √ — 0 1 2 3 4 5 6 7 8 9

C2683 Mac + PC ⑧
Agfa Pi & Symbols: Math & Technical 12

ΑΒΔΕΦΓΗΙΚΛΜΝΟΠΩΡΣΤΥΘΨΧΞΖ
αβϑδεφγηισφκλμνοπωρτυθψχξζ

C2684 Mac + PC ⑧
Agfa Pi & Symbols: Math & Technical 13

ΑΒΔΕΦΓΗΙΚΛΜΝΟΠΩΡΣΤΥΘΨΧΞΖ
αβϑδεφγηισκλφμνοπωρτυθψχξζ

C2685 Mac + PC ⑧
Agfa Pi & Symbols: Math & Technical 14

ABCDEFGHIJKLMNOPQRSTUVWXYZ:;?-)!/%]
abcdefghijklmnopqrstuvwxyz'*&,.0123456789

C2686 Mac + PC ⑧
Agfa Pi & Symbols: Math & Technical 15

ABCDEFGHIJKLMNOPQRSTUVWXYZ:;?-/%)!
abcdefghijklmnopqrstuvwxyz'*&,.0123456789]

C2687 Mac + PC ⑧
Agfa Pi & Symbols: Math & Technical 16

ABCDEFGHIJKLMNOPQRSTUVWXYZ'/%&,!*
abcdefghijklmnopqrstuvwxyz:;?-).0123456789]

C2688 Mac + PC ⑧
Agfa Pi & Symbols: Math & Technical 17

ABCDEFGHIJKLMNOPQRSTUVWXYZ'/%&,!*
abcdefghijklmnopqrstuvwxyz0123456789.'.-:;?)]

BT1429 Mac + PC ⑧
Math with Greek Pi

ΑΒΨΔΕΦΓΗΙΞΚΛΜΝΟΠΘΡΣΤΘΩϬΧΥΖ
αβψδεϕγηιξκλμνοπϑρστθωφχυζδϖε ∝ ϰ
ς⟩ + ( ) < [″‴ ′ − × ÷ = ± ∓ ° ‾

A912 Mac + PC ⑧
Mathematical Pi

[symbol rows]

▶ Pi
[symbols]

▶ Pi
ΑΒΨΔΕΦΓΗΙΞΚΛΜΝΟΠ
ΘΡΣΤΘΩϬΧΥΖαβψδεϕγη
ιξκλμνοπϑρστθωφχυ ∝ ∅
+ − × ÷ = ± ∪ ⊂ ∇ ∋ ⊇ ∈ ⊆ ⊏

▶ Pi
ΑΒΨΔΕΦΓΗΙΞΚΛΜΝΟΠΘ6
ΡΣΤΘΩΧΥΖ≥αβψδεϕγηιξκ
λμνοπϑρστθωφχυζℏℵ≪≤≦
≲≶≥≦<>"+×÷±°'∀∇≧α=

▶ Pi
ABCDEFGHIJKLMNOP
QRSTUVWXYZ⊗□◀●
◐□■■▲△*☆◆○△L ╚
⊗⊖⊘□▼ ⁇ ⋮ ⋰ ⋱ ⋮⋮ ⋰ ∡ ✶

▶ Pi
[mathematical symbols]

▶ Pi
𝔄𝔅ℭ𝔇𝔈𝔉𝔊ℌℑ𝔍𝔎𝔏𝔐𝔑𝔒
𝔓𝔔ℜ𝔖𝔗𝔘𝔙𝔚𝔛𝔜ℨ𝔞𝔟𝔠𝔡𝔢𝔣𝔤
𝔥𝔦𝔧𝔨𝔩𝔪𝔫𝔬𝔭𝔮𝔯𝔰𝔱𝔲𝔳𝔴𝔵𝔶𝔷𝒜𝒽
𝒞𝒟𝒠𝒢𝒥𝒦ℒ𝒞𝓂𝓌𝒰𝒱𝒴

C2689 Mac + PC ⑧
Agfa Pi & Symbols: Medical & Pharmaceutical 1

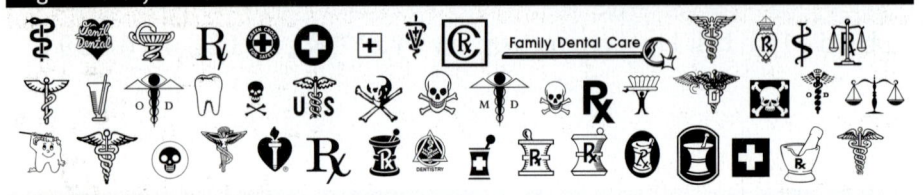

C2690 Mac + PC ⑧
Agfa Pi & Symbols: Medical & Pharmaceutical 2

A088 Mac + PC ⑧
MICR

1 2 3 4 5 6 7 8 9 0 ⑆ ⑇ ⑈ ⑉

OCR:
MICR, OCRA, OCRB

© FSI 1993

C2691 Mac + PC
Agfa Pi & Symbols: Military & Patriotic 1

C2692 Mac + PC
Agfa Pi & Symbols: Military & Patriotic 2

A485 Mac + PC 1990: Robert Slimbach
Minion Ornaments

Minion Expert:
Minion Expert Regular, Expert Italic, Expert Semibold, Expert Semibold Italic, Expert Bold, Expert Bold Italic, Expert Black, Expert Display Regular, Expert Display Italic, Ornaments, Swash Italic, Swash Display Italic, Swash Semibold Italic

M641 Mac + PC
Monotype Pi Fonts

Monotype Pi Fonts:
Almanac (Zodiac Symbols), Botanical, Circle Frame Pos. & Neg., Directions, Sports One & Two, Square Frame Pos. & Neg., Transport, Vacation

C2693 Mac + PC
Agfa Pi & Symbols: Musical

BT1430 Mac + PC
Newspaper Pi

C2694 Mac + PC
Agfa Pi & Symbols: Numerics 1

© FSI 1993

C2695 Mac + PC ⑧
Agfa Pi & Symbols: Numerics 2

① ② ③ ④ ⑤ ⑥ ⑦ ⑧ ⑨ ⑩ ① ② ③ ④ ⑤ ⑥
⑦ ⑧ ⑨ ⑩ ⑪ ⑫ ⑬ ⑭ ⑮ ⑯ ⑰ ⑱ ⑲ ⑳ ㉑ ㉒
㉓ ㉔ ㉕ ㉖ ㉗ ㉘ ㉙ ㉚ ㉛ ㉜ ㉝ ㉞ ㉟ ㊱ ㊲ ㊳

C2696 Mac + PC ⑧
Agfa Pi & Symbols: Numerics 3

❶ ❷ ❸ ❹ ❺ ❻ ❼ ❽ ❾ ❿ ⓫ ⓬ ⓭ ⓮ ⓯ ⓰ ⓱
⓲ ⓳ ⓴ 21 22 23 24 25 26 27 28 29 30 31 32 33 34
35 36 37 38 39 40 41 42 43 44 45 46 47 48 49 50 51

C2697 Mac + PC ⑧
Agfa Pi & Symbols: Numerics 4

❶ ❷ ❸ ❹ ❺ ❻ ❼ ❽ ❾ ❿ ❶ ❷ ❸ ❹ ❺ ❻
❼ ❽ ❾ ❿ ⓫ ⓬ ⓭ ⓮ ⓯ ⓰ ⓱ ⓲ ⓳ ⓴ 21 22
23 24 25 26 27 28 29 30 31 32 33 34 35 36 37 38

C2698 Mac + PC ⑧
Agfa Pi & Symbols: Numerics 5

0 1 2 3 4 5 6 7 8 9 0 1 2 3 4 5 6
7 8 9 1 2 3 4 5 6 7 8 9 1 2 3 4
5 6 7 8 9 10 1 2 3 4 5 6 7 8 9 10

C2699 Mac + PC ⑧
Agfa Pi & Symbols: Numerics 6

0123456789 / 0123456789 / *0123*
456789 0123456789 % ¢ * $, . ¢ - ¢
0123456789

C2700 Mac + PC ⑧
Agfa Pi & Symbols: Numerics 7

0123456789 0123456789 0123456789
0123456789 0123456789 **0123456789**

C2701 Mac + PC ⑧
Agfa Pi & Symbols: Numerics 8

0123456789 0123456789 0123456
789 *0123456789* 0123456789
123456789

C2702 Mac + PC (8)
Agfa Pi & Symbols: Numerics 9

½ ¼ ¾ ⅘ ⅝ ⅞ $\frac{15}{64}$ $\frac{36}{64}$ $\frac{7}{8}$ $\frac{7}{8}$

C2703 Mac + PC (8)
Agfa Pi & Symbols: Numerics 10

0213456789 0123456789 *0123456789* 0123456789 *0123456789* 0123456789 ①②③④⑤⑥⑦⑧⑨

C2704 Mac + PC (8)
Agfa Pi & Symbols: Numerics 11

$\frac{3}{4}$ $\frac{3}{4}$ $\frac{1}{3}$ $\frac{2}{3}$ $\frac{1}{2}$ $\frac{1}{3}$ $\frac{2}{3}$ $\frac{1}{4}$ $\frac{1}{4}$ $\frac{4}{5}$ $\frac{1}{5}$ $\frac{2}{5}$ $\frac{3}{5}$ $\frac{1}{6}$ $\frac{3}{8}$ $\frac{1}{8}$ $\frac{3}{8}$ $\frac{5}{8}$ $\frac{3}{8}$ $\frac{1}{2}$ $\frac{1}{4}$ $\frac{3}{4}$ $\frac{1}{5}$ $\frac{2}{5}$ $\frac{3}{5}$ $\frac{4}{5}$ $\frac{1}{6}$

$\frac{5}{6}$ $\frac{1}{8}$ $\frac{7}{8}$ $\frac{3}{4}$ $\frac{1}{32}$ $\frac{31}{32}$ $\frac{27}{32}$ $\frac{5}{32}$ $\frac{7}{10}$ $\frac{7}{32}$ $\frac{9}{32}$ $\frac{11}{16}$ $\frac{7}{32}$ $\frac{13}{32}$ $\frac{15}{32}$ $\frac{17}{16}$ $\frac{9}{16}$ $\frac{11}{10}$ $\frac{1}{10}$

$\frac{9}{10}$ $\frac{3}{32}$ $\frac{1}{16}$ $\frac{5}{16}$ $\frac{29}{32}$ $\frac{3}{10}$ $\frac{25}{32}$ $\frac{3}{16}$ $\frac{23}{32}$ $\frac{19}{32}$ $\frac{13}{16}$ $\frac{15}{16}$

A088 Mac + PC
OCR

OCR:
MICR, OCRA, OCRB

A088 Mac + PC (8)
OCRA

abcdefghijklmnopqrstuvwxyz[']ABCDEFGH
IJKLMNOPQRSTUVWXYZ{*}1234567890ÄÖÜÅØÆ
(.,;:?!⇔&-)

OCR:
MICR, OCRA, OCRB

A088 Mac + PC (8)   1968: Adrian Frutiger
OCRB

ABCDEFGHIJKLMNOPQRSTUVWXYZ{ÄÖÜÅØÆIJ}
abcdefghijklmnopqrstuvwxyz[ßåøæij]0
123456789(.,;:?!$&-*)

OCR:
MICR, OCRA, OCRB
aaa EF522
OCRB, Reg, BT6416

FB1052 Mac + PC
Bureau Ornaments™

Bureau Ornaments™:
City Ornaments™, Town Ornaments™, Village Ornaments™

TF668 Mac + PC ⑧ 1989: Joseph Treacy/Carol Treacy
TF Puzzle™

TF Crossword™:
TF Puzzle™, TF Solution™

C2708 Mac + PC ⑧
Agfa Pi & Symbols: Religious

M2836 Mac + PC ⑧
Rococo Ornaments

Rococo Ornaments:
Rococo Ornaments, Arabesque Ornaments

M2836 Mac + PC ⑧
Rococo Ornaments

Rococo Ornaments:
Rococo Ornaments, Arabesque Ornaments

C2709 Mac ⑧
Agfa Pi & Symbols: Seals 1

C2710 Mac + PC ⑧
Agfa Pi & Symbols: Seals 2

TF668 Mac + PC ⑧ — 1989: Joseph Treacy/Carol Treacy
TF Solution™

A B C D E F G H I J K L M N O P Q R S T U V W X Y Z

Ą Ć Ď Ę ß Ā Ö Ř Š Ť Ū Ł Ń Ő X̌ Ý Ź Ÿ Ě & Ǔ Č Ä Ö Ü Å

Ø Æ Œ Ç 1 2 3 4 5 6 7 8 9 0

TF Crossword™:
TF Puzzle™, TF Solution™

A106 Mac + PC ⑧ — 1986: Cleo Huggins
Sonata™

C2711 Mac ⑧
Agfa Pi & Symbols: Special Alphabets 1

A B C D E F G H I J K L M N O P Q R S T U
V W X Y Z a b c d e f g h i j k l m n o p q r s t u v w x y z

C2712 Mac + PC ⑧
Agfa Pi & Symbols: Special Alphabets 2

A B C D E F G H I J K L M N O P Q R S T U V
W X Y Z a b c d e f g h i j k l m n o p q r s t u v w x y z

© FSI 1993

& 30

C2713 Mac + PC ⑧
Agfa Pi & Symbols: Special Alphabets 3

ABCDEFGHIJKLMNOPQRS
TUVWXYZßSabcdefghijklmno
pqrstuvwxyz

C2714 Mac ⑧
Agfa Pi & Symbols: Special Alphabets 4

ABCDEFGHIJKLMNOPQRSTUV
WXYZABCDEFGHIJKLMNOPQ
RSTUVWXYZ

C2715 Mac + PC ⑧
Agfa Pi & Symbols: Special Alphabets 5

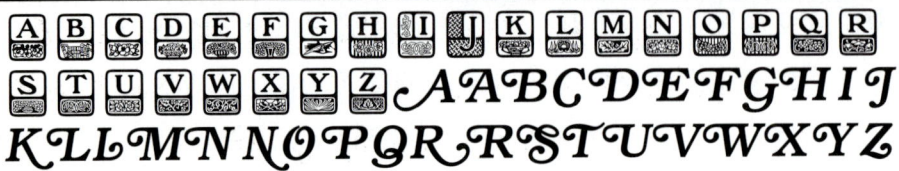

ABCDEFGHIJKLMNOPQR
STUVWXYZ AABCDEFGHIJ
KLLMNOPQRRSTUVWXYZ

C2716 Mac + PC ⑧
Agfa Pi & Symbols: Special Alphabets 6

ABCDEFGHIJKLMNOPQ
RSTUVWXYZ ABCDEFGH
IJKLMNOPQRSTUVWXYZ

C2717 Mac + PC ⑧
Agfa Pi & Symbols: Special Alphabets 7

ABCDEFGHIJKLMNOPQR
STUVWXYZ ⒶⒷⒸⒹⒺⒻⒼⒽⒾ
ⒿⓀⓁⓂⓃⓄⓅⓆⓇⓈⓉⓊⓋⓌⓍⓎⓏ

C2718 Mac + PC ⑧
Agfa Pi & Symbols: Special Alphabets 8

ABCDEFGHIJKLMNO
PQRSTUVWXYZ ⒶⒷⒸⒹⒺⒻⒼ
ⓊⓋⓌⓍⓎⓏ,.⓪①②③④⑤⑥⑦⑧⑨;CTRL SPACEBAR TAB

C2719 Mac ⑧
Agfa Pi & Symbols: Special Alphabets 9

ABCDEFGHIJKLMNOPQRSTUVWXYZ
abcdefghijklmnopqrstuvwxyz*!"$%&()
0123456789 +,-.:;=[ÉÖÏáäçƒÿŸüé£§ß]

© FSI 1993

C2720 Mac + PC ⑧
Agfa Pi & Symbols: Special Alphabets 10

ABCDEFGHIJKLMNOPQRSTUVWXYZ
abcde»ßÄÄÇÉÖÜÂÊÁËÈÍÎÏÌÓÔÒÚÛ
áäçéêèëîïòöôùüÿ!"$%&*()0123.=[:;]

C2721 Mac + PC ⑧
Agfa Pi & Symbols: Special Alphabets 11

A B C D E F G H I J K L M N O P Q R S
T U V W X Y Z 0 1 2 3 4 5 6 7 8 9

M6412 Mac + PC ⑧
Sport Pi One, Two

► One

► Two

Monotype Pi Fonts:
Almanac (Zodiac Symbols), Botanical, Circle Frame Pos. & Neg., Directions, Sports One & Two, Square Frame Pos. & Neg., Transport, Vacation

M6412 Mac + PC ⑧
Square Frame, Pos., Neg.

A B C D E F G H I J K L M N O P Q R
S T U V W X Y Z 0 1 2 3 4 5 6 7 8 9
0 1 2 3 4 5 6 7 8 9 0 1 2 3 4 5 6 7 8 9

► Positive

► Negative

Monotype Pi Fonts:
Almanac (Zodiac Symbols), Botanical, Circle Frame Pos. & Neg., Directions, Sports One & Two, Square Frame Pos. & Neg., Transport, Vacation

© FSI 1993

M1527 Mac + PC ⑧
Symbol

ΑΒΧΔΕΦΓΗΙϑΚΛΜΝΟΠΘΡΣΤΥςΩΞΨΖ
αβχδεφγηιφκλμνοπθρστυϖξψζ[♣].!↵
∉(,;:?∃&–*)—{↓→∈}1234567890

Courier: Courier, Symbol

BT1432 Mac + PC ⑧
Symbol Proportional

ΑΒΧΔΕΦΓΗΙΚΛΜΝΟΠΘΡΣΤΥΩΞΨΖ
αβχδεφγηιφκλμνοπθρστυϖϑξψζ!∀#∃
%&()*⊥+,−.0123456789:;=≅[∴]{~}

C2722 Mac + PC ⑧
Agfa Pi & Symbols: Television 1

C2723 Mac + PC ⑧
Agfa Pi & Symbols: Television 2

FB1052 Mac + PC ⑧ 🖉 1991: David Berlow
Town Ornaments™

Bureau Ornaments™:
City Ornaments™, Town Ornaments™, Village Ornaments™

C2724 Mac ⑧
Agfa Pi & Symbols: Transporation 1

© FSI 1993

& 33

C2725 Mac + PC ⑧
Agfa Pi & Symbols: Transporation 2

M6412 Mac + PC ⑧
Transportation Pi

Monotype Pi Fonts:
Almanac (Zodiac Symbols), Botanical, Circle Frame Pos. & Neg., Directions, Sports One & Two, Square Frame Pos. & Neg., Transport, Vacation

---

ET6389 Mac + PC ⑧
Troubador Initials

Abelard/Troubador:
Abelard, Troubador, Troubador Initials

BT1431 Mac + PC ⑧
Universal Math 1

ΑΒΨΔΕΦΓΗΙΞΚΛΜΝΟΠΘΡΣΤΘΩΧΥΖ
αβψδεφγηιξκλμνοπϑρστθωφχυϐϰζς·°/
>‴≦λ″∅+−×÷=±∓′∞α≤≧

A138 Mac + PC ⑧
Universal Greek + Math Pi

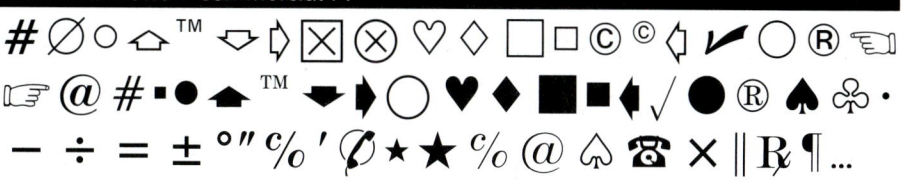

ΑΒΨΔΕΦΓΗΙΞΚΛΜΝΟΠΘΡΣΠΣΤΘΩΧ
ΥΖαβψδεφγηιξκλμνοπϑρστθωφχυϐζ≦]{
}⟨⟩∫<‴>″+−×÷=±∓°′≳∼√[≡ℏ∂·(∝)

Universal News/Commercial Pi & Universal Greek/Math Pi:
Universal Greek + Math Pi, Universal News + Commercial Pi

A138 Mac + PC ⑧
Universal News + Commercial Pi

Universal News/Commercial Pi & Universal Greek/Math Pi:
Universal Greek + Math Pi, Universal News + Commercial Pi

A138 Mac + PC ⑧
Universal Greek + Math Pi

Universal News/Commercial Pi & Universal Greek/Math Pi:
Universal Greek + Math Pi, Universal News + Commercial Pi

A258 Mac + PC ⑧ ✎ 1989: Robert Slimbach
Utopia Ornaments

Utopia Expert:
Utopia Expert Regular, Utopia Expert Italic, Utopia Expert Semi Bold, Utopia Expert Semi Bold Italic, Utopia Expert Bold, Utopia Expert Bold Italic, Utopia Expert Black, Utopia Ornaments, Utopia Titling

M6412 Mac + PC ⑧
Vacation Pi

Monotype Pi Fonts:
Almanac (Zodiac Symbols), Botanical, Circle Frame Pos. & Neg., Directions, Sports One & Two, Square Frame Pos. & Neg., Transport, Vacation

FB1052 Mac + PC ⑧ ✎ 1991: David Berlow
Village Ornaments™

Bureau Ornaments™:
City Ornaments™, Town Ornaments™, Village Ornaments™

G460 Mac + PC ⑧
Vine Leaves™, Folio One

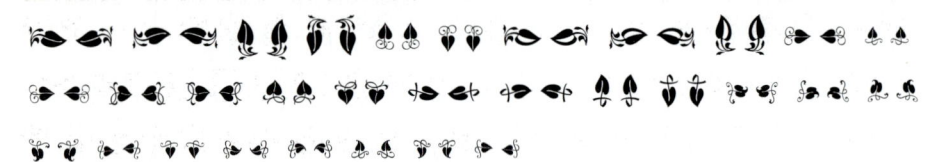

G6341 Mac + PC ⑧ ✎ 1993: (1905)
Vine Leaves®, II

▶ BH    ▶ CH

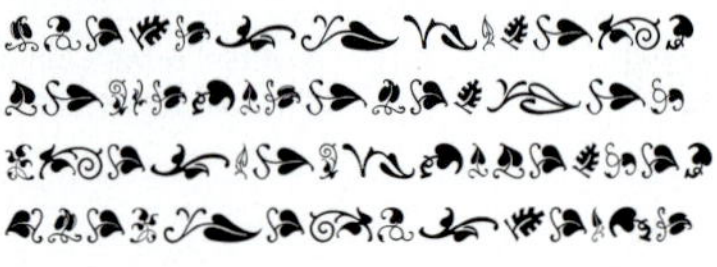

© FSI 1993

▼ G6341 Mac + PC Vine Leaves®, II

▶ XH

A2772 Mac + PC ⑧
Warning Pi

Linotype Audio Pi:
Audio Pi, Warning Pi

A424 Mac + PC ⑧ ✎ 1990: Buker, Lind, Redick
Wood Type Ornaments 1

Wood Type Ornaments 1:
Cottonwood, Ironwood, Mesquite, Ponderosa, Wood Type Ornaments 1

A922 Mac + PC ⑧ ✎ 1990: Buker, Lind, Redick
Wood Type Ornaments 2

Wood Type Ornaments 2:
Birch, Blackoak, Madrone, Poplar, Willow, Wood Type Ornaments 2

A125 Mac + PC ⑧ ✎ 1979: Hermann Zapf
ITC Zapf Dingbats®

ITC Zapf Chancery/ITC Dingbats:
ITC Zapf Chancery, ITC Zapf Dingbats
a*a*a* BT6832
ITC Zapf Chancery, ITC Zapf Dingbats

winter en plots begon je heel hard te huilen en ik schrok en ik zette je recht op de rand van het bed en ik trok je T-shirt weer goed en je lachte door je tranen heen en je zei:

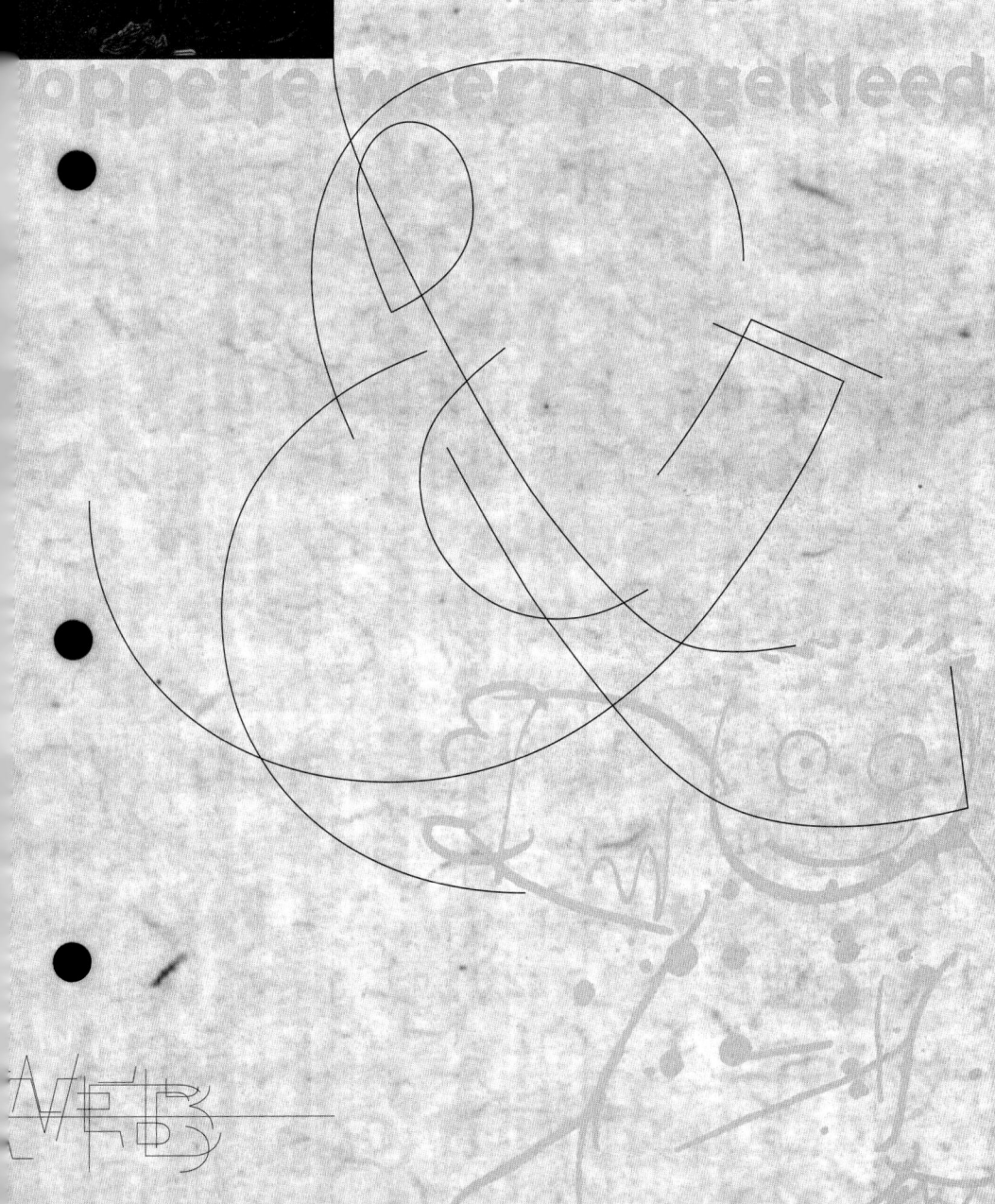

"oppetre weer aangekleed."

Yves Peters, Gent, B

English

Welcome to FontBook's non-latin and accented section. These are organized into the following categories:
Eastern European · Cyrillic · Arabic, Greek & Hebrew · Asian · Phonetic · Additional
Due to the complex nature of these fonts, the following reference information is provided on encoding standards, keyboard drivers and language support. Please note that different manufacturers may support the same languages but use different code pages and/or different keyboard layouts, and therefore fonts are not always compatible with each other.

Language Support

ce: the Central European Standard from Apple for Polish, Czech, Slovakian, Serbian, Latvian, Lithuanian, Hungarian, Croatian, Slovenian, German, Finnish and Estonian.
cyr: English, plus the Cyrillic languages: Russian, Belorussian, Ukrainian, Macedonian, Bulgarian and Serbian
cyr-f: all Cyrillic languages plus French
cyr-gr: all Cyrillic languages plus German
cyr-k: all Cyrillic languages
cyr-lh: all Cyrillic languagues and Moldavian
cyr-tur: Altaic, Azerbaijanian, Bashkirish, Karakalpakish, Kazakhish, Kirgizish, Kumykish, Nogaian, Tatarish, Chuvashish, Turkmenian and Usbekian and Russian
ee: Polish, Sorbian, Czech, Slovakian, Slovanian, Croatian, Rumanian, Albanian, Hungarian, German, English, Finnish and Irish
turk: Turkish, English and all other languages covered by the Adobe Standard (except Icelandic)
UNI: Accents for Polish, Czech, Croatian, Hungarian, Rumanian, Turkish, universally usable

FontFonts, Adobe and ParaType fonts all support Adobe/ParaType Encoding.

Keyboard drivers

All foreign language packages from Linotype contain keyboard drivers for either Macintosh or Windows 3.x for switching keyboard layouts according to the supported languages. MacCampus fonts marked with (+T) contain keyboard drivers. The user can change the keyboard layout per hot key and menu while an application is running.

ParaWin/ParaMac from ParaType

All ParaType fonts are supplied with menu driven keyboard drivers for Windows 3.x (ParaWin) and Macintosh (ParaMac). The user can change between the keyboard layout while an application is running. The keyboard layout of ParaType fonts allows the user to write multilingual texts with the same font. In addition to the layouts supplied with ParaWin it is possible to produce custom layouts for any font. ParaWin enables six different keyboard layouts to be simultanously available. ParaWin is also available as a separate product (PG 6616 P).

In the "Special Pack" section you will find font packages for working with foreign languages.

Should you need additional languages (Japanese, Chinese, etc), just call FontShop!

Deutsch

Willkommen zu den nicht-lateinischen und osteuropäischen Schriften des FontBook. Sie unterteilen sich in folgende Kategorien :
Osteuropäisch · Kyrillisch · Arabisch, Griechisch & Hebräisch · Asiatisch · Phonetisch · Andere
Im folgenden liefern wir Ihnen Informationen über unterstützte Sprachen und Tastaturtreiber. Bitte beachten Sie, daß verschiedene Hersteller möglicherweise die gleichen Sprachen unterstützen, aber unterschiedliche Code Pages und/ oder Tastaturbelegungen benutzen und sie deshalb nicht unbedingt untereinander kompatibel sind.

Unterstützte Sprachen

ce: Central European Standard von Apple für Polnisch, Tschechisch, Slowakisch, Serbisch, Litauisch, Lettisch, Ungarisch, Kroatisch, Slowenisch, Deutsch, Finnisch und Estnisch
cyr: Englisch & alle slawisch-kyrillischen Sprachen: Russisch, Weißrussisch, Ukrainisch, Makedonisch, Bulgarisch und Serbisch
cyr-f: die slawisch-kyrillischen Sprachen und Französisch
cyr-gr: die slawisch-kyrillischen Sprachen und Deutsch
cyr-k: alle slawisch-kyrillischen Sprachen
cyr-lh: alle slawisch-kyrillischen Sprachen und Moldawisch
cyr-tur: die Turksprachen der ehemaligen UdSSR: Altaisch, Aserbaidschanisch, Baschkirisch, Karakalpakisch, Kasachisch, Kirgisisch, Kumykisch, Nogaiisch, Tatarisch, Tschuwaschisch, Turkmenisch, Usbekisch und Russisch
ee: Polnisch, Sorbisch, Tschechisch, Slowakisch, Slowenisch, Kroatisch, Rumänisch, Albanisch, Ungarisch, Deutsch, Englisch, Finnisch und Irisch
turk: Türkisch, Englisch und alle anderen Sprachen, die der Adobe-Standard abdeckt (außer Isländisch)
UNI: Fliegende Akzente für Polnisch, Tschechisch, Kroatisch, Ungarisch, Rumänisch, Türkisch, universell einsetzbar

FontFonts, Adobe- und ParaType-Fonts entsprechen alle dem Adobe/ParaType-Encoding.

Tastaturtreiber

Alle Fremdsprachenpakete von Linotype enthalten spezielle Tastaturtreiber für Macintosh und Windows 3.x, mit denen sprachspezifische Tastaturbelegungen angesprochen werden. MacCampus-Fonts, die mit (+T) gekennzeichnet sind, enthalten Tastaturtreiber. Der Anwender kann per Hot-Key und Menü bei laufender Anwendung die Tastaturbelegung ändern.

ParaWin/ParaMac von ParaType

Mit den ParaType-Fonts wird ein menügesteuerter Tastaturtreiber für Windows 3.x (ParaWin) bzw. Macintosh (ParaMac) geliefert. Der Anwender kann per Hot-Key bei laufender Anwendung die Tastaturbelegung ändern. Die Zeichenbelegung der ParaType-Fonts gestattet es, mehrsprachige Dokumente mit einer Schrift zu schreiben. Zusätzlich zu vorgefertigten, im Lieferumfang enthaltenen Layouts können mit ParaWin per Maus selbstdefinierte Belegungen für jeden beliebigen Font erstellt werden. Sechs verschiedene Tastaturbelegungen stehen dann unter Windows simultan zur Verfügung. ParaWin ist auch als separates Programm erhältlich (PG 6616 P).

Bei „Special Packs" finden Sie günstige Schriftenpakete zum Arbeiten mit Fremdsprachen.

LH6288 Mac + PC
Antique Olive East A

ĄÁÄÂĂĆÇČĐĎÉÎĹĽŁŇÔÓŐÖŔŘŠŞŢŤŤŮÚŰÜÝŹ
ŻŽąáâäăçčćd'ëëęd'ÍíĺľłňńñŏóőöŕřŚšşţťúůüű
ýžźżßABCDEFGHIJKLMNOPabcdefghijklmn

▶ Light
ĄÁÄÂĂĆÇČĐĎÉÎĹĽŁŇÔÓŐÖŔŘŠ
ŞŢŤŤŮÚŰÜÝŹŻŽąáâäăçčćd'ëëę
d'ÍíĺľłňńñŏóőöŕřŚšşţťúůüűýžźżß
ABCDEFGHIJKLabcdefghijklmn

▶ Roman
ĄÁÄÂĂĆÇČĐĎÉÎĹĽŁŇÔÓŐÖŔ
ŘŠŞŢŤŤŮÚŰÜÝŹŻŽąáâäăçčćd'
ëëęd'ÍíĺľłňńñŏóőöŕřŚšşţťúů
üűýžźżßABCDEFGabcdefgh

▶ Italic
ĄÁÄÂĂĆÇČĐĎÉÎĹĽŁŇÔÓŐÖŔŘ
ŠŞŢŤŤŮÚŰÜÝŹŻŽąáâäăçčćd'
ëëęd'ÍíĺľłňńñŏóőöŕřŚšşţťúůüű
ýžźżßABCDEFGabcdefghijkl

▶ Bold
ĄÁÄÂĂĆÇČĐĎÉÎĹĽŁŇÔÓŐÖ
ŔŘŠŞŢŤŤŮÚŰÜÝŹŻŽąáâäăçčć
d'ëëęd'ÍíĺľłňńñŏóőöŕřŚšşţtú
ůüűýžźżßABCDEFGabcdefg

▶ Black
ĄÁÄÂĂĆÇČĐĎÉÎĹĽŁŇÔÓŐÖ
ŔŘŠŞŢŤŤŮÚŰÜÝŹŻŽąáâäăçč
ćd'ëëęd'ÍíĺľłňńñŏóőöŕřŚšşţ
ťúůüűýžźżßABCDEabcdefg

K496 Mac
Avant Turk

ÄÁÀÂĂÇËÉÈÊĞIÍÎĨİÖÓÒÔŐŢŞÜÚÙÛŰ
äáàâăçëéèêğıíîĩïöóòôőşţüúùûű¿¡
ABCDEFGHIJKLMNabcdefghijklmno

▶ Bold
ÄÁÀÂĂÇËÉÈÊĞIÍÎĨİÖÓÒÔŐŢ
ŞÜÚÙÛŰäáàâăçëéèêğıíîĩïöó
òôőşţüúùûű¿¡ABCDEFGHIJKL
MNOPQRSTabcdefghijklmno

▶ Bold Oblique
ÄÁÀÂĂÇËÉÈÊĞIÍÎĨİÖÓÒÔŐŢ
ŞÜÚÙÛŰäáàâăçëéèêğıíîĩïöó
òôőşţüúùûű¿¡ABCDEFGHIJKL
MNOPQRSabcdefghijklmno

▶ Plain
ÄÁÀÂĂÇËÉÈÊĞIÍÎĨİÖÓÒÔŐŢ
ŞÜÚÙÛŰäáàâăçëéèêğıíîĩïöó
òôőşţüúùûű¿¡ABCDEFGHIJK
LMNOPQabcdefghijklmnop

▶ Oblique
ÄÁÀÂĂÇËÉÈÊĞIÍÎĨİÖÓÒÔŐŢ
ŞÜÚÙÛŰäáàâăçëéèêğıíîĩïöó
òôőşţüúùûű¿¡ABCDEFGHIJK
LMNOPQabcdefghijklmnop

PG6605 Mac + PC
Courier East Europe

ĄÁÂĂÄĆÇČĎĐÉĚËÍÎĹĽŁŃÓÔŐÖŔŘŠŚŞŤŢŮÚŰÜÝŻŽ
Źáâăäąćçčéęëěd'đíîíľłńňóôőöřŕšśşťţůúűü
ýžźżßABCDEFGHIJKLMabcdefghijklmnopqrs

▶ Regular
ĄÁÂĂÄĆÇČĎĐÉĚËÍÎĹĽŁŃÓÔÕ
ŔŘŠŚŞŤŢŮÚŰÜÝŹŻáâăäąćçč
éęëěd'đíîíľłńňóôőöřŕšśşť
ţůúűüýžźżßABCDEFGabcdef

▶ Bold
ĄÁÂĂÄĆÇČĎĐÉĚËÍÎĹĽŁŃÓÔÕ
ŔŘŠŚŞŤŢŮÚŰÜÝŹŻáâăäąćçč
éęëěd'đíîíľłńňóôőöřŕšśşť
ţůúűüýžźżßABCDEFGabcdef

PG6609 Mac + PC — Courier Turk

ÀÁÂÃÄÅÇÈÉÊËÌÍÎÏİÒÓÔÕÖØŞŠÙÚÛÜÝŸÆŒàáâãäå
çèéêëğìíîïñòóôõöøšşùúûüÿßæœABCDEFGHIJ
KLMNOPQRSTUVWXYZabcdefghijklmnopqrstu

▶ Regular
ÀÁÂÃÄÅÇÈÉÊËÌÍÎÏİÒÓÔÕÖØŞ
ŠÙÚÛÜÝŸÆŒàáâãäåçèéêëğìíî
ïñòóôõöøšşùúûüÿßæœABCDE
FGHIJKLMNOabcdefghijklm

▶ Bold
ÀÁÂÃÄÅÇÈÉÊËÌÍÎÏİÒÓÔÕÖØŞ
ŠÙÚÛÜÝŸÆŒàáâãäåçèéêëğìíî
ïñòóôõöøšşùúûüÿßæœABCDE
FGHIJKLMNOPabcdefghijkl

LH6285 Mac + PC — Excelsior East A

ĄÁÄÂĂĆÇČĐĎÉÎŁĹĽŇÔÓŐÖŔŘŠŞŢŤŤ
ŮÚŰÜÝŹŻŽąáâäăčćčďďëëęďĺíľľłňńńőóöŕř
ŚšşţťúůüűýžźżßABCDEFGHabcdefghijklm

▶ Roman
ĄÁÄÂĂĆÇČĐĎÉÎŁĹĽŇÔÓ
ŐÖŔŘŠŞŢŤŤŮÚŰÜÝŹŻŽąá
âäăčćčďďëëęďĺíľľłňńńőóöŕřŚ
šşţťúůüűýžźżßABCDabcdefg

▶ Italic
ĄÁÄÂĂĆÇČĐĎÉÎŁĹĽŇÔÓ
ŐÖŔŘŠŞŢŤŤŮÚŰÜÝŹŻŽąá
âäăčćčďďëëęďĺíľľłňńńőóöŕřŚ
šşţťúůüűýžźżßABCDabcdef

▶ Bold
ĄÁÄÂĂĆÇČĐĎÉÎŁĹĽŇÔÓ
ŐÖŔŘŠŞŢŤŤŮÚŰÜÝŹŻŽąá
âäăčćčďďëëęďĺíľľłňńńőóöŕřŚ
šşţťúůüűýžźżßABCDabcdefg

K950 Mac — GAccents

ÄÅÁĄÂÀÃÇĐÉĘÊËÈÍÎÏİĮŁÑÓÔÒÕÖØŢ
ÚÚÛÙŸÆŒáàâäãåąçđéèêëíîïİįłñóòôô
õøţúùûüÿæœßABCDEFGabcdefghijkl

▶ Light
ÄÅÁĄÂÀÃÇĐÉĘÊËÈÍÎÏİĮŁÑÓÔ
ÕÖØŢÚÚÛÙŸÆŒáàâäãåąçđéè
êëíîïİįłñóòôôõøţúùûüÿæœßABC
DEFGHIJKLMNabcdefghijklmno

▶ Light Italic
ÄÅÁĄÂÀÃÇĐÉĘÊËÈÍÎÏİĮŁÑÓÔ
ÕÖØŢÚÚÛÙŸÆŒáàâäãåąçđéè
êëíîïİįłñóòôôõøţúùûüÿæœßABC
DEFGHIJKLMNabcdefghijklmno

▶ Bold
ÄÅÁĄÂÀÃÇĐÉĘÊËÈÍÎÏİĮŁÑÓ
ÒÕÖØŢÚÚÛÙŸÆŒáàâäãåąç
đéèêëíîïİįłñóòôôõøţúùûüÿæ
œßABCDEFGHIJabcdefghijkl

▶ Bold Italic
ÄÅÁĄÂÀÃÇĐÉĘÊËÈÍÎÏİĮŁÑÓ
ÒÕÖØŢÚÚÛÙŸÆŒáàâäã
ąçđéèêëíîïİįłñóòôôõøţúùûüÿ
æœßABCDEFGHabcdefghijk

K654 Mac — Galata

ÄÅÁÀÂĂÇËÉÈÊĞIÍÎİÏÖÓÒÔÕŐŞÜÚÙÛŰ
äáàâăçëéèêğıíîiïöóòôõőşüúùûű¿¡ABCDEF
GHIJKLMNOPQRabcdefghijklmnopqrst

© FSI 1993

▼ K654 Mac Galata

▶ Plain
ÄÁÀÂÃÇËÉÈÊĞÍÎÏÏÖÓÒÔŐŢŞ
ÜÚÙÛŰäáàâãçëéèêğíîïïöóòôő
şţüúùûű¿¡ABCDEFGHIJKLMNOP
QRSTUVWXYZabcdefghijklmn

▶ Oblique
ÄÁÀÂÃÇËÉÈÊĞÍÎÏÏÖÓÒÔŐŢŞ
ÜÚÙÛŰäáàâãçëéèêğíîïïöóòôő
şţüúùûű¿¡ABCDEFGHIJKLMNOP
QRSTUVWXYZabcdefghijklmn

▶ Bold
ÄÁÀÂÃÇËÉÈÊĞÍÎÏÏÖÓÒÔŐŢŞ
ÜÚÙÛŰäáàâãçëéèêğíîïïöóòôő
şţüúùûű¿¡ABCDEFGHIJKLMNO
PQRSTUVWXYZabcdefghijklm

▶ Bold Oblique
ÄÁÀÂÃÇËÉÈÊĞÍÎÏÏÖÓÒÔŐŢŞ
ÜÚÙÛŰäáàâãçëéèêğíîïïöóòôő
şţüúùûű¿¡ABCDEFGHIJKLMNO
PQRSTUVWXYZabcdefghijklm

Eastern Europe

K493 Mac + PC (PL) +T
Gazeta
ÄĄÀÁÂĆÉĖĘĒÊËÈÍÎĨÌŁŃÑÖÓÔÒŚÚÛ
ÜÙŸŹŻŒáàâäąćéèêëęéèíîĩìłńñóòôö
śúùûüÿźżœßABCDEFGabcdefghijklmn

▶ Plain
ÄĄÀÁÂĆÉĖĘĒÊËÈÍÎĨÌŁŃÑÖÓ
ÔÒŚÚÛÜÙŸŹŻŒáàâäąćéèê
ëęéèíîĩìłńñóòôöśúùûüÿźżœßA
BCDEFGHIJabcdefghijklmnop

▶ Oblique
ÄĄÀÁÂĆÉĖĘĒÊËÈÍÎĨÌŁŃÑÖÓ
ÔÒŚÚÛÜÙŸŹŻŒáàâäąćéèê
ëęéèíîĩìłńñóòôöśúùûüÿźżœßA
BCDEFGHIJKabcdefghijklmno

▶ Bold
ÄĄÀÁÂĆÉĖĘĒÊËÈÍÎĨÌŁŃÑÖÓ
ÔÒŚÚÛÜÙŸŹŻŒáàâäąćéèê
ëęéèíîĩìłńñóòôöśúùûüÿźżœß
ABCDEFGHIJKabcdefghijkl

▶ Bold Oblique
ÄĄÀÁÂĆÉĖĘĒÊËÈÍÎĨÌŁŃÑÖÓ
ÔÒŚÚÛÜÙŸŹŻŒáàâäąćéèê
ëęéèíîĩìłńñóòôöśúùûüÿźżœß
ABCDEFGHIJabcdefghijklm

K6578 Mac (PL) +T
Gazeta Light/Black
ÄĄÀÁÂĆÉĖĘĒÊËÈÍÎĨÌŁŃÑÖÓÔÒŚÚÛÜÙŸŹ
ŻŒáàâäąćéèêëęéèíîĩìłńñóòôöśúùûüÿźżœ
ßABCDEFGHIJKLMabcdefghijklmnopqrstu

▶ Light
ÄĄÀÁÂĆÉĖĘĒÊËÈÍÎĨÌŁŃÑÖÓÔ
ÒŚÚÛÜÙŸŹŻŒáàâäąćéèêê
ęéèíîĩìłńñóòôöśúùûüÿźżœßABC
DEFGHIJKLMabcdefghijklmno

▶ Light Oblique
ÄĄÀÁÂĆÉĖĘĒÊËÈÍÎĨÌŁŃÑÖÓÔ
ÒŚÚÛÜÙŸŹŻŒáàâäąćéèêê
ęéèíîĩìłńñóòôöśúùûüÿźżœßABC
DEFGHIJKLMNabcdefghijklm

▶ Black
ÄĄÀÁÂĆÉĖĘĒÊËÈÍÎĨÌŁŃÑ
ÖÓÔÒŚÚÛÜÙŸŹŻŒáàâä
ąćéèêëęéèíîĩìłńñóòôöś
úùûüÿźżœßABCDEabcdef

▶ Black Oblique
ÄĄÀÁÂĆÉĖĘĒÊËÈÍÎĨÌŁŃÑ
ÖÓÔÒŚÚÛÜÙŸŹŻŒáàâä
ąćéèêëęéèíîĩìłńñóòôöś
úùûüÿźżœßABCDEabcdef

K6573 Mac ce +T
HCentral
ÄĀĄÁČĆĎĐÉĒĖĚĘĢIĪÍĶĻĹĽŁŅŃŇŐÕŌŎ
ÓÔŘŔŖŠŚŤŪŮÜÚŰŲÝŹŻŽāáąăčćďđéėēě
ęġíįīļľĺķņńňóôöõōőŕřŗšśťūůüúűųýźżžABabc

© FSI 1993 ▼

Eastern Europe

K6573 Mac — HCentral

▶ Plain
ÄĀĄÁĆČĎĐÉĒĚĘGJĪĺĶĻĽŁ
ŃŇŇÕŌÖÓÔŘŖŘŚŠŤÚŪŮ
ÚŰŲÝŹŽŻāąąäčćďéēěęģíįīĮ
ļĺĺķņňóôöōōőŕŗśšťüūůűųýźžż

▶ Oblique
ÄĀĄÁĆČĎĐÉĒĚĘGJĪĺĶĻĽŁ
ŃŇŇÕŌÖÓÔŘŖŘŚŠŤÚŪŮ
ÚŰŲÝŹŽŻāąąäčćďéēěęģíįīĮ
ļĺĺķņňóôöōōőŕŗśšťüūůűųýźžż

▶ Bold
ÄĀĄÁĆČĎĐÉĒĚĘGJĪĺĶĻĽ
ŁŃŇŇÕŌÖÓÔŘŖŘŚŠŤÚŪŮ
ÚŰŲÝŹŽŻāąąäčćďéēěęģíįī
įļĺĺķņňóôöōōőŕŗśšťüūůűųý

▶ Bold Oblique
ÄĀĄÁĆČĎĐÉĒĚĘGJĪĺĶĻĽŁ
ŁŃŇŇÕŌÖÓÔŘŖŘŚŠŤÚŪŮ
ÚŰŲÝŹŽŻāąąäčćďéēěęģíįī
įļĺĺķņňóôöōōőŕŗśšťüūůűųý

K931 Mac — HCzech (CS) +T

ÄÁÀÃÂČÉĚÊËÈĎD'ÍÍĨÌĽĹŇÓÕÔÒŘŔ
ŠŤÚÛÙŮÝŽáàâäãáčdd'éèêëěíîĩìľňóò
ôõřŕšťt'úùûůýžßABCDEFabcdefghijklm

▶ Plain
ÄÁÀÃÂČÉĚÊËÈĎD'ÍÍĨÌĽĹŇÓÓ
ÔÒŘŔŠŤÚÛÙŮÝŽáàâäãáčdd'
éèêëěíîĩìľňóòôõřŕšťt'úùûůýžß
ABCDEFGHIJKabcdefghijklmn

▶ Oblique
ÄÁÀÃÂČÉĚÊËÈĎD'ÍÍĨÌĽĹŇÓÓ
ÔÒŘŔŠŤÚÛÙŮÝŽáàâäãáčdd'
éèêëěíîĩìľňóòôõřŕšťt'úùûůýžß
ABCDEFGHIJKabcdefghijklmn

▶ Bold
ÄÁÀÃÂČÉĚÊËÈĎD'ÍÍĨÌĽĹŇÓ
ÕÔÒŘŔŠŤÚÛÙŮÝŽáàâäãáčd
d'éèêëěíîĩìľňóòôõřŕšťt'úùûů
ýžßABCDEFGHIabcdefghijkl

▶ Bold Oblique
ÄÁÀÃÂČÉĚÊËÈĎD'ÍÍĨÌĽĹŇÓ
ÕÔÒŘŔŠŤÚÛÙŮÝŽáàâäãáčd
d'éèêëěíîĩìľňóòôõřŕšťt'úùûů
ýžßABCDEFGHabcdefghijkl

K933 Mac — HCzech & TCzech (CS) +T

HCzech & TCzech

LH6284 Mac + PC — Helvetica East A ee

ĄÁÄÂĂĆÇČĎĐÉÎŁĹĽŃÔÓŐÖŔŘŠŞŢŤŮ
ÚŰÜÝŹŻŽąáâäăçčćďďëęęďíìĺľłńňŕňőóöŕśŚ
šşţťúůüűýžźżßABCDEFGHabcdefghijklmn

▶ 35 Thin
ĄÁÄÂĂĆÇČĎĐÉÎŁĹĽŃÔÓŐÖŔŘ
ŠŞŢŤŮÚŰÜÝŹŻŽąáâäăçčćďďë
ęęďíìĺľłńňŕňőóöŕśŚšşţťúůüűýžźżßA
BCDEFGHIJabcdefghijklmnopqrs

▶ 36 Thin Oblique
ĄÁÄÂĂĆÇČĎĐÉÎŁĹĽŃÔÓŐÖŔŘ
ŠŞŢŤŮÚŰÜÝŹŻŽąáâäăçčćďďë
ęęďíìĺľłńňŕňőóöŕśŚšşţťúůüűýžźżßA
BCDEFGHIJabcdefghijklmnopqrs

▶ 55 Roman
ĄÁÄÂĂĆÇČĎĐÉÎŁĹĽŃÔÓŐÖŔ
ŘŠŞŢŤŮÚŰÜÝŹŻŽąáâäăçčć
ďďëęęďíìĺľłńňŕňőóöŕśŚšşţťúůüű
ýžźżßABCDEabcdefghijklmno

▶ 56 Roman Oblique
ĄÁÄÂĂĆÇČĎĐÉÎŁĹĽŃÔÓŐÖŔ
ŘŠŞŢŤŮÚŰÜÝŹŻŽąáâäăçčć
ďďëęęďíìĺľłńňŕňőóöŕśŚšşţťúůüű
ýžźżßABCDEabcdefghijklmno

© FSI 1993

▼ LH6284 Mac + PC Helvetica East A

▶ 75 Bold
ĄÁÄÂĂĆÇČĎDÉÎĹĽŁŃÔÓŐÖ
ŔŘŠŞŢŤŦÚÜŰÝŹŻŽąáâäăç
čćďđěëęď'íîľl'łńňñőóöŕřŚšşţť
úůüűýźżžßABCabcdefghijkl

▶ 76 Bold Oblique
ĄÁÄÂĂĆÇČĎDÉÎĹĽŁŃÔÓŐÖ
ŔŘŠŞŢŤŦÚÜŰÝŹŻŽąáâäăç
čćďđěëęď'íîľl'łńňñőóöŕřŚšşţť
úůüűýźżžßABCDabcdefghijkl

Eastern Europe

K456 Mac
Helvetica Light /Black & Times Ten Czech

Helvetica & Times Ten Czech

(CS) +T

K454 Mac
Helvetica Light/Black

(CS) +T

ÄĀÀÃÂČÉĒÊËÈĎD'ÍÍÎÏÌĹĽŇÓÕ
ÔÒŘŔŠŤÚÛÙŮÝŹŽáàâäãáčďd'
éèêëěéíîïìl'ňóòôõřŕšťúùûůýžßABCDEFGHabcdefghijklm

▶ Light
ÄĀÀÃÂČÉĒÊËÈĎD'ÍÍÎÏÌĹĽŇÓÔ
ÔÒŘŔŠŤÚÛÙŮÝŹŽáàâäãáčďd'
éèêëěéíîïìl'ňóòôõřŕšťúùûůýžßA
BCDEFGHIJKLMabcdefghijkl

▶ Light Oblique
ÄĀÀÃÂČÉĒÊËÈĎD'ÍÍÎÏÌĹĽŇÓÔ
ÔÒŘŔŠŤÚÛÙŮÝŹŽáàâäãáčďd'
éèêëěéíîïìl'ňóòôõřŕšťúùûůýžßA
BCDEFGHIJKLabcdefghijklmn

▶ Black
ÄĀÀÃÂČÉĒÊËÈĎD'ÍÍÎÏÌĹĽ
ŇÓÕÔÒŘŔŠŤÚÛÙŮÝŹŽáà
âäãáčďd'éèêëěéíîïìl'ňóòô
õřŕšťúùûůýžßABCDabcd

▶ Black Oblique
ÄĀÀÃÂČÉĒÊËÈĎD'ÍÍÎÏÌĹĽ
ŇÓÕÔÒŘŔŠŤÚÛÙŮÝŹŽáà
âäãáčďd'éèêëěéíîïìl'ňóòô
õřŕšťúùûůýžßABCDabcd

K340 Mac
Kurland

(LV)

ÄĀÀÃÂÁČÉĒÊËÈĢĪÍÎÏÌĶĻŅÑÖŌÕÓÔ
ÒŖŠÜŪÚÛÙŸŽŒáàâäãāčéèêëēģîíîïīķļñņó
òôöõōŗšúùûüūyžœßABCDEFabcdefghijkl

▶ Plain
ÄĀÀÃÂÁČÉĒÊËÈĢĪÍÎÏÌĶĻŅÑ
ÖŌÕÓÔÒŖŠÜŪÚÛÙŸŽŒáàâäã
āčéèêëēģîíîïīķļñņóòôöõōŗšúùûüūy
žœßABCDEFGHIJKabcdefghijkl

▶ Italic
ÄĀÀÃÂÁČÉĒÊËÈĢĪÍÎÏÌĶĻŅÑÖŌ
ÕÓÔÒŖŠÜŪÚÛÙŸŽŒáàâäãāčé
èêëēģîíîïīķļñņóòôöõōŗšúùûüūyžœß
ABCDEFGHIJKabcdefghijklmno

▶ Bold
ÄĀÀÃÂÁČÉĒÊËÈĢĪÍÎÏÌĶĻŅ
ÑÖŌÕÓÔÒŖŠÜŪÚÛÙŸŽŒáà
âäãāčéèêëēģîíîïīķļñņóòôöõōŗšúù
ûüūyžœßABCDEFGHIabcdefg

▶ Bold Italic
ÄĀÀÃÂÁČÉĒÊËÈĢĪÍÎÏÌĶĻŅÑ
ÖŌÕÓÔÒŖŠÜŪÚÛÙŸŽŒáàâ
āčéèêëēģîíîïīķļñņóòôöõōŗšúùûü
ūyžœßABCDEFGHIabcdefghijkl

© FSI 1993

Eastern Europe

K345 Mac — Kurland & Livland (LV)

Kurland & Livland

K341 Mac — Livland (LV)

ÄĀÀÃÂÁĆČÉĒÈÊËĘĢĪÍÎĨĪĶĻŅÑÖŌÕÓÔ
ÒŖŠÜŪÚÛÙŸŽŒåàâäãǎáćéèêëęģíîìĩīķļ
ñņóòôöõōŗšúùûüūÿžœßABCDEabcdef

▶ Plain
ÄĀÀÃÂÁĆČÉĒÈÊËĘĢĪÍÎĨĪĶĻŅÑÖ
ÕÓÔÒŖŠÜŪÚÛÙŸŽŒáàâä
ãǎćéèêëęģíîìĩīķļñņóòôöõōŗšúù
ûüūÿžœßABCDEFGabcdefghij

▶ Oblique
ÄĀÀÃÂÁĆČÉĒÈÊËĘĢĪÍÎĨĪĶĻŅÑÖ
ÕÓÔÒŖŠÜŪÚÛÙŸŽŒáàâä
ãǎćéèêëęģíîìĩīķļñņóòôöõōŗšúù
ûüūÿžœßABCDEFGabcdefghij

▶ Bold
ÄĀÀÃÂÁĆČÉĒÈÊËĘĢĪÍÎĨĪĶĻŅ
ÖÕÓÔÒŖŠÜŪÚÛÙŸŽŒáàâ
äãǎćéèêëęģíîìĩīķļñņóòôöõōŗš
úùûüūÿžœßABCDEFabcdefg

▶ Bold Oblique
ÄĀÀÃÂÁĆČÉĒÈÊËĘĢĪÍÎĨĪĶĻŅ
ÖÕÓÔÒŖŠÜŪÚÛÙŸŽŒáàâ
äãǎćéèêëęģíîìĩīķļñņóòôöõōŗš
úùûüūÿžœßABCDEFabcdefg

PG6606 Mac + PC — Newton East Europe (ee)

AÁÂÃÄĄĆÇČĎĐÉĚËÍÎŁĹĽŇÓÔŐÖŔŘŠŚ
ŞŢŤŮÚÚŰÜÝŽŹŻáâãäąćçčéęëěďíîĺľłńňóô
őöŕŕššşţťůúűüýžźżßABCDEFGabcdefghijkl

▶ Book
AÁÂÃÄĄĆÇČĎĐÉĚËÍÎŁĹĽŇ
ÓÔŐÖŔŘŠŚŞŢŤŮÚÚŰÜÝŽŹ
Żáâãäąćçčéęëěďíîĺľłńňóôőöŕ
ŕššşţťůúűüýžźżßABCDabcdefg

▶ Italic
AÁÂÃÄĄĆÇČĎĐÉĚËÍÎŁĹ ĽŇÓ
ÔŐÖŔŘŠŚŞŢŤŮÚÚŰÜÝŽŹŻáâ
ãäąćçčéęëěďíîĺľłńňóôőöŕŕššşţ ť
ůúűüýžźżßABCDEFabcdefghijkl

▶ Bold
AÁÂÃÄĄĆÇČĎĐÉĚËÍÎŁĹĽŇ
ÓÔŐÖŔŘŠŚŞŢŤŮÚÚŰÜÝŽŹ
Żáâãäąćçčéęëěďíîĺľłńňóôőöŕŕ
ššşţťůúűüýžźżßABCDabcdefghi

▶ Bold Italic
AÁÂÃÄĄĆÇČĎĐÉĚËÍÎŁĹ ĽŇÓ
ÔŐÖŔŘŠŚŞŢŤŮÚÚŰÜÝŽŹŻáâ
ãäąćçčéęëěďíîĺľłńňóôőöŕŕššşţ
ťůúűüýžźżßABCDEFabcdefghijk

PG6610 Mac + PC — Newton Turk (turk)

AÁÂÃÄÅÇÈÉÊËĞÌÍÎÏİÒÓÔÕÖØŞŠÙÚÛÜ
ŸÆŒàáâãäåçèéêëğìíîïıñòóôõöøšşùúûüÿßæ
œABCDEFGHIJKLMabcdefghijklmnopqrs

▶ Book
AÁÂÃÄÅÇÈÉÊËĞÌÍÎÏİÒÓÔÕ
ÖØŞŠÙÚÛÜŸÆŒàáâãäåçèé
êëğìíîïıñòóôõöøšşùúûüÿßæœA
BCDEFGHIJKabcdefghijklm

▶ Italic
AÁÂÃÄÅÇÈÉÊËĞÌÍÎÏİÒÓÔÕÖ
ØŞŠÙÚÛÜŸÆŒàáâãäåçèéêë
ğìíîïıñòóôõöøšşùúûüÿßæœABCD
EFGHIJKLMNabcdefghijklmn

© FSI 1993

▼ PG6610 Mac + PC   Newton Turk

▶ Bold
ÀÁÂÃÄÅÇÈÉÊËÌÍÎÏİÒÓÔÕ
ÖØŞŠÙÚÛÜŸÆŒàáâãäåçèé
êëğìíîïñòóôõöøšşùúûüÿßæœAB
CDEFGHIJKLabcdefghijklmn

▶ Bold Italic
*ÀÁÂÃÄÅÇÈÉÊËÌÍÎÏİÒÓÔÕÖ
ØŞŠÙÚÛÜŸÆŒàáâãäåçèéêëğ
ìíîïñòóôõöøšşùúûüÿßæœABCDE
FGHIJKLMNOabcdefghijklmn*

Eastern Europe

K6576 Mac
PAccents   UNI

ÄÅÁĄÂÀÃÇĐÉĘÊËÈÍÎÏİĻŃÓÔÒÕÖØŢÜ ÚÛÙŸÆŒáàâäãåąçđéèêëíîïįļńóòôöõøŗúùû üÿæœßABCDEFGHIJKLMabcdefghijklmno

▶ Regular
ÄÅÁĄÂÀÃÇĐÉĘÊËÈÍÎÏİĻŃ
ÓÔÒÕÖØŢÜÚÛÙŸÆŒáàâä
åąçđéèêëíîïįļńóòôöõøŗúùûüÿæ
œßABCDEFGHIJabcdefghijkl

▶ Italic
*ÄÅÁĄÂÀÃÇĐÉĘÊËÈÍÎÏİĻŃÓ
ÔÒÕÖØŢÜÚÛÙŸÆŒáàâäãåąç
đéèêëíîïįļńóòôöõøŗúùûüÿæœßAB
CDEFGHIJKLMabcdefghijklmno*

▶ Bold
**ÄÅÁĄÂÀÃÇĐÉĘÊËÈÍÎÏİĻŃ
ÓÔÒÕÖØŢÜÚÛÙŸÆŒáàâã
äåąçđéèêëíîïįļńóòôöõøŗúùûü
ÿæœßABCDEFGHabcdefghij**

▶ Bold Italic
***ÄÅÁĄÂÀÃÇĐÉĘÊËÈÍÎÏİĻŃÓ
ÔÒÕÖØŢÜÚÛÙŸÆŒáàâäã
ąçđéèêëíîïįļńóòôöõøŗúùûüÿæ
œßABCDEFGHIJKabcdefghijk***

K343 Mac
Pannonica   Ⓗ ⓇⓄ Ⓣ®

ÄÁÀÂĂÇËÉÈÊĞÍÎÌÏÖÓÒÔŐŢŞÜÚÙÛ Űäáàâăçëéèêğíîìïöóòôőşţüúùûű¿¡ABC DEFGHIJKLMNOPQabcdefghijklmnop

▶ Plain
ÄÁÀÂĂÇËÉÈÊĞÍÎÌÏÖÓÒÔŐŢ
ŞÜÚÙÛŰäáàâăçëéèêğíîìïöóò
ôőşţüúùûű¿¡ABCDEFGHIJKLM
NOPQRSTUVWXYZabcdefghij

▶ Oblique
*ÄÁÀÂĂÇËÉÈÊĞÍÎÌÏÖÓÒÔŐŢ
ŞÜÚÙÛŰäáàâăçëéèêğíîìïöóò
ôőşţüúùûű¿¡ABCDEFGHIJKLM
NOPQRSTUVWXYZabcdefghij*

▶ Bold
**ÄÁÀÂĂÇËÉÈÊĞÍÎÌÏÖÓÒÔŐŢ
ŞÜÚÙÛŰäáàâăçëéèêğíîìïöóò
ôőşţüúùûű¿¡ABCDEFGHIJK
LMNOPQRSTUVWXYZabcde**

▶ Bold Oblique
***ÄÁÀÂĂÇËÉÈÊĞÍÎÌÏÖÓÒÔŐŢ
ŞÜÚÙÛŰäáàâăçëéèêğíîìïöóò
ôőşţüúùûű¿¡ABCDEFGHIJK
LMNOPQRSTUVWXYZabcde***

K2789 Mac
Pannonica Light/Black   Ⓗ ⓇⓄ Ⓣ®

ÄÁÀÂĂÇËÉÈÊĞÍÎÌÏÖÓÒÔŐŢŞÜÚÙÛŰäá àâăçëéèêğíîìïöóòôőşţüúùûű¿¡ABCDEFGH IJKLMNOPQRSTUVWXYZabcdefghijklmn

▶ Light
ÄÁÀÂĂÇËÉÈÊĞÍÎÌÏÖÓÒÔŐŢŞ
ÜÚÙÛŰäáàâăçëéèêğíîìïöóòô
şţüúùûű¿¡ABCDEFGHIJKLMN
OPQRSTUVWXYZabcdefghijkl

▶ Light Oblique
*ÄÁÀÂĂÇËÉÈÊĞÍÎÌÏÖÓÒÔŐŢŞ
ÜÚÙÛŰäáàâăçëéèêğíîìïöóòô
şţüúùûű¿¡ABCDEFGHIJKLMN
OPQRSTUVWXYZabcdefghijkl*

© FSI 1993   ▼

Eastern Europe

▼ K2789 Mac Pannonica Light/Black

▶ Black
ÄÁÀÂĂÇËÉÈÊĞÍÎÌÏÖÓÒÔ ŐŢŞÜÚÙÛŰäáàâăçëéèêğ íîìïöóòôőşţüúùûű¿¡ABCD EFGHIJKLMabcdefghijkl

▶ Black Oblique
ÄÁÀÂĂÇËÉÈÊĞÍÎÌÏÖÓÒÔ ŐŢŞÜÚÙÛŰäáàâăçëéèêğ íîìïöóòôőşţüúùûű¿¡ABCD EFGHIJKLMabcdefghijkl

K450 Mac — Pannonica & Thourque
(H) (RO) (TR)

Pannonica & Thourque

PG6607 Mac + PC — Petersburg East Europe ee

ĄÁÂÃÄĆÇČĎĐÉËĚÍÎĹĽŁŃÓÔÕÖŔŘŠŚ ŞŢŤŮÚŰÜÝŹŽŻáâãäąćçčéęëěďđíîĺľłńňóôő öŕřśšşşťťůúűüýźžżßABCDEFGHabcdefghijkl

▶ Book
ĄÁÂÃÄĆÇČĎĐÉËĚÍÎĹĽŃÓ ÔÕÖŔŘŠŚŞŢŤŮÚŰÜÝŹŽŻá âãäąćçčéęëěďđíîĺľłńňóôőöŕřśšşť ťůúűüýźžżßABCDEFabcdefghij

▶ Italic
ĄÁÂÃÄĆÇČĎĐÉËĚÍÎĹĽŃÓÔ ÕÖŔŘŠŚŞŢŤŮÚŰÜÝŹŽŻáâãäą ćçčéęëěďđíîĺľłńňóôőöŕřśšşťťůúű üýźžżßABCDEFGHabcdefghijklm

▶ Bold
ĄÁÂÃÄĆÇČĎĐÉËĚÍÎĹĽŃ ÓÔÕÖŔŘŠŚŞŢŤŮÚŰÜÝŹŽ Żáâãäąćçčéęëěďđíîĺľłńňóôőöŕř śšşťťůúűüýźžżßABCDabcdefg

▶ Bold Italic
ĄÁÂÃÄĆÇČĎĐÉËĚÍÎĹĽŃÓ ÔÕ ÖŔŘŠŚŞŢŤŮÚŰÜÝŹŽŻáâ ãäąćçčéęëěďđíîĺľłńňóôőöŕřśšş ťťůúűüýźžżßABCDEabcdefghi

PG6611 Mac + PC — Petersburg Turk turk

ÀÁÂÃÄÅÇÈÉËĞÌÍÎÏÑÒÓÔÕÖØŞŠÙÚÛ ÜŸÆŒàáâãäåçèéêêğìíîïñòóôõöøšşùúûüÿßæ œABCDEFGHIJKLMNabcdefghijklmnopq

▶ Book
ÀÁÂÃÄÅÇÈÉËĞÌÍÎÏÒÓÔÕ ÖØŞŠÙÚÛÜŸÆŒàáâãäåçèéê êğìíîïñòóôõöøšşùúûüÿßæœABC DEFGHIJKLMabcdefghijklmn

▶ Italic
ÀÁÂÃÄÅÇÈÉËĞÌÍÎÏÒÓÔÕÖØ ŞŠÙÚÛÜŸÆŒàáâãäåçèéêêğìíî ñòóôõöøšşùúûüÿßæœABCDEFG HIJKLMNOPabcdefghijklmnopq

▶ Bold
ÀÁÂÃÄÅÇÈÉËĞÌÍÎÏÒÓÔÕ ÖØŞŠÙÚÛÜŸÆŒàáâãäåçèé êêğìíîïñòóôõöøšşùúûüÿßæœA BCDEFGHIJKabcdefghijklmn

▶ Bold Italic
ÀÁÂÃÄÅÇÈÉËĞÌÍÎÏÒÓÔÕÖ ØŞŠÙÚÛÜŸÆŒàáâãäåçèéêê ğìíîïñòóôõöøšşùúûüÿßæœABC DEFGHIJKLMabcdefghijklmn

PG6608 Mac + PC — Pragmatica East Europe ee

ĄÁÂÃÄĆÇČĎĐÉËĚÍÎĹĽŁŃÓÔÕÖŔŘŠŚŞŢŤ ŮÚŰÜÝŹŽŻáâãäąćçčéęëěďđíîĺľłńňóôőöŕ řśšşťťůúűüýźžżßABCDEFGHIabcdefghijkl

© FSI 1993

▼

▼ PG6608 Mac + PC Pragmatica East Europe

► Book
AÁÂÄĆÇČĎĐÉËĚÍÎŁĹŃÓÔ
ŐÖŔŘŚŞŠŢŤÚÛŰÜÝŹŻŽáâä
ąćçčéęëěd'ďíîĺľ'łńňóôőöŕřśşš
t'ťůúűüýźżžßABCDEFabcdefg

► Italic
AÁÂÄĆÇČĎĐÉËĚÍÎŁĹŃÓÔ
ŐÖŔŘŚŞŠŢŤÚÛŰÜÝŹŻŽáâä
ąćçčéęëěd'ďíîĺľ'łńňóôőöŕřśşš
t'ťůúűüýźżžßABCDEFabcdefg

► Bold
AÁÂÄĆÇČĎĐÉËĚÍÎŁĹŃÓ
ÔŐÖŔŘŚŞŠŢŤÚÛŰÜÝŹŻŽáâ
äąćçčéęëěd'ďíîĺľ'łńňóôőö
ŕřśşšt'ťůúűüýźżžßABCabcd

► Bold Italic
AÁÂÄĆÇČĎĐÉËĚÍÎŁĹŃÓ
ÔŐÖŔŘŚŞŠŢŤÚÛŰÜÝŹŻŽáâ
äąćçčéęëěd'ďíîĺľ'łńňóôőö
ŕřśşšt'ťůúűüýźżžßABCabcd

Eastern Europe

PG6612 Mac + PC   turk
Pragmatica Turk

ÀÁÂÃÄÅÇÈÉÊËĞÌÍÎÏİÒÓÔÕÖØŞŠÙÚÛÜŸÆ
Œàáâãäåçèéêëğìíîïıñòóôõöøšşùúûüÿßæœ
ABCDEFGHIJKLMNabcdefghijklmnopqrst

► Book
ÀÁÂÃÄÅÇÈÉÊËĞÌÍÎÏİÒÓÔÕÖØŞ
ŠÙÚÛÜŸÆŒàáâãäåçèéêëğìíî
ïıñòóôõöøšşùúûüÿßæœABCD
EFGHIJKLMNOabcdefghijklm

► Italic
ÀÁÂÃÄÅÇÈÉÊËĞÌÍÎÏİÒÓÔÕÖØŞ
ŠÙÚÛÜŸÆŒàáâãäåçèéêëğìíî
ïıñòóôõöøšşùúûüÿßæœABCD
EFGHIJKLMNOabcdefghijklm

► Bold
ÀÁÂÃÄÅÇÈÉÊËĞÌÍÎÏİÒÓÔÕ
ÖØŞŠÙÚÛÜŸÆŒàáâãäåçèé
êëğìíîïıñòóôõöøšşùúûüÿßæ
œABCDEFGHIJabcdefghijkl

► Bold Italic
ÀÁÂÃÄÅÇÈÉÊËĞÌÍÎÏİÒÓÔÕ
ÖØŞŠÙÚÛÜŸÆŒàáâãäåçèé
êëğìíîïıñòóôõöøšşùúûüÿßæ
œABCDEFGHIJabcdefghijkl

K1098 Mac   UNI
TAccents & HAccents & TPlusChars & HPlusChars
TAccents & HAccents & TPlusChars & HPlusChars

K281 Mac   UNI
TAccents & HAccents

ÄÅÁĄÂÀÃÇĐÉĘÊËÈÍÎÏİŁÑÓÔÒÕÖØŢ
ÜÚÛÙŸÆŒáàâäãåąçđéèêëíîïïłñóòôöõ
øţúùûüÿæœßABCDEFGHabcdefghijkl

► H Plain
ÄÅÁĄÂÀÃÇĐÉĘÊËÈÍÎÏİŁÑÓÔ
ÒÕÖØŢÜÚÛÙŸÆŒáàâäãåąç
đéèêëíîïïłñóòôöõøţúùûüÿæœß
ABCDEFGHIJabcdefghijklmno

► H Oblique
ÄÅÁĄÂÀÃÇĐÉĘÊËÈÍÎÏİŁÑÓÔ
ÒÕÖØŢÜÚÛÙŸÆŒáàâäãåąç
đéèêëíîïïłñóòôöõøţúùûüÿæœß
ABCDEFGHIJabcdefghijklmno

► H Bold
ÄÅÁĄÂÀÃÇĐÉĘÊËÈÍÎÏİŁÑÓ
ÔÒÕÖØŢÜÚÛÙŸÆŒáàâäã
åąçđéèêëíîïïłñóòôöõøţúùûüÿ
æœßABCDEFGHIJabcdefghi

► H Bold Oblique
ÄÅÁĄÂÀÃÇĐÉĘÊËÈÍÎÏİŁÑÓ
ÔÒÕÖØŢÜÚÛÙŸÆŒáàâäã
åąçđéèêëíîïïłñóòôöõøţúùûüÿ
æœßABCDEFGHIJabcdefghi

© FSI 1993
▼

Eastern Europe

▼ K281 Mac TAccents & HAccents

▶ T Plain
ÄÅÁĄÂÀÃÇĐÉĘÊËÈÍÎÏÌŁÑÓÔ
ÒÕÖØŢÚÙÛÙŸÆŒáàâãåąçđé
êëèñîíìłñóòôõöøţúùûüÿæœßABCD
EFGHIJabcdefghijklmnopqrstuv

▶ T Italic
*ÄÅÁĄÂÀÃÇĐÉĘÊËÈÍÎÏÌŁÑÓÒÒ
ÕÖØŢÚÚÛÙŸÆŒáàâãåąçđéè
ëíîïìłñóòôõöøţúùûüÿæœßABCDEF
GHIJabcdefghijklmnopqrstuvwxy*

▶ T Bold
**ÄÅÁĄÂÀÃÇĐÉĘÊËÈÍÎÏÌŁÑÓ
ÒÕÖØŢÚÚÛÙŸÆŒáàâãåą
çđéêëèñîíìłñóòôõöøţúùûüÿæœßA
BCDEFGHIJabcdefghijklmnop**

▶ T Bold Italic
***ÄÅÁĄÂÀÃÇĐÉĘÊËÈÍÎÏÌŁÑÓ
ÒÕÖØŢÚÚÛÙŸÆŒáàâãåą
çđéêëèñîíìłñóòôõöøţúùûüÿæœßA
BCDEFGHIJabcdefghijklmnop***

K6574 Mac   ce + T
TCentral & HCentral

   TCentral & HCentral

K6572 Mac   ce + T
TCentral

ÄĀĄÁČĆĎĐÉĒĖĚĘĢĪÍĶĻĽŁŅŃŇŐÕŌÖ
ÓÔŖŘŖŠŚŤŪŮÜÚŰŲÝŹŽŻāáąäčćďđéēėěęģíįī
łļĽĺķņńňóôöõōőŕřŗšśťüūůűųúýźžżABCDEabcdef

▶ Plain
ÄĀĄÁČĆĎĐÉĒĖĚĘĢĪÍĶĻĽŁ
ŅŃŇŐÕŌÖÓÔŖŘŖŠŚŤŪŮÜÚ
ŰŲÝŹŽŻāáąäčćďđéēėěęģíįīłļĽĺķņ
ńňóôöõōőŕřŗšśťüūůűųúýźžżABCD

▶ Italic
*ÄĀĄÁČĆĎĐÉĒĖĚĘĢĪÍĶĻĽŁŅ
ŇŐÕŌÖÓÔŖŘŖŠŚŤŪŮÜÚŰŲ
ÝŹŽŻāáąäčćďđéēėěęģíįīłļĽĺķņńňó
ôöõōőŕřŗšśťüūůűųúýźžżABCDEF*

▶ Bold
**ÄĀĄÁČĆĎĐÉĒĖĚĘĢĪÍĶĻĽ
ŁŅŃŇŐÕŌÖÓÔŖŘŖŠŚŤŪŮ
ÜÚŰŲÝŹŽŻāáąäčćďđéēėěęģíįī
łļĽĺķņńňóôöõōőŕřŗšśťüūůűųúýźž**

▶ Bold Italic
***ÄĀĄÁČĆĎĐÉĒĖĚĘĢĪÍĶĻĽŁ
ŅŃŇŐÕŌÖÓÔŖŘŖŠŚŤŪŮÜÚ
ŰŲÝŹŽŻāáąäčćďđéēėěęģíįīłļĽĺķņ
ńňóôöõōőŕřŗšśťüūůűųúýźžżABC***

K932 Mac   CS + T
TCzech

ÄÁÀÃÂČÉĚÊËÈĎĎ'ÍÍÎÏÌĽĹŇÓÕÔÒŘŔŠ
ŤÚÛÙŮÝŽáàâäãáčďđ'éěêëéíîîïľňóòôõřŕšť
ťúùûůýžßABCDEFGHIabcdefghijklmnopq

▶ Plain
ÄÁÀÃÂČÉĚÊËÈĎĎ'ÍÍÎÏÌĽĹŇÓ
ÕÔÒŘŔŠŤÚÛÙŮÝŽáàâäáčďđ'é
ěêëéíîîľňóòôõřŕšťťúùûůýžßABC
DEFGHIJKLMabcdefghijklmnop

▶ Italic
*ÄÁÀÃÂČÉĚÊËÈĎĎ'ÍÍÎÏÌĽĹŇÓÕ
ÔÒŘŔŠŤÚÛÙŮÝŽáàâäáčďđ'éèê
ëéíîîľňóòôõřŕšťťúùûůýžßABCD
EFGHIJKLMNOabcdefghijklmno*

▶ Bold
**ÄÁÀÃÂČÉĚÊËÈĎĎ'ÍÍÎÏÌĽĹŇ
ÓÕÔÒŘŔŠŤÚÛÙŮÝŽáàâäáč
ďđ'éěêëéíîîľňóòôõřŕšťťúùûůýž
ßABCDEFGHIJKabcdefghijkl**

▶ Bold Italic
***ÄÁÀÃÂČÉĚÊËÈĎĎ'ÍÍÎÏÌĽĹŇÓ
ÕÔÒŘŔŠŤÚÛÙŮÝŽáàâäáčďđ'
éěêëéíîîľňóòôõřŕšťťúùûůýžßAB
CDEFGHIJKLabcdefghijklmno***

© FSI 1993

K342 Mac
Thourque

(H) (RO) (TR)

Eastern Europe

ÄÁÀÂĂÇËÉÈÊĞÍÎÏÖÓÒÔŐŢŞÜÚÙÛ
ŰäáàâăçëéèêğíîïöóòôőşţüúùûűABCDEFG
HIJKLMNOPQRSTUVWXYZabcdefghijk

▶ Plain
ÄÁÀÂĂÇËÉÈÊĞÍÎÏÖÓÒÔŐŢ
ŞÜÚÙÛŰäáàâăçëéèêğíîïöóòôőşţ
üúùûűABCDEFGHIJKLMNOPQ
RSTUVWXYZabcdefghijklmnop

▶ Italic
ÄÁÀÂĂÇËÉÈÊĞÍÎÏÖÓÒÔŐŢŞ
ÜÚÙÛŰäáàâăçëéèêğíîïöóòôőşţü
úùûűABCDEFGHIJKLMNOPQR
STUVWXYZabcdefghijklmnopqrst

▶ Bold
ÄÁÀÂĂÇËÉÈÊĞÍÎÏÖÓÒÔŐ
ŢŞÜÚÙÛŰäáàâăçëéèêğíîïöóòôő
şţüúùûűABCDEFGHIJKLMN
OPQRSTUVWXYZabcdefghijk

▶ Bold Italic
ÄÁÀÂĂÇËÉÈÊĞÍÎÏÖÓÒÔŐŢ
ŞÜÚÙÛŰäáàâăçëéèêğíîïöóòôőşţ
üúùûűABCDEFGHIJKLMNOP
QRSTUVWXYZabcdefghijklmno

K455 Mac
Times Ten Czech

✎ 1988: (Stanley Morison, Victor Lardent, 1931-35)   (CS) +T

ÄÁÀÃÂČÉÉĚÊËÈĎD'ÍÍÎÏÌĽ'ĹŇÓÕÔ
ÒŘŔŠŤÚÚÛÙŮÝŹáàâäãáčdd'éèêëěéíîï
ľ'ňóòôõřŕšťt'úùûůýžßABCDEabcdefghij

▶ Plain
ÄÁÀÃÂČÉÉĚÊËÈĎD'ÍÍÎÏÌĽ'Ĺ
ŇÓÕÔÒŘŔŠŤÚÚÛÙŮÝŹáàâä
ãáčdd'éèêëěéíîïľ'ňóòôõřŕšťt'úùû
ůýžßABCDEFGHIabcdefghijk

▶ Italic
ÄÁÀÃÂČÉÉĚÊËÈĎD'ÍÍÎÏÌĽ'Ĺ
ŇÓÕÔÒŘŔŠŤÚÚÛÙŮÝŹáàâä
ãáčdd'éèêëěéíîïľ'ňóòôõřŕšťt'úùû
ůýžßABCDEFGHabcdefghijkl

▶ Bold
ÄÁÀÃÂČÉÉĚÊËÈĎD'ÍÍÎÏÌĽ'Ĺ
ŇÓÕÔÒŘŔŠŤÚÚÛÙŮÝŹáàâä
ãáčdd'éèêëěéíîïľ'ňóòôõřŕšťt'úù
ûůýžßABCDEFGHabcdefghij

▶ Bold Italic
ÄÁÀÃÂČÉÉĚÊËÈĎD'ÍÍÎÏÌĽ'Ĺ
ŇÓÕÔÒŘŔŠŤÚÚÛÙŮÝŹáàâä
ãáčdd'éèêëěéíîïľ'ňóòôõřŕšťt'úù
ûůýžßABCDEFGHabcdefghij

LH6283 Mac + PC
Times Ten East A

ee

ĄÁÄÂĂĆÇČĐĎÉÎŁĽĹŇÔÓŐÖŔŘŠŞŢŤ
ŤŮÚÚÜÝŹŻŽąáâäăçččďdëěęďĺľłńňőóöŕ
řŚšşţťúůüűýžźżßABCDEFGHabcdefghijklm

▶ Roman
ĄÁÄÂĂĆÇČĐĎÉÎŁĽĹŇÔÓ
ŐÖŔŘŠŞŢŤŤŮÚÚÜÝŹŻŽąá
âäăçččďdëěęďĺľłńňőóöŕřŚšşţť
úůüűýžźżßABCDEFabcdefghij

▶ Italic
ĄÁÄÂĂĆÇČĐĎÉÎŁĽĹŇÔÓ
ŐÖŔŘŠŞŢŤŤŮÚÚÜÝŹŻŽąáâ
äăçččďdëěęďĺľłńňőóöŕřŚšşţťú
ůüűýžźżßABCDEFGabcdefghi

▶ Bold
ĄÁÄÂĂĆÇČĐĎÉÎŁĽĹŇÔÓ
ŐÖŔŘŠŞŢŤŤŮÚÚÜÝŹŻŽąá
âäăçččďdëěęďĺľłńňőóöŕřŚšşţ
ťúůüűýžźżßABCDEFGabcdefg

▶ Bold Italic
ĄÁÄÂĂĆÇČĐĎÉÎŁĽĹŇÔÓ
ŐÖŔŘŠŞŢŤŤŮÚÚÜÝŹŻŽąá
âäăçččďdëěęďĺľłńňőóöŕřŚšşţ
ťúůüűýžźżßABCDEFabcdefghi

© FSI 1993

Eastern Europe

K282 Mac — UNI
TPlusChars & HPlusChars

ĂĀĄÅÄĂB'ČĊČĆĎDĐ'ĎĐĒĔĖĚËĘĒF'ĠĢĞǦĦḦĪĬİĮĻ
ĴĶḰĽĻŁĹĽḾŃŅÕŌŎÖŐṔPPQŔŘŞŚŜŠṢŤŢṮŢŰŨŬ
ŮŲŰṼV̆Ṽ̌V̊ŴẂŸẎỲÝŶỸȲŹŻŽąāăǎąàb'ččçćďdd'ḑ
ďďěēĕẽěçəf'ğġģǧħḧīĭịįļĵķḱļ'ḿńņ

▶ H Plain
ĂĀĄÅÄĂB'ČĊČĆĎDĐ'ĎĐĒĔ
ĖĚĘĒF'ĠĢĞǦĦḦĪĬİĮĻĴĶḰĽĻŁĹĽ
ḾŃŅÕŌŎÖŐąāăǎąàb'ččçćďdd
d'ďďěēĕẽěçəf'ğġģǧħḧīĭịįļĵk

▶ T Plain
ĂĀĄÅÄĂB'ČĊČĆĎDĐ'ĎĐĒĔĖĚ
ĘĒF'ĠĢĞǦĦḦĪĬİĮĻĴĶḰĽĻŁĹĽ
ḾŃŅÕŌŎÖŐąāăǎąàb'ččçćďdd'ḑ
ďďěēĕẽěçəf'ğġģǧħḧīĭịįļĵk'ḱḿń

K490 Mac + PC — (PL) +T
Trybuna

ÄÀÁÂĆÉÈĘËÊÈÍÎÏÌŁŃÑÖÓÔÒŚÚÛ
ÜÙŸŹŻŒáàâäąćéèêëęėíîïìłñńóòôöśúùû
üÿźżœßABCDEFGHIJabcdefghijklmnopqr

▶ Plain
ÄÀÁÂĆÉÈĘËÊÈÍÎÏÌŁŃÑÖÓ
ÔÒŚÚÛÜÙŸŹŻŒáàâäąćéèêëę
ėíîïìłñńóòôöśúùûüÿźżœßABCDE
FGHIJKLMNOPabcdefghijklmno

▶ Italic
*ÄÀÁÂĆÉÈĘËÊÈÍÎÏÌŁŃÑÖÓ
ÒŚÚÛÜÙŸŹŻŒáàâäąćéèêëęėí
îïìłñńóòôöśúùûüÿźżœßABCDEFG
HIJKLMNOPabcdefghijklmnopqr*

▶ Bold
**ÄÀÁÂĆÉÈĘËÊÈÍÎÏÌŁŃÑ
ÓÒŚÚÛÜÙŸŹŻŒáàâäąćéèê
ëęėíîïìłñńóòôöśúùûüÿźżœßAB
CDEFGHIJKLabcdefghijklmn**

▶ Bold Italic
***ÄÀÁÂĆÉÈĘËÊÈÍÎÏÌŁŃÑÖÓ
ÒŚÚÛÜÙŸŹŻŒáàâäąćéèêëęė
íîïìłñńóòôöśúùûüÿźżœßABCDE
FGHIJKLMNOabcdefghijklmno***

K495 Mac + PC — (PL) +T
Trybuna & Gazeta

Trybuna & Gazeta

PG6158 Mac + PC — cyr / cyr-gr
Academy

АБВГДЕЖЗИЙКЛМНОПРСТУФХЦЧ
ШЩЪЫЬЭЮЯабвгдежзийклмнопрстуфхцч
шщъыьэюяљњћкў џ ђ ґ є ABCDEFGabcdefghijkl

▶ Regular
АБВГДЕЖЗИЙКЛМНОПРС
ТУФХЦЧШЩЪЫЬЭЮЯабвгд
ежзийклмнопрстуфхцчшщъыьэюяљ
њћкў џ ђ ґ єABCDEFGabcdefghijklm

▶ Italic
*АБВГДЕЖЗИЙКЛМНОПРСТ
УФХЦЧШЩЪЫЬЭЮЯабвгде
жзийклмнопрстуфхцчшщъыьэюя
љњћкў џ ђ ґ єABCDEFGabcdefghijk*

▶ Bold
**АБВГДЕЖЗИЙКЛМНОПРС
ТУФХЦЧШЩЪЫЬЭЮЯабвг
дежзийклмнопрстуфхцчшщъыьэ
юяљњћкў џ ђ ґ єABCDEFabcdefghi**

Baltica
PG6159 Mac + PC — cyr / cyr-gr — Cyrillic

АБВГДЕЖЗИЙКЛМНОПРСТУФХЦЧШЩ
ЪЫЬЭЮЯабвгдежзийклмнопрстуфхцчшщ
ъыьэюяѕ њћкўџђгєABCDEFabcdefghijklmn

▶ Regular
АБВГДЕЖЗИЙКЛМНОПРС
ТУФХЦЧШЩЪЫЬЭЮЯабвг
дежзийклмнопрстуфхцчшщ
ъыьэюяѕ њћкўџђгєABCabcd

▶ Italic
АБВГДЕЖЗИЙКЛМНОПРСТ
УФХЦЧШЩЪЫЬЭЮЯабвгде
жзийклмнопрстуфхцчшщъы
ьэюяѕ њћкўџ ђгєABCabcdefg

▶ Bold
АБВГДЕЖЗИЙКЛМНОПРС
ТУФХЦЧШЩЪЫЬЭЮЯабвг
дежзийклмнопрстуфхцчшщ
ъыьэюя љњћкўџђгєABCabc

Baskerville Cyrillic
LH6287 Mac + PC — cyr-LH

АБВГДЕЖЗИЙКЛМНОПРСТУФХЦЧ
ШЩЫЬЭЮЯабвгдежзийклмнопрстуфхц
чшщъыьэюяѣàèëѳґѕҗѝòỳрр̀ѵѵжа́е́є́и́ıїо́ў́ъ̀

▶ Upright
АБВГДЕЖЗИЙКЛМНОПР
СТУФХЦЧШЩЫЬЭЮЯаб
вгдежзийклмнопрстуфхцчш
щъыьэюяѣàèëѳґѕҗѝòỳрр̀ѵж

▶ Inclined
АБВГДЕЖЗИЙКЛМНОПРС
ТУФХЦЧШЩЫЬЭЮЯаб
вгдежзийклмнопрстуфхцчшщ
ъыьэюяѣàèëѳґѕҗѝòỳрр̀ѵѵжа́е́є́и́ı́

▶ Bold
АБВГДЕЖЗИЙКЛМНОПР
СТУФХЦЧШЩЫЬЭЮЯаб
вгдежзийклмнопрстуфхцчш
щъыьэюяѣàèëѳґѕҗѝòỳрр̀ѵ

Bodoni
PG6160 Mac + PC — cyr / cyr-gr

АБВГДЕЖЗИЙКЛМНОПРСТУФХЦЧШЩ
ЪЫЬЭЮЯЂҐЄЉЊЋЎЏабвгдежзийклмноп
рстуфхцчшщъыьэюяљњћкўџђгєABCDabcdef

▶ Regular
АБВГДЕЖЗИЙКЛМНОПРСТ
УФХЦЧШЩЪЫЬЭЮЯабвгде
жзийклмнопрстуфхцчшщъыю
яљњћкўџђгєABCDEFabcdefghij

▶ Italic
АБВГДЕЖЗИЙКЛМНОПРСТУ
ФХЦЧШЩЪЫЬЭЮЯабвгдежз
ийклмнопрстуфхцчшщъыьэю
яљњћкўџђгєABCDEFGabcdefgh

▶ Bold
АБВГДЕЖЗИЙКЛМНОПРС
ТУФХЦЧШЩЪЫЬЭЮЯабвг
дежзийклмнопрстуфхцчшщ
ъыьэюяљњћкўџђгєABCabcdef

▶ Bold Italic
АБВГДЕЖЗИЙКЛМНОПРС
ТУФХЦЧШЩЪЫЬЭЮЯабвгд
ежзийклмнопрстуфхцчшщ
ъыьэюяљњћкўџђгєABCabcde

© FSI 1993

Cyrillic

▼ PG6160 Mac + PC **Bodoni**

▶ Condensed
АБВГДЕЖЗИЙКЛМНОПРСТУФХЦЧШЩ
ЪЫЬЭЮЯЋГЄЉЊЂЎЏабвгдежзийклмноп
рстуфхцчшщъыьэюяљњћкÿцђгєABCDEFGH
IJKLMNOPQRSTUVWXYZÄËÏÖÜabcdefghi

PG6161 Mac + PC cyr / cyr-gr
Compact

АБВГДЕЖЗИЙКЛМНОПРСТУФХЦЧШЩЪЫЬЭЮЯЋГЄЉЊЂЎЏабвгдежзий
клмнопрстуфхцчшщъыьэюяљњћкÿцђгєABCDEFGHIJKLMNOPQRSTUVW
XYZÄËÏÖÜabcdefghijklmnopqrstuvwxyzäëïöüßNº

▶ Regular
АБВГДЕЖЗИЙКЛМНОПРСТУФХЦЧШЩЪЫЬ
ЭЮЯЋГЄЉЊЂЎЏабвгдежзийклмнопрстуфх
цчшщъыьэюяљњћкÿцђгєABCDEFGHIJKLMN
OPQRSTUVWXYZÄËÏÖÜabcdefghijklmnopqrs

▶ Italic
*АБВГДЕЖЗИЙКЛМНОПРСТУФХЦЧШЩЪЫЬ
ЭЮЯЋГЄЉЊЂЎЏабвгдежзийклмнопрстуфх
цчшщъыьэюяљњћкÿцђгєABCDEFGHIJKLMN
OPQRSTUVWXYZÄËÏÖÜabcdefghijklmnopqrs*

▶ Bold
**АБВГДЕЖЗИЙКЛМНОПРСТУФХЦЧ
ШЩЪЫЬЭЮЯЋГЄЉЊЂЎЏабвгдеж
зийклмнопрстуфхцчшщъыьэюял
њћкÿцђгєABCDEFGHIJKLMNOPQRS**

▶ Bold Italic
***АБВГДЕЖЗИЙКЛМНОПРСТУФХЦЧ
ШЩЪЫЬЭЮЯЋГЄЉЊЂЎЏабвгдеж
зийклмнопрстуфхцчшщъыьэюял
њћкÿцђгєABCDEFGHIJKLMNOPQRS***

PG6617 Mac + PC cyr / cyr-gr / cyr-f
Courier

АБВГДЕЖЗИЙКЛМНОПРСТУФХЦЧШЩЪЫЬЭЮЯЋГЄЉЊ
ЂЎЏабвгдежзийклмнопрстуфхцчшщъыьэюяљњ
ћкÿцђгєABCDEFGHIJKLabcdefghijklmnopqr

▶ Regular
АБВГДЕЖЗИЙКЛМНОПРСТУФХ
ЦЧШЩЪЫЬЭЮЯЋГЄЉЊЂЎЏабвг
дежзийклмнопрстуфхцчшщ
ъыьэюяљњћкÿцђгєABCabcd

▶ Italic
*АБВГДЕЖЗИЙКЛМНОПРСТУФХ
ЦЧШЩЪЫЬЭЮЯЋГЄЉЊЂЎЏабвг
дежзийклмнопрстуфхцчшщ
ъыьэюяљњћкÿцђгєABCabcd*

▶ Bold
**АБВГДЕЖЗИЙКЛМНОПРСТУФХ
ЦЧШЩЪЫЬЭЮЯЋГЄЉЊЂЎЏабвг
дежзийклмнопрстуфхцчшщ
ъыьэюяљњћкÿцђгєABCabcd**

▶ Bold Italic
***АБВГДЕЖЗИЙКЛМНОПРСТУФХ
ЦЧШЩЪЫЬЭЮЯЋГЄЉЊЂЎЏабвг
дежзийклмнопрстуфхцчшщ
ъыьэюяљњћкÿцђгєABCabcd***

PG6162 Mac + PC cyr / cyr-gr
Display 1

АБВГДЕЖЗИЙКЛМНОПРСТУФХЦЧШЩЪЫЬ
ЭЮЯЋГЄЉЊЂЎЏабвгдежзийклмнопрстуф
хцчшщъыьэюяљњћкÿцђгєABCDEabcdefghij

▶ Adver Gothic
АБВГДЕЖЗИЙКЛМНОПРС
ТУФХЦЧШЩЪЫЬЭЮЯаб
вгдежзийклмнопрстуфхц
чшщъыьэюяљњћкÿцђгєA

▶ Futura Eugenia
АБВГДЕЖЗИЙКЛМНОПРСТ
УФХЦЧШЩЪЫЬЭЮЯЋГ
ЄЉЊЂЎЏабвгдежзийклмнопрс
туфхцчшщъыьэюяљњћкÿ

© FSI 1993

FF Dolores Cyrillic

FF6274 Mac + PC — 1993: Tobias Frere-Jones — cyr / cyr-gr

АБВГДЕЖЗИЙКЛМНОПРСТУФХЦЧШЪ
ЬЫЭЮЯаб'вгдежзийклмнопрстуфхцчш
щъыьэюяяљњҌќўџѓєABCDEFGabcdefghijk

▶ Light
АБВГДЕЖЗИЙКЛМНОПРСТУФ
ЦЧШЩЪЫЬЭЮЯЋЄЉЊҌЌЎЏа
б'вгдежзийклмнопрстуфхцчш
щъыьэюяљњҌќўџѓєABCDabcdefg

▶ Regular
АБВГДЕЖЗИЙКЛМНОПРСТУ
ФХЦЧШЩЪЫЬЭЮЯаб'вгдеж
зийклмнопрстуфхцчшщъыь
эюяљњҌќўџЋЄabcDEabcdefgh

▶ Bold
АБВГДЕЖЗИЙКЛМНОПР
СТУФХЦЧШЩЪЫЬЭЮЯа
б'вгдежзийклмнопрстуфх
цчшщъыьэюяљњҌЌЎЏҌЄ

▶ Extra Bold
АБВГДЕЖЗИЙКЛМНО
ПРСТУФХЦЧШЩЪЫЬЭ
ЮЯаб'вгдежзийклмно
прстуфхцчшщъыьэюяљ

▶ Black
АБВГДЕЖЗИЙКЛМ
НОПРСТУФХЦЧШЩ
ЪЫЬЭЮЯаб'вгдежзи
йклмнопрстуфхцчш

Excelsior Cyrillic

LH6286 Mac + PC — cyr-LH

АБВГДЕЖЗИЙКЛМНОПРСТУФХЦЧШ
ЩЫЬЭЮЯабвгдежзийклмнопрстуфхцчш
щъыьэюяѣѐѐёѳѓѓѕжиòỳṕѵvжáééúíїóўъыїэ

▶ Upright
АБВГДЕЖЗИЙКЛМНОПР
СТУФХЦЧШЩЫЬЭЮЯаб
вгдежзийклмнопрстуфхцч
шщъыьэюяѣѐѐёѳѓѕжиòỳṕ

▶ Inclined
АБВГДЕЖЗИЙКЛМНОПР
СТУФХЦЧШЩЫЬЭЮЯаб
вгдежзийклмнопрстуфхцч
шщъыьэюяѣѐѐёѳѓѕжиòỳṕ

▶ Bold
АБВГДЕЖЗИЙКЛМНОПР
СТУФХЦЧШЩЫЬЭЮЯаб
вгдежзийклмнопрстуфхцч
шщъыьэюяѣѐѐёѳѓѕжиòỳṕ

Faktor™

K497 Mac + PC — cyr-K + T

АБВГДЕЖЗИЙКЛМНОПРСТУФХЦЧШЩ
ЪЫЬЭЮЯабвгдежзийклмнопрстуфхц
чшщъыьэюяЄЫЁЯА́Э́И́Ю́О́У́І́Ѣ́V̌V̌ѲѢ́áч

▶ Cond. Extra Bold
АБВГДЕЖЗИЙКЛМНОПРСТУФХ
ЦЧШЩЪЫЬЭЮЯабвгдежзийк
лмнопрстуфхцчшщъыьэюяЄЫ
ЁЯА́Э́И́Ю́О́У́І́Ѣ́V̌V̌ѲѢ́áчéзёийо

▶ Cond. Extra Bold Oblique
АБВГДЕЖЗИЙКЛМНОПРСТУФХ
ЦЋЩЪЫЬЭЮЯабвгдежзийкл
мнопрстуфхцђшщъыьэсяЄЫЁ
ЯА́Э́И́Ю́О́У́І́Ѣ́V̌V̌ИЉѢ́áчéзёийо

© FSI 1993

Free Set
PG6163 Mac + PC — cyr / cyr-gr

АБВГДЕЖЗИЙКЛМНОПРСТУФХЦЧШЩЪЫЬЭЮЯЂГЄЉЊЋЎЏабвгдежзийклмнопрстуфхцчшщъыьэюялњњћкўџђгєABCDEFabcdefghij

▶ Regular
АБВГДЕЖЗИЙКЛМНОПРСТУ
ФХЦЧШЩЪЫЬЭЮЯабвгдеж
зийклмнопрстуфхцчшщъыьэю
ялњњћкўџђгєABCDEFabcdefghi

▶ Bold
АБВГДЕЖЗИЙКЛМНОПРСТ
УФХЦЧШЩЪЫЬЭЮЯабвгде
жзийклмнопрстуфхцчшщ
ъыьэюялњњћкўџђгєABCabcde

Furturis
PG6164 Mac + PC — cyr / cyr-gr

АБВГДЕЖЗИЙКЛМНОПРСТУФХЦЧШЩЪЫЬЭЮЯЂГЄЉЊЋЎЏабвгдежзийклмнопрстуфхцчшщъыьэюялњњћкўџђгєABCDEabcdefgh

▶ Regular
АБВГДЕЖЗИЙКЛМНОПРСТУ
ФХЦЧШЩЪЫЬЭЮЯЂГЄЉЊЋЎ
Џабвгдежзийклмнопрстуфхцчш
щъыьэюялњњћкўџђгєABCDabcde

▶ Extra
АБВГДЕЖЗИЙКЛМНОПРСТ
УФХЦЧШЩЪЫЬЭЮЯЂГЄЉ
ЊЋЎЏабвгдежзийклмноп
рстуфхцчшщъыьэюялњњћк

▶ Extra Bold
АБВГДЕЖЗИЙКЛМНОПР
СТУФХЦЧШЩЪЫЬЭЮЯ
ЂГЄЉЊЋЎЏабвгдежзий
клмнопрстуфхцчшщъыьэ

URW™ Garamond Cyrillic
K901 Mac + PC — (Claude Garamond, 1532) — cyr-K + T

АБВГДЕЖЗИЙКЛМНОПРСТУФХЦЧШЩЪЫЬЭЮЯабвгдежзийклмнопрстуфхцчшщъыьэюяЀЁЂЃЄЅІЇЈЉЊЋЌЍЎЏ

▶ Plain
АБВГДЕЖЗИЙКЛМНОПРСТ
УФХЦЧШЩЪЫЬЭЮЯабвгде
жзийклмнопрстуфхцчшщъыь
эюяЀЁЂЃЄЅІЇЈЉЊЋЌЍЎЏѲѢ

▶ Italic
*АБВГДЕЖЗИЙКЛМНОПРСТУ
ФХЦЧШЩЪЫЬЭЮЯабвгджзи
йклмнопрстуфхцчшщъыьэюяЀ
ЁЂЃЄЅІЇЈЉЊЋЌЍЎЏѲѢачéзњúú*

▶ Bold
**АБВГДЕЖЗИЙКЛМНОПР
СТУФХЦЧШЩЪЫЬЭЮЯаб
вгдежзийклмнопрстуфхцчш
щъыьэюяЀЁЂЃЄЅІЇЈЉЊЋЌЍ**

▶ Bold Inclined
***АБВГДЕЖЗИЙКЛМНОПР
СТУФХЦЧШЩЪЫЬЭЮЯаб
вгдежзийклмнопрстуфхцчш
щъыьэюяЀЁЂЃЄЅІЇЈЉЊЋЌЍ***

K6368 Mac — Glagol
Croatian/Square Glagolica

ⰊⰋⰍⰎⰏⰐⰑⰒⰓⰔⰕⰖⰗⰘⰙⰚⰛⰜⰝⰞⰟⰠⰡⰢⰣⰤⰥⰦⰧⰨⰩⰪⰫⰬⰭⰮ

LH6281 Mac + PC — Helvetica Cyrillic
cyr-LH

АБВГДЕЖЗИЙКЛМНОПРСТУФХЦЧШЩЫЬЭЮЯабвгдежзийклмнопрстуфхцчшщъыьэюяѣàèëѳґѕжйòỳрр́ѵѵжа́е́є́и́ї́і́о́у́ъ́ы́э́

▶ Upright
АБВГДЕЖЗИЙКЛМНОПРСТУФХЦЧШЩЫЬЭЮЯабвгдежзийклмнопрстуфхцчшщъыьэюяѣàèëѳґѕжйòỳрр́ѵѵжа́е́є́и́ї́і́о́

▶ Inclined
АБВГДЕЖЗИЙКЛМНОПРСТУФХЦЧШЩЫЬЭЮЯабвгдежзийклмнопрстуфхцчшщъыьэюяѣàèëѳґѕжйòỳрр́ѵѵжа́е́є́и́ї́і́

▶ Bold
АБВГДЕЖЗИЙКЛМНОПРСТУФХЦЧШЩЫЬЭЮЯабвгдежзийклмнопрстуфхцчшщъыьэюяѣàèëѳґѕжйòỳрр́ѵѵжа́

▶ Bold Inclined
АБВГДЕЖЗИЙКЛМНОПРСТУФХЦЧШЩЫЬЭЮЯабвгдежзийклмнопрстуфхцчшщъыьэюяѣàèëѳґѕжйòỳрр́ѵѵжа́

LH6289 Mac + PC — Helvetica Inserat Cyrillic
cyr-LH

АБВГДЕЖЗИЙКЛМНОПРСТУФХЦЧШЩЫЬЭЮЯабвгдежзийклмнопрстуфхцчшщъыьэюяѣàèëѳґѕжйòỳрр́ѵѵжа́е́є́и́ї́і́о́у́ъ́ы́э́ю́я́

PG6165 Mac + PC — Journal
cyr / cyr-gr

АБВГДЕЖЗИЙКЛМНОПРСТУФХЦЧШЩЪЫЬЭЮЯЂЄЉЊЋЎЏабвгдежзийклмнопрстуфхцчшщъыьэюяљњћкÿџђгєABCabcdef

▶ Regular
АБВГДЕЖЗИЙКЛМНОПРСТУФХЦЧШЩЪЫЬЭЮЯабвгдежзийклмнопрстуфхцчшщъыьэюяљњћкÿџђгєABabcd

▶ Italic
АБВГДЕЖЗИЙКЛМНОПРСТУФХЦЧШЩЪЫЬЭЮЯабвгдежзийклмнопрстуфхцчшщъыьэюяљњћкÿџђгєABabcde

▶ Bold
АБВГДЕЖЗИЙКЛМНОПРСТУФХЦЧШЩЪЫЬЭЮЯабвгдежзийклмнопрстуфхцчшщъыьэюяљњћкÿџђгєABab

Journal Sans

PG6166 Mac + PC — cyr / cyr-gr

АБВГДЕЖЗИЙКЛМНОПРСТУФХЦЧШЩЪЫ
ЬЭЮЯЂГЄЉЊЋЎЏабвгдежзийклмнопрсту
фхцчшщъыьэюяљњћкўџђгєABCDEabcdefg

▶ Regular
АБВГДЕЖЗИЙКЛМНОПРСТУ
ФХЦЧШЩЪЫЬЭЮЯабвгдежз
ийклмнопрстуфхцчшщъыьэю
љњћкўџђгєABCDEabcdefghijkl

▶ Italic
АБВГДЕЖЗИЙКЛМНОПРСТУ
ФХЦЧШЩЪЫЬЭЮЯабвгдеж
зийклмнопрстуфхцчшщъыьз
юяљњћкўџђгєABCDEFabcdef

▶ Bold
АБВГДЕЖЗИЙКЛМНОПРСТУ
ФХЦЧШЩЪЫЬЭЮЯабвгдежз
ийклмнопрстуфхцчшщъыьэю
яљњћкўџђгєABCDEabcdefghi

Kirill & Glagol

K6695 Mac — Glagolitic

Kirill & Glagol

Kirill

K6694 Mac — Bulgarian Round Glagolitic

Kolomna

K2990 Mac — cyr-K + T

АБВГДЕЖЗИЙКЛМНОПРСТУФХЦЋБЩЪЫЭ
ЮЯaßгдежзийклмнопрстуфхцħшщъыьэє
яЯÉЫЁЯ́А́ЭЙЮÓÝÍЄ́V́VНЬҔӨáчéзЁ́ы́ióëív́ýюb

Ladoga 2

K259 Mac — cyr-K + T

АБВГДЕЖЗИЙКЛМНОПРСТУФХЦЋБЩЪЫ
ЬЭЮAабвгдежзийклмнопрстуфхцħшщъыьэ
єяЯÉЫЁЯ́А́ЭЙЮÓÝÍЄ́V́VНЬҔӨáчéзЁ́ы́ióëív́ýю

▶ Regular
АБВГДЕЖЗИЙКЛМНОПРСТ
УФХЦЋБЩЪЫЬЭЮАабвгде
жзийклмнопрстуфхцħшщъы
ьэєЯÉЫЁЯ́А́ЭЙЮÓÝÍЄ́V́VН

▶ Oblique
АБВГДЕЖЗИЙКЛМНОПРСТ
УФХЦЋБЩЪЫЬЭЮАабвгде
жзийклмнопрстуфхцħшщъы
ьэєЯÉЫЁЯ́А́ЭЙЮÓÝÍЄ́V́VН

© FSI 1993

K2758 Mac + PC cyr-K + T
Ladoga 4

Cyrillic

АБВГДЕЖЗИЙКЛМНОПРСТУФХЦЋЂЩЪЫ
ЬЭЮАабвгдежзийклмнопрстуфхцћшщъыьэ
єяÉЫЁЯ́А́ЭЙЮО́У́ІЄ́V́VНЈЂӨа́чéз́ếйы́іо́ëív́ýю

▶ Regular
АБВГДЕЖЗИЙКЛМНОПРСТ
УФХЦЋЂЩЪЫЬЭЮАабвгде
жзийклмнопрстуфхцћшщъы
ьэєяÉЫЁЯ́А́ЭЙЮО́У́ІЄ́V́VНЈ

▶ Oblique
АБВГДЕЖЗИЙКЛМНОПРСТ
УФХЦЋЂЩЪЫЬЭЮАабвгде
жзийклмнопрстуфхцћшщъы
ьэєяÉЫЁЯ́А́ЭЙЮО́У́ІЄ́V́VНЈ

▶ Bold
АБВГДЕЖЗИЙКЛМНОПРСТ
УФХЦЋЂЩЪЫЬЭЮАабвгд
ежзийклмнопрстуфхцћш
щъыьэєяÉЫЁЯ́А́ЭЙЮО́У́ІЄ́

▶ Bold Oblique
АБВГДЕЖЗИЙКЛМНОПРСТ
УФХЦЋЂЩЪЫЬЭЮАабвгд
ежзийклмнопрстуфхцћш
щъыьэєяÉЫЁЯ́А́ЭЙЮО́У́ІЄ́

K2801 Mac cyr-tur + T
Ladoga CyrTurk

АБВГДЕЖЗИЙКЛМНОПРСТУФХЦҺЧЩЪЫЬ
ЭЮӐабвгдежзийклмнопрстуфхцһшщъыьэә
ÉЫЁЯ́А́ЭЙЮО́У́ІЄ́V́VНҢЁ̆Ө́а́чéз́ếйы́іо́ëív́ýю̆ĕv

▶ Regular
АБВГДЕЖЗИЙКЛМНОПРСТ
УФХЦҺЧЩЪЫЬЭЮӐабвгде
жзийклмнопрстуфхцһшщъы
ьэәÉЫЁЯ́А́ЭЙЮО́У́ІЄ́V́VНĚ

▶ Oblique
АБВГДЕЖЗИЙКЛМНОПРСТ
УФХЦҺЧЩЪЫЬЭЮӐабвгде
жзийклмнопрстуфхцһшщъы
ьэәÉЫЁЯ́А́ЭЙЮО́У́ІЄ́V́VНĚ

▶ Bold
АБВГДЕЖЗИЙКЛМНОПРСТ
УФХЦҺЧЩЪЫЬЭЮӐабвгде
жзийклмнопрстуфхцһшщ
ъыьэәÉЫЁЯ́А́ЭЙЮО́У́ІЄ́V

▶ Bold Oblique
АБВГДЕЖЗИЙКЛМНОПРСТ
УФХЦҺЧЩЪЫЬЭЮӐабвгде
жзийклмнопрстуфхцһшщ
ъыьэәÉЫЁЯ́А́ЭЙЮО́У́ІЄ́V

K6810 Mac cyr-K + T
Ladoga Black

АБВГДЕЖЗИЙКЛМНОПРСТУФХЦЋЂЩЪЫЬЭ
ЮАабвгдежзийклмнопрстуфхцћшщъыьэєяÉ
ЫЁЯ́А́ЭЙЮО́У́ІЄ́V́VНЈЂӨа́чéз́ếйы́іо́ëív́ýюѣьvөiá

▶ Black
АБВГДЕЖЗИЙКЛМНОП
РСТУФХЦЋЂЩЪЫЬЭЮ
Аабвгдежзийклмнопрс
туфхцћшщъыьэєяÉЫЁ

▶ Black Oblique
АБЦДЕФГЋИЙКЛМНОПЭ
РСТУВЩХЫЗЬабцде
фгћийклмнопэрст
увщхызГшiККіЛы

K1612 Mac cyr-K + T
Ladoga Narrow

АБВГДЕЖЗИЙКЛМНОПРСТУФХЦЧШЩЪЫЬ
ЭЮЯабвгдежзийклмнопрстуфхцчшщъыьэюя
ÉЫЁЯ́А́ЭЙЮО́У́ІЄ́V́VӨЂӨа́чéз́ếйы́іо́ëív́ýюѣv

© FSI 1993

Cyrillic

▼ K1612 Mac **Ladoga Narrow**

▶ Narrow
АБВГДЕЖЗИЙКЛМНОПРСТУФХЦЏЋ
ЋЏЉЊЬЭЮЯабвгдежзийклмнопрст
уфхцџчшщъыьэюяÉЍЁÁÁЭЍЌÓÝÍЁ
V́V̀НЂӨӘче́з̀е́ы̀іо́ёі́ў́ю̀ёьво́ія

▶ NarrowOblique
*АБВГДЕЖЗИЙКЛМНОПРСТУФХЦЏ
ЋЏЉЊЬЭЮЯабвгдежзийклмнопрст
уфхцџчшщъыьэюяÉЍЁÁÁЭЍЌÓÝÍЁ
V́V̀ӨЂӨӘче́з̀е́ы̀іо́ёі́ў́ю̀ёьво́ія*

PG6167 Mac + PC   cyr / cyr-gr
Lazurski

АБВГДЕЖЗИЙКЛМНОПРСТУФХЦЧШЩ ЪЫЬЭЮЯЂГЄЉЊЋЎЏабвгдежзийклмноп рстуфхцчшщъыьэюяљњћкўџѓєABCDabcdef

▶ Regular
АБВГДЕЖЗИЙКЛМНОПРСТУ
ФХЦЧШЩЪЫЬЭЮЯЂГЄЉЊ
ЋЎЏабвгдежзийклмнопрстуф
хцчшщъыьэюяљњћкўџѓєABabc

▶ Italic
*АБВГДЕЖЗИЙКЛМНОПРСТУФХ
ЦЧШЩЪЫЬЭЮЯЂГЄЉЊЋЎЏаб
вгдежзийклмнопрстуфхцчшщ
ъыьэюяљњћкўџѓєABCDEabcdefg*

▶ Bold
**АБВГДЕЖЗИЙКЛМНОПРСТ
УФХЦЧШЩЪЫЬЭЮЯЂГЄЉ
ЊЋЎЏабвгдежзийклмнопрс
туфхцчшщъыьэюяљњћкўџ**

▶ Bold Italic
***АБВГДЕЖЗИЙКЛМНОПРСТ
УФХЦЧШЩЪЫЬЭЮЯЂГЄЉ
ЊЋЎЏабвгдежзийклмнопрс
туфхцчшщъыьэюяљњћкўџѓ***

FF6272 Mac + PC   ⑨   ✎ 1993: Martin Wenzel   cyr / cyr-gr
FF Marten Cyrillic

АБВГДЕЖЗИЙКЛМНОПРСТУФХЦЧШЩЪЫЬЭЮЯабвгдежз ийклмнопрстуфхцчшщъыьэюяљњћкўџѓєABCabc

▶ Regular
АБВГДЕЖЗИЙКЛМНОПРСТУФХЦЧШЩЪЫЬЭЮЯЂГ
ЄЉЊЋЎЏабвгдежзийклмнопрстуфхцчшщъ
ыьэюяљњћкўџѓєABCDEFGHIJKLMNOPQRSTUU
WXYZÄËÏÖÜabcdefghijklmnopqrstuvwxyzäëïöü

▶ Grotesque
АБВГДЕЖЗИЙКЛМНОПРСТУФХЦЧШЩЪЫЬЭЮЯЂГ
ЄЉЊЋЎЏабвгдежзийклмнопрстуфхцчшщъ
ыьэюяљњћкўџѓєABCDEFGHIJKLMNOPQRSTUU
WXYZÄËÏÖÜabcdefghijklmnopqrstuvwxyzäëïöü

▶ Rough
АБВГДЕЖЗИЙКЛМНОПРСТУФХЦЧШЩЪЫЬЭЮЯЂГ
ЄЉЊЋЎЏабвгдежзийклмнопрстуфхцчшщъ
ыьэюяљњћкўџѓєABCDEFGHIJKLMNOPQRSTUU
WXYZÄËÏÖÜabcdefghijklmnopqrstuvwxyzäëïöü

▶ Grotesque Rough
АБВГДЕЖЗИЙКЛМНОПРСТУФХЦЧШЩЪЫЬЭЮЯЂГ
ЄЉЊЋЎЏабвгдежзийклмнопрстуфхцчшщъ
ыьэюяљњћкўџѓєABCDEFGHIJKLMNOPQRSTUU
WXYZÄËÏÖÜabcdefghijklmnopqrstuvwxyzäëïöü

K6408 Mac   cyr-K + T
Mashinka

АБВГДЕЖЗИЙКЛМНОПРСТУФХЦЋЋЩЪЫЬЭ ЮЯАабвгдежзийклмнопрстуфхцѣшщъы ьэєяÉЍЁÁÁЭЍЌÓÝÍЁV́V̀ҢЂӨӘче́з̀е́ы̀іо́ё

▶ Plain
АБВГДЕЖЗИЙКЛМНОПРСТУФХЦ
ЋЋЩЪЫЬЭЮАабвгдежзийклмн
опрстуфхцѣшщъыьэєяÉЍЁÁÁ
ЭЍЌÓÝÍЁV́V̀НЂӨӘче́з̀е́ы̀іо́ё і́v̀

▶ Oblique
*АБВГДЕЖЗИЙКЛМНОПРСТУФХЦ
ЋЋЩЪЫЬЭЮАабвгдежзийклмн
опрстуфхцѣшщъыьэєяÉЍЁÁÁ
ЭЍЌÓÝÍЁV́V̀НЂӨӘче́з̀е́ы̀іо́ё і́v̀*

▼ K6408 Mac Mashinka

▶ Bold
АБВГДЕЖЗИЙКЛМНОПРСТУФХЦ
ЂЩЫЬЭЮАабвгдежзийклмн
опрстуфхцќшщыьэсяЕ́ЫЁЯ́А́
Э́Й́Ю́О́У́І́Є́V̀V̀ЊЂО́а́ч́е́з́ѐй́ю́о̀ё̀і́v́

▶ Bold Oblique
АБВГДЕЖЗИЙКЛМНОПРСТУФХЦ
ЂЩЫЬЭЮАабвгдежзийклмн
опрстуфхцќшщыьэсяЕ́ЫЁЯ́А́
Э́Й́Ю́О́У́І́Є́V̀V̀ЊЂО́а́ч́е́з́ѐй́ю́о̀ё̀і́v́

Cyrillic

K451 Mac + PC   Old Church Slavonic
Method™

ѦБВГДЕЖЅИЗКЛМНОПРСТОУФХЦЧШЩЪЫ
ЬѢЮѪабвгдежѕзклмнопрстоуфхцчшщъыьѣ
ижѧꙖЄѣѧэпоѡѵѵѴ̈НЃѲѲ́ч̀ѐѐѐѥѝѝо́о́ѷїїѣѣѧѵѻꙇѧ

▶ Regular
ѦБВГДЕЖЅИЗКЛМНОПРСТОУФХ
ЦЧШЩЪЫЬѢЮѪабвгдежѕзклмноп
рстоуфхцчшщъыьѣижѧꙖЄѣѧэпоѡѵ
ѴНЃѲѲ́ч̀ѐѐѐѥѝѝо́о́ѷїїѣѣѧѵѻꙇѧ

▶ Two
./°˙˙˙˙˙:;абцдефгћижклмнопрст
оувцчхызнѓаѧѧамчѣѥєѣйѝй̈Ӹȯó̈ѻѻ
ӝѻ̈ѻю̈˙иҥѧѣѣыичшӱжиах˙мо
ѧк←Ҡжыш

▶ Plus
ЕЙЮ́ӦУ̀̇Ӏ͞ӑч̌ӗй̈ю̆о̆ш̆̈к̆ˇо̆йо̆ӥѥѥт̆а́ѥѐє̆ѣѐӣ́ы̆̓ы̆̓ы
о́ѻѵ̀̌ѵ̀̌̃ӳ̆ӧ̆ѻ̈ѳ

▶ Antik
ѦБВГДЕЖЅИЗКЛМНОПРСТОУФХ
ЦЧШЩЪЫЬѢЮѪабвгдежѕзклмноп
рстоуфхцчшщъыьѣижѧꙖЄѣѧэпоѡѵ
ѴНЃѲѲ́ч̀ѐѐѐѥѝѝо́о́ѷїїѣѣѧѵѻꙇѧ

A6430 Mac   cyr
Minion Cyrillic

АБВГДЕЖЗИЙЛМНОПРСТУФХЦЧШЩ
ЪЫЬЭЮЯабвгдежзийклмнопрстуфхцчш
щъыьэюяABCDEFGHIJKabcdefghijklmnop

▶ Regular
АБВГДЕЖЗИЙЛМНОПРСТУФ
ХЦЧШЩЪЫЬЭЮЯабвгдежзий
клмнопрстуфхцчшщъыьэюяAB
CDEFGHIJKLMabcdefghijklmno

▶ Italic
АБВГДЕЖЗИЙЛМНОПРСТУФ
ХЦЧШЩЪЫЬЭЮЯабвгдежзийк
лмнопрстуфхцчшщъыьэюяABC
DEFGHIJKLMabcdefghijklmnopqr

▶ Semibold
АБВГДЕЖЗИЙЛМНОПРСТУФ
ХЦЧШЩЪЫЬЭЮЯабвгдежзи
йклмнопрстуфхцчшщъыьэюя
ABCDEFGHIJabcdefghijklmnop

▶ Semibold Italic
АБВГДЕЖЗИЙЛМНОПРСТУФ
ХЦЧШЩЪЫЬЭЮЯабвгдежзий
клмнопрстуфхцчшщъыьэюяAB
CDEFGHIJKabcdefghijklmnopqrs

▶ Bold
АБВГДЕЖЗИЙЛМНОПРСТУ
ФХЦЧШЩЪЫЬЭЮЯабвгдежз
ийклмнопрстуфхцчшщъыьэю
яABCDEFGHIJabcdefghijklmno

▶ Bold Italic
АБВГДЕЖЗИЙЛМНОПРСТУФ
ХЦЧШЩЪЫЬЭЮЯабвгдежзи
йклмнопрстуфхцчшщъыьэюя
ABCDEFGHIJabcdefghijklmnopq

PG6618 Mac + PC   cyr / cyr-gr
Mono Condensed

АБВГДЕЖЗИЙКЛМНОПРСТУФХЦЧШЩЪЫЬЭЮЯЃЄЉ
ЋЎЏабвгдежзийклмнопрстуфхцчшщъыьэюяљ
ћкўџѓгєABCDEFGHIJKLMabcdefghijklmnopq

Cyrillic

▼ PG6618 Mac + PC **Mono Condensed**

▶ Regular
АБВГДЕЖЗИЙКЛМНОПРСТУФХЦЧШЩЬЫ
ЭЮЯЂГЄЉЊЋЎЏабвгдежзийклмнопрс
туфхцчшщьыэюяљњђкўџгєABCDEF
GHIJKLMNOPQRSTUabcdefghijklmn

▶ Italic
АБВГДЕЖЗИЙКЛМНОПРСТУФХЦЧШЩЬЫ
ЭЮЯЂГЄЉЊЋЎЏабвгдежзийклмнопрс
туфхцчшщьыэюяљњђкўџгєABCDEF
GHIJKLMNOPQRSTUabcdefghijklmn

▶ **Bold**
АБВГДЕЖЗИЙКЛМНОПРСТУФХЦЧШЩЬЫ
ЭЮЯЂГЄЉЊЋЎЏабвгдежзийклмнопрс
туфхцчшщьыэюяљњђкўџгєABCDEF
GHIJKLMNOPQRSTUabcdefghijklmn

▶ ***Bold Italic***
АБВГДЕЖЗИЙКЛМНОПРСТУФХЦЧШЩЬЫ
ЭЮЯЂГЄЉЊЋЎЏабвгдежзийклмнопрс
туфхцчшщьыэюяљњђкўџгєABCDEF
GHIJKLMNOPQRSTUabcdefghijklmn

K260 Mac cyr-K + T
Moskva 2

АБВГДЕЖЗИЙКЛМНОПРСТУФХЦЧШЩ
ЪЫЬЭЮЯабвгдежзийклмнопрстуфхцчшщъ
ыьэюяÉЫЁЯ́А́ЭЙЮ́О́УЍÍЄ́V́VΘÆΘáчéзéйы

▶ Plain
АБВГДЕЖЗИЙКЛМНОПРС
ТУФХЦЧШЩЪЫЬЭЮЯабвгде
жзийклмнопрстуфхцчшщъыьэ
юяÉЫЁЯ́А́ЭЙЮ́О́УЍÍЄ́V́VΘ

▶ **Bold**
АБВГДЕЖЗИЙКЛМНОПРС
ТУФХЦЧШЩЪЫЬЭЮЯабвг
дежзийклмнопрстуфхцчшщ
ыьэюяÉЫЁЯ́А́ЭЙЮ́О́УЍÍЄ́V́

K6369 Mac cyr-K + T
Moskva 4

АБВГДЕЖЗИЙКЛМНОПРСТУФХЦЧШЩ
ЪЫЬЭЮЯабвгдежзийклмнопрстуфхцчшщъ
ыьэюяÉЫЁЯ́А́ЭЙЮ́О́УЍÍЄ́V́VΘÆΘáчéзéйы

▶ Plain
АБВГДЕЖЗИЙКЛМНОПРС
ТУФХЦЧШЩЪЫЬЭЮЯабвгде
жзийклмнопрстуфхцчшщъыьэ
юяÉЫЁЯ́А́ЭЙЮ́О́УЍÍЄ́V́VΘ

▶ *Italic*
АБВГДЕЖЗИЙКЛМНОПРС
ТУФХЦЧШЩЪЫЬЭЮЯабвгде
жзийклмнопрстуфхцчшщъыьэ
юяÉЫЁЯ́А́ЭЙЮ́О́УЍÍЄ́V́VΘ

▶ **Bold**
АБВГДЕЖЗИЙКЛМНОПРС
ТУФХЦЧШЩЪЫЬЭЮЯабвг
дежзийклмнопрстуфхцчшщ
ыьэюяÉЫЁЯ́А́ЭЙЮ́О́УЍÍЄ́V́

▶ ***Bold Italic***
АБВГДЕЖЗИЙКЛМНОПРС
ТУФХЦЧШЩЪЫЬЭЮЯабвг
дежзийклмнопрстуфхцчшщ
ыьэюяÉЫЁЯ́А́ЭЙЮ́О́УЍÍЄ́V́

K344 Mac cyr-K + T
Moskva & Ladoga

Moskva & Ladoga

PG6169 Mac + PC cyr / cyr-gr
Mysl

АБВГДЕЖЗИЙКЛМНОПРСТУФХЦЧШЩ
ЪЫЬЭЮЯЂГЄЉЊЋЎЏабвгдежзийклмно
прстуфхцчшщъыьэюялњђкўџгєABCabcdef

© FSI 1993
▼
Cyrillic 22

▼ PG6169 Mac + PC **Mysl**   Cyrillic

▶ Regular
АБВГДЕЖЗИЙКЛМНОПРС
ТУФХЦЧШЩЪЫЬЭЮЯабвгд
ежзийклмнопрстуфхцчшщъы
ьэюяљњћкўџђѓєABCDabcdefg

▶ Italic
*АБВГДЕЖЗИЙКЛМНОПРС
ТУФХЦЧШЩЪЫЬЭЮЯабвг
дежзийклмнопрстуфхцчишщ
ыьэюяљњћкўџђѓєABCDabcdef*

▶ Bold
**АБВГДЕЖЗИЙКЛМНОПРСТ
УФХЦЧШЩЪЫЬЭЮЯабвгде
жзийклмнопрстуфхцчшщъь
эюяљ њћкўџђѓєABCDabcdefg**

▶ Bold Italic
***АБВГДЕЖЗИЙКЛМНОПР
СТУФХЦЧШЩЪЫЬЭЮЯаб
вгдежзийклмнопрстуфхцчи
щъыьэюяљњћкўџђѓєABCabcd***

PG6275 Mac + PC   cyr / cyr-gr / cyr-f
Newton

АБВГДЕЖЗИЙКЛМНОПРСТУФХЦЧШ
ЩЪЫЬЭЮЯабвгдежзийклмнопрстуфхцч
шщъыьэюяљњћкўџђѓєABCDEFabcdefghijk

▶ Regular
АБВГДЕЖЗИЙКЛМНОПР
СТУФХЦЧШЩЪЫЬЭЮЯа
бвгдежзийклмнопрстуфхцч
шщъыьэюяABCDEabcdefghij

▶ Italic
*АБВГДЕЖЗИЙКЛМНОПРС
ТУФХЦЧШЩЪЫЬЭЮЯабвг
дежзийклмнопрстуфхцчшщъ
ыьэюяABCDEabcdefghijklmno*

▶ Bold
**АБВГДЕЖЗИЙКЛМНОПР
СТУФХЦЧШЩЪЫЬЭЮЯа
бвгдежзийклмнопрстуфхцч
шщъыьэюяABCDEabcdefghijkl**

▶ Bold Italic
***АБВГДЕЖЗИЙКЛМНОПРС
ТУФХЦЧШЩЪЫЬЭЮЯабв
гдежзийклмнопрстуфхцчшщъ
ыьэюяABCDEabcdefghijklmno***

▶ Extra Bold
**АБВГДЕЖЗИЙКЛМНОП
РСТУФХЦЧШЩЪЫЬЭ
ЮЯабвгдежзийклмнопрс
туфхцчшщъыьэюяABCDE**

PG6176 Mac + PC   cyr / cyr-gr / cyr-f
Petersburg

АБВГДЕЖЗИЙКЛМНОПРСТУФХЦЧШ
ЩЪЫЬЭЮЯабвгдежзийклмнопрстуфхцчш
щъыьэюяљњћкўџђѓєABCDEFGabcdefghijkl

▶ Regular
АБВГДЕЖЗИЙКЛМНОПР
СТУФХЦЧШЩЪЫЬЭЮЯа
бвгдежзийклмнопрстуфхцч
шщъыьэюяABCDEabcdefghijkl

▶ Italic
*АБВГДЕЖЗИЙКЛМНОПРСТ
УФХЦЧШЩЪЫЬЭЮЯабвгде
жзийклмнопрстуфхцчшщъыэ
юяABCDEFGHIJabcdefghijklmn*

▶ Bold
**АБВГДЕЖЗИЙКЛМНОПР
СТУФХЦЧШЩЪЫЬЭЮЯа
бвгдежзийклмнопрстуфхцч
шщъыьэюяABCDEabcdefghijkl**

▶ Bold Italic
***АБВГДЕЖЗИЙКЛМНОПРС
ТУФХЦЧШЩЪЫЬЭЮЯабв
гдежзийклмнопрстуфхцчш
щъыьэюяABCDEFabcdefghijk***

© FSI 1993

Cyrillic

PG6170 Mac + PC   cyr / cyr-gr / cyr-f
Pragmatica

АБВГДЕЖЗИЙКЛМНОПРСТУФХЦЧШЩЪЫ
ЬЭЮЯЂГЄЉЊЋЎЏабвгдежзийклмнопрст
уфхцчшщъыьэюяљњћќўџђгєABCDabcdefg

▶ Regular
АБВГДЕЖЗИЙКЛМНОПРСТ
УФХЦЧШЩЪЫЬЭЮЯЂГЄЉ
ЊЋЎЏабвгдежзийклмнопрс
туфхцчшщъыьэюяABCabcde

▶ Italic
*АБВГДЕЖЗИЙКЛМНОПРСТУ
ФХЦЧШЩЪЫЬЭЮЯ ЂГЄЉ
ЊЋЎЏабвгдежзийклмнопрс
туфхцчшщъыьэюяABCabcde*

▶ Bold
**АБВГДЕЖЗИЙКЛМНОПРС
ТУФХЦЧШЩЪЫЬЭЮЯабв
гдежзийклмнопрстуфхцч
шщъыьэюяABCDEabcdefg**

▶ Bold Italic
***АБВГДЕЖЗИЙКЛМНОПРС
ТУФХЦЧШЩЪЫЬЭЮЯабв
гдежзийклмнопрстуфхцч
шщъыьэюяABCDEabcdefg***

PG6171 Mac + PC   cyr / cyr-gr
Quant Antiqua

АБВГДЕЖЗИЙКЛМНОПРСТУФХЦЧШЩ
ЪЫЬЭЮЯЂГЄЉЊЋЎЏабвгдежзийклмноп
рстуфхцчшщъыьэюяABCabcdefghijklmnopqr

▶ Regular
АБВГДЕЖЗИЙКЛМНОПРСТ
УФХЦЧШЩЪЫЬЭЮЯЂГЄЉ
ЊЋЎЏабвгдежзийклмнопрсту
фхцчшщъыьэюяABCabcdefghij

▶ Italic
*АБВГДЕЖЗИЙКЛМНОПРСТ
УФХЦЧШЩЪЫЬЭЮЯäГЄйЎ
абвгдежзийклмнопрстуфхц
шщъыьэюяABCabcdefghijklm*

▶ Bold
**АБВГДЕЖЗИЙКЛМНОПР
СТУФХЦЧШЩЪЫЬЭЮЯä
ГЄйЎабвгдежзийклмнопрс
туфхцчшщъыьэюяABCabcd**

K900 Mac   cyr-K + T
URW Roman Cyrillic

АБВГДЕЖЗИЙКЛМНОПРСТУФХЦЧ
ШЩЪЫЬЭЮЯабвгдежзийклмнопрсту
фхцчшщъыьэюяЀЁЍЀЯ́А́Ӭ́Й́Ю́О̀Ӯ́І́Ѐ́V́

▶ Plain
АБВГДЕЖЗИЙКЛМНОПРСТ
УФХЦЧШЩЪЫЬЭЮЯабвгде
жзийклмнопрстуфхцчшщъь
эюяЀЁЍЀЯ́А́Ӭ́Й́Ю́О̀Ӯ́І́Ѐ́V́VѲҌ

▶ Italic
*АБВГДЕЖЗИЙКЛМНОПРСТУ
ФХЦЧШЩЪЫЬЭЮЯабвгдежзи
йклмнопрстуфхцчшщъыьэюяЀ
ЁЍЀЯ́А́Ӭ́Й́Ю́О̀Ӯ́І́Ѐ́V́VѲҌѲа́че́зы́й*

▶ Semi Bold
**АБВГДЕЖЗИЙКЛМНОПРСТ
УФХЦЧШЩЪЫЬЭЮЯабвгде
жзийклмнопрстуфхцчшщъы
эюяЀЁЍЀЯ́А́Ӭ́Й́Ю́О̀Ӯ́І́Ѐ́V́VѲҌ**

▶ Semi Bold Italic
***АБВГДЕЖЗИЙКЛМНОПРСТ
УФХЦЧШЩЪЫЬЭЮЯабвгде
жзийклмнопрстуфхцчшщъыьэ
юяЀЁЍЀЯ́А́Ӭ́Й́Ю́О̀Ӯ́І́Ѐ́V́VѲҌ***

© FSI 1993

K2860 Mac — Roman Cyr Turk
cyr-tur + T
Cyrillic

АБВГДЕЖЗИЙКЛМНОПРСТУФХЦЬҺЧЩЪ
ЫЬЭЮЯАабвгдежзийклмнопрстуфхцһшщъы
ьэяяЕ́Ы́Ё́Я́А́Э́Й́Ю́О́У́Ї̀Ѐ̀VVНЁӨа́че́э́ѐй́ы́і́о́ё́ı̀v

▶ Plain
АБВГДЕЖЗИЙКЛМНОПРСТ
УФХЦЬҺЧЩЪЫЬЭЮЯАабвгде
жзийклмнопрстуфхцһшщъыь
эяяЕ́Ы́Ё́Я́А́Э́Й́Ю́О́У́Ї̀Ѐ̀VVНЁӨ

▶ Italic
*АБВГДЕЖЗИЙКЛМНОПРСТУ
ФХЦЬҺЧЩЪЫЬЭЮЯАабвгдежзий
клмнопрстуфхцһшщъыьэяяЕ́Ы́Ё́
Я́А́Э́Й́Ю́О́У́Ї̀Ѐ̀VVНЁӨа́че́э́ѐй́ы́і́о́ё́*

▶ Bold
**АБВГДЕЖЗИЙКЛМНОПРСТ
УФХЦЬҺЧЩЪЫЬЭЮЯАабвгде
жзийклмнопрстуфхцһшщъыь
эяяЕ́Ы́Ё́Я́А́Э́Й́Ю́О́У́Ї̀Ѐ̀VVНЁӨ**

▶ Bold Italic
***АБВГДЕЖЗИЙКЛМНОПРСТ
УФХЦЬҺЧЩЪЫЬЭЮЯАабвгде
жзийклмнопрстуфхцһшщъыьэ
яяЕ́Ы́Ё́Я́А́Э́Й́Ю́О́У́Ї̀Ѐ̀VVНЁӨ***

PG6172 Mac + PC — Schoolbook
cyr / cyr-gr

АБВГДЕЖЗИЙКЛМНОПРСТУФХЦЧШЩ
ЪЫЬЭЮЯЂҐЄЉЊЋЎЏабвгдежзийклмноп
рстуфхцчшщъыьэюяљњћкўџђгєABCabcdefg

▶ Regular
АБВГДЕЖЗИЙКЛМНОПРС
ТУФХЦЧШЩЪЫЬЭЮЯабв
гдежзийклмнопрстуфхцчш
щъыьэюяљњћкўџђгєABabc

▶ Italic
*АБВГДЕЖЗИЙКЛМНОПР
СТУФХЦЧШЩЪЫЬЭЮЯ
абвгдежзийклмнопрстуфхц
чшщъыьэюяљњћкўџђгєABab*

▶ Bold
**АБВГДЕЖЗИЙКЛМНОП
РСТУФХЦЧШЩЪЫЬЭЮЯа
бвгдежзийклмнопрстуфхцч
шщъыьэюяљњћкўџђгєAabc**

▶ Bold Italic
***АБВГДЕЖЗИЙКЛМНОП
РСТУФХЦЧШЩЪЫЬЭЮ
Яабвгдежзийклмнопрстуф
хцчшщъыьэюяљњћкўџђгє***

PG6173 Mac + PC — Script 1
cyr / cyr-gr

*АБВГДЕЖЗИЙКЛМНОПРСТУФХЧ
ШЩЪЫЬЭЮЯЂҐЄЉЊЋЎЏабвгдежзийклмно
прстуфхцчшщъыьэюяљњћкўџђгєABCDabcdefghijkl*

▶ Astron
*АБВГДЕЖЗИЙКЛМНОПР
СТУФХЦЧШЩЪЫЬЭЮЯЂҐЄ
ЉЊЋЎЏабвгдежзийклмнопрстуфх
цчшщъыьэюяљњћкўџђгєABCabcdefgh*

▶ Decor
АБВГДЕЖЗИЙКЛМНОПРСТУ
ФХЦЧШЩЪЫЬЭЮЯЂҐЄЉЊЋЎ
Џабвгдежзийклмнопрстуфхцчшщъыьэюяљњћ
кўџђгєABCDEFGHIJabcdefghijklmnopqrst

▶ Parsek
АБВГДЕЖЗИЙКЛМНОПР
СТУФХЦЧШЩЪЫЬЭЮЯ
ЂҐЄЉЊЋЎЏабвгдежзийклмнопрс
туфхцчшщъыьэюяљњћкўџђгєABabcd

▶ Zhikharev
АБВГДЕЖЗИЙКЛМНОПРСТУФ
ХЦЧШЩЪЫЬЭЮЯЂҐЄЉЊЋЎЏаб
вгдежзийклмнопрстуфхцчшщъыьэюя
љњћкўџђгєABCDEFGabcdefghijklmno

© FSI 1993

Cyrillic

Script 2
PG6619 Mac + PC — cyr / cyr-gr

бБвГDjЗИЙКЛМНОПРСТУФХЦЧШЩ
ґЫЬЭЮѕТУабвгдежзийклмнопрстуфхцчш
щъыьэюяякґABCDEFGHIJabcdefghijklmnop

▶ BetinaScript
бБвГDjЗИЙКЛМНОПРСТУФХ
ЦЧШЩЫЬЭЮѕТУабвгдежзийкл
мнопрстуфхцчшщъыьэюяякґABCD
EFGHIJKLMNOabcdefghijklmnopq

▶ BetinaScript Bold
бБвГDjЗИЙКЛМНОПРСТУФХ
ЦЧШЩЫЬЭЮѕТУабвгдежзийкл
мнопрстуфхцчшщъыьэюяякґABCD
EFGHIJKLMNOabcdefghijklmnopq

▶ Corrida
АБВГДЕЖЗИЙКЛ
МНОПРСТУФХЦ
ШЩЪЫЬЭЮЯЋГЕЉЊ
ЂЌЏабвгдежзийклмнопрстуф

▶ Inform
АБВГДЕЖЗИЙКЛМНОПРСТУФХЦЧШЩ
ЪЫЬЭЮЯЋГЕЉЊЂЌЏабвгдежзийклм
нопрстуфхцчшщъыьэюяљњћкўџђгєABCDEFGHIJKLMabcdefghijklmnopqrs

▶ Inform Bold
АБВГДЕЖЗИЙКЛМНОПРСТУФХЦЧШ
ЩЪЫЬЭЮЯЋГЕЉЊЂЌЏабвгдежзий
клмнопрстуфхцчшщъыьэюяљњћк
ўџђгєABCDEFGHIJKLMabcdefghijklm

Text
PG6174 Mac + PC — cyr / cyr-gr

АБВГДЕЖЗИЙКЛМНОПРСТУФХЦЧШЩЪ
ЫЬЭЮЯЋГЄЉЊЂЌЏУЦабвгдежзийклмнопрс
туфхцчшщъыьэюяљњћкўџђгєABCDabcdefg

▶ Regular
АБВГДЕЖЗИЙКЛМНОПРСТУ
ФХЦЧШЩЪЫЬЭЮЯабвгдежзи
йклмнопрстуфхцчшщъыьэюяљ
њћкўџђгєABCDEFGabcdefghijkl

▶ Italic
АБВГДЕЖЗИЙКЛМНОПРСТУ
ФХЦЧШЩЪЫЬЭЮЯабвгдежз
ийклмнопрстуфхцчшщъыьэю
яљњћкўџђгєABCDEFGabcdefg

▶ Bold
АБВГДЕЖЗИЙКЛМНОПРСТ
УФХЦЧШЩЪЫЬЭЮЯабвгде
жзийклмнопрстуфхцчшщъы
ьэюяљњћкўџђгєABCDabcdef

Times Cyrillic
LH6282 Mac + PC — cyr-LH

АБВГДЕЖЗИЙКЛМНОПРСТУФХЦЧШ
ЩЫЬЭЮЯабвгдежзийклмнопрстуфхцчш
щъыьэюяѣàèё̈ǵѓѧ̈ѫѩо̀у̀ р̀р̀v̀v̌жа́є́є́и́ії́ї́о̂у̂ъ̆ы̆і́э̀

▶ Upright
АБВГДЕЖЗИЙКЛМНОПР
СТУФХЦЧШЩЫЬЭЮЯабвг
дежзийклмнопрстуфхцчшщ
ыьэюяѣàèё̈ǵѓѧ̈ѫѩо̀у̀р̀р̀v̀v̌жа́є́

▶ Inclined
*АБВГДЕЖЗИЙКЛМНОПР
СТУФХЦЧШЩЫЬЭЮЯабвг
дежзийклмнопрстуфхцчшщ
ыьэюяѣàèё̈ǵѓѧ̈ѫѩо̀у̀р̀р̀v̀v̌жа́є́*

© FSI 1993
Cyrillic 26

▼ LH6282   Mac + PC   Times Cyrillic

▶ Bold
АБВГДЕЖЗИЙКЛМНОПР
СТУФХЦЧШЩЪЫЬЭЮЯабвг
дежзийклмнопрстуфхцчшщъ
ыьэюяѣàèёӧґѣжйоѵррѵvжáé

▶ Bold Inclined
*АБВГДЕЖЗИЙКЛМНОПР
СТУФХЦЧШЩЪЫЬЭЮЯабвгд
ежзийклмнопрстуфхцчшщъ
ыьэюяѣàèёӧґѣжйоѵррѵvжáé*

M623   Mac + PC   cyr-K
Times New Roman Cyrillic

АБВГДЕЖЗИЙКЛМНОПСТУФХЦ
ЧШЩЪЫЬЭЮЯабвгдежзийклмнопр
стуфхцчшщъыьэюяњы́ќѐциб́ѵѳѯє́ђjáћ

▶ Regular
АБВГДЕЖЗИЙКЛМНОПСТ
УФХЦЧШЩЪЫЬЭЮЯабвгд
ежзийклмнопрстуфхцчшщъы
эюяњы́ќѐциб́ѵѳѯє́ђjáħóéѓу́ю ў

▶ Inclined
*АБВГДЕЖЗИЙКЛМНОПСТ
УФХЦЧШЩЪЫЬЭЮЯабвгде
жзийклмнопрстуфхцчшщъыьэ
юяњы́ќъциб́ѵѳѯє́ђjáħóéѓу́ю ўџ*

▶ Bold
**АБВГДЕЖЗИЙКЛМНОПСТ
УФХЦЧШЩЪЫЬЭЮЯабвгд
ежзийклмнопрстуфхцчшщъыьэ
юяњы́ќѐциб́ѵѳѯє́ђjáħóéѓу́ю ўɡ**

▶ Bold Inclined
***АБВГДЕЖЗИЙКЛМНОПСТ
УФХЦЧШЩЪЫЬЭЮЯабвгде
жзийклмнопрстуфхцчшщъыьэ
юяњы́ќъциб́ѵѳѯє́ђjáħóéѓу́ю ўџ***

FF6273   Mac + PC   ⑨   cyr / cyr-gr
FF Trixie Cyrillic

АБВГДЕЖЗИЙḰЛМНОПРСТУФХЦЧШЩЪЫЬЭЮ
ЯЂЃЄЉЊЋЎЏабвгдежзийклмнопрстуфх
цчшщъыьэюяљњћќўџѓѓєABCDEabcdefg

▶ Light
АБВГДЕЖЗИЙḰЛМНОПРСТУФХЦЧШ
ЩЪЫЬЭЮЯЂЃЄЉЊЋЎЏабвгдежзий
клмнопрстуфхцчшщъыьэюяљњћ
ќўџђѓєABCDEFGHIJabcdefghi

▶ Plain
АБВГДЕЖЗИЙḰЛМНОПРСТУФХЦЧШ
ЩЪЫЬЭЮЯЂЃЄЉЊЋЎЏабвгдежзий
клмнопрстуфхцчшщъыьэюяљњћ
ќўџђѓєABCDEFGHIJabcdefghi

▶ Cameo
АБВГДЕЖЗИЙḰЛМНОПРСТУФХЦЧШ
ЩЪЫЬЭЮЯЂЃЄЉЊЋЎЏабвгдежзий
клмнопрстуфхцчшщъыьэюяљњћ
ќўџђѓєABCDEFGHIJabcdefghi

© FSI 1993

Xenia
PG6175 Mac + PC — cyr / cyr-gr

АБВГДЕЖЗИЙКЛМНОПРСТУФХЦЧШЩЪЫЬЭ
ЮЯЂҐЄЉЊЋЎЏабвгдежзийклмнопрстуфхц
чшщъыьэюяљњћкўџђгєABCDEFGabcdefghij

▶ Regular
АБВГДЕЖЗИЙКЛМНОПРС
ТУФХЦЧШЩЪЫЬЭЮЯабв
гдежзийклмнопрстуфхцч
шщъыьэюяABCDEabcdef

▶ Condensed
АБВГДЕЖЗИЙКЛМНОПРСТУФ
ХЦЧШЩЪЫЬЭЮЯабвгдежзи
йклмнопрстуфхцчшщъыьэю
яљњћкўџђгєABCDEabcdefghi

▶ Extended
АБВГДЕЖЗИЙКЛМНОП
РСТУФХЦЧШЩЪЫЬЭ
ЮЯабвгдежзийклмно
прстуфхцчшщъыьэю

▶ Extended Bold
АБВГДЕЖЗИЙКЛМН
ОПРСТУФХЦЧШЩЪ
ЫЬЭЮЯабвгдежзи
йклмнопрстуфхцч

Agora Times
K2966 Mac + PC — Modern and Classical Greek

ΑΒΓΔΕΖΗΘΙΚΛΜΝΞΟΠΡΣΤΥΦΧΨΩαβγ
δεζηθιλμνξοπρστυφχψωςΉΏΈΉΫάὰâήώὲὲ
ἐίὶῖῆόὸôöύὺûüϋϛΉΏμδΣΠπΩἠῶΔΆΏὼϋΫΐ

▶ Plain
ΑΒΓΔΕΖΗΘΙΚΛΜΝΞΟΡΣΤ
ΥΦΧΨΩαβγδεζηθιλμνξοπρστυ
φχψωςΉΏΈΉΫάὰâήώὲὲἐίὶῖῆό
ὸôöύὺûüϋϛΉΏμδΣΠπΩἠῶΔΆΏ

▶ Italic
ΑΒΓΔΕΖΗΘΙΚΛΜΝΞΟΡΣΤ
ΥΦΧΨΩαβγδεζηθιλμνξοπρστυ
φχψωςΉΏΈΉΫάὰâήώὲὲἐίὶῖῆό
ὸôöύὺûüϋϛΉΏμδΣΠπΩἠῶΔΆΏ

▶ Bold
ΑΒΓΔΕΖΗΘΙΚΛΜΝΞΟΡΣΤ
ΥΦΧΨΩαβγδεζηθιλμνξοπρστυ
φχψωςΉΏΈΉΫάὰâήώὲὲἐίὶῖῆ
όὸôöύὺûüϋϛΉΏμδΣΠπΩἠῶΔΆΏ

▶ Bold Italic
ΑΒΓΔΕΖΗΘΙΚΛΜΝΞΟΡΣΤ
ΥΦΧΨΩαβγδεζηθιλμνξοπρστυ
φχψωςΉΏΈΉΫάὰâήώὲὲἐίὶῖῆ
όὸôöύὺûüϋϛΉΏμδΣΠπΩἠῶΔΆΏ

LS337 Mac
Arabic & Farsi

Arabic and Farsi

لكقفغغظططضصستُّآىىومنممللكقفغغظططضصصشسسززرذدخ
‎غىم.م.ملخلحتجتحخج جحتمى . . . مم مىىج ث ـ ة بىإبؤأأ يه ه.
بلابلا«ژڈپ...قـمج ٹ پڤ»ىہچٹ پىكؤچ صگ ضلّ ضلاؐ , گلمخلحلج

▶ Baghdad

مزىىق نكغوط لاقس فىىقمد ظنضروا زصىئ
فزشخط مزسلكغهظلاقص ضزنىج مشقطخ
لاوزضى زد ُزمەق معًا صنمور خطً
زفو زغوس ضول رفـقـعد زظنـضصـہ

▶ Geezah

لاقسىىقمد ظذ . ل زىئ
ىمشقـطـ خ مزىق نلكغ ط
مزسلكغ ظلاقص ُ زىج
ـمقك هعا ذم ر خىظ زشخط

▶ Kufi Standard

وس ىىمد ظذضول زصىئ
ضزىج ىسط ُ مزى نكغوط
ىظً ىس خط مزسكغط و
وىصى زذ ُزممىك معا صخمور

▶ Nadeem

خ مزىق نلكوط لاقس فىىقمد ظنضروا زصىئ
فزشخط مزسلكظلاقص ضزنىج مشقط
لاوزضى زد ُزمەق معا صنمور خطً
زلكضك زفو زوس ضول رفـقعد زظنـضصـہ

LH6827 Mac + PC
Baskerville Greek Monotonic

Modern Greek

ΑΒΓΔΕΖΗΘΙΚΛΜΝΞΠΟΡΣΤΥΦΧΨΩαβ
γδεζηθικλμνξπορσςτυφχψωΆΈΌΎΩάέήίό
ύώϋϊΰABCDEFGHIJKLabcdefghijklmnopq

▶ Upright
ΑΒΓΔΕΖΗΘΙΚΛΜΝΞΠΟΡΣ
ΤΥΦΧΨΩαβγδεζηθικλμνξπο
ρσςτυφχψωΆΈΌΎΩάέήίόύώ
ϋϊΰABCDEFGHIJabcdefghijkl

▶ Inclined
ΑΒΓΔΕΖΗΘΙΚΛΜΝΞΠΟΡΣΤΥ
ΦΧΨΩαβγδεζηθικλμνξπορσςτυφχψ
ωΆΈΌΎΩάέήίόύώϋϊΰABCDEFG
HIJKLMNOPabcdefghijklmnopq

▶ Bold
ΑΒΓΔΕΖΗΘΙΚΛΜΝΞΠΟΡΣ
ΤΥΦΧΨΩαβγδεζηθικλμνξπο
ρσςτυφχψωΆΈΌΎΩάέήίόύ
ώϋϊΰABCDEFGHabcdefghijk

LH6290 Mac + PC
New Century Schoolbook Greek Polytonic

Classical Greek

ΑΒΓΔΕΖΗΘΙΚΛΜΝΞΠΟΡΣΤΥΦΧΨΩαβ
γδεζηθικλμνξπορσςτυφχψωΆΈΌΎΩάέήί
όύώϋϊΰΑΒἔἰΕὖΗΙὢΚἃΜΝΟΡἰὓὢΤἰὓῤΧΥΖ

▶ Upright
ΑΒΓΔΕΖΗΘΙΚΛΜΝΞΠΟΡΣΤ
ΥΦΧΨΩαβγδεζηθικλμνξπορ
ςτυφχψωΆΈΌΎΩάέήίόύώϋϊ
ΰΑΒἔἰΕὖΗΙὢάἐἠἰὁὺὢ᾽ἀῇὃ῎ῆὃ῀

▶ Inclined
ΑΒΓΔΕΖΗΘΙΚΛΜΝΞΠΟΡΣ
ΤΥΦΧΨΩαβγδεζηθικλμνξπορ
σςτυφχψωΆΈΌΎΩάέήίόύώϋϊΰ
ΑΒἔἰΕὖΗΙὢάἐἠἰὁὺὢ᾽ἀῇὃ῎ῆὄἇῆ

▶ Bold
ΑΒΓΔΕΖΗΘΙΚΛΜΝΞΠΟΡ
ΣΤΥΦΧΨΩαβγδεζηθικλμν
ξπορσςτυφχψωΆΈΌΎΩά
έήίόύώϋϊΰΑΒἔἰΕὖΗΙὢάἐἠ

LH6291 Mac + PC — Modern Greek
New Century Schoolbook Greek Monotonic

ΑΒΓΔΕΖΗΘΙΚΛΜΝΞΠΟΡΣΤΥΦΧΨΩαβγδ
εζηθικλμνξπορσςτυφχψωΆΈΌΎΩάέήίόύώ
ϋϊΰABCDEFGHIJKLabcdefghijklmnopqrst

▶ Upright
ΑΒΓΔΕΖΗΘΙΚΛΜΝΞΠΟΡΣΤ
ΥΦΧΨΩαβγδεζηθικλμνξπορ
σςτυφχψωΆΈΌΎΩάέήίόύώϊϋ
ΰABCDEFGHabcdefghijklmn

▶ Inclined
ΑΒΓΔΕΖΗΘΙΚΛΜΝΞΠΟΡΣ
ΤΥΦΧΨΩαβγδεζηθικλμνξπορ
σςτυφχψωΆΈΌΎΩάέήίόύώϊϋΰ
ABCDEFGHabcdefghijklmno

▶ Bold
ΑΒΓΔΕΖΗΘΙΚΛΜΝΞΠΟΡ
ΣΤΥΦΧΨΩαβγδεζηθικλμν
ξπορσςτυφχψωΆΈΌΎΩά
έήίόύώϊϋΰABCDEabcdefg

K6407 Mac — Modern Greek + T
GrCourier

```
ΑΒΓΔΕΖΗΘΙΚΛΜΝΠΟΡΤΥΨΧΩαβγδεζηθι
κλμνξπορσςτυφχψωABCDEFGHIJKLMN
OPQRSTUVWXYZabcdefghijklmnopqr
```

▶ Regular
```
ΑΒΓΔΕΖΗΘΙΚΛΜΝΠΟΡΤΥΨΧΩαβ
γδεζηθικλμνξπορσςτυφχψω
ABCDEFGHIJKLMNOPQRSTUVW
XYZabcdefghijklmnopqrst
```

▶ Italic
```
ΑΒΓΔΕΖΗΘΙΚΛΜΝΠΟΡΤΥΨΧΩαβ
γδεζηθικλμνξπορσςτυφχψω
ABCDEFGHIJKLMNOPQRSTUVW
XYZabcdefghijklmnopqrst
```

▶ Bold
```
ΑΒΓΔΕΖΗΘΙΚΛΜΝΠΟΡΤΥΨΧΩαβ
γδεζηθικλμνξπορσςτυφχψω
ABCDEFGHIJKLMNOPQRSTUVW
XYZabcdefghijklmnopqrst
```

▶ Bold Italic
```
ΑΒΓΔΕΖΗΘΙΚΛΜΝΠΟΡΤΥΨΧΩαβ
γδεζηθικλμνξπορσςτυφχψω
ABCDEFGHIJKLMNOPQRSTUVW
XYZabcdefghijklmnopqrst
```

LH6828 Mac + PC — Modern Greek
Helvetica Greek Monotonic

ΑΒΓΔΕΖΗΘΙΚΛΜΝΞΠΟΡΣΤΥΦΧΨΩαβγδεζη
θικλμνξπορσςτυφχψωΆΈΌΎΩάέήίόύώϊϋΰ
ABCDEFGHIJKLMNOPabcdefghijklmnopqr

▶ Upright
ΑΒΓΔΕΖΗΘΙΚΛΜΝΞΠΟΡΣΤΥ
ΦΧΨΩαβγδεζηθικλμνξπορς
τυφχψωΆΈΌΎΩάέήίόύώϊϋΰ
ABCDEFGHIJKabcdefghijklm

▶ Inclined
ΑΒΓΔΕΖΗΘΙΚΛΜΝΞΠΟΡΣΤΥ
ΦΧΨΩαβγδεζηθικλμνξπορς
τυφχψωΆΈΌΎΩάέήίόύώϊϋΰ
ABCDEFGHIJKabcdefghijkl

▶ Bold
ΑΒΓΔΕΖΗΘΙΚΛΜΝΞΠΟΡΣΤΥ
ΦΧΨΩαβγδεζηθικλμνξπορς
τυφχψωΆΈΌΎΩάέήίόύώϊϋΰ
ABCDEFGHIJKabcdefghijkl

▶ Bold Inclined
ΑΒΓΔΕΖΗΘΙΚΛΜΝΞΠΟΡΣΤΥ
ΦΧΨΩαβγδεζηθικλμνξπορς
τυφχψωΆΈΌΎΩάέήίόύώϊϋΰ
ABCDEFGHIJKabcdefghijkl

LH6829 Mac + PC — Classical Greek
Helvetica Greek Polytonic

ΑΒΓΔΕΖΗΘΙΚΛΜΝΞΟΠΡΣΤΥΦΧΨΩαβγδεζη
θικλμνξοπρσςτυφχψωΆΈΌΎΩάέήίόύώϊϋ
ΑΒἒἲἘὒΉΙὼΚἄΜΝΟΡἲὒὣΤἳὔρΧΥΖἀἐἠἰὀὐὠ῀ᾶ

▶ Upright
ΑΒΓΔΕΖΗΘΙΚΛΜΝΞΟΠΡΣΤΥ
ΦΧΨΩαβγδεζηθικλμνξοπρς
τυφχψωΆΈΌΎΩάέήίόύώϊϋ
ΑΒἒἲἘὒΉΙὼΚἄΜΝΟΡἲὒὣΤἳὔρ

▶ Inclined
ΑΒΓΔΕΖΗΘΙΚΛΜΝΞΟΠΡΣΤΥ
ΦΧΨΩαβγδεζηθικλμνξοπρς
τυφχψωΆΈΌΎΩάέήίόύώϊϋ
ΑΒἒἲἘὒΉΙὼΚἄΜΝΟΡἲὒὣΤἳὔρ

▶ Bold
ΑΒΓΔΕΖΗΘΙΚΛΜΝΞΟΠΡΣΤΥ
ΦΧΨΩαβγδεζηθικλμνξοπρς
τυφχψωΆΈΌΎΩάέήίόύώϊϋ
ΑΒἒἲἘὒΉΙὼΚἄΜΝΟΡἲὒὣΤἳὔρ

▶ Bold Inclined
ΑΒΓΔΕΖΗΘΙΚΛΜΝΞΟΠΡΣΤΥ
ΦΧΨΩαβγδεζηθικλμνξοπρς
τυφχψωΆΈΌΎΩάέήίόύώϊϋ
ΑΒἒἲἘὒΉΙὼΚἄΜΝΟΡἲὒὣΤἳὔρ

LS338 Mac — Hebrew
Laser Hebrew

יצּוּשׁשׂסּרּקּפּנּמלּכחהגּטדשׁבא
׃ןךּף+שׂﭏ׃ﭏוּﭏנּ׃=׃׃ׁ׃׃׃׃0123456789KL**ℒ**S**ℭℸℳ**BK
𝔘𝔔𝔔𝔙𝔞σθ*TWdef†.:,?-×

K355 Mac — Modern Greek + T
Modern Greek

ΑΒΓΔΕΖΗΘΙΚΛΜΝΞΟΠΡΣΤΥΦΧΨΩαβγδεζ
ηθικλμνξοπρσςτυφχψωΆΈΌΎΩάέήίόύώϊϋ
ABCDEFGHIJKLMNOabcdefghijklmnopqrst

▶ Olympia Plain
ΑΒΓΔΕΖΗΘΙΚΛΜΝΞΟΠΡΣΤΥ
ΦΧΨΩαβγδεζηθικλμνξοπρςς
υφχψωΆΈΌΎΩάέήίόύώϊϋΑΒ
CDEFGHIJKLMabcdefghijklm

▶ Olympia Oblique
ΑΒΓΔΕΖΗΘΙΚΛΜΝΞΟΠΡΣΤΥ
ΦΧΨΩαβγδεζηθικλμνξοπρςς
υφχψωΆΈΌΎΩάέήίόύώϊϋΑΒ
CDEFGHIJKLMabcdefghijklm

▶ Olympia Bold
ΑΒΓΔΕΖΗΘΙΚΛΜΝΞΟΠΡΣΤΥ
ΦΧΨΩαβγδεζηθικλμνξοπρς
τυφχψωΆΈΌΎΩάέήίόύώϊϋ
ABCDEFGHIJabcdefghijklm

▶ Olympia BoldOblique
ΑΒΓΔΕΖΗΘΙΚΛΜΝΞΟΠΡΣΤΥ
ΦΧΨΩαβγδεζηθικλμνξοπρς
τυφχψωΆΈΌΎΩάέήίόύώϊϋ
ABCDEFGHIJabcdefghijklm

▶ Tiryns Roman
ΑΒΓΔΕΖΗΘΙΚΛΜΝΞΟΠΡΣΤ
ΥΦΧΨΩαβγδεζηθικλμνξοπρς
τυφχψωΆΈΌΎΩάέήίόύώϊϋΑ
BCDEFGHIJKLMNOabcdefghij

▶ Tiryns Italic
ΑΒΓΔΕΖΗΘΙΚΛΜΝΞΟΠΡΣΤ
ΥΦΧΨΩαβγδεζηθικλμνξοπρς
τυφχψωΆΈΌΎΩάέήίόύώϊϋΑ
BCDEFGHIJKLMNOabcdefghij

▶ Tiryns Bold
ΑΒΓΔΕΖΗΘΙΚΛΜΝΞΟΠΡΣΤ
ΥΦΧΨΩαβγδεζηθικλμνξοπρς
τυφχψωΆΈΌΎΩάέήίόύώϊϋΑ
BCDEFGHIJKLMNOabcdefg

▶ Tiryns Bold Italic
ΑΒΓΔΕΖΗΘΙΚΛΜΝΞΟΠΡΣΤ
ΥΦΧΨΩαβγδεζηθικλμνξοπρς
τυφχψωΆΈΌΎΩάέήίόύώϊϋΑ
BCDEFGHIJKLMNOabcdefg

© FSI 1993

K2757 Mac — Parmenides
Classical Greek

ΑΒΓΔΕΖΗΘΙΚΛΜΝΞΠΟΡΣΤΥΦΧΨΩαβγδεζ
ηθικλμνξπορσςτυφχψωÂĤÉΩ̂ÔΎ̀Ĥ̀Ὺ̀ῺΗΈΈΊΩΙ
ΌΌ̀Ύ̀ϋ̃ι̃α̂ά̂ώ̂α̂̓ά̂̓ά̓ὰᾶἐ̓ά̓ώἔἒΕ̄ί̓ὺῖϊ̄όὃὂΰῢϋ̃ύ̃ϋ̃̀ὰ̣

▶ **One**
ΑΒΓΔΕΖΗΘΙΚΛΜΝΞΠΟΡΣΤΥ
ΦΧΨΩαβγδεζηθικλμνξπορσςτυφ
χψωÂĤÉΩ̂ÔΎ̀Ĥ̀Ὺ̀ῺΗΈΈΊΩΙΌΌ̀Ύ̀ϋ̃ι̃
αάώα̂̓ά̂̓ά̓ὰᾶἐ̓ά̓ώἔἒΕ̄ί̓ὺῖϊ̄όὃὂΰῢϋ̃

▶ **Two**
ΑΒΓΔΕΖΗΘΙΚΛΜΝΞΠΟΡΣΤΥ
ΦΧΨΩαβγδεζηθικλμνξπορσςτυφ
χψεψζάὰὰήώέὲΕ̄ίὺῖϊ̄ῆόὃὂΰῢϋ̃ςμδ
πήῶωϋϋ̃ύ̃ἨΩ̂ΕΗΎἨΩ̂ΣΠΔΑὨΥ̓

LH6831 Mac + PC — Souvenir Greek Polytonic
Classical Greek

ΑΒΓΔΕΖΗΘΙΚΛΜΝΞΟΠΡΣΤΥΦΧΨΩαβγδ
εζηθικλμνξπορσςτυφχψωΆΈΌΎΏάέήίόύώ
ϋϊ̈ΑΒἒἲΕὺΗΙὠΚἂΜΝΟΡϊὖὦΤϊϋ̈ρ̇ΧΥΖάἐήὶὀ

▶ **Light**
ΑΒΓΔΕΖΗΘΙΚΛΜΝΞΠΟΡΣΤΥ
ΦΧΨΩαβγδεζηθικλμνξπορσςτυ
φχψωΆΈΌΎΏάέήίόύώϋϊ̈ΑΒἒἲ
ΕὺΗΙὠΚἂΜΝΟΡϊὖὦΤϊϋ̈ρ̇ΧΥΖάἐ

▶ **Demi**
ΑΒΓΔΕΖΗΘΙΚΛΜΝΞΟΠΡΣ
ΤΥΦΧΨΩαβγδεζηθικλμνξπ
ορσςτυφχψωΆΈΌΎΏάέήί
όύώϋϊ̈ΑΒἒἲΕὺΗΙὠΚἂΜΝΟ

LH6830 Mac + PC — Souvenir Greek Monotonic
Modern Greek

ΑΒΓΔΕΖΗΘΙΚΛΜΝΞΟΠΡΣΤΥΦΧΨΩαβγ
δεζηθικλμνξπορσςτυφχψωΆΈΌΎΏάέήίό
ύώϋϊ̈ABCDEFGHIJKLabcdefghijklmnopq

▶ **Light**
ΑΒΓΔΕΖΗΘΙΚΛΜΝΞΠΟΡΣΤΥ
ΦΧΨΩαβγδεζηθικλμνξπορσςτυ
φχψωΆΈΌΎΏάέήίόύώϋϊ̈AB
CDEFGHIJKLabcdefghijklmno

▶ **Demi**
ΑΒΓΔΕΖΗΘΙΚΛΜΝΞΟΠΡΣ
ΤΥΦΧΨΩαβγδεζηθικλμνξπ
ορσςτυφχψωΆΈΌΎΏάέήίό
ύώϋϊ̈ABCDEFGabcdefghij

LH6321 Mac + PC — Times Greek Polytonic
Classical Greek

ΑΒΓΔΕΖΗΘΙΚΛΜΝΞΟΠΡΣΤΥΦΧΨΩαβ
γδεζηθικλμνξπορσςτυφχψωΆΈΌΎΏάέήί
όύώϋϊ̈ABCDEFGHIJKLMNOPQRSTUV

▶ **Upright**
ΑΒΓΔΕΖΗΘΙΚΛΜΝΞΠΟΡΣΤ
ΥΦΧΨΩαβγδεζηθικλμνξπορσ
ςτυφχψωΆΈΌΎΏάέήίόύώϊ
ϋABCDEFGHIJKLMNOPQR

▶ *Inclined*
ΑΒΓΔΕΖΗΘΙΚΛΜΝΞΟΠΡΣ
ΤΥΦΧΨΩαβγδεζηθικλμνξπορ
σςτυφχψωΆΈΌΎΏάέήίόύώϊ
ϋABCDEFGHIJKLMNOPQR

▶ **Bold**
ΑΒΓΔΕΖΗΘΙΚΛΜΝΞΟΠΡΣ
ΤΥΦΧΨΩαβγδεζηθικλμνξπο
ρσςτυφχψωΆΈΌΎΏάέήίόύώ
ϋϊ̈ABCDEFGHIJKLMNOP

▶ ***Bold Inclined***
ΑΒΓΔ ΕΖΗΘΙΚΛΜΝΞΟΠΡΣ
ΤΥΦΧΨΩαβγδεζηθικλμνξπο
ρσςτυφχψωΆΈΌΎΏάέήίόύώ
ϋϊ̈ABCDEFGHIJKLMNOP

© FSI 1993

LH6826 Mac + PC
Times Ten Greek Monotonic

Modern Greek

ΑΒΓΔΕΖΗΘΙΚΛΜΝΞΠΟΡΣΤΥΦΧΨΩαβγ
δεζηθικλμνξπορσςτυφχψωΆΈΌΎΩάέήίόύ
ώϋΐϋΰΑΒε̃ι̃ΕϋΗΙὡΚὰἐἠἰὀὺὠ˜ᾶἠὁ˜ἠὁ˜ᾶἠἰὑὠ˜ᾶ

▶ Upright
ΑΒΓΔΕΖΗΘΙΚΛΜΝΞΠΟΡΣΤ
ΥΦΧΨΩαβγδεζηθικλμνξπορσ
ςτυφχψωΆΈΌΎΩάέήίόύώϋΐϋΰ
ΑΒε̃ι̃ΕϋΗὰἐἠἰὀὺὠ˜ᾶἠὁ˜ἠὁ˜ᾶἠἰ

▶ Inclined
ΑΒΓΔΕΖΗΘΙΚΛΜΝΞΠΟΡΣ
ΤΥΦΧΨΩαβγδεζηθικλμνξπορ
σςτυφχψωΆΈΌΎΩάέήίόύώϋΐ
ΰΑΒε̃ι̃ΕϋΗὰἐἠἰὀὺὠ˜ᾶἠὁ˜ἠὁ˜ᾶἠἰ

▶ Bold
ΑΒΓΔΕΖΗΘΙΚΛΜΝΞΠΟΡΣ
ΤΥΦΧΨΩαβγδεζηθικλμνξπο
ρσςτυφχψωΆΈΌΎΩάέήίόύώ
ϋΐϋΰΑΒε̃ι̃ΕϋΗὰἐἠἰὀὺὠ˜ᾶἠὁ˜ἠὁ˜

▶ Bold Inclined
ΑΒΓΔΕΖΗΘΙΚΛΜΝΞΠΟΡΣ
ΤΥΦΧΨΩαβγδεζηθικλμνξπορ
σςτυφχψωΆΈΌΎΩάέήίόύώϋΐ
ΰΑΒε̃ι̃ΕϋΗὰἐἠἰὀὺὠ˜ᾶἠὁ˜ἠὁ˜ᾶἠ

M977 Mac + PC
Times New Roman Greek

Modern Greek

ΑΒΓΔΕΖΗΘΙΚΛΜΝΞΠΟΡΣΤΥΘΧΨΩαβγ
δεζηθικλμνξπορσςτυφχψωΆΈΌΎΩάέήίόύ
ώϋΐϋΰΑBCDEFGHIJKLabcdefghijklmnopqr

▶ Regular
ΑΒΓΔΕΖΗΘΙΚΛΜΝΞΠΟΡΣΤ
ΥΘΧΨΩαβγδεζηθικλμνξπορς
τυφχψωΆΈΌΎΩάέήίόύώϋΐϋΰΑ
BCDEFGHIJKabcdefghijklmn

▶ Regular Inclined
ΑΒΓΔΕΖΗΘΙΚΛΜΝΞΠΟΡΣΤ
ΥΘΧΨΩαβγδεζηθικλμνξπορςτυ
φχψωΆΈΌΎΩάέήίόύώϋΐϋΰΑBCD
EFGHIJKLMNabcdefghijklmno

▶ Bold
ΑΒΓΔΕΖΗΘΙΚΛΜΝΞΠΟΡΣΤ
ΥΘΧΨΩαβγδεζηθικλμνξπορς
τυφχψωΆΈΌΎΩάέήίόύώϋΐϋΰΑ
BCDEFGHIJKabcdefghijklmn

▶ Bold Inclined
ΑΒΓΔΕΖΗΘΙΚΛΜΝΞΠΟΡΣΤ
ΥΘΧΨΩαβγδεζηθικλμνξπορςτυ
φχψωΆΈΌΎΩάέήίόύώϋΐϋΰΑBCD
EFGHIJKLMNabcdefghijklmno

K6801 Mac
New Baskerville South Asia

Indian Transliteration

ÄĀČḌGĠḤĪJ̄ḶṀṂÑṄŅŌṚṢŚṢŚṬṬŪŪZŽ
ŹẒẒáàâāãāãā̄ɔčḍĕéèēëə̄eġġḥḥḥ ḥ hí ìîīïīij̄ j̄ḷḷ
ṁṁṅñṇóòôōöṓṙṛŕ̄ŕ̄ŕ̄śṣṣṣṭṭúùûūüūūu̯ẇẏẓ́ẓ́ẓ́

▶ Plain
ÄĀČḌGĠḤĪJ̄ḶṀṂÑṄŅŌṚṢŚ
ṢŚṬṬŪŪZŽŹẒẒáàâāãāãāɔčḍĕéè
ēëə̄eġġḥḥḥhíìîīïīij̄j̄ḷḷṁṁṅñṇóó
òôōöṓṙṛŕ̄ŕ̄ŕ̄śṣṣṣṭṭúùûūüūūu̯ẇẏẓ́ẓ́ẓ́

▶ Italic
ÄĀČḌGĠḤĪJ̄ḶṀṂÑṄŅŌṚṢŚṢŚṬ
ṬŪŪZŽŹẒẒáàâāãāãāɔčḍĕéèēëə̄eġġ
ḥḥḥhíìîīïīij̄j̄ḷḷṁṁṅñṇóòôōöṓṙṛŕ̄ŕ̄ŕ̄śṣ
ṣṣṭṭúùûūüūūu̯ẇẏẓ́ẓ́ẓ́ẓ́βKhkhABCD

▶ Bold
ÄĀČḌGĠḤĪJ̄ḶṀṂÑṄŅŌṚṢŚ
ṢŚṬṬŪŪZŽŹẒẒáàâāãāãāɔčḍĕéè
ēëə̄eġġḥḥḥhíìîīïīij̄j̄ḷḷṁṁṅñṇóó
òôōöṓṙṛŕ̄ŕ̄ŕ̄śṣṣṣṭṭúùûūüūūu̯ẇẏẓ́ẓ́ẓ́

▶ Bold Italic
ÄĀČḌGĠḤĪJ̄ḶṀṂÑṄŅŌṚṢŚṢŚṬ
ṬŪŪZŽŹẒẒáàâāãāãāɔčḍĕéèēëə̄eə
gġḥḥḥhíìîīïīij̄j̄ḷḷṁṁṅñṇóòôōöṓṙṛ
ŕ̄ŕ̄ŕ̄śṣṣṣṭṭúùûūüūūu̯ẇẏẓ́ẓ́ẓ́βKhkhAB

© FSI 1993
Arabic, Greek/Asian

Asian

K6802 MAC — Indian Transliteration
Stempel Garamond South Asia

ÄĀČḌGĠHĪJĽĻMṀÑṄŅÖRṢŠṢ́ṢŢṬÜŪZ̲
ŽŹZ̧Z̲áàáäãāàā̃ɔčďéèēëē̃əgġḥhḫh̲ĥîíïįīĩĩĭǰļḷm̱
ṁṅñṇŏóòōöõŗŕṛṝŗ́ṛ́śṣšs̱ṣ́ṭṭúùúüùū̃ũṉ̇ w̉ỳz̲žźẓßſ

► Plain
ÄĀČḌGĠHĪJĽĻMṀÑṄŅÖR
ṢŠṢ́ṢŢṬÜŪZ̲ŽŹZ̧Z̲áàáäãāàā̃ɔčďé
èēëē̃əgġḥhḫh̲ĥîíïįīĩĩĭǰļḷm̱ṁṅñṇŏ
óòōöõŗŕṛṝŗ́ṛ́śṣšs̱ṣ́ṭṭúùúüùū̃ũṉ̇ w̉ỳzž

► Italic
ÄĀČḌGĠHĪJĽĻMṀÑṄŅÖRṢ
ŠṢ́ṢŢṬÜŪZ̲ŽŹZ̧Z̲áàáäãāàā̃ɔčďé
èēëē̃əgġḥhḫh̲ĥîíïįīĩĩĭǰļḷm̱ṁṅñṇŏ
óòōöõŗŕṛṝŗ́ṛ́śṣšs̱ṣ́ṭṭúùúüùū̃ũṉ̇ w̉ỳzž

► Bold
ÄĀČḌGĠHĪJĽĻMṀÑṄŅÖR
ṢŠṢ́ṢŢṬÜŪZ̲ŽŹZ̧Z̲áàáäãāàā̃ɔč
ďéèēëē̃əgġḥhḫh̲ĥîíïįīĩĩĭǰļḷm̱ṁṅ
ñṇŏóòōöõŗŕṛṝŗ́ṛ́śṣšs̱ṣ́ṭṭúùúüùū̃ũṉ̇

► Bold Italic
ÄĀČḌGĠHĪJĽĻMṀÑṄŅÖRṢ
ŠṢ́ṢŢṬÜŪZ̲ŽŹZ̧Z̲áàáäãāàā̃ɔčďé
èēëē̃əgġḥhḫh̲ĥîíïįīĩĩĭǰļḷm̱ṁṅñṇŏ
óòōöõŗŕṛṝŗ́ṛ́śṣšs̱ṣ́ṭṭúùúüùū̃ũṉ̇ w̉ỳz

K2859 MAC — South Asia Transliteration
South Asia Roman

ÄĀČḌGHĪJĽĻMṀÑṄŅÖRṢŠṢ́ṢŢÜŪZ̲ŽŹ
ZZ̧áàáäãāàā̃ɔčd̲zéèēëē̃əghḥĥîíïįīĩĩĭǰļm̱ṁṅñṇó
òōöõŗŕṛṝŗ́ṛ́śṣšs̱ṣ́ṭṭúùúüùūũ̃ w̉ỳz̲žźẓßKhkhABC

► Plain
ÄĀČḌGHĪJĽĻMṀÑṄŅÖRṢŠṢ́ṢŢ
ÜŪZ̲ŽŹZZ̧áàáäãāàā̃ɔčd̲zéèēëē̃əg
ḥĥîíïįīĩĩĭǰļm̱ṁṅñṇóòōöõŗŕṛṝŗ́ṛ́śṣšs̱ṣ́ṭṭú
ùúüùūũ̃ w̉ỳz̲žźẓßKhkhABCabcdef

► Italic
ÄĀČḌGHĪJĽĻMṀÑṄŅÖRṢŠṢ́ṢŢU
ŪZ̲ŽŹ ZZ̧áàáäãāàā̃ɔčd̲zéèēëē̃əghḥ
ĥîíïįīĩĩĭǰļm̱ṁṅñṇóòōöõŗŕṛṝŗ́ṛ́śṣšs̱ṣ́ṭṭúùú
üùūũ̃ w̉ỳz̲žźẓßKhkhABCDabcdefg

► Bold
ÄĀČḌGHĪJĽĻMṀÑṄŅÖRṢŠṢ́Ṣ
ŢÜŪZ̲ŽŹZZ̧áàáäãāàā̃ɔčd̲zéèēëē̃
əgḥĥîíïįīĩĩĭǰļm̱ṁṅñṇóòōöõŗŕṛṝŗ́ṛ́
śṣšs̱ṣ́ṭṭúùúüùūũ̃ w̉ỳz̲žźẓßKhkhA

► Bold Italic
ÄĀČḌGHĪJĽĻMṀÑṄŅÖRṢŠṢ́Ṣ
ŢÜŪZ̲ŽŹZZ̧áàáäãāàā̃ɔčd̲zéèēë
ē̃əgḥĥîíïįīĩĩĭǰļm̱ṁṅñṇóòōöõŗŕṛṝŗ́ṛ́ś
ṣšs̱ṣ́ṭṭúùúüùūũ̃ w̉ỳz̲žźẓßKhkhABabc

LS934 MAC + PC — Thai
Laser Thai

ศภฤคลงชบผ๐๒๓ ๔๖๗๘๕ซวฌฬ%ใฉฏฎโฌณฆฯบ
ฯญๆฑธฮไลต๊ไฟแก๊าดเราสกนยๆพหะอไผฒิ๋ม
1234567890

► Sukanya
ศภฤคลงชบผ๐๒๓ ๔๖๗๘๕ซวฌฬ%ใฉฏฎโ
ฌณฆฯบฯญๆฑธฮไลต๊ไฟแก๊าดเราสกน
ยๆพหะอไผฒิ๋ม

► Thai Key Caps
ⁿ๒๑๐๕๐๐๕ ญษจ°๐๖⁺ค๓⁺°๒๙ษ‡๔๖ᵐฯฆ!¹°ๅ
°ๅ°๊ⁿ๒๘%ๆๆ   5ษ° ใฟแก๊าดเราสก
           นยๆพหะอไป๛ผ

© FSI 1993
Asian 34

LS935 Mac + PC — Vietnamese

ạọụảỏầÈ ĐẸỖ

LS2855 Mac + PC — Laser IPA

abcdefghijklmnopqrstuvwxyzaβçðeɸɢɦiʒʃʃ
mɲɔʁθʀʃʈʌɣχʏzɾɾɐɒtɕʊʎɟəçɖtsɪəʎʧʃɨˌσʤʞ
œɐdzɳɰɟɡəɰøɴˤɦɖʍθœʢʔωˤɬʒɾldʐʠʡæ·

▶ Roman
abcdefghijklmnopqrstuvwxyzaβç
ðeɸɢɦiʒʃʃmɲɔʁθʀʃʈʌɣχʏzɾɐɒtɕʊʎ
ɟəçɖtsɪəʎʧʃɨˌσʤʞœɐdzɳɰɟɡəɰø
ɴˤɦɖʍθœʢʔωˤɬʒɾldʐʠʡæ·ʒ·ʁʒʢ

▶ Plus
abcdefghijklmnopqrstuvwxyzaβçðeɸɢɦ
iʒ☆ɫmɲɔʁθʀʃʈʌɣχʏzɾɐɒtɕʊʎɟəçɪəʎ☆zɨ
ɰɸɟɡəɰøɴˤɦɖʍθœœɒʔωˤɬʒɾdʃɟʡæ·ʒʁʒ
ʊʘɦɖʜɦˈʒʃɬɒɮɻʎɬ˦ʕʕʱˬʕ

▶ Sans
abcdefghijklmnopqrstuvwxyzaβçðeɸɢɦ
iʒ☆ɫmɲɔʁθʀʃʈʌɣχʏzɾɐɒtɕʊʎɟəçɪəʎ☆zɨ
ɰɸɟɡəɰøɴˤɦɖʍθœœɒʔωˤɬʒɾdʃɟʡæ·ʒʁʒ
ʊʘɦɖʜɦˈʒʃɬɒɮɻʎɬ˦ʕʕʱˬʕ

C2705 Mac + PC — Agfa Pi & Symbols: Phonetics 1

ʊʜ,β''ʃɾɛɕtʒɚᴧɓʁɫɻpɒɳɯɡɞʘqɪʂtðɲɰχʎz
-ɬɞʒʁɾɑɦĸlɯɲŋǫǿʀʂʈʉʋχʌzθ˧ɪγ

C2706 Mac + PC — Agfa Pi & Symbols: Phonetics 2

ᷓ ᷄ . ᷆ ᷇ ᷈ ᷉ ꜛ ꜜ ᷋ ᷌ ᷍ ᷎ ᷏ · ́ ̀ ̂ ̃ ̄ ̅ ̆ ̇ ̈ ̉ ̊ ̋ ̌ ̍ ̎ ̏

C2707 Mac + PC — Agfa Pi & Symbols: Phonetics 3

e i ? ə z ? ɸ \ ə ʌ ʒ ɜ̃ æ ɔ ɐ m ɟ ʎ ʒ ɫ ĝ ʒ ɜ̃
ɜ ɛ

Stone Phonetic
A2868 Mac + PC — Phonetics

abcdefghijklmnopqrstuvwxyzaʙçðɛɸɢ
ʜɪɟɪʟɯɴɔʼɾʀʃθʊʋχʏʒɵɒçɛɕ~ɬɟʝʒɥɵʎɯdɯ
ʍᵊƥɓzøʕɫʏʄǁǂɽɖʁɱʈʏʉɦɗɣɕɧʝⱼʟẓɨɳɦkʔ

▶ Sans
abcdefghijklmnopqrstuvwxyza
ʙçðɛɸɢʜɪɟɪʟɯɴɔʼɾʀʃθʊʋχʏʒɵɒ
çɛɕ~ɬɟʝʒɥɵʎɯdɯʍᵊƥɓzøʕɫʏʄǁǂ
ɽɖʁɱʈʏʉɦɗɣɕɧʝⱼʟẓɨɳɦkʔˤʷⁿˢ

▶ Sans Alternate

▶ Serif
abcdefghijklmnopqrstuvwxy
zaʙçðɛɸɢʜɪɟɪʟɯɴɔʼɾʀʃθʊʋχʏʒ
ɵɒçɛɕ~ɬɟʝʒɥɵʎɯdɯʍᵊƥɓzøʕɫʏ
ʄǁǂɽɖʁɱʈʏʉɦɗɣɕɧʝⱼʟẓɨɳɦkʔ

▶ Serif Alternate

Times Phonetic
A6065 Mac + PC — Phonetics

abcdefghijklmnopqrstuvwxyzaʙçðɛɸɢʜ
ɪɟɪʟɯɴɔʼɾʀʃθʊʋχʏʒɵɒçɛɕ~ɬɟʝʒɥɵʎɯdɯ
ʍᵊƥɓzøʕɫʏʄǁǂɽɖʁɱʈʏʉɦɗɣɕɧʝⱼʟẓɨɳɦkʔˤʷ

▶ Regular
abcdefghijklmnopqrstuvwxyz
aʙçðɛɸɢʜɪɟɪʟɯɴɔʼɾʀʃθʊʋχʏʒɵ
ɒçɛɕ~ɬɟʝʒɥɵʎɯdɯʍᵊƥɓzøʕɫʏʄ
ǁǂɽɖʁɱʈʏʉɦɗɣɕɧʝⱼʟẓɨɳɦkʔˤʷⁿ

▶ Alternate

HEsperanto
K6192 Mac + PC — Esperanto

abcdefghijklmnopqrstuvwxyz[äöüßåŝĵĝĉ]AB
CDEFGHIJKLMNOPQRSTUVWXYZ12345
67890(.,;:?!$&-*){ÄÖÜÅŜĴĜĈ}

▶ Regular
The quick brown fox jumps over a Dog. Zwei Boxkämpfer jagen Eva durch Sylt portez ce vieux Whiskey blond qui fume

▶ Oblique
The quick brown fox jumps over a Dog. Zwei Boxkämpfer jagen Eva durch Sylt portez ce vieux Whiskey blond qui fume

▶ Bold
The quick brown fox jumps over a Dog. Zwei Boxkämpfer jagen Eva durch Sylt portez ce vieux Whiskey blond

▶ Bold Oblique
The quick brown fox jumps over a Dog. Zwei Boxkämpfer jagen Eva durch Sylt portez ce vieux Whiskey blond

Lesebuch & HEsperanto

© FSI 1993

K6192 Mac + PC — Esperanto
Lesebuch & HEsperanto
Lesebuch & HEsperanto

K6192 Mac + PC
Lesebuch

abcdefghijklmnopqrstuvwxyz[äöüßåøæœç]
ABCDEFGHIJKLMNOPQRSTUVWXYZ
1234567890(.,;:?!$&-*){ÄÖÜÅØÆŒÇ}

▶ Regular
The quick brown fox jumps over a Dog. Zwei Boxkämpfer jagen Eva durch Sylt portez ce vieux Whiskey blond qui fume

▶ Oblique
The quick brown fox jumps over a Dog. Zwei Boxkämpfer jagen Eva durch Sylt portez ce vieux Whiskey blond qui fume

▶ Bold
The quick brown fox jumps over a Dog. Zwei Boxkämpfer jagen Eva durch Sylt portez ce vieux Whiskey blond

▶ Bold Oblique
The quick brown fox jumps over a Dog. Zwei Boxkämpfer jagen Eva durch Sylt portez ce vieux Whiskey blond

Lesebuch & HEsperanto

© FSI 1993

Neville Brody, London, UK

FUSE © @ …

FU 5000   Mac + PC
FUSE 1 ⟶ 4 designers, 4 typefaces, 4 A2 posters, 1 brochure

▶ **F State**
  Neville Brody

▶ **F Stealth**
  Malcolm Garrett

▶ **F Maze 91**
  Ian Swift

▶ **Can you …?**
  Phil Baines

FU 5001   Mac + PC
FUSE 2 ⟶ 4 designers, 4 typefaces, 4 A2 posters, 1 brochure

▶ **F Linear Konstrukt**
  Max Kisman

▶ **F Decoder**
  Gerard Unger

▶ **F Niwida**
  Erik van Blokland

▶ **F Flixel**
  Just van Rossum

© FSI 1993
Fuse 1

FU 5002 Mac + PC

FUSE 3 ⇢ 4 designers, 4 typefaces, 4 A2 posters, 1 brochure

▶ **F Grid**
⌽ Erik Spiekermann

▶ **F Dear John**
⌽ Barbara Butterweck

ABCDEFGHIJKLMNOPQRSTUVXYZ

▶ **F InTegel**
⌽ Martin Wenzel

▶ **F Moonbase Alpha**
⌽ Cornel Windlin

abcdefghijklmnopqrstuvwxyz (äüöß¢)
ABCDEFGHIJKLMNOPQRSTUVWXYZ (ÄÜÖÇ)
0123456789 (!$%+/=?.¢¤*@)

FU 5003 Mac + PC

FUSE 4 ⇢ 4 designers, 4 typefaces, 4 A2 posters, 1 brochure

▶ **F Caustic Biomorph**
⌽ Barry Deck

ABCDEFGHIJKLMNO
PQRSTUVWXYZ
0123456789 ..:;?!FAX

▶ **F Lushus**
⌽ Jefferey Keedy

ABCDEFGHIJKLMNOPQRS
TUVWXYZ ····4·!·

▶ **F Uck'N Pretty**
⌽ Rick Valicenti

abcdefghijklmnopqrstuvwxyz
a ❤ 4V ST

▶ **F Yurnacular**
⌽ David Berlow

© FSI 1993

Fuse 2

FU 5004 Mac + PC

FUSE 5 ⟶ 4 designers, 4 typefaces, 4 A2 posters, 1 A2 infoposter + 1 bonus font

▶ **F Flo Motion**
✎ Peter Saville

abcdefghijklmnopqrstuvwxyz(äüöc)
ABCDEFGHIJKLMNOPQRSTUVW
XYZ (ÄÜÖÇ) 01234567890 (!?Œ)

FUSE

▶ **F Scratched Out**
✎ Pierre di Sciullo

▶ **F Spherize**
✎ Lo Breier / Florian Fossel

▶ **F Alphabet**
✎ Paul Elliman

Bonusfont
▶ **F Virtual**

FU 5005 Mac + PC

FUSE 6 ⟶ 4 designers, 4 typefaces, 4 A2 posters, 1 A2 infoposter + 1 bonus font

▶ **F Box**
✎ Paul Sych

▶ **F Dr. NOB**
✎ Ian Anderson

▶ **F Morsig**
✎ Rick Vermeulen

▶ **F Schirft**
✎ Martin Wenzel

Bonusfont
▶ **F Code**

© FSI 1993

Fuse 3

FU 5006 Mac + PC

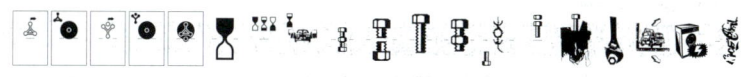

FUSE 7 ⇢ 4 designers, 4 typefaces, 4 A2 posters, 1 A2 infoposter + 2 bonus fonts

▶ **F Fingers**
✎ David Carson

▶ **F Illiterate**
✎ Phil Bicker

▶ **F Moga-dischu**
✎ Cornel Windlin

▶ **F Reactor**
✎ Tobias Frere-Jones

Bonusfonts
▶ **F Crash**
▶ **F Crash-Cameo**

FU 5007 Mac + PC

FUSE 8 ⇢ 4 designers, 4 typefaces, 4 A2 posters, 1 A2 infoposter + 3 bonus fonts

▶ **F Ushaw**
✎ Phil Baines

▶ **F Creation 6**
✎ Dave Crow

▶ **F Goodevil**
✎ Tibor Kalman

▶ **F X-Pain**
✎ Chu Uroz

Bonusfonts
▶ **F Religion**
▶ **F Obedience**
▶ **F Loss of Faith**

F QUATERLY:
- 4 designers
- 4 typefaces
- 4 A2 poster
- 1 A2 infoposter

© FSI 1993
Fuse 4

rock & roll

a farhill production for fsi, june 1993

guitaxed!
a farhill tape

'Grunge Type'

Retromusic also has dramatic influences on the quality of type

farhill types

Peter Verheul, The Hague, NL

This page is designed by using only homemade typefaces

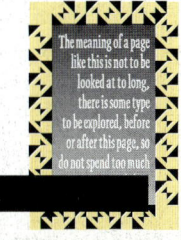

Fonts on CD-ROM

(GB) (USA) (CDN) (AUS) (NZ)

Most typefaces shown in the FontBook are available in CD-ROM format, either as complete 'open' libraries or in 'unlockable' form, for both Mac and PC.

Some advantages of CD:
1. Single weights are often available, as well as complete family packages.
2. Prices are often lower than the floppy-disk equivalent.
3. Utilities, screen-fonts and other software may be available on the CD-ROM.
4. Fonts and software are 'unlocked' the same day – usually within minutes of your call.
5. Substantial environmental benefits when fonts are unlocked: no packaging, no floppy disks, no transportation impact.
6. Some manufacturers offer discounted drives with their CD's.

Call FontShop for details.

(F) (B) (CH) (CDN)

Presque toutes les polices de caractères reprises dans ce livre sont disponible sur CD-ROM, en tant que bibliothèques complètes 'ouvertes' ou sous forme 'vérrouilé', pour Mac et PC.

Les avantages du CD:
1. L'achat de familles complètes et de graisses est possible sur le système CD-ROM.
2. Le prix des polices de caractères est moins cher que leur équivalent sur disquette.
3. Utilitaires, polices d'écran et d'autres logiciels sont disponibles sur le CD-ROM.
4. L'achat d'un système sur CD-ROM permet d'avoir vos polices dans l'heure.
5. Autres avantage: Pas d'emballage, pas de disquettes ni frais de transport.
6. Quelques fabricants offrent leur CD-ROM plus lecteur à des prix avantageux.

Contactez FontShop pour de plus amples informations.

(I)

Quasi tutti i caratteri illustrati nel FontBook sono disponibili per Mac e PC anche sul CD-ROM.

Vantaggi del CD:
1. È possibile acquistare un singolo font, oppure tutti i fonts che compongono la famiglia.
2. I prezzi sono spesso inferiori ai corrispondenti prodotti su floppy-disk.
3. Utilities, screen fonts e altro software sono spesso forniti su CD-ROM.
4. I codici di accesso per fonts e software sono forniti il giorno stesso.
5. Ulteriori vantaggi: niente imballaggio, nessun floppy disk, nessun rischio di danneggiamento durante il trasporto.
6. Alcuni produttori offrono il lettore CD a prezzi scontati.

Chiamate FontShop per qualsiasi informazione.

(NL) (B)

Vrijwel alle lettertypes opgenomen in het FontBook zijn beschikbaar op CD-ROM, als volledig 'geopende' bibliotheken of in 'ongrendelbare' vorm, beide voor Mac en PC.

De voordelen van een CD:
1. Volledige letterfamilies alsook hun gewichten zijn afzonderlijk verkrijgbaar.
2. De prijs per letterfamilie is goedkoper dan hun equivalent op diskette.
3. Utilities, screen fonts en andere software kunnen beschikbaar zijn op de CD-ROM.
4. Lettertypes en software zijn beschikbaar voor een CD-ROM gebruiker binnen het uur.
5. Andere voordelen bij het gebruik van een CD-ROM: geen verpakking, geen diskettes, geen transportkosten.
6. Enkele fabrikanten bieden CD-ROMS met drive aan tegen goedkopere prijzen.

Geef een seintje aan uw plaatselijke FontShop voor meer details.

(D) (A) (CH)

Die meisten der im FontBook gezeigten Schriften gibt es auf CD-ROM. Sie sind erhältlich als komplett geöffnete Bibliotheken oder in sukzessiver Freischaltung, sowohl für Mac als auch für PC.

Die Vorteile der CD:
1. In der Mehrzahl sind sowohl Einzelschnitte als auch Pakete mit kompletten Familien erhältlich.
2. Die Paketpreise liegen meistens unter denen der Diskettenversion.
3. Auf der CD können mitunter auch Utilities, Bildschirmfonts und andere Software gespeichert sein.
4. Schriften und Software werden noch am selben Tag freigeschaltet – normalerweise sogar innerhalb weniger Minuten.
5. CDS sind umweltfreundlich: keine Disketten, keine Verpackung, kein Transport.
6. Einige Hersteller bieten CDs komplett mit Laufwerken zu besonders günstigen Preisen an.

Rufen Sie FontShop an, wenn Sie irgendwelche Fragen haben.

IT IS
STILL A MATTER
OF CONJECTURE WHETHER
JOHANN GUTENBERG WAS THE FIRST TO
CONCEIVE THE PRINCIPLE OF CASTING MOVABLE [I.E., SEPARATE]
METAL TYPES WHICH HE COULD ARRANGE IN WORDS AND SENTENCES SO
THAT HE COULD IMPRESS THEIR FACES ON PAPER. THERE IS, HOWEVER, HARDLY A DOUBT,
JUDGING AT LEAST FROM THE EVIDENCE AVAILABLE, THAT HE WAS THE
FIRST TO MAKE PRACTICAL USE OF THE IDEA, AND THAT IT
IS DUE TO HIS INGENIOUS APPLICATION OF IT
THAT THE PROFOUND ART OF
TYPOGRAPHY WAS
BORN.

FREDERIC W. GOUDY
"TYPOLOGIA"
1940

Paul H. Neville, Boston, USA

Explanations

Special packages

Our Special Pack section offers compendium packs plus some font utilities to help make your life easier.

Compendium font packs are great value – bundles of original high-quality typefaces, all fully licenced, produced by the leading manufacturers. Some packs are designed for a specific design application, in other cases they are in the form of a 'starter pack' with a wide selection of typeface styles. But in all cases they are exceptionally good value.

Our font utilities help you put your typefaces to work by enabling better screen display, simpler font selection, improved printing, and so on.

Icon explanations
*SYSTEM REQUIREMENTS
(ICONS ON DARK BACKGROUND)*

MICROSOFT WINDOWS-COMPATIBLE PRODUCTS

Windows 3.x general system requirements apply in terms of printers, graphic cards and other peripherals.

2MB memory is the recommended minimum RAM; where many fonts and font utilities (such as ATM) are used, a minimum of 4MB is recommended. Each font requires an average 70k of disk storage space (fonts generally need 40k - 100k depending on their complexity).

IBM OS/2-COMPATIBLE PRODUCTS

OS/2 1.3 and 2.x general system requirements apply in terms of printers, graphic cards and other peripherals. OS/2 has ATM built-in, so directly supports installation and use of PostScript Type 1 fonts. OS/2 v. 2.1 users can use TrueType fonts during Windows 3.1 sessions.

MS-DOS AND PC-DOS-COMPATIBLE PRODUCTS

The following system requirements apply:
Processor: 286 or higher
DOS version 3.1 or higher
RAM: minimum 640k
System components: hard disk and floppy drive, supported graphics card (Hercules, MGA, CGA, EGA, VGA)

APPLE MACINTOSH-COMPATIBLE PRODUCTS

System 6.0 or higher with ATM allows on-screen scaling of outline PostScript Type 1 fonts. TrueType fonts are directly supported by System 7.x

Font Formats

POSTSCRIPT TYPE 1

The industry-standard format for scaleable typefaces. Huge choice of typeface designs, with excellent quality. PostScript printers work directly with Type 1 fonts, other printers need ATM present.

TRUETYPE

A font format for scaleable typefaces developed by Apple and Microsoft.

SPEEDO

Several DOS Applications such as Framework IV, Harvard Graphics 3.0, Lotus 1-2-3 and WordPerfect 6.0 can handle this format directly. If you use WordPerfect 5.x and BT FaceLift for WordPerfect you may also use Speedo format fonts.

FONTWARE

You may use Bitstream's fontware products in conjunction with Ventura Publisher (includes Bitstream Fontware 2.0), MS Word 5.0 (requires 'Fontware Installation Kit for MS Word 5.0', BT2556), Multimate IV (includes Bitstream FontWare), Lotus Manuscript (includes Bitstream Fontware) and other applications for which a Fontware Installation Kit is available or which directly supports the Fontware format.

Font Utilities

ADOBE TYPE MANAGER (ATM)

ATM allows the use of PostScript Type 1 typefaces under Windows 3.x and on the Macintosh. (There are also special versions for WordPerfect, DOS and Windows). ATM creates on-the-fly screen display for any size of any face as requested by the user. ATM also enables PostScript Type 1 typefaces to be printed on non-PostScript printers (such as HP DeskJet and LaserJet series). ATM peacefully coexists with TrueType that is built into Windows 3.x and Mac System 7.x.

BISTREAM FACELIFT

Facelift 2.0 is Bitstream's alternative to ATM. In addition to ATM's capabilities, FaceLift provides type effects, type grouping, type styles such as outline, filling pattern, shading and the capability of using different alphabets. Both Type 1 and Speedo font formats can be handled.

Font Packs

A 6620

Adobe Type Basics

Font	font format	medium	system	utility
Helvetica, *Helvetica*, **Helvetica**, ***Helvetica***	✎	💾	Windows 3.0/3.1	
Times, *Times*, **Times**, ***Times***			OS/2 1.3/2.x	
Courier, *Courier*, **Courier**, ***Courier***	✎	💾	Mac 7.0 ↓6.0.3	
Συμβολ (Symbol)				
ITC Avant Garde / *ITC Avant Garde* / **ITC Avant Garde** / ***ITC Avant Garde***				
ITC Bookman / *ITC Bookman* / **ITC Bookman** / ***ITC Bookman***				
Helvetica Narrow / *Helvetica Narrow* / **Helvetica Narrow** / ***Helvetica Narrow***				
New Century Schoolb. / *New Century Schoolb.* / **New Century Schoolb.** / ***New Century Schoolb.***				
Palatino, *Palatino*, **Palatino**, ***Palatino***				
ITC Zapf Chancery				
✆✉❼✆✿✂❈☞✺ ITC Zapf Dingbats				
Americana / **Americana**				
Barmeno, **Medium**, **Bold**, **Extra Bold**				
Blackoak				
Adobe Caslon, *Italic*, **Semibold**, ***Semib. Italic***				
Adobe Garamond, *Italic*, **Bold**, ***Bold Italic***				
Formata, *Italic*, **Medium**, ***Medium Italic***				
Kaufmann				
LITHOS, **BLACK**				
Parisian				
Park Avenue				
Tekton / **Tekton**				
TRAJAN BOLD				
⬚◉⦿⊙✦✢✤⚞⚟ Carta				
❦❧✾❡❈✿❀ Poetica Ornaments				
✺❋✾❀⟿❏ Wood Type Ornaments				

+ ATM

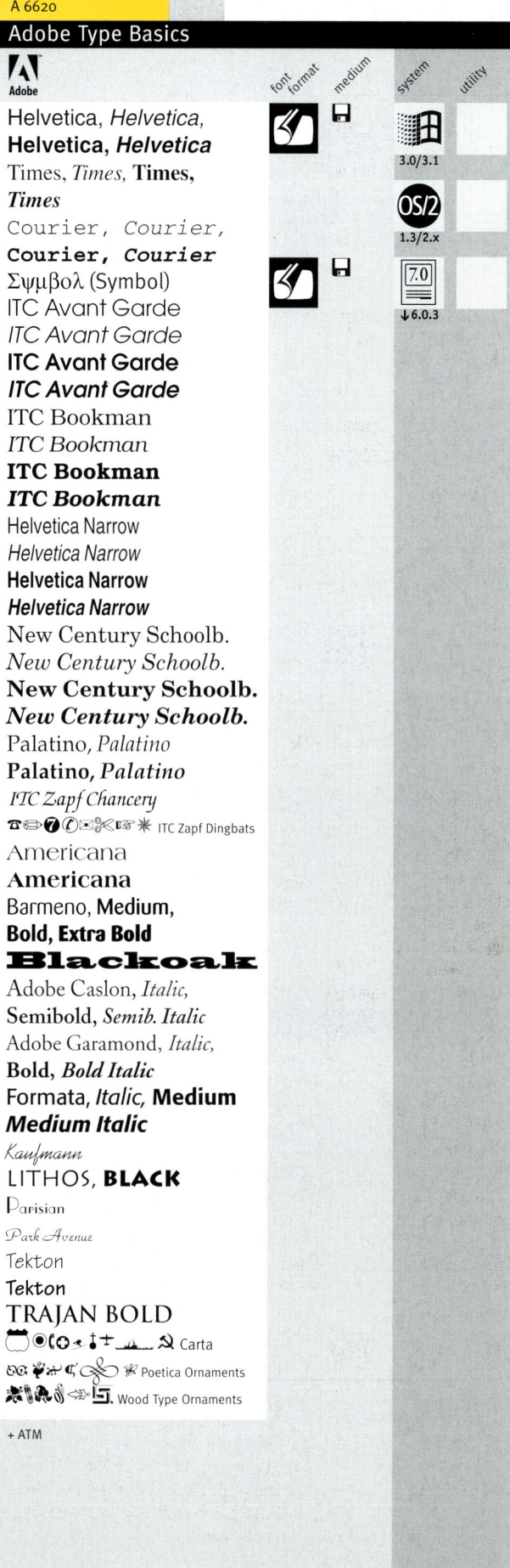

A 6620 PC
A 6620 Mac

Adobe Type Library
Adobe Type Basics

© FSI 1993 ▼

Special Packs 1

Font Packs

A 6179
Adobe Type Set Value Pack

Adobe

- AG Oldface Outline
- **Barmeno Extra Bold**
- *Bellevue*
- *Biffo*
- **Blackoak**
- Bodoni Poster Compressed
- Carta
- CASTELLAR
- **Colossalis Bold**
- COPPERPLATE 33BC
- Dom Casual
- Gill Sans Condensed
- **Gill Sans Ultra Bold**
- Goudy Text Lombardic Capitals
- **Berthold Imago Bold**
- IRONWOOD
- Joanna
- *Joanna*
- Letter Gothic
- LITHOS
- MESQUITE
- Minion Ornament
- *Nuptial Script*
- *Pepita*
- Prestige Elite
- **Rockwell Bold**
- Runic Condensed
- **STENCIL**
- Willow
- Wood Type Ornaments

+ ATM

A 6179 PC
A 6179 Mac

A 459
Adobe Plus Pack

Adobe

- ITC Avant Garde
- *ITC Avant Garde*
- **ITC Avant Garde**
- ***ITC Avant Garde***
- ITC Bookman
- *ITC Bookman*
- **ITC Bookman**
- ***ITC Bookman***
- Helvetica Narrow
- *Helvetica Narrow*
- **Helvetica Narrow**
- ***Helvetica Narrow***
- New Century Schoolb.
- *New Century Schoolb.*
- **New Century Schoolb.**
- ***New Century Schoolb.***
- Palatino
- *Palatino*
- **Palatino**

* or PostScript output device

A 459 PC
A 459 Mac

© FSI 1993

Special Packs 2

Font Packs

Palatino
ITC Zapf Chancery
✆✇❼☍✄☞✳ ITC Zapf Dingbats

A 6927
Adobe Wild Type

CRITTER
CUTOUT
Giddyup
🐾🌿🦌🎣 Giddyup Thangs
MYTHOS
Quake
RAD
STUDZ
TOOLBOX
Birch
Myriad Headline
Myriad Sketch
Myriad Tilt
Utopia Headline

+ ATM

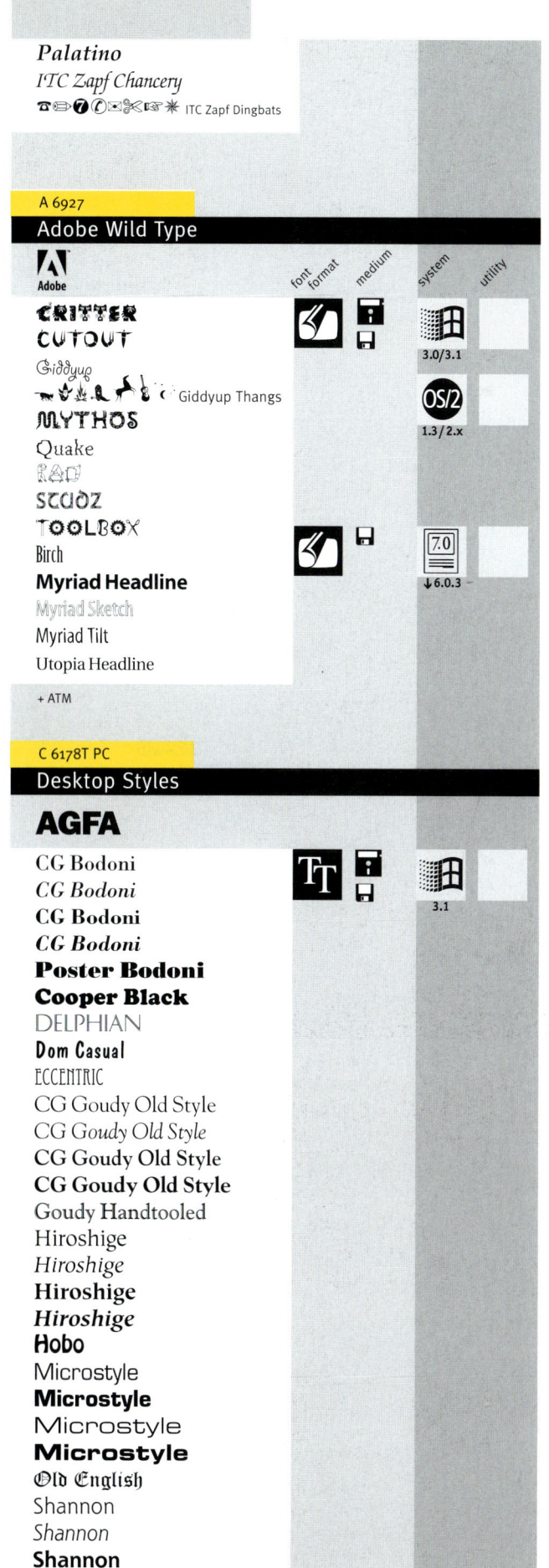

A 6927 PC
A 6927 Mac

C 6178T PC
Desktop Styles

AGFA

CG Bodoni
CG Bodoni
CG Bodoni
CG Bodoni
Poster Bodoni
Cooper Black
DELPHIAN
Dom Casual
ECCENTRIC
CG Goudy Old Style
CG Goudy Old Style
CG Goudy Old Style
CG Goudy Old Style
Goudy Handtooled
Hiroshige
Hiroshige
Hiroshige
Hiroshige
Hobo
Microstyle
Microstyle
Microstyle
Microstyle
Old English
Shannon
Shannon
Shannon
Shannon

© FSI 1993

Font Packs

Signet Roundhand
CG Times
CG Times
CG Times
CG Times
Typo Roman
uncial
Univers
Univers
Univers
Univers

C 6650T PC
Discovery TrueType Pack

AGFA

Bernhard Modern
Bernhard Fashion
Cooper Black
Artistik,
Broadway
Revue Shadow,
Dom Casual
Signet Roundhand,
ECCENTRIC
CG Poster Bodoni
Old English
Goudy Handtooled
Carmine Tango,
DELPHIAN
Nadianne Book, **Medium**
Nadianne Bold
Wile Roman, *Italic,* **Bold,**
Wile Bold Italic
Garth Graphic, *Italic,*
Bold, ***Bold Italic***
Garth Graphic Condensed
Garth Graphic Condensed
Shannon Book, *Oblique,*
Bold, Extra Bold
Border and Ornaments 1·4·5

Communications 1·2·3·6

Games and Sports 1·3·4

Holiday
Industry and Engineering 1·2

Transportation 1·2

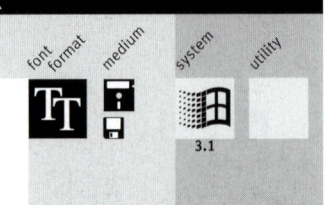

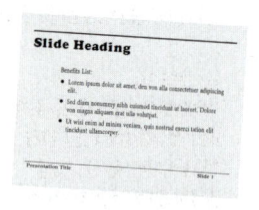

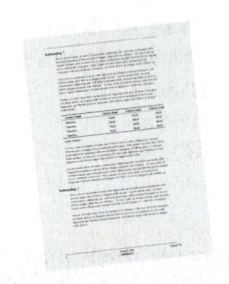

© FSI 1993
Special Packs 4

Font Packs

BT 6152
Font Pack 1 for Microsoft Windows

Bitstream

Geometric 706
Geometric 706
Geometric 706
Geometric 706
Humanist 521
Humanist 521
Humanist 777
Humanist 777
Humanist 777
Humanist 777
Imperial
Imperial
Imperial
Revival 565
Revival 565
Revival 565
Revival 565
Square Slabserif
Square Slabserif
Square Slabserif
Bitstream Oz Handicraft
Clarendon
English 157
Fraktur
Freehand 575
Freehand 591
Humanist 970
Humanist 970
HUXLEY VERTICAL
Impress
Incised 901
Incised 901
INFORMAL 011
INFORMAL 011
Nuptial
Poster Bodoni
Poster Bodoni
Staccato 555
UMBRA
Vineta

BT 6152T PC
BT 6152 PC

BT 6249
Font Pack 2 for Microsoft Windows

Bitstream

Geometric 415, *Italic*, **Bold**, ***Bold Italic***
Square 721
Zapf Elliptical 711, *Italic*, **Bold**, ***Bold Italic***
American Text
BT Cooper
Broadway
Brush 738
DAVIDA BOLD
Embassy

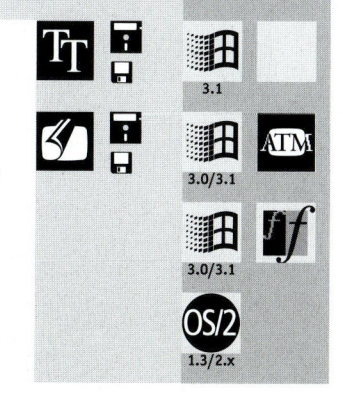

BT 6249T PC
BT 6249 PC

© FSI 1993
Special Packs 5

Font Packs

Exotic 350 Demi Bold
Handel Gothic
Hobo
VAG Rounded
Zurich Condensed

BT 6475T PC
The Flintstone Font Pack

Bitstream

FLINTSTONE
BEDROCK
Impress
BT Cooper
Swiss 721 light

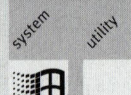

BT 6476
The Star Trek Font Pack

Bitstream

STARFLEET
ᴀᴇᴛʀᴏᴋᴀᴀᴛᴀ Star Trek Pi
Star Trek
Star Trek
Venetian
Square Condensed

BT 6476T PC
BT 6476 Mac

BT 6805
Star Trek the Next Generation Font Pack

Bitstream

STAR TREK NEXT
STAR TREK GEN
Crillee Italic
⚙️⚜️🛸 Symbols
Swiss 911 Ultra Compressed
Transitional 521

BT 6805T PC
BT 6805 Mac

BT 6806T PC
Looney Tunes Font Pack

Bitstream

LOONEY TUNES
LOONEY TUNES TILT
Incised 901 Bold
STENCIL
Freehand 471
Aachen

© FSI 1993

Special Packs 6

Font Packs

BT 6474T PC
Winter Holiday Font Pack

Bitstream

Holiday Pi
Cloister Black
Shelley Allegro
Freeform
Snowcap

FF 6306
FF Fun

Font*Shop*

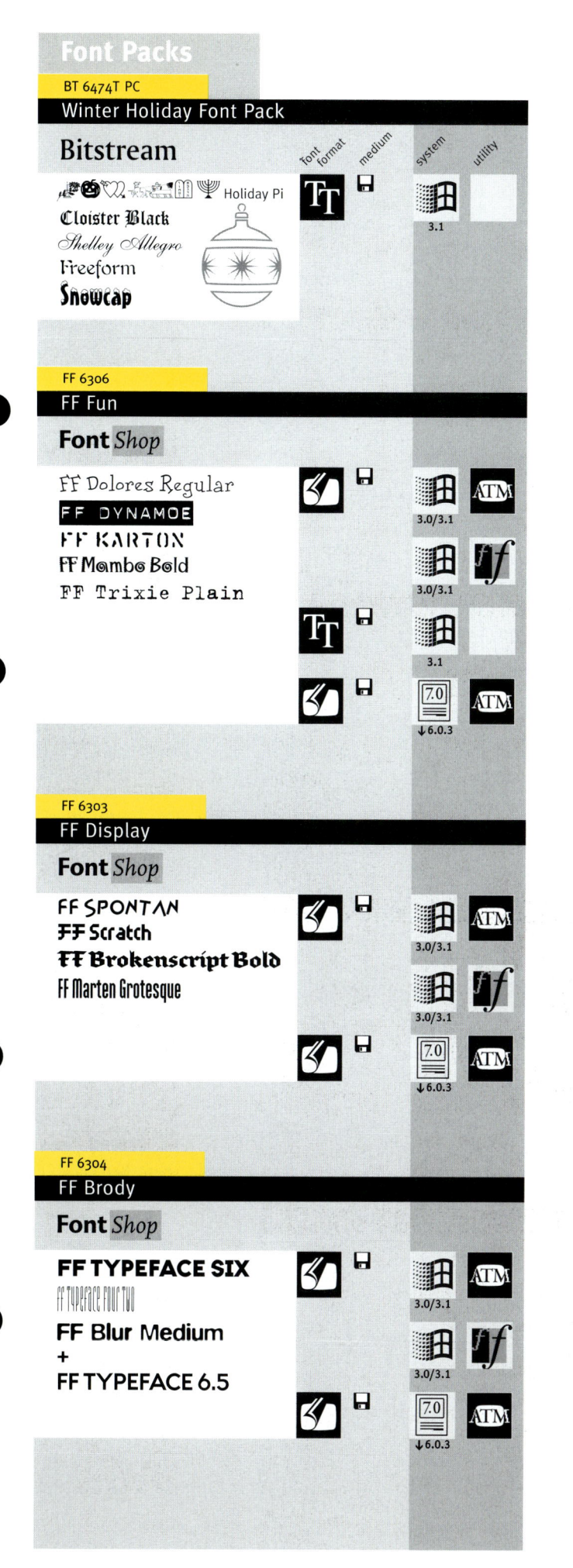

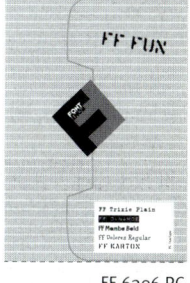

FF Dolores Regular
FF DYNAMOE
FF KARTON
FF Mambo Bold
FF Trixie Plain

FF 6306 PC
FF 6306T PC
FF 6306 Mac

FF 6303
FF Display

Font*Shop*

FF SPONTAN
FF Scratch
FF Brokenscript Bold
FF Marten Grotesque

FF 6303 PC
FF 6303 Mac

FF 6304
FF Brody

Font*Shop*

FF TYPEFACE SIX
FF TYPEFACE FOUR TWO
FF Blur Medium
+
FF TYPEFACE 6.5

FF 6304 PC
FF 6304 Mac

© FSI 1993

Font Packs

FF 6302
FF Text

Font Shop

FF Advert
FF Advert
FF Scala
FF Scala

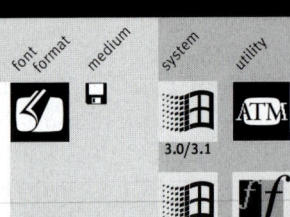

FF 6302 PC
FF 6302 Mac

M 6677
100 Great TrueType Faces

Monotype

Abadi Condensed Light,
Roman, **Bold**, **Extra Bold**
Albertus
Arial Condensed Light,
Condensed, **Condensed Bold**
Arial Light, *Italic*,
Black, Black Italic
Baskerville
Baskerville
Bell, **Bold**, *Italic*
Bembo, *Italic*, Semi Bold,
Semi Bold Italic, **Bold**,
Bold Italic
Centaur, *Italic*, **Bold**,
Bold Italic
Colonna
Ellington, *Italic*, **Bold**,
Bold Italic
ENGRAVERS
Engravers Old English
Footlight Light, *Light Italic*,
Bold, *Bold Italic*
Garamond, **Bold**, *Italic*
Gill Sans Light, *Light Italic*,
Regular, *Italic*, **Bold**,
***Bold Italic*, Extra Bold,
Ultra Bold**
Gill Sans Condensed, **Condensed Bold, Extra Condensed Bold**
Goudy Old Style, *Italic*
Goudy Catalogue, **Bold**
Joanna
Joanna
Kino
Lydian
Lydian Cursive
Matura Script Capitalis
News Gothic, *Italic*, **Bold**,
Condensed, **Condensed Bold**
Nimrod, **Bold**,
Italic, ***Bold Italic***

M 6677T PC
M 6677T Mac

© FSI 1993
Special Packs 8

Font Packs

Onyx
PERPETUA TITLING
PERPETUA TITLING
Photina, *Italic*, **Bold**, ***Bold Italic***
Placard Condensed
Plantin Light, *Light Italic*, Regular, *Italic*, Semi Bold, *Semi Bold Italic*, **Bold**, ***Bold Italic***
Plantin Condensed Bold
Rockwell Light, *Light Italic*, Regular, *Italic*, **Bold**, ***Bold Italic***
Rockwell Condensed
Swing Bold
20thCentury Condensed Bold
123ABC²/₇ffi, *123²/₇ffi*, **13²/₇ffi**, ***123ffifl*** Plantin Expert

M 6678
Font Option Pack 1

Monotype

Braggadocio
Centaur
Centaur
Clarendon
Ellington
Ellington
Ellington
News Gothic
News Gothic
Times Roman

M 6678T PC
M 6678T Mac

M 6679
Font Option Pack 2

Monotype

Biffo Script
Bodoni
Bodoni
Bodoni
CASTELLAR
Placard
Rockwell
Script
20th Century
20th Century Condensed

M 6679T PC
M 6679T Mac

Font Packs

M 6680
Font Option Pack 3
Monotype

- **Clearface Gothic**
- Goudy Old Style
- Goudy
- *Monoline Script*
- *New Berolina*
- Old Style Outline
- PERPETUA TITLING
- Placard Condensed
- **Rockwell**
- Rockwell

M 6680T PC
M 6680T Mac

M 6681
Font Option Pack 4
Monotype

- **Arial Extra Bold**
- ***Arial Extra Bold Italic***
- **Arial Condensed**
- Bembo
- *Blado*
- Nimrod
- **Nimrod**
- Onyx
- *Pepita*
- **Plantin**

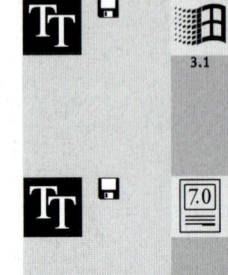

M 6681T PC
M 6681T Mac

M 6682
Font Option Pack 5
Monotype

- Garamond
- *Garamond*
- Gill Sans
- *Gill Sans*
- **Gill Sans**
- Gill Sans
- Klang
- *Mercurius Script*
- Old English Text
- *Palace Script*

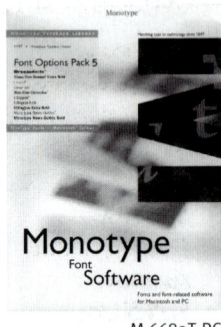

M 6682T PC
M 6682T Mac

© FSI 1993
Special Packs 10

Font Packs

M 6683
Font Option Pack 6

Monotype

ENGRAVERS
ENGRAVERS
Engravers Old English
FELIX
Figaro
Forte
Gill Sans
Gill Sans
Gill Sans
Goudy Extra

M 6683T PC
M 6683T Mac

SX 6689T PC
Office Collection

/// s.a.x. software

Courier
Courier
Courier
Letter Gothic
Letter Gothic
Letter Gothic
Prestige Elite
Prestige Elite
Prestige Elite
DIN/ISO 3098
Tile

SX 6690T PC
TrueType Deco

/// s.a.x. software

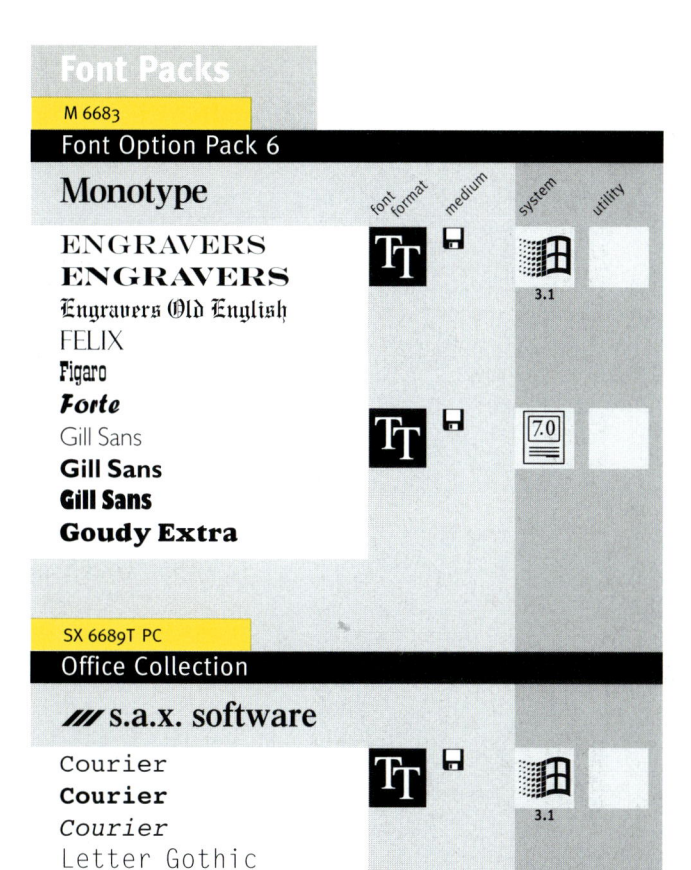

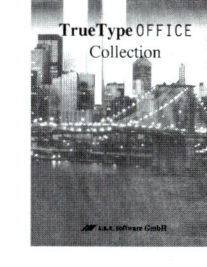

ALGERIAN
Broadway
Broadway Engraved
Brush
Commercial Script
DAVIDA
Fette Fraktur
Kaufmann
STENCIL
Arnold Böcklin
Stentor
Stymie
Vivaldi
Binner
Bodoni Ultra
Sans Kyrillisch (3 Schnitte)
Sans Greek

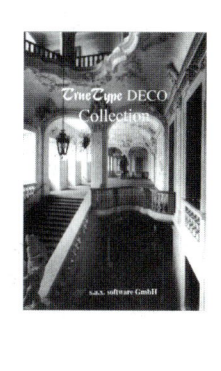

© FSI 1993

Special Packs 11

Type Sets

A 1537
Adobe Type Set Letters, Memos & Faxes

ITC Berkeley Oldstyle
ITC Berkeley Oldstyle
ITC Berkeley Oldstyle
ITC Berkeley Oldstyle
Glypha 45
Glypha 45
Glypha 65
Glypha 65
Lucida Sans
Lucida Sans

+ ATM

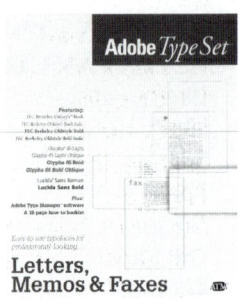

A 1537 PC
A 1537 Mac

A 1538
Adobe Type Set Overheads & Slides

Formata
Formata
Formata
Formata
ITC Stone Serif
ITC Stone Serif
ITC Stone Serif
Tekton
☎︎✉︎➆✆︎✂︎✄︎✈︎ ITC Zapf Dingbats

+ ATM

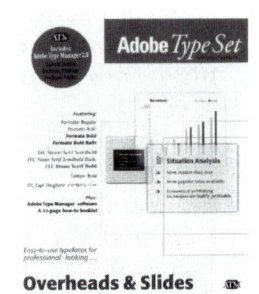

A 1538 PC
A 1538 Mac

A 1539
Adobe Type Set Invitations & Awards

Arcadia
CHARLEMAGNE
Cochin
Cochin
COPPERPLATE 33BC
𝔉𝔢𝔱𝔱𝔢 𝔉𝔯𝔞𝔨𝔱𝔲𝔯
Snell Roundhand
🍎◉⚜︎✝︎⚓︎ Carta

+ ATM

A 1539 PC
A 1539 Mac

© FSI 1993

Special Packs 12

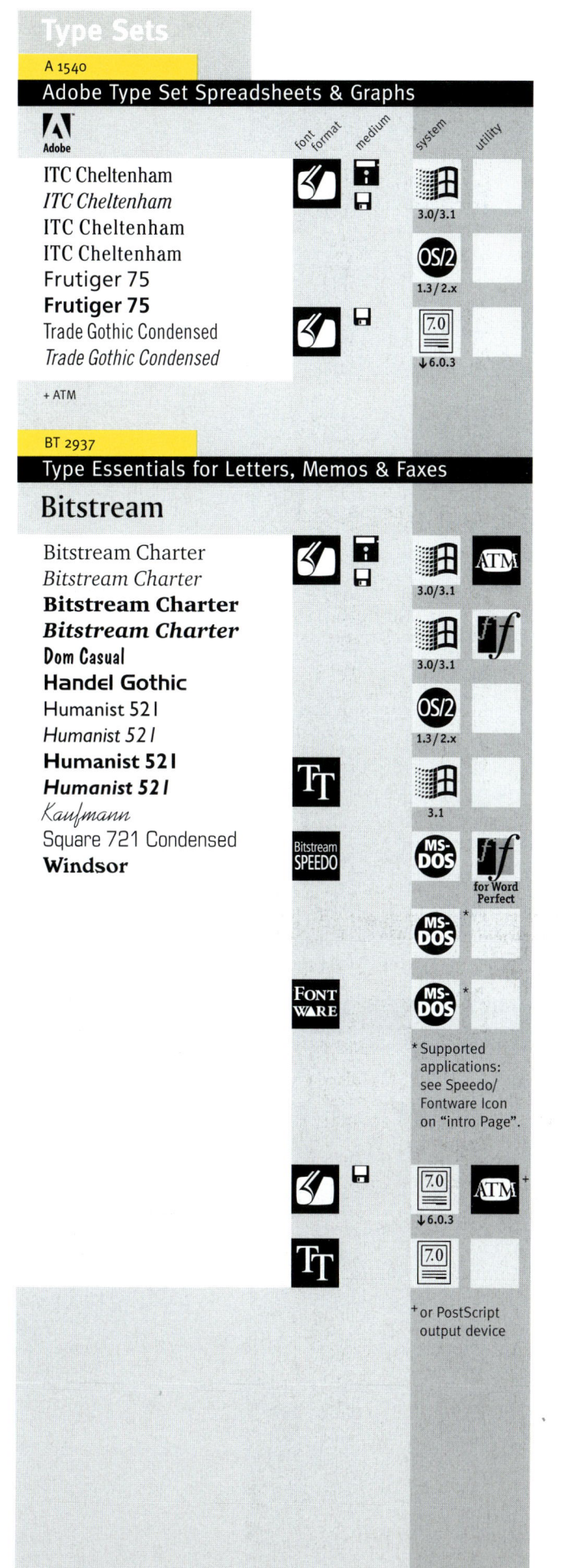

Type Sets

A 1540
Adobe Type Set Spreadsheets & Graphs

Adobe

ITC Cheltenham
ITC Cheltenham
ITC Cheltenham
ITC Cheltenham
Frutiger 75
Frutiger 75
Trade Gothic Condensed
Trade Gothic Condensed

+ ATM

A 1540 PC
A 1540 Mac

BT 2937
Type Essentials for Letters, Memos & Faxes

Bitstream

Bitstream Charter
Bitstream Charter
Bitstream Charter
Bitstream Charter
Dom Casual
Handel Gothic
Humanist 521
Humanist 521
Humanist 521
Humanist 521
Kaufmann
Square 721 Condensed
Windsor

* Supported applications: see Speedo/Fontware Icon on "intro Page".

\+ or PostScript output device

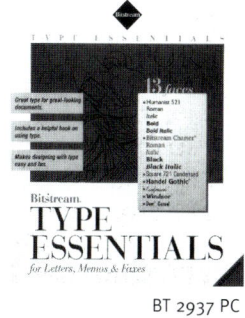

BT 2937 PC
BT 2937 Mac

© FSI 1993

Special Packs 13

Type Sets

BT 2938
Type Essentials for Spreadsheets, Graphs & Presentations

Bitstream

- Exotic 350
- Pica 10 Pitch
- Raleigh
- **Raleigh**
- **Seagull**
- Swiss 721 Condensed
- *Swiss 721 Condensed*
- **Swiss 721 Condensed**
- ***Swiss 721 Condensed***
- Zapf Elliptical
- *Zapf Elliptical*
- **Zapf Elliptical**
- ***Zapf Elliptical***

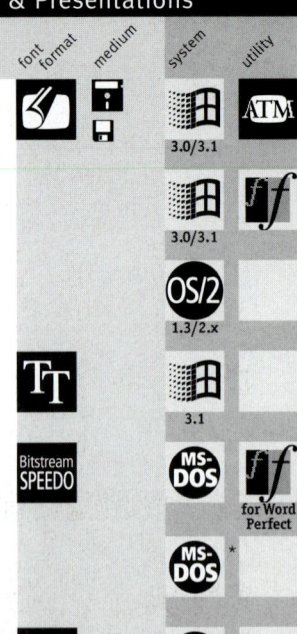

BT 2938 PC
BT 2938 Mac

* Supported applications: see Speedo/Fontware Icon on "intro Page".

⁺ or PostScript output device

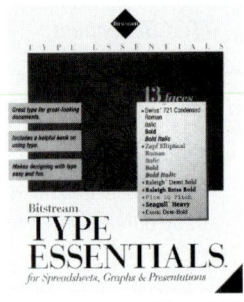

BT 2939
Type Essentials for Newsletters, Brochures & Announcements

Bitstream

- Incised 901
- **Incised 901**
- *Incised 901*
- ***Incised 901***
- Goudy Old Style
- *Goudy Old Style*
- **Goudy Old Style**
- ***Goudy Old Style***
- **Schadow Black Condensed**
- **Broadway**
- *Ribbon 131 Bold*
- American Text
- P. T. Barnumum

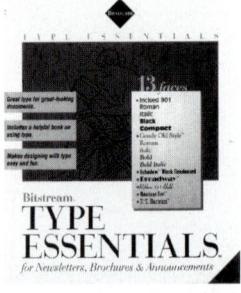

BT 2939 PC
BT 2939 Mac

© FSI 1993

Special Packs 14

Type Sets

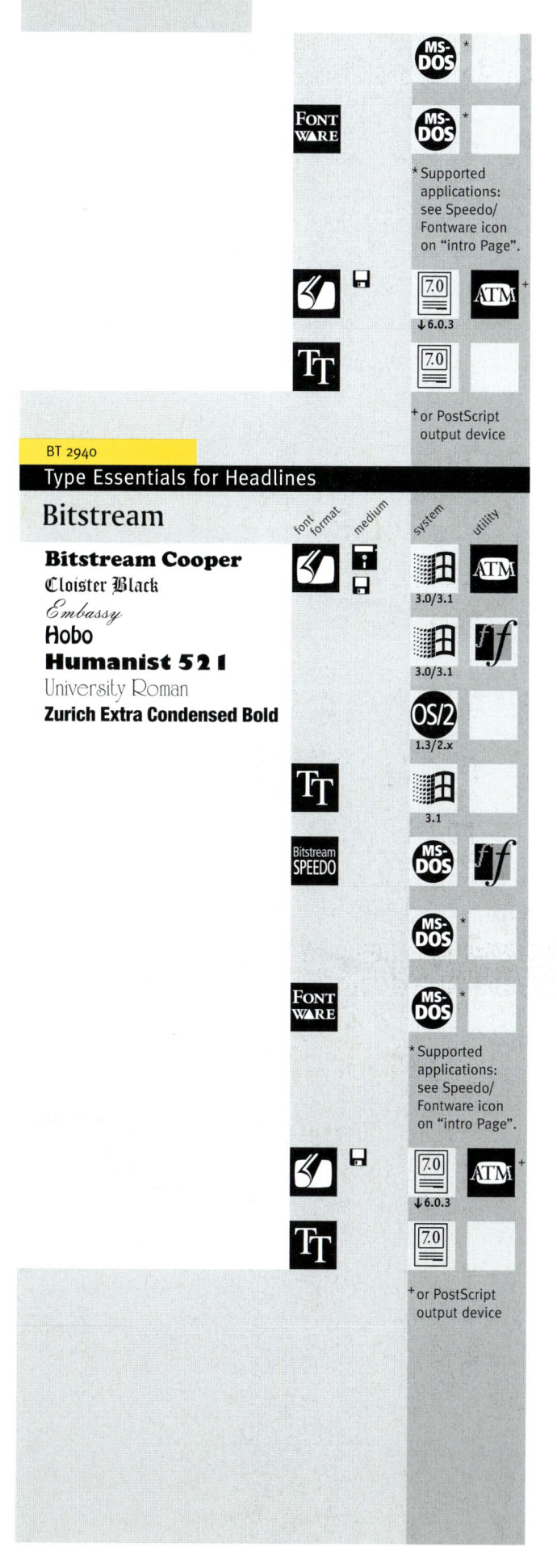

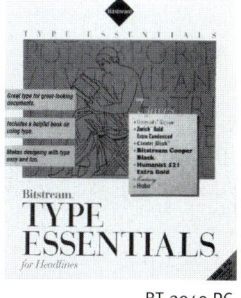

*Supported applications: see Speedo/Fontware icon on "intro Page".

+ or PostScript output device

BT 2940
Type Essentials for Headlines

Bitstream

Bitstream Cooper
Cloister Black
Embassy
Hobo
Humanist 521
University Roman
Zurich Extra Condensed Bold

BT 2940 PC
BT 2940 Mac

*Supported applications: see Speedo/Fontware icon on "intro Page".

+ or PostScript output device

Type Sets

M 2529
Monotype Desktop Solution
Designing Forms and Catalogues

Monotype

font / format / medium	system	utility

Amasis
Amasis
Amasis
Amasis
Arial
Arial
Arial
Arial
Arial Condensed
Arial Condensed
Arial Condensed
Arial Condensed

M 2529T PC
M 2529 PC
M 2529T Mac
M 2529 Mac

M 2530
Monotype Desktop Solution
Designing Newsletters and Booklets

Monotype

Abadi Condensed
Abadi Condensed
Abadi Condensed
Abadi Condensed
Plantin
PLANTIN EXPERT: ¼fflRp
Plantin
PLANTIN EXPERT: ¼fflRp
Plantin
PLANTIN EXPERT: ¼fflRp
Plantin
PLANTIN EXPERT: ¼fflRp

M 2530T PC
M 2530 PC
M 2530T Mac
M 2530 Mac

© FSI 1993

Special Packs 16

Font Packs

M 2531

Monotype Desktop Solution
Designing Reports and Presentations

Monotype

Photina
Photina
Photina
Photina
News Gothic
News Gothic
News Gothic
News Gothic
News Gothic

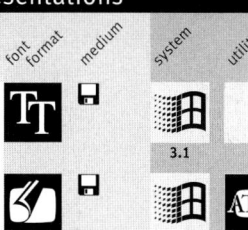

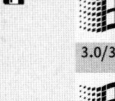

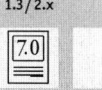

M 2531T PC
M 2531 PC
M 2531T Mac
M 2531 Mac

© FSI 1993

Special Packs 17

Font Packs

PG 6620
ParaType TypeSet

ParaType

cyr / cyr-gr

Inform
AdverGothic
MonoCondensed
Futuris
Bodoni
Didona
Standard Poster
Xenia
Courier
Pragmatica
Petersburg
Newton
Xenia Western

+ keyboard utility ParaWin/ParaMac

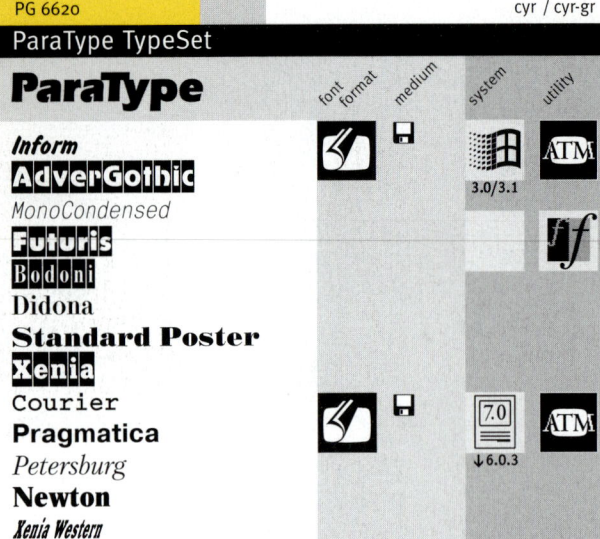

PG 6620 PC
PG 6620 Mac

PG 6820
Cyrillic TrueType Set 1

ParaType

cyr / cyr-gr

Newton Regular
Newton Italic
Newton Bold
Newton Bold Italic
Courier Regular
Courier Bold
Betina Script
Betina Bold
Zikharev Regular

+ keyboard utility ParaWin/ParaMac

PG 6820T PC
PG 6820T Mac

PG 6821
Cyrillic TrueType Set 2

ParaType

cyr / cyr-gr

Pragmatica Regular
Pragmatica Italic
Pragmatica Bold
Pragmatica Bold Italic
Astron Regular
Corrida Regular
Decor Regular
Inform Regular
Inform Bold
Parsek Regular

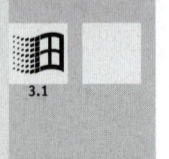

+ keyboard utility ParaWin/ParaMac

PG 6821T PC
PG 6821T Mac

© FSI 1993

Special Packs 18

non latin

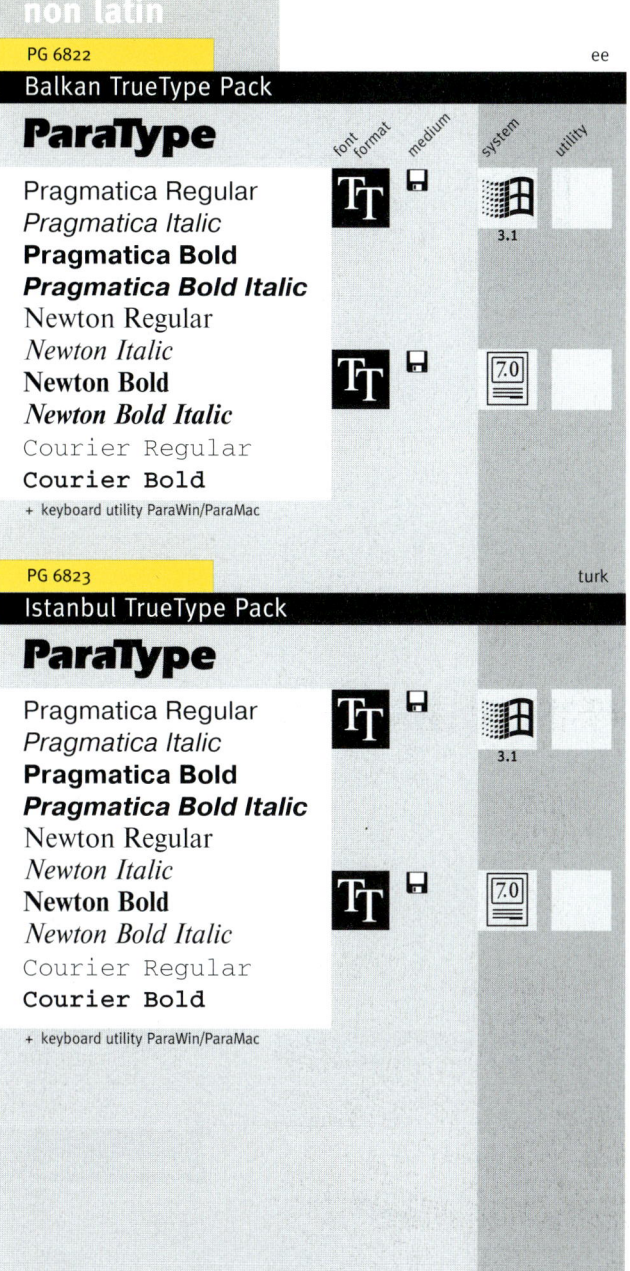

PG 6822   ee
Balkan TrueType Pack

ParaType

font format   medium   system   utility

Pragmatica Regular
Pragmatica Italic
Pragmatica Bold
Pragmatica Bold Italic
Newton Regular
Newton Italic
Newton Bold
Newton Bold Italic
Courier Regular
Courier Bold

+ keyboard utility ParaWin/ParaMac

TT 💾 🪟 3.1

TT 💾 📄 7.0

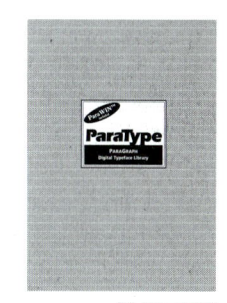

PG 6822T PC
PG 6822T Mac

PG 6823   turk
Istanbul TrueType Pack

ParaType

Pragmatica Regular
Pragmatica Italic
Pragmatica Bold
Pragmatica Bold Italic
Newton Regular
Newton Italic
Newton Bold
Newton Bold Italic
Courier Regular
Courier Bold

+ keyboard utility ParaWin/ParaMac

TT 💾 🪟 3.1

TT 💾 📄 7.0

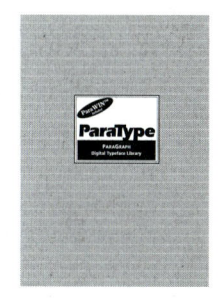

PG 6823T PC
PG 6823T Mac

© FSI 1993

Special Packs 19

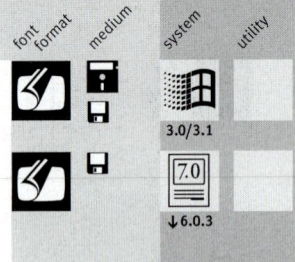

Font Utilities

A 347/642
Adobe Type Manager (ATM)

	font format	medium	system	utility
Helvetica / *Helvetica* / **Helvetica** / ***Helvetica***	🖋	💾	🪟 3.0/3.1	
Times / *Times* / **Times** / ***Times***	🖋	💾	7.0 ↓6.0.3	
Courier / *Courier* / **Courier** / ***Courier***				
Σψμβολ Symbol				

A 347 Mac
A 642 PC

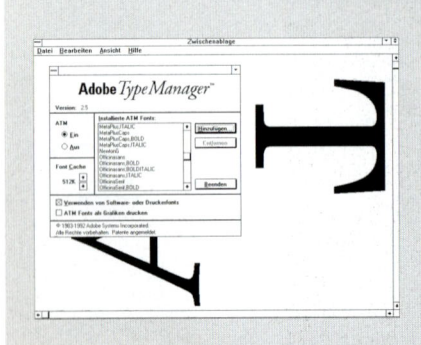

A 6256 PC
Adobe Type Manager (ATM) for WordPerfect

	font format	medium	system	utility
Helvetica / *Helvetica* / **Helvetica** / ***Helvetica***	🖋	💾	🪟 3.0/3.1	Word Perfect 5.1
Times / *Times* / **Times** / ***Times***			MS-DOS	Word Perfect 5.0/5.1
Courier (4 Schnitte)			MS-DOS	Letter Perfect 1.0
ΑΒαβΣψμ ℘ολ Symbol			MS-DOS	Word Perfect Works
Adobe Garamond / *Adobe Garamond*				
Bellevue			MS-DOS	Plan Perfect 5.0/5.1
Bodoni Poster				
Franklin Gothic Condensed				
LITHOS BOLD				
Rockwell Bold				

© FSI 1993

Special Packs 20

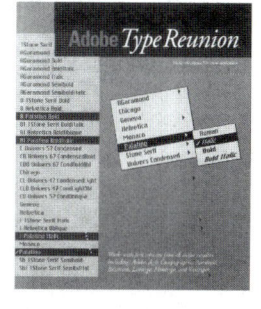

Font Utilities

A 6613 Mac
Adobe Super ATM

ITC Symbol
Bellevue
Madrone
COTTONWOOD
❄︎✁☎✈︎✉︎★✍︎ ITC Zapf Dingbats
Serif MULTIPLE **MASTER**
Sans **MULTIPLE MASTER**

↓ 6.0.2

A 461 Mac
Adobe Type Reunion

↓ 6.0.1

© FSI 1993

Special Packs 21

Font Utilities

A 466
Adobe TypeAlign

medium / system / utility

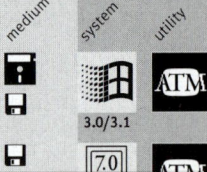

3.0/3.1
↓6.0.2

A 466 PC
A 466 Mac

BT 2516 PC
FaceLift

Bitstream

Swiss 721
Swiss 721
Swiss 721
Swiss 721
Dutch 801
Dutch 801
Dutch 801
Dutch 801
Park Avenue
Bitstream Cooper
Brush Script

font format

Bitstream SPEEDO

3.0/3.1

3.0/3.1

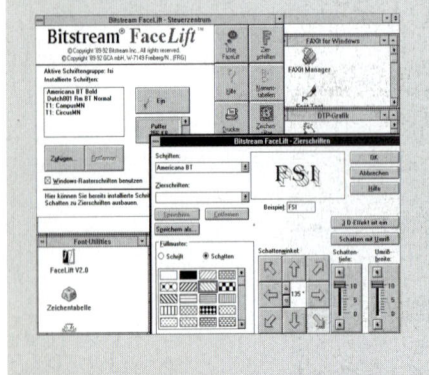

BT 2554 PC
FaceLift 2.0 for WordPerfect

Bitstream

Swiss, *Italic,* **Bold,**
Bold Italic
Dutch, *Italic,* **Bold,**
Bold Italic
Bodoni, *Italic,* **Bold,**
Bold Italic
Bitstream Oz Handicraft
Revue
Swiss 721 Bold Condensed
Swiss 721 Black Condensed
Park Avenue

Bitstream SPEEDO

MS-DOS — Word Perfect 5.0/5.1
MS-DOS — Letter Perfect 1.0
MS-DOS — Plan Perfect 5.0/5.1

© FSI 1993
Special Packs 22

Font Utilities

Bitstream Cooper
Brush Script
Formal Script 421
Monospace 821
☎☞✆✉✳ ITC Zapf Dingbats
Σψμβολ Symbol Proportional
Σψμβολ Symbol Monospaced

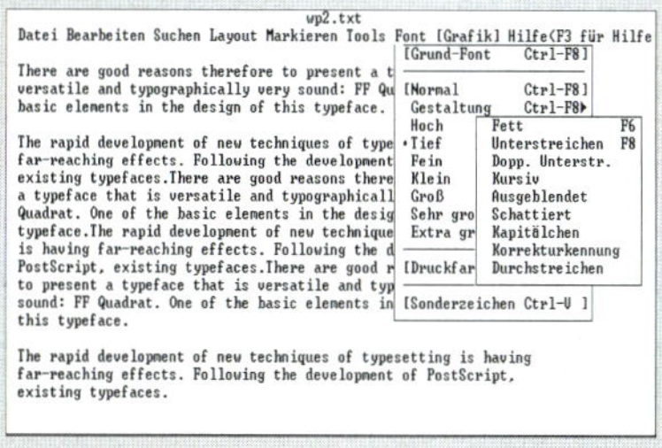

FG 6316 Mac
Suitcase

FIFTH GENERATION SYSTEMS, INC

medium   system   utility
7.0
↓6.0.3

SUITCASE

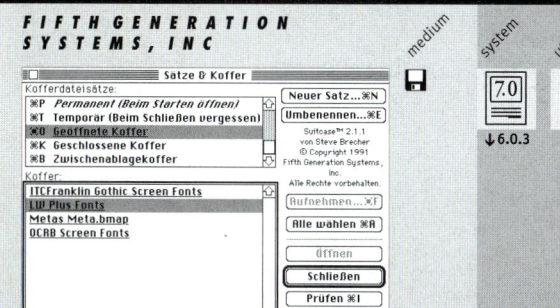

K 6575 Mac
CE Utilities

A collection of keyboard drivers for fonts following the Apple CE standard. It allowss access to ALL additional characters in CE fonts.

M 6577
Font Mixer

Monotype

Times New Roman (Superfont)

3.0/3.1

7.0
↓6.0.3

ATM

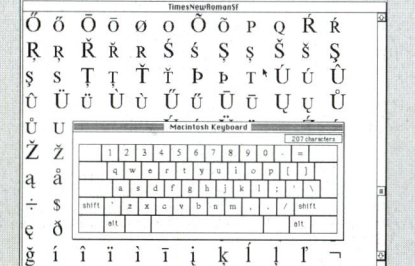

© FSI 1993

Font-Packs

PG 6616 PC
ParaWin

ParaType

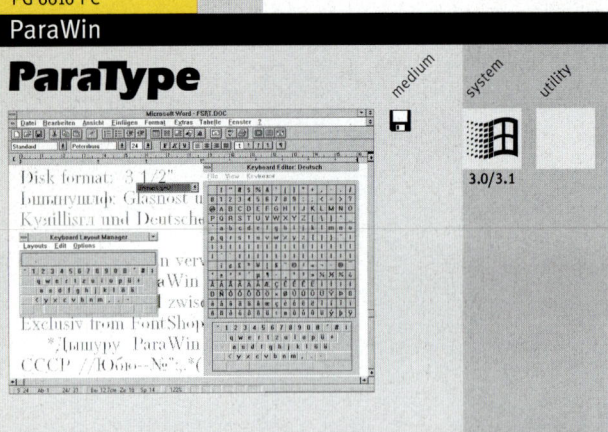

ParaWin is a menu driven keyboard driver for Windows 3.x. It is possible to produce custom layouts for any font. ParaWin enables six different keyboard layouts to be available simultaneously. In addition the user can change between the keyboard layouts while an application is running.

medium — system 3.0/3.1 — utility

PG 6929 PC
ParaWord

ParaType

ParaWord localisation kit contains a Russian spell checker with over 300 000 words, hyphenator, alphabetical sorting, text identification and import/export filters (MS Word for DOS/Mac).

system 3.0/3.1 — Win Word V 2.0

© FSI 1993
Special Packs 24

Abcd

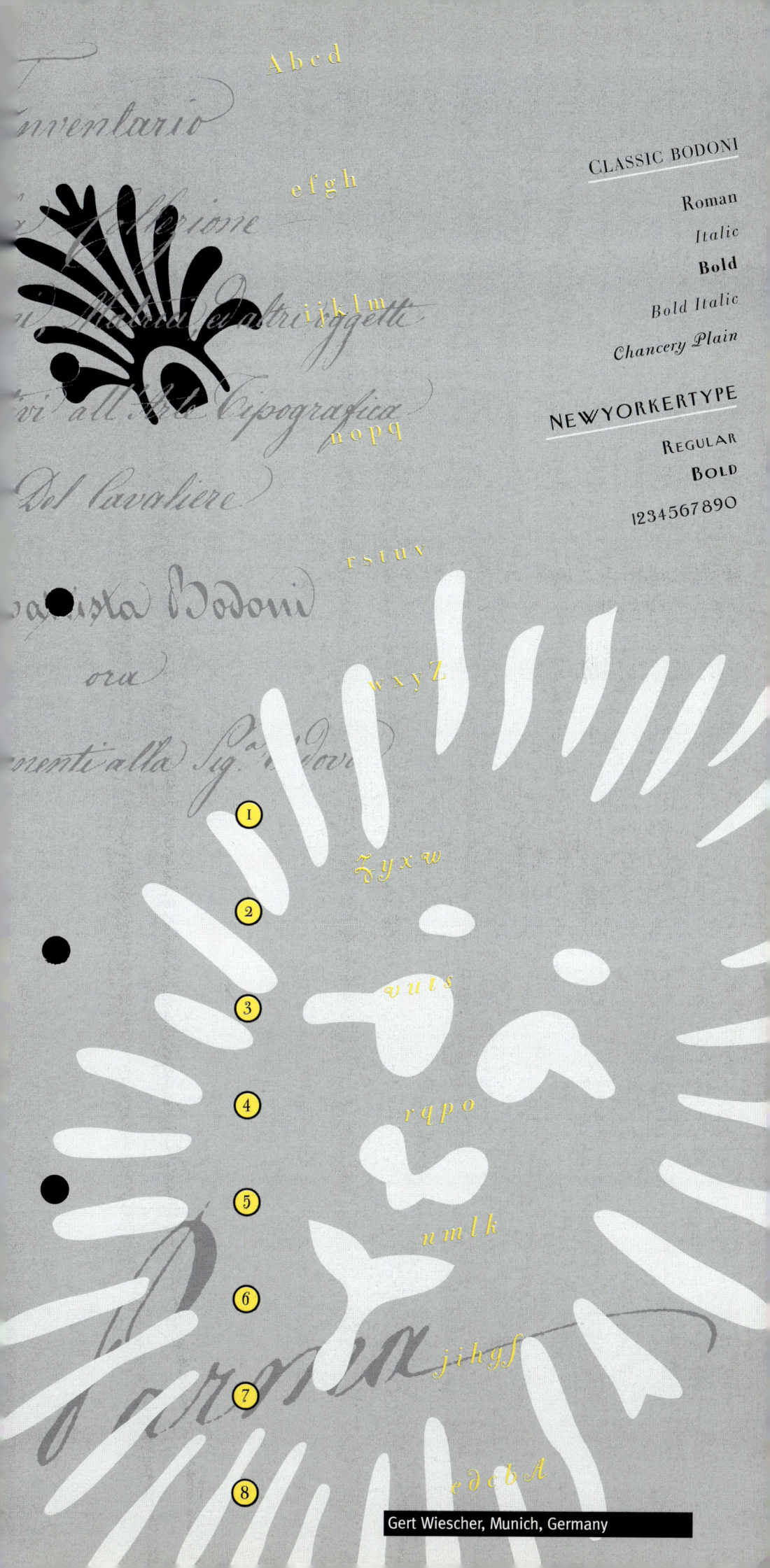

efgh

ijklm

nopq

CLASSIC BODONI

Roman
Italic
Bold
Bold Italic
Chancery Plain

NEWYORKERTYPE

Regular
Bold
1234567890

rstuv

wxyz

zyxw

vuts

rqpo

umlk

jihgf

edcbA

① ② ③ ④ ⑤ ⑥ ⑦ ⑧

Gert Wiescher, Munich, Germany

Trademarks

Adobe, Adobe Garamond, Adobe Type Manager, Carta, Charlemagne, Cottonwood, Ironwood, Juniper, Lithos, Mesquite, PostScript, Sonata, Trajan & Utopia are registered trademarks in the USA and other countries, & Adobe Font Folio, Adobe Type Align, Font Foundry, Adobe Type Reunion, Adobe Caslon, Adobe Expert Collection, Adobe Originals, Adobe Type Set, Birch, Blackoak, Madrone, Minion, Myriad, Poetica, Ponderosa, Poplar, Tekton, & Willow are trademarks of Adobe Systems, Inc.

Agfa, CG, Rotis & Garth Graphic are registered trademarks and Agfa Nadianne, Shannon & Agfa Wile are trademarks of Miles Inc.

A*I Barrel, A*I Box Gothic, A*I French XXX Condensed, A*I Oz Brush, A*I Painter, A*I Oz Poster, A*I Prospera and A*I Tuscan Egyptian are trademarks of Alphabets, Inc.

Amigo, Hiroshige, Marigold, Oxford, Pelican & Visigoth are trademarks of AlphaOmega Typography, Inc.

Apple & Macintosh are registered trademarks of Apple Computer, Inc.

Printbar is a trademark of Bear Rock Technologies, Inc.

Baxter, Childs, Eusebius, Goudy Claremont, Goudy Saks, Hermosa, Jenson-Eusebius, Kennerley, Recherché, Spiral, Beatty Victoriana & Wanted are trademarks of Richard Beatty Designs.

Berling is a trademark of Berlingska Stilgjuteri AB.

Berthold Akzidenz Grotesk, Block, Berthold Bodoni, Berthold City, Formata, Berthold Imago & Nofret are registered trademarks, and AG Book, AG Old Face, Barmeno, Berthold Baskerville Book, Bellevue, Boton, Boulevard, Christiana, Colossalis, Comenius, Concorde, Concorde Nova, Cosmos, Delta Jaeger, Englische Schreibschrift, Berthold Garamond, Normande, Palette, Poppl-Exquisit, Poppl-Pontifex, Poppl-Residenz, Post Antiqua, Post Mediaeval, Berthold Script & Berthold Walbaum Book are trademarks of H. Berthold AG.

Lucida is a registered trademark of Bigelow & Holmes, Inc.

Bitstream Amerigo, Bitstream Arrus, Bremen, Bitstream Carmina, Bitstream Charter, Bitstream Cooper, Bitstream Iowan Oldstyle, Bitstream Lucian, Mister Earl, Bitstream Oranda & Bitstream Oz Handicraft are trademarks or registered trademarks of Bitstream, Inc.

Mantinia is a trademark of Carter & Cone Type, Inc.

Admark, Bulldog, Column, Congress Sans, Eurocrat, Monkton, Poseidon & Veronan are trademarks or registered trademarks of ClubType Limited.

Abelard, Barbara, Electric Hand, Electric Marlborough, Electric Uncial, Flourish, Italian Electric, Leonardo, Lutahline, Maskerade, Petroglyph, Renaissance, Tagliente, Troubador, Santa Barbara & Serpents are trademarks of The Electric Typographer.

Postscript Error and BrainDamage are trademarks of The FontShop Catalog Production Team, used by permission of the FontShop Price List Production Team.

Arbitrary Sans, Citizen, Elektrix, Emigré, Emperor, Exocet, Journal, Keedy Sans, Lunatix, Matrix, Modular, Motion, Oakland, Oblong, Quartet, Remedy, Senator, Template Gothic, Totally Gothic, Totally Glyphic, Triplex, Universal & Variex are trademarks of Emigré Graphics, or are trademarks licensed for use by Emigré Graphics.

Aardvark, Belucian, Berlizio, Bodega, Bremen, Bureau Agency, Bureau Eagle, Bureau Empire, Bureau Grotesque, Bureau Roxy, City Ornaments, Clicker, Commerce, FBI Condensed Classics, Garage Gothic, Hoffmann, Ironmonger, Munich, Phaistos, Romeo, Scamp, Town Ornaments, Village Ornaments & Wessex are trademarks of The Font Bureau, Inc., or are trademarks licensed for use by The Font Bureau Inc.

Blippo & Handel Gothic are trademarks of Fotostar International Inc.

FF Advert, FF BeoSans, FF Beowolf, FF Berlinsans, FF Blur, FF Brokenscript, FF Carolus Magnus, FF Confidential, FF Cutout, FF Dig, FF Disturbance, FF Dog, FF Dolores, FF Dome, FF Double Digits, FF Double Dutch, FF DuBrush, FF DuChirico, FF DuDuchamp, FF DuGauguin, FF DuTurner, FF Erikrighthand, FF Flèches, FF Flightcase, FontZine, Fudoni, Fuse, FSI, FF Gothic, FF Hands, FF Hip, FF InstantTypes, FF Jacque, FF Johannes G, FF Justlefthand, FF Karton, FF Kath, FF Kipp, FF Kisman, FF Koberger, FF Mambo, FF Marten, FF Meta, FF Network, FF Newberlin, FF NewYorkerType, FF Pop, FF Quadraat, FF Rosetta, FF Scala, FF Schoensperger, FF Schulbuch, FF Schulschrift, FF Scratch, FF ScribeType, FF Spontan, FF Stamp Gothic, FF Tokyo, FF Trixie, FF Typeface Four, FF Typeface Seven, FF Typeface Six, FF Typeface Six-point-five, FF Tyson, FF Vortex, FF World & FF Wunderlich are trademarks of FontShop International.

LaserJet is a registered trademark of the Hewlett-Packard Company.

Accolade, Claridge, Congress, Raleigh, Seagull, Stratford and Worcester Round are trademarks of International Graphic Marketing, S.A.

ITC Anna, ITC BeesKnees, ITC Legacy, ITC Mendoza, ITC Mona Lisa Recut, ITC Mona Lisa Solid, ITC Officina, ITC Ozwald & ITC Syndor are trademarks & ITC American Typewriter, ITC Avant Garde Gothic, ITC Bauhaus, ITC Benguiat, ITC Benguiat Gothic, ITC Berkeley Oldstyle, ITC Bolt, ITC Bookman, ITC Busorama, ITC Caslon 224, ITC Century, ITC Cheltenham, ITC Clearface, ITC Cushing, ITC Élan, ITC Eras, ITC Esprit, ITC Fenice, ITC Flora, ITC Franklin Gothic, ITC Galliard, ITC Gamma, ITC Garamond, ITC Giovanni, ITC Golden Type, ITC Gorilla, ITC Goudy Sans, ITC Grizzly, ITC Grouch, ITC Isadora, ITC Isbell, ITC Jamille, ITC Kabel, ITC Korinna, ITC Leawood, ITC Lubalin Graph, ITC Machine, ITC Mixage, ITC Modern 216, ITC New Baskerville, ITC Newtext, ITC Novarese, ITC Pacella, ITC Panache, ITC Pioneer, ITC Quay Sans, ITC Quorum, ITC Ronda, ITC Serif Gothic, ITC Slimbach, ITC Souvenir, ITC Stone, ITC Symbol, ITC Tiepolo, ITC Tiffany, ITC Tom's Roman, ITC Usherwood, ITC Veljovic, ITC Weidemann, ITC Zapf Book, ITC Zapf Chancery, ITC Zapf Dingbats & ITC Zapf International are registered trademarks of International Typeface Corporation, Inc.

Advertiser's Gothic, Alternate Gothic, American Text, Americana, Arsis, Balloon, Bank Gothic, Baskerville Old Face, Bernhard Antique, Bernhard Fashion, Bernhard Modern, Bernhard Tango, Bookman, Broadway Engraved, Brody, Brush, Century Schoolbook, Cheltenham Old Style, Clearface Gothic, Cleland Border, Cloister, Commercial Script, Cooper Black, Della Robbia, Dom, Empire, Engraver's Old English, Franklin Gothic, Gallia, Goudy Handtooled, Gothic Outline, Huxley Vertical, Kaufmann, Latin, Liberty, Lydian, Miehle, Murray Hill, News Gothic, Old Towne No. 536, Onyx, Park Avenue, Phenix, Piranesi, P. T. Barnum, Romana, Skjald, Spartan, Stymie, Thompson Quillscript, Thunderbird, Tower, Typo Upright & Wedding Text are trademarks or registered trademarks of Kingsley/ATF Type Corporation.

Albertan, Bodoni No. 175, Bodoni No. 2175, Bodoni No. 26, Caslon Oldstyle No. 337, Caslon No. 637, Caslon No. 537, Deepdene, Figures Square, Flash, Fleurons, Folio One, Forum, Francis, Globe Gothic, Goudy, Goudy Oldstyle No. 394, Goudy Thirty No. 392, Goudy Village, Granjon Folio, Hadriano, Initials, Jenson, Kaatskill, Metropolitan, Pabst Oldstyle No. 45, Spire, Swing Bold, & Vine Leaves are trademarks or registered trademarks of Lanston Type Company Inc.

Aachen, Academy, Annlie, Aquinas, Aquitaine, Letraset Arta, Artiste, Balmoral, Becka, Belshaw, Belwe, Belwe Mono, Bergell, Bertram, Bible, Bickley, Bitmax, Blackmoor, Bottleneck, Bramley, Brighton, Bronx, Burlington, Cabaret, Camellia, Campaign, Cancelleresca, Candice, Carousel, Caxton, Challenge, Champers, Charlotte, Chesterfield, Chromium, Cikulus, Citation, Claude Sans, Conference, Compacta, Coptek, Cortez, Countdown, Crillee, Croissant, Data 70, Demian, Digitek, Diskus, Dolmen, Einhorn, Elefont, Elysium, Emphasis, Enviro, Epokha, Equinox, Fashion Compressed, Fashion Engraved, Fine Hand, Follies, Forest Shaded, Frankfurter, Freestyle, Galadriel, Glastonbury, Greyton, Hadfield, Harlow, Harvey, Hawthorn, Hazel, Heliotype, Highlight, Horatio, Horndon, Ignatius, Indy, Informal, Isis, Italia, Jazz, Julia Script, Kanban, Kapitellia, Klee, Knightsbridge, L.C.D., La Bamba, Lambada, Laser, Latino, Laura, Lazybones, Le Griffe, Lexikos, Limehouse, Lindsay, Line Out, Lotus, Magnus, Malibu, Mastercard, Mekanik, Nevison Casual, Octopuss, Odessa, Odin, One Stroke, Orlando, Paddington, Papyrus, Pendry, Piccadilly, Plaza, Pleasure, Pneuma, Prague, Premier, Princetown, Pritchard, Pump, Quadrus, Quixley, Rage, Ragtime, Rapier, Refracta, Regatta, Retro, Revue, Robotik, Romic, Ru'ach, Rubber Stamp, Rundfunk, Santa Fe, Savoye, Scriba, Scriptek, Shatter, Sinaloa, Skid Row, Slipstream, Spotlight, Springfield, Squire, Stentor, Stilla, Strobos, Superstar, Tango, Tannhäuser, Teknik, Tiger Rag, Tropica, Ulysses, University Roman, Van Dijk, Varga, Vermont, Vienna, Vivaldi, Wade Sans, Waterloo, Westwood, Willow & Young Baroque are trademarks, & Letraset is a registered trademark of Esselte Pendaflex Corporation in the USA, Letraset Canada Ltd. in Canada, and Esselte Letraset Ltd. elsewhere.

Trademarks

DeStijl, Florens, Hardwood, Kryptic, Manito, Silhouette, Spring, Spumoni, Tomboy and Wendy are trademarks of LetterPerfect, Inc.

Ad Sans, Aldus, Angro, Antique No. 3, Arcadia, Aurelia, Auriol, Aurora, Avenir, Basilia, Bison, PMN Caecilia, Caledonia, Carolina, Cascade, Clairvaux, Clarendon, Cochin, Codex, Corona, Demos, Linotype Didot, Digi Grotesk N, Digi Grotesk S, Diotima, Doric, Duc de Berry, Eckmann, Edison, Egyptienne F, Electra, Excelsior, Fairfield, Flyer, Frutiger, Garamond 3, Glypha, Granjon, Guardi, Hanseatic, Helvetica, Heraldus, Herculanum, Hogarth, Hollander, Industria, Insignia, Janson Text, Kabel, Kapitellia, Kuenstler Script, Linoletter, Linoscript, Linotext, Linotype Centennial, London Text, Marconi, Maximus, Medici, Melior, Memphis, Méridien, Metro, Minister, Linotype Modern, Monanti, Neuland, Neuzeit, Neuzeit Grotesk, New Caledonia, Nikis, Olympia, Olympian, Omnia, Ondine, Optima, Palatino, Peignot, Praxis, Present, Primer, Profil, Raleigh, Rotation, Sabon, Salut, San Marco, Schreibmaschineschrift, Shelley, Sierra, Snell Roundhand, Spartan, Stempel Garamond, Swift, Syntax, Texttype, Times, Trade Gothic, Trump Mediaeval, Unica, Univers, Vario, Vectora, Versailles, Wilhelm Klingspor Gothic & Wilke are trademarks or registered trademarks of Linotype-Hell AG and/or its subsidiary companies.

Bodoni Campanile, Coronet, Delphian, Mandate, Radiant, Tempo & Umbra are trademarks of Ludlow Industries (UK) Ltd.

Today Sans Serif, Vega, Vega TV, Vega VW and Zapf Renaissance are trademarks of Mannesmann Scangraphic GmbH.

Access, American Uncial, Anatol, Art Deco, Art World, Brio, Campus, Card Camio, Carplate, Chinon, Circus, Classic Script, Comic Script, Dubbeldik, Enroute, Fidelio, Fumo Dropshadow, Galba, GlowWorm, Hansson Stencil, Hotel, Jackson, Latina, Milton, Orator, Organda, Ortem, Polka, Rondo, Roslyn, Saphir, Sayer Interview, Sayer Script, Sayer Spiritual, Squash, Sully Jonquieres, Swaak Centennial, Tzigane, Watch & Zambesi are trademarks of Mecanorma or trademarks licensed for use by Mecanorma.

Abadi, Albertus, Arial, Monotype Baskerville, Bell, Bembo, Monotype Bodoni, Calisto, Cantoria, Centaur, Monotype Century, Monotype Century Schoolbook, Clarion, Ehrhardt, Ellington, Figaro, Footlight, Monotype Garamond, Gill Sans, Grotesque, Monotype Janson, Joanna, Klang, Nimrod, Pepita, Perpetua, Photina, Placard, Plantin, Poliphilus, Rockwell, Times New Roman, Van Dijck and Monotype Walbaum are registered trademarks of the Monotype Corporation plc. registered in the U.S. Patent and Trademark Office; Amasis, Apollo, Ashley Script, Bernard, Biffo, Binny Old Style, Blado, Monotype Bodoni Book, Braggadocio, Calvert, Castellar, Monotype Century Old Style, Monotype Clearface, Monotype Clearface Gothic, Colonna, Columbus, Coronet, Monotype Courier 12, Dante, Dorchester Script, Monotype Egyptian 72, Monotype Engravers Old English, Monotype Engravers, Falstaff, Felix, Festival, Footlight, Forte, Gloucester Old Style, Monotype Goudy Catalogue, Monotype Goudy Modern, Monotype Goudy Old Style, Monotype Goudy Text, Headline Bold, Horley Old Style, Imprint, Inflex Bold, Ionic, Monotype Italian Old Style, Kino, Matura, Mercurius Script, Monotype Modern, Monoline Script, Neographic, New Berolina, New Clarendon, Monotype News Gothic, News Plantin, Octavian, Old English, Monotype Old Style, Monotype Old Style Bold Outline, Onyx, Palace Script, Monotype Runic, Sabon, Monotype Scotch Roman, Monotype Script, Monotype Spartan, Spectrum, Swing Bold, Victoria Titling & Zeitgeist are trademarks of the Monotype Corporation plc.

Athenaeum, Egiziano, Estro, Eurostile, Fiorello, Fluidum, Neon, Orlando, Quirinus, Ritmo, Section, Stop & Torino are trademarks of Società Nebiolo S.A.

Allegro, Amalthea, Bauer Bodoni, Beton, Candida, Charme, Folio, Futura, Gillies Gothic, Impressum, Koloss, Lucian, Phyllis, Schneidler, Serifa, Slogan, Stempel Schneidler, Volta & Weiss are trademarks or registered trademarks of Fundicion Tipografica Neufville S.A.

Antique Olive, Banco, Choc, Mistral & Vendôme are registered trademarks of M. Olive.

Aster, New Aster & Simoncini Garamond are trademarks, & Life is a registered trademark of Officine Simoncini S.P.A.

Stratford is a trademark of V. Pacella.

PL is a trademark of Photo Lettering, Inc.

Pasquale is a trademark of Tony Stan.

Fry's Baskerville, Grotesque No. 9, Impact, Playbill & Windsor are trademarks or registered trademarks of Stephenson Blake (Holdings) Ltd.

Loyalist & Regency Gothic are trademarks of Stylus Fonts.

Amazone, Amsterdam Garamont & Libra are trademarks of Tetterode Nederland (Lettergieterij Amsterdam).

TF Akimbo, TF Ardent, TF Avian, TF Bryn Mawr, TF Forever, TF Guestcheck, TF Habitat, TF Hôtelmoderne, TF Puzzle, TF Raincheck, TF Simper and TF Solution are trademarks of TreacyFaces, Inc.

Cortada, Ebu Script, Frankie, Mayayo, Me Mima and Neeskens are trademarks of Type-ø-Tones.

Adroit & Souvenir Gothic are trademarks and Heldustry is a registered trademark of TypeSpectra, Inc.

Mirarae is a trademark of Carol Twombly.

Adminster, Caslon Graphique and Flange are trademarks of Typsettra Limited.

Berling is a trademark of Verbum AB.

Amelia, Baker Signet, Davida, Egyptian 505, Flyer, Friz Quadrata, Maximus, Orbit-B, Russell Square, Shotgun, Serpentine & Vineta are trademarks of Visual Graphics Corporation.

Motter Femina is a trademark of Vorarlberger GmbH.

Aurora, Impuls, Reporter & Schadow are trademarks or registered trademarks of Johannes Wagner.

Sassoon is a registered trademark of A. Williams & R. Sassoon.

WTC Our Bodoni is a trademark of World Typeface Corporation, Inc.

All other trademarks are the property of their respective owners.

Publisher	FontShop International
Typographic Editor	Ed Cleary
Design	Erik Spiekermann
Cover	Erik Spiekermann
Special Pages	Martin Wenzel, Just van Rossum
Icons	Petr van Blokland, Johannes Erler
Typefaces	FF Meta, FF Dingbats *et al*
Divider pages	David Berlow, Erik van Blokland, Alexander Branczyk, Lo Breier, Neville Brody, Ed Cleary, Factor Design, Tobias Frere-Jones, Val Fullard, Lucas de Groot, Marianne van Ham, Rian Hughes, Claudia Kipp, Max Kisman, Manfred Klein, Alessio Leonardi, Martin Majoor, Paul Neville, Yves Peters, Just van Rossum, Pierre di Sciullo, Fred Smeijers, Erik Spiekermann, Paul Sych, Jeremy Tankard, Gerard Unger, Peter Verheul, Gert Wiescher, Cornel Windlin, Martin Wunderlich
Text	Ed Cleary, Jürgen Siebert, Erik Spiekermann
Database	Ed Cleary
Organisation	Beth Russell
Administration & Proofreading	Ugla Marekowa, Beth Russell, Jürgen Siebert, Dirk Sievers, Joan Spiekermann, Erik Spiekermann, Karen van Warmerdam, Andreas Zießnitz
Systems operator	Andreas Pieper
Programming	Petr van Blokland, Peter Kriens, Andreas Pieper
Typesetting	Johannes Hoenlinger, Andreas Pieper, Amy Ramsey, Just van Rossum, Martin Wenzel, Ulf Wrede
Production	Uwe Otto, Andreas Pieper, Beth Russell
Film output	Andreas Pieper, Johannes Hoenlinger, CitySatz
Printing & Finishing	Main-Echo Kirsch GmbH & Co., Aschaffenburg
Special thanks to	Klaus Dünser, Rudy Geeraerts, Bart de Boever, Michael Gorman, Stuart Jensen, David Michealides, Petra Weitz

**… and this year's
FontBook Award
for Always Smiling Even Under the Most Chaotic Conditions
goes to Beth Russell!**

15. 1. 1985

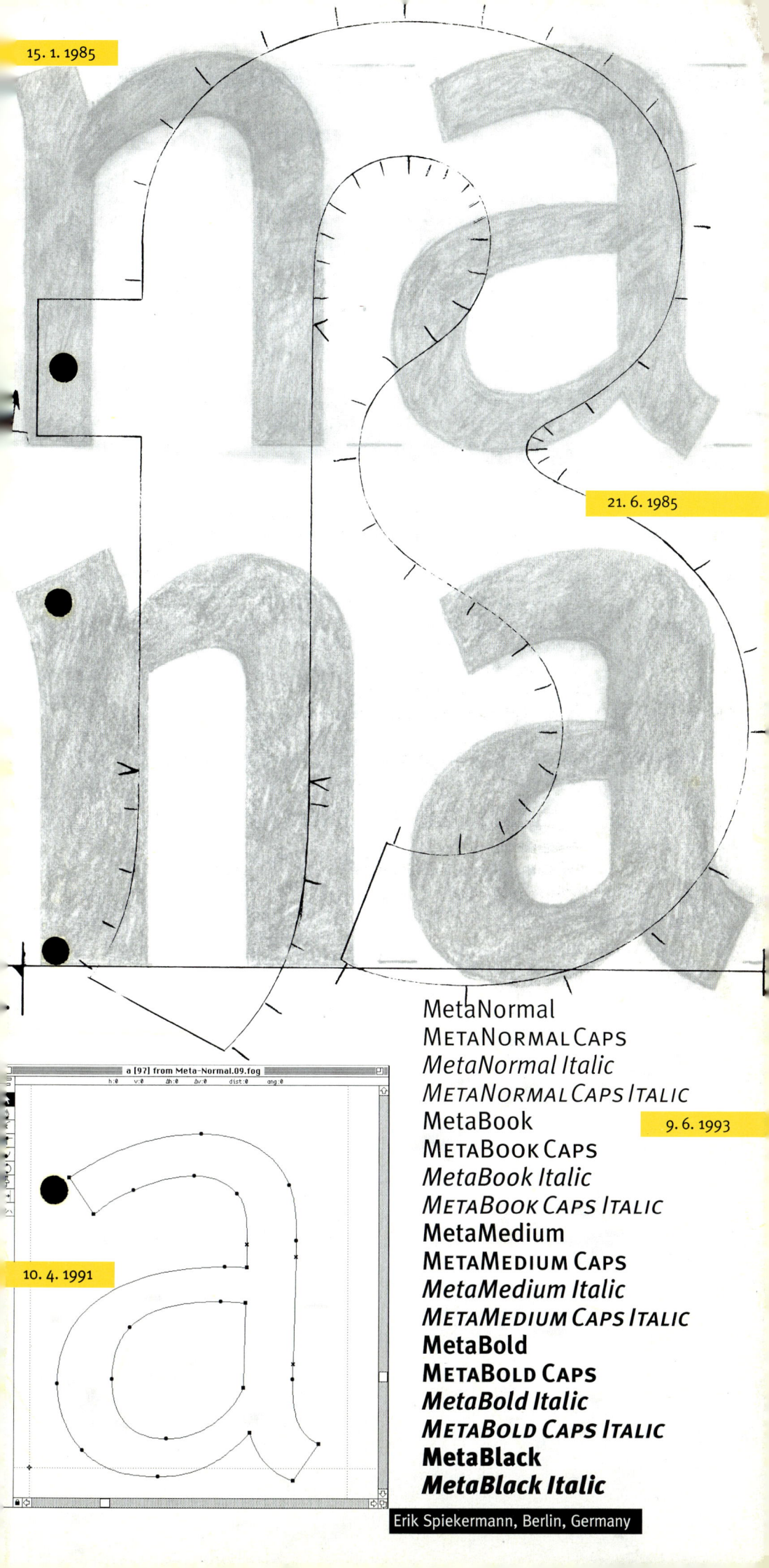

21. 6. 1985

9. 6. 1993

10. 4. 1991

MetaNormal
MetaNormal Caps
MetaNormal Italic
MetaNormal Caps Italic
MetaBook
MetaBook Caps
MetaBook Italic
MetaBook Caps Italic
MetaMedium
MetaMedium Caps
MetaMedium Italic
MetaMedium Caps Italic
MetaBold
MetaBold Caps
MetaBold Italic
MetaBold Caps Italic
MetaBlack
MetaBlack Italic

Erik Spiekermann, Berlin, Germany

Addresses

→ **FontShop Austria**
Seidengasse 26
A-1070 Wien
(0222) 523 2946
Fax (0222) 523 2947-22

→ **FontShop Benelux**
Maaltecenter Blok D
Derbystraat 119
B-9051 St.-Denijs-Westrem
(09) 220 6598
(09) 221 3208
(09) 222 5721
(03404) 323 66
(03404) 249 52
Fax (09) 220 3445

→ **FontShop Canada**
401 Wellington Street West
Toronto, Ontario M5V 1E8
MAC: 1-800-36-FONTS
PC: 1-800-46-FONTS
Local 416-348-9837
Fax 416-593-4318

→ **FontShop France**
6, Rue de Berri
F-75000 Paris
(1) 4 299 9561
Fax (1) 4 299 9501

→ **FontShop Germany**
Bergmannstraße 102
D-10961 Berlin
(030) 69 58 95
Fax (030) 692 88 65

→ **FontShop Italy**
Via Masotto 21
I-20133 Milano
(02) 7010 0555
Fax (02) 7010 0585

→ **FontWorks UK**
65-69 East Road
GB-London N1 6AH
(071) 490 5390
(071) 490 2002
Fax (071) 490 5391

→ **FontShop US**
720 South Dearborn #701
Chicago, Illinois 60605
MAC: 1-800-36-FONTS
PC: 1-800-46-FONTS
Fax 416-593 4318